The Oxford Dictionary of

Synonyms
and Antonyms

The Oxford Dictionary of

Synonyms
and Antonyms

THIRD EDITION

OXFORD
UNIVERSITY PRESS

OXFORD
UNIVERSITY PRESS

Great Clarendon Street, Oxford, OX2 6DP
United Kingdom

Oxford University Press is a department of the University of Oxford.
It furthers the University's objective of excellence in research, scholarship,
and education by publishing worldwide. Oxford is a registered trade mark of
Oxford University Press in the UK and in certain other countries

First Edition published in 1999
Second Edition published in 2007
Third Edition published in 2014

Published in the United States of America by Oxford University Press
198 Madison Avenue, New York, NY 10016, United States of America

British Library Cataloguing in Publication Data
Data available

Library of Congress Control Number: 2013951374

ISBN 978-0-19-870518-5

Printed and bound in Great Britain by Clays Ltd, Elcograf S.p.A.

Contents

Introduction

A dictionary of synonyms and antonyms contains lists of words that have a similar meaning to another word. It can help you to express yourself more clearly, find a word that is on the tip of your tongue, or avoid repeating a word that you have already used. It can also be a very useful resource for crossword puzzles and other word games.

Extra help is provided by the boxed Word Links—words related in different ways to a selection of key entries. Under **bird**, for example, you will find the words **avian** (meaning 'relating to birds') and **ornithology** (meaning 'the study of birds').

New to this Third Edition are words such as **podcast**, **staycation**, **redact**, **chilled**, **coruscating**, **nemesis**, and **disruptive** (in the sense of 'innovative').

In addition, there is a useful centre section designed to improve your knowledge of the English language even further: a supplement of commonly confused words explains the crucial differences between similar words that are often mixed up, and a Wordfinder section offers more sources of vocabulary in the form of thematic lists—from chemical elements and clothing to phobias and flowers.

To explore language further, visit Oxford Dictionaries Online at www.oxforddictionaries.com. This free site, which is regularly updated, allows you to search our largest dictionary of current English, as well as dictionaries of French, German, Italian, and Spanish. It also offers fascinating information on usage, grammar, and writing, a Word of the Day, a language blog, and more.

Guide to the dictionary

Here is an explanation of the main features that you will find in this dictionary.

Entry word (known as a *headword*)

colourful *adjective* **1 bright**, vivid, vibrant, brilliant, radiant, gaudy, garish, multicoloured, psychedelic; *informal* jazzy. **2** *a colourful account* **vivid**, graphic, lively, animated, dramatic, fascinating, interesting, stimulating, scintillating, evocative.
- OPPOSITES drab, dull.

Example of use

Numbered sense of the entry word

Word closest in meaning to the entry word (in **bold** type)

Words meaning the opposite of the entry word

horse *noun* **mount**, charger, cob, nag, hack, colt, stallion, mare, filly; *N. Amer.* bronco; *Austral./NZ* moke; *informal* gee-gee.

Label showing the level of English in which the following synonym is used

Labels showing the region of the world in which the following synonyms are used

> **WORD LINKS**
> **equine** relating to horses
> **equestrian** relating to horse riding

Word links providing extra vocabulary related to the entry word

root *noun* **1 source**, origin, cause, reason, basis, foundation, bottom, seat. **2** *his Irish roots* **origins**, beginnings, family, birth, heritage.
● *verb* **rummage**, hunt, search, rifle, delve, forage, dig, poke.
□ **root out** eradicate, eliminate, weed out, destroy, wipe out, stamp out, abolish, end, put a stop to.

Different parts of speech of the entry word

Phrase for which synonyms are given

Labels

Most of the synonyms in this dictionary are part of standard English, but some are used only in certain contexts or types of writing. These are grouped at the end of their sense, preceded by one of the following labels, as appropriate:

informal	normally used only in speech or informal writing or email (e.g. **barmy** or **gawp**)
formal	normally used only in writing, especially in official documents (e.g. **dwelling**)
dated	no longer used by most people (e.g. **navvy**)
old use	not in ordinary use today, though sometimes used to give an old-fashioned effect (e.g. **comely**)
historical	only used today to refer to things that are no longer part of modern life (e.g. **alms**)
literary	found only or mainly in works of literature (e.g. **plenteous**)
technical:	normally used only in technical language (e.g. **occlude**)
derogatory	meant to convey a low opinion or to insult someone (e.g. **pleb**)

Geographical labels

English is spoken throughout the world, and while most of the words used in standard British English are also used in other varieties, there are some words which are only found in one type of English. If a word has the geographical label *Brit.* in this dictionary, this means that it is used in standard British English but not in American English, although it may be found in other varieties such as Australian English. The labels *US* and *N. Amer.*, on the other hand, mean that the word is typically American and is not standard in British English, though it may be found elsewhere.

Subject labels

These are used to show that a word or sense is connected with a particular subject or specialist activity such as *Medicine* or *Computing*.

Abbreviations used in this dictionary

Austral.	Australian
Brit.	British
Canad.	Canadian
N. Amer.	North American
NZ	New Zealand
US	United States

Trademarks

This dictionary includes some words which have, or are asserted to have, proprietary status as trademarks or otherwise. Their inclusion does not imply that they have acquired for legal purposes a non-proprietary or general significance, nor any other judgement concerning their legal status. In cases where the editorial staff have some evidence that a word has proprietary status this is indicated in the entry for that word by the label *trademark*, but no judgement concerning the legal status of such words is made or implied thereby.

Aa

abandon *verb* **1** *he abandoned his wife* **desert**, leave, turn your back on, cast aside, finish with, jilt, throw over; *informal* walk/run out on, dump, ditch; *literary* forsake. **2** *she had abandoned painting* **give up**, stop, have done with; *informal* pack in, quit; *Brit.* jack in. **3** *they abandoned the car* **leave (behind)**, vacate, dump, quit, evacuate, discard, jettison. **4** *the party abandoned those policies* **renounce**, relinquish, dispense with, discard, give up, drop; *informal* ditch, scrap, junk; *formal* forswear.
- OPPOSITES keep.
● *noun* **uninhibitedness**, recklessness, lack of restraint, lack of inhibition.
- OPPOSITES self-control.

abate *verb* **subside**, die down/away/out, lessen, ease (off), let up, decrease, diminish, fade, weaken.
- OPPOSITES intensify.

abbreviate *verb* **shorten**, reduce, cut, contract, condense, compress, abridge, summarize, precis.
- OPPOSITES lengthen, expand.

abbreviation *noun* **short form**, contraction, acronym, initialism.

abdicate *verb* **resign**, retire, stand down, step down, renounce the throne.

abdomen *noun* **stomach**, belly, gut, middle; *informal* tummy, guts.

> **WORD LINKS**
> **abdominal**, **ventral** relating to the abdomen

abdominal *adjective* **gastric**, intestinal, stomach, duodenal, visceral, coeliac, ventral.

abduct *verb* **kidnap**, carry off, seize, capture, run away/off with, take hostage; *informal* snatch.

aberration *noun* **anomaly**, deviation, abnormality, irregularity, variation, freak, oddity, peculiarity, curiosity, mistake.

abhor *verb* **hate**, detest, loathe, despise, shudder at; *formal* abominate.
- OPPOSITES love, admire.

abhorrent *adjective* **hateful**, detestable, loathsome, abominable, repellent, repugnant, repulsive, revolting, vile, odious, disgusting, horrible, horrid, horrifying, awful, heinous.
- OPPOSITES admirable.

abide *verb* **1** *(informal) I can't abide smoke* **stand**, bear; *Brit. informal* stick. **2** *one memory will abide* **continue**, remain, survive, last, persist, live on.
□ **abide by** comply with, obey, observe, follow, keep to, adhere to, stick to, go along with, heed, accept.

abiding *adjective* **enduring**, lasting, everlasting, perpetual, eternal, unending, permanent.

ability *noun* **1** **capacity**, capability, power, potential, faculty, facility, wherewithal, means. **2** **talent**, skill, aptitude, expertise, savoir faire, prowess, accomplishment, competence, proficiency, flair, gift, knack, genius; *informal* know-how.
- OPPOSITES inability.

able *adjective* **intelligent**, clever, talented, skilful, skilled, expert, accomplished, gifted, proficient, apt, adroit, adept, capable, competent; *informal* genius.
- OPPOSITES incompetent.

abnormal *adjective* **unusual**, uncommon, atypical, untypical, unexpected, unrepresentative, irregular, anomalous, deviant, aberrant, freak, strange, odd, peculiar, eccentric, bizarre, weird, unnatural, perverted, twisted, warped; *informal* funny, freaky, kinky.
- OPPOSITES normal.

a

abnormality noun **deformity**, defect, malformation, oddity, strangeness, irregularity, anomaly, deviation, aberration.

abolish verb **put an end to**, get rid of, scrap, cancel, end, remove, dissolve, stop, ban; informal do away with, axe, ditch.

abominable adjective **loathsome**, detestable, hateful, obnoxious, despicable, contemptible, disgusting, revolting, repellent, repulsive, repugnant, abhorrent, reprehensible, atrocious, execrable, foul, vile, wretched, horrible, awful, dreadful, appalling, nauseating; informal terrible, shocking, God-awful; Brit. informal beastly.
- OPPOSITES good, admirable.

abort verb the crew aborted the take-off **halt**, stop, end, call off, abandon, discontinue, terminate; informal pull the plug on.

abortion noun **termination**, miscarriage.

abortive adjective **unsuccessful**, failed, vain, ineffective, ineffectual, unproductive, futile, useless, unavailing.
- OPPOSITES successful.

abound verb **be plentiful**, be abundant, be numerous, be thick on the ground; informal grow on trees, be two/ten a penny.

about preposition **regarding**, concerning, referring to, with regard to, with respect to, relating to, on, dealing with, on the subject of.
● adverb **approximately**, roughly, around, in the region of, circa, of the order of, or so, or thereabouts, more or less; Brit. getting on for; N. Amer. informal in the ballpark of.

above preposition **1 over**, higher (up) than, on top of, on. **2 superior to**, senior to, over, higher (up) than, more powerful than, in charge of, commanding.
- OPPOSITES below.
● adverb **overhead**, on/at the top, high up, on high, up above, (up) in the sky.

□ **above all** most importantly, most of all, chiefly, primarily, first and foremost, essentially, in essence, at bottom; informal at the end of the day, when all is said and done.

abrasion noun **1 graze**, cut, scrape, scratch, gash, laceration. **2 erosion**, wearing away/down.

abrasive adjective **1 rough**, coarse, harsh, scratchy, chafing. **2 curt**, brusque, sharp, harsh, caustic, grating.
- OPPOSITES gentle.

abridge verb **shorten**, cut (down), edit, abbreviate, condense, compress, truncate, prune, summarize, precis, synopsize; (**abridged**) concise.
- OPPOSITES extend.

abridgement noun **summary**, synopsis, precis, abstract, outline, résumé, digest, cut-down version.

abroad adverb **overseas**, out of the country, to/in foreign parts, to/in a foreign country/land.

abrupt adjective **1 sudden**, rapid, quick, hasty, unexpected, unanticipated, unforeseen, precipitate. **2 curt**, brusque, blunt, short, rude, sharp, terse, brisk, unceremonious.
- OPPOSITES gradual, gentle.

abscond verb **run away**, run off, escape, bolt, flee, make off, take flight, take off, decamp; informal scarper, vamoose, do a bunk, do a runner.

absence noun **1 non-attendance**, absenteeism, truancy, leave, holiday, vacation, sabbatical. **2 lack**, want, non-existence, unavailability, scarcity, shortage, dearth.
- OPPOSITES presence.

absent adjective **1 away**, off, out, elsewhere, off duty, on holiday, on leave, playing truant; informal AWOL. **2 non-existent**, lacking, missing. **3 distracted**, preoccupied, inattentive, vague, absorbed, dreamy, faraway, blank, empty, vacant.
- OPPOSITES present.
□ **absent yourself** stay away, be absent, go away, leave, withdraw.

absent-minded *adjective* **forgetful**, distracted, scatterbrained, preoccupied, inattentive, vague; *informal* with a mind/memory like a sieve.

absolute *adjective* **1** *absolute silence* | *an absolute disgrace* **complete**, total, utter, out-and-out, outright, perfect, pure, thorough, unqualified, unreserved, downright, unmitigated, sheer, unadulterated. **2** *absolute power* **unlimited**, unrestricted, unrestrained, infinite, total, supreme, unconditional. **3** *an absolute ruler* **autocratic**, dictatorial, all-powerful, omnipotent, supreme.
- OPPOSITES partial, qualified, limited.

absolutely *adverb* **completely**, totally, utterly, perfectly, entirely, wholly, fully, quite, thoroughly, unreservedly, definitely, certainly, unquestionably, undoubtedly, without (a) doubt, without question, in every way/respect, one hundred per cent.

absorb *verb* **1** **soak up**, suck up, draw up/in, take up/in, mop up. **2** **engross**, captivate, occupy, preoccupy, engage, rivet, grip, hold, immerse, involve, enthral, spellbind, fascinate.

absorbent *adjective* **spongy**, sponge-like, porous, permeable.

absorbing *adjective* **fascinating**, interesting, captivating, gripping, engrossing, compelling, compulsive, enthralling, riveting, spellbinding; *informal* unputdownable.
- OPPOSITES boring.

absorption *noun* **1** **soaking up**, sucking up. **2** **involvement**, immersion, raptness, preoccupation, captivation, fascination, enthralment.

abstain *verb* **refrain**, desist, forbear, give up, renounce, avoid, eschew, forgo, go/do without, refuse, decline; *informal* cut out.

abstemious *adjective* **moderate**, restrained, temperate, self-disciplined, self-restrained, self-denying, sober, austere, ascetic, puritanical, spartan.
- OPPOSITES self-indulgent.

abstinence *noun* **self-denial**, self-restraint, teetotalism, temperance, sobriety, abstemiousness.

abstract *adjective* **theoretical**, conceptual, intellectual, metaphysical, philosophical, academic.
- OPPOSITES actual, concrete.
  ● *noun* **summary**, synopsis, precis, résumé, outline, abridgement; *N. Amer.* wrap-up.

abstruse *adjective* **obscure**, arcane, esoteric, rarefied, recondite, difficult, hard, cryptic, over/above your head, incomprehensible, unfathomable, impenetrable.

absurd *adjective* **irrational**, illogical, inappropriate, ridiculous, ludicrous, farcical, comical, stupid, idiotic, asinine, hare-brained, foolish, silly, pointless, senseless, preposterous; *informal* crazy, cockeyed; *Brit. informal* barmy, daft.
- OPPOSITES sensible.

abundance *noun* **plenty**, plentifulness, plethora, profusion, exuberance, riot, cornucopia, superabundance.
- OPPOSITES scarcity.

abundant *adjective* **plentiful**, copious, ample, profuse, large, huge, great, bumper, prolific, overflowing, teeming, superabundant; *informal* galore.
- OPPOSITES scarce.

abuse *verb* **1** **misuse**, exploit, take advantage of. **2** **mistreat**, maltreat, ill-treat, hurt, harm, beat, molest, interfere with. **3** **insult**, be rude to, swear at, shout at, vilify, curse.
  ● *noun* **1** **misuse**, exploitation. **2** **mistreatment**, maltreatment, ill-treatment, molestation. **3** **insults**, expletives, swear words, swearing, name-calling, invective, vilification, curses.

abusive *adjective* **1** **insulting**, rude, offensive, derogatory, defamatory, slanderous, libellous. **2** **violent**, brutal, cruel, harsh, oppressive.
- OPPOSITES polite.

abysmal *adjective* **terrible**, dreadful, awful, appalling, frightful, atrocious, disgraceful, deplorable, lamentable;

informal rotten, pathetic, pitiful, woeful, useless, lousy, dire, poxy, the pits; *Brit. informal* chronic, shocking.

abyss *noun* **chasm**, crevasse, gulf, pit, void.

academic *adjective* **1 educational**, scholastic. **2 scholarly**, learned, literary, intellectual, erudite, high-brow, bookish, studious. **3 theoretical**, hypothetical, notional, speculative, conjectural, irrelevant, beside the point.
● *noun* **scholar**, intellectual, don, professor, man/woman of letters, thinker; *informal* egghead; *Brit. informal* boffin.

academy *noun* **college**, school, university, institute.

accelerate *verb* **1 speed up**, go faster, gain momentum, increase speed, pick up speed, gather speed. **2 hasten**, quicken, speed up, further, advance, expedite; *informal* crank up.
- OPPOSITES decelerate, delay.

accent *noun* **1 pronunciation**, intonation, enunciation, articulation, inflection. **2 emphasis**, stress, priority, importance, prominence.

accentuate *verb* **focus attention on**, draw attention to, point up, underline, underscore, accent, highlight, spotlight, foreground, bring to the fore, emphasize, stress.

accept *verb* **1 receive**, take, get, obtain, acquire, pick up. **2 agree to**, accede to, consent to, acquiesce in, concur with, endorse, comply with, go along with, defer to, put up with, recognize, acknowledge, admit. **3 believe**, trust, credit, be convinced of, have faith in; *informal* buy, swallow.
- OPPOSITES reject.

acceptable *adjective* **satisfactory**, adequate, reasonable, fair, good enough, sufficient, tolerable, passable.

acceptance *noun* **1 receipt**, receiving, taking. **2 respect**, acknowledgement, belief, toleration, consent, agreement, assent, compliance, acquiescence.

accepted *adjective* **recognized**, acknowledged, established, traditional,

orthodox, agreed, approved, customary, normal, standard.
- OPPOSITES unorthodox.

access *noun* **1** *a side access* **entrance**, entry, approach, path, drive, way in. **2** *they were denied access* **admission**, admittance, entry.

accessible *adjective* **approachable**, attainable, reachable, obtainable, available, understandable, comprehensible, intelligible; *informal* get-at-able.

accessory *noun* **1 extra**, add-on, addition, supplement, attachment, fitment. **2 accomplice**, abetter, collaborator, co-conspirator, henchman, associate.

accident *noun* **1 mishap**, misadventure, disaster, tragedy, catastrophe, calamity. **2 crash**, collision, smash, bump, derailment; *N. Amer.* wreck; *informal* smash-up, pile-up; *Brit. informal* shunt. **3 chance**, fate, fortune, luck, good luck, fluke, coincidence.

accidental *adjective* **1 chance**, coincidental, unexpected, incidental, fortuitous, serendipitous. **2 unintentional**, unintended, unplanned, inadvertent, unwitting, unpremeditated.
- OPPOSITES intentional.

acclaim *verb* **praise**, applaud, cheer, commend, approve, welcome, hail, celebrate, eulogize; *formal* laud.
- OPPOSITES criticize.
● *noun* **praise**, applause, tributes, plaudits, approval, admiration, congratulations, commendation, eulogies.
- OPPOSITES criticism.

acclimatize *verb* **adjust**, adapt, get used, familiarize yourself, find your feet, get your bearings; *N. Amer.* acclimate.

accommodate *verb* **1** *refugees were accommodated in army camps* **lodge**, house, put up, billet, board. **2** *the cottages accommodate six people* **hold**, take, have room for, sleep, seat. **3** *we tried to accommodate her* **help**, assist, oblige, cater for, fit in with, satisfy, meet the needs of.

accommodating *adjective* **obliging**, cooperative, helpful, amenable, hospitable, flexible.

accommodation noun **housing**, homes, lodging(s), (living) quarters, rooms, billet, shelter, a roof over your head; *informal* digs, pad; *formal* residence, dwelling, abode.

accompaniment noun **1** *a musical accompaniment* **backing**, support, background, soundtrack. **2** *wine is a good accompaniment to cheese* **complement**, addition, adjunct, accessory, companion.

accompany verb **1 escort**, go with, travel with, keep someone company, chaperone, partner, show, see, usher, conduct. **2 occur with**, go along with, go together with, attend, be linked with, go hand in hand with. **3** *he accompanied the choir on the piano* **back**, play along with, support.

accomplice noun **partner in crime**, abetter, accessory, collaborator, co-conspirator, henchman, associate; *informal* sidekick.

accomplish verb **achieve**, succeed in, realize, attain, manage, bring off, carry through, execute, effect, perform, complete.

accomplished adjective **expert**, skilled, skilful, masterly, virtuoso, master, proficient, polished, practised, consummate, talented, gifted, able, capable; *informal* mean, nifty, crack, ace.

accomplishment noun **1 achievement**, success, act, deed, exploit, effort, feat, coup. **2 talent**, skill, gift, ability.

accord verb **1 give**, grant, present, award, confer on, bestow on. **2 correspond**, agree, tally, match, concur, be in harmony, be in tune.
- OPPOSITES disagree, differ.
● noun **1** *a peace accord* **pact**, treaty, agreement, settlement, deal, entente, protocol. **2** *the two sides failed to reach accord* **agreement**, consensus, unanimity, harmony.
- OPPOSITES disagreement.
□ **of your own accord** voluntarily, of

your own free will, of your own volition, by choice, willingly, freely, readily.

account noun **1 description**, report, version, story, statement, explanation, tale, chronicle, narrative, history, record, log. **2 financial record**, ledger, balance sheet, financial statement; (**accounts**) books. **3** *his background is of no account* **importance**, import, significance, consequence, value.
□ **account for 1** explain, answer for, give reasons for, justify. **2** constitute, make up, comprise, represent, be responsible for, produce.

accountability noun **responsibility**, liability, answerability.

accountable adjective **responsible**, liable, answerable, to blame.

accumulate verb **gather**, collect, amass, stockpile, pile up, build up, store (up), hoard, lay in/up, increase, accrue, run up.
- OPPOSITES disperse.

accumulation noun **mass**, build-up, pile, collection, stock, store, stockpile, hoard.

accuracy noun **correctness**, precision, exactness, fidelity, truth, truthfulness, authenticity, realism.

accurate adjective **1 correct**, precise, exact, right, factual, literal, faithful, true, truthful, on the mark, authentic, realistic; *Brit. informal* spot on, bang on; *N. Amer. informal* on the money, on the button. **2 well aimed**, on target, unerring, deadly, true.

accusation noun **allegation**, charge, indictment, impeachment, claim, assertion, imputation.

accuse verb **1 charge**, indict, impeach, prefer charges against, arraign. **2 blame**, hold responsible, condemn, criticize, denounce; *informal* point the finger at.

accustom verb **adapt**, adjust, acclimatize, habituate, familiarize, become reconciled, get used to, come to terms with, learn to live with; *N. Amer.* acclimate.

a

accustomed *adjective* **customary**, established, habitual, usual, normal, regular, routine; *literary* wonted.

ache *noun* **pain**, twinge, pang, soreness, tenderness, irritation, discomfort, burning, throbbing, cramp.
● *verb* **hurt**, be sore, be painful, be tender, burn, be in pain, throb.

achieve *verb* **attain**, reach, realize, bring off, pull off, accomplish, carry through, fulfil, complete, succeed in, manage, effect; *informal* wrap up, swing.

achievement *noun* **1 attainment**, realization, accomplishment, fulfilment, implementation, completion. **2 feat**, exploit, triumph, coup, accomplishment, act, action, deed, effort, work, handiwork.

acid *adjective* **1 sour**, acidic, tart, sharp, vinegary. **2 sharp**, sharp-tongued, catty, sarcastic, scathing, cutting, biting, stinging, caustic; *informal* bitchy.
– OPPOSITES sweet.

acknowledge *verb* **1 admit**, accept, grant, agree, own, allow, concede, confess, recognize. **2 greet**, salute, address, nod to, wave to, say hello to. **3 answer**, reply to, respond to.
– OPPOSITES deny, ignore.

acquaint *verb* **familiarize**, make aware of, inform of, advise of, brief; *informal* fill in on, clue in on.

acquaintance *noun* **1** *a business acquaintance* **contact**, associate, colleague. **2** *my acquaintance with George* **association**, relationship. **3** *some acquaintance with the language* **familiarity with**, knowledge of, experience of, awareness of, understanding of, grasp of.

acquire *verb* **get**, obtain, come by, receive, collect, gain, buy, earn, win, come into, secure, pick up, procure; *informal* get your hands on, get hold of, land, bag, score.
– OPPOSITES lose.

acquisition *noun* **purchase**, addition, investment, possession, accession; *informal* buy.

acquit *verb* **1 clear**, exonerate, find innocent, absolve, discharge, free, release; *informal* let off (the hook). **2** *the boys acquitted themselves well* **behave**, conduct yourself, perform, act.
– OPPOSITES convict.

acrid *adjective* **pungent**, bitter, sharp, harsh, stinging, burning.

acrimonious *adjective* **bitter**, angry, rancorous, harsh, vicious, nasty, bad-tempered, ill-natured.

act *verb* **1 take action**, take steps, take measures, move. **2 behave**, conduct yourself, react. **3** *I'll act as lookout* **function**, work, serve, operate. **4 perform**, play, appear; *informal* tread the boards.
● *noun* **1 deed**, action, step, move, gesture, feat, exploit. **2 law**, decree, statute, bill, edict, ruling, order. **3 performance**, turn, routine, number, sketch. **4 pretence**, show, front, facade, masquerade, charade, pose; *informal* put-on.

acting *adjective* **temporary**, interim, caretaker, pro tem, provisional, stop-gap; *N. Amer. informal* pinch-hitting.
– OPPOSITES permanent.

action *noun* **1 deed**, act, undertaking, feat, exploit, behaviour, conduct, activity. **2 measures**, steps, initiatives, activism, campaigning, pressure. **3 operation**, working, effect, influence, process, power. **4 battle**, combat, hostilities, fighting, conflict, active service. **5 lawsuit**, suit, case, prosecution, litigation, proceedings.

activate *verb* **start (up)**, switch on, turn on, set going, trigger (off), set off, energize.

active *adjective* **1 busy**, lively, dynamic, vigorous, sprightly, spry, mobile; *informal* on the go, full of beans. **2 hard-working**, industrious, tireless, energetic, diligent, enthusiastic, keen, committed, devoted, zealous. **3 working**, operative, functioning, operational, in action, in operation, in force; *informal* (up and) running.
– OPPOSITES inactive.

activity noun **1 action**, bustle, movement, life, hurly-burly; *informal* toing and froing, comings and goings. **2 pursuit**, occupation, hobby, pastime, recreation, diversion, venture, undertaking, enterprise, project, scheme.

actor, actress noun **performer**, player, thespian, star, starlet; *Brit. informal* luvvy.

actual adjective **real**, true, genuine, authentic, bona fide, confirmed, definite, hard, concrete; *informal* real live.
- OPPOSITES imaginary.

actually adverb **really**, in (actual) fact, in point of fact, as a matter of fact, in reality, in truth, if truth be told, to tell the truth.

acute adjective **1 severe**, dire, terrible, grave, serious, desperate, urgent, pressing. **2 excruciating**, sharp, severe, stabbing, agonizing, racking, searing. **3 quick**, astute, shrewd, sharp, keen, penetrating, razor-sharp, quick-witted, agile, nimble, intelligent, canny, discerning, perceptive.
- OPPOSITES mild, dull.

adamant adjective **unshakeable**, unwavering, unswerving, immovable, resolute, resolved, determined, firm, dead set.

adapt verb **1** *the policy can be adapted* **modify**, alter, change, adjust, remodel, reorganize, customize, tailor; *informal* tweak. **2** *he adapts well to new surroundings* **adjust**, conform, acclimatize, accommodate, get used to, get accustomed, habituate yourself.

add verb **1 attach**, append, tack on, join on. **2** *they added the figures up* **total**, count (up), reckon up, tally; *Brit.* tot up.
- OPPOSITES subtract.
  □ **add to** increase, augment, magnify, amplify, enhance, intensify, heighten, deepen, exacerbate, aggravate, compound, reinforce. **add up to** amount to, come to, run to, make, total, equal, number.

addict noun **1 abuser**; *informal* junkie, druggy, -head, freak; *N. Amer. informal* hophead. **2** *(informal)* **enthusiast**, fan, lover, devotee, aficionado; *informal* buff, freak, nut, fanatic.

addicted adjective **dependent**, obsessed, fixated, fanatical, passionate, a slave to; *informal* hooked.

addiction noun **dependency**, dependence, habit, obsession, infatuation, passion, love, mania, enslavement.

addictive adjective **habit-forming**, compulsive; *Brit. informal* moreish.

addition noun **1 adding**, inclusion, incorporation, introduction. **2 add-on**, extra, adjunct, appendage, supplement, rider, addendum, postscript, appendix.
- OPPOSITES subtraction.
  □ **in addition** see **additionally**.

additional adjective **extra**, added, supplementary, further, more, spare, other, new, fresh.

additionally adverb **also**, in addition, besides, too, as well, on top (of that), furthermore, moreover, into the bargain, to boot, to say nothing of.

address noun **1 house**, flat, apartment, home, location, whereabouts; *formal* residence, dwelling, domicile. **2 speech**, lecture, talk, presentation, dissertation, sermon, oration.
  ● verb **speak to**, talk to, give a talk to, lecture, make a speech to, hold forth to.

adept adjective **expert**, proficient, accomplished, skilful, practised, masterly, consummate.
- OPPOSITES inept.

adequate adjective **1** *he has adequate financial resources* **sufficient**, enough. **2** *an adequate service* **satisfactory**, acceptable, passable, reasonable, tolerable, fair, average, not bad, all right, middling; *informal* OK.
- OPPOSITES insufficient, inadequate.

adhere verb **stick**, cling, bond, hold.
  □ **adhere to** abide by, stick to, hold to, comply with, conform to, follow, obey, heed, observe, respect, uphold, fulfil.

adherent noun **follower**, supporter, upholder, defender, advocate, disciple,

devotee, member.
- OPPOSITES opponent.

adjacent *adjective* **adjoining**, neighbouring, next-door, abutting; *formal* contiguous.
 □ **adjacent to** next to, by the side of, bordering on, beside, alongside, touching.

adjoining *adjective* **connecting**, connected, interconnecting, bordering, abutting, attached, adjacent, neighbouring, next-door.

adjourn *verb* **suspend**, break off, discontinue, interrupt, recess, postpone, put off/back, defer, delay, hold over.

adjust *verb* **1 modify**, alter, regulate, tune, fine-tune, balance, tailor, customize, rearrange, change, reshape; *informal* tweak. **2** *she adjusted to her new life* **adapt**, become accustomed, get used, accommodate, acclimatize, habituate yourself, assimilate, come to terms with, fit in with; *N. Amer.* acclimate.

adjustable *adjective* **alterable**, adaptable, modifiable, variable, convertible, multiway, versatile.

administer *verb* **1 manage**, direct, control, operate, regulate, coordinate, conduct, handle, run, organize, govern, steer. **2 dispense**, issue, give out, provide, apply, offer, distribute, deliver, hand out, deal out, dole out.

administration *noun* **1 management**, direction, control, conduct, operation, running, coordination, governance, supervision, regulation. **2 government**, regime, executive, cabinet, authority, directorate, council, leadership, management, incumbency, term of office.

administrative *adjective* **managerial**, executive, operational, organizational, supervisory, directorial, governmental, regulatory.

administrator *noun* **manager**, director, executive, controller, official, coordinator, supervisor.

admirable *adjective* **commendable**, praiseworthy, laudable, creditable, exemplary, worthy, deserving, respectable, worthwhile, good, sterling, fine, excellent.
- OPPOSITES deplorable.

admiration *noun* **respect**, approval, appreciation, (high) regard, esteem, recognition.
- OPPOSITES scorn.

admire *verb* **1 respect**, think highly of, look up to, have a high opinion of, hold in high regard, rate highly, esteem, prize, approve of. **2 adore**, love, worship, be taken with, be attracted to, idolize, hero-worship; *informal* carry a torch for, have a thing about.
- OPPOSITES despise.

admirer *noun* **fan**, devotee, enthusiast, aficionado, supporter, adherent, follower, disciple.

admission *noun* **1 confession**, acknowledgement, acceptance, concession, disclosure, divulgence. **2 admittance**, entry, entrance, access, entrée, acceptance, initiation.

admit *verb* **1** *Paul admitted that he was angry* **confess**, acknowledge, concede, grant, accept, allow, own, reveal, disclose, divulge. **2** *he admitted the offence* **confess (to)**, plead guilty to, own up to. **3 let in**, accept, receive, initiate, take on.
- OPPOSITES deny.

admittance *noun* **entry**, admission, entrance, access, entrée.
- OPPOSITES exclusion.

adolescence *noun* **teenage years**, teens, youth, later childhood.

adolescent *noun* **teenager**, youth, juvenile; *informal* teen, teeny-bopper.
 ● *adjective* **teenage**, young, pubescent, immature, childish, juvenile, infantile, puerile; *informal* teen.
- OPPOSITES mature.

adopt *verb* **take on**, embrace, take up, espouse, assume, follow, choose, endorse, approve.
- OPPOSITES abandon.

adore *verb* **love**, be devoted to, dote on, cherish, treasure, prize, think the world

of, admire, look up to, revere, worship.
- OPPOSITES hate.

adorn verb **decorate**, embellish, array, ornament, bedeck, trim, enhance.
- OPPOSITES disfigure.

adrift adjective **1 lost**, off course, drifting, disorientated, confused, (all) at sea, rootless, unsettled. **2** (informal) **loose**, free, detached, unsecured, unfastened.

adult adjective **mature**, grown-up, fully grown, fully developed, of age.
- OPPOSITES immature.

advance verb **1 move forward**, press on, push on, attack, make progress, make headway, gain ground, forge ahead. **2** the move advanced his career **promote**, further, forward, help, aid, assist, boost. **3** technology has advanced **progress**, develop, evolve, make strides, move forward (in leaps and bounds), move on. **4 lend**, loan, put up, come up with; Brit. informal sub.
- OPPOSITES retreat.
● noun **1 progress**, (forward) movement, attack. **2 breakthrough**, development, step forward, (quantum) leap.
● adjective **early**, prior.
□ **in advance** beforehand, before, ahead of time, earlier, previously, in readiness.

advanced adjective **1 state-of-the-art**, modern, sophisticated, up to date, up to the minute, cutting-edge, new, the latest, pioneering, innovative, progressive, trendsetting. **2 higher-level**, higher, tertiary.
- OPPOSITES primitive, elementary.

advantage noun **1 upper hand**, edge, lead, sway, whip hand, superiority, dominance, supremacy. **2 benefit**, value, good/strong point, asset, plus, bonus, boon, blessing, virtue, profit, good.
- OPPOSITES disadvantage.

advantageous adjective **1 superior**, dominant, powerful, fortunate, lucky, favourable. **2 beneficial**, of benefit, helpful, of assistance, useful, of value, profitable, in someone's interests.

- OPPOSITES disadvantageous.

adventure noun **1 exploit**, escapade, undertaking, experience, incident. **2 excitement**, thrills, action, stimulation, risk, danger.

adventurous adjective **1 intrepid**, daring, daredevil, bold, fearless, brave; informal gutsy. **2 risky**, dangerous, perilous, hazardous, exciting.
- OPPOSITES cautious, safe.

adversary noun **opponent**, rival, enemy, nemesis, antagonist, challenger, contender, competitor, opposition, competition; literary foe.
- OPPOSITES ally.

adverse adjective **1** adverse weather **unfavourable**, inclement, bad, poor, untoward, inauspicious, unpropitious. **2** adverse side effects **harmful**, dangerous, injurious, detrimental, deleterious, inimical. **3** an adverse response **hostile**, unfavourable, antagonistic, unfriendly, negative.
- OPPOSITES favourable, beneficial.

adversity noun **misfortune**, bad luck, trouble, difficulty, hardship, disaster, suffering, sorrow, misery, woe, trials and tribulations.

advertise verb **publicize**, make public, announce, broadcast, proclaim, trumpet, promote, market; informal push, plug, hype; N. Amer. informal ballyhoo, flack.

advertisement noun **announcement**, commercial, promotion, blurb, write-up; informal ad, push, plug; Brit. informal advert.

advice noun **guidance**, counselling, counsel, help, direction, recommendations, guidelines, suggestions, hints, tips, pointers.

advisable adjective **wise**, sensible, prudent, expedient, politic, in your (best) interests.

advise verb **1 counsel**, give guidance, guide, offer suggestions, give hints/tips/pointers. **2 recommend**, advocate, suggest, urge. **3 inform**, notify, give notice, apprise, warn.

adviser noun **counsellor**, aide, mentor, guide, consultant, confidant, confidante, guru.

advocate noun **champion**, upholder, supporter, apologist, backer, promoter, proponent, campaigner, lobbyist; N. Amer. booster.
- OPPOSITES critic.
● verb **recommend**, champion, uphold, support, back, promote, campaign for, urge, subscribe to, speak for, argue for, lobby for.
- OPPOSITES oppose.

affair noun **1 event**, incident, episode, case, matter, business. **2 business**, concern, matter, responsibility, problem; Brit. informal lookout. **3 (affairs) transactions**, activities, dealings, undertakings, ventures, business. **4 relationship**, romance, fling, dalliance, liaison, involvement, amour; informal hankypanky; Brit. informal carry-on.

affect[1] verb **1 influence**, have an effect on, have an impact on, act on, change, alter, modify. **2 move**, touch, hit (hard), make an impression on, upset, trouble, distress, disturb, shake (up).

affect[2] verb **put on**, assume, take on, adopt, feign.

affectation noun **pretension**, pretentiousness, affectedness, artificiality, posturing, airs (and graces); Brit. informal side.

affection noun **fondness**, love, liking, soft spot, tenderness, warmth, devotion, caring, attachment, friendship.

affectionate adjective **fond**, loving, adoring, devoted, caring, tender, warm, friendly, demonstrative; informal touchy-feely, lovey-dovey.
- OPPOSITES cold.

affiliate verb **associate**, unite, combine, join (up), join forces, link up, ally, align, amalgamate, merge.

affinity noun **empathy**, rapport, sympathy, accord, harmony, similarity, relationship, bond, closeness, understanding; informal chemistry.
- OPPOSITES aversion.

affirm verb **declare**, state, assert, proclaim, pronounce, attest, swear, maintain, avow.
- OPPOSITES deny.

affirmative adjective **positive**, assenting, consenting, approving, favourable.
- OPPOSITES negative.

afflict verb **trouble**, burden, distress, beset, harass, worry, oppress, torment, plague, bedevil.

affluent adjective **wealthy**, rich, prosperous, well off, well-to-do, of means; informal well heeled, rolling in it, made of money, loaded.
- OPPOSITES poor.

afford verb **1 pay for**, find the money for, run to, stretch to, stand, manage, spare. **2 give**, offer, supply, provide, furnish, yield.

afraid adjective **1 frightened**, scared, terrified, fearful, nervous, petrified, intimidated, cowardly, faint-hearted; informal scared stiff, chicken; N. Amer. informal spooked. **2 reluctant**, hesitant, unwilling, slow, shy. **3** I'm afraid I'm late **sorry**.
- OPPOSITES brave, confident.

after preposition **following**, subsequent to, at the end of, in the wake of.

aftermath noun **consequences**, aftereffects, results, repercussions, upshot.

afterwards adverb **later**, later on, subsequently, then, next, after this/that, in due course.

again adverb **once more**, another time, afresh, anew.

against preposition **opposed to**, in opposition to, hostile to, antagonistic towards, unsympathetic to, at odds with, in disagreement with; informal anti.

age noun **1 old age**, maturity, advancing years, elderliness, seniority, senescence. **2 era**, epoch, period, time, generation.
● verb **1 mature**, mellow, ripen, soften, season, weather. **2 grow old**, decline, wither, fade.

agency noun **business**, organization, company, firm, office, bureau.

agenda noun **programme**, schedule, to-do list, timetable, plan.

agent noun **1 representative**, intermediary, middleman, negotiator, go-between, proxy, broker, emissary, envoy, spokesperson, delegate; *informal* rep. **2 spy**, secret agent, operative, mole; *N. Amer. informal* spook, G-man.

aggravate verb **1 worsen**, make worse, exacerbate, inflame, compound. **2** (*informal*) **annoy**, antagonize, irritate, exasperate, nettle, provoke, get on someone's nerves; *Brit.* rub up the wrong way; *informal* needle, hack off, get someone's goat; *Brit. informal* wind up; *N. Amer. informal* tick off.
- OPPOSITES alleviate, improve.

aggregate noun **total**, sum, grand total, combined score.

aggression noun **hostility**, belligerence, force, violence, attack.

aggressive adjective **1** *aggressive behaviour* **violent**, confrontational, antagonistic, combative, pugnacious. **2** *aggressive foreign policy* **warmongering**, warlike, warring, belligerent, bellicose, hawkish, militaristic, expansionist; *informal* gung-ho. **3** *an aggressive campaign* **assertive**, forceful, pushy, vigorous, energetic, dynamic, audacious; *informal* in-your-face, feisty.
- OPPOSITES peaceable, peaceful.

agile adjective **1 nimble**, lithe, supple, graceful, fit, acrobatic, sprightly, spry. **2 alert**, sharp, acute, shrewd, astute, perceptive, quick.
- OPPOSITES clumsy.

agitate verb **1 upset**, fluster, ruffle, disconcert, unnerve, disquiet, disturb, distress, unsettle, worry, perturb, trouble; *informal* rattle, faze. **2 shake**, whisk, beat, stir.

agonizing adjective **excruciating**, painful, acute, searing, severe, harrowing, torturous.

agony noun **suffering**, torture, pain, torment, anguish.

agree verb **1 concur**, see eye to eye, be in sympathy, be as one, be unanimous. **2** *they agreed to a ceasefire* **consent**, assent, acquiesce, allow, approve; *formal* accede. **3 match (up)**, correspond, conform, coincide, fit, tally, be consistent; *informal* square. **4 decide on**, settle, arrive at, negotiate, shake hands on.
- OPPOSITES disagree.

agreeable adjective **1** *an agreeable atmosphere* **pleasant**, pleasing, enjoyable, pleasurable, nice, appealing, relaxing, friendly, congenial. **2** *an agreeable man* **likeable**, amiable, affable, pleasant, nice, friendly, good-natured, sociable, genial. **3 willing**, amenable, in agreement.
- OPPOSITES unpleasant.

agreement noun **1 accord**, concurrence, consensus, assent, acceptance, consent, acquiescence. **2 contract**, treaty, pact, concordat, accord, settlement, understanding, bargain. **3 correspondence**, consistency, compatibility, accord, similarity, resemblance, likeness.
- OPPOSITES discord, dissimilarity.

agricultural adjective **farm**, farming, agrarian, rural, rustic, countryside.
- OPPOSITES urban.

agriculture noun **farming**, cultivation, husbandry, agribusiness, agronomy.

> **WORD LINKS**
> **agrarian** relating to agriculture

aid noun **1** *with the aid of his colleagues* **assistance**, support, help, backing, cooperation, a helping hand. **2** *humanitarian aid* **relief**, assistance, support, subsidy, funding, donations, grants; *historical* alms.
- OPPOSITES hindrance.
- ● verb **help**, assist, be of service, support, encourage, further, boost, promote, facilitate.
- OPPOSITES hinder.

aide noun **assistant**, helper, adviser, supporter, right-hand man/woman, adjutant, deputy, second (in command), lieutenant.

ailing *adjective* **1 ill**, sick, unwell, sickly, poorly, weak, in poor/bad health, infirm. **2 failing**, weak, poor, fragile, unstable.
- OPPOSITES healthy.

ailment *noun* **illness**, disease, disorder, affliction, malady, complaint, infirmity; *informal* bug, virus.

aim *verb* **1** *he aimed the rifle* **point**, direct, train, sight, line up. **2** *she aimed at the target* **take aim**, fix on, zero in on, draw a bead on. **3** *this food is aimed at children* **target**, intend, direct, design, tailor, market, pitch. **4 intend**, mean, hope, want, plan, propose.
● *noun* **objective**, object, goal, end, target, design, desire, intention, intent, plan, purpose, ambition, aspiration, wish, dream, hope.

aimless *adjective* **purposeless**, pointless, directionless, undirected, random.
- OPPOSITES purposeful.

air *noun* **1 breeze**, draught, wind, gust/puff of wind; *literary* zephyr. **2** *an air of defiance* **look**, appearance, impression, aspect, manner, tone, feel, atmosphere, mood.
● *verb* **1 express**, voice, make public, articulate, give vent to, state, declare. **2 ventilate**, freshen, refresh, cool.

> **WORD LINKS**
> **aerial** relating to air

airless *adjective* **stuffy**, close, muggy, humid, stifling, suffocating, oppressive, unventilated.
- OPPOSITES airy.

airy *adjective* **spacious**, uncluttered, light, bright, well ventilated, fresh.
- OPPOSITES airless, stuffy.

aisle *noun* **passage**, passageway, lane, path, gangway, walkway.

akin *adjective* **similar**, related, close, near, comparable, equivalent, connected, alike, analogous.
- OPPOSITES unlike.

alarm *noun* **1 fear**, anxiety, apprehension, distress, agitation, consternation, fright, panic, trepidation. **2 warning**, danger signal, siren, bell, detector, sensor.
- OPPOSITES calmness, composure.
● *verb* **frighten**, scare, panic, unnerve, distress, agitate, upset, disconcert, shock, disturb; *informal* rattle, spook; *Brit. informal* put the wind up.

alcoholic *adjective* **intoxicating**, strong, hard, stiff, fermented, brewed, distilled.
● *noun* **drunkard**, dipsomaniac, drunk, heavy drinker, problem drinker, alcohol-abuser; *informal* lush, alky, dipso, soak, wino; *Austral./NZ informal* hophead.

alert *adjective* **1 vigilant**, watchful, attentive, observant, wide awake, on the lookout, on your guard/toes; *informal* keeping your eyes open/peeled. **2 quick-witted**, sharp, bright, quick, perceptive, on your toes; *informal* on the ball, quick on the uptake, all there, with it.
- OPPOSITES inattentive.
● *noun* **1 vigilance**, watchfulness, attentiveness, alertness. **2 warning**, notification, notice, siren, alarm, signal.
● *verb* **warn**, notify, inform, apprise, forewarn, put on your guard; *informal* tip off.

alien *adjective* **foreign**, unfamiliar, unknown, peculiar, exotic, strange.
- OPPOSITES native, familiar.
● *noun* **1 foreigner**, foreign national, non-native, immigrant, émigré, stranger. **2 extraterrestrial**, ET; *informal* little green man.

alienate *verb* **isolate**, distance, estrange, cut off, turn away, drive apart, set at variance/odds, drive a wedge between.

alienation *noun* **isolation**, detachment, estrangement, distance, separation.

alight *adjective* **burning**, ablaze, on fire, in flames, blazing, lit.

align *verb* **1 line up**, range, rank, straighten, even up, arrange, coordinate. **2** *he aligned himself with the workers* **ally**, affiliate, associate, side, join forces, team up, band together, throw in your lot.

alike *adjective* **similar**, (much) the same, analogous, corresponding, indistinguishable, identical, uniform, interchangeable; *informal* much of a muchness.
- OPPOSITES different.
● *adverb great minds think alike* **similarly**, the same, correspondingly, analogously, identically.
- OPPOSITES differently.

alive *adjective* **1 active**, in existence, functioning, in operation, operative, on the map. **2 alert**, awake, aware, conscious, mindful, heedful, sensitive.
- OPPOSITES dead, unaware.

allay *verb* **reduce**, diminish, decrease, lessen, alleviate, assuage, ease, relieve, soothe, soften, calm.
- OPPOSITES increase, intensify.

allegation *noun* **claim**, assertion, charge, accusation, contention.

allege *verb* **claim**, assert, accuse, contend, state, declare, maintain.

alleged *adjective* **reported**, supposed, so-called, claimed, professed, purported, ostensible, unproven.
- OPPOSITES confirmed.

allegiance *noun* **loyalty**, faithfulness, fidelity, obedience, adherence, devotion; *historical* fealty.
- OPPOSITES disloyalty, treachery.

alleviate *verb* **ease**, relieve, take the edge off, deaden, dull, lessen, reduce, moderate, allay, assuage, soothe, help, soften.
- OPPOSITES aggravate.

alley *noun* **passage**, passageway, alleyway, backstreet, lane, path, pathway, walk.

alliance *noun* **association**, union, league, confederation, federation, syndicate, consortium, cartel, coalition, partnership, relationship, marriage, cooperation.

allied *adjective* **associated**, united, related, connected, interconnected, linked, cooperating, in league, affiliated, combined, coupled, married.
- OPPOSITES unrelated, independent.

allocate *verb* **allot**, assign, set aside, earmark, consign, distribute, apportion, share out, dole out, give out.

allocation *noun* **1 allotment**, assignment, distribution, sharing out, doling out, giving out. **2 allowance**, allotment, consignment, quota, share, ration; *informal* cut; *Brit. informal* whack.

allow *verb* **1 permit**, let, enable, authorize, give leave, license, entitle, consent to, assent to, acquiesce in, agree to, approve; *informal* give the go-ahead to, give the thumbs up to, OK, give the green light to; *formal* accede to. **2 set aside**, allocate, allot, earmark, designate, reserve.
- OPPOSITES prevent, forbid.

allowance *noun* **1 allocation**, allotment, quota, share, ration, grant, limit. **2 payment**, contribution, grant, handout, subsidy, maintenance.

all right *adjective* **1 satisfactory**, acceptable, adequate, passable, reasonable; *informal* so-so, OK. **2 unhurt**, uninjured, unharmed, in one piece, safe (and sound), alive and well; *informal* OK. **3 permissible**, permitted, allowed, acceptable, legal, lawful, authorized, approved, in order; *informal* OK, legit, cool.
- OPPOSITES unsatisfactory.
● *adverb* **satisfactorily**, adequately, fairly well, passably, acceptably, reasonably, well, fine; *informal* OK.

allude *verb* **refer**, touch on, suggest, hint, imply, mention (in passing), intimate.

allusion *noun* **reference**, mention, suggestion, intimation, hint.

ally *noun* **associate**, colleague, friend, confederate, partner, supporter.
- OPPOSITES enemy, opponent.
● *verb* **unite**, combine, join (up), join forces, band together, team up, collaborate, side, align yourself.

almost *adverb* **nearly**, (just) about, practically, virtually, all but, as good as, close to, not quite; *informal* pretty nearly/much/well; *literary* well nigh, nigh on.

alone *adjective & adverb* **by yourself**, on your own, unaccompanied, solo, single, isolated, solitary, lonely, deserted, abandoned, friendless; *Brit. informal* on your tod.
- OPPOSITES accompanied.

aloof *adjective* **distant**, detached, unfriendly, remote, unapproachable, reserved, unforthcoming, uncommunicative; *informal* stand-offish.
- OPPOSITES friendly.

also *adverb* **too**, as well, besides, in addition, additionally, furthermore, further, moreover, into the bargain, on top (of that), what's more, to boot.

alter *verb* **change**, make/become different, adjust, adapt, amend, modify, revise, rework, redo, transform; *informal* tweak.

alteration *noun* **change**, adjustment, adaptation, modification, amendment, transformation.

alternate *verb* **1 be interspersed**, follow one another, take turns, take it in turns, oscillate, see-saw. **2 rotate**, swap, exchange, interchange.
● *adjective* **every other**, every second, alternating.

alternative *adjective* **1 different**, other, second, substitute, replacement, standby, emergency, reserve, backup, auxiliary, fallback; *N. Amer.* alternate. **2 unorthodox**, unconventional, nonconformist, radical, revolutionary, avant-garde; *informal* offbeat, way-out, edgy.
● *noun* **(other) option**, (other) choice, substitute, replacement.

altogether *adverb* **1 completely**, totally, entirely, absolutely, wholly, fully, thoroughly, utterly, perfectly, one hundred per cent, in all respects. **2 in all**, all told, in total.

always *adverb* **1** *he's always late* **every time**, all the time, without fail, consistently, invariably, regularly, habitually, unfailingly. **2** *she's always complaining* **continually**, continuously, constantly, forever, all the time, day and night; *informal* 24-7. **3** *the place will always*

be dear to me **forever**, for good, for evermore, for ever and ever, until the end of time, eternally.
- OPPOSITES never, seldom.

amalgamate *verb* **combine**, merge, unite, join, fuse, blend, meld, mix, incorporate.
- OPPOSITES separate.

amass *verb* **gather**, collect, assemble, accumulate, stockpile, hoard.

amateur *noun* **non-professional**, non-specialist, layman, layperson, dilettante, dabbler.
● *adjective* **non-professional**, unpaid, non-specialist, lay, unqualified, inexperienced.
- OPPOSITES professional, expert.

amateurish *adjective* **incompetent**, inept, inexpert, unprofessional, amateur, clumsy, crude, second-rate; *Brit. informal* bodged.

amaze *verb* **astonish**, astound, surprise, stun, stagger, nonplus, shock, startle, stop someone in their tracks, leave open-mouthed, dumbfound; *informal* bowl over, flabbergast; *Brit. informal* knock for six; (**amazed**) thunderstruck, at a loss for words, speechless; *informal* gobsmacked.

amazement *noun* **astonishment**, surprise, shock, speechlessness, awe, wonder.

amazing *adjective* **astonishing**, astounding, surprising, stunning, staggering, breathtaking, awesome, awe-inspiring, sensational, remarkable, spectacular, stupendous, phenomenal, extraordinary, incredible, unbelievable; *informal* mind-blowing; *literary* wondrous.

ambassador *noun* **envoy**, emissary, representative, diplomat, minister, consul, attaché.

ambiguous *adjective* **vague**, unclear, ambivalent, double-edged, equivocal, inconclusive, enigmatic, cryptic.
- OPPOSITES clear.

ambition *noun* **1 drive**, determination, enterprise, initiative, eagerness, motivation, a sense of purpose; *informal* get-up-and-go. **2 aspiration**, desire, dream, intention, goal, aim, objective, plan.

ambitious *adjective* **1 aspiring**, determined, motivated, driven, energetic, committed, purposeful, power-hungry; *informal* go-ahead, go-getting. **2 challenging**, exacting, demanding, formidable, difficult, hard, tough.

ambush *verb* **surprise**, waylay, trap, ensnare, attack, jump on, pounce on; *N. Amer.* bushwhack.

amend *verb* **revise**, alter, change, modify, adapt, adjust, edit, rewrite, redraft, rephrase, reword.

amends *plural noun*
□ **make amends for** make up for, atone for, pay for, make good.
□ **make amends to** compensate, recompense, indemnify, make it up to.

amenity *noun* **facility**, service, resource, convenience, comfort.

amiable *adjective* **friendly**, affable, amicable, cordial, good-natured, nice, pleasant, agreeable, likeable, genial, good-humoured, companionable.
– OPPOSITES unfriendly, disagreeable.

amnesty *noun* **pardon**, reprieve, forgiveness, release, discharge; *informal* let-off.

amount *noun* **quantity**, number, total, aggregate, sum, quota, size, mass, weight, volume.
□ **amount to 1** add up to, come to, run to; *Brit.* tot up to. **2** constitute, comprise, be tantamount to.

ample *adjective* **1 enough**, sufficient, adequate, plenty of, more than enough, abundant, copious, profuse, lavish, liberal, generous; *informal* galore. **2 spacious**, full, capacious, roomy, voluminous, loose-fitting, baggy, sloppy.
– OPPOSITES insufficient.

amplify *verb* **1 make louder**, turn up, increase, raise. **2 expand**, enlarge on, elaborate on, develop, flesh out.

amuse *verb* **1 make someone laugh**, entertain, delight, divert, cheer (up),

please, charm, tickle; *Brit. informal* crack up, crease up. **2 occupy**, engage, busy, absorb, engross, entertain.
– OPPOSITES bore.

amusement *noun* **1 mirth**, merriment, hilarity, glee, delight. **2 entertainment**, pleasure, leisure, relaxation, fun, enjoyment, interest. **3 activity**, entertainment, diversion, pastime, recreation, game, sport.

amusing *adjective* **funny**, comical, humorous, light-hearted, jocular, witty, droll, entertaining, diverting.

analogy *noun* **similarity**, parallel, correspondence, likeness, resemblance, correlation, relation, comparison.
– OPPOSITES dissimilarity.

analyse *verb* **examine**, inspect, survey, study, scrutinize, investigate, probe, explore, evaluate, break down.

analysis *noun* **examination**, inspection, study, scrutiny, breakdown, investigation, exploration, evaluation.

analytical, analytic *adjective* **systematic**, logical, scientific, methodical, precise, meticulous, rigorous, investigative, enquiring.

anarchy *noun* **lawlessness**, disorder, chaos, pandemonium, mayhem, riot, revolution.
– OPPOSITES order.

anatomy *noun* **structure**, make-up, composition, constitution, form, body, physique.

ancestor *noun* **forefather**, forebear, predecessor, antecedent, progenitor, parent, grandparent.
– OPPOSITES descendant.

ancestry *noun* **ancestors**, forebears, forefathers, progenitors, antecedents, family tree, lineage, genealogy, parentage, blood.

ancient *adjective* **1** *ancient civilizations* **early**, prehistoric, primeval, primordial, primitive, bygone. **2** *an ancient custom* **old**, age-old, venerable, time-worn, time-honoured, archaic, antique, obsolete. **3** *I feel ancient* **antiquated**, antediluvian, geriatric; *informal* out of

the ark; *Brit. informal* past its/your sell-by date, superannuated.
- OPPOSITES contemporary, recent.

anecdote noun **story**, tale, urban myth, narrative, reminiscence; *informal* yarn.

angelic adjective **innocent**, pure, virtuous, saintly, cherubic, adorable.

anger noun **annoyance**, vexation, temper, indignation, rage, fury, wrath, outrage; *literary* ire.
● verb **annoy**, irk, vex, enrage, incense, infuriate, rile, provoke, outrage.
- OPPOSITES pacify, placate.

angle noun **1 gradient**, slope, slant, inclination. **2 corner**, point, fork, nook, crook, edge. **3 perspective**, point of view, viewpoint, standpoint, position, aspect, slant, direction, approach, tack.
● verb **tilt**, slant, twist, swivel, lean, tip, turn.

angry adjective **furious**, irate, vexed, wrathful, irked, enraged, incensed, seething, infuriated, in a temper, fuming, apoplectic, outraged, cross; *informal* (hopping) mad, up in arms, foaming at the mouth, steamed up, in a paddy; *Brit. informal* shirty; *N. Amer. informal* sore.
- OPPOSITES pleased.
□ **get angry** lose your temper, go berserk, flare up; *informal* hit the roof, go through the roof, go up the wall, see red, go off the deep end, fly off the handle, blow your top, blow a fuse/gasket, lose your rag, flip (your lid), have a fit, foam at the mouth, go ballistic; *Brit. informal* go spare, do your nut.

anguish noun **agony**, pain, torment, torture, suffering, distress, woe, misery, sorrow, heartache.
- OPPOSITES happiness.

animal noun **1 creature**, beast, (living) thing; (**animals**) wildlife, fauna. **2** *the man was an animal* **beast**, brute, monster, devil, fiend; *informal* swine, bastard, pig.

> **WORD LINKS**
> **zoological** relating to animals
> **zoology** study of animals

animate verb **enliven**, energize, invigorate, liven up, inspire, fire, rouse, stir, galvanize, stimulate, excite, move, revitalize, revive, rejuvenate.
● adjective **living**, alive, live, breathing, sentient.
- OPPOSITES inanimate.

animated adjective **lively**, spirited, energetic, full of life, excited, enthusiastic, eager, alive, vigorous, vibrant, vivacious, exuberant, ebullient, bouncy, bubbly, perky; *informal* bright-eyed and bushy-tailed, full of beans, bright and breezy, chirpy, chipper.
- OPPOSITES lethargic, lifeless.

animosity noun **hostility**, antipathy, antagonism, rancour, enmity, resentment, hatred, loathing, ill feeling/will, dislike, bad blood, animus.
- OPPOSITES goodwill, friendship.

annihilate verb **destroy**, obliterate, eradicate, wipe out, wipe off the face of the earth; *informal* rub out, snuff out.
- OPPOSITES create.

announce verb **make public**, make known, report, declare, state, give out, publicize, broadcast, publish, advertise, circulate, proclaim, release, disclose, divulge.

announcement noun **1 statement**, declaration, proclamation, pronouncement, bulletin, communiqué; *N. Amer.* advisory. **2 declaration**, notification, reporting, publishing, broadcasting, disclosure.

annoy verb **irritate**, bother, vex, make cross, exasperate, irk, anger, antagonize, nettle, rankle with; *Brit.* rub up the wrong way; *informal* aggravate, peeve, miff, rile, needle, get (to), bug, hack off, wind up; *Brit. informal* nark, get on someone's wick; *N. Amer. informal* tee off, tick off.
- OPPOSITES please.

annoyance noun **irritation**, exasperation, vexation, indignation, anger, displeasure, chagrin.

annoyed adjective **irritated**, cross, angry, vexed, exasperated, irked, piqued, displeased, put out, disgruntled, nettled; *informal* aggravated, peeved, miffed, riled, hacked off, hot under the collar, narked, shirty; *Brit. informal* not best pleased; *N. Amer. informal* teed off, ticked off, sore.

annoying *adjective* **irritating**, infuriating, exasperating, maddening, trying, tiresome, troublesome, irksome, vexing, galling; *informal* aggravating.

annual *adjective* **yearly**, once-a-year, year-long, twelve-month.

annually *adverb* **yearly**, once a year, each year, per annum.

annul *verb* **declare invalid**, declare null and void, nullify, invalidate, void, repeal, revoke.

anomaly *noun* **oddity**, peculiarity, abnormality, irregularity, inconsistency, aberration, quirk.

anonymous *adjective* **unnamed**, nameless, unidentified, unknown, incognito, unsigned.

answer *noun* **1 reply**, response, rejoinder, reaction, retort, riposte; *informal* comeback. **2 solution**, remedy, way out, explanation.
- OPPOSITES question.
● *verb* **reply**, respond, rejoin, retort, riposte.
□ **answer for** pay for, be punished for, suffer for, make amends for.

answerable *adjective* **accountable**, responsible, liable.

antagonistic *adjective* **hostile**, opposed, antipathetic, ill-disposed, resistant, in disagreement; *informal* anti.

antagonize *verb* **provoke**, intimidate, alienate, anger, annoy, irritate.
- OPPOSITES pacify.

anthem *noun* **hymn**, song, chorale, chant, psalm, canticle.

anthology *noun* **collection**, selection, compendium, compilation, miscellany, treasury.

anticipate *verb* **1 expect**, foresee, predict, be prepared for, bargain on, reckon on; *N. Amer. informal* figure on.

2 look forward to, await, long for, can't wait for.

anticipation *noun* **expectation**, expectancy, prediction, hope, excitement, suspense.

anticlimax *noun* **let-down**, disappointment, comedown, non-event, disillusionment, bathos; *Brit.* damp squib; *informal* washout.

antics *plural noun* **capers**, pranks, larks, high jinks, skylarking, horseplay, clowning; *Brit. informal* monkey tricks.

antidote *noun* **remedy**, cure, solution, countermeasure, corrective.

antipathy *noun* **hostility**, antagonism, animosity, aversion, animus, distaste, dislike, hatred, abhorrence, loathing.
- OPPOSITES affinity, liking.

antiquated *adjective* **outdated**, outmoded, outworn, behind the times, old, old-fashioned, anachronistic, antediluvian; *informal* out of the ark, superannuated, clunky.
- OPPOSITES modern.

antique *noun* **collector's item**, museum piece, period piece, antiquity.
● *adjective* **antiquarian**, old, collectable, vintage, classic.
- OPPOSITES modern.

antisocial *adjective* **1** *antisocial behaviour* **objectionable**, offensive, unacceptable, disruptive, rowdy. **2** *I'm feeling a bit antisocial* **unsociable**, unfriendly, uncommunicative, reclusive, misanthropic.
- OPPOSITES acceptable, sociable.

anxiety *noun* **worry**, concern, apprehension, unease, fear, disquiet, doubts, nervousness, nerves, tension, stress, angst; *informal* butterflies (in your stomach), the jitters, collywobbles.

anxious *adjective* **1 worried**, concerned, apprehensive, fearful, uneasy, disturbed, fretful, agitated, nervous, on edge, worked up, jumpy, tense, distraught; *informal* uptight, with butterflies in your stomach, jittery, twitchy; *N. Amer. informal* antsy. **2** *she was anxious for news* **eager**, keen,

itching, impatient, desperate.
- OPPOSITES unconcerned.

apart adverb
□ **apart from** except for, but for, aside from, with the exception of, excepting, excluding, bar, barring, besides, other than; informal outside of.

apartment noun **1** flat, suite, penthouse; Austral. home unit. **2 suite (of rooms)**, rooms, quarters, accommodation.

apathetic adjective **uninterested**, indifferent, unenthusiastic, unconcerned, unmoved, uninvolved, unemotional, lukewarm, half-hearted, unresponsive, lethargic; informal couldn't-care-less.
- OPPOSITES enthusiastic.

aperture noun **opening**, hole, gap, slit, slot, vent, crevice, chink, crack; technical orifice.

apologetic adjective **sorry**, regretful, contrite, remorseful, penitent, repentant.
- OPPOSITES unrepentant.

apologize verb **say sorry**, express regret, ask forgiveness, ask for pardon, eat humble pie.

apology noun **regrets**, expression of regret.
□ **apology for** travesty of, poor imitation of, poor substitute for, pale shadow of; informal excuse for.

appal verb **horrify**, shock, dismay, distress, outrage, scandalize, disgust, revolt, sicken, nauseate, offend, make someone's blood run cold.

appalling adjective **1** an appalling crime **horrific**, shocking, horrible, terrible, awful, dreadful, ghastly, hideous, horrendous, frightful, atrocious, abominable, outrageous. **2** your schoolwork is appalling **dreadful**, terrible, atrocious, deplorable, hopeless, lamentable; informal rotten, crummy, woeful, useless, lousy, abysmal, dire; Brit. informal chronic, shocking.

apparatus noun **equipment**, gear, kit, tackle, mechanism, appliance, device, instrument, machine, tool.

apparent adjective **1 evident**, plain, obvious, clear, manifest, visible, discernible, noticeable, perceptible, unmistakable, patent. **2 seeming**, ostensible, outward, superficial.
- OPPOSITES unclear, real.

appeal verb **ask**, request, call, petition, plead, entreat, beg, implore, beseech.
□ **appeal to** attract, interest, fascinate, please, tempt, lure, draw; informal float someone's boat.
● noun **1 plea**, request, petition, entreaty, cry, call, cri de coeur. **2 attraction**, allure, charm, fascination, magnetism, pull.

appealing adjective **attractive**, engaging, alluring, enchanting, captivating, bewitching, fascinating, tempting, enticing, irresistible, charming; Brit. informal tasty.

appear verb **1 become visible**, come into view, materialize, turn up, show up. **2** differences were beginning to appear **be revealed**, emerge, surface, manifest itself, become apparent/evident, come to light, arrive, arise, crop up, show up. **3** they appeared completely devoted **seem**, look, give the impression of being, come across as, strike someone as.
- OPPOSITES vanish.

appearance noun **1** her dishevelled appearance **look**, air, aspect, looks, mien, expression, behaviour. **2** an appearance of respectability **impression**, air, (outward) show, semblance, illusion, facade, front, pretence. **3 occurrence**, manifestation, emergence, arrival, development, materialization.

appease verb **placate**, conciliate, pacify, mollify, reconcile, win over; informal sweeten.
- OPPOSITES provoke.

appendix noun **supplement**, addendum, postscript, codicil, coda, epilogue, afterword, tailpiece.

appetite noun **1 hunger**, taste, palate, stomach. **2** my appetite for learning **desire**, liking, hunger, thirst, longing, yearning, passion, enthusiasm, keenness, eagerness; *informal* yen.

appetizing *adjective* **mouth-watering**, inviting, tempting, tasty, delicious, flavoursome, toothsome, delectable; *informal* scrumptious, scrummy, yummy, moreish.

applaud *verb* **1 clap**, give a standing ovation, put your hands together; *informal* give someone a big hand. **2 praise**, congratulate, commend, salute, welcome, celebrate, approve of.
- OPPOSITES boo, criticize.

appliance *noun* **device**, machine, instrument, gadget, tool, contraption, apparatus, mechanism, contrivance, labour-saving device; *informal* gizmo.

applicable *adjective* **relevant**, appropriate, pertinent, apposite, material, fitting, suitable, apt.
- OPPOSITES inappropriate, irrelevant.

applicant *noun* **candidate**, interviewee, contender, entrant, claimant, petitioner, prospective student/employee, job-seeker.

application *noun* **1 request**, appeal, petition, approach, claim, demand. **2 implementation**, use, exercise, employment, execution, enactment. **3 hard work**, diligence, industry, effort, commitment, dedication, devotion, perseverance, persistence, concentration.

apply *verb* **1** *300 people applied for the job* **put in**, bid, try, audition, seek, solicit, claim, request, ask, petition. **2** *the Act did not apply to Scotland* **be relevant**, pertain, appertain, relate, concern, affect, involve, cover, touch, deal with, have a bearing on. **3 implement**, put into practice, introduce. **4 put on**, rub in/on, work in, spread, smear on, slap on. **5 exert**, administer, use, exercise, employ, utilize, bring to bear.
□ **apply yourself** work hard, exert yourself, make an effort, be industrious, show dedication, buckle down, persevere, persist, concentrate; *informal* put your back into it, knuckle down, get stuck in.

appoint *verb* **nominate**, name, designate, install, commission, engage, co-opt, select, choose, elect, vote in.

appointed *adjective* **1 scheduled**, arranged, prearranged, specified, agreed, designated, set, allotted, fixed. **2 furnished**, decorated, fitted out, supplied.

appointment *noun* **1 meeting**, engagement, interview, consultation, rendezvous, date, assignation; *literary* tryst. **2 nomination**, naming, designation, installation, commissioning, engagement, co-option, selection, election. **3 job**, post, position, situation, place, office.

appraisal *noun* **assessment**, evaluation, estimation, judgement, summing-up, consideration.

appreciate *verb* **1 value**, admire, respect, think highly of, think much of, be grateful for, be glad of. **2 recognize**, realize, know, be aware of, be conscious of, be sensitive to, understand, sympathize with. **3 increase**, gain, grow, rise, go up, soar.
- OPPOSITES disparage, depreciate.

appreciation *noun* **1 knowledge**, awareness, enjoyment, love, feeling, discrimination, sensitivity. **2 gratitude**, thanks, gratefulness. **3 acknowledgement**, recognition, realization, knowledge, awareness, consciousness, understanding. **4 review**, critique, criticism, analysis, assessment, evaluation, judgement; *Brit. informal* crit. **5 increase**, gain, growth, rise, inflation, escalation.
- OPPOSITES ingratitude, depreciation.

appreciative *adjective* **1** *we are appreciative of your support* **grateful**, thankful, obliged, indebted. **2** *an appreciative audience* **admiring**, enthusiastic, approving, complimentary.

apprehension *noun* **1 anxiety**, worry, unease, nervousness, nerves, misgivings, disquiet, concern, trepidation. **2 arrest**, capture, seizure, detention.
- OPPOSITES confidence.

apprehensive *adjective* **anxious**, worried, uneasy, nervous, concerned, fearful.
- OPPOSITES confident.

apprentice *noun* **trainee**, learner, probationer, novice, beginner, tyro, starter, pupil, student; *informal* rookie; *N. Amer. informal* tenderfoot, greenhorn.
- OPPOSITES veteran.

approach *verb* **1 move towards**, near, come near, close in on, close with, gain on. **2 speak to**, talk to, sound out, make a proposal to, proposition, appeal to. **3 tackle**, address, manage, set about, go about, start work on.
- OPPOSITES leave.
  ● *noun* **1 method**, procedure, technique, modus operandi, style, way, strategy, tactic, system, means, line of action. **2 proposal**, submission, application, appeal, plea, request, overture, proposition. **3 advance**, arrival, appearance. **4 driveway**, drive, road, path, entry, way.

approachable *adjective* **1 friendly**, welcoming, pleasant, agreeable, affable, sympathetic, congenial. **2 accessible**, reachable, attainable; *informal* get-at-able.
- OPPOSITES aloof, inaccessible.

appropriate *adjective* **suitable**, proper, fitting, seemly, apt, right, convenient, opportune, relevant, apposite.
- OPPOSITES inappropriate.
  ● *verb* **seize**, commandeer, requisition, expropriate, usurp, take over, hijack, steal; *informal* swipe, nab; *Brit. informal* pinch, nick.

approval *noun* **1 acceptance**, agreement, consent, assent, permission, rubber stamp, sanction, blessing, endorsement, ratification, authorization; *informal* the go-ahead, the green light, the OK, the thumbs up. **2 favour**, liking, appreciation, admiration, regard, esteem, respect.
- OPPOSITES refusal, disapproval.

approve *verb* **agree to**, accept, consent to, assent to, give your blessing to, bless, ratify, sanction, endorse, authorize, validate, pass, rubber-stamp; *informal* give the go-ahead to, give the green light to, give the OK to, give the thumbs-up to.
- OPPOSITES refuse.
  □ **approve of** agree with, hold with, endorse, support, be in favour of, favour, think well of, like, take kindly to, admire.

approximate *adjective* **estimated**, rough, imprecise, inexact, broad, loose; *N. Amer. informal* ballpark.
- OPPOSITES precise.
  □ **approximate to** roughly equal, come near/close to, approach, border on, verge on, resemble, be similar to.

approximately *adverb* **roughly**, about, around, circa, round about, more or less, nearly, almost, approaching; *Brit.* getting on for; *informal* pushing; *N. Amer. informal* in the ballpark of.

apt *adjective* **1 suitable**, fitting, appropriate, relevant, apposite, felicitous; *Brit. informal* spot on. **2 inclined**, given, likely, liable, prone. **3 clever**, quick, bright, sharp, smart, able, gifted, talented; *informal* genius.
- OPPOSITES inappropriate.

aptitude *noun* **talent**, gift, flair, bent, skill, knack, facility, ability, capability, potential, capacity, faculty.

arbitrary *adjective* **random**, unpredictable, capricious, subjective, whimsical, wanton, motiveless, irrational, groundless, unjustified.

arbitration *noun* **adjudication**, judgement, mediation, conciliation, intervention.

arbitrator *noun* **adjudicator**, arbiter, judge, referee, umpire, mediator, go-between.

arc *noun* **curve**, arch, bow, curl, crescent, semicircle, half-moon.

arch *noun* **archway**, vault, span.
  ● *verb* **curve**, arc, bend, bow, crook, hunch.

architect *noun* **designer**, planner, originator, author, creator, founder, inventor.

architecture noun **building**, planning, design, construction.

archive noun **1** *the family archives* **records**, papers, documents, files, annals, chronicles, history. **2** *the National Sound Archive* **record office**, registry, repository, museum, library. ● verb **file**, log, catalogue, document, record, register, store.

ardent adjective **passionate**, fervent, zealous, wholehearted, intense, fierce, enthusiastic, keen, eager, avid, committed, dedicated.
- OPPOSITES apathetic.

arduous adjective **tough**, difficult, hard, heavy, laborious, onerous, taxing, strenuous, back-breaking, demanding, challenging, punishing, gruelling; *informal* killing; *Brit. informal* knackering.
- OPPOSITES easy.

area noun **1** **district**, zone, region, sector, quarter, locality, neighbourhood; *informal* neck of the woods; *Brit. informal* manor; *N. Amer. informal* turf. **2** *the dining area* **space**, section, part, place, room, footprint. **3** *specific areas of knowledge* **field**, sphere, realm, domain, sector, province, territory.

arena noun **1** **stadium**, amphitheatre, ground, field, ring, rink, pitch, court; *N. Amer.* bowl, park. **2** **scene**, sphere, realm, province, domain, forum, territory, world.

argue verb **1** **claim**, maintain, insist, contend, assert, hold, reason, allege. **2** **quarrel**, disagree, dispute, row, squabble, bicker, have words, cross swords, fight, wrangle.

argument noun **1** **quarrel**, disagreement, difference of opinion, squabble, dispute, altercation, fight, wrangle; *Brit.* row; *informal* slanging match, tiff, set-to; *Brit. informal* barney. **2** **reasoning**, justification, explanation, case, defence, vindication, evidence, reasons, grounds.

arid adjective **dry**, waterless, parched, scorched, desiccated, desert, barren, infertile.
- OPPOSITES wet, fertile.

arise verb **1** *many problems arose* **come about**, happen, occur, come into being, emerge, crop up, come to light, become apparent, appear, turn up, surface, spring up. **2** *injuries arising from defective products* **result**, stem, originate, proceed, follow, ensue, be caused by.

aristocrat noun **nobleman**, noblewoman, lord, lady, peer (of the realm), patrician; *informal* aristo; *Brit. informal* toff, nob.
- OPPOSITES commoner.

aristocratic adjective **noble**, titled, upper-class, blue-blooded, high-born, patrician; *informal* upper crust, top drawer; *Brit. informal* posh.
- OPPOSITES common.

arm verb **equip**, provide, supply, furnish, issue, fit out.

armaments plural noun **arms**, weapons, weaponry, firearms, guns, ordnance, artillery, munitions, materiel.

armistice noun **truce**, ceasefire, peace, suspension of hostilities.

armoured adjective **armour-plated**, steel-plated, ironclad, bulletproof, bombproof, reinforced, toughened.

arms plural noun **weapons**, weaponry, firearms, guns, ordnance, artillery, armaments, munitions.

army noun **1** **armed force**, military force, land force(s), military, soldiery, infantry, militia, troops, soldiers. **2** *an army of tourists* **crowd**, swarm, horde, mob, gang, throng, mass, flock, herd, pack.

> **WORD LINKS**
> **military**, **martial** relating to armies

aroma noun **smell**, odour, fragrance, scent, perfume, bouquet, nose.

aromatic adjective **fragrant**, scented, perfumed, fragranced.

around preposition **1** **surrounding**, enclosing, on all sides of. **2** **approximately**, about, round about, circa, roughly, more or less, nearly, almost,

a

approaching; *Brit.* getting on for; *N. Amer. informal* in the ballpark of.

arouse *verb* **1 provoke**, trigger, stir up, engender, cause, whip up, rouse, inflame, agitate, incite, galvanize, electrify, stimulate, inspire, fire up. **2 wake (up)**, awaken, bring to/round, rouse.
- OPPOSITES allay.

arrange *verb* **1 set out**, (put in) order, lay out, align, position, present, display, exhibit, group, sort, organize, tidy. **2 organize**, fix (up), plan, schedule, contrive, determine, agree. **3** *he arranged the piece for a full orchestra* **adapt**, set, score, orchestrate.

arrangement *noun* **1 positioning**, presentation, grouping, organization, alignment. **2 preparation**, plan, provision, planning. **3 agreement**, deal, understanding, bargain, settlement, pact. **4** *an arrangement of Beethoven's symphonies* **adaptation**, orchestration, scoring, interpretation.

array *noun* **range**, collection, selection, assortment, variety, arrangement, line-up, display, exhibition.
● *verb* **arrange**, assemble, group, order, range, place, position, set out, lay out, spread out, display, exhibit.

arrest *verb* **1 detain**, apprehend, seize, capture, take into custody; *informal* pick up, pull in, collar; *Brit. informal* nick. **2 stop**, halt, check, block, curb, prevent, obstruct, stem, slow, interrupt, delay.
- OPPOSITES release.
● *noun* **detention**, apprehension, seizure, capture.

arresting *adjective* **striking**, eye-catching, conspicuous, impressive, imposing, spectacular, dramatic, breathtaking, stunning, awe-inspiring.
- OPPOSITES inconspicuous.

arrival *noun* **coming**, appearance, entrance, entry, approach, advent.
- OPPOSITES departure.

arrive *verb* **come**, turn up, get here/there, make it, appear; *informal* show (up), roll in/up, blow in.
- OPPOSITES depart, leave.

arrogant *adjective* **haughty**, conceited, self-important, cocky, supercilious, condescending, full of yourself, overbearing, imperious, proud; *informal* high and mighty, too big for your boots.
- OPPOSITES modest.

art *noun* **1 fine art**, design, artwork, aesthetics. **2 skill**, craft, technique, knack, facility, aptitude, talent, flair, mastery, expertise.

article *noun* **1 object**, thing, item, piece, artefact, device, implement. **2 report**, account, story, essay, feature, item, piece (of writing), column. **3 clause**, section, paragraph, point, item.

articulate *adjective* **eloquent**, fluent, effective, persuasive, lucid, expressive, silver-tongued, clear, coherent.
- OPPOSITES unintelligible.
● *verb* **express**, voice, vocalize, put in words, communicate, state.

artificial *adjective* **1 synthetic**, fake, imitation, mock, ersatz, man-made, manufactured, plastic, simulated, faux; *informal* pretend. **2 insincere**, feigned, false, unnatural, contrived, put-on, forced, laboured, hollow; *informal* pretend, phoney.
- OPPOSITES natural, genuine.

artistic *adjective* **1 creative**, imaginative, inventive, sensitive, perceptive, discerning. **2 attractive**, aesthetic, beautiful, stylish, ornamental, decorative, graceful, subtle, expressive.

ascent *noun* **1** *the ascent of the Matterhorn* **climbing**, scaling, conquest. **2** *the ascent grew steeper* **slope**, incline, gradient, hill, climb.
- OPPOSITES descent, drop.

ascertain *verb* **find out**, discover, get to know, work out, make out, fathom (out), learn, deduce, divine, establish, determine; *informal* figure out.

ashamed *adjective* **1 sorry**, shamefaced, sheepish, guilty, contrite, remorseful, regretful, apologetic, mortified, red-faced, repentant, penitent, rueful, chagrined. **2 reluctant**, loath, unwilling, afraid, embarrassed.
- OPPOSITES proud.

ask verb **1 enquire**, want to know, question, interrogate, quiz. **2** *they'll ask a few questions* **put (forward)**, pose, raise, submit. **3 request**, demand, seek, solicit, apply, petition, call, appeal.
- OPPOSITES answer.

asleep adjective **sleeping**, napping, dozing, drowsing; *informal* snoozing, dead to the world; *humorous* in the land of Nod.
- OPPOSITES awake.

aspect noun **1 feature**, facet, side, characteristic, particular, detail. **2 point of view**, position, standpoint, viewpoint, perspective, angle, slant. **3** *his face had a sinister aspect* **appearance**, look, air, mien, demeanour, expression.

aspiration noun **desire**, hope, dream, wish, longing, yearning, aim, ambition, expectation, goal, target.

aspire verb
□ **aspire to** desire, aim for, hope for, dream of, long for, yearn for, set your heart on, wish for, want, seek, set your sights on.

aspiring adjective **would-be**, hopeful, budding, potential, prospective; *informal* wannabe.

assassin noun **murderer**, killer, gunman, executioner; *informal* hit man.

assassinate verb **murder**, kill, eliminate, liquidate, execute; *N. Amer.* terminate; *informal* hit.

assault verb **attack**, hit, strike, beat up; *informal* lay into, rough up, do over.
● noun **1 violence**, battery; *Brit.* grievous bodily harm, GBH, actual bodily harm, ABH. **2 attack**, strike, onslaught, offensive, charge, push, thrust, raid.

assemble verb **1 gather**, collect, get together, congregate, convene, meet, muster, rally, round up, marshal. **2 construct**, build, erect, set up, make, manufacture, fabricate, put together, connect.
- OPPOSITES disperse, dismantle.

assembly noun **1 gathering**, meeting, congregation, convention, council, rally, group, crowd; *informal* get-together. **2 construction**, manufacture, building, fabrication, erection.

assert verb **1 declare**, state, maintain, contend, argue, claim, insist. **2** *you should assert your rights* **insist on**, stand up for, uphold, defend, press/push for.

assertion noun **declaration**, contention, statement, claim, opinion, protestation.

assertive adjective **confident**, self-confident, bold, decisive, forceful, insistent, emphatic, determined, strong-willed, commanding, pushy; *informal* feisty.
- OPPOSITES timid.

assess verb **evaluate**, judge, gauge, rate, estimate, appraise, weigh up, calculate, value, work out, determine; *informal* size up.

asset noun **1 benefit**, advantage, blessing, good/strong point, strength, forte, virtue, recommendation, attraction, resource. **2** *the seizure of all their assets* **property**, resources, estate, holdings, funds, valuables, possessions, effects, belongings.
- OPPOSITES liability.

assign verb **1 allocate**, give, set, charge with, entrust with. **2 appoint**, promote, delegate, nominate, commission, post, co-opt; *Military* detail. **3 earmark**, designate, set aside, reserve, appropriate, allot, allocate.

assignation noun **rendezvous**, date, appointment, meeting; *literary* tryst.

assignment noun **task**, job, duty, responsibility, mission, errand, undertaking, commission.

assist verb **1 help**, aid, lend a (helping) hand to, support, back (up), work with, cooperate with. **2** *the aim was to assist cashflow* **facilitate**, aid, ease, promote, boost, speed, benefit, encourage, further.
- OPPOSITES hinder.

assistance noun **help**, aid, a (helping) hand, support, backing, reinforcement.
- OPPOSITES hindrance.

assistant noun **helper**, aide, deputy, lieutenant, second (in command), number two, right-hand man/woman, PA, auxiliary, attendant, henchman; informal sidekick, gofer; Brit. informal dogsbody, skivvy.

associate verb **1 link**, connect, relate, bracket, identify, equate. **2 mix**, keep company, mingle, socialize, go around, have dealings; informal hobnob, hang out/around/round.
- OPPOSITES avoid.
● noun **partner**, colleague, co-worker, workmate, collaborator, comrade, ally; informal crony.

associated adjective **related**, connected, linked, similar, corresponding, attendant, accompanying, incidental.
- OPPOSITES unrelated.

association noun **1 alliance**, consortium, coalition, union, league, guild, syndicate, federation, confederation, cartel, cooperative, partnership. **2 relationship**, relation, interrelation, connection, interconnection, interdependence, link, bond.

assorted adjective **various**, miscellaneous, mixed, varied, diverse, different, sundry.
- OPPOSITES uniform.

assortment noun **variety**, mixture, array, mix, miscellany, selection, medley, melange, ragbag, potpourri.

assume verb **1 presume**, suppose, take it (as given), take for granted, take as read, conclude, infer, think, fancy, imagine, surmise, believe, understand, gather, suspect; N. Amer. figure. **2 affect**, adopt, put on. **3 accept**, shoulder, bear, undertake, take on/up. **4 seize**, take (over), appropriate, wrest, usurp.

assumed adjective **false**, fictitious, fake, bogus, invented, made-up; informal pretend, phoney.
- OPPOSITES genuine.

assumption noun **supposition**, presumption, inference, conjecture, belief, surmise, hypothesis, theory, suspicion, guess.

assurance noun **1 promise**, word (of honour), pledge, vow, oath, undertaking, guarantee, commitment. **2 confidence**, self-confidence, self-assurance, self-possession, nerve, poise; informal cool. **3 insurance**, indemnity, protection, security, cover.

assure verb **1 reassure**, convince, satisfy, persuade. **2 promise**, guarantee, swear, confirm, certify, vow, give your word. **3 ensure**, secure, guarantee, seal, clinch; informal sew up.

assured adjective **1 confident**, self-confident, self-assured, self-possessed, poised, composed, imperturbable, unruffled; informal unflappable, together. **2 guaranteed**, certain, sure, secure, reliable, dependable; informal sure-fire.
- OPPOSITES nervous, uncertain.

astonish verb **amaze**, astound, stagger, startle, stun, surprise, confound, dumbfound, nonplus, take aback, leave open-mouthed; informal flabbergast, bowl over; Brit. informal knock for six.

astonishing adjective **amazing**, astounding, staggering, surprising, breathtaking, remarkable, extraordinary, incredible, unbelievable, phenomenal; informal mind-boggling.
- OPPOSITES unremarkable.

astound verb **amaze**, astonish, stagger, surprise, startle, stun, confound, dumbfound, take aback, leave open-mouthed; informal flabbergast, bowl over; Brit. informal knock for six.

astounding adjective **amazing**, astonishing, staggering, surprising, breathtaking, remarkable, extraordinary, incredible, unbelievable, phenomenal; informal mind-boggling.
- OPPOSITES unremarkable.

astute adjective **shrewd**, sharp, acute, quick, clever, intelligent, bright, smart, canny, perceptive, perspicacious; informal quick on the uptake.
- OPPOSITES stupid.

asylum noun **refuge**, sanctuary, shelter, protection, immunity, a safe haven.

athletic adjective **muscular**, fit, strapping, well built, strong, sturdy, powerful, brawny, burly.

atmosphere noun **1 air**, sky; literary the heavens, the ether. **2** a relaxed atmosphere **ambience**, spirit, air, mood, feel, feeling, character, tone, aura, quality, environment, climate; informal vibe.

> **WORD LINKS**
> **meteorology** study of the atmosphere

atrocious adjective **1 wicked**, cruel, brutal, barbaric, vicious, monstrous, vile, inhuman, fiendish. **2 appalling**, awful, dreadful, terrible, miserable; informal abysmal, dire, rotten, lousy; Brit. informal shocking.
- OPPOSITES admirable, superb.

atrocity noun **1** a number of atrocities **outrage**, horror, violation, abuse, crime. **2** scenes of hardship and atrocity **wickedness**, cruelty, brutality, barbarity, viciousness, savagery, inhumanity.

attach verb **1 fasten**, fix, affix, join, secure, stick, connect, tie, link, couple, pin, hitch. **2** they attach importance to research **ascribe**, assign, attribute, accredit, impute. **3** the medical officer attached to HQ **assign**, appoint, allocate, second.
- OPPOSITES detach.

attached adjective
□ **attached to** fond of, devoted to, keen on; informal mad about, crazy about.

attachment noun **1 bond**, closeness, devotion, loyalty, fondness for, love for, affection for, feeling for, sympathy for. **2 accessory**, fitting, extension, add-on.

attack verb **1 assault**, beat up, set upon, mug, charge, pounce on, raid, rush, storm; informal lay into, do over, work over, rough up; Brit. informal duff up. **2 criticize**, censure, condemn, denounce, revile, vilify, impugn, disparage; informal knock, slam, lay into; Brit. informal slate, slag off, rubbish.
- OPPOSITES defend, praise.
● noun **1 assault**, onslaught, offensive,

strike, blitz, raid, incursion, sortie, foray, charge, invasion. **2 criticism**, censure, condemnation, vilification, disparagement; Brit. informal slating. **3 fit**, seizure, spasm, convulsion, paroxysm, bout, episode.
- OPPOSITES defence, praise.

attacker noun **assailant**, assaulter, mugger, aggressor, raider, invader.
- OPPOSITES victim.

attain verb **achieve**, accomplish, reach, obtain, gain, secure, get, win, earn, realize, fulfil; informal clinch, bag, wrap up.

attempt verb **try**, strive, aim, venture, endeavour, seek, have a go, bid.
● noun **try**, effort, endeavour, venture, bid, go; informal crack, shot, stab.

attend verb **1 be present at**, sit in on, take part in, appear at, turn up at, visit, go to; informal show up at. **2 pay attention**, listen, be attentive, concentrate.
□ **attend to 1** deal with, see to, look after, manage, organize, sort out, handle, take care of, tackle. **2** care for, look after, minister to, see to, tend, treat, help.

attendance noun **1 presence**, appearance, attention. **2 audience**, turnout, house, gate, crowd.
- OPPOSITES absence.

attendant noun **assistant**, aide, companion, escort, steward, equerry, servant, retainer, valet, maid.
● adjective **accompanying**, associated, concomitant, related, connected, resulting, consequent.

attention noun **1 consideration**, contemplation, deliberation, thought, study, observation, mind, investigation, action. **2 awareness**, notice, scrutiny, eye, gaze. **3** medical attention **care**, ministrations, treatment, therapy, relief, aid, assistance.

attentive adjective **1** an attentive pupil **alert**, perceptive, observant, acute, aware, heedful, focused, studious, diligent, conscientious, earnest. **2** the most attentive of husbands **considerate**, conscientious, thoughtful, kind, caring,

solicitous, understanding, sympathetic.
- OPPOSITES inattentive.

attic noun **loft**, roof space, garret.

attitude noun **1 view**, viewpoint, outlook, perspective, stance, standpoint, position, frame of mind, approach, opinion. **2** *an attitude of prayer* **posture**, position, pose, stance.

attract verb **1 appeal to**, fascinate, charm, captivate, interest, tempt, entice, lure, bewitch, beguile, seduce. **2 draw**, pull, magnetize.
- OPPOSITES repel.

attraction noun **1 appeal**, attractiveness, pull, desirability, fascination, allure, charisma, charm. **2** *the town's main attractions* **entertainment**, activity, diversion, amenity, service. **3** *magnetic attraction* **pull**, draw, force.
- OPPOSITES repulsion.

attractive adjective **1 good-looking**, beautiful, pretty, handsome, lovely, stunning, striking, desirable, gorgeous, prepossessing, fetching; *Scottish & N. English* bonny; *informal* drop-dead gorgeous, hunky; *Brit. informal* fit; *N. Amer. informal* cute; *old use* comely. **2 appealing**, inviting, tempting, pleasing, interesting.
- OPPOSITES unattractive, ugly.

attribute verb **ascribe**, assign, accredit, credit, put down, chalk up, pin on.
● noun **quality**, characteristic, trait, feature, element, aspect, property, sign, hallmark, mark.

audible adjective **perceptible**, discernible, detectable, distinct, clear.
- OPPOSITES inaudible, faint.

audience noun **1 spectators**, listeners, viewers, onlookers, concertgoers, theatregoers, crowd, public, throng, gallery, congregation, turnout. **2 meeting**, interview, consultation, conference, hearing, reception.

augment verb **increase**, add to, supplement, enhance, build up, raise, boost, up, hike up, enlarge, swell, expand, extend.
- OPPOSITES decrease, reduce.

august adjective **distinguished**, respected, eminent, venerable, illustrious, prestigious, renowned, celebrated, honoured, acclaimed, esteemed.

aura noun **atmosphere**, ambience, air, quality, character, mood, feeling; *informal* vibe.

auspicious adjective **favourable**, promising, encouraging, fortunate, opportune, timely, advantageous, good.
- OPPOSITES inauspicious, unfavourable.

austere adjective **1 severe**, stern, strict, harsh, dour, grim, cold, frosty, unfriendly. **2 spartan**, frugal, ascetic, puritanical, abstemious, strict, simple, hard. **3** *an austere building* **plain**, simple, basic, functional, unadorned, bleak, bare, clinical.
- OPPOSITES easy-going, ornate.

authentic adjective **1 genuine**, real, bona fide, true, legitimate; *informal* pukka, kosher; *Austral./NZ informal* dinkum. **2 accurate**, factual, true, truthful, reliable, trustworthy, honest, faithful.
- OPPOSITES fake, unreliable.

authenticate verb **verify**, validate, prove, substantiate, corroborate, confirm, support, back up.
- OPPOSITES disprove.

author noun **1 writer**, novelist, poet, playwright, dramatist, columnist, reporter, wordsmith; *informal* scribe, scribbler. **2 creator**, originator, founder, father, architect, designer, producer.

authoritarian adjective **strict**, autocratic, dictatorial, despotic, tyrannical, domineering, imperious, illiberal, undemocratic; *informal* bossy.
- OPPOSITES democratic, liberal.
● noun **disciplinarian**, autocrat, dictator, despot, tyrant.
- OPPOSITES democrat, liberal.

authoritative adjective **1 reliable**, dependable, trustworthy, accurate, authentic, valid, definitive, classic. **2 commanding**, masterful, assertive, self-assured, self-confident.
- OPPOSITES unreliable.

authority noun **1** *a rebellion against those in authority* **power**, command, control, charge, dominance, jurisdiction, rule; *informal* clout. **2** *the authority to arrest drug traffickers* **right**, authorization, power, mandate, prerogative, licence. **3** *they need parliamentary authority* **permission**, authorization, consent, sanction, assent, agreement, approval, clearance; *informal* the go-ahead. **4** (**the authorities**) **officials**, officialdom, government, administration, establishment, police; *informal* the powers that be. **5 expert**, specialist, professional, master, connoisseur, pundit, doyen(ne), guru.

authorize verb **1** *they authorized further action* **permit**, sanction, allow, approve, consent to, assent to; *informal* give the go-ahead to, OK. **2** *the troops were authorized to fire* **empower**, give authority, mandate, commission, entitle.
- OPPOSITES forbid.

authorized adjective **approved**, sanctioned, accredited, recognized, licensed, certified, official, legal, legitimate.
- OPPOSITES unauthorized, unofficial.

automatic adjective **1 mechanized**, powered, mechanical, automated, computerized, electronic, robotic. **2 instinctive**, involuntary, unconscious, reflex, knee-jerk, subconscious, spontaneous, impulsive, unthinking, mechanical; *informal* gut. **3 inevitable**, unavoidable, inescapable, certain.
- OPPOSITES manual, conscious, deliberate.

autonomous adjective **self-governing**, independent, sovereign, free.
- OPPOSITES dependent.

autonomy noun **self-government**, self-rule, home rule, self-determination, independence, sovereignty, freedom.
- OPPOSITES dependence.

auxiliary adjective **additional**, supplementary, extra, reserve, backup, emergency, fallback, second.

available adjective **obtainable**, accessible, to/at hand, to be had, on sale, untaken, unsold, free, vacant, unoccupied; *informal* up for grabs, on tap.

avalanche noun *an avalanche of enquiries* **barrage**, flood, deluge, torrent, wave, onslaught.

avant-garde adjective **experimental**, modern, cutting-edge, progressive, unorthodox, unconventional; *informal* edgy, offbeat, way-out.
- OPPOSITES conservative, traditional.

avarice noun **greed**, acquisitiveness, covetousness, materialism.
- OPPOSITES generosity.

average noun **mean**, median, mode, norm, standard, rule, par.
● adjective **1** *the average temperature* **mean**, median. **2** *a woman of average height* **normal**, standard, typical, ordinary, common, regular.
- OPPOSITES abnormal, unusual.
□ **on average** normally, usually, ordinarily, generally, typically, for the most part, as a rule, by and large, overall, on the whole.

averse adjective **opposed**, hostile, antagonistic, resistant, disinclined, reluctant, loath; *informal* anti.
- OPPOSITES keen.

aversion noun **dislike**, hatred, loathing, abhorrence, distaste, antipathy, hostility, reluctance, disinclination.
- OPPOSITES liking.

avert verb **1 turn aside**, turn away, shift, redirect. **2 prevent**, avoid, stave off, ward off, head off, forestall.

avid adjective **keen**, eager, enthusiastic, ardent, passionate, zealous, devoted.
- OPPOSITES apathetic.

avoid verb **1 keep away from**, steer clear of, give a wide berth to. **2 evade**, dodge, sidestep, escape, run away from; *informal* duck, wriggle out of, get out of. **3** *book early to avoid disappointment* **prevent**, preclude, stave off, forestall, head off, ward off. **4** *avoid alcohol* **refrain from**, abstain from, desist from, steer clear of, eschew.
- OPPOSITES confront, face.

await verb **1 wait for**, expect, look forward to, anticipate. **2 be in store for**, lie ahead of, be waiting for, be round the corner.

awake verb **wake up**, wake, awaken, waken, stir, come to, come round, rouse, call.
● adjective **1 sleepless**, wide awake, restless, insomniac. **2** too few are awake to the dangers **aware of**, conscious of, mindful of, alert to.
- OPPOSITES asleep, oblivious.

awaken verb **1** see **awake** (verb).
2 arouse, kindle, bring out, trigger, stir up, stimulate, revive.

award verb **give**, grant, accord, confer on, bestow on, present to, decorate with.
● noun **1 prize**, trophy, medal, decoration, reward; informal gong. **2 grant**, scholarship, endowment; Brit. bursary.

aware adjective **1** she is aware of the dangers **conscious of**, mindful of, informed about, acquainted with, familiar with, alive to, alert to; informal wise to, in the know about. **2** environmentally aware **sensitive**, enlightened, knowledgeable, (well) informed; informal clued up; Brit. informal switched-on.
- OPPOSITES ignorant.

awareness noun **consciousness**, recognition, realization, perception, understanding, grasp, appreciation, knowledge, familiarity.

away adverb **elsewhere**, abroad, gone, off, out, absent, on holiday, on vacation.

awe noun **wonder**, wonderment, admiration, reverence, respect, fear, dread.

awesome adjective **breathtaking**, awe-inspiring, magnificent, amazing, stunning, staggering, imposing, formidable, intimidating; informal mind-boggling, mind-blowing, brilliant.
- OPPOSITES unimpressive.

awful adjective **1** the place smells awful **disgusting**, terrible, dreadful, ghastly, horrible, vile, foul, revolting, repulsive, repugnant, sickening, nauseating; informal gross; Brit. informal beastly. **2** an awful book **dreadful**, terrible, frightful, atrocious, lamentable; informal

crummy, pathetic, rotten, woeful, lousy, appalling, abysmal, dismal, dire; Brit. informal rubbish. **3** I feel awful **ill**, unwell, sick, nauseous, off colour, poorly; Brit. informal grotty, ropy; Austral./NZ informal crook.
- OPPOSITES delightful, excellent, well.

awfully adverb **1** (informal) an awfully nice man **very**, extremely, really, immensely, exceedingly, thoroughly, dreadfully, terrifically, terribly, exceptionally, remarkably, extraordinarily; N. English right; informal seriously; Brit. informal jolly, dead, well; N. Amer. informal real, mighty; informal, dated frightfully. **2** we played awfully **terribly**, dreadfully, atrociously, appallingly; informal abysmally, diabolically.

awkward adjective **1 difficult**, tricky, cumbersome, unwieldy; Brit. informal fiddly. **2 unreasonable**, uncooperative, unhelpful, difficult, obstructive, contrary, perverse, obstinate, stubborn; Brit. informal bloody-minded, bolshie; N. Amer. informal balky. **3** an awkward time **inconvenient**, inappropriate, inopportune, difficult. **4** he put her in an awkward position **embarrassing**, uncomfortable, unenviable, delicate, tricky, problematic, troublesome, humiliating, compromising; informal sticky. **5** she felt awkward **uncomfortable**, uneasy, tense, nervous, edgy, self-conscious, embarrassed. **6** his awkward movements **clumsy**, ungainly, uncoordinated, graceless, inelegant, gauche, gawky, stiff, unskilful, inept, blundering; informal ham-fisted, cack-handed; Brit. informal all (fingers and) thumbs.
- OPPOSITES easy, amenable, convenient, graceful.

axe noun **hatchet**, chopper, cleaver; historical battleaxe.
● verb **1 cancel**, withdraw, drop, scrap, cut, discontinue, end; informal ditch, dump, pull the plug on. **2 dismiss**, make redundant, lay off, get rid of; informal sack, fire.

axle noun **shaft**, spindle, rod.

Bb

babble *verb* **prattle**, rattle on, gabble, chatter, jabber, twitter, burble, blather; *informal* yatter, blabber, jaw, gas, shoot your mouth off; *Brit. informal* witter, rabbit, chunter, natter, waffle.

baby *noun* **infant**, newborn, child; *Scottish & N. English* bairn; *technical* neonate; *informal* sprog, tot, bundle of joy; *literary* babe.
● *adjective* **miniature**, mini, little, toy, pocket, fun-size, midget, dwarf; *Scottish* wee; *N. Amer.* vest-pocket; *informal* teeny, teensy, tiddly, bite-sized; *Brit. informal* titchy.

babyish *adjective* **childish**, infantile, juvenile, puerile, immature.
- OPPOSITES mature.

back *noun* **1 spine**, backbone, spinal column, vertebral column. **2 rear**, end, rear end, tail end; *Nautical* stern. **3 reverse**, other side, underside; *informal* flip side.
- OPPOSITES front.
● *verb* **1 sponsor**, finance, fund, subsidize, underwrite; *informal* pick up the bill for. **2 support**, endorse, sanction, approve of, give your blessing to, smile on, favour, advocate, promote, champion; *informal* throw your weight behind. **3 bet on**, gamble on, stake money on. **4 reverse**, draw back, step back, pull back, retreat, withdraw.
- OPPOSITES oppose, advance.
● *adjective* **1 rear**, rearmost, hind, hindmost, posterior. **2 past**, old, previous, earlier.
- OPPOSITES front, future.
□ **back down** give in, concede defeat, surrender, yield, submit, climb down. **back out of** renege on, withdraw from, pull out of, fail to honour. **back up 1** substantiate, corroborate, confirm, support, bear out, endorse, lend weight to. **2** support, stand by, side with, take someone's part.

> **WORD LINKS**
> **dorsal**, **lumbar** relating to the back
> **supine** lying on your back

backbone *noun* **1 spine**, spinal column, vertebral column, vertebrae. **2 mainstay**, cornerstone, foundation. **3 strength of character**, strength of will, firmness, resolution, resolve, grit, determination, fortitude, mettle, spirit.

backer *noun* **1 sponsor**, investor, underwriter, financier, patron, benefactor; *informal* angel. **2 supporter**, defender, advocate, promoter; *N. Amer.* booster.

backfire *verb* **rebound**, boomerang, come back, fail; *informal* blow up in someone's face.

background *noun* **1 backdrop**, backcloth, surrounding(s), setting, scene, framework. **2 social circumstances**, family circumstances, environment, class, culture, tradition. **3 experience**, record, history, past, training, education.
- OPPOSITES foreground.

backing *noun* **1 support**, endorsement, approval, blessing, assistance, aid, help. **2 sponsorship**, finance, funding, subsidy, patronage.

backlash *noun* **adverse reaction**, counterblast, repercussion, comeback, retaliation, reprisal.

backup *noun* **help**, support, assistance, aid, reserve, reinforcements.
● *adjective* **reserve**, spare, substitute, replacement, standby, fallback, emergency.

backward *adjective* **1 rearward**, towards the rear, behind you, reverse. **2 retrograde**, regressive, for the worse, in the wrong direction, downhill, negative. **3 underdeveloped**, undeveloped, primitive. **4 hesitant**, reticent, reluctant, shy, diffident, timid,

self-effacing, unassertive.
- OPPOSITES forward, advanced.

backwards adverb **towards the rear**, rearwards, behind you.
- OPPOSITES forwards.

bad adjective **1** *bad workmanship* **unsatisfactory**, substandard, poor, inferior, second-rate, second-class, inadequate, deficient, imperfect, defective, faulty, shoddy, negligent, disgraceful, awful, terrible, appalling, dreadful, frightful, atrocious, abysmal; *informal* crummy, rotten, pathetic, useless, woeful, lousy, diabolical; *Brit. informal* duff, rubbish. **2** *the alcohol had a bad effect* **harmful**, damaging, detrimental, injurious, hurtful, destructive, deleterious, inimical. **3** *the bad guys* **wicked**, evil, sinful, criminal, immoral, corrupt, villainous; *informal* crooked, bent. **4** *you bad girl!* **naughty**, badly behaved, disobedient, wayward, wilful, defiant, unruly, undisciplined. **5** *bad news* **unpleasant**, disagreeable, unwelcome, unfavourable, unfortunate, grim, distressing, gloomy. **6** *a bad time to arrive* **unfavourable**, inauspicious, unpropitious, inopportune, unfortunate, disadvantageous, inappropriate, unsuitable. **7** *a bad accident* **serious**, severe, grave, critical, acute. **8** *the meat's bad* **rotten**, off, decayed, putrid, rancid, curdled, sour, mouldy. **9** *a bad knee* **injured**, wounded, diseased; *informal* gammy; *Brit. informal* knackered; *Austral./NZ informal* crook.
- OPPOSITES good, beneficial, virtuous, favourable.

badge noun **1** **brooch**, pin, emblem, crest, insignia; *N. Amer.* button. **2** *a badge of success* **sign**, symbol, indication, signal, mark, hallmark, trademark.

badger verb **pester**, harass, hound, harry, nag, bother, go on at; *informal* hassle, bug.

badly adverb **1** **poorly**, unsatisfactorily, inadequately, incorrectly, faultily, defectively, shoddily, amateurishly, carelessly, incompetently, inexpertly. **2** **unfavourably**, ill, critically,

disapprovingly. **3** **naughtily**, disobediently, wilfully, mischievously. **4** **cruelly**, wickedly, unkindly, harshly, shamefully, unfairly, unjustly, wrongly. **5** **unfavourably**, unsuccessfully, adversely, unfortunately. **6** **severely**, seriously, gravely, acutely, critically.
- OPPOSITES well.

bad-tempered adjective **irritable**, irascible, tetchy, testy, grumpy, grouchy, crotchety, in a (bad) mood, cantankerous, curmudgeonly, ill-tempered, ill-humoured, peevish, cross, fractious, petulant, pettish, crabby, quarrelsome, dyspeptic; *informal* snappish, on a short fuse; *Brit. informal* shirty, stroppy, ratty; *N. Amer. informal* cranky, ornery.
- OPPOSITES good-humoured, affable.

baffle verb **puzzle**, perplex, bewilder, mystify, confuse; *informal* flummox, stump, beat, fox.

bag noun **suitcase**, case, valise, holdall, grip, rucksack, haversack, satchel, handbag.
● verb **1** **catch**, land, capture, trap, net, snare. **2** **get**, secure, obtain, acquire, pick up, win, achieve; *informal* land, net.

baggage noun **luggage**, suitcases, cases, bags, belongings.

baggy adjective **loose**, roomy, generously cut, sloppy, voluminous, full.
- OPPOSITES tight.

bail noun **surety**, security, indemnity, bond, guarantee, pledge.
□ **bail out 1** eject, parachute to safety. **2** rescue, save, relieve, finance, help (out), aid.

bait noun **enticement**, lure, decoy, snare, trap, inducement, siren, carrot, attraction; *informal* come-on.
● verb **taunt**, tease, goad, pick on, torment, persecute, harass; *informal* needle; *Brit. informal* wind up.

balance noun **1** **stability**, equilibrium, steadiness, footing. **2** **fairness**, justice, impartiality, parity, equity, evenness, uniformity, comparability. **3** **remainder**, outstanding amount, rest, residue, difference.

- OPPOSITES instability, bias.
● *verb* **1 steady**, stabilize, poise, level. **2 counterbalance**, balance out, offset, counteract, compensate for, make up for. **3 correspond**, agree, tally, match up, coincide. **4 weigh (up)**, compare, evaluate, consider, assess.

bald *adjective* **1 hairless**, smooth, shaven, depilated. **2 plain**, simple, direct, blunt, unadorned, unvarnished, unembellished, stark; *informal* upfront.
- OPPOSITES hairy.

ball *noun* **sphere**, globe, orb, globule, spheroid.

ballot *noun* **vote**, poll, election, referendum, show of hands, plebiscite.

ban *verb* **prohibit**, forbid, veto, proscribe, outlaw, make illegal, bar, debar, prevent, exclude, banish.
- OPPOSITES permit, admit.
● *noun* **prohibition**, embargo, veto, boycott, bar, proscription, moratorium, injunction.

banal *adjective* **unoriginal**, unimaginative, uninspired, trite, hackneyed, clichéd, platitudinous, commonplace, stereotyped, overused, stale, boring, dull, obvious, predictable, tired, pedestrian; *informal* corny, old hat.
- OPPOSITES original.

band[1] *noun* **1 loop**, wristband, headband, ring, hoop, circlet, belt, sash, girdle, strap, strip, tape, circle. **2 stripe**, strip, line, belt, bar, streak, border, swathe.

band[2] *noun* **1 gang**, group, mob, pack, troop, troupe, company, set, party, crew, body, team; *informal* bunch. **2 pop group**, ensemble, group, orchestra; *informal* combo.

bandage *noun* **dressing**, covering, plaster, compress, gauze, lint.
● *verb* **bind**, dress, cover, strap (up).

bandit *noun* **robber**, thief, raider, mugger, pirate, outlaw, hijacker, looter, marauder, gangster; *literary* brigand; *historical* rustler, highwayman, footpad.

bang *noun* **1 crash**, crack, thud, thump, bump, boom, blast, clap, report, explosion. **2 blow**, bump, knock, hit, smack, crack, thump; *informal* bash, whack.
● *verb* **1 hit**, strike, beat, thump, hammer, knock, rap, pound, thud, punch, bump, smack, crack, slap, slam; *informal* bash, whack, clobber, clout, wallop. **2 crash**, boom, pound, explode, detonate, burst, blow up.

banish *verb* **1 exile**, expel, deport, eject, repatriate, transport, extradite, evict, throw out, exclude, shut out, ban. **2 dispel**, dismiss, disperse, scatter, dissipate, drive away, chase away, shut out.

bank[1] *noun* **1 edge**, shore, side, embankment, levee, margin, verge, brink. **2 slope**, rise, incline, gradient, ramp, mound, pile, heap, ridge, hillock, knoll, bar, shoal, mass, drift. **3 array**, row, line, tier, group, series.
● *verb* **1 pile up**, heap up, stack up, amass. **2 tilt**, lean, tip, slant, incline, angle, list, camber, pitch.

bank[2] *noun* **store**, reserve, stock, stockpile, supply, pool, fund, cache, hoard, deposit.
● *verb* **deposit**, pay in, save.

bankrupt *adjective* **insolvent**, ruined; *Brit.* in administration, in receivership; *informal* bust, broke, belly up, wiped out.
- OPPOSITES solvent.

banner *noun* **1 placard**, sign, poster, notice. **2 flag**, standard, ensign, colour(s), pennant, pennon, banderole.

banquet *noun* **feast**, dinner; *informal* spread, blowout; *Brit. informal* nosh-up, slap-up meal.

banter *noun* **repartee**, witty conversation, raillery, wordplay, cut and thrust, badinage, persiflage.
● *verb* **joke**, jest; *informal* josh, wisecrack.

baptize *verb* **1 christen**. **2** *they were baptized into the church* **admit**, initiate, enrol, recruit. **3 name**, call, dub.

bar *noun* **1 rod**, stick, pole, batten, shaft, rail, spar, strut, crosspiece, beam. **2 block**, slab, cake, tablet, wedge,

ingot. **3 counter**, table, buffet. **4 inn**, tavern, hostelry; *Brit.* pub, public house; *Brit. informal* local, boozer. **5 obstacle**, impediment, hindrance, obstruction, block, hurdle, barrier.
– OPPOSITES aid.
● *verb* **1 bolt**, lock, fasten, secure, block, barricade, obstruct. **2 prohibit**, debar, preclude, forbid, ban, exclude, obstruct, prevent, hinder, block, stop.

barbarian *noun* **savage**, heathen, brute, beast, philistine, boor, yahoo, oaf, lout, vandal; *Brit. informal* yob.

barbaric *adjective* **1 cruel**, brutal, barbarous, brutish, savage, vicious, wicked, ruthless, vile, inhuman. **2 uncultured**, uncivilized, barbarian, philistine, boorish, loutish; *Brit. informal* yobbish.
– OPPOSITES civilized.

bare *adjective* **1 naked**, unclothed, undressed, uncovered, stripped, with nothing on, nude; *informal* without a stitch on, in the altogether; *Brit. informal* starkers; *Scottish informal* in the scud; *N. Amer. informal* buck naked. **2 empty**, unfurnished, clear, undecorated, unadorned, bleak, austere. **3 basic**, essential, bare-bones, fundamental, plain, straightforward, simple, unembellished, pure, stark, bald, cold, hard.
– OPPOSITES dressed.

barely *adverb* **hardly**, scarcely, only just, narrowly, by the skin of your teeth, by a hair's breadth; *informal* by a whisker; *Brit. informal* at a push.

bargain *noun* **1 agreement**, arrangement, understanding, deal, contract, pact. **2 good value**; *informal* good buy, cheap buy, snip, steal, giveaway.
● *verb* **haggle**, negotiate, discuss terms, deal, barter.
□ **bargain for/on** expect, anticipate, be prepared for, allow for, plan for, reckon with, envisage, foresee, predict, count on, reckon on; *N. Amer. informal* figure on. **into the bargain** in addition, as well, also, moreover, besides, on top, to boot, for good measure.

bark¹ *verb* **1 woof**, yap. **2 shout**, snap, bawl, yell, roar, bellow, thunder; *informal* holler.
– OPPOSITES whisper.

bark² *noun* **rind**, skin, peel, covering.

barracks *plural noun* **garrison**, camp, encampment, depot, billet, quarters, fort, cantonment.

barrage *noun* **1 bombardment**, gunfire, shelling, salvo, volley, fusillade; *historical* broadside. **2 deluge**, stream, storm, torrent, onslaught, flood, spate, tide, avalanche, hail, blaze. **3 dam**, barrier, weir, dyke, embankment, wall.

barrel *noun* **cask**, keg, butt, vat, tun, drum, hogshead, firkin.

> **WORD LINKS**
> **cooper** person who makes barrels

barren *adjective* **unproductive**, infertile, unfruitful, sterile, arid, desert, waste, lifeless, empty.
– OPPOSITES fertile.

barricade *noun* **barrier**, roadblock, blockade, obstacle, obstruction.
● *verb* **seal up**, close up, block off, shut off/up, defend, protect, fortify, occupy.

barrier *noun* **1 fence**, railing, barricade, hurdle, bar, blockade, roadblock. **2** *a barrier to international trade* **obstacle**, obstruction, hurdle, stumbling block, bar, impediment, hindrance, curb.

barter *verb* **1 swap**, trade, exchange, sell. **2 haggle**, bargain, negotiate, deal.

base¹ *noun* **1 foundation**, bottom, foot, support, stand, pedestal, plinth, rest. **2 basis**, foundation, bedrock, starting point, source, origin, root(s), core, key component. **3 headquarters**, camp, site, station, settlement, post, centre.
– OPPOSITES top.
● *verb* **1 found**, build, construct, form, ground; (**be based on**) derive from, spring from, stem from, depend on. **2 locate**, situate, position, install, station, site.

base² *adjective* **sordid**, ignoble, low, mean, immoral, unscrupulous, unprincipled, dishonest, dishonourable,

shameful, shabby, contemptible, despicable.
- OPPOSITES noble.

bashful adjective **shy**, reserved, diffident, inhibited, retiring, reticent, reluctant, shrinking, self-effacing, unassertive, timid, nervous, self-conscious.
- OPPOSITES bold, confident.

basic adjective **1 fundamental**, essential, bare-bones, vital, primary, principal, cardinal, elementary, intrinsic, central, pivotal, critical, key, focal. **2 plain**, simple, unsophisticated, straightforward, adequate, spartan, stark, severe, austere, limited, meagre, rudimentary, patchy, sketchy, minimal, crude, makeshift; informal bog-standard.
- OPPOSITES unimportant, luxurious.

basically adverb **fundamentally**, essentially, first and foremost, primarily, at heart, at bottom, intrinsically, inherently, principally, chiefly, above all, mostly, mainly, on the whole, by and large; informal at the end of the day.

basics plural noun **fundamentals**, essentials, first principles, foundations, preliminaries, groundwork, essence, basis, core; informal nitty-gritty, brass tacks, nuts and bolts, ABC.

basin noun **bowl**, dish, pan, container, receptacle, vessel.

basis noun **1** the basis of his method **foundation**, support, base, reasoning, rationale, defence, reason, grounds, justification. **2** the basis of discussion **starting point**, base, point of departure, beginning, premise, fundamental point/principle, cornerstone, core, heart. **3** on a part-time basis **footing**, condition, status, position, arrangement.

bask verb **1 laze**, lie, lounge, relax, sprawl, loll, luxuriate. **2 revel**, wallow, delight, take pleasure, enjoy, relish, savour.

bass adjective **low**, deep, resonant, sonorous, rumbling, booming, resounding.
- OPPOSITES high.

batch noun **group**, quantity, lot, bunch, cluster, raft, set, collection, bundle, pack, consignment, shipment.

bathe verb **1 swim**, take a dip. **2 clean**, wash, rinse, wet, soak, steep. **3 envelop**, cover, flood, fill, wash, pervade, suffuse.

baton noun **stick**, rod, staff, wand, truncheon, club, mace.

batter verb **beat up**, hit repeatedly, pummel, pound, rain blows on, buffet, belabour, thrash; informal knock about/around, lay into, do over.

battle noun **1** he was killed in the battle **fight**, engagement, armed conflict, clash, struggle, skirmish, fray, war, campaign, crusade, warfare, combat, action, hostilities; informal scrap, dogfight, shoot-out. **2** a legal battle **conflict**, clash, struggle, disagreement, argument, dispute, tussle.
● verb **fight**, combat, contend with, resist, withstand, stand up to, confront, war, feud, struggle, strive, work.

battlefield noun **battleground**, field of battle, field of operations, combat zone, lines, front, theatre of war.

bawdy adjective **ribald**, indecent, risqué, racy, earthy, rude, suggestive, titillating, naughty, improper, indelicate, vulgar, crude, smutty; informal raunchy.

bawl verb **1 shout**, yell, roar, bellow, screech, scream, shriek, bark, thunder; informal yammer, holler. **2 cry**, sob, weep, wail, whine, howl; Scottish informal greet.
- OPPOSITES whisper.

bay[1] noun **cove**, inlet, gulf, sound, bight, basin, fjord.

bay[2] noun **alcove**, recess, niche, nook, opening, inglenook.

bazaar noun **1 market**, marketplace, souk, mart. **2 fete**, fair, fund-raiser; Brit. jumble sale, bring-and-buy sale, car boot sale; N. Amer. rummage sale, tag sale.

be verb **1 exist**, live, be alive, breathe, be extant. **2 occur**, happen, take place, come about, arise, fall; literary come to

b

pass, befall, betide. **3 be situated**, be located, be found, be present, be set, be positioned, be placed, be installed, sit, lie.

beach noun **sands**, seaside, seashore, coast; *literary* strand, littoral.
● verb **land**, ground, strand, run ashore.

beached adjective **stranded**, run aground, ashore, marooned, high and dry, stuck.
- OPPOSITES afloat.

beacon noun **signal**, light, fire, danger signal, bonfire, lighthouse.

bead noun **1 ball**, pellet, pill, globule, sphere, spheroid, orb, round; (**beads**) necklace, rosary, chaplet. **2** *beads of sweat* **droplet**, drop, drip, blob, pearl, dot.

beaker noun **cup**, tumbler, glass, mug, drinking vessel.

beam noun **1 plank**, timber, joist, rafter, lintel, spar, girder, support. **2 ray**, shaft, stream, streak, pencil, flash, gleam, glint. **3 grin**, smile.
- OPPOSITES frown.
● verb **1 broadcast**, transmit, relay, disseminate, direct, send, aim. **2 shine**, radiate, glare, gleam. **3 grin**, smile.
- OPPOSITES frown.

bear[1] verb **1 carry**, bring, transport, move, convey, take, fetch; *informal* tote. **2 display**, be marked with, show, carry, exhibit. **3 withstand**, support, sustain, stand, take, carry, hold up, cope with, handle. **4 harbour**, foster, entertain, cherish, nurse. **5** *I can't bear sport* **endure**, tolerate, put up with, stand, abide, countenance, stomach; *informal* hack, swallow; *Brit. informal* stick, wear; *formal* brook. **6 give birth to**, bring forth, deliver, have, produce, spawn. **7 produce**, yield, give, provide, supply.
□ **bear fruit** yield results, succeed, be effective, be profitable, work; *informal* pay off, do the trick. **bear out** confirm, corroborate, substantiate, endorse, vindicate, give credence to, support, justify, prove. **bear up** remain cheerful,

cope, manage, get by, muddle through.
bear with be patient with, make allowances for, tolerate, put up with, endure.

bear[2] noun

> **WORD LINKS**
> **ursine** relating to bears

bearable adjective **tolerable**, endurable, supportable, sustainable.

bearer noun **1 carrier**, porter. **2 bringer**, messenger, agent, conveyor, emissary.

bearing noun **1 posture**, stance, carriage, gait, demeanour, manner, mien, air, aspect, attitude, style; *Brit.* deportment. **2** *this has no bearing on the matter* **relevance**, pertinence, connection, relation, relationship, import, significance, application. **3 direction**, orientation, course, trajectory, heading, tack, path. **4** *I lost my bearings* **orientation**, sense of direction, whereabouts, location, position.
- OPPOSITES irrelevance.

beast noun **1 creature**, animal; *N. Amer. informal* critter. **2 monster**, brute, savage, barbarian, animal, swine, ogre, fiend, sadist, demon, devil.

beat verb **1 hit**, strike, batter, thump, bang, hammer, punch, knock, thrash, pound, pummel, slap, rain blows on, assault; *informal* wallop, belt, bash, whack, clout, clobber. **2 throb**, pulse, pulsate, pump, palpitate, pound, thump, thud, hammer, drum. **3 flap**, flutter, thrash, wave, vibrate. **4 whisk**, mix, blend, whip. **5 defeat**, conquer, vanquish, trounce, rout, overpower, overcome; *informal* lick, thrash, whip; *US informal* own. **6 exceed**, surpass, better, improve on, eclipse, transcend, top, trump, cap.
● noun **1 rhythm**, pulse, metre, time, measure, cadence, stress, accent. **2 pounding**, banging, thumping, thudding, hammering, crashing. **3 pulse**, pulsation, vibration, throb, palpitation, reverberation, pounding, thump, thud, hammering, drumming. **4 circuit**, round, route, path.

□ **beat off** repel, fight off, fend off, stave off, repulse, drive away/back, push back. **beat up** assault, attack, mug; *informal* knock about/around, do over, work over, rough up; *Brit. informal* duff up.

beautiful *adjective* **attractive**, pretty, handsome, good-looking, fetching, lovely, charming, graceful, elegant, appealing, winsome, ravishing, gorgeous, stunning, glamorous; *Scottish & N. English* bonny; *informal* tasty, knockout, drop-dead gorgeous; *Brit. informal* smashing; *N. Amer. informal* cute, foxy; *Austral./NZ informal* beaut, spunky; *old use* comely.
- OPPOSITES ugly.

beautify *verb* **adorn**, embellish, enhance, decorate, ornament, prettify, glamorize; *informal* do up, tart up.

beauty *noun* **1 attractiveness**, prettiness, good looks, loveliness, appeal, winsomeness, charm, grace, elegance, exquisiteness, glamour; *literary* pulchritude. **2 belle**, vision, goddess, picture, Venus; *informal* babe, looker, lovely, stunner, knockout, bombshell, bit of all right.
- OPPOSITES ugliness.

because *conjunction* **since**, as, seeing that, in view of the fact that, in that. □ **because of** on account of, as a result of, as a consequence of, owing to, due to, thanks to, by virtue of; *formal* by reason of.

beckon *verb* **1 gesture**, signal, wave, gesticulate, motion. **2 entice**, invite, tempt, lure, charm, attract, draw, call.

become *verb* **1** *she became rich* **grow**, get, turn, come to be, get to be. **2** *he became a tyrant* **turn into**, change into, be transformed into, be converted into. **3** *he became Foreign Secretary* **be appointed**, be assigned as, be nominated, be elected. **4 suit**, flatter, look good on, set off; *informal* do something for. □ **become of** happen to, be the fate of, be the lot of, overtake.

becoming *adjective* **flattering**, fetching, attractive, pretty, elegant, handsome, well chosen, stylish, fashionable, tasteful.

bed *noun* **1 couch**, berth, billet, cot; *informal* the sack. **2** *a flower bed* **patch**, plot, border, strip. **3 base**, foundation, footing, support, basis.
● *verb* **embed**, set, fix, insert, inlay, implant, bury, plant.
□ **go to bed** retire; *informal* hit the sack, hit the hay, turn in.

bedraggled *adjective* **dishevelled**, disordered, untidy, unkempt, tousled; *N. Amer. informal* mussed.
- OPPOSITES neat.

before *preposition* **1 prior to**, previous to, earlier than, preparatory to, in advance of, ahead of, pre-. **2 in front of**, in the presence of. **3 in preference to**, rather than, sooner than.
- OPPOSITES after.
● *adverb* **previously**, before now/then, until now/then, up to now/then, earlier, formerly, hitherto, in the past.
- OPPOSITES afterwards, later.

beforehand *adverb* **in advance**, in readiness, ahead of time, before, before now/then, earlier (on), previously, already, sooner.
- OPPOSITES afterwards.

beg *verb* **1 ask for money**, seek charity; *informal* sponge, cadge, scrounge, bum. **2** *we begged for mercy* **plead for**, request, ask for, appeal for, call for, sue for, solicit, seek. **3** *he begged her not to go* **implore**, entreat, plead with, appeal to, pray to, call on, petition; *literary* beseech.

beggar *noun* **tramp**, vagrant, vagabond, mendicant; *N. Amer.* hobo; *informal* scrounger, sponger, cadger, freeloader; *Brit. informal* dosser; *N. Amer. informal* bum; *Austral./NZ informal* bagman.

begin *verb* **1 start**, commence, set about, go about, embark on, launch into, get down to, take up, initiate, set in motion, get going, get off the ground, lead off, institute, inaugurate,

b

open; *informal* get cracking on, kick off. **2 appear**, arise, become apparent, spring up, crop up, turn up, come into existence, originate, start, commence, develop.
- OPPOSITES finish, end.

beginner *noun* **novice**, learner, starter, (raw) recruit, newcomer, tyro, fresher, probationer, apprentice, trainee; *N. Amer. informal* rookie, new kid (on the block), tenderfoot, greenhorn.
- OPPOSITES expert, veteran.

beginning *noun* **1 start**, commencement, creation, birth, inception, conception, origination, origin, genesis, germ, emergence, rise, dawn, launch, onset, outset, day one; *informal* kick-off. **2 opening**, start, commencement, first part, introduction, preamble.
- OPPOSITES end, conclusion.

begrudge *verb* **envy**, resent, grudge, be jealous of, be envious of, mind, object to.

behalf *noun*
□ **on behalf of 1** representing, as a representative of, as a spokesperson for, for, in the name of, in place of, on the authority of. **2** in the interests of, in support of, for the benefit of, for the good of, for the sake of.

behave *verb* **1** *she behaved badly* **act**, conduct yourself, acquit yourself. **2** *the children behaved themselves* **act correctly**, be good, be well behaved, mind your manners; *informal* mind your Ps and Qs.
- OPPOSITES misbehave.

behaviour *noun* **conduct**, actions, manners, ways, deportment, bearing, etiquette.

behind *preposition* **1 at the back of**, at the rear of, beyond, on the far side of; *N. Amer.* in back of. **2 after**, following, at the back/rear of, hard on the heels of, in the wake of. **3 responsible for**, at the bottom of, the cause of, the perpetrator of, the organizer of, to blame for, guilty of. **4 supporting**, backing, for, on the side of, in agreement with; *informal* rooting for.

being *noun* **1 existence**, living, life, reality, lifeblood, vital force. **2 soul**, spirit, nature, essence, psyche, heart, bosom, breast. **3 creature**, life form, organism, living thing, individual, person, human.

belated *adjective* **late**, overdue, behindhand, delayed, tardy, unpunctual.
- OPPOSITES early.

beleaguered *adjective* **1 besieged**, blockaded, surrounded, encircled, hemmed in, under attack. **2 troubled**, harassed, hard-pressed, in difficulties, under pressure, in a tight corner; *informal* up against it.

belief *noun* **1 opinion**, view, conviction, judgement, thinking, idea, theory, thought, feeling. **2 faith**, trust, reliance, confidence, credence. **3 ideology**, principle, ethic, tenet, doctrine, teaching, dogma, creed, credo.
- OPPOSITES disbelief, doubt.

believe *verb* **1** *I don't believe you* **trust**, have confidence in, consider honest, consider truthful. **2** *do you believe that story?* **accept**, be convinced by, give credence to, credit, trust, put confidence in; *informal* swallow, buy, go for. **3 think**, be of the opinion that, have an idea that, imagine, assume, presume, take it, understand, gather; *informal* reckon, figure.
- OPPOSITES doubt.
□ **believe in** have faith in, trust in, have every confidence in, cling to, set (great) store by, value, be convinced by, be persuaded by; *informal* swear by, rate.

believer *noun* **disciple**, follower, supporter, adherent, devotee, upholder, worshipper.
- OPPOSITES infidel, sceptic.

belittle *verb* **disparage**, denigrate, run down, deprecate, play down, trivialize, minimize; *informal* do down, pooh-pooh.

belligerent *adjective* **1 hostile**, aggressive, threatening, antagonistic, pugnacious, bellicose, truculent, confrontational, contentious, militant, combative, argumentative; *informal*

spoiling for a fight; *Brit. informal* stroppy, bolshie; *N. Amer. informal* scrappy. **2** *the belligerent states* **warring**, combatant, fighting, battling.
- OPPOSITES peaceable.

bellow *verb* **roar**, shout, bawl, thunder, boom, bark, yell, shriek, howl, scream; *informal* holler.
- OPPOSITES whisper.

belly *noun* **stomach**, abdomen, paunch, middle, midriff, girth; *informal* tummy, gut, insides.

belong *verb* **1** **be owned by**, be the property of, be held by, be in the hands of. **2** **be a member of**, be in, be affiliated to, be allied to, be associated with. **3** **be part of**, be attached to, go with. **4** **fit in**, be suited to; *informal* go, click.

belongings *plural noun* **possessions**, effects, worldly goods, chattels, property; *informal* gear, tackle, kit, things, stuff, bits and pieces; *Brit. informal* clobber.

beloved *adjective* **darling**, dear, precious, adored, cherished, treasured, prized, valued, idolized.
● *noun* **sweetheart**, love, darling, dearest, lover, girlfriend, boyfriend; *informal* steady, baby, angel, honey, pet.

below *preposition* **1** **beneath**, under, underneath, lower than. **2** **less than**, lower than, under, not as much as, smaller than. **3** **inferior to**, subordinate to, under, beneath.
- OPPOSITES above, over.

belt *noun* **1** **sash**, girdle, band, strap, cummerbund. **2** **region**, strip, stretch, zone, area, district, sector, territory.

bemused *adjective* **bewildered**, confused, puzzled, perplexed, baffled, mystified, nonplussed, dumbfounded, at sea, at a loss; *informal* flummoxed, bamboozled, fazed.

bench *noun* **1** **seat**, form, pew, stall, settle. **2** **workbench**, worktop, counter.

benchmark *noun* **standard**, point of reference, guide, guideline, norm, touchstone, yardstick, barometer, model, gauge, criterion, specification.

bend *verb* **1** **curve**, crook, flex, angle, hook, bow, arch, buckle, warp, contort, distort, deform, twist. **2** **turn**, curve, incline, swing, veer, fork, change course, curl, loop. **3** **stoop**, bow, crouch, hunch, lean down/over.
- OPPOSITES straighten.
● *noun* **curve**, turn, corner, kink, angle, arc, twist.

beneath *preposition* **1** **under**, underneath, below, at the foot of, at the bottom of, lower than. **2** **inferior to**, below, lower than, subordinate to. **3** **unworthy of**, unbecoming to, degrading to.
- OPPOSITES above.
● *adverb* **underneath**, below, further down, lower down.
- OPPOSITES above.

benefactor *noun* **patron**, supporter, backer, sponsor, donor, contributor, subscriber; *informal* angel.

beneficial *adjective* **advantageous**, favourable, helpful, useful, of assistance, valuable, salutary, worthwhile, fruitful, productive, profitable, rewarding, gainful.
- OPPOSITES disadvantageous.

beneficiary *noun* **recipient**, payee, heir, heiress, inheritor.

benefit *noun* **1** **good**, sake, welfare, well-being, advantage, comfort, ease, convenience, help, aid, assistance, service. **2** **advantage**, profit, plus point, boon, blessing, reward; *informal* perk. **3** **social security payment**, welfare, charity; *informal* the dole.
- OPPOSITES detriment, disadvantage.
● *verb* **1** **help**, be advantageous to, be beneficial to, profit, do good to, be of service to, serve, be useful to, be helpful to, aid, assist. **2** **profit**, gain, reap reward, make the most of, exploit, turn to your advantage, put to good use.
- OPPOSITES disadvantage, harm.

benevolent *adjective* **kind**, kindly, kind-hearted, good-natured, compassionate, caring, altruistic, humanitarian, philanthropic, beneficent, well meaning, benign.
- OPPOSITES unkind.

benign adjective **1 kindly**, kind, warm-hearted, good-natured, friendly, genial, tender-hearted, gentle, sympathetic, compassionate, caring, well disposed, benevolent. **2 mild**, temperate, gentle, balmy, soft, pleasant, favourable, healthy. **3** (Medicine) **harmless**, non-malignant, non-cancerous.
- OPPOSITES unkind, malignant.

bent adjective **1 twisted**, crooked, warped, contorted, deformed, mis-shapen, out of shape, bowed, arched, curved, angled, hooked, kinked; N. Amer. informal pretzeled. **2 corrupt**, dishonest, fraudulent, criminal, untrustworthy.
- OPPOSITES straight.
● noun **inclination**, leaning, tendency, talent, gift, flair, aptitude, facility, skill.
□ **bent on** intent on, determined on, set on, insistent on, resolved on.

bequeath verb **leave**, will, hand down, pass on, entrust, make over, grant, transfer, give, bestow on, confer on.

bequest noun **legacy**, estate, inheritance, endowment, settlement.

bereavement noun **death in the family**, loss, passing (away), demise; formal decease.

berserk adjective **mad**, crazy, insane, out of your mind, hysterical, frenzied, crazed, demented, maniacal, manic, frantic, raving, wild, out of control, amok, on the rampage; informal off your head, off the deep end, ape, bananas, bonkers; Brit. informal spare; N. Amer. informal postal.

berth noun **1 bunk**, bed, cot, couch, hammock. **2 mooring**, dock, pier, jetty, quay.
● verb **dock**, moor, land, tie up, make fast.

beseech verb **implore**, beg, entreat, plead with, appeal to, call on, importune, pray to, ask, petition.

beside preposition **alongside**, by/at the side of, next to, parallel to, abreast of, adjacent to, next door to, neighbouring.
□ **beside yourself** distraught, overcome, out of your mind, frantic, desperate, distracted, at your wits' end, frenzied, hysterical.

besides preposition **in addition to**, as well as, over and above, on top of, apart from, other than, aside from, not counting, excluding, leaving aside; N. Amer. informal outside of.

besiege verb **1 lay siege to**, beleaguer, blockade. **2 surround**, mob, harass, pester, badger. **3 overwhelm**, bombard, inundate, deluge, flood, swamp, snow under.

best adjective **finest**, premier, greatest, top, foremost, leading, pre-eminent, supreme, superlative, unrivalled, second to none, without equal, unsurpassed, unparalleled, unbeatable, optimum, ultimate, incomparable, record-breaking; informal star, number-one, a cut above the rest, top-drawer.
● noun only the best will do **finest**, choicest, top, cream, choice, prime, elite, crème de la crème, flower, jewel in the crown; informal tops, pick of the bunch.
- OPPOSITES worst.

bestow verb **confer on**, grant, accord, afford, endow with, present, award, give, donate, entrust with, vouchsafe.

bet verb **1 wager**, gamble, stake, risk, venture, hazard, chance; Brit. informal punt, have a flutter. **2** (informal) **be certain**, be sure, be convinced, be confident, expect, predict, guess.
● noun **1 wager**, gamble, stake, ante; Brit. informal punt, flutter. **2** (informal) your best bet is to go early **option**, choice, alternative, course of action, plan.

betray verb **1 be disloyal to**, be unfaithful to, break faith with, play someone false, inform on/against, give away, denounce, sell out, stab in the back; informal split on, rat on, stitch up, do the dirty on, sell down the river; Brit. informal grass on, shop, sneak on; N. Amer. informal rat out, drop a/the dime on, finger; Austral./NZ informal dob in, point the bone at. **2 reveal**, disclose, divulge, tell, give away, leak, bring out into the open.

betrayal noun **disloyalty**, treachery, bad faith, breach of faith, breach of trust, faithlessness, duplicity, deception, double-dealing, stab in the back, double-cross, sell-out.
- OPPOSITES loyalty.

better adjective **1 superior**, finer, of higher quality, preferable; informal a cut above, streets ahead, head and shoulders above, ahead of the pack/field. **2 healthier**, fitter, stronger, well again, cured, healed, recovered, recovering, on the road to recovery, on the mend.
- OPPOSITES worse, inferior.
● verb **1 surpass**, improve on, beat, exceed, top, cap, trump, eclipse. **2 improve**, ameliorate, raise, advance, further, lift, upgrade, enhance.
- OPPOSITES worsen.

between preposition **1 in the middle of**, with one on either side, among; old use betwixt. **2 connecting**, linking, joining, uniting, allying.

beware verb **watch out**, look out, mind out, be alert, be on your guard, keep your eyes open/peeled, keep an eye out, take care, be careful, be cautious, watch your step, guard against.

bewilder verb **baffle**, mystify, bemuse, perplex, puzzle, confuse; informal flummox, faze, stump, beat.

bewildered adjective **baffled**, mystified, bemused, perplexed, puzzled, confused, nonplussed, at sea, at a loss, disorientated; informal flummoxed, bamboozled; N. Amer. informal discombobulated.

bewitch verb **captivate**, enchant, entrance, enrapture, charm, beguile, delight, fascinate, enthral, cast a spell on.

beyond preposition **1 on the far side of**, on the other side of, further away than, behind, past, after. **2 later than**, past, after. **3 greater than**, more than, exceeding, in excess of, above, upwards of.

bias noun **prejudice**, partiality, favouritism, partisanship, unfairness, one-sidedness, discrimination, leaning, tendency, inclination.
- OPPOSITES impartiality.
● verb **prejudice**, influence, colour, sway, predispose, distort, skew, slant.

biased adjective **prejudiced**, partial, partisan, one-sided, bigoted, discriminatory, distorted, warped, twisted, skewed.
- OPPOSITES impartial.

bid verb **offer**, put up, tender, proffer, propose.
● noun **1 offer**, tender, proposal. **2 attempt**, effort, endeavour, try; informal crack, go, shot, stab.

bidding noun **command**, order, direction, instruction, decree, injunction, demand, beck and call.

big adjective **1 large**, sizeable, substantial, considerable, great, huge, immense, enormous, extensive, colossal, massive, mammoth, vast, gigantic, cosmic, giant, spacious; informal jumbo, whopping, thumping, bumper, mega; Brit. informal whacking, ginormous; formal commodious. **2 well built**, sturdy, brawny, burly, broad-shouldered, muscular, bulky, hulking, strapping, hefty, tall, huge, fat, stout; informal hunky, beefy. **3 elder**, older, grown-up, adult, mature, grown. **4 important**, significant, major, momentous, weighty, far-reaching, key, vital, crucial. **5 that was big of you generous**, kind, kindly, caring, compassionate, loving.
- OPPOSITES small, minor.

bigoted adjective **prejudiced**, biased, partial, one-sided, sectarian, discriminatory, opinionated, dogmatic, intolerant, narrow-minded, blinkered, illiberal.
- OPPOSITES open-minded.

bill noun **1 invoice**, account, statement, list of charges; humorous the damage; N. Amer. check; informal tab. **2 draft law**, proposal, measure. **3 programme**, line-up; N. Amer. playbill. **4** (N. Amer.) **banknote**, note;

US informal greenback. **5 poster**, advertisement, notice, announcement, flyer, leaflet, handbill; informal ad; Brit. informal advert.
● verb **1 invoice**, charge, debit. **2 advertise**, announce, schedule, programme, timetable; N. Amer. slate. **3** he was billed as the new Sean Connery **describe**, call, style, label, dub, promote, talk up; informal hype.

billow verb **1 puff out**, balloon (out), swell, fill (out). **2 swirl**, spiral, roll, undulate, eddy, pour, flow.

bind verb **1 tie up**, fasten together, secure, make fast, attach, rope, lash, tether. **2 bandage**, dress, cover, wrap, strap up, tape up. **3 trim**, hem, edge, border, fringe.
- OPPOSITES untie.

binding adjective **irrevocable**, unalterable, inescapable, unbreakable, contractual, compulsory, obligatory, mandatory, incumbent.

binge noun (informal) **bout**, spell, fling, spree, orgy, drinking bout; informal bender, session; Scottish informal skite; N. Amer. informal jag.

bird noun fowl, chick, fledgling, nestling.

> **WORD LINKS**
> **avian** relating to birds
> **ornithology** study of birds

birth noun **1 childbirth**, delivery, nativity. **2 beginning(s)**, emergence, genesis, dawn, dawning, rise, start. **3 ancestry**, lineage, blood, descent, parentage, family, extraction, origin, stock.
- OPPOSITES death, end.
□ **give birth to** have, bear, produce, be delivered of, bring into the world; informal drop.

> **WORD LINKS**
> **antenatal** before birth
> **post-natal** after birth
> **obstetrics** branch of medicine concerned with birth

bit noun **piece**, portion, section, part, chunk, lump, hunk, fragment, scrap, shred, crumb, grain, speck, spot, drop, pinch, dash, morsel, mouthful, bite, sample, iota, jot, whit, atom, particle, trace, touch, suggestion, hint, tinge; informal smidgen, tad.

bite verb **1 chew**, sink your teeth into, munch, crunch, champ. **2 grip**, hold, get a purchase. **3 take effect**, work, act, have results.
● noun **1 chew**, munch, nibble, gnaw, nip, snap. **2 mouthful**, piece, bit, morsel, snack. **3 piquancy**, pungency, spiciness, tang, zest; informal kick, punch, zing.

biting adjective **1 vicious**, harsh, cruel, savage, cutting, sharp, bitter, scathing, caustic, acerbic, acid, acrimonious, spiteful, venomous, vitriolic; informal bitchy, catty. **2 freezing**, icy, arctic, bitter, piercing, penetrating, raw.
- OPPOSITES mild.

bitter adjective **1 sharp**, acid, acrid, tart, sour, vinegary. **2 acrimonious**, hostile, angry, rancorous, spiteful, vicious, vitriolic, savage, ferocious, nasty. **3** a bitter woman **resentful**, embittered, aggrieved, spiteful, jaundiced, sullen, sour. **4 freezing**, icy, arctic, biting, piercing, penetrating, raw.
- OPPOSITES sweet, mild.

bizarre adjective **strange**, peculiar, odd, funny, fantastic, extraordinary, curious, outlandish, eccentric, unconventional, unorthodox, weird, outré, surreal; informal wacky, oddball, way out, freaky; N. Amer. informal wacko.
- OPPOSITES normal.

black adjective **1 dark**, pitch-black, coal-black, jet-black, ebony, inky, sable. **2** a black day **tragic**, dark, disastrous, calamitous, catastrophic, cataclysmic, fateful. **3** a black mood **miserable**, unhappy, sad, wretched, heartbroken, grief-stricken, sorrowful, anguished, desolate, despairing, disconsolate, downcast, dejected, gloomy; informal blue. **4 macabre**, cynical, unhealthy, ghoulish, weird, morbid, gruesome; informal sick.
- OPPOSITES white, bright.

◻ **black out** faint, lose consciousness, pass out, swoon.

blacklist *verb* **boycott**, ostracize, avoid, embargo, ignore, refuse to employ.

blackmail *noun* **extortion**, demanding money with menaces, threats, intimidation.
● *verb* **1 extort money from**, threaten, hold to ransom, intimidate. **2 coerce**, pressure, force, dragoon; *informal* lean on, twist someone's arm.

blame *verb* **1 hold responsible**, hold accountable, condemn, accuse, find/consider guilty. **2** *they blame youth crime on unemployment* **attribute to**, ascribe to, impute to, lay at the door of, put down to; *informal* pin.
- OPPOSITES absolve.
● *noun* **responsibility**, guilt, accountability, liability, culpability, fault.

blameless *adjective* **innocent**, guiltless, above reproach, irreproachable, unimpeachable, in the clear, exemplary, impeccable, unblemished; *informal* squeaky clean.
- OPPOSITES guilty.

bland *adjective* **1 uninteresting**, dull, boring, tedious, monotonous, ordinary, run-of-the-mill, drab, dreary, unexciting, lacklustre, flat, stale, trite. **2 tasteless**, flavourless, plain, insipid, weak, watery, thin, wishy-washy.
- OPPOSITES interesting, tangy.

blank *adjective* **1 empty**, unmarked, unused, clear, free, bare, clean, plain. **2 expressionless**, deadpan, wooden, stony, impassive, inscrutable, glazed, fixed, lifeless.
- OPPOSITES expressive.
● *noun* **space**, gap, void.

blanket *noun* *a blanket of cloud* **covering**, layer, coating, carpet, cloak, mantle, veil, pall, shroud.
● *verb* **cover**, coat, carpet, cloak, shroud, swathe, envelop.

blasé *adjective* **indifferent**, unconcerned, casual, nonchalant, offhand, uninterested, unimpressed, unmoved, uncaring; *informal* laid-back.

blasphemous *adjective* **sacrilegious**, profane, irreligious, irreverent, impious, ungodly, godless.
- OPPOSITES reverent.

blasphemy *noun* **profanity**, sacrilege, irreligion, irreverence, taking the Lord's name in vain, impiety, desecration.
- OPPOSITES reverence.

blast *noun* **1 explosion**, detonation, discharge, burst. **2 gust**, rush, gale, squall, flurry. **3** *the shrill blast of the trumpets* **blare**, wail, roar, screech, shriek, hoot, honk, beep.
● *verb* **1 blow up**, bomb, blow (to pieces), dynamite, explode, fire, shoot, blaze, let fly, discharge. **2 blare**, boom, roar, thunder, bellow, shriek, screech.

blatant *adjective* **flagrant**, glaring, obvious, undisguised, open, overt, outright, naked, shameless, barefaced, unashamed, brazen.
- OPPOSITES discreet, inconspicuous.

blaze *noun* **1 fire**, flames, conflagration, inferno, holocaust. **2** *a blaze of light* **glare**, flash, burst, flare, streak, radiance, brilliance, beam, glitter.
● *verb* **1 burn**, be alight, be on fire, be in flames. **2 shine**, flash, flare, glare, gleam, glitter, glisten. **3 fire**, shoot, blast, let fly.

bleach *verb* **turn white**, whiten, turn pale, blanch, lighten, fade.
- OPPOSITES darken.

bleak *adjective* **1 bare**, exposed, desolate, stark, desert, lunar, open, empty, windswept. **2 unpromising**, unfavourable, dim, gloomy, black, grim, discouraging, disheartening, depressing, dismal.
- OPPOSITES lush, promising.

bleary *adjective* **blurry**, unfocused, fogged, clouded, misty, watery, rheumy.
- OPPOSITES clear.

blemish *noun* **imperfection**, flaw, defect, fault, discoloration, stain, scar, mark, spot.
● *verb* **mar**, spoil, impair, disfigure, deface, mark, stain, scar, blight, tarnish.
- OPPOSITES enhance.

b

blend verb **1 mix**, mingle, combine, merge, fuse, amalgamate, stir, whisk, fold in. **2 harmonize**, go (well), fit (in), be in tune, be compatible, coordinate, match, complement, suit.
● noun **mixture**, mix, melange, combination, synthesis, compound, amalgam, fusion, alloy.

bless verb **1 consecrate**, sanctify, dedicate to God, make holy; formal hallow. **2 endow**, bestow, furnish, give, favour, confer on. **3 sanction**, consent to, endorse, agree to, approve, back, support; informal give the green light to, OK.
- OPPOSITES curse, oppose.

blessed adjective **holy**, sacred, hallowed, consecrated, sanctified, ordained, canonized, beatified.
- OPPOSITES cursed.

blessing noun **1 benediction**, dedication, consecration, grace, invocation, intercession. **2 sanction**, endorsement, approval, consent, assent, agreement, backing, support; informal the green light, OK. **3 advantage**, godsend, boon, benefit, help, bonus, plus, stroke of luck, windfall.
- OPPOSITES condemnation.

blight noun **1** potato blight **disease**, canker, infestation, fungus, mildew, mould. **2** the blight of aircraft noise **curse**, scourge, affliction, plague, menace, misfortune, bane, trouble, nuisance, pest.
● verb **ruin**, wreck, spoil, mar, frustrate, disrupt, undo, scotch, destroy, shatter, devastate, demolish; informal mess up, foul up, put paid to, put the kibosh on, stymie; Brit. informal scupper.

blind adjective **1 sightless**, unsighted, visually impaired, unseeing. **2 uncritical**, unreasoned, unthinking, unquestioning, mindless, undiscerning, indiscriminate. **3** blind to the realities of the situation **unaware of**, oblivious to, ignorant of, unmindful of, heedless of, insensible to, indifferent to.
● noun **screen**, shade, sunshade, curtain, awning, canopy, louvre, jalousie, shutter.

blindly adverb **1 impetuously**, impulsively, recklessly, heedlessly. **2 uncritically**, unquestioningly, unthinkingly, mindlessly, indiscriminately.

bliss noun **joy**, happiness, pleasure, delight, ecstasy, elation, rapture, euphoria, seventh heaven.
- OPPOSITES misery.

blitz noun **bombing**, air raid, air strike, bombardment, barrage, attack, assault.

bloated adjective **swollen**, distended, bulging, puffed out, inflated, dilated.

blob noun **drop**, droplet, globule, bead, bubble, spot, dab, blotch, blot, dot, smudge; informal splodge.

bloc noun **group**, alliance, coalition, federation, confederation, league, union, axis, association.

block noun **1 chunk**, hunk, lump, wedge, cube, brick, ingot, slab, piece. **2 building**, complex, structure, development. **3 obstacle**, bar, barrier, impediment, hindrance, check, hurdle.
● verb **1 clog**, stop up, choke, plug, bung up, obstruct, gum up, dam up, congest, jam. **2 hinder**, hamper, obstruct, impede, inhibit, halt, stop, bar, check, prevent, fend off, hold off, repel.
- OPPOSITES clear, aid.
□ **block out** keep out, exclude, stop, conceal, blot out, blank out, obliterate.

blockage noun **obstruction**, stoppage, block, jam, congestion, bottleneck.

blonde, **blond** adjective **fair**, light, yellow, flaxen, golden.
- OPPOSITES dark.

blood noun **1 lifeblood**, gore, vital fluid. **2 ancestry**, lineage, descent, parentage, family, birth, extraction, origin, stock.

> **WORD LINKS**
> **haematology** branch of medicine concerned with blood

bloodshed noun **slaughter**, massacre, killing, wounding, carnage, butchery, bloodletting, bloodbath.

bloodthirsty *adjective* **murderous**, homicidal, violent, vicious, barbarous, barbaric, savage, brutal, cut-throat.

bloody *adjective* **1 bloodstained**, blood-soaked, gory, bleeding. **2 vicious**, ferocious, savage, fierce, brutal, cruel, murderous, gory.

bloom *verb* **1 flower**, blossom, open, mature. **2 flourish**, thrive, prosper, progress, burgeon; *informal* be in the pink.
- OPPOSITES wither, decline.

blossom *noun* **flower**, bloom, bud.
● *verb* **1 bloom**, flower, open, mature. **2 develop**, grow, mature, progress, evolve, burgeon, flourish, thrive, prosper, bloom.
- OPPOSITES wither, decline.

blot *noun* **1 patch**, dab, smudge, blotch, mark, dot, spot; *Brit. informal* splodge. **2 blemish**, taint, stain, blight, flaw, fault. **3** *a blot on the landscape* **eyesore**, monstrosity, carbuncle, mess; *informal* sight.
□ **blot out 1 conceal**, hide, obscure, exclude, obliterate, shadow, eclipse. **2 erase**, blank out, wipe out, eradicate.

blow[1] *verb* **1 gust**, puff, flurry, blast, roar, bluster, rush, storm. **2 sweep**, carry, toss, drive, push, force, drift, flutter, waft, float, glide, whirl. **3** *he blew the trumpet* **sound**, blast, toot, play, pipe, trumpet.
□ **blow out extinguish**, put out, snuff, douse, quench, smother. **blow up 1 explode**, detonate, go off, ignite, erupt, bomb, blast, destroy. **2 inflate**, pump up, fill up, puff up, swell, expand, distend.

blow[2] *noun* **1 stroke**, knock, bang, hit, punch, thump, smack, crack, rap; *informal* whack, bash, clout, wallop. **2 upset**, disaster, setback, misfortune, disappointment, calamity, catastrophe, thunderbolt, bombshell, shock, surprise, jolt.

blue *adjective* **azure**, cobalt, sapphire, navy, indigo, sky-blue, ultramarine, aquamarine, turquoise, cyan.

blueprint *noun* **plan**, design, diagram, drawing, sketch, layout, model, template, pattern, example, guide, prototype, pilot.

bluff[1] *noun* **trick**, deception, fraud, ruse, pretence, sham, fake, hoax, charade; *informal* put-on.
● *verb* **pretend**, sham, fake, feign, lie, deceive, delude, mislead, trick, fool, hoodwink, dupe, hoax; *informal* con, kid, have on.

bluff[2] *adjective* **plain-spoken**, straightforward, blunt, direct, no-nonsense, frank, open, candid, forthright, unequivocal; *informal* upfront.
- OPPOSITES guarded.

blunder *noun* **mistake**, error, gaffe, slip, oversight, faux pas; *informal* slip-up, boo-boo; *Brit. informal* clanger, boob, howler; *N. Amer. informal* blooper.
● *verb* **1 make a mistake**, err, miscalculate, bungle, trip up; *informal* slip up, screw up, blow it, goof; *Brit. informal* boob. **2 stumble**, lurch, stagger, flounder, grope.

blunt *adjective* **1** *a blunt knife* **dull**, worn. **2** *a broad leaf with a blunt tip* **rounded**, flat, stubby. **3 straightforward**, frank, plain-spoken, candid, direct, bluff, forthright, unequivocal, brusque, abrupt, curt, bald, brutal, harsh, stark; *informal* upfront.
- OPPOSITES sharp, subtle.
● *verb* **dull**, deaden, dampen, numb, take the edge off, weaken, allay, diminish, lessen.
- OPPOSITES intensify.

blur *verb* **cloud**, fog, obscure, dim, make hazy, make fuzzy, soften, dull, numb, deaden, mute.

blurred *adjective* **indistinct**, fuzzy, hazy, misty, foggy, clouded, cloudy, faint, unclear, vague, indefinite, unfocused.
- OPPOSITES sharp, clear.

blurt *verb*
□ **blurt out burst out with**, exclaim, call out, divulge, disclose, reveal, betray, let slip, give away; *informal* blab, let on, spill the beans.

blush *verb* **redden**, go pink, go red, flush, colour, burn up.

● *noun* **flush**, rosiness, redness, pinkness, bloom, high colour, glow.

blustery *adjective* **stormy**, gusty, blowy, windy, squally, wild.
- OPPOSITES calm.

board *noun* **1 plank**, beam, panel, slat, batten, timber. **2 committee**, council, panel, directorate, commission.
● *verb* **1 get on**, go aboard, enter, mount, ascend, embark, catch.
2 lodge, live, reside, stay, be housed; *N. Amer.* room; *informal* put up.

boast *verb* **1 brag**, crow, swagger, swank, show off, blow your own trumpet, sing your own praises; *informal* talk big, lay it on thick; *Austral./NZ informal* skite. **2** *the hotel boasts a fine restaurant* **have**, possess, own, enjoy, pride yourself/itself on, offer.
● *noun* **1 brag**, exaggeration, overstatement; *informal* swank; *Austral./NZ informal* skite. **2 pride**, joy, pride and joy, apple of someone's eye, wonder, delight.

boastful *adjective* **bragging**, swaggering, bumptious, swollen-headed, puffed up, full of yourself, cocky, conceited, arrogant; *informal* swanky, big-headed.
- OPPOSITES modest.

bob *verb* **move up and down**, bounce, toss, skip, dance, wobble, jiggle, joggle, jolt, jerk.

bodily *adjective* **physical**, corporeal, corporal, mortal, material, tangible, concrete, real, actual, incarnate.
- OPPOSITES spiritual, mental.
● *adverb* **forcefully**, forcibly, violently, completely, entirely.

body *noun* **1 figure**, frame, form, physique, anatomy, skeleton. **2 torso**, trunk. **3 corpse**, carcass, skeleton, remains; *informal* stiff; *Medicine* cadaver. **4 main part**, core, heart, hub. **5 association**, organization, assembly, delegation, committee, executive, company, society, corporation, group.

WORD LINKS
corporal, **corporeal** relating to the body

bog *noun* **marsh**, swamp, mire, quagmire, morass, slough, fen, wetland.
□ **bog down** mire, stick, entangle, ensnare, embroil, hamper, hinder, impede, obstruct, swamp, overwhelm.

bogus *adjective* **fake**, spurious, false, fraudulent, sham, counterfeit, forged, feigned; *informal* phoney, pretend.
- OPPOSITES genuine.

boil[1] *verb* **simmer**, bubble, stew, seethe, froth, foam.

boil[2] *noun* **swelling**, spot, pimple, blister, gathering, pustule, carbuncle, abscess.

boisterous *adjective* **lively**, animated, exuberant, spirited, noisy, loud, rowdy, unruly, wild, uproarious, unrestrained, uninhibited, uncontrolled, rough, disorderly, riotous; *informal* rumbustious.
- OPPOSITES restrained.

bold *adjective* **1 daring**, intrepid, brave, courageous, valiant, valorous, fearless, dauntless, audacious, daredevil, adventurous, heroic, plucky; *informal* gutsy, spunky. **2 striking**, vivid, bright, strong, eye-catching, prominent, gaudy, lurid, garish.
- OPPOSITES timid, faint.

bolster *verb* **strengthen**, reinforce, boost, fortify, support, prop up, buoy up, shore up, buttress, maintain, help, augment, increase.

bolt *noun* **1** *the bolt on the door* **bar**, lock, catch, latch, fastener. **2** *nuts and bolts* **pin**, rivet, peg, screw.
● *verb* **1** *he bolted the door* **lock**, bar, latch, fasten, secure. **2** *the lid was bolted down* **pin**, rivet, peg, screw, fasten, fix. **3 dash**, dart, run, sprint, hurtle, rush, fly, shoot; *informal* tear, scoot, leg it. **4 gobble**, gulp, wolf, guzzle, devour; *informal* demolish, polish off, shovel down; *N. Amer. informal* scarf, snarf.

bomb *noun* **explosive**, incendiary (device), missile, projectile.
● *verb* **blow up**, blast, shell, blitz, strafe, pound, bombard, attack, assault, destroy, demolish.

bombard verb **1 shell**, pound, blitz, strafe, bomb, batter, blast, pelt. **2 swamp**, inundate, flood, deluge, snow under, overwhelm.

bombardment noun **assault**, attack, bombing, shelling, strafing, blitz, air raid, cannonade, fusillade, barrage, broadside.

bonanza noun **windfall**, godsend, blessing, bonus, stroke of luck; *informal* jackpot.

bond noun **1 friendship**, relationship, fellowship, partnership, association, affiliation, alliance, attachment, tie, connection, link. **2 promise**, pledge, vow, oath, word (of honour), guarantee, assurance, agreement, contract, pact, deal.
● verb **join**, fasten, fix, affix, attach, secure, bind, stick, fuse.

bonus noun **1 advantage**, plus, benefit, extra, boon, blessing, godsend, stroke of luck, attraction. **2 gratuity**, handout, gift, present, reward, prize, incentive; *informal* perk, sweetener.
- OPPOSITES disadvantage.

bony adjective **skinny**, thin, lean, gaunt, scrawny, spare, skin and bone, skeletal, emaciated, underweight.
- OPPOSITES plump.

book noun **1 volume**, tome, publication, title, novel, treatise, manual. **2 notepad**, notebook, pad, exercise book, logbook, ledger, journal, diary; *Brit.* jotter, pocketbook; *N. Amer.* scratch pad.
● verb **reserve**, prearrange, order; *informal* bag.
□ **book in** register, check in, enrol.

> **WORD LINKS**
> **bibliography** list of books

booklet noun **pamphlet**, brochure, leaflet, tract; *N. Amer.* folder, mailer.

boom noun **1 roar**, rumble, thunder, crashing, drumming, pounding, echoing, resonance, reverberation. **2 increase**, growth, advance, boost, escalation, improvement, upsurge, upturn.

- OPPOSITES slump.
● verb **1 roar**, rumble, thunder, crash, roll, clap, explode, bang, resound, blare, echo, resonate, reverberate. **2 shout**, yell, bellow, roar, thunder, bawl; *informal* holler. **3 flourish**, thrive, prosper, burgeon, progress, improve, pick up, expand.

boorish adjective **coarse**, uncouth, rude, vulgar, uncivilized, unrefined, oafish, ignorant, uncultured, philistine, rough, thuggish, loutish, Neanderthal; *Brit. informal* yobbish; *Austral. informal* ocker.
- OPPOSITES refined.

boost verb **increase**, raise, escalate, improve, strengthen, inflate, push up, promote, advance, foster, stimulate, encourage, facilitate, help, assist, aid; *informal* hike, bump up.
- OPPOSITES decrease.
● noun **1** *a boost to your morale* **uplift**, lift, spur, encouragement, help, inspiration, stimulus, fillip; *informal* shot in the arm. **2** *a boost in sales* **increase**, expansion, upturn, upsurge, rise, escalation, improvement, advance, growth, boom; *informal* hike.
- OPPOSITES decrease.

boot verb **kick**, punt, tap, propel, drive, knock.

booth noun **1 stall**, stand, kiosk. **2** *a phone booth* **cubicle**, kiosk, box, compartment, enclosure, cabin.

booty noun **loot**, plunder, haul, spoils, ill-gotten gains, pickings; *informal* swag.

border noun **1 edge**, margin, perimeter, circumference, periphery, rim, fringe, verge, sides. **2 frontier**, boundary, borderline, perimeter.
● verb **1 surround**, enclose, encircle, edge, fringe, bound, flank. **2 edge**, fringe, hem, trim, pipe, finish. **3 adjoin**, abut, be next to, be adjacent to, touch.
□ **border on** verge on, approach, come close to, be comparable to, approximate to, be tantamount to.

bore¹ verb **drill**, pierce, perforate, puncture, punch, tunnel, burrow, mine, dig, gouge, sink.

bore[2] verb **weary**, pall on, tire, fatigue, send to sleep, leave cold; *informal* turn off.
- OPPOSITES interest.
  - ● noun **tedious person/thing**, tiresome person/thing, bother, nuisance, pest, annoyance, trial, thorn in your flesh/side; *informal* drag, pain (in the neck), headache, hassle.

boredom noun **tedium**, ennui, apathy, weariness, dullness, monotony, repetitiveness, flatness, dreariness.
- OPPOSITES interest, excitement.

boring adjective **tedious**, dull, dreary, monotonous, repetitive, uneventful, unimaginative, characterless, featureless, colourless, lifeless, uninteresting, unexciting, lacklustre, humdrum, mind-numbing, soul-destroying, wearisome, tiresome; *informal* deadly; *Brit. informal* samey; *N. Amer. informal* dullsville.
- OPPOSITES interesting, exciting.

borrow verb **1 loan**, lease, hire; *informal* cadge, scrounge, bum, touch someone for; *N. Amer. informal* mooch; *Austral./NZ informal* bludge. **2 adopt**, take on, acquire, embrace, copy, imitate.
- OPPOSITES lend.

boss (informal) noun **head**, chief, principal, director, president, chief executive, chair, manager, supervisor, foreman, overseer, controller, employer, owner, proprietor; *Brit. informal* gaffer, governor; *N. Amer. informal* head honcho.
  - ● verb **order around**, dictate to, bully, push around/about, call the shots, lay down the law; *informal* bulldoze, walk all over, railroad.

bossy adjective (informal) **domineering**, pushy, overbearing, imperious, officious, high-handed, authoritarian, dictatorial, autocratic; *informal* high and mighty.
- OPPOSITES submissive.

bother verb **1** no one bothered her **disturb**, trouble, inconvenience, pester, badger, harass, molest, plague; *informal* hassle, bug; *N. English informal* mither; *N. Amer. informal* ride. **2** don't bother about me **mind**, care, worry, concern yourself, trouble yourself. **3** something was bothering him **worry**, trouble, concern, perturb, disturb, disquiet; *informal* rattle.
  - ● noun **1 trouble**, effort, exertion, inconvenience, fuss, pains; *informal* hassle. **2 nuisance**, pest, palaver, rigmarole, job, trial, bind, bore, drag, inconvenience, trouble; *informal* hassle, headache, pain (in the neck). **3** a spot of bother in the public bar **disorder**, fighting, trouble, disturbance, commotion, uproar; *informal* hoo-ha, aggro, argy-bargy, kerfuffle.

bottle noun **flask**, carafe, decanter, pitcher, flagon, magnum, demijohn, phial.
  - □ **bottle up** suppress, repress, restrain, hold in, smother, contain, conceal, hide; *informal* keep a lid on.

bottom noun **1 foot**, lowest part, base, foundation. **2 underside**, underneath, undersurface, underbelly. **3 floor**, bed, depths. **4 farthest point**, extremity, far end. **5** (Brit.) **buttocks**, rear (end), rump, seat, derrière; *informal* behind, backside; *Brit. informal* bum, jacksie; *N. Amer. informal* butt, fanny; *humorous* posterior.
- OPPOSITES top, surface.
  - ● adjective **lowest**, last, bottommost.
- OPPOSITES top.

bounce verb **1 rebound**, spring back, ricochet; *N. Amer.* carom. **2 bound**, leap, jump, spring, bob, hop, skip, gambol, trip, prance.
  - ● noun **1 springiness**, resilience, elasticity, give. **2 vitality**, vigour, energy, vivacity, liveliness, animation, sparkle, verve, spirit; *informal* get-up-and-go, pep, zing.

bound[1] adjective **1 tied**, restrained, fixed, fastened, secured. **2 certain**, sure, very likely, destined. **3** bound by the Official Secrets Act **constrained**, obliged, compelled, required, obligated.
- OPPOSITES free.

bound² *verb* **leap**, jump, spring, vault, bounce, hop, skip, dance, prance, gambol, gallop.

bound³ *verb* **1 limit**, restrict, confine, circumscribe, demarcate, delimit. **2 enclose**, surround, encircle, circle, border, close in/off, hem in.

boundary *noun* **1 border**, frontier, borderline, partition, dividing line. **2** *the boundary of his estate* **limits**, confines, bounds, margins, edges, fringes, border, periphery, perimeter.

boundless *adjective* **limitless**, untold, immeasurable, abundant, inexhaustible, endless, infinite, interminable, unfailing, ceaseless, everlasting.
- OPPOSITES limited.

bouquet *noun* **1 posy**, nosegay, spray, corsage, buttonhole, garland, wreath, arrangement. **2 aroma**, nose, smell, fragrance, perfume, scent, odour.

bourgeois *adjective* **middle-class**, conservative, conformist, conventional, propertied, provincial, suburban, small-town.
- OPPOSITES proletarian.

bout *noun* **1 spell**, period, stretch, stint, session, burst, flurry, spurt. **2 attack**, fit, spasm. **3 contest**, fight, match, round, competition, meeting, encounter; *Brit.* clash.

bow¹ *verb* **1 incline your head**, bend, stoop, bob, curtsy, kneel, genuflect. **2** *the mast bowed in the wind* **bend**, buckle, curve, flex. **3** *the government bowed to foreign pressure* **give in**, submit, yield, surrender, succumb, capitulate.
● *noun* **nod**, bob, obeisance, curtsy, genuflection, salaam.

bow² *noun* **prow**, front, stem, nose, head.

bowels *plural noun* **1 intestines**, entrails, viscera, innards, digestive system; *Medicine* gut; *informal* guts, insides. **2 interior**, inside, core, belly, depths, recesses; *informal* innards.

bowl¹ *verb* **throw**, pitch, hurl, toss, lob, fling, roll, launch, propel; *informal* chuck, sling, bung.

bowl² *noun* **dish**, basin, pot, crock, vessel, receptacle.

box¹ *noun* **1 carton**, pack, packet, case, crate, chest, coffer, casket. **2** *a telephone box* **booth**, kiosk, cubicle, compartment, cabin, hut.
● *verb* **pack**, package, parcel, encase, bundle, crate.

box² *verb* **fight**, spar, battle, brawl; *informal* scrap.

boxer *noun* **fighter**, pugilist, prizefighter; *informal* bruiser, scrapper.

boy *noun* **lad**, youth, young man, stripling; *Scottish & N. English* laddie.

boycott *verb* **shun**, snub, spurn, avoid, ostracize, blacklist, blackball, reject, veto, send to Coventry.
● *noun* **ban**, veto, embargo, prohibition, moratorium, sanction, restriction, avoidance, rejection.

boyfriend *noun* **lover**, sweetheart, beloved, darling, partner; *informal* fella, fancy man; *N. Amer. informal* squeeze; *dated* beau; *literary* swain.

brace *noun* **prop**, strut, stay, support, bracket.
● *verb* **1 support**, shore up, prop up, hold up, buttress, reinforce. **2 steady**, secure, stabilize, poise, fix. **3** *brace yourself for disappointment* **prepare**, get ready, gear up, nerve, steel, fortify; *informal* psych yourself up.

bracing *adjective* **invigorating**, refreshing, stimulating, energizing, exhilarating, restorative, rejuvenating.

bracket *noun* **1 support**, prop, stay, batten, rest, mounting, rack, frame. **2 group**, category, grade, classification, division.

brag *verb* **boast**, crow, swagger, swank, show off, blow your own trumpet, sing your own praises; *informal* talk big.

brain *noun* **intelligence**, intellect, brainpower, cleverness, wit(s), reasoning, wisdom, judgement, understanding, sense; *informal* nous, grey matter; *N. Amer. informal* smarts.

b

b

> **WORD LINKS**
> **cerebral** relating to the brain

brake noun curb, check, restraint, constraint, control, limit.
● verb **slow (down)**, decelerate, reduce speed.
– OPPOSITES accelerate.

branch noun **1 bough**, limb, arm, offshoot, twig. **2 division**, subdivision, section, subsection, department, unit, sector, wing, office, bureau, agency, subsidiary.
● verb **1 fork**, divide, split, bifurcate. **2** narrow paths branched off the road **diverge**, split off, fan out, radiate.

brand noun **1 make**, line, label, marque, trade name, trademark, proprietary name. **2 type**, kind, sort, variety, class, category, genre, style, ilk; N. Amer. stripe.
● verb **1 mark**, stamp, burn, sear. **2 stigmatize**, characterize, label, mark out, denounce, discredit, vilify.

brandish verb **flourish**, wave, shake, wield, swing, swish.

brash adjective **1 self-assertive**, pushy, cocky, self-confident, arrogant, bold, audacious, brazen. **2 garish**, gaudy, loud, flamboyant, showy, tasteless; informal flashy, tacky.
– OPPOSITES meek.

brave adjective **courageous**, intrepid, bold, plucky, heroic, fearless, daring, audacious, dauntless, valiant, valorous, doughty, indomitable, stout-hearted; informal game, gutsy.
– OPPOSITES cowardly.
● verb **endure**, put up with, bear, withstand, weather, suffer, face, confront, defy.

bravery noun **courage**, boldness, heroism, intrepidity, nerve, daring, fearlessness, audacity, pluck, valour; informal guts; Brit. informal bottle.

brawl noun **fight**, skirmish, scuffle, tussle, fray, melee, fracas, fisticuffs; informal scrap, set-to; Brit. informal punch-up.

brawny adjective **strong**, muscular, muscly, well built, powerful, strapping, burly, sturdy; informal beefy, hulking.
– OPPOSITES puny, weak.

brazen adjective **bold**, shameless, unashamed, unrepentant, unabashed, defiant, impudent, impertinent, cheeky, barefaced, blatant, flagrant.

breach noun **1 contravention**, violation, infringement, infraction, transgression. **2 break**, rupture, split, crack, fracture, opening, gap, hole, fissure. **3 rift**, severance, estrangement, parting, parting of the ways, split, falling-out, schism.
● verb **1 break (through)**, burst, rupture. **2 contravene**, break, violate, infringe, defy, disobey, flout.

breadth noun **1 width**, broadness, thickness, span, diameter. **2 range**, extent, scope, depth, reach, compass, scale.

break verb **1 shatter**, smash, crack, snap, fracture, fragment, splinter, split, burst; informal bust. **2 stop working**, break down, give out, go wrong, malfunction, crash; informal go kaput, conk out; Brit. informal pack up. **3 violate**, contravene, infringe, breach, defy, flout, disobey. **4** the film broke box-office records **beat**, surpass, exceed, better, cap, top, outdo, outstrip. **5** he tried to break the news gently **reveal**, disclose, divulge, impart, tell, announce, release.
– OPPOSITES repair, obey.
● noun **1 interval**, interruption, gap, disruption, stoppage, cessation, halt, stop. **2 rest**, respite, recess, pause, intermission; informal breather, time out. **3 gap**, opening, space, hole, breach, chink, crack, fracture, fissure, tear, split.
□ **break down 1 stop working**, give out, go wrong, malfunction, crash; informal go kaput, conk out; Brit. informal pack up. **2 fail**, collapse, founder, fall through. **3 burst into tears**, lose control, be overcome, go to pieces; informal crack up, lose it. **4 analyse**, categorize, classify, sort, itemize, organize, divide, separate, split. **break off 1 snap**

off, pull off, sever, detach. **2** end, terminate, stop, cease, call a halt to, suspend, discontinue; *informal* pull the plug on. **break out 1** escape, abscond, flee, get free. **2** flare up, start suddenly, erupt, burst out. **break up 1** end, finish, stop, terminate, adjourn; *N. Amer.* recess. **2** disperse, scatter, disband, part company. **3** split up, separate, part (company), divorce.

breakdown noun **1 failure**, collapse, disintegration, foundering. **2 nervous breakdown**, collapse. **3 malfunction**, failure, crash. **4 analysis**, itemization, classification, examination, investigation, explanation.

break-in noun **burglary**, robbery, theft, raid, breaking and entering; *informal* smash-and-grab.

breakthrough noun **advance**, development, step forward, success, improvement, discovery, innovation, revolution, quantum leap.
- OPPOSITES setback.

breast noun **chest**, bosom, bust; *informal* boobs, knockers.

breath noun **inhalation**, exhalation, gulp of air, puff, gasp; *Medicine* respiration.

breathe verb **1 inhale**, exhale, respire, draw breath, puff, pant, blow, gasp, wheeze; *Medicine* inspire, expire. **2 whisper**, murmur, purr, sigh.

> **WORD LINKS**
> **respiratory** relating to breathing

breathless adjective **1 out of breath**, panting, puffing, gasping, wheezing, winded; *informal* out of puff. **2 eager**, agog, open-mouthed, excited, on the edge of your seat, on tenterhooks.

breathtaking adjective **spectacular**, magnificent, awe-inspiring, awesome, astonishing, amazing, stunning, thrilling; *informal* sensational, out of this world.

breed verb **1 reproduce**, produce offspring, procreate, multiply, mate. **2 bring up**, rear, raise, nurture.

3 cause, produce, bring about, give rise to, occasion, arouse, stir up, generate, foster.
● noun **1** *a breed of cow* **variety**, stock, strain, race, species. **2** *a new breed of journalist* **type**, kind, sort, variety, class, genre, generation.

breeding noun **(good) manners**, gentility, refinement, cultivation, polish, urbanity; *informal* class.

breeze noun **gentle wind**, puff of air, gust, draught; *literary* zephyr.

breezy adjective **1 windy**, fresh, brisk, blowy, blustery, gusty. **2 jaunty**, cheerful, cheery, brisk, carefree, easy, casual, relaxed, informal, light-hearted, upbeat.

brevity noun **conciseness**, concision, succinctness, pithiness, incisiveness, shortness, compactness.

brew verb **1 ferment**, make, prepare, infuse; *Brit. informal* mash. **2 develop**, loom, be imminent, be on the horizon, be in the offing, be just around the corner.
● noun **1** *home brew* **beer**, ale. **2** *a hot reviving brew* **drink**, beverage, infusion. **3 mixture**, mix, blend, combination, amalgam, cocktail.

bribe verb **buy off**, pay off, suborn; *informal* grease someone's palm, keep someone sweet, square; *Brit. informal* nobble.
● noun **inducement**; *informal* bung, backhander, pay-off, kickback, sweetener.

bribery noun **corruption**; *N. Amer.* payola; *informal* palm-greasing, graft, hush money.

> **WORD LINKS**
> **venal** susceptible to bribery

bridge noun **1 viaduct**, flyover, overpass, aqueduct. **2 link**, connection, bond, tie.
● verb **span**, cross (over), extend across, traverse, arch over, straddle.

> **WORD LINKS**
> **pontine** relating to bridges

brief adjective **1 concise**, succinct, short, pithy, compact, thumbnail, potted, condensed, to the point, terse, summary. **2 short**, flying, fleeting, hasty, hurried, quick, cursory, perfunctory, temporary, short-lived, ephemeral, transient, transitory.
- OPPOSITES long.
● noun **1** my brief is to reorganize the project **instructions**, directions, directive, remit, mandate. **2** a barrister's brief **case**, summary, argument, contention, dossier.
● verb **inform**, tell, update, notify, advise, prepare, prime, instruct; informal fill in, put in the picture.

briefly adverb **1 concisely**, succinctly, tersely. **2 momentarily**, temporarily, fleetingly. **3** briefly, the plot is as follows **in short**, to cut a long story short, in brief, in a word, in a nutshell, in essence.

briefs plural noun **underpants**, pants, knickers, bikini briefs; N. Amer. shorts; informal panties; Brit. informal kecks.

brigade noun **squad**, team, group, band, party, crew, force, outfit.

bright adjective **1 shining**, brilliant, dazzling, glaring, sparkling, flashing, glittering, gleaming, glistening, coruscating, shimmering, radiant, glowing, luminous, shiny, glossy, lustrous. **2 sunny**, cloudless, clear, fair, fine. **3** bright colours **vivid**, brilliant, intense, strong, vibrant, bold, gaudy, lurid, garish. **4 clever**, intelligent, quick-witted, smart, canny, astute, perceptive, ingenious; informal brainy, genius.
- OPPOSITES dull, cloudy, dark, stupid.

brighten verb **1 illuminate**, light up, lighten. **2 cheer up**, perk up, liven up, rally, feel heartened; informal buck up.

brilliance noun **1 brightness**, vividness, intensity, sparkle, glitter, blaze, luminosity, radiance. **2 genius**, intelligence, talent, ability, prowess, skill, expertise, aptitude, flair, wisdom, intellect. **3 splendour**, magnificence, grandeur, resplendence, glory.
- OPPOSITES dullness, stupidity.

brilliant adjective **1 bright**, shining, sparkling, blazing, coruscating, dazzling, vivid, intense, glaring, luminous, radiant. **2 clever**, bright, intelligent, smart, able, talented, gifted, skilful, astute; informal brainy, genius. **3** her brilliant career **superb**, glorious, illustrious, successful, impressive, remarkable, exceptional, excellent, outstanding, distinguished.
- OPPOSITES dim, stupid, undistinguished.

brim noun **1 peak**, visor, shield. **2 rim**, lip, brink, edge.
● verb **be full (up)**, overflow, run over, well over.

bring verb **1 fetch**, carry, bear, take, convey, transport, shift. **2 escort**, conduct, guide, lead, usher. **3 cause**, produce, create, bring about, generate, precipitate, occasion, provoke, lead to, give rise to, result in.
□ **bring in** introduce, launch, inaugurate, initiate, institute. **bring off** achieve, accomplish, bring about, succeed in, pull off, carry off, manage. **bring out** launch, establish, begin, start, found, set up, market, publish, issue. **bring up 1** rear, raise, nurture, look after. **2** mention, raise, broach, introduce, air, suggest.

brink noun **1 edge**, verge, margin, rim, lip, border, boundary. **2** on the brink of war **verge**, threshold, point, edge.

brisk adjective **1 quick**, rapid, fast, swift, speedy, hurried, energetic, lively; informal nippy. **2 no-nonsense**, businesslike, decisive, brusque, abrupt, short, sharp, curt, blunt, terse; informal snappy.
- OPPOSITES leisurely.

bristle noun **1 hair**, whisker; (**bristles**) stubble, five o'clock shadow. **2 spine**, prickle, quill, barb.
● verb **1 rise**, stand up, stand on end. **2 take offence**, bridle, take umbrage, be offended. **3 be crowded**, be full, be packed, be jammed, be covered, overflow; informal be thick, be chockfull.

brittle *adjective* **breakable**, fragile, crisp, crumbly, delicate.
- OPPOSITES flexible.

broach *verb* **bring up**, raise, introduce, mention, touch on, air.

broad *adjective* **1 wide**, extensive, vast, immense, great, spacious, expansive, sizeable, sweeping. **2 comprehensive**, inclusive, extensive, wide, all-embracing, unlimited. **3** *a broad outline* **general**, non-specific, rough, approximate, basic, loose, vague.
- OPPOSITES narrow, limited.

broadcast *verb* **1 transmit**, relay, air, beam, show, televise, screen, telecast, videocast, podcast. **2 report**, announce, publicize, advertise, make public, proclaim, spread, circulate, promulgate.
● *noun* **transmission**, programme, show, telecast, videocast, podcast, production.

broaden *verb* **1** *her smile broadened* **widen**, expand, stretch (out), spread. **2** *the government tried to broaden its political base* **expand**, enlarge, extend, widen, swell, increase, add to, develop.
- OPPOSITES narrow, restrict.

broad-minded *adjective* **liberal**, tolerant, freethinking, indulgent, progressive, permissive, unshockable, unprejudiced, unbiased.
- OPPOSITES intolerant.

brochure *noun* **booklet**, prospectus, catalogue, pamphlet, leaflet, circular, mailshot; *N. Amer.* folder.

broken *adjective* **1 smashed**, shattered, fragmented, splintered, crushed, snapped, in bits, in pieces, cracked, split, fractured; *informal* in smithereens. **2 faulty**, damaged, defective, not working, malfunctioning, out of order, broken down, down; *informal* kaput, bust, acting up; *Brit. informal* knackered. **3 interrupted**, disturbed, fitful, disrupted, discontinuous, intermittent. **4 halting**, hesitating, disjointed, faltering, imperfect.

broken-hearted *adjective* **heartbroken**, grief-stricken, desolate, devastated, inconsolable, miserable, wretched, forlorn, heavy-hearted, woeful.
- OPPOSITES overjoyed.

broker *noun* **dealer**, agent, middleman, intermediary, mediator, factor, liaison, stockbroker.
● *verb* **arrange**, organize, orchestrate, work out, settle, clinch, negotiate, mediate.

brood *noun* **offspring**, young, family, litter, clutch, progeny.
● *verb* **think**, ponder, contemplate, meditate, ruminate, muse, worry, dwell on, fret, agonize.

brook *noun* **stream**, rill; *N. English* beck; *Scottish & N. English* burn; *N. Amer. & Austral./NZ* creek.

brotherly *adjective* **fraternal**, friendly, comradely, affectionate, amicable, kind, devoted, loyal.

brow *noun* **1 forehead**, temple. **2 summit**, peak, top, crest, crown, head, pinnacle, apex.

browbeat *verb* **bully**, intimidate, force, coerce, compel, dragoon, bludgeon, pressure, pressurize, tyrannize, terrorize; *informal* bulldoze, railroad.

brown *adjective* **1 hazel**, chestnut, chocolate, coffee, brunette, sepia, mahogany, tan, café au lait, caramel. **2 tanned**, suntanned, bronzed, swarthy.
● *verb* **grill**, toast, singe, sear, barbecue, sauté.

browse *verb* **look through**, scan, skim, glance, peruse, thumb, leaf, flick, dip into.

bruise *noun* **contusion**, bump, swelling, lump, mark, injury, welt.
● *verb* **contuse**, injure, mark, discolour, make black and blue, blemish, damage, spoil.

brush¹ *noun* **1 broom**, sweeper, besom, whisk. **2 clean**, sweep, wipe, dust. **3** *a brush with the law* **encounter**, clash, confrontation, conflict, altercation, incident; *informal* run-in, to-do; *Brit. informal* spot of bother.

b

● *verb* **1 sweep**, clean, buff, polish, scrub. **2 groom**, comb, neaten, tidy, smooth, arrange. **3** *his lips brushed her cheek* **touch**, stroke, caress, skim, sweep, graze, contact, kiss.
□ **brush aside** disregard, ignore, dismiss, shrug off, wave aside, reject, spurn, laugh off, make light of; *informal* pooh-pooh. **brush up (on)** revise, read up, go over, improve, polish up, enhance, hone, perfect; *informal* bone up on; *Brit. informal* swot up (on).

brush² *noun* **undergrowth**, scrub, brushwood, shrubs, bushes; *N. Amer.* underbrush, chaparral.

brusque *adjective* **curt**, abrupt, blunt, short, sharp, brisk, peremptory, gruff, discourteous, impolite, rude.
- OPPOSITES polite.

brutal *adjective* **savage**, violent, cruel, vicious, ferocious, barbaric, wicked, murderous, bloodthirsty, cold-blooded, callous, ruthless, heartless, merciless, sadistic, inhuman.
- OPPOSITES gentle.

bubbly *adjective* **1 fizzy**, sparkling, effervescent, gassy, aerated, carbonated, frothy, foamy. **2 vivacious**, animated, ebullient, lively, high-spirited, bouncy, merry, happy, cheerful, sunny; *informal* chirpy.
- OPPOSITES still.

buckle *noun* **clasp**, clip, catch, hasp, fastener.
● *verb* **1 fasten**, do up, hook, secure, clasp, clip. **2 bend**, warp, twist, distort, contort, deform, crumple, collapse, give way.

budding *adjective* **promising**, up-and-coming, rising, in the making, aspiring, future, fledgling, developing.

budge *verb* **1 move**, shift, stir, go. **2 persuade**, convince, influence, sway, bend.

budget *noun* **1 financial plan**, forecast. **2** *the defence budget* **allowance**, allocation, quota, funds, resources, capital.
● *verb* **allocate**, allot, allow, earmark, designate, set aside.

buff¹ *verb* **polish**, burnish, shine, smooth, rub.

buff² *noun* *(informal)* **enthusiast**, fan, devotee, lover, admirer, expert, aficionado, authority; *informal* freak, nut, addict.

buffer *noun* **cushion**, bulwark, shield, barrier, guard, safeguard.

buffet¹ *noun* **1 cold table**, self-service meal, smorgasbord. **2 cafe**, cafeteria, snack bar, canteen, restaurant.

buffet² *verb* **batter**, pound, lash, strike, hit, beat.

bug *noun* **1** *(informal)* **illness**, disease, sickness, disorder, upset, ailment, infection, virus; *Brit. informal* lurgy. **2 insect**, minibeast; *informal* creepy-crawly, beastie. **3 listening device**, hidden microphone, wire, wiretap, tap. **4 fault**, error, defect, flaw, virus; *informal* glitch, gremlin.
● *verb* **eavesdrop on**, spy on, tap, monitor.

build *verb* **construct**, erect, put up, assemble, make, create, fashion, model, shape.
- OPPOSITES demolish, dismantle.
● *noun* **physique**, frame, body, figure, form, shape, stature, proportions; *informal* vital statistics.
□ **build up 1** increase, grow, mount up, intensify, strengthen. **2** boost, strengthen, increase, improve, augment, raise, enhance, swell. **3** accumulate, amass, collect, gather.

building *noun* **structure**, construction, edifice, pile, property, premises, establishment.

> **WORD LINKS**
> **architectural** relating to building

build-up *noun* **increase**, growth, expansion, enlargement, escalation, accumulation, development.

bulbous *adjective* **bulging**, round, fat, rotund, swollen, distended, bloated.

bulge *noun* **swelling**, bump, lump, hump, protrusion, protuberance.
● *verb* **swell**, stick out, project, protrude, stand out, puff out, balloon (out), fill out, distend.

bulk *noun* **1 size**, volume, dimensions, proportions, mass, scale. **2 majority**, mass, generality, main part, lion's share, preponderance.

bulky *adjective* **unwieldy**, cumbersome, unmanageable, awkward, ponderous, outsize, oversized; *informal* hulking.

bullet *noun* **ball**, shot, pellet; *informal* slug; (**bullets**) lead.

bulletin *noun* **1 report**, dispatch, story, newsflash, statement, announcement, message, communication, communiqué. **2 newsletter**, news-sheet, proceedings, newspaper, magazine, gazette, review.

bully *noun* **persecutor**, oppressor, tyrant, tormentor, intimidator, bully boy, thug, attack dog.
● *verb* **1** *the others bully him* **persecute**, oppress, tyrannize, browbeat, intimidate, dominate, terrorize; *informal* push around/about. **2** *she was bullied into helping* **coerce**, pressure, press, push, prod, browbeat, dragoon, strong-arm; *informal* bulldoze, railroad, lean on.

bump *noun* **1 jolt**, crash, smash, smack, crack, bang, thud, thump, clang, knock, clunk, boom; *informal* whack, wallop. **2 swelling**, lump, bulge, injury, contusion, hump, knob.
● *verb* **1 hit**, crash into, smash into, slam into, bang, knock, run into, plough into, ram, collide with, strike; *N. Amer.* impact. **2 bounce**, jolt, jerk, rattle, shake.

bumper *adjective* **exceptional**, large, abundant, rich, bountiful, good, plentiful, record, successful; *informal* whopping.
- OPPOSITES meagre.

bumpy *adjective* **1 uneven**, rough, rutted, pitted, potholed, lumpy, rocky. **2 bouncy**, rough, uncomfortable, jolting, lurching, jerky, jarring, bone-shaking.
- OPPOSITES smooth.

bunch *noun* **1 bouquet**, posy, nosegay, spray, wreath, garland. **2 cluster**, clump, knot, group, bundle.
● *verb* **cluster**, huddle, gather, congregate, collect, amass, group, crowd.

bundle *noun* **collection**, roll, clump, wad, parcel, sheaf, bale, pile, stack, heap, mass, bunch; *informal* load, wodge.
● *verb* **1 tie**, parcel, wrap, swathe, roll, fold, bind, pack. **2** *he was bundled into a van* **push**, shove, thrust, throw, propel, jostle, manhandle.

bungle *verb* **mishandle**, mismanage, mess up, spoil, ruin; *informal* blow, botch, fluff, make a hash of, screw up; *Brit. informal* make a pig's ear of; *N. Amer. informal* goof up.

bungling *adjective* **incompetent**, blundering, amateurish, inept, unskilful, clumsy, awkward, bumbling; *informal* ham-fisted, cack-handed.

buoy *noun* **float**, marker, beacon.

buoyant *adjective* **1 floating**, floatable. **2 cheerful**, cheery, happy, light-hearted, carefree, joyful, bubbly, bouncy, sunny, upbeat.
- OPPOSITES gloomy.

burden *noun* **responsibility**, onus, obligation, duty, liability, trouble, care, problem, difficulty, worry, strain.
● *verb* **oppress**, trouble, worry, weigh down, overload, encumber, saddle, tax, afflict.

bureau *noun* **1 desk**, writing table, secretaire. **2 department**, agency, office, division, branch, section, station, unit.

bureaucracy *noun* **1 red tape**, rules and regulations, protocol, officialdom, paperwork. **2 civil service**, government, administration, establishment, system, powers that be, authorities.

bureaucrat *noun* **official**, administrator, civil servant, minister, functionary, mandarin; *derogatory* apparatchik.

burgeon *verb* **grow**, increase, rocket, mushroom, expand, escalate, swell, boom, flourish, thrive, prosper.

burglar *noun* **housebreaker**, thief, intruder, robber, raider, looter.

burglary *noun* **housebreaking**, breaking and entering, break-in, theft, raid, stealing, robbery, larceny, looting; *informal* smash-and-grab; *N. Amer. informal* heist.

burgle verb **rob**, loot, steal from, raid.

burial noun **funeral**, interment, committal, inhumation, entombment, obsequies, exequies.
- OPPOSITES exhumation.

burly adjective **strapping**, well built, strong, muscular, muscly, hefty, sturdy, brawny; *informal* hunky, beefy.
- OPPOSITES puny.

burn verb **1 be on fire**, be alight, blaze, go up (in smoke), be in flames, smoulder, glow. **2 set fire to**, set alight, set light to, kindle, ignite, touch off, incinerate, cremate; *informal* torch. **3 scorch**, singe, sear, char, blacken, brand.

burning adjective **1 on fire**, blazing, flaming, fiery, glowing, red-hot, smouldering. **2** *a burning desire* **intense**, passionate, deep-seated, profound, strong, ardent, fervent, urgent, fierce, consuming. **3** *burning issues* **important**, crucial, critical, vital, essential, pivotal, urgent, pressing, compelling.

burrow noun **warren**, tunnel, hole, dugout, lair, set, den, earth.
● verb **tunnel**, dig, excavate, mine, bore, channel.

burst verb **1** *one balloon burst* **split (open)**, rupture, break, tear. **2** *a shell burst* **explode**, blow up, detonate, go off. **3** *smoke burst through the hole* **gush**, erupt, surge, rush, stream, flow, pour, spurt, jet. **4** *he burst into the room* **charge**, plunge, barge, plough, hurtle, career, rush, dash, tear.
● noun **1 rupture**, puncture, breach, split, blowout. **2 explosion**, detonation, blast, eruption, bang. **3** *a burst of gunfire* **volley**, salvo, barrage, hail, rain. **4** *a burst of activity* **outbreak**, eruption, flare-up, blaze, attack, fit, rush, storm, surge, spurt.

bury verb **1 inter**, lay to rest, entomb. **2 hide**, conceal, cover, enfold, sink. **3** *the bullet buried itself in the wood* **embed**, sink, implant, submerge, lodge.

- OPPOSITES exhume.

bush noun **1 shrub**, thicket; (**bushes**) undergrowth, shrubbery. **2** *the bush* **wilds**, wilderness, backwoods; *N. Amer.* backcountry; *Austral./NZ* outback, backblocks; *N. Amer. informal* boondocks.

bushy adjective **thick**, shaggy, curly, fuzzy, bristly, fluffy, woolly.

business noun **1 work**, occupation, profession, career, employment, job, position. **2 trade**, commerce, dealing, traffic, dealings, transactions, negotiations. **3 firm**, company, concern, enterprise, venture, organization, operation, undertaking; *informal* outfit. **4** *it's none of your business* **concern**, affair, responsibility, duty. **5** *an odd business* **affair**, matter, case, circumstance, situation, event, incident.

businesslike adjective **professional**, efficient, organized, slick, methodical, systematic, orderly, structured, disciplined, practical, pragmatic.

businessman, businesswoman noun **executive**, entrepreneur, industrialist, merchant, dealer, trader, manufacturer, tycoon, employer, broker, buyer, seller, tradesman, retailer, supplier.

bust noun **1 bosom**, breasts, chest; *informal* boobs, knockers. **2 sculpture**, carving, effigy, statue, head and shoulders.

bustle verb **rush**, dash, hurry, scurry, scuttle, scamper, scramble; *informal* scoot, beetle, buzz.
● noun **activity**, action, liveliness, excitement, tumult, commotion, hubbub, hurly-burly, whirl; *informal* toing and froing.

bustling adjective **busy**, crowded, swarming, teeming, humming, buzzing, hectic, lively.

busy adjective **1** *I'm very busy* **hard at work**, involved, rushed off your feet, hard-pressed, pushed; *informal* on the go, hard at it; *Brit. informal* on the hop. **2** *I'm sorry, she's busy* **unavailable**, engaged, occupied, absorbed, engrossed, immersed, preoccupied,

working; *informal* tied up. **3** *a busy day* **hectic**, active, lively, full, eventful, energetic, tiring.
- OPPOSITES idle, free, quiet.
● *verb* **occupy**, involve, engage, concern, absorb, engross, immerse, distract.

but *conjunction* **1 however**, nevertheless, nonetheless, even so, yet, still.
2 whereas, conversely.
● *preposition* **except (for)**, apart from, other than, besides, aside from, with the exception of, bar.
◻ **but for** except for, if it were not for, notwithstanding, barring.

butt[1] *verb* **ram**, headbutt, bump, poke, prod, push, shove, thrust.
◻ **butt in** interrupt, intrude, break in, cut in, interfere, put your oar in; *informal* poke your nose in; *Brit. informal* chip in.

butt[2] *noun* **target**, victim, object, dupe, laughing stock.

butt[3] *noun* **1 stock**, end, handle, hilt, haft. **2 stub**, end, stump; *informal* fag end, dog end.

buttocks *plural noun* **bottom**, rear (end), rump, seat, derrière, cheeks; *informal* behind, backside; *Brit. informal* bum; *N. Amer. informal* butt, fanny; *humorous* posterior.

buttress *verb* **strengthen**, shore up, reinforce, fortify, support, bolster, underpin, cement, uphold, defend, back up.

buy *verb* **purchase**, acquire, obtain, get, pick up, snap up, invest in; *informal* get hold of, score.
- OPPOSITES sell.
● *noun* (*informal*) **purchase**, deal, bargain, investment, acquisition.

buyer *noun* **purchaser**, customer, consumer, shopper, investor; (**buyers**) clientele, market.

buzz *noun* **hum**, murmur, drone, whirr.

bypass *noun* **ring road**, detour, diversion, alternative route; *Brit.* relief road.
● *verb* **1 go round**, go past, make a detour round, avoid. **2 ignore**, sidestep, avoid, evade, escape, elude, skirt, dodge, circumvent, get round, go over the head of, pass over; *informal* short-circuit, duck.

bystander *noun* **onlooker**, passer-by, observer, spectator, eyewitness.

Cc

cab noun **taxi**, taxi cab; *Brit.* minicab, hackney carriage; *N. Amer.* hack.

cabin noun **1 berth**, stateroom, compartment. **2 hut**, log cabin, shanty, shack, chalet; *Scottish* bothy; *N. Amer.* cabana.

cabinet noun **cupboard**, bureau, chest of drawers.

cable noun **1** *a thick cable moored the ship* **rope**, cord, line, guy; *Nautical* hawser. **2** *electric cables* **wire**, lead, cord, power line; *Brit.* flex.

cache noun **hoard**, store, stockpile, stock, supply, reserve, arsenal; *informal* stash.

cadence noun **rhythm**, tempo, metre, beat, pulse, intonation, modulation, lilt.

cafe noun **snack bar**, cafeteria, coffee bar/shop, tea room/shop, bistro, brasserie; *N. Amer.* diner, lunchroom.

cafeteria noun **self-service restaurant**, canteen, cafe, buffet, refectory, mess hall.

cage noun **enclosure**, pen, pound, coop, hutch, birdcage, aviary.
● *verb* **confine**, shut in/up, pen, coop up, enclose.

cagey adjective (*informal*) **secretive**, guarded, tight-lipped, reticent, evasive; *informal* playing your cards close to your chest.

cajole verb **persuade**, wheedle, coax, talk into, prevail on; *informal* sweet-talk, soft-soap.

cake noun **1 bun**, pastry, gateau, slice. **2 bar**, tablet, block, slab, lump, wedge.
● *verb* *boots caked with mud* **coat**, encrust, plaster, cover.

calamity noun **disaster**, catastrophe, tragedy, cataclysm, accident, misfortune, misadventure.

calculate verb **1 compute**, work out, reckon, figure, add up/together, count up, tally, total; *Brit.* tot up. **2 intend**, mean, design.

calculated adjective **deliberate**, premeditated, planned, pre-planned, preconceived, intentional, intended.
– OPPOSITES unintentional.

calculating adjective **cunning**, crafty, wily, sly, scheming, devious, disingenuous.

calculation noun **1 computation**, reckoning, adding up, counting up, working out; *Brit.* totting up. **2 assessment**, judgement, forecast, projection, prediction.

calendar noun **schedule**, diary, programme, timetable, agenda.

calibre noun **1 quality**, standard, level, merit, distinction, stature, excellence, ability, expertise, talent, capability. **2 bore**, diameter, gauge.

call verb **1 cry**, cry out, shout, yell, sing out, exclaim, shriek, scream, roar; *informal* holler. **2 wake (up)**, awaken, rouse; *Brit. informal* knock up. **3 phone**, telephone, give someone a call; *Brit.* ring (up), give someone a ring; *informal* call up, give someone a buzz; *Brit. informal* give someone a bell. **4 summon**, send for, order. **5 pay a visit to**, visit, call/drop/look in on, drop/stop by, pop into, nip over to. **6 convene**, summon, assemble. **7 name**, christen, baptize, designate, style, term, dub. **8 describe as**, regard as, look on as, think of as, consider to be.
● *noun* **1 cry**, shout, yell, exclamation, shriek, scream, roar; *informal* holler. **2** *the call of the barn owl* **cry**, song. **3 phone call**, telephone call; *Brit.* ring; *informal* buzz; *Brit. informal* bell. **4 appeal**, plea, request. **5** *there's no call for that kind of language* **need**, necessity, reason, justification, excuse. **6** *there's no call for expensive wine*

demand, desire, market. **7 attraction**, appeal, lure, allure, pull, draw.
□ **call for 1** require, need, necessitate, make necessary, demand, be grounds for, justify, warrant. **2** ask for, request, seek, apply for, appeal for, demand, insist on, order. **call off** cancel, abandon, scrap, drop, axe; *informal* scrub; *N. Amer. informal* redline. **call up** enlist, recruit, conscript; *US* draft.

calling *noun* **profession**, occupation, job, vocation, career, métier, work, line of work, employment, trade, craft.

callous *adjective* **heartless**, unfeeling, uncaring, cold, cold-hearted, hard, hardbitten, as hard as nails, hard-hearted, insensitive, unsympathetic.
- OPPOSITES kind, compassionate.

calm *adjective* **1 relaxed**, composed, self-possessed, serene, tranquil, unruffled, unperturbed, unflustered, untroubled, unexcitable, level-headed, unemotional, phlegmatic, imperturbable; *informal* unflappable, laid-back, chilled. **2 windless**, still, quiet, tranquil, smooth.
- OPPOSITES excited, nervous, stormy.
● *noun* **1** *his usual calm deserted him* **composure**, coolness, calmness, self-possession, sangfroid, serenity, tranquillity; *informal* cool, unflappability. **2** *calm prevailed* **tranquillity**, stillness, quiet, peace.
□ **calm down 1** soothe, pacify, placate, mollify; *Brit.* quieten (down). **2** compose yourself, regain your composure, control yourself, pull yourself together, simmer down, cool down/off, take it easy; *Brit.* quieten down; *informal* get a grip, keep your shirt on; *N. Amer. informal* decompress.

camouflage *noun* **disguise**, mask, screen, cover, cloak, front, facade, blind, concealment, subterfuge.
● *verb* **disguise**, hide, conceal, mask, screen, cover (up).

camp *noun* **1 campsite**, encampment, camping ground, bivouac, base, settlement. **2 faction**, wing, group, lobby, caucus, bloc.

campaign *noun* **1** *Napoleon's Russian campaign* **operation(s)**, manoeuvre(s), offensive, attack, war, battle, crusade. **2** *the campaign to reduce vehicle emissions* **effort**, drive, push, struggle, movement, crusade, operation, strategy.
● *verb* **fight**, battle, push, press, strive, struggle, lobby, agitate.

cancel *verb* **1 call off**, abandon, scrap, drop, axe; *informal* scrub; *N. Amer. informal* redline. **2 annul**, invalidate, declare null and void, void, revoke, rescind, retract, withdraw.
□ **cancel out** neutralize, negate, nullify, wipe out, balance (out), make up for, compensate for, offset.

cancer *noun* **(malignant) growth**, tumour, malignancy; *technical* carcinoma, sarcoma.

WORD LINKS

carcinogenic causing cancer
oncology branch of medicine concerned with cancer

---

candid *adjective* **frank**, forthright, direct, blunt, outspoken, plain-spoken, open, honest, truthful, sincere; *informal* upfront; *N. Amer. informal* on the up and up.
- OPPOSITES guarded.

candidate *noun* **applicant**, contender, competitor, entrant, claimant, nominee, interviewee, examinee, possible; *Brit. informal* runner.

canny *adjective* **shrewd**, astute, smart, sharp, discerning, discriminating, perceptive, clever, judicious, wise.
- OPPOSITES foolish.

canopy *noun* **awning**, shade, sunshade, covering.

canvass *verb* **1 campaign**, electioneer. **2 poll**, question, survey, interview, consult.

canyon *noun* **ravine**, gorge, gully, chasm, abyss, gulf; *N. Amer.* gulch, coulee.

cap *noun* **1 lid**, top, stopper, cork, bung; *N. Amer.* stopple. **2 limit**, ceiling, curb, check.

● *verb* **1 top**, crown, cover, coat, tip. **2 limit**, restrict, curb, control, peg.

capability *noun* **ability**, capacity, power, potential, competence, aptitude, faculty, skill, talent, flair; *informal* know-how.
- OPPOSITES inability.

capable *adjective* **able**, competent, effective, proficient, accomplished, experienced, skilful, talented, gifted; *informal* useful.
- OPPOSITES incapable, incompetent.

capacity *noun* **1 volume**, size, dimensions, measurements, proportions. **2 ability**, capability, power, potential, competence, aptitude, faculty, skill, talent, flair. **3 role**, function, position, post, job, office.

cape¹ *noun* **cloak**, mantle, shawl, poncho, pashmina.

cape² *noun* **headland**, promontory, point, head, horn, mull, peninsula.

capital *noun* **money**, finance(s), funds, cash, wherewithal, means, assets, wealth, resources, deep pockets.

capitalism *noun* **private enterprise**, free enterprise, the free market, private ownership.
- OPPOSITES communism.

capitalize *verb*
□ **capitalize on** take advantage of, profit from, make the most of, exploit, develop; *informal* cash in on.

capitulate *verb* **surrender**, give in, yield, concede defeat, give up (the struggle), submit, lay down your arms, throw in the towel/sponge.
- OPPOSITES resist.

capricious *adjective* **fickle**, volatile, unpredictable, temperamental, mercurial, impulsive, changeable, unreliable, erratic, wayward, whimsical, flighty.
- OPPOSITES consistent.

capsize *verb* **overturn**, turn over, turn upside down, upend, flip/tip over, keel over, turn turtle.

capsule *noun* **1 pill**, tablet, lozenge, pastille; *informal* tab. **2 module**, craft, probe.

captain *noun* **1** *the ship's captain* **commander**, master; *informal* skipper. **2** *the team captain* **leader**, head, chief; *informal* boss, skipper.

caption *noun* **title**, heading, legend, description.

captivate *verb* **enthral**, charm, enchant, bewitch, fascinate, beguile, entrance, delight, attract, allure.
- OPPOSITES bore.

captive *noun* **prisoner**, convict, detainee, hostage, prisoner of war, internee.
● *adjective* **confined**, caged, incarcerated, locked up, jailed, imprisoned, interned, detained.
- OPPOSITES free.

captivity *noun* **imprisonment**, incarceration, confinement, detention, internment.
- OPPOSITES freedom.

capture *verb* **1 catch**, apprehend, seize, arrest, take prisoner, take into custody, detain. **2 occupy**, invade, conquer, seize, take.
- OPPOSITES release, liberate.
● *noun* **arrest**, apprehension, detention, seizure.

car *noun* **1 motor**, motor car, automobile; *informal* wheels; *N. Amer. informal* auto. **2 carriage**, coach; *Brit.* saloon.

carcass *noun* **corpse**, dead body, remains; *Medicine* cadaver; *informal* stiff.

care *noun* **1 safe keeping**, supervision, custody, charge, protection, responsibility, guardianship. **2 discretion**, caution, sensitivity, thought, regard, consideration. **3 worry**, anxiety, trouble, concern, stress, pressure, strain.
- OPPOSITES neglect, carelessness.
● *verb* **be concerned**, worry (yourself), trouble/concern yourself, bother, mind, be interested; *informal* give a damn/hoot.
□ **care for 1** love, be fond of, be devoted to, treasure, adore, dote on, think the world of, worship. **2** look after, take care of, tend, attend to, minister to, nurse.

career noun **profession**, occupation, vocation, calling, life's work, employment.
● verb **hurtle**, rush, shoot, race, speed, charge, hare, fly; informal belt, tear; Brit. informal bucket.

carefree adjective **unworried**, untroubled, blithe, nonchalant, happy-go-lucky, free and easy, easy-going, relaxed; informal laid-back.
– OPPOSITES troubled.

careful adjective **1** be careful on the stairs **cautious**, alert, attentive, watchful, vigilant, wary, on your guard, circumspect. **2** careful with money **prudent**, thrifty, economical, sparing, frugal. **3** careful consideration of the facts **attentive**, conscientious, painstaking, meticulous, diligent, assiduous, scrupulous, methodical.
– OPPOSITES careless.

careless adjective **1** careless motorists **inattentive**, negligent, heedless, irresponsible, impetuous, reckless. **2** careless work **shoddy**, slapdash, slipshod, scrappy, slovenly, sloppy, negligent, lax, slack, disorganized, hasty, hurried. **3** a careless remark **thoughtless**, insensitive, indiscreet, unguarded, incautious, inadvertent.
– OPPOSITES careful.

caress verb **stroke**, touch, fondle, brush, feel, skim.

caretaker noun **janitor**, attendant, porter, custodian, concierge; N. Amer. superintendent.
● adjective **temporary**, acting, provisional, substitute, interim, stand-in, fill-in, stopgap; N. Amer. informal pinch-hitting.

cargo noun **freight**, load, haul, consignment, delivery, shipment, goods, merchandise.

caricature noun **cartoon**, parody, satire, lampoon, burlesque; informal send-up, take-off.
● verb **parody**, satirize, lampoon, make fun of, mock, ridicule; informal send up, take off.

carnage noun **slaughter**, massacre, murder, butchery, bloodbath, bloodletting, holocaust.

carnival noun **festival**, fiesta, fete, fair, gala, Mardi Gras.

carp verb **complain**, find fault, quibble, grumble, grouse, whine; informal nitpick, gripe, moan, bitch, whinge.

carpenter noun **woodworker**, joiner, cabinetmaker; Brit. informal chippy.

carriage noun **1** a railway carriage **coach**, car; Brit. saloon. **2** a horse and carriage **wagon**, coach. **3** posture, bearing, gait; Brit. deportment.

carry verb **1** convey, transfer, transport, move, take, bring, bear, fetch; informal cart, hump, lug. **2** transmit, conduct, relay, communicate, convey, beam, send. **3** approve, pass, accept, endorse, ratify. **4** be audible, travel, reach, be heard.
□ **carry on** continue, keep (on), go on, persist in; informal stick with/at. **carry out 1** conduct, perform, execute, implement. **2** keep, honour, fulfil, observe, abide by, comply with, adhere to, stick to.

carton noun **box**, package, cardboard box, case, container, pack, packet.

cartoon noun **1** animation, animated film, comic strip, graphic novel. **2** caricature, parody, lampoon, satire; informal take-off, send-up.

cartridge noun **cassette**, magazine, canister, case, container.

carve verb **1** sculpt, cut, hew, whittle, chisel, shape, fashion. **2** engrave, incise, score, cut. **3** slice, cut up, chop.
□ **carve up** divide, break up, partition, apportion, subdivide, split up, share out.

cascade noun **waterfall**, cataract, falls, rapids, white water, flood, torrent.
● verb **pour**, gush, surge, spill, stream, flow, issue, spurt, jet.

case[1] noun **1** a classic case of overreaction **instance**, example, occurrence, occasion, demonstration, illustration. **2** is that the case? **situation**, position, state of affairs, circumstances, conditions, facts; *Brit.* state of play; *informal* score. **3 assignment**, job, project, investigation, exercise. **4** *he lost his case* **lawsuit**, legal action, trial, legal proceedings, litigation. **5** *the case against animal testing* **argument**, defence, justification, vindication, exposition, thesis.

case² noun **1 container**, box, canister, holder. **2 casing**, cover, sheath, envelope, sleeve, jacket, shell. **3** (*Brit.*) **suitcase**, travel bag, valise; (**cases**) luggage, baggage. **4 cabinet**, cupboard.

cash noun **1 money**, currency, bank notes, coins, change; *N. Amer.* bills; *informal* dough, loot; *Brit. informal* dosh, brass; *N. Amer. informal* dinero. **2 finance**, money, resources, funds, assets, means, wherewithal.

cashier noun **clerk**, teller, banker, treasurer, bursar, purser.

cask noun **barrel**, keg, butt, tun, vat, drum, hogshead; *historical* firkin.

cast verb **1 throw**, toss, fling, pitch, hurl, lob; *informal* chuck, sling, bung. **2 direct**, shoot, throw, fling, send. **3 register**, record, enter, file. **4 emit**, give off, throw, send out, radiate. **5 mould**, fashion, form, shape, forge. ● noun **1 mould**, die, matrix, shape, casting, model. **2 actors**, performers, players, company, troupe, dramatis personae, characters.

caste noun **class**, rank, level, order, stratum, echelon, status.

castle noun **fortress**, fort, stronghold, fortification, keep, citadel, palace, chateau, tower.

casual adjective **1** *a casual attitude* **unconcerned**, uncaring, indifferent, lackadaisical, nonchalant, offhand, flippant, easy-going, free and easy, blithe, carefree, devil-may-care; *informal* laid-back. **2** *a casual remark* **offhand**, spontaneous, unthinking, unconsidered, impromptu, throwaway, unguarded; *informal* off-the-cuff. **3** *a casual glance* **cursory**, perfunctory, superficial, passing, fleeting. **4** *casual work* **temporary**, freelance, irregular, occasional. **5** *a*

casual meeting **chance**, accidental, unplanned, unintended, unexpected, unforeseen. **6** *a casual atmosphere* **relaxed**, friendly, informal, easy-going, free and easy; *informal* laid-back.
- OPPOSITES serious, deliberate, formal.

casualty noun **victim**, sufferer, fatality, death, loss, wounded person, injured person.

cat noun **feline**, tomcat, tom, kitten; *informal* pussy (cat), puss, kitty; *Brit. informal* moggie, mog.

> **WORD LINKS**
> **feline** relating to cats

catalogue noun **directory**, register, index, list, listing, record, schedule, archive, inventory.
● verb **classify**, categorize, index, list, archive, record, itemize.

catastrophe noun **disaster**, calamity, cataclysm, ruin, tragedy, fiasco, debacle.

catch verb **1 seize**, grab, snatch, grasp, grip, clutch, intercept, trap, receive, get. **2 capture**, apprehend, seize, arrest, take prisoner, trap, snare, net; *informal* nab, collar; *Brit. informal* nick. **3 become trapped**, become entangled, snag, jam, wedge, lodge, get stuck. **4 discover**, find, come across, stumble on, chance on, surprise. **5 contract**, go/come down with, be taken ill with, develop, pick up, succumb to.
- OPPOSITES drop, release.
● noun **1 haul**, net, bag, yield. **2 latch**, lock, fastener, clasp, hasp. **3 snag**, disadvantage, drawback, stumbling block, hitch, complication, problem, trap, trick.
◻ **catch on** (*informal*) **1 become popular**, take off, boom, flourish, thrive. **2 understand**, comprehend, learn, see the light; *informal* cotton on, latch on.

catching adjective (*informal*) **infectious**, contagious, communicable; *dated* infective.

catchy adjective **memorable**, unforgettable, haunting, appealing, popular.
- OPPOSITES forgettable.

categorical *adjective* **unqualified**, unconditional, unequivocal, absolute, explicit, unambiguous, definite, direct, emphatic, positive, out-and-out.

category *noun* **class**, classification, group, grouping, bracket, heading, set, type, sort, kind, grade, order, rank.

cater *verb*
□ **cater for 1** provide (food) for, feed, serve, cook for. **2** *a resort catering for older holidaymakers* serve, provide for, meet the needs/wants of, accommodate. **3** *we cater for all tastes* take into account, take into consideration, allow for, consider, bear in mind, make provision for, have regard for.

cattle *plural noun* **cows**, oxen, herd, livestock.

> **WORD LINKS**
> **bovine** relating to cattle

cause *noun* **1** *the cause of the fire* **source**, root, origin, beginning(s), starting point, originator, author, creator, agent. **2** *there is no cause for alarm* **reason**, grounds, justification, call, need, necessity, occasion, excuse. **3** *raising money for good causes* **principle**, ideal, belief, conviction, object, aim, objective, purpose, charity.
● *verb* **bring about**, give rise to, lead to, result in, create, produce, generate, engender, spawn, bring on, precipitate, prompt, provoke, trigger, make happen, induce, inspire, promote, foster.

caustic *adjective* **1** **corrosive**, acid, burning. **2** **sarcastic**, cutting, biting, mordant, sharp, scathing, sardonic, scornful, trenchant, acerbic, vitriolic.

caution *noun* **1** **care**, attention, alertness, circumspection, discretion, prudence. **2** **warning**, admonishment, injunction, reprimand, rebuke; *informal* telling-off, dressing-down; *Brit. informal* ticking-off.
● *verb* **1** *advisers cautioned against tax increases* **advise**, warn, counsel, urge. **2** *he was cautioned by the police* **warn**, admonish, reprimand; *informal* tell off; *Brit. informal* tick off.

cautious *adjective* **careful**, attentive, alert, judicious, circumspect, prudent, tentative, guarded.
- OPPOSITES reckless.

cave *noun* **cavern**, grotto, pothole, chamber, gallery, hollow.

> **WORD LINKS**
> **speleology**, **potholing** exploration of caves
> **spelunking** (N. Amer.)

cavity *noun* **space**, chamber, hollow, hole, pocket, gap, crater, pit.

cease *verb* **stop**, come/bring to an end, come/bring to a halt, end, halt, conclude, terminate, finish, wind up, discontinue, suspend, break off.
- OPPOSITES start, continue.

ceaseless *adjective* **continual**, constant, continuous, incessant, unending, endless, never-ending, interminable, non-stop, unremitting, relentless, unrelenting, sustained, persistent, eternal, perpetual.
- OPPOSITES intermittent.

celebrate *verb* **1** **commemorate**, observe, mark, keep, honour, remember. **2** **enjoy yourself**, make merry, have fun, have a good time, have a party; *N. Amer.* step out; *informal* party, whoop it up, have a ball. **3** **perform**, observe, officiate at, preside at.

celebrated *adjective* **acclaimed**, admired, highly rated, esteemed, exalted, vaunted, eminent, great, distinguished, prestigious, illustrious, notable.
- OPPOSITES unsung.

celebration *noun* **1** **commemoration**, observance, marking, keeping. **2** **merrymaking**, jollification, revelry, revels, festivities; *informal* partying. **3** **party**, function, gathering, festivities, festival, fete, carnival, jamboree; *informal* do, bash, rave; *Brit. informal* rave-up. **4** **performance**, observance, officiation, solemnization.

celebrity *noun* **1** **fame**, prominence, renown, stardom, popularity, distinction, prestige, stature, repute,

reputation. **2 famous person**, VIP, personality, big name, household name, star, superstar; *informal* celeb, megastar.
- OPPOSITES obscurity.

celestial adjective **1 (in) space**, heavenly, astronomical, extraterrestrial, stellar, planetary. **2 heavenly**, holy, saintly, divine, godly, godlike, ethereal, angelic.

celibate adjective **unmarried**, single, chaste, pure, virginal.

cell noun **1 room**, cubicle, chamber, dungeon, compartment, lock-up. **2 unit**, squad, detachment, group.

cellar noun **basement**, vault, crypt.

cement noun **adhesive**, glue, fixative, gum, paste.

cemetery noun **graveyard**, churchyard, burial ground, necropolis, garden of remembrance, mass grave; *Scottish* kirkyard.

censor verb **cut**, edit, expurgate, redact, sanitize, clean up, ban, delete.

censorious adjective **critical**, overcritical, hypercritical, disapproving, condemnatory, judgemental, moralistic, fault-finding, reproachful.

censure verb **condemn**, criticize, attack, reprimand, rebuke, admonish, upbraid, reproach.
- OPPOSITES defend, praise.
● *noun* **condemnation**, criticism, attack, reprimand, rebuke, admonishment, reproof, disapproval, reproach.
- OPPOSITES approval, praise.

central adjective **1** *a central position* **middle**, centre, halfway, midway, mid. **2** *central London* **inner**, innermost, middle, mid. **3 main**, chief, principal, primary, foremost, key, crucial, vital, essential, basic, fundamental, core; *informal* number-one.
- OPPOSITES side, outer.

centralize verb **concentrate**, consolidate, amalgamate, condense, unify, focus.
- OPPOSITES devolve.

centre noun **middle**, nucleus, heart, core, hub.
- OPPOSITES edge.
● *verb the story centres on a doctor* **focus**, concentrate, pivot, revolve, be based.

ceremonial adjective **formal**, official, state, public, ritual, ritualistic, stately, solemn.
- OPPOSITES informal.

ceremony noun **1 rite**, ritual, observance, service, event, function. **2 pomp**, protocol, formality, formalities, niceties, decorum, etiquette, pageantry, ceremonial.

certain adjective **1** *I'm certain he's guilty* **sure**, confident, positive, convinced, in no doubt, satisfied. **2** *it is certain that more changes are in the offing* **unquestionable**, sure, definite, beyond question, indubitable, undeniable, indisputable. **3** *they are certain to win* **sure**, bound, destined. **4** *certain defeat* **inevitable**, assured, unavoidable, inescapable, inexorable. **5** *there is no certain cure* **reliable**, dependable, foolproof, guaranteed, sure, infallible; *informal* sure-fire.
- OPPOSITES doubtful, unlikely, possible.

certainly adverb **definitely**, surely, assuredly, unquestionably, beyond/without question, undoubtedly, without doubt, indubitably, undeniably, irrefutably, indisputably.

certainty noun **1 confidence**, sureness, conviction, assurance. **2 inevitability**, foregone conclusion; *informal* sure thing; *Brit. informal* (dead) cert.
- OPPOSITES doubt, possibility.

certificate noun **guarantee**, document, authorization, authentication, accreditation, credentials, testimonial.

certify verb **1 verify**, guarantee, attest, validate, confirm, endorse. **2 accredit**, recognize, license, authorize, approve.

cessation noun **end**, termination, halt, finish, stoppage, conclusion, winding up, pause, suspension.
- OPPOSITES start, resumption.

chain noun **1 fetters**, shackles, irons, manacles, handcuffs; *informal* cuffs, bracelets. **2 series**, succession, string, sequence, train, course.
● verb **secure**, fasten, tie, tether, hitch, restrain, shackle, fetter, manacle, handcuff.

chairman, chairwoman noun **chair**, chairperson, president, chief executive, leader, master of ceremonies, MC.

challenge noun **1 dare**, provocation, offer. **2 problem**, difficult task, test, trial.
● verb **1 question**, dispute, take issue with, call into question, protest against, oppose. **2 dare**, defy, invite, throw down the gauntlet to. **3 test**, tax, strain, make demands on, stretch.

challenging adjective **demanding**, testing, taxing, exacting, hard, difficult, stimulating.
- OPPOSITES easy.

champion noun **1 winner**, title-holder, gold medallist, prizewinner; *informal* champ, number one. **2 advocate**, proponent, promoter, supporter, defender, upholder, backer; *N. Amer.* booster.
● verb **advocate**, promote, defend, uphold, support, espouse, stand up for, campaign for, lobby for, fight for.
- OPPOSITES oppose.

chance noun **1 possibility**, prospect, probability, likelihood, risk, threat, danger. **2** *I gave her a chance to answer* **opportunity**, opening, occasion, window; *N. Amer. & Austral./NZ* show; *Brit. informal* look-in. **3** *he took an awful chance* **risk**, gamble, leap in the dark. **4 coincidence**, accident, fate, destiny, providence, happenstance, good fortune, luck, fluke.
- OPPOSITES certainty.
● adjective **accidental**, fortuitous, fluky, coincidental.
□ **by chance** by accident, fortuitously, accidentally, coincidentally, unintentionally, inadvertently.

change verb **1 alter**, make/become different, adjust, adapt, amend, modify, revise, vary, transform, metamorphose, evolve. **2 exchange**, substitute, swap, switch, replace, alternate.
● noun **1 alteration**, modification, variation, revision, amendment, adjustment, adaptation, metamorphosis, transformation, evolution. **2 replacement**, exchange, substitution, swap, switch.

changeable adjective **variable**, varying, changing, fluctuating, irregular, erratic, inconsistent, unstable, unsettled, inconstant, fickle, capricious, temperamental, volatile, mercurial, unpredictable.
- OPPOSITES constant.

channel noun **1 strait(s)**, sound, narrows, passage. **2 duct**, gutter, conduit, trough, sluice, drain. **3 means**, medium, instrument, mechanism, agency, vehicle, route, avenue.
● verb **convey**, transmit, conduct, direct, relay, pass on, transfer.

chant noun **shout**, cry, call, slogan, chorus, refrain.
● verb **shout**, chorus, repeat, call.

chaos noun **disorder**, disorganization, confusion, mayhem, bedlam, pandemonium, havoc, turmoil, anarchy, lawlessness; *Brit.* a shambles; *informal* all hell broken loose; *Brit. informal* an omnishambles.
- OPPOSITES order.

chaotic adjective **disorderly**, disorganized, in confusion, in turmoil, topsyturvy, anarchic, lawless; *Brit. informal* shambolic.

chap noun *(Brit.)* **man**, boy, individual, character; *informal* fellow, guy, geezer; *Brit. informal* bloke, lad; *N. Amer. informal* dude, hombre.

chapter noun **1 section**, part, division, topic, stage, episode. **2 period**, phase, page, stage, epoch, era.

character noun **1 personality**, nature, quality, disposition, temperament, mentality, make-up, spirit, identity, tone, feel. **2 integrity**, honour, moral strength/fibre, strength, backbone, resolve, grit, will power; *informal* guts; *Brit. informal* bottle. **3 reputation**, (good) name, standing, position, status. **4 eccentric**, oddity, crank, original, individualist, madcap, nonconformist; *informal* oddball. **5 person**, man, woman, soul, creature, individual, customer; *informal* cookie; *Brit. informal* bod, guy. **6 letter**, figure, symbol, mark, device, sign, hieroglyph.

characteristic *noun* **attribute**, feature, quality, property, trait, aspect, idiosyncrasy, peculiarity, quirk.
● *adjective* **typical**, usual, normal, distinctive, representative, particular, special, peculiar, idiosyncratic.
- OPPOSITES abnormal.

characterize *verb* **1 distinguish**, mark, typify, set apart. **2 portray**, depict, present, represent, describe, categorize, class, brand.

charade *noun* **pretence**, act, masquerade, show, facade, pantomime, farce, travesty, mockery, parody.

charge *verb* **1 ask**, demand, bill, invoice. **2 accuse**, indict, arraign, prosecute, try, put on trial; *N. Amer.* impeach. **3 entrust**, burden, encumber, saddle, tax. **4 attack**, storm, assault, assail, descend on; *informal* lay into, tear into. **5 rush**, storm, stampede, push, plough, launch yourself, go headlong; *informal* steam; *N. Amer. informal* barrel. **6** *charge your glasses!* **fill (up)**, top up, load (up), arm.
● *noun* **1 fee**, payment, price, rate, tariff, fare, levy. **2 accusation**, allegation, indictment, arraignment; *N. Amer.* impeachment. **3 attack**, assault, offensive, onslaught, drive, push. **4** *the child was in her charge* **care**, protection, safe keeping, control, custody, hands.

charisma *noun* **charm**, presence, (force of) personality, strength of character, (animal) magnetism, appeal, allure.

charismatic *adjective* **charming**, magnetic, compelling, inspiring, captivating, mesmerizing, appealing, alluring, glamorous.

charitable *adjective* **1 philanthropic**, generous, open-handed, giving, munificent, benevolent, altruistic, unselfish,

public-spirited, humanitarian, non-profit-making. **2 magnanimous**, generous, liberal, tolerant, sympathetic, understanding, lenient, indulgent, forgiving.
- OPPOSITES commercial, mean.

charity *noun* **1 voluntary organization**, charitable institution, fund, trust, foundation. **2 aid**, financial assistance, welfare, relief, donations, handouts, gifts, largesse; *historical* alms. **3 philanthropy**, humanitarianism, altruism, public-spiritedness, social conscience, benevolence. **4 goodwill**, compassion, consideration, concern, kindness, sympathy, indulgence, tolerance, leniency.

charm *noun* **1 appeal**, attraction, fascination, beauty, loveliness, allure, seductiveness, magnetism, charisma; *informal* pulling power. **2 spell**, incantation, formula; *N. Amer.* mojo, hex. **3 talisman**, trinket, amulet, mascot, fetish.
● *verb* **1 delight**, please, win (over), attract, captivate, lure, fascinate, enchant, beguile. **2 coax**, cajole, wheedle; *informal* sweet-talk, soft-soap.

charming *adjective* **delightful**, pleasing, endearing, lovely, adorable, appealing, attractive, good-looking, alluring, winning, fetching, captivating, enchanting, entrancing.

chart *noun* **graph**, table, diagram, plan, map; *Computing* graphic.
● *verb* **1 plot**, tabulate, graph, record, register, represent. **2 follow**, trace, outline, describe, detail, record, document.

charter *noun* **1** *a Royal charter* **authority**, authorization, sanction, dispensation, permit, licence, warrant. **2** *the UN Charter* **constitution**, code, principles.
● *verb* **hire**, lease, rent, book.

chase *verb* **1 pursue**, run after, follow, hunt, track, trail; *informal* tail. **2** *she chased away the dogs* **drive**, send, scare; *informal* send packing. **3** *she chased away all thoughts of him* **dispel**, banish, dismiss, drive away, shut out, put out of your mind.

● *noun* **pursuit**, hunt, trail.

chat *noun* **talk**, conversation, gossip; *informal* jaw, gas, confab; *Brit. informal* natter, chinwag; *Austral. informal* convo.
● *verb* **talk**, gossip; *informal* gas, jaw, chew the rag/fat; *Brit. informal* natter, have a chinwag; *N. Amer. informal* shoot the breeze/bull.

chatter *verb* **prattle**, chat, gossip, jabber, babble; *informal* yatter; *Brit. informal* natter, chunter, rabbit on.
● *noun* **prattle**, chat, gossip, patter, jabber, babble; *informal* chit-chat, yattering; *Brit. informal* nattering, chuntering, rabbiting on.

chatty *adjective* **talkative**, communicative, effusive, gossipy, loquacious, voluble; *informal* mouthy, gabby.
- OPPOSITES taciturn.

cheap *adjective* **1 inexpensive**, low-priced, low-cost, economical, competitive, affordable, reasonable, budget, economy, bargain, cut-price, reduced, discounted; *informal* dirt cheap.
2 poor-quality, second-rate, substandard, inferior, vulgar, shoddy, trashy, tawdry; *informal* tacky; *Brit. informal* naff. **3 despicable**, contemptible, immoral, unscrupulous, unprincipled, cynical.
- OPPOSITES expensive.

cheat *verb* **swindle**, defraud, deceive, trick, dupe, hoodwink, double-cross, gull; *informal* rip off, diddle, con, pull a fast one on; *N. Amer. informal* sucker.
● *noun* **swindler**, fraudster, confidence trickster, double-dealer, double-crosser, fraud, fake, charlatan; *informal* con artist.

check *verb* **1 examine**, inspect, look at/over, scrutinize, study, investigate, probe, look into, enquire into; *informal* check out, give something a/the once-over. **2 make sure**, confirm, verify. **3 halt**, stop, arrest, bar, obstruct, foil, thwart, curb, block.
● *noun* **1 examination**, inspection, scrutiny, perusal, study, investigation, test, check-up; *informal* once-over.
2 control, restraint, constraint, curb, limitation.
□ **check in** register, book in, report.
check out pay the bill, settle up, leave.

cheek *noun* **impudence**, impertinence, insolence, rudeness, disrespect; *informal* brass neck, lip, mouth, chutzpah; *Brit. informal* backchat; *N. Amer. informal* sass, back talk.

cheeky *adjective* **impudent**, impertinent, insolent, rude, disrespectful; *informal* brass-necked, lippy, mouthy, fresh; *N. Amer. informal* sassy, nervy.
- OPPOSITES respectful, polite.

cheer *verb* **1 applaud**, hail, salute, shout for, clap, put your hands together for, bring the house down for; *informal* holler for, give someone a big hand; *N. Amer. informal* ballyhoo. **2 please**, raise/lift someone's spirits, brighten, buoy up, hearten, gladden, perk up, encourage; *informal* buck up.
- OPPOSITES boo, depress.
● *noun* **hurrah**, hurray, whoop, bravo, shout; (**cheers**) acclaim, applause, ovation.
- OPPOSITES boo.
□ **cheer up** perk up, brighten up, rally, revive, bounce back, take heart; *informal* buck up.

cheerful *adjective* **1 happy**, jolly, merry, bright, sunny, joyful, in good/high spirits, buoyant, cheery, animated, smiling, good-humoured; *informal* chipper, chirpy, full of beans. **2 pleasant**, attractive, agreeable, bright, sunny, friendly, welcoming.
- OPPOSITES sad, gloomy.

cheerless *adjective* **gloomy**, dreary, dull, dismal, bleak, drab, sombre, dark, dim, dingy, funereal, austere, stark, unwelcoming, uninviting, depressing.

chemist *noun* **pharmacist**, dispenser; *N. Amer.* druggist; *old use* apothecary.

cherish *verb* **1 adore**, love, dote on, be devoted to, revere, think the world of, care for, look after, protect, keep safe. **2 treasure**, prize, hold dear. **3 harbour**, entertain, nurse, cling to, foster.
- OPPOSITES hate.

chest noun **1 breast**, upper body, torso, trunk, front. **2 box**, case, casket, crate, trunk, coffer, strongbox.

> **WORD LINKS**
> **pectoral**, **thoracic** relating to the chest

chew verb **munch**, champ, chomp, crunch, gnaw, bite, masticate.

chic adjective **stylish**, smart, elegant, sophisticated, fashionable; *informal* trendy; *Brit. informal* swish; *N. Amer. informal* kicky, tony.
- OPPOSITES unfashionable.

chief noun **1** *a Highland chief* **leader**, chieftain, head, ruler, master, commander. **2** *the chief of the central bank* **head**, chief executive, chief executive officer, CEO, president, chairman, chairwoman, principal, governor, director, manager; *informal* boss, (head) honcho; *Brit. informal* gaffer, guv'nor.
● adjective **1 head**, leading, principal, premier, highest, supreme, arch. **2 main**, principal, primary, prime, first, cardinal, central, key, crucial, essential; *informal* number-one.
- OPPOSITES subordinate, minor.

chiefly adverb **mainly**, in the main, primarily, principally, predominantly, mostly, for the most part, usually, typically, commonly, generally, on the whole, largely.

child noun **youngster**, baby, infant, toddler, minor, juvenile, junior, descendant; *Scottish & N. English* bairn; *informal* kid, kiddie, nipper, tiny, tot; *derogatory* brat.

> **WORD LINKS**
> **paediatrics** branch of medicine concerned with children

childbirth noun **labour**, delivery, birthing; *old use* confinement.

childhood noun **youth**, early years/life, infancy, babyhood, boyhood, girlhood, minority.
- OPPOSITES adulthood.

childish adjective **immature**, babyish, infantile, juvenile, puerile, silly.
- OPPOSITES mature.

childlike adjective **youthful**, innocent, unsophisticated, naive, trusting, artless, unaffected, uninhibited, natural, spontaneous.
- OPPOSITES adult.

chill noun **1 coldness**, chilliness, coolness, nip. **2 cold**, dose of flu, fever. **3 shiver**, frisson.
- OPPOSITES warmth.
● verb **scare**, frighten, petrify, terrify, alarm, make someone's blood run cold; *informal* scare the pants off; *Brit. informal* put the wind up.
- OPPOSITES warm.
● adjective **cold**, chilly, cool, fresh, wintry, frosty, icy, arctic, bitter, freezing; *informal* nippy; *Brit. informal* parky.

chilly adjective **1 cold**, cool, crisp, fresh, wintry, frosty, icy; *informal* nippy; *Brit. informal* parky. **2 unfriendly**, unwelcoming, cold, cool, frosty; *informal* stand-offish.
- OPPOSITES warm.

china noun **crockery**, dishes, plates, cups and saucers, tableware, porcelain, dinnerware, dinner service, tea service.

chink noun **gap**, crack, space, hole, aperture, fissure, cranny, cleft, split, slit.

chip noun **1 fragment**, sliver, splinter, shaving, shard, flake. **2 nick**, crack, scratch. **3 counter**, token; *N. Amer.* check.
● verb **1 nick**, crack, scratch. **2** *chip off the old plaster* **cut**, hack, chisel, carve, hew, whittle.

chivalrous adjective **gallant**, gentlemanly, honourable, respectful, considerate, courteous, polite, gracious, well mannered.
- OPPOSITES rude.

choice noun **1** *freedom of choice* **selection**, choosing, picking, pick, preference, decision, say, vote. **2** *you have no other choice* **option**, alternative, course of action. **3** *an extensive choice* **range**, variety, selection, assortment.
● adjective **superior**, first-class, first-rate, prime, premier, grade A, best, finest, select, quality, top, top-quality,

high-grade, prize; *informal* A1, top-notch.
- OPPOSITES inferior.

choke *verb* **1 gag**, retch, cough, fight for breath. **2 suffocate**, asphyxiate, smother, stifle, strangle, throttle; *informal* strangulate. **3 clog (up)**, bung up, stop up, block, obstruct.

choose *verb* **1 select**, pick (out), opt for, plump for, settle on, prefer, decide on, fix on, elect, adopt. **2 wish**, want, desire, please, like.

choosy *adjective (informal)* **fussy**, finicky, fastidious, over-particular, hard to please; *informal* picky, pernickety; *N. Amer. informal* persnickety.

chop *verb* **cut (up)**, cube, dice, hew, split, fell; *N. Amer.* hash.
□ **chop off** cut off, sever, lop, shear.

choppy *adjective* **rough**, turbulent, heavy, heaving, stormy, tempestuous, squally.
- OPPOSITES calm.

chore *noun* **task**, job, duty, errand, burden; *informal* hassle.

christen *verb* **1** *she was christened Sara* **baptize**, name, give the name of, call. **2** *a group christened 'The Magic Circle'* **call**, name, dub, style, term, label, nickname.

chronic *adjective* **1** *a chronic illness* **persistent**, long-standing, long-term, incurable. **2** *chronic economic problems* **constant**, continuing, persistent, long-lasting, severe, serious, acute, grave, dire. **3** *a chronic liar* **inveterate**, hardened, dyed-in-the-wool, incorrigible, compulsive; *informal* pathological.
- OPPOSITES acute, temporary.

chronicle *noun* **record**, account, history, annals, archive(s), log, diary, journal.
● *verb* **record**, write down, set down, document, report.

chubby *adjective* **plump**, tubby, flabby, rotund, portly, chunky; *Brit. informal* podgy; *N. Amer. informal* zaftig, corn-fed.
- OPPOSITES skinny.

chuck *verb (informal)* **1 throw**, toss, fling, hurl, pitch, cast, lob; *informal* sling, bung. **2 throw away**, throw out, discard, dispose of, get rid of, dump, bin, jettison; *informal* ditch, junk; *N. Amer. informal* trash. **3 give up**, leave, resign from; *informal* quit, pack in; *Brit. informal* jack in. **4 jilt**, finish with, break off with, leave; *informal* dump, ditch, give someone the elbow; *Brit. informal* give someone the push.

chuckle *verb* **laugh**, chortle, giggle, titter, snigger.

chum *noun (informal)* **friend**, companion, playmate, classmate, schoolmate, workmate; *informal* pal, crony; *Brit. informal* mate; *N. Amer. informal* buddy.
- OPPOSITES enemy.

chunk *noun* **lump**, hunk, wedge, block, slab, square, nugget, brick, cube; *informal* wodge; *N. Amer. informal* gob.

churlish *adjective* **rude**, ill-mannered, discourteous, ungracious, impolite, inconsiderate, surly, sullen.
- OPPOSITES polite.

churn *verb* **disturb**, stir up, agitate, beat.

cinema *noun* **1 the movies**, the pictures, multiplex; *informal* the flicks. **2** *British cinema* **films**, film, movies, pictures, motion pictures.

circa *preposition* **approximately**, (round) about, around, in the region of, roughly, something like, or so, or thereabouts, more or less; *informal* as near as dammit; *N. Amer. informal* in the ballpark of.
- OPPOSITES exactly.

circle *noun* **1 ring**, band, hoop, circlet, halo, disc. **2 group**, set, crowd, band, company, clique, coterie, club, society; *informal* gang, bunch.
● *verb* **1** *seagulls circled above* **wheel**, revolve, rotate, whirl, spiral. **2** *satellites circling the earth* **go round**, travel round, circumnavigate, orbit. **3** *the abbey was circled by a wall* **surround**, encircle, ring, enclose.

circuit noun **1** *two circuits of the track* **lap**, turn, round, circle. **2** *(Brit.) a racing circuit* **track**, racetrack, course, route, stadium.

circuitous adjective **roundabout**, indirect, winding, meandering, twisting, tortuous.
- OPPOSITES direct.

circular adjective **round**, ring-shaped.
● noun **leaflet**, pamphlet, handbill, flyer, advertisement, notice.

circulate verb **1** **spread**, communicate, disseminate, make known, make public, broadcast, publicize, distribute. **2** **socialize**, mingle, mix, wander, stroll.

circumspect adjective **cautious**, wary, careful, chary, guarded, on your guard; *informal* cagey.
- OPPOSITES unguarded.

circumstances plural noun **situation**, conditions, state of affairs, position, the lie of the land, (turn of) events, factors, facts, background, environment, context.

cite verb **quote**, mention, refer to, allude to, instance, specify, name.

citizen noun **1** *a British citizen* **subject**, national, passport holder. **2** *the citizens of Edinburgh* **inhabitant**, resident, native, townsman, townswoman, taxpayer; *formal* denizen.

city noun **town**, municipality, metropolis, conurbation, urban area; *Scottish* burgh; *informal* big smoke; *N. Amer. informal* burg.

> **WORD LINKS**
> **urban**, **civic**, **metropolitan** relating to cities

civic adjective **municipal**, city, town, urban, metropolitan, public, community.

civil adjective **1** **secular**, non-religious, lay. **2** **non-military**, civilian. **3** **polite**, courteous, well mannered, gentlemanly, chivalrous, ladylike.
- OPPOSITES religious, military, rude.

civilization noun **1** **human development**, advancement, progress, enlightenment, culture, refinement, sophistication. **2** **culture**, society, nation, people.

civilize verb **enlighten**, improve, educate, instruct, refine, cultivate, socialize.

civilized adjective **1** *civilized society* **advanced**, developed, sophisticated, enlightened, educated, cultured, cultivated. **2** *civilized behaviour* **polite**, courteous, well mannered, civil, refined, polished.
- OPPOSITES unsophisticated, rude.

claim verb **1** **assert**, declare, profess, protest, maintain, insist, contend, allege. **2** **request**, ask for, apply for, demand.
● noun **1** **assertion**, declaration, profession, protestation, insistence, contention, allegation. **2** **application**, request, demand.

clamour noun **noise**, din, racket, rumpus, uproar, shouting, commotion, hubbub; *Brit.* row; *informal* hullabaloo.

clamp verb **fasten**, secure, fix, attach, clench, grip, hold, press, clasp, screw, bolt.

clan noun **family**, house, dynasty, tribe.

clandestine adjective **secret**, covert, furtive, surreptitious, stealthy, cloak-and-dagger, underhand; *Military* black; *informal* hush-hush.

clap verb **applaud**, give someone a round of applause, put your hands together; *informal* give someone a (big) hand; *N. Amer. informal* give it up.
● noun **1** **round of applause**, handclap; *informal* hand. **2** **crack**, peal, crash, bang, boom.

clarify verb **make clear**, shed/throw light on, illuminate, elucidate, explain, interpret, spell out, clear up.
- OPPOSITES confuse.

clarity noun **1** *the clarity of his explanation* **lucidity**, precision, coherence, transparency, simplicity. **2** *the clarity of the image* **sharpness**, clearness, crispness, definition. **3** *the clarity of the water* **transparency**, clearness, limpidity, translucence.

clash noun **1 fight**, battle, confrontation, skirmish, engagement, encounter, conflict. **2 argument**, altercation, confrontation, quarrel, disagreement, dispute; informal run-in, slanging match. **3 crash**, clang, bang, clatter, clangour.
● verb **1 fight**, battle, confront, skirmish, contend, come to blows. **2 disagree**, differ, wrangle, dispute, cross swords, lock horns, be at loggerheads. **3 conflict**, coincide, overlap. **4 bang**, strike, clang, crash.

clasp verb **grasp**, grip, clutch, hold, squeeze, seize, grab, embrace, hug.
● noun **1 fastener**, catch, clip, pin, buckle. **2 grasp**, grip, squeeze, embrace, hug.

class noun **1 kind**, sort, type, variety, genre, category, grade, rating, classification. **2 group**, grouping, rank, stratum, level, echelon, status, caste.
● verb **classify**, categorize, group, grade, order, rate, bracket, designate, label, rank.

classic adjective **1 definitive**, authoritative, outstanding, first-rate, first-class, best, finest, excellent, superior, masterly. **2 typical**, archetypal, quintessential, model, representative, perfect, prime, textbook. **3 timeless**, traditional, simple, elegant, understated.
● noun **definitive example**, model, epitome, paradigm, exemplar, masterpiece, master work.

classification noun **categorization**, classifying, grouping, grading, ranking, organization, sorting, codification.

classify verb **categorize**, group, grade, rank, order, organize, sort, type, codify, bracket.

classy adjective (informal) **stylish**, high-class, superior, exclusive, chic, elegant, smart, sophisticated; Brit. upmarket; N. Amer. high-toned; informal posh, ritzy, plush, swanky; Brit. informal swish.

clause noun **section**, paragraph, article, passage, subsection, chapter,

condition, proviso, rider.

claw noun **talon**, nail, pincer.
● verb **scratch**, lacerate, tear, rip, scrape, dig into.

clean adjective **1 washed**, scrubbed, cleansed, cleaned, laundered, spotless, unstained, unsullied, unblemished, immaculate, pristine, disinfected, sterilized, sterile, aseptic, decontaminated. **2 blank**, empty, clear, plain, unused, new, pristine, fresh, unmarked. **3 pure**, clear, fresh, unpolluted, uncontaminated.
- OPPOSITES dirty, polluted.
● verb **wash**, cleanse, wipe, sponge, scrub, mop, rinse, scour, swab, shampoo, launder, dry-clean.
- OPPOSITES dirty.

cleanse verb **1 clean (up)**, wash, bathe, rinse, disinfect. **2** cleansing the environment of traces of lead **rid**, clear, free, purify, purge.

clear adjective **1 understandable**, comprehensible, intelligible, plain, uncomplicated, explicit, lucid, coherent, simple, straightforward, unambiguous, clear-cut. **2 obvious**, evident, plain, sure, definite, unmistakable, manifest, indisputable, unambiguous, patent, incontrovertible, visible, conspicuous, overt, blatant, glaring. **3 transparent**, limpid, translucent, crystal clear, pellucid. **4 bright**, cloudless, unclouded, blue, sunny, starry. **5 unobstructed**, passable, open, unrestricted, unhindered.
- OPPOSITES incoherent, vague, cloudy.
● verb **1 disappear**, go away, stop, die away, fade, wear off, lift, settle, evaporate, dissipate, decrease, lessen, shift. **2 unblock**, unstop, clean out. **3 evacuate**, vacate, empty, leave. **4 remove**, strip, take away, carry away, tidy away/up. **5 go over**, pass over, sail over, jump (over), vault (over), leap (over). **6 acquit**, declare innocent, find not guilty, absolve, exonerate; informal let off (the hook).
□ **clear up 1** tidy (up), put in order, straighten up, clean up, fix. **2** solve, resolve, straighten out, find an/the

answer to, get to the bottom of, explain; *informal* crack, figure out, suss out.

clearance *noun* **1 removal**, clearing, demolition. **2 authorization**, permission, consent, approval, leave, sanction, licence, dispensation; *informal* the go-ahead. **3 space**, room (to spare), headroom, margin, leeway.

clear-cut *adjective* **definite**, distinct, precise, specific, explicit, unambiguous, unequivocal, black and white.
- OPPOSITES vague.

clearly *adverb* **1 intelligibly**, plainly, distinctly, comprehensibly, legibly, audibly. **2 obviously**, evidently, patently, unquestionably, undoubtedly, without doubt, plainly, undeniably.

cleft *noun* **split**, crack, fissure, crevice.

clench *verb* **grip**, grasp, grab, clutch, clasp, clamp, hold tightly, seize, squeeze.

clergyman, clergywoman *noun* **priest**, cleric, minister, preacher, chaplain, padre, father, pastor, vicar, rector, parson, curate; *Scottish* kirkman.

clerical *adjective* **1 office**, desk, administrative, secretarial, white-collar. **2 ecclesiastical**, church, priestly, religious, spiritual, holy.

clever *adjective* **1 intelligent**, bright, smart, astute, quick-witted, shrewd, talented, gifted, capable, able, competent; *informal* brainy, genius. **2** *a clever scheme* **ingenious**, canny, cunning, crafty, artful, slick, neat. **3** *she was clever with her hands* **skilful**, dexterous, adroit, adept, deft, nimble, handy, skilled, talented, gifted.
- OPPOSITES stupid.

cliché *noun* **platitude**, hackneyed phrase, commonplace, banality, truism, stock phrase; *informal* old chestnut.

click *verb* **1 clack**, snick, snap, clink. **2 become clear**, fall into place, make sense, dawn on someone, register, get through, sink in. **3 take to each other**, get along, be compatible, be likeminded, see eye to eye, be on the same

wavelength; *informal* hit it off. **4 go down well**, prove popular, be a hit, succeed, resonate, work, take off.

client *noun* **customer**, buyer, purchaser, shopper, patient, patron; *Brit. informal* punter.

cliff *noun* **precipice**, rock face, crag, bluff, ridge, escarpment, scar, scarp.

climate *noun* **1 (weather) conditions**, weather. **2 atmosphere**, mood, spirit, ethos, feeling, ambience, environment.

climax *noun* **peak**, pinnacle, height, high point, top, zenith, culmination.
- OPPOSITES anticlimax, nadir.

climb *verb* **1 ascend**, mount, scale, scramble up, clamber up, shin up, conquer. **2 rise**, ascend, go up, gain height, soar, rocket. **3** *the road climbs steeply* **slope (upwards)**, rise, go uphill, incline.
- OPPOSITES descend.
□ **climb down** back down, retreat, give in, backtrack, eat your words, eat humble pie, do a U-turn, row back; *N. Amer. informal* eat crow.

clinch *verb* **1** *he clinched the deal* **secure**, settle, conclude, close, confirm, seal, finalize, wrap up; *informal* sew up. **2** *these findings clinched the matter* **settle**, decide, determine, resolve.

cling *verb* **stick**, adhere, hold.
□ **cling (on) to** hold on, clutch, grip, grasp, clasp, hang on, embrace, hug.

clinical *adjective* **1 detached**, impersonal, dispassionate, indifferent, uninvolved, distant, remote, aloof, cold. **2 plain**, stark, austere, spartan, bleak, bare, functional, basic, institutional.
- OPPOSITES emotional.

clip[1] *noun* **fastener**, clasp, hasp, catch, hook, buckle, lock.
● *verb* **fasten**, attach, fix, join, pin, staple, tack.

clip[2] *verb* **1 trim**, prune, cut, snip, crop, shear, lop. **2 hit**, strike, graze, glance off, nudge, scrape.
● *noun* **1 extract**, excerpt, snippet, fragment, trailer. **2 trim**, cut, crop, haircut.

clique noun **coterie**, set, circle, ring, in-crowd, group, gang, fraternity.

cloak noun **1 cape**, robe, wrap, mantle. **2** *a cloak of secrecy* **cover**, veil, mantle, shroud, screen, blanket.
● verb **conceal**, hide, cover, veil, shroud, mask, obscure, cloud, envelop, swathe, surround.

clog verb **block**, obstruct, congest, jam, choke, bung up, plug, stop up.

close[1] *adjective* **1 near**, nearby, adjacent, neighbouring, adjoining, abutting, at hand. **2 neck and neck**, even, nip and tuck. **3 intimate**, dear, bosom, close-knit, inseparable, devoted, faithful, special, firm. **4** *a close resemblance* **noticeable**, marked, distinct, pronounced, strong. **5 careful**, detailed, thorough, minute, search-ing, painstaking, meticulous, rigorous. **6 humid**, muggy, stuffy, airless, heavy, sticky, sultry, stifling.
- OPPOSITES far, distant.

close[2] *verb* **1** *she closed the door* **shut**, pull to, push to, slam. **2** *close the hole* **block**, stop up, plug, seal, bung up, clog up, choke, obstruct. **3 end**, conclude, finish, terminate, wind up. **4 shut down**, close down, cease production, cease trading, be wound up, go out of business; *informal* fold, go to the wall, go bust. **5 clinch**, settle, secure, seal, confirm, pull off, conclude, finalize; *informal* wrap up.
- OPPOSITES open, start.
● noun **end**, finish, conclusion.
- OPPOSITES beginning.

closet noun **cupboard**, wardrobe, cabinet, locker.
● adjective **secret**, covert, private, sur-reptitious, clandestine.
● verb **shut away**, sequester, seclude, cloister, confine, isolate.

clot noun **lump**, clump, mass, thrombo-sis; *informal* glob; *Brit. informal* gob.
● verb **coagulate**, set, congeal, thicken, solidify.

cloth noun **1 fabric**, material, textile(s), stuff. **2 rag**, wipe, duster, flannel; *Austral.* washer.

clothe verb **dress**, attire, robe, garb, costume, swathe, deck (out), turn out, fit out, rig (out); *informal* get up.

clothes plural noun **clothing**, garments, attire, garb, dress, wear, costume, wardrobe; *informal* gear, togs; *Brit. informal* clobber; *N. Amer. informal* threads; *formal* apparel.

> **WORD LINKS**
> **sartorial** relating to clothes
> **clothier**, **couturier**, **tailor** person who sells or makes clothes

clothing noun see **clothes**.

cloud noun *a cloud of exhaust smoke* **mass**, billow, mantle, blanket, pall.
● verb **confuse**, muddle, obscure.

cloudy adjective **1 overcast**, dark, grey, black, leaden, murky, gloomy, sunless, starless. **2 murky**, muddy, milky, dirty, turbid.
- OPPOSITES clear, sunny.

clown noun **1 joker**, comedian, comic, wag, wit, jester. **2 fool**, idiot, buffoon, dolt, ignoramus; *informal* moron, ass, numbskull, halfwit, fathead; *Brit. infor-mal* prat, berk, twit, twerp.

club[1] noun **1 society**, association, group, circle, league, guild, union. **2 nightclub**, bar; *informal* disco. **3 team**, squad, side.

club[2] noun **stick**, cudgel, truncheon, bludgeon, baton, mace, bat; *N. Amer.* blackjack, nightstick; *Brit. informal* cosh.
● verb **hit**, beat, strike, cudgel, bludg-eon, batter; *informal* clout, clobber; *Brit. informal* cosh.

clue noun **hint**, indication, sign, signal, pointer, lead, tip, evidence.

clump noun **1** *a clump of trees* **cluster**, thicket, group, bunch. **2** *a clump of earth* **lump**, clod, mass, chunk.

clumsy adjective **1 awkward**, uncoor-dinated, ungainly, graceless, lum-bering, inelegant, inept, unskilful, accident-prone, all fingers and thumbs; *informal* cack-handed, ham-fisted, but-terfingered; *N. Amer. informal* klutzy.

2 unwieldy, cumbersome, bulky, awkward.
- OPPOSITES graceful.

cluster noun **bunch**, clump, mass, knot, group, clutch, huddle, crowd.
● verb **congregate**, gather, collect, group, assemble, huddle, crowd.

clutch verb **grip**, grasp, clasp, cling to, hang on to, clench, hold, grab, snatch.

clutter noun **disorder**, chaos, mess, disarray, untidiness, confusion, litter, rubbish, junk.
● verb **litter**, mess up, be strewn, be scattered, cover, bury.

coach[1] noun **1** *a journey by coach* **bus**; *dated* omnibus, charabanc. **2** *a railway coach* **carriage**, wagon; *N. Amer.* car.

coach[2] noun **instructor**, trainer, teacher, tutor, mentor, guru.
● verb **instruct**, teach, tutor, school, educate, drill, train.

coagulate verb **congeal**, clot, thicken, solidify, harden, set, dry.

coalition noun **alliance**, union, partnership, bloc, federation, league, association, confederation, consortium, syndicate, amalgamation, merger.

coarse adjective **1 rough**, scratchy, prickly, wiry, harsh. **2** *coarse manners* **uncouth**, oafish, loutish, boorish, rude, impolite, ill-mannered, vulgar, common, rough. **3** *a coarse remark* **vulgar**, crude, rude, off colour, lewd, smutty, indelicate.
- OPPOSITES soft, refined, polite.

coast noun **shore**, coastline, seashore, seaboard, shoreline, seaside; *literary* strand.
● verb **freewheel**, cruise, taxi, drift, glide, sail.

WORD LINKS
littoral relating to a coast or seashore

coat noun **1 fur**, hair, wool, fleece, hide, pelt, skin. **2 layer**, covering, coating, skin, film, deposit.
● verb **cover**, surface, plate, spread, daub, smear, plaster, cake.

coax verb **persuade**, wheedle, cajole, get round, inveigle, manoeuvre; *informal* sweet-talk, soft-soap, twist someone's arm.

cocky adjective **arrogant**, conceited, overconfident, swollen-headed, self-important, full of yourself, egotistical, presumptuous, boastful; *informal* too big for your boots.
- OPPOSITES modest.

code noun **1 cipher**. **2 convention**, etiquette, protocol, ethic. **3 law(s)**, rules, regulations, constitution, system.

coerce verb **pressure**, press, push, constrain, force, compel, oblige, browbeat, bully, threaten, intimidate, dragoon, twist someone's arm; *informal* railroad, steamroller, lean on.

cogent adjective **convincing**, persuasive, compelling, strong, forceful, powerful, potent, effective, sound, telling, coherent, clear, lucid, logical, well argued.

coherent adjective **logical**, reasoned, rational, sound, cogent, consistent, clear, lucid, articulate, intelligible.
- OPPOSITES muddled.

coil verb **wind**, loop, twist, curl, spiral, twine, wrap.

coin verb **invent**, create, make up, conceive, originate, think up, dream up.

WORD LINKS
numismatic relating to coins

coincide verb **1 occur simultaneously**, happen together, co-occur, coexist. **2 tally**, correspond, agree, accord, match up, be compatible, dovetail, mesh; *informal* square.
- OPPOSITES differ.

coincidence noun **accident**, chance, providence, happenstance, fate, luck, fortune, fluke.

coincidental adjective **accidental**, chance, fluky, random, fortuitous, unintentional, unplanned.

cold adjective **1 chilly**, chill, cool, freezing, icy, wintry, frosty, raw, bitter; *informal* nippy; *Brit. informal* parky.

2 unfriendly, inhospitable, unwelcoming, cool, frigid, frosty, distant, formal, stiff.
- OPPOSITES hot, warm.

collaborate verb **1 cooperate**, join forces, work together, combine, pool resources, club together. **2 fraternize**, conspire, collude, cooperate, consort.

collaborator noun **1 co-worker**, partner, associate, colleague, confederate, assistant. **2 sympathizer**, traitor, quisling, fifth columnist.

collapse verb **1 cave in**, fall in, subside, fall down, give (way), crumple, crumble, disintegrate. **2 faint**, pass out, black out, lose consciousness. **3 go to pieces**, break down, be overcome; informal crack up. **4 fail**, break down, fall through, fold, founder; informal flop, fizzle out, flatline.
● noun **1 cave-in**, disintegration. **2 breakdown**, failure.

colleague noun **co-worker**, fellow worker, workmate, teammate, associate, partner, collaborator, ally, confederate.

collect verb **1** he collected up the rubbish **gather**, accumulate, assemble, amass, stockpile, pile up, heap up, store (up), hoard, save. **2** a crowd soon collected **gather**, assemble, meet, muster, congregate, convene, converge. **3 fetch**, pick up, go/come and get, call for, meet.
- OPPOSITES distribute, disperse.

collected adjective **calm**, cool, self-possessed, self-controlled, composed, poised, serene, tranquil, relaxed; informal laid-back.
- OPPOSITES excited.

collection noun **1 hoard**, pile, heap, stock, store, stockpile, accumulation, reserve, supply, bank, pool, fund; informal stash. **2 group**, crowd, body, gathering, knot, cluster. **3 anthology**, selection, compendium, compilation, miscellany, treasury. **4 appeal**; informal whip-round.

collective adjective **common**, shared, joint, combined, mutual, communal, pooled, united, allied, cooperative, collaborative.
- OPPOSITES individual.

collide verb **crash**, hit, strike, run into, bump into.

collision noun **crash**, accident, smash; N. Amer. wreck; informal pile-up; Brit. informal shunt, prang.

colloquial adjective **informal**, conversational, everyday, familiar, popular, casual, idiomatic, slangy, vernacular.
- OPPOSITES formal.

colonize verb **settle (in)**, people, populate, occupy, take over, invade.

colony noun **territory**, dependency, protectorate, satellite, settlement, outpost, province.

colossal adjective **huge**, massive, enormous, gigantic, giant, mammoth, vast, cosmic, immense, monumental, mountainous; informal monster, whopping, humongous; Brit. informal ginormous.
- OPPOSITES tiny.

colour noun **1 hue**, shade, tint, tone, coloration. **2 paint**, pigment, colourant, dye, stain.
● verb **1 tint**, dye, stain, tinge. **2 influence**, affect, taint, warp, skew, distort.

> **WORD LINKS**
> **chromatic** relating to colour

colourful adjective **1 bright**, vivid, vibrant, brilliant, radiant, gaudy, garish, multicoloured, psychedelic; informal jazzy. **2** a colourful account **vivid**, graphic, lively, animated, dramatic, fascinating, interesting, stimulating, scintillating, evocative.
- OPPOSITES drab, dull.

column noun **1 pillar**, post, support, upright, pier, pile. **2 article**, piece, feature. **3 line**, file, queue, procession, convoy; informal crocodile.

comb verb **1 groom**, brush, untangle, smooth, straighten, neaten, tidy, arrange. **2 search**, scour, explore, sweep.

combat noun **battle**, fighting, action, hostilities, conflict, war, warfare.

● *verb* **fight**, battle, tackle, attack, counter, resist.

combative *adjective* **aggressive**, pugnacious, antagonistic, quarrelsome, argumentative, hostile, truculent, belligerent; *informal* spoiling for a fight.
- OPPOSITES conciliatory.

combination *noun* **mixture**, mix, blend, fusion, amalgamation, amalgam, merger, marriage, synthesis.

combine *verb* **1 mix**, blend, fuse, amalgamate, integrate, merge, marry. **2 unite**, collaborate, join forces, get together, team up.

come *verb* **1** *come and listen* **approach**, advance, draw close/closer, draw near/nearer. **2** *they came last night* **arrive**, get here/there, make it, appear, turn up, materialize; *informal* show (up), roll up. **3** *they came to a stream* **reach**, arrive at, get to, come across, run across, happen on, chance on, come upon, stumble on, end up at; *informal* wind up at. **4** *she comes from Belgium* **be from**, be a native of, hail from, live in, reside in. **5 happen**, occur, take place, come about, fall, crop up.
- OPPOSITES go, leave.
□ **come about** happen, occur, take place, transpire, fall, arise. **come across** meet, run into, run across, come upon, chance on, stumble on, happen on, discover, encounter, find; *informal* bump into. **come on** progress, develop, shape up, take shape, come along, turn out, improve.

comeback *noun* **return**, recovery, resurgence, rally, upturn; *Brit.* fightback.

comedian *noun* **1 comic**, comedienne, funny man/woman, humorist, stand-up; *N. Amer.* tummler. **2 joker**, wit, wag, comic, clown; *informal* laugh, hoot.

comedy *noun* **humour**, fun, hilarity, funny side, laughs, jokes.
- OPPOSITES tragedy.

comfort *noun* **1 ease**, repose, luxury, prosperity. **2 consolation**, condolence, sympathy, commiseration, support, reassurance, cheer.

- OPPOSITES discomfort.
● *verb* **console**, support, reassure, soothe, calm, cheer, hearten.
- OPPOSITES distress, depress.

comfortable *adjective* **1 affluent**, prosperous, well-to-do, pleasant, luxurious, opulent. **2 cosy**, snug, warm, pleasant, agreeable, homely; *informal* comfy. **3 loose**, loose-fitting, roomy, casual; *informal* comfy.

comforting *adjective* **soothing**, reassuring, calming, heartening, cheering.
- OPPOSITES upsetting.

comic *adjective* **humorous**, funny, amusing, hilarious, comical, zany, witty, droll.
- OPPOSITES serious.
● *noun* **comedian**, comedienne, funny man/woman, humorist, wit, joker.

comical *adjective* **1 funny**, humorous, droll, witty, comic, amusing, entertaining; *informal* wacky. **2 absurd**, silly, ridiculous, laughable, ludicrous, preposterous, foolish; *informal* crazy.
- OPPOSITES serious.

coming *adjective* **forthcoming**, imminent, impending, approaching.
● *noun* **approach**, advance, advent, arrival, appearance, emergence.

command *verb* **1 order**, tell, direct, instruct, call on, require, charge, enjoin, ordain; *old use* bid. **2 be in charge of**, be in command of, head, lead, control, direct, manage, supervise, oversee; *informal* head up.
● *noun* **1 order**, instruction, direction, directive, injunction, decree, edict, dictate, mandate, commandment, fiat. **2** *he had 160 men under his command* **authority**, control, charge, power, direction, dominion, guidance, leadership, rule, government, management, supervision, jurisdiction. **3 knowledge**, mastery, grasp, comprehension, understanding.

commander *noun* **leader**, head, chief, overseer, director, controller; *informal* boss, skipper, head honcho; *Brit. informal* gaffer, guv'nor.

commanding *adjective* **dominant**, controlling, superior, powerful, advantageous, favourable.

commemorate *verb* **celebrate**, remember, recognize, acknowledge, observe, mark, pay tribute to, pay homage to, honour, salute.

commence *verb* **begin**, inaugurate, start, initiate, launch into, open, get the ball rolling, get going, get under way, get off the ground, set about, embark on; *informal* kick off.
- OPPOSITES conclude.

commend *verb* **1 praise**, compliment, congratulate, applaud, salute, honour, sing the praises of, pay tribute to. **2 recommend**, endorse, vouch for, speak for, support, back.
- OPPOSITES criticize.

commendable *adjective* **admirable**, praiseworthy, creditable, laudable, meritorious, exemplary, honourable, respectable.
- OPPOSITES reprehensible.

comment *noun* **1 remark**, observation, statement, pronouncement, judgement, reflection, opinion, view. **2 discussion**, debate, interest. **3 note**, annotation, commentary, footnote, gloss, explanation.
● *verb* **remark**, observe, say, state, note, point out, mention, interject; *formal* opine.

commentary *noun* **1 narration**, description, report, review, voice-over. **2 explanation**, elucidation, interpretation, analysis, assessment, review, criticism, notes, comments.

commentator *noun* **1 reporter**, narrator, journalist, newscaster. **2 analyst**, pundit, critic, columnist, leader-writer, opinion-former, monitor, observer.

commerce *noun* **trade**, trading, business, dealing, buying and selling, traffic, trafficking.

commercial *adjective* **1 trade**, trading, business, mercantile, sales. **2 profit-making**, materialistic, mercenary.

commission *noun* **1 percentage**, share, premium, fee, bonus, royalty; *informal* cut, rake-off, slice; *Brit. informal* whack. **2 contract**, engagement, assignment, booking, job. **3 committee**, board, council, panel, body.
● *verb* **1 engage**, contract, book, employ, hire, recruit, take on, retain, appoint. **2 order**, place an order for, pay for.

commit *verb* **1 carry out**, do, perpetrate, engage in, execute, accomplish, be responsible for; *informal* pull off. **2 entrust**, consign, assign, deliver, hand over. **3 consign**, send, confine.

commitment *noun* **1 responsibility**, obligation, duty, liability, engagement, tie. **2 dedication**, devotion, allegiance, loyalty. **3 promise**, vow, pledge, undertaking.

committed *adjective* **devoted**, dedicated, motivated, driven, staunch, loyal, faithful, devout, firm, steadfast, unwavering, passionate, ardent, sworn.
- OPPOSITES apathetic.

common *adjective* **1** *a common occurrence* **frequent**, regular, everyday, normal, usual, ordinary, familiar, standard, commonplace, average, unexceptional, typical. **2** *a common belief* **widespread**, general, universal, popular, mainstream, prevalent, rife, established, conventional, accepted. **3 collective**, communal, shared, community, public, popular, general. **4 uncouth**, vulgar, coarse, rough, uncivilized, unsophisticated, unrefined, inferior, plebeian; *informal* plebby.
- OPPOSITES unusual, rare.

commonplace *adjective* see **normal** (sense 1).

common sense *noun* **good sense**, native wit, good judgement, level-headedness, prudence, wisdom; *informal* horse sense, nous; *Brit. informal* common; *N. Amer. informal* smarts.
- OPPOSITES stupidity.

commotion *noun* **disturbance**, uproar, disorder, confusion, rumpus, fuss, furore, hue and cry, stir, storm, chaos, havoc, pandemonium.

communal *adjective* **1** *a communal kitchen* **shared**, joint, common, public, general. **2** *they farm on a communal basis* **collective**, cooperative, community.
- OPPOSITES private, individual.

communicate *verb* **1** **liaise**, be in touch, be in contact, have dealings, talk, speak, interface. **2** **convey**, tell, relay, transmit, impart, pass on, report, recount, relate. **3** **transmit**, spread, transfer, pass on.

communication *noun* **1** **contact**, dealings, relations, connection, correspondence, dialogue, conversation. **2** **message**, statement, announcement, report, dispatch, bulletin, disclosure, communiqué, letter, correspondence.

communicative *adjective* **forthcoming**, expansive, expressive, unreserved, vocal, outgoing, frank, open, candid, talkative, chatty.

communist *noun & adjective* **collectivist**, Bolshevik, Marxist, Maoist, Soviet; *informal, derogatory* red, Commie.

community *noun* **society**, population, populace, people, public, residents, inhabitants, citizens.

compact[1] *adjective* **1** **dense**, tightly packed, compressed, thick, tight, firm, solid. **2** **neat**, small, handy, portable, fun-size. **3** **concise**, succinct, condensed, brief, pithy, to the point, short and sweet; *informal* snappy.
- OPPOSITES loose, bulky, lengthy.
● *verb* **compress**, condense, pack down, tamp (down), flatten.

compact[2] *noun* **treaty**, pact, accord, agreement, contract, bargain, deal, settlement.

companion *noun* **comrade**, fellow, partner, associate, escort, compatriot, confederate, friend; *informal* pal, chum, crony; *Brit. informal* mate; *N. Amer. informal* buddy.

company *noun* **1** **firm**, business, corporation, establishment, agency, office, house, institution, concern, enterprise, consortium, syndicate; *informal* outfit. **2** **companionship**, fellowship, society, presence. **3** **unit**, section, detachment, corps, squad, platoon.

comparable *adjective* **1** **similar**, close, near, approximate, equivalent, proportionate. **2** *nobody is comparable with him* **equal to**, as good as, in the same league as, on a level with, a match for.
- OPPOSITES incomparable.

compare *verb* **1** **contrast**, balance, set against, weigh up. **2** **liken**, equate, class with, bracket with. **3** **be as good as**, be comparable to, bear comparison with, be the equal of, match up to, be on a par with, be in the same league as, come close to, rival.

comparison *noun* **resemblance**, likeness, similarity, correspondence.

compartment *noun* **bay**, locker, recess, alcove, cell, cubicle, pod, pigeonhole, cubbyhole.

compass *noun* **scope**, range, extent, reach, span, breadth, ambit, limits, parameters, bounds.

compassion *noun* **sympathy**, empathy, understanding, fellow feeling, pity, care, concern, sensitivity, kindness.
- OPPOSITES indifference, cruelty.

compassionate *adjective* **sympathetic**, understanding, pitying, caring, sensitive, warm, loving, kind.
- OPPOSITES unsympathetic, uncaring.

compatible *adjective* **well matched**, (well) suited, like-minded, in tune, in harmony, in keeping, consistent, consonant; *informal* on the same wavelength.

compel *verb* **force**, pressure, coerce, dragoon, press, push, oblige, require, make; *informal* lean on, railroad, put the screws on.

compelling *adjective* **1** **enthralling**, captivating, gripping, riveting, spellbinding, mesmerizing, absorbing. **2** **convincing**, persuasive, cogent, irresistible, powerful, strong.
- OPPOSITES boring, weak.

compensate *verb* **1** **recompense**, repay, pay back, reimburse, remunerate, indemnify. **2 balance (out)**, counterbalance, counteract, offset, make up for, cancel out.

compensation noun **recompense**, repayment, reimbursement, remuneration, redress, amends, damages; *N. Amer. informal* comp.

compete verb **1 take part**, participate, be a contestant, play, enter, go in for. **2** *they had to compete with other firms* **contend**, vie, battle, jockey, go head to head, pit yourself against, challenge, take on.

competence noun **1** *my technical competence* **ability**, capability, proficiency, accomplishment, expertise, skill, prowess; *informal* know-how. **2** *the competence of the system* **adequacy**, suitability, fitness.

competent adjective **1 able**, capable, proficient, adept, accomplished, skilful, skilled, expert. **2 fit**, suitable, suited, appropriate, qualified, empowered, authorized.

competition noun **1 contest**, tournament, championship, match, game, heat; *Brit.* clash. **2 rivalry**, competitiveness, conflict; *informal* keeping up with the Joneses. **3 opposition**, rivals, other side, field, enemy.

competitive adjective **1** *a competitive player* **ambitious**, zealous, keen, combative, aggressive, driven, motivated; *informal* go-ahead. **2** *a highly competitive industry* **ruthless**, aggressive, fierce, cut-throat; *informal* dog-eat-dog. **3** *competitive prices* **reasonable**, moderate, keen, low, cheap, budget, bargain, rock-bottom, bargain-basement.

competitor noun **1 contestant**, contender, challenger, participant, entrant, player. **2 rival**, challenger, opponent, competition, opposition.

compile verb **assemble**, put together, make up, collate, compose, organize, arrange, gather, collect.

complacency noun **smugness**, self-satisfaction, self-congratulation, self-regard.

complacent adjective **smug**, self-satisfied, self-congratulatory, resting on your laurels, pleased with yourself.

complain verb **protest**, grumble, whine, bleat, carp, cavil, grouse, make a fuss, object, find fault; *informal* whinge, gripe, moan, bitch.

complaint noun **1 protest**, objection, grievance, grouse, grumble, criticism; *informal* gripe, whinge. **2 disorder**, disease, illness, sickness, ailment, infection, condition, problem, upset, trouble.

complement noun **1 accompaniment**, companion, addition, supplement, accessory, finishing touch. **2 amount**, contingent, capacity, allowance, quota.
● verb **accompany**, go with, round off, set off, suit, harmonize with, enhance, complete.

complementary adjective **harmonious**, compatible, corresponding, matching, reciprocal.

complete adjective **1 entire**, whole, full, total, uncut, unabridged, unexpurgated. **2 finished**, ended, concluded, completed; *informal* wrapped up, sewn up. **3 absolute**, utter, out-and-out, total, downright, prize, perfect, unqualified, unmitigated, sheer; *N. Amer.* full-bore.
- OPPOSITES partial, unfinished.
● verb **1 finish**, end, conclude, finalize, wind up, clinch; *informal* wrap up. **2 finish off**, round off, top off, crown, cap, add the finishing touch.

completely adverb **totally**, entirely, wholly, thoroughly, fully, utterly, absolutely, perfectly, downright.

complex adjective **1 compound**, composite, multiplex. **2 complicated**, involved, intricate, convoluted, elaborate, difficult; *Brit. informal* fiddly.
- OPPOSITES simple.
● noun **1 network**, system, nexus, web. **2** *(informal)* **obsession**, fixation, preoccupation, neurosis; *informal* hang-up, thing.

complexion noun **1 skin**, skin colour/tone, colouring. **2 kind**, nature, character, colour, persuasion, outlook.

complicate verb **make (more) difficult**, make complicated, mix up, confuse, muddle, obscure.
- OPPOSITES simplify.

complicated adjective **complex**, involved, intricate, convoluted, elaborate, difficult, knotty, tortuous, labyrinthine, Byzantine; *Brit. informal* fiddly.
- OPPOSITES simple, straightforward.

complication noun **difficulty**, problem, issue, obstacle, hurdle, stumbling block, snag, catch, hitch; *Brit.* spanner in the works; *informal* headache.

compliment noun **tribute**, accolade, commendation, pat on the back; (**compliments**) praise, acclaim, admiration, flattery, congratulations; *N. Amer. informal* kudos.
- OPPOSITES criticism, insult.
● verb **praise**, pay tribute to, flatter, commend, acclaim, applaud, salute, congratulate.
- OPPOSITES criticize.

complimentary adjective **1 flattering**, appreciative, congratulatory, admiring, approving, favourable, glowing. **2 free (of charge)**, gratis; *informal* on the house.
- OPPOSITES critical.

comply verb **obey**, observe, abide by, adhere to, conform to, follow, respect, go along with.
- OPPOSITES disobey.

component noun **part**, piece, bit, element, constituent, ingredient, unit, module.

compose verb **1 write**, devise, make up, think up, produce, invent, pen, author. **2 organize**, arrange, construct, set out. **3 make up**, constitute, form, comprise. □ **compose yourself** calm down, control yourself, regain your composure, pull yourself together, steady yourself; *informal* get a grip.

composed adjective **calm**, collected, cool (as a cucumber), self-possessed, poised, serene, relaxed, at ease, unruffled, unperturbed; *informal* unflappable, together, laid-back, chilled.

composition noun **1 make-up**, constitution, configuration, structure, formation, anatomy, organization. **2 work (of art)**, creation, opus, piece. **3 writing**, creation, formulation, compilation. **4 essay**, paper, study, piece of writing; *N. Amer.* theme. **5 arrangement**, layout, proportions, balance, symmetry.

composure noun **self-control**, self-possession, calm, equanimity, equilibrium, serenity, tranquillity, poise, presence of mind, sangfroid, placidness, impassivity; *informal* cool.

compound noun **amalgam**, blend, mixture, mix, alloy.
● adjective **composite**, complex, multiple.
- OPPOSITES simple.
● verb **1 mix**, combine, blend. **2 aggravate**, exacerbate, worsen, add to, augment, intensify, heighten, increase.

comprehend verb **understand**, grasp, see, take in, follow, make sense of, fathom; *informal* work out, figure out, get.

comprehensible adjective **intelligible**, understandable, lucid, coherent, accessible, self-explanatory, clear, plain, straightforward.
- OPPOSITES incomprehensible.

comprehension noun **understanding**, grasp, mastery, conception, knowledge, awareness.
- OPPOSITES ignorance.

comprehensive adjective **inclusive**, all-inclusive, complete, full, thorough, extensive, all-embracing, blanket, exhaustive, detailed, sweeping, wholesale, broad, wide-ranging.
- OPPOSITES limited.

compress verb **1 squeeze**, press, squash, crush, compact. **2 shorten**, abridge, condense, abbreviate, contract, telescope, summarize, precis.
- OPPOSITES expand, pad out.

comprise verb **1** *the country comprises twenty states* **consist of**, be made up of, be composed of, contain. **2** *this breed comprises half the herd* **make up**, constitute, form, account for.

compromise noun **agreement**, understanding, settlement, terms, deal, trade-off, bargain, middle ground.
● verb **1 meet each other halfway**, come to an understanding, make a deal, make concessions, find a happy medium, strike a balance. **2 undermine**, weaken, damage, harm, jeopardize, prejudice.

compulsion noun **1** he is under no compulsion to go **obligation**, pressure, coercion. **2 urge**, impulse, need, desire, drive, obsession, fixation, addiction.

compulsive adjective **1** a compulsive desire **irresistible**, uncontrollable, compelling, overwhelming. **2** compulsive eating **obsessive**, obsessional, addictive, uncontrollable. **3 inveterate**, chronic, incorrigible, incurable, hopeless, persistent, habitual; informal pathological. **4 fascinating**, compelling, gripping, riveting, engrossing, enthralling, captivating.

compulsory adjective **obligatory**, mandatory, required, requisite, necessary, binding, enforced, prescribed.
- OPPOSITES optional.

compute verb **calculate**, work out, reckon, determine, evaluate, add up, total.

comrade noun **companion**, friend, colleague, associate, partner, ally; Brit. informal mate; N. Amer. informal buddy.

conceal verb **1** clouds concealed the sun **hide**, screen, cover, obscure, block out, blot out, mask. **2** he concealed his true feelings **keep secret**, hide, disguise, mask, veil, bottle up; informal keep a/the lid on.
- OPPOSITES reveal, confess.

concede verb **1 admit**, acknowledge, accept, allow, grant, recognize, own, confess, agree. **2 surrender**, yield, give up, relinquish, hand over.
- OPPOSITES deny.

conceit noun **vanity**, pride, arrogance, egotism, self-importance, narcissism, self-admiration.

- OPPOSITES humility.

conceited adjective **vain**, proud, arrogant, egotistic, self-important, narcissistic, full of yourself, swollen-headed, boastful, cocky, self-satisfied, smug; informal big-headed, stuck-up.

conceivable adjective **imaginable**, possible, plausible, credible, believable, feasible.

conceive verb **1 think up**, think of, dream up, devise, formulate, design, create, develop; informal cook up. **2 imagine**, envisage, visualize, picture.

concentrate verb **1 focus on**, pay attention to, give your attention to, put your mind to, keep your mind on, be absorbed in, be engrossed in, be immersed in. **2 collect**, gather, congregate, converge, mass, rally.

concentrated adjective **1 strenuous**, concerted, intensive, all-out, intense. **2 condensed**, reduced, undiluted, strong.
- OPPOSITES half-hearted, diluted.

concentration noun **close attention**, attentiveness, application, single-mindedness, absorption.
- OPPOSITES inattention.

concept noun **idea**, notion, conception, abstraction, theory, hypothesis.

conception noun **1 pregnancy**, fertilization, impregnation, insemination. **2 inception**, genesis, origination, creation, invention, beginning, origin. **3 plan**, idea, notion, scheme, project, proposal, intention, aim.

concern verb **1 be about**, deal with, cover, relate to, pertain to. **2 affect**, involve, be relevant to, apply to, have a bearing on, impact on. **3 worry**, disturb, trouble, bother, perturb, unsettle.
● noun **1 anxiety**, worry, disquiet, apprehensiveness, unease, misgiving, issue. **2 care**, consideration, solicitude, sympathy. **3 responsibility**, business, affair, duty, job; informal bailiwick; Brit. informal lookout. **4** issues of concern to women **interest**, importance, relevance, significance. **5 firm**, business, company, enterprise, operation,

corporation; *informal* outfit.
- OPPOSITES indifference.

concerned adjective **1 worried**, anxious, upset, troubled, uneasy, bothered. **2 interested**, involved, affected, implicated.
- OPPOSITES unconcerned.

concerning preposition **about**, regarding, relating to, with reference to, referring to, with regard to, as regards, touching, in connection with, re, apropos.

concerted adjective **1** *a concerted effort* **strenuous**, vigorous, intensive, all-out, intense, concentrated. **2** *concerted action* **joint**, united, collaborative, collective, combined, cooperative.

concession noun **1 compromise**, accommodation, trade-off, sop. **2 reduction**, cut, discount, deduction, rebate; *informal* break. **3 right**, privilege, licence, permit, franchise, warrant.

concise adjective **succinct**, pithy, brief, abridged, condensed, abbreviated, compact, potted.
- OPPOSITES lengthy.

conclude verb **1 finish**, end, come/ bring to an end, draw to a close, close, wind up, terminate, stop, cease; *informal* wrap up. **2 settle**, clinch, finalize, tie up; *informal* sew up. **3 deduce**, infer, gather, judge, decide, surmise; *N. Amer.* figure.
- OPPOSITES begin.

conclusion noun **1 end**, ending, finish, close. **2 settlement**, clinching, completion, arrangement. **3 deduction**, inference, interpretation, judgement, verdict.
- OPPOSITES beginning.

conclusive adjective **incontrovertible**, undeniable, indisputable, irrefutable, unquestionable, convincing, certain, decisive, definitive, definite, positive, categorical, unequivocal.
- OPPOSITES unconvincing.

concoct verb **make up**, dream up, fabricate, invent, devise, formulate, hatch, brew; *informal* cook up.

concrete adjective **1 solid**, material, real, physical, tangible. **2 definite**, specific, firm, positive, conclusive, definitive.
- OPPOSITES abstract, imaginary.

concur verb **agree**, be in agreement, accord, be in sympathy, see eye to eye, be of the same mind, be of the same opinion.
- OPPOSITES disagree.

condemn verb **1 censure**, criticize, denounce, deplore, decry; *informal* slam; *Brit. informal* slate, slag off. **2** *his illness condemned him to a lonely childhood* **doom**, destine, damn, sentence.
- OPPOSITES praise.

condense verb **abridge**, compress, summarize, shorten, cut, abbreviate, edit.
- OPPOSITES expand.

condescend verb **1 patronize**, talk down to, look down your nose at, look down on. **2** *he condescended to see us* **deign**, stoop, lower yourself, demean yourself, consent.

condescending adjective **patronizing**, supercilious, superior, disdainful, lofty, haughty; *informal* snooty, stuck-up; *Brit. informal* toffee-nosed.

condition noun **1 state**, shape, order, fitness, health, form; *Brit. informal* nick, fettle. **2 circumstances**, surroundings, environment, situation, state of affairs, position. **3 disorder**, problem, complaint, illness, disease, ailment, malady. **4 stipulation**, constraint, prerequisite, precondition, requirement, term, proviso.
● verb **train**, teach, educate, guide, accustom, adapt, habituate, mould.

conditional adjective **qualified**, dependent, contingent, with reservations, limited, provisional, provisory.

condone verb **disregard**, accept, allow, let pass, turn a blind eye to, overlook, forget, forgive, pardon, excuse.
- OPPOSITES condemn.

conducive adjective **favourable**, beneficial, advantageous, opportune,

encouraging, promising, convenient, good, helpful, instrumental.
- OPPOSITES unfavourable.

conduct noun **1 behaviour**, actions, deeds, doings, exploits. **2 management**, running, direction, control, supervision, regulation, administration, organization, coordination, handling.
● verb **1 manage**, direct, run, administer, organize, coordinate, orchestrate, handle, carry out/on. **2 escort**, guide, lead, usher, steer. **3 transmit**, convey, carry, channel.
☐ **conduct yourself** behave, act, acquit yourself, bear yourself.

confer verb **1 bestow**, present, grant, award, honour with. **2 consult**, talk, speak, converse, have a chat, deliberate, compare notes.

conference noun **meeting**, congress, convention, seminar, discussion, council, forum, summit.

confess verb **1 admit**, acknowledge, reveal, disclose, divulge, own up, plead guilty, accept the blame; informal come clean. **2** I confess I don't know **acknowledge**, admit, concede, grant, allow, own.
- OPPOSITES deny.

confide verb **reveal**, disclose, divulge, impart, declare, vouchsafe, tell, confess.

confidence noun **1 trust**, belief, faith, credence. **2 self-assurance**, self-confidence, self-possession, assertiveness, self-belief, conviction.
- OPPOSITES distrust, doubt.

confident adjective **1 sure**, certain, positive, convinced, in no doubt, satisfied. **2 self-assured**, assured, self-confident, positive, assertive, self-possessed.

confidential adjective **private**, personal, intimate, quiet, secret, sensitive, classified, restricted; informal hush-hush.

confine verb **1 enclose**, incarcerate, imprison, intern, hold captive, cage, lock up, coop up, kettle. **2 restrict**, limit.

confirm verb **1 corroborate**, verify, prove, substantiate, justify, vindicate, bear out. **2 affirm**, reaffirm, assert, assure someone, repeat. **3 ratify**, approve, endorse, validate, sanction, authorize.
- OPPOSITES contradict, deny.

confiscate verb **impound**, seize, commandeer, requisition, appropriate, expropriate, take, sequestrate.

conflict noun **1 dispute**, quarrel, squabble, disagreement, clash, feud, discord, friction, strife, antagonism, hostility. **2 war**, campaign, fighting, engagement, struggle, hostilities, warfare, combat. **3** a conflict between work and home life **clash**, incompatibility, friction, mismatch, variance, contradiction.
- OPPOSITES agreement, peace, harmony.
● verb **clash**, be incompatible, be at odds, differ, diverge, disagree, collide.

conflicting adjective **contradictory**, incompatible, inconsistent, irreconcilable, contrary, opposite, opposing, clashing.

conform verb **1** visitors have to conform to our rules **comply with**, abide by, obey, observe, follow, keep to, stick to, adhere to, uphold, heed, accept, go along with. **2 fit in**, behave (yourself), toe the line, obey the rules; informal play by the rules.
- OPPOSITES flout, rebel.

confound verb **baffle**, bewilder, mystify, bemuse, perplex, puzzle, confuse, dumbfound, throw; informal flabbergast, flummox.

confront verb **1 challenge**, square up to, face (up to), come face to face with, meet, accost, stand up to, tackle. **2 face**, bedevil, beset, plague, bother, trouble, threaten. **3** they must confront these issues **tackle**, address, face (up to), get to grips with, grapple with, deal with, sort out.
- OPPOSITES evade.

confrontation noun **conflict**, clash, fight, battle, encounter, head-to-head;

informal set-to, run-in, dust-up, showdown.

confuse verb **1 bewilder**, baffle, mystify, bemuse, perplex, puzzle, nonplus; informal flummox, faze. **2** the authors have confused the issue **complicate**, muddle, blur, obscure, cloud. **3** some confuse strokes with heart attacks **mix up**, muddle up, mistake for.
- OPPOSITES enlighten, simplify.

confused adjective **1 puzzled**, bemused, bewildered, perplexed, baffled, mystified; informal flummoxed. **2 disorientated**, bewildered, muddled, addled, befuddled, demented, senile. **3** a confused recollection **vague**, unclear, indistinct, imprecise, blurred, hazy, dim. **4 disorderly**, disorganized, untidy, jumbled, mixed up, chaotic, topsy-turvy, tangled; informal higgledy-piggledy; Brit. informal shambolic.
- OPPOSITES clear, lucid.

confusion noun **1 bewilderment**, bafflement, perplexity, puzzlement, bemusement, mystification, befuddlement, disorientation, uncertainty. **2 disorder**, disarray, muddle, mess, chaos, mayhem, pandemonium, turmoil; informal a shambles; Brit. informal an omnishambles.
- OPPOSITES clarity, order.

congeal verb **coagulate**, clot, thicken, cake, set, gel.

congenial adjective **agreeable**, pleasant, friendly, amicable, amiable, nice.
- OPPOSITES unfriendly, unpleasant.

congested adjective **blocked**, clogged, choked, jammed, obstructed, crowded, overcrowded, overflowing, packed; informal snarled up, gridlocked.
- OPPOSITES clear.

congratulate verb **compliment**, wish someone happiness, pay tribute to, pat on the back, take your hat off to, praise, applaud, salute, honour.
- OPPOSITES criticize.

congratulations plural noun **best wishes**, compliments, greetings, felicitations; N. Amer. informal kudos.

congregate verb **assemble**, gather, collect, come together, convene, rally, muster, meet, cluster, group.
- OPPOSITES disperse.

conjure verb **1 produce**, magic, summon. **2** the picture that his words conjured up **bring to mind**, call to mind, evoke, summon up, suggest.

connect verb **1 attach**, join, fasten, fix, link, hook (up), secure, hitch, stick. **2 associate**, link, couple, identify, relate to.
- OPPOSITES detach.

connection noun **1 link**, relationship, relation, interconnection, interdependence, association, bond, tie, tie-in, correspondence. **2** he has the right connections **contact**, friend, acquaintance, ally, colleague, associate, relation.

connive verb **1 ignore**, overlook, disregard, pass over, take no notice of, turn a blind eye to. **2 conspire**, collude, collaborate, plot, scheme.

conniving adjective **scheming**, cunning, calculating, devious, wily, sly, artful, manipulative, Machiavellian, deceitful.

connotation noun **overtone**, undertone, undercurrent, implication, nuance, hint, echo, association.

conquer verb **1 defeat**, beat, vanquish, triumph over, overcome, overwhelm, overpower, overthrow, subdue, subjugate. **2** Peru was conquered by Spain **seize**, take (over), appropriate, capture, occupy, invade, annex, overrun. **3 overcome**, get the better of, control, master, deal with, cope with, rise above; informal lick; US informal own.

conquest noun **1 defeat**, overthrow, subjugation. **2 seizure**, takeover, capture, occupation, invasion, annexation.

conscience noun **moral sense**, morals, sense of right and wrong, standards, values, principles, ethics, beliefs, scruples, qualms.

conscientious adjective **diligent**, industrious, punctilious, painstaking, dedicated, careful, meticulous,

thorough, attentive, hard-working, rigorous, scrupulous.
- OPPOSITES casual.

conscious adjective **1 aware**, awake, responsive; informal with us. **2 deliberate**, purposeful, knowing, considered, calculated, wilful, premeditated.
- OPPOSITES unaware, unconscious.

consecutive adjective **successive**, succeeding, in succession, running, in a row, straight; informal on the trot.

consensus noun **1 agreement**, unanimity, harmony, accord, unity, solidarity. **2** the consensus was that they should act **general opinion**, common view.
- OPPOSITES disagreement.

consent noun **agreement**, assent, acceptance, approval, permission, authorization, sanction; informal go-ahead, green light, OK.
- OPPOSITES dissent.
● verb **agree**, assent, submit, allow, sanction, approve, go along with.
- OPPOSITES forbid, refuse.

consequence noun **1 result**, upshot, outcome, effect, repercussion, ramification, product, end result. **2** the past is of no consequence **importance**, import, significance, account, value, concern.
- OPPOSITES cause.

consequent adjective **resulting**, resultant, ensuing, consequential, following, subsequent.

consequently adverb **as a result**, as a consequence, so, thus, therefore, accordingly, hence, for this/that reason, because of this/that.

conservation noun **preservation**, protection, safe keeping, husbandry, upkeep, maintenance, repair, restoration.

conservative adjective **1 right-wing**, reactionary, traditionalist, old-fashioned, dyed-in-the-wool, hidebound, unadventurous, set in your ways; informal stick-in-the-mud. **2 conventional**, sober, modest, sensible, restrained; informal square.
- OPPOSITES socialist, radical.

conserve verb **preserve**, protect, save, safeguard, keep, look after, sustain, husband.
- OPPOSITES squander.

consider verb **1 think about**, contemplate, reflect on, mull over, ponder, deliberate on, chew over, meditate on, ruminate on, evaluate, weigh up, appraise, take account of, bear in mind; informal size up. **2 deem**, think, believe, judge, rate, count, find, regard as, hold to be, reckon to be, view as, see as.

considerable adjective **sizeable**, substantial, appreciable, significant, plentiful, goodly; informal tidy.
- OPPOSITES paltry.

considerably adverb **greatly**, (very) much, a great deal, a lot, lots, significantly, substantially, appreciably, markedly, noticeably; informal plenty.

considerate adjective **attentive**, thoughtful, solicitous, kind, unselfish, caring, polite, sensitive.

consideration noun **1 thought**, deliberation, reflection, contemplation, examination, inspection, scrutiny, analysis, discussion, attention. **2 factor**, issue, matter, concern, aspect, feature. **3 attentiveness**, concern, care, thoughtfulness, solicitude, understanding, respect, sensitivity.

considering preposition **bearing in mind**, taking into consideration, taking into account, in view of, in the light of.

consist verb
□ **consist of** be composed of, be made up of, be formed of, comprise, include, contain.

consistent adjective **1 constant**, regular, uniform, steady, stable, even, unchanging. **2** her injuries were consistent with a knife attack **compatible**, in tune, in line, corresponding to, conforming to, consonant with.
- OPPOSITES irregular, incompatible.

consolation noun **comfort**, solace, sympathy, pity, commiseration, relief, encouragement, reassurance.

console *verb* **comfort**, sympathize with, commiserate with, show compassion for, help, support, cheer (up), hearten, encourage, reassure, soothe.
- OPPOSITES upset.

consolidate *verb* **1 strengthen**, secure, stabilize, reinforce, fortify. **2 combine**, unite, merge, integrate, amalgamate, fuse, synthesize.

consort *verb*
□ **consort with** associate with, keep company with, mix with, socialize with, fraternize with, have dealings with.

conspicuous *adjective* **obvious**, evident, apparent, visible, noticeable, clear, plain, marked, patent, blatant.
- OPPOSITES inconspicuous.

conspiracy *noun* **plot**, scheme, intrigue, plan, collusion.

conspire *verb* **1 plot**, scheme, intrigue, manoeuvre, plan. **2 combine**, unite, join forces, work together.

constant *adjective* **1** *constant noise* **continuous**, persistent, sustained, ceaseless, unceasing, perpetual, incessant, never-ending, eternal, endless, non-stop. **2** *a constant speed* **consistent**, regular, steady, uniform, even, invariable, unvarying, unchanging. **3 faithful**, loyal, devoted, true, fast, firm, unswerving.
- OPPOSITES intermittent, variable, fickle.

consternation *noun* **dismay**, distress, disquiet, discomposure, surprise, alarm, fear, fright, shock.

constitute *verb* **1 comprise**, make up, form, account for. **2 amount to**, be tantamount to, be equivalent to, represent. **3 establish**, inaugurate, found, create, set up.

constitution *noun* **1 composition**, make-up, structure, construction, arrangement, configuration, formation, anatomy. **2 health**, condition, strength, stamina, build, physique.

constraint *noun* **1 restriction**, limitation, curb, check, restraint, control. **2 inhibition**, uneasiness, embarrassment, self-consciousness, awkwardness.
- OPPOSITES freedom, ease.

constrict *verb* **narrow**, tighten, compress, contract, squeeze, strangle.
- OPPOSITES expand, dilate.

construct *verb* **1 build**, erect, put up, set up, assemble, fabricate. **2 formulate**, create, form, put together, devise, compose, work out, frame.
- OPPOSITES demolish.

construction *noun* **1 structure**, building, edifice, work. **2 interpretation**, explanation, analysis, reading, meaning; *informal* take.

constructive *adjective* **useful**, helpful, productive, positive, practical, valuable, profitable, worthwhile.

consult *verb* **1 seek advice from**, ask, call (on), turn to; *informal* pick someone's brains. **2 confer**, talk things over, communicate, deliberate, compare notes. **3 refer to**, look at, check.

consultant *noun* **adviser**, expert, specialist, authority.

consultation *noun* **1 discussion**, talk(s), dialogue, debate, negotiation, deliberation. **2 meeting**, talk, discussion, interview, audience, hearing.

consume *verb* **1 eat**, devour, swallow, gobble up, wolf down, guzzle, drink. **2 use (up)**, expend, deplete, exhaust, spend. **3 destroy**, demolish, lay waste, raze, devastate, gut, ruin, wreck. **4 eat up**, devour, grip, overwhelm, absorb, obsess, preoccupy.

consumer *noun* **buyer**, purchaser, customer, shopper, user.

contact *noun* **1 communication**, correspondence, connection, relations, dealings, touch. **2 connection**, link, acquaintance, associate, friend.
● *verb* **get in touch with**, communicate with, approach, notify, speak to, write to, come forward; *informal* get hold of.

contagious *adjective* **infectious**, communicable, transmittable, transmissible; *informal* catching.

contain *verb* **1 hold**, carry, enclose, accommodate, have room for. **2 include**, comprise, incorporate, involve, consist of, be made up of, be composed of. **3 restrain**, control, curb, rein in, suppress, stifle, swallow, bottle up, keep in check.

container *noun* **receptacle**, vessel, holder, repository.

contaminate *verb* **pollute**, taint, poison, stain, adulterate, defile, debase, corrupt.
- OPPOSITES purify.

contemplate *verb* **1 look at**, gaze at, stare at, view, regard, examine, inspect, observe, survey, study, eye. **2 think about**, ponder, reflect on, consider, mull over, muse on, dwell on, deliberate over, meditate on, ruminate on, chew over. **3 envisage**, consider, think about, have in mind, intend, plan, propose.

contemplative *adjective* **thoughtful**, pensive, reflective, meditative, ruminative, introspective, brooding, deep/lost in thought.

contemporary *adjective* **1** *contemporary sources* **of the time**, contemporaneous, concurrent, coexisting, coeval. **2** *contemporary society* **modern**, present-day, present, current. **3** *a very contemporary design* **modern**, up to date, up to the minute, fashionable, recent; *informal* trendy.
- OPPOSITES former, old-fashioned.

contempt *noun* **scorn**, disdain, derision, disgust, disrespect.
- OPPOSITES respect.

contemptible *adjective* **despicable**, detestable, beneath contempt, reprehensible, deplorable, unspeakable, disgraceful, shameful, ignominious, abject, low, mean, cowardly, discreditable, worthless, shabby, cheap.
- OPPOSITES admirable.

contemptuous *adjective* **scornful**, disdainful, derisive, mocking, sneering, scoffing, condescending, dismissive.
- OPPOSITES respectful.

contend *verb* **1 compete**, vie, battle, tussle, struggle, jostle, strive. **2 assert**, maintain, hold, claim, argue, insist, allege.
◽ **contend with** cope with, struggle with, grapple with, deal with, take on, handle.

content[1] *adjective* **satisfied**, contented, pleased, gratified, fulfilled, happy, glad, cheerful, at ease, at peace, relaxed, comfortable, untroubled.
- OPPOSITES dissatisfied.
● *verb* **satisfy**, comfort, gratify, gladden, please, soothe, placate, appease, mollify.

content[2] *noun* **1 amount**, proportion, level. **2 constituents**, ingredients, components. **3 subject matter**, theme, argument, thesis, message, substance, material, ideas.

contented *adjective* see **content**[1] (adjective).

contentious *adjective* **controversial**, debatable, disputed, open to debate, moot, vexed.

contentment *noun* **contentedness**, content, satisfaction, fulfilment, happiness, pleasure, cheerfulness, ease, comfort, well-being, peace.

contest *noun* **1 competition**, match, tournament, rally, race, game, bout. **2 fight**, battle, tussle, struggle, competition, race.
● *verb* **1** *he will contest the seat* **compete for**, contend for, vie for, fight for. **2** *the parties contesting the election* **compete in**, take part in, fight, enter. **3 oppose**, challenge, take issue with, question, call into question, object to.
- OPPOSITES accept.

contestant *noun* **competitor**, participant, player, contender, candidate, entrant.

context *noun* **circumstances**, conditions, frame of reference, factors, state of affairs, situation, background, scene, setting.

contingency *noun* **eventuality**, possibility, chance event, incident, occurrence, accident, emergency.

continual adjective **1** *continual breakdowns* **frequent**, regular, repeated, constant, recurrent, recurring, habitual. **2** *continual pain* **constant**, continuous, unremitting, unrelenting, non-stop, sustained, chronic, uninterrupted, incessant, ceaseless, unceasing, neverending, unbroken, perpetual.
- OPPOSITES occasional, temporary.

continue verb **1 carry on**, go on, keep on, persist, persevere, proceed, pursue, keep at; *informal* stick at. **2** *we hope to continue this relationship* **maintain**, keep up, sustain, keep going, keep alive, preserve, perpetuate. **3** *his willingness to continue in office* **remain**, stay, carry on, keep going. **4** *we continued our conversation* **resume**, pick up, take up, carry on with, return to, revisit.
- OPPOSITES stop.

continuous adjective **continual**, persistent, sustained, ceaseless, unceasing, unremitting, unrelenting, perpetual, incessant, never-ending, eternal, endless, non-stop, unbroken, uninterrupted.
- OPPOSITES intermittent.

contort verb **twist**, bend out of shape, distort, misshape, warp, buckle, deform.

contract noun **agreement**, arrangement, commitment, settlement, understanding, compact, covenant, deal, bargain.
● verb **1 shrink**, diminish, reduce, decrease, dwindle, decline. **2 tighten**, tense, flex, constrict, draw in. **3 engage**, take on, hire, commission, employ. **4 catch**, pick up, come/go down with, develop.
- OPPOSITES expand, relax, lengthen.

contraction noun **1 shrinking**, shrinkage, decline, decrease, diminution, dwindling. **2 tightening**, tensing, flexing. **3 abbreviation**, short form, shortening.

contradict verb **1 deny**, refute, rebut, dispute, challenge, counter. **2 argue with**, go against, challenge, oppose.

- OPPOSITES confirm, agree with.

contradiction noun **1 conflict**, clash, disagreement, inconsistency, mismatch. **2 denial**, refutation, rebuttal, countering.
- OPPOSITES agreement, confirmation.

contradictory adjective **inconsistent**, incompatible, irreconcilable, opposed, opposite, contrary, conflicting, at variance.

contraption noun **device**, gadget, apparatus, machine, appliance, mechanism, invention, contrivance; *informal* gizmo, widget; *Brit. informal* gubbins.

contrary adjective **1 opposite**, opposing, contradictory, clashing, conflicting, antithetical, incompatible, irreconcilable. **2 perverse**, awkward, difficult, uncooperative, obstinate, pig-headed, intractable; *Brit. informal* bloodyminded, stroppy; *N. Amer. informal* balky.
- OPPOSITES compatible, accommodating.
● noun **opposite**, reverse, converse, antithesis.

contrast noun **1 difference**, dissimilarity, disparity, divergence, variance, distinction, comparison. **2 opposite**, antithesis, foil, complement.
- OPPOSITES similarity.
● verb **1 differ**, be at variance, be contrary, conflict, be at odds, disagree, clash. **2 compare**, juxtapose, measure, distinguish, differentiate.
- OPPOSITES resemble, liken.

contribute verb **give**, donate, put up, grant, provide, supply; *informal* chip in; *Brit. informal* stump up.
□ **contribute to** play a part in, be instrumental in, have a hand in, be conducive to, make for.

contribution noun **gift**, donation, offering, present, handout, grant, subsidy.

contributor noun **donor**, benefactor, supporter, backer, patron, sponsor.

contrite adjective **remorseful**, repentant, penitent, regretful, sorry, apologetic, rueful, sheepish, hangdog, ashamed, shamefaced.

contrive verb **1 create**, engineer, manufacture, devise, concoct, construct, fabricate, hatch. **2 manage**, find a way, engineer a way, arrange.
- OPPOSITES fail.

contrived adjective **forced**, strained, laboured, overdone, unnatural, artificial, false, affected.
- OPPOSITES natural.

control noun **1 power**, authority, command, dominance, sway, management, direction, leadership, rule, government, sovereignty, supremacy. **2 limit**, limitation, restriction, restraint, check, curb, regulation. **3 self-control**, self-restraint, composure, calm; informal cool.
● verb **1 run**, manage, direct, preside over, supervise, command, rule, govern, lead, dominate. **2** she struggled to control her temper **restrain**, keep in check, curb, hold back, suppress, repress. **3** public spending was controlled **limit**, restrict, curb, cap.

controversial adjective **disputed**, contentious, moot, debatable, arguable, vexed.

controversy noun **dispute**, disagreement, argument, debate, contention, quarrel, war of words, storm; Brit. row.

convalesce verb **recuperate**, get better, recover, get well, get back on your feet.

convene verb **1** he convened a meeting **summon**, call, order. **2** the committee convened **assemble**, gather, meet, come together; formal foregather.

convenience noun **1 advantage**, benefit, expedience, suitability. **2 ease of use**, usefulness, utility, accessibility, availability.
- OPPOSITES inconvenience.

convenient adjective **1 suitable**, favourable, advantageous, appropriate, opportune, timely, expedient. **2 nearby**, handy, well situated, practical, useful, accessible.

convention noun **1 custom**, usage, practice, tradition, etiquette, protocol.

2 agreement, accord, protocol, pact, treaty. **3 conference**, meeting, congress, assembly, gathering.

conventional adjective **1 orthodox**, traditional, established, accepted, customary, received, prevailing, normal, standard, regular, ordinary, usual, typical. **2 conservative**, traditional, conformist, old-fashioned; informal square, stick-in-the-mud. **3 unoriginal**, formulaic, predictable, unadventurous, run-of-the-mill, routine, pedestrian.
- OPPOSITES unorthodox, original.

converge verb **meet**, intersect, cross, connect, link up, join, merge.
- OPPOSITES diverge.
□ **converge on** meet at, arrive at, close in on, bear down on, descend on, approach, move towards.

conversation noun **discussion**, talk, chat, gossip, tête-à-tête, exchange, dialogue; Brit. informal chinwag, natter; Austral. informal convo.

conversion noun **change**, transformation, metamorphosis, alteration, adaptation, modification, redevelopment, rebuilding, remodelling.

convert verb **1 change**, transform, alter, adapt, turn, modify, redevelop, remodel, rebuild, reorganize, metamorphose. **2 win over**, convince, persuade, claim, redeem, save, reform, re-educate, proselytize, evangelize.

convey verb **1 transport**, carry, bring, take, fetch, move. **2 communicate**, pass on, impart, relate, relay, transmit, send. **3 express**, get across/over, put across/over, communicate, indicate.

convict verb **find guilty**, sentence.
- OPPOSITES acquit.
● noun **prisoner**, inmate, criminal, offender, felon; informal jailbird, con, (old) lag.

conviction noun **1 beliefs**, opinions, views, persuasion, ideals, position, stance, values. **2 assurance**, confidence, certainty.
- OPPOSITES diffidence.

convince verb **1** he convinced me I was wrong **assure**, persuade, satisfy, prove to. **2** *I convinced her to marry me* **persuade**, induce, prevail on, talk into, talk round, win over, coax, cajole.

convincing adjective **1 persuasive**, powerful, strong, forceful, compelling, cogent, plausible, irresistible, telling. **2** *a convincing win* **resounding**, emphatic, decisive, conclusive.
- OPPOSITES unconvincing.

convivial adjective **friendly**, genial, affable, amiable, congenial, agreeable, cordial, warm, sociable, outgoing, gregarious, cheerful.

convoy noun **group**, fleet, cavalcade, motorcade, cortège, caravan, line.

cook verb **prepare**, make, put together; *informal* fix, rustle up; *Brit. informal* knock up.

> **WORD LINKS**
> **culinary** relating to cooking

cool adjective **1 chilly**, chill, bracing, cold, brisk, crisp, fresh; *informal* nippy; *Brit. informal* parky. **2 unenthusiastic**, lukewarm, tepid, indifferent, uninterested, apathetic. **3 unfriendly**, distant, remote, aloof, cold, chilly, frosty, unwelcoming; *informal* stand-offish. **4 calm**, collected, composed, self-possessed, poised, serene, relaxed, at ease, unruffled, unperturbed; *informal* unflappable, together, laid-back, chilled.
- OPPOSITES warm, enthusiastic, friendly.
 ● noun **1 chill**, chilliness, coldness, coolness. **2** *(informal)* **self-control**, control, composure, self-possession, calmness, aplomb, poise.
- OPPOSITES warmth.
 ● verb **chill**, refrigerate, freeze.
- OPPOSITES warm.

cooperate verb **1 collaborate**, work together, pull together, join forces, team up, unite, combine, pool resources. **2 assist**, help, lend a hand, be of service, do your bit; *informal* play ball.

cooperation noun **1 collaboration**, joint action, combined effort, teamwork, give and take, compromise.

2 assistance, help.

cooperative adjective **1 collaborative**, collective, combined, joint, shared, united, concerted. **2 helpful**, eager to help, obliging, accommodating, willing.

coordinate verb **organize**, arrange, order, synchronize, bring together, orchestrate.

cope verb **1 manage**, survive, look after yourself, fend for yourself, shift for yourself, get by/through, hold your own. **2** *his inability to cope with the situation* **deal with**, handle, manage, address, face (up to), confront, tackle, get to grips with.

copious adjective **abundant**, plentiful, ample, profuse, extensive, generous, lavish, liberal, overflowing, in abundance, numerous, many; *informal* galore; *literary* plenteous.
- OPPOSITES sparse.

copy noun **1 duplicate**, facsimile, photocopy; *trademark* Xerox. **2 replica**, reproduction, imitation, likeness, forgery, fake, counterfeit.
 ● verb **1 duplicate**, photocopy, xerox, photostat, reproduce. **2 reproduce**, replicate, forge, fake, counterfeit. **3 imitate**, reproduce, emulate, mimic; *informal* rip off.

cord noun **string**, thread, line, rope, cable, wire, twine, yarn.

cordon noun **barrier**, line, chain, ring, circle.
 □ **cordon off** close off, seal off, fence off, separate off, isolate, enclose, encircle, surround.

core noun **1** *the earth's core* **centre**, interior, middle, nucleus. **2** *the core of the argument* **heart**, nucleus, nub, kernel, meat, essence, crux, pith, substance; *informal* nitty-gritty.

corner noun **1 bend**, curve, turn, junction; *Brit.* hairpin bend. **2 district**, region, area, quarter; *informal* neck of the woods.
 ● verb **1 surround**, trap, hem in, pen in, kettle, cut off. **2 gain control of**, take over, dominate, monopolize, capture; *informal* sew up.

corporation noun **company**, firm, business, concern, operation, conglomerate, group, chain, multinational.

corpse noun **dead body**, carcass, remains; *informal* stiff; *Medicine* cadaver.

correct adjective **1 right**, accurate, exact, true, perfect; *informal* spot on. **2 proper**, decent, right, respectable, decorous, seemly, suitable, appropriate, accepted.
- OPPOSITES wrong, improper.
● verb **rectify**, right, put right, set right, amend, remedy, repair, reform, cure.

correction noun **rectification**, righting, amendment, repair, remedy, cure.

correctly adverb **1 accurately**, right, perfectly, exactly, precisely. **2 properly**, decorously, with decorum, decently, fittingly, appropriately, well.

correspond verb **1 be consistent**, correlate, agree, accord, coincide, tally, tie in, match; *informal* square. **2** *a rank corresponding to a British sergeant* **be equivalent**, be analogous, be comparable, equate. **3 exchange letters**, write, communicate.

correspondence noun **1 parallel**, correlation, agreement, consistency, conformity, similarity, resemblance, comparability. **2 letters**, messages, mail, post, communication.

correspondent noun **reporter**, journalist, columnist, writer, contributor, commentator.

corresponding adjective **equivalent**, related, parallel, matching, comparable, analogous.

corrupt adjective **1 dishonest**, unscrupulous, criminal, fraudulent, illegal, unlawful; *informal* crooked; *Brit. informal* bent. **2 immoral**, depraved, degenerate, debauched, vice-ridden, perverted, dissolute.
- OPPOSITES honest, ethical, pure.
● verb **deprave**, pervert, lead astray, debauch, defile, pollute, sully.

corruption noun **1 dishonesty**, unscrupulousness, double-dealing, fraud, misconduct, bribery, venality; *N. Amer.* payola; *informal* graft, sleaze. **2 immorality**, depravity, vice, degeneracy, perversion, debauchery, wickedness, evil, sin.
- OPPOSITES honesty, morality.

cosmetic adjective **superficial**, surface, skin-deep, outward, external.
- OPPOSITES fundamental.

cosmopolitan adjective **1 multicultural**, multiracial, international, worldwide, global. **2 sophisticated**, cultivated, cultured, worldly, suave, urbane.

cost noun **1 price**, fee, tariff, fare, toll, levy, charge, payment, value, rate, outlay; *humorous* damage. **2 sacrifice**, loss, toll, harm, damage, price. **3** *we need to cover our costs* **expenses**, outgoings, overheads, expenditure, spend, outlay.
● verb **1 be priced at**, sell for, be valued at, fetch, come to, amount to; *informal* set someone back, go for. **2 price**, value, put a price/value/figure on.

costly adjective **1 expensive**, dear, high-cost, overpriced; *informal* steep, pricey. **2 catastrophic**, disastrous, calamitous, ruinous, damaging, harmful, deleterious.
- OPPOSITES cheap.

costume noun **clothes**, garments, outfit, ensemble, dress, clothing, attire, garb, uniform, livery; *formal* apparel.

cosy adjective **1 snug**, comfortable, warm, homely, welcoming, safe, sheltered, secure; *informal* comfy. **2 intimate**, relaxed, informal, friendly.

cottage noun **lodge**, chalet, cabin, shack, shanty; *(in Russia)* dacha; *Scottish* bothy; *Austral. informal* weekender.

cough verb **hack**, hawk, bark, clear your throat.
● noun **bark**, hack; *informal* frog in your throat.

council noun **1** the town council **authority**, government, administration, executive, chamber, assembly; *Brit.* corporation. **2** the Schools Council **committee**, board, commission, assembly, panel, synod.

counsel noun **1 advice**, guidance, counselling, recommendations, suggestions, direction. **2 barrister**, lawyer; *Scottish* advocate; *N. Amer.* attorney, counselor(-at-law).
● verb **advise**, recommend, advocate, encourage, warn, caution, guide.

count verb **1 add up**, reckon up, total, tally, calculate, compute; *Brit.* tot up. **2 include**, take into account/consideration, take account of, allow for. **3 consider**, think, feel, regard, look on as, view as, hold to be, judge, deem. **4 matter**, be important, be of consequence, be significant, signify, carry weight, rate.
□ **count on** rely on, depend on, bank on, be sure of, have confidence in, believe in, put your faith in, take for granted, take as read.

counter verb **1 respond to**, parry, hit back at, answer. **2 oppose**, dispute, argue against/with, contradict, challenge, contest.
- OPPOSITES support.
□ **counter to** against, in opposition to, contrary to, at variance with, in defiance of, in conflict with, at odds with.

counteract verb **offset**, counterbalance, balance (out), cancel out, work against, countervail, neutralize, nullify, prevent.

counterfeit adjective **fake**, pirate, bogus, forged, imitation; *informal* phoney.
- OPPOSITES genuine.
● noun **fake**, forgery, copy, reproduction, imitation, fraud, sham; *informal* phoney.
- OPPOSITES original.
● verb **fake**, forge, copy, reproduce, imitate, falsify.

counterpart noun **equivalent**, opposite number, peer, equal, parallel, complement, analogue, match, twin, mate, fellow.

countless adjective **innumerable**, numerous, untold, legion, numberless, limitless, incalculable; *informal* umpteen; *N. Amer. informal* gazillions of.
- OPPOSITES few.

country noun **1 nation**, state, kingdom, realm, land, territory, province. **2 people**, public, population, populace, citizens, nation; *Brit. informal* Joe Public. **3 terrain**, land, territory, landscape, countryside, scenery, surroundings, environment. **4 countryside**, provinces, rural areas, backwoods, hinterland; *Austral./NZ* outback, bush, back country; *informal* sticks.

countryside noun see **country** (sense 3), **country** (sense 4).

county noun **shire**, province, territory, region, district, area.

coup noun **1 takeover**, coup d'état, overthrow, palace revolution, rebellion, uprising. **2 success**, triumph, feat, masterstroke, accomplishment, achievement, scoop.

couple noun **1 pair**, duo, twosome, two, brace. **2 husband and wife**, twosome, partners, lovers; *informal* item.
● verb **1 combine**, accompany, ally, mix, incorporate, add to. **2 connect**, attach, join, fasten, fix, link, secure, hook (up).
- OPPOSITES detach.

coupon noun **voucher**, token, ticket, slip.

courage noun **bravery**, pluck, valour, fearlessness, nerve, daring, audacity, boldness, grit, heroism, gallantry; *informal* guts; *Brit. informal* bottle.
- OPPOSITES cowardice.

courageous adjective **brave**, plucky, fearless, intrepid, valiant, heroic, undaunted, dauntless; *informal* gutsy, have-a-go.
- OPPOSITES cowardly.

course noun **1 route**, way, track, path, line, trail, trajectory, bearing, heading. **2 procedure**, plan (of action), course

of action, practice, approach, technique, policy, strategy, tactic. **3 racecourse**, racetrack, track. **4 course of study**, curriculum, syllabus, classes, lectures, studies. **5 programme**, series, sequence, system, schedule, regime.
● *verb* **flow**, pour, stream, run, rush, gush, cascade, flood, roll.
□ **of course** naturally, as you would expect, needless to say, as a matter of course, obviously, it goes without saying.

court *noun* **1 court of law**, law court, bench, bar, tribunal, assizes. **2 household**, retinue, entourage, train, courtiers, attendants.
● *verb* **1 cultivate**, flatter, curry favour with, wine and dine; *informal* butter up. **2 seek**, pursue, go after, strive for, solicit. **3 risk**, invite, attract, bring on yourself. **4** *(dated)* **woo**, go out with, date, go steady with.

> **WORD LINKS**
> **forensic** relating to a court of law

courteous *adjective* **polite**, well mannered, civil, respectful, well behaved, gracious, obliging, considerate.
- OPPOSITES rude.

courtesy *noun* **politeness**, good manners, civility, respect, grace, consideration, thought.

cove *noun* **bay**, inlet, fjord.

cover *verb* **1 protect**, shield, shelter, hide, conceal, mask, screen, veil, obscure, spread over, extend over, overlay. **2 cake**, coat, encrust, plaster, smother, blanket, carpet, shroud. **3 deal with**, consider, take in, include, involve, incorporate, embrace.
- OPPOSITES reveal.
● *noun* **1** *a protective cover* **covering**, sleeve, wrapping, wrapper, envelope, sheath, housing, jacket, casing, cowling, canopy. **2** *a manhole cover* **lid**, top, cap. **3** *a book cover* **binding**, jacket, dust jacket, dust cover, wrapper. **4 coating**, coat, covering, layer, carpet, blanket, film, sheet, veneer, crust, skin, cloak, mantle, veil, pall, shroud. **5 shelter**, protection, refuge, sanctuary.

covert *adjective* **secret**, furtive, clandestine, surreptitious, stealthy, cloak-and-dagger, backstairs, hidden, concealed, private, undercover, underground; *Military* black; *informal* hush-hush.
- OPPOSITES overt.

covet *verb* **desire**, yearn for, crave, have your heart set on, long for, hanker after/for, hunger after/for, thirst for.

coward *noun* **mouse**, baby; *informal* chicken, scaredy-cat, yellow-belly, sissy; *Brit. informal* big girl's blouse; *N. Amer. informal* pantywaist.

cowardly *adjective* **faint-hearted**, lily-livered, spineless, craven, timid, timorous, fearful; *informal* yellow, chicken, gutless, yellow-bellied.
- OPPOSITES brave.

cower *verb* **cringe**, shrink, flinch, crouch, blench.

coy *adjective* **demure**, shy, modest, bashful, diffident, self-effacing, shrinking.
- OPPOSITES brazen.

crack *noun* **1** *a crack in the glass* **split**, break, chip, fracture, rupture. **2** *a crack between two rocks* **space**, gap, crevice, fissure, cleft, cranny, chink. **3 bang**, report, explosion, detonation, clap, crash. **4** *a crack on the head* **blow**, bang, hit, knock, rap, bump, smack, slap; *informal* bash, whack, clout.
● *verb* **1 break**, split, fracture, rupture, snap. **2 break down**, give way, cave in, go to pieces, give in, yield, succumb. **3 hit**, strike, smack, slap, beat, thump, knock, rap; *informal* bash, whack, clobber, clout, clip. **4** *(informal)* **decipher**, interpret, decode, break, solve.

cradle *noun* **1 crib**, Moses basket, cot, carrycot. **2 birthplace**, fount, fountainhead, source, spring, origin.
● *verb* **hold**, support, cushion, pillow, nurse, rest.

craft *noun* **1 activity**, occupation, trade, profession, work, line of work, job. **2 cunning**, craftiness, guile, wiliness, artfulness, deviousness, slyness, trickery, duplicity, dishonesty, deceit, deceitfulness, deception, intrigue, subterfuge, wiles, ploys, ruses, schemes, tricks. **3 vessel**, ship, boat, aircraft, spacecraft.

craftsman, **craftswoman** noun artisan, artist, skilled worker, technician, expert, master.

crafty adjective **cunning**, wily, sly, artful, devious, tricky, scheming, calculating, shrewd, canny, dishonest, deceitful.
- OPPOSITES honest.

cram verb **1** wardrobes crammed with clothes **fill**, stuff, pack, jam, fill to overflowing, overload, crowd, throng. **2** he crammed his clothes into a case **push**, thrust, shove, force, ram, jam, stuff, pack, pile, squash, squeeze, compress. **3 revise**, study; informal swot, mug up, bone up.

cramp noun **spasm**, pain, shooting pain, twinge, pang, convulsion.
● verb **hinder**, impede, inhibit, hamper, constrain, hamstring, interfere with, restrict, limit, slow.

cramped adjective **1 poky**, uncomfortable, confined, restricted, constricted, small, tiny, narrow, crowded, congested. **2 small**, crabbed, illegible, unreadable, indecipherable.
- OPPOSITES spacious.

crash verb **1** the car crashed into a tree **smash into**, collide with, be in collision with, hit, strike, ram, cannon into, plough into, meet head-on; N. Amer. impact. **2** he crashed his car **smash**, wreck; Brit. write off; Brit. informal prang; N. Amer. informal total. **3 fall**, drop, plummet, plunge, sink, dive, tumble. **4** (informal) **fail**, fold, collapse, go under, go bankrupt; informal go bust, go to the wall, flatline.
● noun **1 accident**, collision, smash; N. Amer. wreck; informal pile-up; Brit. informal shunt, prang. **2 bang**, smash, smack, crack, bump, thud, explosion. **3 failure**, collapse, liquidation, bankruptcy.

crate noun **packing case**, chest, tea chest, box, container.

crater noun **hollow**, bowl, basin, hole, cavity, depression, dip; Geology caldera.

crave verb **long for**, yearn for, hanker after, desire, want, hunger for, thirst for, pine for; informal be dying for.

craving noun **longing**, yearning, desire, hankering, hunger, thirst, appetite.

crawl verb **1 creep**, worm your way, go on all fours, wriggle, slither, squirm. **2** (informal) **grovel**, kowtow, pander, toady, bow and scrape, fawn; informal suck up, lick someone's boots.

craze noun **fad**, fashion, trend, vogue, enthusiasm, mania, passion, rage; informal thing.

crazy adjective (informal) **1 mad**, insane, out of your mind, deranged, demented, crazed, lunatic, unbalanced, unhinged; Brit. sectionable; informal mental, off your head, round the bend; Brit. informal barmy, crackers, barking (mad), potty, round the twist. **2** a crazy idea **stupid**, foolish, idiotic, silly, absurd, ridiculous, ludicrous, preposterous, asinine; informal cockeyed, half-baked; Brit. informal barmy, daft. **3** he's crazy about her **passionate**, very keen, enamoured, infatuated, smitten, enthusiastic, fanatical; informal wild, mad, nuts; Brit. informal potty.
- OPPOSITES sane, sensible.

cream noun **1 lotion**, ointment, moisturizer, cosmetic, salve, rub. **2 best**, finest, pick, flower, crème de la crème, elite, A-list.
- OPPOSITES dregs.
● adjective **off-white**, creamy, ivory.

creamy adjective **smooth**, thick, velvety, rich, buttery.

crease noun **fold**, line, crinkle, ridge, furrow, groove, corrugation, wrinkle, crow's foot.
● verb **crumple**, wrinkle, crinkle, line, scrunch up, rumple, ruck up, pucker.

create verb **1 produce**, generate, bring into being, make, fashion, build, construct. **2 bring about**, give rise to, lead to, result in, cause, breed, generate, engender, produce. **3 establish**, found, initiate, institute, constitute, inaugurate, launch, set up, form.
- OPPOSITES destroy, abolish.

creation noun **1 establishment**, formation, foundation, initiation, institution, inauguration, constitution, setting up. **2 the world**, the universe, the cosmos, nature, the natural world. **3 work**, work of art, production, opus, oeuvre, achievement, concoction, invention; *informal* brainchild.
- OPPOSITES abolition, destruction.

creative adjective **inventive**, imaginative, innovative, experimental, original, artistic, inspired, visionary.
- OPPOSITES unimaginative.

creator noun **maker**, producer, author, designer, deviser, originator, inventor, architect.

creature noun **animal**, beast, brute, living thing, living being; *N. Amer. informal* critter.

credentials plural noun **1 suitability**, eligibility, attributes, qualifications, record, experience, background. **2 documents**, identity papers, ID, passport, testimonial, reference, certification.

credibility noun **plausibility**, believability, credence, trustworthiness, reliability, dependability, integrity.

credible adjective **believable**, plausible, conceivable, persuasive, convincing, tenable, probable, possible, feasible, reasonable.

credit noun **praise**, commendation, acclaim, acknowledgement, recognition, kudos, glory, respect, appreciation.
● verb **1** (*Brit.*) *you wouldn't credit it!* **believe**, accept, give credence to, trust, have faith in. **2 ascribe to**, attribute to, put down to.

credulous adjective **gullible**, naive, easily taken in, impressionable, unsuspecting, unsuspicious, innocent, inexperienced, unsophisticated, wide-eyed.
- OPPOSITES suspicious.

creed noun **1** *people of many creeds* **faith**, religion, belief, religious persuasion. **2** *his political creed* **beliefs**, principles, articles of faith, tenets, ideology, credo, doctrines, teachings.

creek noun **inlet**, bay, estuary, fjord; *Scottish* firth.

creep verb **tiptoe**, steal, sneak, slink, edge, inch, skulk, prowl.

creepy adjective (*informal*) **frightening**, eerie, disturbing, sinister, weird, menacing, threatening; *informal* spooky, scary.

crest noun **1 tuft**, comb, plume, crown. **2 summit**, peak, top, ridge, pinnacle, brow, crown, apex. **3 insignia**, emblem, coat of arms, arms, badge, device, regalia.

crestfallen adjective **downhearted**, downcast, despondent, disappointed, disconsolate, disheartened, discouraged, dispirited, dejected, sad, dismayed, unhappy, forlorn.
- OPPOSITES cheerful.

crevice noun **crack**, fissure, interstice, cleft, chink, cranny, slit, split.

crew noun **1** *the ship's crew* **company**, complement, sailors, hands. **2** *a film crew* **team**, squad, company, unit, party, gang.

crime noun **1 offence**, unlawful act, illegal act, felony, violation, misdemeanour. **2 lawbreaking**, delinquency, wrongdoing, criminality, misconduct, illegality, villainy, vice.

criminal noun **lawbreaker**, felon, offender, malefactor, villain, delinquent, culprit, miscreant, wrongdoer; *informal* crook.
● adjective **1 unlawful**, illegal, illicit, lawless, delinquent, corrupt, felonious, nefarious; *informal* crooked; *Brit. informal* bent. **2** (*informal*) **deplorable**, shameful, reprehensible, disgraceful, inexcusable, outrageous, scandalous.
- OPPOSITES lawful.

cringe verb **1 cower**, shrink, recoil, shy away, flinch, quail, blench, tremble, quiver, quake. **2 wince**, shudder, squirm, feel embarrassed/mortified.

cripple verb **1 disable**, paralyse, immobilize, incapacitate, handicap. **2 damage**, weaken, hamper, paralyse, ruin, destroy, wipe out, bring to a standstill, put out of action, put out of business.

crippled *adjective* **disabled**, paralysed, incapacitated, physically handicapped, lame, immobilized, bedridden, confined to a wheelchair; *euphemistic* physically challenged.

crisis *noun* **1 emergency**, disaster, catastrophe, calamity, meltdown, predicament, plight, dire straits. **2 critical point**, turning point, crossroads, head, point of no return, moment of truth; *informal* crunch.

crisp *adjective* **1 crunchy**, crispy, brittle, breakable, dry. **2 invigorating**, brisk, cool, fresh, refreshing, exhilarating.
- OPPOSITES soft.

criterion *noun* **standard**, measure, gauge, test, benchmark, yardstick, touchstone, barometer.

critic *noun* **1 reviewer**, commentator, analyst, judge, pundit, expert. **2 detractor**, attacker, fault-finder.

critical *adjective* **1 disapproving**, disparaging, scathing, fault-finding, judgemental, negative, unfavourable, censorious; *informal* nit-picking, picky. **2 serious**, grave, precarious, touch-and-go, in the balance, desperate, dire, acute, life-and-death. **3 crucial**, vital, essential, all-important, paramount, fundamental, key, pivotal.
- OPPOSITES complimentary.

criticism *noun* **1 fault-finding**, censure, condemnation, disapproval, disparagement; *informal* flak, a bad press, panning; *Brit. informal* stick. **2 evaluation**, assessment, appraisal, appreciation, analysis, critique, judgement, commentary.
- OPPOSITES praise.

criticize *verb* **find fault with**, censure, condemn, attack, disparage, denigrate, run down; *informal* knock, pan, pull to pieces; *Brit. informal* slag off, slate, rubbish; *N. Amer. informal* trash.
- OPPOSITES praise.

crook *noun* see **criminal** (noun).

crooked *adjective* **1 winding**, twisting, zigzag, meandering, tortuous,

serpentine. **2 bent**, twisted, misshapen, deformed, malformed, contorted, warped, bowed, distorted. **3 lopsided**, askew, awry, off-centre, out of true, at an angle, slanting, squint; *Scottish* agley; *Brit. informal* skew-whiff, wonky. **4** *(informal)* **dishonest**, criminal, illegal, unlawful, nefarious, fraudulent, corrupt; *informal* shady; *Brit. informal* bent.
- OPPOSITES straight.

crop *noun* **harvest**, yield, fruits, produce, vintage.
● *verb* **1 cut**, clip, trim, shear, shave, lop off, chop off, hack off, dock. **2 graze on**, browse on, feed on, nibble, eat.
□ **crop up** happen, occur, arise, turn up, pop up, emerge, materialize, surface, appear, come to light.

cross *noun* **1** *we all have our crosses to bear* **burden**, trouble, worry, trial, tribulation, affliction, curse, misfortune, woe; *informal* hassle, headache. **2** *a cross between a yak and a cow* **mixture**, blend, combination, amalgam, hybrid, cross-breed, mongrel.
● *verb* **1 travel across**, traverse, negotiate, navigate, cover. **2 intersect**, meet, join, connect. **3 oppose**, resist, defy, obstruct, contradict, argue with, stand up to. **4 hybridize**, cross-breed, interbreed, cross-fertilize, cross-pollinate.
● *adjective* **angry**, annoyed, irate, vexed, irritated, in a bad mood, put out, exasperated; *informal* hot under the collar, peeved; *Brit. informal* shirty, ratty, not best pleased; *N. Amer. informal* sore, ticked off.
- OPPOSITES pleased.
□ **cross out** delete, strike out, score out, cancel, obliterate.

crossing *noun* **1 junction**, crossroads, intersection, interchange, level crossing. **2 journey**, passage, voyage.

crouch *verb* **squat**, bend (down), hunker down, hunch over, stoop, duck, cower.

crow *verb* **boast**, brag, blow your own trumpet, swagger, swank, gloat.

crowd *noun* **1 horde**, throng, mass, multitude, host, army, herd, swarm,

troop, mob, rabble; *informal* gaggle.
2 *they're a nice crowd* **group**, set, circle,
clique; *informal* gang, bunch, crew, lot.
3 *a capacity crowd* **audience**, spectators, listeners, viewers, house, turnout,
attendance, gate, congregation.
● *verb* **1 cluster**, flock, swarm, mill,
throng, huddle, gather, assemble,
congregate, converge. **2 surge**, throng,
push, jostle, elbow your way, squeeze,
pile, cram.

crowded *adjective* **packed**, full, filled to
capacity, full to bursting, congested,
overflowing, teeming, swarming,
thronged, populous, overpopulated,
busy; *informal* jam-packed, stuffed,
chock-a-block, chock-full, bursting at
the seams, full to the gunwales, wall-
to-wall, mobbed; *Austral./NZ informal*
chocker.
- OPPOSITES deserted.

crown *noun* **1 coronet**, diadem, tiara,
circlet. **2 monarch**, sovereign, king,
queen, emperor, empress, monarchy,
royalty. **3 top**, crest, summit, peak,
pinnacle, tip, brow, apex.
● *verb* *the post at Harvard crowned his
career* **round off**, cap, be the climax
of, be the culmination of, top off, complete, perfect.

crucial *adjective* **1 pivotal**, critical,
key, decisive, life-and-death. **2 all-
important**, of the utmost importance,
of the essence, critical, paramount,
essential, vital.
- OPPOSITES insignificant, unimportant.

crude *adjective* **1 unrefined**, unpurified,
unprocessed, untreated, coarse, raw,
natural. **2 primitive**, simple, basic,
homespun, rudimentary, rough and
ready, makeshift, improvised, unsophisticated. **3 vulgar**, rude, dirty, naughty,
smutty, indecent, obscene, coarse;
informal blue.
- OPPOSITES refined.

cruel *adjective* **1** *a cruel man* **brutal**,
savage, inhuman, barbaric, vicious,
sadistic, monstrous, callous, ruthless,
merciless, heartless, pitiless, implacable, unkind, inhumane. **2** *her death

was a cruel blow* **harsh**, severe, bitter,
heartbreaking, heart-rending, painful,
agonizing, traumatic.
- OPPOSITES compassionate.

cruise *noun* **(boat) trip**, voyage, sail.
● *verb* **1 sail**, voyage. **2 drive slowly**,
drift; *informal* mosey, tootle; *Brit. informal* pootle.

crumb *noun* **fragment**, bit, morsel, particle, speck, scrap, shred, atom, trace,
mite, jot, ounce; *informal* smidgen, tad.

crumble *verb* **1 disintegrate**, fall apart,
fall to pieces, collapse, decompose,
break up, decay, become dilapidated,
deteriorate, degenerate. **2 break up**,
crush, fragment, pulverize.

crumple *verb* **1 crush**, scrunch up,
screw up, squash, squeeze. **2 crease**,
wrinkle, crinkle, rumple. **3 collapse**,
give way, cave in, go to pieces, break
down, crumble.

crunch *verb* **munch**, chomp, champ,
bite into, crush, grind.

crusade *noun* **campaign**, drive, push,
movement, effort, struggle, battle, war,
offensive.
● *verb* **campaign**, fight, battle, do battle, strive, struggle, agitate, lobby.

crush *verb* **1 squash**, squeeze, press,
pulp, mash, mangle, pulverize.
2 crease, crumple, rumple, wrinkle,
scrunch up. **3 suppress**, put down,
quell, stamp out, repress, subdue,
extinguish. **4 demoralize**, deflate,
flatten, squash, devastate, shatter,
mortify, humiliate.
● *noun* **crowd**, throng, horde, swarm,
press, mob.

crust *noun* **covering**, layer, coating,
surface, topping, sheet, film, skin, shell,
scab.

cry *verb* **1 weep**, shed tears, sob, wail,
snivel, whimper; *Scottish* greet; *informal*
blub, blubber; *Brit. informal* grizzle.
2 call, shout, exclaim, sing out, yell,
bawl, bellow, roar; *informal* holler.
- OPPOSITES laugh.
● *noun* **call**, shout, exclamation, yell,
bawl, bellow, roar; *informal* holler.
□ **cry off** *(informal)* back out, pull out,

cancel, withdraw, change your mind; *informal* get cold feet, cop out.

crypt noun **tomb**, vault, burial chamber, sepulchre, catacomb.

cryptic adjective **enigmatic**, mysterious, mystifying, puzzling, obscure, abstruse, arcane, unintelligible.
- OPPOSITES clear.

cuddle verb **1 hug**, embrace, clasp, hold in your arms, caress, pet, fondle; *informal* canoodle, smooch. **2 snuggle**, nestle, curl, nuzzle.

cudgel noun **club**, truncheon, bludgeon, baton, shillelagh, mace; *N. Amer.* blackjack, nightstick; *Brit. informal* cosh.
● verb **club**, bludgeon, beat, batter, bash; *Brit. informal* cosh.

cue noun **signal**, sign, indication, prompt, reminder.

culminate verb **come to a climax**, come to a head, climax, end, finish, conclude, build up to, lead up to.

culmination noun **climax**, peak, pinnacle, high point, height, summit, zenith, apotheosis, apex, apogee.

culpable adjective **to blame**, guilty, at fault, in the wrong, answerable, accountable, responsible.
- OPPOSITES innocent.

culprit noun **guilty party**, offender, wrongdoer, miscreant, criminal, lawbreaker, felon, delinquent; *informal* baddy, crook.

cult noun **1 sect**, group, movement. **2 obsession**, fixation, idolization, devotion, worship, veneration.

cultivate verb **1 farm**, work, till, plough, dig. **2 grow**, raise, rear, tend, plant, sow. **3 woo**, court, curry favour with, ingratiate yourself with; *informal* get in someone's good books. **4 improve**, better, refine, educate, develop, enrich.

cultivated adjective see **cultured**.

cultural adjective **1 social**, lifestyle, sociological, anthropological, racial, ethnic. **2 aesthetic**, artistic, intellectual, educational, civilizing.

culture noun **1** *a lover of culture* **the arts**, high art. **2** *a man of culture* **education**, cultivation, enlightenment, discernment, discrimination, taste, refinement, sophistication. **3 civilization**, society, way of life, lifestyle, customs, traditions, heritage, values. **4 philosophy**, ethic, outlook, approach, rationale.

cultured adjective **cultivated**, artistic, enlightened, civilized, educated, well read, learned, discerning, discriminating, refined, sophisticated; *informal* arty.
- OPPOSITES ignorant.

cunning adjective **1 crafty**, wily, artful, devious, Machiavellian, sly, scheming, canny, dishonest, deceitful. **2 clever**, shrewd, astute, canny, ingenious, imaginative, enterprising, inventive, resourceful, creative, original, inspired, brilliant.
- OPPOSITES honest, stupid.
● noun **1 guile**, craftiness, deviousness, trickery, duplicity. **2 ingenuity**, imagination, inventiveness, enterprise, resourcefulness.

curator noun **custodian**, keeper, conservator, guardian, caretaker.

curb noun **restraint**, restriction, check, brake, control, limit.
● verb **restrain**, hold back, keep in check, control, rein in, contain; *informal* keep a lid on.

cure verb **1 heal**, restore to health, make well/better. **2 rectify**, remedy, put/set right, right, fix, mend, repair, solve, sort out, eliminate, end. **3 preserve**, smoke, salt, dry, pickle.
● noun **remedy**, medicine, medication, antidote, treatment, therapy.

curiosity noun **1 interest**, inquisitiveness, attention, spirit of enquiry; *informal* nosiness. **2 oddity**, curio, novelty, rarity.

curious adjective **1 intrigued**, interested, eager, inquisitive. **2 strange**, odd, peculiar, funny, unusual, queer, bizarre, weird, eccentric, extraordinary, abnormal, anomalous.

- OPPOSITES uninterested, normal.

curl *verb* **spiral**, coil, wreathe, twirl, swirl, wind, curve, twist (and turn), snake, corkscrew, twine, entwine, wrap.
● *noun* **1 ringlet**, corkscrew, kink, lock. **2** *a curl of smoke* **spiral**, coil, twirl, swirl, twist, corkscrew.

curly *adjective* **wavy**, curling, curled, frizzy, kinky, corkscrew.
- OPPOSITES straight.

currency *noun* **1 money**, legal tender, cash, banknotes, notes, coins; *N. Amer.* bills. **2 popularity**, circulation, exposure, acceptance, prevalence.

current *adjective* **1 contemporary**, present-day, modern, topical, live, burning. **2 prevalent**, common, accepted, in circulation, popular, widespread. **3 valid**, usable, up to date. **4 incumbent**, present, in office, in power, reigning.
- OPPOSITES past, former.
● *noun* **1 flow**, stream, draught, jet, tide. **2 course**, progress, progression, flow, tide, movement.

curse *noun* **1 jinx**, malediction; *N. Amer.* hex; *formal* imprecation, anathema. **2 affliction**, burden, misery, ordeal, evil, scourge. **3 swear word**, expletive, oath, profanity, four-letter word, dirty word, obscenity; *informal* cuss word.
● *verb* **1 afflict**, trouble, plague, bedevil. **2 swear**, take the Lord's name in vain, blaspheme; *informal* cuss, turn the air blue, eff and blind.

cursed *adjective* **damned**, doomed, ill-fated, ill-starred, jinxed.

cursory *adjective* **brief**, hasty, hurried, quick, rapid, passing, perfunctory, desultory, casual.
- OPPOSITES thorough.

curt *adjective* **terse**, brusque, abrupt, clipped, blunt, short, sharp, rude, ungracious; *informal* snappy.
- OPPOSITES expansive.

curtail *verb* **reduce**, shorten, cut, cut down, decrease, trim, restrict, limit, curb, rein in/back, cut short, truncate; *informal* slash.
- OPPOSITES increase, extend.

curve *noun* **bend**, turn, loop, arc, arch, bow, curvature.
● *verb* **bend**, turn, loop, wind, meander, snake, arc, arch.

curved *adjective* **bent**, arched, bowed, rounded, crescent.
- OPPOSITES straight.

cushion *noun* *a cushion against inflation* **protection**, buffer, shield, defence, bulwark.
● *verb* **1** *cushioned from the outside world* **protect**, shield, shelter, cocoon. **2** *cushion the blow* **soften**, lessen, diminish, mitigate, alleviate, take the edge off, dull, deaden.

custody *noun* **care**, guardianship, charge, supervision, safe keeping, responsibility, protection.
◻ **in custody** in prison, in jail, imprisoned, incarcerated, under lock and key, on remand; *informal* behind bars, doing time, inside; *Brit. informal* banged up.

custom *noun* **1** *local customs* **tradition**, practice, usage, way, convention, formality, ritual, mores. **2** *it was his custom to sleep in a chair* **habit**, practice, routine, way; *formal* wont.

customary *adjective* **usual**, traditional, normal, conventional, habitual, familiar, accepted, accustomed, routine, established, time-honoured, prevailing.
- OPPOSITES unusual.

customer *noun* **consumer**, buyer, purchaser, patron, client, shopper; *Brit. informal* punter.

cut *verb* **1 gash**, slash, lacerate, slit, wound, scratch, graze, nick. **2 slice**, chop, dice, cube, carve; *N. Amer.* hash. **3 carve**, engrave, incise, etch, score, chisel, whittle. **4 reduce**, cut back/down on, decrease, lessen, mark down, discount, lower; *informal* slash. **5 shorten**, abridge, condense, abbreviate, truncate, edit, censor. **6 delete**, remove, take out, excise.
● *noun* **1 gash**, slash, laceration, incision, wound, scratch, graze, nick. **2 piece**, joint, fillet, section. **3** *(informal)* **share**, portion, quota, percentage;

informal slice (of the cake). **4 reduction**, cutback, decrease, lessening; *N. Amer.* rollback. **5 style**, design, line, fit.

cutback *noun* **reduction**, cut, decrease, economy, saving; *N. Amer.* rollback.
- OPPOSITES increase.

cute *adjective* **endearing**, adorable, lovable, sweet, lovely, appealing, engaging, delightful, dear; *informal* twee; *Brit. informal* dinky.

cutting *noun* **clipping**, article, piece, column, paragraph.
● *adjective* **hurtful**, wounding, barbed, sharp, scathing, caustic, sarcastic,

snide, spiteful, malicious, vicious, cruel; *informal* bitchy.

cycle *noun* **1** *the cycle of birth, death, and rebirth* **circle**, round, pattern, rhythm, loop. **2** *a cycle of three plays* **series**, sequence, set, succession, run.

cynic *noun* **sceptic**, doubter, doubting Thomas, pessimist, prophet of doom.
- OPPOSITES idealist, optimist.

cynical *adjective* **sceptical**, doubtful, distrustful, suspicious, disbelieving, pessimistic, negative, world-weary, disillusioned, disenchanted, jaundiced.
- OPPOSITES idealistic, optimistic.

Dd

dab *verb* **pat**, press, touch, blot, swab, daub, wipe.
● *noun* **drop**, spot, smear, splash, bit.

dabble *verb* **toy with**, dip into, flirt with, tinker with, play with.

daft *adjective (Brit. informal)* **absurd**, preposterous, ridiculous, ludicrous, idiotic, stupid, foolish, asinine, senseless, inane; *informal* crazy, cockeyed, half-baked; *Brit. informal* barmy.
- OPPOSITES sensible.

daily *adjective* **everyday**, day-to-day; *formal* quotidian.
● *adverb* **every day**, once a day, day after day.

dainty *adjective* **1 delicate**, fine, elegant, exquisite, graceful. **2 fastidious**, fussy, particular, finicky; *informal* choosy, picky; *Brit. informal* faddy.
- OPPOSITES unwieldy.

dam *noun* **barrage**, barrier, wall, embankment, barricade, obstruction.
● *verb* **block (up)**, obstruct, bung up, close, hold back.

damage *noun* **1 harm**, destruction, vandalism, injury, ruin, devastation. **2** *she won £4,000 damages* **compensation**, recompense, restitution, redress, reparation(s); *N. Amer. informal* comp.
● *verb* **harm**, injure, deface, spoil, impair, vandalize, ruin, destroy, wreck; *N. Amer. informal* trash.
- OPPOSITES repair.

damaging *adjective* **harmful**, detrimental, injurious, hurtful, destructive, environmentally unfriendly, ruinous, deleterious.
- OPPOSITES beneficial.

damn *verb* **condemn**, censure, criticize, attack, denounce.
- OPPOSITES praise.

damning *adjective* **incriminating**, damaging, condemnatory, conclusive, irrefutable.

damp *adjective* **moist**, humid, muggy, clammy, sweaty, dank, wet, rainy, drizzly, showery, misty, foggy, dewy.
- OPPOSITES dry.
● *noun* **moisture**, liquid, wet, wetness, dampness, humidity.

dampen *verb* **1 moisten**, damp, wet, soak. **2 lessen**, decrease, diminish, reduce, moderate, cool, suppress, stifle, inhibit.
- OPPOSITES dry, heighten.

dance *verb* **1 trip**, sway, twirl, whirl, pirouette, gyrate, jive; *informal* bop, trip the light fantastic; *N. Amer. informal* get down. **2** *the girls danced round me* **caper**, cavort, frolic, skip, prance, gambol, leap, hop, jig, bounce.
● *noun* **ball**; *N. Amer.* prom, hoedown; *informal* disco, rave, hop, bop.

danger *noun* **1 peril**, hazard, risk, jeopardy, endangerment, menace. **2 possibility**, chance, risk, probability, likelihood, threat.
- OPPOSITES safety.

dangerous *adjective* **1 menacing**, threatening, treacherous. **2 hazardous**, perilous, risky, unsafe, unpredictable, precarious, insecure; *informal* dicey, hairy; *Brit. informal* dodgy.
- OPPOSITES harmless, safe.

dangle *verb* **hang**, swing, droop, wave, trail, stream.

dank *adjective* **damp**, musty, chilly, clammy.
- OPPOSITES dry.

dapper *adjective* **smart**, spruce, trim, debonair, neat, well dressed, elegant; *informal* snappy, natty; *N. Amer. informal* spiffy, fly.
- OPPOSITES scruffy.

dare *verb* **1 be brave enough**, have the courage, venture, have the nerve, risk, take the liberty of; *N. Amer.* take a flyer; *informal* stick your neck out.

2 challenge, defy, invite, bid, provoke, goad.
● *noun* **challenge**, invitation, wager, bet.

daring *adjective* **bold**, audacious, intrepid, fearless, brave, heroic, dashing; *informal* gutsy.
- OPPOSITES cowardly, timid.
● *noun* **boldness**, audacity, temerity, fearlessness, bravery, courage, pluck; *informal* nerve, guts; *Brit. informal* bottle; *N. Amer. informal* moxie.
- OPPOSITES cowardice.

dark *adjective* **1** *a dark room* **dingy**, gloomy, shadowy, murky, grey, poorly lit, inky, black. **2** *dark hair* **brunette**, dark brown, sable, jet-black, ebony. **3** *dark skin* **swarthy**, dusky, olive, black, ebony. **4** *dark thoughts* **gloomy**, dismal, negative, downbeat, bleak, grim, fatalistic, black. **5** *a dark look* **angry**, forbidding, threatening, ominous, moody, brooding, sullen, scowling, glowering. **6** *dark deeds* **evil**, wicked, sinful, bad, iniquitous, ungodly, vile, foul, monstrous; *informal* dirty, shady, crooked.
- OPPOSITES bright, light, blonde, pale.
● *noun* **night**, night-time, darkness, nightfall, blackout.

darken *verb* **grow dark**, make dark, blacken, grow dim, cloud over, lour.
- OPPOSITES lighten.

darkness *noun* **1** *lights shone in the darkness* **dark**, blackness, gloom, dimness, murk, shadow, shade. **2** *darkness fell* **night**, night-time, dark. **3** *the forces of darkness* **evil**, wickedness, sin, ungodliness, the Devil.

darling *noun* **1** **dear**, dearest, love, sweetheart, beloved; *informal* honey, angel, pet, sweetie, baby, poppet. **2** **favourite**, idol, hero, heroine; *Brit. informal* blue-eyed boy/girl.
● *adjective* **1** **dear**, dearest, precious, beloved. **2** **adorable**, charming, cute, sweet, enchanting, dear, delightful; *Scottish & N. English* bonny.

dart *verb* **1** **dash**, rush, tear, shoot, sprint, bound, scurry, scamper; *informal*

scoot, whip. **2** **direct**, cast, throw, shoot, send, flash.

dash *verb* **1** **rush**, race, run, sprint, career, charge, shoot, hurtle, hare, fly, speed, zoom; *informal* tear, belt; *Brit. informal* bomb; *N. Amer. informal* barrel. **2** **hurl**, smash, fling, slam, throw, toss, cast; *informal* chuck, sling. **3** **shatter**, destroy, wreck, ruin, demolish, scotch, frustrate, thwart; *informal* put paid to; *Brit. informal* scupper.
- OPPOSITES dawdle.
● *noun* **1** **rush**, race, run, sprint, bolt, dart, leap, charge, bound. **2** **pinch**, touch, sprinkle, taste, spot, drop, dab, splash; *informal* smidgen, tad.

dashing *adjective* **debonair**, stylish, dapper, devil-may-care, raffish, flamboyant, swashbuckling.

data *noun* **facts**, figures, statistics, details, particulars, information.

date *noun* **1** **day**, occasion, time, year, age, period, era, epoch. **2** **appointment**, meeting, engagement, rendezvous, commitment, assignation; *literary* tryst. **3** *(informal)* **partner**, escort, girlfriend, boyfriend.
● *verb* **1** **age**, grow old, become dated, show its age, be of its time. **2** *(informal)* **go out with**, take out, go with, see; *informal* go steady with; *dated* court, woo.
□ **date from** be from, originate in, come from, belong to, go back to.

> **WORD LINKS**
> **chronological** relating to dates

dated *adjective* **old-fashioned**, outdated, outmoded, unfashionable, passé, behind the times, archaic, obsolete, antiquated; *informal* old hat, out of the ark.
- OPPOSITES modern.

daunt *verb* **discourage**, deter, demoralize, put off, dishearten, intimidate, overawe, awe.

daunting *adjective* **intimidating**, forbidding, challenging, formidable, unnerving, disconcerting, discouraging, disheartening, demoralizing, dismaying, scary, frightening, alarming.

dawdle *verb* **linger**, take your time, be slow, waste time, dally, amble, stroll, trail, move at a snail's pace; *informal* dilly-dally.
- OPPOSITES hurry.

dawn *noun* **1 daybreak**, sunrise, first light, daylight, cockcrow, first thing; *N. Amer.* sunup. **2 beginning**, start, birth, inception, genesis, emergence, advent, appearance, arrival, rise, origin.
- OPPOSITES dusk.
● *verb* **1** *Thursday dawned crisp and sunny* **begin**, break, arrive, emerge. **2** *a bright new future has dawned* **begin**, start, commence, be born, appear, arrive, emerge, arise, rise, unfold, develop. **3** *the reality dawned on him* **become evident**, register, cross someone's mind, suggest itself, occur to, come to, strike, hit.

day *noun* **1 daytime**, daylight (hours), waking hours. **2 period**, time, date, age, era, generation.
- OPPOSITES night.

> **WORD LINKS**
> **diurnal** relating to the day

daze *verb* **dumbfound**, stupefy, stun, shock, stagger, bewilder, take aback, nonplus; *informal* flabbergast; *Brit. informal* knock for six.
● *noun* **stupor**, trance, haze, spin, whirl, muddle, jumble.

dazzle *verb* **1 blind**, confuse, disorient. **2 overwhelm**, overcome, impress, move, stir, touch, awe, overawe; *informal* bowl over, blow away, knock out.

dead *adjective* **1 passed on**, passed away, departed, late, lost, perished, fallen, killed, lifeless, extinct; *informal* six feet under, pushing up daisies; *formal* deceased. **2 obsolete**, extinct, defunct, disused, abandoned, superseded, vanished, archaic, ancient. **3 not working**, out of order, inoperative, inactive, broken, defective; *informal* kaput, conked out, on the blink, bust; *Brit. informal* knackered. **4 boring**,

uninteresting, unexciting, uninspiring, dull, flat, quiet, sleepy, slow, lifeless; *informal* one-horse; *N. Amer. informal* dullsville.
- OPPOSITES alive, living, lively.
● *adverb* **1 completely**, absolutely, totally, utterly, deadly, perfectly, entirely, quite, thoroughly. **2 directly**, exactly, precisely, immediately, right, straight, due.

deaden *verb* **1 numb**, dull, blunt, alleviate, mitigate, diminish, reduce, lessen, ease, soothe, relieve, assuage. **2 muffle**, mute, smother, stifle, damp (down), soften, cushion.
- OPPOSITES intensify, amplify.

deadline *noun* **time limit**, finishing date, target date, cut-off point.

deadlock *noun* **stalemate**, impasse, checkmate, stand-off, standstill, gridlock.

deadly *adjective* **1 fatal**, lethal, mortal, life-threatening, noxious, toxic, poisonous. **2** *deadly enemies* **mortal**, irreconcilable, implacable, bitter, sworn. **3** *his aim is deadly* **unerring**, unfailing, perfect, true, accurate; *Brit. informal* spot on.
- OPPOSITES harmless.

deafening *adjective* **ear-splitting**, thunderous, crashing, uproarious, almighty, booming.
- OPPOSITES low, soft.

deal *noun* **agreement**, understanding, pact, bargain, covenant, contract, treaty, arrangement, compromise, settlement, terms.
● *verb* **1 trade in**, buy and sell, purvey, supply, market, traffic in. **2 distribute**, give out, share out, divide out, hand out, pass out, pass round, dispense, allocate.
□ **deal with 1** cope with, handle, manage, treat, take care of, take charge of, take in hand, sort out, tackle, take on, control. **2** concern, be about, have to do with, discuss, consider, cover, tackle, explore, investigate, examine.

dealer *noun* **trader**, merchant, salesman/woman, seller, vendor, purveyor, pedlar, distributor, supplier, shop-keeper, retailer, wholesaler, tradesman, tradesperson; *Brit.* stockist.

dear *adjective* **1** *a dear friend* **beloved**, precious, close, intimate, bosom. **2** *her pictures were too dear to part with* **precious**, treasured, valued, prized, cherished, special. **3 endearing**, adorable, lovable, appealing, engaging, charming, captivating, lovely, delightful, sweet, darling. **4 expensive**, costly, high-priced, overpriced, exorbitant, extortionate; *Brit.* over the odds; *informal* pricey.
- OPPOSITES disagreeable, cheap.
● *noun* **darling**, dearest, love, beloved, sweetheart, precious; *informal* sweetie, sugar, honey, baby, pet, poppet.

dearly *adverb* **very much**, a great deal, greatly, profoundly, deeply.

dearth *noun* **lack**, scarcity, shortage, shortfall, deficiency, insufficiency, inadequacy, absence.
- OPPOSITES surfeit.

death *noun* **1 dying**, demise, end, passing, loss of life; *formal* decease. **2 end**, finish, termination, extinction, extinguishing, collapse, destruction.
- OPPOSITES life, birth.

> **WORD LINKS**
> **fatal**, **lethal**, **mortal** causing death

deathly *adjective* **deathlike**, ghostly, ghastly, ashen, white, pale, pallid.

debacle *noun* **fiasco**, failure, catastrophe, disaster; *informal* fail.

debase *verb* **degrade**, devalue, demean, cheapen, prostitute, discredit, drag down, tarnish, blacken, disgrace, dishonour, shame.
- OPPOSITES enhance.

debatable *adjective* **arguable**, questionable, open to question, disputable, controversial, contentious, doubtful, dubious, uncertain, borderline, moot.

debate *noun* **discussion**, argument, dispute, talks.
● *verb* **1 discuss**, talk over/through, talk about, thrash out, argue, dispute. **2 consider**, think over/about, chew

over, mull over, weigh up, ponder, deliberate.

debauched *adjective* **dissolute**, dissipated, degenerate, decadent, profligate, immoral, lecherous, lewd, licentious.
- OPPOSITES wholesome.

debris *noun* **ruins**, remains, rubble, wreckage, detritus, refuse, rubbish, waste, scrap, flotsam and jetsam.

debt *noun* **1 bill**, account, dues, arrears, charges. **2 indebtedness**, obligation, gratitude, appreciation.

decay *verb* **1 decompose**, rot, putrefy, go bad, go off, spoil, fester, perish. **2 deteriorate**, degenerate, decline, go downhill, slump, slide, go to rack and ruin, go to seed; *informal* go to the dogs.
● *noun* **1 decomposition**, putrefaction, rot. **2 deterioration**, degeneration, decline, weakening, crumbling, disintegration, collapse.

deceit *noun* **deception**, deceitfulness, duplicity, double-dealing, lies, fraud, cheating, trickery.
- OPPOSITES honesty.

deceitful *adjective* **dishonest**, untruthful, insincere, false, disingenuous, untrustworthy, unscrupulous, unprincipled, two-faced, duplicitous, fraudulent, double-dealing; *informal* sneaky, tricky, crooked; *Brit. informal* bent.
- OPPOSITES honest.

deceive *verb* **trick**, cheat, defraud, swindle, hoodwink, hoax, dupe, take in, mislead, delude, fool; *informal* con, pull the wool over someone's eyes; *N. Amer. informal* sucker, goldbrick.

decency *noun* **1 propriety**, decorum, good taste, respectability, morality, virtue, modesty. **2 courtesy**, politeness, good manners, civility, consideration, thoughtfulness.

decent *adjective* **1** *a decent burial* **proper**, correct, right, appropriate, suitable, respectable, decorous, modest, seemly, accepted; *informal* pukka. **2** *a job with decent pay* **satisfactory**, reasonable, fair, acceptable, adequate,

sufficient, not bad, all right, tolerable, passable, suitable; *informal* OK. **3** *(Brit. informal)* **kind**, generous, thoughtful, considerate, obliging, courteous, polite, well mannered, neighbourly, hospitable, pleasant, agreeable, amiable.
- OPPOSITES improper, unsatisfactory.

deception *noun* **1 deceit**, duplicity, double-dealing, fraud, cheating, trickery, guile, bluff, lying, pretence, treachery. **2 trick**, sham, fraud, pretence, hoax, ruse, scheme, dodge, cheat, swindle; *informal* con, set-up, scam.

deceptive *adjective* **misleading**, confusing, illusory, distorted, ambiguous.

decide *verb* **1 resolve**, determine, make up your mind, choose, opt, plan, aim, intend, have in mind, set your sights on. **2 settle**, resolve, determine, work out, answer; *informal* sort out. **3 adjudicate**, arbitrate, judge, pronounce on, give a verdict on, rule on.

decidedly *adverb* **distinctly**, clearly, markedly, obviously, noticeably, unmistakably, patently, manifestly, definitely, positively.

decision *noun* **1 resolution**, conclusion, settlement, choice, option, selection. **2 verdict**, finding, ruling, judgement, adjudication, sentence.

decisive *adjective* **1 resolute**, firm, strong-minded, strong-willed, determined, purposeful. **2 deciding**, conclusive, determining, key, pivotal, critical, crucial.

declaration *noun* **1 announcement**, statement, communication, pronouncement, proclamation; *N. Amer.* advisory. **2 assertion**, profession, affirmation, acknowledgement, revelation, disclosure, confirmation, testimony, avowal, protestation.

declare *verb* **1 announce**, proclaim, state, reveal, air, voice, articulate, express, vent, set forth, publicize, broadcast. **2 assert**, profess, affirm, maintain, state, contend, claim, argue, insist, avow.

decline *verb* **1 turn down**, reject, brush aside, refuse, rebuff, spurn, repulse, dismiss, pass up, say no; *informal* give something a miss. **2 decrease**, reduce, lessen, diminish, dwindle, contract, shrink, fall off, tail off, drop, fall, go down. **3 deteriorate**, degenerate, decay, crumble, collapse, slump, slip, slide, go downhill, worsen; *informal* go to the dogs.
- OPPOSITES accept, increase, improve.
● *noun* **1 reduction**, decrease, downturn, downswing, diminution, ebb, drop, slump, plunge. **2 deterioration**, degeneration, degradation, shrinkage, erosion.
- OPPOSITES rise, improvement.

decompose *verb* **decay**, rot, putrefy, go bad, go off, spoil, perish, deteriorate, degrade, break down.

decor *noun* **decoration**, furnishing, colour scheme.

decorate *verb* **1 ornament**, adorn, trim, embellish, garnish, furnish, enhance. **2 paint**, wallpaper, paper, refurbish, renovate, redecorate; *informal* do up, give something a facelift, give something a makeover. **3 give a medal to**, honour, cite, reward.

decoration *noun* **1 ornamentation**, adornment, trimming, embellishment, beautification. **2 ornament**, bauble, trinket, knick-knack. **3 medal**, award, prize; *Brit. informal* gong.

decorative *adjective* **ornamental**, fancy, ornate, attractive, pretty, showy.
- OPPOSITES functional.

decorum *noun* **1 propriety**, seemliness, decency, good taste, correctness, politeness, good manners. **2 etiquette**, protocol, good form, custom, convention.
- OPPOSITES impropriety.

decrease *verb* **lessen**, reduce, drop, diminish, decline, dwindle, fall off, plummet, plunge.
- OPPOSITES increase.
● *noun* **reduction**, drop, decline, downturn, cut, cutback, diminution.
- OPPOSITES increase.

d

decree noun **1** *a presidential decree* **order**, command, commandment, edict, proclamation, law, statute, act. **2** *a court decree* **judgement**, verdict, adjudication, finding, ruling, decision.
● verb **order**, direct, command, rule, dictate, pronounce, proclaim, ordain.

decrepit adjective **dilapidated**, rickety, run down, tumbledown, ramshackle, derelict, ruined, in (a state of) disrepair, gone to rack and ruin, on its last legs, decayed, crumbling.

dedicate verb **1 commit**, devote, pledge, give (up), sacrifice, set aside. **2 inscribe**, address, offer. **3 devote**, assign, bless, consecrate, sanctify.

dedicated adjective **1 committed**, devoted, enthusiastic, keen, staunch, firm, steadfast, loyal, faithful. **2 specialized**, custom-built, customized, purpose-built, exclusive.
- OPPOSITES half-hearted.

dedication noun **1 commitment**, devotion, loyalty, allegiance, application, resolve, conscientiousness, perseverance, persistence. **2 inscription**, message.
- OPPOSITES apathy.

deduce verb **conclude**, reason, work out, infer, understand, assume, presume, surmise, reckon; *informal* figure out, put two and two together; *Brit. informal* suss out.

deduct verb **subtract**, take away, take off, debit, dock, stop; *informal* knock off.
- OPPOSITES add.

deduction noun **1 subtraction**, removal, debit. **2 stoppage**, tax, expenses, rebate, discount, concession. **3 conclusion**, inference, supposition, hypothesis, assumption, presumption, suspicion.

deed noun **1 act**, action, feat, exploit, achievement, accomplishment, endeavour. **2 document**, contract, instrument.

deep adjective **1 cavernous**, yawning, gaping, huge, extensive, bottomless, fathomless. **2 intense**, heartfelt, wholehearted, deep-seated, sincere, genuine,

earnest, enthusiastic, great. **3 profound**, serious, intelligent, intellectual, learned, wise, scholarly. **4** *he was deep in concentration* **rapt**, absorbed, engrossed, preoccupied, intent, immersed, lost, gripped. **5 obscure**, complex, mysterious, unfathomable, opaque, abstruse, esoteric, enigmatic. **6 low-pitched**, low, bass, rich, resonant, booming, sonorous. **7 dark**, intense, rich, strong, vivid.
- OPPOSITES shallow, superficial, high.

deeply adverb **profoundly**, greatly, enormously, extremely, very, strongly, intensely, keenly, acutely, thoroughly, completely, entirely, seriously.

deface verb **vandalize**, disfigure, spoil, ruin, damage; *N. Amer. informal* trash.

defeat verb **1 beat**, conquer, win against, triumph over, get the better of, vanquish, rout, trounce, overcome, overpower; *informal* lick, thrash; *US informal* own. **2 thwart**, frustrate, foil, ruin, scotch, derail; *informal* put paid to, stymie; *Brit. informal* scupper.
● noun **loss**, conquest, rout; *informal* thrashing, hiding, drubbing, licking.
- OPPOSITES victory.

defect noun **fault**, flaw, imperfection, deficiency, deformity, blemish, mistake, error.

defective adjective **faulty**, flawed, imperfect, unsound, inoperative, malfunctioning, out of order, broken; *informal* on the blink; *Brit. informal* duff.
- OPPOSITES perfect.

defence noun **1 protection**, guarding, security, fortification, resistance. **2 armaments**, weapons, weaponry, arms, the military, the armed forces. **3 justification**, vindication, explanation, mitigation, excuse, alibi, denial, rebuttal, plea, pleading, argument, case.
- OPPOSITES attack, prosecution.

defenceless adjective **vulnerable**, helpless, powerless, weak, undefended, unprotected, unguarded, unarmed, exposed, open to attack.

defend *verb* **1 protect**, guard, safeguard, secure, shield, fortify, watch over. **2 justify**, vindicate, explain, argue for, support, back, stand by, make a case for, stick up for.
- OPPOSITES attack, criticize.

defender *noun* **1 protector**, guardian, guard, custodian. **2 supporter**, upholder, backer, champion, advocate, apologist.

defensive *adjective* **1 defending**, protective. **2 self-justifying**, oversensitive, prickly, paranoid, neurotic; *informal* twitchy.

defer *verb* **postpone**, put off, delay, hold over/off, put back, shelve, suspend; *N. Amer.* table; *informal* put on ice, put on the back burner.

defiance *noun* **resistance**, opposition, non-compliance, disobedience, insubordination, rebellion, disregard, contempt, insolence.
- OPPOSITES obedience.

defiant *adjective* **disobedient**, resistant, obstinate, uncooperative, non-compliant, recalcitrant, insubordinate; *Brit. informal* stroppy, bolshie.
- OPPOSITES cooperative.

deficiency *noun* **1 lack**, insufficiency, shortage, inadequacy, deficit, shortfall, scarcity, dearth. **2 defect**, fault, flaw, failing, weakness, shortcoming, limitation.
- OPPOSITES surplus, strength.

deficit *noun* **shortfall**, deficiency, shortage, debt, arrears, loss.
- OPPOSITES surplus.

define *verb* **1 explain**, give the meaning of, spell out, expound, interpret, describe. **2 determine**, establish, fix, specify, designate, decide, stipulate, set out.

definite *adjective* **specific**, explicit, express, precise, exact, clear, clear-cut, unambiguous, certain, sure, positive, conclusive, decisive, firm, unequivocal, unmistakable, proven, decided, marked, distinct, identifiable.
- OPPOSITES vague, ambiguous.

definitely *adverb* **certainly**, surely, for sure, unquestionably, without doubt, undoubtedly, undeniably, clearly, positively, absolutely, unmistakably.

definition *noun* **1 meaning**, sense, interpretation, explanation, description. **2 clarity**, sharpness, focus, crispness, resolution.

definitive *adjective* **1 conclusive**, final, unqualified, absolute, categorical, positive, definite. **2 authoritative**, best, ultimate, classic, standard, recognized, accepted, exhaustive.

deflect *verb* **divert**, turn away, draw away, distract, fend off, parry, stave off.

deformed *adjective* **misshapen**, distorted, malformed, contorted, out of shape, twisted, crooked, warped, buckled, gnarled, disfigured, mutilated, mangled.

defraud *verb* **swindle**, cheat, rob, deceive, dupe, hoodwink, double-cross, trick; *informal* con, do, sting, diddle, rip off, shaft, pull a fast one on, put one over on, sell a pup to; *N. Amer. informal* sucker, snooker, stiff; *Austral. informal* pull a swifty on.

deft *adjective* **skilful**, adept, adroit, dexterous, agile, nimble, handy, able, capable, skilled, proficient, accomplished, expert, polished, slick, professional.
- OPPOSITES clumsy.

defy *verb* **disobey**, flout, disregard, ignore, break, violate, contravene, breach, challenge, fly in the face of, confront.
- OPPOSITES obey.

degenerate *adjective* **corrupt**, perverted, decadent, dissolute, dissipated, debauched, immoral, unprincipled, disreputable.
● *verb* **deteriorate**, decline, worsen, slip, slide, go downhill; *informal* go to the dogs.
- OPPOSITES improve.

degrade *verb* **demean**, debase, humiliate, humble, belittle, mortify, dehumanize, brutalize.
- OPPOSITES dignify.

degree noun **level**, standard, grade, stage, mark, amount, extent, measure, intensity, strength, proportion.

deign verb **condescend**, stoop, lower yourself, demean yourself, humble yourself, consent.

dejected adjective **downcast**, downhearted, despondent, disconsolate, dispirited, crestfallen, disheartened, depressed; informal down in the mouth, down in the dumps.
- OPPOSITES cheerful.

delay verb **1 detain**, hold up, make late, slow up/down, bog down, hinder, hamper, impede, obstruct. **2 linger**, drag your feet, hold back, dawdle, waste time, stall, hesitate, dither, shilly-shally; informal dilly-dally. **3 postpone**, put off, defer, hold over, adjourn, reschedule.
- OPPOSITES hurry, advance.
  ● noun **1 hold-up**, wait, interruption, stoppage. **2** the delay of his trial **postponement**, deferral, adjournment.

delegate noun **representative**, envoy, emissary, commissioner, agent, deputy.
  ● verb **assign**, entrust, pass on, hand on/over, turn over, devolve.

delegation noun **deputation**, mission, commission, contingent, legation.

delete verb **remove**, cut (out), take out, edit out, excise, cancel, cross out, strike out, obliterate, rub out, erase.
- OPPOSITES add.

deliberate adjective **1 intentional**, calculated, conscious, intended, planned, wilful, premeditated. **2 careful**, cautious, measured, regular, even, steady. **3 methodical**, systematic, careful, painstaking, meticulous, thorough.
- OPPOSITES accidental, hasty.
  ● verb **think**, think about/over, ponder, consider, contemplate, reflect on, muse on, meditate on, ruminate on, mull over; N. Amer. think on.

deliberately adverb **1 intentionally**, on purpose, purposely, by design, knowingly, wittingly, consciously, wilfully. **2 carefully**, cautiously, slowly, steadily, evenly.

deliberation noun **thought**, consideration, reflection, contemplation, discussion.

delicacy noun **1 fineness**, delicateness, fragility, thinness, lightness, flimsiness. **2 difficulty**, trickiness, sensitivity, ticklishness, awkwardness. **3 care**, sensitivity, tact, discretion, diplomacy, subtlety. **4 treat**, luxury, titbit, speciality.

delicate adjective **1** delicate embroidery **fine**, intricate, dainty, exquisite, graceful. **2** a delicate shade of blue **subtle**, soft, pale, muted, pastel, light. **3** delicate china cups **fragile**, dainty. **4** his wife is very delicate **sickly**, unhealthy, frail, feeble, weak. **5** a delicate issue **difficult**, tricky, sensitive, ticklish, awkward, touchy, embarrassing; informal sticky, dicey. **6** the matter needs delicate handling **careful**, sensitive, tactful, diplomatic, discreet, kid-glove, subtle. **7** a delicate mechanism **sensitive**, light, precision.
- OPPOSITES coarse, strong, robust.

delicious adjective **delectable**, mouthwatering, appetizing, tasty, flavoursome; informal scrumptious, moreish; N. Amer. informal finger-licking.
- OPPOSITES unpalatable.

delight verb **charm**, enchant, captivate, entrance, thrill, entertain, amuse, divert; informal send, tickle pink, bowl over.
- OPPOSITES dismay, disgust.
  ● noun **pleasure**, happiness, joy, glee, excitement, amusement, bliss, ecstasy.
- OPPOSITES displeasure.
  □ **delight in** love, relish, savour, adore, lap up, take pleasure in, enjoy, revel in.

delighted adjective **pleased**, glad, happy, thrilled, overjoyed, ecstatic, elated, on cloud nine, walking on air, in seventh heaven, jumping for joy, gleeful, cock-a-hoop; informal over the moon, tickled pink, as pleased as Punch, on top of the world, as happy as Larry; Brit. informal chuffed; N. English informal made up; Austral. informal wrapped.

delightful *adjective* **1** *a delightful evening* **lovely**, enjoyable, amusing, entertaining, pleasant, pleasurable. **2** *a delightful girl* **charming**, enchanting, captivating, bewitching, appealing, sweet, endearing, cute, adorable, delectable.

deliver *verb* **1 bring**, take, convey, carry, transport, send, distribute, dispatch, ship. **2 state**, utter, give, read, broadcast, pronounce, announce, declare, proclaim, hand down, return. **3 administer**, deal, inflict, give; *informal* land.

delivery *noun* **1 conveyance**, carriage, transportation, transport, distribution, dispatch, shipping. **2 consignment**, load, shipment. **3 speech**, pronunciation, enunciation, articulation, elocution.

delusion *noun* **misapprehension**, misconception, false impression, misunderstanding, mistake, error, misconstruction, illusion, fantasy, fancy.

delve *verb* **1 rummage**, search, hunt, scrabble about, root about, ferret, fish about, dig, rifle through. **2 investigate**, enquire, probe, explore, research, look into, go into.

demand *noun* **1** *I gave in to her demands* **request**, call, command, order, dictate. **2** *the demands of a young family* **requirement**, need, claim, commitment, imposition. **3 market**, call, appetite, desire.
● *verb* **1 call for**, ask for, request, push for, press for, seek, claim, insist on. **2 order**, command, enjoin, require. **3 ask**, enquire, question, query. **4 require**, need, necessitate, call for, involve, entail. **5 insist on**, stipulate, expect, look for.

demanding *adjective* **1 difficult**, challenging, taxing, exacting, tough, hard, onerous, formidable, arduous, gruelling, back-breaking, punishing. **2 nagging**, trying, tiresome, hard to please, high-maintenance.
- OPPOSITES easy.

demeaning *adjective* **degrading**, humiliating, shameful, undignified, menial; *informal* infra dig.

demeanour *noun* **manner**, air, attitude, appearance, look, mien, bearing, carriage, behaviour, conduct.

demise *noun* **1 death**, dying, passing, end. **2 end**, break-up, disintegration, fall, downfall, collapse, overthrow.
- OPPOSITES birth.

democratic *adjective* **elected**, representative, parliamentary, popular, egalitarian, self-governing.

demolish *verb* **1 knock down**, pull down, tear down, destroy, flatten, raze to the ground, dismantle, level, bulldoze, blow up. **2 destroy**, ruin, wreck, overturn, explode, drive a coach and horses through; *informal* shoot full of holes.
- OPPOSITES build.

demonstrate *verb* **1 indicate**, prove, show, establish, confirm, verify. **2 reveal**, manifest, indicate, illustrate, signify, signal, denote, show, display, exhibit. **3 protest**, march, parade, picket, strike.

demonstration *noun* **1 exhibition**, presentation, display. **2 manifestation**, indication, sign, mark, proof, testimony. **3 protest**, march, rally, mass lobby, sit-in; *informal* demo.

demonstrative *adjective* **expressive**, open, forthcoming, communicative, unreserved, emotional, effusive, affectionate, loving, warm, friendly, approachable; *informal* touchy-feely.
- OPPOSITES reserved.

demoralized *adjective* **dispirited**, disheartened, downhearted, dejected, downcast, low, depressed, dismayed, daunted, discouraged.

demure *adjective* **modest**, reserved, shy, unassuming, decorous, decent, proper.
- OPPOSITES brazen.

den *noun* **1 lair**, burrow, hole, shelter, hiding place, hideout. **2 study**, studio, workshop, retreat, sanctuary, hideaway; *informal* hidey-hole.

d

denial noun **1 contradiction**, rebuttal, repudiation, refutation, disclaimer. **2 refusal**, withholding.

denomination noun **1 religious group**, sect, cult, movement, persuasion, order, creed, school, church. **2 value**, unit, size.

denote verb **indicate**, be a mark of, signify, signal, designate, symbolize, represent.

denounce verb **1 condemn**, attack, censure, decry, stigmatize, deprecate, disparage, revile, damn. **2 expose**, betray, inform on, incriminate, implicate, cite, accuse.

dense adjective **1** *a dense forest* **thick**, crowded, compact, solid, tight, overgrown, impenetrable, impassable. **2** *dense smoke* **thick**, heavy, opaque, murky. **3** (informal) **stupid**, brainless, foolish, slow, simple-minded, empty-headed, obtuse; informal thick, dim, dopey.
- OPPOSITES sparse, thin.

dent noun **knock**, indentation, dint, depression, hollow, crater, pit; N. Amer. informal ding.
● verb **knock**, dint, mark; N. Amer. informal ding.

deny verb **1 contradict**, rebut, repudiate, refute, challenge, contest. **2 refuse**, turn down, reject, rebuff, decline, veto, dismiss; informal give the thumbs down to.
- OPPOSITES confirm, allow, accept.

depart verb **1 leave**, go away, withdraw, absent yourself, quit, exit, decamp, retreat, retire, make off; informal make tracks, take off, split; Brit. informal sling your hook. **2 deviate**, diverge, digress, stray, veer, differ, vary.
- OPPOSITES arrive.

department noun **division**, section, sector, unit, branch, wing, office, bureau, agency, ministry.

departure noun **1 leaving**, going, leave-taking, withdrawal, exit. **2 deviation**, divergence, digression, shift, variation. **3 change**, innovation, novelty.

depend verb **1** *her career depends on this* **be dependent on**, hinge on, hang on, rest on, rely on. **2** *my family depends on me* **rely on**, lean on, count on, bank on, trust (in), pin your hopes on.

dependable adjective **reliable**, trustworthy, trusty, faithful, loyal, stable, sensible, responsible.

dependent adjective **1 addicted**, reliant; informal hooked. **2 reliant**, needy, helpless, infirm, invalid, incapable, debilitated, disabled.
- OPPOSITES independent.
□ **dependent on 1 conditional on**, contingent on, based on, subject to, determined by, influenced by. **2 reliant on**, relying on, counting on, sustained by.

depict verb **1 portray**, show, represent, picture, illustrate, reproduce, render. **2 describe**, detail, relate, present, set forth, set out, outline.

deplete verb **reduce**, decrease, diminish, exhaust, use up, consume, expend, drain, empty.
- OPPOSITES augment.

deplore verb **1 abhor**, find unacceptable, frown on, disapprove of, take a dim view of, take exception to, condemn, denounce. **2 regret**, lament, mourn, bemoan, bewail, complain about, grieve over, sigh over.
- OPPOSITES applaud.

deploy verb **1 position**, station, post, place, install, locate, base. **2 use**, utilize, employ, take advantage of, exploit, call on.

deport verb **expel**, banish, extradite, repatriate.
- OPPOSITES admit.

depose verb **overthrow**, unseat, dethrone, topple, remove, supplant, displace, oust.

deposit noun **1 layer**, covering, coating, blanket, accumulation, sediment. **2 seam**, vein, lode, layer, stratum, bed. **3 down payment**, advance payment, prepayment, instalment, retainer, security.

● *verb* **1 put down**, place, set down, unload, rest, drop; *informal* dump, park, plonk; *N. Amer. informal* plunk. **2 leave (behind)**, precipitate, dump, wash up, cast up. **3 lodge**, bank, house, store, stow.

depot *noun* **1 terminal**, terminus, station, garage, headquarters, base. **2 storehouse**, warehouse, store, repository, depository, cache, arsenal, armoury, dump.

depress *verb* **1 sadden**, dispirit, cast down, get down, dishearten, demoralize, crush, weigh down on. **2 slow down**, weaken, impair, inhibit, restrict. **3 reduce**, lower, cut, cheapen, discount, deflate, diminish, depreciate, devalue. **4 press**, push, hold down.
- OPPOSITES cheer, boost, raise.

depressed *adjective* **1 sad**, unhappy, miserable, gloomy, dejected, downhearted, downcast, down, despondent, dispirited, low, morose, dismal, desolate; *informal* blue, down in the dumps, down in the mouth. **2 weak**, inactive, flat, slow, slack, sluggish, stagnant. **3 poverty-stricken**, poor, disadvantaged, deprived, needy, distressed, run down.
- OPPOSITES cheerful.

depressing *adjective* **dismal**, sad, unhappy, sombre, gloomy, grave, bleak, black, melancholy, dreary, grim, cheerless.

depression *noun* **1 unhappiness**, sadness, melancholy, melancholia, misery, sorrow, gloom, despondency, low spirits. **2 recession**, slump, decline, downturn. **3 hollow**, indentation, dent, cavity, dip, pit, crater, basin, bowl.

deprivation *noun* **1 poverty**, impoverishment, privation, hardship, destitution, need, want. **2 dispossession**, withholding, withdrawal, removal, seizure.
- OPPOSITES prosperity.

deprive *verb* **dispossess**, strip, divest, relieve, rob, cheat out of.

deprived *adjective* **disadvantaged**, underprivileged, poverty-stricken, impoverished, poor, destitute, needy.
- OPPOSITES privileged.

depth *noun* **1 deepness**, drop, height. **2 extent**, range, scope, breadth, width. **3 profundity**, wisdom, understanding, intelligence, discernment, penetration, insight, awareness. **4 intensity**, richness, vividness, strength, brilliance.

deputize *verb* **stand in**, sit in, fill in, cover, substitute, replace, take someone's place, take over, hold the fort, step into the breach.

deputy *noun* **second in command**, number two, assistant, aide, lieutenant, proxy, stand-in, replacement, substitute, representative, reserve.

derelict *adjective* **dilapidated**, ramshackle, run down, tumbledown, in ruins, falling down, disused, abandoned, deserted.
● *noun* **tramp**, vagrant, down and out, homeless person, drifter, beggar; *informal* dosser, bag lady.

derision *noun* **mockery**, ridicule, jeers, sneers, taunts, disdain, disparagement, denigration, insults.

derogatory *adjective* **disparaging**, disrespectful, demeaning, critical, pejorative, negative, unfavourable, uncomplimentary, unflattering, insulting, defamatory, slanderous, libellous.
- OPPOSITES complimentary.

descend *verb* **1 go down**, come down, drop, fall, sink, dive, plummet, plunge, nosedive. **2 slope**, dip, slant, go down, fall away. **3 alight**, disembark, get down, get off, dismount.
- OPPOSITES climb, board.
□ **descend on** flock to, besiege, surround, take over, invade, swoop on, occupy.

descent *noun* **1 dive**, drop, fall, plunge, nosedive. **2 slope**, incline, dip, drop, gradient. **3 decline**, slide, fall, degeneration, deterioration. **4 ancestry**, parentage, ancestors, family, extraction, origin, derivation, birth, lineage, stock, blood, roots, origins.

describe *verb* **1 report**, recount, relate, narrate, tell of, set out, detail, give a rundown of. **2 portray**, depict, paint, define, characterize, call, label, class, brand. **3 mark out**, delineate, outline, trace, draw.

description noun **1 account**, report, narrative, story, portrayal, portrait, sketch, details. **2 designation**, labelling, naming, dubbing, characterization, definition, classification, branding. **3 sort**, variety, kind, type.

desert[1] verb **1 abandon**, leave, jilt, leave high and dry, leave in the lurch, leave behind, strand, maroon; *informal* walk/run out on, dump, ditch; *literary* forsake. **2 abscond**, defect, run away, decamp, flee, turn tail, take French leave; *Military* go AWOL.

desert[2] noun **wasteland**, wastes, wilderness, dust bowl.

deserted adjective **1 abandoned**, jilted, cast aside, neglected, stranded, marooned, forlorn; *literary* forsaken. **2 empty**, uninhabited, unoccupied, abandoned, evacuated, desolate, lonely, godforsaken.
- OPPOSITES populous.

deserve verb **merit**, earn, warrant, rate, justify, be worthy of, be entitled to.

deserved adjective **well earned**, merited, warranted, justified, rightful, due, fitting, just, proper.

deserving adjective **worthy**, commendable, praiseworthy, admirable, estimable, creditable.

design noun **1 plan**, blueprint, drawing, sketch, outline, map, plot, diagram, draft. **2 pattern**, motif, device, style, theme, layout.
● verb **1 invent**, create, think up, come up with, devise, formulate, conceive; *informal* dream up. **2 intend**, aim, mean.

designate verb **1 appoint**, nominate, delegate, select, choose, pick, elect, name, identify, assign. **2 classify**, class, label, tag, name, call, term, dub.

desirable adjective **1 attractive**, sought-after, in demand, popular, enviable; *informal* to die for, must-have.

2 advantageous, advisable, wise, sensible, recommended, beneficial, preferable. **3 (sexually) attractive**, beautiful, pretty, appealing, seductive, alluring, irresistible; *informal* sexy.
- OPPOSITES unattractive.

desire noun **1 wish**, want, aspiration, yearning, longing, craving, hankering, hunger; *informal* yen, itch. **2 lust**, passion, sensuality, sexuality, libido, lasciviousness.
● verb **want**, wish for, long for, yearn for, crave, hanker after, be desperate for, be bent on, covet, aspire to.

desolate adjective **1 bleak**, stark, bare, dismal, grim, wild, inhospitable, deserted, uninhabited, empty, abandoned, godforsaken, isolated, remote. **2 miserable**, unhappy, despondent, depressed, disconsolate, devastated, despairing, inconsolable, wretched, broken-hearted.

despair noun **desperation**, anguish, unhappiness, despondency, depression, misery, wretchedness, hopelessness.
- OPPOSITES hope, joy.
● verb **lose hope**, give up, lose heart, be discouraged, be despondent, be demoralized.

despatch verb & noun see **dispatch**.

desperate adjective **1 despairing**, hopeless, anguished, distressed, wretched, desolate, forlorn, distraught, at your wits' end, at the end of your tether. **2 last-ditch**, last-gasp, eleventh-hour, do-or-die, final, frantic, frenzied, wild. **3 grave**, serious, critical, acute, urgent, pressing, drastic, extreme.

desperation noun **hopelessness**, despair, distress, anguish, agony, torment, misery.

despise verb **detest**, hate, loathe, abhor, deplore, scorn, disdain, deride, sneer at, revile, spurn, shun.
- OPPOSITES adore, respect.

despite preposition **in spite of**, notwithstanding, regardless of, in the face of, in the teeth of, undeterred by, for all, even with.

destined *adjective* **1 fated**, ordained, predestined, doomed, meant, intended. **2** *computers destined for Pakistan* **heading**, bound, en route, scheduled, headed.

destiny *noun* **1 future**, fate, fortune, doom, lot, nemesis. **2 providence**, fate, God, the stars, luck, fortune, chance, karma, kismet.

destitute *adjective* **penniless**, poor, impoverished, poverty-stricken, impecunious, indigent, down and out; *Brit.* on the breadline; *informal* (flat) broke, on your uppers; *Brit. informal* stony broke, skint; *formal* penurious.
- OPPOSITES rich.

destroy *verb* **1 demolish**, knock down, level, raze to the ground, fell, blow up. **2 spoil**, ruin, wreck, blight, devastate, wreak havoc on. **3 kill**, put down, put to sleep, slaughter, cull. **4 annihilate**, wipe out, obliterate, eliminate, eradicate, liquidate, exterminate; *informal* take out; *N. Amer. informal* waste.
- OPPOSITES build.

destruction *noun* **1 devastation**, carnage, ruin, chaos, wreckage. **2** *the destruction of the countryside* **wrecking**, ruining, annihilation, obliteration, elimination, eradication, devastation. **3 killing**, slaughter, extermination, culling.
- OPPOSITES preservation.

destructive *adjective* **devastating**, ruinous, damaging, harmful, environmentally unfriendly, detrimental, injurious, hurtful, deleterious.

detach *verb* **disconnect**, separate, unfasten, disengage, uncouple, isolate, remove, loose, unhitch, unhook, free, pull off, cut off, break off, split off, sever.
- OPPOSITES attach, join.

detached *adjective* **1 disconnected**, separated, separate, unfastened, disengaged, uncoupled, isolated, loosened, unhitched, unhooked, free, severed, cut off. **2 dispassionate**, disinterested, objective, outside, neutral, unbiased, impartial.

detachment *noun* **1 objectivity**, dispassion, disinterest, neutrality, impartiality. **2 unit**, squad, detail, troop, contingent, task force, party, platoon.

detail *noun* **1 feature**, respect, particular, characteristic, specific, aspect, fact, point, element. **2 triviality**, technicality, nicety, fine point. **3 unit**, detachment, squad, troop, contingent, outfit, task force, party, platoon.
● *verb* **describe**, relate, catalogue, list, spell out, itemize, identify, specify.

detailed *adjective* **comprehensive**, full, complete, thorough, exhaustive, all-inclusive, elaborate, minute, precise, itemized, blow-by-blow.
- OPPOSITES general.

detain *verb* **1 hold**, take into custody, confine, imprison, intern, arrest, apprehend, seize; *informal* pick up; *Brit. informal* nick. **2 delay**, hold up, make late, keep, slow up/down, hinder.
- OPPOSITES release.

detect *verb* **1 notice**, perceive, discern, become aware of, note, make out, spot, recognize, identify, catch, sense. **2 discover**, uncover, turn up, unearth, dig up, root out, expose. **3 catch**, hunt down, track down, find out, expose, reveal, unmask, smoke out.

detective *noun* **investigator**, police officer; *informal* private eye, sleuth; *N. Amer. informal* gumshoe.

detention *noun* **custody**, imprisonment, incarceration, internment, captivity, remand, arrest, quarantine.
- OPPOSITES release.

deter *verb* **1 discourage**, dissuade, put off, scare off, dishearten, demoralize, daunt, intimidate. **2 prevent**, stop, avert, stave off, ward off.
- OPPOSITES encourage.

deteriorate *verb* **worsen**, decline, degenerate, fail, go downhill, wane.
- OPPOSITES improve.

determination *noun* **resolution**, resolve, will power, strength of character, dedication, single-mindedness, perseverance, persistence, tenacity,

d

staying power, doggedness; *informal* guts.

determine *verb* **1 control**, decide, regulate, direct, dictate, govern. **2 resolve**, decide, make up your mind, choose, elect, opt. **3 specify**, set, fix, decide on, settle, establish, ordain, prescribe, decree. **4 ascertain**, find out, discover, learn, establish, calculate, work out; *informal* figure out.

determined *adjective* **resolute**, purposeful, adamant, single-minded, unswerving, unwavering, persevering, persistent, tenacious, dedicated, dogged.
- OPPOSITES irresolute.

deterrent *noun* **disincentive**, discouragement, damper, curb, check, restraint, inhibition.
- OPPOSITES incentive.

detest *verb* **hate**, abhor, loathe, regard with disgust, be unable to bear, have an aversion to, find intolerable, disdain, despise.
- OPPOSITES love.

detrimental *adjective* **harmful**, damaging, injurious, hurtful, inimical, deleterious, destructive, pernicious, undesirable, unfavourable, environmentally unfriendly.
- OPPOSITES beneficial.

devastate *verb* **1 destroy**, ruin, wreck, lay waste, ravage, demolish, raze to the ground, level, flatten. **2 shatter**, shock, stun, daze, dumbfound, traumatize, distress; *informal* knock sideways; *Brit. informal* knock for six.

devastation *noun* **destruction**, ruin, desolation, wreckage, ruins.

develop *verb* **1 grow**, expand, spread, advance, progress, evolve, mature. **2 initiate**, instigate, set in motion, originate, invent, form. **3 expand**, augment, broaden, supplement, reinforce, enhance, refine, improve, polish, perfect. **4 start**, begin, emerge, erupt, break out, arise, break, unfold.

development *noun* **1 evolution**, growth, expansion, enlargement,

spread, progress. **2 event**, change, circumstance, incident, occurrence. **3 estate**, complex, site.

deviate *verb* **diverge**, digress, drift, stray, veer, swerve, get sidetracked, branch off, differ, vary.

device *noun* **1 implement**, gadget, utensil, tool, appliance, apparatus, instrument, machine, mechanism, contrivance, contraption; *informal* gizmo. **2 ploy**, tactic, move, stratagem, scheme, manoeuvre, plot, trick, ruse.

devil *noun* **1 Satan**, Beelzebub, Lucifer, the Prince of Darkness; *informal* Old Nick. **2 evil spirit**, demon, fiend. **3 brute**, beast, monster, fiend, villain, sadist, barbarian, ogre.

> **WORD LINKS**
> **diabolical**, **diabolic**, **satanic** relating to the Devil

devious *adjective* **1 underhand**, dishonest, crafty, cunning, conniving, scheming, sneaky, furtive; *informal* crooked, shady; *Brit. informal* dodgy. **2 circuitous**, roundabout, indirect, meandering, tortuous.
- OPPOSITES honest, direct.

devise *verb* **conceive**, think up, dream up, work out, formulate, concoct, hatch, contrive, design, invent, coin; *informal* cook up.

devoid *adjective*
□ **devoid of** empty of, free of, bereft of, lacking, deficient in, without, wanting in; *informal* minus.

devote *verb* **dedicate**, allocate, assign, allot, commit, give (over), consign, pledge, set aside, earmark, reserve.

devoted *adjective* **dedicated**, committed, devout, loyal, faithful, true, staunch, steadfast, fond, loving.

devotee *noun* **enthusiast**, fan, lover, aficionado, admirer, supporter, disciple; *informal* buff, freak, nut, fanatic.

devotion *noun* **1 loyalty**, fidelity, commitment, allegiance, dedication, fondness, love, care. **2 piety**, spirituality, godliness, holiness, sanctity.

devour verb **1 gobble**, guzzle, gulp down, bolt, wolf; *informal* polish off; *Brit. informal* scoff. **2 consume**, engulf, envelop.

devout adjective **dedicated**, devoted, committed, loyal, sincere, fervent, pious, reverent, God-fearing, dutiful, churchgoing.

diagnose verb **identify**, determine, distinguish, recognize, interpret, detect, pinpoint.

diagnosis noun **1 identification**, detection, recognition, determination, discovery, pinpointing. **2 opinion**, judgement, verdict, conclusion.

diagonal adjective **crosswise**, crossways, slanting, slanted, oblique, angled, cornerways, cornerwise.

diagram noun **drawing**, representation, plan, outline, figure, chart, graph.

dialogue noun **conversation**, talk, discussion, chat, tête-à-tête, exchange, debate, conference, consultation; *informal* confab; *Austral. informal* convo.

diary noun **1 appointment book**, engagement book, personal organizer; *trademark* Filofax. **2 journal**, memoir, chronicle, log, logbook, history, annal, record, weblog, blog; *N. Amer.* daybook.

dictate verb **1 prescribe**, lay down, impose, set down, order, command, decree, ordain, direct. **2 determine**, control, govern, decide, influence, affect.
☐ **dictate to** give orders to, order about/around, lord it over; *informal* boss about/around, push about/around.

dictator noun **autocrat**, despot, tyrant, absolute ruler.
- OPPOSITES democrat.

dictatorial adjective **domineering**, autocratic, authoritarian, oppressive, imperious, overweening, overbearing, peremptory; *informal* bossy, high-handed.

dictionary noun **lexicon**, glossary, vocabulary.

WORD LINKS
lexicography writing of dictionaries

die verb **1 pass away**, pass on, perish; *informal* give up the ghost, kick the bucket, croak, bite the dust, flatline; *Brit. informal* snuff it, peg out, pop your clogs; *N. Amer. informal* buy the farm. **2 lessen**, subside, drop, ease (off), let up, moderate, abate, fade, peter out, wane, ebb. **3** (*informal*) *the engine died* **fail**, cut out, give out, break down, stop; *informal* conk out, go kaput; *Brit. informal* pack up.
- OPPOSITES live.

diet noun **1** *a healthy diet* **food**, nutrition, eating habits. **2** *she's on a diet* **dietary regime**, regimen, restricted diet, fast.
● verb **be on a diet**, slim, lose weight, watch your weight; *N. Amer.* reduce; *N. Amer. informal* slenderize.

differ verb **1** *the second set of data differed from the first* **contrast with**, be different to, vary from, deviate from, conflict with, run counter to, be at odds with, contradict. **2 disagree**, conflict, be at variance/odds, be in dispute, not see eye to eye.
- OPPOSITES resemble, agree.

difference noun **1 dissimilarity**, contrast, distinction, differentiation, variance, variation, divergence, disparity, contradiction. **2 disagreement**, difference of opinion, dispute, argument, quarrel; *Brit.* row. **3** *I'll pay the difference* **balance**, remainder, rest.
- OPPOSITES similarity.

different adjective **1 dissimilar**, unlike, contrasting, differing, varying, disparate, poles apart, incompatible, mismatched; *informal* like chalk and cheese. **2 changed**, altered, transformed, new, unfamiliar, unknown, strange. **3 distinct**, separate, individual, independent. **4** (*informal*) **unusual**, out of the ordinary, unfamiliar, novel, new, fresh, original, unconventional, exotic.
- OPPOSITES similar, ordinary.

d

difficult *adjective* **1** *a difficult job* **laborious**, strenuous, arduous, hard, tough, demanding, punishing, gruelling, backbreaking, exhausting, tiring; *informal* hellish, killing, no picnic. **2** *a difficult problem* **hard**, complicated, complex, puzzling, perplexing, baffling, problematic, thorny, ticklish. **3** *a difficult child* **troublesome**, tiresome, trying, exasperating, awkward, demanding, contrary, recalcitrant, uncooperative, fussy.
- OPPOSITES easy, simple, cooperative.

difficulty *noun* **1** **strain**, stress, trouble, problems, struggle; *informal* hassle. **2** **problem**, complication, snag, hitch, issue, obstacle, hurdle, stumbling block, pitfall; *Brit.* spanner in the works; *informal* headache. **3** *he got into difficulties* **trouble**, predicament, plight, hard times; *informal* fix, scrape, jam.
- OPPOSITES ease.

diffident *adjective* **shy**, bashful, modest, self-effacing, unassuming, meek, unconfident, insecure, unassertive, timid, shrinking, reticent.
- OPPOSITES confident.

dig *verb* **1** *she began to dig the soil* **turn over**, work, break up. **2** *he dug a hole* **excavate**, dig out, quarry, hollow out, scoop out, bore, burrow, mine. **3** **poke**, prod, jab, stab, shove, ram, push, thrust, drive, stick. **4** **delve**, probe, search, enquire, look, investigate, research.
● *noun* **1** **poke**, prod, jab, stab, shove, push. **2** *(informal)* **snide remark**, cutting remark, jibe, taunt, sneer, insult; *informal* wisecrack, put-down.
□ **dig up** exhume, disinter, unearth.

digest *verb* **assimilate**, absorb, take in, understand, comprehend, grasp.
● *noun* **summary**, synopsis, abstract, precis, résumé, summation.

dignified *adjective* **stately**, noble, majestic, distinguished, regal, imposing, impressive, grand, solemn, formal, ceremonious, decorous, sedate.

dignity *noun* **1** **stateliness**, nobility, majesty, impressiveness, grandeur, magnificence, ceremoniousness, formality, decorum, propriety, respectability, worthiness, integrity, solemnity, gravitas. **2** **self-respect**, pride, self-esteem, self-worth.

dilapidated *adjective* **run down**, tumbledown, ramshackle, in disrepair, shabby, battered, rickety, crumbling, in ruins, ruined, decaying, decrepit, neglected, uncared-for, gone to rack and ruin.

dilemma *noun* **quandary**, predicament, catch-22, vicious circle, plight, conflict; *informal* fix, tight spot/corner; (**in a dilemma**) between the devil and the deep blue sea, between a rock and a hard place.

diligent *adjective* **industrious**, hardworking, assiduous, conscientious, particular, punctilious, meticulous, painstaking, rigorous, careful, thorough, sedulous.
- OPPOSITES lazy.

dilute *verb* **1** *dilute the bleach with water* **make weaker**, water down, thin, doctor, adulterate; *informal* cut. **2** *the original plans have been diluted* **tone down**, moderate, weaken, water down, compromise.

dim *adjective* **1** *the dim light* **faint**, weak, feeble, soft, pale, dull, subdued, muted. **2** *long dim corridors* **dark**, badly lit, dingy, dismal, gloomy, murky. **3** *a dim figure* **indistinct**, ill-defined, vague, shadowy, nebulous, blurred, fuzzy. **4** *dim memories* **vague**, imprecise, imperfect, unclear, indistinct, sketchy, hazy. **5** see **stupid** (sense 1).
- OPPOSITES bright, distinct, clear.
● *verb* **1** **turn down**, lower, soften, subdue. **2** **fade**, dwindle, dull.
- OPPOSITES brighten.

dimension *noun* **1** **size**, measurements, proportions, extent, length, width, breadth, depth. **2** **aspect**, feature, element, angle, facet, side.

diminish *verb* **1** **subside**, lessen, decline, reduce, decrease, dwindle, fade, slacken off, let up. **2** *new laws diminished the courts' authority* **reduce**,

decrease, lessen, curtail, cut, limit, curb.
- OPPOSITES increase.

din noun **noise**, racket, rumpus, cacophony, hubbub, uproar, commotion, clangour, clatter, clamour; Brit. row; informal hullaballoo.
- OPPOSITES silence.

dine verb **eat**, have dinner, have lunch.

dingy adjective **gloomy**, dark, dull, dim, dismal, dreary, drab, sombre, grim, cheerless, dirty, grimy, shabby, seedy, run down.
- OPPOSITES bright.

dinner noun **main meal**, lunch, evening meal, supper, feast, banquet; Brit. tea.

dip verb **1 immerse**, submerge, plunge, dunk, bathe, sink. **2 sink**, set, drop, fall, descend. **3 decrease**, fall, drop, fall off, decline, diminish, dwindle, slump, plummet, plunge. **4 slope down**, descend, go down, drop (away), fall away.
- OPPOSITES rise, increase.
● noun **1 swim**, bathe, paddle. **2 slope**, incline, decline, descent, hollow, depression, basin. **3 decrease**, fall, drop, downturn, decline, falling-off, slump, reduction.
□ **dip into 1** draw on, use, spend. **2** browse through, skim through, look through, flick through.

diplomacy noun **1 statesmanship**, statecraft, negotiation(s), discussion(s), talks. **2 tact**, tactfulness, sensitivity, discretion, soft skills.

diplomat noun **ambassador**, attaché, consul, chargé d'affaires, envoy, emissary.

diplomatic adjective **tactful**, sensitive, subtle, delicate, polite, discreet, judicious, politic.
- OPPOSITES tactless.

dire adjective **terrible**, dreadful, appalling, frightful, awful, grim, sore, alarming, acute, grave, serious, urgent, pressing, wretched, desperate, parlous.

direct adjective **1 straight**, short, quick. **2 non-stop**, through, unbroken,

uninterrupted. **3 frank**, candid, straightforward, open, blunt, plain-spoken, outspoken, forthright, no-nonsense, matter-of-fact; informal upfront.
● verb **1 manage**, govern, run, administer, control, conduct, handle, be in charge of, preside over, lead, head, rule. **2 aim**, target, address to, intend for, mean for, design for. **3 give directions**, show the way, point someone in the direction of. **4 instruct**, tell, command, order, require; old use bid.

direction noun **1 way**, route, course, line, bearing, orientation. **2 running**, management, administration, conduct, handling, supervision, superintendence, command, rule, leadership. **3 instruction**, order, command, rule, regulation, requirement.

directive noun **instruction**, direction, command, order, injunction, decree, dictum, edict.

directly adverb **1** they flew directly to New York **straight**, as the crow flies. **2** directly after breakfast **immediately**, right (away), straight (away), without delay, promptly. **3** the houses directly opposite **exactly**, right, immediately, diametrically; informal bang. **4 frankly**, candidly, openly, bluntly, forthrightly, without beating about the bush.

director noun **manager**, head, chief, principal, leader, governor, president, chair, chief executive; informal boss, gaffer.

dirt noun **1 grime**, filth, muck, dust, mud, pollution; Brit. informal gunge. **2** a dirt road **earth**, soil, clay, loam.

dirty adjective **1 soiled**, grimy, grubby, filthy, mucky, stained, unwashed, greasy, muddy, dusty, polluted, contaminated, foul, unhygienic; Brit. informal manky, grotty. **2 obscene**, indecent, rude, naughty, vulgar, smutty, coarse, crude, filthy, off colour, pornographic, explicit, X-rated; informal blue; euphemistic adult. **3 malevolent**, hostile, black, angry, disapproving.
- OPPOSITES clean.

● *verb* **soil**, stain, muddy, blacken, mess (up), mark, spatter, smudge, smear, splatter, sully, pollute, foul.

disability *noun* **handicap**, incapacity, impairment, infirmity, defect, abnormality, condition, disorder, affliction.

disable *verb* **1 incapacitate**, put out of action, debilitate, handicap, cripple, lame, maim, immobilize, paralyse. **2 deactivate**, defuse, disarm, make safe.

disabled *adjective* **handicapped**, incapacitated, infirm, crippled, lame, paralysed, immobilized, bedridden; *euphemistic* physically challenged, differently abled.
- OPPOSITES able-bodied.

disadvantage *noun* **1 drawback**, snag, downside, fly in the ointment, catch, nuisance, handicap, trouble; *informal* minus. **2 detriment**, prejudice, harm, loss, hurt.
- OPPOSITES advantage.

disagree *verb* **1 be of a different opinion**, not see eye to eye, take issue, challenge, contradict, differ, dissent, be in dispute, clash. **2 differ**, be dissimilar, be different, be at variance/odds, vary, contradict each other, conflict. **3** *the food disagreed with her* **make ill**, make unwell, upset, nauseate.
- OPPOSITES agree.

disagreeable *adjective* **unpleasant**, distasteful, off-putting, unpalatable, nasty, objectionable, disgusting, horrible, offensive, repulsive, obnoxious, odious, repellent, revolting, vile, foul.
- OPPOSITES pleasant.

disagreement *noun* **dissent**, difference of opinion, controversy, discord, division, dispute, quarrel.
- OPPOSITES agreement.

disappear *verb* **1 vanish**, be lost to view/sight, recede, fade away, melt away, clear. **2 die out**, cease to exist, end, go, pass away, pass into oblivion, vanish, perish.
- OPPOSITES materialize.

disappoint *verb* **let down**, fail, dissatisfy, upset, dismay, sadden, disenchant,

disillusion, shatter someone's illusions.

disappointed *adjective* **upset**, saddened, let down, displeased, dissatisfied, disheartened, downhearted, discouraged, crestfallen, disenchanted, disillusioned; *informal* choked, cut up; *Brit. informal* gutted, as sick as a parrot.
- OPPOSITES delighted.

disappointment *noun* **1 sadness**, sorrow, regret, dismay, displeasure, dissatisfaction, disenchantment, disillusionment. **2 let-down**, non-event, anticlimax; *Brit.* damp squib; *informal* washout.
- OPPOSITES delight.

disapproval *noun* **disfavour**, objection, dislike, dissatisfaction, distaste, displeasure, criticism, censure, condemnation, denunciation.
- OPPOSITES approval.

disapprove *verb*
□ **disapprove of** object to, have a poor opinion of, take exception to, dislike, take a dim view of, look askance at, frown on, be against, not believe in, deplore, censure, condemn, denounce.

disarm *verb* **1 lay down your arms**, demobilize, disband, demilitarize. **2 defuse**, disable, deactivate, make safe. **3 win over**, charm, persuade, soothe, mollify, appease, placate.
- OPPOSITES arm, antagonize.

disarmament *noun* **demilitarization**, demobilization, disbandment, decommissioning, arms reduction, arms limitation.

disarming *adjective* **winning**, charming, irresistible, persuasive, soothing, conciliatory, mollifying.

disarray *noun* **disorder**, confusion, chaos, untidiness, disorganization, a mess, a muddle; *informal* a shambles; *Brit. informal* an omnishambles.
- OPPOSITES tidiness.

disaster *noun* **1 catastrophe**, calamity, cataclysm, tragedy, act of God, accident. **2 misfortune**, mishap, misadventure, setback, reversal, stroke of bad luck, blow. **3 failure**, fiasco, catastrophe; *informal* flop, washout,

dead loss, fail.
- OPPOSITES success.

disastrous adjective **catastrophic**, calamitous, cataclysmic, tragic, devastating, ruinous, terrible, awful.

disbelief noun **incredulity**, incredulousness, scepticism, doubt, cynicism, suspicion, distrust.

discard verb **dispose of**, throw away/out, get rid of, toss out, jettison, dispense with, scrap, reject, drop; informal ditch, bin, junk; Brit. informal get shot of; N. Amer. informal trash.
- OPPOSITES keep.

discharge verb **1 dismiss**, eject, expel, throw out, make redundant, release, let go; Military cashier; informal sack, fire. **2 free**, set free, release, let out, liberate. **3 emit**, give off, let out, send out, exude, leak, secrete, excrete, release. **4 fire**, shoot, let off, set off, loose off, trigger, launch. **5 unload**, offload, put off, remove. **6 carry out**, perform, execute, conduct, fulfil, complete.
- OPPOSITES recruit, imprison.
● noun **1 dismissal**, release, removal, ejection, expulsion; Military cashiering; informal the sack, the boot. **2 leak**, leakage, emission, secretion, excretion, suppuration, pus. **3 carrying out**, performance, execution, conduct, fulfilment, accomplishment, completion.

disciple noun **follower**, adherent, believer, admirer, devotee, acolyte, apostle, supporter, advocate.

discipline noun **1 control**, regulation, direction, order, authority, strictness. **2 good behaviour**, order, control, obedience. **3 field (of study)**, branch of knowledge, subject, area, speciality.
● verb **1 train**, drill, teach, school, coach. **2 punish**, penalize, bring to book, reprimand, rebuke; Brit. informal carpet.

disclose verb **reveal**, make known, divulge, tell, impart, communicate, pass on, release, make public, broadcast, publish.
- OPPOSITES conceal.

discolour verb **stain**, mark, soil, dirty, streak, smear, tarnish, spoil.

discomfort noun **1 pain**, aches and pains, soreness, aching, twinge, pang, throb, cramp. **2 inconvenience**, difficulty, problem, trial, tribulation, hardship. **3 embarrassment**, discomfiture, unease, awkwardness, discomposure, confusion, nervousness, distress, anxiety.

disconnect verb **1 detach**, disengage, uncouple, unhook, unhitch, undo, unfasten, unyoke. **2 separate**, cut off, divorce, sever, isolate, dissociate, remove. **3 deactivate**, shut off, turn off, switch off, unplug.
- OPPOSITES attach, connect.

discontent noun **dissatisfaction**, disaffection, grievances, unhappiness, displeasure, resentment, envy, restlessness, unrest, unease.
- OPPOSITES satisfaction.

discontented adjective **dissatisfied**, disgruntled, disaffected, unhappy, aggrieved, displeased, resentful, envious, restless, frustrated; informal fed up.
- OPPOSITES satisfied.

discordant adjective **tuneless**, inharmonious, off-key, dissonant, harsh, jarring, grating, jangly, jangling, strident, shrill, cacophonous.
- OPPOSITES harmonious.

discount noun **reduction**, deduction, markdown, price cut, concession, rebate.
● verb **1 disregard**, pay no attention to, take no notice of, dismiss, ignore, overlook; informal pooh-pooh. **2 reduce**, mark down, cut, lower; informal knock down.

discourage verb **1 dissuade**, deter, put off, talk out of. **2 dishearten**, dispirit, demoralize, disappoint, put off, unnerve, daunt, intimidate. **3 prevent**, deter, stop, avert, inhibit, curb.
- OPPOSITES encourage.

discover verb **1 find**, locate, come across/upon, stumble on, chance on, uncover, unearth, turn up. **2 find out**, learn, realize, ascertain, work out, recognize; *informal* figure out; *Brit. informal* twig.

discovery noun **1 finding**, location, uncovering, unearthing. **2 realization**, recognition, revelation, disclosure. **3 breakthrough**, finding, find, innovation.

discredit verb **1 bring into disrepute**, disgrace, dishonour, blacken the name of, put/show in a bad light, compromise, smear, tarnish; *N. Amer.* slur. **2 disprove**, invalidate, explode, refute; *informal* debunk.
- OPPOSITES honour, prove.
● noun **dishonour**, disgrace, shame, humiliation, ignominy.

discreet adjective **tactful**, circumspect, diplomatic, judicious, sensitive, careful, cautious, strategic.

discrepancy noun **difference**, disparity, variation, deviation, divergence, disagreement, inconsistency, mismatch, conflict.
- OPPOSITES correspondence.

discretion noun **1 tact**, diplomacy, delicacy, sensitivity, good sense, prudence, circumspection. **2** *at the discretion of the council* **choice**, option, preference, disposition, pleasure, will, inclination.

discriminate verb **1 differentiate**, distinguish, draw a distinction, tell the difference, tell apart, separate. **2** *policies that discriminate against women* **be biased**, be prejudiced, treat differently, treat unfairly, put at a disadvantage, victimize, pick on.

discriminating adjective **discerning**, perceptive, judicious, selective, tasteful, refined, sensitive, cultivated, cultured.
- OPPOSITES indiscriminate.

discrimination noun **1 prejudice**, bias, bigotry, intolerance, favouritism, partisanship. **2 discernment**, judgement, perceptiveness, (good) taste, refinement, sensitivity, cultivation.
- OPPOSITES impartiality.

discuss verb **1 talk over**, talk about, talk through, debate, confer about.

2 examine, explore, study, analyse, go into, deal with, consider, tackle.

discussion noun **1 conversation**, talk, chat, dialogue, conference, debate, exchange of views, consultation, deliberation; *informal* confab; *Austral. informal* convo. **2 examination**, exploration, study, analysis, treatment, consideration.

disdain noun **contempt**, scorn, derision, disrespect, condescension, superciliousness, hauteur, haughtiness.
- OPPOSITES respect.
● verb **scorn**, deride, regard with contempt, sneer at, look down your nose at, look down on, despise.

disease noun **illness**, sickness, ill health, infection, ailment, malady, disorder, condition, problem; *informal* bug, virus; *Brit. informal* lurgy.

> **WORD LINKS**
> **pathological** relating to disease

diseased adjective **unhealthy**, ill, sick, unwell, ailing, infected, septic, rotten, bad.

disgrace noun **1 dishonour**, shame, discredit, ignominy, disrepute, infamy, scandal, stigma, humiliation, loss of face. **2 scandal**, discredit, reproach, stain, blemish, blot, black mark, outrage, affront.
- OPPOSITES honour, credit.
● verb **shame**, bring shame on, dishonour, discredit, stigmatize, taint, sully, tarnish, stain, blacken.
- OPPOSITES honour.

disgraceful adjective **shameful**, scandalous, contemptible, dishonourable, discreditable, disreputable, reprehensible, blameworthy, unworthy, ignoble.
- OPPOSITES admirable.

disgruntled adjective **dissatisfied**, discontented, fed up, put out, aggrieved, resentful, displeased, unhappy, disappointed, annoyed; *informal* hacked off, browned off; *Brit. informal* cheesed off, narked, not best pleased; *N. Amer. informal* sore, ticked off.
- OPPOSITES contented.

disguise verb **camouflage**, conceal, hide, cover up, mask, screen, veil, paper over.
- OPPOSITES expose.

disgust noun **revulsion**, repugnance, aversion, distaste, abhorrence, loathing, hatred.
- OPPOSITES delight.
● verb **revolt**, repel, repulse, sicken, nauseate, horrify, appal, shock, turn someone's stomach, scandalize, outrage, offend, affront; N. Amer. informal gross out.
- OPPOSITES delight.

disgusting adjective **1** the food was disgusting **revolting**, repulsive, sickening, nauseating, stomach-turning, off-putting; N. Amer. vomitous; informal gross, sick-making. **2** I find racism disgusting **outrageous**, objectionable, abhorrent, repellent, loathsome, offensive, appalling, shocking, horrifying, scandalous, monstrous, detestable; informal sick.
- OPPOSITES delightful.

dish noun **1 bowl**, plate, platter, salver, pot. **2 recipe**, meal, course, fare.
□ **dish out** distribute, dispense, issue, hand out/round, give out, pass round, deal out, dole out, allocate.

dishevelled adjective **untidy**, unkempt, scruffy, messy, disarranged, rumpled, bedraggled, tousled, tangled, windswept; N. Amer. informal mussed (up).
- OPPOSITES tidy.

dishonest adjective **fraudulent**, cheating, underhand, devious, treacherous, unfair, dirty, criminal, illegal, unlawful, false, untruthful, deceitful, lying, corrupt, dishonourable, untrustworthy, unscrupulous; informal crooked, shady, sharp; Brit. informal bent; Austral./NZ informal shonky.
- OPPOSITES honest.

dishonourable adjective **disgraceful**, shameful, discreditable, ignoble, reprehensible, shabby, shoddy, despicable, contemptible, base, low.

disintegrate verb **break up**, crumble, break apart, fall apart, fall to pieces,

collapse, fragment, shatter, splinter.

disinterested adjective **unbiased**, unprejudiced, impartial, neutral, detached, objective, dispassionate, non-partisan.

dislike verb **find distasteful**, regard with distaste, be averse to, have an aversion to, disapprove of, object to, take exception to, have no taste for, hate, despise.
- OPPOSITES like.
● noun **distaste**, aversion, disfavour, antipathy, disgust, abhorrence, hatred.
- OPPOSITES liking.

disloyal adjective **unfaithful**, faithless, false, untrue, inconstant, two-faced, double-dealing, double-crossing, deceitful, treacherous, subversive, seditious, unpatriotic; informal back-stabbing, two-timing; literary perfidious.

dismal adjective **1** a dismal look **gloomy**, glum, melancholy, morose, doleful, woebegone, forlorn, dejected, downcast. **2** a dismal hall **dim**, dingy, dark, gloomy, dreary, drab, dull.
- OPPOSITES cheerful, bright.

dismantle verb **take apart**, take to pieces/bits, pull to pieces, disassemble, break up, strip (down).
- OPPOSITES build.

dismay noun **alarm**, distress, concern, consternation, disquiet.
- OPPOSITES pleasure, relief.
● verb **concern**, distress, disturb, worry, alarm, disconcert, take aback, unnerve, unsettle.
- OPPOSITES encourage.

dismiss verb **1 give someone their notice**, discharge, lay off, make redundant; informal sack, fire. **2 send away**, let go, release, disband, discharge. **3 banish**, set aside, put out of your mind, brush aside, reject, repudiate, spurn; informal pooh-pooh.

disobedient adjective **naughty**, insubordinate, defiant, unruly, wayward, badly behaved, delinquent, rebellious, mutinous, troublesome, wilful.
- OPPOSITES obedient.

disobey verb **defy**, go against, flout, contravene, infringe, transgress, violate, disregard, ignore, pay no heed to.

disorder noun **1 untidiness**, mess, disarray, chaos, confusion, clutter, jumble, a muddle; *informal* a shambles; *Brit. informal* an omnishambles. **2 unrest**, disturbance, turmoil, mayhem, violence, fighting, fracas, rioting, lawlessness, anarchy, breach of the peace. **3 disease**, infection, complaint, condition, affliction, malady, sickness, illness, ailment.
- OPPOSITES tidiness, peace.

disorderly adjective **1 untidy**, disorganized, topsy-turvy, at sixes and sevens, messy, jumbled, cluttered, in disarray, chaotic; *informal* like a bomb's hit it, higgledy-piggledy; *Brit. informal* shambolic. **2 unruly**, riotous, disruptive, troublesome, disobedient, lawless.
- OPPOSITES tidy, peaceful.

disorganized adjective **unmethodical**, unsystematic, undisciplined, unstructured, haphazard, chaotic, muddled, hit-or-miss, sloppy, slapdash, slipshod; *Brit. informal* shambolic.
- OPPOSITES organized.

disown verb **reject**, cast off/aside, abandon, renounce, repudiate, deny, turn your back on, wash your hands of, disinherit.

dispatch verb **1 send (off)**, post, mail, forward. **2 deal with**, finish, conclude, settle, discharge, perform. **3 kill**, put to death, massacre, wipe out, exterminate, eliminate, murder, assassinate, execute.
● noun **message**, report, communication, communiqué, bulletin, statement, letter, news, intelligence.

dispel verb **banish**, drive away/off, chase away, scatter, eliminate, dismiss, allay, ease, quell.

dispense verb **1 distribute**, pass round, hand out, dole out, dish out, share out. **2 administer**, deliver, issue, deal out, mete out. **3** *dispensing medicines* **prepare**, make up, supply, provide.
◻ **dispense with 1** waive, omit, drop, leave out, forgo, do away with; *informal* give something a miss. **2** get rid of, throw away/out, dispose of, discard; *informal* ditch, scrap, dump, chuck out/away; *Brit. informal* get shot of.

disperse verb **1 break up**, split up, disband, scatter, leave, go their separate ways, drive away/off, chase away. **2 dissipate**, dissolve, melt away, fade away, clear, lift. **3 scatter**, distribute, spread, disseminate.
- OPPOSITES assemble, gather.

displace verb **1 dislodge**, dislocate, move out of place/position, shift. **2 replace**, take the place of, supplant, supersede, oust, remove, depose.

display verb **1 exhibit**, show, arrange, array, present, lay out, set out. **2 show off**, parade, highlight, reveal, showcase. **3 manifest**, be evidence of, reveal, demonstrate, show.
- OPPOSITES conceal.
● noun **1 exhibition**, exposition, array, arrangement, presentation, demonstration, spectacle, show, parade. **2 manifestation**, expression, show, proof, demonstration, evidence.

displease verb **annoy**, irritate, anger, incense, irk, vex, nettle, put out, upset, exasperate.

dispose verb
◻ **dispose of** throw away, throw out, get rid of, discard, jettison, scrap; *informal* dump, junk, ditch, chuck (out/away); *Brit. informal* get shot of; *N. Amer. informal* trash.

disposition noun **1 temperament**, nature, character, constitution, make-up, mentality. **2 arrangement**, positioning, placement, configuration, set-up, line-up, layout.

disprove verb **refute**, prove false, rebut, debunk, give the lie to, demolish; *informal* shoot full of holes, blow out of the water.

dispute noun **1 debate**, discussion, argument, controversy, disagreement, dissent, conflict. **2 quarrel**, argument, altercation, squabble, falling-out,

disagreement, difference of opinion, clash; *Brit.* row.
- OPPOSITES agreement.
● *verb* **1 debate**, discuss, exchange views, quarrel, argue, disagree, clash, fall out, wrangle, bicker, squabble. **2 challenge**, contest, question, call into question, quibble over, contradict, argue about, disagree with, take issue with.
- OPPOSITES accept.

disqualify *verb* **rule out**, bar, exclude, prohibit, debar, preclude.

disregard *verb* **ignore**, take no notice of, pay no attention to, discount, overlook, turn a blind eye to, shut your eyes to, gloss over, brush off/aside, shrug off.
- OPPOSITES heed.
● *noun* **indifference**, non-observance, inattention, heedlessness, neglect, contempt.
- OPPOSITES attention.

disrupt *verb* **interrupt**, disturb, interfere with, play havoc with, upset, unsettle, obstruct, impede, hold up, delay.

disruptive *adjective* **1 troublesome**, disturbing, upsetting, unsettling, unruly, badly behaved, rowdy, disorderly, undisciplined, unmanageable, uncontrollable, uncooperative, attention-seeking.
- OPPOSITES well behaved. **2 innovative**, groundbreaking, inventive, ingenious, pioneering, revolutionary, radical, experimental, original, new, novel, fresh, unusual; *informal* edgy.

dissatisfied *adjective* **discontented**, disappointed, disaffected, displeased, disgruntled, aggrieved, unhappy.
- OPPOSITES contented.

dissent *verb* **disagree**, differ, demur, be at variance/odds, take issue, protest, object.
- OPPOSITES agree, conform.
● *noun* **disagreement**, difference of opinion, argument, dispute, resistance, objection, protest, opposition.
- OPPOSITES agreement, conformity.

dissident *noun* **dissenter**, objector, protester, rebel, revolutionary, subversive, agitator, refusenik.
- OPPOSITES conformist.
● *adjective* **dissenting**, opposing, objecting, protesting, rebellious, revolutionary, subversive, nonconformist.
- OPPOSITES conformist.

dissimilar *adjective* **different**, differing, unalike, variant, diverse, divergent, heterogeneous, disparate, unrelated, distinct, contrasting.

dissociate *verb* **separate**, detach, disconnect, sever, cut off, divorce, isolate, alienate.
- OPPOSITES associate.

dissolve *verb* **1 break down**, liquefy, melt, deliquesce, disintegrate. **2 disband**, disperse, bring to an end, end, terminate, discontinue, break up, close down, wind up/down, suspend, adjourn. **3 annul**, nullify, void, invalidate, revoke.

dissuade *verb* **discourage**, deter, prevent, stop, talk out of, persuade against, advise against, argue out of.
- OPPOSITES encourage.

distance *noun* **1 interval**, space, span, gap, extent, length, range, reach. **2 aloofness**, remoteness, detachment, unfriendliness, reserve, reticence, formality; *informal* stand-offishness.
- OPPOSITES proximity.

distant *adjective* **1 faraway**, far-off, far-flung, remote, out of the way, outlying. **2 bygone**, remote, ancient, prehistoric. **3 vague**, faint, dim, indistinct, sketchy, hazy. **4 aloof**, reserved, remote, detached, unapproachable, unfriendly; *informal* stand-offish. **5 distracted**, absent, faraway, detached, vague.
- OPPOSITES near, close, recent.

distasteful *adjective* **unpleasant**, disagreeable, displeasing, undesirable, objectionable, offensive, unsavoury, unpalatable.
- OPPOSITES agreeable.

distinct *adjective* **1** *two distinct categories* **discrete**, separate, different, unconnected, distinctive, contrasting.

2 *the tail has distinct black tips* **clear**, well defined, unmistakable, easily distinguishable, recognizable, visible, obvious, pronounced, prominent, striking.
- OPPOSITES similar.

distinction *noun* **1 difference**, contrast, variation, division, differentiation, discrepancy. **2 merit**, worth, greatness, excellence, quality, repute, renown, honour, credit.
- OPPOSITES similarity.

distinctive *adjective* **distinguishing**, characteristic, typical, individual, particular, peculiar, unique, exclusive, special.
- OPPOSITES common.

distinctly *adverb* **1 decidedly**, markedly, definitely, unmistakably, manifestly, patently. **2 clearly**, plainly, intelligibly, audibly.

distinguish *verb* **1 differentiate**, tell apart, discriminate between, tell the difference between. **2 discern**, see, perceive, make out, detect, recognize, identify. **3 separate**, set apart, make distinctive, make different, single out, mark off.

distinguished *adjective* **eminent**, famous, renowned, prominent, well known, great, esteemed, respected, notable, illustrious, acclaimed, celebrated.
- OPPOSITES unknown, obscure.

distorted *adjective* **1 twisted**, warped, contorted, buckled, deformed, malformed, misshapen, disfigured, crooked, out of shape. **2 misrepresented**, perverted, twisted, falsified, misreported, misstated, garbled, inaccurate, biased, prejudiced.

distract *verb* **divert**, sidetrack, draw away, lead astray, disturb, put off.

distracted *adjective* **preoccupied**, inattentive, vague, abstracted, absent-minded, faraway, in a world of your own, troubled, harassed, worried; *informal* miles away, not with it.
- OPPOSITES attentive.

distraction *noun* **1 diversion**, interruption, disturbance, interference. **2 amusement**, entertainment, diversion, recreation, pastime, leisure pursuit.

distraught *adjective* **distressed**, frantic, fraught, overcome, overwrought, beside yourself, out of your mind, desperate, hysterical, worked up, at your wits' end; *informal* in a state.
- OPPOSITES calm.

distress *noun* **1 anguish**, suffering, pain, agony, torment, heartache, heartbreak, sorrow, sadness, unhappiness. **2** *a ship in distress* **danger**, peril, difficulty, trouble, jeopardy, risk.
- OPPOSITES happiness.
● *verb* **upset**, pain, trouble, worry, perturb, disturb, disquiet, agitate, torment.
- OPPOSITES comfort.

distribute *verb* **1 give out**, deal out, dole out, dish out, hand out/round, share out, divide out/up, parcel out, apportion, allocate, allot. **2** *the newsletter is distributed free* **circulate**, issue, deliver, disseminate, publish.
- OPPOSITES collect.

distribution *noun* **1** *the distribution of aid* **giving out**, dealing out, doling out, handing out/round, issuing, allocation, sharing out, dividing up/out, parcelling out. **2** *centres of food distribution* **supply**, delivery, dispersal, transportation.

district *noun* **area**, region, quarter, sector, zone, territory, locality, neighbourhood, community.

distrust *noun* **mistrust**, suspicion, wariness, scepticism, doubt, cynicism, misgivings, qualms.
- OPPOSITES trust.
● *verb* **mistrust**, be suspicious of, be wary of, be chary of, regard with suspicion, suspect, be sceptical of, doubt, be unsure of/about, have misgivings about.
- OPPOSITES trust.

disturb *verb* **1 interrupt**, intrude on, butt in on, barge in on, distract, disrupt, bother, trouble, pester, harass. **2 move**, rearrange, mix up, interfere with, mess up. **3 perturb**, trouble,

concern, worry, upset, fluster, disconcert, dismay, alarm, distress, unsettle.
- OPPOSITES calm, reassure.

disturbance noun **1 disruption**, distraction, interference, inconvenience,
upset, annoyance, irritation, intrusion.
2 riot, fracas, brawl, street fight, free-
for-all, commotion, disorder.
- OPPOSITES order.

disturbed adjective **1 disrupted**,
interrupted, fitful, intermittent,
broken. **2 troubled**, distressed, upset,
distraught, unbalanced, unstable, disordered, dysfunctional, maladjusted, neurotic, unhinged; informal screwed up.
- OPPOSITES uninterrupted.

ditch noun **trench**, trough, channel,
dyke, drain, gutter, gully, watercourse.

dive verb **1 plunge**, plummet, nosedive, jump, fall, drop, pitch. **2 leap**,
jump, lunge, throw/fling yourself, go
headlong.
● noun **1 plunge**, nosedive, jump, fall,
drop, swoop. **2 lunge**, spring, jump,
leap.

diverge verb **1 separate**, part, fork,
divide, split, bifurcate, go in different
directions. **2 differ**, be different, be dissimilar, disagree, be at variance/odds,
conflict, clash.
- OPPOSITES converge, agree.

diverse adjective **various**, sundry, varied, varying, miscellaneous, assorted,
mixed, diversified, divergent, different,
differing, distinct, unlike, dissimilar.
- OPPOSITES similar.

diversion noun **1 detour**, deviation,
alternative route, re-routing, redirec-
tion. **2 distraction**, disturbance,
smokescreen; informal red herring.
3 entertainment, amusement, pastime, delight, fun, recreation, pleasure.

diversity noun **variety**, miscellany,
assortment, mixture, mix, range, array,
multiplicity, variation, difference.
- OPPOSITES uniformity.

divert verb **1 re-route**, redirect, change
the course of, deflect, channel. **2 distract**, sidetrack, disturb, draw away,
put off. **3 amuse**, entertain, distract,

delight, enchant, interest, fascinate,
absorb, engross, rivet, grip.

divide verb **1** he divided his kingdom
into four **split (up)**, cut up, carve up,
dissect, bisect, halve, quarter. **2** a
curtain divided her cabin from the galley
separate, segregate, partition, screen
off, section off, split off. **3 diverge**,
separate, part, branch (off), fork, split
(in two). **4 share out**, ration out,
parcel out, deal out, dole out, dish out,
distribute. **5 disunite**, drive apart, drive
a wedge between, break up, split (up),
separate, isolate, alienate.
- OPPOSITES unify, converge, unite.

divine[1] adjective **godly**, angelic, heavenly, celestial, holy, sacred.
- OPPOSITES mortal.

divine[2] verb **guess**, surmise, deduce,
infer, discern, discover, perceive; informal figure (out); Brit. informal suss.

division noun **1** the division of the island
dividing (up), breaking up, break-
up, carving up, splitting, dissection,
partitioning, separation, segregation.
2 the division of his estates **sharing out**,
dividing up, parcelling out, dishing out,
allocation, allotment, splitting up, carving up. **3 dividing line**, divide, boundary, border, demarcation line, gap, gulf.
4 section, subsection, subdivision,
category, class, group, grouping, set.
5 department, branch, arm, wing.
6 disunity, disunion, conflict, discord,
disagreement, alienation, isolation.
- OPPOSITES unification.

divorce noun **1 dissolution**, annulment,
decree nisi, separation. **2** the divorce
between the church and people **separation**, division, split, gulf, disunity,
alienation, schism.
- OPPOSITES marriage.
● verb **1 split up**, get a divorce,
separate. **2** religion cannot be divorced
from morality **separate**, divide, detach,
isolate, alienate, set apart, cut off.

divulge verb **disclose**, reveal, tell, communicate, pass on, publish, give away,
let slip.
- OPPOSITES conceal.

dizzy adjective **giddy**, light-headed, faint, unsteady, shaky, muzzy, wobbly; informal woozy.

do verb **1** she does most of the work **carry out**, undertake, discharge, execute, perform, accomplish, achieve, bring about, engineer; informal pull off. **2** they can do as they please **act**, behave, conduct yourself. **3** suffice, be adequate, be satisfactory, fill/fit the bill, serve. **4** a portrait I am doing **make**, create, produce, work on, design, manufacture.
□ **do away with** abolish, get rid of, eliminate, discontinue, stop, end, terminate, drop, abandon, give up; informal scrap. **do without** forgo, dispense with, abstain from, refrain from, eschew, give up, cut out, renounce, manage without.

docile adjective **compliant**, obedient, pliant, submissive, deferential, unassertive, cooperative, amenable, accommodating, biddable.
– OPPOSITES disobedient, wilful.

dock[1] noun **harbour**, marina, port, wharf, quay, pier, jetty, landing stage.
● verb **moor**, berth, put in, tie up, anchor.

dock[2] verb **1** **deduct**, subtract, remove, debit, take off/away; informal knock off. **2** **reduce**, cut, decrease. **3** **cut off**, cut short, shorten, crop, lop.

doctor noun **physician**, medical practitioner, general practitioner, GP, clinician, consultant; informal doc, medic; Brit. informal quack.
● verb **1** **adulterate**, tamper with, lace; informal spike. **2** **falsify**, tamper with, interfere with, alter, change, forge, fake; Brit. informal fiddle.

doctrine noun **creed**, credo, dogma, belief, teaching, ideology, tenet, maxim, canon, principle.

document noun **paper**, certificate, deed, form, contract, agreement, report, record.
● verb **record**, register, report, log, chronicle, authenticate, verify.

dodge verb **1** he dodged the police **elude**, evade, avoid, escape, run away from, lose, shake (off); informal give someone the slip. **2** the minister tried to dodge the debate **avoid**, evade, get out of, back out of, sidestep; informal duck, wriggle out of. **3** **dart**, duck, dive, swerve, veer.
● noun a clever dodge | a tax dodge **ruse**, scheme, tactic, stratagem, ploy, subterfuge, trick, hoax, cheat, deception, fraud; informal scam; Brit. informal wheeze.

dog noun **hound**, canine, man's best friend, mongrel; informal pooch, mutt; Austral. informal bitzer.
● verb **plague**, beset, bedevil, blight, trouble.

> **WORD LINKS**
> **canine** relating to dogs

dogged adjective **tenacious**, determined, resolute, stubborn, obstinate, purposeful, persistent, persevering, single-minded, tireless.
– OPPOSITES half-hearted.

dogmatic adjective **opinionated**, assertive, insistent, emphatic, adamant, doctrinaire, authoritarian, imperious, dictatorial, uncompromising.

dole verb
□ **dole out** deal out, share out, divide up, allocate, distribute, dispense, hand out, give out, dish out.

domain noun **1** **realm**, kingdom, empire, dominion, province, territory, land. **2** **field**, area, sphere, discipline, province, world.

domestic adjective **1** **family**, home, household. **2** **domesticated**, homely, home-loving. **3** **tame**, pet, domesticated; Brit. house-trained. **4** **national**, state, home, internal.

dominant adjective **1** **ruling**, governing, controlling, presiding, commanding. **2** **assertive**, authoritative, forceful, domineering, commanding, controlling, pushy. **3** **main**, principal, prime, chief, primary, central, key, crucial, core.
– OPPOSITES subservient, subsidiary.

dominate *verb* **1 control**, influence, command, be in charge of, rule, govern, direct. **2 overlook**, command, tower above/over, loom over.

domination *noun* **control**, power, command, authority, dominion, rule, supremacy, superiority, ascendancy, sway, mastery.

domineering *adjective* **overbearing**, authoritarian, imperious, high-handed, peremptory, autocratic, dictatorial, despotic, strict, harsh; *informal* bossy.

don *verb* **put on**, get dressed in, dress (yourself) in, get into, slip into/on, change into.

donate *verb* **give**, contribute, gift, subscribe, grant, present, endow; *informal* chip in, stump up.

donation *noun* **gift**, contribution, subscription, present, handout, grant, offering.

donor *noun* **giver**, contributor, benefactor, benefactress, subscriber, supporter, backer, patron, sponsor.
- OPPOSITES beneficiary.

doom *noun* **destruction**, downfall, ruin, extinction, annihilation, death, nemesis.
● *verb* **destine**, fate, predestine, preordain, mean, condemn, sentence.

doomed *adjective* **ill-fated**, ill-starred, cursed, jinxed, damned; *literary* star-crossed.

dose *noun* **measure**, portion, draught, dosage.

dot *noun* **spot**, speck, fleck, speckle, full stop, decimal point.
● *verb* **1 spot**, fleck, mark, spatter. **2 scatter**, pepper, sprinkle, strew, spread.

dote *verb*
□ **dote on** adore, love dearly, be devoted to, idolize, treasure, cherish, worship.

double *adjective* **dual**, duplex, twin, binary, duplicate, coupled, matching, twofold, in pairs.
- OPPOSITES single.

● *noun* **lookalike**, twin, clone, duplicate, exact likeness, replica, copy, facsimile, doppelgänger; *informal* spitting image, dead ringer.

doubt *noun* **1 uncertainty**, indecision, hesitation, irresolution, hesitancy, vacillation, lack of conviction. **2 scepticism**, distrust, mistrust, suspicion, cynicism, wariness, reservations, misgivings, suspicions.
- OPPOSITES certainty, trust.
● *verb* **disbelieve**, distrust, mistrust, suspect, be suspicious of, have misgivings about.
□ **in doubt 1** doubtful, uncertain, unconfirmed, unknown, undecided, unresolved, in the balance, up in the air; *informal* iffy. **2** irresolute, hesitant, doubtful, unsure, uncertain, in two minds, undecided, in a quandary/dilemma. **no doubt** doubtless, undoubtedly, indubitably, without (a) doubt, unquestionably, undeniably, clearly, plainly, obviously, patently.

doubtful *adjective* **1 hesitant**, in doubt, unsure, uncertain, in two minds, in a quandary, in a dilemma. **2 in doubt**, uncertain, open to question, unsure, debatable, up in the air, inconclusive, unconfirmed. **3 unlikely**, improbable. **4 distrustful**, mistrustful, sceptical, suspicious, having reservations, wary, chary, leery. **5 questionable**, dubious, suspect, suspicious.
- OPPOSITES confident, certain.

doubtless *adverb* **undoubtedly**, no doubt, unquestionably, indisputably, undeniably, certainly, surely, of course.

douse *verb* **1 drench**, soak, saturate, wet. **2 extinguish**, put out, quench, smother.

dowdy *adjective* **unfashionable**, frumpy, old-fashioned, shabby, frowzy; *Brit. informal* mumsy.
- OPPOSITES fashionable.

downfall *noun* **ruin**, ruination, undoing, defeat, overthrow, nemesis, destruction, annihilation, end, collapse, fall, crash, failure.
- OPPOSITES rise.

d

downgrade *verb* **demote**, reduce, relegate.
- OPPOSITES promote.

downright *adjective* **complete**, total, absolute, utter, thorough, out-and-out, outright, sheer, arrant, pure.
● *adverb* **thoroughly**, utterly, positively, profoundly, really, completely, totally, entirely.

drab *adjective* **1 colourless**, grey, dull, washed out, dingy, dreary, dismal, cheerless, gloomy, sombre. **2 uninteresting**, dull, boring, tedious, monotonous, dry, dreary.
- OPPOSITES bright, interesting.

draft *noun* **1 version**, sketch, attempt, effort, outline, plan. **2 cheque**, order, money order, bill of exchange.

drag *verb* **haul**, pull, tug, heave, lug, draw, trail.
● *noun* **1 pull**, resistance, tug. **2** *(informal)* **bore**, nuisance, bother, trouble, pest, annoyance, trial; *informal* pain (in the neck), bind, headache, hassle.

drain *verb* **1** *a valve for draining the tank* **empty (out)**, void, clear (out), evacuate, unload. **2** *drain off any surplus liquid* **draw off**, extract, siphon off, pour out, pour off, bleed, tap, filter, discharge. **3** *the water drained away* **flow**, pour, trickle, stream, run, rush, gush, flood, surge, leak, ooze, seep, dribble. **4 use up**, exhaust, deplete, consume, expend, get through, sap, milk, bleed. **5 drink**, gulp (down), guzzle, quaff, swallow, finish off, toss off; *informal* sink, down, swig, swill (down), knock back.
- OPPOSITES fill.
● *noun* **1 sewer**, channel, ditch, culvert, duct, pipe, gutter. **2 strain**, pressure, burden, load, demand.

drama *noun* **1 play**, show, piece, theatrical work, stage show, dramatization. **2 acting**, the theatre, the stage, dramatic art, stagecraft, dramaturgy. **3 incident**, scene, spectacle, crisis, disturbance, row, commotion, excitement, thrill, sensation, dramatics, theatrics, histrionics.

dramatic *adjective* **1 theatrical**, thespian, dramaturgical. **2 considerable**, substantial, significant, remarkable, extraordinary, exceptional, phenomenal. **3 exciting**, stirring, action-packed, sensational, spectacular, startling, unexpected, tense, gripping, riveting, thrilling, hair-raising, lively. **4 striking**, impressive, imposing, spectacular, breathtaking, dazzling, sensational, awesome, awe-inspiring, remarkable. **5 exaggerated**, theatrical, ostentatious, actressy, stagy, showy, melodramatic.
- OPPOSITES unremarkable, boring.

dramatize *verb* **1 adapt**, turn into a play/film. **2 exaggerate**, overdo, overstate, magnify, amplify, inflate, sensationalize, embroider, colour, aggrandize, embellish, elaborate; *informal* blow up (out of all proportion).

drape *verb* **wrap**, cover, envelop, shroud, wind, swathe, festoon, hang.

drastic *adjective* **extreme**, serious, desperate, radical, far-reaching, momentous, substantial.
- OPPOSITES moderate.

draught *noun* **1 current of air**, wind, breeze, gust, puff, waft. **2 gulp**, drink, swallow, mouthful; *informal* swig.

draw *verb* **1 sketch**, outline, rough out, illustrate, render, represent, trace, portray, depict. **2 pull**, haul, drag, tug, heave, lug, tow; *informal* yank. **3 move**, go, come, proceed, progress, pass, drive, inch, roll, glide, cruise, sweep. **4 pull out**, take out, produce, fish out, extract, withdraw, unsheathe. **5 attract**, win, capture, catch, engage, lure, entice, bring in.
● *noun* **1 raffle**, lottery, sweepstake, sweep, tombola, ballot. **2 tie**, dead heat, stalemate. **3 attraction**, lure, allure, pull, appeal, temptation, charm, fascination.
□ **draw on** call on, have recourse to, turn to, look to, exploit, use, employ, utilize, bring into play. **draw out** prolong, protract, drag out, spin out, string out, extend, lengthen. **draw up**

compose, formulate, frame, write down, draft, prepare, think up, devise, work out, create, invent, design.

drawback *noun* **disadvantage**, snag, downside, stumbling block, catch, hitch, pitfall, issue, fly in the ointment, weak spot/point, weakness, imperfection; *informal* minus.
- OPPOSITES benefit.

drawing *noun* **sketch**, picture, illustration, representation, portrayal, depiction, diagram, outline.

> **WORD LINKS**
> **graphic** relating to drawing

dread *verb* **fear**, be afraid of, worry about, be anxious about, shudder at the thought of.
● *noun* **fear**, apprehension, trepidation, anxiety, panic, alarm, terror, disquiet, unease.

dreadful *adjective* **1** *a dreadful accident* **terrible**, frightful, horrible, grim, awful, horrifying, shocking, distressing, appalling, harrowing, ghastly, gruesome, fearful, horrendous, tragic. **2** *a dreadful meal* **very bad**, frightful, shocking, awful, abysmal, dire, atrocious, disgraceful, deplorable; *informal* woeful, rotten, lousy, ropy; *Brit. informal* duff, rubbish. **3** *a dreadful flirt* **outrageous**, shocking, real, awful, terrible, inordinate, incorrigible.
- OPPOSITES wonderful, excellent.

dream *noun* **1 daydream**, reverie, trance, daze, stupor. **2 ambition**, aspiration, hope, goal, aim, objective, intention, desire, wish, daydream, fantasy. **3 delight**, joy, marvel, wonder, gem, treasure.
- OPPOSITES nightmare.
● *verb* **1 fantasize**, daydream, wish, hope, long, yearn, hanker. **2 daydream**, be in a trance, be lost in thought, be preoccupied, be abstracted, stare into space, be in cloud cuckoo land.
□ **dream up** think up, invent, concoct, devise, hatch, come up with.

dreary *adjective* **dull**, uninteresting, tedious, boring, unexciting, unstimulating, uninspiring, soul-destroying, monotonous, uneventful.
- OPPOSITES exciting.

drench *verb* **soak**, saturate, wet through, douse, steep, flood, drown.

dress *noun* **1** *a long blue dress* **frock**, gown, robe, shift. **2** *full evening dress* **clothes**, clothing, garments, garb, attire, costume, outfit; *informal* get-up, gear; *Brit. informal* clobber; *formal* apparel.
● *verb* **1 clothe**, attire, deck out, garb; *informal* get up. **2 decorate**, trim, adorn, arrange, prepare. **3 bandage**, cover, bind, wrap.
- OPPOSITES undress.

> **WORD LINKS**
> **sartorial** relating to dress

dribble *verb* **1 drool**, slaver, slobber. **2 trickle**, drip, roll, run, drizzle, ooze, seep, leak.

drift *verb* **1 be carried**, be borne, float, bob, glide, coast, waft. **2 wander**, meander, stray, stroll, dawdle, float, roam. **3 stray**, digress, wander, deviate, get sidetracked. **4 pile up**, bank up, heap up, accumulate, gather, amass.
● *noun* **1 movement**, shift, flow, transfer, gravitation. **2 gist**, meaning, sense, significance, thrust, import, tenor, intention, direction. **3 pile**, heap, bank, mound, mass, accumulation.

drill *noun* **1 training**, instruction, coaching, teaching, (physical) exercises; *informal* square-bashing. **2 procedure**, routine, practice, programme, schedule, method, system.
● *verb* **1 bore**, pierce, puncture, perforate. **2 train**, instruct, coach, teach, discipline, exercise.

drink *verb* **1 swallow**, gulp (down), quaff, guzzle, imbibe, sip, drain; *informal* swig, down, knock back. **2 drink alcohol**, tipple, indulge, carouse; *informal* hit the bottle, booze; *Brit. informal* bevvy.
● *noun* **1 beverage**, liquid refreshment; *Brit. informal* bevvy. **2 alcohol**, intoxicating liquor, spirits; *informal*

booze, the hard stuff, the bottle, grog.
3 swallow, gulp, mouthful, draught,
sip; *informal* swig, slug.

drip *verb* **drop**, dribble, leak, trickle, run,
splash, sprinkle.
● *noun* **drop**, dribble, spot, trickle,
splash, bead.

drive *verb* **1 operate**, handle, manage,
pilot, steer, work. **2 go by car**, motor.
3 run, chauffeur, give someone a lift,
take, ferry, transport, convey. **4 power**,
propel, move, push. **5 hammer**, screw,
ram, sink, plunge, thrust, knock.
6 force, compel, prompt, precipitate,
oblige, coerce, pressure, spur, prod.
● *noun* **1 excursion**, outing, trip,
jaunt, tour, ride, run, journey; *informal*
spin. **2 motivation**, ambition, single-
mindedness, determination, will power,
dedication, doggedness, tenacity,
enthusiasm, zeal, commitment, energy,
vigour; *informal* get-up-and-go. **3 campaign**, crusade, movement, effort,
push, initiative.

droop *verb* **hang down**, wilt, dangle,
sag, flop, sink, slump, drop.

drop *verb* **1 let fall**, let go of, release.
2 fall, descend, plunge, plummet, dive,
sink, dip, tumble. **3 decrease**, lessen,
reduce, fall, decline, dwindle, sink,
slump. **4 abandon**, give up, discontinue, finish with, renounce, reject,
forgo, relinquish, dispense with, leave
out; *informal* dump, pack in, quit.
- OPPOSITES rise, increase.
● *noun* **1 droplet**, blob, globule, bead.
2 small amount, little, bit, dash, spot,
dribble, sprinkle, trickle, splash, mouthful; *informal* smidgen, tad. **3 decrease**,
reduction, decline, fall-off, downturn,
slump. **4 cliff**, precipice, slope, descent,
incline.
□ **drop off** fall asleep, doze (off), nap,
drowse; *informal* nod off, drift off,
snooze, take forty winks. **drop out**
leave, give up, withdraw, retire, pull
out, abandon something, fall by the
wayside; *informal* quit, pack in, jack in.

drug *noun* **1 medicine**, medication,
remedy, cure, antidote. **2 narcotic**,

stimulant, hallucinogen; *informal* dope,
gear.
● *verb* **1 anaesthetize**, poison, knock
out; *informal* dope. **2 tamper with**,
lace, poison; *informal* dope, spike,
doctor.

WORD LINKS

pharmacology branch of medicine
concerned with drugs
pharmacy (*Brit.* **chemist**; *N. Amer.*
drugstore) shop selling drugs

drum *noun* **canister**, barrel, cylinder,
tank, bin, can.
● *verb* **1 tap**, beat, rap, thud, thump,
tattoo, thrum. **2 instil**, drive, din, hammer, drill, implant, ingrain, inculcate.
□ **drum up** round up, gather, collect,
summon, attract, canvass, solicit,
petition.

drunk *adjective* **intoxicated**, inebriated,
drunken, tipsy, under the influence;
informal tight, merry, plastered,
sloshed, pickled, tanked (up), ratted,
three sheets to the wind, squiffy; *Brit.
informal* legless, paralytic, Brahms
and Liszt, tiddly; *N. Amer. informal*
loaded.
- OPPOSITES sober.
● *noun* **drunkard**, alcoholic, dipsomaniac, inebriate; *informal* boozer, soak,
wino, alky.

dry *adjective* **1 arid**, parched, waterless,
dehydrated, desiccated, withered,
shrivelled, wizened. **2 dull**, uninteresting, boring, unexciting, tedious, dreary,
monotonous, unimaginative, sterile;
informal deadly. **3 wry**, subtle, laconic,
ironic, sardonic, sarcastic, cynical.
- OPPOSITES wet, moist.
● *verb* **1 parch**, scorch, bake, sear,
dehydrate, desiccate, wither, shrivel.
2 wipe, towel, rub dry, drain.
- OPPOSITES wet, moisten.

dual *adjective* **double**, twofold, duplex,
binary, twin, matching, paired,
coupled.
- OPPOSITES single.

dub *verb* **name**, call, nickname, label,
christen, term, tag.

dubious *adjective* **1 doubtful**, uncertain, unsure, hesitant, sceptical, suspicious; *informal* iffy. **2 suspicious**, suspect, untrustworthy, unreliable, questionable; *informal* shady; *Brit. informal* dodgy.
- OPPOSITES certain, trustworthy.

duck *verb* **1 bob down**, bend down, stoop, crouch, squat, hunch down, hunker down. **2** *(informal)* **shirk**, dodge, evade, avoid, elude, escape, sidestep.

duct *noun* **tube**, channel, canal, vessel, conduit, pipe, outlet, inlet, flue, shaft, vent.

due *adjective* **1** *their fees were due* **owing**, owed, payable, outstanding, overdue, unpaid, unsettled. **2** *the chancellor's statement is due today* **expected**, anticipated, scheduled, awaited, required. **3 deserved**, merited, warranted, justified, owing, appropriate, fitting, right, rightful, proper. **4 proper**, correct, suitable, appropriate, adequate, sufficient.
● *noun* **fee**, subscription, charge, payment, contribution, levy.
● *adverb* **directly**, straight, exactly, precisely, dead.
☐ **due to 1** *her death was due to an infection* **attributable to**, caused by, because of, down to. **2** *the train was cancelled due to staff shortages* **because of**, owing to, on account of, as a consequence of, as a result of, thanks to.

duel *noun* **1 single combat**, fight, confrontation, head-to-head; *informal* shoot-out. **2 contest**, match, game, meet, encounter, clash.

dull *adjective* **1 uninteresting**, boring, tedious, monotonous, unimaginative, uneventful, featureless, colourless, lifeless, unexciting, uninspiring, flat, bland, stodgy, dreary; *informal* deadly; *N. Amer. informal* dullsville. **2 overcast**, cloudy, gloomy, dark, dismal, dreary, sombre, grey, murky, sunless. **3 drab**, dreary, sombre, dark, subdued, muted. **4 muffled**, muted, quiet, soft, faint, indistinct, stifled. **5 unintelligent**, stupid, slow, brainless, mindless, foolish, idiotic; *informal* dense, dim, half-witted, thick.
- OPPOSITES interesting, bright.
● *verb* **lessen**, decrease, diminish, reduce, dampen, blunt, deaden, allay, ease.
- OPPOSITES intensify.

duly *adverb* **1 properly**, correctly, appropriately, suitably, fittingly. **2 at the right time**, on time, punctually.

dumb *adjective* **1 mute**, speechless, tongue-tied, silent, at a loss for words. **2** *(informal)* **stupid**, unintelligent, ignorant, dense, brainless, foolish, slow, dull, simple; *informal* thick, dim; *Brit. informal* daft.
- OPPOSITES talkative, clever.

dummy *noun* **mannequin**, model, figure.
● *adjective* **simulated**, practice, trial, mock, make-believe; *informal* pretend.

dump *noun* **1 tip**, rubbish dump, dumping ground. **2** *(informal)* **hovel**, slum; *informal* hole, pigsty.
● *verb* **1 put down**, set down, deposit, place, shove, unload, drop, throw down; *informal* stick, park, plonk; *Brit. informal* bung. **2 dispose of**, get rid of, throw away/out, discard, bin, jettison; *informal* ditch, junk.

dune *noun* **bank**, mound, hillock, hummock, knoll, ridge, heap, drift.

duplicate *noun* **copy**, photocopy, facsimile, reprint, replica, reproduction, clone; *trademark* Xerox, photostat.
● *adjective* **matching**, identical, twin, corresponding, equivalent.
● *verb* **1 copy**, photocopy, photostat, xerox, reproduce, replicate, reprint, run off. **2 repeat**, do again, redo, replicate.

durable *adjective* **1 hard-wearing**, wear-resistant, heavy-duty, tough, long-lasting, strong, sturdy, robust, utilitarian. **2 lasting**, long-lasting, long-term, enduring, persistent, abiding, permanent, undying, everlasting.
- OPPOSITES delicate, short-lived.

duration *noun* **length**, time, period, term, span, extent, stretch.

dusk *noun* **twilight**, nightfall, sunset, sundown, evening, close of day, semi-darkness, gloom; *literary* gloaming.
- OPPOSITES dawn.

dust *noun* **dirt**, grime, grit, powder, particles.
● *verb* **1 wipe**, clean, brush, sweep. **2** *dust the cake with icing sugar* **sprinkle**, scatter, powder, dredge, sift, cover.

dusty *adjective* **1 dirty**, grimy, grubby. **2 powdery**, crumbly, chalky, granular, soft, gritty.

dutiful *adjective* **conscientious**, responsible, dedicated, devoted, attentive, obedient, deferential.
- OPPOSITES remiss.

duty *noun* **1** *a sense of duty* **responsibility**, obligation, commitment, allegiance, loyalty. **2** *it was his duty to attend the king* **job**, task, assignment, mission, function, role. **3 tax**, levy, tariff, excise, toll, rate.

dwarf *verb* **1 dominate**, tower over, loom over, overshadow. **2 overshadow**, outshine, surpass, exceed, outclass, outstrip, outdo, top.

dwell *verb* (*formal*) **reside**, live, be housed, lodge, stay; *informal* put up; *formal* abide.
□ **dwell on** linger over, mull over, muse on, brood about/over, think about, be preoccupied by, obsess about, harp on about.

dwindle *verb* **diminish**, decrease, reduce, lessen, shrink, wane.
- OPPOSITES increase.

dye *noun* **colouring**, dyestuff, pigment, tint, stain, wash.
● *verb* **colour**, tint, pigment, stain, wash.

dying *adjective* **1 terminally ill**, at death's door, on your deathbed, fading fast, not long for this world, moribund, in extremis. **2 declining**, vanishing, fading, waning; *informal* on the way out.

dynamic *adjective* **energetic**, spirited, active, lively, vigorous, forceful, high-powered, aggressive, enterprising; *informal* go-getting, go-ahead.

dynasty *noun* **family**, house, line, lineage, regime, empire.

Ee

each *adverb* **apiece**, per person, per head, per capita.

eager *adjective* **1 keen**, enthusiastic, avid, ardent, zealous, highly motivated, committed, earnest. **2** *we were eager for news* **anxious**, impatient, agog, longing, yearning, wishing, hoping; *informal* itching, dying, raring.
- OPPOSITES apathetic.

ear *noun* *he has an ear for a good song* **appreciation**, feel, instinct, intuition, sense.

> **WORD LINKS**
> **aural** relating to the ear

early *adjective* **1 advance**, initial, preliminary, first. **2 untimely**, premature, unseasonable. **3 primitive**, ancient, prehistoric, primeval. **4 prompt**, timely, quick, speedy.
- OPPOSITES late, overdue.
● *adverb* **1 in advance**, in good time, ahead of schedule, with time to spare, before the last moment. **2 prematurely**, before the usual time, too soon, ahead of schedule.
- OPPOSITES late.

earmark *verb* **set aside**, keep (back), reserve, designate, assign, allocate.

earn *verb* **1 be paid**, take home, gross, receive, get, make, collect, bring in; *informal* pocket, bank. **2 deserve**, merit, warrant, justify, be worthy of, gain, win, secure, obtain.
- OPPOSITES lose.

earnest *adjective* **1 serious**, solemn, grave, sober, humourless, staid, intense. **2 devout**, heartfelt, wholehearted, sincere, impassioned, fervent, intense.
- OPPOSITES frivolous, half-hearted.

earnings *plural noun* **income**, pay, wages, salary, stipend, remuneration, fees, revenue, yield, profit, takings, proceeds.

earth *noun* **1 world**, globe, planet. **2 land**, ground, terra firma, floor. **3 soil**, clay, dust, dirt, loam, ground, turf.

> **WORD LINKS**
> **terrestrial** relating to the earth
> **geography**, **geology** study of the earth

earthly *adjective* **worldly**, temporal, mortal, human, material, carnal, fleshly, bodily, physical, corporeal, sensual.
- OPPOSITES spiritual, heavenly.

earthquake *noun* **(earth) tremor**, shock, convulsion; *informal* quake.

> **WORD LINKS**
> **seismic** relating to earthquakes
> **seismology** study of earthquakes

earthy *adjective* **1 down-to-earth**, unsophisticated, unrefined, simple, plain, unpretentious, natural. **2 bawdy**, ribald, racy, rude, crude, coarse, indelicate, indecent; *informal* raunchy; *Brit. informal* fruity.

ease *noun* **1 effortlessness**, no trouble, simplicity. **2 naturalness**, casualness, informality, composure, nonchalance, insouciance. **3 affluence**, wealth, prosperity, luxury, plenty, comfort, enjoyment, well-being.
- OPPOSITES difficulty.
● *verb* **1 relieve**, alleviate, soothe, moderate, dull, deaden, numb. **2** *the rain eased off* **let up**, abate, subside, die down, slacken off, diminish, lessen. **3 calm**, quieten, pacify, soothe, comfort, console. **4 slide**, slip, squeeze, guide, manoeuvre, inch, edge.
- OPPOSITES aggravate, intensify.

easily *adverb* **effortlessly**, comfortably, simply, without difficulty, readily, without a hitch.

easy *adjective* **1 uncomplicated**, undemanding, effortless, painless, trouble-free, simple, straightforward, elementary, plain sailing; *informal* a piece of cake, child's play, a cinch. **2 natural**, casual, informal, unceremonious, unreserved, unaffected, easy-going, amiable, affable, genial, good-humoured, carefree, nonchalant, unconcerned; *informal* laid-back. **3 quiet**, tranquil, serene, peaceful, untroubled, contented, relaxed, comfortable, secure, safe; *informal* cushy. **4 an easy pace leisurely**, unhurried, comfortable, undemanding, easy-going, gentle, sedate, moderate, steady.
- OPPOSITES difficult, demanding.

easy-going *adjective* **relaxed**, even-tempered, placid, happy-go-lucky, carefree, imperturbable, undemanding, patient, tolerant, lenient, broad-minded, understanding; *informal* laid-back, unflappable.
- OPPOSITES intolerant.

eat *verb* **1 consume**, devour, swallow, partake of, munch, chomp; *informal* tuck into, put away. **2 have a meal**, feed, snack, breakfast, lunch, dine; *informal* graze.

eavesdrop *verb* **listen in**, spy, overhear; *informal* snoop, earwig.

ebb *verb* **1 recede**, go out, retreat. **2 diminish**, dwindle, wane, fade (away), peter out, decline, flag.
- OPPOSITES flow, increase.

ebullient *adjective* **exuberant**, buoyant, cheerful, cheery, merry, jolly, sunny, jaunty, animated, sparkling, vivacious, irrepressible; *informal* bubbly, bouncy, upbeat, chirpy, full of beans.
- OPPOSITES depressed.

eccentric *adjective* **unconventional**, abnormal, anomalous, odd, strange, peculiar, weird, bizarre, outlandish, idiosyncratic, quirky; *informal* oddball, kooky, cranky.
- OPPOSITES conventional.
● *noun* **oddity**, free spirit, misfit; *informal* oddball, weirdo.

echo *noun* **reverberation**, reflection, ringing, repetition, repeat.
● *verb* **1 reverberate**, resonate, resound, reflect, ring, vibrate. **2 repeat**, restate, reiterate, imitate, parrot, mimic, reproduce, recite.

eclipse *verb* **outshine**, overshadow, surpass, exceed, outclass, outstrip, outdo, transcend.

economic *adjective* **1 financial**, monetary, budgetary, commercial, fiscal. **2 profitable**, moneymaking, lucrative, remunerative, fruitful, productive.
- OPPOSITES unprofitable.

economical *adjective* **1 cheap**, inexpensive, low-cost, budget, economy, cut-price, bargain. **2 thrifty**, provident, prudent, sensible, frugal.
- OPPOSITES expensive, spendthrift.

economize *verb* **save (money)**, cut costs, cut back, make cutbacks, retrench, scrimp.

economy *noun* **1 wealth**, financial resources, financial management. **2 thrift**, thriftiness, prudence, careful budgeting, economizing, saving, restraint, frugality.
- OPPOSITES extravagance.

ecstasy *noun* **rapture**, bliss, joy, elation, euphoria, rhapsodies.
- OPPOSITES misery.

ecstatic *adjective* **enraptured**, elated, euphoric, rapturous, joyful, overjoyed, blissful; *informal* over the moon, on top of the world.

eddy *noun* **swirl**, whirlpool, vortex.
● *verb* **swirl**, whirl, spiral, wind, twist.

edge *noun* **1 border**, boundary, extremity, fringe, margin, side, lip, rim, brim, brink, verge, perimeter. **2 sharpness**, severity, bite, sting, sarcasm, malice, spite, venom. **3 advantage**, lead, head start, the whip hand, the upper hand, dominance.
- OPPOSITES middle.
● *verb* **1 border**, fringe, skirt, surround, enclose, encircle, bound. **2 trim**, decorate, finish, border, fringe. **3 creep**, inch, work your way, ease yourself, sidle, steal.

edgy *adjective* **tense**, nervous, on edge, anxious, apprehensive, uneasy, unsettled, twitchy, jumpy, nervy, keyed up, restive; *informal* uptight, wired.
- OPPOSITES calm.

edit *verb* **correct**, check, copy-edit, improve, polish, modify, adapt, revise, rewrite, reword, shorten, condense, cut, abridge; censor, redact, suppress.

edition *noun* **issue**, number, volume, printing, impression, publication, programme, version.

educate *verb* **teach**, school, tutor, instruct, coach, train, inform, enlighten.

educated *adjective* **informed**, literate, schooled, tutored, well read, learned, knowledgeable, enlightened, intellectual, academic, erudite, scholarly, cultivated, cultured.
- OPPOSITES uneducated.

education *noun* **1 teaching**, schooling, tuition, tutoring, instruction, coaching, training, guidance, enlightenment. **2 learning**, knowledge, literacy, scholarship, enlightenment.

educational *adjective* **1 academic**, scholastic, learning, teaching, pedagogic. **2 instructive**, instructional, educative, informative, illuminating, enlightening; *formal* edifying.

eerie *adjective* **uncanny**, sinister, ghostly, unnatural, unearthly, supernatural, other-worldly, strange, abnormal, weird, freakish; *informal* creepy, scary, spooky.

effect *noun* **1** *the effect of these changes* **result**, consequence, upshot, outcome, repercussions, end result, aftermath, footprint. **2** *the effect of the drug* **impact**, action, effectiveness, power, potency, strength, success. **3** *the dead man's effects* **belongings**, possessions, worldly goods, chattels, property; *informal* things, stuff; *Brit. informal* clobber.
- OPPOSITES cause.
● *verb* **achieve**, accomplish, carry out, manage, bring off, execute, conduct, engineer, perform, do, cause, bring about, produce.

effective *adjective* **1 successful**, effectual, potent, powerful, helpful, beneficial, advantageous, valuable, useful. **2 convincing**, compelling, strong, forceful, persuasive, plausible, credible, logical, reasonable, cogent. **3 operative**, in force, in effect, valid, official, legal, binding. **4 virtual**, practical, essential, actual.
- OPPOSITES ineffective.

effervescent *adjective* **fizzy**, sparkling, carbonated, aerated, gassy, bubbly.
- OPPOSITES still.

efficiency *noun* **1 economy**, productivity, cost-effectiveness, organization, order, orderliness, regulation. **2 competence**, capability, ability, proficiency, expertise, skill, effectiveness.
- OPPOSITES inefficiency, incompetence.

efficient *adjective* **1 economic**, productive, effective, cost-effective, streamlined, organized, methodical, systematic, orderly. **2 competent**, capable, able, proficient, skilful, skilled, effective, productive, organized, businesslike.
- OPPOSITES inefficient, incompetent.

effort *noun* **1 attempt**, try, endeavour; *informal* shot, stab, bash. **2 achievement**, accomplishment, feat, undertaking, enterprise, work, result, outcome. **3 exertion**, energy, work, application; *informal* elbow grease; *Brit. informal* graft.

egg *noun* **ovum**, gamete; **(eggs)** roe, spawn.
□ **egg on** urge, goad, incite, provoke, push, drive, spur on, prod.

> **WORD LINKS**
> **ovoid** egg-shaped

egotistic, egoistic *adjective* **self-centred**, selfish, egocentric, self-interested, self-seeking, self-absorbed, self-obsessed, narcissistic, vain, conceited, self-important, boastful.

eject *verb* **1 emit**, spew out, discharge, disgorge, give off, send out, belch, vent. **2 expel**, throw out, remove, oust, evict, banish; *informal* kick out, turf out, boot out.

elaborate *adjective* **1 complicated**, complex, intricate, involved, detailed. **2 ornate**, decorated, embellished, adorned, ornamented, fancy, fussy, busy.
- OPPOSITES simple, plain.
● *verb* **expand on**, enlarge on, add to, flesh out, develop, fill out, amplify.

elastic *adjective* **1 stretchy**, elasticated, springy, flexible, pliable, supple. **2 adaptable**, flexible, adjustable, accommodating, variable, fluid, versatile.
- OPPOSITES rigid.

elated *adjective* **thrilled**, delighted, overjoyed, ecstatic, euphoric, jubilant, rapturous, in raptures, walking on air, on cloud nine, in seventh heaven; *informal* on top of the world, over the moon, tickled pink.
- OPPOSITES miserable.

elder *adjective* **older**, senior.
● *noun* **leader**, patriarch, father.

elderly *adjective* **aged**, old, ageing, long in the tooth, grey-haired, in your dotage; *informal* getting on, over the hill.
- OPPOSITES youthful.

elect *verb* **1 vote in**, vote for, return, cast your vote for, choose, pick, select. **2 choose**, decide, opt, prefer, vote.

election *noun* **ballot**, vote, poll; *Brit.* by-election; *US* primary.

> **WORD LINKS**
> **psephology** study of elections

electric *adjective* the atmosphere was electric **exciting**, charged, electrifying, thrilling, dramatic, dynamic, stimulating, galvanizing.

electrify *verb* **excite**, thrill, stimulate, arouse, rouse, inspire, stir (up), exhilarate, galvanize, fire (with enthusiasm), fire someone's imagination, invigorate, animate; *N. Amer.* light a fire under.

elegance *noun* **1 style**, grace, taste, sophistication, refinement, dignity, poise. **2 neatness**, simplicity, aptness.

elegant *adjective* **1 stylish**, graceful, tasteful, sophisticated, classic, chic, smart, poised, cultivated, polished, cultured. **2** *an elegant solution* **neat**, simple, apt.
- OPPOSITES inelegant.

element *noun* **1 component**, constituent, part, section, portion, piece, segment, aspect, factor, feature, facet, ingredient, strand, detail, member. **2 trace**, touch, hint, smattering, soupçon. **3** (**elements**) **weather**, climate, weather conditions.

elementary *adjective* **1** *an elementary astronomy course* **basic**, rudimentary, preparatory, introductory. **2** *a lot of the work is elementary* **easy**, simple, straightforward, uncomplicated, undemanding, painless, child's play, plain sailing; *informal* a piece of cake.
- OPPOSITES advanced, difficult.

elevate *verb* **1 raise**, lift (up), raise up/aloft, hoist, hike up, haul up. **2 promote**, upgrade, move up, raise; *informal* kick upstairs.
- OPPOSITES lower, demote.

elevated *adjective* **1 raised**, overhead, in the air, high up. **2 lofty**, grand, fine, sublime, inflated, pompous, bombastic. **3 high**, high-ranking, lofty, exalted, grand, noble.

elicit *verb* **obtain**, draw out, extract, bring out, evoke, induce, prompt, generate, trigger, provoke.

eligible *adjective* **1 entitled**, permitted, allowed, qualified, able. **2 desirable**, suitable, available, single, unmarried, unattached.

eliminate *verb* **1 remove**, get rid of, put an end to, do away with, end, stop, eradicate, destroy, stamp out. **2 knock out**, exclude, rule out, disqualify.

elite *noun* **best**, pick, cream, crème de la crème, A-list, flower, high society, beautiful people, aristocracy, ruling class.
- OPPOSITES dregs.

eloquent *adjective* **articulate**, fluent, expressive, persuasive, well expressed,

effective, lucid, vivid.
- OPPOSITES inarticulate.

elude verb **evade**, avoid, get away from, dodge, escape from, lose, shake off, give the slip to, slip away from, throw off the scent.

elusive adjective **1 difficult to find**, evasive, slippery. **2 indefinable**, intangible, impalpable, fugitive, fleeting, transitory, ambiguous.

emaciated adjective **thin**, skeletal, bony, gaunt, wasted, thin as a rake, scrawny, skinny, scraggy, skin and bone, starved, cadaverous, shrivelled, shrunken, withered.
- OPPOSITES fat.

embargo noun **ban**, bar, prohibition, stoppage, veto, moratorium, restriction, block, boycott.
● verb **ban**, bar, prohibit, stop, outlaw, blacklist, restrict, block, boycott.
- OPPOSITES allow.

embark verb **board (ship)**, go on board, go aboard; informal hop on, jump on.
- OPPOSITES disembark.
□ **embark on** begin, start, undertake, set out on, take up, turn your hand to, get down to, enter into, venture into, launch into, plunge into, engage in.

embarrass verb **humiliate**, shame, put someone to shame, abash, mortify, fluster, discomfit; informal show up.

embarrassed adjective **humiliated**, mortified, red-faced, blushing, abashed, shamed, ashamed, shamefaced, self-conscious, uncomfortable, discomfited, disconcerted, flustered; informal with egg on your face.

embarrassing adjective **humiliating**, shameful, mortifying, ignominious, awkward, uncomfortable, compromising; informal cringeworthy, cringemaking, toe-curling.

embarrassment noun **1 humiliation**, mortification, shame, shamefacedness, awkwardness, self-consciousness, discomfort, discomfiture. **2 difficulty**, predicament, plight, problem, mess; informal bind, pickle, fix.

embellish verb **decorate**, adorn, ornament, beautify, enhance, trim, garnish, gild, deck, bedeck, festoon, emblazon.

embezzle verb **misappropriate**, steal, thieve, pilfer, purloin, appropriate, siphon off, pocket; informal filch; Brit. informal pinch, nick.

emblem noun **symbol**, representation, token, image, figure, mark, sign, crest, badge, device, insignia, coat of arms, shield, logo, trademark.

embody verb **1 personify**, manifest, symbolize, represent, express, epitomize, stand for, typify, exemplify. **2 incorporate**, include, contain.

embrace verb **1 hug**, take/hold in your arms, hold, cuddle, clasp to your bosom, squeeze, clutch, enfold. **2 welcome**, welcome with open arms, accept, take on board, take up, take to your heart, adopt, espouse. **3 include**, take in, comprise, contain, incorporate, encompass, cover, subsume.
● noun **hug**, cuddle, squeeze, clinch, caress.

emerge verb **1 appear**, come out, come into view, become visible, surface, materialize, issue, come forth. **2 become known**, become apparent, be revealed, come to light, come out, turn up, transpire, unfold, turn out, prove to be the case.

emergence noun **appearance**, arrival, coming, materialization, advent, inception, dawn, birth, origination, start, development.

emergency noun **crisis**, disaster, catastrophe, calamity, plight; informal panic stations.
● adjective **1 urgent**, crisis, extraordinary. **2 reserve**, standby, backup, fallback.

emigrate verb **move abroad**, move overseas, leave your country, migrate, relocate, resettle.
- OPPOSITES immigrate.

eminent adjective **illustrious**, distinguished, renowned, esteemed, pre-eminent, notable, noted, noteworthy,

e

great, prestigious, important, outstanding, celebrated, prominent, well known, acclaimed, exalted.
- OPPOSITES unknown.

emission noun **discharge**, release, outpouring, outflow, outrush, leak.

emit verb **1 discharge**, release, give out/off, pour out, radiate, leak, ooze, disgorge, eject, belch, spew out, exude. **2 utter**, voice, let out, produce, give vent to, come out with.

emotion noun **1 feeling**, sentiment, reaction, response, instinct, intuition. **2 passion**, strength of feeling, heart.

emotional adjective **1 passionate**, hot-blooded, ardent, fervent, warm, responsive, excitable, temperamental, demonstrative, sensitive. **2 poignant**, moving, touching, affecting, powerful, stirring, emotive, impassioned, dramatic; informal tear-jerking.
- OPPOSITES cold, clinical.

emphasis noun **1 prominence**, importance, significance, value, stress, weight, accent, attention, priority. **2** the emphasis is on the word 'little' **stress**, accent, weight, beat.

emphasize verb **stress**, underline, highlight, focus attention on, point up, lay stress on, draw attention to, spotlight, foreground.
- OPPOSITES understate.

emphatic adjective **forceful**, firm, vehement, wholehearted, energetic, vigorous, direct, insistent, certain, definite, out-and-out, decided, categorical, unqualified, unconditional, unequivocal, unambiguous, absolute, explicit, downright, outright, clear.

empire noun **1 kingdom**, realm, domain, territory, commonwealth, power. **2 business**, firm, company, corporation, multinational, conglomerate, group, consortium, operation.

> WORD LINKS
> **imperial** relating to an empire

employ verb **1 hire**, engage, recruit, take on, sign up, appoint, retain. **2 occupy**, engage, involve, keep busy, tie up. **3 use**, utilize, make use of, apply, exercise, practise, put into practice, exert, bring into play, bring to bear, draw on, resort to, turn to, have recourse to.
- OPPOSITES dismiss.

employed adjective **working**, in work, in employment, holding down a job, earning, salaried, waged.
- OPPOSITES unemployed.

employee noun **worker**, member of staff, blue-collar worker, white-collar worker, workman, labourer, hand; (**employees**) personnel, staff, workforce.

employment noun **work**, labour, service, job, post, position, situation, occupation, profession, trade, business, line of work.

empower verb **1 authorize**, entitle, permit, allow, license, enable. **2 emancipate**, unshackle, set free, liberate, enfranchise.
- OPPOSITES forbid.

empty adjective **1 vacant**, unoccupied, uninhabited, bare, clear, free. **2 meaningless**, hollow, idle, vain, futile, worthless, useless, ineffectual. **3 futile**, pointless, purposeless, worthless, meaningless, fruitless, valueless, of no value, senseless.
- OPPOSITES full, occupied.
● verb **1 unload**, unpack, clear, evacuate, drain. **2 remove**, take out, extract, tip out, pour out.
- OPPOSITES fill, replace.

emulate verb **imitate**, copy, mirror, echo, follow, model yourself on, take a leaf out of someone's book.

enable verb **allow**, permit, let, equip, empower, make able, fit, authorize, entitle, qualify.
- OPPOSITES prevent.

enact verb **1 make law**, pass, approve, ratify, validate, sanction, authorize. **2 act out**, perform, appear in, stage, mount, put on, present.
- OPPOSITES repeal.

enchanting adjective **captivating**, charming, delightful, adorable, lovely, attractive, appealing, engaging, fetching, irresistible, fascinating.

enclose *verb* **1 surround**, circle, ring, encircle, bound, close in, wall in. **2 include**, insert, put in, send.

> **WORD LINKS**
> **claustrophobia** fear of enclosed spaces

enclosure *noun* **compound**, pen, fold, stockade, ring, paddock, yard, run, coop; *N. Amer.* corral.

encompass *verb* **include**, cover, embrace, incorporate, take in, contain, comprise, involve, deal with.

encounter *verb* **1 experience**, run into, meet, come up against, face, be faced with, confront, suffer. **2 meet**, run into, come across/upon, stumble across/on, chance on, happen on; *informal* bump into.
● *noun* **1 meeting**, chance meeting. **2 battle**, fight, skirmish, clash, scuffle, confrontation, struggle; *informal* run-in, set-to, scrap.

encourage *verb* **1 hearten**, cheer, buoy up, uplift, inspire, motivate, spur on, stir, fire up, stimulate, embolden; *informal* buck up. **2** *she encouraged him to go* **persuade**, coax, urge, press, push, pressure, prod, egg on. **3 support**, back, promote, further, foster, nurture, cultivate, strengthen, stimulate.
- OPPOSITES discourage.

encouragement *noun* **1 support**, cheering up, inspiration, motivation, stimulation, morale-boosting; *informal* a shot in the arm. **2 persuasion**, coaxing, urging, prodding, prompting, inducement, incentive, carrot. **3 backing**, sponsorship, support, promotion, furtherance, fostering, nurture, cultivation, stimulation.

encouraging *adjective* **1 promising**, hopeful, auspicious, favourable, heartening, reassuring, cheering, comforting, welcome, pleasing, gratifying. **2 supportive**, understanding, helpful, positive, enthusiastic.

end *noun* **1 conclusion**, termination, ending, finish, close, resolution, climax, finale, culmination, denouement. **2 extremity**, limit, edge, border, boundary, periphery, point, tip, head, top, bottom. **3 aim**, goal, purpose, objective, object, target, intention, aspiration, wish, desire, ambition.
- OPPOSITES beginning, means.
● *verb* **1 finish**, conclude, terminate, close, stop, cease, culminate, climax. **2 break off**, call off, bring to an end, put an end to, stop, finish, terminate, discontinue, cancel.
- OPPOSITES begin.

endanger *verb* **jeopardize**, risk, put at risk, put in danger, be a danger to, threaten, compromise, imperil.
- OPPOSITES safeguard.

endearing *adjective* **charming**, appealing, attractive, engaging, winning, captivating, enchanting, cute, sweet, delightful, lovely.

endeavour *verb* **try**, attempt, seek, strive, struggle, labour, toil, work.
● *noun* **1 attempt**, try, bid, effort. **2 undertaking**, enterprise, venture, exercise, activity, exploit, deed, act, action, move.

ending *noun* **end**, finish, close, conclusion, resolution, summing-up, denouement, finale.
- OPPOSITES beginning.

endless *adjective* **1 unlimited**, limitless, infinite, inexhaustible, boundless, unbounded, ceaseless, unending, everlasting, constant, continuous, interminable, unfailing, perpetual, eternal, never-ending. **2 countless**, innumerable, numerous, a multitude of; *informal* umpteen, no end of; *literary* myriad.
- OPPOSITES limited, few.

endorse *verb* **support**, back, agree with, approve (of), favour, subscribe to, recommend, champion, uphold, sanction.
- OPPOSITES oppose.

endorsement *noun* **support**, backing, approval, seal of approval, agreement, recommendation, patronage, sanction.

endow verb **1 finance**, fund, pay for, subsidize, sponsor. **2** *he was endowed with great strength* **provide**, supply, furnish, equip, favour, bless, grace.

endowment noun **gift**, present, grant, funding, award, donation, contribution, subsidy, sponsorship, bequest, legacy.

endurance noun **1 toleration**, tolerance, forbearance, patience, acceptance, resignation, stoicism. **2 resistance**, durability, permanence, longevity, strength, toughness, stamina, staying power, fortitude.

endure verb **1 undergo**, go through, live through, experience, cope with, deal with, face, suffer, tolerate, put up with, brave, bear, withstand. **2 last**, live, live on, go on, survive, abide, continue, persist, remain.

enemy noun **opponent**, adversary, rival, nemesis, antagonist, combatant, challenger, competitor, opposition, competition, the other side; *literary* foe.
- OPPOSITES friend, ally.

energetic adjective **1** *an energetic woman* **active**, lively, dynamic, spirited, animated, bouncy, bubbly, sprightly, tireless, indefatigable, enthusiastic; *informal* full of beans. **2** *energetic exercises* **vigorous**, strenuous, brisk, hard, arduous, demanding, taxing, tough, rigorous. **3** *an energetic advertising campaign* **forceful**, vigorous, aggressive, hard-hitting, high-powered, all-out, determined, bold, intensive; *informal* in-your-face.
- OPPOSITES lethargic.

energy noun **vitality**, vigour, strength, stamina, animation, spirit, verve, enthusiasm, zest, exuberance, dynamism, drive; *informal* punch, bounce, oomph, go, get-up-and-go.

enforce verb **1 impose**, apply, administer, carry out, implement, bring to bear, put into effect. **2 force**, compel, coerce, exact.

engage verb **1 capture**, catch, arrest, grab, draw, attract, gain, hold, grip, absorb, occupy. **2 employ**, hire, recruit, take on, enrol, appoint. **3** *the chance to engage in a wide range of pursuits* **participate in**, join in, take part in, partake in/of, enter into, embark on. **4 attack**, fall on, take on, clash with, encounter, meet, fight, do battle with.
- OPPOSITES lose, dismiss.

engagement noun **1 appointment**, meeting, arrangement, commitment, date, assignation, rendezvous. **2 participation**, involvement. **3 battle**, fight, clash, confrontation, encounter, conflict, skirmish, action, hostilities.

engaging adjective **charming**, attractive, appealing, pleasing, pleasant, agreeable, likeable, lovable, sweet, winning, fetching; *Scottish & N. English* bonny.
- OPPOSITES unappealing.

engender verb **cause**, give rise to, bring about, occasion, lead to, result in, produce, create, generate, arouse, rouse, inspire, provoke, kindle, trigger, spark, stir up, whip up.

engine noun **motor**, generator, machine, turbine.

engineer noun **1** *a structural engineer* **designer**, planner, builder. **2** *a repair engineer* **mechanic**, repairer, technician, maintenance man, operator, driver.
● verb **bring about**, arrange, pull off, bring off, contrive, manoeuvre, negotiate, organize, orchestrate, plan, mastermind.

engraving noun **etching**, print, plate, picture, illustration, inscription.

engrossed adjective **absorbed**, involved, interested, occupied, preoccupied, immersed, caught up, riveted, gripped, rapt, fascinated, intent, captivated, enthralled.

engulf verb **swamp**, inundate, flood, deluge, immerse, swallow up, submerge, bury, envelop, overwhelm.

enhance verb **improve**, add to, strengthen, boost, increase, intensify, heighten, magnify, amplify, inflate, build up, supplement, augment.
- OPPOSITES diminish.

enjoy verb **1 like**, be fond of, take pleasure in, be keen on, delight in, relish, revel in, adore, lap up, savour, luxuriate in, bask in; *informal* get a thrill out of. **2 benefit from**, be blessed with, be favoured with, be endowed with, possess, own, boast.
- OPPOSITES dislike, lack.
□ **enjoy yourself** have fun, have a good time, make merry, celebrate, revel; *informal* party, have a whale of a time, let your hair down.

enjoyable adjective **entertaining**, amusing, delightful, pleasant, congenial, convivial, agreeable, pleasurable, satisfying.
- OPPOSITES disagreeable.

enjoyment noun **pleasure**, fun, entertainment, amusement, recreation, relaxation, happiness, merriment, joy, satisfaction, liking.

enlarge verb **1 extend**, expand, grow, add to, amplify, augment, magnify, build up, stretch, widen, broaden, lengthen, elongate, deepen, thicken. **2 swell**, distend, bloat, bulge, dilate, blow up, puff up.
- OPPOSITES reduce, shrink.
□ **enlarge on** elaborate on, expand on, add to, flesh out, add detail to, develop, fill out, embellish, embroider.

enlighten verb **inform**, tell, make aware, open someone's eyes, illuminate; *informal* put someone in the picture.

enlightened adjective **informed**, aware, sophisticated, liberal, open-minded, broad-minded, educated, knowledgeable, civilized, refined, cultured.
- OPPOSITES benighted.

enlightenment noun **insight**, understanding, awareness, education, learning, knowledge, illumination, awakening, instruction, teaching, open-mindedness, broad-mindedness, culture, refinement, cultivation, civilization.

enlist verb **1 join up**, enrol, sign up for, volunteer, register. **2 recruit**, call up,

enrol, sign up, conscript, mobilize; *US* draft. **3 obtain**, engage, secure, win, get.
- OPPOSITES discharge, demobilize.

enormity noun **1 wickedness**, vileness, heinousness, baseness, depravity, outrageousness. **2 immensity**, hugeness, size, extent, magnitude.

enormous adjective **huge**, vast, immense, gigantic, giant, massive, colossal, mammoth, tremendous, extensive, mighty, monumental, mountainous, cosmic; *informal* mega, monster, whopping; *Brit. informal* ginormous.
- OPPOSITES tiny.

enough determiner **sufficient**, adequate, ample, abundant, the necessary; *informal* plenty of.
- OPPOSITES insufficient.
● pronoun **sufficient**, plenty, an adequate amount, as much as necessary, a sufficiency, an ample supply, your fill.

enquire verb **1 ask**, query, question. **2 investigate**, probe, look into, make enquiries, research, examine, explore, delve into; *informal* check out.

enquiry noun **1 question**, query. **2 investigation**, probe, examination, exploration, inquest, hearing.

enrage verb **anger**, infuriate, incense, madden, inflame, antagonize, provoke; *informal* drive mad/crazy, make someone see red, make someone's blood boil.
- OPPOSITES placate.

enraged adjective **furious**, infuriated, irate, incensed, raging, incandescent, fuming, seething, beside yourself; *informal* mad, livid, foaming at the mouth.

enrich verb **enhance**, improve, better, add to, augment, supplement, complement, refine.

enrol verb **1 register**, sign on/up, put your name down, apply, volunteer, enter, join. **2 accept**, admit, take on, sign on/up, recruit, engage.

ensemble noun **1 group**, band, company, troupe, cast, chorus, corps;

informal combo. **2 whole**, unit, body, set, collection, combination, composite, package. **3 outfit**, costume, suit; informal get-up.

ensue verb **result**, follow, develop, succeed, emerge, arise, proceed, stem.

ensure verb **1 make sure**, make certain, see to it, check, confirm, establish, verify. **2 secure**, guarantee, assure, certify.

entail verb **involve**, necessitate, require, need, demand, call for, mean, imply, cause, give rise to, occasion.

enter verb **1 go into**, come into, get into, set foot in, gain access to. **2 penetrate**, pierce, puncture, perforate. **3 join**, enrol in/for, enlist in, volunteer for, sign up for. **4 go in for**, register for, enrol for, sign on/up for, compete in, take part in, participate in. **5 record**, write, put down, take down, note, jot down, register, log. **6 key (in)**, type (in), tap in.
– OPPOSITES leave.

enterprise noun **1 undertaking**, endeavour, venture, exercise, activity, operation, task, business, project, scheme. **2 initiative**, resourcefulness, imagination, ingenuity, inventiveness, originality, creativity. **3 business**, company, firm, venture, organization, operation, concern, establishment; informal outfit.

enterprising adjective **resourceful**, entrepreneurial, imaginative, ingenious, inventive, creative, adventurous, bold; informal go-ahead.

entertain verb **1 amuse**, please, charm, cheer, interest, engage, occupy. **2 receive**, play host/hostess to, throw a party for, wine and dine, feed, fete. **3 consider**, contemplate, think of, hear of, countenance.
– OPPOSITES bore, reject.

entertainment noun **amusement**, pleasure, leisure, recreation, relaxation, fun, enjoyment, diversion, interest.

enthralling adjective **fascinating**, entrancing, enchanting, bewitching, captivating, delightful, absorbing,

engrossing, compelling, riveting, gripping, exciting; informal unputdownable.

enthusiasm noun **keenness**, eagerness, passion, fervour, zeal, zest, gusto, energy, vigour, fire, spirit, interest, commitment, devotion; informal get-up-and-go.
– OPPOSITES apathy.

enthusiast noun **fan**, devotee, supporter, follower, aficionado, lover, admirer; informal buff.

enthusiastic adjective **keen**, eager, avid, ardent, fervent, passionate, zealous, excited, wholehearted, committed, devoted, fanatical, earnest.
– OPPOSITES apathetic.

entice verb **tempt**, lure, attract, appeal to, invite, persuade, beguile, coax, woo, lead on, seduce; informal sweet-talk.

entire adjective **whole**, complete, total, full.

entirely adverb **1 absolutely**, completely, totally, wholly, utterly, quite, altogether, thoroughly. **2 solely**, only, exclusively, purely, merely, just, alone.

entitle verb **1 qualify**, make eligible, authorize, allow, permit, enable, empower. **2 name**, title, call, label, designate, dub.

entity noun **being**, creature, individual, organism, life form, body, object, article, thing.

entrance[1] noun **1 entry**, way in, access, approach, door, portal, gate, opening, mouth, foyer, lobby, porch; N. Amer. entryway. **2 appearance**, arrival, entry, coming. **3 admission**, admittance, (right of) entry, entrée, access.
– OPPOSITES exit, departure.

entrance[2] verb **enchant**, bewitch, beguile, captivate, mesmerize, hypnotize, spellbind, transfix, enthral, engross, absorb, fascinate, stun, electrify, charm, delight; informal bowl over, knock out.

entrant noun **competitor**, contestant, contender, participant, candidate, applicant.

entreat *verb* **implore**, beg, plead with, pray, ask, request, bid, enjoin, appeal to, call on; *literary* beseech.

entrenched, intrenched *adjective* **ingrained**, established, fixed, firm, deep-seated, deep-rooted, unshakeable, ineradicable.

entrust *verb* **1 charge**, give someone the responsibility for, present. **2 assign**, confer on, bestow on, vest in, delegate, give, grant, vouchsafe.

entry *noun* **1 appearance**, arrival, entrance, coming. **2 entrance**, way in, access, approach, door, portal, gate, entrance hall, foyer, lobby; *N. Amer.* entryway. **3 admission**, admittance, entrance, access. **4 item**, record, note, memo, memorandum. **5 submission**, application, entry form.
- OPPOSITES departure, exit.

envelop *verb* **surround**, cover, enfold, engulf, encircle, cocoon, sheathe, swathe, enclose, cloak, veil, shroud.

envious *adjective* **jealous**, covetous, desirous, grudging, begrudging, resentful; *informal* green with envy.

environment *noun* **1 situation**, setting, milieu, background, backdrop, context, conditions, ambience, atmosphere. **2 the natural world**, nature, the earth, the ecosystem, the biosphere, Mother Nature, wildlife, flora and fauna, the countryside.

> **WORD LINKS**
> **ecology** study of the environment

environmentalist *noun* **conservationist**, ecologist, nature-lover, green; *informal* eco-warrior, tree-hugger.

envisage *verb* **1 foresee**, predict, forecast, anticipate, expect, think likely. **2 imagine**, contemplate, picture, conceive of, think of.

envoy *noun* **ambassador**, emissary, diplomat, representative, delegate, spokesperson, agent, intermediary, mediator; *informal* go-between.

envy *noun* **jealousy**, covetousness, resentment, bitterness.

● *verb* **1 be envious of**, be jealous of, be resentful of. **2 covet**, desire, aspire to, wish for, want, long for, yearn for, hanker after, crave.

ephemeral *adjective* **transitory**, transient, fleeting, passing, short-lived, momentary, brief, short, temporary, impermanent, short-term.
- OPPOSITES permanent.

epidemic *noun* **1 outbreak**, plague, pandemic. **2 spate**, rash, wave, eruption, plague, outbreak, craze, upsurge.

episode *noun* **1 incident**, event, occurrence, chapter, experience, occasion, interlude, adventure, exploit. **2 instalment**, chapter, passage, part, portion, section, programme, show. **3 period**, spell, bout, attack, phase; *informal* dose.

epitome *noun* **personification**, embodiment, incarnation, essence, quintessence, archetype, paradigm, exemplar, model.

epoch *noun* **era**, age, period, time, aeon.

equal *adjective* **1 identical**, uniform, alike, like, the same, matching, equivalent, corresponding. **2 impartial**, non-partisan, fair, just, equitable, unprejudiced, non-discriminatory. **3 evenly matched**, even, balanced, level, nip and tuck, neck and neck; *informal* level pegging.
- OPPOSITES different, unequal.
● *noun* **equivalent**, peer, fellow, like, counterpart, match, parallel.
● *verb* **1 be equal to**, be equivalent to, be the same as, come to, amount to, make, total, add up to. **2 match**, reach, parallel, be level with.

equality *noun* **fairness**, equal rights, equal opportunities, impartiality, even-handedness, justice.

equanimity *noun* **composure**, calm, level-headedness, self-possession, presence of mind, serenity, tranquillity, imperturbability, equilibrium, poise, aplomb, sangfroid, nerve; *informal* cool.
- OPPOSITES anxiety.

equate verb **1** *he equates criticism with treachery* **identify**, compare, bracket, class, associate, connect, link, relate. **2 equalize**, balance, even out/up, level, square, tally, match.

equilibrium noun **balance**, stability, poise, symmetry, harmony.
- OPPOSITES imbalance.

equip verb **1** *the boat was equipped with a flare gun* **provide**, furnish, supply, issue, kit out, stock, provision, arm. **2** *the course will equip them for the workplace* **prepare**, qualify, ready, suit, train.

equipment noun **apparatus**, kit, paraphernalia, tools, utensils, implements, hardware, gadgetry, things; *informal* stuff, gear.

equivalent adjective **comparable**, corresponding, commensurate, similar, parallel, analogous.
● noun **counterpart**, parallel, alternative, analogue, twin, opposite number.

equivocal adjective **ambiguous**, indefinite, non-committal, vague, imprecise, inexact, inexplicit, hazy, unclear, ambivalent, uncertain, unsure.
- OPPOSITES definite.

era noun **age**, epoch, period, time, date, day, generation.

eradicate verb **eliminate**, get rid of, remove, obliterate, extinguish, exterminate, destroy, annihilate, kill, wipe out.

erase verb **delete**, rub out, wipe off, blank out, expunge, excise, remove, obliterate, redact.

erect adjective **upright**, straight, vertical, perpendicular, standing (on end), bristling, stiff.
● verb **build**, construct, put up, assemble, put together, fabricate, raise.
- OPPOSITES demolish, dismantle.

erode verb **wear away**, abrade, grind down, crumble, weather, undermine, weaken, deteriorate, destroy.

erosion noun **wearing away**, abrasion, attrition, weathering, dissolution, deterioration, disintegration, destruction.

erotic adjective **sexually arousing**, sexually stimulating, titillating, suggestive, pornographic, sexually explicit; *informal* blue, X-rated; *euphemistic* adult.

errand noun **task**, job, chore, assignment, mission.

erratic adjective **unpredictable**, inconsistent, changeable, variable, inconstant, irregular, fitful, unstable, varying, fluctuating, unreliable.
- OPPOSITES consistent.

error noun **mistake**, inaccuracy, miscalculation, blunder, slip, oversight, misconception, delusion, misprint; *Brit. informal* boob.

erupt verb *fighting erupted* **break out**, flare up, blow up, explode, burst out.

eruption noun **1 discharge**, explosion, lava flow, pyroclastic flow. **2 outbreak**, flare-up, upsurge, outburst, explosion, wave, spate.

escalate verb **1 increase rapidly**, soar, rocket, shoot up, spiral; *informal* go through the roof. **2 grow**, develop, mushroom, increase, heighten, intensify, accelerate.
- OPPOSITES plunge, subside.

escape verb **1 run away**, run off, get away, break out, break free, bolt, make your getaway, slip away, abscond; *informal* vamoose, skedaddle, fly the coop; *Brit. informal* do a runner, do a bunk. **2** *he escaped his pursuers* **get away from**, elude, avoid, dodge, shake off; *informal* give someone the slip. **3** *they cannot escape their duties* **avoid**, evade, elude, cheat, sidestep, circumvent, steer clear of, shirk. **4 leak (out)**, spill (out), seep (out), discharge, flow (out), pour (out).
● noun **1 getaway**, breakout, flight. **2 leak**, spill, seepage, discharge, outflow, outpouring.

escort noun **guard**, bodyguard, protector, minder, attendant, chaperone, entourage, retinue, protection, convoy.
● verb **1 conduct**, accompany, guide, usher, shepherd, take, lead. **2 partner**, accompany, chaperone.

esoteric adjective **abstruse**, obscure, arcane, rarefied, recondite, abstract, enigmatic, cryptic, complex, complicated, incomprehensible, impenetrable, mysterious.

especially *adverb* **1 mainly**, mostly, chiefly, particularly, principally, largely, primarily. **2** *a committee formed especially for the purpose* **expressly**, specially, specifically, exclusively, just, particularly, explicitly. **3** *he is especially talented* **exceptionally**, particularly, unusually, extraordinarily, uncommonly, uniquely, remarkably, outstandingly.

essay *noun* **article**, composition, paper, dissertation, thesis, discourse, study, assignment, treatise, piece, feature; *N. Amer.* theme.

essence *noun* **1 nature**, heart, core, substance, basis, principle, quintessence, soul, spirit, reality; *informal* nitty-gritty. **2 extract**, concentrate, elixir, juice, oil.

essential *adjective* **1 crucial**, key, vital, indispensable, all-important, critical, imperative. **2 basic**, bare-bones, inherent, fundamental, quintessential, intrinsic, underlying, characteristic, innate, primary.
- OPPOSITES unimportant, incidental.
● *noun* **1 necessity**, prerequisite; *informal* must. **2** (**essentials**) **fundamentals**, basics, rudiments, first principles, foundations, essence, basis, core, kernel, crux; *informal* nitty-gritty, nuts and bolts.

establish *verb* **1 set up**, start, initiate, institute, found, create, inaugurate. **2 prove**, demonstrate, show, indicate, determine, confirm.

established *adjective* **accepted**, traditional, orthodox, set, fixed, official, usual, customary, common, normal, general, prevailing, accustomed, familiar, expected, conventional, standard.

establishment *noun* **1 foundation**, institution, formation, inception, creation, installation, inauguration. **2 business**, firm, company, concern, enterprise, venture, organization, operation; *informal* outfit. **3 institution**, place, premises, institute. **4** *criticism of*

the Establishment **the authorities**, the powers that be, the system, the ruling class.

estate *noun* **1 property**, grounds, garden(s), park, parkland, land(s), territory. **2** *an industrial estate* **area**, development, complex. **3 plantation**, farm, holding, forest, vineyard; *N. Amer.* ranch. **4 assets**, capital, wealth, riches, holdings, fortune, property, effects, possessions, belongings.

esteem *noun* **respect**, admiration, acclaim, appreciation, recognition, honour, reverence, estimation, regard.
● *verb* **respect**, admire, value, regard highly, appreciate, like, prize, treasure, revere.

estimate *verb* **1 calculate**, approximate, guess, evaluate, judge, assess, weigh up. **2 consider**, believe, reckon, deem, judge, rate.
● *noun* **calculation**, approximation, estimation, guess, assessment, evaluation, costing, quotation, valuation; *informal* guesstimate.

estrangement *noun* **alienation**, disaffection, parting, separation, divorce, break-up, split, breach.

etch *verb* **engrave**, carve, inscribe, incise, score, mark, scratch.

etching *noun* **engraving**, print, plate.

eternal *adjective* **everlasting**, neverending, endless, perpetual, undying, immortal, abiding, permanent, enduring, constant, continual, continuous, sustained, uninterrupted, unbroken, non-stop, round-the-clock.

eternity *noun* **1 ever**, all time, perpetuity. **2** (*informal*) **a long time**, an age, ages, a lifetime, hours, years, forever.

ethical *adjective* **moral**, morally correct, right-minded, principled, good, just, honourable, fair.

ethics *plural noun* **morals**, morality, values, principles, ideals, standards (of behaviour).

ethnic *adjective* **racial**, race-related, national, cultural, folk, tribal, ethnological.

e

euphoria noun **elation**, happiness, joy, delight, glee, excitement, exhilaration, jubilation, exultation, ecstasy, bliss, rapture.
- OPPOSITES misery.

evacuate verb **1 remove**, move out, take away. **2 leave**, vacate, abandon, move out of, quit, withdraw from, retreat from, flee. **3** *police evacuated the area* **clear**, empty.

evade verb **1 elude**, avoid, dodge, escape (from), steer clear of, sidestep, lose, leave behind, shake off; *informal* give someone the slip. **2 avoid**, dodge, sidestep, bypass, skirt round, fudge; *informal* duck, cop out of.
- OPPOSITES confront.

evaluate verb **assess**, judge, gauge, rate, estimate, appraise, weigh up; *informal* size up.

evaporate verb **1 vaporize**, dry up. **2 end**, pass (away), fizzle out, peter out, wear off, vanish, fade, disappear, melt away.
- OPPOSITES condense, materialize.

evasive adjective **equivocal**, prevaricating, elusive, ambiguous, non-committal, vague, unclear, oblique.

even adjective **1 flat**, smooth, uniform, level, plane. **2 uniform**, constant, steady, stable, consistent, unvarying, unchanging, regular. **3 all square**, drawn, tied, level, neck and neck, nip and tuck; *Brit.* level pegging; *informal* even-steven(s).
- OPPOSITES bumpy, irregular, unequal.

evening noun **dusk**, twilight, nightfall, sunset, sundown, night.

event noun **1 occurrence**, happening, incident, affair, occasion, phenomenon, function, gathering; *informal* do. **2 competition**, contest, tournament, match, fixture, tie, race, game, sport, discipline; *Brit.* clash.

eventful adjective **busy**, action-packed, full, lively, active, hectic.
- OPPOSITES dull.

eventual adjective **final**, ultimate, resulting, ensuing, consequent, subsequent.

eventually adverb **in the end**, in due course, by and by, in time, after a time, finally, at last, ultimately, in the long run, at the end of the day, one day, some day, sometime, sooner or later.

ever adverb **1 at any time**, at any point, on any occasion, under any circumstances, on any account, until now. **2 always**, forever, eternally, continually, constantly, endlessly, perpetually, incessantly.

everlasting adjective **eternal**, endless, never-ending, perpetual, undying, abiding, enduring, infinite.
- OPPOSITES transient, occasional.

everybody pronoun **everyone**, every person, each person, all, one and all, all and sundry, the whole world, the public.
- OPPOSITES nobody.

everyday adjective **1 daily**, day-to-day, ongoing; *formal* quotidian. **2 commonplace**, ordinary, common, usual, regular, familiar, conventional, routine, run-of-the-mill, standard, stock, household, domestic; *Brit.* common or garden.
- OPPOSITES unusual.

everyone pronoun see **everybody**.

everywhere adverb **all over**, all around, in every nook and cranny, far and wide, near and far, high and low, {here, there, and everywhere}, the world over, worldwide; *informal* all over the place; *Brit. informal* all over the shop; *N. Amer. informal* all over the map.
- OPPOSITES nowhere.

evict verb **expel**, eject, remove, dislodge, turn out, throw out, drive out, dispossess; *informal* chuck out, kick out, boot out, throw someone out on their ear; *Brit. informal* turf out.

evidence noun **1 proof**, confirmation, verification, substantiation, corroboration. **2 testimony**, witness statement, declaration, submission; *Law* deposition, affidavit. **3 signs**, indications, marks, traces, suggestions, hints.

evident *adjective* **obvious**, apparent, noticeable, conspicuous, visible, discernible, clear, plain, manifest, patent; *informal* as clear as day.

evidently *adverb* **1 obviously**, clearly, plainly, unmistakably, manifestly, patently. **2 seemingly**, apparently, as far as you can tell, from all appearances, on the face of it, it seems, it appears.

evil *adjective* **1** *an evil deed* **wicked**, bad, wrong, immoral, sinful, vile, iniquitous, villainous, vicious, malicious, malevolent, demonic, diabolical, fiendish, dark, monstrous. **2** *an evil spirit* **harmful**, bad, malign. **3 unpleasant**, disagreeable, nasty, horrible, foul, filthy, vile.
– OPPOSITES good, virtuous.
● *noun* **1** *the evil in our midst* **wickedness**, badness, wrongdoing, sin, sinfulness, immorality, vice, iniquity, corruption, villainy. **2** *nothing but evil will result* **harm**, pain, misery, sorrow, suffering, trouble, disaster, misfortune, woe.
– OPPOSITES good.

evoke *verb* **bring to mind**, put someone in mind of, conjure up, summon (up), invoke, elicit, induce, kindle, awaken, arouse.

evolution *noun* **1 development**, progress, rise, expansion, growth. **2 natural selection**, Darwinism, adaptation, development.

evolve *verb* **develop**, progress, advance, grow, expand, spread.

exacerbate *verb* **aggravate**, worsen, inflame, compound, intensify, increase, heighten, magnify, add to.
– OPPOSITES reduce.

exact *adjective* **1** *an exact description* **precise**, accurate, correct, faithful, close, true, literal, strict, perfect. **2** *an exact record keeper* **careful**, meticulous, painstaking, punctilious, conscientious, scrupulous.
– OPPOSITES inaccurate, careless.
● *verb* **1 demand**, require, impose, extract, compel, force, wring. **2 inflict**, impose, administer, mete out, wreak.

exacting *adjective* **demanding**, stringent, testing, challenging, arduous, laborious, hard, taxing, gruelling, punishing, tough.
– OPPOSITES easy, easy-going.

exactly *adverb* **1 precisely**, entirely, absolutely, completely, totally, just, quite, in every respect. **2 accurately**, precisely, unerringly, faultlessly, perfectly, faithfully.

exaggerate *verb* **overstate**, overemphasize, overestimate, inflate, embellish, embroider, elaborate, overplay, dramatize; *Brit. informal* blow out of all proportion.
– OPPOSITES understate.

examination *noun* **1** *items spread out for examination* **scrutiny**, inspection, perusal, study, investigation, consideration, analysis. **2** *a medical examination* **inspection**, check-up, assessment, appraisal, test, scan. **3** *a school examination* **test**, exam, assessment; *N. Amer.* quiz.

examine *verb* **1 inspect**, scrutinize, investigate, look at, study, appraise, analyse, review, survey; *informal* check out. **2 test**, quiz, question, assess, appraise.

example *noun* **1 specimen**, sample, instance, case, illustration. **2 precedent**, lead, model, pattern, ideal, standard. **3 warning**, lesson, deterrent, disincentive.

exasperate *verb* **infuriate**, anger, annoy, irritate, madden, provoke, irk, vex, gall, get on someone's nerves; *Brit.* rub up the wrong way; *informal* aggravate, rile, bug, hack off; *Brit. informal* nark, get on someone's wick; *N. Amer. informal* tee off, tick off.

excavate *verb* **unearth**, dig up, uncover, reveal, disinter, exhume, dig out, quarry, mine.

exceed *verb* **be more than**, be greater than, be over, go beyond, top, surpass.

excel *verb* **shine**, be excellent, be outstanding, be skilful, be talented, stand out, be second to none.

excellence noun **distinction**, quality, superiority, brilliance, greatness, calibre, eminence.

excellent adjective **very good**, outstanding, superb, exceptional, marvellous, wonderful, splendid; informal terrific, fantastic.
- OPPOSITES inferior.

except preposition **excluding**, not including, excepting, except for, omitting, not counting, but, besides, apart from, aside from, barring, bar, other than; informal outside of.

exception noun **anomaly**, irregularity, deviation, special case, peculiarity, abnormality, oddity.

exceptional adjective **1** the drought was exceptional **unusual**, abnormal, atypical, out of the ordinary, rare, unprecedented, unexpected, surprising. **2** her exceptional ability **outstanding**, extraordinary, remarkable, special, phenomenal, prodigious.
- OPPOSITES normal, average.

excerpt noun **extract**, part, section, piece, portion, snippet, clip, citation, quotation, quote, line, passage, fragment.

excess noun **1 surplus**, surfeit, overabundance, superabundance, superfluity, glut. **2 remainder**, leftovers, extra, rest, residue. **3 overindulgence**, intemperance, immoderation, profligacy, extravagance, self-indulgence.
- OPPOSITES lack, restraint.
● adjective excess oil **surplus**, superfluous, redundant, unwanted, unneeded, excessive, extra.

excessive adjective **1 immoderate**, intemperate, overindulgent, unrestrained, uncontrolled, extravagant. **2 exorbitant**, extortionate, unreasonable, outrageous, uncalled for, inordinate, unwarranted, disproportionate; informal over the top.

exchange noun **1 interchange**, trade, trading, swapping, traffic, trafficking. **2 conversation**, dialogue, chat, talk, discussion.
● verb **trade**, swap, switch, change.

excitable adjective **temperamental**, volatile, mercurial, emotional, sensitive, highly strung, tempestuous, hotheaded, fiery.
- OPPOSITES placid.

excite verb **1 thrill**, exhilarate, animate, enliven, rouse, stir, stimulate, galvanize. **2 provoke**, stir up, rouse, arouse, kindle, trigger, spark off, incite, cause.
- OPPOSITES bore.

excitement noun **1** the excitement of seeing a leopard in the wild **thrill**, pleasure, delight, joy; informal kick, buzz. **2** the excitement in her eyes **exhilaration**, elation, animation, enthusiasm, eagerness, anticipation.

exciting adjective **thrilling**, exhilarating, stirring, rousing, stimulating, intoxicating, electrifying, invigorating, gripping, compelling, powerful, dramatic.

exclaim verb **cry out**, declare, proclaim, blurt out, call out, shout, yell.

exclude verb **1 keep out**, deny access to, shut out, bar, ban, prohibit. **2 rule out**, preclude. **3** be exclusive of, not include.
- OPPOSITES admit, include.

exclusive adjective **1 select**, chic, high-class, elite, fashionable, stylish, elegant, premier; Brit. upmarket; informal posh, classy; Brit. informal swish. **2 sole**, unshared, unique, individual, personal, private. **3** prices exclusive of VAT **not including**, excluding, leaving out, omitting, excepting.
- OPPOSITES inclusive.

excruciating adjective **agonizing**, severe, acute, intense, violent, racking, searing, piercing, stabbing, unbearable, unendurable; informal splitting, killing.

excursion noun **outing**, trip, jaunt, expedition, journey, tour, day out, drive, run; informal spin.

excuse verb **1 forgive**, pardon. **2 justify**, defend, condone, forgive, overlook, disregard, ignore, tolerate, explain, mitigate. **3 let off**, release, relieve, exempt, absolve, free.
- OPPOSITES punish, condemn.

● *noun* **1 justification**, defence, reason, explanation, mitigating circumstances, mitigation. **2 pretext**, pretence; *Brit.* get-out; *informal* story, alibi.

execute *verb* **1 carry out**, accomplish, bring off/about, implement, achieve, complete, engineer; *informal* pull off. **2 put to death**, kill, hang, behead, electrocute, shoot.

execution *noun* **1 implementation**, carrying out, performance, accomplishment, bringing off/about, attainment, realization. **2 killing**, capital punishment, the death penalty.

executive *adjective* **administrative**, managerial, decision-making, law-making, governing, controlling.
● *noun* **1 director**, manager, senior official, administrator; *informal* boss, exec, suit. **2 administration**, management, directorate, government, authority.

exemplary *adjective* **perfect**, ideal, model, faultless, flawless, impeccable, irreproachable.
- OPPOSITES deplorable.

exemplify *verb* **typify**, epitomize, be an example of, be representative of, symbolize, illustrate, demonstrate.

exempt *adjective* **free**, not liable, not subject, immune, excepted, excused, absolved.
● *verb* **excuse**, free, release, exclude, grant immunity, spare, absolve; *informal* let off.

exemption *noun* **immunity**, exception, dispensation, indemnity, exclusion, freedom, release, relief, absolution.

exercise *noun* **1 physical activity**, a workout, working out, movement, training. **2 task**, piece of work, problem, assignment, practice. **3 manoeuvre**, operation, deployment.
● *verb* **1 work out**, do exercises, train. **2 use**, employ, make use of, utilize, practise, apply. **3 concern**, occupy, worry, trouble, bother, disturb, prey on someone's mind.

exert *verb* **bring to bear**, apply, use, utilize, deploy.
□ **exert yourself** work hard, labour, toil, make an effort, endeavour, slog away, push yourself.

exhaust *verb* **1 tire out**, wear out, over-tire, fatigue, weary, drain; *informal* take it out of someone, shatter; *Brit. informal* knacker; *N. Amer. informal* poop, tucker out. **2 use up**, get through, consume, finish, deplete, spend, empty, drain; *informal* blow.
- OPPOSITES invigorate, replenish.

exhausting *adjective* **tiring**, wearying, taxing, wearing, draining, arduous, strenuous, onerous, demanding, gruelling; *informal* killing; *Brit. informal* knackering.

exhaustion *noun* **tiredness**, fatigue, weariness, debility, enervation.

exhibit *verb* **1 put on display**, show, display, unveil, present. **2 show**, reveal, display, manifest, indicate, demonstrate, express, evince, evidence.
● *noun* **item**, piece, artefact, display, collection.

exhibition *noun* **1 exposition**, display, show, showing, presentation. **2 display**, show, demonstration, manifestation, expression.

exhilarating *adjective* **thrilling**, exciting, invigorating, stimulating, intoxicating, electrifying.

exhort *verb* **urge**, encourage, call on, enjoin, charge, press, bid, appeal to, entreat, implore; *literary* beseech.

exile *noun* **1 banishment**, expulsion, deportation, eviction, isolation. **2 expatriate**, émigré, deportee, displaced person, refugee.

exist *verb* **1 live**, be alive, be, be present. **2 prevail**, occur, be found, be in existence, be the case; *formal* obtain. **3 survive**, subsist, live, support yourself, manage, make do, get by, scrape by, make ends meet, eke out a living.

existence *noun* **1 survival**, continuation. **2 way of life**, life, lifestyle, situation.

□ **in existence** existing, alive, surviving, remaining, extant, existent, in circulation, current.

exit noun **1 way out**, door, escape route, egress. **2 turning**, turn-off, junction. **3 departure**, leaving, withdrawal, going, retreat, flight, exodus, escape.
- OPPOSITES entrance, arrival.
● verb **leave**, go out, depart, withdraw, retreat.
- OPPOSITES enter.

exonerate verb **absolve**, clear, acquit, find innocent, discharge; formal exculpate.
- OPPOSITES convict.

exorbitant adjective **extortionate**, excessive, prohibitive, outrageous, unreasonable, inflated; Brit. over the odds; informal steep, stiff, a rip-off; Brit. informal daylight robbery.
- OPPOSITES cheap.

exotic adjective **1** exotic birds **foreign**, non-native, alien, tropical. **2** exotic places **foreign**, faraway, far-off, far-flung, distant. **3 striking**, colourful, eye-catching, unusual, unconventional, extravagant, outlandish.

expand verb **1** metals expand when heated **enlarge**, increase in size, swell, lengthen, stretch, spread, thicken, fill out. **2** the company is expanding **grow**, enlarge, increase in size, extend, augment, broaden, widen, develop, diversify, build up, branch out, spread.
- OPPOSITES contract.
□ **expand on** elaborate on, enlarge on, go into detail about, flesh out, develop.

expanse noun **area**, stretch, sweep, tract, swathe, belt, region, sea, carpet, blanket, sheet.

expansion noun **1** expansion and contraction **enlargement**, swelling, lengthening, elongation, stretching, thickening. **2** the expansion of the company **growth**, increase in size, enlargement, extension, development, diversification, spread.
- OPPOSITES contraction.

expect verb **1 suppose**, presume, imagine, assume, surmise; informal guess, reckon; N. Amer. informal figure. **2 anticipate**, envisage, await, look for, hope for, look forward to, contemplate, bargain for/on, predict, forecast. **3 require**, ask for, call for, want, insist on, demand.

expectation noun **1 supposition**, assumption, presumption, conjecture, calculation, prediction, hope. **2 anticipation**, expectancy, eagerness, excitement, suspense.

expedient adjective **convenient**, advantageous, useful, beneficial, helpful, practical, pragmatic, politic, prudent, judicious.
● noun **measure**, means, method, stratagem, scheme, plan, solution, move, tactic, manoeuvre, device, contrivance, ploy, ruse.

expedition noun **journey**, voyage, tour, safari, trek, mission, quest, hike, trip.

expel verb **throw out**, bar, ban, debar, drum out, banish, exile, deport, evict; informal chuck out.
- OPPOSITES admit.

expense noun **cost**, expenditure, spending, outlay, outgoings, payment, price, charge, fees, overheads, tariff, bill.
- OPPOSITES income, profit.

expensive adjective **costly**, dear, high-priced, overpriced, exorbitant, extortionate; informal steep, stiff, pricey.
- OPPOSITES cheap.

experience noun **1 skill**, practical knowledge, understanding, familiarity, involvement, participation, contact, acquaintance, exposure, background, track record, history; informal know-how. **2 incident**, occurrence, event, happening, episode, adventure.
● verb **undergo**, go through, encounter, face, meet, come across, come up against, come into contact with.

experienced adjective **knowledgeable**, skilful, skilled, expert, proficient, trained, competent, capable, seasoned, practised, mature, veteran.

experiment noun **test**, investigation, trial, examination, observation, research, assessment, evaluation,

appraisal, analysis, study.
● verb **carry out experiments**, test, trial, try out, assess, appraise, evaluate.

experimental adjective **1 exploratory**, investigational, trial, test, pilot, speculative, tentative, preliminary. **2 new**, innovative, creative, radical, avant-garde, alternative, unorthodox, unconventional, cutting-edge; informal edgy.

expert noun **specialist**, authority, professional, pundit, maestro, virtuoso, master, wizard, connoisseur, aficionado; informal ace, pro, hotshot; Brit. informal dab hand; N. Amer. informal maven.
- OPPOSITES amateur.
● adjective **skilful**, skilled, adept, accomplished, experienced, practised, knowledgeable, talented, masterly, virtuoso; informal ace, crack, mean, genius.
- OPPOSITES incompetent.

expertise noun **skill**, prowess, proficiency, competence, knowledge, ability, aptitude, capability; informal know-how.

expire verb **1 run out**, become invalid, become void, lapse, end, finish, stop, terminate. **2 die**, pass away, breathe your last; informal kick the bucket, croak; Brit. informal snuff it, peg out; N. Amer. informal buy the farm.

explain verb **1 describe**, make clear, spell out, put into words, define, elucidate, expound, clarify, throw light on. **2 account for**, give a reason for, excuse.

explanation noun **1 clarification**, description, statement, interpretation, definition, commentary. **2 account**, reason, justification, answer, excuse, defence, vindication.

explicit adjective **1 clear**, plain, straightforward, crystal clear, precise, exact, specific, unequivocal, unambiguous, detailed. **2 graphic**, candid, full-frontal, uncensored.
- OPPOSITES vague.

explode verb **1 blow up**, detonate, go off, burst, erupt. **2 lose your temper**,

blow up; informal fly off the handle, hit the roof, blow your top; Brit. informal go spare; N. Amer. informal blow your lid/stack. **3 increase rapidly**, mushroom, snowball, escalate, burgeon, rocket. **4 disprove**, refute, rebut, repudiate, debunk, give the lie to; informal shoot full of holes, blow out of the water.

exploit verb **1 utilize**, make use of, turn/put to good use, make the most of, capitalize on, benefit from; informal cash in on. **2 take advantage of**, abuse, impose on, treat unfairly, misuse, ill-treat; informal walk (all) over.
● noun **feat**, deed, act, adventure, stunt, escapade, achievement.

exploration noun **investigation**, study, survey, research, inspection, examination, scrutiny, observation.

explore verb **1 travel through**, tour, survey, scout, reconnoitre. **2 investigate**, look into, consider, examine, research, survey, scrutinize, study, review; informal check out.

explosion noun **1 detonation**, eruption, bang, blast, boom. **2 outburst**, flare-up, outbreak, eruption, storm, rush, surge, fit, paroxysm. **3 sudden increase**, mushrooming, snowballing, escalation, multiplication, burgeoning, rocketing.

explosive adjective **1 volatile**, inflammable, flammable, combustible, incendiary. **2 fiery**, stormy, violent, volatile, passionate, tempestuous, turbulent, touchy, irascible. **3 tense**, highly charged, overwrought, dangerous, perilous, hazardous, sensitive, delicate, unstable, volatile.
● noun **bomb**, charge, incendiary (device).

expose verb **1** at low tide the rocks are exposed **reveal**, uncover, lay bare. **2** he was exposed to radiation **lay open**, subject, put at risk of, put in jeopardy of, leave unprotected from. **3** they were exposed to new ideas **introduce to**, bring into contact with, make aware of, familiarize with, acquaint with.

4 uncover, reveal, unveil, unmask, detect, find out, denounce, condemn; *informal* blow the whistle on.
- OPPOSITES cover, protect.

exposure noun **1 frostbite**, cold, hypothermia. **2 uncovering**, revelation, disclosure, unveiling, unmasking, discovery, detection. **3 publicity**, advertising, public attention, media interest; *informal* hype.

express[1] *verb* **communicate**, convey, indicate, show, demonstrate, reveal, put across/over, get across/over, articulate, put into words, voice, give voice to, state, air, give vent to.

express[2] *adjective* **rapid**, swift, fast, high-speed, non-stop, direct.

express[3] *adjective* **1 explicit**, clear, direct, plain, distinct, unambiguous, categorical. **2 sole**, specific, particular, special, specified.
- OPPOSITES vague.

expression noun **1 utterance**, uttering, voicing, declaration, articulation. **2 indication**, demonstration, show, exhibition, token, illustration. **3 look**, appearance, air, manner, countenance, mien. **4 idiom**, phrase, turn of phrase, term, proverb, saying, adage, maxim. **5 emotion**, feeling, spirit, passion, intensity, style.

expressive *adjective* **1 eloquent**, meaningful, demonstrative, suggestive. **2 emotional**, passionate, poignant, moving, stirring, emotionally charged, lyrical.
- OPPOSITES undemonstrative.

expulsion noun **1 removal**, debarment, dismissal, exclusion, ejection, banishment, eviction. **2 discharge**, ejection, excretion, voiding, evacuation, elimination, passing.
- OPPOSITES admission.

exquisite *adjective* **1 beautiful**, lovely, elegant, fine, delicate, fragile, dainty, subtle. **2** *exquisite taste* **discriminating**, discerning, sensitive, fastidious, refined.

extend *verb* **1 expand**, enlarge, increase, lengthen, widen, broaden.

2 continue, carry on, stretch, reach. **3 widen**, expand, broaden, augment, supplement, increase, add to, enhance, develop. **4 prolong**, lengthen, increase, stretch out, protract, spin out, string out. **5 hold out**, reach out, hold forth, stretch out, outstretch, offer, give, proffer.
- OPPOSITES reduce, shorten.
  □ **extend to** include, take in, incorporate, encompass.

extension noun **1 addition**, add-on, adjunct, annex, wing. **2 expansion**, increase, enlargement, widening, broadening, deepening, augmentation, enhancement, development, growth. **3 prolongation**, lengthening, increase.

extensive *adjective* **1 large**, sizeable, substantial, considerable, ample, great, vast. **2 comprehensive**, thorough, exhaustive, broad, wide, wide-ranging, catholic.

extent noun **1 area**, size, expanse, length, proportions, dimensions. **2 degree**, scale, level, magnitude, scope, size, reach, range.

exterior *adjective* **outer**, outside, outermost, outward, external.
- OPPOSITES interior.
  ● *noun* **outside**, external surface, outward appearance, facade.
- OPPOSITES interior.

external *adjective* **outer**, outside, outermost, outward, exterior.
- OPPOSITES internal.

extinct *adjective* **1 vanished**, lost, gone, died out, wiped out, destroyed. **2 inactive**.
- OPPOSITES living, dormant.

extinction noun **dying out**, disappearance, vanishing, extermination, destruction, elimination, eradication, annihilation.

extinguish *verb* **douse**, quench, put out, stamp out, smother, snuff out.
- OPPOSITES light.

extol *verb* **praise**, wax lyrical about, sing the praises of, acclaim, applaud, celebrate, eulogize, rave about, enthuse over; *formal* laud.

- OPPOSITES criticize.

extort verb **extract**, exact, wring, wrest, screw, squeeze.

extortionate adjective **exorbitant**, excessive, outrageous, unreasonable, inordinate, inflated; Brit. informal daylight robbery.

extra adjective **additional**, more, added, supplementary, further, auxiliary, ancillary, subsidiary, secondary.
● adverb **exceptionally**, particularly, specially, especially, extremely.
● noun **addition**, supplement, bonus, adjunct, addendum, add-on.

extract verb **1 take out**, draw out, pull out, remove, withdraw, release, extricate. **2 wrest**, exact, wring, screw, squeeze, obtain by force, extort. **3 squeeze out**, press out, obtain.
- OPPOSITES insert.
● noun **1 excerpt**, passage, citation, quotation. **2 distillation**, distillate, concentrate, essence, juice.

extraordinary adjective **1** an extraordinary coincidence **remarkable**, exceptional, amazing, astonishing, astounding, sensational, stunning, incredible, unbelievable, phenomenal; informal fantastic. **2** extraordinary speed **very great**, tremendous, enormous, immense, prodigious, stupendous, monumental.
- OPPOSITES unremarkable.

extravagant adjective **1 spendthrift**, profligate, wasteful, prodigal, lavish. **2 excessive**, immoderate, exaggerated, gushing, unrestrained, effusive, fulsome. **3 ornate**, elaborate, fancy, over-elaborate, ostentatious, exaggerated; informal flashy.
- OPPOSITES thrifty, moderate.

extreme adjective **1** extreme danger **utmost**, (very) great, greatest (possible), maximum, great, acute, enormous, severe, serious. **2** extreme measures **drastic**, serious, desperate,

dire, radical, far-reaching, draconian; Brit. swingeing. **3 radical**, extremist, immoderate, fanatical, revolutionary, subversive, militant. **4 dangerous**, hazardous, risky, high-risk; informal white-knuckle. **5 furthest**, farthest, utmost, remotest, ultra-.
- OPPOSITES slight, moderate.
● noun **opposite**, antithesis, side of the coin, (opposite) pole, limit, extremity, contrast.

extremely adverb **very**, exceptionally, especially, extraordinarily, tremendously, immensely, hugely, supremely, highly, mightily; informal awfully, terribly, seriously; Brit. informal jolly; N. Amer. informal mighty.
- OPPOSITES slightly.

extremist noun **fanatic**, radical, zealot, fundamentalist, hardliner, militant, activist.
- OPPOSITES moderate.

extrovert adjective **outgoing**, extroverted, sociable, gregarious, lively, ebullient, exuberant, uninhibited, unreserved.
- OPPOSITES introverted.

exuberant adjective **ebullient**, buoyant, cheerful, high-spirited, cheery, lively, vivacious, enthusiastic, irrepressible, energetic, animated, full of life, sparkling; informal bubbly, bouncy, full of beans.

eye verb **look at**, observe, view, gaze at, stare at, regard, contemplate, survey, scrutinize, consider, glance at, watch; informal check out, size up; N. Amer. informal eyeball.

> **WORD LINKS**
>
> **ocular**, **ophthalmic**, **optic** relating to the eye
> **ophthalmology** branch of medicine dealing with the eye

eyewitness noun **observer**, onlooker, witness, bystander, passer-by.

Ff

fable noun **parable**, allegory, myth, legend, story, tale.

fabric noun **1 cloth**, material, textile, stuff. **2 structure**, construction, make-up, organization, framework, essence.

fabricate verb **falsify**, fake, counterfeit, invent, make up.

fabulous adjective **1 stupendous**, prodigious, phenomenal, exceptional, fantastic, breathtaking, staggering, unthinkable, unimaginable, incredible, undreamed of. **2** (informal) a fabulous time. see **excellent**.

facade noun **1 front**, frontage, face, elevation, exterior, outside. **2 show**, front, appearance, pretence, simulation, affectation, act, charade, mask, veneer.

face noun **1 countenance**, physiognomy, features, profile; literary visage, lineaments. **2 expression**, look, appearance, mien, air. **3** he made a face **grimace**, scowl, wince, frown, pout. **4 side**, aspect, surface, plane, facet, wall, elevation.
● verb **1 look out on**, front on to, look towards, look over/across, overlook, be opposite (to). **2 accept**, get used to, adjust to, learn to live with, cope with, deal with, come to terms with, become resigned to. **3 beset**, worry, trouble, confront, torment, plague, bedevil. **4 brave**, face up to, encounter, meet (head-on), confront. **5 cover**, clad, veneer, surface, dress, laminate, coat, line.

facelift noun **renovation**, redecoration, refurbishment, revamp, makeover.

facet noun **aspect**, feature, factor, side, dimension, strand, component, element.

facetious adjective **flippant**, flip, glib, frivolous, tongue-in-cheek, joking, jokey, jocular, playful.
- OPPOSITES serious.

facilitate verb **make easier**, ease, make possible, smooth the way for, enable, assist, help (along), aid, promote, hasten, speed up.
- OPPOSITES impede.

facility noun **1** a wealth of local facilities **amenity**, resource, service, benefit, convenience, equipment. **2** a medical facility **establishment**, centre, station, location, premises, site, post, base. **3 ease**, effortlessness, skill, adroitness, smoothness, fluency, slickness.

fact noun **1** a fact we cannot ignore **reality**, actuality, certainty, truth, verity, gospel. **2** every fact was double-checked **detail**, particular, finding, point, factor, feature, characteristic, aspect; (**facts**) information, data.
- OPPOSITES lie, fiction.

faction noun **1 clique**, coterie, caucus, bloc, camp, group, grouping, splinter group. **2 infighting**, dissent, dispute, discord, strife, conflict, friction, argument, disagreement, disunity, schism.

factor noun **element**, part, component, ingredient, strand, constituent, feature, facet, aspect, characteristic, consideration, influence, circumstance.

factory noun **works**, plant, yard, mill, facility, workshop, shop.

factual adjective **truthful**, true, accurate, authentic, historical, genuine, true-to-life, correct, exact.
- OPPOSITES fictitious.

faculty noun **1 power**, capability, capacity, facility; (**faculties**) senses, wits, reason, intelligence. **2 department**, school.

fad noun **craze**, vogue, trend, fashion, mode, mania, rage.

fade verb **1 grow pale**, become bleached, become washed out, lose colour, discolour, blanch. **2 (grow) dim**, grow faint, fail, dwindle, die away,

wane, disappear, vanish, decline, melt away. **3 decline**, die out, diminish, decay, crumble, collapse, fail.
- OPPOSITES brighten.

fail verb **1 be unsuccessful**, fall through, fall flat, collapse, founder, backfire, miscarry, come unstuck; informal flop, bomb, flatline. **2 be unsuccessful in**, not make the grade; informal flunk. **3 let down**, disappoint, desert, abandon, betray, be disloyal to. **4 break (down)**, stop working, cut out, crash, malfunction, go wrong; informal conk out; Brit. informal pack up. **5 deteriorate**, degenerate, decline, fade. **6 collapse**, crash, go under, go bankrupt, cease trading, be wound up; informal fold, go bust.
- OPPOSITES succeed, pass, improve.

failing noun **fault**, shortcoming, weakness, imperfection, deficiency, defect, flaw, frailty.
- OPPOSITES strength.

failure noun **1 lack of success**, defeat, collapse, foundering. **2 fiasco**, debacle, catastrophe, disaster; informal flop, washout, dead loss. **3 loser**, underachiever, ne'er-do-well, disappointment; informal no-hoper, dud. **4 negligence**, dereliction, omission, oversight. **5 breakdown**, malfunction, crash. **6 collapse**, crash, bankruptcy, insolvency, liquidation, closure.
- OPPOSITES success.

faint adjective **1 indistinct**, vague, unclear, indefinite, ill-defined, imperceptible, pale, light, faded. **2 quiet**, muted, muffled, stifled, feeble, weak, low, soft, gentle. **3 slight**, slender, slim, small, tiny, remote, vague. **4 dizzy**, giddy, light-headed, unsteady; informal woozy.
- OPPOSITES clear, loud, strong.
● verb **pass out**, lose consciousness, black out, keel over, swoon.
● noun **blackout**, fainting fit, loss of consciousness, coma, swoon.

faintly adverb **1 indistinctly**, softly, gently, weakly, in a whisper. **2 slightly**, vaguely, somewhat, quite, fairly, rather, a little, a bit, a touch, a shade.

fair¹ adjective **1 just**, equitable, honest, impartial, unbiased, unprejudiced, neutral, even-handed. **2 fine**, dry, bright, clear, sunny, cloudless. **3 blond(e)**, yellow, golden, flaxen, light. **4 pale**, light, pink, white, creamy. **5 reasonable**, passable, tolerable, satisfactory, acceptable, respectable, decent, all right, good enough, pretty good.
- OPPOSITES inclement, dark, poor.

fair² noun **1 fete**, gala, festival, carnival. **2 market**, bazaar, exchange, sale. **3 exhibition**, display, show, exposition.

fairly adverb **1 justly**, equitably, impartially, without bias, without prejudice, even-handedly, equally. **2 reasonably**, passably, tolerably, adequately, moderately, quite, relatively, comparatively; informal pretty. **3 positively**, really, simply, absolutely.

fairy noun **sprite**, pixie, elf, imp, brownie, puck, leprechaun.

faith noun **1 trust**, belief, confidence, conviction, reliance. **2 religion**, belief, creed, church, persuasion, ideology, doctrine.
- OPPOSITES mistrust.

faithful adjective **1 loyal**, constant, true, devoted, staunch, steadfast, dedicated, committed, trusty, dependable, reliable. **2 accurate**, precise, exact, true, strict, realistic, authentic.
- OPPOSITES disloyal, treacherous.

fake noun **1 forgery**, counterfeit, copy, sham, fraud, hoax, imitation; informal phoney, rip-off. **2 charlatan**, quack, sham, fraud, impostor; informal phoney.
● adjective **1 counterfeit**, forged, fraudulent, sham, pirated, false, bogus; informal phoney, dud. **2 imitation**, artificial, synthetic, simulated, reproduction, replica, ersatz, man-made, dummy, false, mock; informal pretend. **3 feigned**, faked, put-on, assumed, invented, affected.
- OPPOSITES genuine, real, authentic.
● verb **1 forge**, counterfeit, falsify, copy, pirate. **2 feign**, pretend, simulate, put on, affect.

fall verb **1 drop**, descend, plummet, plunge, sink, dive, tumble, cascade. **2 topple over**, tumble over, fall down/over, collapse. **3 subside**, recede, drop, retreat, fall away, go down, sink. **4 decrease**, decline, diminish, fall off, drop off, lessen, dwindle, plummet, plunge, slump, sink. **5 die**, perish, lose your life, be killed, be slain, be lost; informal bite the dust, buy it. **6 surrender**, yield, submit, give in, capitulate, succumb, be taken, be overwhelmed. **7 occur**, take place, happen, come about.
- OPPOSITES rise.
● noun **1 tumble**, trip, spill, topple. **2 decline**, fall-off, drop, decrease, cut, dip, reduction, slump; informal crash. **3 downfall**, collapse, failure, decline, destruction, overthrow, demise. **4 surrender**, capitulation, yielding, submission, defeat. **5 descent**, slope, slant.
- OPPOSITES rise.
□ **fall back** retreat, withdraw, back off, draw back, pull back, move away. **fall back on** resort to, turn to, look to, call on, have recourse to. **fall for** (informal) **1** fall in love with, take a fancy to, be smitten by, be attracted to. **2** be deceived by, be duped by, be fooled by, be taken in by; informal go for, buy, swallow. **fall out** quarrel, argue, fight, squabble, bicker; Brit. row. **fall through** fail, be unsuccessful, come to nothing, miscarry, go awry, collapse, founder, come to grief.

false adjective **1 incorrect**, untrue, wrong, inaccurate, untruthful, fictitious, fabricated, invented, made up, trumped up, counterfeit, forged, fraudulent. **2 disloyal**, faithless, unfaithful, untrue, inconstant, treacherous, double-crossing, deceitful, dishonest, duplicitous. **3 fake**, artificial, imitation, synthetic, simulated, reproduction, replica, ersatz, man-made, dummy, mock; informal pretend.
- OPPOSITES correct, faithful, genuine.

falsify verb **forge**, fake, counterfeit, fabricate, alter, change, doctor, tamper with, manipulate, misrepresent, misreport, distort.

falter verb **hesitate**, delay, drag your feet, stall, waver, vacillate, be indecisive, be irresolute; Brit. hum and haw; informal sit on the fence.

fame noun **renown**, celebrity, stardom, popularity, prominence, distinction, esteem, eminence, repute.
- OPPOSITES obscurity.

familiar adjective **1 well known**, recognized, accustomed, everyday, day-to-day, habitual, customary, routine. **2** are you familiar with the subject? **acquainted**, conversant, versed, knowledgeable, well informed, au fait; informal well up on. **3 overfamiliar**, presumptuous, disrespectful, forward, bold, impudent, impertinent.

familiarity noun **1** a familiarity with politics **acquaintance**, awareness, knowledge, experience, insight, understanding, comprehension. **2 overfamiliarity**, presumption, forwardness, boldness, cheek, impudence, impertinence, disrespect. **3 closeness**, intimacy, friendliness, friendship.

family noun **1 relatives**, relations, (next of) kin, clan, tribe; informal folks. **2 children**, little ones, youngsters; informal kids. **3 species**, order, class, genus, phylum.

famine noun **1 food shortage**, hunger, starvation, malnutrition. **2 shortage**, scarcity, lack, dearth, deficiency, insufficiency, shortfall.
- OPPOSITES plenty.

famished adjective **ravenous**, hungry, starving, starved, empty, unfed; informal peckish.
- OPPOSITES replete.

famous adjective **well known**, prominent, famed, popular, renowned, noted, eminent, distinguished, celebrated, illustrious, legendary.
- OPPOSITES unknown.

fan noun **enthusiast**, devotee, admirer, lover, aficionado, supporter, follower, disciple, adherent; informal buff.

fanatic noun **extremist**, militant, dogmatist, bigot, zealot, radical, diehard; informal maniac.

fanatical adjective **1 zealous**, extremist, extreme, militant, gung-ho, dogmatic, radical, diehard, intolerant, single-minded, blinkered, inflexible, uncompromising. **2 enthusiastic**, eager, keen, fervent, passionate, obsessive, obsessed, fixated, compulsive; informal wild, nuts, crazy; Brit. informal potty.

fancy verb **1** (Brit. informal) **wish for**, want, desire, long for, yearn for, crave, thirst for, hanker after, dream of, covet. **2** (Brit. informal) **be attracted to**, find attractive, be infatuated with, be taken with; informal have a crush on, carry a torch for. **3 imagine**, believe, think, be under the impression; informal reckon.
● adjective **elaborate**, ornate, ornamental, decorative, embellished, intricate, ostentatious, showy, flamboyant, lavish, expensive; informal flashy, snazzy, posh, classy; Brit. informal swish.
- OPPOSITES plain.
● noun **1 whim**, foible, urge, whimsy, fascination, fad, craze, enthusiasm, passion, caprice. **2 fantasy**, dreaming, imagination, creativity.

fantastic adjective **1 fanciful**, extravagant, extraordinary, irrational, wild, absurd, far-fetched, unthinkable, implausible, improbable, unlikely; informal crazy. **2 strange**, weird, bizarre, outlandish, grotesque, surreal, exotic. **3** (informal) **marvellous**, wonderful, sensational, outstanding, superb, excellent; informal terrific, fabulous; Brit. informal brilliant; Austral./NZ informal bonzer.
- OPPOSITES ordinary.

fantasy noun **1 imagination**, fancy, invention, make-believe, creativity, vision, daydreaming, reverie. **2 dream**, daydream, pipe dream, fanciful notion, wish, fond hope, delusion; informal pie in the sky.
- OPPOSITES realism.

far adverb **1 a long way**, a great distance, a good way, afar. **2 much**, considerably, markedly, greatly, significantly, substantially, appreciably, by a long way, by a mile, easily.
● adjective **1 distant**, faraway, far-off, remote, out of the way, far-flung, outlying. **2 further**, opposite.
- OPPOSITES near.

farce noun **mockery**, travesty, parody, sham, pretence, charade, joke; informal shambles.
- OPPOSITES tragedy.

fare noun **1 price**, cost, charge, fee, toll, tariff. **2 food**, meals, cooking, cuisine.
● verb **get on**, get along, cope, manage, do, survive; informal make out.

farewell exclam. **goodbye**, so long, adieu, au revoir, ciao; informal bye, cheerio, see you (later); Brit. informal ta-ta, cheers.
● noun **goodbye**, adieu, leave-taking, parting, departure, send-off.

farm noun **smallholding**, farmstead, plantation, estate, farmland; Brit. grange, croft; Scottish steading; N. Amer. ranch; Austral./NZ station.
● verb **breed**, rear, keep, raise, tend.
☐ **farm out** contract out, outsource, subcontract, delegate.

farming noun **agriculture**, cultivation, husbandry; Brit. crofting.

fascinating adjective **interesting**, captivating, engrossing, absorbing, enchanting, enthralling, spellbinding, riveting, engaging, compelling, compulsive, gripping, charming, attractive, intriguing, diverting, entertaining.
- OPPOSITES boring.

fascination noun **interest**, preoccupation, passion, obsession, compulsion, allure, lure, charm, attraction, appeal, pull, draw.

fashion noun **1 vogue**, trend, craze, rage, mania, fad, style, look, convention, mode; informal thing. **2 clothes**, clothing design, couture; informal the rag trade. **3 manner**, way, method, style, approach, mode.
● verb **construct**, build, make,

manufacture, cast, shape, form, mould, sculpt, forge, hew, carve.

fashionable *adjective* **in vogue**, in fashion, popular, up to date, up to the minute, modern, all the rage, trendsetting, stylish, chic, modish; *informal* trendy, classy, cool; *N. Amer. informal* tony.

fast[1] *adjective* **1 speedy**, quick, swift, rapid, high-speed, accelerated, express, blistering, breakneck, hasty, hurried; *informal* nippy, scorching, supersonic; *Brit. informal* cracking. **2 secure**, fastened, tight, firm, closed, shut, immovable. **3 loyal**, devoted, faithful, firm, steadfast, staunch, true, boon, bosom, inseparable.
- OPPOSITES slow, loose.
  ● *adverb* **1 quickly**, rapidly, swiftly, speedily, briskly, at full tilt, hastily, hurriedly, in a hurry; *informal* double quick, nippily; *N. Amer. informal* lickety-split. **2 securely**, firmly, tight. **3** *he's fast asleep* **deeply**, sound, completely.

fast[2] *verb* **eat nothing**, go without food, go hungry, starve yourself, go on hunger strike.

fasten *verb* **1 bolt**, lock, secure, make fast, chain, seal. **2 attach**, fix, affix, clip, pin, tack, stick, join. **3 tie (up)**, tether, hitch, truss, fetter, lash, anchor, strap, rope.
- OPPOSITES unlock, untie.

fat *adjective* **1 obese**, overweight, plump, stout, chubby, portly, flabby, paunchy, pot-bellied, corpulent; *informal* tubby; *Brit. informal* podgy. **2 fatty**, greasy, oily. **3 thick**, big, chunky, substantial, sizeable.
- OPPOSITES thin, slim, lean.
  ● *noun* **1 blubber**, fatty tissue, adipose tissue, cellulite. **2 oil**, grease, lard, suet, butter, margarine.

fatal *adjective* **1 deadly**, lethal, mortal, death-dealing, terminal, incurable, untreatable, inoperable. **2 disastrous**, devastating, ruinous, catastrophic, calamitous, dire.
- OPPOSITES harmless, beneficial.

fate *noun* **1 destiny**, providence, the stars, chance, luck, serendipity, fortune, karma, kismet. **2 future**, destiny, outcome, end, lot. **3 death**, demise, end, sentence, nemesis.
  ● *verb* **predestine**, preordain, destine, mean, doom.

father *noun* **1** *informal* **dad**, daddy, pop, pa, old man; *informal, dated* pater. **2 originator**, initiator, founder, inventor, creator, author, architect.
  ● *verb* **sire**, spawn, breed, give life to.

> **WORD LINKS**
> **paternal** relating to a father
> **patricide** killing of your father

fatigue *noun* **tiredness**, weariness, exhaustion.
- OPPOSITES energy.
  ● *verb* **tire out**, exhaust, wear out, drain, weary, overtire; *informal* knock out, take it out of; *Brit. informal* knacker.

fatty *adjective* **greasy**, fat, oily, creamy, rich.

fault *noun* **1** *he has his faults* **defect**, failing, imperfection, blemish, flaw, shortcoming, weakness, weak point, vice. **2** *engineers have located the fault* **defect**, flaw, imperfection, bug, error, mistake, inaccuracy, oversight; *informal* glitch. **3 responsibility**, liability, culpability, guilt.
- OPPOSITES strength.
  ● *verb* **find fault with**, criticize, attack, condemn; *informal* knock; *Brit. informal* slag off.
  ▢ **at fault** to blame, blameworthy, culpable, responsible, guilty, in the wrong.

faultless *adjective* **perfect**, flawless, without fault, error-free, impeccable, accurate, precise, exact, correct, exemplary.
- OPPOSITES flawed.

faulty *adjective* **1 malfunctioning**, broken, damaged, defective, not working, out of order; *informal* on the blink, acting up; *Brit. informal* playing up. **2 flawed**, unsound, defective, inaccurate, incorrect, erroneous, wrong.
- OPPOSITES working, sound.

favour *noun* **1 good turn**, service, good deed, act of kindness, courtesy. **2 approval**, approbation, goodwill, kindness, benevolence.
- OPPOSITES disservice, disapproval.
● *verb* **1 advocate**, recommend, approve of, be in favour of, support, back, champion, campaign for, press for, lobby for, promote; *informal* push for. **2 prefer**, go for, choose, opt for, select, pick, plump for, like better, be biased towards. **3 benefit**, be to the advantage of, help, assist, aid, advance, be of service to.
- OPPOSITES oppose.
□ **in favour of** on the side of, pro, for, giving support to, approving of, sympathetic to.

favourable *adjective* **1 approving**, positive, complimentary, full of praise, flattering, glowing, enthusiastic, kind, good; *informal* rave. **2 advantageous**, beneficial, in your favour, good, right, suitable, appropriate, auspicious, promising, encouraging. **3 positive**, affirmative, assenting, approving, encouraging, reassuring.
- OPPOSITES critical, unfavourable.

favourite *adjective* **favoured**, preferred, chosen, choice, best-loved, dearest, pet.
● *noun* **first choice**, pick, preference, pet, darling, the apple of your eye; *informal* golden boy, teacher's pet; *Brit. informal* blue-eyed boy/girl; *N. Amer. informal* fair-haired boy/girl.

fear *noun* **1 terror**, fright, fearfulness, horror, alarm, panic, trepidation, dread, anxiety, angst, apprehension, nervousness. **2 phobia**, aversion, antipathy, dread, nightmare, horror, terror; *informal* hang-up.
● *verb* **1 be afraid of**, be fearful of, be scared of, be apprehensive of, dread, live in fear of, be terrified of. **2 suspect**, be afraid, have a sneaking suspicion, be inclined to think, have a hunch.

fearful *adjective* **1 afraid**, scared, frightened, scared stiff, scared to death, terrified, petrified, nervous, apprehensive,

uneasy, anxious, timid; *informal* jittery. **2 terrible**, dreadful, awful, appalling, frightful, ghastly, horrific, horrible, shocking, gruesome.
- OPPOSITES unafraid.

fearless *adjective* **brave**, courageous, bold, audacious, intrepid, valiant, plucky, heroic, daring, unafraid; *informal* gutsy.
- OPPOSITES timid, cowardly.

feasible *adjective* **practicable**, practical, workable, achievable, attainable, realizable, viable, realistic, possible; *informal* doable.
- OPPOSITES impracticable.

feast *noun* **banquet**, dinner, treat; *informal* spread; *Brit. informal* beanfeast, slap-up meal.
● *verb* **gorge**, dine, binge; (**feast on**) devour, consume, partake of, eat your fill of; *informal* stuff your face with, pig out on.

feat *noun* **achievement**, accomplishment, coup, triumph, undertaking, enterprise, venture, exploit, operation, exercise, endeavour, effort.

feather *noun* **plume**, quill; (**feathers**) plumage, down.

feature *noun* **1 characteristic**, attribute, quality, property, trait, hallmark, aspect, facet, factor, ingredient, component, element. **2** *her delicate features* **face**, countenance, physiognomy; *informal* mug; *Brit. informal* mush, phizog; *literary* lineaments, visage. **3 centrepiece**, special attraction, highlight, focal point, focus, conversation piece. **4 article**, piece, item, report, story, column.
● *verb* **1 present**, promote, make a feature of, spotlight, highlight, showcase, foreground. **2 star**, appear, participate.

federation *noun* **confederation**, confederacy, association, league, alliance, coalition, union, syndicate, guild, consortium.

fee *noun* **payment**, wage, salary, price, charge, bill, tariff, rate; (**fees**) remuneration, dues, earnings, pay; *formal* emolument.

feeble *adjective* **1 weak**, weakened, debilitated, enfeebled, frail, decrepit, infirm, delicate, sickly, ailing, unwell, poorly. **2 ineffective**, unconvincing, implausible, unsatisfactory, poor, weak, flimsy, lame. **3 cowardly**, faint-hearted, spineless, timid, timorous, fearful, unassertive, weak, ineffectual; *informal* sissy, chicken; *Brit. informal* wet. **4 faint**, dim, weak, pale, soft, subdued, muted.
- OPPOSITES strong.

feed *verb* **1 cater for**, provide for, cook for, dine, nourish. **2 eat**, graze, browse, crop. **3 supply**, provide, give, deliver. ● *noun* **fodder**, food, provender.

feel *verb* **1 touch**, stroke, caress, fondle, finger, paw, handle. **2** *she felt a breeze on her back* **perceive**, sense, detect, discern, notice, be aware of, be conscious of. **3** *he will not feel any pain* **experience**, undergo, go through, bear, endure, suffer. **4 grope**, fumble, scrabble. **5 believe**, think, consider it right, be of the opinion, hold, maintain, judge; *informal* reckon, figure. ● *noun* **1 texture**, finish, touch, consistency. **2 atmosphere**, ambience, aura, mood, feeling, air, impression, spirit; *informal* vibes. **3 aptitude**, knack, flair, bent, talent, gift, ability.

feeling *noun* **1 sensation**, sense, perception, awareness, conscious- ness. **2 (sneaking) suspicion**, notion, inkling, hunch, impression, intuition, instinct, funny feeling, fancy, idea. **3 love**, affection, fondness, tenderness, warmth, emotion, passion, desire. **4 mood**, (tide of) opinion, attitude, sentiment, emotion, belief, views, consensus. **5 compassion**, sympathy, empathy, fellow feeling, concern, pity, sorrow, commiseration. **6** *he hurt her feelings* **sensibilities**, sensitivities, self-esteem, pride. **7 atmosphere**, ambience, aura, air, mood, impres- sion, spirit; *informal* vibes. **8 aptitude**, knack, flair, bent, talent, feel, gift, ability.

felicitous *adjective* **apt**, well chosen, fitting, suitable, appropriate, apposite, pertinent, germane, relevant.
- OPPOSITES inappropriate.

fell *verb* **1 cut down**, chop down, hack down, saw down, clear. **2 knock down**, knock to the ground, floor, rugby- tackle, strike down, knock out; *informal* deck, flatten, lay out.

fellow *noun* **1** (*informal*) **man**, boy, per- son, individual, character; *informal* guy, lad; *Brit. informal* chap, bloke; *N. Amer. informal* dude. **2 companion**, friend, comrade, partner, associate, co-worker, colleague; *informal* pal, buddy; *Brit. informal* mate.

fellowship *noun* **1 companionship**, comradeship, camaraderie, friendship, sociability, solidarity. **2 association**, organization, society, club, league, union, guild, alliance, fraternity, brotherhood.

feminine *adjective* **womanly**, ladylike, soft, gentle, tender, delicate, pretty.
- OPPOSITES masculine.

fence *noun* **barrier**, paling, railing, enclosure, barricade, stockade. ● *verb* **1 enclose**, surround, encircle. **2 confine**, pen in, coop up, shut in/up, kettle; *N. Amer.* corral.

fend *verb*
□ **fend off** ward off, head off, stave off, hold off, repel, repulse, resist, fight off. **fend for yourself** take care of yourself, look after yourself, shift for yourself, cope alone, stand on your own two feet, get by.

ferocious *adjective* **1** *ferocious animals* **fierce**, savage, wild, predatory, ravening, aggressive, dangerous. **2** *a ferocious attack* **brutal**, vicious, violent, bloody, barbaric, savage, frenzied.
- OPPOSITES gentle, mild.

ferry *verb* **transport**, convey, carry, run, ship, shuttle.

fertile *adjective* **1 productive**, fruitful, fecund, rich, lush. **2 creative**, inventive, innovative, visionary, original, ingen- ious, prolific.
- OPPOSITES barren.

fertilizer noun **plant food**, dressing, manure, muck, guano, compost.

fervent adjective **impassioned**, passionate, intense, vehement, ardent, sincere, heartfelt, enthusiastic, zealous, fanatical, wholehearted, avid, eager, keen, committed, dedicated, devout.
- OPPOSITES apathetic.

fervour noun **passion**, ardour, intensity, zeal, vehemence, emotion, warmth, avidity, eagerness, keenness, enthusiasm, excitement, animation, vigour, energy, fire, spirit.
- OPPOSITES apathy.

festival noun **celebration**, festivity, fete, fair, gala, carnival, fiesta, jamboree, feast day, holiday, holy day.

festive adjective **jolly**, merry, joyous, joyful, happy, jovial, light-hearted, cheerful, jubilant, celebratory.

festoon verb **decorate**, adorn, ornament, trim, deck (out), hang, loop, drape, swathe, garland, wreathe, bedeck; informal do up/out, get up.

fetch verb **1 go and get**, go for, call for, summon, pick up, collect, bring, carry, convey, transport. **2 sell for**, bring in, raise, realize, yield, make, command; informal go for.

fetching adjective **attractive**, appealing, sweet, pretty, lovely, delightful, charming, captivating, enchanting; Scottish & N. English bonny; Brit. informal fit.

feud noun **vendetta**, conflict, quarrel, row, rivalry, hostility, strife.
● verb **quarrel**, fight, clash, argue, squabble, dispute.

fever noun **1 feverishness**, high temperature; Medicine pyrexia; informal temperature. **2 excitement**, mania, frenzy, agitation, passion.

> **WORD LINKS**
> **febrile** having a fever

feverish adjective **1 febrile**, fevered, hot, burning. **2 frenzied**, frenetic, hectic, agitated, excited, restless, nervous, worked up, overwrought, frantic, furious, hysterical, wild, uncontrolled, unrestrained.

few determiner **not many**, hardly any, scarcely any, a small number of, a handful of, a couple of, one or two.
- OPPOSITES many.
● adjective **scarce**, scant, meagre, sparse, in short supply, thin on the ground, few and far between.
- OPPOSITES plentiful.

fiasco noun **failure**, disaster, catastrophe, debacle, farce, mess; informal flop, washout, fail, shambles; Brit. informal cock-up.
- OPPOSITES success.

fibre noun **thread**, strand, filament, wisp, yarn.

fickle adjective **capricious**, flighty, giddy, changeable, volatile, mercurial, erratic, unpredictable, unreliable, unsteady.
- OPPOSITES constant.

fiction noun **1 novels**, stories, literature, creative writing. **2 fabrication**, invention, lie, fib, tall story, untruth, falsehood, fantasy, nonsense.
- OPPOSITES fact.

fictitious adjective **false**, fake, fabricated, bogus, spurious, assumed, affected, adopted, invented, made up; informal pretend, phoney.
- OPPOSITES genuine.

fiddle noun **fraud**, swindle, confidence trick; informal racket, scam.
● verb **1 fidget**, play, toy, finger, handle. **2 adjust**, tinker, play about/around, fool about/around, meddle, interfere, tamper; informal tweak, mess about/around; Brit. informal muck about/around. **3 falsify**, manipulate, massage, rig, distort, misrepresent, doctor, tamper with, interfere with; informal fix, cook (the books).

fidelity noun **1 faithfulness**, loyalty, constancy, allegiance, commitment, devotion. **2 accuracy**, exactness, precision, correctness, strictness, closeness, authenticity.
- OPPOSITES disloyalty.

fidget *verb* **1 wriggle**, squirm, twitch, jiggle, shuffle, be agitated; *informal* be jittery. **2 play**, fuss, toy, twiddle, fool about/around; *informal* fiddle, mess about/around.

fidgety *adjective* **restless**, restive, on edge, uneasy, nervous, nervy, keyed up, anxious, agitated; *informal* jittery, twitchy.

field *noun* **1 meadow**, pasture, paddock, grassland; *literary* lea, mead, greensward. **2 pitch**, ground; *Brit. informal* park. **3 area**, sphere, discipline, province, department, domain, territory, branch, subject. **4 scope**, range, sweep, reach, extent. **5 competitors**, entrants, competition, applicants, candidates, runners.
● *verb* **1 catch**, stop, retrieve, return, throw back. **2 deal with**, handle, cope with, answer, reply to, respond to.

fiendish *adjective* **1 wicked**, cruel, vicious, evil, malevolent, villainous, brutal, savage, barbaric, barbarous, inhuman, murderous, ruthless, merciless. **2 cunning**, clever, ingenious, crafty, canny, wily, devious. **3 difficult**, complex, challenging, complicated, intricate.

fierce *adjective* **1 ferocious**, savage, vicious, aggressive. **2 aggressive**, cutthroat, keen, intense, strong, relentless, dog-eat-dog. **3 intense**, powerful, vehement, passionate, impassioned, fervent, ardent. **4 powerful**, strong, violent, forceful, stormy, howling, raging, tempestuous.
- OPPOSITES gentle, mild.

fiery *adjective* **1 burning**, blazing, on fire, flaming, ablaze. **2 bright**, brilliant, vivid, intense, rich. **3 passionate**, impassioned, excitable, spirited, quick-tempered, volatile, explosive, impetuous.

fight *verb* **1 brawl**, exchange blows, scuffle, grapple, wrestle, tussle, spar; *informal* scrap; *Brit. informal* have a punch-up; *N. Amer. informal* roughhouse. **2 do battle**, serve your country, go to war, take up arms, engage, meet,

clash, skirmish. **3 wage**, engage in, conduct, prosecute, undertake. **4 quarrel**, argue, bicker, squabble, fall out, feud, wrangle; *Brit.* row; *informal* scrap. **5 campaign**, strive, battle, struggle, crusade, agitate, lobby, push, press. **6 oppose**, contest, confront, challenge, appeal against, take a stand against, dispute, resist. **7 repress**, restrain, suppress, stifle, smother, hold back, fight back, keep in check, curb, choke back; *informal* keep the lid on, cork up.
● *noun* **1 brawl**, scuffle, disturbance, fisticuffs, fracas, melee, skirmish, clash, tussle; *informal* scrap, dust-up; *Brit. informal* punch-up; *N. Amer. informal* rough house; *dated* affray. **2 boxing match**, bout, match, contest. **3 battle**, engagement, conflict, struggle, war, campaign, crusade, action, hostilities. **4 argument**, quarrel, squabble, wrangle, disagreement, falling-out, dispute, feud; *Brit.* row; *informal* tiff, spat, scrap; *Brit. informal* barney, ding-dong. **5 struggle**, battle, campaign, push, effort. **6** *she had no fight left in her* **will**, resistance, spirit, pluck, grit, strength, backbone, determination, resolution, resolve.

fighter *noun* **1 soldier**, fighting man/woman, warrior, combatant, serviceman, servicewoman; (**fighters**) troops, personnel, militia. **2 boxer**, pugilist, prizefighter, wrestler.

figurative *adjective* **metaphorical**, non-literal, symbolic, allegorical, representative, emblematic.
- OPPOSITES literal.

figure *noun* **1 statistic**, number, quantity, amount, level, total, sum; (**figures**) data, statistics. **2 digit**, numeral, character, symbol. **3 price**, cost, amount, value, valuation. **4 shape**, outline, form, silhouette, proportions, physique, build, frame. **5 person**, personage, individual, character, personality, celebrity. **6 shape**, pattern, design, motif. **7 diagram**, illustration, drawing, picture, plate.
● *verb he figures in many myths* **feature**, appear, be featured, be mentioned, be referred to.

□ **figure out** (*informal*) work out, fathom, puzzle out, decipher, make sense of, think through, get to the bottom of, understand, comprehend, see, grasp, get the hang of; *informal* twig, crack; *Brit. informal* suss out.

file[1] *noun* **1 folder**, portfolio, binder. **2 dossier**, document, record, report, data, information, documentation, archives.
● *verb* **1 categorize**, classify, organize, put in order, order, arrange, catalogue, store, archive. **2 bring**, press, lodge.

file[2] *noun* **line**, column, row, queue, string, chain, procession; *Brit. informal* crocodile.
● *verb* **walk in a line**, queue, march, parade, troop.

file[3] *verb* **smooth**, buff, rub down, polish, shape, scrape, abrade, rasp, manicure.

fill *verb* **1 fill up**, top up, charge. **2 crowd into**, throng, pack (into), occupy, squeeze into, cram (into). **3 stock**, pack, load, supply, replenish. **4 block up**, stop (up), plug, seal, caulk. **5 pervade**, permeate, suffuse, penetrate, infuse. **6 occupy**, hold, take up.
- OPPOSITES empty, clear, leave.

filling *noun* **stuffing**, padding, wadding, filler, contents.
● *adjective* **substantial**, hearty, ample, satisfying, square, heavy, stodgy.

film *noun* **1 layer**, coat, coating, covering, cover, skin, patina, tissue. **2 movie**, picture, feature film, motion picture, video, DVD. **3 cinema**, movies, the pictures, films, the silver screen, the big screen.
● *verb* **1 photograph**, record on film, shoot, capture on film, video. **2 cloud**, mist, haze, blur.

filter *noun* **strainer**, sifter, sieve, gauze, mesh, net.
● *verb* **1 sieve**, strain, sift, clarify, purify, refine, treat. **2 seep**, percolate, leak, trickle, ooze, leach.

filth *noun* **dirt**, muck, grime, mud, sludge, slime, excrement, excreta, ordure, sewage, pollution.

filthy *adjective* **1 dirty**, mucky, grimy, foul, squalid, sordid, soiled, stained, polluted, contaminated, unwashed. **2 obscene**, rude, vulgar, dirty, smutty, improper, coarse, bawdy, lewd; *informal* blue. **3 bad**, foul, irritable, grumpy, grouchy, cross; *informal* snappy; *Brit. informal* shirty, stroppy; *N. Amer. informal* cranky, ornery.
- OPPOSITES clean, pleasant.

final *adjective* **1 last**, closing, concluding, finishing, end, ultimate, eventual. **2 irrevocable**, unalterable, absolute, conclusive, irrefutable, incontrovertible, indisputable, unchallengeable, binding.
- OPPOSITES first, provisional.

finale *noun* **climax**, culmination, end, ending, finish, close, conclusion, termination, denouement.
- OPPOSITES opening.

finally *adverb* **1 eventually**, ultimately, in the end, after a long time, at (long) last, in the long run, in the fullness of time. **2 lastly**, last, in conclusion. **3 conclusively**, irrevocably, decisively, definitively, for ever, for good, once and for all.

finance *noun* **1 financial affairs**, money matters, economics, commerce, business, investment. **2 funds**, money, capital, cash, resources, assets, reserves, funding.
● *verb* **fund**, pay for, back, capitalize, endow, subsidize, invest in, sponsor; *N. Amer. informal* bankroll.

financial *adjective* **monetary**, money, economic, pecuniary, fiscal, banking, commercial, business, investment.

find *verb* **1 locate**, spot, pinpoint, unearth, obtain, search out, track down, root out, come across/upon, run across/into, chance on, happen on, stumble on, encounter; *informal* bump into. **2 discover**, invent, come up with, hit on. **3 realize**, become aware, discover, observe, notice, note, learn. **4 consider**, think, feel to be, look on as, view as, see as, judge, deem, regard as. **5 judge**, deem, rule, declare, pronounce.

f

- OPPOSITES lose.

● *noun* **1 discovery**, acquisition. **2 bargain**, godsend, boon, catch, asset; *informal* good buy.

□ **find out** discover, become aware of, learn, detect, discern, observe, notice, note, get/come to know, realize, bring to light; *informal* figure out, cotton on, tumble; *Brit. informal* twig, suss.

fine¹ *adjective* **1** *fine wines* **good**, choice, select, excellent, first-class, first-rate, great, exceptional, outstanding, splendid, magnificent, exquisite, superb, wonderful, superlative, prime, quality, special, superior, of distinction, premium, classic, vintage; *informal* A1, top-notch. **2** *a fine fellow* **worthy**, admirable, praiseworthy, laudable, upright, upstanding, respectable. **3 all right**, acceptable, suitable, good (enough), passable, satisfactory, adequate, reasonable, tolerable; *informal* OK. **4 healthy**, well, good, all right, (fighting) fit, blooming, thriving, in good shape/condition; *informal* OK, in fine fettle, in the pink. **5 fair**, dry, bright, clear, sunny, cloudless, balmy. **6 keen**, quick, alert, sharp, razor-sharp, acute, bright, brilliant, astute, clever, intelligent. **7 elegant**, stylish, expensive, smart, chic, fashionable, fancy, sumptuous, lavish, opulent; *informal* flashy. **8 flyaway**, wispy, delicate, thin, light. **9 sheer**, light, lightweight, thin, flimsy, diaphanous, filmy, see-through. **10 subtle**, ultra-fine, nice, hair-splitting.

fine² *noun* **penalty**, forfeit, damages, fee, excess charge.

finger *noun* **digit**.

● *verb* **touch**, feel, handle, stroke, rub, caress, fondle, toy with, play (about/around) with, fiddle with.

finish *verb* **1 complete**, end, conclude, close, terminate, wind up, round off, achieve, accomplish, fulfil; *informal* wrap up, sew up. **2 consume**, eat, devour, drink, finish off, polish off, use (up), exhaust, empty, drain, get through; *informal* down. **3 end**, come to an end, stop, conclude, come to a close, cease.

- OPPOSITES start.

● *noun* **1 end**, ending, completion, conclusion, close, termination, finale, denouement. **2 surface**, texture, coating, covering, lacquer, glaze, veneer, gloss, patina, sheen, lustre.

- OPPOSITES start.

□ **finish off 1** kill, execute, terminate, exterminate, liquidate, get rid of; *informal* wipe out, bump off, dispose of; *N. Amer. informal* waste. **2** overwhelm, overcome, defeat, get the better of, bring down; *informal* drive to the wall.

finite *adjective* **limited**, restricted, determinate, fixed.

- OPPOSITES infinite.

fire *noun* **1 blaze**, conflagration, inferno, flames, burning, combustion. **2 dynamism**, energy, vigour, animation, vitality, exuberance, zest, elan, passion, zeal, spirit, verve, vivacity, enthusiasm; *informal* go, get-up-and-go, oomph. **3 gunfire**, firing, shooting, bombardment, shelling, volley, salvo, hail.

● *verb* **1 launch**, shoot, discharge, let fly with. **2 shoot**, discharge, let off, set off. **3** *(informal)* **dismiss**, discharge, give someone their notice, lay off, let go; *informal* sack. **4 stimulate**, stir up, excite, awaken, rouse, inflame, animate, inspire, motivate.

□ **catch fire** ignite, catch light, burst into flames, go up in flames. **set on fire** ignite, light, set fire to, set alight.

> **WORD LINKS**
>
> **arson** crime of setting fire to property
> **pyromania** obsessive desire to set fire to things

firm¹ *adjective* **1 hard**, solid, unyielding, resistant, compacted, compressed, dense, stiff, rigid, set. **2 secure**, stable, steady, strong, fixed, fast, tight, immovable, rooted, stationary, motionless. **3 resolute**, determined, decided, resolved, steadfast, adamant, emphatic, insistent, single-minded, wholehearted, unfaltering, unwavering, unflinching, unswerving, unbending, committed. **4 close**, good, boon, intimate, inseparable, dear, special,

constant, devoted, loving, faithful, long-standing, steady, steadfast. **5 definite**, fixed, settled, decided, cut-and-dried, established, confirmed, agreed.
- OPPOSITES soft, unstable.

firm² noun **business**, company, concern, enterprise, organization, corporation, conglomerate, office, bureau, agency, consortium; *informal* outfit, operation.

first adjective **1 earliest**, initial, opening, introductory. **2 fundamental**, basic, rudimentary, primary, key, cardinal, central, chief, vital, essential. **3 foremost**, principal, highest, greatest, paramount, top, main, overriding, central, core; *informal* number-one. **4 top**, best, prime, premier, winning, champion.
- OPPOSITES last.
● adverb **at first**, to begin with, first of all, at the outset, initially.
● noun **novelty**, innovation, departure, break with tradition.

fish verb **1 go fishing**, angle, trawl. **2 search**, delve, look, hunt, grope, fumble, ferret, rummage.
◻ **fish out** pull out, haul out, remove, extricate, extract, retrieve, rescue, save.

> **WORD LINKS**
> **piscine** relating to fish
> **ichthyology** study of fish

fit¹ adjective **1 suitable**, appropriate, suited, apposite, fitting, good enough, apt. **2 competent**, able, capable, ready, prepared, equipped. **3 healthy**, well, in good health, in (good) shape, in trim, in good condition, fighting fit, athletic, muscular, strapping, strong, robust, hale and hearty.
- OPPOSITES unsuitable, incapable.
● verb **1 lay**, install, put in, position, place, fix, arrange. **2 equip**, provide, supply, fit out, furnish. **3 join**, connect, piece together, attach, unite, link. **4 be appropriate to**, suit, match, correspond to, tally with, go with, accord with. **5 qualify**, prepare, make ready, train.
◻ **fit in** conform, be in harmony, blend in, be in line, be assimilated.

fit² noun **1 convulsion**, spasm, paroxysm, seizure, attack. **2 outbreak**, outburst, attack, bout, spell. **3 tantrum**, frenzy; *informal* paddy.

fitness noun **1 good health**, strength, robustness, vigour, athleticism, toughness, stamina. **2 suitability**, capability, competence, ability, aptitude, readiness, preparedness.

fitting noun **1 attachment**, part, piece, component, accessory, apparatus. **2 furnishings**, furniture, fixtures, fitments, equipment.
● adjective **apt**, appropriate, suitable, apposite, fit, proper, right, seemly, correct.
- OPPOSITES unsuitable.

fix verb **1 fasten**, attach, affix, secure, connect, couple, link, install, stick, glue, pin, nail, screw, bolt, clamp, clip. **2 lodge**, stick, embed. **3 focus**, direct, level, point, train. **4 repair**, mend, put right, get working, restore. **5 arrange**, organize, contrive, manage, engineer; *informal* swing, wangle. **6** (*informal*) **arrange**, put in order, adjust, style, groom, comb, brush; *informal* do. **7** (*informal*) **prepare**, cook, make, get; *informal* rustle up; *Brit. informal* knock up. **8 decide on**, select, choose, settle, set, arrange, establish, allot, designate, name, appoint, specify. **9** (*informal*) **rig**, tamper with, skew, influence; *informal* fiddle.
● noun (*informal*) **1 predicament**, plight, difficulty, awkward situation, corner, tight spot, mess; *informal* pickle, jam, hole, scrape, bind. **2 fraud**, swindle, trick, charade, sham; *informal* set-up, fiddle.

fixation noun **obsession**, preoccupation, mania, addiction, compulsion; *informal* thing, bug, bee in your bonnet.

fixed adjective **predetermined**, set, established, arranged, specified, decided, agreed, determined, confirmed, prescribed, definite, defined, explicit, precise.

fizz *verb* **bubble**, sparkle, effervesce, froth.
● *noun* **1 bubbles**, sparkle, fizziness, effervescence, gassiness, froth. **2 crackle**, buzz, hiss, white noise.

fizzy *adjective* **sparkling**, effervescent, carbonated, gassy, bubbly, frothy.
- OPPOSITES still, flat.

flag[1] *noun* **banner**, standard, ensign, pennant, streamer, colours; *Brit.* pendant.
● *verb* **indicate**, identify, point out, mark, label, tag, highlight.
□ **flag down** hail, wave down, stop, halt.

flag[2] *verb* **1 tire**, grow tired, wilt, weaken, grow weak, droop. **2 fade**, decline, wane, ebb, diminish, decrease, lessen, dwindle.
- OPPOSITES revive.

flagrant *adjective* **blatant**, glaring, obvious, conspicuous, barefaced, shameless, brazen, undisguised.

flair *noun* **1 aptitude**, talent, gift, instinct, ability, facility, knack, skill. **2 style**, elegance, panache, dash, elan, poise, taste; *informal* class.

flake *noun* **sliver**, wafer, shaving, paring, chip, fragment, scrap, shred.
● *verb* **peel (off)**, chip, blister, come off.

flamboyant *adjective* **1 ostentatious**, exuberant, confident, lively, animated, vibrant, vivacious. **2 colourful**, bright, vibrant, vivid, dazzling, bold, showy, gaudy, garish, loud; *informal* jazzy, flashy.
- OPPOSITES restrained.

flame *noun* **1 fire**, blaze, conflagration, inferno. **2** *(informal)* **sweetheart**, boyfriend, girlfriend, lover, partner.
□ **in flames** on fire, burning, alight, flaming, blazing.

flank *noun* **1 side**, haunch, quarter, thigh. **2 side**, wing, sector, face, aspect.
● *verb* **edge**, bound, line, border, fringe.

flap *verb* **1** *ducks flapped their wings* **beat**, flutter, agitate, vibrate, wag,

thrash, flail. **2** *the flag flapped in the breeze* **flutter**, wave, fly, blow, swing, ripple, stir.
● *noun* **1 beat**, stroke, flutter, movement. **2** *(informal)* **panic**, fluster; *informal* state, stew, tizzy; *N. Amer. informal* twit.

flare *noun* **1 blaze**, flame, flash, burst, flicker. **2 signal**, beacon, rocket, light, torch.
● *verb* **1 blaze**, flash, flare up, flame, burn, flicker. **2 spread**, splay, broaden, widen, dilate.

flash *verb* **1 shine**, flare, blaze, gleam, glint, sparkle, burn, blink, wink, flicker, shimmer, twinkle, glimmer, glisten. **2** *(informal)* **show off**, flaunt, flourish, display, parade. **3 zoom**, streak, tear, shoot, dash, dart, fly, whistle, hurtle, rush, bolt, race, speed, career; *informal* belt, zap; *Brit. informal* bomb; *N. Amer. informal* barrel.
● *noun* **flare**, blaze, burst, gleam, glint, sparkle, flicker, shimmer, twinkle, glimmer.

flashy *adjective* *(informal)* **ostentatious**, flamboyant, showy, conspicuous, extravagant, expensive, vulgar, tasteless, brash, garish, loud, gaudy; *informal* snazzy, fancy, swanky, flash, glitzy.
- OPPOSITES understated.

flat[1] *adjective* **1 level**, horizontal, smooth, even, plane. **2 calm**, still, glassy, smooth, placid, like a millpond. **3 stretched out**, prone, spreadeagled, prostrate, supine, recumbent. **4 monotonous**, toneless, lifeless, droning, boring, dull, tedious, uninteresting, unexciting. **5 inactive**, slow, sluggish, slack, quiet, depressed. **6** *(Brit.)* **run down**, dead, used up, expired. **7 deflated**, punctured, burst, blown. **8 fixed**, set, invariable, regular, constant. **9 outright**, direct, absolute, definite, positive, straight, plain, explicit, categorical.
- OPPOSITES sloping, rough, uneven.
● *adverb* **stretched out**, outstretched, spreadeagled, sprawling, prone, prostrate.

flat² noun **apartment**, suite, penthouse, rooms.

flatten verb **1 level**, even out, smooth out, make/become flat. **2 squash**, compress, press down, crush, compact, trample. **3 demolish**, raze (to the ground), tear down, knock down, destroy, wreck, devastate.
- OPPOSITES crumple.

flatter verb **1 compliment**, praise, express admiration for, fawn on, humour, wheedle, blarney; informal sweet-talk, soft-soap, butter up, play up to. **2 honour**, gratify, please, delight; informal tickle pink. **3 suit**, become, look good on, go well with; informal do something for.
- OPPOSITES insult, offend.

flattering adjective **1 complimentary**, praising, favourable, admiring, appreciative, fulsome, honeyed, obsequious, ingratiating, sycophantic. **2 pleasing**, gratifying, an honour. **3 becoming**, enhancing.
- OPPOSITES unflattering.

flattery noun **praise**, adulation, compliments, blandishments, honeyed words, fawning, blarney; informal sweet talk, soft soap, buttering up.

flaunt verb **show off**, display, make a great show of, put on show/display, parade, draw attention to, brag about, crow about, vaunt; informal flash.

flavour noun **1 taste**, savour, tang, smack. **2 flavouring**, seasoning, taste, tang, relish, bite, piquancy, spice. **3 character**, quality, feel, feeling, ambience, atmosphere, air, mood, tone, spirit. **4 impression**, suggestion, hint, taste.
● verb **season**, spice (up), add piquancy to, ginger up, enrich, infuse.

flaw noun **defect**, blemish, fault, imperfection, deficiency, weakness, weak spot/point, failing; Computing bug; informal glitch.
- OPPOSITES strength.

flawed adjective **1 faulty**, defective, unsound, imperfect, blemished, broken, cracked, scratched; Brit. informal duff. **2 unsound**, distorted, inaccurate, incorrect, erroneous, fallacious, wrong.
- OPPOSITES flawless.

flawless adjective **perfect**, unblemished, unmarked, unimpaired, whole, intact, sound, unbroken, undamaged, mint, pristine, impeccable, immaculate, accurate, correct, faultless, error-free, exemplary, model, ideal, copybook.
- OPPOSITES flawed.

flee verb **run away**, run off, run for it, make off, take off, take to your heels, make a break for it, bolt, beat a (hasty) retreat, make a quick exit, escape; informal beat it, clear off/out, skedaddle, scram; Brit. informal scarper.

fleet noun **navy**, naval force, (naval) task force, armada, flotilla, squadron, convoy.

fleeting adjective **brief**, short-lived, quick, momentary, cursory, transient, ephemeral, passing, transitory.
- OPPOSITES lasting.

flesh noun **1 tissue**, skin, muscle, fat, meat, body. **2 pulp**, marrow, meat. **3** the pleasures of the flesh **the body**, human nature, physicality, sensuality, sexuality.

flexibility noun **1 pliability**, suppleness, elasticity, stretchiness, springiness, spring, resilience, bounce; informal give. **2 adaptability**, adjustability, versatility, open-endedness, freedom, latitude. **3 willingness to compromise**, give and take, amenability, cooperation, tolerance.
- OPPOSITES rigidity.

flexible adjective **1 bendy**, pliable, supple, pliant, plastic, elastic, stretchy, springy, resilient, bouncy. **2 adaptable**, adjustable, variable, versatile, open-ended, open. **3 accommodating**, amenable, willing to compromise, cooperative, tolerant.
- OPPOSITES rigid, inflexible.

flick noun **jerk**, snap, flip, whisk.
● verb **1 click**, snap, flip, jerk, throw. **2 swish**, twitch, wave, wag, waggle, shake.
□ **flick through** thumb through, leaf

through, flip through, skim, scan, look through, browse through, dip into, glance at/through.

flicker verb **1 glimmer**, flare, dance, gutter, twinkle, sparkle, wink, flash. **2 flutter**, quiver, tremble, shiver, shudder, jerk, twitch.

flight noun **1 aviation**, flying, air transport, aeronautics. **2 flock**, swarm, cloud, throng. **3 escape**, getaway, hasty departure, exit, exodus, breakout, bolt, disappearance; *Brit. informal* flit.

flimsy adjective **1 insubstantial**, fragile, frail, rickety, ramshackle, makeshift, jerry-built, shoddy. **2 thin**, light, fine, filmy, floaty, diaphanous, sheer, delicate, gossamer, gauzy. **3 weak**, feeble, poor, inadequate, insufficient, thin, unsubstantial, unconvincing, implausible.
- OPPOSITES sturdy.

flinch verb **1 wince**, start, shudder, quiver, jerk. **2** *he never flinched from his duty* **shrink from**, recoil from, shy away from, dodge, evade, avoid, duck, baulk at.

fling verb **throw**, hurl, toss, sling, launch, pitch, lob; *informal* chuck, heave.
● noun **1 good time**, party, spree, fun and games; *informal* binge, bash, night on the town. **2 affair**, love affair, relationship, romance, liaison, entanglement, involvement.

flip verb **1 overturn**, turn over, tip over, roll (over), upturn, capsize, upend, invert, knock over, keel over, topple over, turn turtle. **2 flick**, click, throw, push, pull.
□ **flip through** thumb through, leaf through, flick through, skim through, scan, look through, browse through, dip into, glance at/through, peruse, run your eye over.

flippant adjective **frivolous**, facetious, tongue-in-cheek, disrespectful, irreverent, cheeky; *informal* flip, saucy; *N. Amer. informal* sassy.
- OPPOSITES serious.

flirt noun **tease**, coquette, heartbreaker.
□ **flirt with 1** tease, lead on, toy with. **2** dabble in, toy with, trifle with, play with, tinker with, dip into, scratch the surface of.

float verb **1 stay afloat**, stay on the surface, be buoyant, be buoyed up. **2 hover**, levitate, be suspended, hang, defy gravity. **3 drift**, glide, sail, slip, slide, waft. **4 launch**, offer, sell, introduce.
- OPPOSITES sink.

floating adjective **1 uncommitted**, undecided, undeclared, wavering; *informal* sitting on the fence. **2 unsettled**, transient, temporary, migrant, wandering, nomadic, migratory, itinerant.

flock noun **1 herd**, drove. **2 flight**, swarm, cloud, gaggle, skein.
● verb **1** *people flocked around her* **gather**, collect, congregate, assemble, converge, mass, crowd, throng, cluster, swarm. **2** *tourists flock to the place* **stream**, go in large numbers, swarm, crowd, troop.

flog verb **whip**, thrash, lash, scourge, birch, cane, beat.

flood noun **1 inundation**, deluge, torrent, overflow, flash flood; *Brit.* spate. **2 gush**, outpouring, torrent, rush, stream, surge, cascade. **3 succession**, series, string, barrage, volley, battery, avalanche, torrent, stream, storm.
● verb **1** *the town was flooded* **inundate**, swamp, deluge, immerse, submerge, drown, engulf. **2** *the river could flood* **overflow**, burst its banks, brim over, run over. **3 glut**, swamp, saturate, oversupply. **4 pour**, stream, flow, surge, swarm, pile, crowd.

floor noun **1 ground**, flooring. **2 storey**, level, deck, tier, stage.
● verb **1 knock down**, knock over, fell, rugby-tackle; *informal* deck, lay out. **2** *(informal)* **baffle**, defeat, confound, perplex, puzzle, disconcert; *informal* throw, beat, stump.

flop verb **1 collapse**, slump, crumple, sink, drop. **2 hang (down)**, dangle, droop, sag, loll. **3** *(informal)*

be unsuccessful, fail, fall flat, founder; *informal* bomb, flatline; *N. Amer. informal* tank.
● *noun (informal)* **failure**, disaster, fiasco, debacle, catastrophe; *Brit.* damp squib; *informal* washout, fail, also-ran.
- OPPOSITES success.

floppy *adjective* **limp**, flaccid, slack, flabby, relaxed, drooping, droopy, loose, flowing.
- OPPOSITES erect, stiff.

flounder *verb* **1** *floundering in the water* **struggle**, thrash, flail, twist and turn, splash, stagger, stumble, reel, lurch, blunder. **2** *she floundered, not knowing what to say* **struggle**, be out of your depth, be confused; *informal* scratch your head, be flummoxed, be fazed, be floored.

flourish *verb* **1** *ferns flourish in the shade* **grow**, thrive, prosper, do well, burgeon, increase, multiply, proliferate, run riot. **2** *the arts flourished* **thrive**, prosper, bloom, be in good health, be vigorous, be in its heyday, make progress, advance, expand; *informal* go places. **3** *brandish*, wave, shake, wield, swing, display, show off.
- OPPOSITES wither, decline.

flout *verb* **defy**, refuse to obey, disobey, break, violate, fail to comply with, fail to observe, contravene, infringe, breach, commit a breach of, transgress against, ignore, disregard; *informal* cock a snook at.
- OPPOSITES observe.

flow *verb* **1** **pour**, run, course, circulate, stream, swirl, surge, sweep, gush, cascade, roll, rush, trickle, seep, ooze, dribble. **2** **result**, proceed, arise, follow, ensue, stem, originate, emanate, spring.
● *noun* **movement**, motion, current, circulation, stream, swirl, surge, gush, rush, spate, tide, trickle, ooze.

flower *noun & verb* **bloom**, blossom.

WORD LINKS
floral relating to flowers
florist person who sells flowers

---

fluctuate *verb* **vary**, change, shift, alter, waver, swing, oscillate, alternate, rise and fall.

fluent *adjective* **articulate**, eloquent, silver-tongued, communicative, natural, effortless.
- OPPOSITES inarticulate.

fluid *noun* **liquid**, solution, liquor, gas, vapour.
● *adjective* **1** **free-flowing**, runny, liquid, liquefied, melted, molten, gaseous. **2** **smooth**, fluent, flowing, effortless, easy, continuous, graceful, elegant.
- OPPOSITES solid.

flurry *noun* **1** **swirl**, whirl, eddy, shower, gust. **2** **burst**, outbreak, spurt, fit, spell, bout, rash, eruption.

flush *verb* **1** **blush**, redden, go pink, go red, go crimson, go scarlet, colour (up). **2** **rinse**, wash, sluice, swill, cleanse, clean; *Brit. informal* sloosh. **3** **chase**, force, drive, dislodge, expel.
● *noun* **blush**, colour, rosiness, pinkness, ruddiness, bloom.
- OPPOSITES pallor.

flutter *verb* **1** *butterflies fluttered around* **flit**, hover, dance. **2** *a robin fluttered its wings* **flap**, beat, quiver, agitate, vibrate, ruffle. **3** *she fluttered her eyelashes* **flicker**, bat. **4** *flags fluttered* **flap**, wave, ripple, undulate, quiver, fly.

fly *verb* **1** **wing**, glide, soar, wheel, take wing, take to the air, hover, swoop. **2** **pilot**, operate, control, manoeuvre, steer. **3** *the ship flew a French flag* **display**, show, exhibit, hoist, raise, wave. **4** **dash**, race, rush, bolt, zoom, dart, speed, hurry, career, hurtle; *informal* tear.

foam *noun* **froth**, spume, surf, spray, fizz, effervescence, bubbles, head, lather, suds.
● *verb* **froth**, fizz, effervesce, bubble, lather, ferment, boil, seethe.

focus *noun* **1** **centre**, focal point, central point, centre of attention, hub, pivot, nucleus, heart, cornerstone, linchpin. **2** **subject**, theme, concern, subject matter, topic, point, essence, gist.

● *verb* **bring into focus**, aim, point, turn.

□ **focus on** concentrate, centre, zero in, zoom in, address yourself to, pay attention to, pinpoint, revolve around.

fog *noun* **mist**, smog, murk, haze; *informal* pea-souper.

foggy *adjective* **1 misty**, smoggy, hazy, murky. **2** *a foggy memory* **muddled**, confused, dim, hazy, shadowy, cloudy, blurred, obscure, vague, indistinct, unclear.
- OPPOSITES clear.

foil[1] *verb* **thwart**, frustrate, stop, defeat, block, prevent, obstruct, hinder, snooker, scotch; *informal* put paid to; *Brit. informal* scupper.
- OPPOSITES assist.

foil[2] *noun* **contrast**, complement, antithesis.

fold *verb* **1 double**, crease, turn, bend, tuck, pleat. **2 fail**, collapse, founder, go bankrupt, cease trading, be wound up, be shut (down); *informal* crash, go bust, go under, go to the wall, go belly up, flatline.
● *noun* **crease**, knife-edge, wrinkle, crinkle, pucker, furrow, pleat.

folk *noun* (*informal*) **1 people**, individuals, [men, women, and children], (living) souls, citizenry, inhabitants, residents, populace, population. **2 relatives**, relations, family, people; *informal* peeps.

follow *verb* **1 come behind**, come after, go behind, go after, walk behind. **2 accompany**, go along with, go around with, travel with, escort, attend; *informal* tag along with. **3 shadow**, trail, stalk, track; *informal* tail. **4 obey**, comply with, conform to, adhere to, stick to, keep to, act in accordance with, abide by, observe. **5 understand**, comprehend, take in, grasp, fathom, see; *informal* make head or tail of, figure out; *Brit. informal* suss out. **6 be a fan of**, be a supporter of, support, watch, keep up with.
- OPPOSITES lead, flout.

follower *noun* **1 disciple**, apostle, defender, champion, believer, worshipper. **2 fan**, enthusiast, admirer, devotee, lover, supporter, adherent.
- OPPOSITES leader, opponent.

following *noun* **admirers**, supporters, backers, fans, adherents, devotees, public, audience.
- OPPOSITES opposition.
● *adjective* **next**, ensuing, succeeding, subsequent, successive.
- OPPOSITES preceding.

folly *noun* **foolishness**, foolhardiness, stupidity, idiocy, lunacy, madness, rashness, recklessness, irresponsibility.
- OPPOSITES wisdom.

fond *adjective* **1** *she was fond of dancing* **keen on**, partial to, enthusiastic about, attached to; *informal* into. **2 adoring**, devoted, doting, loving, caring, affectionate, indulgent. **3 unrealistic**, naive, foolish, over-optimistic, absurd, vain.
- OPPOSITES indifferent, uncaring.

fondle *verb* **caress**, stroke, pat, pet, finger, tickle, play with.

food *noun* **nourishment**, sustenance, nutriment, fare, cooking, cuisine, foodstuffs, refreshments, meals, provisions, rations; *informal* eats, grub, nosh; *literary* viands; *dated* victuals.

> **WORD LINKS**
> **alimentary** relating to food

fool *noun* **1 idiot**, ass, halfwit, blockhead, dunce, simpleton; *informal* nincompoop, clod, dimwit, dummy, fathead, numbskull; *Brit. informal* nitwit, twit, clot, berk, prat, pillock, wally, dork, twerp, charlie; *N. Amer. informal* schmuck; *Austral./NZ informal* drongo. **2** *she made a fool of me* **laughing stock**, dupe, gull; *informal* stooge, sucker, mug, fall guy; *N. Amer. informal* sap.
- OPPOSITES genius.
● *verb* **1 deceive**, trick, hoax, dupe, take in, mislead, delude, hoodwink, bluff, gull; *informal* bamboozle, take for a ride, have on; *N. Amer. informal* sucker; *Austral. informal* pull a swifty

on. **2 pretend**, make believe, put on an act, act, sham, fake, joke, jest; *informal* kid; *Brit. informal* have on.

foolish *adjective* **stupid**, idiotic, senseless, mindless, unintelligent, thoughtless, imprudent, unwise, ill-advised, rash, reckless, foolhardy; *informal* dumb, dim, dim-witted, half-witted, moronic, thick, hare-brained; *Brit. informal* barmy, daft, potty.
- OPPOSITES sensible, wise.

foolproof *adjective* **infallible**, dependable, reliable, trustworthy, certain, sure, guaranteed, safe, sound, tried and tested, watertight, airtight, flawless, perfect; *informal* sure-fire.

foot *noun* **1 paw**, hoof, trotter, pad. **2 bottom**, base, lowest part, end, foundation.

> **WORD LINKS**
> **chiropody**, **podiatry** medical treatment of the feet

footing *noun* **1** *a solid financial footing* **basis**, base, foundation. **2** *on an equal footing* **standing**, status, position, condition, arrangement, basis, relationship, terms.

forbid *verb* **prohibit**, ban, outlaw, make illegal, veto, proscribe, embargo, bar, debar, rule out.
- OPPOSITES permit.

forbidden *adjective* **prohibited**, verboten, taboo, illegal, illicit, against the law.

forbidding *adjective* **threatening**, ominous, menacing, sinister, daunting, off-putting.

force *noun* **1 strength**, power, energy, might, effort. **2 coercion**, compulsion, constraint, duress, pressure, oppression, harassment, intimidation, violence; *informal* arm-twisting. **3 power**, potency, weight, effectiveness, persuasiveness, validity, strength, significance, influence, authority; *informal* punch. **4 body**, group, outfit, party, team, detachment, unit, squad.
● *verb* **1 compel**, coerce, make, constrain, oblige, impel, drive, pressure,

pressurize, press-gang, bully; *informal* lean on, twist someone's arm. **2 break open**, knock/smash/break down, kick in. **3 propel**, push, thrust, shove, drive, press, pump.
☐ **in force** effective, in operation, operative, valid, current, binding.

forced *adjective* **1 enforced**, compulsory, obligatory, mandatory, involuntary, imposed, required. **2 strained**, unnatural, artificial, false, feigned, simulated, contrived, laboured, affected, hollow; *informal* phoney, pretend, put on.
- OPPOSITES voluntary, natural.

forceful *adjective* **1 dynamic**, energetic, assertive, authoritative, vigorous, powerful, strong, pushy; *informal* in-your-face, go-ahead, feisty. **2 convincing**, cogent, compelling, strong, powerful, persuasive, coherent.
- OPPOSITES weak.

forecast *verb* **predict**, prophesy, foretell, foresee.
● *noun* **prediction**, prophecy, prognostication, prognosis.

foreign *adjective* **alien**, overseas, non-native, imported, distant, external, far-off, exotic, strange.
- OPPOSITES domestic, native.

foreigner *noun* **alien**, foreign national, non-native, stranger, outsider, immigrant, settler, newcomer, incomer.
- OPPOSITES native, national.

> **WORD LINKS**
> **xenophobia** irrational dislike or fear of foreigners

foremost *adjective* **leading**, principal, premier, prime, top, greatest, best, supreme, pre-eminent, outstanding, most important, most notable; *N. Amer.* ranking; *informal* number-one.
- OPPOSITES minor.

foresee *verb* **anticipate**, expect, envisage, predict, forecast, foretell, prophesy.

foresight *noun* **forethought**, planning, far-sightedness, vision, anticipation,

f

prudence, care, caution; *N. Amer.* forehandedness.
- OPPOSITES hindsight.

foretell *verb* **predict**, forecast, prophesy, foresee, anticipate, envisage, warn of.

forever *adverb* **1 for always**, evermore, for ever and ever, for good, for all time, until the end of time, eternally; *N. Amer.* forevermore; *informal* until the cows come home. **2 always**, continually, constantly, perpetually, incessantly, endlessly, persistently, repeatedly, regularly; *informal* 24-7.

forfeit *verb* **lose**, be deprived of, surrender, relinquish, sacrifice, give up, renounce, forgo.
● *noun* **penalty**, sanction, punishment, penance, fine, confiscation, loss, forfeiture, surrender.

forge *verb* **1 hammer out**, beat out, fashion. **2 build**, construct, form, create, establish, set up. **3 fake**, falsify, counterfeit, copy, imitate, pirate.

forged *adjective* **fake**, false, counterfeit, imitation, copied, pirate, bogus; *informal* phoney, dud.
- OPPOSITES genuine.

forgery *noun* **fake**, counterfeit, fraud, imitation, replica, copy, pirate copy; *informal* phoney.

forget *verb* **1 fail to remember**, be unable to remember. **2 leave behind**, fail to take/bring, travel/leave home without. **3** *I forgot to close the door* **neglect**, fail, omit.
- OPPOSITES remember.

forgetful *adjective* **1 absent-minded**, amnesiac, vague, scatterbrained, disorganized, dreamy, abstracted, with a mind/memory like a sieve; *informal* scatty. **2** *forgetful of the time* **heedless**, careless, inattentive to, negligent about, oblivious to, unconcerned about, indifferent to.

forgive *verb* **1 pardon**, excuse, exonerate, absolve. **2 excuse**, overlook, disregard, ignore, make allowances for, turn a blind eye to, condone, indulge, tolerate.
- OPPOSITES blame, resent.

forgiveness *noun* **pardon**, absolution, exoneration, indulgence, clemency, mercy, reprieve, amnesty; *informal* let-off.
- OPPOSITES punishment.

forgiving *adjective* **merciful**, lenient, compassionate, magnanimous, humane, soft-hearted, forbearing, tolerant, indulgent, understanding.
- OPPOSITES merciless, vindictive.

forgo, forego *verb* **do without**, go without, give up, waive, renounce, surrender, relinquish, part with, drop, sacrifice, abstain from, refrain from, eschew, cut out; *informal* swear off; *formal* forswear, abjure.

fork *verb* **split**, branch, divide, separate, part, diverge, go in different directions, bifurcate.

forlorn *adjective* **1 unhappy**, sad, miserable, sorrowful, dejected, despondent, disconsolate, wretched, down, downcast, dispirited, downhearted, crestfallen, depressed, melancholy, gloomy, glum, mournful, despairing, doleful, woebegone; *informal* blue, down in the mouth, down in the dumps, fed up. **2 hopeless**, useless, futile, pointless, purposeless, vain, unavailing.
- OPPOSITES happy.

form *noun* **1 shape**, configuration, formation, structure, construction, arrangement, appearance, exterior, outline, format, layout, design. **2 body**, shape, figure, frame, physique, anatomy; *informal* vital statistics. **3 manifestation**, appearance, embodiment, incarnation, semblance, shape, guise. **4 kind**, sort, type, class, category, variety, genre, brand, style. **5 questionnaire**, document, coupon, slip. **6 class**, year; *N. Amer.* grade. **7 condition**, fettle, shape, health; *Brit. informal* nick.
● *verb* **1 make**, construct, build, manufacture, fabricate, assemble, put together, create, fashion, shape. **2 formulate**, devise, conceive, work out, think up, lay, draw up, put together, produce, fashion, concoct, forge, hatch; *informal* dream up. **3 set**

up, establish, found, launch, create, institute, start, inaugurate. **4 materialize**, come into being/existence, emerge, develop, take shape, gather, accumulate, collect, amass. **5 arrange**, draw up, line up, assemble, organize, sort, order. **6 comprise**, make, make up, constitute, compose, add up to.
- OPPOSITES dissolve, disappear.

formal adjective **1 ceremonial**, ritualistic, ritual, official, conventional, traditional, stately, solemn, ceremonious. **2 aloof**, reserved, remote, detached, unapproachable, stiff, stuffy, correct, proper; informal stand-offish. **3 official**, legal, authorized, approved, certified, endorsed, sanctioned, licensed, recognized.
- OPPOSITES informal, casual, unofficial.

formality noun **1 ceremony**, ritual, protocol, decorum, solemnity. **2 aloofness**, reserve, remoteness, detachment, unapproachability, stiffness, stuffiness, correctness; informal stand-offishness.
- OPPOSITES informality.

format noun **design**, style, appearance, look, form, shape, size, arrangement, plan, structure, scheme, composition, configuration.

formation noun **1** the formation of the island **emergence**, genesis, development, evolution, shaping, origin. **2** the formation of a new government **establishment**, setting up, institution, foundation, creation, inauguration. **3 configuration**, arrangement, grouping, pattern, array, alignment, order.
- OPPOSITES destruction, dissolution.

former adjective **1 one-time**, erstwhile, sometime, as was, ex-, previous, preceding, earlier, prior, last; formal quondam. **2 earlier**, old, past, bygone, olden, long ago, gone by, long past, of old. **3 first-mentioned**, first.
- OPPOSITES future, current, latter.

formerly adverb **previously**, earlier, before, until now/then, once, once upon a time, at one time, in the past, as was.

formidable adjective **1 intimidating**, daunting, indomitable, forbidding, alarming, frightening, awesome, fearsome; humorous redoubtable. **2 accomplished**, masterly, virtuoso, expert, impressive, powerful, terrific, superb; informal tremendous, nifty, crack, ace, wizard, magic, mean, wicked, deadly.

formula noun **1 form of words**, set expression, rubric, phrase, saying. **2 recipe**, prescription, blueprint, plan, policy, method, procedure.

formulate verb **1 devise**, conceive, work out, think up, lay, draw up, form, concoct, contrive, forge, hatch, prepare, develop. **2 express**, phrase, word, define, specify, put into words, frame, couch, put, articulate, say.

fort noun **fortress**, castle, citadel, bunker, stronghold, fortification, bastion.

forte noun **strength**, strong point, speciality, strong suit, talent, skill, gift; informal thing.

forthcoming adjective **1 coming**, upcoming, approaching, imminent, impending, future. **2 communicative**, talkative, chatty, informative, expansive, expressive, frank, open, candid.
- OPPOSITES past, current, reticent.

forthright adjective **frank**, direct, straightforward, honest, candid, open, sincere, outspoken, straight, blunt, plain-spoken, no-nonsense, bluff, matter-of-fact, to the point; informal upfront.
- OPPOSITES secretive, evasive.

fortify verb **1 strengthen**, secure, barricade, protect, buttress, shore up. **2 invigorate**, strengthen, energize, enliven, animate, vitalize, buoy up; informal pep up, buck up.
- OPPOSITES weaken.

fortitude noun **courage**, bravery, endurance, resilience, mettle, strength of character, backbone, grit; informal guts; Brit. informal bottle.

fortress noun **fort**, castle, citadel, bunker, stronghold, fortification.

fortunate adjective **1 lucky**, favoured, blessed, leading a charmed life, in luck; *Brit. informal* born with a silver spoon in your mouth, jammy. **2 favourable**, advantageous, happy.
- OPPOSITES unfavourable, unlucky.

fortunately adverb **luckily**, as luck would have it, happily, mercifully, thankfully.

fortune noun **1 chance**, accident, coincidence, serendipity, destiny, providence; *N. Amer.* happenstance. **2 luck**, fate, destiny, predestination, the stars, karma, kismet, lot. **3** *an upswing in their fortunes* **circumstances**, state of affairs, condition, position, situation. **4 wealth**, money, riches, assets, resources, means, deep pockets, possessions, property, estate.

forum noun **meeting**, assembly, gathering, rally, conference, seminar, convention, symposium.

forward adverb **1 ahead**, forwards, onwards, onward, on, further. **2 towards the front**, out, forth, into view, up.
- OPPOSITES backwards, back.
● adjective **1 onward**, advancing. **2 front**, advance, foremost, leading. **3 future**, forward-looking, for the future, anticipatory. **4 bold**, brazen, cheeky, shameless, familiar, overfamiliar, presumptuous; *informal* fresh.
- OPPOSITES backward, rear.
● verb **1 send on**, post on, redirect, readdress, pass on. **2 send**, dispatch, transmit, carry, convey, deliver, ship.

foster verb **1 encourage**, promote, further, nurture, help, aid, assist, support, back. **2 bring up**, rear, raise, care for, take care of, look after, provide for.

foul adjective **1 disgusting**, revolting, repulsive, repugnant, abhorrent, loathsome, offensive, sickening, nauseating; *informal* ghastly, gruesome, gross. **2 contaminated**, polluted, infected, tainted, impure, filthy, dirty, unclean. **3 vulgar**, crude, coarse, filthy, dirty, obscene, indecent, naughty, offensive; *informal* blue.

- OPPOSITES pleasant.
● verb **1 dirty**, pollute, contaminate, poison, taint, sully. **2 tangle up**, entangle, snarl, catch, entwine.

found verb **establish**, set up, start, begin, get going, institute, inaugurate, launch.

foundation noun **1 footing**, foot, base, substructure, underpinning. **2 justification**, grounds, evidence, basis. **3 institution**, establishment, charitable body, agency.

founder[1] noun **originator**, creator, (founding) father, architect, developer, pioneer, author, inventor, mastermind.

founder[2] verb **1 sink**, go to the bottom, go down, be lost at sea. **2 fail**, be unsuccessful, fall flat, fall through, collapse, backfire, meet with disaster; *informal* flop, bomb, flatline.
- OPPOSITES succeed.

fountain noun **1 jet**, spray, spout, spurt, cascade, water feature. **2 source**, fount, well, reservoir, fund, mine.

foyer noun **entrance hall**, hallway, entry, porch, reception area, atrium, concourse, lobby, anteroom; *N. Amer.* entryway.

fracas noun **disturbance**, brawl, melee, rumpus, skirmish, struggle, scuffle, scrum, clash, fisticuffs, altercation; *informal* scrap, scrap-up, set-to, shindy, shindig; *Brit. informal* punch-up, bust-up, ruck; *N. Amer. informal* rough house; *Law, dated* affray.

fraction noun **1** *a fraction of the population* **tiny part**, fragment, snippet, snatch. **2** *he moved a fraction closer* **bit**, little, touch, soupçon, trifle, mite, shade, jot; *informal* smidgen, tad.
- OPPOSITES whole.

fractious adjective **grumpy**, bad-tempered, irascible, irritable, crotchety, grouchy, cantankerous, tetchy, testy, ill-tempered, peevish, cross, pettish, waspish, crabby, crusty; *Brit. informal* shirty, stroppy, narky, ratty; *N. Amer. informal* cranky, ornery.

fracture noun **break**, crack, split, rupture, fissure.
● verb **break**, crack, split, rupture, snap, shatter, fragment, splinter.

fragile adjective **1 breakable**, delicate, brittle, flimsy, dainty, fine. **2 tenuous**, shaky, insecure, vulnerable, flimsy. **3 weak**, delicate, frail, debilitated, ill, unwell, poorly, sickly.
- OPPOSITES sturdy, robust.

fragment noun **1 piece**, bit, particle, speck, chip, shard, sliver, splinter, flake. **2 snatch**, snippet, scrap, bit.
● verb **break up**, crack open, shatter, splinter, fracture, disintegrate, fall to pieces, fall apart.

fragrance noun **1 sweet smell**, scent, perfume, bouquet, aroma, nose. **2 perfume**, scent, eau de toilette.

fragrant adjective **sweet-scented**, sweet-smelling, scented, perfumed, aromatic.
- OPPOSITES smelly.

frail adjective **1** *a frail old lady* **weak**, delicate, feeble, infirm, ill, unwell, sickly, poorly. **2** *a frail structure* **fragile**, easily damaged, delicate, flimsy, insubstantial, unsteady, unstable, rickety.
- OPPOSITES strong, robust.

frame noun **1 framework**, structure, substructure, skeleton, casing, chassis, shell. **2 body**, figure, form, shape, physique, anatomy, build.
● verb **1 mount**, set in a frame. **2 formulate**, draw up, draft, shape, compose, put together, form, devise.
□ **frame of mind** mood, state of mind, humour, temper, disposition.

framework noun **1 frame**, structure, skeleton, chassis, support, scaffolding. **2 structure**, shape, fabric, order, scheme, system, organization, anatomy; *informal* make-up.

frank adjective **1 candid**, direct, forthright, plain, plain-spoken, straight, to the point, matter-of-fact, open, honest; *informal* upfront. **2 undisguised**, open, unconcealed, naked, unmistakable, clear, obvious, transparent, patent, evident.

- OPPOSITES evasive.

frankly adverb **1 to be frank**, to be honest, to tell the truth, in all honesty. **2 candidly**, directly, plainly, straightforwardly, forthrightly, openly, honestly, without beating about the bush, bluntly.

frantic adjective **panic-stricken**, panicky, beside yourself, at your wits' end, distraught, overwrought, worked up, frenzied, frenetic, fraught, feverish, desperate; *informal* in a state, tearing your hair out; *Brit. informal* having kittens, in a flat spin.
- OPPOSITES calm.

fraternity noun **1 brotherhood**, fellowship, kinship, friendship, mutual support, solidarity, community. **2 profession**, community, trade, set, circle. **3** *(N. Amer.)* **society**, club, association, group.

fraud noun **1 deception**, sharp practice, cheating, swindling, trickery, embezzlement, deceit, double-dealing, chicanery. **2 swindle**, racket, deception, trick, cheat, hoax; *informal* scam, con, rip-off, sting, fiddle; *N. Amer. informal* hustle. **3 impostor**, fake, sham, charlatan, swindler, fraudster, confidence trickster; *informal* phoney.

fraudulent adjective **dishonest**, cheating, swindling, corrupt, criminal, deceitful, double-dealing, duplicitous; *informal* crooked, shady, dirty; *Brit. informal* bent, dodgy; *Austral./NZ informal* shonky.
- OPPOSITES honest.

fraught adjective **1** *a world fraught with danger* **full of**, filled with, rife with. **2 anxious**, worried, stressed, upset, distraught, overwrought, worked up, agitated, distressed, desperate, frantic, panic-stricken, panicky, beside yourself, at your wits' end, at the end of your tether.

frayed adjective **1 worn**, threadbare, tattered, ragged, the worse for wear; *informal* tatty; *N. Amer. informal* raggedy. **2 strained**, fraught, tense, edgy, stressed.

freak noun **1 aberration**, abnormality, oddity, monster, monstrosity, mutant, chimera. **2 anomaly**, aberration, rarity, oddity, one-off, fluke, twist of fate. **3** (informal) **eccentric**, misfit, oddity, crank; informal oddball, weirdo, nut; Brit. informal nutter; N. Amer. informal wacko, kook. **4** (informal) **enthusiast**, fan, devotee, lover, aficionado; informal nut, fanatic, addict, maniac.
● adjective **unusual**, anomalous, aberrant, atypical, unrepresentative, irregular, exceptional, isolated.

free adjective **1 free of charge**, without charge, for nothing, complimentary, gratis; informal for free, on the house. **2** free of any pressures **without**, unencumbered by, unaffected by, clear of, rid of, exempt from, not liable to, safe from, immune to, excused. **3 unoccupied**, not busy, available, off duty, off work, on holiday, on leave, at leisure, with time to spare. **4 vacant**, empty, available, unoccupied, not in use. **5 independent**, self-governing, self-determining, sovereign, autonomous, democratic. **6 on the loose**, at liberty, at large, loose, unrestrained. **7** you are free to leave **able**, in a position, allowed, permitted. **8 unobstructed**, unimpeded, unrestricted, unhampered, clear, open. **9** she was free with her money **generous**, liberal, open-handed, unstinting.
- OPPOSITES busy, occupied, confined.
● verb **1 release**, set free, let go, liberate, set loose, untie. **2 extricate**, release, get out, cut free, pull free, rescue.
- OPPOSITES confine, trap.

freedom noun **1 liberty**, liberation, release, deliverance. **2 independence**, self-government, self-determination, self-rule, home rule, sovereignty, autonomy, democracy. **3** freedom from political accountability **exemption**, immunity, dispensation, impunity. **4 right**, entitlement, privilege, prerogative, discretion, latitude, elbow room, licence, free rein, a free hand, carte blanche.

- OPPOSITES captivity, obligation.

freely adverb **1 openly**, candidly, frankly, directly, without beating about the bush, without mincing your words. **2 voluntarily**, willingly, readily, of your own accord, of your own free will, without being told to.

freeze verb **1 ice over**, ice up, solidify. **2 stand still**, stop dead in your tracks, go rigid, become motionless, become paralysed. **3 fix**, hold, peg, set, limit, restrict, cap.
- OPPOSITES thaw.

freezing adjective **1 icy**, bitter, chill, frosty, glacial, arctic, wintry, sub-zero, raw, biting. **2 frozen**, numb with cold, chilled to the bone/marrow.
- OPPOSITES balmy, hot.

freight noun **goods**, cargo, merchandise.

frenzied adjective **frantic**, wild, frenetic, hectic, feverish, fevered, mad, crazed, manic, furious, uncontrolled.
- OPPOSITES calm.

frenzy noun **hysteria**, madness, mania, delirium, wild excitement, fever, lather, passion, panic, fury, rage.

frequent adjective **recurrent**, recurring, repeated, periodic, continual, habitual, regular, successive, numerous, several.
- OPPOSITES occasional.
● verb **visit**, patronize, spend time in, visit regularly, haunt; informal hang out at.
- OPPOSITES avoid.

frequently adverb **often**, all the time, habitually, regularly, customarily, routinely, again and again, repeatedly, recurrently, continually; N. Amer. oftentimes.

fresh adjective **1 new**, modern, original, novel, different, innovative. **2 recently made**, just picked, crisp, raw, natural, unprocessed. **3 refreshed**, rested, restored, energetic, vigorous, invigorated, lively, sprightly, bright, alert, bouncing, perky; informal full of beans, bright-eyed and bushy-tailed. **4 bracing**, brisk, strong, invigorating, chilly, cool; informal nippy; Brit. informal

parky. **5 cool**, crisp, refreshing, invigorating, pure, clean, clear. **6** (*informal*) **impudent**, impertinent, insolent, presumptuous, forward, cheeky, disrespectful, rude; *informal* mouthy, saucy, lippy; *N. Amer. informal* sassy.
- OPPOSITES stale, old.

fret *verb* **worry**, be anxious, distress yourself, upset yourself, concern yourself, agonize, lose sleep.

friction *noun* **1 rubbing**, chafing, grating, rasping, scraping, resistance, drag, abrasion. **2 discord**, disagreement, dissension, dispute, conflict, hostility, animosity, antipathy, antagonism, resentment, acrimony, bitterness, bad feeling.
- OPPOSITES harmony.

friend *noun* **companion**, comrade, confidant, confidante, familiar, intimate, soul mate, playmate, playfellow, ally, associate; *informal* pal, chum; *Brit. informal* mate; *N. Amer. informal* buddy, amigo, compadre, homeboy.
- OPPOSITES enemy.

friendly *adjective* **1** *a friendly woman* **amiable**, companionable, sociable, gregarious, comradely, neighbourly, hospitable, easy to get on with, affable, genial, cordial, warm, affectionate, convivial; *informal* chummy, pally; *Brit. informal* matey. **2** *friendly conversation* **amicable**, cordial, pleasant, easy, relaxed, casual, informal, close, intimate, familiar.
- OPPOSITES hostile.

friendship *noun* **1** *lasting friendships* **relationship**, attachment, association, bond, tie, link, union. **2** *ties of friendship* **friendliness**, affection, camaraderie, comradeship, companionship, fellowship, closeness, affinity, unity, intimacy.
- OPPOSITES hostility.

fright *noun* **1 fear**, terror, horror, alarm, panic, dread, trepidation, dismay, nervousness. **2 scare**, shock, surprise, turn, jolt, start.

frighten *verb* **scare**, startle, alarm, terrify, petrify, shock, chill, panic, unnerve, intimidate; *informal* spook;

Brit. informal put the wind up.

frightening *adjective* **terrifying**, horrifying, alarming, startling, chilling, spine-chilling, hair-raising, blood-curdling, disturbing, unnerving, intimidating, daunting, eerie, sinister, fearsome, nightmarish, menacing; *informal* scary, spooky, creepy.

frightful *adjective* **horrible**, horrific, ghastly, horrendous, awful, dreadful, terrible, nasty; *informal* horrid.

fringe *noun* **1 edge**, border, margin, extremity, perimeter, periphery, rim, limits, outskirts. **2 edging**, border, trimming, frill, flounce, ruffle.
- OPPOSITES middle.
● *adjective* **alternative**, avant-garde, experimental, innovative, left-field, radical.
- OPPOSITES mainstream.

frisky *adjective* **lively**, bouncy, bubbly, perky, active, energetic, animated, playful, coltish, skittish, spirited, high-spirited, in high spirits, exuberant; *informal* full of beans.

frivolous *adjective* **flippant**, glib, facetious, joking, jokey, light-hearted, fatuous, inane; *informal* flip.
- OPPOSITES serious.

front *noun* **1 fore**, foremost part, forepart, nose, head, bow, prow, foreground. **2 frontage**, face, facing, facade. **3 head**, beginning, start, top, lead. **4 appearance**, air, face, manner, exterior, veneer, (outward) show, act, pretence. **5 cover**, blind, disguise, facade, mask, cloak, screen, smokescreen, camouflage.
- OPPOSITES back.
● *adjective* **leading**, lead, first, foremost.
- OPPOSITES back, last.
□ **in front** ahead, to/at the fore, at the head, up ahead, in the lead, leading, coming first, at the head of the queue; *informal* up front.

frontier *noun* **border**, boundary, borderline, dividing line, perimeter, limit, edge.

frosty *adjective* **1 cold**, freezing, frozen, icy, bitter, chill, wintry, arctic; *informal* nippy; *Brit. informal* parky. **2 unfriendly**, cold, frigid, icy, glacial, inhospitable, unwelcoming, forbidding, hostile, stony.
- OPPOSITES warm, friendly.

froth *noun* **foam**, head, bubbles, frothiness, fizz, effervescence, lather, suds.
● *verb* **bubble**, fizz, effervesce, foam, lather, churn, seethe.

frown *verb* **scowl**, glower, glare, lour, make a face, look daggers, give someone a black look, knit your brows; *informal* give someone a dirty look.
- OPPOSITES smile.
□ **frown on** disapprove of, take a dim view of, take exception to, object to, look askance at, not take kindly to.

frugal *adjective* **1 thrifty**, economical, careful, cautious, prudent, provident, sparing, abstemious, austere, self-denying, ascetic, spartan. **2 meagre**, scanty, scant, paltry, skimpy, plain, simple, spartan, inexpensive, cheap, economical.
- OPPOSITES extravagant, lavish.

fruitful *adjective* **productive**, constructive, useful, worthwhile, helpful, beneficial, valuable, rewarding, profitable, advantageous.
- OPPOSITES barren, futile.

fruition *noun* **fulfilment**, realization, actualization, materialization, achievement, attainment, accomplishment, success, completion, consummation, conclusion, close, finish, perfection, maturity.

fruitless *adjective* **futile**, vain, in vain, to no avail, to no effect, idle, pointless, useless, worthless, hollow, ineffectual, ineffective, unproductive, unrewarding, profitless, unsuccessful, unavailing, abortive.
- OPPOSITES fruitful, productive.

frustrate *verb* **1 thwart**, defeat, foil, block, stop, counter, spoil, check, forestall, scotch, derail, snooker; *informal* stymie; *Brit. informal* scupper. **2 exasperate**, infuriate, discourage,

dishearten, disappoint.
- OPPOSITES further, satisfy.

fudge *verb* **evade**, avoid, dodge, skirt, duck, gloss over, cloud, hedge, beat about the bush, equivocate.

fuel *verb* **1 power**, fire, drive, run. **2 fan**, feed, stoke up, inflame, intensify, stimulate, encourage, provoke, incite, sustain.

fugitive *noun* **escapee**, runaway, deserter, absconder, refugee.

fulfil *verb* **1 achieve**, attain, realize, make happen, succeed in, bring to completion, bring to fruition, satisfy. **2 carry out**, perform, accomplish, execute, do, discharge, conduct. **3 meet**, satisfy, comply with, conform to, fill, answer.

fulfilled *adjective* **satisfied**, content, contented, happy, pleased, at peace.
- OPPOSITES discontented.

full *adjective* **1 filled**, brimming, brimful, packed, loaded, crammed, crowded, bursting, overflowing, congested; *informal* jam-packed, wall-to-wall, chock-a-block, chock-full, awash. **2 replete**, full up, satisfied, sated, satiated; *informal* stuffed. **3 eventful**, interesting, exciting, lively, action-packed, busy, active. **4 comprehensive**, thorough, exhaustive, all-inclusive, all-encompassing, all-embracing, in-depth, complete, entire, whole, unabridged, uncut. **5 plump**, rounded, buxom, shapely, ample, curvaceous, voluptuous; *informal* busty, curvy, well endowed; *N. Amer. informal* zaftig. **6 loose-fitting**, loose, baggy, voluminous, roomy, capacious, billowing.
- OPPOSITES empty.

fully *adverb* **completely**, entirely, wholly, totally, perfectly, quite, altogether, thoroughly, in all respects, (up) to the hilt.
- OPPOSITES partly.

fumble *verb* **grope**, fish, scrabble, feel.

fume *noun* **smoke**, vapour, gas, exhaust, pollution.
● *verb* **be furious**, seethe, be livid, be incensed, boil, be beside yourself, spit;

informal foam at the mouth, see red.

fumigate *verb* **disinfect**, purify, sterilize, sanitize, decontaminate, cleanse, clean out.

fun *noun* **1 enjoyment**, entertainment, amusement, pleasure, jollification, merrymaking, recreation, leisure, relaxation, a good time; *informal* living it up, a ball. **2 merriment**, cheerfulness, jollity, joviality, high spirits, mirth, laughter, hilarity, light-heartedness, levity. **3** *he became a figure of fun* **ridicule**, derision, mockery, scorn, contempt.
- OPPOSITES boredom.
● *adjective (informal)* **enjoyable**, entertaining, amusing, pleasurable, pleasant, agreeable, convivial.
□ **make fun of** tease, poke fun at, ridicule, mock, laugh at, parody, caricature, satirize; *informal* take the mickey out of, send up; *N. Amer. informal* goof on.

function *noun* **1 purpose**, task, use, role. **2 responsibility**, duty, role, province, activity, assignment, task, job, mission. **3 social event**, party, social occasion, affair, gathering, reception, soirée; *N. Amer.* levee; *informal* do, bash.
● *verb* **1 work**, go, run, be in working/running order, operate. **2 act**, serve, operate, perform, do duty.

functional *adjective* **1 practical**, useful, utilitarian, workaday, serviceable, no-frills. **2 working**, in working order, functioning, in service, in use, going, running, operative; *informal* up and running.

fund *noun* **1 collection**, kitty, reserve, pool, purse, savings, coffers. **2 money**, cash, wealth, means, assets, resources, savings, capital, reserves, deep pockets, the wherewithal; *informal* dosh; *Brit. informal* lolly.
● *verb* **finance**, pay for, back, capitalize, subsidize, endow, invest in, sponsor; *N. Amer. informal* bankroll.

fundamental *adjective* **basic**, underlying, core, rudimentary, root, primary, prime, cardinal, principal, chief, key,

central, vital, essential.
- OPPOSITES secondary, incidental.

fundamentally *adverb* **essentially**, in essence, basically, at heart, at bottom, deep down, profoundly, primarily, above all.

funeral *noun* **burial**, interment, entombment, committal, laying to rest, cremation.

funny *adjective* **1 amusing**, humorous, witty, comic, comical, hilarious, hysterical, riotous, uproarious, farcical; *informal* rib-tickling, priceless. **2 strange**, peculiar, odd, weird, bizarre, curious, freakish, quirky, unusual. **3 suspicious**, suspect, dubious, untrustworthy, questionable; *informal* fishy; *Brit. informal* dodgy.
- OPPOSITES serious.

furious *adjective* **1 very angry**, enraged, infuriated, irate, incensed, fuming, ranting, raving, seething, beside yourself, outraged; *informal* hopping mad, wild, livid. **2 fierce**, heated, passionate, fiery, tumultuous, turbulent, tempestuous, violent, stormy, acrimonious.
- OPPOSITES pleased, calm.

furnish *verb* **1 fit out**, appoint, equip; *Brit. informal* do out. **2** *they furnished us with waterproofs* **supply**, provide, equip, issue, kit out; *informal* fix up.

furore *noun* **commotion**, uproar, outcry, fuss, upset, brouhaha, stir; *informal* to-do, hoo-ha, hullabaloo.

further *adverb* see **furthermore**.
● *adjective* **additional**, more, extra, supplementary, new, fresh.
● *verb* **promote**, advance, forward, develop, facilitate, aid, assist, help, boost, encourage.
- OPPOSITES impede.

furthermore *adverb* **moreover**, further, what's more, also, additionally, in addition, besides, as well, too, on top of that, into the bargain.

furthest *adjective* **most distant**, remotest, farthest, furthermost, farthermost, outer, outermost, extreme.
- OPPOSITES nearest.

furtive *adjective* **surreptitious**, secretive, secret, clandestine, hidden, covert, conspiratorial, cloak-and-dagger, sneaky; *Military* black; *informal* shifty.
- OPPOSITES open.

fury *noun* **1 rage**, anger, wrath, outrage; *literary* ire. **2 ferocity**, violence, turbulence, tempestuousness, savagery, severity, intensity, vehemence, force.

fuss *noun* **1 commotion**, excitement, stir, confusion, disturbance, brouhaha, uproar, furore, storm in a teacup; *informal* hoo-ha, to-do, song and dance, performance. **2 protest**, complaint, objection, argument; *Brit.* row. **3 trouble**, bother, inconvenience, effort, exertion, labour; *informal* hassle.
● *verb* **worry**, fret, be agitated, be worked up, make a big thing out of it, make a mountain out of a molehill; *informal* flap, be in a tizzy.

fussy *adjective* **1 particular**, finicky, fastidious, hard to please, faddish; *informal* pernickety, choosy, picky; *Brit. informal* faddy; *N. Amer. informal* persnickety. **2 over-elaborate**, ornate, fancy, busy, cluttered.

futile *adjective* **fruitless**, vain, pointless, useless, ineffectual, forlorn, hopeless.
- OPPOSITES useful.

future *noun* **1** *plans for the future* **time to come**, what lies ahead, the hereafter. **2** *her future lay in acting* **destiny**, fate, fortune, prospects, chances.
- OPPOSITES past.
● *adjective* **1 later**, to come, following, forthcoming, ensuing, succeeding, subsequent, coming, impending, approaching. **2** *her future husband to be*, destined, intended, planned, prospective.
- OPPOSITES previous, past.

fuzzy *adjective* **1 frizzy**, fluffy, woolly, downy. **2 blurred**, indistinct, unclear, out of focus, misty. **3 unclear**, imprecise, unfocused, nebulous, vague, hazy, loose, woolly.
- OPPOSITES smooth, sharp, clear.

Gg

gadget noun **device**, appliance, apparatus, instrument, implement, tool, utensil, contrivance, contraption, machine, mechanism, invention; informal gizmo.

gaffe noun **blunder**, mistake, error, slip, faux pas, indiscretion, solecism; informal slip-up, howler, boo-boo; Brit. informal boob, clanger; N. Amer. informal blooper.

gag[1] verb **1 silence**, muzzle, suppress, stifle, censor, curb, restrain. **2 retch**, heave.

gag[2] noun (informal) **joke**, quip, jest, witticism; informal crack, wisecrack, one-liner.

gain verb **1 obtain**, get, secure, acquire, come by, procure, attain, achieve, earn, win, capture; informal land. **2** they stood to gain from the deal **profit**, make money, benefit, do well out of. **3** she gained weight **put on**, increase in, build up. **4** they're gaining on us **catch up (with)**, catch, reduce someone's lead, narrow the gap.
- OPPOSITES lose.
● noun **1 profit**, earnings, income, yield, return, reward, advantage, benefit; informal take. **2 increase**, addition, rise, increment, advance.
- OPPOSITES loss.

gainful adjective **profitable**, paid, well paid, remunerative, lucrative, money-making, rewarding, fruitful, worthwhile, useful, productive, constructive, beneficial, advantageous, valuable.

gait noun **walk**, step, stride, pace, tread, way of walking, bearing, carriage; Brit. deportment.

gala noun **festival**, fair, fete, carnival, pageant, jubilee, jamboree, celebration.

gale noun **1 high wind**, blast, squall, storm, tempest, hurricane, tornado, cyclone, whirlwind, typhoon. **2 peal**, howl, hoot, shriek, roar, fit, paroxysm.

gallant adjective **1 brave**, courageous, valiant, bold, plucky, daring, fearless, intrepid, heroic, stout-hearted; informal gutsy, spunky. **2 chivalrous**, gentlemanly, courteous, polite, attentive, respectful, gracious, considerate, thoughtful.
- OPPOSITES cowardly, discourteous.

gamble verb **1 bet**, place a bet, wager, hazard; Brit. informal punt, have a flutter. **2 take a chance**, take a risk; N. Amer. take a flyer; informal stick your neck out; Brit. informal chance your arm.
● noun I took a gamble **risk**, chance, leap in the dark, speculation, lottery, pot luck.

game noun **1 pastime**, diversion, entertainment, amusement, distraction, recreation, sport, activity. **2 match**, contest, fixture, meeting, tie; Brit. clash.
● adjective **willing**, prepared, ready, disposed, interested, eager, keen, enthusiastic.

gang noun **band**, group, crowd, pack, horde, throng, mob, herd, swarm, troop; informal bunch, gaggle, load.

gangster noun **hoodlum**, racketeer, thug, villain, criminal, Mafioso; informal mobster, crook, tough; N. Amer. informal hood.

gaol noun & verb see **jail**.

gap noun **1 opening**, aperture, space, breach, chink, slit, crack, crevice, cleft, cavity, hole, interstice. **2 pause**, intermission, interval, interlude, break, breathing space, breather, respite, hiatus, lull; N. Amer. recess. **3 omission**, blank, lacuna. **4** the gap between rich and poor **chasm**, gulf, separation, contrast, difference, disparity, divergence, imbalance.

gape verb **1 stare**, goggle, gaze, ogle; *informal* rubberneck; *Brit. informal* gawp. **2 open**, yawn, part, split.

gaping adjective **wide**, broad, vast, yawning, cavernous.

garbage (*N. Amer.*) noun **1 waste**, refuse, rubbish, detritus, litter, junk, scrap, scraps, leftovers, remains; *N. Amer.* trash. **2 nonsense**, rubbish, balderdash, claptrap, twaddle, dross; *informal* hogwash, baloney, tripe, bilge, bull, bunk, poppycock, rot, piffle; *Brit. informal* tosh, codswallop.

garble verb **mix up**, muddle, jumble, confuse, obscure, distort.

garden noun park, estate, grounds.

> **WORD LINKS**
> **horticultural** relating to gardens

garish adjective **gaudy**, lurid, loud, harsh, showy, glittering, brash, tasteless, vulgar; *informal* flashy.
- OPPOSITES drab, tasteful.

garments plural noun **clothes**, clothing, dress, garb, wardrobe, costume, attire; *informal* gear, togs; *Brit. informal* clobber; *N. Amer. informal* threads; *formal* apparel.

garnish verb **decorate**, adorn, ornament, trim, dress, embellish.
● noun **decoration**, adornment, ornament, embellishment, enhancement, finishing touch.

garrison noun **1 troops**, forces, militia, soldiers, force, detachment, unit. **2 base**, camp, station, barracks, fort, command post.
● verb **station**, post, deploy, base, site, place, billet.

garrulous adjective **talkative**, loquacious, voluble, verbose, chatty, gossipy, effusive, expansive, forthcoming, conversational, communicative; *informal* mouthy, having the gift of the gab.
- OPPOSITES taciturn.

gash noun **cut**, laceration, slash, slit, split, wound, injury.
● verb **cut**, lacerate, slash, slit, split, wound, injure.

gasp verb **1 catch your breath**, gulp, draw in your breath. **2 pant**, puff, puff and blow, wheeze, breathe hard/heavily, choke, fight for breath.
● noun **gulp**, pant, puff.

gate noun **barrier**, turnstile, gateway, doorway, entrance, exit, door, portal; *N. Amer.* entryway.

gather verb **1 congregate**, assemble, meet, collect, get together, convene, muster, rally, converge. **2 summon**, call together, bring together, assemble, convene, rally, round up, muster, marshal. **3 harvest**, reap, crop, pick, pluck, collect. **4 understand**, believe, be led to believe, conclude, infer, assume, take it, surmise, hear, learn, discover. **5 pleat**, pucker, tuck, fold, ruffle.
- OPPOSITES disperse.

gathering noun **assembly**, meeting, convention, rally, council, congress, congregation, audience, crowd, group, throng, mass; *informal* get-together.

gauche adjective **awkward**, gawky, inelegant, graceless, ungraceful, clumsy, ungainly, maladroit, inept, unsophisticated.
- OPPOSITES elegant, sophisticated.

gaudy adjective **garish**, lurid, loud, glaring, harsh, showy, glittering, ostentatious, tasteless; *informal* flashy, tacky.
- OPPOSITES drab, tasteful.

gauge noun **meter**, measure, indicator, dial, scale, display.
● verb **1 measure**, calculate, compute, work out, determine, ascertain, count, weigh, quantify, put a figure on. **2 assess**, evaluate, determine, estimate, form an opinion of, appraise, weigh up, judge, guess; *informal* size up.

gaunt adjective **haggard**, drawn, thin, lean, skinny, spindly, spare, bony, angular, raw-boned, pinched, hollow-cheeked, scrawny, scraggy, as thin as a rake, cadaverous, skeletal, emaciated, skin and bone, wasted, withered; *informal* like a bag of bones.
- OPPOSITES plump.

gaze *verb* **stare**, gape, look fixedly, goggle, eye, scrutinize, ogle; *informal* rubberneck; *Brit. informal* gawp; *N. Amer. informal* eyeball.
● *noun* **stare**, gape, fixed look, regard, scrutiny.

gear *noun* **1 equipment**, apparatus, paraphernalia, tools, utensils, implements, instruments, rig, tackle; *Brit. informal* clobber. **2** (*informal*) **belongings**, possessions, effects, paraphernalia, bits and pieces; *informal* things, stuff, kit; *Brit. informal* clobber, gubbins. **3** (*informal*) **clothes**, clothing, garments, outfits, attire, garb, wardrobe; *informal* togs; *Brit. informal* clobber, kit; *N. Amer. informal* threads; *formal* apparel.

gem *noun* **1 jewel**, precious stone, semiprecious stone; *informal* rock, sparkler. **2 masterpiece**, classic, treasure, prize, find; *informal* one in a million, the bee's knees.

genealogy *noun* **lineage**, line (of descent), family tree, bloodline, pedigree, ancestry, heritage, parentage, family, stock, blood, roots.

general *adjective* **1** *suitable for general use* **widespread**, common, extensive, universal, wide, popular, public, mainstream. **2** *a general pay increase* **comprehensive**, overall, across the board, blanket, global, universal, mass, wholesale. **3 usual**, customary, habitual, traditional, normal, conventional, typical, standard, regular, accepted, prevailing, routine, established, everyday. **4** *a general description* **broad**, rough, loose, approximate, unspecific, vague, imprecise, inexact.
- OPPOSITES restricted, unusual, detailed.

generally *adverb* **1 normally**, in general, as a rule, by and large, mainly, mostly, for the most part, predominantly, on the whole, usually. **2 widely**, commonly, extensively, universally, popularly.

generate *verb* **create**, make, produce, engender, spawn, precipitate, prompt, provoke, trigger, spark off, stir up, induce.

generation *noun* **1 age**, age group, peer group. **2 crop**, batch, wave, range.

generosity *noun* **liberality**, lavishness, magnanimity, bounty, munificence, open-handedness, largesse, unselfishness, altruism, charity.
- OPPOSITES meanness, selfishness.

generous *adjective* **1 liberal**, lavish, magnanimous, giving, open-handed, bountiful, unselfish, ungrudging, free, unstinting, munificent; *literary* bounteous. **2 plentiful**, copious, ample, liberal, large, abundant, rich.
- OPPOSITES mean, selfish, meagre.

genesis *noun* **origin**, source, root, beginning, start.

genial *adjective* **friendly**, affable, cordial, amiable, warm, easy-going, approachable, sympathetic, good-natured, good-humoured, cheerful, hospitable, companionable, sociable, convivial, outgoing, gregarious; *informal* chummy, pally; *Brit. informal* matey.
- OPPOSITES unfriendly.

genius *noun* **1 brilliance**, intelligence, intellect, ability, cleverness, brains. **2 talent**, gift, flair, aptitude, facility, knack, ability, expertise, capacity, faculty. **3 brilliant person**, mastermind, Einstein, intellectual, brain, prodigy; *informal* egghead, bright spark; *Brit. informal* brainbox, clever clogs; *N. Amer. informal* brainiac.
● *adjective* (*informal*) **ingenious**, clever, canny, cunning, crafty, artful, slick, neat.

genre *noun* **category**, class, classification, group, set, type, sort, kind, variety.

genteel *adjective* **refined**, respectable, well mannered, courteous, polite, proper, correct, seemly, well bred, ladylike, gentlemanly, dignified, gracious.
- OPPOSITES uncouth.

gentle *adjective* **1 kind**, tender, sympathetic, considerate, understanding, compassionate, humane, mild, placid, serene. **2 light**, soft, quiet, low. **3 gradual**, slight, easy, slow, imperceptible.
- OPPOSITES brutal, strong, loud, steep.

g

genuine *adjective* **1 authentic**, real, actual, original, bona fide, true; *informal* pukka, the real McCoy, the real thing, kosher; *Austral./NZ informal* dinkum. **2 sincere**, honest, truthful, straightforward, direct, frank, candid, open, natural; *informal* straight, upfront.
- OPPOSITES bogus, insincere.

germ *noun* **1 microbe**, microorganism, bacillus, bacterium, virus; *informal* bug. **2** *the germ of an idea* **start**, beginnings, seed, embryo, bud, root, origin, source.

gesture *noun* **1 signal**, sign, motion, indication, gesticulation. **2 action**, act, deed, move.
● *verb* **signal**, motion, gesticulate, wave, indicate, give a sign.

get *verb* **1 obtain**, acquire, come by, receive, gain, earn, win, be given; *informal* get hold of, score. **2 become**, grow, turn, go. **3 fetch**, collect, go/come for, call for, pick up, bring, deliver, convey. **4 capture**, catch, arrest, apprehend, seize; *informal* collar, grab, pick up; *Brit. informal* nick. **5 contract**, develop, go down with, catch, fall ill with. **6 hear**, catch, make out, follow, take in. **7 understand**, comprehend, grasp, see, fathom, follow. **8 arrive**, reach, make it, turn up, appear, present yourself, come along; *informal* show up. **9 persuade**, induce, prevail on, influence, talk into. **10 prepare**, get ready, cook, make; *informal* fix, rustle up; *Brit. informal* knock up.
- OPPOSITES give.
□ **get across** communicate, get over, impart, convey, transmit, make clear, express. **get along** be friendly, be compatible, get on, agree, see eye to eye; *informal* hit it off. **get away** escape, run away/off, break free, bolt, flee, make off, take off, decamp; *informal* skedaddle, scarper; *Brit. informal* do a bunk, do a runner. **get by** manage, cope, survive, exist, subsist, muddle through/along, scrape by, make ends meet, make do; *informal* make out. **get out of** evade, dodge, shirk, avoid, escape, sidestep; *informal*

wriggle out of. **get round** cajole, persuade, wheedle, coax, prevail on, win over, bring round, sway, inveigle; *informal* sweet-talk, butter up. **get up** get out of bed, rise, stir, rouse yourself; *informal* surface.

ghastly *adjective* **1 terrible**, frightful, horrible, grim, awful, horrifying, shocking, appalling, gruesome, horrendous, monstrous. **2** *(informal)* **unpleasant**, objectionable, disagreeable, distasteful, awful, terrible, dreadful, frightful, detestable, vile; *informal* horrible, horrid.
- OPPOSITES pleasant.

ghost *noun* **spectre**, phantom, wraith, spirit, presence, apparition; *informal* spook.

> **WORD LINKS**
> **spectral** relating to a ghost

ghostly *adjective* **supernatural**, unearthly, spectral, phantom, unnatural, eerie, weird, uncanny; *informal* spooky.

giant *noun* **colossus**, mammoth, monster, leviathan, ogre.
- OPPOSITES dwarf.
● *adjective* **huge**, colossal, massive, enormous, gigantic, mammoth, vast, immense, monumental, mountainous, titanic, towering, gargantuan; *informal* mega, monster, whopping; *Brit. informal* ginormous.
- OPPOSITES miniature.

giddy *adjective* **1 dizzy**, light-headed, faint, unsteady, wobbly, reeling; *informal* woozy. **2 flighty**, silly, frivolous, skittish, irresponsible, scatty; *informal* dizzy.

gift *noun* **1 present**, handout, donation, offering, bonus, award, endowment; *informal* prezzie. **2 talent**, flair, aptitude, facility, knack, bent, ability, skill, capacity, faculty.

gifted *adjective* **talented**, skilled, accomplished, expert, able, proficient, intelligent, clever, bright, brilliant, precocious; *informal* crack, ace, genius.
- OPPOSITES inept.

gigantic *adjective* **huge**, enormous, vast, giant, massive, colossal, mammoth, immense, monumental, mountainous, cosmic, gargantuan; *informal* mega, monster, whopping, humongous; *Brit. informal* ginormous.
- OPPOSITES tiny.

giggle *verb & noun* **titter**, snigger, chuckle, chortle, laugh.

girl *noun* **young woman**, young lady, miss; *Scottish & N. English* lass, lassie; *Irish* colleen; *informal* chick; *Brit. informal* bird; *N. Amer. informal* gal, broad, dame, babe; *Austral./NZ informal* sheila.

girlfriend *noun* **sweetheart**, lover, partner, significant other, girl, woman; *informal* steady; *Brit. informal* bird; *N. Amer. informal* squeeze.

give *verb* **1 donate**, contribute, present with, award, grant, bestow, hand (over), bequeath, leave, make over. **2 convey**, pass on, impart, communicate, transmit, send, deliver, relay. **3 sacrifice**, give up, relinquish, devote, dedicate. **4 organize**, arrange, lay on, throw, host, hold, have. **5 perform**, execute, make, do. **6 utter**, let out, emit, produce, make.
- OPPOSITES receive, take.
- ❑ **give away** betray, inform on; *informal* split on, rat on; *Brit. informal* grass on, shop; *N. Amer. informal* finger; *Austral./NZ informal* dob in. **give in/up** capitulate, concede defeat, admit defeat, give up, surrender, yield, submit. **give off** emit, produce, send out, throw out, discharge, release. **give up** stop, cease, discontinue, desist from, abstain from, cut out, renounce, forgo; *informal* quit; *Brit. informal* jack in.

glad *adjective* **1 pleased**, happy, gratified, delighted, thrilled, overjoyed; *informal* over the moon; *Brit. informal* chuffed; *N. English informal* made up. **2** *I'd be glad to help* **willing**, eager, happy, pleased, delighted, ready, prepared.
- OPPOSITES dismayed, reluctant.

gladly *adverb* **with pleasure**, happily, cheerfully, willingly, readily, eagerly, freely, ungrudgingly.

glamorous *adjective* **1 beautiful**, elegant, chic, stylish, fashionable. **2 exciting**, glittering, glossy, colourful, exotic; *informal* glitzy, jet-setting.
- OPPOSITES dowdy, dull.

glamour *noun* **1** *she had undeniable glamour* **beauty**, allure, elegance, chic, style, charisma, charm, magnetism. **2** *the glamour of TV* **allure**, attraction, fascination, charm, magic, romance, excitement, thrill; *informal* glitz, glam.

glance *verb* **1 look briefly**, look quickly, peek, peep, glimpse, catch a glimpse. **2** *I glanced through the report* **read quickly**, scan, skim, leaf, flick, flip, thumb, browse.

glare *verb* **scowl**, glower, look daggers, frown, lour; *informal* give someone a dirty look.
- *noun* **1 scowl**, glower, angry stare, frown, black look; *informal* dirty look. **2 blaze**, dazzle, shine, beam, brilliance.

glaring *adjective* **1 dazzling**, blinding, blazing, strong, harsh. **2 obvious**, conspicuous, unmistakable, inescapable, unmissable, striking, flagrant, blatant.

glaze *verb* **cover**, coat, varnish, lacquer, polish.
- *noun* **coating**, topping, varnish, lacquer, polish.

gleam *verb* **shine**, glint, glitter, shimmer, glimmer, sparkle, twinkle, flicker, wink, glisten, flash.
- *noun* **flash**, glimmer, glint, shimmer, twinkle, sparkle, flicker, beam, ray, shaft.

glide *verb* **1** *a gondola glided past* **slide**, slip, sail, float, drift, flow. **2** *seagulls gliding over the waves* **soar**, wheel, plane, fly.

glimpse *noun* **glance**, brief/quick look, sight, sighting, peek, peep.
- *verb* **catch sight of**, sight, spot, notice, discern, spy, pick out, make out.

glitter *verb* **sparkle**, twinkle, glint, shimmer, glimmer, wink, flash, shine.
- *noun* **sparkle**, twinkle, glint, shimmer, glimmer, flicker, flash.

g

global *adjective* **1 worldwide**, international, world, intercontinental, universal. **2 comprehensive**, overall, general, all-inclusive, all-encompassing, universal, broad.

gloom *noun* **1 darkness**, dark, murk, shadows, shade. **2 despondency**, depression, dejection, melancholy, unhappiness, sadness, misery, woe, despair.
- OPPOSITES light, happiness.

gloomy *adjective* **1 dark**, shadowy, murky, sunless, dim, dingy. **2 despondent**, depressed, downcast, downhearted, dejected, dispirited, disheartened, demoralized, crestfallen, glum, melancholy; *informal* down in the mouth, down in the dumps. **3 pessimistic**, depressing, downbeat, disheartening, disappointing, unfavourable, bleak, black.
- OPPOSITES bright, cheerful.

glorious *adjective* **wonderful**, marvellous, magnificent, superb, sublime, spectacular, lovely, fine, delightful; *informal* stunning, fantastic, terrific, tremendous, sensational, heavenly, divine, gorgeous, fabulous, awesome.
- OPPOSITES undistinguished.

glory *noun* **1 honour**, distinction, prestige, fame, renown, kudos, eminence, acclaim, celebrity, praise, recognition. **2 magnificence**, splendour, grandeur, majesty, greatness, nobility, opulence, beauty, elegance.
- OPPOSITES shame.
● *verb we gloried in our independence* **delight**, triumph, revel, rejoice, exult, relish, savour, be proud of; *informal* get a kick out of.

gloss *noun* **shine**, sheen, lustre, gleam, patina, polish, brilliance, shimmer.
□ **gloss over** conceal, cover up, hide, disguise, mask, veil, play down, minimize, understate.

glossy *adjective* **shiny**, gleaming, lustrous, brilliant, glistening, glassy, polished, lacquered, glazed.
- OPPOSITES dull.

glow *verb* **1 shine**, gleam, glimmer, flicker, flare. **2 smoulder**, burn.
● *noun* **radiance**, light, gleam, glimmer.

glowing *adjective* **1 bright**, radiant, incandescent, luminous, smouldering; *literary* lambent. **2 rosy**, pink, red, ruddy, flushed, blushing, burning. **3 vivid**, vibrant, bright, brilliant, rich, intense, radiant. **4 complimentary**, favourable, enthusiastic, admiring, rapturous, fulsome; *informal* rave.

glue *noun* **adhesive**, gum, paste, cement; *N. Amer.* mucilage; *N. Amer. informal* stickum.
● *verb* **stick**, gum, paste, fix, seal, cement.

glum *adjective* **gloomy**, downcast, dejected, despondent, crestfallen, disheartened, depressed, doleful, miserable, woebegone; *informal* fed up, down in the dumps, down in the mouth.
- OPPOSITES cheerful.

go *verb* **1** *he's gone into town* **travel**, move, proceed, make your way, journey, advance, progress, pass. **2** *the road goes to London* **lead**, stretch, reach, extend. **3 leave**, depart, take yourself off, go away, withdraw, absent yourself, exit, set off, start out, get under way, be on your way; *Brit.* make a move; *informal* make tracks. **4 be used up**, be spent, be exhausted, be consumed. **5 become**, get, turn, grow. **6 turn out**, work out, develop, progress, result, end (up); *informal* pan out. **7 match**, harmonize, blend, be complementary, coordinate, be compatible. **8 function**, work, run, operate.
● *noun* (*informal*) **1 here, have a go** **try**, attempt, effort, bid; *informal* shot, stab, crack. **2 turn**, opportunity, chance, stint, spell, time.
□ **go down 1** sink, founder. **2** decrease, fall, drop, decline, plummet, plunge, slump. **go in for** take part in, participate in, engage in, get involved in, join in, enter into, undertake, practise, pursue, espouse, adopt, embrace. **go into** investigate, examine, enquire into, look into, research, probe,

explore, delve into, consider, review, analyse. **go off 1** explode, detonate, blow up. **2** *(Brit.)* go bad, go stale, go sour, turn, spoil, go rancid. **go on 1** last, continue, carry on, run on, proceed, endure, persist, take. **2** talk at length, ramble, rattle on, chatter, prattle; *Brit. informal* witter, rabbit. **3** happen, take place, occur, transpire; *N. Amer. informal* go down. **go out 1** be turned off, be extinguished, stop burning. **2** see, take out, be someone's boyfriend/girlfriend, be in a relationship with; *informal* date, go with. **go through 1** undergo, experience, face, suffer, live through, endure. **2** search, look, hunt, rummage, rifle. **3** examine, study, scrutinize, inspect, look over, scan, check.

goal noun **objective**, aim, end, target, intention, plan, purpose, ambition, aspiration.

gobble verb **guzzle**, bolt, gulp, devour, wolf; *informal* tuck into, put away, demolish; *Brit. informal* scoff; *N. Amer. informal* scarf (down/up).

god noun **deity**, goddess, divine being, divinity, immortal.

> **WORD LINKS**
>
> **divine** relating to God or a god
> **theology** study of God

golden adjective **blonde**, yellow, fair, flaxen.
- OPPOSITES dark.

gone adjective **1 away**, absent, off, out, missing. **2 past**, over (and done with), no more, done, finished, ended, forgotten. **3 used up**, consumed, finished, spent, depleted.

good adjective **1 fine**, superior, excellent, superb, outstanding, magnificent, exceptional, marvellous, wonderful, first-rate, first-class, quality; *informal* great, ace, terrific, fantastic, fabulous, class, awesome, wicked; *Brit. informal* brilliant. **2 virtuous**, righteous, upright, upstanding, moral, ethical, principled, law-abiding, blameless, honourable, decent, respectable, trustworthy;

informal squeaky clean. **3 well behaved**, obedient, dutiful, polite, courteous, respectful. **4 capable**, able, proficient, adept, adroit, accomplished, skilful, talented, masterly, expert; *informal* mean, wicked, nifty; *N. Amer. informal* crackerjack. **5 close**, intimate, dear, bosom, special, best, firm, loyal. **6 enjoyable**, pleasant, agreeable, pleasurable, delightful, lovely, amusing. **7** *it was good of you to come* **kind**, generous, charitable, gracious, noble, altruistic, unselfish. **8 convenient**, suitable, appropriate, fitting, fit, opportune, timely, favourable. **9** *milk is good for you* **wholesome**, healthy, nourishing, nutritious, beneficial. **10 tasty**, appetizing, flavoursome, palatable, succulent; *informal* scrumptious, scrummy, yummy; *Brit. informal* moreish. **11 valid**, genuine, authentic, legitimate, sound, bona fide, convincing, compelling. **12 fine**, fair, dry, bright, clear, sunny, cloudless, calm, warm, mild.
- OPPOSITES bad, wicked, naughty.
● noun **1 virtue**, righteousness, goodness, morality, integrity, honesty, truth, honour. **2** *it's for your own good* **benefit**, advantage, profit, gain, interest, welfare, well-being.
- OPPOSITES wickedness, disadvantage.
□ **for good** forever, permanently, for always, (for) evermore, for ever and ever; *N. Amer.* forevermore; *informal* for keeps.

goodbye exclam. **farewell**, adieu, au revoir, ciao, adios; *informal* bye, bye-bye, so long, see you (later); *Brit. informal* cheerio, cheers, ta-ta.

good-looking adjective **attractive**, beautiful, pretty, handsome, lovely, stunning, striking, arresting, gorgeous, prepossessing, fetching; *Scottish & N. English* bonny; *informal* tasty, easy on the eye; *Brit. informal* fit; *N. Amer. informal* cute, foxy; *old use* comely.
- OPPOSITES ugly.

goodness noun **1 virtue**, good, righteousness, morality, integrity, rectitude, honesty, honour, decency, respectability, nobility, worth, merit. **2 kindness**, humanity, benevolence, tenderness, warmth, affection, love, goodwill, sympathy, compassion, care, concern, understanding, generosity, charity.

goods *plural noun* **merchandise**, wares, stock, commodities, produce, products, articles.

goodwill *noun* **kindness**, compassion, goodness, benevolence, consideration, charity, decency, neighbourliness.
- OPPOSITES hostility.

gorge *noun* **ravine**, canyon, gully, defile, couloir, chasm, gulf; *S. English* chine; *N. English* gill; *N. Amer.* gulch, coulee.
□ **gorge yourself** stuff yourself, guzzle, overindulge; *informal* pig yourself, pig out, stuff your face.

gorgeous *adjective* **1 good-looking**, attractive, beautiful, pretty, handsome, lovely, stunning; *Scottish & N. English* bonny; *informal* fanciable, tasty, hot; *Brit. informal* fit; *N. Amer. informal* cute, foxy; *old use* comely. **2 spectacular**, splendid, superb, wonderful, grand, impressive, awe-inspiring, awesome, stunning, breathtaking; *informal* sensational, fabulous, fantastic. **3 resplendent**, magnificent, sumptuous, luxurious, elegant, dazzling, brilliant.
- OPPOSITES ugly, drab.

gossip *noun* **1 news**, rumours, scandal, hearsay, tittle-tattle; *informal* dirt, buzz; *N. Amer. informal* scuttlebutt. **2 chat**, talk, conversation, chatter, heart-to-heart, tête-à-tête; *informal* jaw, gas; *Brit. informal* natter, chinwag; *N. Amer. informal* gabfest. **3 gossipmonger**, busybody, scandalmonger, rumour-monger, muckraker.
● *verb* **1 talk**, whisper, tell tales, spread rumours; *informal* dish the dirt. **2** *people sat around gossiping* **chat**, talk, converse; *informal* gas, chew the fat, chew the rag, jaw; *Brit. informal* natter, chinwag; *N. Amer. informal* shoot the breeze.

gourmet *noun* **gastronome**, epicure, epicurean, connoisseur; *informal* foodie.

govern *verb* **1 rule**, preside over, control, be in charge of, command, run, head, manage, oversee, supervise. **2 determine**, decide, control, constrain, regulate, direct, rule, dictate, shape, affect.

government *noun* **administration**, executive, regime, authority, council, powers that be, cabinet, ministry.

governor *noun* **leader**, ruler, chief, head, administrator, principal, director, chairman, chairwoman, chair, superintendent, commissioner, controller; *informal* boss.

gown *noun* **dress**, frock, robe, habit, costume.

grab *verb* **seize**, grasp, snatch, take hold of, grip, clasp, clutch, catch.

grace *noun* **1 elegance**, poise, finesse, polish, fluency, smoothness, suppleness. **2** *he had the grace to apologize* **courtesy**, decency, (good) manners, politeness, respect. **3** *he fell from grace* **favour**, approval, approbation, acceptance, esteem, regard, respect.
- OPPOSITES awkwardness.
● *verb* **adorn**, embellish, decorate, ornament, enhance.

graceful *adjective* **elegant**, fluid, fluent, easy, polished, supple.

gracious *adjective* **courteous**, polite, civil, well mannered, tactful, diplomatic, kind, considerate, thoughtful, obliging, accommodating, hospitable.

grade *noun* **1** *hotels within the same grade* **category**, class, classification, ranking, quality, grouping, group, bracket. **2** *his job is of the lowest grade* **rank**, level, standing, position, class, status, order, echelon. **3 mark**, score, assessment, evaluation, appraisal. **4** (*N. Amer.*) **year**, form, class.
● *verb* **classify**, class, categorize, bracket, sort, group, arrange, pigeonhole, rank, evaluate, rate, value.

gradient *noun* **slope**, incline, hill, rise, ramp, bank; *N. Amer.* grade.

gradual *adjective* **1 slow**, steady, measured, unhurried, cautious, piecemeal,

step-by-step, bit-by-bit, progressive, continuous. **2 gentle**, moderate, slight, easy.
- OPPOSITES abrupt, steep.

gradually *adverb* **slowly**, steadily, slowly but surely, cautiously, gently, gingerly, piecemeal, bit by bit, by degrees, progressively, systematically.

graft *noun* **transplant**, implant.
● *verb* **1 splice**, join, insert, fix. **2 transplant**, implant.

grain *noun* **1 kernel**, seed. **2 granule**, particle, speck, bit, scrap, crumb, fragment, morsel. **3 trace**, hint, tinge, suggestion, shadow, soupçon, ounce, iota, jot, scrap, shred; *informal* smidgen. **4 texture**, weave, pattern, nap.

grand *adjective* **1 magnificent**, imposing, impressive, awe-inspiring, splendid, resplendent, majestic, monumental, palatial, stately; *Brit.* upmarket; *N. Amer.* upscale; *informal* fancy, posh; *Brit. informal* swish. **2 ambitious**, bold, epic, big, extravagant. **3 august**, distinguished, illustrious, eminent, venerable, dignified, proud. **4** *(informal)* **excellent**, marvellous, splendid, first-class, first-rate, wonderful, outstanding; *informal* superb, terrific, great, super; *Brit. informal* brilliant.
- OPPOSITES humble, poor.

grandeur *noun* **splendour**, magnificence, glory, resplendence, majesty, greatness, stateliness, pomp, ceremony.

grant *verb* **1** *he granted them leave of absence* **allow**, permit, agree to, accord, afford, vouchsafe. **2** *he granted them £20,000* **give**, award, bestow on, confer on, present with, endow with. **3 admit**, accept, concede, allow, appreciate, recognize, acknowledge, confess.
- OPPOSITES refuse, deny.
● *noun* **award**, bursary, endowment, scholarship, allowance, subsidy, contribution, handout, donation, gift.

graphic *adjective* **1 visual**, pictorial, illustrative, diagrammatic. **2 vivid**, explicit, detailed, realistic, descriptive,
powerful, colourful, lurid, shocking.
- OPPOSITES vague.

grapple *verb* **1 wrestle**, struggle, tussle, scuffle, battle. **2 deal**, cope, get to grips, tackle, confront, face.

grasp *verb* **1 grip**, clutch, clasp, clench, squeeze, catch, seize, grab, snatch. **2 understand**, comprehend, take in, see, apprehend, assimilate, absorb; *informal* get, take on board; *Brit. informal* twig.
● *noun* **1 grip**, hold, squeeze. **2 reach**, scope, power, range, sights. **3 understanding**, comprehension, awareness, grip, knowledge, mastery, command.

grasping *adjective* **greedy**, acquisitive, avaricious, rapacious, mercenary, materialistic; *informal* tight-fisted, tight, money-grubbing.

grate *verb* **1 shred**, pulverize, mince, grind, crush, crumble. **2 grind**, rub, rasp, scrape, jar, creak.

grateful *adjective* **thankful**, appreciative, indebted, obliged, in someone's debt, beholden.

gratitude *noun* **thanks**, gratefulness, thankfulness, appreciation, indebtedness, recognition, acknowledgement.

grave[1] *noun* **tomb**, burial place, last resting place, vault, mausoleum, sepulchre.

grave[2] *adjective* **1 serious**, important, weighty, profound, significant, momentous, critical, urgent, pressing, dire, terrible, dreadful. **2 solemn**, serious, sober, unsmiling, grim, sombre, dour.
- OPPOSITES trivial, light-hearted.

graveyard *noun* **cemetery**, churchyard, burial ground, necropolis, garden of remembrance; *Scottish* kirkyard.

gravity *noun* **1 seriousness**, importance, significance, weight, consequence, magnitude, acuteness, urgency, dreadfulness. **2 solemnity**, seriousness, sobriety, severity, grimness, sombreness, dourness.

graze[1] *verb* **feed**, eat, crop, nibble, browse.

graze² verb **1 scrape**, skin, scratch, chafe, scuff, rasp. **2 touch**, brush, shave, skim, kiss, scrape, clip, glance off.
● noun **scratch**, scrape, abrasion.

grease noun **oil**, fat, lubricant.

greasy adjective **oily**, fatty, buttery, oleaginous, slippery, slick, slimy, slithery; informal slippy.

great adjective **1 considerable**, substantial, significant, serious, exceptional, extraordinary. **2 large**, big, extensive, expansive, broad, wide, vast, immense, huge, enormous, massive, cosmic; informal humongous, whopping; Brit. informal ginormous. **3 prominent**, eminent, distinguished, illustrious, celebrated, acclaimed, admired, esteemed, renowned, notable, famous, well known, leading, top, major. **4 magnificent**, imposing, impressive, awe-inspiring, grand, splendid, majestic. **5 expert**, skilful, skilled, adept, accomplished, talented, fine, masterly, master, brilliant, virtuoso, marvellous, outstanding, first-class, superb; informal crack, class. **6 keen**, eager, enthusiastic, devoted, ardent, fanatical, passionate, dedicated, committed. **7 enjoyable**, delightful, lovely, excellent, marvellous, wonderful, fine, splendid; informal terrific, fantastic, fabulous, super, cool; Brit. informal brilliant.
- OPPOSITES little, small, minor, modest.

greatly adverb **very much**, extremely, considerably, substantially, significantly, markedly, seriously, materially, enormously, vastly, immensely, tremendously, mightily.

greatness noun **1 eminence**, distinction, celebrity, fame, prominence, renown, importance. **2 brilliance**, genius, prowess, talent, expertise, mastery, artistry, skill, proficiency, flair.

greed noun **1 avarice**, acquisitiveness, covetousness, materialism, mercenariness; informal money-grubbing. **2 gluttony**, hunger, voracity, self-indulgence; informal piggishness.

3 desire, appetite, hunger, thirst, craving, longing, yearning, hankering; informal itch.
- OPPOSITES generosity, temperance, indifference.

greedy adjective **1 gluttonous**, ravenous, voracious; informal piggish, piggy. **2 avaricious**, acquisitive, covetous, grasping, materialistic, mercenary; informal money-grubbing.

green adjective **1** olive green, pea green, emerald green, lime green, avocado, pistachio, bottle green, Lincoln green, jade. **2 verdant**, grassy, leafy. **3 environmental**, ecological, conservationist, eco-, eco-friendly. **4 inexperienced**, callow, raw, unseasoned, untried, naive, innocent, unworldly; informal wet behind the ears.

greet verb **1 say hello to**, address, salute, hail, welcome, meet, receive. **2** the decision was greeted with outrage **receive**, respond to, react to, take.

greeting noun **1 hello**, salutation, welcome, reception. **2 best wishes**, good wishes, congratulations, compliments, regards, respects.
- OPPOSITES farewell.

grey adjective **1 silvery**, gunmetal, slate, charcoal, smoky. **2 cloudy**, overcast, dull, dark, sunless, murky, gloomy, cheerless. **3 pale**, wan, ashen, pasty, pallid, colourless, waxen. **4 characterless**, colourless, nondescript, flat, bland, dull, boring, tedious, monotonous. **5** a grey area **ambiguous**, doubtful, unclear, uncertain, indefinite, debatable.

grief noun **sorrow**, misery, sadness, anguish, pain, distress, heartache, heartbreak, agony, woe, desolation.
- OPPOSITES joy.

grievance noun **complaint**, objection, grumble, grouse, ill feeling, bad feeling, resentment; informal gripe.

grieve verb **1 mourn**, sorrow, cry, sob, weep. **2 sadden**, upset, distress, pain, hurt, wound, break someone's heart.
- OPPOSITES rejoice.

grim *adjective* **1 stern**, forbidding, uninviting, unsmiling, dour, formidable. **2 dreadful**, ghastly, horrible, terrible, awful, appalling, frightful, shocking, grisly, gruesome, depressing, distressing, upsetting. **3 bleak**, dismal, dingy, wretched, miserable, depressing, cheerless, joyless, gloomy, uninviting.
- OPPOSITES amiable, pleasant.

grin *verb* & *noun* **smile**, beam, smirk.

grind *verb* **1 crush**, pound, pulverize, mill, crumble. **2 rub**, grate, scrape. **3 sharpen**, whet, hone, put an edge on, mill, machine, polish, smooth.
● *noun* **drudgery**, toil, labour, donkey work, exertion, chores; *informal* slog.

grip *verb* **1 grasp**, clutch, clasp, take hold of, clench, cling to, grab, seize, squeeze. **2 engross**, enthral, absorb, rivet, spellbind, fascinate, mesmerize.
● *noun* **1 grasp**, hold. **2 traction**, purchase, friction, adhesion. **3 control**, power, hold, stranglehold, clutches, influence.

gripping *adjective* **engrossing**, enthralling, absorbing, riveting, captivating, spellbinding, fascinating, compelling, thrilling, exciting, action-packed, dramatic.
- OPPOSITES boring.

groan *verb* **1 moan**, cry. **2 complain**, grumble, moan, mutter; *informal* grouse, bellyache, bitch, whinge. **3 creak**, grate, rasp.
● *noun* **1 moan**, cry. **2 complaint**, grumble, grievance, moan, muttering; *informal* grouse, gripe, whinge. **3 creaking**, creak, grating, grinding.

groom *verb* **1 curry**, brush, clean, rub down. **2 brush**, comb, arrange, do; *informal* fix. **3 prepare**, prime, condition, coach, train, drill, teach, school.

groove *noun* **furrow**, channel, trench, trough, rut, gutter, canal, hollow, indentation.

grope *verb* **fumble**, scrabble, fish, ferret, rummage, feel, search, hunt.

gross *adjective* **1** (*informal*) **disgusting**, repulsive, revolting, foul, nasty, obnoxious, sickening, nauseating, stomach-churning. **2 thorough**, complete, utter, out and out, shameful, serious, unacceptable, flagrant, blatant, obvious, barefaced, shameless, brazen. **3 total**, full, overall, combined, before deductions, before tax.
- OPPOSITES pleasant, net.
● *verb* **earn**, make, bring in, take, get, receive; *informal* rake in.

grotesque *adjective* **1 misshapen**, deformed, distorted, twisted, monstrous, hideous, freakish, unnatural, abnormal, strange; *informal* weird. **2 outrageous**, monstrous, shocking, appalling, preposterous, ridiculous, ludicrous, unbelievable, incredible.

ground *noun* **1 floor**, earth, terra firma; *informal* deck. **2 earth**, soil, turf, land, terrain. **3 stadium**, pitch, field, arena, track; *Brit. informal* park. **4** *the mansion's grounds* **estate**, gardens, park, land, property, surroundings, territory. **5** *grounds for dismissal* **reason**, cause, basis, foundation, justification, rationale, argument, occasion, excuse, pretext.
● *verb* **1 base**, found, establish, root, build, form. **2** *she was well grounded in the classics* **teach**, instruct, coach, tutor, educate, school, train, drill.

group *noun* **1 category**, class, classification, grouping, cluster, set, batch, type, sort, kind, variety, family. **2 crowd**, party, body, band, company, gathering, congregation, assembly, collection, cluster, clump, knot, flock, pack, troop, gang; *informal* bunch. **3 band**, ensemble, act; *informal* line-up, combo, outfit.
● *verb* **1 categorize**, classify, class, catalogue, sort, bracket, pigeonhole. **2 assemble**, collect, organize, place, arrange, range, line up, lay out.

grovel *verb* **1 prostrate yourself**, lie, kneel, cringe. **2 be obsequious**, fawn on, kowtow, bow and scrape, toady, dance attendance on, ingratiate yourself with; *informal* crawl, creep, suck up to, lick someone's boots.

grow verb **1 enlarge**, get bigger, get larger, get taller, expand, increase in size, extend, spread, swell, multiply, snowball, mushroom, balloon, build up, mount up, pile up. **2 sprout**, germinate, spring up, develop, bud, bloom, flourish, thrive, run riot. **3 cultivate**, produce, propagate, raise, rear, farm. **4 become**, get, turn, begin to be.
- OPPOSITES shrink, decline.

grown-up adjective **adult**, mature, of age, fully grown, independent.
● noun **adult**, woman, man, grown man/woman.
- OPPOSITES child.

growth noun **1 enlargement**, increase in size, expansion, extension, swelling, multiplication, mushrooming, snowballing, rise, escalation, build-up, development. **2 tumour**, malignancy, cancer, lump, swelling.

grubby adjective **dirty**, grimy, filthy, mucky, unwashed, stained, soiled; informal cruddy, yucky; Brit. informal manky.
- OPPOSITES clean.

grudge noun **grievance**, resentment, bitterness, rancour, ill will, animosity, antipathy, antagonism; informal a chip on your shoulder.

gruelling adjective **exhausting**, tiring, taxing, draining, demanding, exacting, difficult, arduous, strenuous, back-breaking, punishing, crippling; informal murderous; Brit. informal knackering.

gruesome adjective **grisly**, ghastly, frightful, horrid, horrifying, hideous, horrible, grim, awful, dreadful, terrible, horrific; informal sick, sick-making, gross.
- OPPOSITES pleasant.

grumble verb **complain**, grouse, whine, mutter, carp, make a fuss; informal moan, bellyache, bitch, whinge; N. English informal mither.
● noun **complaint**, grouse, grievance, protest; informal grouch, moan, whinge, beef, gripe.

grumpy adjective **bad-tempered**, crabby, tetchy, touchy, irascible, cantankerous, curmudgeonly, surly, fractious; informal grouchy; Brit. informal ratty; N. Amer. informal cranky, ornery.
- OPPOSITES good-humoured.

guarantee noun **1 warranty**. **2 promise**, assurance, word (of honour), pledge, vow, oath, commitment. **3 collateral**, security, surety, bond.
● verb **1 promise**, swear, pledge, vow, give your word, give an assurance, give an undertaking. **2 underwrite**, stand surety.

guard verb **protect**, defend, shield, secure, cover, mind, stand guard over, watch, keep an eye on.
● noun **1 sentry**, sentinel, nightwatchman, protector, defender, guardian, lookout, watch. **2 warder**, warden, keeper, jailer; informal screw. **3 cover**, shield, screen, fender, bumper, buffer.

guarded adjective **cautious**, careful, circumspect, wary, chary, reluctant, non-committal; informal cagey.

guardian noun **protector**, defender, preserver, custodian, warden, guard, keeper, curator, caretaker, steward, trustee.

> **WORD LINKS**
> **tutelary** relating to a guardian

guerrilla noun **rebel**, irregular, partisan, freedom fighter, revolutionary, terrorist.

guess verb **1 estimate**, reckon, judge, speculate, conjecture, hypothesize, surmise. **2** (informal) **suppose**, think, imagine, expect, suspect, dare say; informal reckon.
● noun **hypothesis**, theory, conjecture, surmise, estimate, belief, opinion, supposition, speculation, suspicion, impression, feeling.

guest noun **1 visitor**, caller, company. **2 client**, customer, resident, boarder, lodger, patron, diner, holidaymaker, tourist.
- OPPOSITES host.

guidance noun **1 advice**, counsel, instruction, suggestions, tips, hints, pointers, guidelines. **2 direction**, control, leadership, management, supervision.

guide noun **1 escort**, attendant, courier, leader, usher. **2 outline**, template, example, exemplar, model, pattern, guideline, yardstick, precedent. **3 guidebook**, travel guide, vade mecum, companion, handbook, manual, directory, A to Z, instructions, directions; *informal* bible.
● verb **1 lead**, conduct, show, usher, shepherd, direct, steer, pilot, escort. **2 direct**, steer, manage, conduct, run, be in charge of, govern, preside over, supervise, oversee. **3 advise**, counsel, direct.

guild noun **association**, society, union, league, organization, company, fellowship, club, order, lodge.

guilt noun **1 culpability**, blameworthiness, responsibility. **2 remorse**, shame, regret, contrition, self-reproach, a guilty conscience.
- OPPOSITES innocence.

guilty adjective **1 culpable**, to blame, at fault, in the wrong, responsible. **2 ashamed**, guilt-ridden, consciencestricken, remorseful, sorry, contrite, repentant, penitent, regretful, rueful, shamefaced.
- OPPOSITES innocent.

gulf noun **1 bay**, inlet, cove, bight, fjord, estuary, sound; *Scottish* firth. **2 gap**, divide, separation, difference, contrast.

gullible adjective **credulous**, naive, easily deceived, impressionable, unsuspecting, ingenuous, innocent, inexperienced, green; *informal* wet behind the ears.
- OPPOSITES suspicious.

gulp verb **1 swallow**, quaff, swill down; *informal* swig, down, knock back. **2 gobble**, guzzle, devour, bolt, wolf; *informal* shovel down; *Brit. informal* scoff. **3** *she gulped back her tears* **choke**

back, fight/hold back, suppress, stifle, smother.
● noun **mouthful**, swallow, draught; *informal* swig.

gum noun **glue**, adhesive, paste, cement; *N. Amer.* mucilage; *N. Amer. informal* stickum.
● verb **stick**, glue, paste, cement, attach.

gun noun **firearm**, side arm, handgun, weapon; *informal* shooter; *N. Amer. informal* piece, shooting iron.

gunman noun **armed criminal**, assassin, sniper, terrorist, gunfighter; *informal* hit man, gunslinger; *N. Amer. informal* shootist.

guru noun **1 spiritual teacher**, tutor, sage, mentor, spiritual leader, master. **2 expert**, authority, pundit, leading light, master, specialist.
- OPPOSITES disciple.

gush verb **surge**, stream, spout, spurt, jet, rush, pour, spill, cascade, flood; *Brit. informal* sloosh.
● noun **surge**, stream, spout, spurt, jet, rush, outpouring, spill, outflow, cascade, flood, torrent.

gushing adjective **effusive**, overenthusiastic, extravagant, fulsome, lavish, unrestrained; *informal* over the top.

gust noun **flurry**, blast, puff, blow, rush, squall.

gut noun **1 stomach**, belly, abdomen, paunch, intestines, viscera; *informal* tummy, insides, innards. **2** *(informal) he has a lot of guts* **courage**, bravery, backbone, nerve, pluck, spirit, daring, grit, fearlessness, determination; *Brit. informal* bottle; *N. Amer. informal* moxie.
● adjective *(informal)* **instinctive**, intuitive, deep-seated, involuntary, spontaneous, unthinking, knee-jerk.
● verb **1 clean (out)**, disembowel, draw; *formal* eviscerate. **2 strip**, empty, devastate, lay waste, ravage, ruin, wreck.

> **WORD LINKS**
> **visceral** relating to the gut

g

gutter noun **drain**, trough, trench, ditch, sluice, sewer, channel, conduit, pipe.

guy noun (informal) **man**, fellow; informal lad; Brit. informal chap, bloke, geezer; N. Amer. informal dude, hombre.

guzzle verb **1 gobble**, bolt, wolf, devour; informal tuck into, shovel down, hoover up; Brit. informal scoff; N. Amer. informal snarf, scarf. **2 gulp down**, quaff, swill; informal knock back, swig, slug, neck.

gyrate verb **rotate**, revolve, wheel, turn, whirl, circle, pirouette, twirl, swirl, spin, swivel.

Hh

habit *noun* **1 custom**, practice, routine, way; *formal* wont. **2** *(informal)* **addiction**, dependence, craving, fixation.

habitual *adjective* **1 constant**, persistent, continual, continuous, perpetual, non-stop, endless, never-ending; *informal* eternal. **2 inveterate**, confirmed, compulsive, incorrigible, hardened, ingrained, chronic, regular. **3 customary**, accustomed, regular, usual, normal, characteristic; *literary* wonted.
- OPPOSITES occasional.

hack *verb* **cut**, chop, hew, lop, saw, slash.

hackneyed *adjective* **overused**, overdone, overworked, worn out, time-worn, stale, tired, threadbare, trite, banal, clichéd.
- OPPOSITES original.

haggard *adjective* **drawn**, tired, exhausted, drained, careworn, gaunt, pinched, hollow-cheeked, hollow-eyed.

haggle *verb* **barter**, bargain, negotiate, wrangle.

hail[1] *noun* **barrage**, volley, shower, stream, salvo.

hail[2] *verb* **1 call out to**, shout to, address, greet, salute, say hello to. **2 flag down**, wave down. **3 acclaim**, praise, applaud. **4** *he hails from Australia* **come**, be, be a native of.

hair *noun* **1 head of hair**, shock of hair, mane, mop, locks, tresses, curls. **2 hairstyle**, haircut; *informal* hairdo. **3 fur**, wool, coat, fleece, pelt, mane.

hairdresser *noun* **hairstylist**, coiffeur, coiffeuse, barber.

hairy *adjective* **1 shaggy**, bushy, long-haired, woolly, furry, fleecy. **2 bearded**, unshaven, stubbly, bristly; *formal* hirsute. **3** *(informal)* **risky**, dangerous, perilous, hazardous, tricky; *informal* dicey; *Brit. informal* dodgy.

half-hearted *adjective* **unenthusiastic**, cool, lukewarm, tepid, apathetic.
- OPPOSITES enthusiastic.

halfway *adjective* **midway**, middle, mid, central, centre, intermediate.
● *adverb* **midway**, in the middle, in the centre, part of the way.

hall *noun* **1 entrance hall**, hallway, entry, entrance, lobby, foyer, vestibule, atrium. **2 assembly room**, meeting room, chamber, auditorium, theatre, house.

hallucination *noun* **delusion**, illusion, figment of the imagination, mirage, chimera, fantasy.

halt *verb* **1** *halt at the barrier* **stop**, come to a halt, come to a stop, come to a standstill, pull up, draw up. **2** *a strike halted production* **stop**, bring to a stop, put a stop to, suspend, arrest, check, curb, stem, staunch, block, stall.
● *noun* **1 stop**, standstill. **2 stoppage**, break, pause, interval, interruption.
- OPPOSITES start.

halting *adjective* **hesitant**, faltering, hesitating, stumbling, stammering, stuttering, broken, imperfect.
- OPPOSITES fluent.

hammer *verb* **beat**, batter, bang, pummel, pound, knock, thump.

hamper *verb* **hinder**, obstruct, impede, inhibit, delay, slow down, hold up, interfere with, handicap, hamstring.
- OPPOSITES help.

hand *noun* **1 fist**, palm; *informal* paw, mitt. **2 handwriting**, writing, script. **3 worker**, employee, workman, labourer, operative, craftsman.
● *verb* **pass**, give, present, let someone have.

> **WORD LINKS**
> **manual** relating to the hands

handbook *noun* **manual**, instructions, ABC, A to Z, companion, guide, guidebook, vade mecum.

handcuff *verb* **manacle**, shackle, clap/put someone in irons; *informal* cuff.
● *noun* (**handcuffs**) **manacles**, shackles, irons; *informal* cuffs, bracelets.

handful *noun* **few**, small number, small amount, small quantity, sprinkling, smattering, one or two, some, not many.
- OPPOSITES lot.

handicap *noun* **1 disability**, infirmity, defect, impairment, affliction. **2 impediment**, hindrance, obstacle, barrier, constraint, disadvantage, stumbling block.
- OPPOSITES benefit, advantage.
● *verb* **hamper**, impede, hinder, impair, hamstring, restrict, constrain.
- OPPOSITES help.

handle *verb* **1 hold**, pick up, grasp, grip, lift, finger. **2 control**, drive, steer, operate, manoeuvre. **3 deal with**, manage, tackle, take care of, look after, take charge of, attend to, see to, sort out. **4 trade in**, deal in, buy, sell, supply, peddle, traffic in.
● *noun* **grip**, haft, hilt, stock, shaft.

handsome *adjective* **1 good-looking**, attractive, striking; *informal* hunky, dishy, tasty, fanciable; *Brit. informal* fit; *N. Amer. informal* cute. **2 substantial**, considerable, sizeable, princely, generous, lavish, ample, bumper; *informal* tidy, whopping; *Brit. informal* ginormous.
- OPPOSITES ugly.

handy *adjective* **1 useful**, convenient, practical, neat, easy to use, userfriendly, helpful, functional. **2 ready**, to hand, within reach, accessible, readily available, nearby, at the ready. **3 skilful**, skilled, dexterous, deft, adept, proficient.

hang *verb* **1** *lights hung from the trees* **be suspended**, dangle, swing, sway, hover, float. **2** *hang the picture at eye level* **suspend**, put up, pin up, display. **3 decorate**, adorn, drape, festoon, deck out.

4 send to the gallows, execute, lynch; *informal* string up.

hang-up *noun* **neurosis**, phobia, preoccupation, fixation, obsession, inhibition, mental block; *informal* complex, thing, issue, bee in your bonnet.

hanker *verb* **yearn**, long, wish, hunger, thirst, lust, ache; *informal* itch.

haphazard *adjective* **random**, disorderly, indiscriminate, chaotic, hit-and-miss, aimless, chance; *informal* higgledy-piggledy.
- OPPOSITES methodical.

hapless *adjective* **unfortunate**, unlucky, unhappy, wretched, miserable.
- OPPOSITES lucky.

happen *verb* **1 occur**, take place, come about, arise, develop, result, transpire; *N. Amer. informal* go down; *literary* come to pass. **2** *I happened to be in London* **chance**, have the good/bad luck.

happening *noun* **occurrence**, event, incident, episode, affair.

happily *adverb* **1 cheerfully**, contentedly, cheerily, merrily, joyfully. **2 gladly**, willingly, readily, freely. **3 fortunately**, luckily, thankfully, mercifully, as luck would have it.

happiness *noun* **pleasure**, contentment, well-being, satisfaction, cheerfulness, good spirits, merriment, joy, joyfulness, delight, elation, jubilation.
- OPPOSITES sadness.

happy *adjective* **1 cheerful**, cheery, merry, joyful, jovial, jolly, carefree, in good spirits, in a good mood, pleased, contented, content, satisfied, gratified, delighted, sunny, radiant, elated, jubilant; *literary* blithe. **2 glad**, pleased, delighted, more than willing. **3 fortunate**, lucky, timely, convenient.
- OPPOSITES sad, unhappy, unfortunate.

harass *verb* **persecute**, intimidate, hound, pester, bother; *informal* hassle, bug; *N. Amer. informal* ride.

harassed *adjective* **stressed**, hard-pressed, careworn, worried, troubled; *informal* hassled.
- OPPOSITES carefree.

harassment noun **persecution**, intimidation, victimization, trouble, bother; informal hassle.

harbour noun **port**, dock, haven, marina, mooring, wharf, anchorage, waterfront.
● verb **1 shelter**, conceal, hide, shield, protect, give asylum to. **2 bear**, hold, nurse, foster.

hard adjective **1 firm**, solid, rigid, stiff, unbreakable, unyielding, compacted, compressed, tough, strong. **2 arduous**, strenuous, tiring, exhausting, back-breaking, gruelling, heavy, laborious, demanding, uphill; Brit. informal knackering. **3 industrious**, diligent, assiduous, conscientious, energetic, keen, enthusiastic, indefatigable. **4 difficult**, puzzling, complicated, complex, intricate, knotty, thorny, problematic. **5 harsh**, unpleasant, grim, austere, difficult, bad, bleak, tough. **6 forceful**, heavy, strong, sharp, violent, powerful.
- OPPOSITES soft, easy, gentle.
● adverb **1 forcefully**, roughly, heavily, sharply, violently. **2 diligently**, industriously, assiduously, conscientiously, energetically, doggedly; informal like mad, like crazy. **3 closely**, intently, critically, carefully, searchingly.

harden verb **1 solidify**, set, stiffen, thicken, cake, congeal. **2 toughen**, desensitize, inure, season, train, numb.
- OPPOSITES soften.

hardened adjective **inveterate**, seasoned, habitual, chronic, compulsive, confirmed, incorrigible.

hardly adverb **scarcely**, barely, only just, just.

hardship noun **difficulty**, privation, destitution, poverty, austerity, need, distress, suffering, adversity.
- OPPOSITES prosperity, ease.

hardware noun **equipment**, apparatus, gear, paraphernalia, tackle, kit, machinery.

hardy adjective **robust**, healthy, fit, strong, sturdy, tough, rugged.
- OPPOSITES delicate.

harm noun **injury**, damage, mischief, detriment, disservice.
- OPPOSITES good.
● verb **1 hurt**, injure, wound, lay a finger on, mistreat, ill-treat, maltreat. **2 damage**, spoil, affect, undermine, ruin.
- OPPOSITES heal, help.

harmful adjective **damaging**, injurious, detrimental, dangerous, unhealthy, unwholesome, environmentally unfriendly, hurtful, destructive, hazardous.
- OPPOSITES beneficial.

harmless adjective **1 safe**, innocuous, gentle, mild, non-toxic. **2 inoffensive**, innocuous, innocent, blameless, gentle.
- OPPOSITES harmful, objectionable.

harmonious adjective **1 melodious**, tuneful, musical, sweet-sounding, mellifluous, dulcet, euphonious. **2 friendly**, amicable, cordial, amiable, congenial, peaceful, in harmony, in tune. **3 balanced**, coordinated, pleasing, tasteful.
- OPPOSITES discordant, hostile.

harmonize verb **1 coordinate**, go together, match, blend, mix, balance, tone in, be compatible, be harmonious, suit each other, set each other off. **2 standardize**, coordinate, integrate, synchronize, make consistent, bring into line, systematize.
- OPPOSITES clash.

harmony noun **1 tunefulness**, euphony, melodiousness, unison. **2 accord**, agreement, peace, friendship, fellowship, cooperation, understanding, rapport, unity.
- OPPOSITES dissonance, disagreement.

harrowing adjective **distressing**, traumatic, upsetting, shocking, disturbing, painful, agonizing.

harry verb **harass**, hound, torment, pester, worry, badger, nag, plague; informal hassle, bug.

harsh adjective **1 grating**, rasping, strident, raucous, discordant, jarring, dissonant. **2 garish**, loud, glaring, gaudy, lurid. **3 cruel**, savage, barbarous, merciless, inhumane, ruthless, brutal,

hard-hearted, unfeeling, unrelenting.
4 severe, stringent, firm, stiff, stern,
rigorous, uncompromising, draconian.
5 rude, discourteous, unfriendly, sharp,
bitter, unkind, critical, disparaging.
6 austere, grim, spartan, hard, inhospitable. **7 cold**, freezing, icy, bitter, hard,
severe, bleak.
- OPPOSITES kind, mild, gentle.

harvest noun **crop**, yield, vintage,
produce.
● verb **gather**, bring in, reap, pick,
collect.

hassle (informal) noun **inconvenience**,
bother, nuisance, trouble, annoyance,
irritation, fuss; informal aggravation,
headache, pain in the neck.
● verb **harass**, pester, be on at, badger,
hound, bother, nag, torment; informal
bug; N. English informal mither.

haste noun **speed**, hurriedness, swiftness, rapidity, quickness, briskness,
alacrity; old use celerity.
- OPPOSITES delay.
□ **in haste** quickly, rapidly, fast, speedily, in a rush, in a hurry.

hasten verb **1 hurry**, rush, dash, race,
fly, speed; informal zip, hare, scoot,
hotfoot it; N. Amer. informal hightail.
2 speed up, bring on, precipitate,
advance.
- OPPOSITES dawdle, delay.

hasty adjective **hurried**, rash, impetuous, impulsive, reckless, precipitate,
spur-of-the-moment.
- OPPOSITES considered.

hate verb **1 loathe**, detest, despise,
dislike, abhor, shrink from, be unable
to bear/stand; formal abominate. **2 be
sorry**, be reluctant, be loath.
● noun **hatred**, loathing, abhorrence,
abomination, aversion, disgust.
- OPPOSITES love.

hatred noun see **hate** (noun).

haul verb **drag**, pull, heave, lug, hump.
● noun **booty**, loot, plunder, spoils,
stolen goods; informal swag.

haunt verb **torment**, disturb, trouble,
worry, plague, prey on.
● noun **meeting place**, stamping

ground, spot, venue; informal hang-
out; N. Amer. stomping ground.

haunted adjective **1 possessed**, cursed,
jinxed, eerie. **2 tormented**, anguished,
tortured, obsessed, troubled, worried.

haunting adjective **evocative**, affecting, stirring, powerful, poignant,
memorable.

have verb **1 own**, be in possession of, be
blessed with, boast, enjoy. **2 comprise**,
consist of, contain, include, incorporate, be composed of, be made up of.
3 eat, drink, take. **4 organize**, hold,
give, throw, put on, lay on. **5** I have to
get up at six **must**, be obliged to, be
required to, be compelled to, be forced
to, be bound to.
□ **have on 1** be wearing, be dressed in,
be clothed in, be decked out in, sport.
2 (Brit. informal) play a trick on, play a
joke on, pull someone's leg; Brit. informal wind up; N. Amer. informal put on.

haven noun **refuge**, retreat, shelter,
sanctuary, oasis.

havoc noun **chaos**, mayhem, bedlam,
pandemonium, a shambles.

hazard noun **danger**, risk, peril, menace, jeopardy, threat.

hazardous adjective **risky**, dangerous,
unsafe, perilous, fraught with danger,
high-risk; informal dicey; Brit. informal
dodgy.
- OPPOSITES safe.

haze noun **mist**, fog, cloud, vapour.

hazy adjective **1 misty**, foggy, smoggy,
murky. **2 vague**, dim, nebulous,
blurred, fuzzy.

head noun **1 skull**, cranium; informal
nut. **2 brain(s)**, brainpower, intellect,
intelligence, grey matter; Brit. informal
loaf; N. Amer. informal smarts. **3** a
head for business **aptitude**, talent, gift,
capacity. **4 leader**, chief, controller,
governor, superintendent, commander,
captain, director, manager, principal,
president; informal boss; Brit. informal
gaffer, guv'nor. **5 front**, beginning,
start, top.
● adjective **chief**, principal, leading,

main, first, top, highest.

● *verb* **command**, control, lead, manage, direct, supervise, superintend, oversee, preside over.

□ **head off 1** intercept, divert, redirect, re-route, turn away. **2** forestall, avert, stave off, nip in the bud, prevent, avoid, stop.

headache *noun* **1** sore head, migraine. **2** (*informal*) **problem**, worry, hassle, pain in the neck, bind.

heading *noun* **title**, caption, legend, rubric, headline.

headlong *adverb* **1 head first**, on your head. **2 without thinking**, precipitously, impetuously, rashly, recklessly, hastily.
- OPPOSITES cautiously.

● *adjective* **breakneck**, whirlwind, reckless, precipitous.

headquarters *plural noun* **head office**, HQ, base, nerve centre, mission control.

heady *adjective* **1 potent**, intoxicating, strong. **2 exhilarating**, exciting, stimulating, thrilling, intoxicating.

heal *verb* **1 cure**, make better, restore to health, treat. **2 get better**, be cured, recover, recuperate, mend, be on the mend. **3 put right**, repair, resolve, reconcile, settle; *informal* patch up.

health *noun* **1 well-being**, fitness, good condition, strength, robustness, vigour. **2** *her poor health forced her to retire* **condition**, state of health, physical shape, constitution.
- OPPOSITES illness.

> **WORD LINKS**
> **salubrious** good for the health

healthy *adjective* **1 well**, fit, in good shape, in fine fettle, in tip-top condition, strong, fighting fit; *informal* in the pink. **2 wholesome**, good for you, health-giving, nutritious, nourishing, invigorating, sanitary, hygienic.

heap *noun* **pile**, stack, mound, mountain.

● *verb* **pile (up)**, stack (up), make a mound of.

hear *verb* **1 make out**, catch, get, perceive, overhear. **2 learn**, find out, discover, gather, glean. **3 try**, judge, adjudicate on.

hearing *noun* **1 earshot**, hearing distance. **2 trial**, court case, enquiry, inquest, tribunal.

> **WORD LINKS**
> **auditory**, **aural** relating to hearing

heart *noun* **1 emotions**, feelings, sentiments, soul, mind. **2 compassion**, sympathy, humanity, fellow feeling(s), empathy, understanding, soul, goodwill. **3 enthusiasm**, spirit, determination, resolve, nerve; *Brit. informal* bottle. **4 centre**, middle, hub, core. **5 essence**, crux, core, nub, root, meat, substance, kernel; *informal* nitty-gritty.
□ **at heart** deep down, basically, fundamentally, essentially, in essence, intrinsically. **by heart** from memory, off pat, word for word, verbatim, parrot-fashion, word-perfect.

> **WORD LINKS**
> **cardiac** relating to the heart
> **coronary** relating to the heart's arteries
> **cardiology** branch of medicine concerning the heart

heartache *noun* **anguish**, suffering, distress, unhappiness, grief, misery, sorrow, sadness, heartbreak, pain, hurt, woe.
- OPPOSITES happiness.

heartbreaking *adjective* **distressing**, upsetting, disturbing, heart-rending, tragic, painful, sad, agonizing, harrowing.
- OPPOSITES comforting.

heartfelt *adjective* **sincere**, genuine, from the heart, earnest, profound, deep, wholehearted, honest.
- OPPOSITES insincere.

heartily *adverb* **1 wholeheartedly**, warmly, profoundly, eagerly, enthusiastically. **2 thoroughly**, completely, absolutely, exceedingly, downright; *N. Amer.* quite; *informal* seriously; *Brit.*

h

informal jolly; N. Amer. informal real, mighty.

heartless adjective **unfeeling**, unsympathetic, unkind, uncaring, hard-hearted, cold, callous, cruel, merciless, pitiless, inhuman.
- OPPOSITES compassionate.

hearty adjective **1 exuberant**, jovial, ebullient, cheerful, lively, loud, animated, vivacious, energetic, spirited. **2 wholehearted**, heartfelt, sincere, genuine, real. **3 robust**, healthy, hardy, fit, vigorous, sturdy, strong. **4 substantial**, large, ample, satisfying, filling, generous.

heat noun **1 warmth**, hotness, high temperature. **2 passion**, intensity, vehemence, fervour, excitement, agitation, anger.
- OPPOSITES cold, apathy.
● verb **1 warm (up)**, reheat, cook, keep warm. **2 get hot**, get warm, warm up; Brit. informal hot up.
- OPPOSITES cool.

> **WORD LINKS**
> **thermal** relating to heat

heated adjective **1 vehement**, passionate, impassioned, animated, lively, acrimonious, angry, bitter, furious, fierce. **2 excited**, animated, worked up, wound up, keyed up; informal het up.

heave verb **1 haul**, pull, drag, tug; informal yank. **2** (informal) **throw**, fling, cast, hurl, lob, pitch; informal chuck, sling. **3 let out**, breathe, give, emit, utter. **4 rise and fall**, roll, swell, surge, churn, seethe. **5 retch**, vomit, cough up; Brit. be sick; N. Amer. get sick; informal throw up, puke, chunder, chuck up, hurl, spew; N. Amer. informal barf.

heaven noun **1 paradise**, the hereafter, the next world, the afterworld, nirvana, Zion, Elysium. **2 bliss**, ecstasy, rapture, contentment, happiness, delight, joy, paradise.
- OPPOSITES hell.

> **WORD LINKS**
> **celestial** relating to heaven

heavenly adjective **1 divine**, angelic, holy, celestial. **2 celestial**, cosmic, stellar, sidereal. **3** (informal) **delightful**, wonderful, glorious, sublime, exquisite, beautiful, lovely, gorgeous, enchanting; informal divine, super, fantastic, fabulous.

heavily adverb **1 laboriously**, slowly, ponderously, awkwardly, clumsily. **2 decisively**, conclusively, roundly, soundly, utterly, completely, thoroughly. **3 excessively**, immoderately, copiously, intemperately. **4 densely**, closely, thickly. **5 deeply**, extremely, greatly, exceedingly, tremendously, profoundly.

heavy adjective **1 weighty**, hefty, substantial, ponderous, solid, dense, cumbersome, unwieldy. **2 forceful**, hard, strong, violent, powerful, mighty, sharp, severe. **3 strenuous**, hard, physical, difficult, arduous, demanding, back-breaking, gruelling. **4 intense**, fierce, relentless, severe, serious. **5 substantial**, filling, stodgy, rich, big.
- OPPOSITES light.

hectic adjective **frantic**, frenetic, frenzied, feverish, manic, busy, active, fast and furious.
- OPPOSITES leisurely.

heed verb **pay attention to**, take notice of, take note of, listen to, consider, take to heart, take into account, obey, adhere to, abide by, observe.
- OPPOSITES disregard.
● noun **attention**, notice, note, regard, thought.

hefty adjective **1 burly**, sturdy, strapping, bulky, strong, muscular, big, solid, well built; informal hulking, beefy. **2 powerful**, violent, hard, forceful, mighty. **3 substantial**, sizeable, considerable, stiff, large, heavy; informal whopping.
- OPPOSITES light.

height noun **1 tallness**, stature, elevation, altitude. **2** mountain heights **summit**, top, peak, crest, crown, tip, cap, pinnacle. **3** the height of their fame **highest point**, peak, zenith, pinnacle, climax.

- OPPOSITES width, nadir.

> **WORD LINKS**
> **acrophobia** fear of heights

heighten verb **intensify**, increase, enhance, add to, augment, boost, strengthen, deepen, magnify, reinforce.
- OPPOSITES reduce.

heinous adjective **odious**, wicked, evil, atrocious, monstrous, abominable, detestable, despicable, horrific, terrible, awful, abhorrent, loathsome, hideous, unspeakable, execrable.
- OPPOSITES admirable.

heir, **heiress** noun **successor**, next in line, inheritor, beneficiary, legatee.

hell noun **1 the underworld**, the netherworld, eternal damnation, perdition, hellfire, fire and brimstone, the Inferno, Hades. **2 misery**, torture, agony, purgatory, torment, a nightmare.
- OPPOSITES heaven, bliss.

> **WORD LINKS**
> **infernal** relating to hell

help verb **1 assist**, aid, abet, lend a hand, give assistance, come to the aid of, be of service, do someone a favour, do someone a service, do someone a good turn, rally round, pitch in. **2 support**, contribute to, give money to, donate to, promote, boost, back. **3 relieve**, soothe, ease, alleviate, improve, lessen. **4** *he could not help laughing* **resist**, avoid, refrain from, keep from, stop.
- OPPOSITES hinder, impede.
● noun **1 assistance**, aid, support, succour, benefit, use, advantage, service, solution. **2 relief**, alleviation, improvement, healing.
- OPPOSITES hindrance.

helper noun **assistant**, aide, deputy, auxiliary, supporter, second, mate, right-hand man/woman, attendant.

helpful adjective **1 obliging**, of assistance, supportive, accommodating, cooperative, neighbourly, eager to please. **2 useful**, beneficial, valuable, constructive, informative, instructive. **3 handy**, useful, convenient, practical, easy-to-use, serviceable; *informal* neat, nifty.
- OPPOSITES useless.

helping noun **portion**, serving, piece, slice, share, plateful; *informal* dollop.

helpless adjective **dependent**, incapable, powerless, paralysed, defenceless, vulnerable, exposed, unprotected.
- OPPOSITES independent.

hence adverb **consequently**, as a consequence, for this reason, therefore, so, accordingly, as a result, that being so.

herd noun **drove**, flock, pack, fold, swarm, mass, crowd, horde.

hereditary adjective **1 inherited**, bequeathed, handed down, passed down, family, ancestral. **2 genetic**, inborn, inherited, inbred, innate, in the family, in the blood, in the genes.

heritage noun **1 tradition**, history, past, background, culture, customs. **2 ancestry**, lineage, descent, extraction, parentage, roots, heredity, birth.

hermit noun **recluse**, loner, ascetic; *historical* anchorite, anchoress; *old use* eremite.

hero noun **1 star**, superstar, megastar, idol, celebrity, favourite, darling; *informal* celeb. **2 main character**, starring role, male protagonist, (male) lead, leading man; *informal* good guy.
- OPPOSITES villain.

heroic adjective **brave**, courageous, valiant, intrepid, bold, fearless, daring; *informal* gutsy, spunky.
- OPPOSITES cowardly.

heroine noun **1 star**, superstar, megastar, idol, celebrity, favourite, darling; *informal* celeb. **2 main character**, female protagonist, lead, leading lady, prima donna, diva.

heroism noun **bravery**, courage, valour, daring, fearlessness, pluck; *informal* guts, spunk; *Brit. informal* bottle; *N. Amer. informal* moxie.
- OPPOSITES cowardice.

h

hesitant *adjective* **1 uncertain**, undecided, unsure, doubtful, dubious, ambivalent, in two minds, wavering, vacillating, irresolute, indecisive; *Brit.* havering, humming and hawing; *informal* iffy. **2 timid**, diffident, shy, bashful, insecure, nervous.
- OPPOSITES certain, decisive, confident.

hesitate *verb* **1 pause**, delay, wait, stall, be uncertain, be unsure, be doubtful, be indecisive, vacillate, waver; *Brit.* haver, hum and haw; *informal* dilly-dally. **2** *don't hesitate to ask* **be reluctant**, be unwilling, be disinclined, scruple, have misgivings about, have qualms about, think twice about.

hidden *adjective* **1 concealed**, secret, invisible, unseen, camouflaged. **2 obscure**, unclear, concealed, cryptic, arcane, mysterious, secret, covert, abstruse, deep.
- OPPOSITES visible, obvious.

hide *verb* **1 conceal**, secrete, put out of sight, cache; *informal* stash. **2 conceal yourself**, secrete yourself, take cover, lie low, go to ground; *informal* hole up. **3 obscure**, block out, blot out, obstruct, cloud, shroud, veil, eclipse, camouflage. **4 keep secret**, conceal, cover up, keep quiet about, hush up, suppress, disguise, mask; *informal* keep a/the lid on.
- OPPOSITES reveal.

hideaway *noun* **retreat**, refuge, hiding place, hideout, safe house, den, bolt-hole; *informal* hidey-hole.

hideous *adjective* **1 ugly**, repulsive, repellent, unsightly, revolting, grotesque. **2 horrific**, terrible, appalling, awful, dreadful, frightful, horrible, horrendous, horrifying, shocking, sickening, gruesome, ghastly.
- OPPOSITES beautiful, pleasant.

hiding *noun* (*informal*) **beating**, thrashing, whipping, drubbing; *informal* licking, belting, pasting, walloping.

hierarchy *noun* **ranking**, order, pecking order, grading, ladder, scale.

high *adjective* **1 tall**, lofty, towering, giant, big, multi-storey, high-rise, elevated. **2 high-ranking**, leading, top, prominent, senior, influential, powerful, important, exalted; *N. Amer.* ranking. **3 inflated**, excessive, unreasonable, expensive, exorbitant, extortionate; *informal* steep, stiff. **4 high-pitched**, shrill, piercing, squeaky, penetrating, soprano, treble, falsetto.
- OPPOSITES low, deep.
● *adverb* **at a great height**, high up, way up, at altitude, in the sky, aloft, overhead, to a great height.
- OPPOSITES low.

highlight *noun* **high point**, climax, peak, pinnacle, height, zenith, summit, focus, feature.
● *verb* **spotlight**, call attention to, focus on, underline, show up, bring out, accentuate, accent, stress, emphasize.
- OPPOSITES play down.

hijack *verb* **commandeer**, seize, take over, appropriate, expropriate.

hike *noun* **1 walk**, trek, tramp, trudge, slog, march, ramble. **2 increase**, rise.
● *verb* **1 walk**, trek, tramp, trudge, slog, march, ramble, backpack. **2 increase**, raise, up, put up, push up; *informal* jack up, bump up.

hilarious *adjective* **very funny**, hysterical, uproarious, rib-tickling; *informal* side-splitting, priceless, a scream, a hoot.

hill *noun* **high ground**, hillock, hillside, rise, mound, knoll, hummock, fell, mountain; *Scottish* brae.

hinder *verb* **hamper**, impede, inhibit, thwart, foil, delay, interfere with, slow down, hold back, hold up, restrict, handicap, hamstring.
- OPPOSITES facilitate.

hindrance *noun* **impediment**, obstacle, barrier, obstruction, handicap, hurdle, restraint, restriction, encumbrance, complication, delay, drawback, setback, difficulty, inconvenience, hitch, stumbling block, fly in the ointment, hiccup; *Brit.* spanner in the works.
- OPPOSITES aid, help.

hint noun **1 clue**, inkling, suggestion, indication, sign, signal, intimation. **2 tip**, suggestion, pointer, guideline, recommendation. **3 trace**, touch, suspicion, suggestion, dash, soupçon; *informal* smidgen, tad.
● verb **imply**, insinuate, intimate, suggest, refer to, drive at, mean; *informal* get at.

hire verb **1 rent**, lease, charter. **2 employ**, engage, recruit, appoint, take on, sign up.
- OPPOSITES dismiss.

hiss verb **1 fizz**, whistle, wheeze. **2 jeer**, catcall, whistle, hoot.
- OPPOSITES cheer.
● noun **1 fizz**, whistle, wheeze. **2 jeer**, catcall, whistle, abuse, derision.
- OPPOSITES cheer.

historic adjective **significant**, notable, important, momentous, memorable, groundbreaking; *informal* earth-shattering.

historical adjective **1 documented**, recorded, chronicled, authentic, factual, actual. **2 past**, bygone, ancient, old, former.

history noun **1 the past**, former times, the olden days, yesterday, antiquity. **2 chronicle**, archive, record, report, narrative, account, study. **3 background**, past, life story, experiences, record.

hit verb **1 strike**, smack, slap, beat, punch, thump, thrash, batter, club, pummel, cuff, swat; *informal* whack, wallop, bash, clout, belt, clobber; *Brit. informal* slosh, stick one on; *N. Amer. informal* slug; *Austral./NZ informal* quilt. **2 crash into**, run into, smash into, knock into, bump into, plough into, collide with, meet head-on. **3 devastate**, affect badly, upset, shatter, crush, traumatize; *informal* knock sideways; *Brit. informal* knock for six.
● noun **1 blow**, slap, smack, thump, punch, knock, bang; *informal* whack, wallop, bash, clout, belt; *N. Amer. informal* slug. **2 success**, sell-out, winner, triumph, sensation, best-seller; *informal* smash hit, chart-topper, crowd-puller.
- OPPOSITES failure.
□ **hit back** retaliate, respond, reply, react, counter. **hit it off** (*informal*) get on (well), get along, be compatible, be on the same wavelength, see eye to eye, take to each other; *informal* click. **hit on** discover, come up with, think of, conceive of, dream up, invent, devise.

hitch verb **1 pull**, lift, raise; *informal* yank. **2 harness**, yoke, couple, fasten, connect, attach.
● noun **problem**, difficulty, issue, snag, setback, obstacle, complication; *informal* glitch, hiccup.

hoard noun **cache**, stockpile, store, collection, supply, reserve; *informal* stash.
● verb **stockpile**, store up, put aside, put by, lay by, set aside, cache, save, squirrel away; *informal* salt away.
- OPPOSITES squander.

hoarse adjective **rough**, harsh, croaky, throaty, gruff, husky, grating, rasping.

hoax noun **practical joke**, prank, trick, deception, fraud; *informal* con, spoof, wind-up, scam.

hobble verb **limp**, shamble, totter, dodder, stagger, stumble.

hobby noun **pastime**, leisure activity, sideline, diversion, relaxation, recreation, amusement.

hoist verb **raise**, lift, haul up, heave up, winch up, pull up, elevate.
● noun **crane**, winch, pulley, windlass.

hold verb **1 clasp**, clutch, grasp, grip, clench, cling to, hold on to, embrace, hug, squeeze. **2 detain**, imprison, lock up, keep behind bars, confine, intern, incarcerate. **3 take**, contain, accommodate, fit, have room for. **4 maintain**, consider, take the view, believe, think, feel, deem, be of the opinion, rule, decide; *informal* reckon. **5 convene**, call, summon, conduct, organize, run.
- OPPOSITES release.
● noun **1 grip**, grasp, clasp, clutch. **2 influence**, power, control, grip, dominance, authority, sway.

h

holder noun **1 bearer**, owner, possessor, keeper. **2 container**, receptacle, case, cover, housing, sheath.

hold-up noun **1 delay**, setback, hitch, snag, issue, difficulty, problem, glitch, hiccup, traffic jam, tailback; informal snarl-up. **2 robbery**, raid, armed robbery, mugging; informal stick-up; N. Amer. informal heist.

hole noun **1 opening**, aperture, orifice, gap, space, interstice, fissure, vent, chink, breach, crack, rupture, puncture. **2 pit**, crater, depression, hollow, cavern, cave, chamber. **3 burrow**, lair, den, earth, sett.

holiday noun **vacation**, break, rest, recess, time off, leave, day off, festival, feast day.

hollow adjective **1 empty**, hollowed out, void. **2 sunken**, deep-set, concave, depressed, recessed. **3 worthless**, meaningless, empty, profitless, fruitless, pointless, pyrrhic. **4 insincere**, false, deceitful, hypocritical, sham, untrue.
- OPPOSITES solid, convex.
● noun **1 hole**, pit, cavity, crater, trough, depression, indentation, dip. **2 valley**, vale, dale, dell.
● verb **gouge**, scoop, dig, cut, excavate, channel.

holy adjective **1 saintly**, godly, pious, religious, devout, God-fearing, spiritual. **2 sacred**, consecrated, hallowed, sanctified, venerated, revered.
- OPPOSITES sinful, irreligious.

homage noun **respect**, honour, reverence, worship, admiration, esteem, adulation, tribute.
- OPPOSITES contempt.

home noun **1 residence**, house, accommodation, property, quarters, lodgings, address, place; informal pad; formal abode, dwelling. **2 homeland**, native land, home town, birthplace, roots, fatherland, mother country, motherland. **3 institution**, hospice, shelter, refuge, retreat, asylum, hostel.
● adjective **domestic**, internal, local, national.
- OPPOSITES foreign, international.

homeless adjective **of no fixed abode**, without a roof over your head, on the streets, vagrant, sleeping rough, destitute.

homely adjective **1** (Brit.) **cosy**, comfortable, snug, welcoming, friendly; informal comfy. **2** (N. Amer.) **unattractive**, plain, unprepossessing, ugly; Brit. informal no oil painting.

homicide noun **murder**, manslaughter, killing, slaughter, butchery, assassination.

honest adjective **1** an honest man **upright**, honourable, principled, virtuous, good, decent, law-abiding, trustworthy, scrupulous, ethical, upstanding, right-minded. **2** I haven't been honest with you **truthful**, sincere, candid, frank, open, forthright, straight; informal upfront.
- OPPOSITES dishonest.

honestly adverb **1 fairly**, lawfully, legally, legitimately, honourably, decently, ethically; informal on the level. **2 sincerely**, genuinely, truthfully, truly, wholeheartedly, to be honest, to be frank, in all honesty, in all sincerity.

honesty noun **1 integrity**, uprightness, honour, righteousness, virtue, goodness, probity, trustworthiness. **2 sincerity**, candour, frankness, directness, truthfulness, truth, openness, straightforwardness.
- OPPOSITES dishonesty, insincerity.

honorary adjective **1 titular**, nominal, in name only, unofficial, token. **2** (Brit.) **unpaid**, unsalaried, voluntary, volunteer.

honour noun **1 integrity**, honesty, uprightness, morality, probity, principles, high-mindedness, decency, scrupulousness, fairness, justness. **2 distinction**, privilege, glory, kudos, cachet, prestige. **3 reputation**, good name, character, repute, image, standing, status. **4 privilege**, pleasure, compliment.
- OPPOSITES shame.

h

● *verb* **1 respect**, esteem, admire, look up to, value, cherish, revere, venerate. **2 applaud**, acclaim, praise, salute, recognize, celebrate, pay tribute to. **3 fulfil**, observe, keep, obey, heed, follow, carry out, keep to, abide by, adhere to, comply with, conform to, be true to.
- OPPOSITES disobey, break.

honourable *adjective* **1 honest**, moral, principled, righteous, decent, respectable, virtuous, good, upstanding, upright, noble, fair, trustworthy, law-abiding. **2 illustrious**, distinguished, eminent, great, glorious, prestigious.
- OPPOSITES dishonourable.

hook *noun* **1 peg**, nail. **2 fastener**, clasp, hasp, clip.
● *verb* **1 attach**, hitch, fasten, fix, secure, hang, clasp. **2 catch**, land, net, take, bag.

hooked *adjective* **curved**, hook-shaped, aquiline, angular, bent.
□ **hooked on** (*informal*) addicted to, dependent on, obsessed with, fanatical about, enthusiastic about; *informal* mad about.

hooligan *noun* **lout**, thug, tearaway, vandal, delinquent, ruffian, troublemaker; *Austral.* larrikin; *informal* tough, bruiser; *Brit. informal* yob, yobbo, lager lout; *Scottish informal* ned.

hoop *noun* **ring**, band, circle, wheel, circlet, loop.

hop *verb & noun* **jump**, bound, spring, bounce, skip, leap, prance, caper.

hope *noun* **1 aspiration**, desire, wish, expectation, ambition, aim, plan, dream. **2 optimism**, expectation, confidence, faith, belief.
- OPPOSITES pessimism.
● *verb* **1 expect**, anticipate, look for, be hopeful of, dream of. **2 aim**, intend, be looking, have the intention, have in mind, plan.

hopeful *adjective* **1 optimistic**, full of hope, confident, sanguine, positive, buoyant, bullish, upbeat. **2 promising**, encouraging, heartening, reassuring, favourable, optimistic.

- OPPOSITES pessimistic, discouraging.

hopefully *adverb* **1 optimistically**, full of hope, confidently, buoyantly, expectantly. **2 all being well**, if all goes well, God willing, with luck, touch wood, fingers crossed.

hopeless *adjective* **1 forlorn**, beyond hope, lost, irreparable, irreversible, incurable, impossible, futile. **2 bad**, poor, awful, terrible, dreadful, appalling, atrocious, incompetent; *informal* pathetic, useless, lousy, rotten; *Brit. informal* rubbish.
- OPPOSITES competent.

hopelessly *adverb* **utterly**, completely, irretrievably, impossibly, extremely, totally.

horde *noun* **crowd**, mob, pack, gang, troop, army, swarm, mass, throng.

horizontal *adjective* **level**, flat, parallel.
- OPPOSITES vertical.

horrible *adjective* **1 dreadful**, awful, terrible, shocking, appalling, horrifying, horrific, horrendous, grisly, ghastly, gruesome, harrowing, unspeakable, abhorrent. **2** (*informal*) **nasty**, horrid, disagreeable, obnoxious, disgusting, hateful, odious, objectionable, insufferable.
- OPPOSITES pleasant.

horrific *adjective* **dreadful**, horrendous, horrible, terrible, atrocious, horrifying, shocking, appalling, harrowing, hideous, grisly, ghastly, sickening.

horrify *verb* **shock**, appal, outrage, scandalize, offend, disgust, revolt, nauseate, sicken.

horror *noun* **1 terror**, fear, fright, alarm, panic. **2 dismay**, consternation, alarm, distress, disgust, shock.
- OPPOSITES delight, satisfaction.

horse *noun* **mount**, charger, cob, nag, hack, colt, stallion, mare, filly; *N. Amer.* bronco; *Austral./NZ* moke; *informal* gee-gee.

WORD LINKS
equine relating to horses
equestrian relating to horse riding

hospitable adjective **welcoming**, friendly, sociable, cordial, gracious, accommodating, warm.

hospital noun **infirmary**, clinic, sanatorium, hospice; *Brit.* cottage hospital; *Military* field hospital.

hospitality noun **friendliness**, neighbourliness, sociability, welcome, warmth, kindness, cordiality, generosity.

host noun **presenter**, compère, anchor, anchorman, anchorwoman, announcer.
- OPPOSITES guest.
● verb **present**, introduce, compère, front, anchor.

hostage noun **captive**, prisoner, detainee, internee.

hostile adjective **1 unfriendly**, unkind, unsympathetic, antagonistic, aggressive, confrontational, belligerent. **2 unfavourable**, adverse, bad, harsh, grim, inhospitable, forbidding. **3** *they are hostile to the idea* **opposed**, averse, antagonistic, ill-disposed, unsympathetic, antipathetic, against; *informal* anti.
- OPPOSITES friendly, favourable.

hostility noun **1 antagonism**, unfriendliness, malevolence, venom, hatred, aggression, belligerence. **2 opposition**, antagonism, animosity, antipathy. **3** *a cessation of hostilities* **fighting**, armed conflict, combat, warfare, war, bloodshed, violence.

hot adjective **1** *hot food* **heated**, sizzling, roasting, boiling, scorching, scalding, red-hot. **2** *a hot day* **very warm**, balmy, summery, tropical, scorching, searing, blistering, sweltering, torrid, sultry; *informal* boiling, baking, roasting. **3 spicy**, peppery, fiery, strong, piquant, powerful. **4 fierce**, intense, keen, competitive, cut-throat, ruthless, aggressive, violent. **5** *(informal) she's hot on local history* **knowledgeable**, well informed, au fait, well up, well versed; *informal* clued up.
- OPPOSITES cold, mild.

hotly adverb **vehemently**, vigorously, strenuously, fiercely, heatedly.

hound verb **pursue**, chase, stalk, harry, harass, pester, badger, torment.

house noun **1 residence**, home; *informal* pad; *Brit. informal* gaff; *formal* dwelling, abode, habitation, domicile. **2 family**, clan, tribe, dynasty, line, bloodline, lineage. **3 firm**, business, company, corporation, enterprise, establishment, institution, concern, organization, operation; *informal* outfit. **4 assembly**, legislative body, chamber, council, parliament, congress, senate.
● verb **1 accommodate**, give someone a roof over their head, lodge, quarter, board, billet, take in, sleep, put up. **2 contain**, hold, store, cover, protect, enclose.

household noun **family**, house, occupants, clan, tribe; *informal* brood.
● adjective **domestic**, family, everyday, workaday.

housing noun **1 accommodation**, houses, homes, living quarters; *formal* dwellings. **2 casing**, covering, case, cover, holder, fairing, sleeve.

hovel noun **shack**, slum, shanty, hut; *informal* dump, hole.

hover verb **1 hang**, be poised, be suspended, float, fly, drift. **2 wait**, linger, loiter.

however adverb **nevertheless**, nonetheless, even so, but, for all that, despite that, in spite of that.

howl noun **1 baying**, cry, bark, yelp, yowl. **2 wail**, cry, yell, yelp, bellow, roar, shout, shriek, scream, screech.
● verb **1 bay**, cry, bark, yelp, yowl. **2 wail**, cry, yell, bawl, bellow, shriek, scream, screech, caterwaul, ululate; *informal* holler.

hub noun **centre**, core, heart, focus, focal point, nucleus, kernel, nerve centre.
- OPPOSITES periphery.

huddle verb **1 crowd**, cluster, gather, bunch, throng, flock, collect, group, congregate. **2 curl up**, snuggle, nestle, hunch up.
- OPPOSITES disperse.

● *noun* **group**, cluster, bunch, collection; *informal* gaggle.

hue *noun* **colour**, shade, tone, tint, tinge.

hug *verb* **embrace**, cuddle, squeeze, clasp, clutch, hold tight.
● *noun* **embrace**, cuddle, squeeze, bear hug.

huge *adjective* **enormous**, vast, immense, massive, colossal, prodigious, gigantic, gargantuan, mammoth, monumental, giant, towering, mountainous, cosmic; *informal* mega, monster, astronomical; *Brit. informal* ginormous.
- OPPOSITES tiny.

hull *noun* **framework**, body, shell, frame, skeleton, structure.

hum *verb* **1 purr**, drone, murmur, buzz, whirr, throb. **2 be busy**, be active, be lively, buzz, bustle, be a hive of activity, throb.
● *noun* **murmur**, drone, purr, buzz.

human *adjective* **1 mortal**, flesh and blood, fallible, weak, frail, imperfect, vulnerable, physical, bodily, fleshly. **2 compassionate**, humane, kind, considerate, understanding, sympathetic.
● *noun* **person**, human being, Homo sapiens, man, woman, individual, mortal, (living) soul, earthling; (**humans**) the human race, humanity, humankind, mankind, people.

> **WORD LINKS**
> **anthropology** study of humankind

humane *adjective* **compassionate**, kind, considerate, understanding, sympathetic, tolerant, forbearing, forgiving, merciful, humanitarian, charitable.
- OPPOSITES cruel.

humanitarian *adjective* **1 compassionate**, humane, unselfish, altruistic, generous. **2 charitable**, philanthropic, public-spirited, socially concerned.
● *noun* **philanthropist**, altruist, benefactor, social reformer, good Samaritan, do-gooder.

humanity *noun* **1 humankind**, mankind, man, people, the human race, Homo sapiens. **2 compassion**, brotherly love, fellow feeling, humaneness, kindness, consideration, understanding, sympathy, tolerance.

humble *adjective* **1 meek**, deferential, respectful, submissive, self-effacing, unassertive, modest, unassuming, self-deprecating. **2 lowly**, poor, undistinguished, mean, common, ordinary, simple, modest.
- OPPOSITES proud, arrogant.
● *verb* **humiliate**, demean, lower, degrade, debase, mortify, shame.

humdrum *adjective* **mundane**, dull, dreary, boring, tedious, monotonous, prosaic, routine, everyday, run-of-the-mill, workaday, pedestrian.

humid *adjective* **muggy**, close, sultry, sticky, steamy, clammy, heavy.
- OPPOSITES dry, fresh.

humiliate *verb* **embarrass**, mortify, humble, shame, disgrace, chasten, deflate, crush, squash, demean, take down a peg or two; *informal* show up, put down, cut down to size; *N. Amer. informal* make someone eat crow.
- OPPOSITES dignify.

humiliating *adjective* **embarrassing**, mortifying, humbling, ignominious, inglorious, shaming, undignified, chastening, demeaning, degrading, deflating.

humiliation *noun* **embarrassment**, mortification, shame, indignity, ignominy, disgrace, dishonour, degradation, discredit, loss of face, blow to your pride.

humility *noun* **modesty**, humbleness, meekness, respect, deference, diffidence.
- OPPOSITES pride.

humorous *adjective* **amusing**, funny, comic, comical, entertaining, diverting, witty, jocular, light-hearted, hilarious.
- OPPOSITES serious.

humour *noun* **1 comedy**, funny side, hilarity, absurdity, ludicrousness, satire,

irony. **2 jokes**, jests, quips, witticisms, funny remarks, wit, comedy; *informal* gags, wisecracks. **3 mood**, temper, disposition, spirits.
– OPPOSITES seriousness.
● *verb* **indulge**, accommodate, pander to, cater to, give in to, go along with, flatter, mollify, placate.

hunch *noun* **feeling**, guess, suspicion, impression, inkling, idea, notion, fancy, intuition; *informal* gut feeling.

hunger *noun* **1 lack of food**, starvation, malnutrition, undernourishment. **2 desire**, craving, longing, yearning, hankering, appetite, thirst; *informal* itch.
□ **hunger after/for** desire, crave, long for, yearn for, pine for, ache for, hanker after, thirst for, lust for; *informal* itch for, be dying for, be gagging for.

hungry *adjective* **1 ravenous**, famished, starving, starved, malnourished, undernourished, underfed; *informal* peckish. **2** *they are hungry for success* **eager**, keen, avid, longing, yearning, aching, greedy, craving, desirous of, hankering after; *informal* itching, dying, gagging.
– OPPOSITES full.

hunk *noun* **chunk**, wedge, block, slab, lump, square, gobbet; *Brit. informal* wodge.

hunt *verb* **1 chase**, stalk, pursue, course, track, trail. **2 search**, seek, look high and low, scour the area.
● *noun* **1 chase**, pursuit. **2 search**, quest.

hurdle *noun* **obstacle**, difficulty, problem, barrier, bar, snag, stumbling block, impediment, obstruction, complication, hindrance.

hurl *verb* **throw**, toss, fling, launch, pitch, cast, lob; *informal* chuck, sling, bung.

hurricane *noun* **cyclone**, typhoon, tornado, storm, windstorm, whirlwind, gale, tempest; *Austral.* willy-willy; *N. Amer. informal* twister.

hurried *adjective* **1 quick**, fast, swift, rapid, speedy, brisk, cursory,

perfunctory, brief, short, fleeting. **2 hasty**, rushed, precipitate, spur-of-the-moment.
– OPPOSITES slow.

hurry *verb* **1 be quick**, hurry up, hasten, speed up, run, dash, rush, race, scurry, scramble, scuttle, sprint; *informal* get a move on, step on it, get a wiggle on, hightail it, hotfoot it; *Brit. informal* get your skates on. **2 hustle**, hasten, push, urge.
– OPPOSITES dawdle, delay.
● *noun* **rush**, haste, speed, urgency, hustle and bustle.

hurt *verb* **1 be painful**, ache, be sore, be tender, smart, sting, burn, throb; *informal* be agony. **2 injure**, wound, damage, disable, bruise, cut, gash, graze, scrape, scratch. **3 distress**, pain, wound, sting, upset, sadden, devastate, grieve, mortify.
● *noun* **distress**, pain, suffering, grief, misery, anguish, upset, sadness, sorrow.
● *adjective* **1 injured**, wounded, bruised, grazed, cut, gashed, sore, painful, aching. **2 pained**, aggrieved, offended, distressed, upset, sad, mortified; *informal* miffed.

hurtful *adjective* **upsetting**, distressing, wounding, unkind, cruel, nasty, mean, malicious, spiteful.

hush *verb* **silence**, quieten (down), shush, gag, muzzle; *informal* shut up.
● *noun* **silence**, quiet, stillness, peace, calm, tranquillity.
– OPPOSITES noise.
□ **hush up** keep secret, conceal, hide, suppress, cover up, keep quiet about, sweep under the carpet.

hut *noun* **shack**, shanty, cabin, shelter, shed, lean-to, hovel; *Scottish* bothy; *N. Amer.* cabana.

hybrid *noun* **cross**, cross-breed, mixture, blend, combination, composite, fusion, amalgam.
● *adjective* **composite**, cross-bred, interbred, mixed, blended, compound.

hygiene *noun* **cleanliness**, sanitation, sterility, purity, disinfection.

hygienic *adjective* **sanitary**, clean, germ-free, disinfected, sterilized, sterile, antiseptic, aseptic.
- OPPOSITES insanitary.

hypocritical *adjective* **sanctimonious**, pious, self-righteous, holier-than-thou, superior, insincere, two-faced.

hysteria *noun* **frenzy**, feverishness, hysterics, agitation, mania, panic, alarm, distress.
- OPPOSITES calm.

hysterical *adjective* **1 overwrought**, overemotional, out of control, frenzied, frantic, wild, beside yourself, manic, delirious; *informal* in a state. **2** *(informal)* **very funny**, hilarious, uproarious, rib-tickling; *informal* side-splitting, priceless, a scream, a hoot.
- OPPOSITES calm.

h

I i

ice *noun* **1** icicles, black ice, frost, permafrost, hoar (frost); *literary* rime. **2 ice cream**, water ice, sorbet; *N. Amer.* sherbet. **3 coldness**, coolness, frostiness, iciness, hostility, unfriendliness.

> **WORD LINKS**
> **glacial** relating to ice

icy *adjective* **1 iced (over)**, frozen, frosty, slippery, treacherous; *literary* rimy. **2 freezing**, chill, biting, bitter, raw, arctic. **3 unfriendly**, hostile, forbidding, cold, chilly, frosty, stern.

idea *noun* **1 concept**, notion, conception, thought. **2 plan**, scheme, design, proposal, proposition, suggestion, aim, intention, objective, goal. **3 thought**, theory, view, opinion, feeling, belief. **4 sense**, feeling, suspicion, fancy, inkling, hunch, notion. **5 estimate**, approximation, guess, conjecture; *informal* guesstimate.

ideal *adjective* **perfect**, faultless, exemplary, classic, archetypal, quintessential, model, ultimate, utopian, fairy-tale.
● *noun* **1** *an ideal to aim at* **model**, pattern, archetype, exemplar, example, perfection, epitome, last word. **2** *liberal ideals* **principle**, standard, value, belief, conviction, ethos.

idealistic *adjective* **Utopian**, visionary, romantic, quixotic, unrealistic, impractical.

identical *adjective* **(exactly) the same**, indistinguishable, twin, duplicate, interchangeable, alike, matching.
- OPPOSITES different.

identification *noun* **1 recognition**, singling out, pinpointing, naming. **2 determination**, establishing, ascertainment, discovery, diagnosis. **3 ID**, papers, documents, credentials, card, pass, badge.

identify *verb* **1 recognize**, pick out, spot, point out, pinpoint, put your finger on, name. **2 determine**, establish, ascertain, make out, discern, distinguish. **3** *we identify sport with glamour* **associate**, link, connect, relate. **4** *he identified with the team captain* **empathize**, sympathize, understand, relate to, feel for.

identity *noun* **individuality**, self, personality, character, originality, distinctiveness, uniqueness.

ideology *noun* **belief**; doctrine, creed, theory.

idiomatic *adjective* **colloquial**, everyday, conversational, vernacular, natural.

idiosyncrasy *noun* **peculiarity**, oddity, eccentricity, mannerism, quirk, characteristic.

idiot *noun* **fool**, ass, halfwit, blockhead, dunce, simpleton; *informal* nincompoop, clod, dimwit, dummy, fathead, numbskull; *Brit. informal* nitwit, twit, clot, berk, prat, pillock, wally, dork, twerp, charlie, moron; *N. Amer. informal* schmuck; *Austral./NZ informal* drongo.
- OPPOSITES genius.

idle *adjective* **1 lazy**, indolent, slothful, shiftless, work-shy. **2 unemployed**, jobless, out of work, redundant, unoccupied; *Brit. informal* on the dole. **3 unoccupied**, spare, empty, unfilled. **4 frivolous**, trivial, trifling, minor, insignificant, unimportant, empty, meaningless, vain.
- OPPOSITES industrious, busy.

idol *noun* **1 icon**, effigy, statue, figurine, totem. **2 hero**, heroine, star, superstar, icon, celebrity, darling; *informal* pin-up, heart-throb.

idolize *verb* **hero-worship**, worship, revere, venerate, look up to, exalt; *informal* put on a pedestal.

if *conjunction* **provided**, providing, on condition that, presuming, supposing, assuming, as long as, in the event that.

ignite *verb* **1 catch fire**, burst into flames, explode. **2 light**, set fire to, set alight, kindle.
- OPPOSITES extinguish.

ignorance *noun* **1 lack of knowledge**, lack of education, unenlightenment. **2 unfamiliarity**, incomprehension, inexperience, innocence.
- OPPOSITES education, knowledge.

ignorant *adjective* **1 uneducated**, unschooled, illiterate, uninformed, unenlightened, inexperienced, unsophisticated. **2 unaware**, unconscious, unfamiliar, unacquainted, uninformed; *informal* in the dark.
- OPPOSITES educated, knowledgeable.

ignore *verb* **1 snub**, look right through, cold-shoulder, take no notice of, pay no attention to, cut (dead); *informal* blank. **2 disregard**, take no account of, fail to observe, disobey, defy, overlook, brush aside, turn a blind eye to.
- OPPOSITES acknowledge, obey.

ill *adjective* **1 unwell**, sick, poorly, peaky, indisposed, nauseous, queasy; *informal* rough, under the weather; *Brit. informal* grotty; *Austral./NZ informal* crook. **2 ill effects harmful**, damaging, detrimental, deleterious, adverse, injurious, destructive, dangerous.
- OPPOSITES well, beneficial.
 ● *noun* **problem**, trouble, difficulty, misfortune, trial, tribulation; *informal* headache, hassle.
 ● *adverb* **1 barely**, scarcely, hardly, only just. **2 inadequately**, insufficiently, poorly, badly.

illegal *adjective* **unlawful**, illicit, illegitimate, criminal, fraudulent, corrupt, dishonest, outlawed, banned, forbidden, prohibited, proscribed, unlicensed, unauthorized; *informal* crooked, shady; *Brit. informal* bent, dodgy.
- OPPOSITES legal.

illegible *adjective* **unreadable**, indecipherable, unintelligible.

illegitimate *adjective* **illegal**, unlawful, illicit, criminal, felonious, fraudulent, corrupt, dishonest; *informal* crooked, shady; *Brit. informal* bent, dodgy.
- OPPOSITES legal, legitimate.

illicit *adjective* **illegal**, unlawful, criminal, outlawed, banned, forbidden, prohibited, proscribed, unlicensed, unauthorized, improper, disapproved of.
- OPPOSITES legal.

illness *noun* **sickness**, poor health, disease, ailment, disorder, complaint, indisposition, malady, affliction, infection; *informal* bug, virus.
- OPPOSITES health.

illogical *adjective* **irrational**, unreasonable, erroneous, invalid, spurious, fallacious, specious.

illuminating *adjective* **informative**, enlightening, revealing, explanatory, instructive, helpful, educational.
- OPPOSITES confusing.

illumination *noun* **light**, lighting, radiance, gleam, glow, glare.

illusion *noun* **1 delusion**, misapprehension, misconception, false impression, mistaken impression, fantasy, dream, fancy. **2 appearance**, impression, semblance. **3 mirage**, hallucination, apparition, figment of the imagination, trick of the light.

illusory *adjective* **false**, imagined, imaginary, fanciful, unreal, sham, fallacious.
- OPPOSITES genuine.

illustrate *verb* **1 decorate**, ornament, accompany, support. **2 explain**, elucidate, clarify, demonstrate, show, point up; *informal* get across/over.

illustration *noun* **1 picture**, drawing, sketch, figure, plate, image, print. **2 example**, sample, case, instance, exemplification, demonstration.

image *noun* **1 likeness**, depiction, portrayal, representation, painting, picture, portrait, drawing, photograph. **2 conception**, impression, perception, notion, idea. **3 persona**, profile, face.

WORD LINKS
iconography study of images

imaginary adjective **unreal**, non-existent, fictional, pretend, make-believe, invented, made-up, illusory.
- OPPOSITES real.

imagination noun **1 mind's eye**, fancy. **2 creativity**, vision, inventiveness, resourcefulness, ingenuity, originality.

imaginative adjective **creative**, visionary, inventive, resourceful, ingenious, original, innovative.

imagine verb **1 visualize**, envisage, picture, see in your mind's eye, dream up, think up/of, conceive. **2 assume**, presume, expect, take it (as read), suppose.

imbue verb **permeate**, saturate, suffuse, inject, inculcate, fill.

imitate verb **1 copy**, emulate, follow, echo, ape, parrot; informal rip off. **2 mimic**, do an impression of, impersonate, parody, caricature; informal take off, send up.

imitation noun **1 copy**, simulation, reproduction, replica, forgery. **2 emulation**, copying. **3 impersonation**, impression, parody, caricature; informal take-off, send-up, spoof.
● adjective **artificial**, synthetic, mock, fake, simulated, man-made, manufactured, substitute, ersatz.
- OPPOSITES real.

immaculate adjective **1 clean**, spotless, shining, shiny, gleaming, perfect, pristine, mint, flawless, faultless, unblemished; informal tip-top, A1. **2** his immaculate record **impeccable**, unsullied, spotless, unblemished, untarnished; informal squeaky clean.
- OPPOSITES dirty, damaged.

immature adjective **childish**, babyish, infantile, juvenile, puerile, callow.

immediate adjective **1 instant**, instantaneous, prompt, swift, speedy, rapid, quick. **2 current**, present, urgent, pressing. **3 nearest**, close, next-door, adjacent, adjoining.
- OPPOSITES delayed.

immediately adverb **1 straight away**, at once, right away, instantly, (right) now, directly, forthwith, there and then; informal pronto. **2 directly**, right, exactly, precisely, squarely, just, dead; informal slap bang; N. Amer. informal smack dab.
- OPPOSITES later.

immense adjective **huge**, massive, vast, enormous, gigantic, colossal, monumental, towering, giant, mammoth, cosmic; informal monster, whopping (great); Brit. informal ginormous.
- OPPOSITES tiny.

immerse verb **1 dip**, submerge, dunk, duck, sink. **2 absorb**, engross, occupy, engage, involve, bury, preoccupy; informal lose.

immigrant noun **newcomer**, settler, incomer, migrant, non-native, foreigner, foreign national, alien, expatriate.
- OPPOSITES native.

imminent adjective **near**, close (at hand), impending, approaching, coming, forthcoming, on the way, expected, looming.
- OPPOSITES distant.

immobile adjective **motionless**, still, stock-still, static, stationary, rooted to the spot, rigid, frozen, transfixed.

immodest adjective **indecorous**, improper, indecent, indelicate, immoral, forward, bold, brazen, shameless.

immoral adjective **wicked**, bad, wrong, unethical, unprincipled, unscrupulous, dishonest, corrupt, sinful, impure.
- OPPOSITES moral, ethical.

immortal adjective **1 undying**, deathless, eternal, everlasting, imperishable, indestructible. **2 timeless**, perennial, classic, time-honoured, enduring, evergreen.
- OPPOSITES mortal, ephemeral.

immovable adjective **1 fixed**, secure, set firm, set fast, stuck, jammed, stiff. **2 motionless**, unmoving, stationary, still, stock-still, rooted to the spot,

transfixed, paralysed, frozen.
- OPPOSITES mobile.

immune adjective **resistant**, not subject, not liable, not vulnerable, protected from, safe from, secure against.
- OPPOSITES susceptible, liable.

immunity noun **1 resistance**, protection, defence. **2 exemption**, exception, freedom, indemnity, privilege, prerogative, licence, impunity, protection.
- OPPOSITES susceptibility, liability.

immunize verb **vaccinate**, inoculate, inject.

impact noun **1 collision**, crash, smash, bump, knock. **2 effect**, influence, footprint, consequences, repercussions, ramifications.
● verb **1 crash into**, smash into, collide with, hit, strike, smack into, bang into. **2** *interest rates impacted on spending* **affect**, influence, hit, have an effect, make an impression.

impair verb **weaken**, damage, harm, undermine, diminish, reduce, lessen, decrease.
- OPPOSITES improve, enhance.

impart verb **communicate**, pass on, convey, transmit, relay, relate, tell, make known, report, announce.

impartial adjective **unbiased**, unprejudiced, neutral, non-partisan, disinterested, detached, dispassionate, objective.
- OPPOSITES biased, partisan.

impasse noun **deadlock**, dead end, stalemate, stand-off, standstill.

impatient adjective **1 restless**, agitated, nervous, anxious. **2 anxious**, eager, keen; *informal* itching, dying. **3 irritated**, annoyed, angry, tetchy, snappy, cross, curt, brusque.
- OPPOSITES patient.

impeccable adjective **flawless**, faultless, unblemished, spotless, stainless, perfect, exemplary, irreproachable; *informal* squeaky clean.
- OPPOSITES imperfect.

impede verb **hinder**, obstruct, hamper, hold back/up, delay, interfere with,

disrupt, retard, slow (down).
- OPPOSITES facilitate.

impediment noun **1 hindrance**, obstruction, obstacle, barrier, bar, block, check, curb, restriction, problem, issue. **2 defect**, impairment, stammer, stutter, lisp.

impending adjective **imminent**, close (at hand), near, approaching, coming, brewing, looming, threatening.

impenetrable adjective **1 unbreakable**, indestructible, solid, thick, unyielding. **2 impassable**, dense, thick, overgrown. **3 incomprehensible**, unfathomable, unintelligible, baffling, bewildering, confusing, opaque.

imperative adjective **vital**, crucial, critical, essential, pressing, urgent.

imperceptible adjective **unnoticeable**, undetectable, indiscernible, invisible, inaudible, impalpable, slight, small, subtle, faint.

imperfect adjective **faulty**, flawed, defective, inferior, second-rate, shoddy, substandard, damaged, blemished, torn, broken, cracked, scratched; *Brit. informal* duff.

imperious adjective **peremptory**, highhanded, overbearing, domineering, authoritarian, dictatorial, authoritative, bossy, arrogant; *informal* pushy, high and mighty.

impersonal adjective **aloof**, distant, remote, detached, unemotional, unsentimental, cold, cool, indifferent, unconcerned, formal, stiff, businesslike, matter-of-fact; *informal* starchy, stand-offish.

impersonate verb **imitate**, mimic, do an impression of, ape, parody, caricature, satirize, lampoon, masquerade as, pose as, pass yourself off as; *informal* take off, send up.

impertinent adjective **rude**, insolent, impolite, ill-mannered, disrespectful, impudent, cheeky, presumptuous, forward.
- OPPOSITES polite, respectful.

impetuous *adjective* **impulsive**, rash, hasty, reckless, foolhardy, imprudent, ill-considered, spontaneous, impromptu, spur-of-the-moment.

impetus *noun* **1 momentum**, drive, thrust, energy, force, power, push. **2 motivation**, stimulus, incentive, inspiration, driving force.

implant *verb* **1 insert**, embed, bury, inject, transplant, graft. **2 instil**, inculcate, introduce, plant, sow.

implausible *adjective* **unlikely**, improbable, questionable, doubtful, debatable, unconvincing, far-fetched.
- OPPOSITES convincing.

implement *noun* **tool**, utensil, instrument, device, apparatus, gadget, contraption, appliance; *informal* gizmo.
● *verb* **execute**, apply, put into effect, put into practice, carry out/through, perform, enact, fulfil.
- OPPOSITES abolish, cancel.

implicate *verb* **incriminate**, involve, connect, embroil, enmesh.

implication *noun* **1 suggestion**, inference, insinuation, innuendo, intimation, imputation. **2 consequence**, result, ramification, repercussion, reverberation, effect. **3 incrimination**, involvement, connection, entanglement, association.

implicit *adjective* **1 implied**, inferred, understood, hinted at, suggested, unspoken, unstated, tacit, taken for granted. **2 inherent**, latent, underlying, inbuilt, incorporated. **3 absolute**, complete, total, wholehearted, utter, unqualified, unconditional, unshakeable, unquestioning, firm.
- OPPOSITES explicit.

implore *verb* **plead with**, beg, entreat, appeal to, ask, request, call on, exhort, urge.

imply *verb* **1 insinuate**, suggest, infer, hint, intimate, give someone to understand, make out. **2 involve**, entail, mean, point to, signify, indicate, presuppose.

impolite *adjective* **rude**, bad-mannered, ill-mannered, discourteous, uncivil, disrespectful, insolent, impudent, impertinent, cheeky; *informal* lippy.

import *verb* **bring in**, buy in, ship in.
- OPPOSITES export.
● *noun* **1 importance**, significance, consequence, momentousness, magnitude, substance, weight, note, gravity, seriousness. **2 meaning**, sense, essence, gist, drift, message, thrust, substance, implication.
- OPPOSITES insignificance.

importance *noun* **1 significance**, momentousness, moment, import, consequence, note, weight, seriousness, gravity. **2 status**, eminence, prestige, worth, influence, power, authority.
- OPPOSITES insignificance.

important *adjective* **1 significant**, consequential, momentous, of great import, major, valuable, necessary, crucial, vital, essential, pivotal, decisive, far-reaching, historic. **2 powerful**, influential, well connected, high-ranking, prominent, eminent, notable, distinguished, esteemed, respected, great, prestigious.
- OPPOSITES insignificant.

impose *verb* **1** *he imposed his ideas on everyone* **foist**, force, inflict, press, saddle someone with. **2 levy**, charge, apply, enforce, set, establish, institute, introduce, bring into effect.
- OPPOSITES abolish.
□ **impose on** take advantage of, exploit, take liberties with, bother, trouble, disturb, inconvenience, put out, put to trouble.

imposing *adjective* **impressive**, spectacular, striking, dramatic, commanding, arresting, awesome, formidable, splendid, grand, majestic.
- OPPOSITES modest.

imposition *noun* **1 imposing**, foisting, forcing, inflicting. **2 levying**, charging, application, enforcement, enforcing, setting, establishment, introduction. **3 burden**, encumbrance, liberty, bother, worry; *informal* hassle.

impossible *adjective* **1 impracticable**, non-viable, unworkable, unattainable, unachievable, unobtainable, hopeless, out of the question; *informal* like herding cats. **2 unbearable**, intolerable, unendurable. **3** (*informal*) **unreasonable**, difficult, awkward, intolerable, unbearable, exasperating, maddening, infuriating.
- OPPOSITES possible.

impostor *noun* **impersonator**, deceiver, hoaxer, fraudster, fake, fraud; *informal* phoney.

impound *verb* **confiscate**, appropriate, take possession of, seize, commandeer, expropriate, requisition, take over.

impracticable *adjective* **unworkable**, unfeasible, non-viable, unachievable, unattainable, impractical; *informal* like herding cats.
- OPPOSITES practicable.

impractical *adjective* **1 unrealistic**, unworkable, unfeasible, non-viable, ill-thought-out, absurd, idealistic, fanciful, romantic, starry-eyed, pie-in-the-sky; *informal* cockeyed, crackpot, crazy. **2 unsuitable**, not sensible, inappropriate, unserviceable.
- OPPOSITES realistic, practical.

imprecise *adjective* **1 vague**, loose, indistinct, inaccurate, non-specific, sweeping, broad, general, hazy, fuzzy, woolly, nebulous, ambiguous, equivocal, uncertain. **2 inexact**, approximate, rough; *N. Amer. informal* ballpark.
- OPPOSITES exact.

impress *verb* **make an impression on**, have an impact on, influence, affect, move, stir, rouse, excite, inspire, dazzle, awe.
- OPPOSITES disappoint.
  □ **impress on** emphasize to, stress to, bring home to, instil in, inculcate into, drum into.

impression *noun* **1 feeling**, sense, fancy, (sneaking) suspicion, inkling, intuition, hunch, notion, idea. **2 opinion**, view, image, picture, perception, reaction, judgement, verdict,

estimation. **3 impact**, effect, influence. **4 indentation**, dent, mark, outline, imprint. **5 impersonation**, imitation, caricature; *informal* take-off.

impressionable *adjective* **easily influenced**, suggestible, susceptible, persuadable, pliable, malleable, pliant, ingenuous, trusting, naive, gullible.

impressive *adjective* **magnificent**, majestic, imposing, splendid, spectacular, grand, awe-inspiring, stunning, breathtaking.

imprint *verb* **stamp**, print, impress, mark, emboss.
 ● *noun* **impression**, print, mark, stamp, indentation.

imprison *verb* **incarcerate**, send to prison, jail, lock up, put away, intern, detain, hold prisoner, hold captive; *informal* send down; *Brit. informal* bang up.

imprisonment *noun* **custody**, incarceration, internment, confinement, detention, captivity; *informal* time; *Brit. informal* porridge.

improbable *adjective* **1 unlikely**, doubtful, dubious, debatable, questionable, uncertain. **2 unconvincing**, unbelievable, implausible, unlikely.

impromptu *adjective* **unrehearsed**, unprepared, unscripted, extempore, extemporized, improvised, spontaneous, unplanned; *informal* off-the-cuff.

improper *adjective* **1 unacceptable**, unprofessional, irregular, unethical, dishonest. **2 unseemly**, unfitting, unbecoming, unladylike, ungentlemanly, inappropriate, indelicate, indecent, immodest, indecorous, immoral. **3 indecent**, risqué, suggestive, naughty, dirty, filthy, vulgar, crude, rude, obscene, lewd; *informal* blue, raunchy, steamy.
- OPPOSITES proper, seemly.

improve *verb* **1 make better**, ameliorate, upgrade, refine, enhance, boost, build on, raise. **2 get better**, advance, progress, develop, make headway, make progress, pick up, look up, move forward. **3 recover**, get better,

recuperate, rally, revive, be on the mend.
- OPPOSITES worsen, deteriorate.

improvement noun **advance**, development, upgrade, refinement, enhancement, betterment, amelioration, boost, augmentation, rally, recovery, upswing.

improvise verb **1 extemporize**, ad-lib; informal speak off the cuff, play it by ear, busk it, wing it. **2 contrive**, devise, throw together, cobble together, rig up; informal whip up, rustle up; Brit. informal knock up.

impulse noun **1 urge**, instinct, drive, compulsion, itch, whim, desire, fancy, notion. **2 spontaneity**, impetuosity, recklessness, rashness.

impulsive adjective **1 hasty**, sudden, quick, precipitate, impetuous, impromptu, spontaneous, snap, unplanned, unpremeditated, thoughtless, rash, reckless. **2 impetuous**, instinctive, passionate, intuitive, emotional, devil-may-care.
- OPPOSITES cautious, premeditated.

inaccurate adjective **inexact**, imprecise, incorrect, wrong, erroneous, faulty, imperfect, defective, unreliable, false, mistaken, untrue; Brit. informal adrift.

inactivity noun **inaction**, inertia, idleness, non-intervention, negligence, apathy, indolence, laziness, slothfulness.
- OPPOSITES action.

inadequate adjective **1 insufficient**, deficient, poor, scant, scarce, sparse, in short supply, paltry, meagre. **2 incapable**, incompetent, ineffective, inefficient, inept, unfit; informal not up to scratch.

inadvertently adverb **accidentally**, by accident, unintentionally, by mistake, mistakenly, unwittingly.
- OPPOSITES intentionally.

inappropriate adjective **unsuitable**, unfitting, unseemly, unbecoming, improper, out of place/keeping, inapposite; informal out of order.

inaudible adjective **unclear**, indistinct, faint, muted, soft, low, muffled, whispered, muttered, murmured, mumbled.

inaugurate verb **1 initiate**, begin, start, institute, launch, get going, get under way, establish, bring in, usher in; informal kick off. **2 install**, instate, swear in, invest, ordain, crown.

incapable adjective **incompetent**, inept, inadequate, ineffective, ineffectual, unfit, unqualified; informal not up to it.
- OPPOSITES competent.

incense verb **enrage**, infuriate, anger, madden, outrage, exasperate, antagonize, provoke; informal make someone see red.
- OPPOSITES placate.

incensed adjective **enraged**, furious, infuriated, irate, raging, incandescent, fuming, seething, beside yourself, outraged; informal mad, hopping mad, wild, livid.

incentive noun **inducement**, motivation, motive, reason, stimulus, spur, impetus, encouragement, carrot; informal sweetener.
- OPPOSITES deterrent.

incident noun **1 event**, occurrence, episode, happening, affair, business, adventure, exploit, escapade. **2 disturbance**, commotion, clash, confrontation, scene, accident, fracas, contretemps; Brit. row. **3** the journey was not without incident **excitement**, adventure, drama, crisis, danger.

incidental adjective **1 secondary**, subsidiary, minor, peripheral, background, by-the-by, unimportant, insignificant, tangential. **2 chance**, accidental, random, fluky, fortuitous, serendipitous, coincidental, unlooked-for.
- OPPOSITES essential.

incidentally adverb **1 by the way**, by the by, in passing, speaking of which; informal as it happens. **2 by chance**, by accident, accidentally, fortuitously, by a fluke, by happenstance.

incite *verb* **1 stir up**, whip up, encourage, stoke up, fuel, kindle, inflame, instigate, provoke, excite, trigger, spark off. **2 provoke**, encourage, urge, goad, spur on, egg on, drive, prod, prompt; *informal* put up to.
- OPPOSITES discourage, deter.

inclination *noun* **tendency**, propensity, leaning, predisposition, predilection, impulse, bent, liking, taste, penchant, preference.
- OPPOSITES aversion.

incline *verb* **1 predispose**, lead, make, dispose, prejudice, prompt, induce. **2** *I incline to the opposite view* **tend**, lean, swing, veer, gravitate, be drawn, prefer, favour, go for. **3 bend**, bow, nod, bob, lower, dip.
● *noun* **slope**, gradient, pitch, ramp, bank, ascent, rise, hill, dip, descent; *N. Amer.* grade.

inclined *adjective* **1 disposed**, minded, of a mind. **2 prone**, given, in the habit of, liable, apt.

include *verb* **1 incorporate**, comprise, encompass, cover, embrace, take in, number, contain. **2 allow for**, count, take into account, take into consideration. **3 add**, insert, put in, append, enter.
- OPPOSITES exclude, leave out.

inclusive *adjective* **all-in**, comprehensive, overall, full, all-round, umbrella, catch-all, all-encompassing.
- OPPOSITES exclusive, limited.

income *noun* **earnings**, salary, wages, pay, remuneration, revenue, receipts, takings, profits, proceeds, yield, dividend; *N. Amer.* take.
- OPPOSITES expenditure, outgoings.

incoming *adjective* **1 arriving**, approaching, inbound, inward, returning, homeward. **2 new**, next, future, elect, designate.
- OPPOSITES outward, outgoing.

incompatible *adjective* **mismatched**, unsuited, poles apart, irreconcilable, inconsistent, conflicting, opposed, opposite, contradictory, at odds, at variance.

- OPPOSITES harmonious, consistent.

incompetent *adjective* **inept**, unskilled, inexpert, amateurish, unprofessional, bungling, blundering, clumsy; *informal* useless, not up to it.

incomplete *adjective* **1 unfinished**, uncompleted, partial, half-finished. **2 deficient**, insufficient, partial, sketchy, fragmentary, scrappy, bitty.
- OPPOSITES completed, full.

incomprehensible *adjective* **unintelligible**, impenetrable, unclear, indecipherable, unfathomable, abstruse, difficult, involved; *Brit. informal* double Dutch.
- OPPOSITES intelligible, clear.

inconsistent *adjective* **1 erratic**, changeable, unpredictable, variable, unstable, fickle, unreliable, volatile; *informal* up and down. **2 incompatible**, conflicting, at odds, at variance, irreconcilable, out of keeping, contrary.

inconvenience *noun* **trouble**, nuisance, bother, problem, disruption, difficulty, disturbance; *informal* aggravation, hassle, headache, pain, pain in the neck.
● *verb* **trouble**, bother, put out, put to any trouble, disturb, impose on.

inconvenient *adjective* **awkward**, difficult, inopportune, badly timed, unsuitable, inappropriate, unfortunate.

incorporate *verb* **1 absorb**, include, subsume, assimilate, integrate, swallow up. **2 include**, contain, embrace, build in, offer, boast. **3 blend**, mix, combine, fold in, stir in.

incorrect *adjective* **1 wrong**, erroneous, mistaken, untrue, false, fallacious, flawed; *informal* wide of the mark. **2 inappropriate**, unsuitable, unacceptable, improper, unseemly; *informal* out of order.
- OPPOSITES correct.

increase *verb* **1 grow**, get bigger, get larger, enlarge, expand, swell, rise, climb, mount, intensify, strengthen, extend, spread, widen. **2 add to**, make larger, make bigger, augment, supplement, top up, build up, extend,

raise, swell, inflate, intensify, heighten; *informal* up, bump up.
● *noun* **growth**, rise, enlargement, expansion, extension, increment, gain, addition, augmentation, surge; *informal* hike.
- OPPOSITES decrease.

incredible *adjective* **1 unbelievable**, unconvincing, far-fetched, implausible, improbable, inconceivable, unimaginable. **2 wonderful**, marvellous, spectacular, remarkable, phenomenal, prodigious, breathtaking; *informal* fantastic, terrific.

incur *verb* **bring on yourself**, expose yourself to, lay yourself open to, run up, earn, sustain, experience.

indecent *adjective* **1 obscene**, dirty, filthy, rude, naughty, vulgar, smutty, pornographic; *informal* blue; *euphemistic* adult. **2 unseemly**, improper, unbecoming, inappropriate.

independence *noun* **1 self-government**, self-rule, home rule, self-determination, sovereignty, autonomy. **2 impartiality**, neutrality, disinterestedness, detachment, objectivity.

independent *adjective* **1 self-governing**, self-ruling, self-determining, sovereign, autonomous, non-aligned, free. **2 separate**, different, unconnected, unrelated, discrete. **3 private**, non-state-run, private-sector, fee-paying, privatized, deregulated, denationalized. **4 impartial**, unbiased, unprejudiced, neutral, disinterested, uninvolved, detached, dispassionate, objective, non-partisan.
- OPPOSITES related, biased.

independently *adverb* **alone**, on your own, separately, individually, unaccompanied, solo, unaided, unassisted, without help, by your own efforts, under your own steam, single-handedly.

index *noun* **list**, listing, inventory, catalogue, register, directory, database.

indicate *verb* **1 point to**, be a sign of, be evidence of, demonstrate, show, testify to, be symptomatic of, denote, mark, signal, reflect, signify, suggest,
imply. **2 state**, declare, make known, communicate, announce, put on record. **3 specify**, designate, stipulate, show.

indication *noun* **sign**, signal, indicator, symptom, mark, demonstration, pointer, guide, hint, clue, omen, warning.

indicator *noun* **measure**, gauge, meter, barometer, guide, index, mark, sign, signal.

indictment *noun* **charge**, accusation, arraignment, prosecution, citation, summons; *N. Amer.* impeachment.

indifference *noun* **detachment**, lack of concern, disinterest, lack of interest, nonchalance, boredom, unresponsiveness, impassivity, coolness.
- OPPOSITES concern.

indifferent *adjective* **1 detached**, unconcerned, uninterested, uncaring, casual, nonchalant, offhand, unenthusiastic, unimpressed, unmoved, impassive, cool. **2 mediocre**, ordinary, average, middle-of-the-road, uninspired, undistinguished, unexceptional, pedestrian, forgettable, amateurish; *informal* no great shakes, not up to much.
- OPPOSITES enthusiastic, brilliant.

indignant *adjective* **aggrieved**, affronted, displeased, resentful, angry, annoyed, offended, exasperated; *informal* peeved, irked, put out; *Brit. informal* narked, not best pleased; *N. Amer. informal* sore.

indirect *adjective* **1 incidental**, secondary, subordinate, ancillary, collateral, concomitant, contingent. **2 roundabout**, circuitous, meandering, winding, tortuous. **3 oblique**, implicit, implied.

individual *adjective* **1 single**, separate, discrete, independent, lone. **2 unique**, characteristic, distinctive, distinct, particular, idiosyncratic, peculiar, personal, special. **3 original**, exclusive, different, unusual, novel, unorthodox, out of the ordinary.
- OPPOSITES multiple, shared, ordinary.
● *noun* **person**, human being, soul,

creature, character; *informal* type, sort, customer.

individually *adverb* **separately**, singly, one by one, one at a time, independently.

induce *verb* **1 persuade**, convince, prevail on, get, make, prompt, encourage, cajole into, talk into. **2 bring about**, cause, produce, create, give rise to, generate, engender.
- OPPOSITES dissuade.

indulge *verb* **1 satisfy**, gratify, fulfil, feed, yield to, give in to, go along with. **2 pamper**, spoil, overindulge, coddle, mollycoddle, cosset, pander to, wait on hand and foot.

indulgence *noun* **1 satisfaction**, gratification, fulfilment. **2 self-gratification**, self-indulgence, overindulgence, intemperance, excess, extravagance, hedonism. **3 extravagance**, luxury, treat, non-essential, extra, frill. **4 pampering**, coddling, mollycoddling, cosseting. **5 tolerance**, forbearance, understanding, compassion, sympathy, leniency.
- OPPOSITES asceticism, intolerance.

indulgent *adjective* **generous**, permissive, easy-going, liberal, tolerant, forgiving, forbearing, lenient, kind, kindly, soft-hearted.
- OPPOSITES strict.

industrialist *noun* **manufacturer**, factory owner, captain of industry, magnate, tycoon.

industry *noun* **1 manufacturing**, production, construction, trade, commerce. **2 business**, trade, field, line of business, profession. **3 activity**, energy, effort, endeavour, hard work, industriousness, diligence, application.

ineffective *adjective* **1 unsuccessful**, unproductive, unprofitable, ineffectual, unavailing, to no avail, fruitless, futile. **2 ineffectual**, inefficient, inadequate, incompetent, incapable, unfit, inept; *informal* useless, hopeless.
- OPPOSITES effective.

inefficient *adjective* **1 ineffective**, ineffectual, incompetent, inept, disorganized. **2 uneconomical**, wasteful,

unproductive, time-wasting, slow, unsystematic.

inequality *noun* **imbalance**, inequity, inconsistency, disparity, discrepancy, dissimilarity, difference, bias, prejudice, discrimination, unfairness.

inevitable *adjective* **unavoidable**, inescapable, inexorable, assured, certain, sure.
- OPPOSITES avoidable.

inevitably *adverb* **unavoidably**, necessarily, automatically, naturally, as a matter of course, of necessity, inescapably, certainly, surely; *informal* like it or not.

inexpensive *adjective* **cheap**, affordable, low-cost, economical, competitive, reasonable, budget, economy, bargain, cut-price, reduced.

inexperienced *adjective* **inexpert**, untrained, unqualified, unskilled, unseasoned, naive, new, callow, immature; *informal* wet behind the ears, wide-eyed.

infamous *adjective* **notorious**, disreputable, scandalous.
- OPPOSITES reputable.

infancy *noun* **beginnings**, early days, early stages, emergence, dawn, outset, birth, inception.
- OPPOSITES end.

infant *noun* **baby**, newborn, young child, tiny tot, little one; *Medicine* neonate; *Scottish & N. English* bairn, wean; *informal* tiny, sprog.

infect *verb* **contaminate**, pollute, taint, foul, poison, blight.

infection *noun* **1 disease**, virus, illness, ailment, disorder, sickness; *informal* bug. **2 contamination**, poison, bacteria, germs; *Medicine* sepsis.

infectious *adjective* **communicable**, contagious, transmittable, transmissible, transferable; *informal* catching.

inferior *adjective* **1 second-class**, lower-ranking, subordinate, junior, minor, lowly, humble, menial, beneath someone. **2 second-rate**, mediocre, substandard, low-grade, unsatisfactory, shoddy, poor; *informal* crummy, lousy.

- OPPOSITES superior.
● *noun* **subordinate**, junior, underling, minion.

infertility *noun* **barrenness**, sterility, childlessness.

infested *adjective* **overrun**, swarming, teeming, crawling, alive, plagued.

infiltrate *verb* **penetrate**, insinuate yourself into, worm your way into, sneak into, slip into, creep into, invade.

infiltrator *noun* **spy**, secret agent, plant, intruder, interloper, subversive, informer, mole, fifth columnist; *N. Amer. informal* spook.

infinite *adjective* **boundless**, unbounded, unlimited, limitless, never-ending, incalculable, untold, countless, uncountable, innumerable, numberless, immeasurable, cosmic.
- OPPOSITES limited.

inflame *verb* **1 enrage**, incense, anger, madden, infuriate, exasperate, provoke, antagonize; *informal* make someone see red. **2 aggravate**, exacerbate, intensify, worsen, compound.
- OPPOSITES placate.

inflamed *adjective* **swollen**, red, hot, burning, itchy, sore, painful, tender, infected.

inflate *verb* **1 blow up**, pump up, fill, puff up/out, dilate, distend, swell, bloat. **2 increase**, raise, boost, escalate, put up; *informal* hike up, jack up.
- OPPOSITES deflate, lower.

inflated *adjective* **1 high**, sky-high, excessive, unreasonable, outrageous, exorbitant, extortionate; *Brit.* over the odds; *informal* steep. **2 exaggerated**, immoderate, overblown, overstated.
- OPPOSITES low, modest.

inflict *verb* **1 give**, administer, deal out, mete out, exact, wreak. **2 impose**, force, thrust, foist.

influence *noun* **1 effect**, impact, control, spell, hold. **2** *a good influence on her* **example to**, role model for, inspiration to. **3 power**, authority, sway, leverage, weight, pull; *informal* clout.

● *verb* **1 affect**, have an impact on, determine, guide, control, shape, govern, decide, change, alter. **2 sway**, bias, prejudice, manipulate, persuade, induce.

influential *adjective* **powerful**, controlling, important, authoritative, leading, significant, instrumental, guiding.

inform *verb* **1 tell**, notify, apprise, advise, impart to, communicate to, let someone know, brief, enlighten, send word to. **2** *he informed on two colleagues* **betray**, give away, denounce, incriminate, report; *informal* rat, squeal, split, snitch, tell, blow the whistle; *Brit. informal* grass, shop; *N. Amer. informal* finger; *Austral./NZ informal* dob in.

informal *adjective* **1 unofficial**, casual, relaxed, easy-going, low-key. **2 colloquial**, vernacular, idiomatic, popular, familiar, everyday; *informal* slangy, chatty. **3 casual**, relaxed, comfortable, everyday; *informal* comfy.
- OPPOSITES formal.

information *noun* **facts**, particulars, details, figures, statistics, data, knowledge, intelligence; *informal* info, gen.

informative *adjective* **instructive**, illuminating, enlightening, revealing, explanatory, factual, educational, edifying.

informed *adjective* **knowledgeable**, enlightened, educated, briefed, up to date, up to speed, in the picture, in the know, au fait; *informal* clued up.
- OPPOSITES ignorant.

infuriate *verb* **enrage**, incense, provoke, anger, madden, exasperate; *informal* make someone see red; *Brit. informal* wind up.
- OPPOSITES please.

ingenious *adjective* **inventive**, creative, imaginative, original, innovative, pioneering, resourceful, enterprising, inspired, clever; *informal* genius.
- OPPOSITES unimaginative.

ingredient *noun* **constituent**, component, element, item, part, strand, unit, feature, aspect, attribute.

inhabit *verb* **live in**, occupy, settle, people, populate, colonize.

inhabitant *noun* **resident**, occupant, occupier, settler, local, native; (**inhabitants**) population, populace, people, public, community, citizenry, townsfolk, townspeople.

inhale *verb* **breathe in**, draw in, suck in, sniff in, drink in, gasp.
- OPPOSITES exhale.

inherit *verb* **be bequeathed**, be left, be willed, come into, succeed to, assume, take over.

inheritance *noun* **legacy**, bequest, endowment, birthright, heritage, patrimony.

> **WORD LINKS**
> **hereditary** relating to inheritance

inhibit *verb* **impede**, hinder, hamper, hold back, discourage, interfere with, obstruct, slow down, retard.
- OPPOSITES assist, allow.

inhibited *adjective* **reserved**, reticent, guarded, self-conscious, insecure, withdrawn, repressed, undemonstrative, shy, diffident, bashful; *informal* uptight.

initial *adjective* **beginning**, opening, commencing, starting, first, earliest, primary, preliminary, preparatory, introductory, inaugural.
- OPPOSITES final.

initially *adverb* **at first**, at the start, at the outset, in/at the beginning, to begin with, to start with, originally.

initiate *verb* **1 begin**, start (off), commence, institute, inaugurate, launch, instigate, establish, set up. **2** *he was initiated into a religious cult* **introduce**, admit, induct, install, swear in, ordain, invest.
- OPPOSITES end, expel.

initiative *noun* **1 enterprise**, resourcefulness, inventiveness, imagination, ingenuity, originality, creativity. **2 advantage**, upper hand, edge, lead, start. **3 scheme**, plan, strategy, measure, proposal, step, action.

inject *verb* **1 administer**, take; *informal* shoot (up), mainline, fix. **2 inoculate**, vaccinate. **3 insert**, introduce, feed, push, force, shoot. **4 introduce**, instil, infuse, imbue, breathe.

injection *noun* **1 inoculation**, vaccination, immunization, booster; *informal* jab, shot. **2 addition**, introduction, investment, dose, infusion, insertion.

injunction *noun* **order**, ruling, direction, directive, command, instruction, mandate.

injure *verb* **1 hurt**, wound, damage, harm, disable, break; *Medicine* traumatize. **2 damage**, mar, spoil, weaken, ruin, blight, blemish, tarnish, blacken.

injured *adjective* **1 hurt**, wounded, damaged, sore, bruised, broken, fractured; *Medicine* traumatized; *Brit. informal* gammy. **2 upset**, hurt, wounded, offended, reproachful, pained, aggrieved.
- OPPOSITES healthy.

injury *noun* **1 wound**, bruise, cut, gash, scratch, graze; *Medicine* trauma, lesion. **2 harm**, hurt, damage, pain, suffering. **3 offence**, abuse, injustice, disservice, affront, insult.

injustice *noun* **1 unfairness**, onesidedness, inequity, bias, prejudice, discrimination, intolerance, exploitation, corruption. **2 wrong**, offence, crime, sin, outrage, scandal, disgrace, affront.

inland *adjective* **interior**, inshore, internal, upcountry.
- OPPOSITES coastal.

inlet *noun* **1 cove**, bay, bight, creek, estuary, fjord, sound; *Scottish* firth. **2 vent**, flue, shaft, duct, channel, pipe.

inmate *noun* **1 patient**, inpatient, resident, occupant. **2 prisoner**, convict, captive, detainee, internee.

inner *adjective* **1 central**, innermost; *N. Amer.* downtown. **2 internal**, interior, inside, innermost. **3 hidden**, secret, deep, underlying, veiled.
- OPPOSITES outer.

innocence *noun* **1 guiltlessness**, blamelessness. **2 naivety**, credulity, inexperience, gullibility, ingenuousness.

innocent adjective **1 guiltless**, blameless, clean, irreproachable, above reproach, honest, upright, law-abiding. **2 harmless**, innocuous, safe, inoffensive, unobjectionable. **3 naive**, ingenuous, trusting, credulous, impressionable, easily led, inexperienced, unsophisticated, artless.
- OPPOSITES guilty.

innovation noun **change**, alteration, upheaval, reorganization, restructuring, novelty, departure.

innovative adjective **original**, new, novel, fresh, unusual, experimental, inventive, disruptive, ingenious, pioneering, groundbreaking, revolutionary, radical; informal edgy.

inquest noun **enquiry**, investigation, probe, examination, review, hearing.

inquire see enquire.

inquiry see enquiry.

insane adjective **1 mad**, of unsound mind, certifiable, psychotic, schizophrenic, unhinged; Brit. sectionable; informal crazy, raving mad, bonkers, loony, round the bend; Brit. informal crackers, off your trolley; N. Amer. informal nutso. **2 stupid**, idiotic, nonsensical, absurd, ridiculous, ludicrous, preposterous; informal crazy, mad; Brit. informal daft, barmy.
- OPPOSITES sane.

insect noun **bug**; informal creepy-crawly; Brit. informal minibeast.

> **WORD LINKS**
> **entomology** study of insects

insecure adjective **1 unconfident**, uncertain, unsure, doubtful, diffident, hesitant, self-conscious, anxious, fearful. **2 unprotected**, unguarded, vulnerable, unsecured. **3 unstable**, rickety, wobbly, shaky, unsteady, precarious.
- OPPOSITES confident, stable.

insecurity noun **lack of confidence**, uncertainty, self-doubt, diffidence, hesitancy, nervousness, self-consciousness, anxiety, worry, unease.

insert verb **put**, place, push, thrust, slide, slip, load, fit, slot, install; informal pop, stick, bung.
- OPPOSITES extract, remove.

inside noun **1 interior**, centre, core, middle, heart. **2 (insides) stomach**, gut, bowels, intestines; informal tummy, belly, guts.
● adjective **1 inner**, interior, internal, innermost. **2 confidential**, classified, restricted, privileged, private, secret, exclusive; informal hush-hush.
- OPPOSITES outside.

insight noun **intuition**, perception, understanding, comprehension, appreciation, judgement, discernment, vision, imagination, wisdom; informal nous.

insignificant adjective **unimportant**, trivial, trifling, negligible, inconsequential, of no account, paltry, petty, insubstantial; informal piddling.

insincere adjective **false**, fake, hollow, artificial, feigned, pretended, put-on, disingenuous, hypocritical, cynical; informal phoney, pretend.

insist verb **1 stand firm**, stand your ground, be resolute, be determined, hold out, persist, be emphatic, lay down the law, not take no for an answer; informal stick to your guns, put your foot down. **2 demand**, command, order, require. **3 maintain**, assert, protest, swear, declare, repeat.

insistent adjective **persistent**, determined, tenacious, unyielding, dogged, unrelenting, importunate, relentless, inexorable.

inspect verb **examine**, check, scrutinize, investigate, vet, test, monitor, survey, study, look over; informal check out, give something a/the once-over.

inspection noun **examination**, check-up, survey, scrutiny, exploration, investigation; informal once-over, going-over.

inspector noun **examiner**, scrutineer, investigator, surveyor, assessor, supervisor, monitor, watchdog, ombudsman, auditor.

inspiration noun **1 stimulus**, motivation, encouragement, influence, spur, fillip; informal shot in the arm. **2 creativity**, invention, innovation, ingenuity, imagination, originality, insight, vision. **3 bright idea**, revelation; informal brainwave; N. Amer. informal brainstorm.

inspire verb **1 stimulate**, motivate, encourage, influence, move, spur, energize, galvanize. **2 give rise to**, lead to, bring about, prompt, spawn, engender. **3 arouse**, awaken, prompt, induce, ignite, trigger, kindle, produce, bring out.

inspired adjective **outstanding**, wonderful, marvellous, excellent, magnificent, coruscating, exceptional, first-class, virtuoso, superlative; informal tremendous, superb, awesome, out of this world, genius; Brit. informal brilliant.

inspiring adjective **inspirational**, encouraging, heartening, uplifting, stirring, rousing, electrifying, moving.

instability noun **unreliability**, uncertainty, unpredictability, insecurity, volatility, capriciousness, changeability, variability, inconsistency, mutability.
- OPPOSITES stability.

install verb **1 put**, place, station, site, insert. **2 swear in**, induct, inaugurate, invest, appoint, ordain, consecrate, anoint, enthrone, crown. **3 ensconce**, position, settle, seat, plant, sit (down); informal plonk, park.
- OPPOSITES remove.

instalment noun **1 payment**, repayment, tranche, portion. **2 part**, episode, chapter, issue, programme, section, segment, volume.

instance noun **example**, occasion, occurrence, case, illustration, sample.

instant adjective **1 immediate**, instantaneous, on-the-spot, prompt, swift, speedy, rapid, quick; informal snappy. **2 prepared**, pre-cooked, microwaveable.
- OPPOSITES delayed.
  ● noun **moment**, minute, second, split second, trice, twinkling of an eye, flash; informal jiffy.

instantly adverb **immediately**, at once, straight away, right away, instantaneously, forthwith, there and then, here and now, this/that minute, this/that second.

instead adverb **as an alternative**, in lieu, alternatively, rather, on second thoughts; N. Amer. alternately.

instinct noun **1 inclination**, urge, drive, compulsion, intuition, feeling, sixth sense, nose. **2 talent**, gift, ability, aptitude, skill, flair, feel, knack.

instinctive adjective **intuitive**, natural, instinctual, innate, inborn, inherent, unconscious, subconscious, automatic, reflex, knee-jerk; informal gut.

institute noun **organization**, establishment, institution, foundation, centre, academy, school, college, university, society, association, federation, body.
  ● verb **set up**, inaugurate, found, establish, organize, initiate, set in motion, get under way, get off the ground, start, launch.
- OPPOSITES abolish, end.

institution noun **1 establishment**, organization, institute, foundation, centre, academy, school, college, university, society, association, body. **2 (residential) home**, hospital, asylum, prison. **3** the institution of marriage **practice**, custom, convention, tradition.

institutional adjective **organized**, established, bureaucratic, conventional, procedural, formal, formalized, systematic, systematized, structured, regulated.

instruct verb **1 order**, direct, command, tell, mandate; old use bid. **2 teach**, coach, train, educate, tutor, guide, school, show.

instruction noun **1 order**, command, directive, direction, decree, injunction, mandate, commandment; old use bidding. **2** read the instructions **directions**, handbook, manual, guide, advice, guidance. **3 tuition**, teaching, coaching, schooling, lessons, classes, lectures, training, drill, guidance.

instructor noun **trainer**, coach, teacher, tutor, adviser, counsellor, guide.

instrument noun **1 implement**, tool, utensil, device, apparatus, gadget. **2 gauge**, meter, indicator, dial, display. **3 agent**, cause, agency, channel, medium, means, vehicle.

instrumental adjective
□ **be instrumental in** play a part in, contribute to, be a factor in, have a hand in, promote, advance, further.

insufficient adjective **inadequate**, deficient, poor, scant, scanty, not enough, too little, too few.

insulate verb **1 wrap**, sheathe, cover, encase, enclose, lag, soundproof. **2 protect**, save, shield, shelter, screen, cushion, cocoon.

insult verb **abuse**, be rude to, call someone names, slight, disparage, discredit, malign, defame, denigrate, offend, hurt, humiliate; informal bad-mouth; Brit. informal slag off.
- OPPOSITES compliment.
● noun **jibe**, affront, slight, slur, barb, indignity, abuse, aspersions; informal dig, put-down.

insulting adjective **abusive**, rude, offensive, disparaging, belittling, derogatory, deprecating, disrespectful, uncomplimentary; informal bitchy, catty.

insurance noun **indemnity**, assurance, protection, security, cover, safeguard, warranty.

insure verb **provide insurance for**, indemnify, cover, assure, protect, underwrite, warrant.

intact adjective **whole**, entire, complete, unbroken, undamaged, unscathed, unblemished, unmarked, in one piece.
- OPPOSITES damaged.

integral adjective **1 essential**, fundamental, component, basic, intrinsic, inherent, vital, necessary. **2 built-in**, inbuilt, integrated, inboard, fitted. **3 unified**, integrated, comprehensive,

holistic, joined-up, all-embracing.
- OPPOSITES peripheral, supplementary.

integrate verb **combine**, amalgamate, merge, unite, fuse, blend, consolidate, meld, mix, incorporate, assimilate, homogenize, desegregate.
- OPPOSITES separate.

integrity noun **1 honesty**, probity, rectitude, uprightness, fairness, honour, sincerity, truthfulness, trustworthiness. **2 unity**, coherence, cohesion, solidity. **3 soundness**, strength, sturdiness, solidity, durability, stability, rigidity.
- OPPOSITES dishonesty.

intellect noun **mind**, brain(s), intelligence, reason, judgement, grey matter, brain cells.

intellectual adjective **1 mental**, cerebral, rational, conceptual, theoretical, analytical, logical, cognitive. **2 learned**, academic, erudite, bookish, highbrow, scholarly, donnish.

intelligence noun **1 intellect**, cleverness, brainpower, judgement, reasoning, acumen, wit, insight, perception. **2 information**, facts, details, particulars, data, knowledge.

intelligent adjective **clever**, bright, quick-witted, smart, astute, sharp, insightful, perceptive, penetrating, educated, knowledgeable, enlightened; informal brainy, genius.

intelligible adjective **comprehensible**, understandable, accessible, digestible, user-friendly, clear, coherent, plain, unambiguous.

intend verb **plan**, mean, have in mind, aim, propose, hope, expect, envisage.

intense adjective **1 extreme**, great, acute, fierce, severe, high, exceptional, extraordinary, harsh, strong, powerful, violent; informal serious. **2 passionate**, impassioned, zealous, vehement, fervent, earnest, eager, committed.
- OPPOSITES mild, apathetic.

intensify verb **escalate**, increase, step up, raise, strengthen, reinforce, pick up, build up, heighten, deepen, extend, expand, amplify, magnify,

aggravate, exacerbate, worsen, inflame, compound.
- OPPOSITES abate.

intensity noun **1 strength**, power, force, severity, ferocity, fierceness, harshness, violence. **2 passion**, ardour, fervour, vehemence, fire, emotion, eagerness.

intensive adjective **thorough**, thoroughgoing, in-depth, rigorous, exhaustive, vigorous, detailed, minute, meticulous, painstaking, methodical, extensive.
- OPPOSITES cursory.

intent noun **aim**, intention, purpose, objective, goal.
● adjective **1** *he was intent on proving his point* **bent**, set, determined, insistent, resolved, hell-bent, keen, committed to, determined to. **2 attentive**, absorbed, engrossed, fascinated, enthralled, rapt, focused, concentrating, preoccupied.
- OPPOSITES distracted.

intention noun **aim**, purpose, intent, objective, goal.

intentional adjective **deliberate**, done on purpose, wilful, calculated, conscious, intended, planned, meant, knowing.

inter verb **bury**, lay to rest, consign to the grave, entomb.
- OPPOSITES exhume.

intercept verb **stop**, head off, cut off, catch, seize, block, interrupt.

intercourse noun **1 dealings**, relations, relationships, contact, interchange, communication, networking. **2 sexual intercourse**, sex, sexual relations, mating, copulation, fornication; *technical* coitus.

interdict noun **prohibition**, ban, bar, veto, embargo, moratorium, injunction.

interest noun **1 attentiveness**, attention, regard, notice, curiosity, enjoyment, delight. **2** *this will be of interest* **concern**, consequence, importance, import, significance, note, relevance, value. **3 hobby**, pastime, leisure

pursuit, amusement, recreation, diversion, passion. **4 stake**, share, claim, investment, involvement, concern.
- OPPOSITES boredom.
● verb **appeal to**, be of interest to, attract, intrigue, amuse, divert, entertain, arouse someone's curiosity, whet someone's appetite; *informal* tickle someone's fancy.

interested adjective **1 attentive**, fascinated, riveted, gripped, captivated, agog, intrigued, curious, keen, eager. **2 concerned**, involved, affected.

interesting adjective **absorbing**, engrossing, fascinating, riveting, gripping, compelling, captivating, engaging, enthralling, appealing, entertaining, stimulating, diverting, intriguing.

interfere verb **butt in**, barge in, intrude, meddle, tamper, encroach; *informal* poke your nose in, stick your oar in.
□ **interfere with** impede, obstruct, stand in the way of, hinder, inhibit, restrict, constrain, hamper, handicap, disturb, disrupt, influence, affect, confuse.

interference noun **1 intrusion**, intervention, involvement, meddling, prying. **2 disruption**, disturbance, static, noise.

interior adjective **1 inside**, inner, internal, inland, upcountry, central. **2 internal**, home, domestic, national, state, civil, local. **3 inner**, mental, spiritual, psychological, private, personal, secret.
● noun **1 inside**, depths, recesses, bowels, belly, heart. **2 centre**, heartland.
- OPPOSITES exterior.

intermediary noun **mediator**, go-between, negotiator, arbitrator, peacemaker, middleman, broker.

intermediate adjective **halfway**, in-between, middle, mid, midway, intervening, transitional.

intermittent adjective **sporadic**, irregular, fitful, spasmodic, discontinuous, isolated, random, patchy, scattered, occasional, periodic.
- OPPOSITES continuous.

internal adjective **1 inner**, interior, inside, central. **2 domestic**, home, interior, civil, local, national, state.
- OPPOSITES external, foreign.

international adjective **global**, worldwide, world, intercontinental, universal, cosmopolitan, multiracial, multinational.
- OPPOSITES national, local.

interpret verb **1 explain**, elucidate, expound, clarify. **2 understand**, construe, take (to mean), see, regard. **3 decipher**, decode, translate, understand.

interpretation noun **1 explanation**, elucidation, exposition, clarification, analysis. **2 meaning**, understanding, explanation, inference. **3 rendition**, execution, presentation, performance, reading, playing, singing.

interrupt verb **1 cut in (on)**, break in (on), barge in (on), intrude, intervene; informal butt in (on), chime in (on); Brit. informal chip in (on). **2 suspend**, discontinue, adjourn, break off, stop, halt; informal put on ice.

interruption noun **1 cutting in**, barging in, interference, intervention, intrusion, disturbance; informal butting in. **2 suspension**, breaking off, discontinuance, stopping.

interval noun **intermission**, interlude, break, recess, time out.

intervene verb **intercede**, involve yourself, get involved, step in, interfere, intrude.

interview noun **meeting**, discussion, interrogation, cross-examination, debriefing, audience, talk, chat; informal grilling.
● verb **talk to**, question, quiz, interrogate, cross-examine, debrief, poll, canvass, sound out; informal grill, pump.

interviewer noun **questioner**, interrogator, examiner, assessor, journalist, reporter, inquisitor.

intimacy noun **closeness**, togetherness, rapport, attachment, familiarity, friendliness, affection, warmth.
- OPPOSITES formality.

intimate[1] adjective **1 close**, bosom, dear, cherished, fast, firm. **2 friendly**, warm, welcoming, hospitable, relaxed, informal, cosy, comfortable. **3 personal**, private, confidential, secret, inward. **4 detailed**, thorough, exhaustive, deep, in-depth, profound.
- OPPOSITES distant, formal, cold.

intimate[2] verb **1 announce**, state, make known, disclose, reveal, divulge, let it be known. **2 imply**, suggest, hint at, indicate, insinuate.

intimidate verb **frighten**, menace, scare, terrorize, threaten, browbeat, bully, harass, hound; informal lean on.

intricate adjective **complex**, complicated, convoluted, tangled, elaborate, ornate, detailed.
- OPPOSITES simple.

intrigue verb **interest**, fascinate, arouse someone's curiosity, attract, engage.
● noun **plotting**, conniving, scheming, machination, double-dealing, subterfuge.

intriguing adjective **interesting**, fascinating, absorbing, engaging.

introduce verb **1 institute**, initiate, launch, inaugurate, establish, found, bring in, set in motion, start, begin, get going. **2 present**, make known, acquaint with. **3 insert**, inject, put, force, shoot, feed. **4 instil**, infuse, inject, add.
- OPPOSITES end, remove.

introduction noun **1 institution**, establishment, initiation, launch, inauguration, foundation. **2 presentation**, meeting, audience. **3 foreword**, preface, preamble, prologue, prelude; informal intro.
- OPPOSITES ending, epilogue.

introductory adjective **1 opening**, initial, starting, initiatory, first, preliminary. **2 elementary**, basic, rudimentary, entry-level.
- OPPOSITES final, advanced.

intrude verb **encroach**, impinge, trespass, infringe, invade, violate, disturb, disrupt.

intruder *noun* **trespasser**, interloper, invader, infiltrator, burglar, house-breaker; *informal* gatecrasher.

intuition *noun* **1 instinct**, feeling, insight, sixth sense. **2 hunch**, feeling in your bones, inkling, sneaking suspicion, premonition; *informal* gut feeling.

intuitive *adjective* **instinctive**, innate, inborn, inherent, natural, unconscious, subconscious; *informal* gut.

invade *verb* **1 occupy**, conquer, capture, seize, take (over), annex, overrun, storm. **2 intrude on**, violate, encroach on, infringe on, trespass on, disturb, disrupt.
- OPPOSITES leave, liberate.

invader *noun* **attacker**, conqueror, raider, marauder, occupier, intruder, trespasser.

invalid[1] *adjective* **ill**, sick, ailing, infirm, incapacitated, bedridden, frail, sickly, poorly.
- OPPOSITES healthy.
● *verb* **disable**, incapacitate, hospital-ize, put out of action, lay up.

invalid[2] *adjective* **1 void**, null and void, not binding, illegitimate, inapplicable. **2 false**, fallacious, spurious, unsound, wrong, untenable.

invaluable *adjective* **indispensable**, irreplaceable, all-important, crucial, vital, worth its weight in gold, priceless.
- OPPOSITES dispensable.

invariably *adverb* **always**, at all times, without fail, without exception, consist-ently, habitually, unfailingly.

invasion *noun* **1 occupation**, conquer-ing, capture, seizure, annexation, takeover. **2 violation**, infringement, interruption, encroachment, distur-bance, disruption, breach.
- OPPOSITES withdrawal.

invent *verb* **1 originate**, create, design, devise, develop. **2 make up**, fabricate, concoct, hatch, contrive, dream up; *informal* cook up.

invention *noun* **1 origination**, crea-tion, development, design, discovery. **2 innovation**, contraption, contrivance, device, gadget. **3 fabrication**, concoc-tion, (piece of) fiction, story, tale, lie, untruth, falsehood, fib.

inventive *adjective* **creative**, original, innovative, imaginative, resourceful, unusual, fresh, novel, new, ground-breaking, disruptive, unorthodox, unconventional.
- OPPOSITES unimaginative.

inventor *noun* **originator**, creator, designer, deviser, developer, author, architect, father.

inventory *noun* **list**, listing, catalogue, record, register, checklist, log, archive.

invest *verb* **put in**, plough in, put up, advance, expend, spend; *informal* lay out.
□ **invest in** put money into, sink money into, plough money into, fund, back, finance, underwrite.

investigate *verb* **enquire into**, look into, go into, probe, explore, scrutinize, analyse, study, examine; *informal* check out, suss out.

investigation *noun* **examination**, enquiry, study, inspection, exploration, analysis, research, scrutiny, probe, review.

investigator *noun* **researcher**, exam-iner, analyst, inspector, scrutineer, detective.

investment *noun* **1 investing**, specula-tion, outlay, funding, backing, financ-ing, underwriting. **2 stake**, payment, outlay, venture, proposition.

invidious *adjective* **1 unpleasant**, awk-ward, difficult, undesirable, unenviable. **2 unfair**, unjust, unwarranted.

invigorate *verb* **revitalize**, energize, refresh, revive, enliven, liven up, perk up, wake up, animate, galvanize, fortify, rouse, exhilarate; *informal* buck up, pep up.
- OPPOSITES tire.

invincible *adjective* **invulnerable**, indestructible, unconquerable, unbeat-able, indomitable, unassailable, impregnable.
- OPPOSITES vulnerable.

i

invisible *adjective* **unseen**, imperceptible, undetectable, inconspicuous, unnoticed, unobserved, hidden, out of sight.
- OPPOSITES visible.

invitation *noun* **request**, call, summons; *informal* invite.

invite *verb* **1 ask**, summon. **2 ask for**, request, call for, appeal for, solicit, seek. **3 cause**, induce, provoke, ask for, encourage, lead to, bring on yourself, arouse.

inviting *adjective* **tempting**, enticing, alluring, attractive, appealing, appetizing, mouth-watering, intriguing, seductive.
- OPPOSITES repellent.

invoke *verb* **1 cite**, refer to, resort to, have recourse to, turn to. **2 pray to**, call on, appeal to. **3 bring forth**, bring out, elicit, conjure up, generate.

involuntary *adjective* **1 reflex**, automatic, instinctive, unintentional, uncontrollable. **2 compulsory**, obligatory, mandatory, forced, prescribed.
- OPPOSITES deliberate, optional.

involve *verb* **1 entail**, require, necessitate, demand, call for. **2 include**, take in, incorporate, encompass, comprise, cover.
- OPPOSITES preclude, exclude.

involved *adjective* **1** *social workers involved in the case* **associated**, connected, concerned. **2** *he had been involved in burglaries* **implicated**, caught up, mixed up. **3 complicated**, intricate, complex, elaborate, convoluted, confusing. **4 engrossed**, absorbed, immersed, caught up, preoccupied, intent.

involvement *noun* **1 participation**, collaboration, collusion, complicity, association, connection, entanglement. **2 attachment**, friendship, intimacy, commitment.

inwards *adverb* **inside**, towards the inside, into the interior, inward, within.

iota *noun* **(little) bit**, mite, speck, scrap, shred, ounce, jot.

iron *adjective* **1 ferric**, ferrous. **2 uncompromising**, unrelenting, unyielding, unbending, rigid, steely.
- OPPOSITES flexible.
□ **iron out 1** resolve, straighten out, sort out, clear up, put right, solve, rectify; *informal* fix. **2** eliminate, eradicate, reconcile, resolve.

ironic *adjective* **1 sarcastic**, sardonic, satirical, dry, wry, double-edged, mocking, derisive, scornful; *Brit. informal* sarky. **2 paradoxical**, funny, strange.

irony *noun* **1 sarcasm**, mockery, ridicule, derision, scorn; *Brit. informal* sarkiness. **2 paradox**.

irrational *adjective* **unreasonable**, illogical, groundless, baseless, unfounded, unjustifiable.
- OPPOSITES rational, logical.

irrefutable *adjective* **indisputable**, undeniable, unquestionable, incontrovertible, incontestable, beyond question, beyond doubt, conclusive, definite, definitive, decisive.

irregular *adjective* **1 uneven**, crooked, misshapen, lopsided, asymmetrical, twisted. **2 rough**, bumpy, uneven, pitted, rutted, lumpy, knobbly, gnarled. **3 inconsistent**, unsteady, uneven, fitful, patchy, variable, varying, changeable, inconstant, erratic, unstable, spasmodic, intermittent. **4 improper**, illegitimate, unethical, unprofessional; *informal* shady, dodgy. **5 guerrilla**, underground, paramilitary, partisan, mercenary, terrorist.
● *noun* **guerrilla**, paramilitary, militiaman, resistance fighter, partisan, mercenary, terrorist.

irrelevant *adjective* **beside the point**, immaterial, unconnected, unrelated, peripheral, extraneous.

irreparable *adjective* **irreversible**, irrevocable, irrecoverable, unrepairable, beyond repair.

irrepressible *adjective* **ebullient**, exuberant, buoyant, breezy, jaunty, high-spirited, vivacious, animated, full of life, lively; *informal* bubbly, bouncy, peppy, chipper, chirpy, full of beans.

irresistible *adjective* **1 captivating**, enticing, alluring, enchanting, fascinating, seductive. **2 uncontrollable**, overwhelming, overpowering, ungovernable, compelling.

irresponsible *adjective* **reckless**, rash, careless, unwise, imprudent, ill-advised, injudicious, hasty, impetuous, foolhardy, foolish, unreliable, undependable, untrustworthy.

irreverent *adjective* **disrespectful**, impertinent, cheeky, flippant, rude, discourteous.
- OPPOSITES respectful.

irrevocable *adjective* **irreversible**, unalterable, unchangeable, immutable, final, binding, permanent, set in stone.

irritable *adjective* **bad-tempered**, short-tempered, irascible, tetchy, testy, grumpy, grouchy, crotchety, cantankerous, fractious, curmudgeonly.
- OPPOSITES good-humoured.

irritate *verb* **1 annoy**, bother, vex, make cross, exasperate, infuriate, anger, madden; *Brit.* rub up the wrong way; *informal* aggravate, peeve, rile, needle, get (to), bug, hack off; *Brit. informal* nark, get on someone's wick; *N. Amer. informal* tee off, tick off. **2 inflame**, hurt, chafe, scratch, scrape, rub.
- OPPOSITES delight, soothe.

irritation *noun* **annoyance**, exasperation, vexation, indignation, anger, displeasure, chagrin.
- OPPOSITES delight.

island *noun* **isle**, islet, atoll; *Brit.* holm; (**islands**) archipelago.

> **WORD LINKS**
> **insular** relating to an island

isolate *verb* **separate**, segregate, detach, cut off, shut away, alienate, distance, cloister, seclude, cordon off, seal off, close off, fence off.
- OPPOSITES integrate.

isolated *adjective* **1 remote**, out of the way, outlying, off the beaten track, in the back of beyond, godforsaken, inaccessible, cut-off; *informal* in the middle of nowhere, in the sticks; *N. Amer. informal* jerkwater. **2 solitary**, lonely, secluded, reclusive, hermit-like; *N. Amer.* lonesome. **3 unique**, lone, solitary, unusual, exceptional, untypical, freak; *informal* one-off.
- OPPOSITES accessible.

isolation *noun* **1 solitariness**, loneliness, friendlessness. **2 remoteness**, inaccessibility.
- OPPOSITES contact.

issue *noun* **1 matter**, question, point at issue, affair, case, subject, topic, situation. **2 problem**, difficulty, complication, snag, hitch, catch, drawback, pitfall, stumbling block; *informal* headache, hiccup. **3 edition**, number, instalment, copy, impression. **4 issuing**, release, publication, distribution.
● *verb* **1 release**, put out, deliver, publish, broadcast, circulate, distribute. **2 supply**, provide, furnish, arm, equip, fit out, rig out, kit out; *informal* fix up.
□ **take issue with** disagree with, challenge, dispute, (call into) question.

itch *noun* **1 tingling**, irritation, itchiness, prickle. **2** (*informal*) **longing**, yearning, craving, ache, hunger, thirst, urge, hankering; *informal* yen.
● *verb* **1 tingle**, be irritated, be itchy, sting, hurt, be sore. **2** (*informal*) **long**, yearn, ache, burn, crave, hanker for/after, hunger, thirst, be eager, be desperate; *informal* be dying.

item *noun* **1 thing**, article, object, piece, element, constituent, component, ingredient. **2 issue**, matter, affair, case, subject, topic, question, point. **3 report**, story, article, piece, write-up, bulletin, feature, review.

itinerary *noun* **route**, plan, schedule, timetable, programme.

Jj

jab verb & noun **poke**, prod, dig, elbow, nudge, thrust, stab, push.

jacket noun **wrapping**, wrapper, sleeve, cover, covering, sheath.

jagged adjective **spiky**, barbed, ragged, rough, uneven, irregular, serrated.
- OPPOSITES smooth.

jail noun **prison**, lock-up, detention centre; N. Amer. penitentiary, jailhouse; informal clink, cooler, the slammer, inside; Brit. informal nick; N. Amer. informal can, pen, slam, pokey.
● verb **imprison**, incarcerate, lock up, put away, detain; informal send down, put behind bars, put inside; Brit. informal bang up.
- OPPOSITES acquit, release.

jam verb **1 stuff**, shove, force, ram, thrust, press, push, wedge, stick, cram. **2 crowd**, pack, pile, press, squeeze, sandwich, cram, throng, mob, fill, block, clog, congest. **3 stick**, become stuck, catch, seize (up).
● noun **tailback**, hold-up, queue, congestion, bottleneck; N. Amer. gridlock; informal snarl-up.

jar¹ noun **pot**, container, crock.

jar² verb **1 jolt**, jerk, shake, vibrate. **2 grate**, set someone's teeth on edge, irritate, annoy, get on someone's nerves. **3 clash**, conflict, contrast, be incompatible, be at variance, be at odds.

jargon noun **slang**, idiom, cant, argot, gobbledegook; informal lingo, geek-speak, -speak, -ese.

jaunt noun **trip**, outing, excursion, tour, drive, ride, run; informal spin, junket.

jaws plural noun **mouth**, maw, muzzle, mandibles; informal chops.

jealous adjective **1 envious**, covetous, resentful, grudging, green with envy. **2 suspicious**, distrustful, possessive, proprietorial, overprotective.

3 protective, vigilant, watchful, mindful, careful.
- OPPOSITES trusting.

jealousy noun **envy**, resentment, bitterness; humorous the green-eyed monster.

jeer verb **taunt**, mock, ridicule, deride, insult, abuse, heckle, catcall (at), boo (at), whistle at, scoff at, sneer at; Brit. barrack.
- OPPOSITES applaud, cheer.
● noun **taunt**, sneer, insult, shout, jibe, boo, catcall, derision, teasing, scoffing, abuse, scorn, heckling, catcalling; Brit. barracking.
- OPPOSITES applause, cheer.

jeopardize verb **threaten**, endanger, imperil, risk, compromise, prejudice.
- OPPOSITES safeguard.

jeopardy noun **danger**, peril, risk.

jerk noun **1 yank**, tug, pull, wrench. **2 jolt**, lurch, bump, judder, jump, bounce, jounce, shake.
● verb **1 yank**, tug, pull, wrench, wrest, drag, snatch. **2 jolt**, lurch, bump, judder, bounce, jounce.

jerky adjective **convulsive**, spasmodic, fitful, twitchy, shaky.
- OPPOSITES smooth.

jet noun **1 stream**, spurt, spray, fountain, rush, spout, gush, surge, burst. **2 nozzle**, head, spout.

jettison verb **dump**, drop, ditch, throw out, get rid of, discard, dispose of, scrap.

jetty noun **pier**, landing (stage), quay, wharf, dock, breakwater, groyne, mole; N. Amer. levee.

jewel noun **1 gem**, gemstone, (precious) stone; informal sparkler, rock. **2 showpiece**, pride (and joy), cream, crème de la crème, jewel in the crown, prize, pick.

jibe *noun* **taunt**, sneer, jeer, insult, barb; *informal* dig, put-down.

jilt *verb* **leave**, walk out on, throw over, finish with, break up with, stand up, leave at the altar; *informal* chuck, ditch, dump, drop, run out on, give someone the push/elbow, give someone the big E.

jingle *noun & verb* **clink**, chink, tinkle, jangle, ring.

jinx *noun* **curse**, spell, the evil eye, black magic, voodoo, bad luck; *N. Amer.* hex.
● *verb* **curse**, cast a spell on; *Austral.* point the bone at; *N. Amer.* hex.

job *noun* **1 position**, post, situation, appointment, occupation, profession, trade, career, work, vocation, calling, métier. **2 task**, piece of work, assignment, mission, project, undertaking, operation, duty, chore, errand, responsibility, charge, role, function; *informal* department.

jobless *adjective* **unemployed**, out of work, unwaged, redundant, laid off; *Brit. informal* on the dole; *Canad. informal* on pogey; *Austral./NZ informal* on the wallaby track.
- OPPOSITES employed.

jog *verb* **1 run**, trot, lope. **2 nudge**, prod, poke, push, bump, jar.

join *verb* **1** *the two parts are joined with clay* **connect**, unite, couple, fix, affix, attach, fasten, stick, glue, fuse, weld, amalgamate, bond, link, yoke, merge, secure, make fast, tie, bind. **2** *the path joins a major road* **meet**, touch, reach. **3** *he joined the search party* **help in**, participate in, get involved in, contribute to, enlist in, join up, sign up, band together, get together, team up.
- OPPOSITES separate, leave.

joint *noun* **join**, junction, intersection, link, connection, weld, seam, coupling.
● *adjective* **common**, shared, communal, collective, mutual, cooperative, collaborative, concerted, combined, united, allied.
- OPPOSITES separate.

jointly *adverb* **together**, in partnership, in cooperation, cooperatively, in conjunction, in combination, mutually, in league.

joke *noun* **1 witticism**, jest, quip, pun; *informal* gag, wisecrack, crack, funny, one-liner. **2 trick**, prank, stunt, hoax, jape; *informal* leg-pull, spoof, wind-up. **3** *(informal)* **laughing stock**, figure of fun, Aunt Sally. **4** *(informal)* **farce**, travesty.
● *verb* **tell jokes**, jest, banter, quip; *informal* wisecrack, josh.

joker *noun* **comedian**, comedienne, comic, humorist, wit, jester, prankster, practical joker, clown.

jolly *adjective* **cheerful**, happy, cheery, good-humoured, jovial, merry, sunny, joyful, light-hearted, in high spirits, buoyant, bubbly, genial; *informal* chipper, chirpy, perky; *literary* blithe.
- OPPOSITES miserable.

jolt *verb* **1 push**, jar, bump, knock, bang, shake, jog. **2 bump**, bounce, jerk, rattle, lurch, shudder, judder, jounce. **3 startle**, surprise, shock, stun, shake; *informal* rock, knock sideways.
● *noun* **bump**, bounce, shake, jerk, lurch, jounce.

jostle *verb* **1 push**, shove, elbow, barge into, bang into, bump against, knock against. **2** *photographers jostled for position* **struggle**, vie, jockey, scramble, fight.

journal *noun* **1 periodical**, magazine, gazette, review, newsletter, newssheet, bulletin, newspaper, paper, daily, weekly, monthly, quarterly. **2 diary**, log, logbook, weblog, blog, chronicle, history, yearbook; *N. Amer.* daybook.

journalist *noun* **reporter**, correspondent, columnist; *Brit.* pressman; *informal* news hound, hack, hackette, stringer, journo.

journey *noun* **trip**, expedition, tour, trek, travels, voyage, cruise, ride, drive, crossing, passage, flight, odyssey, pilgrimage, safari, globetrotting; *old use* peregrinations.
● *verb* **travel**, go, voyage, sail, cruise,

j

fly, hike, trek, ride, drive, make your way.

jovial *adjective* **cheerful**, jolly, happy, cheery, jocular, good-humoured, convivial, genial, good-natured, affable, outgoing, smiling, merry, sunny; *literary* blithe.
- OPPOSITES miserable.

joy *noun* **delight**, pleasure, jubilation, triumph, exultation, rejoicing, happiness, elation, euphoria, bliss, ecstasy, rapture.
- OPPOSITES misery.

joyful *adjective* **1 cheerful**, happy, jolly, merry, sunny, joyous, cheery, smiling, jovial, mirthful, gleeful, pleased, delighted, thrilled, jubilant, elated, ecstatic; *informal* over the moon, on cloud nine. **2** *joyful news* **pleasing**, happy, good, cheering, gladdening, welcome, gratifying, heart-warming.
- OPPOSITES sad.

jubilant *adjective* **overjoyed**, exultant, triumphant, joyful, cock-a-hoop, elated, thrilled, gleeful, euphoric, ecstatic; *informal* over the moon, on cloud nine.
- OPPOSITES despondent.

jubilee *noun* **anniversary**, commemoration, celebration, festival.

judge *noun* **1 justice**, magistrate, recorder, sheriff; *N. Amer.* jurist; *Brit. informal* beak. **2 adjudicator**, referee, umpire, arbiter, assessor, examiner, moderator, scrutineer.
● *verb* **1 conclude**, decide, consider, believe, think, deduce, infer, gauge, estimate, guess, surmise, conjecture, regard as, rate as, class as; *informal* reckon, figure. **2** *she was judged innocent* **pronounce**, decree, rule, find. **3 adjudicate**, arbitrate, moderate, referee, umpire. **4 assess**, evaluate, appraise, examine, review.

judgement *noun* **1 sense**, discernment, perception, discrimination, understanding, powers of reasoning, reason, logic. **2 opinion**, view, estimate, appraisal, conclusion, diagnosis, assessment, impression, conviction, perception, thinking. **3** *a court judgement*

verdict, decision, adjudication, ruling, pronouncement, decree, finding, sentence.

judgemental *adjective* **critical**, censorious, disapproving, disparaging, deprecating, negative, overcritical.

judicious *adjective* **wise**, sensible, prudent, shrewd, astute, canny, discerning, sagacious, strategic, politic, expedient.
- OPPOSITES ill-advised.

jug *noun* **pitcher**, ewer, crock, jar, urn, carafe, flask, flagon, decanter; *N. Amer.* creamer.

juice *noun* **liquid**, fluid, sap, extract, concentrate, essence.

juicy *adjective* **1 succulent**, tender, moist, ripe. **2** *(informal)* **sensational**, fascinating, intriguing, exciting, graphic, lurid.
- OPPOSITES dry.

jumble *noun* **heap**, muddle, mess, tangle, confusion, disarray, chaos, hotchpotch; *N. Amer.* hodgepodge; *informal* shambles.
● *verb* **mix up**, muddle up, disorganize, disorder, tangle, confuse.

jump *verb* **1 leap**, spring, bound, vault, hop, skip, caper, dance, prance. **2** *pretax profits jumped* **rise**, go up, shoot up, soar, surge, climb, increase; *informal* skyrocket. **3** *the noise made her jump* **start**, jolt, flinch, recoil, shudder.
● *noun* **1 leap**, spring, bound, hop, skip. **2 rise**, leap, increase, upsurge, upswing; *informal* hike. **3 start**, jerk, spasm, shudder.

jumper *noun* *(Brit.)* **sweater**, pullover, jersey; *informal* woolly.

jumpy *adjective* *(informal)* **nervous**, on edge, edgy, tense, anxious, restless, fidgety, keyed up, overwrought; *informal* jittery, uptight, het up; *N. Amer. informal* antsy.
- OPPOSITES calm.

junction *noun* **crossroads**, intersection, interchange, T-junction, turn, turn-off, exit; *Brit.* roundabout; *N. Amer.* turnout, cloverleaf.

junior *adjective* **younger**, minor, subordinate, lower, lesser, low-ranking, inferior, secondary.
- OPPOSITES senior, older.

junk *noun (informal)* **rubbish**, clutter, odds and ends, bric-a-brac, refuse, litter, scrap, waste, debris; *N. Amer.* trash.

just *adjective* **1** *a just society* **fair**, fair-minded, equitable, even-handed, impartial, unbiased, objective, neutral, disinterested, unprejudiced, honourable, upright, decent, principled. **2** *a just reward* **deserved**, well deserved, well earned, merited, rightful, due, proper, fitting, appropriate, defensible, justified, justifiable.
- OPPOSITES unfair.
● *adverb* **1** **exactly**, precisely, absolutely, completely, totally, entirely, perfectly, utterly, thoroughly; *informal* dead. **2** **narrowly**, only just, by a hair's breadth, by the skin of your teeth, barely, scarcely, hardly; *informal* by a whisker.

justice *noun* **1** **fairness**, justness, fair play, fair-mindedness, equity, right, even-handedness, honesty, morality. **2** *the justice of his case* **validity**, justification, soundness, well-foundedness, legitimacy. **3** **judge**, magistrate, recorder, sheriff; *N. Amer.* jurist.

> **WORD LINKS**
> **judicial** relating to a system of justice

justifiable *adjective* **valid**, legitimate, warranted, well founded, justified, just, reasonable, tenable, defensible, sound, warrantable.
- OPPOSITES unjustifiable, unwarranted.

justification *noun* **grounds**, reason, basis, rationale, premise, vindication, explanation, defence, argument, case.

justify *verb* **1** **give grounds for**, give reasons for, explain, account for, defend, vindicate, excuse, exonerate. **2** **warrant**, be good reason for.

jut *verb* **stick out**, project, protrude, bulge out, overhang, beetle.

juvenile *adjective* **1** **young**, teenage, adolescent, junior. **2** **childish**, immature, puerile, infantile, babyish.
- OPPOSITES adult, mature.
● *noun* **child**, youngster, teenager, adolescent, minor, junior; *informal* kid.
- OPPOSITES adult.

Kk

keel *verb*
□ **keel over 1** capsize, turn turtle, turn upside down, founder, overturn, turn over, tip over. **2** collapse, faint, pass out, black out, swoon.

keen *adjective* **1** *I'm keen to help* **eager**, anxious, intent, impatient, determined; *informal* raring, itching, dying. **2** *a keen birdwatcher* **enthusiastic**, avid, ardent, fervent, conscientious, committed, dedicated, motivated. **3** *a girl he was keen on* **attracted to**, interested in, fond of, taken with, smitten with, enamoured of; *informal* struck on. **4** *a keen mind* **acute**, penetrating, astute, incisive, sharp, perceptive, piercing, razor-sharp, shrewd, discerning, clever, intelligent, brilliant, bright, smart, wise, insightful. **5** *a keen sense of duty* **intense**, acute, fierce, passionate, burning, fervent, strong, powerful.
- OPPOSITES reluctant, unenthusiastic.

keep *verb* **1** *I kept the forms* **retain**, hold on to, save, store, put by/aside, set aside; *informal* hang on to. **2** *keep calm* **remain**, stay. **3** *he keeps going on about it* **persist in**, keep on, carry on, continue, insist on. **4** *keep the rules* **comply with**, obey, observe, conform to, abide by, adhere to, stick to, heed, follow, carry out, act on, make good, honour, keep to, stand by. **5** *keeping the old traditions* **preserve**, keep alive/up, carry on, perpetuate, maintain, uphold. **6** *he stole to keep his family* **provide for**, support, feed, maintain, sustain, take care of, look after. **7** *she keeps rabbits* **breed**, rear, raise, tend, farm, own.
● *noun* **maintenance**, upkeep, sustenance, board (and lodging), food, livelihood.

keeper *noun* **curator**, custodian, guardian, conservator, administrator, overseer, steward, caretaker, attendant, concierge.

keeping *noun* **care**, custody, charge, guardianship, possession, trust, protection.
□ **in keeping with** consistent with, in harmony with, in accord with, in agreement with, in line with, in character with, compatible with, appropriate to, befitting, suitable for.

key *noun* **1** *the key to the mystery* **answer**, clue, solution, explanation, basis, foundation. **2** *the key to success* **means**, way, route, path, passport, secret, formula.
● *adjective* **crucial**, central, essential, indispensable, pivotal, critical, vital, principal, prime, major, leading, main, important.

kick *verb* **boot**, punt.
● *noun (informal) I get a kick out of driving* **thrill**, excitement, stimulation, tingle, frisson; *informal* buzz, high; *N. Amer. informal* charge.
□ **kick off** *(informal)* start, commence, begin, get going, get off the ground, get under way, open, set in motion, launch, initiate, introduce, inaugurate.

kid *noun (informal)* **child**, youngster, baby, toddler, tot, infant, boy, girl, minor, juvenile, adolescent, teenager, youth, stripling; *Scottish* bairn; *informal* kiddie, nipper, kiddiewink; *Brit. informal* sprog; *N. Amer. informal* rug rat; *Austral./NZ* ankle-biter; *derogatory* brat.

kidnap *verb* **abduct**, carry off, capture, seize, snatch, take hostage.

kill *verb* **murder**, assassinate, eliminate, terminate, dispatch, execute, slaughter, exterminate, butcher, massacre; *informal* bump off, do away with, do in, top, take out, blow away; *N. Amer. informal* rub out, waste; *literary* slay.

killer *noun* **murderer**, assassin, butcher, gunman, terminator, executioner; *informal* hit man.

killing noun **murder**, assassination, homicide, manslaughter, execution, slaughter, massacre, butchery, bloodshed, carnage, extermination, genocide.

kin noun **relatives**, relations, family, kith and kin, kindred, kinsfolk, kinsmen, kinswomen, people; informal folks.

kind[1] noun **sort**, type, variety, style, form, class, category, genre, genus, species.

kind[2] adjective **kindly**, good-natured, kind-hearted, warm-hearted, caring, affectionate, loving, warm, considerate, obliging, compassionate, sympathetic, understanding, benevolent, benign, altruistic, unselfish, generous, charitable, philanthropic, helpful, thoughtful, humane; Brit. informal decent.
- OPPOSITES unkind.

kindle verb **1 light**, ignite, set light to, set fire to; informal torch. **2 rouse**, arouse, wake, awaken, stimulate, inspire, stir (up), excite, fire, trigger, activate, spark off.
- OPPOSITES extinguish.

kindly adjective **benevolent**, kind, kind-hearted, warm-hearted, generous, good-natured, gentle, warm, compassionate, caring, loving, benign, well meaning, considerate.
- OPPOSITES unkind, cruel.

kindness noun **kindliness**, affection, warmth, gentleness, concern, care, consideration, altruism, unselfishness, compassion, sympathy, benevolence, generosity.
- OPPOSITES unkindness.

king noun **ruler**, sovereign, monarch, Crown, His Majesty, emperor, prince, potentate.

kingdom noun **realm**, domain, dominion, country, empire, land, territory, nation, (sovereign) state, province.

kiss verb informal peck, smooch, canoodle, neck, pet; Brit. informal snog; N. Amer. informal buss; formal osculate.
● noun informal peck, smack, smacker, smooch; Brit. informal snog; N. Amer.

informal buss.

kit noun **1 equipment**, tools, implements, instruments, gadgets, utensils, appliances, gear, tackle, hardware, paraphernalia; informal things, stuff; Military accoutrements. **2** (informal) **clothes**, clothing, garments, outfit, dress, costume, attire, garb, strip; informal gear, get-up, rig-out. **3** a tool kit **set**, selection, collection, pack.
□ **kit out** equip, fit (out/up), furnish, supply, provide, issue, dress, clothe, attire, rig out, deck out; informal fix up.

knack noun **1 gift**, talent, flair, instinct, genius, ability, capability, capacity, aptitude, bent, facility, trick; informal the hang of something. **2 tendency**, habit, liability, propensity.

knickers plural noun (Brit.) **underpants**, briefs; Brit. pants; informal panties, undies; Brit. informal smalls; dated drawers; historical bloomers.

knife verb **stab**, hack, gash, slash, lacerate, cut, bayonet, wound.

knit verb **unite**, unify, bond, fuse, coalesce, merge, meld, blend, join, link.

knob noun **lump**, bump, protrusion, protuberance, bulge, swelling, knot, nodule, boss.

knock verb **1 bang**, tap, rap, thump, pound, hammer, beat, strike, hit; informal bash. **2 collide with**, bump into, run into, crash into, smash into, plough into; N. Amer. impact.
● noun **tap**, rap, rat-tat, knocking, bang, banging, pounding, hammering, thump, thud.
□ **knock down 1 fell**, floor, flatten, knock over, rugby-tackle, run over/down. **2 demolish**, pull down, tear down, destroy, raze, level, flatten, bulldoze. **knock out** knock unconscious, floor, prostrate; informal lay out, KO, fell.

knot noun a knot of people **cluster**, group, band, huddle, bunch, circle, ring.
● verb **tie**, fasten, secure, bind, do up.

knotted adjective **tangled**, matted, snarled, unkempt, tousled; informal mussed up.

k

know verb 1 *she doesn't know I'm here* **be aware**, realize, be conscious, be cognizant. 2 *I know the rules* **be familiar with**, be conversant with, be acquainted with, be versed in, have a grasp of, understand, comprehend; *informal* be clued up on. 3 *do you know her?* **be acquainted with**, have met, be familiar with; *Scottish* ken.

know-how noun *(informal)* **expertise**, skill, proficiency, knowledge, understanding, mastery, technique; *informal* savvy.

knowing adjective **significant**, meaningful, expressive, suggestive, eloquent, superior.

knowledge noun 1 **understanding**, comprehension, grasp, command, mastery, familiarity, acquaintance; *informal* know-how. 2 **learning**, erudition, education, scholarship, schooling, wisdom. 3 **awareness**, consciousness, realization, cognition, apprehension, perception, appreciation, cognizance.
- OPPOSITES ignorance.

> **WORD LINKS**
> **gnostic** relating to knowledge

knowledgeable adjective 1 **well informed**, learned, well read, (well) educated, erudite, scholarly, cultured, cultivated, enlightened. 2 *he's knowledgeable about art* **conversant with**, familiar with, well acquainted with, au fait with, up on, up to date with, abreast of; *informal* clued up on.
- OPPOSITES ignorant.

known adjective **recognized**, well known, widely known, noted, celebrated, notable, notorious, acknowledged.

kudos noun **prestige**, cachet, glory, honour, status, standing, distinction, admiration, respect, esteem.

k

Commonly confused words

There are many words in English which look or sound alike but have quite different meanings. These words are very easy to confuse and most spellcheckers will not be able to help in those situations in which a word is spelled correctly but used in the wrong context. This section provides a quick-reference guide to the differences between those pairs of words that commonly cause problems.

Word 1	Meaning	Word 2	Meaning
accept	to agree to receive or do	except	not including; apart from
access	the means to enter somewhere or opportunity to use something	excess	an amount that is too much
adverse	unfavourable or harmful	averse	strongly disliking or opposed
advice	recommendations about what to do	advise	to recommend something
affect	to change or make a difference to	effect	a result; to bring about a result
aisle	a passage between rows of seats	isle	an island
all together	all in one place or all at once	altogether	in total; completely; on the whole
allusion	an indirect reference	illusion	a false idea or belief
aloud	out loud	allowed	permitted
altar	sacred table in a church	alter	to change
amoral	not concerned with right or wrong	immoral	not following accepted moral standards
ante-	before (e.g. *antedate*)	anti-	against (e.g. *antidepressant*)
appraise	to assess	apprise	to inform someone
assent	approval or agreement	ascent	an act of going up something
augur	to be a sign of a good or bad outcome	auger	a tool for boring holes
aural	relating to the ears or hearing	oral	relating to the mouth; spoken
balmy	pleasantly warm	barmy	crazy
bare	naked; to uncover	bear	to carry; to tolerate
base	the lowest or supporting part; a centre of operations	bass	the lowest male singing voice; the deep low-frequency part of sound
bated	with bated breath (i.e. in great suspense)	baited	taunted

Word 1	Meaning	Word 2	Meaning
bazaar	a Middle Eastern market	bizarre	very strange
berth	a bunk in a ship, train, etc.	birth	the process of being born
blanch	make or become white or pale	blench	flinch through fear or pain
born	having started life	borne	carried
brake	a device for stopping a vehicle; to stop a vehicle	break	to separate into pieces; a pause
breach	a gap in a barrier; an act that breaks a rule or agreement	breech	the back part of a rifle or gun barrel
broach	to raise a subject for discussion	brooch	a piece of jewellery
canvas	a type of strong cloth	canvass	to ask for people's votes
cannon	a large heavy gun	canon	a rule or law; a list of books; a clergyman
censure	to criticize severely	censor	to ban parts of a book or film; an official who does this
chord	a group of musical notes	cord	a length of string; a cord-like body part
climactic	forming a climax	climatic	relating to climate
coarse	rough	course	a direction
complacent	smugly self-satisfied	complaisant	willing to please
complement	to add to so as to improve; an addition that improves something	compliment	to politely congratulate or praise; a polite expression of praise
complementary	combining to form a whole or to improve something	complimentary	praising; given free of charge
council	a group of people who manage or advise	counsel	advice; to advise
councillor	a member of a council	counsellor	a person giving guidance on personal problems
credible	believable; convincing	credulous	too ready to believe things
cue	a signal for action; a wooden rod	queue	a line of people or vehicles
curb	to control or put a limit on; a control or limit	kerb	(in British English) the stone edge of a pavement
currant	a dried grape	current	happening now; a flow of water, air, or electricity
defuse	to make a situation less tense	diffuse	to spread over a wide area
dependant	a person who relies on another for support	dependent	determined; relying on

Word 1	Meaning	Word 2	Meaning
desert	a waterless, empty area	dessert	the sweet course of a meal
discreet	careful not to attract attention or give offence	discrete	separate and distinct
disinterested	impartial	uninterested	not interested
draught	a current of air	draft	a first version of a piece of writing; to write such a version
draw	to produce a picture; to pull; an even score at the end of a game	drawer	a sliding storage compartment
dual	having two parts	duel	a fight or contest between two people
elicit	to draw out a response or reaction	illicit	forbidden by law or rules
emigrant	a person who leaves their country to settle permanently in another	immigrant	a person who has come to live permanently in a foreign country
emotional	showing strong feeling	emotive	arousing strong feeling
empathy	the ability to understand another person's feelings	sympathy	the feeling of being sorry for someone
ensure	to make certain that something will happen	insure	to pay money in order to receive financial compensation if a person dies or property is damaged
envelop	to cover or surround	envelope	a paper container for a letter
exceptional	unusual or unusually good	exceptionable	causing disapproval or offence
exercise	physical activity; to do physical activity	exorcize	to drive out an evil spirit
faint	to lose consciousness; not clearly seen, heard, or smelled	feint	a pretended attacking movement; to make such a movement
fawn	a young deer; light brown	faun	a mythical being, part man, part goat
flair	a natural ability or talent	flare	a brief burst of flame or light; to gradually become wider
flaunt	to display in a way intended to attract attention	flout	to openly fail to follow a rule
flounder	to have trouble doing something	founder	to fail
forbear	to stop yourself from doing something	forebear	an ancestor

Word 1	Meaning	Word 2	Meaning
foreword	an introduction to a book	forward	onwards; ahead
freeze	to turn to ice	frieze	a decoration along a wall
Gallic	French	Gaelic	Celtic
grisly	causing horror or disgust	grizzly	a type of bear
hanger	a person who hangs something, or a frame to hang clothes on	hangar	a building in which aircraft are kept
historic	famous or important in history	historical	relating to history
hoard	a store of money or valuable objects	horde	a large crowd of people
hummus or houmous	a chickpea dip	humus	a substance found in soil
imply	to suggest indirectly	infer	to draw a conclusion about something not directly stated
incredible	impossible to believe	incredulous	unwilling or unable to believe something
internment	imprisonment	interment	burial
its	belonging to it	it's	short for *it is* or *it has*
judicial	relating to a law court or judge	judicious	sensible
lama	a Buddhist monk	llama	an animal related to the camel
licence	a permit to own or do something	license	to grant a licence or authorize something
lightening	getting lighter	lightning	a high-voltage electrical discharge; very quick
loath	reluctant or unwilling	loathe	to hate
loose	to unfasten or set free; not fixed in place	lose	to have something taken away; to be unable to find
meter	a measuring device	metre	a unit of measurement; rhythm in poetry
militate	to make it very difficult for something to happen or exist	mitigate	to make something less severe
muscle	tissue that moves a body part	mussel	a shellfish
omit	to leave out	emit	to give out light, heat, gas, etc.
pain	an unpleasant feeling	pane	a sheet of glass
palate	the roof of the mouth	palette	a board for mixing colours
pedal	a foot-operated lever; to work the pedals of a bicycle	peddle	to sell goods or spread an idea

Word 1	Meaning	Word 2	Meaning
peninsula	piece of land jutting out into the sea	peninsular	relating to a peninsula
perpetrate	to carry out a bad or illegal act	perpetuate	to make something continue for a long time
pole	a long, thin piece of wood; each of the two opposite points of a magnet	poll	the process of voting in an election
pore	a tiny opening; to study or read something closely	pour	to flow in a steady stream
practice	the use of an idea or method; the work or business of a doctor, dentist, etc.	practise	to do something repeatedly to improve your skill; to carry something out regularly
prescribe	to authorize the use of a medicine; to order authoritatively	proscribe	to officially forbid something
principal	most important; the most important person in an organization	principle	a law or theory on which something is based; a belief
prophecy	a prediction of a future event	prophesy	to predict a future event
quiet	making little or no noise	quite	moderately; completely
reign	period that a monarch rules; to rule as a monarch	rein	a strap used to control a horse; also used in the phrase a free rein
role	a part played by an actor	roll	to move by turning over and over; a rolling movement
sceptic	a person who tends to question accepted opinions	septic	infected with bacteria
shear	to cut the wool off a sheep	sheer	nothing but; to change course quickly
sight	the ability to see	site	a location
silicon	an element used in electronics	silicone	a substance used in cosmetic implants
stationary	not moving	stationery	paper and writing materials
storey	a level of a building	story	a tale or account
straight	without a curve or bend	strait	a narrow passage of water; (straits) trouble or difficulty
summary	a brief statement of the main points	summery	typical of summer
swat	to hit or crush	swot	to study hard
tail	the rear or end part	tale	a story

Word 1	Meaning	Word 2	Meaning
team	a group of people playing or working together	teem	to be full of something; to pour down
their	belonging to them	there	in, at, or to that place
titillate	to interest or excite, especially sexually	titivate	to make more attractive
to	in the direction of	too	excessively; in addition
toe	part of the foot; also in toe the line	tow	to pull something along behind a vehicle or boat
tortuous	full of twists and turns; complicated	torturous	full of pain or suffering
vain	having too high an opinion of yourself	vein	a tube that carries blood around the body
venal	open to bribery	venial	(of a sin) slight and able to be forgiven
waive	to choose not to insist on a right	wave	to move to and fro; a ridge of water
who's	short for *who is* or *who has*	whose	belonging to which person
wreath	an arrangement of flowers	wreathe	to surround or encircle
your	belonging to you	you're	short for *you are*

Wordfinder

Contents

Animals

Amphibians

axolotl	fire salamander	horned toad	newt	tree frog
bullfrog	flying frog	marsh frog	salamander	
cane toad	frog	natterjack toad	toad	

Birds

albatross	buzzard	dabchick	goldcrest	house martin
Arctic tern	Canada goose	dipper	golden eagle	hummingbird
auk	canary	dodo	goldfinch	ibis
avocet	capercaillie	dotterel	goose	jackdaw
barnacle goose	caracara	dove	goshawk	jay
barn owl	cassowary	duck	great tit	kestrel
Bewick's swan	chaffinch	dunlin	grebe	kingfisher
bird of paradise	chicken	dunnock	green	kite
bittern	chiffchaff	eagle	woodpecker	kittiwake
blackbird	chough	eagle owl	greenfinch	kiwi
blackcap	coal tit	egret	grouse	kookaburra
black swan	cockatiel	eider duck	guillemot	lammergeier
bluebird	cockatoo	emperor penguin	guineafowl	lapwing
blue tit	condor	emu	gull	lark
booby	coot	falcon	harrier	linnet
bowerbird	cormorant	fantail	hawfinch	lovebird
brambling	corncrake	fieldfare	hawk	lyrebird
budgerigar	crane	finch	hen	macaw
bullfinch	crossbill	flamingo	heron	magpie
bunting	crow	flycatcher	hobby	mallard
bustard	cuckoo	fulmar	hoopoe	martin
butcher-bird	curlew	gannet	hornbill	merlin

moa
mockingbird
moorhen
mynah bird
nightingale
nightjar
nuthatch
osprey
ostrich
ouzel
owl
oystercatcher
parakeet
parrot
partridge

peacock
peewit
pelican
penguin
peregrine falcon
petrel
pheasant
pigeon
pipit
plover
ptarmigan
puffin
quail
raven
red kite

redpoll
redstart
redwing
rhea
ring ouzel
roadrunner
robin
rook
sandpiper
seagull
shag
shearwater
shelduck
shrike
skua

skylark
snipe
sparrow
sparrowhawk
spoonbill
starling
stonechat
stork
storm petrel
sunbird
swallow
swan
swift
tern
thrush

tit
toucan
turkey
vulture
wagtail
warbler
waxwing
weaver bird
woodcock
woodlark
woodpecker
wren
yellowhammer

Crustaceans

barnacle
crab
crawfish
crayfish

crevette
fiddler crab
ghost crab
goose barnacle

hermit crab
horseshoe crab
king prawn
krill

land crab
langoustine
lobster
prawn

shrimp
spider crab
woodlouse

Dinosaurs

allosaurus
ankylosaur
apatosaurus
brachiosaurus
brontosaurus
carnosaur

coelurosaur
deinonychus
diplodocus
dromaeosaur
duck-billed
dinosaur

hadrosaur
iguanodon
megalosaurus
pliosaur
protoceratops
pteranodon

pterodactyl
raptor
saurischian
sauropod
seismosaurus
stegosaurus

theropod
triceratops
tyrannosaurus
velociraptor

Fish

anchovy
angelfish
anglerfish
archerfish
barbel
barracouta
barracuda
basking shark
bass
beluga
blenny
bluefin
boxfish
bream
brill
brisling
bullhead
butterfly fish
carp
catfish
charr
chub
clownfish

cod
coelacanth
coley
conger eel
dab
dace
damselfish
dogfish
dorado
dory
Dover sole
eel
electric eel
electric ray
fighting fish
filefish
flatfish
flathead
flounder
flying fish
garfish
goby
goldfish

gourami
grayling
great white shark
grouper
gudgeon
gulper eel
guppy
gurnard
haddock
hake
halfbeak
halibut
hammerhead
herring
hoki
huss
John Dory
koi carp
lamprey
lanternfish
lemon sole
loach
lumpsucker

lungfish
mackerel
mako
manta
marlin
megamouth
minnow
monkfish
moray eel
mudskipper
mullet
needlefish
nurse shark
oarfish
orfe
parrotfish
perch
pike
pilchard
pilotfish
pipefish
piranha
plaice

pollack
porbeagle
porcupine fish
puffer fish
rabbitfish
rainbow trout
ray
roach
sailfish
salmon
sardine
sawfish
scorpionfish
sea horse
shad
shark
skate
skipjack tuna
skipper
smelt
snapper
sockeye salmon
sole

sprat
stargazer
stickleback
stingray
stonefish
sturgeon

sunfish
surgeonfish
swordfish
swordtail
tench
tetra

thresher
tiger shark
tope
triggerfish
trout
tuna

tunny
turbot
weever
whaler
whale shark
whitebait

whitefish
whiting
wobbegong
wrasse
zander

Insects

ant
ant lion
aphid
assassin bug
bark beetle
bedbug
bee
beetle
blackfly
blowfly
bluebottle
boll weevil
bombardier
　beetle
borer
botfly
bumblebee
butterfly
caddis fly
carpet beetle
chafer

chigger
cicada
click beetle
cockchafer
cockroach
Colorado beetle
crane fly
cricket
daddy-long-legs
damselfly
death-watch
　beetle
devil's coach-
　horse
dragonfly
dung beetle
earwig
firefly
flea
fluke
fly

froghopper
fruit fly
furniture beetle
gadfly
gall wasp
glow-worm
gnat
goliath beetle
grasshopper
greenbottle
greenfly
honeybee
hornet
horsefly
housefly
hoverfly
lacewing
ladybird
leafcutter ant
leafhopper
leaf miner

leatherjacket
leech
locust
louse
mantis
mason bee
May bug
mayfly
mealy bug
midge
mosquito
moth
pond skater
praying mantis
rhinoceros beetle
robber fly
sandfly
sawfly
scale insect
scarab
scorpion fly

sexton beetle
silverfish
springtail
stag beetle
stick insect
stink bug
termite
thrips
thunderbug
thunderfly
tsetse fly
warble fly
wasp
water beetle
water boatman
weevil
whirligig
whitefly
witchetty grub

Mammals

aardvark
alpaca
angora
anteater
antelope
ape
armadillo
ass
aurochs
baboon
badger
baleen whale
Barbary ape
bat
beaked whale
bear
beaver
beluga
bison
blue whale
boar
bobcat
bottlenose
　dolphin

bottlenose whale
bowhead whale
buffalo
bushbaby
camel
capuchin monkey
capybara
caribou
cat
chamois
cheetah
chimpanzee
chinchilla
chipmunk
civet
coati
colobus
cougar
cow
coyote
coypu
deer
dingo
dog

dolphin
donkey
dormouse
dromedary
duck-billed
　platypus
dugong
echidna
eland
elephant
elephant seal
elk
ermine
fallow deer
fennec
ferret
fin whale
flying fox
fox
fur seal
gazelle
gemsbok
gerbil
gibbon

giraffe
gnu
goat
gopher
gorilla
grampus
grizzly bear
guinea pig
hamster
hare
harp seal
hartebeest
hedgehog
hippopotamus
hog
horse
howler monkey
humpback whale
hyena
hyrax
ibex
impala
jackal
jaguar

killer whale
kinkajou
Kodiak bear
kudu
langur
laughing hyena
lemming
lemur
leopard
leopard seal
lion
llama
loris
lynx
macaque
manatee
mandrill
margay
marmoset
marsupial
marten
meerkat
mink
minke whale

mole	oryx	porpoise	sheep	vervet monkey
mongoose	otter	possum	shrew	vole
monkey	ox	potto	skunk	walrus
moose	panda	puma	sloth	wapiti
mouse	pangolin	rabbit	snow leopard	warthog
mule	panther	raccoon	sperm whale	waterbuck
muntjac	peccary	rat	spider monkey	water buffalo
musk deer	pig	reindeer	spiny anteater	weasel
musk ox	pilot whale	rhinoceros	springbok	whale
narwhal	pine marten	roe deer	squirrel	wild boar
ocelot	pipistrelle	rorqual	squirrel monkey	wildcat
okapi	platypus	sea cow	stoat	wildebeest
opossum	polar bear	seal	tapir	wolverine
orang-utan	polecat	sea lion	tiger	yak
orca	porcupine	serval	vampire bat	zebra

Reptiles

adder	constrictor	Gila monster	moloch	skink
alligator	coral snake	glass lizard	monitor lizard	slow-worm
anaconda	corn snake	grass snake	pit viper	smooth snake
axolotl	crocodile	horned toad	puff adder	snake
basilisk	diamondback	iguana	python	taipan
boa constrictor	terrapin	Komodo dragon	rattlesnake	terrapin
bushmaster	galliwasp	leatherback	reticulated	tortoise
caiman	garter snake	lizard	python	turtle
chameleon	gecko	loggerhead turtle	rinkhals	viper
cobra	gharial	mamba	sidewinder	whip snake

Shellfish and Other Molluscs

abalone	cowrie	nerite	periwinkle	slug
argonaut	cuttlefish	nudibranch	piddock	snail
auger shell	limpet	octopus	quahog	squid
cephalopod	mitre	ormer	ramshorn snail	triton
clam	murex	oyster	razor shell	whelk
cockle	mussel	paua	scallop	winkle
conch	nautilus	pearl oyster	sea slug	

Spiders and Other Arachnids

bird-eating spider	funnel-web spider	money spider	spider mite	wolf spider
black widow	harvestman	raft spider	tarantula	
camel spider	harvest mite	redback	tick	
chigger	jigger	red spider mite	trapdoor spider	
crab spider	mite	scorpion	whip scorpion	

Male and Female Animals

antelope: *buck, doe*	cattle: *bull, cow*	elephant: *bull, cow*	goose: *gander, goose*	leopard: *leopard, leopardess*
badger: *boar, sow*	chicken: *cock, hen*	ferret: *jack, gill*	hare: *buck, doe*	lion: *lion, lioness*
bear: *boar, sow*	deer: *stag, doe*	fish: *cock, hen*	horse: *stallion, mare*	otter: *dog, bitch*
bird: *cock, hen*	dog: *dog, bitch*	fox: *dog, vixen*	kangaroo: *buck, doe*	pheasant: *cock, hen*
buffalo: *bull, cow*	donkey: *jackass, jenny*	goat: *billy goat, nanny*		pig: *boar, sow*
cat: *tom, queen*	duck: *drake, duck*			

rabbit: *buck, doe* sheep: *ram, ewe* tiger: *tiger,* whale: *bull, cow* zebra: *stallion,*
seal: *bull, cow* swan: *cob, pen* *tigress* wolf: *dog, bitch* *mare*

Young Animals

calf (*antelope,* *fox, leopard, lion,* filly (*female horse*) *weasel*) *seal, wolf*)
buffalo, camel, *tiger, walrus,* foal (*horse, zebra*) kitten (*cat,* puppy (*coyote,*
cattle, elephant, *wolf*) fry (*fish*) *cougar, rabbit,* *dog*)
elk, giraffe, cygnet (*swan*) gosling (*goose*) *skunk*) smolt (*salmon*)
rhinoceros, seal, duckling (*duck*) joey (*kangaroo,* lamb (*sheep*) squab (*pigeon*)
whale) eaglet (*eagle*) *wallaby, possum*) leveret (*hare*) tadpole (*frog,*
chick (*chicken,* elver (*eel*) kid (*goat, roe* owlet (*owl*) *toad*)
hawk, pheasant) eyas (*hawk*) *deer*) parr (*salmon*) whelp (*dog, wolf*)
colt (*male horse*) fawn (*caribou,* kit (*beaver, ferret,* piglet (*pig*)
cub (*badger, bear,* *deer*) *fox, mink,* pup (*dog, rat,*

Collective Names for Animals

band (*gorillas*) cry (*hounds*) knot (*toads*) parliament (*owls*) stare (*owls*)
bask (*crocodiles*) descent labour (*moles*) pod (*seals*) string (*horses*)
bellowing (*woodpeckers*) leap (*leopards*) pride (*lions*) stud (*mares*)
(*bullfinches*) down (*hares*) litter (*kittens, pigs*) rookery (*rooks*) swarm (*bees, flies*)
bevy (*roe deer,* drove (*bullocks*) mob (*kangaroos*) safe (*ducks*) tiding (*magpies*)
quails, larks, exaltation (*larks*) murder (*crows*) school (*whales,* trip (*goats*)
pheasants) flight (*birds*) murmuration *dolphins,* troop (*baboons*)
bloat flock (*sheep*) (*starlings*) *porpoises*) turmoil
(*hippopotami*) gaggle (*geese on* muster (*peacocks,* shoal (*fish*) (*porpoises*)
brood (*chickens*) *land*) *penguins*) shrewdness (*apes*) turn (*turtles*)
bury (*rabbits*) herd (*cattle,* obstinacy (*buffalo*) siege (*herons*) unkindness
busyness (*ferrets*) *elephants*) pack (*hounds,* skein (*geese in* (*ravens*)
charm (*finches*) hive (*bees*) *grouse*) *flight*) watch
cloud (*gnats*) hover (*trout*) pandemonium skulk (*foxes*) (*nightingales*)
covey (*partridges*) kennel (*dogs*) (*parrots*) sloth (*bears*) yoke (*oxen*)
crash (*rhinoceros*) kindle (*kittens*) parade (*elephants*) span (*mules*) zeal (*zebras*)

Chemical Elements

*Metal

*actinium (Ac) *calcium (Ca) *fermium (Fm) krypton (Kr) neon (Ne)
*aluminium (Al) *californium (Cf) fluorine (F) *lanthanum (La) *neptunium (Np)
*americium (Am) carbon (C) *francium (Fr) *lawrencium (Lr) *nickel (Ni)
argon (Ar) *cerium (Ce) *gadolinium (Gd) *lead (Pb) *niobium (Nb)
arsenic (As) chlorine (Cl) *gallium (Ga) *lithium (Li) nitrogen (N)
astatine (At) *chromium (Cr) germanium (Ge) *lutetium (Lu) *nobelium (No)
*barium (Ba) *cobalt (Co) *gold (Au) *magnesium (Mg) *osmium (Os)
*berkelium (Bk) *copper (Cu) *hafnium (Hf) *manganese (Mn) oxygen (O)
*beryllium (Be) *curium (Cm) hassium (Hs) meitnerium (Mt) *palladium (Pd)
*bismuth (Bi) darmstadtium helium (He) *mendelevium phosphorus (P)
bohrium (Bh) (Ds) *holmium (Ho) (Md) *platinum (Pt)
boron (B) dubnium (Db) hydrogen (H) *mercury (Hg) *plutonium (Pu)
bromine (Br) *dysprosium (Dy) *indium (In) *molybdenum *polonium (Po)
*cadmium (Cd) einsteinium (Es) iodine (I) (Mo) *potassium (K)
*caesium (Cs) *erbium (Er) *iridium (Ir) *neodymium *praseodymium
*europium (Eu) *iron (Fe) (Nd) (Pr)

*promethium (Pm)
*protactinium (Pa)
*radium (Ra)
radon (Rn)
*rhenium (Re)
*rhodium (Rh)

roentgenium (Rg)
*rubidium (Rb)
*ruthenium (Ru)
rutherfordium (Rf)
*samarium (Sm)
*scandium (Sc)
seaborgium (Sg)

selenium (Se)
silicon (Si)
*silver (Ag)
*sodium (Na)
*strontium (Sr)
sulphur (S)
*tantalum (Ta)
*technetium (Tc)

tellurium (Te)
*terbium (Tb)
*thallium (Tl)
*thorium (Th)
*thulium (Tm)
*tin (Sn)
*titanium (Ti)
*tungsten (W)

*uranium (U)
*vanadium (V)
*xenon (Xe)
*ytterbium (Yb)
*yttrium (Y)
*zinc (Zn)
*zirconium (Zr)

Clothing

Clothes

anorak
apron
ballgown
bandeau
basque
bell-bottoms
belt
Bermuda shorts
bib
bikini
blazer
bloomers
blouse
blouson
boa
bodice
body
body stocking
body warmer
bolero
bomber jacket
bow tie
bra
braces
breeches
burka/burkha/ burqa
burnous
cagoule
cape
capri pants
cardigan
cargo pants
carpenter trousers
catsuit
chador
chinos
churidars
coat
combat trousers
cords

corset
cravat
crinoline
crop top
culottes
cummerbund
cut-offs
dashiki
denims
dhoti
dinner jacket
dirndl
djellaba
djibba
dolman
domino
donkey jacket
doublet
dress
dressing gown
dress shirt
duffel coat
dungarees
flannels
flares
fleece
flying jacket
frock coat
gilet
glove
gown
greatcoat
guernsey
gymslip
haik
hair shirt
hipsters
hoody/hoodie
hose
hot pants
housecoat
hula skirt

jacket
jeans
jellaba
jerkin
jersey
jibba
jilbab
jodhpurs
jogging pants
jumper
jumpsuit
kaftan
kagoul
kameez
kilt
kimono
knickers
lederhosen
leggings
leg warmers
leotard
loden
loincloth
lumberjacket
lungi
mac
mackintosh/ macintosh
maillot
mandarin jacket
mantilla
mantle
maxi
maxidress
mess jacket
midi
mini
miniskirt
mitt
mitten
morning coat
muff

muffler
nightdress
nightshirt
oilskins
overalls
overcoat
overtrousers
palazzo pants
pantaloons
panties
pants
pantyhose
parka
pedal pushers
peignoir
pencil skirt
peplum
petticoat
pinafore
pinafore dress
plastron
plus fours
polo neck
polo shirt
poncho
pullover
pyjamas
raincoat
reefer jacket
robe
roll-neck
ruff
safari jacket
sailor suit
salopettes
sari
sarong
sash
scarf
serape/sarape
shawl
sheath dress

sheepskin
shell suit
shift
shirt dress
shirtwaister
shorts
skinny-rib
ski pants
skirt
skort
slacks
slip
smock
smoking jacket
sock
stirrup pants
stock
stocking
stole
suit
sundress
suspenders
sweater
sweatpants
sweatshirt
swimming costume
swimming trunks
swimsuit
T-shirt
tabard
tailcoat
tails
tank top
tee
tie
tights
toga
top
topcoat
tracksuit

trench coat	tunic	twinset	vest	windcheater
trews	turtleneck	ulster	V-neck	yashmak
trousers	tutu	underpants	waistcoat	
trouser suit	tux/tuxedo	underskirt	waterproof	
trunks	tweeds	veil	waxed jacket	

Footwear

beetle-crusher	Dr Martens	lace-up	plimsoll	stiletto
boot	(trademark)	loafer	pump	thong
bootee	espadrille	moccasin	sabot	top boot
brogue	flip-flop	moon boot	sandal	trainer
carpet slipper	galosh	mukluk	shoe	wader
chappal	gumboot	mule	slingback	walking boot
clog	half-boot	overshoe	slip-on	wedge
court shoe	high-low	Oxford	slipper	wellington boot
cowboy boot	hobnail boot	patten	sneaker	
deck shoe	jackboot	peep-toe	snow boot	
desert boot	jelly shoe	platform	step-in	

Headgear

balaclava	cloth cap	garland	mob cap	sun hat
bandeau	cocked hat	glengarry	mortar board	tam-o'-shanter
baseball cap	coif	hard hat	nightcap	tarboosh
beanie	coolie hat	headband	panama	ten-gallon hat
bearskin	coronet	headscarf	pillbox hat	tiara
beret	cowl	helmet	pixie hat	top hat
biretta	crash helmet	hijab	pork-pie hat	topi
boater	crown	homburg	sailor hat	topper
bobble hat	deerstalker	hood	skullcap	toque
bonnet	derby	jester's cap	slouch hat	tricorne
bowler	diadem	jockey cap	snood	trilby
busby	Dolly Varden	Juliet cap	sola topi	turban
cap	dunce's cap	keffiyeh	sombrero	veil
chaplet	fedora	kepi	sou'wester	wimple
circlet	fez	mantilla	Stetson (trademark)	wreath
cloche	flat cap	mitre	stovepipe hat	zucchetto

Food and Drink

Bread and Bread Rolls

bagel	ciabatta	focaccia	muffin	poppadom
baguette	cob	French stick	nan/naan	pumpernickel
bannock	cornbread	fruit loaf	panettone	puri
bap	cottage loaf	granary bread	panino	rye
bloomer	crumpet	(trademark)	paratha	soda bread
bridge roll	damper	hoagie	petit pain	sourdough
brioche	farl	malt loaf	pikelet	split tin
bun	farmhouse loaf	matzo	pitta	stollen
chapatti	flatbread	milk loaf	pone	

Cakes, Biscuits, and Desserts

angel cake
apfelstrudel
baba
baked Alaska
Bakewell tart
baklava
banana split
banoffi/
 banoffee pie
Bath bun
Bath Oliver
Battenberg
beignet
biscotti
Black Forest
 gateau
blancmange
bombe
bourbon
brack
brandy snap
bread pudding
bread-and-butter
 pudding
Brown Betty
brownie
bun
butterfly cake
cabinet pudding
cassata
charlotte
charlotte russe
cheesecake
chocolate chip
clafoutis

cobbler
compote
cookie
cream cracker
cream puff
crème brûlée
crème caramel
crêpe
crêpe Suzette
crispbread
croquembouche
crumble
crumpet
cupcake
custard cream
custard pie
custard tart
Danish pastry
devil's food cake
digestive
doughnut
drop scone
dumpling
Dundee cake
Eccles cake
eclair
egg custard
Eskimo pie
 (trademark)
Eve's pudding
fairy cake
fancy
flapjack
Florentine
flummery

fool
fortune cookie
frangipane
fruit cocktail
fruit salad
garibaldi
gateau
gelato
Genoa cake
gingerbread
ginger nut
ginger snap
granita
halwa
hot cross bun
ice cream
jelly
junket
Knickerbocker
 Glory
kulfi
lady's finger
langue de chat
lardy cake
macaroon
Madeira cake
madeleine
maid of honour
marble cake
matzo
meringue
milk pudding
millefeuille
mince pie
Mississippi mud

pie
mousse
muffin
Nice biscuit
oatcake
pancake
panettone
panforte
parfait
parkin
pavlova
peach Melba
petit four
plum duff
plum pudding
popover
pound cake
profiterole
queen of
 puddings
ratafia
rice pudding
rock cake
roly-poly
rusk
Sachertorte
sago pudding
Sally Lunn
sandwich
savarin
scone
seed cake
semolina pudding
shortbread
shortcake

simnel cake
sorbet
soufflé
sponge
sponge pudding
spotted dick
steamed pudding
stollen
streusel
strudel
summer pudding
sundae
Swiss roll
syllabub
tapioca pudding
tart
tarte Tatin
tartlet
tartufo
tipsy cake
tiramisu
torte
treacle tart
trifle
turnover
tutti-frutti
upside-down cake
Victoria sponge
waffle
water biscuit
water ice
whip
yogurt
yule log
zabaglione

Cheeses

asiago
Bel Paese (trademark)
blue vinny
Boursin (trademark)
Brie
Caerphilly
Camembert
Chaumes
Cheddar
Cheshire
chèvre
cottage cheese
cream cheese

crowdie/
 crowdy
curd cheese
Danish blue
Derby
Dolcelatte
 (trademark)
Double
 Gloucester
Dunlop
Edam
Emmental
feta/fetta

fontina
fromage blanc
fromage frais
Gloucester
Gorgonzola
Gouda
Gruyère
halloumi
havarti
Jarlsberg (trademark)
Lancashire
Leicester
Limburger

Manchego
mascarpone
Monterey Jack
mozzarella
paneer/panir
Parmesan
Parmigiano
 Reggiano
pecorino
Port Salut
provolone
quark
Red Leicester

ricotta
Romano
Roquefort
 (trademark)
sage Derby
scamorza
Stilton
taleggio
Tilsit
Wensleydale

Fruit and Nuts

almond
apple

apricot
avocado

banana
betel nut

bilberry
blackberry

blackcurrant
blueberry

boysenberry
Brazil nut
breadfruit
butternut
cantaloupe
Cape gooseberry
carambola
cashew
cherimoya
cherry
chestnut
Chinese
  gooseberry
citron
clementine
cloudberry
cobnut
coconut
cola nut
cowberry
crab apple
cranberry
currant
damson
date
elderberry
fig
filbert
galia melon
gooseberry
gourd
grape
grapefruit
greengage
groundnut
guava
hazelnut
honeydew melon
huckleberry
jackfruit
jujube
kiwi fruit
kumquat
lemon
lime
loganberry
loquat
lychee
macadamia
mandarin
mango
melon
minneola
monkey nut
mulberry
nectarine
olive
orange
ortanique
papaya
passion fruit
pawpaw
peach
peanut
pear
pecan
persimmon
pineapple
pine nut
pistachio
plum
pomegranate
pomelo
prickly pear
pumpkin
quince
rambutan
raspberry
redcurrant
salmonberry
sapodilla
satsuma
serviceberry
sharon fruit
sloe
star anise
starfruit
strawberry
tamarillo
tangerine
tayberry
tiger nut
Ugli fruit (trademark)
walnut
water chestnut
watermelon
whortleberry

Pasta

agnolotti
angel hair
cannelloni
capelli
capellini
cappelletti
conchiglie
ditalini
farfalle
farfalline
fettuccine
fusilli
lasagne
linguine
macaroni
noodles
precchiette
orzo
pappardelle
penne
pipe
radiatori
ravioli
rigatoni
spaghetti
spaghettini
strozzapreti
tagliatelle
tagliolini
tortelli
tortellini
tortelloni
tortiglioni
vermicelli
ziti

Sweets and Confectionery

aniseed ball
barley sugar
bonbon
brittle
bullseye
butterscotch
candy
candyfloss
caramel
chew
chocolate
coconut ice
comfit
cracknel
crystallized fruit
dolly mixtures
dragée
Easter egg
fondant
fruit drop
fruit gum
fruit pastille
fudge
gobstopper
gulab jamun
gumdrop
halva
humbug
jalebi
jelly
jelly baby
jelly bean
jujube
Kendal mint cake
laddu
liquorice
liquorice allsort
lollipop
lolly
marshmallow
marzipan
mint
nougat
pastille
pear drop
peppermint
peppermint
  cream
Pontefract cake
praline
rock
sherbet
sugared almond
toffee
toffee apple
truffle
Turkish delight
walnut whip
wine gum

Vegetables

aduki/adzuki
  bean
alfalfa
artichoke
asparagus
aubergine
bamboo shoots
bean
beet
beetroot
black bean
black-eyed bean
borlotti bean
breadfruit
broad bean
broccoli
Brussels sprout
butter bean
butternut squash
cabbage
calabrese
cannellini bean
capsicum
carrot
cassava
cauliflower
celeriac
celery
chard
chervil
chickpea
chicory
Chinese leaves
corn on the cob
cos lettuce
courgette
cress
cucumber
curly kale
eggplant
endive
fennel
flageolet bean
French bean
garlic

gherkin
globe artichoke
gourd
haricot bean
Jerusalem
  artichoke
kale
kidney bean
kohlrabi
leek
lentil
lettuce
lima bean

lollo rosso
mangetout
marrow
marrowfat pea
mooli
mung bean
mushroom
mustard
okra
onion
pak choi
parsnip
pea

pepper
petits pois
pimiento
pinto bean
plantain
potato
pumpkin
radicchio
radish
rocket
runner bean
salsify
samphire

savoy cabbage
shallot
snow pea
soybean
spinach
spinach beet
spring greens
spring onion
squash
string bean
sugar pea
sugar snap pea
swede

sweetcorn
sweet pepper
sweet potato
tomato
turnip
vegetable
  spaghetti
water chestnut
watercress
waxpod
yam
zucchini

Alcoholic Drinks

absinthe
advocaat
alcopop
ale
amaretto
amontillado
aquavit
Armagnac
barley wine
beer
bitter
bock
bourbon
brandy
brown ale
burgundy
Calvados
cassis
cava
champagne

chartreuse
cherry brandy
cider
claret
cocktail
cognac
crème de
  menthe
curaçao
fine
  champagne
fino
genever
gin
ginger wine
grappa
hock
ice beer
Irish coffee
Irish whiskey

kirsch
kümmel
kvass
lager
Liebfraumilch
light ale
liqueur
Madeira
malmsey
malt
malt whisky
manzanilla
maraschino
Marsala
mead
mescal
mild
milk stout
moscato
muscat

muscatel
oloroso
ouzo
pale ale
palm wine
pastis
perry
Pils
Pilsner/Pilsener
port
porter
poteen
raki
ratafia
retsina
rosé
rum
rye
sack
sake

schnapps
Scotch whisky
scrumpy
Sekt
shandy
sherry
single malt
slivovitz
sloe gin
Spumante
stout
tequila
Tia Maria
triple sec
vermouth
vinho verde
vodka
whiskey
whisky
wine

Non-alcoholic Drinks

barley water
bitter lemon
buttermilk
cafe au lait
caffè latte
caffè
  macchiato
camomile tea
cappuccino
cherryade

citron pressé
club soda
  (trademark)
cocoa
coffee
cola
cordial
cream soda
crush
dandelion and

  burdock
decaf
decaffeinated
  coffee
drinking
  chocolate
Earl Grey
espresso
filter coffee
fruit juice

fruit tea
ginger ale
ginger beer
green tea
gunpowder tea
herbal tea
horchata
hot chocolate
iced tea
Indian tea

infusion
isotonic drink
jasmine tea
lassi
latte
lemon tea
lemonade
limeade
malted milk
maté

milkshake	peppermint tea	sarsaparilla	sports drink	tonic water
mineral water	prairie oyster	seltzer	spring water	yerba maté
mint tea	pressé	sherbet	squash	
mocha	robusta	smoothie	St Clements	
mochaccino	root beer	soda water	tea	
orangeade	rosehip tea	soya milk	tisane	

Phobias

air travel:
aerophobia
American people
and things:
Americophobia
animals:
zoophobia
beards:
pogonophobia
beating:
mastigophobia
bed: *clinophobia*
bees: *apiphobia*
birds:
ornithophobia
blood:
haemophobia
blushing:
erythrophobia
bridges:
gephyrophobia
burial alive:
taphephobia
cancer:
carcinophobia
cats: *ailurophobia*
childbirth:
tocophobia
children:
paedophobia
Chinese people
and things:
Sinophobia
clouds:
nephophobia
cold:
cheimaphobia
colour:
chromophobia
computers:
cyberphobia
corpses:
necrophobia
crowds:
demophobia

dampness:
hygrophobia
darkness:
scotophobia
dawn: *eosophobia*
death:
thanatophobia
depth:
bathophobia
dirt: *mysophobia*
disease:
pathophobia
dogs: *cynophobia*
dreams:
oneirophobia
drink: *potophobia*
dust: *koniophobia*
electricity:
electrophobia
English people
and things:
Anglophobia
everything:
panophobia,
pantophobia
faeces:
coprophobia
feathers:
pteronophobia
fever: *febriphobia*
fire: *pyrophobia*
fish: *ichthyophobia*
flesh: *selaphobia*
floods: *antlophobia*
flowers:
anthophobia
food: *cibophobia*,
sitophobia
foreigners:
xenophobia
French people
and things:
Francophobia,
Gallophobia
fur: *doraphobia*

German people
and things:
Germanophobia,
Teutophobia
germs:
spermophobia
ghosts:
phasmophobia
God: *theophobia*
gold: *aurophobia*,
chrysophobia
hair: *trichophobia*
heat:
thermophobia
heaven:
uranophobia
hell: *hadephobia*,
stygiophobia
high buildings:
batophobia
high places:
hypsophobia
home: *oikophobia*
homosexuals:
homophobia
horses:
hippophobia
ice: *cryophobia*
idleness:
thassophobia
illness:
nosophobia
imperfection:
atelophobia
infinity:
apeirophobia
insanity:
lyssophobia,
maniphobia
insects:
entomophobia
insect stings:
cnidophobia
Italian people
and things:

Italophobia
lakes: *limnophobia*
light: *photophobia*
lightning:
astrapophobia
loneliness:
autophobia,
ermitophobia
machinery:
mechanophobia
magic:
rhabdophobia
marriage:
gametophobia
men: *androphobia*
metal:
metallophobia
mice: *musophobia*
microbes:
bacillophobia
mites:
acarophobia
mobs:
ochlophobia
motion:
kinetophobia
music:
musicophobia
needles:
belonephobia
new things:
neophobia
night:
nyctophobia
nudity:
gymnophobia
open places:
agoraphobia
pain: *algophobia*
pins: *enetophobia*
pleasure:
hedonophobia
poison: *toxiphobia*
poverty:
peniaphobia

precipices:
cremnophobia
priests:
hierophobia
punishment:
poinephobia
religious works of
art: *iconophobia*
responsibility:
hypegiaphobia
rivers:
potamophobia
robbers:
harpaxophobia
ruin: *atephobia*
Russian people
and things:
Russophobia
Satan:
Satanophobia
scabies:
scabiophobia
Scottish people
and things:
Scotophobia
sex: *erotophobia*
shadows:
sciophobia
sharpness:
acrophobia
shock:
hormephobia
sin:
hamartophobia
sleep:
hypnophobia
slime:
blennophobia
small things:
microphobia
smell:
olfactophobia,
osmophobia
smothering:
pnigerophobia

snakes:
  ophidiophobia
snow:
  chionophobia
solitude:
  eremophobia
sourness:
  acerophobia
speech:
  glossophobia,
  phonophobia
speed:

  tachophobia
spiders:
  arachnophobia
stars:
  siderophobia
stealing:
  kleptophobia
stuttering:
  laliophobia,
  lalophobia
sun: *heliophobia*
swallowing:

  phagophobia
taste:
  geumatophobia
technology:
  technophobia
thunder:
  brontophobia,
  keraunophobia,
  tonitrophobia
time:
  chronophobia
touch:

  haptophobia
travel: *hodophobia*
venereal disease:
  syphilophobia
voids:
  kenophobia
vomiting:
  emetophobia
water:
  hydrophobia
waves:
  cymophobia

weakness:
  asthenophobia
wind:
  anemophobia
women:
  gynophobia
words: *logophobia*
work: *ergophobia*
writing:
  graphophobia

Plants

Flowering Plants and Shrubs

acacia
acanthus
aconite
African violet
agapanthus
aloe
alstroemeria
alyssum
amaranth
amaryllis
anemone
aquilegia
arrowgrass
arum lily
asphodel
aspidistra
aster
astilbe
aubretia
avens
azalea
balsam
banksia
bedstraw
begonia
belladonna
bellflower
bergamot
betony
bilberry
bindweed
bird's-foot trefoil
black-eyed Susan
blackthorn
bleeding heart
bluebell
boneset
borage

bougainvillea
bramble
broom
bryony
buddleia
bugloss
bulrush
burdock
burnet
busy Lizzie
buttercup
cactus
calceolaria
calendula
camellia
camomile
campanula
campion
candytuft
Canterbury bell
carnation
catmint
ceanothus
celandine
chickweed
chicory
Chinese lantern
chives
choisya
chokeberry
Christmas cactus
Christmas rose
chrysanthemum
cicely
cinquefoil
clematis
clove pink
clover

cockscomb
coltsfoot
columbine
comfrey
convolvulus
coreopsis
cornflower
corydalis
cotoneaster
cottonweed
cow parsley
cowslip
cranesbill
crocus
crown imperial
crown of thorns
cuckoo pint
cyclamen
daffodil
dahlia
daisy
damask rose
dandelion
daphne
deadly
  nightshade
delphinium
dianthus
dill
dittany
dock
dog rose
duckweed
echinacea
edelweiss
eglantine
elder
evening primrose

eyebright
feverfew
figwort
firethorn
flax
forget-me-not
forsythia
foxglove
frangipani
freesia
fritillary
fuchsia
furze
gardenia
gentian
geranium
gladiolus
glory-of-the-snow
gloxinia
golden rod
gorse
grape hyacinth
groundsel
guelder rose
gypsophila
harebell
hawkweed
hawthorn
heartsease
heather
hebe
helianthemum
helianthus
heliotrope
hellebore
hemlock
heuchera
hibiscus

hogweed
holly
hollyhock
honesty
honeysuckle
hosta
hyacinth
hydrangea
iris
jacaranda
japonica
jasmine
jonquil
kingcup
knapweed
knotgrass
laburnum
lady's mantle
lady's tresses
larkspur
lavatera
lavender
lemon balm
lilac
lily
lily of the valley
lobelia
London pride
loosestrife
lords and ladies
lotus
lovage
love-in-a-mist
love-lies-bleeding
lungwort
lupin
madonna lily
magnolia

mahonia
mallow
mandrake
marguerite
marigold
marshwort
may
mayflower
meadow rue
meadow saffron
meadowsweet
Michaelmas daisy
milfoil
mimosa
mint
mistletoe
mock orange
montbretia
morning glory
musk rose
myrtle
narcissus
nasturtium
nettle
nicotiana
nigella
night-scented

stock
nightshade
old man's beard
oleander
orchid
ox-eye daisy
oxlip
pansy
Parma violet
parsley
pasque flower
passion flower
pelargonium
pennyroyal
penstemon
peony
peppermint
periwinkle
petunia
phlox
pimpernel
pink
pitcher plant
plantain
plumbago
poinsettia
polyanthus

poppy
potentilla
prickly pear
primrose
primula
privet
pulsatilla
pyracantha
pyrethrum
ragwort
ramsons
red-hot poker
rhododendron
rock rose
rose
rosebay
  willowherb
rose of Sharon
safflower
St John's wort
salvia
samphire
saxifrage
scabious
scarlet pimpernel
scilla
sedum

shamrock
shrimp plant
snapdragon
snow-in-summer
snowdrop
soapwort
sorrel
speedwell
spikenard
spiraea
spurge
spurrey
squill
starwort
stock
stonecrop
streptocarpus
sunflower
sweet pea
sweet william
tansy
teasel
thistle
thrift
toadflax
tradescantia
trefoil

tulip
valerian
Venus flytrap
verbena
veronica
vervain
vetch
viburnum
violet
viper's bugloss
wallflower
water lily
willowherb
winter jasmine
wintergreen
wisteria
witch hazel
wolfsbane
woodruff
wormwood
yarrow
yucca
zinnia

Trees and Shrubs

acacia
acer
alder
almond
apple
apricot
araucaria
ash
aspen
azalea
balsa
balsam fir
bamboo
banksia
banyan
baobab
basswood
bay tree
beech
beefwood
bergamot
birch
blackthorn
bottlebrush
bottle tree
bo tree
box
box elder

bristlecone pine
broom
buckeye
buckthorn
butternut
cacao
calabash
camellia
camphor tree
candelabra tree
candleberry
candlenut
carambola
carob
cassava
cassia
casuarina
cedar
cherimoya
cherry
chestnut
cinnamon
citron
coco de mer
coconut palm
cola
coolibah
copper beech

cork oak
coromandel
crab apple
cypress
dogwood
dragon tree
ebony
elder
elm
eucalyptus
euonymus
ficus
fig
filbert
fir
firethorn
flame tree
frangipani
fuchsia
gean
ginkgo
gorse
grapefruit
greengage
guava
gum tree
hawthorn
hazel

hemlock fir
hickory
holly
holm oak
honeysuckle
hornbeam
horse chestnut
hydrangea
ilex
iroko
ironbark
ironwood
jacaranda
jackfruit
jack pine
japonica
jasmine
juniper
kalmia
kapok
kermes oak
laburnum
larch
laurel
lemon
Leyland cypress
leylandii
lilac

lime
linden
liquidambar
locust
lodgepole pine
logwood
macadamia
magnolia
mahogany
maidenhair tree
mango
mangosteen
mangrove
maple
mastic
may
mimosa
mirabelle
monkey puzzle
mountain ash
mulberry
myrtle
nutmeg
nux vomica
oak
oleaster
olive
osier

pagoda tree
palm
papaya
paper mulberry
paperbark
pawpaw
pear
persimmon
pine
pistachio
pitch pine
plane
plum
pomegranate

pomelo
poplar
privet
pussy willow
quassia
quince
rambutan
red cedar
redwood
rhododendron
robinia
rosewood
rowan
rubber plant

rubber tree
sallow
sandalwood
sapele
sapodilla
sassafras
satinwood
senna
sequoia
service tree
silver birch
Sitka cypress
slippery elm
smoke tree

soapberry
spindle
spruce
star anise
stinkwood
storax
sumac
sycamore
tallow tree
tamarind
tamarisk
tea
teak
tea tree

thuja
tulip tree
tulipwood
umbrella tree
viburnum
walnut
weeping willow
wellingtonia
whitebeam
willow
witch hazel
wych elm
yew

label *noun* **1 tag**, ticket, tab, sticker, marker, docket. **2 description**, designation, name, epithet, nickname, sobriquet, title.
● *verb* **1 tag**, ticket, mark, stamp. **2 categorize**, classify, class, describe, designate, identify, mark, stamp, brand, call, name, term, dub.

laborious *adjective* **1 arduous**, hard, heavy, difficult, strenuous, gruelling, punishing, exacting, tough, onerous, challenging, painstaking, time-consuming. **2 laboured**, strained, forced, stiff, stilted, unnatural, artificial, ponderous.
- OPPOSITES easy, effortless.

labour *noun* **1 work**, toil, exertion, effort, industry, drudgery; *informal* slog, grind; *old use* travail. **2 workers**, employees, labourers, workforce, staff. **3 childbirth**, birth, delivery; *technical* parturition.
● *verb* **work (hard)**, toil, slave (away), struggle, strive, exert yourself, endeavour, try hard; *informal* slog away, plug away.

laboured *adjective* **1** *laboured breathing* **strained**, difficult, forced, laborious. **2** *a laboured metaphor* **contrived**, forced, unconvincing, unnatural, artificial, overdone.
- OPPOSITES natural, easy.

labourer *noun* **workman**, worker, manual worker, blue-collar worker, (hired) hand, roustabout, drudge, menial; *Austral./NZ* rouseabout; *dated* navvy.

labyrinthine *adjective* **1 maze-like**, winding, twisting, serpentine, meandering. **2 complicated**, intricate, complex, involved, tortuous, convoluted, elaborate, confusing, puzzling, mystifying, bewildering, baffling.

lace *verb* **1 fasten**, do up, tie up, secure, knot. **2 flavour**, mix, blend, fortify, strengthen, season, spice (up), liven up,

doctor, adulterate; *informal* spike.

laceration *noun* **gash**, cut, wound, injury, tear, slash, scratch, scrape, abrasion, graze.

lack *noun* **absence**, want, need, deficiency, dearth, shortage, shortfall, scarcity, paucity.
- OPPOSITES abundance.
● *verb* **be without**, be in need of, be short of, be deficient in, be low on, be pressed for, need; *informal* be strapped for.

lacklustre *adjective* **uninspired**, uninspiring, unimaginative, dull, humdrum, colourless, bland, insipid, flat, dry, lifeless, tame, prosaic, dreary, tedious.
- OPPOSITES inspired.

lad *noun* (*informal*) **1 boy**, schoolboy, youth, youngster, juvenile, stripling; *informal* kid, nipper; *Scottish informal* laddie; *derogatory* brat. **2 (young) man**, fellow; *informal* guy, geezer; *Brit. informal* chap, bloke; *N. Amer. informal* dude, hombre.

laden *adjective* **loaded**, burdened, weighed down, overloaded, piled high, full, packed, stuffed, crammed; *informal* chock-full, chock-a-block.

lady *noun* **1 woman**, female, girl; *Scottish & N. English* lass, lassie; *N. Amer. informal* dame, broad; *Austral. informal* sheila. **2 noblewoman**, aristocrat, duchess, countess, peeress, viscountess, baroness.

ladylike *adjective* **genteel**, polite, refined, well bred, cultivated, polished, decorous, proper, respectable, well mannered, cultured, sophisticated, elegant; *Brit. informal* posh.

lag *verb* **fall behind**, trail, bring up the rear, dawdle, hang back, delay, loiter, linger, dally, straggle.

laid-back *adjective* (*informal*) **relaxed**, easy-going, free and easy, casual,

nonchalant, blasé, cool, calm, unconcerned, leisurely, unhurried; *informal* unflappable, chilled.
- OPPOSITES uptight.

lake noun **pool**, pond, tarn, reservoir, lagoon, waterhole; *Scottish* loch; *Anglo-Irish* lough; *N. Amer.* bayou.

lame adjective **1 limping**, hobbling, crippled, disabled, incapacitated; *informal* gammy. **2 feeble**, weak, thin, flimsy, poor, unconvincing, implausible, unlikely.

lament verb **1 mourn**, grieve, sorrow, weep, cry, wail, keen. **2 complain about**, bewail, bemoan, deplore.
- OPPOSITES celebrate, welcome.

lamentable adjective **deplorable**, regrettable, terrible, awful, wretched, woeful, dire, disastrous, desperate, grave, appalling, dreadful, pitiful, shameful, unfortunate; *formal* egregious.
- OPPOSITES wonderful.

land noun **1 dry land**, terra firma, coast, coastline, shore. **2 grounds**, fields, property, acres, acreage, estate, real estate. **3 country**, nation, state, realm, kingdom, province, region, territory, area, domain.
● verb **1 disembark**, go ashore, debark, alight, get off, berth, dock, moor, (drop) anchor, tie up, put in, touch down, come to rest. **2** *(informal)* **get**, obtain, acquire, secure, gain, net, win, achieve, attain, bag, carry off.
- OPPOSITES embark, take off.

> **WORD LINKS**
> **terrestrial** relating to land

landlord, **landlady** noun **1 owner**, proprietor, lessor, householder, landowner. **2 licensee**, innkeeper, hotelier; *Brit.* publican; *humorous* mine host.
- OPPOSITES tenant.

landmark noun **1 feature**, sight, monument, building. **2** *a landmark in Indian history* **turning point**, milestone, watershed.

landscape noun **scenery**, country, countryside, topography, terrain,

view, panorama.

landslide noun **1 landslip**, rockfall, mudslide, avalanche. **2 decisive victory**, runaway victory, overwhelming majority; *informal* whitewash.

lane noun **road**, street, track, trail, alley, alleyway, passage, path.

language noun **1 speech**, speaking, talk, discourse, communication, words, vocabulary. **2 tongue**, mother tongue, native tongue, dialect, patois; *informal* lingo, geekspeak. **3 wording**, phrasing, phraseology, style, vocabulary, terminology, expressions, turn of phrase, parlance.

> **WORD LINKS**
> **linguistic** relating to language

languish verb **1 deteriorate**, decline, go downhill, wither, droop, wilt, fade. **2 waste away**, rot, be abandoned, be neglected, be forgotten, suffer.
- OPPOSITES thrive.

lap[1] verb **1 drink**, lick up, sup, swallow, slurp, gulp. **2 splash**, wash, swish, slosh, break, plash; *literary* purl.
□ **lap up** relish, revel in, savour, delight in, wallow in, glory in, enjoy.

lap[2] noun **circuit**, leg, circle, round, stretch.

lapse noun **1 failure**, slip, error, mistake, blunder, fault, omission; *informal* slip-up. **2 decline**, fall, deterioration, degeneration, backsliding, regression. **3 interval**, gap, pause, interlude, lull, hiatus, break.
● verb **1 expire**, run out, (come to an) end, cease, stop, terminate. **2 revert**, relapse, drift, slide, slip, sink.

large adjective **big**, great, sizeable, substantial, considerable, huge, extensive, voluminous, vast, cosmic, prodigious, massive, immense, enormous, colossal, king-size(d), heavy, mammoth, gigantic, giant, fat, stout, strapping, bulky, burly; *informal* jumbo, mega, whopping.
- OPPOSITES small.

largely adverb **mostly**, mainly, to a large/great extent, chiefly, predominantly, primarily, principally, for the most part, in the main, on the whole.

lash verb **1 beat against**, dash against, pound, batter, hammer against, strike, hit, drum. **2 fasten**, bind, tie (up), tether, hitch, knot, rope.
□ **lash out 1** criticize, attack, condemn, censure; *informal* lay into, dis; *Brit. informal* slag off, have a go at. **2** hit out at, strike, let fly at, take a swing at, set on, turn on, round on, attack; *informal* lay into, pitch into.

last¹ adjective **1 final**, closing, concluding, end, ultimate, terminal, later, latter. **2 rearmost**, hindmost, endmost, furthest (back). **3 previous**, preceding, prior, former, latest, most recent.
- OPPOSITES first, next.

last² verb **1** *the hearing lasted for six days* **continue**, go on, carry on, keep on/going, take. **2** *he won't last long as manager* **survive**, endure, hold on/out, keep going, persevere, persist, stay, remain; *informal* stick it out, hang on, go the distance.
- OPPOSITES end.

lasting adjective **enduring**, longlasting, long-lived, abiding, continuing, long-term, permanent, durable, stable, secure, long-standing, eternal, undying, everlasting, unending, never-ending.
- OPPOSITES passing, ephemeral.

late adjective **1 behind schedule**, tardy, overdue, delayed, belated, behindhand. **2 dead**, departed, lamented, passed on/away; *formal* deceased. **3 recent**, fresh, new, up to date, latter-day, current.
- OPPOSITES punctual, early.

lately adverb **recently**, not long ago, of late, latterly, in recent times.

latent adjective **dormant**, untapped, undiscovered, hidden, concealed, undeveloped, unrealized, unfulfilled, potential.

later adjective **subsequent**, following, succeeding, future, upcoming, to come, ensuing, next.

- OPPOSITES earlier, preceding.
● adverb **subsequently**, eventually, then, next, later on, afterwards, at a later date, in the future, in due course, by and by, in a while, in time; *formal* thereafter.

latest adjective **most recent**, newest, up to the minute, current, state-of-the-art, cutting-edge; *informal* in, with it, trendy, hip, hot, happening, cool.
- OPPOSITES old.

latitude noun **freedom**, scope, leeway, (breathing) space, flexibility, liberty, independence, free rein, licence.
- OPPOSITES restriction.

latter adjective **1 later**, closing, end, concluding, final. **2 last-mentioned**, second, last, final.
- OPPOSITES earlier, former.

laudable adjective **praiseworthy**, commendable, worthy, deserving, creditable, estimable, exemplary.
- OPPOSITES shameful.

laugh verb **chuckle**, chortle, guffaw, giggle, titter, snigger, roar, split your sides; *informal* be in stitches, be rolling in the aisles, crease up, fall about, crack up; *Brit. informal* kill yourself.
● noun **1 chuckle**, chortle, guffaw, giggle, titter, snigger, roar, shriek. **2** *(informal)* **joke**, prank, jest; *informal* lark, hoot, scream.
□ **laugh at** ridicule, mock, deride, scoff at, jeer at, sneer at, jibe at, make fun of, poke fun at, taunt, tease; *informal* take the mickey out of. **laugh off** dismiss, make a joke of, make light of, shrug off, brush aside; *informal* poohpooh.

laughter noun **1 laughing**, chuckling, chortling, guffawing, giggling, tittering, sniggering. **2 amusement**, entertainment, humour, mirth, merriment, gaiety, hilarity, jollity, fun.

launch verb **1 propel**, fire, shoot, throw, hurl, fling, pitch, lob, let fly; *informal* chuck, heave, sling. **2 start**, begin, initiate, put in place, set up, inaugurate, introduce; *informal* kick off.

lavatory noun **toilet**, WC, convenience, privy, latrine; *Brit.* cloakroom; *N. Amer.* washroom, bathroom, rest room, men's/ladies' room, comfort station; *Brit. informal* loo, bog, the Ladies, the Gents, khazi; *N. Amer. informal* can, john; *Austral./NZ informal* dunny.

lavish adjective **1 sumptuous**, luxurious, gorgeous, costly, expensive, opulent, grand, splendid, rich, fancy; *informal* posh, bling-bling. **2 generous**, liberal, bountiful, unstinting, unsparing, free, munificent, extravagant, abundant, copious, plentiful, prolific, excessive, wasteful, prodigal; *literary* plenteous.
- OPPOSITES meagre, frugal.
● verb **shower**, heap, pour, deluge, throw at, squander, dissipate.
- OPPOSITES begrudge, stint.

law noun **1 regulation**, statute, act, bill, decree, edict, rule, ruling, dictum, command, order, directive, dictate, diktat, fiat, by-law; **(laws)** legislation, constitution, code; *N. Amer. formal* ordinance. **2 principle**, rule, precept, commandment, belief, creed, credo, maxim, tenet, doctrine, canon.

> **WORD LINKS**
> **legal, legislative** relating to laws

lawful adjective **legitimate**, legal, licit, permissible, permitted, allowable, allowed, rightful, sanctioned, authorized, warranted; *informal* legit.
- OPPOSITES illegal.

lawyer noun solicitor, barrister, advocate, counsel, Queen's Counsel, QC; *N. Amer.* attorney, counselor(-at-law); *informal* brief, legal eagle.

lax adjective **slack**, slipshod, negligent, remiss, careless, sloppy, slapdash, offhand, casual.
- OPPOSITES strict.

lay¹ verb **1 put (down)**, place, set (down), deposit, rest, position, shove; *informal* stick, dump, park, plonk; *Brit. informal* bung. **2** *we laid plans for the voyage* **devise**, arrange, prepare, work out, hatch, design, plan, scheme, plot, conceive, put together, draw up,

produce, develop, formulate; *informal* cook up. **3** *I'd lay money on it* **bet**, wager, gamble, stake.
□ **lay down 1** relinquish, surrender, give up, abandon. **2** formulate, set down, draw up, frame, ordain, dictate, decree, enact, pass, decide, determine. **lay in** stock up with, stockpile, store (up), amass, hoard, put aside/away/by, garner, squirrel away; *informal* salt away, stash away. **lay off 1** make redundant, dismiss, let go, discharge, give notice to; *informal* sack, fire. **2** *(informal)* give up, stop, refrain from, abstain from, desist from, cut out; *informal* pack in, leave off, quit. **lay on** provide, supply, furnish, line up, organize, prepare, produce, make available; *informal* fix up.

lay² adjective **1** *a lay preacher* **non-ordained**, non-clerical. **2** *science books for a lay audience* **non-expert**, non-professional, non-specialist, non-technical, amateur, unqualified, untrained.

layer noun **sheet**, stratum, level, tier, seam, coat, coating, film, covering, blanket, skin.

layout noun **arrangement**, design, plan, formation, format, configuration, composition, organization, geography, structure.

laze verb **relax**, unwind, loaf around/about, lounge around/about, loll around/about, lie around/about, take it easy, idle; *informal* hang around, chill (out), veg (out).

lazy adjective **1 idle**, indolent, slothful, bone idle, work-shy, shiftless. **2 slow**, slow-moving, languid, leisurely, lethargic, sluggish, torpid.
- OPPOSITES industrious.

lead verb **1 guide**, conduct, show (the way), usher, escort, steer, shepherd, accompany, see, take. **2** *what led you to believe him?* **cause**, induce, prompt, move, persuade, drive, make. **3 control**, preside over, head, command, govern, run, manage, rule, be in charge of; *informal* head up. **4 be ahead**, be winning, be in front, be in the lead,

be first, outrun, outstrip, outpace, leave behind, outdo, outclass, beat. **5** *I want to lead a normal life* **live**, have, spend, follow, pass, enjoy.
- OPPOSITES follow.
● *noun* **1 first place**, winning position, vanguard. **2** *a 3–0 lead* **margin**, advantage, gap, edge. **3 example**, model, pattern, standard, guidance, direction, role model. **4 leading role**, starring role, title role, principal role. **5 leash**, tether, rope, chain. **6 clue**, pointer, hint, tip, tip-off, suggestion, indication.
● *adjective* **leading**, first, top, foremost, front, pole, head, chief, principal, premier.
□ **lead to** result in, cause, bring on/about, give rise to, create, produce, occasion, effect, generate, contribute to, promote, provoke, stir up, spark off.

leader *noun* **chief**, head, principal, commander, captain, controller, superior, chairman, chair, director, manager, superintendent, supervisor, overseer, master, mistress, prime minister, president, premier, governor, ruler, monarch, sovereign; *informal* boss, skipper, gaffer, guv'nor, number one.
- OPPOSITES follower, supporter.

leadership *noun* **1** *the leadership of the Party* **control**, rule, command, dominion, headship, directorship, premiership, chairmanship, governorship, captaincy. **2** *firm leadership* **guidance**, direction, authority, management, supervision, government.

leading *adjective* **main**, chief, top, front, major, prime, principal, foremost, key, central, dominant, greatest, pre-eminent, star.
- OPPOSITES subordinate, minor.

leaf *noun* **1** (**leaves**) **foliage**, greenery. **2 page**, sheet, folio.
● *verb* *I leafed through a magazine* **flick**, flip, thumb, skim, browse, glance, riffle, scan, run your eye over, peruse.

leaflet *noun* **pamphlet**, booklet, brochure, handbill, circular, flyer, handout; *N. Amer.* folder, dodger.

league *noun* **1 alliance**, confederation, confederacy, federation, union, association, coalition, consortium, affiliation, cooperative, partnership, fellowship, syndicate. **2 class**, group, category, level, standard.
□ **in league** collaborating, cooperating, in alliance, allied, conspiring, hand in glove; *informal* in cahoots.

leak *verb* **1 seep**, escape, ooze, drip, dribble, drain, run. **2 disclose**, divulge, reveal, make public, tell, expose, release, let slip.
● *noun* **1 hole**, opening, puncture, perforation, gash, slit, break, crack, chink, fissure, rupture, tear. **2 escape**, leakage, discharge, seepage. **3 disclosure**, revelation, exposé.

lean¹ *verb* **1 rest**, recline, be propped. **2 slant**, incline, bend, tilt, slope, tip, list. **3** (**lean towards**) **tend towards**, incline towards, gravitate towards, favour, prefer, have a preference for, have an affinity with. **4** (**lean on**) **depend on**, rely on, count on, bank on, trust in, have faith in.

lean² *adjective* **1 thin**, slim, slender, skinny, spare, angular, spindly, wiry, lanky. **2 meagre**, sparse, poor, mean, inadequate, insufficient, paltry.
- OPPOSITES fat, abundant.

leaning *noun* **inclination**, tendency, bent, propensity, penchant, preference, predisposition, predilection, proclivity.

leap *verb* **1 jump**, vault, spring, bound, hop, clear. **2 rise**, soar, rocket, skyrocket, shoot up, escalate.
● *noun* **rise**, surge, upsurge, escalation, upswing, upturn.

learn *verb* **1 master**, grasp, take in, absorb, assimilate, digest, familiarize yourself with; *informal* get the hang of. **2 memorize**, learn by heart, learn parrot-fashion, get off pat. **3 discover**, find out, become aware, be informed, hear, understand, gather; *informal* get wind of.

learned *adjective* **scholarly**, erudite, knowledgeable, widely read, cultured, intellectual, academic, literary,

bookish, highbrow; *informal* brainy, genius.
- OPPOSITES ignorant.

learner *noun* **beginner**, novice, starter, trainee, apprentice, pupil, student, fledgling, neophyte, tyro; *informal* rookie, greenhorn.
- OPPOSITES expert, veteran.

learning *noun* **study**, knowledge, education, schooling, tuition, teaching, scholarship, erudition, understanding, wisdom.
- OPPOSITES ignorance.

lease *verb* **rent (out)**, hire (out), charter (out), let (out), sublet.

leave[1] *verb* **1 go away**, depart, withdraw, retire, take your leave, pull out, quit, decamp, flee, escape, abandon, desert, vacate; *informal* vamoose, push off, shove off, clear out/off, split, make tracks, do a bunk. **2 set off**, set sail, get going. **3 abandon**, desert, jilt, leave in the lurch, leave high and dry, throw over; *informal* dump, ditch, walk/run out on. **4 resign**, retire, step down, give up, drop out; *informal* quit, jack in. **5 leave behind**, forget, lose, mislay. **6 entrust**, hand over, pass on, refer, delegate. **7 bequeath**, will, endow, hand down.
- OPPOSITES arrive.
□ **leave out** miss out, omit, overlook, forget, skip, exclude, drop, pass over.

leave[2] *noun* **1 permission**, consent, authorization, sanction, dispensation, approval, clearance, blessing, agreement, assent; *informal* the go-ahead, the green light. **2 holiday**, vacation, break, furlough, sabbatical, leave of absence; *informal* vac.

lecherous *adjective* **lustful**, licentious, lascivious, libidinous, lewd, salacious, prurient; *informal* randy; *formal* concupiscent.

lecture *noun* **1 speech**, talk, address, discourse, presentation, oration. **2 reprimand**, scolding, rebuke, reproach; *informal* dressing-down, telling-off, talking-to, tongue-lashing.
● *verb* **1 talk**, speak, discourse, hold forth, teach; *informal* spout, sound off. **2 reprimand**, scold, rebuke, reproach, take to task, berate, upbraid, remonstrate with, castigate; *informal* tell off, bawl out; *Brit. informal* tick off, carpet.

leeway *noun* **freedom**, scope, latitude, space, room, liberty, flexibility, licence, free hand, free rein.

left *adjective* **left-hand**, sinistral; *Nautical* port; *Heraldry* sinister.
- OPPOSITES right.

left-wing *adjective* **socialist**, communist, leftist, Labour; *informal* Commie, lefty, red, pinko.
- OPPOSITES right-wing, conservative.

leg *noun* **1 limb**, member, shank; *informal* pin, peg.. **2 part**, stage, section, phase, stretch, lap.

legacy *noun* **bequest**, inheritance, endowment, gift, birthright, estate, heirloom.

legal *adjective* **1 lawful**, legitimate, legalized, valid, permissible, permitted, sanctioned, authorized, licensed, allowed, allowable, above board, acceptable, constitutional; *informal* legit. **2** *the legal system* **judicial**, juridical, forensic.
- OPPOSITES illegal.

legend *noun* **1 myth**, saga, epic, folk tale, folk story, fable; (**legends**) lore, folklore, mythology. **2 celebrity**, star, superstar, icon, phenomenon, luminary, giant, hero; *informal* celeb, megastar. **3 caption**, inscription, dedication, slogan, heading, title.

legendary *adjective* **1 fabled**, mythical, traditional, fairy-tale, storybook, mythological, fictional, fictitious. **2 famous**, celebrated, famed, renowned, acclaimed, illustrious, esteemed, honoured, exalted, venerable, eminent, distinguished, great.

legion *noun* **horde**, throng, multitude, crowd, mass, mob, gang, swarm, flock, herd, army.

legislation *noun* **law**, rules, rulings, regulations, acts, bills, statutes; *N. Amer. formal* ordinances.

legislature *noun* **parliament**, senate, congress, council, chamber, house.

legitimate *adjective* **1** *the legitimate use of such weapons* **legal**, lawful, authorized, permitted, sanctioned, approved, licensed; *informal* legit. **2** *the legitimate heir* **rightful**, lawful, genuine, authentic, real, true, proper; *informal* kosher. **3** *a legitimate excuse* **valid**, sound, admissible, acceptable, well founded, justifiable, reasonable, sensible, just, fair, bona fide.
- OPPOSITES illegal, invalid.

leisure *noun* **free time**, spare time, time off, rest, recreation, relaxation, R & R.
- OPPOSITES work.

leisurely *adjective* **unhurried**, relaxed, easy, gentle, sedate, comfortable, restful, undemanding, slow.
- OPPOSITES hurried.

lend *verb* **1 loan**, advance; *Brit. informal* sub. **2 add**, impart, give, bestow, confer, provide, supply, furnish, contribute.
- OPPOSITES borrow.

length *noun* **1 extent**, distance, span, reach, area, expanse, range. **2 period**, duration, stretch, span, term. **3** *a length of silk* **piece**, strip, section, swatch.
□ **at length 1 in detail**, in depth, thoroughly, for a long time, for ages, for hours, interminably, endlessly. **2 eventually**, in time, finally, at (long) last, in the end, ultimately.

lengthen *verb* **extend**, elongate, increase, prolong, draw out, protract, spin out.
- OPPOSITES shorten.

lengthy *adjective* **(very) long**, long-lasting, protracted, extended, long-drawn-out, prolonged, interminable, time-consuming, long-winded.
- OPPOSITES short.

lenient *adjective* **merciful**, forgiving, forbearing, tolerant, charitable, humane, indulgent, magnanimous, clement.
- OPPOSITES severe.

lessen *verb* **1 reduce**, decrease, minimize, moderate, diminish, allay, assuage, alleviate, dull, deaden, take the edge off. **2 decrease**, decline, subside, slacken, abate, fade, die down, let up, ease off, tail off, drop (off/away), dwindle, ebb, wane, recede.
- OPPOSITES increase.

lesser *adjective* **1 less important**, minor, secondary, subsidiary, peripheral. **2 subordinate**, inferior, second-class, subservient, lowly, humble.
- OPPOSITES greater, superior.

lesson *noun* **1 class**, session, seminar, tutorial, lecture, period. **2 warning**, deterrent, caution, example, message, moral.

let *verb* **1 allow**, permit, give permission to, give leave to, authorize, license, empower, enable, entitle; *informal* give the go-ahead to, OK. **2 rent (out)**, lease, hire (out), sublet.
- OPPOSITES prevent, prohibit.
□ **let down fail**, disappoint, disillusion, abandon, desert, leave in the lurch. **let go release**, loose your hold on, relinquish. **let off 1 detonate**, discharge, explode, set off, fire (off), launch. **2** *(informal)* **pardon**, forgive, acquit, absolve, exonerate, clear, vindicate; *informal* let someone off the hook. **3 excuse**, exempt, spare. **let out 1 release**, liberate, (set) free, let go, discharge, set/turn loose. **2 utter**, emit, give (vent to), produce, issue, express, voice, release. **3 reveal**, make known, tell, disclose, mention, divulge, let slip, give away, let it be known, blurt out. **let up** *(informal)* **1 lessen**, decrease, subside, abate, ease, moderate, die down, diminish, tail off. **2 relax**, ease up, slow down, pause, break (off), take a break, rest, stop.

let-down *noun* **disappointment**, anticlimax, comedown, non-event, fiasco; *informal* washout, damp squib.

lethal *adjective* **fatal**, deadly, mortal, terminal, life-threatening, murderous, poisonous, toxic, noxious, venomous, dangerous.
- OPPOSITES harmless, safe.

lethargic *adjective* **sluggish**, inert, inactive, slow, lifeless, languid, listless,

apathetic, weary, tired, fatigued, enervated.
- OPPOSITES energetic.

letter *noun* **1 character**, sign, symbol, figure. **2 message**, note, line, missive, dispatch, communication; *formal* epistle; (**letters**) correspondence, post, mail.

> **WORD LINKS**
> **epistolary** relating to letter-writing

level *adjective* **1** *a level surface* **flat**, smooth, even, uniform, plane, flush, horizontal. **2** *a level voice* **steady**, even, uniform, regular, constant, unchanging. **3** *the scores were level* **equal**, even, drawn, tied, all square, neck and neck, level pegging, on a par, evenly matched; *informal* even-stevens, nip and tuck.
- OPPOSITES uneven, unequal.
● *noun* **1 rank**, position, degree, grade, stage, standard, class, group, set, classification. **2** *a high level of employment* **quantity**, amount, extent, measure, degree, volume.
● *verb* **1 even off**, even out, flatten, smooth (out). **2 raze (to the ground)**, demolish, flatten, bulldoze, destroy. **3 equalize**, equal, even (up), make level. **4 aim**, point, direct, train, focus, turn.
□ **on the level** (*informal*) **genuine**, straight, honest, above board, fair, true, sincere, straightforward; *informal* upfront; *N. Amer. informal* on the up and up.

lever *noun* **handle**, arm, switch, crowbar, bar, jemmy.
● *verb* **prise**, force, wrench; *N. Amer.* pry; *informal* jemmy.

leverage *noun* **1 force**, purchase, grip, hold, anchorage. **2** *more leverage in negotiations* **influence**, power, authority, weight, sway, pull, control, say, advantage, pressure; *informal* clout, muscle, teeth.

levy *verb* **impose**, charge, exact, raise, collect.
● *noun* **tax**, tariff, toll, excise, duty.

liability *noun* **1 responsibility**, accountability. **2** (**liabilities**) **obligations**, debts, arrears, dues, commitments. **3** *he became a liability on and off the field* **hindrance**, handicap, nuisance, inconvenience, embarrassment, impediment, disadvantage, millstone, encumbrance, burden.
- OPPOSITES asset.

liable *adjective* **1 responsible**, accountable, answerable, blameworthy, at fault. **2 likely**, inclined, tending, apt, prone, given, subject, susceptible, vulnerable, exposed, in danger of, at risk of.

liaise *verb* **cooperate**, collaborate, communicate, network, interface, link up; *informal* hook up.

liaison *noun* **1 cooperation**, contact, association, connection, collaboration, communication, alliance, partnership. **2 love affair**, relationship, romance, attachment, fling.

liar *noun* **fibber**, deceiver, perjurer, dissembler, faker, hoaxer, impostor.

libel *noun* **defamation (of character)**, character assassination, calumny, misrepresentation, scandalmongering, slur, smear; *informal* mud-slinging.
● *verb* **defame**, malign, blacken someone's name, sully someone's reputation, smear, cast aspersions on, drag someone's name through the mud/mire, denigrate, traduce; *N. Amer.* slur.

libellous *adjective* **defamatory**, denigratory, disparaging, derogatory, false, untrue, insulting, scurrilous.

liberal *adjective* **1 tolerant**, unprejudiced, broad-minded, open-minded, enlightened, permissive, free (and easy), easy-going, libertarian, indulgent, lenient. **2** *a liberal social agenda* **progressive**, advanced, modern, forward-looking, forward-thinking, enlightened, reformist, radical; *informal* go-ahead. **3** *a liberal interpretation of the law* **flexible**, broad, loose, rough, free, non-literal. **4 abundant**, copious, ample, plentiful, lavish, generous, open-handed, unsparing, unstinting, free, munificent.

- OPPOSITES reactionary, strict.

liberate verb **(set) free**, release, let out, let go, set loose, save, rescue, emancipate; *historical* enfranchise.
- OPPOSITES imprison, enslave.

liberty noun **freedom**, independence, immunity, self-determination, autonomy, emancipation, sovereignty, self-government, self-rule, civil liberties, human rights.
- OPPOSITES slavery.
  □ **at liberty 1** free, loose, on the loose, at large, on the run, out. **2** able, free, entitled, permitted.

licence noun **1 permit**, certificate, document, documentation, authorization, warrant, credentials, pass, papers. **2 franchise**, consent, sanction, warrant, charter, concession. **3 freedom**, liberty, free rein, latitude, independence, scope, carte blanche; *informal* a blank cheque.

license verb **permit**, allow, authorize, give authority to, give permission to, certify, accredit, empower, entitle, enable, sanction.
- OPPOSITES ban.

lid noun **cover**, top, cap, covering, stopper.

lie¹ noun **untruth**, falsehood, fib, fabrication, deception, invention, (piece of) fiction, falsification, white lie; *informal* tall story, whopper; *humorous* terminological inexactitude.
- OPPOSITES truth.
  ● verb **tell a lie**, fib, dissemble, perjure yourself.

WORD LINKS
mendacious telling lies

lie² verb **1** *he was lying on the bed* **recline**, lie down, be recumbent, be prostrate, be supine, be prone, be stretched out, sprawl, rest, repose, lounge, loll. **2** *her bag lay on the chair* **be**, be situated, be positioned, be located, be placed, be found, be sited, be arranged, rest.
- OPPOSITES stand.

life noun **1 existence**, being, living, animation, sentience, creation, viability.

2 living creatures, fauna, flora, the ecosystem, the biosphere, the ecosphere. **3 way of life**, lifestyle, situation, fate, lot. **4 lifetime**, lifespan, days, time (on earth), existence. **5 vitality**, animation, liveliness, vivacity, verve, high spirits, exuberance, zest, enthusiasm, energy, vigour, dynamism, elan, gusto, bounce, spirit, fire. **6 biography**, autobiography, history, chronicle, account, memoirs, diary.
- OPPOSITES death.

WORD LINKS
animate, **vital** having life

lifeless adjective **1 dead**, stiff, cold, inert, inanimate; *formal* deceased. **2 barren**, sterile, bare, desolate, stark, bleak, arid, infertile, uninhabited. **3 lacklustre**, apathetic, lethargic, uninspired, dull, colourless, characterless, wooden.
- OPPOSITES alive, lively.

lifelike adjective **realistic**, true to life, faithful, detailed, vivid, graphic, natural, naturalistic, representational.

lifestyle noun **way of life**, life, situation, conduct, behaviour, ways, habits, mores.

lifetime noun **lifespan**, life, days, time (on earth), existence, career.

lift verb **1 raise**, hoist, heave, haul up, heft, elevate, hold high, pick up, grab, take up, winch up, jack up; *informal* hump. **2** *the fog had lifted* **clear**, rise, disperse, dissipate, disappear, vanish, dissolve. **3** *the ban has been lifted* **cancel**, remove, withdraw, revoke, rescind, end, stop, terminate.
  ● noun *the goal will give his confidence a lift* **boost**, fillip, impetus, encouragement, spur, push; *informal* shot in the arm.
  □ **lift off** take off, become airborne, be launched, take to the air, blast off.

light¹ noun **1 illumination**, brightness, shining, gleam, brilliance, radiance, luminosity, luminescence, incandescence, blaze, glare, glow, lustre; *literary* refulgence, effulgence. **2 lamp**,

lantern, torch, beacon, candle, bulb.
3 daylight, daytime, day, sunlight.
- OPPOSITES darkness.
● *adjective* **1 bright**, well lit, sunny.
2 pale, pastel, delicate, subtle, faded,
bleached.
- OPPOSITES dark.
● *verb* **1 set fire to**, ignite, kindle.
2 illuminate, irradiate, floodlight; *literary* illumine.

> **WORD LINKS**
> **optics** study of the behaviour of light

light² *adjective* **1 lightweight**, portable, underweight. **2 flimsy**, thin, lightweight, floaty, gauzy, diaphanous, filmy. **3** *a light dinner* **small**, modest, simple, insubstantial, frugal. **4** *light duties* **easy**, simple, undemanding, untaxing; *informal* cushy. **5** *a light touch* **gentle**, delicate, dainty, soft, faint, careful, sensitive, subtle. **6** *light entertainment* **undemanding**, middle-of-the-road, mainstream, lightweight, lowbrow, mass-market, superficial, frivolous, trivial.
- OPPOSITES heavy.

lighten¹ *verb* **1 brighten**, light up, illuminate, irradiate; *literary* illumine. **2 bleach**, whiten, blanch.
- OPPOSITES darken.

lighten² *verb* **1 reduce**, lessen, decrease, diminish, ease, alleviate, relieve. **2 cheer (up)**, brighten, gladden, lift, boost, buoy (up), revive, restore, revitalize.
- OPPOSITES increase.

light-hearted *adjective* **carefree**, cheerful, cheery, happy, merry, glad, playful, blithe, bright, entertaining, amusing, diverting; *informal* upbeat; *dated* gay, sportive.
- OPPOSITES miserable.

lightly *adverb* **1 softly**, gently, faintly, delicately. **2 sparingly**, sparsely, moderately, slightly, subtly. **3 carelessly**, airily, readily, heedlessly, uncaringly, unthinkingly, thoughtlessly, flippantly.

lightweight *adjective* **1 thin**, light, filmy, flimsy, insubstantial, summery.

2 trivial, insubstantial, superficial, shallow, undemanding, frivolous.
- OPPOSITES heavy, serious.

like¹ *verb* **1 be fond of**, have a soft spot for, care about, think well/highly of, admire, respect; be attracted to, fancy, be keen on, be taken with; *informal* rate. **2 enjoy**, have a taste for, care for, be partial to, take pleasure in, be keen on, appreciate, love, adore, relish; *informal* have a thing about, be into, be mad about, be hooked on. **3** *feel free to say what you like* **choose**, please, wish, want, see/think fit, care to, will.
- OPPOSITES hate.

like² *preposition* **1 similar to**, the same as, identical to, akin to, resembling. **2 in the manner of**, in the same way/manner as, in a similar way to. **3 such as**, for example, for instance, namely, in particular, viz.. **4 characteristic of**, typical of, in character with.
- OPPOSITES unlike.

likeable *adjective* **pleasant**, friendly, agreeable, affable, amiable, genial, personable, nice, good-natured, engaging, appealing, endearing, convivial, congenial.
- OPPOSITES unpleasant.

likelihood *noun* **probability**, chance, prospect, possibility, odds, risk, threat, danger, hope, promise.

likely *adjective* **1 probable**, possible, odds-on, expected, anticipated; *informal* on the cards. **2 plausible**, reasonable, feasible, acceptable, believable, credible, tenable. **3 suitable**, promising, appropriate.
- OPPOSITES unlikely, implausible.

liken *verb* **compare**, equate, set beside.
- OPPOSITES contrast.

likeness *noun* **1 resemblance**, similarity, similitude, correspondence. **2 representation**, image, depiction, portrayal, picture, drawing, sketch, painting, portrait, photograph, study.
- OPPOSITES dissimilarity.

likewise *adverb* **1 also**, equally, in addition, too, as well, to boot, besides, moreover, furthermore. **2 the same**, similarly, correspondingly.

liking *noun* **fondness**, love, affection, penchant, soft spot, attachment, taste, passion, preference, partiality, predilection, weakness.
- OPPOSITES dislike.

limb *noun* **1 arm**, **leg**, wing, appendage; *old use* member. **2 branch**, bough.

limelight *noun* **attention**, interest, scrutiny, the public eye, publicity, prominence, the spotlight, fame, celebrity.
- OPPOSITES obscurity.

limit *noun* **1 boundary (line)**, border, frontier, bound, edge, perimeter, margin. **2 maximum**, ceiling, cap, cut-off point.
● *verb* **restrict**, curb, cap, (hold in) check, restrain, circumscribe, regulate, control, govern, ration.

limitation *noun* **1 restriction**, curb, restraint, control, check. **2 imperfection**, flaw, defect, failing, shortcoming, weak point, deficiency, frailty, weakness.
- OPPOSITES strength.

limited *adjective* **restricted**, circumscribed, finite, small, tight, slight, in short supply, short, meagre, scanty, sparse, inadequate, insufficient, paltry, poor, minimal.
- OPPOSITES limitless, ample.

limp[1] *verb* **hobble**, hop, lurch, stagger, shuffle, totter, shamble.

limp[2] *adjective* **soft**, flaccid, loose, slack, lax, floppy, drooping, droopy, sagging.
- OPPOSITES firm.

line *noun* **1 stroke**, dash, score, underline, underscore, slash, stripe, strip, band, belt; *Brit.* oblique. **2 wrinkle**, furrow, crease, crinkle, crow's foot. **3** *the Bentley's classic lines* **contour**, outline, configuration, shape, design, profile, silhouette. **4** *the county line* **boundary**, limit, border, frontier, touchline, margin, perimeter. **5 cord**, rope, cable, wire, thread, string. **6 file**, rank, column, string, train, procession, row, queue; *Brit. informal* crocodile. **7 course**, direction, route, track,

path, trajectory.
● *verb* **1 furrow**, wrinkle, crease, score. **2 border**, edge, fringe, bound.
□ **in line 1** in a queue, in a row, in a file. **2** in agreement, in accord, in accordance, in harmony, in step, in compliance. **3** level, aligned, alongside, abreast, side by side. **line up** assemble, get together, organize, prepare, arrange, fix up, lay on, book, schedule, timetable.

lineage *noun* **ancestry**, family, parentage, birth, descent, extraction, genealogy, roots, origins.

lined *adjective* **1 ruled**, feint, striped, banded. **2 wrinkled**, wrinkly, furrowed, wizened.

line-up *noun* **1 cast**, bill, programme. **2 team**, squad, side, configuration.

linger *verb* **1 wait (around)**, stand (around), remain, loiter; *informal* stick around, hang around. **2 persist**, continue, remain, stay, endure, carry on, last.

lining *noun* **backing**, facing, padding, insulation.

link *noun* **connection**, relationship, association, linkage, tie-up, tie, bond, attachment, affiliation.
● *verb* **1 join**, connect, fasten, attach, bind, secure, fix, tie, couple, yoke. **2** *the evidence linking him with the body* **associate**, connect, relate, bracket.
- OPPOSITES separate.

lion *noun*

> **WORD LINKS**
> **leonine** relating to lions

lip *noun* **edge**, rim, brim, border, verge, brink.

liquid *noun* **fluid**, moisture, solution, liquor, juice, sap.
● *adjective* **fluid**, liquefied, melted, molten, thawed, dissolved, runny.
- OPPOSITES solid.

liquor *noun* **1 alcohol**, spirits, drink; *informal* booze, the hard stuff, hooch, moonshine. **2 stock**, broth, bouillon, juice, liquid.

list[1] *noun* **catalogue**, inventory, record, register, roll, file, index, directory, checklist.
● *verb* **record**, register, enter, itemize, enumerate, catalogue, file, log, minute, categorize, inventory, classify, group, sort, rank, index.

list[2] *verb* **lean (over)**, tilt, tip, heel (over), pitch, incline, slant, slope, bank, careen, cant.

listen *verb* **1 pay attention**, be attentive, attend, concentrate, keep your ears open, prick up your ears; *informal* be all ears. **2 heed**, take heed of, take notice/note of, bear in mind, take into consideration/account.

listless *adjective* **lethargic**, lifeless, enervated, languid, inactive, inert, sluggish, apathetic, passive, supine, indifferent, uninterested, impassive.
- OPPOSITES energetic.

literal *adjective* **1 strict**, technical, original, true. **2 word for word**, verbatim, exact, accurate, faithful.
- OPPOSITES figurative.

literary *adjective* **1 artistic**, poetic, dramatic. **2 scholarly**, intellectual, academic, bookish, erudite, well read, cultured.

literate *adjective* **(well) educated**, well read, widely read, scholarly, learned, knowledgeable, cultured, cultivated.
- OPPOSITES ignorant.

literature *noun* **1 writing**, poetry, drama, plays, prose. **2 publications**, reports, studies, material, documentation, leaflets, pamphlets, brochures, handouts, publicity, advertising; *informal* bumf.

lithe *adjective* **agile**, graceful, supple, flexible, lissom, loose-limbed, nimble.
- OPPOSITES clumsy.

litigation *noun* **legal proceedings**, legal action, case, lawsuit, suit, prosecution, indictment.

litter *noun* **rubbish**, refuse, junk, waste, debris, detritus; *N. Amer.* trash, garbage.
● *verb* **cover**, clutter up, mess up,

be scattered/strewn around.

little *adjective* **1 small**, compact, miniature, tiny, minute, minuscule, toy, fun-size, baby, undersized, dwarf, midget; *Scottish* wee; *informal* teeny-weeny; *Brit. informal* titchy, dinky; *N. Amer. informal* vest-pocket. **2 short**, small, slight, petite, diminutive, tiny, elfin; *Scottish* wee; *informal* pint-sized. **3 young**, younger, baby. **4 brief**, short, quick, hasty, cursory. **5 minor**, unimportant, insignificant, trivial, trifling, petty, paltry, inconsequential, negligible.
- OPPOSITES big, large, elder, major.
● *adverb* **1 hardly**, barely, scarcely, not much, only slightly. **2 rarely**, seldom, infrequently, hardly (ever), scarcely ever, not much.
- OPPOSITES well, often.
□ **a little 1** some, a bit of, a touch of, a dash of, a taste of, a spot of, a hint of, a dribble of, a splash of, a pinch of, a sprinkling of, a speck of; *informal* a smidgen of, a tad of. **2** a short time, a while, a bit, an interval, a short period, a minute, a moment, a second, an instant; *informal* a sec, a mo, a jiffy. **3** slightly, somewhat, a little bit, quite, to some degree.

live[1] *verb* **1 exist**, be alive, be, have life, breathe, draw breath, walk the earth. **2 reside**, have your home, lodge, inhabit, occupy; *Scottish* stay; *formal* dwell; *old use* abide, bide. **3** *she had lived a difficult life* **experience**, spend, pass, lead, have, go through, undergo. **4** *he lived by scavenging* **survive**, make a living, eke out a living, subsist, support yourself, sustain yourself, make ends meet, keep body and soul together.
- OPPOSITES die.

live[2] *adjective* **1 living**, alive, conscious, animate, vital. **2** *a live rail* **electrified**, charged, powered up, active, switched on. **3** *a live grenade* **unexploded**, explosive, active, primed. **4** *a live issue* **topical**, current, controversial, hot, burning, pressing, important, relevant.
- OPPOSITES dead, inanimate.

livelihood noun **(source of) income**, living, subsistence, bread and butter, job, work, employment, occupation.

lively adjective **1 energetic**, active, animated, dynamic, full of life, outgoing, spirited, sprightly, high-spirited, vivacious, enthusiastic, vibrant, buoyant, exuberant, boisterous, effervescent, cheerful; informal chirpy, full of beans. **2 busy**, crowded, bustling, hectic, buzzing, vibrant, colourful. **3** a lively debate **stimulating**, interesting, vigorous, animated, spirited, heated.
- OPPOSITES quiet, dull.

livid adjective (informal) **furious**, enraged, very angry, infuriated, irate, incensed, fuming, ranting, raving, seething, beside yourself, outraged; informal hopping mad, wild.

living noun **1 livelihood**, (source of) income, subsistence, keep, daily bread, bread and butter, job, work, employment, occupation. **2 way of life**, lifestyle, life, conduct, behaviour, activities, habits.
● adjective **1 alive**, live, animate, sentient, breathing, existing. **2** a living language **current**, contemporary.
- OPPOSITES dead, extinct.

load noun **1 cargo**, freight, consignment, delivery, shipment, goods, pack, bundle, parcel. **2** a heavy teaching load **commitment**, responsibility, duty, obligation, burden, onus.
● verb **1 fill (up)**, pack, stock, stack, stow, store, bundle, place, put, deposit, pile, stuff, cram; old use lade. **2 burden**, weigh down, saddle, oppress, charge, overburden, overwhelm, encumber, tax, strain, trouble, worry. **3** he loaded the gun **prime**, charge, set up, prepare. **4** load the cassette into the camcorder **insert**, put, place, slot, slide.

loaded adjective **1 full**, filled, laden, packed, stuffed, crammed, brimming, stacked; informal chock-full, chock-a-block. **2** a politically loaded word **charged**, emotive, sensitive, delicate.

loaf verb **laze**, lounge, loll, idle; informal hang around; Brit. informal hang about,

mooch about/around; N. Amer. informal bum around.

loan noun **credit**, advance, mortgage, overdraft; Brit. informal sub.
● verb **lend**, advance.

loath adjective **reluctant**, unwilling, disinclined, averse, opposed, resistant.
- OPPOSITES eager, willing.

loathe verb **hate**, detest, abhor, despise, abominate, not be able to bear/stand, execrate.
- OPPOSITES love.

loathing noun **hatred**, hate, detestation, abhorrence, abomination, antipathy, aversion, dislike, disgust, repugnance.

loathsome adjective **hateful**, detestable, abhorrent, repulsive, odious, repugnant, repellent, disgusting, revolting, sickening, nauseating, abominable, despicable, contemptible, reprehensible, vile, horrible, nasty, obnoxious, gross, foul, execrable; informal horrid; literary noisome.

lobby noun **1 entrance (hall)**, hallway, hall, vestibule, foyer, reception. **2** the anti-hunt lobby **pressure group**, interest group, movement, campaign, crusade, faction, camp, ginger group.
● verb **1 approach**, contact, petition, appeal to, pressurize, importune. **2 campaign**, crusade, press, push, ask, call, demand, promote, advocate, champion.

local adjective **1** the local council **district**, regional, town, municipal, provincial, parish. **2** a local restaurant **neighbourhood**, nearby, near, at hand, close by, handy, convenient. **3** a local infection **confined**, restricted, contained, localized.
- OPPOSITES national, widespread.
● noun **resident**, native, inhabitant, parishioner.
- OPPOSITES outsider.

locate verb **1 find**, pinpoint, track down, unearth, sniff out, smoke out, search out, uncover, run to earth. **2 situate**, site, position, place, base, put, build, establish, station.

location noun **position**, place, situation, site, locality, locale, spot, whereabouts, scene, setting, area, environment, venue, address; technical locus.

lock[1] noun **bolt**, catch, fastener, clasp, hasp, latch.
● verb **1 bolt**, fasten, secure, padlock, latch, chain. **2 join**, interlock, link, engage, combine, connect, couple. **3 become stuck**, stick, jam, seize. **4 clasp**, clench, grasp, embrace, hug, squeeze.
- OPPOSITES unlock, open.
□ **lock up** imprison, jail, incarcerate, intern, send to prison, put behind bars, put under lock and key, cage, pen, coop up; informal send down, put away, put inside.

lock[2] noun **strand**, tress, curl, ringlet, hank, tuft, wisp, coil, tendril.

locker noun **cupboard**, cabinet, chest, safe, box, case, coffer, storeroom.

lodge noun **1 gatehouse**, cottage, house, cabin, hut. **2** a Masonic lodge **section**, branch, wing, group; N. Amer. chapter.
● verb **1 submit**, register, enter, put forward, advance, lay, present, tender, proffer, put on record, record, table, file. **2** the bullet lodged in his back **become embedded**, get stuck, stick, catch, get caught, wedge. **3 reside**, board, stay, live, stop; N. Amer. room; literary sojourn. **4 deposit**, put, bank, stash, store, stow, put away.

lodging noun **accommodation**, rooms, chambers, living quarters, a roof over your head, housing, shelter; informal digs; N. Amer. informal crib; formal residence, dwelling, abode.

lofty adjective **1 tall**, high, towering. **2** lofty ideals **noble**, exalted, high, high-minded, worthy, grand, fine, elevated. **3** lofty disdain **haughty**, arrogant, disdainful, supercilious, condescending, patronizing, scornful, contemptuous, self-important, conceited, snobbish; informal stuck-up, snooty; Brit. informal toffee-nosed.
- OPPOSITES low, short.

log noun **record**, register, logbook, journal, diary, minutes, ledger, account, tally.
● verb **1 register**, record, note, write down, put in writing, enter, file. **2** the pilot had logged 95 hours **attain**, achieve, chalk up, make, do, go, cover, clock up.

logic noun **1 reason**, judgement, rationality, wisdom, sense, good sense, common sense, sanity. **2** the logic of their argument **reasoning**, rationale, argument.

logical adjective **1 reasoned**, rational, sound, cogent, valid, coherent, clear, systematic, orderly, methodical, analytical, consistent. **2** the logical outcome **natural**, reasonable, sensible, understandable, predictable, unsurprising, likely.
- OPPOSITES illogical.

logo noun **design**, symbol, emblem, trademark, motif, monogram.

loiter verb **linger**, wait, skulk, loaf, lounge, idle; informal hang about/around; Brit. informal mooch about/around.

lone adjective **1 solitary**, single, solo, unaccompanied, sole, isolated. **2** a lone parent **single**, unmarried, separated, divorced, widowed.

loneliness noun **1 isolation**, friendlessness, abandonment, rejection; N. Amer. lonesomeness. **2 solitariness**, solitude, aloneness, separation, seclusion.

lonely adjective **1 isolated**, alone, friendless, with no one to turn to, abandoned, rejected, unloved, unwanted; N. Amer. lonesome. **2 deserted**, uninhabited, desolate, solitary, isolated, remote, out of the way, off the beaten track, secluded, in the back of beyond, godforsaken; informal in the middle of nowhere.

long[1] adjective **lengthy**, extended, prolonged, protracted, long-lasting, drawn-out, endless, lingering, interminable.
- OPPOSITES short, brief.

long[2] *verb* I longed for the holidays **yearn**, pine, ache, hanker for/after, hunger, thirst, itch, be eager, be desperate, crave, dream of; *informal* be dying.

longing *noun* **yearning**, craving, ache, burning, hunger, thirst, hankering, desire, wish, hope, aspiration; *informal* yen, itch.

long-standing *adjective* **well established**, time-honoured, traditional, abiding, enduring.
- OPPOSITES new, recent.

long-suffering *adjective* **patient**, forbearing, tolerant, uncomplaining, philosophical, stoical, forgiving.

long-winded *adjective* **verbose**, wordy, lengthy, long, prolix, interminable, rambling, tortuous, meandering, repetitious, repetitive; *Brit. informal* waffly.
- OPPOSITES concise, succinct.

look *verb* **1 glance**, gaze, stare, gape, peer, peep, peek, watch, observe, view, regard, examine, inspect, eye, scan, scrutinize, survey, study, contemplate, take in, ogle, leer at; *informal* take a gander, rubberneck, get a load of; *Brit. informal* gawp; *N. Amer. informal* eyeball. **2 seem (to be)**, appear (to be), come across/over as.
● *noun* **1 glance**, examination, study, inspection, scrutiny, peep, peek, glimpse; *informal* eyeful, once-over, squint; *Brit. informal* dekko, butcher's, shufti. **2 expression**, mien, countenance. **3 appearance**, air, style, effect, ambience, impression, aspect, manner, demeanour.
□ **look after** take care of, care for, attend to, minister to, tend, mind, keep an eye on, keep safe, guard, supervise, be responsible for, protect, nurse, babysit. **look down on** disdain, scorn, look down your nose at, sneer at, despise. **look for** search for, hunt, try to find, seek, cast about/around for, forage for. **look into** investigate, enquire into, go into, probe, explore, follow up, research, study, examine; *informal* check out; *N. Amer. informal* scope out. **look like** resemble, bear a resem-

blance to, look similar to, take after; *informal* be the (spitting) image of, be a dead ringer for. **look out** beware, watch out, mind out, be on your guard, be alert, be wary, be vigilant, be careful, take care, be cautious, pay attention, keep your eyes open/peeled, keep an eye out, watch your step. **look over** inspect, examine, scrutinize, cast an eye over, take stock of, vet, view, peruse, read through; *informal* give something a/the once-over; *N. Amer.* check out; *N. Amer. informal* eyeball. **look up** improve, get better, pick up, come along/on, progress, make progress, make headway, perk up, rally, take a turn for the better. **look up to** admire, think highly of, hold in high regard, respect, esteem, venerate, revere, idolize.

lookalike *noun* **double**, twin, clone, living image, doppelgänger, replica; *informal* spitting image, dead ringer.

lookout *noun* **1 watchman**, watch, guard, sentry, sentinel, observer. **2** (*Brit. informal*) that's your lookout **problem**, concern, business, affair, responsibility, worry; *informal* pigeon.

loom *verb* **1 emerge**, appear, materialize, take shape. **2 be imminent**, be on the horizon, impend, threaten, brew, be just around the corner.

loop *noun* **coil**, ring, circle, noose, spiral, curl, bend, curve, arc, twirl, whorl, twist, helix.
● *verb* **1 coil**, wind, twist, snake, spiral, curve, bend, turn. **2 fasten**, tie, join, connect, knot, bind.

loophole *noun* **flaw**, discrepancy, inconsistency, ambiguity, omission, excuse, escape clause; *Brit.* get-out.

loose *adjective* **1 not secure**, unsecured, unattached, untied, detached, wobbly, unsteady, dangling, free. **2 free**, at large, at liberty, on the loose. **3 baggy**, roomy, oversized, voluminous, shapeless, sloppy. **4** *a loose interpretation* **vague**, imprecise, approximate, broad, general, rough, liberal.
- OPPOSITES secure, tight.

● verb **1 free**, let loose, release, untie, unchain, unfasten, unleash, relax. **2 relax**, slacken, loosen.
- OPPOSITES confine, tighten.

loosen verb **1 undo**, slacken, unfasten, detach, release, disconnect. **2 weaken**, relax, slacken, loose, let go.
- OPPOSITES tighten.

loot noun **booty**, spoils, plunder, haul; informal swag, boodle.
● verb **plunder**, pillage, ransack, sack, rifle, rob, strip, gut.

lopsided adjective **crooked**, askew, awry, off-centre, uneven, out of true, asymmetrical, tilted, at an angle, slanting; Scottish agley; informal cockeyed; Brit. informal skew-whiff, wonky.
- OPPOSITES even, level.

lord noun **1 noble**, nobleman, peer, aristocrat. **2 master**, ruler, leader, chief, superior, monarch, sovereign, king, emperor, prince, governor, commander.

lorry noun **truck**, wagon, van, juggernaut, trailer, HGV; dated pantechnicon.

lose verb **1 mislay**, misplace, be unable to find, lose track of. **2 escape from**, evade, elude, dodge, avoid, give someone the slip, shake off, throw off, leave behind, outdistance, outrun. **3 waste**, squander, let pass, miss; informal pass up, blow. **4 be defeated**, be beaten; informal come a cropper, go down.
- OPPOSITES find, seize, win.

loser noun (informal) **failure**, underachiever, dead loss, write-off, has-been; informal also-ran, non-starter, no-hoper.

loss noun **1 mislaying**, deprivation, forfeiture, erosion, reduction, depletion. **2 death**, demise, passing away, bereavement. **3 casualty**, fatality, victim, death toll. **4 deficit**, debit, debt.
- OPPOSITES recovery, profit.
□ **at a loss** baffled, mystified, puzzled, perplexed, bewildered, confused, stumped, stuck; informal flummoxed, beaten.

lost adjective **1 missing**, mislaid, misplaced, gone astray. **2 stray**, off course, going round in circles, adrift,

at sea. **3** a lost opportunity **missed**, wasted, squandered, gone by the board; informal down the drain. **4** lost traditions **bygone**, past, former, old, vanished, forgotten, dead. **5** lost species and habitats **extinct**, died out, defunct, vanished, gone, destroyed, wiped out, exterminated. **6** lost in thought **engrossed**, absorbed, rapt, immersed, deep, intent, engaged, wrapped up.

lot pronoun (**a lot/lots**) **a large amount**, a good/great deal, an abundance, a wealth, a profusion, plenty, many, a great many, a large number, a considerable number; informal hundreds, loads, masses, heaps, piles, stacks, tons, oodles; Brit. informal lashings.
● adverb (**a lot**) **a great deal**, a good deal, much, often, frequently, regularly.
● noun **1** (informal) **group**, crowd, circle, crew; informal bunch, gang, mob. **2** an auction lot **item**, article, batch, group, bundle, parcel. **3** his lot in life **fate**, destiny, fortune, situation, circumstances, plight, predicament.

lotion noun **ointment**, cream, balm, rub, moisturizer, lubricant, embrocation, liniment, salve, unguent.

lottery noun **raffle**, (prize) draw, sweepstake, sweep, tombola, lotto, pools.

loud adjective **1 noisy**, blaring, booming, roaring, thunderous, resounding, sonorous, powerful, stentorian, deafening, ear-splitting, piercing, shrill, raucous; Music forte, fortissimo. **2 vociferous**, clamorous, insistent, vehement, emphatic. **3 garish**, gaudy, lurid, showy, flamboyant, ostentatious, vulgar, tasteless; informal flashy.
- OPPOSITES quiet.

loudly adverb **at the top of your voice**, noisily, stridently, vociferously, shrilly.

lounge verb **laze**, lie, loll, recline, relax, rest, take it easy, sprawl, slump, slouch, loaf, idle.
● noun **living room**, sitting room, front room, drawing room; dated parlour.

lout noun **hooligan**, ruffian, thug, boor, oaf, rowdy; informal tough, bruiser;

Brit. informal yob, yobbo.

lovable *adjective* **adorable**, dear, sweet, cute, charming, lovely, likeable, engaging, endearing, winning, winsome.
- OPPOSITES hateful, loathsome.

love *noun* **1 adoration**, devotion, affection, fondness, tenderness, attachment, warmth, passion, desire, lust, yearning, infatuation, besottedness. **2 liking**, taste, zeal, zest, enthusiasm, keenness, fondness, weakness, partiality, predilection, penchant. **3 compassion**, care, regard, concern, altruism, unselfishness, philanthropy, benevolence, humanity. **4 beloved**, loved one, dearest, darling, sweetheart, sweet, angel, honey.
- OPPOSITES hatred.
● *verb* **1 be in love with**, adore, be devoted to, be infatuated with, be smitten with, be besotted with, idolize, worship, think the world of, dote on, care for, hold dear, cherish; *informal* be mad/crazy about, carry a torch for. **2 like**, delight in, relish, enjoy, have a soft spot for, have a weakness for, be addicted to, be taken with; *informal* have a thing about, be hooked on, get a kick out of.
- OPPOSITES hate.

> **WORD LINKS**
> **amatory** relating to love

love affair *noun* **relationship**, affair(e), romance, liaison, fling, amour, entanglement, involvement, intrigue; *Brit. informal* carry-on.

lovely *adjective* **1 beautiful**, pretty, attractive, good-looking, handsome, adorable, charming, engaging, enchanting, gorgeous, alluring, ravishing, glamorous; *Scottish & N. English* bonny; *informal* tasty, stunning, drop-dead gorgeous; *Brit. informal* fit; *N. Amer. informal* cute, foxy; *old use* comely. **2 delightful**, marvellous, magnificent, stunning, splendid, wonderful, superb, pleasant, enjoyable; *informal* terrific, fabulous, heavenly, divine, amazing, glorious.
- OPPOSITES ugly, horrible.

lover *noun* **1 boyfriend**, **girlfriend**, beloved, sweetheart, inamorato/a, mistress, partner, gigolo; *informal* bit on the side, fancy man, fancy woman; *dated* beau; *literary* swain; *old use* paramour. **2 devotee**, admirer, fan, enthusiast, aficionado; *informal* buff, nut.

loving *adjective* **affectionate**, fond, devoted, adoring, doting, caring, tender, warm, close, amorous, passionate.
- OPPOSITES cold, cruel.

low *adjective* **1 short**, small, little, squat, stubby, stunted. **2 cheap**, economical, moderate, reasonable, affordable, modest, bargain, bargain-basement, rock-bottom. **3 scarce**, scant, meagre, sparse, few, little, reduced, depleted, diminished. **4 inferior**, substandard, poor, low-grade, unsatisfactory, inadequate, second-rate. **5 quiet**, soft, faint, gentle, muted, subdued, muffled, hushed. **6 bass**, low-pitched, deep, rumbling, booming, sonorous. **7 depressed**, dejected, despondent, downhearted, downcast, down, miserable, dispirited, gloomy, glum, flat; *informal* fed up, down in the dumps, blue.
- OPPOSITES high, expensive, loud.

lower[1] *adjective* **1 subordinate**, inferior, lesser, junior, minor, secondary, subsidiary, subservient. **2** *her lower lip* **bottom**, nether, bottommost, under.
- OPPOSITES upper.

lower[2] *verb* **1 let down**, take down, drop, let fall. **2 soften**, modulate, quieten, hush, tone down, muffle, turn down, mute. **3 reduce**, decrease, lessen, bring down, cut, slash.
- OPPOSITES raise, increase.

low-key *adjective* **restrained**, modest, understated, muted, subtle, quiet, low-profile, inconspicuous, unobtrusive, discreet.
- OPPOSITES ostentatious, obtrusive.

lowly *adjective* **humble**, low, low-ranking, common, ordinary, plain, modest, simple, obscure.
- OPPOSITES aristocratic, exalted.

loyal *adjective* **faithful**, true, true-blue, devoted, constant, steadfast, staunch, dependable, reliable, trustworthy, trusty, patriotic, unswerving.
- OPPOSITES disloyal, treacherous.

loyalty *noun* **allegiance**, faithfulness, fidelity, obedience, adherence, devotion, steadfastness, staunchness, dedication, commitment, patriotism; *old use* fealty.
- OPPOSITES disloyalty, treachery.

lucid *adjective* **1 clear**, crystal-clear, intelligible, comprehensible, cogent, coherent, articulate. **2 rational**, sane, in possession of your faculties, compos mentis, clear-headed, sober; *informal* all there.
- OPPOSITES confused.

luck *noun* **1 good fortune**, good luck, stroke of luck, fluke; *informal* lucky break. **2 fortune**, fate, serendipity, chance, accident, a twist of fate.
- OPPOSITES bad luck, misfortune.

luckily *adverb* **fortunately**, happily, providentially, by good fortune, as luck would have it, mercifully, thankfully.

lucky *adjective* **1 fortunate**, in luck, favoured, charmed, successful; *Brit. informal* jammy. **2 providential**, fortunate, timely, opportune, serendipitous, chance, fortuitous, accidental.
- OPPOSITES unlucky.

lucrative *adjective* **profitable**, gainful, remunerative, moneymaking, well paid, rewarding, worthwhile.
- OPPOSITES unprofitable.

ludicrous *adjective* **absurd**, ridiculous, farcical, laughable, risible, preposterous, mad, insane, idiotic, stupid, asinine, nonsensical; *informal* crazy.
- OPPOSITES sensible.

luggage *noun* **baggage**, bags, suitcases, cases.

lukewarm *adjective a lukewarm response* **indifferent**, cool, half-hearted, apathetic, tepid, unenthusiastic, uninterested, non-committal.
- OPPOSITES warm.

lull *verb* **soothe**, calm, quiet, still, assuage, allay, ease, quell.
● *noun* **1 pause**, respite, interval, break, suspension, breathing space, hiatus; *informal* let-up, breather. **2** *the lull before the storm* **calm**, stillness, quiet, tranquillity, peace, silence, hush.

lumber[1] *verb* **trundle**, stump, clump, plod, stumble, shamble, shuffle, trudge.

lumber[2] *verb (Brit. informal)* **burden**, saddle, encumber, land.

lumbering *adjective* **clumsy**, awkward, slow, blundering, bumbling, ponderous, ungainly; *informal* clodhopping.
- OPPOSITES nimble, agile.

luminous *adjective* **shining**, bright, brilliant, radiant, dazzling, coruscating, glowing, luminescent, phosphorescent, fluorescent, incandescent.
- OPPOSITES dark.

lump *noun* **1 chunk**, hunk, piece, block, wedge, slab, ball, knob, pat, clod, clump, nugget, gobbet. **2 swelling**, bump, bulge, protuberance, protrusion, growth, nodule, tumour.
● *verb* **combine**, put, group, bunch, throw.

lunatic *noun* **maniac**, psychopath, madman, madwoman, idiot; *informal* loony, nutcase, headcase, psycho; *Brit. informal* nutter; *N. Amer. informal* screwball.
● *adjective* **stupid**, foolish, idiotic, insane, absurd, ridiculous, ludicrous, preposterous, asinine; *informal* crazy, mad; *Brit. informal* barmy, daft.

lung *noun*

> **WORD LINKS**
> **pulmonary** relating to the lungs

lunge *noun Darren made a lunge at his attacker* **thrust**, dive, rush, charge, grab.
● *verb he lunged at her with a knife* **thrust**, dive, spring, launch yourself, rush.

lurch *verb* **1 stagger**, stumble, sway, reel, roll, totter. **2 swing**, list, roll, pitch, veer, swerve.

lure *verb* **tempt**, entice, attract, induce, coax, persuade, inveigle, seduce, beguile, draw.
- OPPOSITES deter, put off.
 ● *noun* **temptation**, attraction, pull, draw, appeal, inducement, allure, fascination, interest, glamour.

lurid *adjective* **1 bright**, vivid, glaring, fluorescent, gaudy, loud. **2** *lurid details* **sensational**, colourful, salacious, graphic, explicit, prurient, shocking, gruesome, gory, grisly; *informal* juicy.

lurk *verb* **skulk**, loiter, lie in wait, hide.

lush *adjective* **1 profuse**, abundant, luxuriant, flourishing, rich, riotous, vigorous, dense, thick, rampant. **2 luxurious**, sumptuous, palatial, opulent, lavish, elaborate, extravagant, fancy; *informal* plush, posh, swanky, bling-bling; *Brit. informal* swish; *N. Amer. informal* swank.
- OPPOSITES sparse, austere.

lust *noun* **1 desire**, longing, passion, libido, sex drive, sexuality, lecherousness, lasciviousness; *Brit. informal* randiness. **2 greed**, desire, craving, eagerness, longing, yearning, hunger, thirst, appetite, hankering.
 □ **lust for/after** crave, desire, want, long for, yearn for, dream of, hanker for/after, hunger for, thirst for, ache for.

luxurious *adjective* **opulent**, sumptuous, grand, palatial, magnificent, extravagant, fancy, de luxe, expensive; *Brit.* upmarket; *informal* plush, posh, classy, swanky, bling-bling; *Brit. informal* swish; *N. Amer. informal* swank.
- OPPOSITES plain, basic.

luxury *noun* **1 opulence**, sumptuousness, grandeur, magnificence, splendour, luxuriousness, affluence. **2 indulgence**, extravagance, treat, extra, frill.
- OPPOSITES simplicity, necessity.

lying *noun* **dishonesty**, fabrication, fibbing, perjury, untruthfulness, mendacity, misrepresentation, deceit, duplicity.
- OPPOSITES honesty.
 ● *adjective* **dishonest**, untruthful, false, mendacious, deceitful, duplicitous, double-dealing, two-faced.
- OPPOSITES honest.

lyrical *adjective* **1 expressive**, emotional, deeply felt, personal. **2 enthusiastic**, effusive, rapturous, ecstatic, euphoric, passionate, impassioned.
- OPPOSITES unenthusiastic.

Mm

machine noun **1 device**, appliance, apparatus, engine, gadget, mechanism, tool, instrument, contraption. **2** an efficient publicity machine **organization**, system, structure, machinery; informal set-up.

machinery noun **1 equipment**, apparatus, plant, hardware, gear, gadgetry, technology. **2** the machinery of local government **workings**, organization, system, structure; informal set-up.

macho adjective **manly**, male, masculine, virile, red-blooded; informal butch, laddish.

mad adjective **1 insane**, crazy, out of your mind, deranged, demented, crazed, lunatic, unbalanced, unhinged, psychotic, non compos mentis; Brit. sectionable; informal mental, off your head, round the bend, nuts, nutty, off your rocker, bonkers, loony, loopy, batty, cuckoo; Brit. informal barmy, crackers, barking (mad), potty, round the twist. **2** (informal) **angry**, furious, infuriated, enraged, fuming, incensed, beside yourself; informal livid, spare; N. Amer. informal sore. **3** a mad scheme **foolish**, insane, stupid, lunatic, idiotic, foolhardy, absurd, ludicrous, silly, asinine, wild, crackbrained, senseless, preposterous; informal crazy, crackpot; Brit. informal daft. **4** (informal) he's mad about her **passionate**, fanatical, ardent, fervent, devoted, infatuated; informal crazy, dotty, nuts, wild, hooked; Brit. informal potty; N. Amer. informal nutso. **5** a mad dash to get ready **frenzied**, frantic, frenetic, feverish, hysterical, wild, hectic, manic.
- OPPOSITES sane, sensible.

madden verb **infuriate**, exasperate, irritate, incense, anger, enrage, provoke, make someone see red, inflame; informal aggravate, make someone's blood boil; Brit. informal nark; N. Amer.

informal tee off, tick off.
- OPPOSITES calm.

madman, **madwoman** noun **lunatic**, maniac, psychotic, psychopath; informal loony, nut, nutcase, head case, psycho; Brit. informal nutter; N. Amer. informal screwball.

madness noun **1 insanity**, mental illness, dementia, derangement, lunacy, mania, psychosis. **2 folly**, foolishness, idiocy, stupidity, foolhardiness. **3 bedlam**, mayhem, chaos, pandemonium, uproar, turmoil.
- OPPOSITES sanity.

magazine noun **journal**, periodical, supplement, fanzine; informal glossy, mag.

magic noun **1 sorcery**, witchcraft, wizardry, necromancy, enchantment, the supernatural, occultism, the occult, black magic, the black arts, voodoo, hoodoo. **2 conjuring (tricks)**, sleight of hand, legerdemain, illusion; formal prestidigitation. **3 allure**, excitement, fascination, charm, glamour.

magical adjective **1 supernatural**, magic, mystical, other-worldly. **2 enchanting**, entrancing, spellbinding, bewitching, fascinating, captivating, alluring, enthralling, charming, lovely, delightful, beautiful, amazing; informal heavenly, gorgeous.

magician noun **1 sorcerer**, sorceress, witch, wizard, warlock, enchanter, enchantress, necromancer; formal thaumaturge. **2 conjuror**, illusionist; formal prestidigitator.

magnanimous adjective **generous**, charitable, benevolent, beneficent, big-hearted, open-handed, munificent, philanthropic, noble, unselfish, altruistic.
- OPPOSITES mean.

magnetic *adjective* **attractive**, irresistible, seductive, charismatic, hypnotic, alluring, fascinating, captivating.

magnificent *adjective* **1 splendid**, spectacular, impressive, striking, glorious, superb, majestic, awe-inspiring, breathtaking, sublime, resplendent, sumptuous, grand, imposing, monumental, palatial, opulent, luxurious, lavish, rich, dazzling, coruscating, beautiful. **2 excellent**, outstanding, marvellous, brilliant, wonderful, virtuoso, fine, superb.
- OPPOSITES uninspiring, ordinary.

magnify *verb* **enlarge**, increase, augment, extend, expand, boost, enhance, maximize, amplify, intensify; *informal* blow up.
- OPPOSITES reduce, minimize.

magnitude *noun* **1 size**, extent, immensity, vastness, hugeness, enormity. **2 importance**, import, significance, consequence.

mail *noun* **post**, letters, correspondence, email.
● *verb* **send**, post, dispatch, forward, ship, email.

maim *verb* **injure**, wound, cripple, disable, incapacitate, mutilate, disfigure, mangle.

main *adjective* **principal**, chief, head, leading, foremost, most important, major, dominant, central, focal, key, prime, primary, first, fundamental, predominant, pre-eminent, paramount.
- OPPOSITES subsidiary, minor.

mainly *adverb* **mostly**, for the most part, in the main, on the whole, largely, by and large, to a large extent, predominantly, chiefly, principally, primarily.

maintain *verb* **1 preserve**, conserve, keep, retain, keep going, prolong, perpetuate, sustain, carry on, continue. **2 look after**, service, care for, take care of, support, provide for, keep. **3 insist**, declare, assert, protest, affirm, profess, avow, claim, contend, argue; *formal* aver.
- OPPOSITES discontinue.

maintenance *noun* **1 preservation**, conservation, prolongation, continuation. **2 servicing**, service, repair, running repairs, care. **3 support**, upkeep, alimony, allowance.

majestic *adjective* **stately**, dignified, distinguished, magnificent, grand, splendid, glorious, impressive, regal, noble, awe-inspiring, monumental, palatial, imposing.
- OPPOSITES modest.

majesty *noun* **stateliness**, dignity, magnificence, pomp, grandeur, splendour, glory, impressiveness, nobility.

major *adjective* **1 greatest**, best, finest, most important, chief, main, prime, principal, leading, foremost, outstanding, pre-eminent. **2 crucial**, vital, important, big, significant, considerable, weighty, serious, key, utmost, great, paramount, prime.
- OPPOSITES minor, trivial.

majority *noun* **1 most**, bulk, mass, best part, lion's share, (main) body, preponderance, predominance. **2 coming of age**, age of consent, adulthood, seniority.
- OPPOSITES minority.

make *verb* **1 construct**, build, erect, assemble, put together, manufacture, produce, fabricate, create, form, forge, fashion, model, improvise. **2 force**, compel, coerce, press, drive, dragoon, pressurize, oblige, require; *informal* railroad, steamroller. **3 cause**, create, bring about, produce, generate, give rise to, effect. **4** *they made him chairman* **appoint**, designate, name, nominate, select, elect, vote in. **5** *he's made a lot of money* **acquire**, obtain, gain, get, secure, win, earn. **6** *he made the tea* **prepare**, concoct, cook, whip up, brew; *informal* fix.
- OPPOSITES destroy.
● *noun* **brand**, marque, label, type, sort, kind, variety.
◻ **make for** contribute to, produce, promote, facilitate, foster. **make off** run away, run off, take to your heels, flee, take off, take flight, bolt; *informal*

clear off, beat it, split, scram; *Brit. informal* scarper, do a runner. **make out 1** see, discern, distinguish, detect, observe, recognize. **2** understand, grasp, follow, work out, interpret, decipher, make head or tail of, catch. **make peace** make up, bury the hatchet, forgive and forget, shake hands. **make up 1** comprise, form, compose, constitute, account for. **2** invent, fabricate, concoct, think up; *informal* cook up. **make up for** offset, counterbalance, counteract, cancel out, compensate for, atone for, make amends for.

make-believe noun **fantasy**, pretence, daydreaming, invention, fabrication, charade, play-acting, masquerade.
● *adjective* **imaginary**, imagined, made-up, fanciful, fictitious; *informal* pretend.
- OPPOSITES real, actual.

maker noun **creator**, manufacturer, constructor, builder, producer.

makeshift adjective **temporary**, provisional, stopgap, standby, rough and ready, improvised, ad hoc.

make-up noun **1 cosmetics**, greasepaint; *informal* warpaint, slap. **2 composition**, constitution, structure, configuration, arrangement. **3 character**, nature, temperament, personality, mentality, persona.

makings plural noun **qualities**, characteristics, ingredients, potential, capacity, capability, stuff.

maladjusted adjective **disturbed**, unstable, neurotic, dysfunctional; *informal* mixed up, screwed up.

male adjective **masculine**, manly, virile, macho.
- OPPOSITES female.

malfunction verb **break down**, fail, stop working, crash, go down; *informal* conk out, go kaput; *Brit. informal* play up, pack up.

malice noun **spite**, malevolence, ill will, vindictiveness, vengefulness, malignity, animus, enmity, rancour.
- OPPOSITES benevolence.

malicious adjective **spiteful**, malevolent, vindictive, vengeful, resentful, malign, nasty, hurtful, cruel, catty, venomous, poisonous, barbed; *informal* bitchy.
- OPPOSITES benevolent.

maltreat verb **ill-treat**, mistreat, abuse, ill-use, mishandle, misuse, persecute, harm, hurt, injure.

man noun **1 male**, gentleman, fellow, youth; *informal* guy, gent, geezer; *Brit. informal* bloke, chap, lad; *N. Amer. informal* dude, hombre. **2 human being**, human, person, mortal, individual, soul. **3 the human race**, Homo sapiens, humankind, humanity, human beings, humans, people, mankind.
● *verb* **1 staff**, crew, occupy. **2 operate**, work, use.

> **WORD LINKS**
> **male, masculine, virile** relating to men

manage verb **1 be in charge of**, run, head, direct, control, preside over, lead, govern, rule, command, supervise, oversee, administer; *informal* head up. **2 accomplish**, achieve, carry out, perform, undertake, deal with, cope with, get through. **3 cope**, get along/on, make do, survive, get by, muddle through/along, make ends meet; *informal* make out, hack it.

manageable adjective **1 achievable**, doable, practicable, feasible, reasonable, attainable, viable. **2 compliant**, tractable, pliant, biddable, docile, amenable, accommodating, acquiescent.

management noun **1 administration**, running, managing, organization, direction, leadership, control, governance, rule, command, supervision, guidance, operation. **2 managers**, employers, directors, board, directorate, executive, administration; *informal* bosses, top brass.
- OPPOSITES employees.

manager noun **executive**, head, supervisor, principal, director, superintendent, foreman, forewoman, overseer, organizer, administrator; *informal* boss, chief, governor; *Brit. informal* gaffer, guv'nor, honcho.

mandate *noun* **1 authority**, approval, ratification, endorsement, sanction, authorization. **2 instruction**, directive, decree, command, order, injunction.

mandatory *adjective* **obligatory**, compulsory, binding, required, requisite, necessary.
- OPPOSITES optional.

mania *noun* **obsession**, compulsion, fixation, fetish, fascination, preoccupation, passion, enthusiasm, desire, urge, craving, craze, fad, rage; *informal* thing.

maniac *noun* **lunatic**, madman, madwoman, psychopath; *informal* loony, nutcase, nut, head case, headbanger, psycho, sicko; *Brit. informal* nutter; *N. Amer. informal* screwball.

manifest *verb* **display**, show, exhibit, demonstrate, betray, present, reveal; *formal* evince.
- OPPOSITES hide.
● *adjective* **obvious**, clear, plain, apparent, evident, patent, distinct, definite, blatant, overt, glaring, transparent, conspicuous, undisguised.

manifestation *noun* **1 display**, demonstration, show, exhibition, presentation. **2 sign**, indication, evidence, symptom, testimony, proof, mark, reflection, example, instance.

manipulate *verb* **1 operate**, work, handle, turn, pull, push, twist, slide. **2 control**, influence, use to your advantage, exploit, twist.

mankind *noun* **the human race**, humankind, humanity, human beings, humans, Homo sapiens, people, man, men and women.

manly *adjective* **virile**, masculine, strong, all-male, red-blooded, muscular, muscly, strapping, well built, rugged, tough, powerful, brawny; *informal* hunky.
- OPPOSITES effeminate.

man-made *adjective* **artificial**, synthetic, manufactured, imitation, ersatz, simulated, mock, fake, faux.
- OPPOSITES natural, real.

manner *noun* **1 way**, fashion, mode, means, method, methodology, system, style, approach, technique, procedure, process. **2** *her unfriendly manner* **behaviour**, attitude, demeanour, air, aspect, mien, bearing, conduct. **3** (**manners**) **social graces**, politeness, Ps and Qs, etiquette, protocol, decorum, propriety, civility.

mannerism *noun* **idiosyncrasy**, quirk, oddity, foible, trait, peculiarity, habit, characteristic.

manoeuvre *verb* **1 steer**, guide, drive, negotiate, jockey, navigate, pilot, direct, move, work. **2 manipulate**, contrive, manage, engineer, fix, organize, arrange, orchestrate, choreograph, stage-manage; *informal* wangle, pull strings.
● *noun* **1 operation**, exercise, move, movement, action. **2 stratagem**, tactic, gambit, ploy, trick, dodge, ruse, scheme, device, plot, machination, artifice, subterfuge, intrigue.

mansion *noun* **country house**, stately home, hall, manor house; *informal* pile.
- OPPOSITES hovel.

manual *noun* **handbook**, instructions, guide, companion, ABC, guidebook, vade mecum; *informal* bible.
● *adjective* **physical**, labouring, blue-collar, hand.

manufacture *verb* **1 make**, produce, mass-produce, build, construct, assemble, put together, turn out, process. **2 make up**, invent, fabricate, concoct, hatch, dream up, think up, contrive; *informal* cook up.
● *noun* **production**, making, manufacturing, mass production, construction, building, assembly.

manufacturer *noun* **maker**, producer, builder, constructor, industrialist.

many *determiner* & *adjective* **numerous**, a lot of, plenty of, countless, innumerable, scores of, untold, copious, abundant; *informal* lots of, umpteen, loads of, masses of, stacks of, heaps of,

m

oodles of, a slew of; *literary* myriad.
- OPPOSITES few.

map noun **plan**, chart, A to Z, atlas.
● *verb* **chart**, plot, draw, record.

> **WORD LINKS**
> **cartography** making of maps

mar *verb* **spoil**, impair, detract from, disfigure, blemish, scar, deface, ruin, damage, wreck, taint, tarnish.
- OPPOSITES enhance.

march *verb* **1 stride**, walk, troop, step, pace, tread, slog, tramp, hike, trudge, parade, file. **2 stalk**, strut, flounce, storm, stomp, sweep.
● *noun* **1 walk**, trek, slog, route march, hike. **2 parade**, procession, cortège, demonstration; *informal* demo.

margin noun **1 edge**, side, verge, border, perimeter, brink, brim, rim, fringe, boundary, periphery, extremity. **2 leeway**, latitude, scope, room, space, allowance.

marginal *adjective* **slight**, small, tiny, minute, insignificant, minimal, negligible.
- OPPOSITES considerable.

marine *adjective* **1 seawater**, sea, saltwater, aquatic. **2 maritime**, nautical, naval, seafaring, seagoing, ocean-going.

mariner noun **sailor**, seaman, seafarer; *informal* matelot, sea dog, old salt; *dated* tar.

marital *adjective* **matrimonial**, conjugal, married, wedded, nuptial.

maritime *adjective* **naval**, marine, nautical, seafaring, seagoing, sea, ocean-going, oceanic, coastal.

mark noun **1 blemish**, streak, spot, fleck, blot, stain, smear, speck, smudge, blotch, bruise, scratch, scar, dent, chip, nick; *informal* splodge. **2 sign**, token, symbol, emblem, badge, indication, characteristic, feature, trait, attribute, quality, hallmark, indicator, symptom, proof. **3 grade**, grading, rating, score, percentage.
● *verb* **1 discolour**, stain, smear, smudge, streak, dirty, scratch, scar,

dent; *informal* splodge. **2 label**, identify, flag, tag, initial, highlight, name, brand. **3 celebrate**, observe, recognize, acknowledge, keep, honour, commemorate, remember, solemnize. **4 represent**, signify, indicate, herald. **5 characterize**, distinguish, identify, typify. **6 assess**, evaluate, appraise, correct; *N. Amer.* grade.

marked *adjective* **noticeable**, pronounced, decided, distinct, striking, clear, unmistakable, obvious, conspicuous, notable.
- OPPOSITES imperceptible.

market noun **shopping centre**, marketplace, bazaar, souk, fair; *N. Amer.* mart.
● *verb* **sell**, retail, merchandise, trade, advertise, promote.

maroon *verb* **strand**, cast away, cast ashore, abandon, desert, leave behind, leave.

marriage noun **1 matrimony**, wedlock, wedding, nuptials, union, match. **2** *a marriage of jazz, pop, and gospel* **union**, fusion, mixture, mix, blend, amalgamation, combination, hybrid.
- OPPOSITES divorce, separation.

> **WORD LINKS**
> **marital, matrimonial, nuptial, conjugal** relating to marriage

marry *verb* **1 get married**, wed, become man and wife; *informal* tie the knot, walk down the aisle, get spliced, get hitched. **2** *the show marries poetry with art* **join**, unite, combine, fuse, mix, blend, merge, amalgamate.
- OPPOSITES divorce, separate.

marsh noun **swamp**, marshland, bog, morass, mire, quagmire, slough, fen.

marshal *verb* **assemble**, gather (together), collect, muster, call together, draw up, line up, array, organize, group, arrange, deploy, position, summon, round up.

martial *adjective* **military**, soldierly, warlike, fighting, militaristic; *informal* gung-ho.

marvel *verb* **be amazed**, be astonished, be in awe, wonder; *informal* be gobsmacked.

● *noun* **wonder**, miracle, sensation, spectacle, phenomenon, prodigy.

marvellous *adjective* **excellent**, splendid, wonderful, magnificent, superb, sensational, glorious, sublime, lovely, delightful; *informal* super, great, amazing, fantastic, terrific, tremendous, fabulous, cracking, awesome, divine, ace, wicked; *Brit. informal* smashing, brilliant.
- OPPOSITES commonplace, awful.

masculine *adjective* **1 virile**, macho, manly, male, muscular, muscly, strong, strapping, well built, rugged, robust, brawny, powerful, red-blooded, vigorous; *informal* hunky, laddish. **2 mannish**, unfeminine, unladylike; *informal* butch.
- OPPOSITES feminine, effeminate.

mash *verb* **pulp**, crush, purée, cream, pound, beat.

mask *noun* **pretence**, semblance, veil, screen, front, facade, veneer, disguise, cover, cloak, camouflage.

● *verb* **hide**, conceal, disguise, cover up, obscure, screen, cloak, camouflage.

mass *noun* **1** *a mass of fallen leaves* **pile**, heap, accumulation, aggregation, mat, tangle. **2** *a mass of cyclists* **crowd**, horde, throng, host, troop, army, herd, flock, swarm, mob, pack, flood, multitude. **3** *the mass of the population* **majority**, most, preponderance, greater part, best/better part, bulk, body.

● *adjective* **widespread**, general, extensive, large-scale, wholesale, universal, indiscriminate.

● *verb* **assemble**, gather together, collect, rally.

massacre *noun* **slaughter**, mass murder, mass execution, ethnic cleansing, genocide, holocaust, annihilation, liquidation, extermination, carnage, butchery, bloodbath, bloodletting.

● *verb* **slaughter**, butcher, murder, kill, annihilate, exterminate, execute, liquidate, eliminate, mow down.

massage *noun* **rub**, rub-down, kneading.

● *verb* **1 rub**, knead, manipulate, pummel, work. **2 alter**, tamper with, manipulate, doctor, falsify, juggle, fiddle with, tinker with, distort, rig; *informal* cook, fiddle.

massive *adjective* **huge**, enormous, vast, immense, mighty, great, colossal, tremendous, gigantic, mammoth, monumental, giant, mountainous; *informal* monster, whopping, astronomical, mega; *Brit. informal* whacking, ginormous.
- OPPOSITES tiny.

master *noun* **1** *(historical)* **lord**, liege, ruler, sovereign, monarch. **2 expert**, genius, maestro, virtuoso, authority; *informal* ace, wizard, whizz, hotshot, pro; *Brit. informal* dab hand; *N. Amer. informal* maven, crackerjack. **3 teacher**, schoolteacher, schoolmaster, tutor, instructor. **4 guru**, teacher, leader, guide, mentor.
- OPPOSITES servant, pupil.

● *verb* **1 overcome**, conquer, beat, quell, suppress, control, triumph over, subdue, vanquish, subjugate, curb, check, defeat, get the better of; *informal* lick. **2** *he'd mastered the technique* **learn**, become proficient in, pick up, grasp, understand; *informal* get the hang of.

● *adjective* **expert**, adept, proficient, skilled, skilful, deft, dexterous, adroit, practised, experienced, masterly, accomplished; *informal* crack, ace; *N. Amer. informal* crackerjack.
- OPPOSITES amateur.

masterful *adjective* **commanding**, powerful, imposing, magisterial, authoritative.
- OPPOSITES weak.

masterly *adjective* **expert**, adept, skilful, skilled, adroit, proficient, deft, dexterous, accomplished, polished, consummate.
- OPPOSITES inept.

mastermind *noun* **genius**, intellect; *informal* brain(s).

● *verb* **plan**, control, direct, be in charge of, run, conduct, organize,

m

arrange, preside over, orchestrate, stage-manage, engineer, manage, coordinate.

masterpiece noun **magnum opus**, chef-d'œuvre, masterwork, pièce de résistance, tour de force, classic.

mastery noun **1 proficiency**, ability, capability, knowledge, understanding, comprehension, command, grasp. **2 control**, domination, command, supremacy, superiority, power, authority, jurisdiction, dominion, sovereignty.

mat noun **rug**, carpet, doormat, runner.

match noun **1 contest**, competition, game, tournament, tie, fixture, meet, friendly, (local) derby, bout, fight; Brit. clash. **2** an exact match **lookalike**, double, twin, duplicate, mate, companion, counterpart, pair, replica, copy, doppelgänger; informal spitting image, dead ringer.
● verb **1 go with**, coordinate with, complement, suit, set off. **2 correspond**, tally, agree, coincide, square. **3 equal**, compare with, be in the same league as, touch, rival, compete with; informal hold a candle to.

matching adjective **corresponding**, equivalent, parallel, analogous, complementary, paired, twin, identical, alike.
- OPPOSITES different, clashing.

mate noun **1** (Brit. informal) **friend**, companion, schoolmate, classmate, workmate; informal pal, chum; N. Amer. informal buddy, amigo, compadre. **2 partner**, husband, wife, spouse, consort, lover; informal better half, other half. **3** a plumber's mate **assistant**, helper, apprentice.
● verb **breed**, couple, copulate, pair.

material noun **1 matter**, substance, stuff, constituents. **2 fabric**, cloth, textiles. **3 information**, data, facts, facts and figures, statistics, evidence, details, particulars, background; informal info.
● adjective **1 physical**, corporeal, fleshly, bodily, tangible, mundane, worldly, earthly, secular, temporal, concrete, real. **2** information material to the

enquiry **relevant**, pertinent, applicable, germane, vital, essential, key.
- OPPOSITES spiritual.

materialize verb **1 happen**, occur, come about, take place, transpire; informal come off; literary come to pass. **2 appear**, turn up, arrive, emerge, surface, pop up; informal show up, fetch up.

maternal adjective **motherly**, protective, caring, nurturing, maternalistic.

matrimonial adjective **marital**, conjugal, married, wedded, nuptial; literary connubial.

matted adjective **tangled**, knotted, tousled, dishevelled, uncombed, unkempt, ratty.

matter noun **1 material**, stuff, substance. **2 affair**, business, situation, concern, incident, episode, subject, topic, issue, question, point at issue, case.
● verb **be important**, make any difference, be of consequence, be relevant, count, signify.

matter-of-fact adjective **unemotional**, practical, down-to-earth, sensible, realistic, unsentimental, pragmatic, businesslike, commonsensical, level-headed, hard-headed, no-nonsense, straightforward.

mature adjective **1 adult**, of age, fully grown, in your prime. **2 grown-up**, sensible, responsible, adult. **3 ripe**, ripened, mellow, seasoned, ready.
- OPPOSITES immature.
● verb **1 grow up**, come of age, reach adulthood. **2 ripen**, mellow, age. **3 develop**, grow, bloom, blossom, evolve.

maturity noun **1 adulthood**, coming of age, manhood, womanhood. **2 responsibility**, sense, wisdom.

maul verb **savage**, attack, claw, scratch, lacerate, mangle, tear.

maverick noun **individualist**, nonconformist, free spirit, original, eccentric, rebel, dissenter, dissident.
- OPPOSITES conformist.

maxim noun **saying**, adage, aphorism, proverb, motto, saw, axiom, dictum, precept, epigram.

maximum adjective **greatest**, highest, biggest, largest, top, most, utmost, supreme.
● noun **upper limit**, limit, utmost, greatest, most, peak, pinnacle, height, ceiling, top.
- OPPOSITES minimum.

maybe adverb **perhaps**, possibly, for all you know; N. English happen; literary perchance.

mayhem noun **chaos**, havoc, bedlam, pandemonium, uproar, turmoil, a riot, anarchy; informal a madhouse.

maze noun **labyrinth**, network, warren, web, tangle, confusion, jungle.

meadow noun **field**, paddock, pasture; literary lea, mead.

meagre adjective **inadequate**, scant, paltry, limited, restricted, sparse, negligible, skimpy, slender, pitiful, miserly, niggardly; informal measly, stingy.
- OPPOSITES abundant.

meal noun **snack**, feast, banquet; informal spread, blowout; Brit. informal nosh-up; formal repast.

> **WORD LINKS**
> **prandial** relating to meals

mean[1] verb **1 signify**, denote, indicate, convey, designate, show, express, spell out, stand for, represent, symbolize, imply, suggest, intimate, portend. **2 intend**, aim, plan, have in mind, set out, want. **3** this will mean war **entail**, involve, necessitate, lead to, result in, give rise to, bring about, cause, engender, produce.

mean[2] adjective **1 miserly**, niggardly, parsimonious, penny-pinching, cheese-paring; informal tight-fisted, stingy, tight; N. Amer. informal cheap. **2 unkind**, nasty, unpleasant, spiteful, malicious, unfair, shabby, horrible, despicable, contemptible, obnoxious, vile, loathsome, base, low; informal rotten.
- OPPOSITES generous, kind.

meaning noun **1 significance**, sense, signification, import, gist, thrust, drift, implication, message. **2 definition**, sense, explanation, interpretation, connotation.

> **WORD LINKS**
> **semantic** relating to meaning

meaningful adjective **1 significant**, relevant, important, telling, expressive, eloquent, pointed, pregnant, revealing, suggestive. **2 sincere**, deep, serious, earnest, significant, important.

meaningless adjective **unintelligible**, incomprehensible, incoherent, senseless, pointless.

means plural noun **1 method**, way, manner, course, agency, channel, avenue, procedure, process, methodology, expedient, solution. **2 money**, resources, capital, income, finance, funds, cash, the wherewithal, deep pockets, assets, wealth, riches, affluence, fortune.

meanwhile, meantime adverb **1 for now**, for the moment, for the present, for the time being, in the meanwhile, in the meantime, in the interim. **2 at the same time**, simultaneously, concurrently.

measure verb **quantify**, gauge, size, count, weigh, evaluate, assess, determine, calculate, compute.
● noun **1 action**, act, course of action, deed, procedure, step, expedient, initiative, programme. **2 statute**, act, bill, law. **3 ruler**, tape measure, gauge, meter, scale. **4** sales are a measure of their success **yardstick**, test, standard, barometer, touchstone, benchmark.

measured adjective **1 regular**, steady, even, rhythmic, unfaltering, slow, dignified, stately, sedate, leisurely, unhurried. **2 careful**, thoughtful, considered, reasoned, calculated.

measurement noun **1 quantification**, evaluation, assessment, calculation, computation, mensuration. **2 size**, dimension, proportions, value, amount, quantity.

m

meat *noun* flesh.

> **WORD LINKS**
> **carnivorous** meat-eating

mechanical *adjective* **1 mechanized**, machine-driven, automated, automatic. **2 automatic**, knee-jerk, unthinking, instinctive, habitual, routine, unemotional, unfeeling.
- OPPOSITES manual.

mechanism *noun* **1 apparatus**, machine, machinery, appliance, device, instrument, tool, contraption, gadget; *informal* gizmo. **2** *a complaints mechanism* **procedure**, process, system, method, means, solution, medium, channel.

meddle *verb* **1 interfere**, intrude, intervene, pry; *informal* poke your nose in. **2 fiddle**, interfere, tamper, mess about; *Brit. informal* muck about.

mediate *verb* **arbitrate**, conciliate, moderate, make peace, intervene, intercede, act as an intermediary, negotiate, liaise, referee.

mediation *noun* **arbitration**, conciliation, reconciliation, intervention, intercession, negotiation, shuttle diplomacy.

mediator *noun* **arbitrator**, arbiter, negotiator, conciliator, peacemaker, go-between, middleman, intermediary, moderator, honest broker, liaison officer, umpire, referee, adjudicator, judge.

medicinal *adjective* **curative**, healing, remedial, therapeutic, restorative, health-giving.

medicine *noun* **medication**, drug, prescription, treatment, remedy, cure, nostrum, panacea, cure-all.

> **WORD LINKS**
> **pharmaceutical** relating to medicines

mediocre *adjective* **average**, ordinary, undistinguished, uninspired, indifferent, unexceptional, unexciting, unremarkable, run-of-the-mill, pedestrian, prosaic, lacklustre, forgettable, amateurish; *informal* so-so.

- OPPOSITES excellent.

meditate *verb* **contemplate**, think, consider, ponder, muse, reflect, deliberate, ruminate, brood, mull over.

medium *noun* *a medium of expression* **means**, method, avenue, channel, vehicle, organ, instrument, mechanism.
● *adjective* **average**, middling, medium-sized, middle-sized, moderate, normal, standard.

meek *adjective* **submissive**, obedient, compliant, tame, biddable, acquiescent, timid, quiet, mild, gentle, docile, shy, diffident, unassuming, self-effacing.
- OPPOSITES assertive.

meet *verb* **1 encounter**, come face to face with, run into, run across, come across/upon, chance on, happen on, stumble across; *informal* bump into. **2 get to know**, be introduced to, make the acquaintance of. **3 assemble**, gather, congregate, convene; *formal* foregather. **4 converge**, connect, touch, link up, intersect, cross, join.

meeting *noun* **1 gathering**, assembly, conference, congregation, convention, forum, summit, rally, consultation, audience, interview, conclave; *informal* get-together. **2 encounter**, contact, appointment, assignation, rendezvous; *literary* tryst. **3** *the meeting of land and sea* **convergence**, confluence, conjunction, union, intersection, crossing. **4** *an athletics meeting* **event**, tournament, meet, rally, competition, match, game, contest.

melancholy *adjective* **sad**, sorrowful, unhappy, gloomy, despondent, dejected, disconsolate, downcast, downhearted, woebegone, glum, miserable, morose, depressed, dispirited, mournful, doleful, lugubrious; *informal* down in the dumps, blue.
- OPPOSITES cheerful.
● *noun* **sadness**, sorrow, unhappiness, depression, despondency, dejection, gloom, misery; *informal* the blues.
- OPPOSITES happiness.

mellow *adjective* **1 sweet-sounding**, dulcet, melodious, mellifluous, soft, smooth, rich. **2 genial**, affable, amiable, good-humoured, good-natured, pleasant, relaxed, easy-going.
- OPPOSITES harsh, rough.

melodious *adjective* **tuneful**, melodic, musical, mellifluous, dulcet, sweet-sounding, harmonious, euphonious, lyrical.
- OPPOSITES discordant.

melodramatic *adjective* **exaggerated**, histrionic, extravagant, overdramatic, overdone, sensationalized, overemotional, theatrical, stagy; *informal* hammy.

melody *noun* **tune**, air, strain, theme, song, refrain.

melt *verb* **1 liquefy**, thaw, defrost, soften, dissolve; *technical* deliquesce. **2 vanish**, disappear, fade, evaporate.
- OPPOSITES freeze, solidify.

member *noun* **subscriber**, associate, fellow, representative.

memento *noun* **souvenir**, keepsake, reminder, remembrance, token, memorial.

memoir *noun* **1 account**, history, record, chronicle, narrative, story, portrayal, depiction, portrait, profile. **2 (memoirs) autobiography**, life story, journal, diary.

memorable *adjective* **unforgettable**, momentous, significant, historic, remarkable, notable, noteworthy, important, outstanding, arresting, indelible, catchy, haunting.

memorial *noun* **1 monument**, cenotaph, mausoleum, statue, plaque, cairn, shrine, tombstone. **2 tribute**, testimonial, remembrance, memento.

memorize *verb* **commit to memory**, remember, learn (by heart), become word-perfect in, get/have off pat.

memory *noun* **1 recollection**, remembrance, reminiscence, recall. **2 commemoration**, remembrance, honour, tribute, recognition, respect.

> **WORD LINKS**
> **mnemonic** helping the memory

menace *noun* **1 threat**, intimidation, malevolence, oppression. **2 danger**, peril, risk, hazard, threat. **3 nuisance**, pest, troublemaker, mischief-maker.
● *verb* **1 threaten**, endanger, put at risk, jeopardize, imperil. **2 intimidate**, threaten, terrorize, frighten, scare, terrify.

menacing *adjective* **threatening**, ominous, intimidating, frightening, forbidding, hostile, sinister, baleful.
- OPPOSITES friendly.

mend *verb* **repair**, fix, restore, sew (up), stitch, darn, patch, renew, renovate; *informal* patch up.
- OPPOSITES break.

menial *adjective* **unskilled**, lowly, humble, low-grade, low-status, humdrum, routine, boring, dull.

mental *adjective* **1 intellectual**, cerebral, cognitive, rational. **2 psychiatric**, psychological, behavioural.
- OPPOSITES physical.

mentality *noun* **way of thinking**, mind set, mind, psychology, attitude, outlook, make-up, disposition, character.

mentally *adverb* **psychologically**, intellectually, in your mind, in your head, inwardly, internally.

mention *verb* **1 allude to**, refer to, touch on, bring up, raise, broach. **2 state**, say, observe, remark, indicate, disclose, divulge, reveal.
● *noun* **reference**, allusion, comment, citation; *informal* namecheck, plug.

mentor *noun* **adviser**, counsellor, guide, guru, consultant, confidant(e), trainer, teacher, tutor, instructor.

menu *noun* **bill of fare**, tariff, carte du jour, set menu, table d'hôte.

mercenary *adjective* **grasping**, greedy, acquisitive, avaricious, materialistic, venal; *informal* money-grubbing.

merchandise *noun* **goods**, wares, stock, commodities, produce, products.

merchant *noun* **trader**, tradesman, dealer, wholesaler, broker, agent, seller, retailer, supplier, buyer, vendor, distributor.

merciful *adjective* **forgiving**, compassionate, pitying, forbearing, lenient, humane, mild, kind, soft-hearted, tender-hearted, sympathetic, humanitarian, liberal, generous, magnanimous.
- OPPOSITES cruel.

merciless *adjective* **ruthless**, remorseless, pitiless, unforgiving, implacable, inexorable, relentless, inhumane, inhuman, unfeeling, severe, cold-blooded, hard-hearted, stony-hearted, heartless, harsh, callous, cruel, brutal.
- OPPOSITES compassionate.

mercy *noun* **pity**, compassion, leniency, clemency, charity, forgiveness, forbearance, kindness, sympathy, indulgence, tolerance, generosity, magnanimity.
- OPPOSITES ruthlessness, cruelty.

merely *adverb* **only**, purely, solely, simply, just, but.

merge *verb* **1 join (together)**, join forces, unite, affiliate, team up. **2 amalgamate**, bring together, join, consolidate, conflate, unite, unify, combine, incorporate, integrate. **3 mingle**, blend, fuse, mix, intermix, intermingle, coalesce.
- OPPOSITES separate.

merger *noun* **amalgamation**, combination, union, fusion, coalition, affiliation, unification, incorporation, consolidation, link-up, alliance.
- OPPOSITES split.

merit *noun* **1 excellence**, quality, calibre, worth, value, distinction, eminence. **2 good point**, strong point, advantage, benefit, value, asset, plus.
- OPPOSITES fault, disadvantage.
● *verb* **deserve**, warrant, justify, earn, rate, be worthy of, be entitled to, have a right to, have a claim to.

merry *adjective* **cheerful**, cheery, in high spirits, sunny, smiling, light-hearted, lively, carefree, joyful, joyous, jolly, convivial, festive, gleeful, happy, laughing; *informal* chirpy.
- OPPOSITES miserable.

mesh *noun* **netting**, net, grille, screen, lattice, gauze.
● *verb* **1 engage**, connect, lock, interlock. **2 harmonize**, fit together, match, dovetail, connect, interconnect.

mess *noun* **1 untidiness**, disorder, disarray, clutter, muddle, jumble, chaos; *informal* shambles; *Brit. informal* tip, omnishambles. **2 plight**, predicament, tight spot, tight corner, difficulty, trouble, quandary, dilemma, problem, muddle, mix-up; *informal* jam, fix, pickle, hole.
□ **mess about/around** potter about, fiddle about/around, play about/around, fool about/around, fidget, toy, trifle, tamper, tinker, interfere, meddle, monkey about/around; *Brit. informal* muck about/around. **mess up 1** dirty, clutter up, jumble, dishevel, rumple; *N. Amer. informal* muss up. **2** bungle, spoil, make a mess of, ruin; *informal* botch, make a hash of, muck up, foul up, screw up, muff.

message *noun* **1 communication**, news, note, memo, email, letter, missive, report, bulletin, communiqué, dispatch. **2** *the message of his teaching* **meaning**, sense, import, idea, point, thrust, moral, gist, essence, implication.

messenger *noun* **courier**, postman, runner, dispatch rider, envoy, emissary, agent, go-between.

messy *adjective* **1 dirty**, filthy, grubby, soiled, grimy, mucky, muddy, stained, smeared, smudged, dishevelled, scruffy, unkempt, rumpled, matted, tousled. **2 untidy**, disordered, in a muddle, chaotic, confused, disorganized, in disarray, cluttered, in a jumble; *informal* like a bomb's hit it; *Brit. informal* shambolic. **3** *a messy legal battle* **complex**, tangled, confused, convoluted, unpleasant, nasty, bitter, acrimonious.
- OPPOSITES clean, tidy.

metaphor *noun* **figure of speech**, image, trope, analogy, comparison, symbol.

method *noun* **1 procedure**, technique, system, practice, routine, modus operandi, process, strategy, tactic, approach, way, manner, mode. **2** *there's no method in his approach* **order**, organization, structure, form, system, logic, planning, design, consistency.
- OPPOSITES disorder.

methodical *adjective* **orderly**, well ordered, well organized, well planned, efficient, businesslike, systematic, structured, logical, disciplined, consistent, scientific.

meticulous *adjective* **careful**, conscientious, diligent, scrupulous, punctilious, painstaking, thorough, studious, rigorous, detailed, perfectionist, fastidious.
- OPPOSITES careless.

midday *noun* **noon**, twelve noon, high noon, noonday.
- OPPOSITES midnight.

middle *noun* **1 centre**, midpoint, halfway point, dead centre, hub, eye, heart, core, kernel. **2 midriff**, waist, belly, stomach; *informal* tummy.
- OPPOSITES edge.
● *adjective* **central**, mid, mean, medium, median, midway, halfway, equidistant.

might *noun* **strength**, force, forcefulness, power, vigour, energy, brawn.

mighty *adjective* **powerful**, forceful, strong, hard, heavy, violent, vigorous, hefty.
- OPPOSITES feeble.

migrant *noun* **immigrant**, emigrant, nomad, itinerant, traveller, transient, wanderer, drifter.
● *adjective* **travelling**, wandering, drifting, nomadic, itinerant, transient.

mild *adjective* **1 gentle**, tender, soft, sympathetic, peaceable, good-natured, quiet, placid, docile, meek. **2** *a mild punishment* **lenient**, light. **3 warm**, balmy, temperate, clement. **4 bland**, tasteless, insipid.
- OPPOSITES harsh, strong, severe.

militant *adjective* **hard-line**, extreme, extremist, committed, zealous, fanatical, radical.
● *noun* **activist**, extremist, partisan, radical, zealot.

military *adjective* **fighting**, service, army, armed, defence, martial.
- OPPOSITES civilian.
● *noun* **(armed) forces**, services, militia, army, navy, air force, marines.

militate *verb*
□ **militate against** work against, hinder, discourage, be prejudicial to, be detrimental to.

milk *verb* **exploit**, take advantage of, suck dry; *informal* bleed, squeeze, fleece.

> **WORD LINKS**
> **lactic** relating to milk

mill *noun* **factory**, plant, works, workshop, shop, foundry.
● *verb* **grind**, pulverize, powder, granulate, pound, crush, press.
□ **mill around/about** wander, drift, swarm, crowd, fill, pack, throng.

mimic *verb* **imitate**, copy, impersonate, do an impression of, ape, caricature, parody; *informal* send up, take off.
● *noun* **impersonator**, impressionist; *informal* copycat.

mince *verb* **grind**, chop up, cut up, dice, crumble; *N. Amer.* hash.

mind *noun* **1 brain**, intelligence, intellect, brains, brainpower, wits, understanding, reasoning, judgement, sense, head; *informal* grey matter; *N. Amer. informal* smarts. **2 attention**, thoughts, concentration. **3 sanity**, mental faculties, senses, wits, reason, reasoning, judgement. **4 intellect**, thinker, brain, scholar, genius.
● *verb* **1 object**, care, be bothered, be annoyed, be upset, take offence, disapprove, look askance; *informal* give/care a damn. **2 be careful of**, watch out for, look out for, beware of. **3 look after**, take care of, keep an eye on, watch, attend to, care for.

WORD LINKS
mental relating to the mind

mindless *adjective* **1 stupid**, idiotic, brainless, asinine, witless, empty-headed; *informal* dumb, dopey, dim, half-witted, fat-headed, boneheaded. **2 unthinking**, thoughtless, senseless, gratuitous, wanton, indiscriminate. **3 mechanical**, routine, tedious, boring, monotonous, mind-numbing.

mine *noun* **1 pit**, colliery, excavation, quarry. **2** *a mine of information* **store**, storehouse, reservoir, repository, gold mine, treasure house, treasury.
● *verb* **quarry**, excavate, dig, extract.

mingle *verb* **1 mix**, blend, intermingle, intermix, interweave, interlace, combine, merge, fuse, unite, join, amalgamate. **2 socialize**, circulate, associate, fraternize, get together; *informal* hobnob.
- OPPOSITES separate.

miniature *adjective* **small**, mini, little, small-scale, baby, toy, fun-size, pocket, diminutive; *informal* pint-sized; *Scottish* wee; *N. Amer.* vest-pocket.
- OPPOSITES giant.

minimal *adjective* **very little**, very small, minimum, the least (possible), nominal, token, negligible.
- OPPOSITES maximum.

minimize *verb* **1 keep down**, keep to a minimum, reduce, decrease, cut (down), lessen, curtail, prune; *informal* slash. **2 belittle**, make light of, play down, underrate, downplay, undervalue.
- OPPOSITES maximize, exaggerate.

minimum *noun* **lowest level**, lower limit, rock bottom, least, lowest.
● *adjective* **minimal**, least, smallest, least possible, slightest, lowest.
- OPPOSITES maximum.

minister *noun* **1 member of the government**, member of the cabinet, Secretary of State. **2 clergyman**, clergywoman, cleric, pastor, vicar, rector, priest, parson, curate; *informal* reverend, padre.

● *verb doctors ministered to the injured* **tend**, care for, take care of, look after, nurse, treat, attend to, see to, help.

ministry *noun* **1 department**, bureau, agency, office. **2 the priesthood**, holy orders, the church.

minor *adjective* **1 slight**, small, unimportant, insignificant, inconsequential, negligible, trivial, trifling, paltry, petty; *N. Amer.* nickel-and-dime; *informal* piffling. **2** *a minor poet* **little known**, unknown, lesser, unimportant, obscure; *N. Amer.* minor-league; *informal* small-time; *N. Amer. informal* two-bit.
- OPPOSITES major, important.
● *noun* **child**, infant, youth, adolescent, teenager, boy, girl; *informal* kid.
- OPPOSITES adult.

mint *verb* **coin**, stamp, strike, cast, make, manufacture.

minute[1] *noun* **1 moment**, short time, little while, second, instant; *informal* sec, jiffy; *Brit. informal* tick, mo, two ticks. **2** (**minutes**) **record(s)**, proceedings, log, notes, transcript, summary.

minute[2] *adjective* **1 tiny**, minuscule, microscopic, miniature; *Scottish* wee; *informal* teeny, teeny-weeny; *Brit. informal* titchy, tiddly. **2** *minute detail* **exhaustive**, painstaking, meticulous, rigorous, thorough.
- OPPOSITES huge.

miracle *noun* **wonder**, marvel, sensation, phenomenon.

miraculous *adjective* **amazing**, astounding, remarkable, extraordinary, incredible, unbelievable, sensational, phenomenal, inexplicable.

mirror *noun* **looking glass**; *Brit.* glass.
● *verb* **reflect**, match, reproduce, imitate, copy, mimic, echo, parallel.

misbehave *verb* **behave badly**, be naughty, be disobedient, get up to mischief, get up to no good, be rude; *informal* carry on, act up.

miscellaneous *adjective* **various**, varied, different, assorted, mixed, sundry, diverse, disparate, heterogeneous.

mischief *noun* **naughtiness**, bad behaviour, misbehaviour, misconduct, disobedience, wrongdoing; *informal* monkey business, shenanigans.

mischievous *adjective* **1 naughty**, bad, badly behaved, troublesome, disobedient, rascally. **2 playful**, wicked, impish, roguish.
- OPPOSITES well behaved.

misconduct *noun* **1 wrongdoing**, criminality, unprofessionalism, malpractice, negligence, impropriety; *formal* maladministration. **2 misbehaviour**, bad behaviour, mischief, misdeeds, naughtiness.

miser *noun* **penny-pincher**, Scrooge; *informal* skinflint, cheapskate; *N. Amer. informal* tightwad.
- OPPOSITES spendthrift.

miserable *adjective* **1 unhappy**, sad, sorrowful, melancholy, dejected, depressed, downhearted, downcast, despondent, disconsolate, wretched, glum, gloomy, forlorn, woebegone, mournful; *informal* blue, down in the dumps. **2** *their miserable surroundings* **dreary**, dismal, gloomy, drab, wretched, depressing, grim, cheerless, bleak, desolate.
- OPPOSITES cheerful, lovely.

miserly *adjective* **mean**, parsimonious, close-fisted, penny-pinching, cheeseparing, grasping, niggardly; *informal* stingy, tight, tight-fisted; *N. Amer. informal* cheap.
- OPPOSITES generous.

misery *noun* **unhappiness**, distress, wretchedness, suffering, angst, anguish, anxiety, torment, pain, grief, heartache, heartbreak, despair, despondency, dejection, depression, gloom, sorrow; *informal* the blues.
- OPPOSITES contentment, pleasure.

misfortune *noun* **problem**, difficulty, setback, trouble, adversity, (stroke of) bad luck, misadventure, mishap, blow, failure, accident, disaster, trial, tribulation.

misguided *adjective* **unwise**, foolish, ill-advised, ill-judged, ill-considered, injudicious, imprudent, unsound, mistaken, misplaced.
- OPPOSITES wise.

mislay *verb* **lose**, misplace, be unable to find.
- OPPOSITES find.

mislead *verb* **deceive**, delude, take in, lie to, fool, hoodwink, misinform; *informal* lead up the garden path, take for a ride; *N. Amer. informal* give someone a bum steer.

misleading *adjective* **deceptive**, confusing, deceiving, equivocal, false.
- OPPOSITES clear, straightforward.

miss *verb* **1 go wide of**, fall short of, pass, overshoot. **2 avoid**, beat, evade, escape, dodge, sidestep, elude, circumvent, bypass. **3 pine for**, yearn for, ache for, long for. **4 fail to attend**, be absent from, play truant from, cut, skip, omit; *Brit. informal* skive off.
- OPPOSITES hit, catch.
  □ **miss out** leave out, exclude, miss (off), fail to mention, pass over, skip, omit, ignore.

missing *adjective* **1 lost**, mislaid, misplaced, absent, gone (astray), unaccounted for. **2 absent**, lacking, wanting.
- OPPOSITES present.

mission *noun* **1 assignment**, commission, expedition, journey, trip, undertaking, operation, project. **2** *her mission in life* **vocation**, calling, goal, aim, quest, purpose, function, task, job, labour, work, duty.

missionary *noun* **evangelist**, apostle, proselytizer, preacher.

mist *noun* **haze**, fog, smog, murk, cloud, vapour, steam, spray, condensation.

mistake *noun* **error**, fault, inaccuracy, omission, slip, blunder, miscalculation, misunderstanding, oversight, misinterpretation, gaffe, faux pas, solecism; *informal* slip-up, boo-boo, howler; *Brit. informal* boob, clanger; *N. Amer. informal* goof.
  □ **make a mistake** make an error, go wrong, err, blunder, miscalculate.

m

mistake for confuse with, mix up with, take for.

mistaken *adjective* **1 inaccurate**, wrong, erroneous, incorrect, off beam, false, fallacious, unfounded, misguided. **2 misinformed**, wrong, in error, under a misapprehension, barking up the wrong tree.
- OPPOSITES correct.

mistimed *adjective* **ill-timed**, badly timed, inopportune, inappropriate, untimely.

mistreat *verb* **ill-treat**, maltreat, abuse, knock about/around, hit, beat, molest, injure, harm, hurt, misuse.

mistrust *verb* **be suspicious of**, be sceptical of, be wary of, be chary of, distrust, have doubts about, have misgivings about, have reservations about, suspect.

misty *adjective* **hazy**, foggy, cloudy, blurred, vague, indistinct.
- OPPOSITES clear.

misunderstand *verb* **misapprehend**, misinterpret, misconstrue, misconceive, mistake, misread, be mistaken, get the wrong idea; *informal* get (hold of) the wrong end of the stick.

misunderstanding *noun* **1 misinterpretation**, misreading, misapprehension, misconception, false impression. **2 disagreement**, difference (of opinion), dispute, falling-out, quarrel, argument, clash.

misuse *verb* **put to wrong use**, misapply, misemploy, abuse, squander, waste, dissipate, misappropriate, embezzle.

mix *verb* **1 blend**, mingle, combine, jumble, fuse, unite, join, amalgamate, incorporate, meld, homogenize; *technical* admix; *literary* commingle. **2 associate**, socialize, keep company, consort, mingle, circulate; *Brit.* rub shoulders; *N. Amer.* rub elbows; *informal* hang out/around, hobnob.
- OPPOSITES separate.
● *noun* **mixture**, blend, combination, compound, fusion, union, amalgamation, medley, selection, assortment, variety.

mixed *adjective* **1 assorted**, varied, variegated, miscellaneous, disparate, diverse, diversified, motley, sundry, jumbled, heterogeneous. **2** *mixed reactions* **ambivalent**, equivocal, contradictory, conflicting, confused, muddled.
- OPPOSITES homogeneous.

mixture *noun* **1 blend**, mix, brew, combination, concoction, composition, compound, alloy, amalgam. **2 assortment**, miscellany, medley, blend, variety, mixed bag, mix, diversity, collection, selection, hotchpotch, ragbag; *N. Amer.* hodgepodge.

mix-up *noun* **confusion**, muddle, misunderstanding, mistake, error.

moan *verb* **1 groan**, wail, whimper, sob, cry. **2 complain**, grouse, grumble, whine, carp; *informal* gripe, grouch, bellyache, bitch, beef, whinge.

mob *noun* **crowd**, horde, multitude, rabble, mass, throng, gathering, assembly.
● *verb* **surround**, crowd round, besiege, jostle.

mobile *adjective* **1 able to move**, able to walk, walking; *informal* up and about. **2** *a mobile library* **travelling**, transportable, portable, movable, itinerant, peripatetic.
- OPPOSITES immobile.

mobilize *verb* **1** *mobilize the troops* **marshal**, deploy, muster, rally, call up, assemble, mass, organize, prepare. **2** *mobilizing support for the party* **generate**, arouse, awaken, excite, stimulate, stir up, encourage, inspire, whip up.

mock *verb* **ridicule**, jeer at, sneer at, deride, make fun of, laugh at, scoff at, tease, taunt; *informal* take the mickey out of; *N. Amer. informal* goof on, rag on.
● *adjective* **imitation**, artificial, manmade, simulated, synthetic, ersatz, fake, reproduction, pseudo, false, spurious; *informal* pretend.
- OPPOSITES genuine.

mocking *adjective* **sneering**, derisive, contemptuous, scornful, sardonic, ironic, sarcastic, satirical.

mode *noun* **1 manner**, way, means, method, system, style, approach. **2** *the camera is in manual mode* **function**, position, operation, setting, option.

model *noun* **1 replica**, copy, representation, mock-up, dummy, imitation, duplicate, reproduction, facsimile. **2 prototype**, archetype, type, paradigm, version, mould, template, framework, pattern, design, blueprint. **3 fashion model**, supermodel, mannequin; *informal* clothes horse.
● *adjective* **1 replica**, toy, miniature, dummy, imitation, duplicate, reproduction, facsimile. **2 ideal**, perfect, exemplary, classic, flawless, faultless, nonpareil.

moderate *adjective* **1 average**, modest, medium, middling, tolerable, passable, adequate, fair; *informal* OK, so-so, bog-standard, fair-to-middling. **2** *moderate prices* **reasonable**, within reason, acceptable, affordable, inexpensive, fair, modest. **3** *moderate views* **middle-of-the-road**, non-extremist, liberal, pragmatic.
- OPPOSITES immoderate, extreme.
● *verb* **1 die down**, abate, let up, calm down, lessen, decrease, diminish, recede, weaken, subside. **2 curb**, control, check, temper, restrain, subdue, tame, lessen, decrease, lower, reduce, diminish, alleviate, allay, appease, ease, soothe, calm, tone down.
- OPPOSITES increase.

moderately *adverb* **somewhat**, quite, fairly, reasonably, comparatively, relatively, to some extent, tolerably, adequately; *informal* pretty.

modern *adjective* **1 present-day**, contemporary, present, current, twenty-first-century, latter-day, recent. **2 fashionable**, up to date, trendsetting, stylish, chic, à la mode, the latest, new, newest, newfangled, advanced; *informal* trendy, cool, in, funky.
- OPPOSITES past, old-fashioned.

modernize *verb* **update**, bring up to date, streamline, rationalize, overhaul, renovate, remodel, refashion, revamp.

modest *adjective* **1 humble**, self-deprecating, self-effacing, unassuming, shy, diffident, reserved, bashful. **2** *modest success* **moderate**, fair, limited, tolerable, passable, adequate, satisfactory, acceptable, unexceptional. **3** *a modest house* **small**, ordinary, simple, plain, humble, inexpensive, unostentatious, unpretentious. **4** *her modest dress* **demure**, decent, seemly, decorous, proper.
- OPPOSITES conceited, grand, indecent.

modesty *noun* **humility**, self-effacement, shyness, bashfulness, self-consciousness, reserve.

modification *noun* **change**, adjustment, alteration, adaptation, refinement, revision, amendment; *informal* tweak.

modify *verb* **1 change**, alter, adjust, adapt, amend, revise, refine; *informal* tweak. **2 moderate**, temper, soften, tone down, qualify.

moist *adjective* **1 damp**, steamy, humid, muggy, clammy, dank, wet, soggy, sweaty, sticky. **2 succulent**, juicy, soft, tender.
- OPPOSITES dry.

moisten *verb* **dampen**, wet, damp, water, humidify.

moisture *noun* **wetness**, wet, water, liquid, condensation, steam, vapour, dampness, damp, humidity.

moment *noun* **1 little while**, short time, bit, minute, instant, (split) second; *informal* sec, jiffy; *Brit. informal* tick, mo, two ticks. **2 point (in time)**, stage, juncture, instant, time, hour, second, minute, day.

momentary *adjective* **brief**, short, short-lived, fleeting, passing, transitory, transient, ephemeral.
- OPPOSITES lengthy.

momentous *adjective* **important**, significant, historic, critical, crucial, decisive, pivotal, consequential, far-reaching; *informal* earth-shattering.
- OPPOSITES insignificant.

m

momentum noun **impetus**, energy, force, driving force, power, strength, thrust, speed, velocity.

monarch noun **sovereign**, ruler, Crown, crowned head, potentate, king, queen, emperor, empress, prince, princess.

monastery noun friary, abbey, priory, cloister.

monetary adjective **financial**, fiscal, pecuniary, money, cash, capital, economic, budgetary.

money noun **cash**, hard cash, means, wherewithal, deep pockets, funds, capital, finances, notes, coins, change, currency, specie; informal dough, bread, loot; Brit. informal dosh, brass, lolly, spondulicks, the readies; N. Amer. informal dinero.

monitor noun **1 detector**, scanner, recorder, sensor, security camera, CCTV. **2** UN monitors **observer**, watchdog, overseer, supervisor, scrutineer. **3** a computer monitor **screen**, display, VDU.
● verb **observe**, watch, track, keep an eye on, keep under surveillance, record, note, oversee; informal keep tabs on.

monkey noun **simian**, primate, ape.
□ **monkey with** tamper with, fiddle with, interfere with, meddle with, tinker with, play with; informal mess with; Brit. informal muck about with.

monotonous adjective **tedious**, boring, uninteresting, unexciting, dull, repetitive, repetitious, unvarying, unchanging, mechanical, mind-numbing, soul-destroying; informal deadly.
- OPPOSITES interesting.

monster noun **1 giant**, mammoth, demon, dragon, colossus, leviathan. **2 fiend**, animal, beast, devil, demon, barbarian, savage, brute; informal swine.

monstrous adjective **1 grotesque**, hideous, ugly, ghastly, gruesome, horrible, horrific, horrifying, grisly, disgusting, repulsive, dreadful, frightening, terrible, terrifying. **2 appalling**, wicked, abominable, terrible, horrible, dreadful, vile, outrageous, unspeakable, despicable, vicious, savage, barbaric, inhuman.
- OPPOSITES beautiful, humane.

monument noun **memorial**, statue, pillar, cairn, column, obelisk, cross, cenotaph, tomb, mausoleum, shrine.

monumental adjective **1 huge**, enormous, gigantic, massive, colossal, mammoth, immense, tremendous, mighty, stupendous. **2 significant**, important, majestic, memorable, remarkable, noteworthy, momentous, grand, awe-inspiring, heroic, epic.
- OPPOSITES tiny.

mood noun **1 frame of mind**, state of mind, humour, temper. **2 bad mood**, temper, bad temper, sulk, low spirits, the doldrums, the blues; Brit. informal paddy. **3 atmosphere**, feeling, spirit, ambience, aura, character, flavour, feel, tone.

moody adjective **temperamental**, emotional, volatile, capricious, erratic, bad-tempered, petulant, sulky, sullen, morose.
- OPPOSITES cheerful.

moon verb **1 waste time**, loaf, idle; Brit. informal mooch. **2 mope**, pine, brood, daydream.

> **WORD LINKS**
> **lunar** relating to the moon

moor[1] verb **tie (up)**, secure, make fast, berth, dock.

moor[2] noun **upland**, heath, moorland; Brit. fell, wold.

mop noun a tousled mop of hair **shock**, mane, tangle, mass.

moral adjective **1 ethical**, good, virtuous, righteous, upright, upstanding, high-minded, principled, honourable, honest, just, noble. **2** moral support **psychological**, emotional, mental.
- OPPOSITES immoral, unethical.
● noun **1 lesson**, message, meaning, significance, import, point, teaching. **2** he's got no morals **moral code**, code of ethics, values, principles, standards, (sense of) morality, scruples.

morale *noun* **confidence**, self-confidence, self-esteem, spirit(s), team spirit, esprit de corps, motivation.

morality *noun* **1 ethics**, rights and wrongs, whys and wherefores. **2 virtue**, good behaviour, righteousness, uprightness, morals, standards, principles, honesty, integrity, propriety, honour, decency.

morbid *adjective* **ghoulish**, macabre, unhealthy, gruesome, unwholesome; *informal* sick.
- OPPOSITES wholesome.

more *determiner* **extra**, further, added, additional, supplementary, increased, new.
- OPPOSITES less, fewer.

moreover *adverb* **besides**, furthermore, what's more, in addition, also, as well, too, to boot, additionally, on top of that, into the bargain.

morning *noun* **1 before lunch**, a.m.; *literary* morn; *Nautical & N. Amer.* forenoon. **2 dawn**, daybreak, sunrise, first light; *N. Amer.* sunup.

mortal *adjective* **1** *all men are mortal* **perishable**, physical, bodily, corporeal, human, fleshly, earthly, impermanent, transient, ephemeral. **2** *a mortal blow* **fatal**, lethal, deadly, death-dealing, murderous, terminal. **3** *mortal enemies* **deadly**, sworn, irreconcilable, bitter, implacable, unrelenting, remorseless.
- OPPOSITES eternal.
● *noun* **human (being)**, person, man, woman, earthling.

mortuary *noun* **morgue**, funeral parlour; *Brit.* chapel of rest.

mostly *adverb* **1 mainly**, for the most part, on the whole, in the main, largely, chiefly, predominantly, principally, primarily. **2 usually**, generally, in general, as a rule, ordinarily, normally, customarily, typically, most of the time, almost always.

mother *noun* **matriarch**, materfamilias; *informal* ma; *Brit. informal* mum, mummy; *N. Amer. informal* mom, mommy; *Brit. informal, dated* mater.

● *verb* **look after**, care for, take care of, nurse, protect, tend, raise, rear, pamper, coddle, cosset, fuss over.

> **WORD LINKS**
> **maternal** relating to a mother
> **matricide** killing of your mother

motherly *adjective* **maternal**, maternalistic, protective, caring, loving, affectionate, nurturing.

motif *noun* **1 design**, pattern, decoration, figure, shape, device, emblem. **2 theme**, idea, concept, subject, topic, leitmotif.

motion *noun* **1 movement**, locomotion, progress, passage, transit, course, travel, orbit. **2 gesture**, movement, signal, sign, indication, wave, nod, gesticulation. **3 proposal**, proposition, recommendation.
● *verb* **gesture**, signal, direct, indicate, wave, beckon, nod.

> **WORD LINKS**
> **kinetic** relating to motion

motivate *verb* **prompt**, drive, move, inspire, stimulate, influence, activate, impel, propel, push, spur (on), encourage, incentivize.

motivation *noun* **motive**, motivating force, incentive, stimulus, stimulation, inspiration, inducement, incitement, spur.

motive *noun* **reason**, motivation, motivating force, rationale, grounds, cause, basis.

motto *noun* **slogan**, maxim, saying, proverb, aphorism, adage, saw, axiom, formula, catchphrase.

mould *noun* **1 cast**, die, matrix, form, shape, template, pattern, frame. **2** *an actress in the Hollywood mould* **pattern**, form, type, style, tradition, school.
● *verb* **1 shape**, form, fashion, model, work, construct, make, create, sculpt, cast. **2 determine**, direct, control, guide, influence, shape, form, fashion, make.

mound *noun* **1 heap**, pile, stack, mountain. **2 hillock**, hill, knoll, rise, hummock, hump; *Scottish* brae.

mount *verb* **1 go up**, ascend, climb (up), scale. **2** *mount a horse* **get on to**, bestride, climb on to, leap on to, hop on to. **3** *mount an exhibition* **put on**, present, install, organize, stage, set up, prepare, launch, set in motion. **4 increase**, grow, rise, escalate, soar, spiral, shoot up, rocket, climb, accumulate, build up, multiply.
- OPPOSITES descend, dismount, fall.
● *noun* **setting**, backing, support, mounting, frame, stand.

mountain *noun* **1 peak**, summit; (**mountains**) range, massif, sierra; *Scottish* ben. **2 lot**; *informal* heap, pile, stack, slew, lots, loads, tons, masses.

mourn *verb* **1 grieve for**, sorrow over, lament for, weep for. **2 deplore**, bewail, bemoan, rue, regret.

mourning *noun* **grief**, grieving, sorrowing, lamentation.

mouth *noun* **1 lips**, jaws, muzzle; *informal* trap, chops, kisser; *Brit. informal* gob; *N. Amer. informal* puss. **2 entrance**, opening. **3 estuary**, delta, firth, outlet, outfall.

> **WORD LINKS**
> **oral** relating to the mouth

move *verb* **1 go**, walk, step, proceed, progress, advance, budge, stir, shift, change position. **2 carry**, transfer, shift, push, pull, lift, slide. **3 progress**, advance, develop, evolve, change, happen. **4 act**, take steps, do something, take measures; *informal* get moving. **5 relocate**, move house, move away/out, change address, go (away), decamp. **6 affect**, touch, impress, shake, upset, disturb. **7 inspire**, prompt, stimulate, motivate, provoke, influence, rouse, induce, incite. **8 propose**, submit, suggest, advocate, recommend, urge.
● *noun* **1 movement**, motion, action, gesture. **2 relocation**, change of house/address, transfer, posting. **3 initiative**, step, action, measure, manoeuvre, tactic, stratagem. **4 turn**, go; *Scottish* shot.

movement *noun* **1 motion**, move, gesture, sign, signal, action. **2 transportation**, shifting, conveyance, moving, transfer. **3 group**, party, faction, wing, lobby, camp. **4 campaign**, crusade, drive, push, initiative.

> **WORD LINKS**
> **kinetic** relating to movement

movie *noun* **film**, picture, motion picture, feature film; *informal* flick.

moving *adjective* **1 in motion**, operating, operational, working, on the move, active, movable, mobile. **2 touching**, poignant, heart-warming, heart-rending, affecting, emotional, inspiring, inspirational, stimulating, stirring.
- OPPOSITES stationary, fixed.

mow *verb* **cut**, trim, crop, clip, shear.

much *determiner* **a lot of**, a great/good deal of, a great/large amount of, plenty of, ample, abundant, plentiful; *informal* lots of, loads of, heaps of, masses of, tons of, stacks of.
- OPPOSITES little.
● *adverb* **1 greatly**, a great deal, a lot, considerably, appreciably. **2 often**, frequently, many times, regularly, habitually, routinely, usually, normally, commonly.
● *pronoun* **a lot**, a great/good deal, plenty; *informal* lots, loads, heaps, masses, tons.

muck *noun* **1 dirt**, grime, filth, mud, mess; *Brit. informal* gunge. **2 dung**, manure, excrement, droppings, ordure.

mud *noun* **dirt**, sludge, ooze, silt, clay, mire, soil.

muddle *verb* **1 confuse**, mix up, jumble (up), disarrange, disorganize, disorder, mess up. **2 bewilder**, confuse, bemuse, perplex, puzzle, baffle, mystify.
● *noun* **mess**, confusion, jumble, tangle, chaos, disorder, disarray, disorganization; *informal* shambles; *Brit. informal* omnishambles.

muddy *adjective* **1 marshy**, boggy, swampy, waterlogged, squelchy, squishy, mucky, slimy, wet, soft. **2 dirty**, filthy, mucky, grimy, soiled.

3 murky, cloudy, turbid.
- OPPOSITES clean, clear.

muffle verb **1 wrap (up)**, swathe, enfold, envelop, cloak. **2 deaden**, dull, dampen, mute, soften, quieten, mask, stifle, smother.

mug noun **beaker**, cup, tankard, glass, stein.
● verb **assault**, attack, set upon, beat up, rob; informal jump.

muggy adjective **humid**, close, sultry, sticky, oppressive, airless, stifling, suffocating, stuffy.
- OPPOSITES fresh.

mull verb
□ **mull over** ponder, consider, think over/about, reflect on, contemplate, chew over; formal cogitate on.

multicoloured adjective **kaleidoscopic**, psychedelic, colourful, many-hued, jazzy, variegated.
- OPPOSITES monochrome.

multiple adjective **numerous**, many, various, different, diverse, several, manifold.
- OPPOSITES single.

multiply verb **increase**, grow, accumulate, proliferate, mount up, mushroom, snowball.
- OPPOSITES decrease.

mumble verb **mutter**, murmur, talk under your breath.

mundane adjective **humdrum**, dull, boring, tedious, monotonous, tiresome, unexciting, uninteresting, uneventful, unremarkable, routine, ordinary.
- OPPOSITES extraordinary.

municipal adjective **civic**, civil, metropolitan, urban, city, town, borough, council.

murder noun **killing**, homicide, assassination, extermination, execution, slaughter, butchery, massacre, manslaughter; literary slaying.
● verb **kill**, put to death, assassinate, execute, butcher, slaughter, massacre, wipe out; informal bump off; N. Amer. informal ice, waste; literary slay.

murderer noun **killer**, assassin, serial killer, butcher; informal hit man, hired gun.

murderous adjective **homicidal**, brutal, violent, savage, ferocious, fierce, vicious, bloodthirsty, barbarous, barbaric, fatal, lethal, deadly.

murky adjective **1 dark**, gloomy, grey, leaden, dull, dim, overcast, cloudy, clouded, sunless, dismal, dreary, bleak. **2 dirty**, muddy, cloudy, turbid.
- OPPOSITES bright, clear.

murmur noun **1 whisper**, mutter, mumble, undertone. **2 hum**, buzz, drone.
● verb **mutter**, mumble, whisper, talk under your breath, talk sotto voce.

muscle noun **1 strength**, power, brawn; informal beef, beefiness. **2** financial muscle **influence**, power, strength, might, force, forcefulness, weight; informal clout.
□ **muscle in** (informal) interfere, force your way in, impose yourself, encroach; informal horn in.

muscular adjective **strong**, brawny, muscly, well built, burly, strapping, sturdy, powerful, athletic; informal hunky, beefy.

muse verb **ponder**, consider, think over/about, mull over, reflect on, contemplate, turn over in your mind, chew over.

musical adjective **tuneful**, melodic, melodious, harmonious, sweet-sounding, dulcet, euphonious, mellifluous.
- OPPOSITES discordant.

must verb **ought to**, should, have (got) to, need to, be obliged to, be required to, be compelled to.

muster verb **1 assemble**, mobilize, rally, raise, summon, gather, call up, call to arms, recruit, conscript; US draft. **2 congregate**, assemble, gather (together), come together, collect, convene, mass, rally. **3** she mustered her courage **summon (up)**, screw up, call up, rally.

mutation noun **1 alteration**, change, transformation, metamorphosis, transmutation. **2 mutant**, freak (of nature), deviant, monstrosity, monster.

mute adjective **1 silent**, speechless, dumb, unspeaking, tight-lipped, taciturn; informal mum. **2 wordless**, silent, dumb, unspoken.

- OPPOSITES voluble, spoken.

muted adjective **1 muffled**, faint, indistinct, quiet, soft, low, distant, faraway. **2 subdued**, pastel, delicate, subtle, understated, restrained.

mutilate verb **1 disfigure**, maim, mangle, dismember, slash, hack up. **2 vandalize**, damage, slash, deface, violate, desecrate.

mutinous adjective **rebellious**, insubordinate, subversive, seditious, insurgent, insurrectionary, disobedient, restive.

mutiny noun **insurrection**, rebellion, revolt, riot, uprising, insurgence, insubordination.
● verb **rise up**, rebel, revolt, riot, strike.

mutter verb **1 murmur**, talk under your breath, talk sotto voce, mumble, whisper. **2 grumble**, complain, grouse, carp, whine; informal moan, whinge.

mutual adjective **reciprocal**, reciprocated, requited, returned, common, joint, shared.

mysterious adjective **1 puzzling**, strange, peculiar, curious, funny, odd, weird, queer, bizarre, mystifying, inexplicable, baffling, perplexing, arcane, esoteric, cryptic, obscure. **2 secretive**, inscrutable, impenetrable, enigmatic, reticent, evasive.

mystery noun **1 puzzle**, enigma, conundrum, riddle, secret, paradox, question mark, closed book. **2 secrecy**, obscurity, uncertainty.

mystic, **mystical** adjective **spiritual**, religious, transcendental, paranormal, other-worldly, supernatural, occult, metaphysical.

mystify verb **bewilder**, puzzle, perplex, baffle, confuse, confound, bemuse, throw; informal flummox, stump, bamboozle.

myth noun **1 folk tale**, folk story, legend, fable, saga, lore, folklore. **2 misconception**, fallacy, old wives' tale, fairy story, fiction; informal cock and bull story.

m

Nn

nadir noun **low point**, all-time low, bottom, rock bottom; informal the pits.
- OPPOSITES zenith.

nag verb **1 harass**, keep on at, go on at, badger, chivvy, hound, plague, criticize, find fault with, moan at, grumble at, henpeck; informal hassle; N. Amer. informal ride. **2 trouble**, worry, bother, torment, niggle, prey on your mind; informal bug.

nail noun **tack**, pin, brad, hobnail, spike, staple, rivet.
● verb **fasten**, fix, attach, secure, affix, pin, tack, hammer.

naive adjective **innocent**, unsophisticated, artless, inexperienced, unworldly, trusting, gullible, credulous, immature, callow, raw, green; informal wet behind the ears.
- OPPOSITES worldly.

naked adjective **nude**, bare, in the nude, stark naked, stripped, unclothed, undressed; informal without a stitch on, in your birthday suit, in the raw/buff, in the altogether; Brit. informal starkers; N. Amer. informal buck naked.
- OPPOSITES dressed.

name noun **title**, designation, tag, nickname, sobriquet, epithet, label, honorific; informal moniker, handle; formal appellation, denomination, cognomen.
● verb **1 call**, dub, label, style, term, title, baptize, christen. **2 nominate**, designate, select, pick, decide on, choose.

> **WORD LINKS**
> **onomastic** relating to names

namely adverb **that is (to say)**, to be specific, specifically, viz., to wit, in other words.

nap noun **sleep**, catnap, siesta, doze, lie-down, rest; informal snooze, forty winks, shut-eye; Brit. informal kip, zizz.

narcotic noun **drug**, sedative, opiate, painkiller, analgesic, palliative.
● adjective **soporific**, sedative, calming, painkilling, pain-relieving, analgesic, anodyne.

narrate verb **tell**, relate, recount, recite, describe, chronicle, report, present.

narrative noun **account**, chronicle, history, description, record, report, story, tale.

narrator noun **storyteller**, chronicler, commentator, presenter, author.
- OPPOSITES listener, audience.

narrow adjective **1 slender**, slim, small, slight, attenuated, tapering, thin, tiny. **2 confined**, cramped, tight, restricted, limited, constricted, small, tiny, inadequate, insufficient.
- OPPOSITES wide, broad.
● verb **reduce**, restrict, limit, decrease, diminish, taper, contract, shrink, constrict.
- OPPOSITES widen.

narrowly adverb **(only) just**, barely, scarcely, hardly, by a hair's breadth; informal by a whisker.

narrow-minded adjective **intolerant**, illiberal, reactionary, conservative, parochial, provincial, insular, small-minded, petty, blinkered, inward-looking, hidebound, prejudiced, bigoted.
- OPPOSITES tolerant.

nasty adjective **1 unpleasant**, disagreeable, disgusting, vile, foul, abominable, revolting, repulsive, repellent, horrible, obnoxious, unsavoury, loathsome, noxious, foul-smelling, smelly, stinking, rank, fetid, malodorous; informal ghastly, horrid, yucky; N. Amer. informal lousy; literary noisome. **2 unkind**, unpleasant, unfriendly, disagreeable, rude, spiteful, malicious, mean, vicious, malevolent, hurtful. **3** a nasty accident **serious**, dangerous, bad, awful,

dreadful, terrible, severe, painful.
- OPPOSITES nice, pleasant.

nation noun **country**, state, land, realm, kingdom, republic, people, race, tribe.

national adjective **1** *national politics* **state**, public, federal, governmental. **2** *a national strike* **nationwide**, country-wide, general, widespread.
- OPPOSITES local, international.
● noun **citizen**, subject, native, resident, inhabitant, voter, passport holder.

nationalism noun **patriotism**, allegiance, xenophobia, chauvinism, jingoism, flag-waving.

nationwide adjective **national**, country-wide, state, general, widespread, extensive.
- OPPOSITES local.

native noun **inhabitant**, resident, local, citizen, national, countryman.
- OPPOSITES foreigner.
● adjective **1** *native species* **indigenous**, original, local, domestic. **2** *native wit* **innate**, inborn, natural, inherent, intrinsic.

natural adjective **1** **unprocessed**, organic, pure, unrefined, additive-free, green, GM-free. **2** *a natural occurrence* **normal**, ordinary, everyday, usual, regular, common, commonplace, typical, routine, standard, logical, understandable, (only) to be expected, predictable. **3** *a natural leader* **born**, instinctive, congenital, pathological. **4** *his natural instincts* **innate**, inborn, inherent, native, inherited, hereditary. **5** *she seemed very natural* **unaffected**, spontaneous, uninhibited, relaxed, unselfconscious, genuine, open, artless, guileless, unpretentious, unstudied.
- OPPOSITES abnormal, artificial, affected.

naturally adverb **of course**, as might be expected, needless to say, obviously, clearly, it goes without saying.

nature noun **1** **the natural world**, the environment, Mother Earth, the universe, the cosmos, wildlife, the countryside, the land. **2** **character**, personality, disposition, temperament, make-up, psyche. **3** **kind**, sort, type, variety, category, class, genre, order, quality, complexion; *N. Amer.* stripe.

naughty adjective **1** **badly behaved**, disobedient, bad, wayward, defiant, unruly, insubordinate, wilful, delinquent, undisciplined, refractory, disruptive, attention-seeking, mischievous, impish. **2** **indecent**, risqué, rude, racy, vulgar, dirty, filthy, smutty, crude, coarse.
- OPPOSITES well behaved, clean.

nausea noun **sickness**, biliousness, queasiness, vomiting, retching.

nautical adjective **maritime**, marine, naval, seafaring, seagoing, sailing.

navigate verb **steer**, pilot, guide, direct, captain; *informal* skipper.

navy noun **fleet**, flotilla, armada.

near adjective **1** **close**, nearby, (close/near) at hand, a stone's throw away, neighbouring, within reach, accessible, handy, convenient; *informal* within spitting distance. **2** **imminent**, in the offing, on its way, coming, impending, looming.
- OPPOSITES far, distant.

nearby adjective **not far away**, not far off, close at hand, close by, near, within reach, neighbouring, local, accessible, convenient, handy.
- OPPOSITES distant.

nearly adverb **almost**, just about, more or less, practically, virtually, all but, as good as, not far off, to all intents and purposes, not quite; *informal* pretty well.

neat adjective **1** **tidy**, orderly, well ordered, in (good) order, spick and span, uncluttered, shipshape, straight, trim. **2** **smart**, spruce, dapper, trim, well groomed, well turned out; *informal* natty. **3** *his neat footwork* **skilful**, deft, dexterous, adroit, adept, expert, nimble, elegant, graceful, accurate; *informal* nifty. **4** *a neat solution* **clever**, ingenious, inventive, imaginative. **5** *neat gin* **undiluted**, straight, pure.
- OPPOSITES untidy.

necessarily adverb **as a consequence**, as a result, automatically, as a matter of course, certainly, incontrovertibly, inevitably, unavoidably, inescapably, of necessity.

necessary adjective **1 obligatory**, required, requisite, compulsory, mandatory, imperative, needed, essential, vital, indispensable, de rigueur; formal needful. **2** a necessary consequence **inevitable**, unavoidable, inescapable, inexorable.

necessity noun **1 essential**, prerequisite, requisite, sine qua non; informal must-have. **2** political necessity forced him to resign **force of circumstance**, obligation, need, exigency.

need verb **require**, be in need of, want, be crying out for, demand, call for, necessitate, entail, involve, lack, be without, be short of.
● noun **1** there's no need to apologize **necessity**, requirement, call, demand. **2** basic human needs **requirement**, necessity, want, requisite, prerequisite, desideratum. **3** my hour of need **difficulty**, trouble, distress, crisis, emergency, urgency, extremity.

needed adjective **necessary**, required, called for, wanted, desired, lacking.
- OPPOSITES optional.

needless adjective **unnecessary**, unneeded, uncalled for, gratuitous, pointless, superfluous, redundant, excessive.
- OPPOSITES necessary.

needy adjective **poor**, deprived, disadvantaged, underprivileged, in need, hard up, poverty-stricken, impoverished, destitute, penniless; informal broke, strapped (for cash); Brit. informal skint; dated needful.
- OPPOSITES wealthy.

negative adjective **1 pessimistic**, defeatist, gloomy, critical, cynical, fatalistic, dismissive, unenthusiastic, apathetic, unresponsive. **2 harmful**, bad, adverse, damaging, detrimental, unfavourable, disadvantageous.

- OPPOSITES positive, optimistic, favourable.

neglect verb **1 fail to look after**, leave alone, abandon, ignore, pay no attention to, let slide, not attend to, be remiss about, be lax about, shirk. **2 fail**, omit, forget.
- OPPOSITES cherish, remember.
● noun **1 disrepair**, dilapidation, shabbiness, abandonment, disuse. **2 negligence**, dereliction (of duty), carelessness, laxity, slackness, irresponsibility.
- OPPOSITES care.

neglected adjective **1** neglected animals **uncared for**, abandoned, mistreated, maltreated. **2** a neglected cottage **derelict**, dilapidated, tumbledown, ramshackle, untended. **3** a neglected masterpiece **disregarded**, forgotten, overlooked, ignored, unrecognized, unnoticed, unsung, underrated.

negligent adjective **neglectful**, remiss, careless, lax, irresponsible, inattentive, thoughtless, uncaring, unmindful, forgetful, slack, sloppy; N. Amer. derelict.
- OPPOSITES dutiful.

negligible adjective **trivial**, trifling, insignificant, unimportant, of no account, minor, inconsequential, minimal, small, slight, infinitesimal, minuscule.
- OPPOSITES significant.

negotiate verb **1 discuss (terms)**, talk, consult, confer, debate, compromise, bargain, haggle. **2 arrange**, broker, work out, thrash out, complete, close, conclude, agree on. **3 get round**, get past, get over, clear, cross, surmount, overcome, deal with, cope with.

negotiation noun **1 discussion(s)**, talks, conference, debate, dialogue, consultation. **2 arrangement**, brokering, settlement, conclusion, completion.

negotiator noun **mediator**, arbitrator, moderator, go-between, middleman, intermediary, representative, spokesperson, broker.

n

neighbourhood noun **1 district**, area, locality, locale, quarter, community; *informal* neck of the woods; *N. Amer. informal* hood. **2 vicinity**, environs.

neighbouring adjective **adjacent**, adjoining, bordering, connecting, next-door, nearby, in the vicinity.
- OPPOSITES remote.

neighbourly adjective **obliging**, helpful, friendly, kind, considerate, amicable, sociable, hospitable, companionable, civil, cordial.
- OPPOSITES unfriendly.

nerve noun **1 confidence**, assurance, courage, bravery, determination, will power, spirit, grit; *informal* guts; *Brit. informal* bottle; *N. Amer. informal* moxie. **2 audacity**, cheek, effrontery, gall, temerity, presumption, impudence, impertinence, arrogance; *informal* face, front, brass neck, chutzpah. **3 (nerves) anxiety**, tension, nervousness, stress, worry, cold feet, apprehension; *informal* butterflies (in your stomach), collywobbles, jitters, the heebie-jeebies.

WORD LINKS
neural relating to nerves in the body

nervous adjective **anxious**, worried, apprehensive, on edge, edgy, tense, stressed, agitated, uneasy, restless, worked up, keyed up, overwrought, jumpy, on tenterhooks, highly strung, nervy, excitable, neurotic; *informal* jittery, twitchy, in a state, uptight, wired, trepidatious; *N. Amer. informal* squirrelly.
- OPPOSITES relaxed, calm.

nestle verb **snuggle**, cuddle, huddle, nuzzle, settle, burrow.

net[1] noun **netting**, mesh, tulle, fishnet, lace, openwork.
● verb **catch**, capture, trap, snare; *informal* nab, bag, collar, bust; *Brit. informal* nick.

net[2] adjective **after tax**, after deductions, take-home, final.
- OPPOSITES gross.
● verb **earn**, make, clear, take home,

bring in, pocket, realize.

network noun **web**, lattice, net, matrix, mesh, criss-cross, grid, maze, labyrinth, warren, tangle.

neurotic adjective **highly strung**, oversensitive, nervous, tense, paranoid, obsessive, fixated, hysterical, overwrought, irrational.
- OPPOSITES stable, calm.

neutral adjective **1 impartial**, unbiased, unprejudiced, objective, open-minded, non-partisan, even-handed, disinterested, dispassionate, detached, non-aligned, unaffiliated, uninvolved. **2 inoffensive**, bland, unobjectionable, unexceptionable, anodyne, uncontroversial, safe, harmless, innocuous. **3 pale**, light, colourless, indeterminate, drab, insipid, nondescript, dull.
- OPPOSITES biased, provocative.

neutralize verb **counteract**, offset, counterbalance, balance, cancel out, nullify, negate.

never-ending adjective **incessant**, continuous, ceaseless, constant, continual, perpetual, uninterrupted, unbroken, steady, unremitting, relentless, persistent, interminable, non-stop, endless, unending.

nevertheless adverb **nonetheless**, even so, however, still, yet, in spite of that, despite that, be that as it may, notwithstanding.

new adjective **1 recent**, up to date, the latest, current, state-of-the-art, contemporary, advanced, cutting-edge, modern, avant-garde. **2 unused**, brand new, pristine, fresh. **3 different**, another, alternative, additional, extra, supplementary, further, unfamiliar, unknown, strange. **4 reinvigorated**, restored, revived, improved, refreshed, regenerated.
- OPPOSITES old, second-hand.

newcomer noun **1 incomer**, immigrant, settler, stranger, outsider, foreigner, alien; *informal* new kid on the block, johnny-come-lately; *Austral. informal* blow-in. **2 beginner**, novice, learner, trainee, apprentice, probationer; *informal* rookie, newbie; *N. Amer. informal* tenderfoot.

newly *adverb* **recently**, only just, lately, freshly, not long ago.

news *noun* **report**, story, account, announcement, press release, communication, communiqué, bulletin, intelligence, information, word, revelation, disclosure, exposé; *Brit.* stop press; *informal* scoop; *literary* tidings.

newspaper *noun* **paper**, journal, gazette, news-sheet, tabloid, broadsheet, periodical; *Brit.* red top; *informal* rag.

next *adjective* **1 following**, succeeding, subsequent, ensuing, upcoming, to come. **2 neighbouring**, adjacent, adjoining, next-door, bordering, connected, closest, nearest; *formal* contiguous, proximate.
- OPPOSITES previous.
● *adverb* **afterwards**, after, then, later, subsequently; *formal* thereafter.

nice *adjective* **1** *have a nice time* **enjoyable**, pleasant, agreeable, good, pleasurable, satisfying, entertaining, amusing; *informal* lovely, great; *N. Amer. informal* neat. **2** *nice people* **pleasant**, likeable, agreeable, personable, good-natured, congenial, amiable, affable, genial, friendly, charming, delightful, engaging, sympathetic, polite, courteous, well mannered, civil, kind, obliging, helpful. **3** *nice weather* **fine**, dry, sunny, warm, mild, clement. **4** *a nice distinction* **subtle**, fine, slight, delicate, precise.
- OPPOSITES unpleasant, nasty.

niche *noun* **1 recess**, alcove, nook, cranny, hollow, bay, cavity, pigeonhole. **2 position**, slot, place, vocation, calling, métier, station, job, level.

nick *noun* **cut**, scratch, incision, notch, chip, dent, indentation.
● *verb* **cut**, scratch, graze, chip, dent.

nickname *noun* **pet name**, diminutive, endearment, tag, label, sobriquet, epithet; *informal* handle, moniker.

night *noun* **night-time**, (hours of) darkness, dark.
- OPPOSITES day.

> **WORD LINKS**
> **nocturnal** occurring or active at night

nightfall *noun* **sunset**, sundown, dusk, twilight, evening, dark; *literary* eventide.
- OPPOSITES dawn.

nightmare *noun* **ordeal**, trial, hell, misery, agony, torture, murder, purgatory, disaster; *informal* the pits.

nil *noun* **nothing**, none, nought, zero; *Tennis* love; *Cricket* a duck.

nimble *adjective* **1 agile**, light, quick, lithe, skilful, deft, dexterous, adroit, sprightly, spry; *informal* nippy. **2** *a nimble mind* **quick**, alert, lively, astute, perceptive, penetrating, discerning, shrewd, sharp, intelligent, bright, smart, clever, brilliant; *informal* quick on the uptake.
- OPPOSITES clumsy.

nip *verb* & *noun* **bite**, nibble, peck, pinch, tweak.

no *adverb* **absolutely not**, of course not, under no circumstances, not at all, never; *informal* nope, no way, not a chance, not on your life; *Brit. informal* no fear; *old use* nay.
- OPPOSITES yes.

noble *adjective* **1 aristocratic**, blue-blooded, patrician, high-born, titled. **2 worthy**, righteous, good, honourable, virtuous, upright. **3 magnificent**, splendid, grand, impressive, stately, imposing, dignified, proud, striking, majestic.
- OPPOSITES humble, lowly.
● *noun* **aristocrat**, nobleman, noblewoman, lord, lady, peer (of the realm), peeress, patrician; *informal* aristo.
- OPPOSITES commoner.

nod *verb* **1 incline**, bob, bow, dip. **2 signal**, gesture, gesticulate, motion, sign, indicate.

noise *noun* **sound**, din, hubbub, clamour, racket, uproar, tumult, commotion, pandemonium; *Brit.* row; *informal* hullabaloo.
- OPPOSITES silence.

n

noisy *adjective* **1 raucous**, rowdy, strident, clamorous, vociferous, boisterous. **2 loud**, blaring, booming, deafening, thunderous, ear-splitting, piercing, cacophonous, tumultuous.
- OPPOSITES quiet, soft.

nominal *adjective* **1 in name only**, titular, formal, official, theoretical, supposed, ostensible, so-called, self-styled. **2 token**, symbolic, minimal; *Brit.* peppercorn.
- OPPOSITES real, considerable.

nominate *verb* **1 propose**, put forward, put up, submit, present, recommend, suggest. **2 appoint**, choose, decide on, select, designate, assign.

nonchalant *adjective* **calm**, composed, unconcerned, cool, imperturbable, casual, blasé, offhand, insouciant; *informal* laid-back.
- OPPOSITES anxious.

non-committal *adjective* **evasive**, equivocal, guarded, circumspect, reserved; *informal* cagey.

nonconformist *noun* **dissenter**, protester, rebel, freethinker, individualist, free spirit, maverick, renegade, schismatic, apostate, heretic.

nondescript *adjective* **undistinguished**, unremarkable, featureless, unmemorable, ordinary, average, run-of-the-mill, mundane, uninteresting, uninspiring, colourless, bland.
- OPPOSITES distinctive.

non-existent *adjective* **imaginary**, imagined, unreal, fictional, fictitious, made up, invented, fanciful, mythical, illusory.
- OPPOSITES real.

nonsense *noun* **1 rubbish**, gibberish, claptrap, balderdash, garbage; *informal* baloney, bosh, tripe, drivel, gobbledegook, mumbo-jumbo, poppycock, twaddle, guff, tosh, bilge, hogwash, piffle; *Brit. informal* cobblers, codswallop, double Dutch, rot. **2 mischief**, misbehaviour; *informal* tomfoolery, monkey business, shenanigans, malarkey; *Brit. informal* monkey tricks, jiggery-pokery.
- OPPOSITES sense.

non-stop *adjective* **continuous**, constant, continual, incessant, ceaseless, uninterrupted, unbroken, never-ending, perpetual, round-the-clock, persistent, steady, unremitting, relentless, interminable.
- OPPOSITES intermittent, occasional.
● *adverb* **continuously**, continually, incessantly, ceaselessly, all the time, constantly, perpetually, persistently, steadily, relentlessly, interminably; *informal* 24-7.

noon *noun* **midday**, twelve o'clock, twelve hundred hours, high noon, noonday.

norm *noun* **standard**, convention, criterion, yardstick, benchmark, touchstone, rule, formula, pattern.
□ **the norm** normal, usual, the rule, standard, typical, average, par for the course, expected.

normal *adjective* **1 usual**, standard, ordinary, customary, conventional, habitual, accustomed, typical, common, regular, routine, traditional, commonplace, everyday. **2 ordinary**, average, run-of-the-mill, middle-of-the-road, conventional, mainstream; *N. Amer.* garden-variety; *Brit. informal* common or garden, bog-standard. **3 sane**, in your right mind, right in the head, of sound mind, compos mentis; *informal* all there.
- OPPOSITES unusual, insane.

normally *adverb* **1 naturally**, conventionally, properly, like everyone else. **2 usually**, ordinarily, as a rule, generally, in general, mostly, on the whole, typically, habitually.

nose *noun* **snout**, muzzle, proboscis, trunk; *informal* beak, conk, schnozz, hooter.
● *verb* **1 pry**, enquire, poke about/around, interfere (in), meddle (in), stick/poke your nose in; *informal* snoop; *Austral./NZ informal* stickybeak. **2 ease**, inch, edge, move, manoeuvre, steer, guide.

WORD LINKS
nasal relating to the nose

nostalgic *adjective* **wistful**, sentimental, emotional, homesick, regretful, dewy-eyed, maudlin.

nosy *adjective* (*informal*) **prying**, inquisitive, curious, spying, eavesdropping, intrusive; *informal* snooping.

notable *adjective* **1 noteworthy**, remarkable, outstanding, important, significant, memorable, marked, striking, impressive, momentous, uncommon. **2 prominent**, well known, famous, famed, noted, of note.
- OPPOSITES unremarkable, unknown.
● *noun* **celebrity**, VIP, dignitary, luminary, star, big name, personage; *informal* celeb, bigwig.

notably *adverb* **1 in particular**, particularly, especially, primarily, principally, chiefly. **2 remarkably**, especially, exceptionally, singularly, particularly, peculiarly, distinctly, significantly, unusually, uncommonly, conspicuously.

notch *noun* **nick**, cut, incision, score, scratch, slit, snick, slot, groove.

note *noun* **1 record**, entry, reminder, comment, jotting. **2 message**, letter, line, missive; *informal* memo; *formal* memorandum, epistle. **3 annotation**, footnote, marginalia. **4** (*Brit.*) **banknote**; *N. Amer.* bill; *US informal* greenback. **5** *the note of hopelessness in her voice* **tone**, hint, indication, sign, element, suggestion, sense.
● *verb* **1 bear in mind**, be mindful of, consider, take notice of, register, be aware, take in, notice, observe, see, perceive. **2 write down**, put down, jot down, take down, scribble, enter, mark, record, register, pencil in.

notebook *noun* **notepad**, exercise book, register, logbook, log, diary, journal, record; *Brit.* jotter, pocketbook; *trademark* Filofax.

noted *adjective* **famous**, famed, well known, renowned, prominent, notable, important, eminent, great, acclaimed, celebrated, distinguished.
- OPPOSITES unknown.

noteworthy *adjective* **notable**, interesting, significant, important, remarkable,

striking, memorable, unique, special, unusual.
- OPPOSITES unexceptional.

nothing *noun* **1 not a thing**, zero; *N. English* nowt; *informal* zilch, sweet FA, not a dicky bird; *N. Amer. informal* zip, nada, diddly-squat. **2 zero**, nought, nil, 0; *Tennis* love; *Cricket* a duck.

notice *verb* **observe**, note, see, discern, detect, spot, perceive, make out; *Brit. informal* clock.
- OPPOSITES overlook.
● *noun* **1 sign**, announcement, advertisement, poster, placard, bill, handbill, flyer. **2 attention**, observation, awareness, consciousness, perception, regard, consideration, scrutiny; *formal* cognizance. **3** *advance notice of the price increase* **notification**, warning, information, news, word.

noticeable *adjective* **obvious**, evident, apparent, manifest, plain, clear, conspicuous, perceptible, discernible, detectable, observable, visible, appreciable, unmistakable, patent.
- OPPOSITES imperceptible.

notify *verb* **inform**, tell, let someone know, advise, apprise, alert, warn.

notion *noun* **idea**, impression, belief, opinion, view, concept, conception, understanding, feeling, suspicion, intuition, inkling.

notorious *adjective* **infamous**, scandalous, disreputable, of ill repute.

nought *noun* **nil**, zero, nothing; *Tennis* love; *Cricket* a duck; *informal* zilch; *N. Amer. informal* zip, nada.

nourish *verb* **feed**, sustain, provide for, care for, nurture.

nourishing *adjective* **nutritious**, wholesome, good for you, nutritive, healthy, health-giving, beneficial.
- OPPOSITES unhealthy.

nourishment *noun* **food**, nutriment, nutrients, nutrition, sustenance.

novel[1] *noun* **story**, tale, narrative, romance, novella.

novel[2] *adjective* **new**, original, unusual, unconventional, unorthodox, different,

fresh, imaginative, innovative, unfamiliar, surprising.
- OPPOSITES traditional.

novelty noun **1 originality**, newness, freshness, unconventionality, innovation, unfamiliarity. **2 knick-knack**, trinket, bauble, toy, trifle, ornament; *N. Amer.* kickshaw.

novice noun **beginner**, learner, newcomer, fledgling, trainee, probationer, student, pupil, apprentice, tyro, neophyte; *informal* rookie, newbie; *N. Amer. informal* tenderfoot, greenhorn.
- OPPOSITES expert, veteran.

now adverb **1 at the moment**, at present, presently, at this moment in time, currently, nowadays, these days, today, in this day and age. **2 at once**, straight away, right away, this minute, this instant, immediately, instantly, directly; *informal* pronto, asap.

noxious adjective **poisonous**, toxic, deadly, harmful, dangerous, environmentally unfriendly, polluting, unhealthy, unpleasant.
- OPPOSITES innocuous.

nuance noun **distinction**, shade, gradation, refinement, degree, subtlety, nicety.

nucleus noun **core**, centre, heart, kernel, nub, hub, middle, focus.

nude adjective **naked**, stark naked, bare, unclothed, undressed, stripped; *informal* without a stitch on, in your birthday suit, in the raw/buff, in the altogether; *Brit. informal* starkers; *N. Amer. informal* buck naked.
- OPPOSITES dressed.

nudge verb **prod**, elbow, dig, poke, jab, jog, push, touch.
● noun **prod**, dig (in the ribs), poke, jab, push.

nuisance noun **annoyance**, inconvenience, bore, bother, irritation, trial, burden, pest; *informal* pain (in the neck), hassle, bind, drag, headache.

nullify verb **annul**, render null and void, invalidate, repeal, reverse, rescind, revoke, cancel, neutralize, negate, counteract.

numb adjective **1 without feeling**, without sensation, dead, numbed, desensitized, frozen, anaesthetized, insensible, insensate. **2 dazed**, stunned, stupefied, paralysed, immobilized.
● verb **1 deaden**, desensitize, anaesthetize, immobilize, freeze. **2 daze**, stun, stupefy, paralyse, immobilize.

number noun **1 numeral**, integer, figure, digit, character. **2 quantity**, total, aggregate, tally, quota. **3 song**, piece, tune, track, dance.
● verb **1 add up to**, amount to, total, come to. **2 include**, count, reckon, deem.

> **WORD LINKS**
> **numerical** relating to numbers

numerous adjective **many**, a number of, a lot of/lots of, several, plenty of, countless, copious, an abundance of, frequent; *informal* umpteen.
- OPPOSITES few.

nurse verb **1 care for**, take care of, look after, tend, minister to. **2** *they nursed old grievances* **harbour**, foster, bear, have, hold (on to), retain.

nurture verb **1 bring up**, care for, take care of, look after, tend, rear, raise. **2** *he nurtured my love of art* **encourage**, promote, stimulate, develop, foster, cultivate, boost, strengthen, fuel.
- OPPOSITES neglect.

nut noun (*informal*) **1 maniac**, lunatic, madman, madwoman; *informal* loony, nutcase, head case; *Brit. informal* nutter; *N. Amer. informal* screwball. **2 enthusiast**, fan, devotee, aficionado; *informal* freak, fanatic, addict, buff.

nutritious adjective **nourishing**, nutritive, wholesome, good for you, healthy, health-giving, beneficial.

Oo

oath noun **1 vow**, pledge, promise, affirmation, word (of honour), guarantee. **2 swear word**, expletive, profanity, four-letter word, dirty word, obscenity, curse; *formal* imprecation.

obedient adjective **compliant**, biddable, acquiescent, good, law-abiding, deferential, governable, docile, submissive.
- OPPOSITES rebellious.

obey verb **1 do as you are told**, defer to, submit to, bow to. **2** *he refused to obey the order* **carry out**, perform, act on, execute, discharge, implement. **3** *rules have to be obeyed* **comply with**, adhere to, observe, abide by, act in accordance with, conform to, respect, follow, keep to, stick to.
- OPPOSITES defy, ignore.

object noun **1 thing**, article, item, entity, device, gadget. **2 target**, butt, focus, recipient, victim. **3 objective**, aim, goal, target, purpose, end, plan, point, ambition, intention, idea.
● verb *they objected to the scheme* **protest about**, oppose, take exception to, take issue with, take a stand against, argue against, quarrel with, condemn, draw the line at, demur at, mind, complain about.
- OPPOSITES approve of, accept.

objection noun **protest**, protestation, complaint, opposition, demurral, counter-argument, disagreement, disapproval, dissent.

objective adjective **1 impartial**, unbiased, unprejudiced, non-partisan, disinterested, neutral, uninvolved, even-handed, fair, dispassionate, detached. **2 factual**, actual, real, empirical, verifiable.
- OPPOSITES subjective, emotional.
● noun **aim**, intention, purpose, target, goal, object, end, idea, plan, ambition.

objectively adverb **impartially**, without bias/prejudice, even-handedly, fairly, dispassionately, with an open mind, without fear or favour.

obligation noun **1 commitment**, duty, responsibility, function, task, job, charge, onus, liability, requirement, debt. **2** *a sense of obligation* **duty**, compulsion, indebtedness, necessity, pressure, constraint.

obligatory adjective **compulsory**, mandatory, prescribed, required, statutory, enforced, binding, requisite, necessary, imperative, de rigueur.
- OPPOSITES optional.

oblige verb **1 compel**, force, require, make, bind, constrain. **2 do someone a favour**, accommodate, help, assist, indulge, humour.

obliged adjective **thankful**, grateful, appreciative, beholden, indebted, in someone's debt.

obliging adjective **helpful**, accommodating, cooperative, agreeable, amenable, generous, kind; *Brit. informal* decent.

obliterate verb **1 destroy**, wipe out, annihilate, demolish; *informal* zap. **2 hide**, obscure, blot out, block, cover, screen.

oblivious adjective **unaware**, unconscious, heedless, unmindful, insensible, ignorant, blind, deaf, impervious.
- OPPOSITES conscious.

obscene adjective **1 pornographic**, indecent, smutty, dirty, filthy, X-rated, explicit, lewd, rude, vulgar, coarse, scatological; *informal* blue; *euphemistic* adult. **2 scandalous**, shocking, outrageous, immoral.

obscure adjective **1 unclear**, uncertain, unknown, mysterious, hazy, vague, indeterminate. **2 abstruse**, oblique, opaque, cryptic, arcane, enigmatic, puzzling, perplexing, baffling, incomprehensible, impenetrable, elliptical.

3 little known, unknown, unheard of, unsung, minor, unrecognized, forgotten.
- OPPOSITES clear, plain, famous.
● verb **1 hide**, conceal, cover, veil, shroud, screen, mask, cloak, block, obliterate, eclipse. **2 confuse**, complicate, obfuscate, cloud, blur, muddy.
- OPPOSITES reveal, clarify.

observant adjective **alert**, sharp-eyed, eagle-eyed, attentive, watchful; informal beady-eyed, on the ball.
- OPPOSITES inattentive.

observation noun **1 monitoring**, watching, scrutiny, survey, surveillance, attention, study. **2 remark**, comment, opinion, impression, thought, reflection.

observe verb **1 notice**, see, note, perceive, discern, spot. **2 watch**, look at, contemplate, view, survey, regard, keep an eye on, scrutinize, keep under surveillance, monitor; informal keep tabs on. **3 remark**, comment, say, mention, declare, announce, state; formal opine. **4 comply with**, abide by, keep, obey, adhere to, heed, honour, fulfil, respect, follow, consent to, accept.

observer noun **spectator**, onlooker, watcher, fly on the wall, viewer, witness.

obsessed adjective **fixated**, possessed, haunted, consumed, infatuated, besotted; informal smitten, hung up.

obsession noun **fixation**, passion, mania, compulsion, fetish, preoccupation, infatuation, hobby horse, phobia, complex, neurosis; informal bee in your bonnet, hang-up, thing.

obsessive adjective **consuming**, all-consuming, compulsive, controlling, fanatical, neurotic, excessive; informal pathological.

obsolete adjective **out of date**, outdated, outmoded, old-fashioned, passé, antiquated, antediluvian, anachronistic, superannuated, archaic, ancient, fossilized, extinct, defunct; informal out of the ark; Brit. informal past its sell-by date.
- OPPOSITES current, modern.

obstacle noun **barrier**, hurdle, stumbling block, obstruction, bar, block, impediment, hindrance, snag, catch, drawback, hitch, fly in the ointment, handicap, difficulty, problem, disadvantage; Brit. spanner in the works.
- OPPOSITES advantage, aid.

obstinate adjective **stubborn**, pig-headed, mulish, self-willed, unyielding, inflexible, unbending, intransigent, intractable; old use contumacious.
- OPPOSITES compliant.

obstruct verb **1 block (up)**, clog (up), cut off, bung up, choke, dam up; technical occlude. **2 impede**, hinder, interfere with, hamper, block, interrupt, hold up, stand in the way of, frustrate, slow down, delay, bring to a standstill, stop, halt.
- OPPOSITES clear, facilitate.

obstruction noun **obstacle**, barrier, stumbling block, impediment, hindrance, difficulty, check, restriction, blockage, stoppage, congestion, bottleneck, hold-up.

obtain verb **get**, acquire, come by, secure, procure, pick up, gain, earn, achieve, attain; informal get hold of, lay your hands on, land.

obtainable adjective **available**, to be had, in circulation, on the market, on offer, in season, at your disposal, accessible; informal up for grabs, on tap.

obvious adjective **clear**, plain, evident, apparent, patent, manifest, conspicuous, pronounced, prominent, distinct, noticeable, unmistakable, perceptible, visible, palpable; informal sticking out a mile.
- OPPOSITES imperceptible.

occasion noun **1 time**, instance, juncture, point, moment, experience, case. **2 event**, affair, function, celebration, party, get-together, gathering; informal do, bash.
● verb **cause**, give rise to, bring about, result in, lead to, prompt, create, engender.

occasional adjective **infrequent**, intermittent, irregular, periodic, sporadic,

odd; *N. Amer.* sometime.
- OPPOSITES regular, frequent.

occasionally *adverb* **sometimes**, from time to time, (every) now and then, (every) now and again, at times, every so often, (every) once in a while, on occasion, periodically.
- OPPOSITES often.

occult *adjective* **supernatural**, magic, magical, satanic, mystical, unearthly, esoteric, psychic.
☐ **the occult** the supernatural, magic, black magic, witchcraft, necromancy, the black arts, occultism.

occupant *noun* **resident**, inhabitant, owner, householder, tenant, leaseholder, lessee; *Brit.* occupier, owner-occupier.

occupation *noun* **1 job**, profession, work, line of work, trade, employment, business, career, métier, calling. **2 pastime**, activity, hobby, pursuit, interest, entertainment, recreation. **3 conquest**, capture, invasion, seizure, annexation, colonization, subjugation.

occupied *adjective* **1 busy**, working, at work, active; *informal* tied up, hard at it, on the go. **2 in use**, full, engaged, taken.

occupy *verb* **1 live in**, inhabit, lodge in, tenant, move into, people, populate, settle; *Scottish* stay in. **2 engage**, busy, distract, absorb, engross, hold, interest, involve, entertain. **3** *the region was occupied by Japan* **capture**, seize, conquer, invade, colonize, annex, subjugate.

occur *verb* **1 happen**, take place, come about, transpire; *N. Amer. informal* go down. **2 be found**, be present, exist, appear, develop, manifest itself.
☐ **occur to** enter your head, cross your mind, come/spring to mind, strike, dawn on, suggest itself.

occurrence *noun* **1 event**, incident, happening, phenomenon, circumstance, episode. **2 existence**, instance, appearance, frequency, incidence, prevalence, rate; *Statistics* distribution.

odd *adjective* **1 strange**, peculiar, queer, funny, bizarre, eccentric, unconventional, outlandish, unusual, weird, curious, abnormal, puzzling, mystifying, baffling, unaccountable; *informal* wacky. **2** *odd jobs* **occasional**, casual, irregular, isolated, sporadic, periodic, miscellaneous, various, varied, sundry. **3** *an odd shoe* **mismatched**, unmatched, unpaired, single, lone, solitary, extra, leftover, spare.
- OPPOSITES normal, ordinary, regular.

odds *plural noun* **likelihood**, probability, chances.
☐ **odds and ends** bits and pieces, bits and bobs, stuff, paraphernalia, sundries, bric-a-brac, knick-knacks, oddments; *informal* junk; *Brit. informal* odds and sods, clobber, gubbins.

odour *noun* **smell**, stench, stink, reek, aroma, bouquet, scent, perfume, fragrance; *Brit. informal* pong, whiff, niff; *N. Amer. informal* funk; *literary* redolence.

> **WORD LINKS**
> **olfactory** relating to odour

odyssey *noun* **journey**, voyage, trip, trek, travels, quest, crusade, pilgrimage.

off *adjective* **1 away**, absent, off duty, on holiday/leave; *N. Amer.* on vacation. **2 cancelled**, postponed, called off. **3 rotten**, bad, stale, mouldy, sour, rancid, turned, spoiled.

offence *noun* **1 crime**, illegal act, misdemeanour, felony, infringement, violation, wrongdoing, sin. **2 annoyance**, resentment, indignation, displeasure, bad feeling, animosity.

offend *verb* **1 upset**, give offence to, affront, hurt someone's feelings, insult, hurt, wound, slight. **2 break the law**, commit a crime, do wrong.

offender *noun* **wrongdoer**, criminal, lawbreaker, crook, villain, miscreant, felon, delinquent, malefactor, culprit, guilty party.

offensive *adjective* **1 insulting**, rude, derogatory, disrespectful, personal,

hurtful, upsetting, wounding, abusive.
2 unpleasant, disagreeable, nasty,
distasteful, objectionable, off-putting,
dreadful, frightful, obnoxious, abominable, disgusting, repulsive, repellent,
vile, foul, horrible, sickening, nauseating; *informal* ghastly, horrid, gross; *Brit.
informal* beastly. **3 hostile**, attacking,
aggressive, invading, incursive, combative, threatening, martial, warlike,
belligerent, bellicose.
- OPPOSITES complimentary, pleasant,
defensive.
  ● *noun* **attack**, assault, onslaught,
  invasion, push, thrust, charge, raid,
  incursion, blitz, campaign.

offer *verb* **1 put forward**, proffer,
give, present, come up with, suggest,
propose, advance, submit, tender.
2 volunteer, step/come forward,
show willing. **3 bid**, tender, put in a
bid/offer of.
- OPPOSITES withdraw, refuse.
  ● *noun* **1 proposal**, proposition,
  suggestion, submission, approach,
  overture. **2 bid**, tender, bidding price.

offering *noun* **contribution**, donation,
gift, present, sacrifice, tribute.

offhand *adjective* **casual**, careless, uninterested, indifferent, cool, nonchalant,
blasé, insouciant, cavalier, glib, perfunctory, cursory, dismissive.

office *noun* **1 place of work**, workplace,
workroom. **2** *the company's Paris office*
branch, division, section, bureau,
department. **3** *the office of President*
post, position, appointment, job, occupation, role, situation, function.

officer *noun* **official**, functionary,
executive.

official *adjective* **1 authorized**,
approved, validated, authenticated,
certified, accredited, endorsed, sanctioned, licensed, recognized, legitimate, legal, lawful, valid, bona fide,
proper; *informal* kosher. **2 ceremonial**,
formal, solemn, bureaucratic.
- OPPOSITES unauthorized, informal.
  ● *noun* **officer**, executive, functionary,
  administrator, bureaucrat, mandarin,

representative, agent; *derogatory*
apparatchik.

officious *adjective* **self-important**,
bumptious, self-assertive, overbearing,
interfering, intrusive, meddlesome,
meddling; *informal* bossy.

offset *verb* **counteract**, balance (out),
even out/up, counterbalance, compensate for, make up for, neutralize, cancel
(out).

offspring *noun* **children**, family, progeny, young, brood, descendants, heirs,
successors; *informal* kids; *Brit. informal*
sprogs, brats.

often *adverb* **frequently**, many times, a
lot, repeatedly, again and again, time
after time, regularly, commonly, generally, ordinarily; *N. Amer.* oftentimes.
- OPPOSITES seldom.

oily *adjective* **greasy**, fatty, buttery, rich,
oleaginous.

ointment *noun* **lotion**, cream, salve,
liniment, embrocation, rub, gel, balm,
emollient, unguent.

OK, okay *(informal) adjective* **1 satisfactory**, all right, acceptable, competent,
adequate, tolerable, passable, reasonable, decent, fair, not bad, average,
middling, moderate, unremarkable,
unexceptional; *informal* so-so, fair-to-
middling. **2 permissible**, allowable,
acceptable, all right, in order, permitted, fitting, suitable, appropriate.
- OPPOSITES unsatisfactory.
  ● *noun* **authorization**, (seal of)
  approval, agreement, consent, assent,
  permission, endorsement, ratification,
  sanction, blessing, leave; *informal* the
  go-ahead, the green light, the thumbs
  up, say-so.

old *adjective* **1** *old people* **elderly**, aged,
older, senior, venerable, in your dotage,
past your prime, long in the tooth,
grizzled, ancient, decrepit, doddery,
senescent, senile; *informal* getting on,
past it, over the hill. **2** *old clothes* **worn**,
shabby, threadbare, frayed, patched,
tattered, moth-eaten, ragged; *informal*
tatty. **3** *the old days* **bygone**, olden,
past, prehistoric, primitive. **4** *old cars*

antique, veteran, vintage, classic.
5 *an old girlfriend* **former**, previous, earlier, past, ex-, one-time, sometime, erstwhile; *formal* quondam.
- OPPOSITES young, new, modern, current.

> WORD LINKS
> **geriatric** relating to old people

old-fashioned *adjective* **out of date**, outdated, dated, out of fashion, outmoded, unfashionable, passé, outworn, behind the times, antiquated, antediluvian, archaic, obsolescent, obsolete, superannuated; *informal* out of the ark, old hat, clunky.
- OPPOSITES modern.

omen *noun* **portent**, sign, signal, token, forewarning, warning, harbinger, presage, indication; *literary* foretoken.

ominous *adjective* **threatening**, menacing, baleful, forbidding, foreboding, fateful, sinister, black, dark, gloomy.
- OPPOSITES promising.

omission *noun* **1 exclusion**, leaving out, deletion, elimination. **2 negligence**, neglect, dereliction, oversight, lapse, failure.

omit *verb* **1 leave out**, exclude, miss out, miss, cut, drop, skip. **2 forget**, neglect, overlook, fail.
- OPPOSITES include, remember.

once *adverb* **1 on one occasion**, one time. **2 formerly**, previously, in the past, once upon a time, in days/times gone by, in the (good) old days, long ago.
● *conjunction* **as soon as**, the moment, when, after.
□ **at once 1** immediately, right away, right now, straight away, instantly, directly, forthwith, without delay, without further ado. **2** at the same time, (all) together, simultaneously, as a group, in unison.

one-sided *adjective* **1 biased**, prejudiced, partisan, partial, slanted, distorted, unfair. **2 unequal**, uneven, unbalanced.
- OPPOSITES impartial, equal.

ongoing *adjective* **in progress**, under way, going on, continuing, proceeding.

onlooker *noun* **eyewitness**, witness, observer, spectator, bystander; *informal* rubberneck.

only *adverb* **1 at most**, at best, just, no more than, hardly, barely, scarcely. **2 exclusively**, solely, purely.
● *adjective* **sole**, single, one (and only), solitary, lone, unique, exclusive.

onset *noun* **start**, beginning, commencement, arrival, appearance, inception, day one, outbreak; *informal* kick-off.
- OPPOSITES end.

onslaught *noun* **attack**, assault, offensive, advance, charge, blitz, bombardment, barrage.

onus *noun* **burden**, responsibility, obligation, duty, weight, load.

ooze *verb* **seep**, discharge, flow, exude, trickle, drip, dribble, drain, leak.

opaque *adjective* **1 non-transparent**, cloudy, filmy, blurred, smeared, misty. **2 obscure**, unclear, unfathomable, incomprehensible, unintelligible, impenetrable; *informal* as clear as mud.
- OPPOSITES transparent, clear.

open *adjective* **1 unlocked**, unlatched, off the latch, ajar, gaping, yawning. **2** *open countryside | open spaces* **unenclosed**, rolling, sweeping, wide open, exposed, spacious, uncrowded, uncluttered, undeveloped. **3** *the position is still open* **available**, free, vacant, unfilled; *informal* up for grabs. **4** *open to abuse* **vulnerable**, subject, susceptible, liable, exposed, an easy target for. **5** *she was very open* **frank**, candid, honest, forthcoming, communicative, forthright, direct, unreserved, plain-spoken, outspoken, blunt; *informal* upfront. **6** *open hostility* **overt**, manifest, conspicuous, plain, undisguised, unconcealed, clear, naked, blatant, flagrant, barefaced, brazen.
- OPPOSITES shut, closed.
● *verb* **1 unfasten**, unlock, unbolt, throw wide. **2 unwrap**, undo, untie. **3 spread out**, unfold, unfurl, unroll,

straighten out. **4 begin**, start, commence, initiate, set in motion, get going, get under way, get off the ground; *informal* kick off.
- OPPOSITES close, shut.

> **WORD LINKS**
> **agoraphobia** fear of open spaces

open-air *adjective* **outdoor**, out-of-doors, outside, alfresco.

opening *noun* **1 hole**, gap, aperture, space, orifice, vent, crack, slit, chink, fissure, cleft, crevice, interstice. **2 beginning**, start, commencement, outset; *informal* kick-off. **3 vacancy**, position, post, job, opportunity.
● *adjective* **first**, initial, introductory, preliminary, maiden, inaugural.
- OPPOSITES final, closing.

openly *adverb* **1 publicly**, blatantly, flagrantly, overtly. **2 frankly**, candidly, explicitly, honestly, sincerely, forthrightly, freely.

open-minded *adjective* **unbiased**, unprejudiced, neutral, objective, disinterested, tolerant, liberal, permissive, broad-minded.
- OPPOSITES prejudiced, narrow-minded.

operate *verb* **1 work**, run, use, handle, control, manage, drive, steer, manoeuvre, function, go, perform. **2 direct**, control, manage, run, handle, be in control/charge of.

operation *noun* **1 functioning**, working, running, performance, action. **2** *a military operation* **action**, exercise, undertaking, enterprise, manoeuvre, campaign. **3 business**, enterprise, company, firm.

operational *adjective* **running**, up and running, working, functioning, operative, in operation, in use, in action, in working order, serviceable, functional.

operative *adjective* **running**, up and running, working, functioning, operational, in operation, in use, in action, in effect.
● *noun* **1 machinist**, operator, mechanic, engineer, worker, workman,

(factory) hand. **2 agent**, secret/undercover agent, spy, mole, plant; *N. Amer. informal* spook.

opinion *noun* **belief**, thought(s), idea, way of thinking, feeling, mind, view, point of view, viewpoint, standpoint, assessment, estimation, judgement, conviction.

opponent *noun* **1 rival**, adversary, competitor, enemy, antagonist, combatant, contender, challenger; *literary* foe. **2 critic**, objector, dissenter.
- OPPOSITES ally, supporter.

opportunity *noun* **chance**, time, occasion, moment, opening, option, window, possibility, scope, freedom; *informal* shot, break, look-in.

oppose *verb* **be against**, object to, be hostile to, disagree with, disapprove of, resist, take a stand against, put up a fight against, fight, counter, challenge, take issue with.
- OPPOSITES support.

opposed *adjective*
☐ **opposed to** against, dead set against, averse to, hostile to, antagonistic to, antipathetic to; *informal* anti.

opposing *adjective* **1 conflicting**, contrasting, opposite, incompatible, irreconcilable, contradictory, clashing, at variance, at odds, opposed. **2 rival**, opposite, enemy, competing.
- OPPOSITES similar, allied.

opposite *adjective* **1 facing**, face to face with, across from. **2 conflicting**, contrasting, incompatible, irreconcilable, contradictory, at variance, at odds, differing. **3 rival**, opposing, competing, enemy.
● *noun* **reverse**, converse, antithesis, contrary.
- OPPOSITES same.

opposition *noun* **1 resistance**, hostility, antagonism, antipathy, objection, dissent, disapproval. **2 opponent(s)**, opposing side, competition, rival(s), adversary.
- OPPOSITES agreement.

oppress *verb* **persecute**, tyrannize, crush, repress, subjugate, subdue, keep down, rule with a rod of iron.

oppression *noun* **persecution**, abuse, ill-treatment, tyranny, repression, suppression, subjugation, cruelty, brutality, injustice.
- OPPOSITES freedom.

oppressive *adjective* **1 harsh**, cruel, brutal, repressive, tyrannical, despotic, draconian, ruthless, merciless, pitiless. **2 muggy**, close, heavy, hot, humid, sticky, airless, stuffy, stifling, sultry.
- OPPOSITES lenient, fresh.

opt *verb* **choose**, select, pick, decide, elect; (**opt for**) go for, settle on, plump for.

optimistic *adjective* **1 positive**, confident, hopeful, sanguine, bullish, buoyant, upbeat. **2 encouraging**, promising, reassuring, favourable.
- OPPOSITES pessimistic, depressing.

optimum *adjective* **best**, most favourable, most advantageous, ideal, perfect, prime, optimal.

option *noun* **choice**, preference, alternative, selection, possibility.

optional *adjective* **voluntary**, non-compulsory, elective, discretionary.
- OPPOSITES compulsory.

opulent *adjective* **luxurious**, sumptuous, palatial, lavishly appointed, rich, splendid, magnificent, grand, fancy; *informal* plush; *Brit. informal* swish; *N. Amer. informal* swank.
- OPPOSITES spartan.

oral *adjective* **spoken**, verbal, unwritten, vocal, uttered.
- OPPOSITES written.

orbit *noun* **circuit**, course, path, track, trajectory, rotation, revolution.
● *verb* **circle**, go round, revolve round, travel round, circumnavigate.

orchestra *noun* **ensemble**, group; *informal* band, combo.

orchestrate *verb* **organize**, arrange, plan, set up, mobilize, mount, stage, mastermind, coordinate, direct.

ordain *verb* **1 confer holy orders on**, admit to the priesthood, appoint, anoint, consecrate. **2 determine**,

predestine, preordain, predetermine, prescribe, designate.

ordeal *noun* **trial**, hardship, suffering, nightmare, trauma, hell, torture, torment, agony.

order *noun* **1** *alphabetical order* **sequence**, arrangement, organization, codification, classification, system, series, succession. **2** *some semblance of order* **tidiness**, neatness, orderliness, method, symmetry, uniformity, regularity, routine. **3** *the police managed to keep order* **peace**, control, law and order, calm. **4** *in good order* **condition**, state, repair, shape, situation; *Brit. informal* nick. **5** *I had to obey orders* **command**, instruction, directive, direction, decree, edict, injunction, dictate. **6** *the lower orders of society* **class**, level, rank, grade, caste. **7** *a religious order* **community**, brotherhood, sisterhood. **8** *the Orange Order* **organization**, association, society, fellowship, fraternity, lodge, guild, league, union, club.
- OPPOSITES chaos.
● *verb* **1 instruct**, tell, command, direct, charge, require, enjoin, ordain, decree, rule. **2 request**, apply for, book, reserve, requisition. **3 organize**, arrange, sort out, lay out, group, classify, categorize, catalogue.

orderly *adjective* **1 neat**, tidy, well ordered, in order, trim, in apple-pie order, shipshape. **2 organized**, efficient, methodical, systematic, coherent, structured, logical. **3 well behaved**, law-abiding, disciplined, peaceful, peaceable.
- OPPOSITES untidy, unruly.

ordinary *adjective* **1 usual**, normal, standard, typical, common, customary, habitual, everyday, regular, routine, day-to-day, quotidian. **2 average**, run-of-the-mill, typical, middle-of-the-road, conventional, humdrum, unremarkable, unexceptional, pedestrian, prosaic, workday; *informal* bog-standard; *Brit. informal* common or garden; *N. Amer. informal* garden-variety.
- OPPOSITES unusual.

organ noun **newspaper**, paper, journal, periodical, magazine, voice, mouthpiece.

organic adjective **1** organic matter **living**, live, animate, biological. **2** organic vegetables **natural**, chemical-free, pesticide-free, bio-. **3** an organic whole **structured**, organized, coherent, integrated, coordinated, ordered, harmonious.

organism noun **living thing**, being, creature, animal, plant, life form.

organization noun **1 planning**, arrangement, coordination, organizing, running, management. **2 structure**, arrangement, plan, pattern, order, form, format, framework, composition. **3 institution**, body, group, company, concern, firm, business, corporation, conglomerate, consortium, syndicate, agency, association, society; informal outfit.

organize verb **1 order**, arrange, sort, assemble, marshal, put straight, group, classify, collate, categorize, catalogue, codify. **2 arrange**, coordinate, sort out, put together, fix up, set up, lay on, orchestrate, see to, mobilize.

orient, orientate verb **1** you need time to orient yourself **acclimatize**, familiarize, adjust, accustom, find your feet, get your bearings. **2 aim**, direct, pitch, design, intend. **3 align**, place, position, arrange.

origin noun **1 beginning**, start, genesis, birth, dawning, dawn, emergence, creation, source, basis, cause, root(s), derivation, provenance. **2 descent**, ancestry, parentage, pedigree, lineage, line (of descent), heritage, birth, extraction, family, roots.

original adjective **1 indigenous**, aboriginal, native, first, earliest, early, ur-. **2 authentic**, genuine, actual, true, bona fide. **3 innovative**, creative, imaginative, inventive, new, novel, fresh, unusual, unconventional, unorthodox, groundbreaking, disruptive, pioneering, unique, distinctive; informal edgy.
● noun **prototype**, source, master.

originally adverb **at first**, in the beginning, to begin with, initially, in the first place, at the outset.

originate verb **1 arise**, have its origin, begin, start, stem, spring, emerge, emanate. **2 invent**, create, devise, think up, dream up, conceive, formulate, form, develop, produce, mastermind, pioneer.

ornament noun **1 knick-knack**, trinket, bauble, gewgaw; N. Amer. informal kickshaw. **2 decoration**, adornment, embellishment, ornamentation, trimming, accessories, frills.

ornamental adjective **decorative**, fancy, ornate, ornamented, attractive.

ornate adjective **elaborate**, decorated, embellished, adorned, ornamented, rococo, fancy, fussy, ostentatious, showy; informal flashy.
- OPPOSITES plain.

orthodox adjective **1 conventional**, mainstream, conformist, established, traditional, traditionalist, prevalent, popular, conservative, received. **2** an orthodox Muslim **observant**, devout, strict.
- OPPOSITES unconventional.

oscillate verb **1 swing to and fro**, swing back and forth, sway. **2 waver**, swing, fluctuate, alternate, see-saw, yo-yo, vacillate.

ostentatious adjective **showy**, conspicuous, flamboyant, gaudy, brash, vulgar, loud, extravagant, fancy, ornate, rococo; informal flash, flashy, bling-bling, over the top, OTT, glitzy.
- OPPOSITES restrained.

ostracize verb **exclude**, shun, spurn, cold-shoulder, reject, ignore, snub, cut dead, blackball, blacklist; Brit. send to Coventry; informal freeze out; Brit. informal blank.

other adjective **1 alternative**, different, distinct, separate, various. **2 more**, further, additional, extra, fresh, new, added, supplementary.

oust verb **expel**, drive out, force out, eject, get rid of, depose, topple, unseat, overthrow, bring down, over-turn, dismiss, dislodge.

outbreak noun **1 eruption**, flare-up, upsurge, rash, wave, spate, burst, flurry. **2 start**, beginning, commencement, onset.

outburst noun **eruption**, explosion, flare-up, storm, outpouring, burst, surge, fit, paroxysm, spasm.

outcome noun **result**, end result, net result, consequence, upshot, conclusion, end product; informal pay-off.

outcry noun **protest**, protestation, complaints, objections, furore, hue and cry, fuss, uproar, opposition, dissent; informal hullabaloo, ructions, stink.

outdated adjective **old-fashioned**, out of date, outmoded, out of fashion, unfashionable, dated, passé, old, behind the times, antiquated; informal out, old hat, square, clunky.
- OPPOSITES modern.

outdo verb **surpass**, outshine, over-shadow, eclipse, outclass, outmanoeu-vre, put in the shade, upstage, exceed, transcend, top, cap, beat, better; informal be a cut above.

outdoor adjective **open-air**, out-of-doors, outside, alfresco.
- OPPOSITES indoor.

outer adjective **1 outside**, outermost, outward, exterior, external, surface. **2 outlying**, distant, remote, faraway, far-flung, furthest.
- OPPOSITES inner.

outfit noun **1 costume**, suit, uniform, ensemble, clothes, clothing, dress, garb; informal get-up, gear; Brit. informal kit. **2** (informal) **organization**, enterprise, company, firm, business, group, body, team; informal set-up.

outgoing adjective **1 extrovert**, uninhibited, unreserved, demonstra-tive, affectionate, warm, sociable, gregarious, convivial, lively, expansive. **2 departing**, retiring, leaving.
- OPPOSITES introverted, incoming.

outgoings plural noun **expenses**, expenditure, spending, outlay,

payments, costs, overheads.

outing noun **trip**, excursion, jaunt, expedition, day out, tour, drive, ride, run; informal spin, junket.

outlaw noun **fugitive**, bandit, robber.
● verb **ban**, bar, prohibit, forbid, make illegal, proscribe.
- OPPOSITES permit.

outlet noun **1 vent**, way out, outfall, opening, channel, conduit, duct. **2 market**, shop, store.

outline noun **1 silhouette**, profile, shape, contours, form, lines. **2 rough idea**, thumbnail sketch, rundown, sum-mary, synopsis, résumé, precis, gist, bare bones.
● verb **rough out**, sketch out, draft, summarize, precis.

outlook noun **1 point of view**, view-point, way of thinking, perspective, attitude, standpoint, stance, frame of mind. **2 view**, vista, prospect, pano-rama. **3 prospects**, future, expecta-tions, prognosis.

out of date adjective **1 old-fashioned**, outmoded, outdated, dated, old, passé, behind the times, obsolete, antiquated, anachronistic, antediluvian; informal old hat, clunky. **2 expired**, lapsed, invalid, void.
- OPPOSITES fashionable, valid, current.

output noun **production**, yield, prod-uct, productivity, work, result.

outrage noun **1 indignation**, fury, anger, rage, wrath, annoyance; literary ire. **2 scandal**, offence, insult, affront, disgrace, atrocity.
● verb **enrage**, infuriate, incense, anger, scandalize, offend, affront, shock.

outrageous adjective **1 shocking**, dis-graceful, scandalous, atrocious, appall-ing, dreadful, insufferable, intolerable. **2 exaggerated**, improbable, preposter-ous, ridiculous, unwarranted.

outright adverb **1 completely**, entirely, wholly, totally, categorically, absolutely, utterly, flatly, unreservedly, out of hand. **2 explicitly**, directly, frankly, candidly, bluntly, plainly, to someone's

face; *Brit. informal* straight up.
3 instantly, instantaneously, immediately, at once, straight away, then and there, on the spot.
● *adjective* **1 complete**, absolute, out-and-out, downright, utter, sheer, categorical. **2 definite**, unequivocal, unmistakable, clear.

outset *noun* **start**, starting point, beginning, inception; *informal* the word go.
- OPPOSITES end.

outside *noun* **exterior**, case, skin, shell, covering, facade.
● *adjective* **1 exterior**, external, outer, outdoor, out-of-doors. **2 independent**, freelance, consultant, external.
● *adverb* **outdoors**, out of doors, alfresco.
- OPPOSITES inside.

outsider *noun* **stranger**, visitor, foreigner, alien, interloper, immigrant, incomer, newcomer.

outskirts *plural noun* **edges**, fringes, margins, suburbs, suburbia, environs, borders, periphery.

outspoken *adjective* **forthright**, direct, candid, frank, straightforward, open, straight from the shoulder, plain-spoken, blunt.

outstanding *adjective* **1 excellent**, marvellous, fine, magnificent, superb, wonderful, superlative, exceptional, pre-eminent, renowned, celebrated; *informal* great, terrific, tremendous, super; *Brit. informal* brilliant; *N. Amer. informal* neat. **2 to be done**, undone, unfinished, incomplete, remaining, pending. **3 unpaid**, unsettled, owing, owed, to be paid, payable, due, overdue; *N. Amer.* delinquent.

outward *adjective* **external**, surface, superficial, seeming, apparent, ostensible.
- OPPOSITES inward.

outweigh *verb* **be greater than**, exceed, be superior to, prevail over, override, supersede, offset, cancel out, outbalance, compensate for.

outwit *verb* **outsmart**, outmanoeuvre, steal a march on, trick, get the better

of; *informal* pull a fast one on, put one over on.

ovation *noun* **applause**, round of applause, cheers, bravos, acclaim, standing ovation; *informal* (big) hand.

over *preposition* **1 above**, on top of, atop, covering. **2 more than**, above, in excess of, upwards of.
- OPPOSITES under.
● *adverb* **1 overhead**, past, by. **2 at an end**, finished, ended, no more, a thing of the past; *informal* finito.

overall *adjective* **total**, all-inclusive, gross, final, inclusive, complete, entire, blanket.
● *adverb* **generally (speaking)**, in general, altogether, all in all, on balance, on average, for the most part, in the main, on the whole, by and large.

overbearing *adjective* **domineering**, dominating, autocratic, tyrannical, despotic, high-handed; *informal* bossy.

overcast *adjective* **cloudy**, sunless, dark, grey, black, leaden, heavy, dull, murky.
- OPPOSITES bright.

overcome *verb* **conquer**, defeat, beat, prevail over, control, get/bring under control, master, get the better of; *informal* lick, best; *US informal* own.
● *adjective* she was overcome with excitement **overwhelmed**, moved, affected, speechless.

overdue *adjective* **1 late**, behind schedule, behind time, delayed, tardy. **2 unpaid**, unsettled, owing, owed, payable, due, outstanding, undischarged; *N. Amer.* delinquent.
- OPPOSITES early, punctual.

overflow *verb* **spill over**, flow over, brim over, well over, flood.
● *noun* **surplus**, excess, extra, remainder, overspill.

overhaul *verb* **service**, maintain, repair, mend, fix up, rebuild, renovate, recondition, refit, refurbish.

overlook *verb* **1 fail to notice**, fail to spot, miss. **2 disregard**, neglect, ignore, pass over, forget, take no notice of, make allowances for, turn a blind eye to, excuse, pardon, forgive. **3 have a view of**, look over/across, look on to, look out on.

overpower verb **overwhelm**, get the better of, overthrow, subdue, suppress, subjugate, repress, bring someone to their knees.

overpowering adjective **overwhelming**, oppressive, unbearable, unendurable, intolerable, shattering.

override verb **1 disallow**, overrule, countermand, veto, quash, overturn, overthrow, cancel, reverse, rescind, revoke, repeal. **2 outweigh**, supersede, take precedence over, take priority over, cancel out, outbalance.

overriding adjective **most important**, top, first (and foremost), predominant, principal, primary, paramount, chief, main, major, foremost, central, key.

overrule verb **countermand**, cancel, reverse, rescind, repeal, revoke, disallow, override, veto, quash, overturn, overthrow.

overrun verb **invade**, storm, occupy, swarm into, surge into, inundate, overwhelm.

overshadow verb **outshine**, eclipse, surpass, exceed, outclass, outstrip, outdo, upstage; informal be head and shoulders above.

overt adjective **undisguised**, unconcealed, plain (to see), clear, conspicuous, obvious, noticeable, manifest, patent, open, blatant.
- OPPOSITES covert.

overtake verb **1 pass**, go past, pull ahead of; Brit. overhaul. **2 outstrip**, surpass, overshadow, eclipse, outshine, outclass, exceed, top, cap. **3 befall**, happen to, come upon, hit, strike, overwhelm, overcome.

overthrow verb **oust**, remove, bring down, topple, depose, displace, unseat, defeat, conquer.
● noun **removal**, ousting, defeat, fall, collapse, demise.

overture noun **1 preliminary**, prelude, introduction, lead-in, precursor, start, beginning. **2 opening move**, approach, advances, feeler, signal.

overturn verb **1 capsize**, turn turtle, keel over, tip over, topple over, upset, turn over, knock over, upend. **2 cancel**, reverse, rescind, repeal, revoke, countermand, disallow, override, overrule, veto, quash, overthrow.

overweight adjective **fat**, obese, stout, plump, portly, chubby, pot-bellied, flabby; informal tubby; Brit. informal podgy.

overwhelm verb **1 trounce**, rout, beat hollow, conquer, crush; informal thrash, lick, wipe the floor with; US informal own. **2 overcome**, move, stir, affect, touch, strike, dumbfound, shake, leave speechless; informal bowl over, knock sideways; Brit. informal knock/hit for six.

overwhelming adjective **1 very large**, enormous, immense, inordinate, massive, huge. **2 very strong**, powerful, uncontrollable, irrepressible, irresistible, overpowering, compelling.

owe verb **be in debt (to)**, be indebted (to), be in arrears (to), be under an obligation (to).

owing adjective **unpaid**, to be paid, payable, due, overdue, undischarged, owed, outstanding, in arrears; N. Amer. delinquent.
□ **owing to** because of, as a result of, on account of, due to, as a consequence of, thanks to, in view of.

own adjective **personal**, individual, particular, private, personalized, unique.
● verb **possess**, keep, hold, be the owner of, have to your name.
□ **own up** confess, admit, acknowledge; informal come clean.

owner noun **possessor**, holder, proprietor, homeowner, freeholder, landlord, landlady.

ownership noun **possession**, freehold, proprietorship, title.

Pp

pace noun **1 step**, stride. **2 gait**, walk, march, tread. **3 speed**, rate, velocity, tempo.
● verb **walk**, step, stride, march, pound.

pacify verb **placate**, appease, calm (down), conciliate, propitiate, assuage, mollify, soothe.
- OPPOSITES enrage.

pack noun **1 packet**, container, package, box, carton, parcel. **2 group**, herd, troop, crowd, mob, band, party, set, gang, rabble, horde, throng, huddle, mass, assembly, gathering, host; informal crew, bunch.
● verb **1 fill**, load, stow, store, bundle, stuff, cram. **2 wrap (up)**, package, parcel, swathe, swaddle, encase, envelop, bundle. **3 throng**, crowd, fill, cram, jam, squash into, squeeze into.

package noun **1 parcel**, packet, box, carton. **2 collection**, bundle, combination, range, complement, raft, platform.
● verb **wrap**, gift-wrap, pack, box, seal.

packed adjective **crowded**, full, filled (to capacity), crammed, jammed, solid, teeming, seething, swarming; informal jam-packed, chock-full, chock-a-block, full to the gunwales, bursting/bulging at the seams.

packet noun **pack**, carton, container, case, package.

pact noun **agreement**, treaty, entente, protocol, deal, settlement, armistice, truce.

pad[1] noun **1 dressing**, pack, wad. **2 notebook**, notepad, writing pad, jotter; N. Amer. scratch pad.

pad[2] verb **creep**, sneak, steal, tiptoe, pussyfoot.

padded adjective **cushioned**, insulated, lined, quilted, stuffed, lagged.

padding noun **1 wadding**, cushioning, stuffing, packing, filling, lining. **2 verbiage**, wordiness; Brit. informal waffle.

paddle[1] noun **oar**, scull.
● verb **row**, pull, scull.

paddle[2] verb **splash (about)**, dabble, wade.

pagan noun & adjective **heathen**, infidel, non-Christian.

page[1] noun **folio**, sheet, side, leaf.

page[2] noun **1 errand boy**, messenger boy; N. Amer. bellboy, bellhop. **2 attendant**, pageboy, train-bearer.
● verb **call (for)**, summon, send for.

pageant noun **parade**, procession, cavalcade, tableau, spectacle, extravaganza, show.

pageantry noun **spectacle**, display, ceremony, magnificence, pomp, splendour, grandeur, show; informal razzle-dazzle, razzmatazz.

pain noun **1 suffering**, agony, torture, torment. **2 ache**, aching, soreness, throbbing, sting, twinge, stab, pang, discomfort, irritation. **3 sorrow**, grief, heartache, heartbreak, sadness, unhappiness, distress, misery, despair, agony, torment, torture. **4** he took pains to hide his feelings **care**, effort, bother, trouble.
● verb **sadden**, grieve, distress, trouble, perturb, oppress, cause anguish to.

> **WORD LINKS**
> **analgesic** pain-relieving drug
> **anaesthetic** drug that stops you feeling pain

painful adjective **1 sore**, hurting, tender, aching, throbbing. **2 disagreeable**, unpleasant, nasty, distressing, upsetting, sad, traumatic, miserable, heartbreaking, agonizing, harrowing.

painfully adverb **distressingly**, disturbingly, uncomfortably, unpleasantly, dreadfully.

painless *adjective* **1 pain-free**, without pain. **2 easy**, trouble-free, straightforward, simple, uncomplicated; *informal* child's play.
- OPPOSITES painful, difficult.

painstaking *adjective* **careful**, meticulous, thorough, assiduous, attentive, conscientious, punctilious, scrupulous, rigorous.
- OPPOSITES slapdash.

paint *noun* **colouring**, colour, tint, dye, stain, pigment, emulsion, gloss.
● *verb* **1 colour**, decorate, whitewash, airbrush, daub, smear. **2 portray**, picture, paint a picture/portrait of, depict, represent.

painting *noun* **picture**, illustration, portrayal, depiction, representation, image, artwork, canvas, oil, watercolour.

pair *noun* **set**, brace, couple, duo, two.
● *verb* **match**, put together, couple, combine.

palace *noun* **castle**, chateau, mansion, stately home, schloss.

palatable *adjective* **1 edible**, tasty, appetizing, delicious, mouth-watering, toothsome, succulent; *informal* scrumptious, yummy, scrummy, moreish. **2 pleasant**, acceptable, agreeable, to your liking.
- OPPOSITES disagreeable.

palatial *adjective* **luxurious**, magnificent, sumptuous, splendid, grand, opulent, lavish, stately, fancy; *Brit.* upmarket; *informal* plush, swanky, posh, ritzy; *Brit. informal* swish.
- OPPOSITES modest.

pale *adjective* **1 white**, pallid, pasty, wan, colourless, anaemic, washed out, peaky, ashen, sickly; *informal* like death warmed up. **2 light**, pastel, muted, subtle, soft, faded, bleached, washed out. **3 dim**, faint, weak, feeble.
- OPPOSITES ruddy, dark.
● *verb* **turn white**, turn pale, blanch, lose colour.

palpable *adjective* **1 tangible**, touchable. **2 perceptible**, visible, noticeable, discernible, detectable, observable, unmistakable, transparent, obvious, clear, plain (to see), evident, apparent, manifest, staring you in the face, written all over someone.
- OPPOSITES imperceptible.

paltry *adjective* **small**, meagre, trifling, insignificant, negligible, inadequate, insufficient, derisory, pitiful, pathetic, miserable, niggardly, beggarly; *informal* measly, piddling, poxy.
- OPPOSITES considerable.

pamper *verb* **spoil**, indulge, overindulge, cosset, mollycoddle, coddle, baby, wait on someone hand and foot.

pamphlet *noun* **brochure**, leaflet, booklet, circular; *N. Amer.* mailer, folder.

pan[1] *noun* **saucepan**, pot, bowl, frying pan, skillet.

pan[2] *verb* **swing (round)**, sweep, move, turn.

panache *noun* **flamboyance**, confidence, self-assurance, style, flair, elan, dash, verve, zest, spirit, brio, vivacity, gusto, liveliness, vitality, energy; *informal* pizzazz, oomph, zip, zing.

panel *noun* **1 console**, dashboard, instruments, controls, dials. **2 group**, team, body, committee, board.

panic *noun* **alarm**, anxiety, fear, fright, trepidation, dread, terror, hysteria, apprehension; *informal* flap, fluster, cold sweat.
- OPPOSITES calm.
● *verb* **1 be alarmed**, be scared, be afraid, take fright, be hysterical, lose your nerve, get worked up; *informal* run around like a headless chicken. **2 frighten**, alarm, scare, unnerve; *Brit. informal* put the wind up.

panorama *noun* **view**, vista, prospect, scenery, landscape, seascape, cityscape, skyline.

panoramic *adjective* **sweeping**, wide, extensive, scenic, commanding.

pant *verb* **breathe heavily**, breathe hard, puff and blow, huff and puff, gasp, heave, wheeze.

p

pants *plural noun* **1** (*Brit.*) **underpants**, briefs, boxer shorts, boxers, knickers; *N. Amer.* shorts, undershorts; *informal* panties; *dated* drawers, bloomers. **2** (*N. Amer.*) **trousers**, slacks; *Brit. informal* trews, strides, kecks; *Austral. informal* daks.

paper *noun* **1** **newspaper**, journal, gazette, periodical, tabloid, broadsheet, daily, weekly; *informal* rag. **2** **exam**, examination, test. **3** **essay**, article, monograph, thesis, work, dissertation, treatise, study, report, analysis; *N. Amer.* theme. **4** **document**, certificate, letter, file, deed, record, archive; (**papers**) paperwork, documentation. **5** *they asked us for our papers* **identification**, identity card, ID, credentials.

parable *noun* **allegory**, moral tale, fable.

parade *noun* **1** **procession**, march, cavalcade, motorcade, spectacle, display, pageant, review, tattoo; *Brit.* march past. **2** **promenade**, walkway, esplanade, mall; *N. Amer.* boardwalk; *Brit. informal* prom.
● *verb* **1** **march**, process, file, troop. **2** **strut**, swagger, stride; *N. Amer.* sashay. **3** **display**, exhibit, make a show of, flaunt, show (off), demonstrate.

paradise *noun* **1** **heaven**, the promised land, the Elysian Fields. **2** **Utopia**, Shangri-La, Eden, idyll. **3** **bliss**, heaven (on earth), ecstasy, delight, joy, happiness.
- OPPOSITES hell.

paradox *noun* **contradiction**, self-contradiction, inconsistency, incongruity, conflict, enigma, puzzle, conundrum.

paragraph *noun* **section**, division, part, portion, segment, passage, clause.

parallel *adjective* **1** **aligned**, side by side, equidistant. **2** **similar**, analogous, comparable, corresponding, like, equivalent, matching.
- OPPOSITES divergent, different.
● *noun* **1** **counterpart**, analogue, equivalent, match, twin, duplicate, mirror. **2** **similarity**, likeness, resemblance, analogy, correspondence, comparison, equivalence, symmetry.
- OPPOSITES divergence, difference.

paralyse *verb* **1** **disable**, cripple, immobilize, incapacitate; (**paralysed**) *Medicine* paraplegic, quadriplegic. **2** **bring to a standstill**, immobilize, bring to a halt, freeze, cripple, disable.

paralysis *noun* **1** **immobility**, powerlessness, incapacity; *Medicine* paraplegia, quadriplegia. **2** **shutdown**, immobilization, stoppage, gridlock, standstill, blockage.

parameter *noun* **framework**, variable, limit, boundary, limitation, restriction, criterion, guideline.

paramount *adjective* **most important**, supreme, chief, overriding, predominant, foremost, prime, primary, principal, main, key, central; *informal* number-one.

paranoid *adjective* **suspicious**, mistrustful, anxious, fearful, insecure, obsessive.

paraphrase *verb* **reword**, rephrase, express differently, rewrite, gloss.

parasite *noun* **hanger-on**, cadger, leech, passenger; *informal* freeloader, sponger, scrounger; *N. Amer. informal* mooch; *Austral./NZ informal* bludger.

parcel *noun* **package**, packet, pack, bundle, box, case, bale.
● *verb* **pack (up)**, package, wrap (up), gift-wrap, tie up, bundle up.

parched *adjective* **1** **(bone) dry**, dried up/out, arid, desiccated, dehydrated, baked, burned, scorched, withered, shrivelled. **2** **dehydrated**, dry; *informal* gasping.

pardon *noun* **1** **forgiveness**, absolution. **2** **reprieve**, amnesty, exoneration, release, acquittal, discharge.
● *verb* **1** **forgive**, absolve. **2** **exonerate**, acquit, reprieve; *informal* let off.
- OPPOSITES blame, punish.

parentage *noun* **origins**, extraction, birth, family, ancestry, lineage, heritage, pedigree, descent, blood, stock, roots.

parish noun **1 district**, community.
2 parishioners, churchgoers, congregation, fold, flock, community.

> **WORD LINKS**
> **parochial** relating to a parish

park noun **1 public garden**, recreation ground, playground. **2 parkland**, grassland, woodland, garden(s), lawns, grounds, estate.
● verb **1 leave**, position, stop, pull up. **2** (informal) **put (down)**, place, deposit, leave, stick, shove, dump; informal plonk; Brit. informal bung.

parliament noun **legislature**, assembly, chamber, house, congress, senate, diet.

parliamentary adjective **legislative**, law-making, governmental, congressional, democratic, elected.

parochial adjective **narrow-minded**, small-minded, provincial, small-town, conservative; N. Amer. informal jerkwater.
- OPPOSITES broad-minded.

parody noun **1 satire**, burlesque, lampoon, pastiche, caricature, imitation; informal spoof, take-off, send-up. **2 distortion**, travesty, misrepresentation, perversion, corruption.

parry verb **1** he parried the blow **ward off**, fend off, deflect, block. **2** I parried her questions **evade**, sidestep, avoid, dodge, field.

parson noun **priest**, minister, clergyman, vicar, rector, cleric, chaplain, pastor, curate; informal reverend, padre.

part noun **1 piece**, amount, portion, proportion, percentage, fraction; informal slice, chunk. **2 component**, bit, constituent, element, module, unit. **3 organ**, limb, member. **4 section**, division, volume, chapter, act, scene, instalment. **5 district**, neighbourhood, quarter, section, area, region. **6 role**, character. **7 involvement**, role, function, hand, responsibility, capacity, participation, contribution; informal bit.
- OPPOSITES whole.
● verb **1 separate**, divide, split, move apart. **2 leave each other**, part company, say goodbye/farewell, say your goodbyes/farewells, go your separate ways, take your leave.
- OPPOSITES join, meet.
  □ **part with** give away, give up, relinquish, forgo, surrender, hand over.
take part participate, join in, get involved, enter, play a part, play a role, be a participant, contribute, have a hand; informal get in on the act.

partial adjective **1 incomplete**, limited, qualified, imperfect, fragmentary, unfinished. **2 biased**, prejudiced, partisan, one-sided, slanted, skewed, coloured, unbalanced.
- OPPOSITES complete, unbiased.
  □ **be partial to** like, love, enjoy, be fond of, be keen on, have a soft spot for, have a taste for, have a penchant for.

partially adverb **somewhat**, to a limited extent, to a certain extent, partly, in part, up to a point, slightly.
- OPPOSITES wholly.

participant noun **participator**, contributor, party, member, entrant, competitor, player, contestant, candidate.

participate verb **take part**, join, engage, get involved, share, play a part, play a role, contribute, partake, have a hand in.

participation noun **involvement**, part, contribution, association.

particle noun **(tiny) bit**, (tiny) piece, speck, spot, fragment, sliver, splinter.

particular adjective **1 specific**, individual, certain, distinct, separate, definite, precise. **2 special**, exceptional, unusual, uncommon, notable, noteworthy, remarkable, unique. **3 fussy**, fastidious, finicky, discriminating, selective; informal pernickety, choosy, picky; Brit. informal faddy.
- OPPOSITES general, indiscriminate.
● noun **detail**, item, point, element, fact, circumstance, feature.

particularly adverb **1 especially**, specially, exceptionally, unusually, remarkably, outstandingly, uncommonly, uniquely. **2 specifically**, explicitly, expressly, in particular, especially, specially.

parting noun **farewell**, leave-taking, goodbye, adieu, departure.

partisan noun **guerrilla**, freedom fighter, resistance fighter, underground fighter, irregular.
● adjective **biased**, prejudiced, one-sided, discriminatory, partial, sectarian, factional.
- OPPOSITES neutral.

partition noun **1 division**, partitioning, separation, break-up. **2 screen**, divider, dividing wall, barrier, panel.
● verb **1 divide**, separate, split up, break up. **2 subdivide**, divide (up), separate, section off, screen off.

partly adverb **in part**, partially, somewhat, a little, up to a point, in some measure, slightly, to some extent.
- OPPOSITES wholly.

partner noun **1 colleague**, associate, co-worker, fellow worker, collaborator, comrade, teammate. **2 accomplice**, confederate, accessory, collaborator, fellow conspirator, helper; informal sidekick. **3 spouse**, husband, wife, lover, girlfriend, boyfriend, fiancé, fiancée, significant other, live-in lover, mate; Brit. informal other half.

partnership noun **1 cooperation**, association, collaboration, coalition, alliance, union, affiliation, connection. **2 company**, association, consortium, syndicate, firm, business, organization.

party noun **1 social gathering**, function, get-together, celebration, reunion, festivity, reception, soirée, social; informal bash, do. **2 group**, company, body, gang, band, crowd, pack, contingent; informal bunch, crew, load. **3 faction**, group, bloc, camp, caucus, alliance.

pass verb **1 go**, proceed, move, progress, make your way, travel. **2 overtake**, go past/by, pull ahead of, leave behind. **3 elapse**, go by, advance, wear on, roll by, tick by. **4** he passed the time reading **occupy**, spend, fill, use (up), employ, while away. **5 hand**, let

someone have, give, reach. **6** her estate passed to her grandson **be transferred**, go, be left, be bequeathed, be handed down/on, be passed on; Law devolve. **7 happen**, occur, take place. **8 come to an end**, fade (away), blow over, run its course, die out/down, finish, end, cease. **9 be successful in**, succeed in, get through; informal sail through, scrape through. **10 approve**, vote for, accept, ratify, adopt, agree to, authorize, endorse, legalize, enact; informal OK.
- OPPOSITES fail, reject.
● noun **permit**, warrant, authorization, licence.
□ **pass out** faint, lose consciousness, black out. **pass up** turn down, reject, refuse, decline, give up, forgo, let pass, miss (out on); informal give something a miss.

passable adjective **1 adequate**, all right, acceptable, satisfactory, not (too) bad, average, tolerable, fair, mediocre, middling, ordinary, indifferent, unremarkable, unexceptional; informal OK, so-so. **2 navigable**, traversable, negotiable, open, clear.

passage noun **1 journey**, voyage, crossing, transit, trip. **2 passing**, progress, advance, course, march, flow. **3 corridor**, hall, hallway. **4 alley**, alleyway, passageway, lane, path, footpath, track, thoroughfare; N. Amer. areaway. **5 extract**, excerpt, quotation, quote.

passenger noun **traveller**, commuter, fare-payer, rider, fare.

passing adjective **1 fleeting**, transient, transitory, ephemeral, brief, short-lived, temporary, momentary. **2 hasty**, rapid, hurried, brief, quick, cursory, superficial, casual, perfunctory, desultory.
● noun **1 passage**, course, progress, advance. **2 death**, demise, passing away, end, loss.

passion noun **1 intensity**, enthusiasm, fervour, eagerness, zeal, vigour, fire, energy, spirit, fanaticism. **2 love**, desire, ardour, lust, lasciviousness, lustfulness. **3 fascination**, love, mania,

obsession, preoccupation, fanaticism, fixation, compulsion, appetite, addiction; *informal* thing.
- OPPOSITES apathy.

passionate *adjective* **1 intense**, impassioned, ardent, fervent, vehement, fiery, heated, emotional, heartfelt, excited. **2 very keen**, very enthusiastic, addicted; *informal* mad, crazy, hooked. **3 amorous**, ardent, hot-blooded, loving, sexy, sensual, erotic, lustful; *informal* steamy, hot, turned on.
- OPPOSITES apathetic, cool.

passive *adjective* **1 inactive**, non-active, non-participative, uninvolved. **2 submissive**, acquiescent, unresisting, compliant, docile.
- OPPOSITES active, resistant.

past *adjective* **1 gone by**, bygone, former, previous, old, of old, olden, long-ago. **2 last**, recent, preceding. **3 previous**, former, foregoing, erstwhile, one-time, sometime, ex-, as was.
- OPPOSITES present, future.
● *noun* **history**, background, past life, life story.

paste *noun* **1 purée**, pulp, mush, spread, pâté. **2 adhesive**, glue, gum; *N. Amer.* mucilage.
● *verb* **stick**, glue, gum, fix, affix.

pastel *adjective* **pale**, soft, light, delicate, muted.
- OPPOSITES dark, bright.

pastime *noun* **hobby**, leisure activity, leisure pursuit, recreation, game, amusement, diversion, entertainment, interest.

pastor *noun* **priest**, minister, parson, clergyman, cleric, chaplain, vicar, rector, curate; *informal* reverend, padre.

pastoral *adjective* **1 rural**, country, rustic, agricultural, bucolic; *literary* Arcadian. **2 priestly**, clerical, ecclesiastical, ministerial.
- OPPOSITES urban, lay.

pasture *noun* **grassland**, grass, grazing, meadow, field; *literary* lea.

pat *verb & noun* **tap**, clap, touch, stroke.

patch *noun* **1 blotch**, mark, spot, smudge, smear, stain, streak, blemish; *informal* splodge. **2 plot**, area, piece, strip, tract, parcel, bed; *Brit.* allotment; *N. Amer.* lot. **3** *(Brit. informal)* **period**, time, spell, phase, stretch.
● *verb* **mend**, repair, sew up, stitch up, cover, reinforce.

patent *adjective* **1 obvious**, clear, plain, evident, manifest, conspicuous, blatant, barefaced, flagrant. **2 proprietary**, patented, licensed, branded.

path *noun* **1 footpath**, pathway, track, trail, bridle path, lane, towpath. **2 route**, way, course, direction, orbit, trajectory. **3 course of action**, route, road, avenue, line, approach, tack.

pathetic *adjective* **1 pitiful**, piteous, moving, touching, poignant, plaintive, wretched, heart-rending, sad. **2** *(informal)* **feeble**, woeful, sorry, poor, weak, pitiful, lamentable, deplorable, contemptible.

pathological *adjective* **1 morbid**, diseased. **2** *(informal)* **compulsive**, obsessive, inveterate, habitual, persistent, chronic, hardened, confirmed.

patience *noun* **1 forbearance**, tolerance, restraint, equanimity, understanding, indulgence. **2 perseverance**, persistence, endurance, tenacity, application, doggedness, staying power.

patient *adjective* **1 forbearing**, uncomplaining, long-suffering, resigned, stoical, calm, imperturbable, tolerant, accommodating, indulgent. **2 persevering**, persistent, tenacious, dogged, determined.
- OPPOSITES impatient.

patriotic *adjective* **nationalistic**, loyalist, loyal, chauvinistic, jingoistic, flag-waving.
- OPPOSITES traitorous.

patrol *noun* **1** *ships on patrol in the straits* **guard**, watch, vigil. **2 squad**, detachment, party, force.
● *verb* **guard**, keep watch on, police, make the rounds of, stand guard (over), defend, safeguard.

p

patron noun **1 sponsor**, backer, benefactor, contributor, subscriber, donor, philanthropist, promoter, friend, supporter; *informal* angel. **2 customer**, client, consumer, user, visitor, guest; *informal* regular.

patronage noun **1 sponsorship**, backing, funding, financing, assistance, support. **2 custom**, trade, business.

patronize verb **1 talk down to**, look down on, condescend to, treat like a child. **2 use**, buy from, shop at, be a customer/client of, deal with, frequent, support.

patronizing adjective **condescending**, supercilious, superior, imperious, scornful; *informal* uppity, high and mighty.

pattern noun **1 design**, decoration, motif, device, marking. **2 system**, order, arrangement, form, method, structure, scheme, plan, format. **3 model**, example, blueprint, criterion, standard, norm, yardstick, touchstone, benchmark.

pause noun **break**, interruption, lull, respite, breathing space, gap, interlude, adjournment, rest, wait, hesitation; *informal* let-up, breather.
● verb **stop**, break off, take a break, adjourn, rest, wait, hesitate; *informal* take a breather.

pave verb **surface**, floor, cover, tile, flag.

pavement noun **footpath**, walkway; *N. Amer.* sidewalk.

pay verb **1 reward**, reimburse, recompense, remunerate. **2 spend**, pay out; *informal* lay out, shell out, fork out, cough up; *N. Amer. informal* ante up, pony up. **3 discharge**, settle, pay off, clear. **4 be profitable**, make money, make a profit. **5 be advantageous to**, benefit, be of advantage to, be beneficial to. **6** *he will pay for his mistakes* **suffer**, be punished, atone, pay the penalty/price.
● noun **salary**, wages, payment, earnings, remuneration, fee, reimbursement, income, revenue, stipend, emolument.
□ **pay back 1** get your revenge on, get back at, get even with, settle the score. **2** repay, pay off, give back, return, reimburse, refund. **pay off** pay (in full), settle, discharge, clear, liquidate.

payable adjective **due**, owed, owing, outstanding, unpaid, overdue; *N. Amer.* delinquent.

payment noun **1 remittance**, settlement, discharge, clearance. **2 instalment**, premium. **3 salary**, wages, pay, earnings, fees, remuneration, reimbursement, income, stipend, emolument.

peace noun **1 quiet**, silence, peace and quiet, hush, stillness, still. **2 serenity**, peacefulness, tranquillity, calm, calmness, composure, ease, contentment, rest, repose. **3 treaty**, truce, ceasefire, armistice.
- OPPOSITES noise, war.

peaceful adjective **1 tranquil**, calm, restful, quiet, still, relaxing, serene, composed, placid, at ease, untroubled, unworried. **2 harmonious**, on good terms, amicable, friendly, cordial, non-violent.
- OPPOSITES noisy.

peacemaker noun **arbitrator**, arbiter, mediator, negotiator, conciliator, go-between, intermediary.

peak noun **1 summit**, top, crest, pinnacle, cap. **2 mountain**, hill, height. **3 height**, high point, pinnacle, summit, top, climax, culmination, apex, zenith, acme.
● verb **reach its height**, climax, culminate.
● adjective **maximum**, greatest, busiest, highest.

peculiar adjective **1 strange**, unusual, odd, funny, curious, bizarre, weird, eccentric, queer, abnormal, unconventional, outlandish, anomalous, out of the ordinary, unexpected, offbeat. **2** *customs peculiar to the area* **distinctive**, exclusive, unique, characteristic, distinct, individual, typical, special.
- OPPOSITES ordinary.

pedant noun **dogmatist**, purist, literalist, formalist, quibbler, hair-splitter;

informal nit-picker.

pedantic adjective **finicky**, fussy, fastidious, dogmatic, purist, hair-splitting, quibbling; informal nit-picking, pernickety.

peddle verb **sell**, hawk, tout, trade, deal in, traffic in.

pedestal noun **plinth**, base, support, mount, stand, pillar, column.
□ **put on a pedestal** idealize, look up to, hold in high regard, think highly of, admire, esteem, revere, worship.

pedestrian noun **walker**, person on foot.
● adjective **dull**, boring, tedious, monotonous, unremarkable, uninspired, unimaginative, unexciting, routine, commonplace, ordinary, everyday, run-of-the-mill, mundane, humdrum; informal bog-standard.
- OPPOSITES exciting.

pedigree noun **ancestry**, lineage, line, descent, genealogy, extraction, parentage, bloodline, family tree.
● adjective **pure-bred**, full-blooded, thoroughbred.

peek verb **1 peep**, look; informal take a gander, have a squint; Brit. informal have a dekko, take a butcher's, take a shufti. **2 appear**, show, peep (out).
● noun **look**, peep, glance, glimpse.

peel verb **1 pare**, skin, hull, shell. **2 flake (off)**, come off, fall off, strip off.
● noun **rind**, skin, covering, zest.

peep verb **peek**, look, sneak a look, glance; informal squint.
● noun **peek**, look, glance; informal squint, dekko.

peer[1] verb **look closely**, squint, gaze.

peer[2] noun **1 aristocrat**, lord, lady, noble, nobleman, noblewoman. **2 equal**, fellow, contemporary.

peeve verb (informal) **irritate**, annoy, vex, anger, irk, gall, pique, put out, nettle; informal aggravate, rile, needle, get to, bug, hack off, get someone's goat, get/put someone's back up; N. Amer. informal tee off, tick off.

peg noun **pin**, nail, dowel.
● verb **1 fix**, pin, attach, fasten, secure. **2 set**, hold, fix, limit, freeze, keep down, hold down.

pen[1] verb **write**, compose, draft, dash off, scribble.

pen[2] noun **enclosure**, fold, pound, compound, stockade, sty, coop; N. Amer. corral.
● verb **confine**, coop, cage, shut, box, lock, trap, kettle, imprison, incarcerate.

penalize verb **1 punish**, discipline. **2 handicap**, disadvantage, discriminate against.
- OPPOSITES reward.

penalty noun **punishment**, sanction, fine, forfeit, sentence.
- OPPOSITES reward.

penance noun **atonement**, expiation, amends, punishment, penalty.

penchant noun **liking**, fondness, preference, taste, appetite, partiality, love, passion, weakness, inclination, bent, proclivity, predilection, predisposition.

pending adjective **1 unresolved**, undecided, unsettled, up in the air, ongoing, outstanding; informal on the back burner. **2 imminent**, impending, about to happen, forthcoming, on the way, coming, approaching, looming, near, on the horizon, in the offing.

penetrate verb **1 pierce**, puncture, enter, perforate, stab, gore. **2 permeate**, pervade, fill, imbue, suffuse, seep through, saturate. **3 register**, sink in, become clear, fall into place; informal click.

penetrating adjective **1 cold**, cutting, biting, keen, sharp, harsh, raw, freezing, chill, bitter. **2 shrill**, strident, piercing, ear-splitting. **3 intent**, searching, piercing, probing, sharp, keen. **4 perceptive**, insightful, keen, sharp, intelligent, clever, smart, incisive, trenchant, astute.
- OPPOSITES mild, soft.

pension noun **old-age pension**, superannuation, allowance, benefit, support, welfare.

p

pensioner *noun* **retired person**, old-age pensioner, OAP, senior citizen; *N. Amer.* senior, retiree, golden ager.

people *plural noun* **1 human beings**, persons, individuals, humans, mortals, living souls, personages, {men, women, and children}; *informal* folk. **2 citizens**, subjects, electors, voters, taxpayers, residents, inhabitants, public, citizenry, nation, population, populace. **3 the common people**, the proletariat, the masses, the populace, the rank and file; *derogatory* the hoi polloi; *informal, derogatory* the proles, the plebs. **4 family**, parents, relatives, relations, folk, kinsfolk, flesh and blood, nearest and dearest; *informal* folks. **5** *(singular)* **race**, ethnic group, tribe, clan, nation.
● *verb* **populate**, settle (in), colonize, inhabit, live in, occupy.

> **WORD LINKS**
> **ethnic** relating to a people
> **anthropology** study of people

pepper *verb* **1 sprinkle**, fleck, dot, spot, stipple. **2 bombard**, pelt, shower, rain down on, strafe, rake, blitz.

perceive *verb* **1 see**, discern, detect, catch sight of, spot, observe, notice; *literary* espy. **2 regard**, look on, view, consider, think of, judge, deem.

perception *noun* **1 impression**, idea, conception, notion, thought, belief. **2 insight**, perceptiveness, understanding, intelligence, intuition, incisiveness.

perceptive *adjective* **insightful**, discerning, sensitive, intuitive, observant, penetrating, intelligent, clever, canny, keen, sharp, astute, shrewd, quick, smart, acute; *informal* on the ball; *N. Amer. informal* heads-up.
- OPPOSITES obtuse.

perch *verb* **1 sit**, rest, alight, settle, land, roost. **2 put**, place, set, rest, balance.

perennial *adjective* **lasting**, enduring, abiding, long-lasting, long-lived, perpetual, continuing, continual, recurring.
- OPPOSITES ephemeral.

perfect *adjective* **1 ideal**, model, faultless, flawless, consummate, exemplary, best, ultimate, copybook. **2 flawless**, mint, as good as new, pristine, immaculate, optimum, prime, peak; *informal* tip-top, A1. **3 exact**, precise, accurate, faithful, true; *Brit. informal* spot on; *N. Amer. informal* on the money. **4 absolute**, complete, total, real, out-and-out, thorough, downright, utter; *Brit. informal* right; *Austral./NZ informal* fair.
● *verb* **improve**, polish (up), hone, refine, brush up, fine-tune.

perfection *noun* **the ideal**, a paragon, the last word, the ultimate; *informal* the tops, the bee's knees.

perform *verb* **1 carry out**, do, execute, discharge, conduct, implement; *informal* pull off. **2 function**, work, operate, run, go, respond, behave, act. **3 stage**, put on, present, mount, act, produce. **4 play**, sing, appear.

performance *noun* **1 show**, production, showing, presentation, staging, concert, recital; *informal* gig. **2 rendition**, interpretation, playing, acting. **3 carrying out**, execution, discharge, completion, fulfilment. **4 functioning**, working, operation, running, behaviour, response.

performer *noun* **actor**, **actress**, artiste, artist, entertainer, trouper, player, musician, singer, dancer, comic, comedian, comedienne.

perfume *noun* **1 scent**, fragrance, eau de toilette, toilet water, cologne, eau de cologne. **2 smell**, scent, fragrance, aroma, bouquet, nose.

perhaps *adverb* **maybe**, for all you know, it could be, it may be, it's possible, possibly, conceivably; *N. English* happen.

peril *noun* **danger**, jeopardy, risk, hazard, menace, threat.
- OPPOSITES safety.

perimeter *noun* **boundary**, border, limits, bounds, edge, margin, fringe(s), periphery.
- OPPOSITES centre.

period *noun* **1 time**, spell, interval, stretch, term, span, phase, bout; *Brit. informal* patch. **2 era**, age, epoch, aeon, time, days, years.

periodic *adjective* **regular**, at fixed intervals, recurrent, recurring, repeated, cyclical, seasonal, occasional, intermittent, sporadic, odd.

periodical *noun* **journal**, magazine, newspaper, paper, review, newsletter, digest, gazette, organ; *informal* mag, glossy.

peripheral *adjective* **secondary**, subsidiary, incidental, tangential, marginal, minor, unimportant, ancillary.
- OPPOSITES central.

perish *verb* **1 die**, lose your life, be killed, fall, be lost; *informal* buy it. **2 go bad**, spoil, rot, decay, decompose.

perk *noun* **fringe benefit**, advantage, bonus, extra, plus; *informal* freebie.

permanent *adjective* **lasting**, enduring, indefinite, continuing, constant, perpetual, indelible, irreparable, irreversible, lifelong, perennial, established, standing, long-term, stable, secure.
- OPPOSITES temporary.

permanently *adverb* **1 forever**, for all time, for good, irreversibly, incurably, irreparably, indelibly; *informal* for keeps. **2 continually**, constantly, perpetually, always.

permission *noun* **authorization**, consent, leave, authority, sanction, licence, dispensation, assent, agreement, approval, blessing, clearance; *informal* the go-ahead, the green light, say-so.
- OPPOSITES ban.

permit *verb* **allow**, let, authorize, give permission, sanction, grant, license, consent to, assent to, agree to; *informal* give the go-ahead to, give the green light to.
- OPPOSITES forbid.
    ● *noun* **authorization**, licence, pass, ticket, warrant, passport, visa.

perpetual *adjective* **1 constant**, permanent, uninterrupted, continuous, unremitting, unending, everlasting, eternal, unceasing, without end, persistent, lasting, abiding. **2 interminable**, incessant, ceaseless, endless, relentless, unrelenting, persistent, continual, continuous, non-stop, never-ending, repeated, unremitting, round-the-clock, unabating; *informal* eternal.
- OPPOSITES temporary, intermittent.

perpetuate *verb* **keep alive**, keep going, preserve, conserve, sustain, maintain, continue, extend.

perplex *verb* **puzzle**, baffle, mystify, bemuse, bewilder, confound, confuse, nonplus, disconcert; *informal* flummox.

perplexing *adjective* **puzzling**, baffling, mystifying, mysterious, bewildering, confusing, disconcerting, worrying.

persecute *verb* **1 oppress**, abuse, victimize, ill-treat, mistreat, maltreat, torment, torture. **2 harass**, hound, plague, badger, harry, intimidate, pick on, pester; *informal* hassle.

persecution *noun* **1 oppression**, victimization, ill-treatment, mistreatment, abuse, discrimination. **2 harassment**, hounding, intimidation, bullying.

persevere *verb* **persist**, continue, carry on, go on, keep on, keep going, struggle on, hammer away, be persistent, keep at it, not take no for an answer, be tenacious, plod on, plough on; *informal* soldier on, hang on, plug away, stick to your guns, stick it out, hang in there.
- OPPOSITES give up.

persist *verb* **1** *he persisted with his questioning* **persevere**, continue, carry on, go on, keep on, keep going, hammer away, keep at it; *informal* soldier on, plug away. **2** *the dry weather persists* **continue**, hold, carry on, last, keep on, remain, linger, stay, endure.
- OPPOSITES give up, stop.

persistence *noun* **perseverance**, tenacity, determination, staying power, endurance, doggedness, stamina; *informal* stickability; *formal* pertinacity.

persistent *adjective* **1 tenacious**, determined, resolute, dogged, tireless, indefatigable, insistent, unrelenting; *formal* pertinacious. **2 constant**, continuous,

continuing, continual, non-stop, never-ending, steady, uninterrupted, unbroken, interminable, incessant, endless, unending, unrelenting. **3** *a persistent cough* **chronic**, nagging, frequent, repeated, habitual.
- OPPOSITES irresolute, intermittent.

person *noun* **human being**, individual, man, woman, human, being, living soul, mortal, creature; *informal* type, sort, beggar, cookie.
□ **in person** physically, in the flesh, personally, yourself.

personal *adjective* **1 distinctive**, characteristic, unique, individual, idiosyncratic. **2 in person**, in the flesh, actual, live, physical. **3 private**, intimate. **4 derogatory**, disparaging, belittling, insulting, rude, disrespectful, offensive, pejorative.

personality *noun* **1 character**, nature, disposition, temperament, make-up, psyche. **2 charisma**, magnetism, character, charm, presence. **3 celebrity**, VIP, star, superstar, big name, somebody, leading light, luminary, notable; *informal* celeb.

personally *adverb* **1 in person**, yourself. **2 for my part**, for myself, as far as I am concerned, from my own point of view, subjectively.

personification *noun* **embodiment**, incarnation, epitome, quintessence, essence, type, symbol, soul, model, exemplification, exemplar, image, representation.

personnel *noun* **staff**, employees, workforce, workers, labour force, manpower, human resources.

perspective *noun* **outlook**, view, viewpoint, point of view, standpoint, position, stand, stance, angle, slant, attitude.

persuade *verb* **1 prevail on**, talk into, coax, convince, get, induce, win over, bring round, influence, sway; *informal* sweet-talk. **2 cause**, lead, move, dispose, incline.
- OPPOSITES dissuade, deter.

persuasion *noun* **1 coaxing**, urging, inducement, encouragement; *informal* sweet-talking. **2 group**, grouping, sect, denomination, party, camp, side, faction, school of thought, belief, creed, faith.

persuasive *adjective* **convincing**, compelling, effective, telling, forceful, powerful, eloquent, impressive, sound, cogent, valid, strong, plausible, credible.
- OPPOSITES unconvincing.

pertain *verb* **1** *developments pertaining to the economy* **concern**, relate to, be connected with, be relevant to, apply to, refer to, have a bearing on, affect, involve, touch on. **2 exist**, be the case, prevail.

pertinent *adjective* **relevant**, to the point, apposite, appropriate, suitable, applicable, material, germane.
- OPPOSITES irrelevant.

perturb *verb* **worry**, upset, disturb, unsettle, concern, trouble, disquiet, disconcert, discomfit, unnerve, alarm, bother; *informal* rattle.
- OPPOSITES reassure.

pervade *verb* **permeate**, spread through, fill, suffuse, imbue, penetrate, filter through, infuse, inform.

pervasive *adjective* **prevalent**, pervading, extensive, ubiquitous, omnipresent, universal, widespread, general.

perverse *adjective* **1 awkward**, contrary, difficult, unreasonable, uncooperative, unhelpful, obstructive, stubborn, obstinate; *Brit. informal* bloody-minded, bolshie. **2 illogical**, irrational, wrong-headed.

perversion *noun* **1 distortion**, misrepresentation, travesty, twisting, corruption, misuse. **2 deviance**, abnormality, depravity.

pervert *verb* **distort**, warp, corrupt, subvert, twist, bend, abuse, divert.
● *noun* **deviant**, degenerate; *informal* perv, dirty old man, sicko.

perverted *adjective* **unnatural**, deviant, warped, twisted, abnormal, unhealthy, depraved, perverse, aberrant, debased, degenerate; *informal* sick, kinky.

pessimist *noun* **defeatist**, fatalist, prophet of doom, alarmist, cynic, sceptic, misery, killjoy, Cassandra; *informal* doom (and gloom) merchant, wet blanket.
- OPPOSITES optimist.

pessimistic *adjective* **gloomy**, negative, cynical, defeatist, downbeat, bleak, fatalistic, depressed.
- OPPOSITES optimistic.

pest *noun* **nuisance**, annoyance, irritant, thorn in your flesh/side, trial, menace, trouble, problem, worry, bother; *informal* pain in the neck, headache.

pester *verb* **badger**, hound, harass, plague, annoy, bother, harry, worry; *informal* hassle, bug.

pet *adjective* **1 tame**, domesticated, companion; *Brit.* house-trained; *N. Amer.* housebroken. **2 favourite**, favoured, cherished, particular, special, personal.
● *verb* **1 stroke**, caress, fondle, pat, tickle. **2 cuddle**, embrace, caress, kiss; *informal* canoodle, neck, smooch; *Brit. informal* snog; *N. Amer. informal* make out.

peter *verb*
□ **peter out** fizzle out, fade (away), die away/out, dwindle, diminish, taper off, tail off, trail away/off, wane, ebb, melt away, evaporate, disappear.

petition *noun* **appeal**, round robin, letter, request, entreaty, application, plea.
● *verb* **appeal to**, request, ask, call on, entreat, beg, implore, plead with, apply to, press, urge.

petrified *adjective* **1 terrified**, horrified, scared/frightened out of your wits, scared/frightened to death. **2 ossified**, fossilized, calcified.

petty *adjective* **1 trivial**, trifling, minor, insignificant, paltry, unimportant, inconsequential, footling, negligible; *informal* piffling. **2 small-minded**, mean, shabby, spiteful.
- OPPOSITES important, magnanimous.

petulant *adjective* **peevish**, bad-tempered, querulous, pettish, fretful, irritable, sulky, tetchy, crotchety, testy, fractious; *informal* grouchy; *Brit. informal* ratty; *N. English informal* mardy; *N. Amer. informal* cranky.
- OPPOSITES good-humoured.

phantom *noun* **ghost**, apparition, spirit, spectre, wraith; *informal* spook.

phase *noun* **stage**, period, chapter, episode, part, step.

phenomenal *adjective* **remarkable**, exceptional, extraordinary, marvellous, miraculous, wonderful, outstanding, unprecedented; *informal* fantastic, terrific, tremendous, stupendous.

phenomenon *noun* **1 occurrence**, event, happening, fact, situation, circumstance, experience, case, incident, episode. **2 marvel**, sensation, wonder, prodigy.

philanderer *noun* **womanizer**, Casanova, Don Juan, Lothario, flirt, ladies' man, playboy; *informal* stud, ladykiller.

philanthropic *adjective* **charitable**, generous, benevolent, humanitarian, public-spirited, altruistic, magnanimous, unselfish, kind.
- OPPOSITES selfish, mean.

philistine *adjective* **uncultured**, lowbrow, uncultivated, uncivilized, uneducated, unenlightened, commercial, materialist, bourgeois, ignorant, crass, boorish, barbarian.
● *noun* **barbarian**, boor, yahoo, materialist.

philosopher *noun* **thinker**, theorist, theoretician, scholar, intellectual, sage.

philosophical *adjective* **1 theoretical**, metaphysical. **2 thoughtful**, reflective, pensive, meditative, contemplative, introspective. **3 stoical**, self-possessed, serene, dispassionate, phlegmatic, long-suffering, resigned.

philosophy *noun* **1 thinking**, thought, reasoning, logic. **2 beliefs**, credo, ideology, ideas, thinking, theories, doctrine, principles, views, outlook.

p

phobia noun **fear**, dread, horror, terror, aversion, antipathy, revulsion; *informal* hang-up.

phone noun **telephone**, mobile; *N. Amer.* cellphone, cell; *Brit. informal* blower.
● verb **call**, telephone; *Brit.* ring, give someone a ring; *informal* call up, give someone a buzz; *Brit. informal* give someone a bell.

phoney (informal) adjective **bogus**, false, fake, fraudulent, counterfeit, forged, imitation, affected, insincere; *informal* pretend; *Brit. informal* cod.
- OPPOSITES authentic.
● noun **1 impostor**, sham, fake, fraud, charlatan; *informal* con artist. **2 fake**, imitation, counterfeit, forgery.

photocopy noun **copy**, duplicate, reproduction, facsimile; *trademark* Xerox, photostat.
● verb **copy**, duplicate, xerox, photostat, reproduce.

photograph noun **picture**, photo, snap, snapshot, shot, print, still, transparency.

photographic adjective **1 pictorial**, graphic, in photographs. **2 detailed**, exact, precise, accurate, vivid.

phrase noun **expression**, construction, term, turn of phrase, idiom, saying.
● verb **express**, put into words, put, word, formulate, couch, frame.

physical adjective **1 bodily**, corporeal, corporal, carnal, fleshly, non-spiritual. **2 manual**, labouring, blue-collar. **3 material**, concrete, tangible, palpable, solid, substantial, real, actual, visible.
- OPPOSITES mental, spiritual.

physician noun **doctor**, medical practitioner, general practitioner, GP, clinician, specialist, consultant; *informal* doc, medic, quack.

pick verb **1 harvest**, gather (in), collect, pluck. **2 choose**, select, single out, opt for, plump for, elect, decide on, settle on, fix on, name, nominate, identify. **3** *pick a fight* **provoke**, start, cause, incite, instigate, prompt.
● noun **best**, finest, choice, choicest, cream, flower, crème de la crème, elite.
◻ **pick on** bully, victimize, torment, persecute, taunt, tease; *informal* get at, needle. **pick out** see, make out, distinguish, discern, spot, perceive, detect, notice, recognize, identify, catch sight of, glimpse. **pick up 1** improve, recover, rally, bounce back, perk up, look up, take a turn for the better, turn the corner, be on the mend, make headway, make progress. **2** lift, take up, raise, hoist, scoop up, gather up, snatch up. **3** arrest, apprehend, detain, take into custody, seize; *informal* nab, run in; *Brit. informal* nick. **4** *he picked up the story in the 1950s* resume, take up, start again, recommence, continue, carry/go on with.

picket noun **1 demonstrator**, striker, protester. **2 demonstration**, picket line, blockade, boycott, strike.

pickup noun **improvement**, recovery, revival, upturn, upswing, rally, resurgence, renewal, turnaround.

picture noun **1 painting, drawing**, sketch, watercolour, print, canvas, portrait, illustration, depiction, likeness, representation, image. **2 photograph**, photo, snap, snapshot, shot, frame, exposure, still, print. **3 concept**, idea, impression, image, vision, visualization, notion. **4 personification**, embodiment, epitome, essence, quintessence, soul, model.
● verb **1 depict**, portray, show, represent, draw, sketch, photograph, paint. **2 visualize**, see (in your mind's eye), imagine, remember.

picturesque adjective **attractive**, pretty, beautiful, lovely, scenic, charming, quaint, pleasing, delightful.
- OPPOSITES ugly.

piece noun **1 bit**, slice, chunk, segment, section, lump, hunk, wedge, slab, block, cake, bar, stick, length. **2 component**, part, bit, constituent, element, section, unit, module. **3 item**, article, specimen. **4 share**, portion, slice, quota, part, percentage, amount, quantity, ration, fraction; *Brit. informal* whack. **5 work (of art)**, artwork, artefact, composition, opus. **6 article**, item, story, report, essay, feature, review, column.

pier *noun* **jetty**, quay, wharf, dock, landing stage.

pierce *verb* **penetrate**, puncture, perforate, prick, spike, stab, drill, bore.

piercing *adjective* **1 shrill**, ear-splitting, high-pitched, penetrating, strident. **2 searching**, probing, penetrating, sharp, keen, shrewd.

pig *noun* **hog**, boar, sow, porker, swine, piglet.

> **WORD LINKS**
> **porcine** relating to pigs

pigment *noun* **colouring**, colour, tint, dye, stain.

pile[1] *noun* **1 heap**, stack, mound, pyramid, mass, collection, accumulation, assemblage, stockpile, hoard. **2** (*informal*) **lot**, mountain, reams, abundance; *informal* load, heap, mass, slew, stack, ton, oodles.
● *verb* **1 heap**, stack, load, fill, charge. **2 crowd**, clamber, pack, squeeze, scramble, struggle.
□ **pile up** accumulate, amass, grow, mount up, build up, multiply, escalate, soar, spiral, rocket, increase.

pile[2] *noun* **nap**, fibres, threads.

pile-up *noun* **crash**, collision, smash, accident; *Brit.* RTA; *N. Amer.* wreck; *Brit. informal* shunt.

pilgrim *noun* **traveller**, wayfarer, worshipper, devotee, believer; *Islam* haji; *old use* palmer.

pilgrimage *noun* **journey**, expedition, mission, hajj, visit, trek, trip, odyssey.

pill *noun* **tablet**, capsule, pellet, lozenge, pastille.

pillar *noun* **1 column**, post, support, upright, pier, pile, prop, stanchion, obelisk. **2 stalwart**, mainstay, bastion, leading light, worthy, backbone, supporter, upholder, champion.

pilot *noun* **1 airman**, airwoman, flyer, captain; *informal* skipper; *dated* aviator. **2 navigator**, helmsman, steersman, coxswain. **3 trial**, sample, experiment.
● *adjective* **experimental**, exploratory, trial, test, sample, preliminary.
● *verb* **navigate**, guide, manoeuvre, steer, control, direct, captain, fly, drive, sail; *informal* skipper.

pin *noun* **1 tack**, safety pin, nail, staple, fastener. **2 bolt**, peg, rod, rivet, dowel. **3 badge**, brooch.
● *verb* **1 attach**, fasten, affix, fix, join, secure, clip, nail. **2 hold**, press, pinion.
□ **pin down** confine, trap, hem in, corner, close in, shut in, pen in. **pin on** blame for, hold responsible for, attribute to, ascribe to, lay something at someone's door; *informal* stick on.

pinch *verb* **nip**, tweak, squeeze, grasp, compress.
● *noun* **1 nip**, tweak, squeeze. **2 bit**, touch, dash, spot, trace, soupçon, speck, taste; *informal* smidgen, tad.

pine *verb* **fade**, waste away, weaken, decline, languish, wilt, sicken.
□ **pine for** long for, yearn for, ache for, sigh for, hunger for, thirst for, itch for, carry a torch for, miss, mourn.

pink *adjective* **rose**, rosy, rosé, pale red, salmon, coral, flushed, blushing.

pinnacle *noun* **1 height**, peak, high point, top, apex, zenith, acme. **2 peak**, needle, crag, tor.
- OPPOSITES nadir.

pinpoint *adjective* **pinpoint accuracy precise**, exact, strict, absolute, complete, scientific.
● *verb* **identify**, determine, distinguish, discover, find, locate, detect, track down, spot, diagnose, recognize, pin down, home in on.

pioneer *noun* **1 settler**, colonist, colonizer, frontiersman, explorer. **2 developer**, innovator, trailblazer, groundbreaker, founding father, architect, creator.
● *verb* **introduce**, develop, launch, instigate, initiate, spearhead, institute, establish, found.

p

pious adjective **religious**, devout, God-fearing, churchgoing, holy, godly, saintly, reverent, righteous.
- OPPOSITES irreligious.

pipe noun **tube**, conduit, hose, main, duct, line, channel, pipeline, drain.
● verb **feed**, siphon, channel, run, convey.

piquant adjective **1** a piquant sauce **spicy**, tangy, peppery, hot, tasty, flavoursome, savoury, pungent, sharp, tart, zesty, strong, salty. **2** a piquant story **intriguing**, stimulating, interesting, fascinating, colourful, exciting, lively, spicy, provocative, racy; informal juicy.
- OPPOSITES bland, dull.

pirate noun **raider**, hijacker, freebooter, marauder; historical privateer, buccaneer; old use corsair.
● verb **steal**, copy, plagiarize, poach, appropriate, bootleg; informal crib, lift, rip off.

pit noun **1 hole**, trough, hollow, excavation, cavity, crater, pothole. **2 coal mine**, colliery, quarry, shaft.
● verb **mark**, pockmark, pock, scar, dent, indent.

pitch noun **1 playing field**, ground, sports field, stadium; Brit. park. **2 tone**, key, modulation, frequency. **3 gradient**, slope, slant, angle, tilt, incline. **4 level**, intensity, point, degree, height, extent. **5 patter**, talk; informal spiel, line.
● verb **1 throw**, toss, fling, hurl, cast, lob, flip; informal chuck, sling, heave, bung. **2 fall**, tumble, topple, plunge, plummet. **3 put up**, set up, erect, raise. **4 lurch**, toss, plunge, roll, reel, sway, rock, list.

pitfall noun **hazard**, danger, risk, peril, difficulty, catch, snag, stumbling block, drawback, issue.

pitiful adjective **1 distressing**, sad, piteous, pitiable, pathetic, heart-rending, moving, touching, tear-jerking, plaintive, poignant, forlorn, poor, sorry, wretched, miserable. **2 paltry**, miserable, meagre, trifling, negligible, pitiable, derisory; informal pathetic, measly; Brit. informal poxy. **3 dreadful**, awful, terrible, appalling, lamentable, hopeless, feeble, pitiable, woeful, inadequate, deplorable, laughable; informal pathetic, useless, lousy, abysmal, dire.

pitiless adjective **merciless**, unmerciful, ruthless, cruel, heartless, remorseless, hard-hearted, cold-hearted, harsh, callous, severe, unsparing, unforgiving, unfeeling, uncaring, unsympathetic, uncharitable.
- OPPOSITES merciful.

pity noun **1 compassion**, commiseration, condolence, sympathy, fellow feeling, understanding. **2** it's a pity you can't go **shame**, misfortune.
- OPPOSITES indifference.
● verb **feel sorry for**, feel for, sympathize with, empathize with, commiserate with, take pity on, be moved by, bleed for.

pivot noun **fulcrum**, axis, axle, swivel, pin, shaft, hub, spindle, hinge, kingpin.
● verb **1 rotate**, turn, swivel, revolve, spin. **2** it all pivoted on his response **depend**, hinge, turn, centre, hang, rely, rest, revolve around.

placate verb **pacify**, calm, appease, mollify, soothe, win over, conciliate, propitiate, make peace with, humour.
- OPPOSITES provoke.

place noun **1 location**, site, spot, setting, position, situation, area, region, locale, venue. **2 country**, state, area, region, town, city. **3 home**, house, flat, apartment, pied-à-terre, accommodation, property, rooms, quarters; informal pad; formal residence, abode, dwelling. **4 situation**, position, circumstances. **5 seat**, chair, space. **6 job**, position, post, appointment, situation, employment. **7 status**, position, standing, rank, niche. **8 responsibility**, duty, job, task, role, function, concern, affair, charge.
● verb **1 put (down)**, set (down), lay, deposit, position, plant, rest, stand, station, situate, leave; informal stick, dump, bung, park, plonk, pop; N. Amer.

informal plunk. **2 rank**, order, grade, class, classify, put. **3 identify**, recognize, remember, put a name to, pin down, locate, pinpoint.
□ **out of place 1** inappropriate, unsuitable, unseemly, improper, untoward, out of keeping, unbecoming. **2** incongruous, out of your element, like a fish out of water, uncomfortable, uneasy. **take place** happen, occur, come about, go on, transpire; *N. Amer. informal* go down. **take the place of** replace, stand in for, substitute for, act for, fill in for, cover for, relieve.

placid *adjective* **1 even-tempered**, calm, tranquil, equable, unexcitable, serene, mild, composed, self-possessed, poised, easy-going, level-headed, steady, unruffled, unperturbed, phlegmatic; *informal* unflappable. **2 quiet**, calm, tranquil, still, peaceful, undisturbed, restful, sleepy.
- OPPOSITES excitable.

plagiarize *verb* **copy**, pirate, steal, poach, appropriate; *informal* rip off, crib; *Brit. informal* pinch, nick.

plague *noun* **1 pandemic**, epidemic, disease, sickness; *dated* contagion; *old use* pestilence. **2 infestation**, invasion, swarm.
● *verb* **1 afflict**, trouble, torment, beset, dog, curse, bedevil. **2 pester**, harass, badger, bother, torment, harry, hound, trouble, nag, molest; *informal* hassle, bug.

plain *adjective* **1 obvious**, clear, evident, apparent, manifest, unmistakable. **2 intelligible**, comprehensible, understandable, clear, lucid, simple, straightforward, user-friendly. **3 candid**, frank, outspoken, forthright, direct, honest, truthful, blunt, bald, unequivocal; *informal* upfront. **4 simple**, ordinary, unadorned, homely, basic, modest, unsophisticated, restrained. **5 unattractive**, unprepossessing, ugly, ordinary; *N. Amer.* homely; *Brit. informal* no oil painting. **6 sheer**, pure, downright, out-and-out.
- OPPOSITES obscure, fancy, attractive.
● *noun* **grassland**, flatland, prairie,

savannah, steppe, tundra, pampas, veld, plateau.

plaintive *adjective* **mournful**, sad, pathetic, pitiful, melancholy, sorrowful, unhappy, wretched, woeful, forlorn.

plan *noun* **1 scheme**, idea, proposal, proposition, project, programme, system, method, strategy, stratagem, solution, formula, recipe. **2 intention**, aim, idea, objective, object, goal, target, ambition. **3 map**, diagram, chart, blueprint, drawing, sketch, impression; *N. Amer.* plat.
● *verb* **1 organize**, arrange, work out, outline, map out, prepare, formulate, frame, develop, devise. **2 intend**, aim, propose, mean, hope. **3 design**, draw up a plan for, sketch out, map out; *N. Amer.* plat.

plane[1] *noun* **level**, degree, standard, stratum, dimension.
● *verb* **skim**, glide.

plane[2] *noun* **aircraft**, airliner, jet, flying machine; *Brit.* aeroplane; *N. Amer.* airplane, ship.

WORD LINKS
aeronautics science of flight

---

plant *noun* **1 flower**, vegetable, herb, shrub, bush, weed; (**plants**) vegetation, greenery, flora. **2 spy**, informant, informer, secret agent, mole, infiltrator, operative; *N. Amer. informal* spook. **3 factory**, works, facility, refinery, mill. **4 machinery**, machines, equipment, apparatus, appliances, gear.
● *verb* **1 sow**, scatter. **2 place**, put, set, position, situate, settle; *informal* plonk. **3 instil**, implant, put, place, introduce, fix, establish, lodge.

WORD LINKS
botany study of plants
herbivorous plant-eating

---

plaster *verb* **1 spread**, smother, smear, cake, coat, bedaub. **2 flatten (down)**, smooth down, slick down.

plastic *adjective* **1 soft**, pliable, pliant, flexible, malleable, workable, mouldable; *informal* bendy. **2 artificial**, false, fake, bogus, insincere; *informal* phoney, pretend.

plate *noun* **1 dish**, platter, salver; *historical* trencher; *old use* charger. **2 plateful**, helping, portion, serving. **3 panel**, sheet, slab. **4 plaque**, sign, tablet. **5 picture**, print, illustration, photograph, photo.
● *verb* **cover**, coat, overlay, laminate, gild.

plateau *noun* **upland**, mesa, highland, tableland.

platform *noun* **1 stage**, dais, rostrum, podium, stand. **2 programme**, manifesto, policies, principles, party line.

platitude *noun* **cliché**, truism, commonplace, old chestnut, banality.

platter *noun* **plate**, dish, salver, tray; *old use* charger.

plausible *adjective* **credible**, believable, reasonable, likely, possible, conceivable, imaginable, convincing, persuasive.
- OPPOSITES unlikely.

play *verb* **1 amuse yourself**, entertain yourself, enjoy yourself, have fun, relax, occupy yourself, frolic, romp, cavort; *informal* mess about/around. **2 take part in**, participate in, be involved in, compete in, do. **3 compete against**, take on, meet. **4 act the part of**, take the role of, appear as, portray, perform.
● *noun* **1 amusement**, relaxation, recreation, diversion, leisure, enjoyment, pleasure, fun. **2 drama**, theatrical work, piece, comedy, tragedy, production, performance.
□ **play down** make light of, make little of, gloss over, downplay, understate, soft-pedal, diminish, trivialize. **play up** (*Brit. informal*) **1** misbehave, be bad, be naughty. **2** malfunction, not work, be defective, be faulty; *informal* be on the blink, act up.

player *noun* **1 participant**, contestant, competitor, contender, sportsman, sportswoman. **2 musician**, performer, artist, virtuoso, instrumentalist. **3 actor**, **actress**, performer, thespian, entertainer, artiste, trouper.

playful *adjective* **1 frisky**, lively, full of fun, frolicsome, high-spirited, exuberant, mischievous, impish; *informal* full of beans. **2 light-hearted**, jokey, teasing, humorous, jocular, facetious, frivolous, flippant.
- OPPOSITES serious.

plea *noun* **appeal**, entreaty, supplication, petition, request, call.

plead *verb* **claim**, use as an excuse, assert, allege, argue.
□ **plead with** beg, implore, entreat, appeal to, ask.

pleasant *adjective* **1 enjoyable**, pleasurable, nice, agreeable, entertaining, amusing, delightful, charming; *informal* lovely, great. **2 friendly**, charming, agreeable, amiable, nice, delightful, sweet, genial, cordial, good-natured, personable, hospitable, polite.

please *verb* **1 make happy**, give pleasure to, delight, charm, amuse, entertain, divert, satisfy, gratify, humour. **2 like**, want, wish, desire, see fit, think fit, choose, will, prefer.
- OPPOSITES annoy.

pleased *adjective* **happy**, glad, delighted, gratified, grateful, thankful, content, contented, satisfied, thrilled; *informal* over the moon, on cloud nine; *Brit. informal* chuffed; *N. English informal* made up; *Austral. informal* wrapped.
- OPPOSITES unhappy.

pleasing *adjective* **1 good**, agreeable, pleasant, pleasurable, satisfying, gratifying, great. **2 friendly**, amiable, pleasant, agreeable, affable, nice, genial, likeable, charming, engaging, delightful; *informal* lovely.

pleasure *noun* **happiness**, delight, joy, gladness, glee, satisfaction, gratification, contentment, enjoyment, amusement, fun, entertainment, relaxation, recreation, diversion.

pledge *noun* **promise**, vow, undertaking, word, commitment, assurance, oath, guarantee.
● *verb* **promise**, vow, undertake, swear, commit yourself, declare, affirm.

plentiful *adjective* **abundant**, copious, ample, profuse, rich, lavish, generous, bountiful, bumper, prolific; *informal* galore.
- OPPOSITES scarce.

plenty *pronoun* **a lot of**, many, a great deal of, a plethora of, enough and to spare, no lack of, a wealth of; *informal* loads of, heaps of, stacks of, masses of, oodles of.
● *noun* **prosperity**, affluence, wealth, opulence, comfort, luxury, abundance.

plethora *noun* **excess**, abundance, superabundance, surplus, glut, surfeit, profusion, enough and to spare.
- OPPOSITES dearth.

pliable *adjective* **1 flexible**, pliant, bendable, supple, workable, plastic; *informal* bendy. **2 malleable**, impressionable, flexible, adaptable, biddable, pliant, tractable, suggestible, persuadable.
- OPPOSITES rigid.

plight *noun* **predicament**, difficult situation, dire straits, trouble, difficulty, bind; *informal* tight corner, tight spot, hole, pickle, jam, fix.

plod *verb* **trudge**, walk heavily, clump, stomp, tramp, lumber, slog.

plot *noun* **1 conspiracy**, intrigue, stratagem, plan, machinations. **2 storyline**, story, scenario, action, thread, narrative. **3 piece of ground**, patch, area, tract, acreage; *Brit.* allotment; *N. Amer.* lot, plat.
● *verb* **1 plan**, scheme, arrange, organize, contrive. **2 conspire**, scheme, intrigue, connive. **3 mark**, chart, map.

plough *verb* **1 till**, furrow, harrow, cultivate, work. **2 crash**, smash, career, plunge, bulldoze, hurtle, cannon.

ploy *noun* **ruse**, tactic, move, device, stratagem, scheme, trick, gambit, plan, manoeuvre, dodge, subterfuge; *Brit. informal* wheeze.

pluck *verb* **1 remove**, pick, pull, extract. **2 pull**, tug, clutch, snatch, grab, catch, tweak, jerk; *informal* yank. **3 strum**, pick, thrum, twang.
● *noun* **courage**, bravery, nerve, daring, spirit, grit; *informal* guts; *Brit. informal* bottle; *N. Amer. informal* moxie.

plug *noun* **1 stopper**, bung, cork; *N. Amer.* stopple. **2** (*informal*) **advertisement**, promotion, commercial, recommendation, mention, good word; *informal* hype, push, puff.
● *verb* **1 stop**, seal, close, block, fill. **2** (*informal*) **publicize**, promote, advertise, mention, bang the drum for, draw attention to; *informal* hype, push.

plumb *verb* **explore**, probe, delve into, search, examine, investigate, fathom, penetrate, understand.
● *adverb* (*informal*) **right**, exactly, precisely, directly, dead, straight; *informal* (slap) bang.

plummet *verb* **plunge**, dive, drop, fall, hurtle, nosedive, tumble.
- OPPOSITES soar.

plump *adjective* **fat**, chubby, rotund, ample, round, stout, portly, overweight; *informal* tubby, roly-poly, pudgy; *Brit. informal* podgy; *N. Amer. informal* zaftig, corn-fed.
- OPPOSITES thin.

plunder *verb* **1 pillage**, loot, rob, raid, ransack, rifle, strip, sack. **2 steal**, seize, thieve, pilfer, embezzle.
● *noun* **booty**, loot, stolen goods, spoils, ill-gotten gains; *informal* swag.

plunge *verb* **1 dive**, jump, throw yourself, immerse yourself. **2 plummet**, nosedive, drop, fall, tumble, descend. **3 charge**, hurtle, career, plough, tear; *N. Amer. informal* barrel. **4 thrust**, stab, sink, stick, ram, drive, push, shove, force.

plus *preposition* **as well as**, together with, along with, in addition to, and, added to, not to mention.
- OPPOSITES minus.
● *noun* **advantage**, good point, asset, pro, benefit, bonus, attraction; *informal* perk.
- OPPOSITES disadvantage.

plush *adjective* (*informal*) **luxurious**, luxury, de luxe, sumptuous, opulent, magnificent, rich, expensive, fancy; *Brit.* upmarket; *informal* posh, classy;

p

Brit. informal swish; *N. Amer. informal* swank.
- OPPOSITES austere.

ply *verb* **1 engage in**, carry on, pursue, conduct, practise. **2 travel**, shuttle, go back and forth. **3** *she plied me with scones* **provide**, supply, shower. **4** *he plied her with questions* **bombard**, assail, pester, plague, harass; *informal* hassle.

pocket *noun* **1 pouch**, compartment. **2 area**, patch, region, cluster.
● *adjective* **small**, little, miniature, mini, fun-size, compact, concise, abridged, portable.
● *verb* **1 acquire**, obtain, gain, get, secure, win, make, earn. **2 steal**, appropriate, purloin, misappropriate, embezzle.

pod *noun* **shell**, husk, hull, case; *N. Amer.* shuck.

podium *noun* **platform**, stage, dais, rostrum, stand.

poem *noun* **verse**, rhyme, lyric, piece of poetry.

poetic *adjective* **expressive**, figurative, symbolic, flowery, artistic, imaginative, creative.

poetry *noun* **poems**, verse, versification, rhyme.

poignant *adjective* **touching**, moving, sad, affecting, pitiful, pathetic, plaintive.

point *noun* **1 tip**, (sharp) end, extremity, prong, spike, tine, nib, barb. **2 pinpoint**, dot, spot, speck. **3 place**, position, location, site, spot. **4 time**, stage, juncture, period, phase. **5 level**, degree, stage, pitch, extent. **6 detail**, item, fact, thing, argument, consideration, factor, element, subject, issue, topic, question, matter. **7 heart of the matter**, essence, nub, core, crux; *informal* nitty-gritty. **8 purpose**, aim, object, objective, goal, intention, use, sense, value, advantage. **9 attribute**, characteristic, feature, trait, quality, property, aspect, side.
● *verb* **aim**, direct, level, train, focus.
□ **point out** identify, show, draw attention to, indicate, specify, detail, mention. **point to** indicate, suggest, evidence, signal, signify, denote.

pointed *adjective* **1 sharp**, spiky, spiked, tapering, barbed. **2 cutting**, biting, incisive, trenchant, acerbic, caustic, scathing, venomous, sarcastic.

pointer *noun* **1 indicator**, needle, arrow, hand. **2 indication**, indicator, clue, hint, sign, signal, evidence. **3 tip**, hint, suggestion, guideline, recommendation.

pointless *adjective* **senseless**, futile, useless, hopeless, unavailing, unproductive, aimless, idle, worthless, valueless.
- OPPOSITES valuable.

poise *noun* **1 grace**, gracefulness, elegance, balance, control. **2 composure**, equanimity, self-possession, aplomb, self-assurance, self-control, sangfroid, dignity, presence of mind; *informal* cool.

poised *adjective* **1 balanced**, suspended, motionless, hanging, hovering. **2 prepared**, ready, braced, geared up, all set, standing by.

poison *noun* **toxin**, venom.
● *verb* **pollute**, contaminate, infect, taint, spoil.

> **WORD LINKS**
> **toxicology** study of poisons

poisonous *adjective* **1 venomous**, deadly. **2 toxic**, noxious, deadly, fatal, lethal, mortal, environmentally unfriendly, polluting. **3 malicious**, malevolent, hostile, spiteful, bitter, venomous, malign.
- OPPOSITES harmless.

poke *verb* **1 prod**, jab, dig, elbow, nudge, shove, jolt, stab, stick. **2** *leave the cable poking out* **stick out**, jut out, protrude, project, extend.
● *noun* **prod**, jab, dig, elbow, nudge.

poky *adjective* **small**, little, tiny, cramped, confined, restricted, boxy.
- OPPOSITES spacious.

pole *noun* **post**, pillar, stanchion, stake, support, prop, stick, paling, staff.

police noun **police force**, police service, police officers, policemen, police-women; Brit. constabulary; informal the cops, the fuzz, the law, the boys in blue; Brit. informal the (Old) Bill; N. Amer. informal the heat.
● verb **1 guard**, watch over, protect, defend, patrol. **2 enforce**, regulate, oversee, supervise, monitor, observe, check.

police officer noun **policeman**, **policewoman**; Brit. constable; N. Amer. patrolman, trooper, roundsman; informal cop; Brit. informal copper, rozzer, bobby; N. Amer. informal uniform.

policy noun **plans**, approach, code, system, guidelines, theory, line, position, stance.

polish verb **1 shine**, wax, buff, rub up/down, gloss, burnish. **2** polish up your essay **perfect**, refine, improve, hone, enhance, brush up, revise, edit, correct, rewrite, go over, touch up.
● noun **sophistication**, refinement, urbanity, suaveness, elegance, style, grace, finesse; informal class.

polished adjective **1 shiny**, glossy, gleaming, lustrous, glassy, waxed, buffed, burnished. **2 expert**, accomplished, masterly, skilful, adept, adroit, dexterous, consummate, superlative, superb.
- OPPOSITES dull, inexpert.

polite adjective **1 well mannered**, civil, courteous, respectful, well behaved, well bred, gentlemanly, ladylike, genteel, gracious, tactful, diplomatic. **2 civilized**, refined, cultured, sophisticated, urbane.
- OPPOSITES rude.

politic adjective **wise**, prudent, sensible, shrewd, astute, judicious, expedient, advantageous, beneficial, profitable.
- OPPOSITES unwise.

political adjective **governmental**, government, constitutional, ministerial, parliamentary, diplomatic, legislative, administrative.

politician noun **legislator**, Member of Parliament, MP, representative,

minister, statesman, stateswoman, senator, congressman, congress-woman; informal politico.

poll noun **1 vote**, ballot, show of hands, referendum, plebiscite, election. **2 survey**, opinion poll, market research, census.
● verb **1 canvass**, survey, ask, question, interview, ballot. **2 get**, gain, register, record, return.

pollute verb **contaminate**, taint, poison, foul, dirty, soil, infect.
- OPPOSITES purify.

pollution noun **contamination**, impurity, dirt, filth, infection.

pomp noun **ceremony**, solemnity, ritual, display, spectacle, pageantry, show, ostentation, splendour, grandeur, magnificence, majesty, stateliness, glory; informal razzmatazz.

pompous adjective **self-important**, overbearing, sententious, grandiose, affected, pretentious, puffed up, haughty, proud, conceited, supercilious, condescending, patronizing.

ponder verb **think about**, contemplate, consider, review, reflect on, mull over, meditate on, muse on, dwell on.

pontificate verb **hold forth**, expound, declaim, preach, lay down the law, sound off, lecture; informal mouth off.

pool¹ noun **puddle**, pond, lake; literary mere.

pool² noun **1 supply**, reserve(s), reservoir, fund, store, bank, stock, cache. **2 fund**, reserve, kitty, pot, bank, purse.
● verb **combine**, group, join, unite, merge, share.

poor adjective **1 poverty-stricken**, penniless, impoverished, impecunious, needy, destitute; Brit. on the breadline; informal hard up, strapped, on your uppers; formal penurious. **2 substandard**, bad, deficient, defective, faulty, imperfect, inferior, unsatisfactory, shoddy, crude, inadequate, unacceptable; informal crummy, rotten; Brit. informal duff. **3 meagre**, scanty, scant, paltry, reduced, modest, sparse, spare,

deficient, insubstantial, skimpy, lean; *informal* measly, stingy. **4 unfortunate**, unlucky, unhappy, hapless, wretched, luckless, ill-fated, ill-starred.
- OPPOSITES rich.

poorly *adverb* **badly**, imperfectly, incompetently, crudely, shoddily, inadequately.
● *adjective* **ill**, unwell, not very well, ailing, indisposed, out of sorts, under par, peaky; *Brit.* off colour; *informal* under the weather, rough; *Brit. informal* ropy, grotty; *Scottish informal* wabbit; *Austral./NZ informal* crook.

pop *verb* **1 go bang**, go off, crack, snap, burst, explode. **2 go**; *informal* tootle, whip; *Brit. informal* nip. **3 put**, place, slip, throw, slide, stick, set, lay, position.
● *noun* **bang**, crack, snap, explosion, report.

populace *noun* **population**, inhabitants, residents, natives, community, country, (general) public, people, nation, common people, masses, multitude, rank and file; *Brit. informal* Joe Public; *derogatory* hoi polloi, common herd, rabble, riff-raff.

popular *adjective* **1 well liked**, sought-after, in demand, commercial, marketable, fashionable, in vogue, all the rage, hot; *informal* in, cool, big. **2 non-specialist**, non-technical, amateur, lay person's, general, middle-of-the-road, accessible, simplified, understandable, mass-market. **3 widespread**, general, common, current, prevailing, standard, ordinary, conventional.

populate *verb* **inhabit**, occupy, people, settle, colonize.

population *noun* **inhabitants**, residents, people, citizens, public, community, populace, society, natives, occupants.

pornographic *adjective* **obscene**, indecent, dirty, smutty, filthy, erotic, titillating, sexy, risqué, X-rated, adult.

porous *adjective* **permeable**, penetrable, absorbent, spongy.
- OPPOSITES impermeable.

port *noun* **harbour**, docks, marina, haven, seaport.

portable *adjective* **transportable**, movable, mobile, wireless, lightweight, compact, handy, convenient.

portend *verb* **presage**, augur, foreshadow, foretell, prophesy, be a sign, warn, be an omen, indicate, herald, signal, bode, promise, threaten, signify, spell, denote.

porter[1] *noun* **carrier**, bearer; *N. Amer.* redcap, skycap.

porter[2] *noun* (*Brit.*) **doorman**, doorkeeper, commissionaire, gatekeeper, concierge, security officer.

portion *noun* **1 part**, piece, bit, section, segment. **2 share**, quota, ration, allocation, tranche; *Brit. informal* whack. **3 helping**, serving, plateful, slice, piece.

portrait *noun* **1 picture**, likeness, painting, drawing, photograph, image. **2 description**, portrayal, representation, depiction, impression, account, profile.

portray *verb* **1 paint**, draw, sketch, picture, depict, represent, illustrate, render, show. **2 describe**, depict, characterize, delineate, put into words. **3 play**, act the part of, take the role of, represent, appear as.

portrayal *noun* **description**, representation, characterization, depiction, delineation, evocation, interpretation.

pose *verb* **1 constitute**, present, offer. **2 raise**, ask, put, submit, advance, propose. **3 posture**, attitudinize, put on airs; *informal* show off, ponce about.
● *noun* **1 posture**, position, stance, attitude. **2 act**, affectation, show, display, front, airs.
□ **pose as** pretend to be, impersonate, pass yourself off as, masquerade as; *formal* personate.

poser[1] *noun* **difficult question**, problem, puzzle, mystery, riddle, conundrum; *informal* dilemma.

poser[2] *noun* **exhibitionist**, poseur; *informal* show-off, pseud.

posh adjective **1** (informal) **smart**, stylish, fancy, high-class, fashionable, chic, luxurious, luxury, exclusive; Brit. upmarket; informal classy, plush, flash; Brit. informal swish; N. Amer. informal swank, tony. **2** (Brit. informal) **upper-class**, aristocratic.

position noun **1 location**, place, situation, spot, site, locality, setting, area, whereabouts, bearings. **2 posture**, stance, attitude, pose. **3 situation**, state, condition, circumstances, predicament, plight. **4 status**, place, level, rank, standing, stature, prestige, reputation. **5 job**, post, situation, appointment, opening, vacancy, placement. **6 viewpoint**, opinion, outlook, attitude, stand, standpoint, stance, perspective, thinking, policy, feelings.
● verb **put**, place, locate, situate, set, site, stand, station, plant, stick; informal plonk, park.

positive adjective **1 affirmative**, favourable, good, enthusiastic, supportive, constructive, useful, productive, helpful, worthwhile, beneficial. **2 optimistic**, hopeful, confident, cheerful, sanguine, buoyant; informal upbeat. **3** positive economic signs **good**, promising, favourable, encouraging, heartening, propitious, auspicious. **4 definite**, certain, reliable, concrete, tangible, clear-cut, explicit, firm, decisive, real, actual. **5 convinced**, sure, confident, satisfied.
- OPPOSITES negative, pessimistic.

positively adverb **1 confidently**, definitely, firmly, categorically, with certainty, conclusively. **2 absolutely**, utterly, downright, simply, virtually; informal plain.

possess verb **1 own**, have (to your name), be in possession of. **2 have**, be blessed with, be endowed with, enjoy, boast. **3 take control of**, take over, bewitch, enchant, enslave.

possession noun **1 ownership**, control, hands, keeping, care, custody, charge. **2** she packed her possessions **belongings**, things, property, worldly goods, goods and chattels, personal effects, stuff, bits and pieces; informal gear, junk; Brit. informal clobber.

possessive adjective **proprietorial**, overprotective, controlling, dominating, jealous, clingy.

possibility noun **1 chance**, likelihood, probability, potentiality, hope, risk, hazard, danger, fear. **2 option**, alternative, choice, course of action, solution. **3 potential**, promise, prospects.

possible adjective **1 feasible**, practicable, viable, attainable, achievable, workable, within reach; informal on, doable. **2 likely**, plausible, imaginable, believable, potential, probable, credible, tenable.
- OPPOSITES impossible, unlikely.

possibly adverb **1 perhaps**, maybe, it is possible, for all you know. **2 conceivably**, under any circumstances, by any means.

post[1] noun **pole**, stake, upright, shaft, prop, support, picket, strut, pillar, stanchion, baluster.
● verb **1 affix**, attach, fasten, display, pin up, put up, stick up. **2 announce**, report, make known, publish.

post[2] noun (Brit.) **1 mail**; informal snail mail. **2 letters**, correspondence, mail.

post[3] noun **1 job**, position, appointment, situation, place, vacancy, opening. **2 assigned position**, station, place, base.
● verb **1 send**, assign, dispatch, consign. **2 put on duty**, mount, station.

poster noun **notice**, placard, bill, sign, advertisement, playbill.

postpone verb **put off**, put back, delay, defer, hold over, reschedule, adjourn, shelve; informal put on ice, put on the back burner.

posture noun **1 position**, pose, attitude, stance, carriage, bearing, comportment; Brit. deportment. **2 attitude**, standpoint, point of view, viewpoint, opinion, position, stance.
● verb **pose**, strike an attitude, attitudinize, strut; informal show off.

p

potent *adjective* **1 powerful**, strong, mighty, formidable, influential, dominant. **2 forceful**, convincing, cogent, compelling, persuasive, powerful, strong.
- OPPOSITES weak.

potential *adjective* **possible**, likely, prospective, future, probable.
● *noun* **possibilities**, potentiality, prospects, promise, capability, capacity.

potion *noun* **concoction**, mixture, brew, elixir, drink, medicine, tonic, philtre.

potter *verb* **amble**, wander, meander, stroll, saunter; *informal* mosey, tootle, toddle; *N. Amer. informal* putter.

pottery *noun* **ceramics**, crockery, earthenware, terracotta, stoneware, china, porcelain.

pouch *noun* **bag**, purse, sack, sac, pocket; *Scottish* sporran.

pounce *verb* **jump**, spring, leap, dive, lunge, swoop, attack.

pound[1] *verb* **1 beat**, strike, hit, batter, thump, pummel, punch, rain blows on, belabour, hammer; *informal* bash, clobber, wallop. **2 beat against**, crash against, batter, dash against, lash, buffet. **3 bombard**, bomb, shell. **4 crush**, grind, pulverize, mash, pulp. **5 stomp**, stamp, clomp, clump, tramp, lumber. **6 throb**, thump, thud, hammer, pulse, race.

pound[2] *noun* **enclosure**, compound, pen, yard, corral.

pour *verb* **1 stream**, flow, run, gush, course, jet, spurt, surge, spill. **2 tip**, splash, spill, decant; *informal* slosh, slop. **3 rain hard**, teem down, pelt down, tip down, rain cats and dogs; *informal* be chucking it down; *Brit. informal* bucket down; *N. Amer. informal* rain pitchforks. **4 crowd**, throng, swarm, stream, flood.

poverty *noun* **1 pennilessness**, destitution, penury, impoverishment, neediness, hardship, impecuniousness, indigence. **2 scarcity**, deficiency, dearth, shortage, paucity, absence, lack, inadequacy.
- OPPOSITES wealth, abundance.

powdery *adjective* **fine**, dry, fine-grained, powder-like, dusty, chalky, floury, sandy, crumbly, friable.

power *noun* **1 ability**, capacity, capability, potential, potentiality, faculty. **2 control**, command, authority, dominance, supremacy, ascendancy, mastery, influence, sway, leverage; *informal* clout, teeth. **3 authority**, right, authorization. **4 state**, country, nation. **5 strength**, might, force, vigour, energy; *Brit. informal* welly. **6 forcefulness**, powerfulness, strength, force, cogency, persuasiveness. **7 driving force**, horsepower, acceleration, torque; *informal* oomph, poke. **8 energy**, electricity.
- OPPOSITES weakness.

WORD LINKS
megalomania obsession with power

powerful *adjective* **1 strong**, muscular, muscly, sturdy, strapping, robust, brawny, burly, athletic, manly, well built, solid; *informal* beefy. **2 intoxicating**, hard, strong, stiff, potent. **3 violent**, forceful, hard, mighty. **4 intense**, keen, fierce, strong, irresistible, overpowering, overwhelming. **5 influential**, strong, important, dominant, commanding, formidable. **6 cogent**, compelling, convincing, persuasive, forceful, potent.
- OPPOSITES weak, gentle.

powerless *adjective* **impotent**, helpless, ineffectual, ineffective, useless, defenceless, vulnerable.

practicable *adjective* **realistic**, feasible, possible, viable, reasonable, sensible, workable, achievable; *informal* doable.

practical *adjective* **1 empirical**, hands-on, actual. **2 feasible**, practicable, realistic, viable, workable, possible, reasonable, sensible; *informal* doable. **3 functional**, sensible, utilitarian. **4 realistic**, sensible, down-to-earth, businesslike, commonsensical, hard-headed, no-nonsense; *informal* hard-nosed.
- OPPOSITES theoretical.

practically adverb **1 almost**, very nearly, virtually, just about, all but, more or less, as good as, to all intents and purposes; *informal* pretty well. **2 realistically**, sensibly, reasonably, rationally, matter-of-factly.

practice noun **1 application**, exercise, use, operation, implementation, execution. **2 custom**, procedure, policy, convention, tradition. **3 training**, rehearsal, repetition, preparation, dummy run, run-through; *informal* dry run. **4 profession**, career, business, work. **5 business**, firm, office, company; *informal* outfit.

practise verb **1 rehearse**, run through, go over/through, work on/at, polish, perfect, refine. **2 train**, rehearse, prepare, go through your paces. **3 carry out**, perform, observe, follow. **4 work in**, pursue a career in, engage in.

practised adjective **expert**, experienced, seasoned, skilled, skilful, accomplished, proficient, talented, able, adept.

pragmatic adjective **practical**, matter-of-fact, sensible, down-to-earth, commonsensical, businesslike, hard-headed, no-nonsense; *informal* hard-nosed.
- OPPOSITES impractical.

praise verb **commend**, applaud, pay tribute to, speak highly of, compliment, congratulate, sing the praises of, rave about.
- OPPOSITES criticize.
● noun **approval**, acclaim, admiration, approbation, plaudits, congratulations, commendation, accolade, compliment, a pat on the back, eulogy; *N. Amer. informal* kudos.
- OPPOSITES criticism.

praiseworthy adjective **commendable**, admirable, laudable, worthy (of admiration), meritorious, estimable, excellent, exemplary.

prance verb **cavort**, dance, jig, trip, caper, jump, leap, spring, bound, skip, hop, frisk, romp, frolic.

prank noun **(practical) joke**, trick, escapade, stunt, caper, jape, game, hoax; *informal* lark, leg-pull.

preach verb **1 give a sermon**, sermonize, evangelize, spread the gospel. **2 proclaim**, teach, spread, propagate, expound. **3 advocate**, recommend, advise, urge, teach, counsel.

> **WORD LINKS**
> **homiletic** relating to preaching

precarious adjective **insecure**, uncertain, unpredictable, risky, hazardous, dangerous, parlous, unsafe, unstable, unsteady, shaky; *informal* dicey, iffy; *Brit. informal* dodgy.
- OPPOSITES safe.

precaution noun **safeguard**, preventive measure, safety measure, insurance; *informal* backstop.

precede verb **1 go before**, come before, lead up to, pave the way for, herald, introduce, usher in. **2 go ahead of**, go in front of, lead the way.
- OPPOSITES follow.

precedence noun **seniority**, superiority, ascendancy, supremacy.
□ **take precedence over** take priority over, outweigh, prevail over, come before.

precedent noun **model**, exemplar, example, pattern, paradigm, criterion, yardstick, standard.

precinct noun **district**, zone, sector, quarter, area.

precious adjective **1 valuable**, costly, expensive, invaluable, priceless. **2 valued**, cherished, treasured, prized, favourite, dear, beloved, special. **3 affected**, pretentious; *informal* la-di-da; *Brit. informal* poncey.

precipitate verb **bring about**, bring on, cause, lead to, give rise to, instigate, trigger, spark off, touch off, provoke, hasten, speed up, accelerate.
● adjective **hasty**, overhasty, rash, hurried, rushed, impetuous, impulsive, precipitous, incautious, imprudent, injudicious, ill-advised, reckless.

P

precipitous *adjective* **1 steep**, sheer, perpendicular, abrupt, sharp, vertical. **2 sudden**, rapid, swift, abrupt, head-long, speedy, quick, fast.

precise *adjective* **1 exact**, accurate, correct, specific, detailed, explicit, careful, meticulous, strict, rigorous. **2** *at that precise moment* **exact**, particular, actual, specific, distinct.
- OPPOSITES inaccurate.

precisely *adverb* **1 exactly**, sharp, on the dot, promptly; *informal* bang (on); *Brit. informal* spot on; *N. Amer. informal* on the button. **2 just**, exactly, in all respects; *informal* to a T.

precision *noun* **exactness**, accuracy, exactitude, correctness, care, meticulousness, scrupulousness, punctiliousness, rigour.

preclude *verb* **prevent**, make it impossible for, rule out, stop, prohibit, debar, bar, hinder, impede, inhibit, exclude.

preconception *noun* **preconceived idea**, presupposition, assumption, presumption, prejudgement, prejudice.

predatory *adjective* **1 predacious**, carnivorous, hunting. **2 exploitative**, wolfish, rapacious, manipulative.

predecessor *noun* **1 forerunner**, precursor, antecedent. **2 ancestor**, forefather, forebear, antecedent.
- OPPOSITES successor, descendant.

predicament *noun* **difficulty**, mess, plight, quandary, muddle, dilemma; *informal* hole, fix, jam, pickle.

predict *verb* **forecast**, foretell, prophesy; *old use* augur.

predictable *adjective* **foreseeable**, to be expected, anticipated, likely, foreseen, unsurprising, reliable; *informal* inevitable.

prediction *noun* **forecast**, prophecy, prognosis, prognostication.

predisposition *noun* **1 susceptibility**, proneness, tendency, liability, inclination, vulnerability. **2 preference**, predilection, inclination, leaning, bent.

predominantly *adverb* **mainly**, mostly, for the most part, chiefly, principally, primarily, in the main, on the whole, largely, by and large, typically, generally, usually.

preface *noun* **introduction**, foreword, preamble, prologue, prelude, front matter; *informal* intro.
● *verb* **precede**, introduce, begin, open, start.

prefer *verb* **like better**, would rather (have), would sooner (have), favour, be more partial to, choose, select, pick, opt for, go for, plump for.

preferable *adjective* **better**, best, more desirable, more suitable, advantageous, superior, preferred, recommended.

preferably *adverb* **ideally**, if possible, for preference, from choice.

preference *noun* **1 liking**, partiality, fondness, taste, inclination, leaning, bent, penchant, predisposition. **2 priority**, favour, precedence, preferential treatment.

pregnant *adjective* **1 expecting**, expectant, carrying a child, with child; *informal* in the family way. **2 meaningful**, significant, suggestive, expressive, charged.

prejudice *noun* **1 preconceived idea**, preconception. **2 bigotry**, bias, partiality, intolerance, discrimination, unfairness, inequality.
● *verb* **1 bias**, influence, sway, predispose, make partial, colour. **2 damage**, be detrimental to, be prejudicial to, injure, harm, hurt, spoil, impair, undermine, compromise.

prejudiced *adjective* **biased**, bigoted, discriminatory, partisan, intolerant, narrow-minded, unfair, unjust, inequitable.
- OPPOSITES impartial.

preliminary *adjective* **preparatory**, introductory, initial, opening, early, exploratory.
- OPPOSITES final.
● *noun* **introduction**, preamble, preface, opening remarks, formalities.

prelude *noun* **preliminary**, overture, opening, preparation, introduction, lead-in, precursor.

premature *adjective* **1 untimely**, too early, before time, unseasonable. **2 rash**, overhasty, hasty, precipitate, impulsive, impetuous; *informal* previous.
- OPPOSITES overdue.

premier *adjective* **leading**, foremost, chief, principal, head, top-ranking, top, prime, primary, first, highest, pre-eminent, senior, outstanding; *N. Amer.* ranking.
● *noun* **head of government**, prime minister, PM, president, chancellor.

premiere *noun* **first performance**, first night, opening night, debut.

premise *noun* **proposition**, assumption, hypothesis, thesis, presupposition, supposition, presumption, assertion.

premises *plural noun* **building(s)**, property, site, office, establishment.

premium *noun* **1 (regular) payment**, instalment. **2 surcharge**, additional payment, extra.
□ **at a premium** scarce, in great demand, hard to come by, in short supply, thin on the ground, like gold dust.

preoccupation *noun* **obsession**, fixation, concern, passion, enthusiasm, hobby horse; *informal* bee in your bonnet.

preoccupied *adjective* **lost in thought**, deep in thought, oblivious, pensive, distracted, absorbed, engrossed, involved, wrapped up, concerned.

preparation *noun* **1** *preparations for the party* **arrangements**, planning, plans, groundwork, spadework, provision. **2 devising**, drawing up, construction, composition, development. **3 mixture**, compound, concoction, solution, medicine, potion.

prepare *verb* **1 get ready**, put together, draw up, produce, arrange, assemble, construct, compose, formulate. **2 cook**, make, get, concoct; *informal* fix, rustle up; *Brit. informal* knock up. **3 get ready**, make preparations, arrange

things, make provision. **4 train**, get into shape, practise, get ready, warm up, limber up. **5** *prepare yourself for a shock* **brace**, ready, tense, steel, steady.

prepared *adjective* **1 ready**, (all) set, equipped, primed, waiting, poised. **2 willing**, ready, disposed, (favourably) inclined, of a mind, minded.

prescribe *verb* **1 advise**, recommend, advocate, suggest. **2 stipulate**, lay down, dictate, order, direct, specify, determine.

presence *noun* **1 existence**, being. **2 attendance**, appearance. **3 aura**, charisma, personality, magnetism.
- OPPOSITES absence.
□ **presence of mind** composure, self-possession, level-headedness, self-assurance, calmness, alertness, quick-wittedness; *informal* cool, unflappability.

present[1] *adjective* **1 in attendance**, here, there, near, nearby, at hand, available. **2 in existence**, detectable, occurring, existing, extant, current.
- OPPOSITES absent.
● *noun* **now**, today, the present time, the here and now, modern times.
- OPPOSITES past, future.
□ **at present** at the moment, just now, right now, at the present time, currently, at this moment in time.

present[2] *verb* **1 hand over**, give (out), confer, bestow, award, grant, accord. **2 submit**, set forth, put forward, offer, tender, table. **3 introduce**, make known, acquaint someone with. **4 host**, introduce, compère; *N. Amer. informal* emcee. **5 represent**, describe, portray, depict.

present[3] *noun* **gift**, donation, offering, contribution, gratuity, tip, handout; *informal* prezzie.

presentation *noun* **1 awarding**, presenting, bestowal, granting. **2 appearance**, arrangement, packaging, layout. **3 demonstration**, talk, lecture, address, speech, show, exhibition, display, introduction, launch, unveiling.

presently adverb **1 soon**, shortly, quite soon, in a short time, in a little while, at any moment/minute/second, before long; N. Amer. momentarily; Brit. informal in a mo. **2 at present**, currently, at the/this moment.

preservation noun **1 conservation**, protection, care. **2 continuation**, conservation, maintenance, upholding, sustaining, perpetuation.

preserve verb **1 conserve**, protect, maintain, care for, look after. **2 continue (with)**, conserve, keep going, maintain, uphold, sustain, perpetuate, prolong. **3 guard**, protect, keep, defend, safeguard, shelter, shield.
- OPPOSITES attack, abandon.
● noun **1** jobs which are no longer the preserve of men **domain**, area, field, sphere, orbit, realm, province, territory; informal turf, bailiwick. **2 sanctuary**, (game) reserve, reservation.

preside verb
□ **preside over** be in charge of, be responsible for, head, manage, administer, control, direct, chair, conduct, officiate at, lead, govern, rule, command, supervise, oversee; informal head up.

press verb **1 push (down)**, depress, hold down, force, thrust, squeeze, compress. **2 iron**, smooth out, flatten. **3 clasp**, hold close, hug, cuddle, squeeze, clutch, grasp, embrace. **4 cluster**, gather, converge, congregate, flock, swarm, crowd. **5 plead**, urge, advance, present, submit, put forward. **6 urge**, put pressure on, pressurize, force, push, coerce, dragoon, steamroller, browbeat; informal lean on, put the screws on, twist someone's arm, railroad, bulldoze. **7** they pressed for a ban **call**, ask, clamour, push, campaign, demand.
● noun **the media**, the newspapers, journalism, reporters, the fourth estate; Brit. dated Fleet Street.

pressing adjective **1 urgent**, critical, crucial, acute, desperate, serious, grave, life-and-death. **2 important**, high-priority, critical, crucial, unavoidable.

pressure noun **1 force**, load, stress, thrust, compression, weight. **2 persuasion**, intimidation, coercion, compulsion, duress, harassment, nagging, badgering. **3 strain**, stress, tension, trouble, difficulty, burden; informal hassle.
● verb **coerce**, push, persuade, force, bulldoze, hound, nag, badger, browbeat, bully, intimidate, dragoon, twist someone's arm; informal railroad, lean on; N. Amer. informal hustle.

pressurize verb **coerce**, pressure, push, persuade, force, bulldoze, hound, nag, badger, browbeat, bully, bludgeon, intimidate, dragoon, twist someone's arm; informal railroad, lean on; N. Amer. informal hustle.

prestige noun **status**, standing, kudos, cachet, stature, reputation, repute, renown, honour, esteem, importance, prominence, distinction.

prestigious adjective **reputable**, distinguished, respected, high-status, esteemed, eminent, highly regarded, renowned, influential.
- OPPOSITES disreputable, obscure.

presume verb **1 assume**, suppose, surmise, imagine, take it, expect. **2 dare**, venture, have the effrontery, be so bold as, go so far as, take the liberty of.

pretence noun **1 make-believe**, acting, faking, play-acting, posturing, deception, trickery. **2 show**, semblance, affectation, appearance, outward appearance, impression, guise, facade.
- OPPOSITES honesty.

pretend verb **put on an act**, act, play-act, put it on, dissemble, sham, feign, fake, dissimulate, make believe, put on a false front, posture, go through the motions, make as if.
● adjective (informal) **mock**, fake, sham, simulated, artificial, false, pseudo; informal phoney.

pretty adjective **attractive**, good-looking, nice-looking, personable, fetching, prepossessing, appealing, charming,

delightful, cute; *Scottish & N. English* bonny; *old use* fair, comely.
- OPPOSITES plain, ugly.
  ● *adverb (informal)* quite, rather, somewhat, fairly.

prevail *verb* **1 win**, triumph, be victorious, carry the day, come out on top, succeed, rule, reign. **2 exist**, be present, be the case, occur, be prevalent, be in force.

prevailing *adjective* **current**, existing, prevalent, usual, common, general, widespread.

prevalent *adjective* **widespread**, frequent, usual, common, current, popular, general.
- OPPOSITES rare.

prevent *verb* **stop**, avert, nip in the bud, foil, inhibit, thwart, prohibit, forbid.
- OPPOSITES allow.

previous *adjective* **1 preceding**, foregoing, prior, past, last. **2 former**, preceding, old, earlier, ex-, past, last, sometime, one-time, erstwhile, as was; *formal* quondam.
- OPPOSITES next.

previously *adverb* **formerly**, earlier (on), before, hitherto, at one time, in the past.

prey *noun* **1 quarry**, kill. **2 victim**, target, dupe; *informal* sucker; *Brit. informal* mug.
- OPPOSITES predator.

price *noun* **1 cost**, charge, fee, fare, amount, sum; *informal* damage. **2 consequence**, result, cost, penalty, toll, sacrifice, downside, drawback, disadvantage, minus.

priceless *adjective* **invaluable**, beyond price, irreplaceable, expensive, costly.
- OPPOSITES worthless, cheap.

prick *verb* **pierce**, puncture, stab, perforate, spike, penetrate, jab.
  ● *noun* jab, sting, pinprick, stab, pinhole, wound.

prickly *adjective* **spiky**, spiked, thorny, barbed, spiny, bristly.

pride *noun* **1 self-esteem**, dignity, honour, self-respect. **2 pleasure**,

joy, delight, gratification, fulfilment, satisfaction, sense of achievement. **3 arrogance**, vanity, self-importance, hubris, conceitedness, egotism, snobbery.
- OPPOSITES shame, humility.

priest *noun* **clergyman**, clergywoman, minister, cleric, pastor, vicar, rector, parson, churchman, churchwoman, father, curate; *N. Amer.* dominie; *informal* reverend, padre.

> **WORD LINKS**
> **clerical**, **sacerdotal** relating to priests

primarily *adverb* **1 first and foremost**, firstly, essentially, in essence, fundamentally, principally, predominantly. **2 mostly**, for the most part, chiefly, mainly, in the main, on the whole, largely, principally, predominantly.

primary *adjective* **main**, chief, key, prime, central, principal, foremost, first, most important, predominant, paramount; *informal* number-one.
- OPPOSITES secondary.

prime[1] *adjective* **1 main**, chief, key, primary, central, principal, foremost, first, most important, paramount, major; *informal* number-one. **2 top-quality**, top, best, first-class, superior, choice, select, finest; *informal* tip-top, A1.
- OPPOSITES secondary, inferior.
  ● *noun* heyday, peak, pinnacle, high point/spot, zenith, flower, bloom, flush.

prime[2] *verb* **brief**, fill in, prepare, advise, instruct, coach, drill, train.

primitive *adjective* **1 ancient**, earliest, first, prehistoric, primordial, primeval. **2 crude**, simple, rough (and ready), basic, rudimentary, makeshift.
- OPPOSITES modern, sophisticated.

prince *noun* **ruler**, sovereign, monarch, crowned head.

principal *adjective* **main**, chief, primary, leading, foremost, first, most important, predominant, dominant, pre-eminent, highest, top; *informal* number-one.
- OPPOSITES minor.

● *noun* **head teacher**, headmaster, headmistress, head, dean, rector, master, mistress, chancellor, vice chancellor, president, provost, warden.

principally *adverb* **mainly**, mostly, chiefly, for the most part, in the main, on the whole, largely, predominantly, primarily.

principle *noun* **1 truth**, concept, idea, theory, fundamental, essential, precept, rule, law. **2 doctrine**, belief, creed, credo, code, ethic. **3 morals**, morality, ethics, ideals, standards, integrity, virtue, probity, honour, decency, conscience, scruples.
□ **in principle 1** in theory, theoretically, on paper, ideally. **2** in general, in essence, on the whole, in the main.

print *verb* **1 publish**, issue, release, circulate, run off, copy, reproduce. **2 imprint**, impress, stamp, mark.
● *noun* **1 type**, printing, letters, lettering, characters, typeface, font. **2 impression**, handprint, fingerprint, footprint. **3 picture**, engraving, etching, lithograph, woodcut. **4 photograph**, photo, snap, snapshot, picture, still, enlargement, reproduction, copy.

prior *adjective* **earlier**, previous, preceding, advance, pre-existing.
- OPPOSITES subsequent.
□ **prior to** before, until, up to, previous to, preceding, earlier than, in advance of.

priority *noun* **1 prime concern**, main consideration, most important thing. **2 precedence**, preference, pre-eminence, predominance, primacy.

prison *noun* **jail**, penal institution; *N. Amer.* jailhouse, penitentiary, correctional facility; *informal* clink, slammer; *Brit. informal* nick; *N. Amer. informal* can, pen.
□ **in prison** behind bars; *informal* inside, doing time; *Brit. informal* doing porridge.

prisoner *noun* **1 convict**, detainee, inmate; *informal* jailbird, con; *Brit. informal* lag; *N. Amer. informal* yardbird. **2 prisoner of war**, POW, internee, captive, hostage.

pristine *adjective* **immaculate**, perfect, in mint condition, as new, spotless, unspoilt.
- OPPOSITES dirty, spoilt.

privacy *noun* **seclusion**, solitude, isolation.

private *adjective* **1 personal**, own, special, exclusive. **2 confidential**, secret, classified, privileged, unofficial, off the record; *informal* hush-hush. **3 intimate**, personal, secret, innermost, undisclosed, unspoken, unvoiced. **4 reserved**, introverted, self-contained, reticent, retiring, unsociable, withdrawn, solitary, reclusive, secretive. **5 secluded**, undisturbed, out of the way, remote, isolated. **6 independent**, non-state, privatized, commercial, private-enterprise.
- OPPOSITES public, open, official.
● *noun* **private soldier**, trooper; *Brit.* sapper, gunner; *US* GI; *Brit. informal* Tommy, squaddie.
□ **in private** in secret, secretly, privately, behind closed doors, in camera, sub rosa.

privilege *noun* **1 advantage**, benefit, prerogative, entitlement, right, concession, freedom, liberty. **2 honour**, pleasure.

privileged *adjective* **1 wealthy**, rich, affluent, prosperous, elite, advantaged. **2 confidential**, private, secret, restricted, classified, not for publication, off the record, inside; *informal* hush-hush.
- OPPOSITES underprivileged, disadvantaged.

prize *noun* **award**, reward, trophy, medal, cup, winnings, purse, honour.
● *adjective* **1 champion**, award-winning, top, best. **2 utter**, complete, total, absolute, real, perfect; *Brit. informal* right.

probability *noun* **likelihood**, prospect, expectation, chance(s), odds, possibility.

probable *adjective* **likely**, odds-on, expected, anticipated, predictable; *informal* on the cards, a safe bet.

- OPPOSITES unlikely.

probably adverb **in all likelihood**, in all probability, as likely as not, ten to one, the chances are, doubtless.

probation noun **trial**, trial period, apprenticeship, training.

probe noun **investigation**, enquiry, examination, inquest, study.
● verb **1 prod**, poke, dig into, delve into, explore, feel around in, examine. **2 investigate**, enquire into, look into, go into, study, examine, explore.

problem noun **1 difficulty**, worry, complication, snag, hitch, drawback, stumbling block, obstacle, hiccup, setback, issue, catch, dilemma, quandary; informal headache, fly in the ointment. **2 nuisance**, bother; informal drag, pain, hassle. **3 puzzle**, question, poser, riddle, conundrum; informal brain-teaser.

problematic adjective **difficult**, troublesome, tricky, awkward, controversial, ticklish, complicated, complex, knotty.
- OPPOSITES easy, straightforward.

procedure noun **course of action**, method, system, strategy, way, approach, formula, solution, mechanism, technique, routine, drill, practice.

proceed verb **1 begin**, make a start, get going, move. **2 go**, make your way, advance, move, progress, carry on, continue, press on, push on.
- OPPOSITES stop.

proceedings plural noun **1 events**, activities, action, happenings, goings-on. **2 report**, transactions, minutes, account, story, record(s). **3 legal action**, litigation, suit, lawsuit, case, prosecution.

proceeds plural noun **profits**, earnings, receipts, returns, takings, income, revenue, profit, yield; Sport gate (money); N. Amer. take.

process noun **1 procedure**, operation, action, activity, exercise, business, job, task, undertaking. **2** a new manufacturing process **method**, system, technique, means.

● verb **deal with**, attend to, see to, sort out, handle, take care of.

procession noun **parade**, march, march past, cavalcade, motorcade, cortège, column, file; Brit. informal crocodile.

proclaim verb **declare**, announce, pronounce, state, make known, give out, advertise, publish, broadcast, trumpet.

prod verb **1 poke**, jab, stab, dig, nudge, elbow. **2 spur**, stimulate, prompt, push, galvanize, persuade, urge, chivvy, remind.

prodigal adjective **wasteful**, extravagant, spendthrift.
- OPPOSITES thrifty.

prodigy noun **genius**, mastermind, virtuoso, wunderkind; informal whizz-kid, whizz.

produce verb **1 manufacture**, make, construct, build, fabricate, put together, assemble, turn out, create, mass-produce. **2 yield**, grow, give, supply, provide, furnish, bear. **3 give birth to**, bear, deliver, bring forth, bring into the world. **4 create**, fashion, turn out, compose, write, pen, paint. **5 pull out**, extract, fish out, present, offer, proffer, show. **6 cause**, bring about, give rise to, occasion, generate, lead to, result in, provoke, precipitate, spark off, trigger. **7 stage**, put on, mount, present, exhibit.
● noun **food**, foodstuff(s), products, crops, harvest.

producer noun **1 manufacturer**, maker, builder, constructor. **2 grower**, farmer. **3 impresario**, manager, administrator, promoter, director.

product noun **1 artefact**, commodity; (**products**) goods, ware(s), merchandise, produce. **2 result**, consequence, outcome, effect, upshot.

production noun **1 manufacture**, making, construction, building, fabrication, assembly, creation, mass production. **2 creation**, origination, fashioning, composition, writing. **3 output**, yield, productivity. **4 performance**, staging, presentation, show, piece, play.

p

productive *adjective* **1 prolific**, inventive, creative. **2 useful**, constructive, profitable, fruitful, valuable, effective, worthwhile, helpful. **3 fertile**, fruitful, rich, fecund.

productivity *noun* **efficiency**, work rate, output, yield, production.

profess *verb* **1 declare**, announce, proclaim, assert, state, affirm, maintain, protest, avow. **2 claim**, pretend, purport, affect, make out.

professed *adjective* **1 claimed**, supposed, ostensible, self-styled, apparent, pretended, purported. **2 declared**, sworn, confirmed, self-confessed.

profession *noun* **career**, occupation, calling, vocation, métier, line of work, job, business, trade, craft.

professional *adjective* **1 white-collar**, non-manual, graduate, qualified, chartered. **2 paid**, salaried. **3 expert**, accomplished, skilful, masterly, fine, polished, skilled, proficient, competent, able, businesslike, deft. **4** *he always behaved in a professional way* **appropriate**, fitting, proper, honourable, ethical.
- OPPOSITES amateur, amateurish.
● *noun* **expert**, virtuoso, old hand, master, maestro, past master; *informal* pro, ace.

profile *noun* **1 outline**, silhouette, side view, contour, shape, form, lines. **2 description**, account, study, portrait, rundown, sketch, outline.

profit *noun* **1 financial gain**, return(s), yield, proceeds, earnings, winnings, surplus; *informal* pay dirt, bottom line. **2 advantage**, benefit, value, use, good; *informal* mileage.
- OPPOSITES loss, disadvantage.
● *verb* **1 make money**, earn; *informal* rake it in, clean up, make a killing; *N. Amer. informal* make a fast buck. **2 benefit**, be advantageous to, be of use to, do someone good, help, be of service to, serve.
- OPPOSITES lose.

profitable *adjective* **1 moneymaking**, profit-making, paying, lucrative, commercial, successful, money-spinning,

gainful. **2 beneficial**, useful, advantageous, valuable, productive, worthwhile, rewarding, fruitful, illuminating, informative, well spent.

profound *adjective* **1 heartfelt**, intense, keen, extreme, acute, severe, sincere, earnest, deep, deep-seated, overpowering, overwhelming. **2 far-reaching**, radical, extensive, sweeping, exhaustive, thoroughgoing. **3 wise**, learned, intelligent, scholarly, discerning, penetrating, perceptive, astute, thoughtful, insightful.
- OPPOSITES superficial.

programme *noun* **1 schedule**, agenda, calendar, timetable, order (of the day), line-up. **2 scheme**, plan, package, strategy, initiative, proposal. **3 broadcast**, production, show, presentation, transmission, performance, telecast, videocast, podcast. **4 course**, syllabus, curriculum.
● *verb* **arrange**, organize, schedule, plan, map out, timetable, line up; *N. Amer.* slate.

progress *noun* **1 (forward) movement**, advance, going, headway, passage. **2 development**, advance, advancement, headway, step forward, improvement, growth.
● *verb* **1 go**, make your way, move, proceed, advance, go on, continue, make headway, work your way. **2 develop**, make progress, advance, make headway, move on, get on, gain ground, improve, get better, come on, come along, make strides.
- OPPOSITES regress.
□ **in progress** under way, going on, ongoing, happening, occurring, taking place, proceeding, continuing.

progression *noun* **1 progress**, advancement, movement, passage, development, evolution, growth. **2 succession**, series, sequence, string, stream, chain, train, row, cycle.

progressive *adjective* **1 continuing**, continuous, ongoing, gradual, step-by-step, cumulative. **2 modern**, liberal, advanced, forward-thinking,

enlightened, pioneering, reforming, reformist, radical; *informal* go-ahead.
- OPPOSITES conservative.

prohibit *verb* **1 forbid**, ban, bar, proscribe, make illegal, outlaw, disallow, veto. **2 prevent**, stop, rule out, preclude, make impossible.
- OPPOSITES allow.

prohibition *noun* **ban**, bar, veto, embargo, boycott, injunction, moratorium, interdict.

project *noun* **1 scheme**, plan, programme, enterprise, undertaking, venture, proposal, idea, concept. **2 assignment**, piece of work, task.
● *verb* **1 forecast**, predict, expect, estimate, calculate, reckon. **2 stick out**, jut (out), protrude, extend, stand out, bulge out. **3 cast**, throw, send, shed, shine.

projection *noun* **1 forecast**, prediction, prognosis, expectation, estimate. **2 outcrop**, outgrowth, overhang, ledge, shelf, prominence, protrusion, protuberance.

proliferate *verb* **increase**, grow, multiply, rocket, mushroom, snowball, burgeon, spread, expand, run riot.
- OPPOSITES decrease, dwindle.

prolific *adjective* **1 plentiful**, abundant, bountiful, profuse, copious, luxuriant, rich, lush, fruitful. **2 productive**, fertile, creative, inventive.
- OPPOSITES meagre.

prolong *verb* **lengthen**, extend, drag out, draw out, protract, spin out, carry on, continue, keep up, perpetuate.
- OPPOSITES shorten.

prominence *noun* **1 fame**, celebrity, eminence, importance, distinction, greatness, prestige, stature, standing. **2** *the press gave prominence to the reports* **wide coverage**, importance, precedence, weight, a high profile, top billing.

prominent *adjective* **1 important**, well known, leading, eminent, distinguished, notable, noteworthy, noted, illustrious, celebrated, famous, renowned; *N. Amer.* major-league.

2 jutting (out), protruding, projecting, protuberant, standing out, sticking out, proud, bulging. **3 conspicuous**, noticeable, obvious, unmistakable, eye-catching, pronounced, salient, striking, dominant, obtrusive.
- OPPOSITES unimportant, inconspicuous.

promise *noun* **1 word (of honour)**, assurance, pledge, vow, guarantee, oath, bond, undertaking, agreement, commitment, contract. **2 potential**, ability, talent, aptitude, possibility.
● *verb* **1 give your word**, swear, pledge, vow, undertake, give an undertaking, guarantee, warrant, contract, give an assurance, commit yourself. **2 indicate**, lead someone to expect, point to, be a sign of, betoken, give hope of, augur, herald, portend, presage.

promising *adjective* **1 good**, encouraging, favourable, hopeful, auspicious, propitious, bright, rosy, heartening. **2 talented**, gifted, budding, up-and-coming, rising, coming, in the making.
- OPPOSITES unfavourable.

promote *verb* **1 upgrade**, give promotion to, elevate, advance, move up. **2 encourage**, further, advance, foster, develop, contribute to, boost, stimulate. **3 advertise**, publicize, give publicity to, beat/bang the drum for, market, merchandise; *informal* push, plug, hype.
- OPPOSITES demote, obstruct.

promotion *noun* **1 upgrading**, preferment, elevation, advancement, step up (the ladder). **2 encouragement**, furtherance, furthering, advancement, contribution to, fostering, boosting, stimulation. **3 advertising**, marketing, publicity, propaganda; *informal* hard sell, plug, hype, puff.

prompt *verb* **1 induce**, make, move, motivate, lead, dispose, persuade, incline, encourage, stimulate, prod, impel, spur on, inspire. **2 give rise to**, bring about, cause, occasion, result in, lead to, elicit, produce, precipitate, trigger, spark off, provoke. **3 remind**,

cue, feed, help out, jog someone's memory.
- OPPOSITES deter.
● *adjective* **quick**, swift, rapid, speedy, fast, expeditious, direct, immediate, instant, early, punctual, in good time, on time.
- OPPOSITES slow, late.
● *adverb* **exactly**, precisely, sharp, on the dot, dead, punctually; *informal* bang on; *N. Amer. informal* on the button, on the nose.

promptly *adverb* **1 punctually**, on time; *informal* on the dot, bang on; *Brit. informal* spot on; *N. Amer. informal* on the button, on the nose. **2 without delay**, straight/right away, at once, immediately, now, as soon as possible, quickly, swiftly, rapidly, speedily, fast; *informal* pronto, asap.
- OPPOSITES late.

prone *adjective* **1 susceptible**, vulnerable, subject, open, liable, given, predisposed, likely, disposed, inclined, apt. **2 lying face down**, on your stomach/front, lying flat, lying down, horizontal, prostrate.

pronounce *verb* **1 say**, enunciate, articulate, utter, voice, sound, vocalize, get your tongue round. **2 declare**, proclaim, judge, rule, decree, ordain.

pronounced *adjective* **noticeable**, marked, strong, conspicuous, striking, distinct, prominent, unmistakable, obvious.
- OPPOSITES slight.

proof *noun* **evidence**, verification, corroboration, demonstration, authentication, confirmation, certification, documentation.
● *adjective* **resistant**, immune, unaffected, impervious.

prop *noun* **1 pole**, post, support, upright, brace, buttress, stay, strut. **2 mainstay**, pillar, anchor, support, cornerstone.
● *verb* **lean**, rest, stand, balance.
□ **prop up 1** hold up, shore up, buttress, support, brace, underpin. **2** subsidize, underwrite, fund, finance.

propaganda *noun* **information**, promotion, advertising, publicity, disinformation; *informal* hype.

propel *verb* **1 move**, power, push, drive. **2 throw**, thrust, toss, fling, hurl, pitch, send, shoot.

proper *adjective* **1 real**, genuine, actual, true, bona fide; *informal* kosher. **2 right**, correct, accepted, conventional, established, official, regular, acceptable, appropriate, suitable, apt. **3 formal**, conventional, correct, orthodox, polite, respectable, seemly.
- OPPOSITES wrong, improper.

property *noun* **1 possessions**, belongings, things, effects, stuff, goods; *informal* gear. **2 building(s)**, premises, house(s), land; *N. Amer.* real estate. **3 quality**, attribute, characteristic, feature, power, trait, hallmark.

prophecy *noun* **prediction**, forecast, prognostication, prognosis, divination.

prophesy *verb* **predict**, foretell, forecast, foresee, prognosticate.

prophet, prophetess *noun* **forecaster**, seer, soothsayer, fortune teller, clairvoyant, oracle.

proportion *noun* **1 part**, portion, amount, quantity, bit, piece, percentage, fraction, section, segment, share. **2 ratio**, distribution, relative amount/number, relationship. **3 balance**, symmetry, harmony, correspondence, correlation, agreement. **4** *men of huge proportions* **size**, dimensions, magnitude, measurements, mass, volume, bulk, expanse, extent.

proportional, proportionate *adjective* **corresponding**, comparable, in proportion, pro rata, commensurate, equivalent, consistent.
- OPPOSITES disproportionate.

proposal *noun* **scheme**, plan, idea, project, programme, motion, proposition, suggestion, submission.

propose *verb* **1 put forward**, suggest, submit, advance, offer, present, move, come up with, nominate, recommend. **2 intend**, mean, plan, have in mind, aim.

proposition noun **1 proposal**, scheme, plan, project, idea, programme. **2 task**, job, undertaking, venture, activity, affair.

proprietor, **proprietress** noun **owner**, possessor, holder, householder, master, mistress, landowner, landlord, landlady, shopkeeper.

prosecute verb **charge**, take to court, take legal action against, sue, try, bring to trial, put on trial, put in the dock, indict; N. Amer. impeach.
- OPPOSITES defend.

prospect noun **likelihood**, hope, expectation, chance, odds, probability, possibility, promise, outlook, lookout.
● verb **search**, look, explore, survey, scout, hunt, dowse.

prospective adjective **potential**, possible, probable, likely, future, eventual, -to-be, soon-to-be, in the making, intending, aspiring, would-be.

prospectus noun **brochure**, syllabus, curriculum, catalogue, programme, list, schedule.

prosper verb **flourish**, thrive, do well, bloom, blossom, burgeon, progress, do all right for yourself, get ahead, get on (in the world), be successful; informal go places.
- OPPOSITES fail.

prosperity noun **success**, affluence, wealth, ease, plenty.
- OPPOSITES hardship, failure.

prosperous adjective **thriving**, flourishing, successful, strong, vigorous, profitable, lucrative, expanding, booming, burgeoning, **affluent**, wealthy, rich, moneyed, well off, well-to-do; informal in the money.
- OPPOSITES ailing, poor.

prostitute noun whore, sex worker, call girl, courtesan; informal working girl; N. Amer. informal hooker, hustler.
● verb **betray**, sacrifice, sell, sell out, debase, degrade, demean, devalue, cheapen, lower, shame, misuse.

protect verb **keep safe**, keep from harm, guard, defend, shield, save, safeguard, preserve, cushion, insulate, shelter, screen, keep, look after.
- OPPOSITES expose, harm.

protection noun **1 defence**, security, safeguard, safety, sanctuary, shelter, refuge, immunity, indemnity. **2 safe keeping**, care, charge, guardianship, support, aegis, patronage. **3 barrier**, buffer, shield, screen, cushion, bulwark, armour, insulation.

protective adjective **1 protecting**, covering, insulated, impermeable, -proof, -resistant. **2 solicitous**, careful, caring, defensive, paternal, maternal, overprotective, possessive.

protector noun **1 defender**, preserver, guardian, champion, patron, custodian. **2 guard**, shield, buffer, cushion, pad, screen.

protest noun **1 objection**, complaint, challenge, dissent, demurral, remonstration, fuss, outcry. **2 demonstration**, rally, vigil, sit-in, occupation, work-to-rule, stoppage, strike, walkout, mutiny, picket, boycott; informal demo.
● verb **1 object**, express opposition, dissent, take issue, take a stand, put up a fight, take exception, complain, express disapproval, disagree, make a fuss, speak out; informal kick up a fuss. **2 insist on**, maintain, assert, affirm, announce, proclaim, declare, profess, avow.

protocol noun **etiquette**, convention, formalities, custom, the rules, procedure, ritual, decorum, the done thing.

prototype noun **original**, master, template, pattern, sample.

protract verb **prolong**, lengthen, extend, draw out, drag out, spin out, stretch out, string out.
- OPPOSITES curtail, shorten.

protracted adjective **prolonged**, extended, long-drawn-out, lengthy, long.
- OPPOSITES short.

proud adjective **1 pleased**, glad, happy, delighted, thrilled, satisfied, gratified. **2** a proud moment **pleasing**, gratifying, satisfying, cheering, heart-warming,

p

happy, glorious. **3 arrogant**, conceited, vain, self-important, full of yourself, overbearing, bumptious, presumptuous, overweening, haughty, high and mighty; *informal* big-headed, too big for your boots, stuck-up.
- OPPOSITES ashamed, humble.

prove *verb* **show (to be true)**, demonstrate, substantiate, corroborate, verify, validate, authenticate, confirm.
- OPPOSITES disprove.

proverb *noun* **saying**, adage, saw, maxim, axiom, motto, aphorism, epigram.

provide *verb* **1 supply**, give, come up with, produce, deliver, donate, contribute; *informal* fork out, lay out. **2** *he was provided with tools* **equip**, furnish, issue, supply, fit out, rig out, kit out, arm, provision; *informal* fix up. **3 offer**, present, afford, give, add, bring, yield, impart, lend.
□ **provide for** feed, nurture, nourish, support, maintain, keep, sustain.

provided, providing *conjunction* **if**, on condition that, provided that, presuming (that), assuming (that), as long as, with/on the understanding that.

provider *noun* **supplier**, donor, giver, contributor, source.

province *noun* **1 territory**, region, state, department, canton, area, district, sector, zone, division. **2 (the provinces) the regions**, the rest of the country, rural areas/districts, the countryside; *informal* the sticks, the middle of nowhere; *N. Amer. informal* the boondocks. **3 domain**, area, department, responsibility, sphere, world, realm, field, discipline, territory; *informal* bailiwick.

provincial *adjective* **1 local**, small-town, rural, country, outlying, backwoods; *informal* one-horse. **2 unsophisticated**, parochial, insular, narrow-minded, inward-looking, suburban, small-town; *N. Amer. informal* corn-fed.
- OPPOSITES cosmopolitan, sophisticated.

provision *noun* **1** *limited provision for young children* **facilities**, services,

amenities, resource(s), arrangements. **2 (provisions) supplies**, food and drink, stores, groceries, foodstuff(s), rations. **3 term**, requirement, specification, stipulation.

provisional *adjective* **interim**, temporary, transitional, changeover, stopgap, short-term, fill-in, acting, working.
- OPPOSITES permanent, definite.

provocation *noun* **goading**, prodding, incitement, harassment, pressure, teasing, taunting, torment; *informal* hassle, aggravation.

provocative *adjective* **annoying**, irritating, maddening, galling, insulting, offensive, inflammatory, incendiary, like a red rag to a bull; *informal* aggravating.

provoke *verb* **1 arouse**, produce, evoke, cause, give rise to, excite, spark off, touch off, kindle, generate, engender, instigate, result in, lead to, bring on, precipitate, prompt, trigger. **2 goad**, spur, prick, sting, prod, incite, rouse, stimulate. **3 annoy**, anger, enrage, irritate, madden, nettle; *Brit.* rub up the wrong way; *informal* aggravate, rile, needle, get/put someone's back up; *Brit. informal* wind up.
- OPPOSITES allay, appease.

prowess *noun* **skill**, expertise, mastery, ability, capability, capacity, talent, aptitude, dexterity, proficiency, finesse; *informal* know-how.
- OPPOSITES inability, ineptitude.

prowl *verb* **steal**, slink, skulk, sneak, stalk, creep; *informal* snoop.

proxy *noun* **deputy**, representative, substitute, delegate, agent, surrogate, stand-in, go-between.

prudent *adjective* **1 wise**, well judged, sensible, politic, judicious, shrewd, sage, sagacious, far-sighted, canny. **2 cautious**, careful, provident, circumspect, thrifty, economical.
- OPPOSITES unwise, extravagant.

prudish *adjective* **puritanical**, priggish, prim, moralistic, censorious, strait-laced, Victorian, stuffy; *informal* goody-goody.

- OPPOSITES permissive.

prune *verb* **1 cut back**, trim, clip, shear, shorten, thin, shape. **2 reduce**, cut (back/down), pare (down), slim down, trim, downsize, axe, shrink; *informal* slash.
- OPPOSITES increase.

pry *verb* **be inquisitive**, poke about/around, ferret about/around, spy, be a busybody; *informal* stick/poke your nose in/into, be nosy, snoop; *Austral./NZ informal* stickybeak.

pseudonym *noun* **pen name**, nom de plume, assumed name, alias, sobriquet, stage name, nom de guerre.

psychiatrist *noun* **psychotherapist**, psychoanalyst, analyst; *informal* shrink.

psychic *adjective* **1 supernatural**, paranormal, other-worldly, metaphysical, extrasensory, magic(al), mystic(al), occult. **2 clairvoyant**, telepathic.
● *noun* **clairvoyant**, fortune teller, medium, spiritualist, telepath, mind-reader.

psychological *adjective* **1 mental**, emotional, inner, cognitive. **2 (all) in the mind**, psychosomatic, emotional, subjective, subconscious, unconscious.
- OPPOSITES physical.

psychology *noun* **mind**, mindset, thought processes, way of thinking, mentality, psyche, attitude(s), make-up, character, temperament; *informal* what makes someone tick.

pub *noun* (*Brit.*) **bar**, inn, tavern, hostelry; *Brit.* public house; *informal* watering hole; *Brit. informal* local, boozer; *N. Amer. historical* saloon.

puberty *noun* **adolescence**, pubescence, youth, teenage years, teens.

public *adjective* **1 state**, national, constitutional, civic, civil, official, social, municipal, nationalized. **2 popular**, general, common, communal, collective, shared, joint, universal, widespread. **3 prominent**, well known, important, leading, eminent, distinguished, celebrated, household, famous; *N. Amer.* major-league. **4 open** (**to the public**), communal, available, free, unrestricted.
- OPPOSITES private, secret.
● *noun* **1 people**, citizens, subjects, electors, electorate, voters, taxpayers, residents, inhabitants, citizenry, population, populace, community, society, country, nation. **2 audience**, spectators, concertgoers, theatregoers, followers, following, fans, devotees, admirers.

> **WORD LINKS**
> **agoraphobia** fear of public places

publication *noun* **1 book**, volume, title, opus, tome, newspaper, paper, magazine, periodical, newsletter, bulletin, journal, report. **2 issuing**, publishing, printing, distribution.

publicity *noun* **1 public attention**, media attention, exposure, glare, limelight, spotlight. **2 promotion**, advertising, propaganda, boost, push; *informal* hype, ballyhoo, puff, build-up, plug.

publicize *verb* **1 make known**, make public, announce, broadcast, spread, promulgate, disseminate, circulate, air. **2 advertise**, promote, build up, talk up, push, beat the drum for, boost; *informal* hype, plug, puff (up).
- OPPOSITES conceal, suppress.

publish *verb* **1 issue**, bring out, produce, print. **2 make known**, make public, publicize, announce, broadcast, issue, put out, distribute, spread, promulgate, disseminate, circulate, air.

pudding *noun* **dessert**, sweet, last course; *Brit. informal* afters, pud.

puerile *adjective* **childish**, immature, infantile, juvenile, babyish, silly, inane, fatuous, foolish.
- OPPOSITES mature.

puff *noun* **1 gust**, blast, flurry, rush, draught, waft, breeze, breath. **2 pull**; *informal* drag, toke.
● *verb* **1 breathe heavily**, pant, blow, gasp. **2 smoke**, draw on, drag on, inhale.

pugnacious *adjective* **combative**, aggressive, antagonistic, belligerent,

p

quarrelsome, argumentative, hostile, truculent.
- OPPOSITES peaceable.

pull verb **1 tug**, haul, drag, draw, tow, heave, jerk, wrench; *informal* yank. **2 strain**, sprain, wrench, tear. **3 attract**, draw, bring in, pull in, lure, seduce, entice, tempt.
- OPPOSITES push.

● noun **1 tug**, jerk, heave; *informal* yank. **2 gulp**, draught, drink, swallow, mouthful, slug; *informal* swig. **3 puff**; *informal* drag, toke. **4 attraction**, draw, lure, magnetism, fascination, appeal, allure.
□ **pull off** achieve, fulfil, succeed in, accomplish, bring off, carry off, clinch, fix. **pull out** withdraw, resign, leave, retire, step down, bow out, back out, give up; *informal* quit. **pull through** get better, get well again, improve, recover, rally, come through, recuperate.

pulp noun **1 mush**, mash, paste, purée, slop, slush, mulch. **2 flesh**, marrow, meat.
● verb **mash**, purée, cream, crush, press, liquidize.

pulse noun **1 heartbeat**, heart rate. **2 rhythm**, beat, tempo, pounding, throb, throbbing, thudding, drumming.
● verb **throb**, pulsate, vibrate, beat, pound, thud, thump, drum, reverberate, echo.

pump verb **1 force**, drive, push, inject, suck, draw. **2 inflate**, blow up, fill up, swell, enlarge, distend, expand, dilate, puff up. **3 spurt**, spout, squirt, jet, surge, spew, gush, stream, flow, pour, spill, well, cascade.

punch[1] verb **hit**, strike, thump, jab, smash; *informal* sock, slug, biff, bop; *Brit. informal* stick one on, slosh; *N. Amer. informal* boff, bust; *Austral./NZ informal* quilt.
● noun **blow**, hit, knock, thump, box, jab, clip; *informal* sock, slug, biff, bop; *N. Amer. informal* boff, bust.

punch[2] verb **perforate**, puncture, pierce, prick, hole, spike, skewer.

punctual adjective **on time**, prompt, on schedule, in (good) time; *informal* on the dot.
- OPPOSITES late.

punctuate verb **break up**, interrupt, intersperse, pepper, sprinkle, scatter.

puncture noun **1 hole**, perforation, rupture, cut, gash, slit, leak. **2 flat tyre**; *informal* flat.
● verb **prick**, pierce, stab, rupture, perforate, cut, slit, deflate.

pungent adjective **strong**, powerful, pervasive, penetrating, sharp, acid, sour, biting, bitter, tart, vinegary, tangy, aromatic, spicy, piquant, peppery, hot, garlicky.
- OPPOSITES bland, mild.

punish verb **discipline**, penalize, correct, sentence, teach someone a lesson; *informal* come down on (like a ton of bricks); *dated* chastise.

punishing adjective **arduous**, demanding, taxing, strenuous, rigorous, stressful, trying, heavy, difficult, tough, exhausting, tiring, gruelling.
- OPPOSITES easy.

punishment noun **penalty**, sanction, penance, discipline, forfeit, sentence.

> **WORD LINKS**
> **penal, punitive** relating to punishment

punitive adjective **penal**, disciplinary, corrective.

puny adjective **1 small**, weak, feeble, slight, undersized, stunted, underdeveloped; *informal* weedy. **2 pitiful**, pitiable, miserable, sorry, meagre, paltry; *informal* pathetic, measly.
- OPPOSITES sturdy.

pupil noun **1 student**, scholar, schoolchild, schoolboy, schoolgirl. **2 disciple**, follower, student, protégé, apprentice, trainee, novice.
- OPPOSITES teacher.

puppet noun **1 marionette**, glove puppet, finger puppet. **2 pawn**, tool, instrument, cat's paw, poodle, mouthpiece, stooge.

purchase *verb* **buy**, acquire, obtain, pick up, procure, pay for, invest in; *informal* get hold of, score.
- OPPOSITES sell.
● *noun* **1 acquisition**, buy, investment, order. **2 grip**, grasp, hold, foothold, toehold, anchorage, support, traction, leverage.
- OPPOSITES sale.

pure *adjective* **1 unadulterated**, undiluted, sterling, solid, unalloyed. **2 clean**, clear, fresh, sparkling, unpolluted, uncontaminated, untainted. **3 virtuous**, moral, good, righteous, honourable, reputable, wholesome, clean, honest, upright, upstanding, exemplary, innocent, chaste, unsullied, undefiled; *informal* squeaky clean. **4 sheer**, utter, absolute, out-and-out, complete, total, perfect.
- OPPOSITES impure, polluted.

purely *adverb* **entirely**, wholly, exclusively, solely, only, just, merely.

purge *verb* **1 cleanse**, clear, purify, rid, empty, strip, scour. **2 remove**, get rid of, eliminate, clear out, sweep out, expel, eject, evict, dismiss, sack, oust, axe, depose, root out, weed out.
● *noun* **removal**, elimination, expulsion, ejection, exclusion, eviction, dismissal.

purify *verb* **clean**, cleanse, refine, decontaminate, filter, clear, freshen, deodorize, sanitize, disinfect, sterilize.

puritanical *adjective* **moralistic**, puritan, strait-laced, stuffy, prudish, prim, priggish, narrow-minded, censorious, austere, severe, ascetic, abstemious; *informal* goody-goody, starchy.
- OPPOSITES permissive.

purity *noun* **1 cleanness**, freshness, cleanliness. **2 virtue**, morality, goodness, righteousness, piety, honour, honesty, integrity, innocence.

purpose *noun* **1 motive**, motivation, grounds, occasion, reason, point, basis, justification. **2 intention**, aim, object, objective, goal, plan, ambition, aspiration. **3 function**, role, use. **4 determination**, resolution, resolve,

steadfastness, single-mindedness, enthusiasm, ambition, motivation, commitment, conviction, dedication.
□ **on purpose** deliberately, intentionally, purposely, wilfully, knowingly, consciously.

purposeful *adjective* **determined**, resolute, steadfast, single-minded, committed.
- OPPOSITES aimless.

purposely *adverb* **deliberately**, intentionally, on purpose, wilfully, knowingly, consciously.

purse *noun* **1 wallet**; N. Amer. change purse, billfold. **2** *(N. Amer.)* **handbag**, shoulder bag, clutch bag; N. Amer. pocketbook. **3 prize**, reward, winnings, stake(s).
● *verb* **press together**, compress, tighten, pucker, pout.

pursue *verb* **1 follow**, run after, chase, hunt, stalk, track, trail, hound. **2 strive for**, work towards, seek, search for, aim at/for, aspire to. **3 engage in**, be occupied in, practise, follow, conduct, ply, take up, undertake, carry on with, continue, proceed with, apply oneself to.

pursuit *noun a range of leisure pursuits* **activity**, hobby, pastime, diversion, recreation, amusement, occupation.

push *verb* **1 shove**, thrust, propel, send, drive, force, prod, poke, nudge, elbow, shoulder, ram, squeeze, jostle. **2 press**, depress, hold down, squeeze, operate, activate. **3 urge**, press, pressure, pressurize, force, coerce, dragoon, browbeat; *informal* lean on, twist someone's arm.
- OPPOSITES pull.
● *noun* **1 shove**, thrust, nudge, bump, jolt, prod, poke. **2** *the army's eastward push* **advance**, drive, thrust, charge, attack, assault, onslaught, onrush, offensive.

pushy *adjective* **assertive**, overbearing, domineering, aggressive, forceful, forward, thrusting, ambitious, driven, overconfident, cocky; *informal* bossy.

put *verb* **1 place**, set, lay, deposit, position, leave, plant, locate, situate,

p

settle, install; *informal* stick, dump, park, plonk, pop; *N. Amer. informal* plunk. **2 express**, word, phrase, frame, formulate, render, convey, state.
□ **put across/over** communicate, convey, get across/over, explain, make clear, spell out. **put off 1** deter, discourage, dissuade, daunt, unnerve, intimidate, scare off; *informal* turn off. **2** postpone, defer, delay, put back, adjourn, hold over, reschedule, shelve; *N. Amer.* table; *informal* put on ice, put on the back burner. **put out 1** annoy, anger, irritate, offend, displease, irk, gall, upset; *informal* rile, miff. **2** inconvenience, trouble, bother, impose on. **3** extinguish, quench, douse, smother, blow out, snuff out. **4** issue, publish, release, bring out, circulate, publicize, post. **put up 1** accommodate, house,

take in, give someone a roof over their head. **2** nominate, propose, put forward, recommend. **3** build, construct, erect, raise. **4** display, pin up, stick up, hang up, post. **5** provide, supply, furnish, give, contribute, donate, pledge, pay; *informal* cough up, shell out; *N. Amer. informal* ante up, pony up. **put up with** tolerate, take, stand (for), accept, stomach, swallow, endure, bear; *informal* abide, lump it; *Brit. informal* stick; *formal* brook.

puzzle *verb* **baffle**, perplex, bewilder, confuse, bemuse, mystify, nonplus; *informal* flummox, stump, beat.
● *noun* **enigma**, mystery, paradox, conundrum, poser, riddle, problem.

puzzling *adjective* **baffling**, perplexing, bewildering, confusing, complicated, unclear, mysterious, enigmatic.

p

quaint *adjective* **1 picturesque**, charming, sweet, attractive, old-fashioned, old-world; *Brit.* twee. **2 unusual**, curious, eccentric, quirky, bizarre, whimsical, unconventional; *informal* offbeat.
- OPPOSITES ugly.

quake *verb* **shake**, tremble, quiver, shudder, sway, rock, wobble, move, heave, convulse.

qualification *noun* **1 certificate**, diploma, degree, licence, document, warrant. **2 modification**, limitation, reservation, stipulation, alteration, amendment, revision, moderation, mitigation, condition, proviso, caveat.

qualified *adjective* **1 certified**, certificated, chartered, licensed, professional. **2 limited**, conditional, restricted, contingent, circumscribed, guarded, equivocal, modified, adapted, amended, adjusted, moderated, reduced.
- OPPOSITES wholehearted.

qualify *verb* **1 be eligible**, meet the requirements, be entitled, be permitted. **2 be certified**, be licensed, pass, graduate, succeed. **3 authorize**, empower, allow, permit, license. **4 modify**, limit, restrict, make conditional, moderate, temper, modulate, mitigate.

quality *noun* **1 standard**, grade, class, calibre, condition, character, nature, form, rank, value, level. **2 excellence**, superiority, merit, worth, value, virtue, calibre, distinction. **3 feature**, trait, attribute, characteristic, point, aspect, facet, side, property.

quantity *noun* **amount**, total, aggregate, sum, quota, mass, weight, volume, bulk.

quarrel *noun* **argument**, disagreement, squabble, fight, dispute, wrangle, clash, altercation, feud, vendetta; *Brit.* row;
informal tiff, slanging match, run-in, spat; *Brit. informal* bust-up.
- OPPOSITES agreement.
● *verb* **argue**, fight, disagree, fall out, differ, be at odds, bicker, squabble, cross swords; *Brit.* row.
- OPPOSITES agree.
□ **quarrel with** fault, criticize, object to, oppose, take exception to, attack, take issue with, impugn, contradict, dispute, controvert; *informal* knock.

quarrelsome *adjective* **argumentative**, disputatious, confrontational, captious, pugnacious, combative, antagonistic, bellicose, belligerent, cantankerous, choleric; *Brit. informal* stroppy.
- OPPOSITES peaceable.

quarry *noun* **prey**, victim, object, goal, target, kill, game, prize.

quarter *noun* **1 district**, area, region, part, side, neighbourhood, precinct, locality, sector, zone, ghetto, community, enclave. **2 source**, direction, place, location. **3** *the servants' quarters* **accommodation**, lodgings, rooms, chambers, home; *informal* pad, digs; *formal* abode, residence, domicile. **4** *riot squads gave no quarter* **mercy**, leniency, clemency, compassion, pity, charity, sympathy, tolerance.
● *verb* **accommodate**, house, board, lodge, put up, take in, install, shelter; *Military* billet.

quash *verb* **1 cancel**, reverse, rescind, repeal, revoke, retract, countermand, withdraw, overturn, overrule. **2 stop**, put an end to, stamp out, crush, put down, check, curb, nip in the bud, squash, suppress, stifle.

queasy *adjective* **nauseous**, bilious, sick, ill, unwell, poorly, green about the gills; *Brit.* off colour.

queen *noun* **monarch**, sovereign, ruler, head of state, Crown, Her Majesty.

queer *adjective* **odd**, strange, unusual, funny, peculiar, curious, bizarre, weird, uncanny, freakish, eerie, unnatural, abnormal, anomalous; *informal* spooky.
- OPPOSITES normal.

quell *verb* **1 put an end to**, put a stop to, crush, put down, check, crack down on, curb, nip in the bud, squash, quash, subdue, suppress, overcome. **2 calm**, soothe, pacify, settle, quieten, silence, allay, assuage, mitigate, moderate.

query *noun* **1 question**, enquiry. **2 doubt**, uncertainty, question (mark), reservation.
● *verb* **1 ask**, enquire, question; *Brit. informal* quiz. **2 challenge**, question, dispute, doubt, have suspicions about, distrust.
- OPPOSITES accept.

quest *noun* **1 search**, hunt, pursuance. **2 expedition**, journey, voyage, trek, travels, odyssey, adventure, exploration, search, crusade, mission, pilgrimage.

question *noun* **1 enquiry**, query, interrogation. **2 doubt**, dispute, argument, debate, uncertainty, reservation. **3 issue**, matter, topic, business, problem, concern, debate, argument, dispute, controversy.
- OPPOSITES answer, certainty.
● *verb* **1 interrogate**, cross-examine, cross-question, quiz, interview, debrief, examine; *informal* grill, pump. **2 query**, challenge, dispute, cast aspersions on, doubt, suspect.
□ **out of the question** impossible, impracticable, unfeasible, unworkable, inconceivable, unimaginable, unrealizable, unsuitable; *informal* not on.

> **WORD LINKS**
> **interrogative** relating to questions

questionable *adjective* **suspicious**, suspect, dubious, irregular, odd, strange, murky, dark, unsavoury, disreputable; *informal* funny, fishy, shady, iffy; *Brit. informal* dodgy.

queue *noun* **row**, column, file, chain, string, procession, waiting list; *N. Amer.* line, wait list.

quick *adjective* **1 fast**, swift, rapid, speedy, brisk, smart, lightning, whirlwind, whistle-stop, breakneck; *informal* nippy, zippy; *literary* fleet. **2 hasty**, hurried, cursory, perfunctory, desultory, superficial, brief. **3 sudden**, instantaneous, instant, immediate, abrupt, precipitate. **4 intelligent**, bright, clever, gifted, able, astute, sharp-witted, smart, alert, sharp, perceptive; *informal* brainy, on the ball, genius.
- OPPOSITES slow, long.

quicken *verb* **1 speed up**, accelerate, step up, hasten, hurry (up). **2 stimulate**, excite, arouse, rouse, stir up, activate, whet, inspire, kindle.

quickly *adverb* **1 fast**, swiftly, briskly, rapidly, speedily, at full tilt, at a gallop, at the double, post-haste, hotfoot; *informal* like (greased) lightning, hell for leather, like blazes, like the wind; *Brit. informal* like the clappers, like billy-o; *N. Amer. informal* lickety-split. **2 immediately**, directly, at once, straight away, right away, instantly, forthwith; *N. Amer.* momentarily; *informal* like a shot, asap, p.d.q., pronto. **3 briefly**, fleetingly, briskly, hastily, hurriedly, cursorily, perfunctorily.

quiet *adjective* **1 silent**, still, hushed, noiseless, soundless, mute, dumb, speechless. **2 soft**, low, muted, muffled, faint, hushed, whispered, suppressed. **3 peaceful**, sleepy, tranquil, calm, still, restful.
- OPPOSITES loud, busy.
● *noun* **silence**, still, hush, restfulness, calm, tranquillity, serenity, peace.

quietly *adverb* **1 silently**, noiselessly, soundlessly, inaudibly. **2 softly**, faintly, in a low voice, in a whisper, in a murmur, under your breath, in an undertone, sotto voce.

quilt *noun* **duvet**, cover(s); *Brit.* eiderdown; *N. Amer.* comforter; *Austral. trademark* Doona.

quirk *noun* **1 idiosyncrasy**, peculiarity, oddity, eccentricity, foible, whim, vagary, habit, characteristic, trait, fad. **2 chance**, fluke, freak, anomaly, twist.

q

quirky *adjective* **eccentric**, idiosyncratic, unconventional, unorthodox, unusual, strange, bizarre, peculiar, zany; *informal* wacky, way-out, offbeat.
- OPPOSITES conventional.

quit *verb* **1 leave**, vacate, exit, depart from. **2** (*informal*) **resign from**, leave, give up, hand in your notice; *informal* chuck, pack in. **3** (*informal*) **give up**, stop, discontinue, drop, abandon, abstain from; *informal* pack in, leave off.

quite *adverb* **1 completely**, entirely, totally, wholly, absolutely, utterly, thoroughly, altogether. **2 fairly**, rather, somewhat, relatively, comparatively, moderately, reasonably; *informal* pretty.

quiz *noun* **competition**, test of knowledge.
● *verb* **question**, interrogate, cross-examine, cross-question, interview; *informal* grill, pump.

quota *noun* **share**, allocation, allowance, ration, portion, slice, percentage; *Brit. informal* whack.

quotation *noun* **1 extract**, quote, citation, excerpt, passage; *N. Amer.* cite. **2 estimate**, quote, price, tender, bid, costing.

quote *verb* **1 recite**, repeat, reproduce, retell, echo. **2 mention**, cite, refer to, name, instance, allude to, point out.
● *noun* see **quotation**.

q

Rr

race¹ *noun* **1 contest**, competition, event, fixture, heat, trial(s). **2** *the race for naval domination* **rivalry**, competition, contention, quest.
● *verb* **1 compete**, contend, run, be pitted against. **2 hurry**, dash, rush, run, sprint, bolt, charge, career, shoot, hurtle, hare, fly, speed, zoom; *informal* tear, belt.

race² *noun* **1 ethnic group**, origin, bloodline, stock. **2 people**, nation.

racial *adjective* **ethnic**, ethnological, race-related, cultural, national, tribal, genetic.

rack *noun* **frame**, framework, stand, holder, trestle, support, shelf.
● *verb* **torment**, afflict, torture, agonize, harrow, plague, persecute, trouble, worry.

racket *noun* **1 noise**, din, hubbub, clamour, uproar, tumult, commotion, rumpus, pandemonium; *Brit.* row; *informal* hullabaloo. **2** *(informal)* **fraud**, swindle, sharp practice; *informal* scam, rip-off.

radiant *adjective* **1 shining**, bright, illuminated, brilliant, gleaming, glowing, ablaze, luminous, lustrous, incandescent, dazzling, coruscating, shimmering. **2 joyful**, elated, thrilled, overjoyed, jubilant, rapturous, ecstatic, euphoric, in seventh heaven, on cloud nine, delighted, very happy; *informal* on top of the world, over the moon.
- OPPOSITES dark, gloomy.

radiate *verb* **1 emit**, give off, discharge, diffuse, scatter, shed, cast. **2 shine**, beam, emanate, pour. **3 fan out**, spread out, branch out/off, extend, issue.

radical *adjective* **1 thorough**, complete, total, comprehensive, exhaustive, sweeping, far-reaching, wide-ranging, extensive, profound, major. **2 fundamental**, basic, deep-seated, essential, structural. **3 revolutionary**, progressive, reformist, revisionist, progressivist, extreme, fanatical, militant.
- OPPOSITES superficial, minor, conservative.

raffle *noun* **lottery**, (prize) draw, sweepstake, sweep, tombola; *N. Amer.* lotto.

rage *noun* **1 fury**, anger, wrath, outrage, indignation, temper, spleen; *formal* ire. **2 craze**, passion, fashion, taste, trend, vogue, fad, mania; *informal* thing.
● *verb* **be angry**, be furious, be enraged, be incensed, seethe, be beside yourself, rave, storm, fume, spit; *informal* be livid, be wild, be steamed up.

ragged *adjective* **1 tattered**, torn, ripped, frayed, worn (out), threadbare, scruffy, shabby; *informal* tatty. **2 jagged**, craggy, rugged, uneven, rough, irregular, indented.

raid *noun* **1 attack**, assault, descent, blitz, incursion, sortie, onslaught, storming. **2 robbery**, burglary, hold-up, break-in, ram raid; *informal* smash-and-grab, stick-up; *N. Amer. informal* heist.
● *verb* **1 attack**, assault, set upon, descend on, swoop on, storm, rush. **2 rob**, hold up, break into, plunder, steal from, pillage, loot, ransack; *informal* stick up.

raider *noun* **robber**, burglar, thief, housebreaker, plunderer, pillager, looter, marauder, attacker, assailant, invader.

railing *noun* **fence**, fencing, rail(s), palisade, balustrade, banister.

rain *noun* **1 rainfall**, precipitation, raindrops, drizzle, mizzle, shower, rainstorm, cloudburst, torrent, downpour, deluge, storm. **2** *a rain of hot ash* **shower**, deluge, flood, torrent, avalanche, flurry, storm, hail.

● *verb* **1 pour (down)**, pelt down, tip down, teem down, beat down, lash down, drizzle, spit; *informal* be chucking it down; *Brit. informal* bucket down. **2** *bombs rained on the city* **fall**, hail, drop, shower.

> **WORD LINKS**
> **pluvial** relating to rain

rainy *adjective* **wet**, showery, drizzly, damp, inclement.
- OPPOSITES dry, fine.

raise *verb* **1 lift (up)**, hold aloft, elevate, uplift, hoist, haul up, hitch up; *Brit. informal* hoick up. **2 increase**, put up, push up, up, mark up, inflate; *informal* hike (up), jack up, bump up. **3 amplify**, louden, magnify, intensify, boost, lift, increase. **4 get**, obtain, acquire, accumulate, amass, collect, fetch, net, make. **5 bring up**, air, present, table, propose, submit, advance, suggest, put forward. **6 give rise to**, occasion, cause, produce, engender, elicit, create, result in, lead to, prompt. **7 bring up**, rear, nurture, educate.
- OPPOSITES lower, reduce.

rake *verb* **1 scrape**, collect, gather. **2 smooth (out)**, level, even out, flatten, comb. **3 rummage**, search, hunt, sift, rifle.

rally *verb* **1 regroup**, reassemble, re-form, reunite, convene, mobilize. **2 recover**, improve, get better, pick up, revive, bounce back, perk up, look up, turn a corner.
● *noun* **1 (mass) meeting**, gathering, assembly, demonstration, march; *informal* demo. **2 recovery**, upturn, improvement, comeback, resurgence.

ram *verb* **1 force**, thrust, plunge, stab, push, sink, dig, stick, cram, jam, stuff. **2 hit**, strike, crash into, collide with, impact, smash into, butt.

ramble *verb* **1 walk**, hike, tramp, trek, backpack. **2 chatter**, babble, prattle, blather, gabble, jabber, twitter, rattle; *Brit. informal* witter, chunter, rabbit.

rambling *adjective* **1 long-winded**, verbose, wordy, prolix, disjointed,

disconnected. **2 sprawling**, spreading, labyrinthine, maze-like.
- OPPOSITES concise, compact.

ramification *noun* **consequence**, result, aftermath, outcome, effect, upshot, development, implication.

ramp *noun* **slope**, bank, incline, gradient, rise, drop.

rampage *verb* **riot**, run amok, go berserk, storm, charge, tear.
□ **go on the rampage** riot, go berserk, get out of control, run amok; *N. Amer. informal* go postal.

rampant *adjective* **uncontrolled**, unrestrained, unchecked, unbridled, out of control, out of hand, widespread, rife, spreading.
- OPPOSITES controlled.

random *adjective* **unsystematic**, unmethodical, arbitrary, unplanned, chance, casual, indiscriminate, non-specific, haphazard, stray, erratic, hit-or-miss.
- OPPOSITES systematic.

range *noun* **1 extent**, limit, reach, span, scope, compass, sweep, area, field, orbit, ambit, horizon, latitude. **2 row**, chain, sierra, ridge, massif. **3 assortment**, variety, diversity, mixture, collection, array, selection, choice.
● *verb* **1 vary**, fluctuate, differ, extend, stretch, reach, go, run, cover. **2 roam**, wander, travel, journey, rove, traverse, walk, hike, trek.

rank[1] *noun* **1 position**, level, grade, echelon, class, status, standing. **2 high standing**, blue blood, high birth, nobility, aristocracy. **3 row**, line, file, column, string, train, procession.
● *verb* **1 classify**, class, categorize, rate, grade, bracket, group, designate, list. **2 line up**, align, order, arrange, dispose, set out, array, range.

rank[2] *adjective* **1 abundant**, lush, luxuriant, dense, profuse, vigorous, overgrown; *informal* jungly. **2 offensive**, nasty, revolting, sickening, obnoxious, foul, fetid, rancid, putrid. **3** *rank stupidity* **downright**, utter, out-and-out, absolute, complete, sheer, blatant, arrant, thorough, unqualified.

r

rankle verb **annoy**, upset, anger, irritate, offend, affront, displease, provoke, irk, vex, pique, nettle, gall; informal rile, miff, peeve, aggravate, hack off; Brit. informal nark; N. Amer. informal tick off.

ransack verb **1 plunder**, pillage, raid, rob, loot, sack, strip, despoil, ravage, devastate. **2 scour**, rifle through, comb, search, turn upside down.

ransom noun **pay-off**, payment, sum, price.

rant verb **shout**, sound off, hold forth, go on, fulminate, spout, bluster; informal mouth off.

rap verb **hit**, knock, strike, smack, bang; informal whack, thwack, bash, wallop.

rapid adjective **quick**, fast, swift, speedy, express, expeditious, brisk, lightning, meteoric, whirlwind, sudden, instantaneous, instant, immediate.
- OPPOSITES slow.

rapport noun **affinity**, close relationship, (mutual) understanding, bond, empathy, sympathy, accord.

rare adjective **1 infrequent**, scarce, sparse, few and far between, occasional, limited, isolated, odd, unaccustomed. **2 unusual**, recherché, uncommon, thin on the ground, like gold dust, unfamiliar, atypical. **3 exceptional**, outstanding, unparalleled, peerless, matchless, unique, unrivalled, beyond compare.
- OPPOSITES common, commonplace.

rarely adverb **seldom**, infrequently, hardly (ever), scarcely.
- OPPOSITES often.

raring adjective **eager**, keen, enthusiastic, impatient, longing, desperate; informal dying, itching.

rarity noun **1 infrequency**, scarcity. **2 curiosity**, oddity, collector's item, rare bird, wonder, nonpareil, one of a kind; Brit. informal one-off.

rash[1] noun **1 spots**, eruption, nettle-rash, hives. **2** a rash of articles in the press **series**, succession, spate, wave, flood, deluge, torrent, outbreak, epidemic, flurry.

rash[2] adjective **reckless**, impulsive, impetuous, hot-headed, daredevil, madcap, hasty, foolhardy, incautious, precipitate, careless, heedless, thoughtless, unthinking, imprudent, foolish.
- OPPOSITES prudent.

rate noun **1 percentage**, ratio, proportion, scale, standard. **2 charge**, price, cost, tariff, fare, fee, remuneration, payment. **3 speed**, pace, tempo, velocity.
● verb **1 assess**, evaluate, appraise, judge, weigh up, estimate, gauge. **2 merit**, deserve, warrant, be worthy of.

rather adverb **1 sooner**, by preference, by choice, more readily. **2 quite**, a bit, a little, fairly, slightly, somewhat, relatively, comparatively; informal pretty.

ratify verb **confirm**, approve, sanction, endorse, agree to, accept, uphold, authorize, formalize, sign.

rating noun **grade**, classification, ranking, position, category, assessment, evaluation, mark, score.

ratio noun **proportion**, relationship, rate, percentage, fraction, correlation.

ration noun **1 allowance**, allocation, quota, share, portion, helping. **2** the garrison ran out of rations **supplies**, provisions, food, stores.
● verb **control**, limit, restrict, conserve.

rational adjective **logical**, reasoned, sensible, reasonable, realistic, cogent, intelligent, shrewd, common-sense, sane, sound.

rationale noun **reason(s)**, thinking, logic, grounds, sense.

rationalize verb **1 justify**, explain (away), account for, defend, vindicate, excuse. **2 streamline**, reorganize, modernize, update, trim, hone, simplify, downsize, prune.

rattle verb **1 clatter**, clank, knock, clunk, clink, jangle, tinkle. **2 unnerve**, disconcert, disturb, fluster, shake, perturb, throw, discomfit; informal faze.

raucous adjective **1 harsh**, strident, screeching, piercing, shrill, grating, discordant, dissonant, noisy, loud,

cacophonous. **2 rowdy**, noisy, boisterous, roisterous, wild.
- OPPOSITES soft, quiet.

ravage verb **lay waste**, devastate, ruin,
destroy, wreak havoc on.

rave verb **1 rant**, rage, lose your temper,
storm, fume, shout; informal fly off
the handle, hit the roof; Brit. informal
go spare; N. Amer. informal flip your
wig. **2 enthuse**, go into raptures, wax
lyrical, rhapsodize, sing the praises
of, acclaim, eulogize, extol; N. Amer.
informal ballyhoo.
- OPPOSITES criticize.

raw adjective **1 uncooked**, fresh,
natural. **2 unprocessed**, untreated,
unrefined, crude, natural. **3 inexperienced**, new, untrained, untried,
untested, callow, green; informal wet
behind the ears. **4 sore**, red, painful,
tender, chafed.
- OPPOSITES cooked, processed.

ray noun **beam**, shaft, stream, streak,
flash, glimmer, flicker, spark.

raze verb **destroy**, demolish, tear down,
pull down, knock down, level, flatten,
bulldoze, wipe out, lay waste.

reach verb **1 extend**, stretch, outstretch, thrust, stick, hold. **2 arrive
at**, get to, come to, end up at. **3** the
temperature reached 75° **attain**, get to,
rise to, fall to, sink to, drop to; informal
hit. **4** ministers reached an agreement
achieve, work out, draw up, put
together, negotiate, thrash out, hammer out. **5 contact**, get in touch with,
get through to, get, speak to; informal
get hold of.
● noun **1 grasp**, range, stretch,
capabilities, capacity. **2 jurisdiction**,
authority, influence, power, scope,
range, compass, ambit.

react verb **respond**, act in response,
reply, answer, behave.

reaction noun **1 response**, answer,
reply, rejoinder, retort, riposte; informal
comeback. **2 backlash**, counteraction.

reactionary adjective **right-wing**, conservative, traditionalist, conventional,
diehard.

- OPPOSITES radical, progressive.

read verb **1 peruse**, study, scrutinize,
look through, pore over, run your eye
over, cast an eye over, leaf through,
scan. **2 understand**, make out, make
sense of, decipher, interpret, construe.
3 register, record, display, show,
indicate.

> **WORD LINKS**
> **literacy** ability to read
> **illiteracy** inability to read

readable adjective **1 legible**, decipher-
able, clear, intelligible, comprehensible.
2 enjoyable, entertaining, interesting, absorbing, gripping, enthralling,
engrossing; informal unputdownable.
- OPPOSITES illegible.

readily adverb **1 willingly**, unhesitat-
ingly, ungrudgingly, gladly, happily,
eagerly. **2 easily**, without difficulty.

readiness noun **willingness**, eagerness,
keenness, enthusiasm, alacrity.
□ **in readiness** (at the) ready, prepared, available, on hand, accessible,
handy.

reading noun **1 perusal**, study,
scanning. **2 learning**, scholarship,
education, erudition. **3 recital**, recitation, performance. **4 lesson**, passage,
excerpt. **5 interpretation**, understanding, explanation, analysis, construction.

ready adjective **1 prepared**, equipped,
all set, organized, primed; informal fit,
psyched up, geared up. **2 completed**,
finished, prepared, organized, done,
arranged, fixed. **3** he's always ready
to help **willing**, prepared, pleased,
inclined, disposed, eager, keen, happy,
glad; informal game. **4** a ready supply
of food **(easily) available**, accessible,
handy, close/near at hand, to/on hand,
convenient, within reach, near, at your
fingertips; informal on tap. **5** a ready
answer **prompt**, quick, swift, speedy,
fast, immediate, unhesitating.
● verb **prepare**, organize, gear up;
informal psych up.

real adjective **1 actual**, true, factual,
non-fictional, historical, material,

physical, tangible, concrete. **2 genuine**, authentic, bona fide, proper, true; *informal* pukka, kosher. **3 sincere**, genuine, true, unfeigned, heartfelt. **4 complete**, utter, thorough, absolute, total, prize, perfect; *Brit. informal* right, proper.
- OPPOSITES imaginary, false.

realism noun **1 pragmatism**, practicality, common sense, level-headedness. **2 authenticity**, accuracy, fidelity, truthfulness, verisimilitude.

realistic adjective **1 practical**, pragmatic, matter-of-fact, down-to-earth, sensible, commonsensical, rational, level-headed; *informal* no-nonsense. **2 achievable**, attainable, feasible, practicable, reasonable, sensible, workable; *informal* doable. **3 authentic**, accurate, true to life, lifelike, truthful, faithful, natural, naturalistic.
- OPPOSITES unrealistic.

reality noun **1 the real world**, real life, actuality, corporeality. **2 fact**, actuality, truth. **3 authenticity**, verisimilitude, fidelity, truthfulness, accuracy.
- OPPOSITES fantasy.

realization noun **1 awareness**, understanding, comprehension, consciousness, appreciation, recognition, discernment. **2 fulfilment**, achievement, accomplishment, attainment.

realize verb **1 register**, perceive, understand, grasp, comprehend, see, recognize, take in; *informal* tumble to; *Brit. informal* twig. **2 fulfil**, achieve, accomplish, make happen, bring to fruition, bring about/off, actualize. **3 make**, clear, gain, earn, return, produce. **4 be sold for**, fetch, go for, make, net.

really adverb **1 in (actual) fact**, actually, in reality, in truth. **2 genuinely**, truly, certainly, honestly, undoubtedly, unquestionably.

realm noun **1 kingdom**, country, land, state, nation, territory, dominion, empire, monarchy, principality. **2** *the realm of academia* **domain**, sphere, area, field, world, province.

reap verb **1 harvest**, cut, pick, gather, garner. **2 receive**, obtain, get, derive, acquire, secure, realize.

rear[1] noun **back (part)**, hind part, end, tail (end), back (end); *Nautical* stern.
● adjective **back**, end, rearmost, hind, last.
- OPPOSITES front.

rear[2] verb **1 bring up**, care for, look after, nurture, parent; *N. Amer.* raise. **2 breed**, raise, keep, grow, cultivate. **3** *houses reared up on either side* **rise**, tower, soar, loom.

reason noun **1 cause**, ground(s), basis, rationale, motive, explanation, justification, defence, vindication, excuse, apologia. **2 rationality**, logic, cognition, reasoning, intellect, thought, understanding; *formal* ratiocination. **3 sanity**, mind, mental faculties, senses, wits; *informal* marbles.
● verb **calculate**, conclude, reckon, think, judge, deduce, infer, surmise; *informal* figure.
□ **reason out** work out, think through, make sense of, get to the bottom of, puzzle out; *informal* figure out.
reason with talk round, bring round, persuade, prevail on, convince.

> **WORD LINKS**
> **rational** relating to reason

reasonable adjective **1 sensible**, rational, logical, fair, just, equitable, intelligent, wise, level-headed, practical, realistic, sound, valid, commonsensical, tenable, plausible, credible, believable. **2 practicable**, sensible, appropriate, suitable. **3 fairly good**, acceptable, satisfactory, average, adequate, fair, tolerable, passable; *informal* OK. **4 inexpensive**, affordable, moderate, low, cheap, within your means.

reassure verb **put someone's mind at rest**, encourage, hearten, buoy up, cheer up, comfort, soothe.
- OPPOSITES alarm.

rebate noun **partial refund**, partial repayment, discount, deduction, reduction.

rebel *noun* **1 revolutionary**, insurgent, insurrectionist, mutineer, guerrilla, terrorist, freedom fighter. **2 nonconformist**, dissenter, dissident, maverick.
- OPPOSITES loyalist, conformist.
● *verb* **revolt**, mutiny, riot, rise up, take up arms.
● *adjective* **1 rebellious**, insurgent, revolutionary, mutinous. **2 defiant**, disobedient, insubordinate, subversive, rebellious, nonconformist, maverick.
- OPPOSITES loyal, obedient.
□ **rebel against** defy, disobey, kick against, challenge, oppose, resist.

rebellion *noun* **1 revolt**, uprising, insurrection, mutiny, revolution, insurgence. **2 defiance**, disobedience, insubordination, subversion, resistance.
- OPPOSITES compliance.

rebellious *adjective* **1 rebel**, insurgent, mutinous, revolutionary. **2 defiant**, disobedient, insubordinate, unruly, mutinous, obstreperous, recalcitrant, intractable; *Brit. informal* bolshie.
- OPPOSITES loyal, obedient.

rebound *verb* **1 bounce (back)**, spring back, ricochet, boomerang. **2 backfire**, misfire, come back on.

rebuff *verb* **reject**, turn down, spurn, refuse, decline, snub, slight, dismiss, brush off.
- OPPOSITES accept.
● *noun* **rejection**, snub, slight, refusal, spurning; *informal* brush-off, kick in the teeth, slap in the face.

rebuke *verb* **reprimand**, reproach, scold, admonish, reprove, chastise, upbraid, berate, take to task; *informal* tell off; *Brit. informal* tick off; *N. Amer. informal* chew out; *formal* castigate.
● *noun* **reprimand**, reproach, scolding, admonition; *informal* telling-off, dressing-down; *Brit. informal* ticking-off.
- OPPOSITES praise.

recalcitrant *adjective* **uncooperative**, intractable, insubordinate, defiant, rebellious, wilful, wayward, headstrong, self-willed, contrary, perverse, difficult, awkward; *Brit. informal* bloody-minded, bolshie, stroppy; *formal* refractory.

- OPPOSITES amenable.

recall *verb* **1 remember**, recollect, call to mind, think back on/to, reminisce about. **2 remind someone of**, bring to mind, call up, conjure up, evoke. **3 call back**, order home, withdraw.
- OPPOSITES forget.
● *noun* **recollection**, remembrance, memory.

recede *verb* **1 retreat**, go back/down/away, withdraw, ebb, subside. **2 diminish**, lessen, dwindle, fade, abate, subside.
- OPPOSITES advance, grow.

receive *verb* **1 be given**, be presented with, be awarded, be sent, be in receipt of, get, obtain, gain, acquire, be paid. **2 hear**, listen to, respond to, react to. **3 experience**, sustain, undergo, meet with, suffer, bear.
- OPPOSITES give, send.

recent *adjective* **new**, the latest, current, fresh, modern, late, contemporary, up to date, up to the minute.
- OPPOSITES old.

recently *adverb* **not long ago**, a little while back, just now, newly, freshly, of late, lately, latterly.

reception *noun* **1 response**, reaction, treatment. **2 party**, function, social occasion, celebration, get-together, gathering, soirée; *N. Amer.* levee; *informal* do.

receptive *adjective* **open-minded**, responsive, amenable, well disposed, flexible, approachable, accessible.
- OPPOSITES unresponsive.

recess *noun* **1 alcove**, bay, niche, nook, corner. **2 break**, adjournment, interlude, interval, rest, holiday, vacation.

recession *noun* **downturn**, depression, slump, slowdown.
- OPPOSITES boom.

recipe *noun* *a recipe for success* **formula**, prescription, blueprint.

reciprocal *adjective* **mutual**, common, shared, give-and-take, joint, corresponding, complementary.

reciprocate verb **requite**, return, give back.

recital noun **1 performance**, concert, recitation, reading. **2 report**, account, listing, catalogue, litany.

recite verb **1 quote**, say, speak, read aloud, declaim, deliver, render. **2 recount**, list, detail, reel off, relate, enumerate.

reckless adjective **rash**, careless, thoughtless, heedless, precipitate, impetuous, impulsive, irresponsible, foolhardy, devil-may-care.
- OPPOSITES cautious.

reckon verb **1 calculate**, compute, work out, figure, count (up), add up, total, tally; Brit. tot up. **2 include**, count, regard as, look on as, consider, judge, think of as, deem, rate. **3 think**, believe, be of the opinion, suppose, assume.
□ **reckon on/with** take into account, take into consideration, bargain for/on, anticipate, foresee, be prepared for, consider.

reckoning noun **calculation**, estimation, computation, working out, addition, count.

reclaim verb **1 get back**, claim back, recover, retrieve, recoup. **2 save**, rescue, redeem, salvage.

recline verb **lie**, lie down/back, lean back, relax, loll, lounge, sprawl, stretch out.

recluse noun **hermit**, ascetic, eremite, loner, lone wolf; historical anchorite.

recognition noun **1 identification**, recollection, remembrance. **2 acknowledgement**, acceptance, admission, confession. **3 appreciation**, gratitude, thanks, congratulations, credit, commendation, acclaim, acknowledgement.

recognize verb **1 identify**, place, know, put a name to, remember, recall, recollect; Scottish & N. English ken. **2 acknowledge**, accept, admit, concede, confess, realize. **3 pay tribute to**, appreciate, be grateful for, acclaim, commend.

recoil verb **1 draw back**, jump back, pull back, flinch, shy away, shrink (back), blench. **2 feel revulsion**, feel disgust, shrink from, wince at.

recollect verb **remember**, recall, call to mind, think of, think back to, reminisce about.
- OPPOSITES forget.

recollection noun **memory**, recall, remembrance, impression, reminiscence.

recommend verb **1 advocate**, endorse, commend, suggest, put forward, propose, nominate, put up, speak favourably of, put in a good word for, vouch for; informal plug. **2 advise**, counsel, urge, exhort, enjoin, prescribe, argue for, back, support.

recommendation noun **1 advice**, counsel, guidance, suggestion, proposal. **2 commendation**, endorsement, good word, testimonial, tip; informal plug.

reconcile verb **1 reunite**, bring (back) together, pacify, appease, placate, mollify; formal conciliate. **2** reconciling his religious beliefs with his career **make compatible**, harmonize, square, make congruent, balance. **3 settle**, resolve, sort out, smooth over, iron out, mend, remedy, heal, rectify; informal patch up. **4** they had to reconcile themselves to drastic losses **accept**, resign yourself to, come to terms with, learn to live with, get used to, make the best of.

reconnoitre verb **survey**, explore, scout (out), find out the lie of the land, investigate, examine, scrutinize, inspect, observe, take a look at, patrol; informal recce, check out.

reconsider verb **rethink**, review, revise, re-evaluate, reassess, have second thoughts, change your mind.

reconstruct verb **rebuild**, remake, recreate, restore, reassemble, remodel, revamp, renovate.

record noun **1 account**, document, data, file, dossier, evidence, report, annals, archive, chronicle, minutes,

transactions, proceedings, transcript, certificate, deed, register, log. **2 disc**, recording, album, LP, single.
● *verb* **1 write down**, take down, note, jot down, put down on paper, document, enter, log, minute, register. **2 indicate**, register, show, display. **3 film**, photograph, tape, tape-record, video-record, videotape.

recount *verb* **tell**, relate, narrate, describe, report, relay, convey, communicate, impart.

recover *verb* **1 get better**, improve, rally, recuperate, convalesce, revive, be on the mend, get back on your feet, pick up, heal, bounce back, pull through. **2 retrieve**, regain, get back, recoup, reclaim, repossess, recapture. **3 salvage**, save, rescue, retrieve.
- OPPOSITES deteriorate.

recovery *noun* **1 improvement**, recuperation, convalescence, rally, revival. **2 retrieval**, repossession, reclamation, recapture.
- OPPOSITES relapse.

recreation *noun* **1 pleasure**, leisure, relaxation, fun, enjoyment, entertainment, amusement, diversion. **2 pastime**, hobby, leisure activity.
- OPPOSITES work.

recruit *verb* **1 enlist**, call up, conscript; *US* draft. **2 muster**, form, raise, mobilize. **3 hire**, employ, take on, enrol, sign up, engage.
- OPPOSITES demobilize.
● *noun* **1 conscript**; *US* draftee; *N. Amer. informal* yardbird. **2 newcomer**, trainee, initiate, joiner, beginner, novice.

rectify *verb* **correct**, (put) right, sort out, deal with, amend, remedy, repair, fix, make good, resolve, settle; *informal* patch up.

recur *verb* **happen again**, reoccur, repeat (itself), come back, return, reappear.

recycle *verb* **reuse**, reprocess, reclaim, recover, salvage.

red *adjective* **1 scarlet**, vermilion, ruby, cherry, cerise, cardinal, carmine, crimson, maroon, magenta, burgundy, claret. **2 flushed**, blushing, pink, rosy, florid, ruddy. **3 auburn**, Titian, chestnut, carroty, ginger.

redeem *verb* **1 save**, deliver from sin, absolve. **2 retrieve**, regain, recover, get back, reclaim, repossess, buy back. **3 exchange**, convert, trade in, cash in.

redolent *adjective* **evocative**, suggestive, reminiscent.

redress *verb* **rectify**, correct, right, compensate for, make amends for, remedy, make good.
● *noun* **compensation**, reparation, restitution, recompense, repayment, amends.

reduce *verb* **1 lessen**, make smaller, lower, decrease, diminish, minimize, shrink, narrow, cut, curtail, contract, shorten, downsize; *informal* chop. **2 bring down**, make cheaper, lower, mark down, slash, discount. **3** *he reduced her to tears* **bring to**, bring to the point of, drive to.
- OPPOSITES increase.

reduction *noun* **1 lessening**, lowering, decrease, diminution, cut, cutback, downsizing. **2 discount**, deduction, cut.

redundancy *noun* **dismissal**, lay-off, sacking, discharge, unemployment.

redundant *adjective* **unnecessary**, not required, unneeded, surplus (to requirements), superfluous.
□ **make redundant** dismiss, lay off, discharge, give someone their notice; *informal* sack, fire.

reel *verb* **1 stagger**, lurch, sway, rock, stumble, totter, wobble, teeter. **2 go round (and round)**, whirl, spin, revolve, swirl, twirl, turn, swim.

refer *verb* **pass**, direct, hand on/over, send on, transfer, entrust, assign.
□ **refer to 1** mention, allude to, touch on, speak of/about, talk of/about, write about, comment on, point out, call attention to. **2** apply to, relate to, pertain to, be relevant to, concern, be connected with. **3** consult, turn to, look at, have recourse to.

r

referee noun **umpire**, judge, adjudicator, arbitrator; informal ref.

reference noun **1 mention**, allusion, quotation, comment, remark. **2 source**, citation, authority, credit. **3 testimonial**, recommendation, character reference, credentials.

referendum noun **(popular) vote**, ballot, poll, plebiscite.

refine verb **1 purify**, filter, distil, process, treat. **2 improve**, perfect, polish (up), hone, fine-tune.

refined adjective **1 purified**, processed, treated. **2 cultivated**, cultured, polished, elegant, sophisticated, urbane, polite, gracious, well bred. **3 discriminating**, discerning, fastidious, exquisite, impeccable, fine.
- OPPOSITES crude, coarse.

reflect verb **1 mirror**, send back, throw back, echo. **2 indicate**, show, display, demonstrate, be evidence of, evince, reveal, betray. **3 think**, consider, review, mull over, ponder, contemplate, deliberate, ruminate, meditate, muse, brood; formal cogitate.

reflection noun **1 image**, likeness. **2 indication**, display, demonstration, manifestation, expression, evidence. **3 thought**, consideration, contemplation, deliberation, pondering, rumination, meditation, musing; formal cogitation.

reform verb **1 improve**, better, ameliorate, correct, rectify, restore, revise, refine, adapt, revamp, redesign, reconstruct, reorganize. **2 mend your ways**, change for the better, turn over a new leaf.
● noun **improvement**, amelioration, refinement, rectification, restoration, adaptation, revision, redesign, revamp, reconstruction, reorganization.

refrain verb **abstain**, desist, hold back, stop yourself, forbear, avoid; informal swear off.

refresh verb **1 reinvigorate**, revitalize, revive, rejuvenate, restore, energize, enliven, perk up, brace, freshen, wake

up, breathe new life into; informal buck up. **2** refresh your memory **jog**, stimulate, prompt, prod.

refreshing adjective **1 invigorating**, revitalizing, reviving, bracing, fortifying, enlivening, stimulating, exhilarating, energizing. **2** a refreshing change of direction **welcome**, stimulating, fresh, new, imaginative, innovative.

refreshment noun **food and drink**, snacks, titbits; informal nibbles.

refuge noun **1 shelter**, protection, safety, security, asylum, sanctuary. **2 place of safety**, shelter, haven, sanctuary, sanctum, retreat, bolt-hole, hiding place.

refugee noun **asylum seeker**, fugitive, displaced person, exile, émigré.

refund verb **repay**, give back, return, pay back, reimburse, compensate, recompense.
● noun **repayment**, reimbursement, compensation, rebate.

refurbish verb **renovate**, recondition, rehabilitate, revamp, overhaul, restore, redecorate, upgrade, refit; informal do up.

refusal noun **non-acceptance**, no, rejection, rebuff; informal knock-back, thumbs down.

refuse[1] verb **1 decline**, turn down, say no to, reject, spurn, rebuff; informal pass up, knock back. **2 withhold**, deny.
- OPPOSITES accept.

refuse[2] noun **rubbish**, waste, litter; N. Amer. garbage, trash; informal dreck, junk.

refute verb **1 disprove**, prove wrong, rebut, explode, debunk, discredit, invalidate; informal shoot full of holes. **2 deny**, reject, repudiate, rebut, contradict.

regain verb **recover**, get back, win back, recoup, retrieve, repossess, take back, retake, recapture, reconquer.

regal adjective **royal**, kingly, queenly, princely, majestic.

regard verb **1 consider**, look on, view, see, think of, judge, deem, estimate,

assess, reckon, rate. **2 look at**, contemplate, eye, gaze at, stare at, observe, view, study, scrutinize.
● *noun* **1 consideration**, care, concern, thought, notice, heed, attention. **2** *doctors are held in high regard* **esteem**, respect, admiration, approval, honour, estimation. **3 (fixed) look**, gaze, stare, observation, contemplation, study, scrutiny. **4** *he sends his regards* **best wishes**, greetings, respects, compliments.

regarding *preposition* **concerning**, as regards, with/in regard to, with respect to, with reference to, relating to, respecting, re, about, apropos, on the subject of, in connection with, vis-à-vis.

regardless *adverb* **anyway**, anyhow, in any case, nevertheless, nonetheless, despite everything, even so, all the same, in any event, come what may.
□ **regardless of** irrespective of, without reference to, without consideration of, discounting, ignoring, notwithstanding, no matter.

regime *noun* **1 government**, administration, leadership, rule, authority, control, command. **2 system**, arrangement, scheme, policy, method, course, plan, programme.

region *noun* **district**, province, territory, division, area, section, sector, zone, belt, quarter.

regional *adjective* **1 geographical**, territorial. **2 local**, provincial, district, parochial, zonal.
- OPPOSITES national.

register *noun* **1 list**, roll, roster, index, directory, catalogue, inventory. **2 record**, chronicle, log, ledger, archive, annals, files.
● *verb* **1 record**, enter, file, lodge, write down, submit, report, note, minute, log. **2 enrol**, put your name down, enlist, sign on/up, apply. **3 indicate**, read, record, show. **4 display**, show, express, exhibit, betray, reveal.

regret *verb* **1 be sorry about**, feel contrite about, feel remorse for, rue, repent of. **2 mourn**, grieve for/over,

weep over, sigh over, lament, bemoan.
- OPPOSITES welcome.
● *noun* **1 remorse**, contrition, repentance, compunction, ruefulness, self-reproach, pangs of conscience. **2 sadness**, sorrow, disappointment, unhappiness, grief.

regrettable *adjective* **unfortunate**, unwelcome, sorry, woeful, disappointing, reprehensible, deplorable, disgraceful.

regular *adjective* **1 uniform**, even, consistent, constant, unchanging, unvarying, fixed. **2 frequent**, repeated, continual, recurrent, periodic, constant, perpetual, numerous. **3 usual**, normal, customary, habitual, routine, typical, accustomed, established.
- OPPOSITES erratic, occasional, unusual.

regulate *verb* **1 control**, adjust, balance, set, synchronize. **2 police**, supervise, monitor, be responsible for, control, manage, direct, govern.

regulation *noun* **1 rule**, order, directive, act, law, by-law, statute, dictate, decree. **2 control**, policing, supervision, superintendence, monitoring, governance, management, administration, responsibility.

rehabilitate *verb* **1 reintegrate**, readapt; *N. Amer. informal* rehab. **2 reinstate**, restore, bring back, pardon, absolve, exonerate, forgive; *formal* exculpate. **3 recondition**, restore, renovate, refurbish, revamp, overhaul, redevelop, rebuild, reconstruct.

rehearsal *noun* **practice**, trial performance, read-through, run-through, drill, training, coaching; *informal* dry run.

rehearse *verb* **1 prepare**, practise, read through, run through/over, go over. **2 train**, drill, prepare, coach. **3 list**, enumerate, itemize, detail, spell out, catalogue, recite, repeat, go over, run through, recap.

reign *verb* **1 be king/queen**, sit on the throne, wear the crown, be supreme, rule. **2** *chaos reigned* **prevail**, exist, be present, be the case, occur, be rife,

be rampant, be the order of the day.
● *noun* **rule**, sovereignty, monarchy, dominion, control.

rein *verb* **restrain**, check, curb, constrain, hold back/in, keep under control, regulate, restrict, control, curtail, limit.
□ **free rein** freedom, a free hand, leeway, latitude, flexibility, liberty, independence, licence, room to manoeuvre, carte blanche. **keep a tight rein on** regulate, discipline, control, keep in line.

reinforce *verb* **1 strengthen**, fortify, bolster up, shore up, buttress, prop up, underpin, brace, support, boost. **2 augment**, increase, add to, supplement, boost, top up.

reinforcement *noun* **1 strengthening**, fortification, bolstering, shoring up, buttressing. **2** *we need reinforcements* **additional troops**, auxiliaries, reserves, support, backup, help.

reinstate *verb* **restore**, put back, bring back, reinstitute, reinstall, re-establish.

reiterate *verb* **repeat**, restate, recapitulate, recap, go over, rehearse.

reject *verb* **1 turn down**, refuse, decline, say no to, spurn; *informal* pass up, give the thumbs down to. **2 rebuff**, spurn, shun, snub, cast off/aside, discard, abandon, desert, turn your back on, cold-shoulder; *informal* give someone the brush-off.
- OPPOSITES accept, welcome.
● *noun* **second**, discard, misshape, faulty item, cast-off.

rejoice *verb* **be happy**, be glad, be delighted, celebrate, make merry; *informal* be over the moon.
- OPPOSITES mourn.
□ **rejoice in** delight in, enjoy, revel in, glory in, relish, savour.

rejoin *verb* **return to**, be reunited with, join again, reach again, regain.

rejuvenate *verb* **revive**, revitalize, regenerate, breathe new life into, revivify, reanimate, resuscitate, refresh, reawaken; *informal* give a shot in the arm to, pep up, buck up.

relapse *verb* **deteriorate**, degenerate, lapse, slip back, slide back, regress, revert, retrogress.
- OPPOSITES improve.

relate *verb* **tell**, recount, narrate, report, describe, recite, rehearse.
□ **relate to 1** connect with, associate with, link with, ally with, couple with. **2** apply to, concern, pertain to, have a bearing on, involve. **3** identify with, get on (well) with, feel sympathy with, have a rapport wit, empathize with, understand; *informal* hit it off with.

related *adjective* **connected**, interconnected, associated, linked, allied, corresponding, analogous, parallel, comparable, equivalent.

relation *noun* **1 connection**, relationship, association, link, tie-in, correlation, correspondence, parallel. **2 relative**, family member, kinsman, kinswoman; (**relations**) family, kin, kith and kin, kindred. **3** *our relations with Europe* **dealings**, communication, relationship, connections, contact, interaction.

relationship *noun* **1 connection**, relation, association, link, correlation, correspondence, parallel. **2 family ties**, kinship, affinity, common ancestry. **3 romance**, affair, love affair, liaison, amour, fling.

relative *adjective* **1 comparative**, respective, comparable. **2 proportionate**, in proportion, commensurate, corresponding.
- OPPOSITES disproportionate.
● *noun* **relation**, member of the family, kinsman, kinswoman; (**relatives**) family, kin, kith and kin, kindred.

relax *verb* **1 rest**, loosen up, ease up/off, slow down, de-stress, unbend, unwind, put your feet up, take it easy; *informal* chill (out); *N. Amer. informal* hang loose, decompress. **2 loosen**, slacken, unclench, weaken, lessen. **3 moderate**, temper, ease, loosen, lighten, dilute, weaken, reduce, decrease; *informal* let up on.
- OPPOSITES tense, tighten.

relaxation noun **recreation**, enjoyment, amusement, entertainment, fun, pleasure, leisure.

relay noun **broadcast**, transmission, showing, feed.

● verb **pass on**, hand on, transfer, repeat, communicate, send, transmit, circulate.

release verb **1 free**, set free, turn loose, let go/out, liberate, discharge. **2 untie**, undo, unfasten, loose, let go, unleash. **3 make public**, make known, issue, put out, publish, broadcast, circulate, launch, distribute.
- OPPOSITES imprison.

relegate verb **downgrade**, demote, lower, put down, move down.
- OPPOSITES upgrade, promote.

relent verb **1 change your mind**, do a U-turn, back-pedal, back down, give way/in, capitulate; Brit. do an about-turn. **2 ease**, slacken, let up, abate, drop, die down, lessen, decrease, subside, weaken, tail off.

relentless adjective **1 persistent**, unfaltering, unremitting, unflagging, untiring, unwavering, dogged, single-minded, tireless, indefatigable. **2 harsh**, cruel, remorseless, unrelenting, merciless, pitiless, implacable, inexorable, unforgiving, unbending, unyielding.

relevant adjective **pertinent**, applicable, apposite, material, apropos, to the point, germane.

reliable adjective **dependable**, trustworthy, good, safe, authentic, faithful, genuine, sound, true, loyal, unfailing; humorous trusty.
- OPPOSITES unreliable.

reliance noun **1 dependence**, need. **2 trust**, confidence, faith, belief, conviction.

relic noun **artefact**, historical object, antiquity, remnant, vestige, remains.

relief noun **1 respite**, remission, interruption, variation, diversion; informal let-up. **2 alleviation**, relieving, palliation, soothing, easing, lessening, mitigation. **3 help**, aid, assistance, charity, succour. **4 replacement**, substitute, deputy, reserve, cover, stand-in, supply, locum, understudy.

relieve verb **1 alleviate**, mitigate, ease, counteract, dull, reduce. **2 replace**, take over from, stand in for, fill in for, substitute for, deputize for, cover for. **3 free**, release, exempt, excuse, absolve, let off.
- OPPOSITES aggravate.

relieved adjective **glad**, thankful, grateful, pleased, happy, easy/easier in your mind, reassured.
- OPPOSITES worried.

religion noun **faith**, belief, worship, creed, church, sect, denomination, cult.

> **WORD LINKS**
> **divinity**, **theology** study of religion

religious adjective **1 devout**, pious, reverent, godly, God-fearing, churchgoing. **2 spiritual**, theological, scriptural, doctrinal, ecclesiastical, church, holy, divine, sacred. **3 scrupulous**, conscientious, meticulous, punctilious, strict, rigorous.
- OPPOSITES atheistic, secular.

relinquish verb **1 renounce**, resign, give up/away, hand over, let go of. **2 leave**, resign from, stand down from, bow out of, give up; informal quit, chuck.
- OPPOSITES retain.

relish noun **1 enjoyment**, gusto, delight, pleasure, glee, appreciation, enthusiasm. **2 condiment**, sauce, dressing.
- OPPOSITES distaste.

● verb **enjoy**, delight in, love, adore, take pleasure in, rejoice in, appreciate, savour, revel in, luxuriate in, glory in.
- OPPOSITES dislike.

reluctance noun **unwillingness**, disinclination, hesitation, wavering, vacillation, doubts, second thoughts, misgivings.

reluctant adjective **unwilling**, disinclined, unenthusiastic, resistant,

r

opposed, hesitant, loath.
- OPPOSITES willing, eager.

rely *verb*
◻ **rely on** depend on, count on, bank on, be confident of, be sure of, have faith in, trust in; *informal* swear by; *N. Amer. informal* figure on.

remain *verb* **1 continue**, endure, last, abide, carry on, persist, stay around, survive, live on. **2 stay**, stay behind, stay put, wait behind, be left, hang on; *informal* hang around/round. **3** *he remained calm* **continue to be**, stay, keep.

remainder *noun* **rest**, balance, residue, others, remnant(s), leftovers, surplus, extra, excess.

remains *plural noun* **1 remainder**, residue, rest, remnant(s), leftovers, scraps, debris, detritus. **2 antiquities**, relics, artefacts. **3 corpse**, body, carcass, bones; *Medicine* cadaver.

remark *verb* **comment**, say, observe, mention, reflect; *formal* opine.
● *noun* **comment**, statement, utterance, observation, reflection.

remarkable *adjective* **extraordinary**, exceptional, outstanding, notable, striking, memorable, unusual, conspicuous, momentous.
- OPPOSITES ordinary.

remedy *noun* **1 treatment**, cure, medicine, medication, medicament, drug. **2 solution**, answer, cure, fix, antidote, panacea.
● *verb* **put right**, set right, rectify, solve, sort out, straighten out, resolve, correct, repair, mend, fix.

remember *verb* **1 recall**, call to mind, recollect, think of, reminisce about, look back on. **2 memorize**, retain, learn off by heart, get off pat. **3 bear in mind**, be mindful of, take into account. **4 commemorate**, pay tribute to, honour, salute, pay homage to.
- OPPOSITES forget.

remembrance *noun* **1 recollection**, reminiscence, recall. **2 commemoration**, memory, recognition.

remind *verb* **jog someone's memory**, prompt.
◻ **remind someone of** make someone think of, cause someone to remember, put someone in mind of, call to mind, evoke.

reminiscent *adjective* **similar to**, comparable with, evocative of, suggestive of, redolent of.

remiss *adjective* **negligent**, neglectful, irresponsible, careless, thoughtless, heedless, lax, slack, slipshod, lackadaisical; *N. Amer.* derelict; *informal* sloppy.
- OPPOSITES careful.

remit *noun* **area of responsibility**, sphere, orbit, scope, ambit, province, brief, instructions, orders; *informal* bailiwick.
● *verb* **1 send**, dispatch, forward, hand over, pay. **2 pardon**, forgive, excuse.

remnant *noun* **remains**, remainder, leftovers, offcut, residue, rest.

remonstrate *verb* **protest**, complain, object, take issue, argue, expostulate..

remorse *noun* **regret**, guilt, contrition, repentance, shame.

remorseful *adjective* **sorry**, regretful, contrite, repentant, penitent, guilt-ridden, conscience-stricken, chastened, self-reproachful.
- OPPOSITES unrepentant.

remote *adjective* **1 isolated**, far-off, faraway, distant, out of the way, off the beaten track, secluded, lonely, inaccessible; *N. Amer.* in the backwoods; *informal* in the middle of nowhere. **2** *a remote possibility* **unlikely**, improbable, doubtful, dubious, faint, slight, slim, small, slender. **3 aloof**, distant, detached, withdrawn, unforthcoming, unapproachable, unresponsive, unfriendly, unsociable, introspective, introverted; *informal* stand-offish.
- OPPOSITES close.

removal *noun* **1 taking away**, withdrawal, abolition. **2 dismissal**, ejection, expulsion, ousting, deposition; *informal* sacking, firing. **3 move**, transfer, relocation.

remove verb **1 take off**, take away, move, take out, pull out, withdraw, detach, undo, unfasten, disconnect. **2 dismiss**, discharge, get rid of, eject, expel, oust, depose, unseat; *informal* sack, fire, kick out. **3 abolish**, withdraw, eliminate, get rid of, do away with, stop, cut; *informal* axe.
- OPPOSITES attach, insert.

renaissance noun **revival**, renewal, resurrection, reawakening, re-emergence, rebirth, reappearance, resurgence.

render verb **1 make**, cause to be/ become, leave, turn. **2 give**, provide, supply, furnish, contribute. **3 act**, perform, play, depict, portray, interpret, represent, draw, paint, execute.

rendezvous noun **meeting**, appointment, assignation; *informal* date; *literary* tryst.
● verb **meet**, come together, gather, assemble.

renegade noun **traitor**, defector, deserter, turncoat, rebel, mutineer.
● adjective **1 treacherous**, traitorous, disloyal, treasonous, rebel, mutinous. **2 apostate**, heretic, heretical, dissident.
- OPPOSITES loyal.

renege verb **default on**, fail to honour, go back on, break, back out of, withdraw from, retreat from, backtrack on, break your word/promise.
- OPPOSITES honour.

renew verb **1 resume**, return to, take up again, come back to, begin again, restart, recommence, continue (with), carry on (with). **2 reaffirm**, repeat, reiterate, restate. **3 revive**, regenerate, revitalize, reinvigorate, restore, resuscitate. **4 renovate**, restore, refurbish, revamp, remodel, modernize; *informal* do up; *N. Amer. informal* rehab.

renounce verb **1 give up**, relinquish, abandon, surrender, waive, forego, desist from, keep off; *informal* say goodbye to. **2 reject**, repudiate, deny, abandon, wash your hands of, turn your back on, disown, spurn, shun.

renovate verb **modernize**, restore, refurbish, revamp, recondition, rehabilitate, update, upgrade, refit; *informal* do up; *N. Amer. informal* rehab.

renown noun **fame**, distinction, eminence, illustriousness, prominence, repute, reputation, prestige, acclaim, celebrity, notability.

renowned adjective **famous**, well known, celebrated, famed, eminent, distinguished, acclaimed, illustrious, prominent, great, esteemed.
- OPPOSITES unknown.

rent noun **hire charge**, rental, payment.
● verb **1 hire**, lease, charter. **2 let (out)**, lease (out), hire (out), charter (out).

repair verb **1 mend**, fix (up), put/set right, restore (to working order), overhaul, renovate; *informal* patch up. **2 rectify**, make good, (put) right, correct, make up for, make amends for, compensate for, redress.
● noun **1 restoration**, mending, overhaul, renovation. **2 mend**, darn, patch. **3** *in good repair* **condition**, working order, state, shape, fettle; *Brit. informal* nick.

repay verb **1 reimburse**, refund, pay back, recompense, compensate, remunerate, settle up with. **2** *he repaid her kindness* **reciprocate**, return, requite, reward.

repeal verb **cancel**, abolish, reverse, rescind, revoke, annul, quash.
- OPPOSITES enact.
● noun **cancellation**, abolition, reversal, rescinding, annulment.

repeat verb **1 say again**, restate, reiterate, go/run through again, recapitulate, recap. **2 recite**, quote, parrot, regurgitate, echo; *informal* trot out. **3 do again**, redo, replicate, duplicate.
● noun **repetition**, replication, duplicate.

repeated adjective **recurrent**, frequent, persistent, continual, incessant, constant, regular, periodic, numerous, (very) many.
- OPPOSITES occasional.

r

repeatedly adverb **frequently**, often, again and again, over and over (again), time and (time) again, many times, persistently, recurrently, constantly, continually, regularly; N. Amer. oftentimes.

repel verb **1 fight off**, repulse, drive back, force back, beat back, hold off, ward off, fend off, keep at bay; Brit. see off. **2 revolt**, disgust, repulse, sicken, nauseate, turn someone's stomach; informal turn off; N. Amer. informal gross out.
- OPPOSITES attract.

repellent adjective **1 revolting**, repulsive, disgusting, repugnant, sickening, nauseating, stomach-turning, vile, nasty, foul, awful, horrible, dreadful, terrible, obnoxious, loathsome, offensive, objectionable, abhorrent, despicable, reprehensible, contemptible, odious, hateful; N. Amer. vomitous; informal ghastly, horrid, gross; literary noisome. **2 impermeable**, impervious, resistant, -proof.

repent verb **feel remorse**, regret, be sorry, rue, reproach yourself, be ashamed, feel contrite, be penitent, be remorseful.

repentant adjective **penitent**, contrite, regretful, rueful, remorseful, apologetic, chastened, ashamed, shamefaced.
- OPPOSITES impenitent.

repercussion noun **consequence**, result, effect, outcome, reverberation, backlash, aftermath, fallout, footprint.

repertoire noun **collection**, range, repertory, list, store, stock, repository, supply.

repetition noun **1 reiteration**, restatement, retelling. **2 repetitiousness**, repetitiveness, tautology.

repetitive, repetitious adjective **recurring**, recurrent, repeated, unvaried, unchanging, routine, mechanical, automatic, monotonous, boring; informal samey.
- OPPOSITES varied.

replace verb **1 put back**, return, restore. **2 take the place of**, succeed, take over from, supersede, stand in for, substitute for, deputize for; informal step into someone's shoes/boots. **3 substitute**, exchange, change, swap.

replacement noun **substitute**, stand-in, fill-in, locum, understudy, relief, cover, proxy, surrogate.

replenish verb **1 refill**, top up, fill up, recharge; N. Amer. freshen. **2 stock up**, restock, restore, replace.
- OPPOSITES empty.

replica noun **copy**, model, duplicate, reproduction, dummy, imitation, facsimile.

reply verb **respond**, answer, write back, rejoin, retort, riposte, counter, come back.
● noun **answer**, response, rejoinder, retort, riposte; informal comeback.

report verb **1 communicate**, announce, divulge, disclose, reveal, relay, describe, narrate, delineate, detail, document, give an account of, make public, publish, broadcast, proclaim, publicize. **2 inform on**; informal shop, tell on, squeal on, rat on; Brit. informal grass on. **3** I reported for duty **present yourself**, arrive, turn up, clock in; informal show up.
● noun **1 account**, record, minutes, proceedings, transcript. **2 news**, information, word, intelligence. **3 story**, account, article, piece, item, column, feature, bulletin, dispatch, communiqué. **4 rumour**, whisper; informal buzz. **5 bang**, crack, explosion, boom.

reporter noun **journalist**, correspondent, newsman, newswoman, columnist; Brit. pressman; informal hack, stringer, journo.

reprehensible adjective **deplorable**, disgraceful, discreditable, despicable, blameworthy, culpable, wrong, bad, shameful, dishonourable, inexcusable, unforgivable, indefensible, unjustifiable.
- OPPOSITES praiseworthy.

represent *verb* **1 stand for**, symbolize, personify, epitomize, typify, embody, illustrate, exemplify. **2 depict**, portray, render, picture, delineate, show, illustrate. **3 appear for**, act for, speak on behalf of.

representation *noun* **1 portrayal**, depiction, delineation, presentation, rendition. **2 likeness**, painting, drawing, picture, illustration, sketch, image, model, figure, statue.

representative *adjective* **1 typical**, archetypal, characteristic, illustrative, indicative. **2 symbolic**, emblematic.
- OPPOSITES atypical.
● *noun* **1 spokesperson**, spokesman, spokeswoman, agent, official, mouthpiece. **2 salesman**, commercial traveller, agent, negotiator; *informal* rep. **3 deputy**, substitute, stand-in, proxy, delegate, ambassador, emissary.

repress *verb* **1 suppress**, quell, quash, subdue, put down, crush, extinguish, stamp out, defeat, contain. **2 oppress**, subjugate, keep down, tyrannize. **3 restrain**, hold back/in, suppress, keep in check, control, curb, stifle, bottle up; *informal* button up, keep the lid on.
- OPPOSITES express.

repression *noun* **1 suppression**, quashing, subduing, crushing, stamping out. **2 oppression**, subjugation, suppression, tyranny, authoritarianism, despotism. **3 restraint**, suppression, control, curbing, stifling.

repressive *adjective* **oppressive**, authoritarian, despotic, tyrannical, dictatorial, fascist, autocratic, totalitarian, undemocratic.

reprieve *verb* **pardon**, spare, amnesty; *informal* let off (the hook).
● *noun* **pardon**, stay of execution, amnesty.

reprimand *verb* **rebuke**, reproach, scold, admonish, reprove, chastise, upbraid, berate, take to task, castigate; *informal* tell off; *Brit. informal* tick off; *N. Amer. informal* chew out.
- OPPOSITES praise.

● *noun* **rebuke**, reproach, scolding, admonition; *informal* telling-off, dressing-down, carpeting; *Brit. informal* ticking-off.

reprisal *noun* **retaliation**, counterattack, comeback, revenge, vengeance, retribution, requital; *informal* a taste of your own medicine.

reproachful *adjective* **disapproving**, reproving, critical, censorious, disparaging, withering, accusatory, admonitory.
- OPPOSITES approving.

reproduce *verb* **1 copy**, duplicate, replicate, photocopy, xerox, photostat, print. **2 repeat**, replicate, recreate, redo, simulate, imitate, emulate, mimic. **3 breed**, procreate, propagate, multiply, proliferate.

reproduction *noun* **1 print**, copy, reprint, duplicate, facsimile, photocopy; *trademark* Xerox. **2 breeding**, procreation, propagation, proliferation.

repudiate *verb* **1 reject**, renounce, disown, abandon, give up, turn your back on, cast off, lay aside, wash your hands of; *formal* forswear; *literary* forsake. **2 deny**, refute, contradict, controvert, rebut, dispute, dismiss, brush aside; *formal* gainsay.
- OPPOSITES embrace.

repugnant *adjective* **abhorrent**, revolting, repulsive, repellent, disgusting, offensive, objectionable, vile, foul, nasty, loathsome, sickening, nauseating, hateful, detestable, execrable, abominable, monstrous, appalling, unsavoury, unpalatable.
- OPPOSITES pleasant.

repulsive *adjective* **disgusting**, revolting, foul, nasty, obnoxious, sickening, nauseating, stomach-churning, vile; *informal* ghastly, gross, horrible; *literary* noisome.
- OPPOSITES attractive.

reputable *adjective* **well thought of**, highly regarded, respected, respectable, of (good) repute, prestigious, established, reliable, dependable, trustworthy.
- OPPOSITES untrustworthy.

r

reputation noun name, good name, character, repute, standing, stature, position, renown, esteem, prestige.

request noun **1 appeal**, entreaty, plea, petition, application, demand, call, solicitation. **2 requirement**, wish, desire, choice.
● verb **ask for**, appeal for, call for, seek, solicit, plead for, beg for, apply for, put in for, demand, petition for, sue for, implore, entreat; literary beseech.

require verb **1 need**, have need of, be short of, want, desire, lack, miss. **2 necessitate**, demand, call for, involve, entail, take. **3 demand**, insist on, call for, ask for, expect. **4 order**, instruct, command, enjoin, oblige, compel, force.

requirement noun **need**, necessity, prerequisite, stipulation, demand, want, essential.

requisition noun **1 order**, request, call, application, claim, demand; Brit. indent. **2 appropriation**, commandeering, seizure, confiscation, expropriation.
● verb **1 commandeer**, appropriate, take over, take possession of, occupy, seize, confiscate, expropriate. **2 request**, order, call for, demand.

rescue verb **1 save**, free, set free, release, liberate, deliver. **2 retrieve**, recover, salvage.
● noun **saving**, rescuing, release, freeing, liberation, deliverance.

research noun **investigation**, experimentation, testing, analysis, fact-finding, examination, scrutiny.
● verb **investigate**, study, enquire into, look into, probe, explore, analyse, examine, scrutinize.

resemblance noun **similarity**, likeness, similitude, correspondence, congruence, conformity, comparability, parallel.
- OPPOSITES dissimilarity.

resemble verb **look like**, be similar to, remind someone of, take after, approximate to, smack of, correspond to, echo, mirror, parallel.
- OPPOSITES differ from.

resent verb **begrudge**, feel aggrieved at/about, feel bitter about, grudge, be resentful of, take exception to, object to, take amiss, take offence at.
- OPPOSITES welcome.

resentful adjective **aggrieved**, indignant, irritated, piqued, put out, in high dudgeon, dissatisfied, disgruntled, discontented, offended, bitter, jaundiced, envious, jealous; informal miffed, peeved; Brit. informal narked; N. Amer. informal sore.

resentment noun **bitterness**, indignation, irritation, pique, dissatisfaction, disgruntlement, discontentment, acrimony, rancour.

reservation noun **1 doubt**, qualm, scruple; (**reservations**) misgivings, scepticism, unease, hesitation, objection. **2 reserve**, enclave, sanctuary, territory, homeland.

reserve verb **1 put aside**, set aside, keep (back), save, hold back, keep in reserve, earmark, retain. **2 book**, order, arrange for, secure, engage, hire.
● noun **1 stock**, store, supply, stockpile, pool, hoard, cache, fund. **2 reinforcements**, extras, auxiliaries. **3 national park**, sanctuary, preserve, reservation. **4 shyness**, diffidence, timidity, taciturnity, inhibition, reticence, detachment, aloofness, distance, remoteness. **5** she trusted him without reserve **reservation**, qualification, condition, limitation, hesitation, doubt.
● adjective **substitute**, stand-in, relief, replacement, fallback, spare, extra.

reserved adjective **1 uncommunicative**, reticent, unforthcoming, aloof, cool, undemonstrative, unsociable, unfriendly, quiet, silent, taciturn, withdrawn, secretive, shy, retiring, diffident, timid, introverted; informal stand-offish. **2 booked**, taken, spoken for, prearranged.
- OPPOSITES outgoing.

reservoir noun **1 lake**, pool, pond, basin. **2 receptacle**, container, holder, tank. **3 stock**, store, stockpile, reserve(s), supply, bank, pool.

reside verb **1 live**, lodge, stay, occupy, inhabit; formal dwell, be domiciled. **2** power resides with the president **be vested in**, be bestowed on, be conferred on, be in the hands of.

residence noun **home**, house, address, quarters, lodgings; informal pad; formal dwelling, abode, domicile.

resident noun **inhabitant**, local, citizen, native, householder, homeowner, occupier, tenant; humorous denizen.

residue noun **remainder**, rest, remnant(s), surplus, extra, excess, remains, leftovers.

resign verb **1 leave**, give notice, stand down, step down; informal quit, pack in. **2 give up**, leave, vacate, renounce, relinquish, surrender.

resignation noun he accepted his fate with resignation **patience**, forbearance, stoicism, fortitude, fatalism, acceptance.

resigned adjective **patient**, long-suffering, uncomplaining, forbearing, stoical, philosophical, fatalistic.

resilient adjective **1 flexible**, pliable, supple, durable, hard-wearing, stout, strong, sturdy, tough. **2 strong**, tough, hardy, quick to recover, buoyant, irrepressible.

resist verb **1 withstand**, be proof against, combat, weather, endure, be resistant to, keep out. **2 oppose**, fight against, object to, defy, kick against, obstruct. **3 refrain from**, abstain from, forbear from, desist from, not give in to, restrain yourself from.

resistance noun **1 opposition**, hostility, struggle, fight, battle, stand, defiance. **2 immunity**, defences.

resistant adjective **1 impervious**, immune, invulnerable, proof, unaffected. **2 opposed**, averse, hostile, inimical, against; informal anti.
- OPPOSITES vulnerable.

resolute adjective **determined**, purposeful, resolved, adamant, single-minded, firm, unswerving, unwavering, steadfast, staunch, stalwart, unfaltering, indefatigable, tenacious, strong-willed, unshakeable.
- OPPOSITES half-hearted.

resolution noun **1 intention**, decision, intent, aim, plan, commitment, pledge, promise. **2 motion**, proposal, proposition. **3 determination**, purpose, purposefulness, resolve, single-mindedness, firmness, will power, strength of character. **4 solution**, answer, end, settlement, conclusion.

resolve verb **1 settle**, sort out, solve, fix, straighten out, deal with, put right, rectify; informal hammer out, thrash out. **2 determine**, decide, make up your mind. **3 vote**, rule, decide formally, agree.
● noun **determination**, purpose, resolution, single-mindedness; informal guts.

resort noun **option**, alternative, choice, possibility, hope, measure, step, recourse, expedient.
□ **resort to** fall back on, have recourse to, turn to, make use of, use, avail yourself of.

resound verb **echo**, reverberate, ring, boom, thunder, rumble, resonate.

resounding adjective **1 reverberating**, resonating, echoing, ringing, sonorous, deep, rich. **2** a resounding success **enormous**, huge, very great, tremendous, terrific, colossal, emphatic, outstanding, remarkable, phenomenal.

resource noun **1 facility**, amenity, aid, help, support, solution. **2 initiative**, resourcefulness, enterprise, ingenuity, inventiveness. **3** we lack resources **assets**, funds, wealth, money, capital, supplies, materials, stores, stocks, reserves, deep pockets.

resourceful adjective **ingenious**, enterprising, inventive, creative, clever, talented, able, capable.

respect noun **1 esteem**, regard, high opinion, admiration, reverence, deference, honour. **2** the report was accurate in every respect **aspect**, regard, feature, way, sense, particular, point, detail.

r

3 (respects) regards, compliments, greetings, best/good wishes.
- OPPOSITES contempt.
● *verb* **1 esteem**, admire, think highly of, have a high opinion of, look up to, revere, honour. **2 show consideration for**, have regard for, observe, be mindful of, be heedful of. **3 abide by**, comply with, follow, adhere to, conform to, act in accordance with, obey, observe, keep (to).
- OPPOSITES despise, disobey.

respectable *adjective* **1 reputable**, upright, honest, honourable, trustworthy, decent, good, well bred, clean-living. **2 fairly good**, decent, fair-sized, reasonable, moderately good, large, sizeable, considerable.
- OPPOSITES disreputable.

respectful *adjective* **deferential**, reverent, dutiful, polite, well mannered, civil, courteous, gracious.
- OPPOSITES rude.

respective *adjective* **separate**, personal, own, particular, individual, specific, special.

respite *noun* **rest**, break, breathing space, interval, lull, pause, time out, relief; *informal* breather, let-up.

respond *verb* **1 answer**, reply, write back, come back, rejoin, retort, riposte, counter. **2 react**, reciprocate, retaliate.

response *noun* **1 answer**, reply, rejoinder, retort, riposte; *informal* comeback. **2 reaction**, reply, retaliation; *informal* comeback.
- OPPOSITES question.

responsibility *noun* **1 duty**, task, function, job, role, onus; *Brit. informal* pigeon. **2 blame**, fault, guilt, culpability, liability, accountability, answerability. **3 trustworthiness**, (common) sense, maturity, reliability, dependability. **4** *managerial responsibility* **authority**, control, power, leadership.

responsible *adjective* **1 in charge of**, in control of, at the helm of, accountable for, liable for. **2 accountable**, answerable, to blame, guilty, culpable, blameworthy, at fault, in the wrong.

3 trustworthy, sensible, mature, reliable, dependable, level-headed, stable.
- OPPOSITES irresponsible.

responsive *adjective* **reactive**, receptive, open to suggestions, amenable, flexible, forthcoming.

rest[1] *verb* **1 relax**, ease up/off, let up, slow down, have/take a break, unbend, unwind, take it easy, put your feet up; *informal* take five, have/take a breather, chill (out). **2** *her hands rested on the rail* **lie**, be laid, repose, be placed, be positioned, be supported by. **3 support**, prop (up), lean, lay, set, stand, position, place, put.
● *noun* **1 relaxation**, repose, leisure, time off; *informal* lie-down. **2 break**, breathing space, interval, interlude, intermission, time off/out, respite, lull, pause; *informal* breather. **3 stand**, base, holder, support, rack, frame, shelf.

rest[2] *noun* **remainder**, residue, balance, others, remnant(s), surplus, excess.

restful *adjective* **relaxing**, quiet, calm, tranquil, soothing, peaceful, leisurely, undisturbed, untroubled.
- OPPOSITES exciting.

restless *adjective* **1 uneasy**, ill at ease, fidgety, edgy, tense, worked up, nervous, nervy, agitated, anxious; *informal* jumpy, jittery, twitchy, uptight. **2** *a restless night* **sleepless**, wakeful, fitful, broken, disturbed, troubled, unsettled.

restoration *noun* **1 reinstatement**, reinstitution, re-establishment, reimposition, return. **2 repair**, renovation, mending, refurbishment, reconditioning, rehabilitation, rebuilding, reconstruction; *N. Amer. informal* rehab.

restore *verb* **1 reinstate**, bring back, reinstitute, reimpose, reinstall, re-establish. **2** *he restored it to its rightful owner* **return**, give back, hand back. **3 repair**, fix, mend, refurbish, recondition, rehabilitate, renovate, revamp, rebuild; *informal* do up; *N. Amer. informal* rehab. **4 reinvigorate**, revitalize, revive, refresh, energize, freshen.

restrain *verb* **control**, check, hold in check, curb, suppress, repress, contain, rein back/in, smother, stifle, bottle up; *informal* keep the lid on.

restrained *adjective* **1 self-controlled**, sober, steady, unemotional, undemonstrative. **2 muted**, soft, discreet, subtle, quiet, unobtrusive, unostentatious, understated, tasteful.
- OPPOSITES impetuous.

restraint *noun* **1 constraint**, check, control, restriction, limitation, curtailment, rein, brake, deterrent. **2 self-control**, self-discipline, control, moderation, judiciousness. **3 subtlety**, taste, discretion, discrimination.

restrict *verb* **1 limit**, keep within bounds, regulate, control, moderate, cut down, curtail. **2 hinder**, interfere with, impede, hamper, obstruct, block, check, curb.

restricted *adjective* **1 cramped**, confined, constricted, small, narrow, tight. **2 limited**, controlled, regulated, reduced.

restriction *noun* **limitation**, constraint, control, regulation, check, curb, reduction, diminution, curtailment.

result *noun* **consequence**, outcome, upshot, sequel, effect, reaction, repercussion, footprint.
- OPPOSITES cause.
● *verb* **follow**, ensue, develop, stem, spring, arise, derive, proceed; (**result from**) be caused by, be brought about by, be produced by, originate in.
☐ **result in** end in, culminate in, lead to, trigger, cause, bring about, occasion, effect, give rise to, produce.

resume *verb* **restart**, recommence, begin again, start again, reopen, renew, return to, continue with, carry on with.
- OPPOSITES suspend, abandon.

résumé *noun* **summary**, precis, synopsis, abstract, outline, abridgement, overview.

resumption *noun* **restart**, recommencement, reopening, continuation, renewal, return, revival.

resurgence *noun* **renewal**, revival, renaissance, recovery, comeback,

reawakening, resurrection, reappearance, re-emergence.

resurrect *verb* **revive**, restore, regenerate, revitalize, breathe new life into, reinvigorate, resuscitate, rejuvenate, re-establish, relaunch.

retain *verb* **keep (possession of)**, keep hold of, hang on to, maintain, preserve, conserve.

retaliate *verb* **fight back**, hit back, respond, react, reply, reciprocate, counter-attack, get back at someone, pay someone back; *informal* get your own back.

retaliation *noun* **revenge**, vengeance, reprisal, retribution, repayment, response, reaction, reply, counter-attack.

retard *verb* **delay**, slow down/up, hold back/up, postpone, detain, decelerate, hinder, impede, check.
- OPPOSITES accelerate.

reticent *adjective* **uncommunicative**, unforthcoming, unresponsive, tight-lipped, quiet, taciturn, silent, reserved.
- OPPOSITES expansive.

retire *verb* **1 give up work**, stop work, be pensioned off; *informal* be put out to grass. **2 withdraw**, go away, exit, leave, take yourself off, absent yourself. **3 go to bed**, call it a day; *informal* turn in, hit the hay/sack.

retiring *adjective* **1 departing**, outgoing. **2 shy**, diffident, self-effacing, unassuming, unassertive, reserved, reticent, quiet, timid, modest.
- OPPOSITES incoming, outgoing.

retort *verb* **answer**, reply, respond, return, counter, riposte, retaliate.
● *noun* **answer**, reply, response, counter, rejoinder, riposte, retaliation; *informal* comeback.

retract *verb* **1 pull in**, pull back, draw in. **2 take back**, withdraw, recant, disavow, disclaim, repudiate, renounce, reverse, revoke, rescind, go back on, backtrack on, row back on; *formal* abjure.

r

retreat *verb* **withdraw**, retire, draw back, pull back/out, fall back, give way, give ground.
- OPPOSITES advance.
● *noun* **1 withdrawal**, retirement, pullback, flight. **2 refuge**, haven, sanctuary, hideaway, hideout, hiding place; *informal* hidey-hole.

retribution *noun* **punishment**, penalty, your just deserts, revenge, reprisal, requital, retaliation, vengeance, an eye for an eye (and a tooth for a tooth), tit for tat, nemesis.

retrieve *verb* **get back**, bring back, recover, recapture, regain, recoup, salvage, rescue.

retrograde *adjective* **for the worse**, regressive, retrogressive, negative, downhill, backward(s), unwelcome.

retrospect *noun*
□ **in retrospect** looking back, on reflection, in/with hindsight.

return *verb* **1 go back**, come back, arrive back, come home. **2 recur**, reoccur, repeat itself, reappear. **3 give back**, hand back, pay back, repay, restore, put back, replace, reinstall, reinstate.
- OPPOSITES leave.
● *noun* **1 recurrence**, reoccurrence, repeat, reappearance. **2 replacement**, restoration, reinstatement, restitution. **3 yield**, profit, gain, revenue, interest, dividend.

revamp *verb* **renovate**, redecorate, refurbish, remodel, refashion, redesign, restyle; *informal* do up, give something a facelift, give something a makeover, vamp up; *Brit. informal* tart up.

reveal *verb* **1 disclose**, make known, make public, broadcast, publicize, circulate, divulge, tell, let slip/drop, give away/out, blurt out, release, leak, bring to light, lay bare, unveil; *informal* let on. **2 show**, display, exhibit, unveil, uncover.
- OPPOSITES conceal, hide.

revel *verb* **celebrate**, make merry; *informal* party, live it up, whoop it up, paint the town red.

● *noun* **celebration**, festivity, jollification, merrymaking, party; *informal* rave, shindig, bash; *Brit. informal* rave-up; *N. Amer. informal* wingding, blast.
□ **revel in** enjoy, delight in, love, like, adore, take pleasure in, relish, lap up, savour; *informal* get a kick out of.

revelation *noun* **disclosure**, announcement, report, admission, confession, divulging, giving away/out, leak, betrayal, publicizing.

revelry *noun* **celebration(s)**, parties, festivity, jollification, merrymaking, carousal, roistering, fun and games; *informal* partying.

revenge *noun* **retaliation**, retribution, vengeance, reprisal, recrimination, an eye for an eye (and a tooth for a tooth), redress.
- OPPOSITES forgiveness.
● *verb* **avenge**, exact retribution for, take reprisals for, get redress for, make someone pay for; *informal* get your own back for.

revenue *noun* **income**, takings, receipts, proceeds, earnings, profit(s), gain, yield.
- OPPOSITES expenditure.

reverberate *verb* **resound**, echo, resonate, ring, boom, rumble.

revere *verb* **respect**, admire, think highly of, esteem, venerate, look up to, be in awe of.
- OPPOSITES despise.

reverence *noun* **high esteem**, high regard, great respect, honour, veneration, homage, admiration, appreciation, deference.
- OPPOSITES scorn.

reverent *adjective* **reverential**, respectful, admiring, devoted, devout, awed, deferential.

reversal *noun* **1 turnaround**, turnabout, about-face, volte-face, change of heart, U-turn, rowback, backtracking; *Brit.* about-turn. **2 swap**, exchange, change, interchange, switch. **3 alteration**, overturning, overthrow, disallowing, overriding, overruling, veto, revocation. **4 setback**, upset, failure, misfortune, mishap, disaster, blow, disappointment, adversity, hardship, affliction, vicissitude, defeat.

reverse *verb* **1 back**, move back/ backwards. **2 turn upside down**, turn over, upend, invert, turn back to front. **3 swap (round)**, change (round), exchange, switch (round), transpose. **4 alter**, change, overturn, overthrow, disallow, override, overrule, veto, revoke, row back on.
● *adjective* **backward(s)**, inverted, transposed, opposite.
● *noun* **1 opposite**, contrary, converse, inverse, antithesis. **2 setback**, reversal, upset, failure, misfortune, mishap, disaster, blow, disappointment, adversity, hardship, affliction, vicissitude, defeat. **3 other side**, back, underside, flip side.
– OPPOSITES front.

revert *verb* **return**, go back, change back, default, relapse.

review *noun* **1 analysis**, evaluation, assessment, appraisal, examination, investigation, enquiry, probe, inspection, study. **2 reconsideration**, reassessment, re-evaluation, reappraisal. **3 criticism**, critique, write-up, assessment, commentary.
● *verb* **1 survey**, study, research, consider, analyse, examine, scrutinize, explore, look into, probe, investigate, inspect, assess, evaluate, appraise, weigh up; *informal* size up. **2 reconsider**, re-examine, reassess, re-evaluate, reappraise, rethink.

reviewer *noun* **critic**, commentator, judge.

revise *verb* **1 reconsider**, review, re-examine, reassess, re-evaluate, reappraise, rethink, change, alter, modify. **2 amend**, correct, edit, rewrite, redraft, rephrase, rework. **3** (*Brit.*) **go over**, reread, memorize, cram; *informal* bone up on; *Brit. informal* swot up (on), mug up (on).

revision *noun* **1 alteration**, adaptation, editing, rewriting, redrafting, correction, updating. **2 reconsideration**, review, re-examination, reassessment, re-evaluation, reappraisal, rethink,

change, modification.

revitalize *verb* **reinvigorate**, re-energize, boost, regenerate, revive, revivify, rejuvenate, reanimate, resuscitate, refresh, stimulate, breathe new life into; *informal* give a shot in the arm to, pep up, buck up.

revival *noun* **1 improvement**, rallying, turn for the better, upturn, upswing, resurgence. **2 comeback**, re-establishment, reintroduction, restoration, reappearance, resurrection, rebirth.
– OPPOSITES downturn.

revive *verb* **1 resuscitate**, bring round, bring back to consciousness; *informal* give the kiss of life to. **2 reinvigorate**, revitalize, refresh, energize, reanimate. **3** *reviving old traditions* **reintroduce**, re-establish, restore, resurrect, bring back.

revoke *verb* **cancel**, repeal, rescind, reverse, annul, nullify, void, invalidate, countermand, retract, withdraw, overrule, override; *formal* abrogate.

revolt *verb* **1 rebel**, rise up, take to the streets, riot, mutiny. **2 disgust**, sicken, nauseate, turn someone's stomach, put off, offend; *informal* turn off; *N. Amer. informal* gross out.
● *noun* **rebellion**, revolution, insurrection, mutiny, uprising, riot, insurgence, coup (d'état).

revolting *adjective* **disgusting**, sickening, nauseating, stomach-turning, repulsive, repugnant, hideous, nasty, foul, offensive; *N. Amer.* vomitous; *informal* ghastly, horrid, gross.
– OPPOSITES attractive, pleasant.

revolution *noun* **1 rebellion**, revolt, insurrection, mutiny, uprising, rising, riot, insurgence, coup (d'état). **2 dramatic change**, sea change, metamorphosis, transformation, innovation, reorganization, restructuring; *informal* shake-up; *N. Amer. informal* shakedown. **3 turn**, rotation, circle, spin, orbit, circuit, lap.

revolutionary *adjective* **1 rebellious**, rebel, insurgent, rioting, mutinous, renegade. **2 new**, novel, original, unusual,

r

unconventional, unorthodox, newfangled, innovatory, disruptive, modern, state-of-the-art, futuristic, pioneering; *informal* edgy.
● *noun* **rebel**, insurgent, mutineer, insurrectionist, agitator.

revolutionize *verb* **transform**, shake up, turn upside down, restructure, reorganize, transmute, metamorphose; *humorous* transmogrify.

revolve *verb* **1 go round**, turn round, rotate, spin. **2 circle**, travel, orbit.

revulsion *noun* **disgust**, repulsion, abhorrence, repugnance, nausea, horror, aversion, abomination, distaste.
- OPPOSITES delight.

reward *noun* **award**, honour, decoration, bonus, premium, bounty, present, gift, payment, recompense, prize; *informal* pay-off.
● *verb* **recompense**, pay, remunerate.
- OPPOSITES punish.

rewarding *adjective* **satisfying**, gratifying, pleasing, fulfilling, enriching, illuminating, worthwhile, productive, fruitful.

rhetoric *noun* **1 oratory**, eloquence, command of language, way with words. **2 wordiness**, verbosity, grandiloquence, bombast, pomposity, extravagant language, purple prose, turgidity; *informal* hot air.

rhetorical *adjective* **1** *a rhetorical device* **stylistic**, oratorical, linguistic, verbal. **2 extravagant**, grandiloquent, highflown, bombastic, grandiose, pompous, pretentious, overblown, turgid, flowery; *informal* highfalutin.

rhyme *noun* **poem**, verse, ode; (**rhymes**) poetry, doggerel.

rhythm *noun* **1 beat**, cadence, tempo, time, pulse. **2 metre**, measure, pattern.

rich *adjective* **1 wealthy**, affluent, moneyed, well off, well-to-do, prosperous; *informal* loaded, well heeled, made of money. **2 sumptuous**, opulent, luxurious, lavish, gorgeous, splendid, magnificent, costly, expensive, fancy, palatial; *informal* plush; *Brit. informal*

swish; *N. Amer. informal* swank. **3** *a garden rich in flowers* **well stocked**, well provided, abounding, crammed, packed, teeming, bursting. **4** *a rich supply* **plentiful**, abundant, copious, ample, profuse, lavish, liberal, generous. **5 fertile**, productive, fruitful, fecund. **6 creamy**, fatty, heavy, full-flavoured. **7** *rich colours* **strong**, deep, full, intense, vivid, brilliant.
- OPPOSITES poor, plain.

riches *plural noun* **money**, wealth, funds, cash, means, assets, capital, resources, deep pockets; *informal* bread, loot; *Brit. informal* dosh, brass, lolly; *N. Amer. informal* bucks.

richly *adverb* **1 sumptuously**, opulently, luxuriously, lavishly, gorgeously, splendidly, magnificently. **2** *the reward she richly deserves* **fully**, amply, well, thoroughly, completely, wholly, totally, entirely, absolutely, utterly.

rid *verb* **clear**, free, purge, empty, strip.
□ **get rid of** dispose of, throw away/out, clear out, discard, scrap, dump, bin, jettison, expel, eliminate; *informal* chuck (away), ditch, junk; *Brit. informal* get shot of; *N. Amer. informal* trash.

riddle *noun* **puzzle**, conundrum, brain-teaser, problem, question, poser, enigma, mystery.

ride *verb* **1 sit on**, mount, control, manage, handle. **2 travel**, move, proceed, drive, cycle, trot, canter, gallop.
● *noun* **trip**, journey, drive, run, excursion, outing, jaunt, lift; *informal* spin.

ridicule *noun* **mockery**, derision, laughter, scorn, scoffing, jeering.
- OPPOSITES respect.
● *verb* **mock**, deride, laugh at, heap scorn on, jeer at, make fun of, scoff at, satirize, caricature, parody.

ridiculous *adjective* **laughable**, absurd, ludicrous, risible, comical, funny, hilarious, amusing, farcical, silly, stupid, idiotic, preposterous.
- OPPOSITES sensible.

rife *adjective* **widespread**, general, common, universal, extensive, ubiquitous, endemic, inescapable.

rifle *verb* **1 rummage**, search, hunt, forage. **2 burgle**, rob, steal from, loot, raid, plunder, ransack.

rift *noun* **1 crack**, split, breach, fissure, fracture, cleft, crevice, opening. **2 disagreement**, estrangement, breach, split, schism, quarrel, falling-out, conflict, feud; *Brit.* row; *Brit. informal* bust-up.

rig[1] *verb* **1 equip**, kit out, fit out, supply, furnish, provide, arm. **2 dress**, clothe, attire, robe, garb, get up; *informal* doll up. **3** *he will rig up a shelter* **set up**, erect, assemble, put together, whip up, improvise, contrive; *Brit. informal* knock up.

rig[2] *verb* **manipulate**, engineer, distort, misrepresent, pervert, tamper with, falsify, fake; *informal* fix; *Brit. informal* fiddle.

right *adjective* **1 just**, fair, equitable, proper, good, upright, righteous, virtuous, moral, ethical, principled, honourable, honest, lawful, legal. **2 correct**, unerring, accurate, exact, precise, valid; *Brit. informal* spot on. **3 suitable**, appropriate, fitting, apposite, apt, correct, proper, desirable, preferable, ideal. **4 opportune**, advantageous, favourable, convenient, good, lucky, fortunate. **5 right-hand**; *Nautical* starboard; *Heraldry* dexter.
- OPPOSITES wrong, left.
● *adverb* **1 completely**, fully, totally, absolutely, utterly, thoroughly, quite. **2 exactly**, precisely, directly, immediately, just, squarely, dead; *informal* (slap) bang, smack, plumb. **3 correctly**, accurately, perfectly.
- OPPOSITES wrong, badly.
● *noun* **1 goodness**, righteousness, virtue, integrity, propriety, probity, morality, truth, honesty, honour, justice, fairness, equity. **2 entitlement**, prerogative, privilege, liberty, authority, power, licence, permission, dispensation, leave, due.
- OPPOSITES wrong.
● *verb* **remedy**, rectify, retrieve, fix, resolve, sort out, settle, square, straighten out, correct, repair, mend, redress.

☐ **right away** at once, straight away, (right) now, this (very) minute, this instant, immediately, instantly, directly, forthwith, without further ado, promptly, quickly, without delay, asap, as soon as possible; *N. Amer.* in short order; *informal* straight off, pronto.

righteous *adjective* **good**, virtuous, upright, upstanding, decent, ethical, principled, moral, honest, honourable, blameless.
- OPPOSITES wicked.

rightful *adjective* **1 legal**, lawful, real, true, proper, correct, recognized, genuine, authentic, acknowledged, approved, valid, bona fide; *informal* legit, kosher. **2 deserved**, merited, due, just, right, fair, proper, fitting, appropriate, suitable.
- OPPOSITES wrongful.

right-wing *adjective* **conservative**, rightist, reactionary, traditionalist, conventional.
- OPPOSITES left-wing.

rigid *adjective* **1 stiff**, hard, taut, firm, inflexible, unbendable, unyielding, inelastic. **2** *a rigid routine* **fixed**, set, firm, inflexible, invariable, hard and fast, cast-iron, strict, stringent, rigorous, uncompromising, intransigent.
- OPPOSITES flexible.

rigorous *adjective* **1 meticulous**, conscientious, punctilious, careful, scrupulous, painstaking, exact, precise, accurate, particular, strict. **2 strict**, stringent, rigid, inflexible, draconian, intransigent, uncompromising. **3** *rigorous conditions* **harsh**, severe, bleak, extreme, demanding.
- OPPOSITES slapdash, lax.

rim *noun* **edge**, brim, lip, border, side, margin, brink, boundary, perimeter, circumference, limits, periphery.

rind *noun* **skin**, peel, zest, integument.

ring[1] *noun* **1 circle**, band, halo, disc. **2 arena**, enclosure, amphitheatre, bowl. **3 gang**, syndicate, cartel, mob, band, circle, organization, association, society, alliance, league.

r

● *verb* **surround**, circle, encircle, enclose, hem in, confine, seal off.

ring² *verb* **1 chime**, sound, peal, toll, clang, bong; *literary* knell. **2 resound**, reverberate, resonate, echo. **3 telephone**, phone (up), call (up); *informal* give someone a buzz; *Brit. informal* give someone a bell, get on the blower to.

rinse *verb* **wash (out)**, clean, cleanse, bathe, dip, drench, splash, swill, sluice.

riot *noun* **disorder**, disturbance, lawlessness, upheaval, uproar, commotion, free-for-all, uprising, insurrection.
● *verb* **(go on the) rampage**, run wild, run amok, run riot, go berserk; *informal* raise hell.

riotous *adjective* **1 unruly**, rowdy, disorderly, uncontrollable, unmanageable, undisciplined, uproarious, tumultuous, violent, wild, lawless, anarchic. **2 boisterous**, lively, loud, noisy, unrestrained, uninhibited, uproarious; *Brit. informal* rumbustious.
- OPPOSITES peaceful.

rip *verb* **tear**, pull, wrench, snatch, drag, pluck; *informal* yank.

ripe *adjective* **1 mature**, full grown, fully developed. **2** *ripe for development* **ready**, fit, suitable, right. **3** *the time is ripe* **opportune**, advantageous, favourable, auspicious, good, right.
- OPPOSITES immature.

ripen *verb* **mature**, mellow, develop.

riposte *noun* **retort**, counter, rejoinder, sally, return, answer, reply, response; *informal* comeback.

rise *verb* **1 climb**, come up, arise, ascend, mount, soar. **2 loom**, tower, soar. **3 go up**, increase, soar, shoot up, surge, leap, jump, rocket, escalate, spiral. **4 get higher**, grow, increase, become louder, swell, intensify. **5 stand up**, get to your feet, get up, jump up, leap up, stir, bestir yourself.
- OPPOSITES fall, descend, drop.
● *noun* **1 increase**, hike, leap, upsurge, upswing, climb. **2 raise**, increase, increment. **3 slope**, incline, hill, elevation, acclivity.

risk *noun* **1 chance**, uncertainty, unpredictability, instability, insecurity. **2 possibility**, chance, probability, likelihood, danger, peril, threat, menace, prospect.
● *verb* **endanger**, jeopardize, imperil, hazard, gamble (with), chance, put at risk, put on the line.

risky *adjective* **dangerous**, hazardous, perilous, unsafe, insecure, precarious, touch-and-go, treacherous, uncertain, unpredictable; *informal* dicey.

rite *noun* **ceremony**, ritual, ceremonial, custom, service, observance, liturgy, worship, office.

ritual *noun* **ceremony**, rite, act, practice, custom, tradition, convention, formality, protocol.
● *adjective* **ceremonial**, prescribed, set, conventional, traditional, formal.

rival *noun* **opponent**, opposition, challenger, competitor, contender, adversary, antagonist, enemy, nemesis; *literary* foe.
- OPPOSITES ally.
● *verb* **match**, compare with, compete with, vie with, equal, emulate, measure up to, touch; *informal* hold a candle to.
● *adjective rival candidates* **competing**, opposing, in competition.

rivalry *noun* **competition**, contention, opposition, conflict, feuding; *informal* keeping up with the Joneses.

river *noun* **1 stream**, brook, watercourse, rivulet, tributary; *Scottish & N. English* burn; *N. English* beck; *S. English* bourn; *N. Amer. & Austral./NZ* creek. **2** *a river of molten lava* **stream**, torrent, flood, deluge, cascade.

> **WORD LINKS**
> **fluvial** relating to rivers

riveting *adjective* **fascinating**, gripping, engrossing, intriguing, absorbing, captivating, enthralling, compelling, spellbinding, mesmerizing; *informal* unputdownable.
- OPPOSITES boring.

road *noun* **1 street**, thoroughfare, roadway, highway, lane; *Brit.* motorway.

2 *the road to recovery* **way**, path, route, course.

roam *verb* **wander**, rove, ramble, drift, walk, traipse, range, travel, tramp, trek; *informal* cruise.

roar *verb* **bellow**, yell, shout, thunder, bawl, howl, scream, cry, bay; *informal* holler.

roaring *adjective* **blazing**, burning, flaming.

rob *verb* **1 burgle**, steal from, hold up, break into, raid, loot, plunder, pillage; *informal* mug; *N. Amer.* burglarize. **2 cheat**, swindle, defraud; *informal* do out of, con out of.

robber *noun* **burglar**, thief, house-breaker, mugger, shoplifter, raider, looter.

robbery *noun* **burglary**, theft, stealing, housebreaking, shoplifting, embezzlement, fraud, hold-up, raid; *informal* mugging, smash-and-grab, stick-up; *N. Amer. informal* heist.

robe *noun* **1 cloak**, kaftan, djellaba, wrap, mantle, cape; *N. Amer.* wrapper. **2** *ceremonial robes* **garb**, vestments, regalia, finery.

robot *noun* **machine**, automaton, android; *informal* bot, droid.

robust *adjective* **1 strong**, vigorous, sturdy, tough, powerful, solid, rugged, hardy, strapping, healthy, (fighting) fit, hale and hearty. **2 durable**, resilient, tough, hard-wearing, long-lasting, sturdy, strong.
- OPPOSITES frail, fragile.

rock[1] *noun* **boulder**, stone, pebble.

rock[2] *verb* **1 move to and fro**, sway, see-saw, roll, pitch, plunge, toss, lurch. **2 stun**, shock, stagger, astonish, startle, surprise, shake, take aback, throw, unnerve, disconcert.

rocky[1] *adjective* **stony**, pebbly, shingly, rough, bumpy, craggy, mountainous.

rocky[2] *adjective* **unsteady**, shaky, unstable, wobbly, tottery, rickety.
- OPPOSITES steady, stable.

rod *noun* **bar**, stick, pole, baton, staff, shaft, strut, rail, spoke.

rogue *noun* **scoundrel**, rascal, good-for-nothing, wretch, villain, criminal, lawbreaker; *informal* crook.

role *noun* **1 part**, character. **2 capacity**, position, function, job, post, office, duty, responsibility.

roll *verb* **1 turn over and over**, spin, rotate, revolve, wheel, trundle, bowl. **2 flow**, run, course, stream, pour, trickle. **3 wind**, coil, fold, curl, twist. **4 rock**, sway, reel, list, pitch, plunge, lurch, toss.
● *noun* **1 cylinder**, tube, scroll, reel, spool, bobbin. **2 turn**, rotation, revolution, spin, whirl. **3 list**, register, directory, record, file, index, catalogue, inventory. **4** *a roll of thunder* **rumble**, reverberation, echo, boom, clap, crack.

romance *noun* **1 love affair**, relationship, liaison, courtship, attachment, amour. **2 story**, tale, legend, fairy tale. **3 mystery**, glamour, excitement, exoticism, mystique, appeal, allure, charm.

romantic *adjective* **1 loving**, amorous, passionate, tender, affectionate; *informal* lovey-dovey. **2 sentimental**, hearts-and-flowers; *informal* slushy, schmaltzy; *Brit. informal* soppy. **3 idyllic**, picturesque, fairy-tale, beautiful, lovely, charming, pretty. **4 idealistic**, unrealistic, fanciful, impractical, head-in-the-clouds, starry-eyed, utopian, rose-tinted.
- OPPOSITES unsentimental, realistic.
● *noun* **idealist**, sentimentalist, dreamer, fantasist.
- OPPOSITES realist.

romp *verb* **play**, frolic, frisk, gambol, skip, prance, caper, cavort.

room *noun* **1 space**, headroom, legroom, area, expanse, extent. **2** *there's very little room for manoeuvre* **scope**, opportunity, capacity, leeway, latitude, freedom.

roomy *adjective* **spacious**, capacious, sizeable, generous, big, large, extensive, voluminous, ample; *formal* commodious.
- OPPOSITES cramped.

r

root *noun* **1 source**, origin, cause, reason, basis, foundation, bottom, seat. **2** *his Irish roots* **origins**, beginnings, family, birth, heritage.
● *verb* **rummage**, hunt, search, rifle, delve, forage, dig, poke.
□ **root out** eradicate, eliminate, weed out, destroy, wipe out, stamp out, abolish, end, put a stop to.

rope *noun* **cord**, cable, line, hawser, string.

roster *noun* **schedule**, list, register, agenda, calendar; *Brit.* rota.

rosy *adjective* **1 pink**, roseate, reddish, glowing, healthy, fresh, radiant, blooming, blushing, flushed, ruddy. **2 promising**, optimistic, auspicious, hopeful, encouraging, favourable, bright, golden.
- OPPOSITES pale, bleak.

rot *verb* **1 decay**, decompose, disintegrate, crumble, perish. **2 go bad**, go off, spoil, moulder, putrefy, fester. **3 deteriorate**, degenerate, decline, decay, go to seed, go downhill; *informal* go to pot, go to the dogs.
● *noun* **decay**, decomposition, mould, mildew, blight, canker.

rotate *verb* **1 revolve**, go round, turn (round), spin, gyrate, whirl, twirl, swivel, circle, pivot. **2 alternate**, take turns, change, switch, interchange, exchange, swap.

rotation *noun* **1 revolving**, turning, spinning, gyration, circling. **2 turn**, revolution, orbit, spin. **3 sequence**, succession, alternation, cycle.

rotten *adjective* **1 decaying**, mouldy, bad, off, decomposing, spoiled, putrid, rancid, festering, fetid. **2 corrupt**, unprincipled, dishonest, dishonourable, unscrupulous, untrustworthy, immoral; *informal* crooked; *Brit. informal* bent.
- OPPOSITES fresh.

rough *adjective* **1 uneven**, irregular, bumpy, stony, rocky, rugged, rutted, pitted. **2 coarse**, bristly, scratchy, prickly, shaggy, hairy, bushy. **3 dry**, leathery, weather-beaten, chapped, calloused, scaly. **4 gruff**, hoarse, harsh,

rasping, husky, throaty, gravelly. **5 violent**, aggressive, belligerent, pugnacious, boisterous, rowdy, disorderly, unruly, riotous. **6 boorish**, loutish, oafish, brutish, coarse, crude, uncouth, vulgar, unrefined, unladylike, ungentlemanly, uncultured. **7 turbulent**, stormy, squally, tempestuous, violent, heavy, choppy. **8 preliminary**, hasty, quick, sketchy, cursory, basic, crude, rudimentary, raw, unpolished, incomplete, unfinished. **9 approximate**, inexact, imprecise, vague, estimated; *N. Amer. informal* ballpark.
- OPPOSITES smooth, gentle, calm, exact.
● *noun* **sketch**, draft, outline, mock-up.

round *adjective* **circular**, spherical, globular, cylindrical.
● *noun* **1 ball**, sphere, globe, orb, circle, disc, ring, hoop. **2** *a policeman on his rounds* **circuit**, beat, route, tour. **3 stage**, level, heat, game, bout, contest. **4 succession**, sequence, series, cycle.
● *verb* **go round**, travel round, skirt, circumnavigate, orbit.
□ **round off** complete, finish off, crown, cap, top, conclude, close, end. **round up** gather together, herd together, muster, marshal, rally, assemble, collect, group; *N. Amer.* corral.

roundabout *adjective* **circuitous**, indirect, meandering, serpentine, tortuous, oblique, circumlocutory.
- OPPOSITES direct.

roundly *adverb* **1 vehemently**, emphatically, fiercely, forcefully, severely, plainly, frankly, candidly. **2 utterly**, completely, thoroughly, decisively, conclusively, heavily, soundly.

rouse *verb* **1 wake (up)**, awaken, arouse; *Brit. informal* knock up. **2 wake up**, awake, come to, get up, rise, bestir yourself. **3 stir up**, excite, galvanize, electrify, stimulate, inspire, move, inflame, agitate, goad, provoke, prompt, whip up.

rousing *adjective* **stirring**, inspiring, exciting, stimulating, moving,

r

electrifying, invigorating, energizing, exhilarating.

rout noun **defeat**, beating, retreat, flight; informal licking, hammering, thrashing, pasting, drubbing.
- OPPOSITES victory.
● verb **defeat**, beat, conquer, vanquish, crush, put to flight, drive off, scatter; informal lick, hammer, clobber, thrash; US informal own.

route noun **way**, course, road, path, direction.

routine noun **1 procedure**, practice, pattern, drill, regime, programme, schedule, plan. **2 act**, performance, number, turn, piece; informal spiel, patter.
● adjective **1 standard**, regular, customary, normal, usual, ordinary, typical, everyday. **2 boring**, tedious, monotonous, humdrum, run-of-the-mill, pedestrian, predictable, hackneyed, unimaginative, unoriginal, banal, trite.
- OPPOSITES unusual.

row[1] noun **1 line**, column, file, queue, procession, chain, string, succession; informal crocodile. **2 tier**, line, rank, bank.
□ **in a row** consecutively, in succession, running, straight; informal on the trot.

row[2] (Brit.) noun **1 argument**, quarrel, squabble, fight, dispute, altercation, falling-out; informal tiff, run-in, slanging match, spat; Brit. informal bust-up. **2 din**, noise, racket, uproar, hubbub, rumpus; informal hullabaloo.
● verb **argue**, quarrel, squabble, bicker, fight, fall out, disagree, have words; informal scrap.

rowdy adjective **unruly**, disorderly, riotous, undisciplined, uncontrollable, ungovernable, disruptive, obstreperous, out of control, rough, wild, boisterous, uproarious, noisy, loud; Brit. informal rumbustious.
- OPPOSITES peaceful.

royal adjective **regal**, kingly, queenly, princely, sovereign.

rub verb **1 massage**, knead, stroke, pat. **2 apply**, smear, spread, work in. **3 chafe**, scrape, pinch.
□ **rub out** erase, delete, remove, obliterate, expunge.

rubbish noun **1 refuse**, waste, litter, scrap, detritus, debris, dross; N. Amer. garbage, trash; informal dreck, junk. **2 nonsense**, gibberish, claptrap, garbage; informal baloney, tripe, drivel, bilge, bunk, piffle, twaddle, poppycock, gobbledegook; Brit. informal codswallop, cobblers, tosh.

rude adjective **1 ill-mannered**, bad-mannered, impolite, discourteous, uncivil, impertinent, insolent, impudent, disparaging, abusive, curt, brusque, offhand. **2 vulgar**, coarse, smutty, dirty, filthy, crude, lewd, obscene, risqué; informal blue; Brit. informal near the knuckle.
- OPPOSITES polite.

rudimentary adjective **1 basic**, elementary, fundamental, essential. **2 primitive**, crude, simple, unsophisticated, rough (and ready), makeshift. **3 vestigial**, undeveloped, incomplete.

rudiments plural noun **basics**, fundamentals, essentials, first principles, foundations; informal nuts and bolts, ABC.

rueful adjective **regretful**, apologetic, sorry, remorseful, shamefaced, sheepish, hangdog, contrite, repentant, penitent, conscience-stricken, self-reproachful, sorrowful, sad.

ruffle verb **1 disarrange**, tousle, dishevel, rumple, mess up; N. Amer. informal muss up. **2 disconcert**, unnerve, fluster, agitate, upset, disturb, discomfit, put off, perturb, unsettle; informal faze, throw, get to.
- OPPOSITES smooth.

rugged adjective **1 rough**, uneven, bumpy, rocky, stony, pitted. **2 robust**, durable, sturdy, strong, tough, resilient. **3 well built**, burly, strong, muscular, muscly, brawny, strapping, tough, hardy, robust, sturdy, solid; informal hunky. **4** his rugged features **strong**,

r

craggy, rough-hewn, manly, masculine.
- OPPOSITES smooth, delicate.

ruin noun **1 disintegration**, decay, disrepair, dilapidation, destruction, demolition, devastation. **2** the ruins of a church **remains**, remnants, fragments, rubble, debris, wreckage. **3 downfall**, collapse, defeat, undoing, failure. **4 bankruptcy**, insolvency, penury, destitution, poverty.
● verb **1 spoil**, wreck, blight, shatter, dash, scotch, mess up, sabotage; informal screw up; Brit. informal scupper. **2 bankrupt**, make insolvent, impoverish, pauperize, wipe out, break, cripple, bring someone to their knees. **3 destroy**, devastate, lay waste, ravage, raze, demolish, wreck, wipe out, flatten.

ruined adjective **derelict**, dilapidated, tumbledown, ramshackle, decrepit, falling to pieces, crumbling, decaying, disintegrating, in ruins.

ruinous adjective **1 disastrous**, devastating, catastrophic, calamitous, crippling, crushing, damaging, destructive, harmful, costly. **2 extortionate**, exorbitant, excessive, sky-high, outrageous, inflated; Brit. over the odds; informal steep.

rule noun **1 regulation**, ruling, directive, order, law, statute, ordinance. **2 procedure**, practice, protocol, convention, norm, routine, custom, habit. **3 principle**, precept, standard, axiom, truth, maxim. **4 government**, jurisdiction, command, power, dominion, control, administration, sovereignty, leadership.
● verb **1 govern**, preside over, control, lead, dominate, run, head, administer. **2 reign**, be on the throne, be in power, govern. **3 decree**, order, pronounce, judge, adjudge, ordain, decide, determine, find.
□ **as a rule** usually, in general, normally, ordinarily, customarily, for the most part, on the whole, by and large, in the main, mostly, commonly, typically. **rule out** exclude, eliminate, disregard, preclude, prohibit, prevent, disallow.

ruler noun **leader**, sovereign, monarch, potentate, king, queen, emperor, empress, prince, princess, crowned head, head of state, president, premier, governor.
- OPPOSITES subject.

ruling noun **judgement**, decision, adjudication, finding, verdict, pronouncement, resolution, decree, injunction.
● adjective **1 governing**, controlling, commanding, supreme. **2 main**, chief, principal, major, dominating, consuming; informal number-one.

rummage verb **search**, hunt, root about/around, ferret about/around, fish about/around, dig, delve, go through, explore, sift through, rifle through.

rumour noun **gossip**, hearsay, talk, tittle-tattle, speculation, word, report, story, whisper; informal the grapevine, the word on the street, the buzz.

run verb **1 sprint**, race, dart, rush, dash, hasten, hurry, scurry, scamper, gallop, jog, trot. **2 flee**, take flight, make off, take off, take to your heels, bolt, make your getaway, escape; informal beat it, clear off/out, scram, leg it; Brit. informal scarper. **3 extend**, stretch, reach, continue. **4 flow**, pour, stream, gush, flood, cascade, roll, course, glide, spill, trickle, drip, dribble, leak. **5 be in charge of**, manage, direct, control, head, govern, supervise, superintend, oversee, organize, coordinate. **6** it's expensive to run a car **maintain**, keep, own, possess, have, use, operate. **7** I left the engine running **operate**, function, work, go.
● noun **1 jog**, sprint, dash, gallop, trot. **2 route**, journey, circuit, round, beat. **3 drive**, ride, turn, trip, excursion, outing, jaunt; informal spin, tootle. **4 series**, succession, sequence, string, streak, spate. **5 enclosure**, pen, coop. **6** a ski run **slope**, track, piste; N. Amer. trail.
□ **run down 1** run over, knock down/over, hit. **2** criticize, denigrate, belittle, disparage, deprecate, find fault with; informal put down, knock, bad-mouth; Brit. informal rubbish, slag off. **run into 1** collide with, hit, strike, crash into,

smash into, plough into, ram. **2** meet (by chance), run across, chance on, stumble on, happen on; *informal* bump into. **3** experience, encounter, meet with, be faced with, be confronted with. **run out 1** be used up, dry up, be exhausted, be finished, peter out. **2** expire, end, terminate, finish, lapse. **run over 1** overflow, spill over, brim over. **2** exceed, go over, overshoot, overreach. **3** review, repeat, run through, go over, reiterate, recapitulate, look over, read through; *informal* recap on. **4** run down, knock down/over, hit.

runaway *noun* **fugitive**, refugee, truant, absconder, deserter.

rundown *noun* **summary**, synopsis, precis, run-through, recap, review, overview, briefing, sketch, outline; *informal* low-down.

run down *adjective* **1 dilapidated**, tumbledown, ramshackle, derelict, crumbling, neglected, uncared-for. **2 unwell**, ill, poorly, unhealthy, peaky, tired, drained, exhausted, worn out, below par, washed out; *Brit.* off colour; *informal* under the weather; *Brit. informal* off; *Austral./NZ informal* crook.

runner *noun* **1 athlete**, sprinter, hurdler, racer, jogger. **2 messenger**, courier, errand boy; *informal* gofer.

running *noun* **1 administration**, management, organization, coordination, orchestration, handling, direction, control, supervision. **2 operation**, working, function, performance.
● *adjective* **1 flowing**, gushing, rushing, moving. **2 in succession**, in a row, in sequence, consecutively, straight, together; *informal* on the trot.

runny *adjective* **liquid**, liquefied, fluid, melted, molten, watery, thin.
- OPPOSITES solid, thick.

rupture *noun & verb* **break**, fracture, crack, burst, split, fissure, breach.

rural *adjective* **country**, rustic, bucolic, pastoral, agricultural, agrarian.
- OPPOSITES urban.

ruse *noun* **ploy**, stratagem, tactic, scheme, trick, gambit, dodge, subterfuge, machination, wile; *Brit. informal* wheeze.

rush *verb* **1 hurry**, dash, run, race, sprint, bolt, dart, gallop, career, charge, shoot, hurtle, hare, fly, speed, zoom, scurry, scuttle, scamper, hasten; *informal* tear, belt, pelt, scoot, zip, whip, hotfoot it; *Brit. informal* bomb. **2 gush**, pour, surge, stream, course, cascade. **3 attack**, charge, storm.
● *noun* **1 dash**, run, sprint, dart, bolt, charge, scramble. **2 hustle and bustle**, commotion, hubbub, hurly-burly, stir. **3 charge**, onslaught, attack, assault.

rushed *adjective* **hasty**, fast, speedy, quick, swift, rapid, hurried.

rust *verb* **corrode**, oxidize, tarnish.

rustic *adjective* **1 rural**, country, pastoral, bucolic, agricultural, agrarian; *literary* Arcadian. **2 plain**, simple, homely, unsophisticated, rough, crude.
- OPPOSITES urban.
● *noun* **peasant**, countryman, countrywoman, bumpkin, yokel, country cousin; *N. Amer. informal* hillbilly, hayseed, hick.

rustle *verb* **1 swish**, whoosh, whisper, sigh. **2 steal**, thieve, take, abduct, kidnap.

rut *noun* **1 furrow**, groove, trough, ditch, hollow, pothole, crater. **2 boring routine**, humdrum existence, groove, dead end.

ruthless *adjective* **merciless**, pitiless, cruel, heartless, hard-hearted, coldhearted, cold-blooded, harsh, callous.
- OPPOSITES merciful.

r

Ss

sabotage noun **vandalism**, wrecking, destruction, damage, obstruction, disruption; *Brit. informal* a spanner in the works.
● *verb* **vandalize**, wreck, damage, destroy, incapacitate, obstruct, disrupt, spoil, ruin, undermine; *Brit. informal* throw a spanner in the works.

sack noun **bag**, pouch, pocket, pack.
● *verb* (*informal*) **dismiss**, discharge, lay off, make redundant, let go, throw out; *informal* fire, give someone the sack; *Brit. informal* give someone their cards.
□ **the sack** (*informal*) dismissal, discharge, redundancy; *informal* the boot, the axe, the heave-ho, the push.

sacred adjective **1 holy**, hallowed, blessed, consecrated, sanctified.
2 religious, spiritual, devotional, church, ecclesiastical.
- OPPOSITES secular, profane.

sacrifice noun **1 offering**, gift, oblation.
2 surrender, giving up, abandonment, renunciation, forfeiture.
● *verb* **1 offer up**, immolate. **2 give up**, forgo, abandon, renounce, relinquish, cede, surrender, forfeit.

sacrilege noun **desecration**, profanity, blasphemy, irreverence, disrespect.

sad adjective **1 unhappy**, sorrowful, depressed, downcast, miserable, down, despondent, wretched, glum, gloomy, doleful, melancholy, mournful, woebegone, forlorn, heartbroken; *informal* blue, down in the mouth, down in the dumps. **2 tragic**, unhappy, miserable, wretched, sorry, pitiful, pathetic, heartbreaking, heart-rending. **3 unfortunate**, regrettable, sorry, deplorable, lamentable, pitiful, shameful, disgraceful.
- OPPOSITES happy, cheerful.

sadden verb **depress**, dispirit, deject, dishearten, grieve, discourage, upset, get down.

saddle verb **burden**, encumber, lumber, land, impose something on.

sadness noun **unhappiness**, sorrow, dejection, depression, misery, despondency, wretchedness, gloom, gloominess, melancholy.

safe adjective **1 secure**, protected, sheltered, guarded, out of harm's way. **2 unharmed**, unhurt, uninjured, unscathed, all right, fine, well, in one piece, out of danger, safe and sound. **3 cautious**, circumspect, prudent, careful, unadventurous, conservative. **4 harmless**, innocuous, non-toxic, non-poisonous.
- OPPOSITES dangerous, harmful.

safeguard noun **protection**, defence, buffer, provision, security, cover, insurance.
● *verb* **protect**, preserve, conserve, save, secure, shield, guard, keep safe.
- OPPOSITES jeopardize.

safety noun **1 welfare**, well-being, protection, security. **2 shelter**, sanctuary, refuge.

sag verb **1 sink**, slump, loll, flop, crumple. **2 dip**, droop, bulge, bag.

saga noun **1 epic**, legend, (folk) tale, romance, narrative, myth. **2 story**, tale, yarn.

sage noun **wise man/woman**, philosopher, scholar, guru, prophet, mystic.

sail verb **1 voyage**, travel, navigate, cruise. **2 set sail**, put to sea, leave, weigh anchor. **3 steer**, pilot, captain; *informal* skipper. **4 glide**, drift, float, flow, sweep, skim, coast, flit, scud.

sailor noun **seaman**, seafarer, mariner, yachtsman, yachtswoman, hand; *informal* old salt, matelot, Jack Tar.

saintly adjective **holy**, godly, pious, religious, devout, spiritual, virtuous, righteous, good, pure.
- OPPOSITES ungodly.

sake noun **1** for the sake of clarity **purpose(s)**, reason(s). **2** for her son's sake **benefit**, advantage, good, well-being, welfare.

salary noun **pay**, wages, earnings, payment, remuneration, fee(s), stipend, income.

sale noun **1 selling**, dealing, trading. **2 deal**, transaction, bargain.
- OPPOSITES purchase.

salty adjective **salt**, salted, saline, briny, brackish.

salubrious adjective **pleasant**, agreeable, nice, select, high-class; Brit. upmarket; informal posh, classy; Brit. informal swish.

salute noun **tribute**, testimonial, homage, honour, celebration (of), acknowledgement (of).
● verb **pay tribute to**, pay homage to, honour, celebrate, acknowledge, take your hat off to.

salvage verb **rescue**, save, recover, retrieve, reclaim.

salvation noun **1 redemption**, deliverance. **2 lifeline**, means of escape, saviour.
- OPPOSITES damnation, ruin.

same adjective **1 identical**, selfsame, very same. **2 matching**, identical, alike, carbon-copy, twin, indistinguishable, interchangeable, corresponding, equivalent, parallel, like, comparable, similar, homogeneous.
- OPPOSITES another, different.
□ **the same** unchanging, unvarying, unvaried, consistent, uniform.

sample noun **1 specimen**, example, snippet, swatch, taste, taster. **2 cross section**, sampling, selection.
● verb **try (out)**, taste, test, put to the test, appraise, evaluate; informal check out.

sanctimonious adjective **self-righteous**, holier-than-thou, pious, moralizing, smug, superior, priggish, hypocritical, insincere; informal goody-goody.

sanction noun **1 penalty**, punishment, deterrent, restriction, embargo, ban, prohibition, boycott. **2 authorization**, consent, leave, permission, authority, dispensation, assent, acquiescence, agreement, approval, endorsement, blessing; informal the thumbs up, the OK, the green light.
- OPPOSITES prohibition.
● verb **authorize**, permit, allow, endorse, approve, accept, back, support; informal OK.
- OPPOSITES prohibit.

sanctuary noun **1 refuge**, haven, oasis, shelter, retreat, bolt-hole, hideaway. **2 safety**, protection, shelter, immunity, asylum. **3 reserve**, wildlife reserve, park.

sane adjective **1 of sound mind**, in your right mind, compos mentis, lucid, rational, balanced, normal; informal all there. **2 sensible**, practical, realistic, prudent, reasonable, rational, level-headed, commonsensical.
- OPPOSITES mad, foolish.

sanguine adjective **optimistic**, hopeful, buoyant, positive, confident, cheerful, bullish; informal upbeat.
- OPPOSITES gloomy.

sanity noun **1 mental health**, reason, rationality, stability, lucidity, sense, wits, mind. **2 sense**, good sense, common sense, wisdom, prudence, rationality.

sap noun **juice**, secretion, fluid, liquid.
● verb **erode**, wear away/down, deplete, reduce, lessen, undermine, drain, bleed.

sarcasm noun **irony**, derision, mockery, ridicule, scorn.

sarcastic adjective **ironic**, sardonic, derisive, scornful, contemptuous, mocking, caustic, scathing, trenchant, acerbic.

sardonic adjective **mocking**, cynical, scornful, derisive, sneering, scathing, caustic, trenchant, cutting, acerbic.

satanic adjective **diabolical**, fiendish, devilish, demonic, ungodly, hellish, infernal, wicked, evil, sinful.
- OPPOSITES godly.

S

satire *noun* **parody**, burlesque, caricature, irony, lampoon, skit; *informal* spoof, take-off, send-up.

satirical *adjective* **mocking**, ironic, sardonic, critical, irreverent, disparaging, disrespectful.

satirize *verb* **mock**, ridicule, deride, make fun of, parody, lampoon, caricature, take off, criticize; *informal* send up, take the mickey out of.

satisfaction *noun* **contentment**, content, pleasure, gratification, fulfilment, enjoyment, happiness, pride.

satisfactory *adjective* **adequate**, all right, acceptable, good enough, sufficient, reasonable, competent, fair, decent, average, passable, fine, in order, up to scratch, up to the mark.

satisfy *verb* **1 fulfil**, gratify, meet, fill, indulge, appease, assuage, quench, slake, satiate. **2 convince**, assure, reassure, put someone's mind at rest. **3 comply with**, meet, fulfil, answer, conform to, measure up to, come up to.
- OPPOSITES frustrate.

saturate *verb* **1 soak**, drench, wet through. **2 flood**, glut, oversupply, overfill, overload.

saturated *adjective* **1 soaked**, soaking (wet), wet through, sopping (wet), sodden, dripping, wringing wet, drenched, soaked to the skin. **2 waterlogged**, flooded, boggy, awash.
- OPPOSITES dry.

sauce *noun* **relish**, condiment, ketchup, dip, dressing, jus, coulis, gravy.

saunter *verb* **stroll**, amble, wander, meander, walk; *informal* mosey, tootle; *formal* promenade.

savage *adjective* **1 vicious**, brutal, cruel, sadistic, ferocious, fierce, violent, barbaric, bloodthirsty, merciless, pitiless. **2 untamed**, wild, feral, undomesticated. **3** *a savage attack on the government* **fierce**, blistering, scathing, searing, stinging, devastating, withering, virulent, vitriolic.
- OPPOSITES mild, tame.

● *noun* **brute**, beast, monster, barbarian, sadist, animal.
● *verb* **maul**, attack, lacerate, claw, bite, tear to pieces.

save *verb* **1 rescue**, set free, free, liberate, deliver, redeem. **2 preserve**, keep, protect, safeguard, salvage, retrieve, reclaim, rescue. **3 put aside**, set aside, put by, keep, conserve, retain, store, hoard, stockpile; *informal* squirrel away. **4 prevent**, avoid, forestall, spare, stop, obviate, avert.

saving *noun* **1 reduction**, cut, decrease, economy. **2 (savings) nest egg**, capital, assets, funds, resources, reserves.

saviour *noun* **rescuer**, liberator, deliverer, champion, protector, redeemer.

savour *verb* **relish**, enjoy, appreciate, delight in, revel in, luxuriate in.
● *noun* **smell**, aroma, fragrance, scent, perfume, bouquet, taste, flavour, tang, smack.

savoury *adjective* **salty**, spicy, tangy, piquant.
- OPPOSITES sweet.
● *noun* **canapé**, hors d'oeuvre, appetizer, titbit.

say *verb* **1 speak**, utter, voice, pronounce. **2 declare**, state, announce, remark, observe, mention, comment, note, add. **3 recite**, repeat, utter, deliver, perform. **4 indicate**, show, read.
● *noun* **influence**, sway, weight, voice, input.

saying *noun* **proverb**, maxim, aphorism, axiom, expression, phrase, formula, slogan, catchphrase.

scale *noun* **1 hierarchy**, ladder, ranking, pecking order, order, spectrum. **2 ratio**, proportion. **3 extent**, size, scope, magnitude, dimensions, range, breadth, degree.
● *verb* **climb**, ascend, clamber up, scramble up, shin (up), mount; *N. Amer.* shinny (up).

scaly *adjective* **dry**, flaky, scurfy, rough, scabrous.

scan *verb* **1 study**, examine, scrutinize, inspect, survey, search, scour, sweep, watch. **2 glance through**, look through, have a look at, run your eye over, cast your eye over, flick through, browse through, leaf through, thumb through.

scandal noun **1 gossip**, rumour(s), slander, libel, aspersions, muckraking; *informal* dirt. **2** *it's a scandal that the hospital has closed* **disgrace**, outrage, sin, (crying) shame.

scandalous adjective **1 disgraceful**, shocking, outrageous, monstrous, criminal, wicked, shameful, appalling, deplorable, inexcusable, intolerable, unforgivable, unpardonable. **2 discreditable**, disreputable, dishonourable, improper, unseemly, sordid. **3 scurrilous**, malicious, slanderous, libellous, defamatory.

scant adjective **little**, little or no, minimal, limited, negligible, meagre, insufficient, inadequate.
- OPPOSITES abundant, ample.

scanty adjective **1 meagre**, scant, minimal, limited, modest, restricted, sparse, tiny, small, paltry, negligible, scarce, in short supply, thin on the ground, few and far between; *informal* measly, piddling, mingy, pathetic. **2 skimpy**, revealing, short, brief, low-cut.
- OPPOSITES ample, plentiful.

scapegoat noun **whipping boy**, Aunt Sally; *informal* fall guy; *N. Amer. informal* patsy.

scar noun **1 mark**, blemish, disfigurement, discoloration, pockmark, pit, lesion, cicatrix. **2** *psychological scars* **trauma**, damage, injury.
● verb **disfigure**, mark, blemish, discolour, mar, spoil.

scarce adjective **in short supply**, scant, scanty, inadequate, lacking, meagre, sparse, hard to come by, at a premium, few and far between, thin on the ground, rare.
- OPPOSITES plentiful.

scarcely adverb **1 hardly**, barely, only just. **2 rarely**, seldom, infrequently, not often, hardly ever; *informal* once in

a blue moon.

scarcity noun **shortage**, dearth, lack, undersupply, insufficiency, paucity, poverty, deficiency, inadequacy, unavailability, absence.

scare verb **frighten**, startle, alarm, terrify, unnerve, worry, intimidate, terrorize, cow; *informal* freak out; *Brit. informal* put the wind up; *N. Amer. informal* spook.
● noun **fright**, shock, start, turn, jump.

scared adjective **frightened**, afraid, fearful, nervous, panicky, terrified; *informal* in a cold sweat; *N. Amer. informal* spooked.

scary adjective (informal) **frightening**, terrifying, hair-raising, spine-chilling, blood-curdling, eerie, sinister; *informal* creepy, spine-tingling, spooky.

scathing adjective **withering**, blistering, searing, devastating, fierce, ferocious, savage, severe, stinging, biting, cutting, virulent, vitriolic, scornful, bitter, harsh.
- OPPOSITES mild.

scatter verb **1 spread**, sprinkle, distribute, strew, disseminate, sow, throw, toss, fling. **2 disperse**, break up, disband, separate, dissolve.
- OPPOSITES gather, assemble.

scavenge verb **search**, hunt, look, forage, rummage, root about/around, grub about/around.

scenario noun **1 plot**, outline, storyline, framework, screenplay, script. **2 situation**, chain of events, course of events.

scene noun **1 location**, site, place, position, spot, locale. **2 background**, setting, context, milieu, backdrop. **3 incident**, event, episode, happening, proceeding. **4 view**, vista, outlook, panorama, landscape, scenery. **5** *she made a scene* **fuss**, exhibition of yourself, performance, tantrum, commotion, disturbance, row; *informal* to-do; *Brit. informal* carry-on. **6** *the political scene* **arena**, stage, sphere, world, milieu, realm. **7 clip**, section, segment, part, sequence, extract.

S

scenery noun **1 landscape**, countryside, country, terrain, setting, surroundings, environment. **2 set**, setting, backdrop.

scenic adjective **picturesque**, pretty, attractive, beautiful, charming, impressive, striking, spectacular, breathtaking, panoramic.

scent noun **1 smell**, fragrance, aroma, perfume, savour, odour. **2 perfume**, fragrance, eau de toilette, toilet water, eau de cologne. **3 spoor**, trail, track.
● verb **smell**, nose out, detect, pick up, sense.

scented adjective **perfumed**, fragranced, fragrant, sweet-smelling, aromatic.

sceptic noun **cynic**, doubter, unbeliever, doubting Thomas.

sceptical adjective **dubious**, doubtful, doubting, cynical, distrustful, suspicious, disbelieving, unconvinced.
– OPPOSITES certain, convinced.

scepticism noun **doubt**, a pinch of salt, disbelief, cynicism, distrust, suspicion, incredulity.

schedule noun **plan**, programme, timetable, scheme, agenda, diary, calendar, itinerary.
● verb **arrange**, organize, plan, programme, timetable, set up, line up; N. Amer. slate.

scheme noun **1 plan**, project, programme, strategy, stratagem, tactic; Brit. informal wheeze. **2 plot**, intrigue, conspiracy, ruse, ploy, stratagem, manoeuvre, subterfuge, machinations; informal racket, scam.
● verb **plot**, conspire, intrigue, connive, manoeuvre, plan.

scheming adjective **cunning**, crafty, calculating, devious, conniving, wily, sly, tricky, artful.
– OPPOSITES ingenuous, honest.

schism noun **division**, split, rift, breach, rupture, break, separation, severance, chasm, gulf, disagreement.

scholar noun **academic**, intellectual, learned person, man/woman of letters, authority, expert; informal egghead; N. Amer. informal pointy-head.

scholarly adjective **learned**, educated, erudite, academic, well read, intellectual, literary, highbrow.
– OPPOSITES uneducated, illiterate.

scholarship noun **1 learning**, knowledge, erudition, education, academic study. **2 grant**, award, endowment; Brit. bursary.

school noun **1 college**, academy, alma mater. **2 department**, faculty, division. **3 tradition**, approach, style, way of thinking, persuasion, creed, credo, doctrine, belief, opinion, point of view.
● verb **train**, teach, tutor, coach, instruct, drill.

> **WORD LINKS**
> **scholastic** relating to schools

science noun the science of criminology **subject**, discipline, field, branch of knowledge, body of knowledge, area of study.

scientific adjective **1 technological**, technical, evidence-based, empirical. **2 systematic**, methodical, organized, ordered, rigorous, exact, precise, accurate, mathematical.

scintillating adjective **brilliant**, dazzling, coruscating, exciting, exhilarating, stimulating, sparkling, lively, vivacious, vibrant, animated, effervescent, witty, clever.
– OPPOSITES dull, boring.

scoff verb **sneer**, jeer, laugh; (**scoff at**) mock, deride, ridicule, dismiss, belittle; informal pooh-pooh.

scoop noun **spoon**, ladle, dipper.
□ **scoop out 1** hollow out, gouge out, dig, excavate. **2** remove, take out, spoon out, scrape out. **scoop up** pick up, gather up, lift, take up, snatch up, grab.

scope noun **1 extent**, range, breadth, reach, sweep, span, area, sphere, realm, compass, orbit, ambit, terms of reference, remit. **2 opportunity**, freedom, latitude, leeway, capacity, room (to manoeuvre).

scorch verb **1 burn**, sear, singe, char, blacken, discolour. **2 dry up**, parch, wither, shrivel, desiccate.

scorching *adjective* **hot**, red-hot, blazing, flaming, fiery, burning, blistering, searing; *informal* boiling, baking, sizzling.
- OPPOSITES freezing, mild.

score *noun* **1 result**, outcome, total, tally, count. **2 rating**, grade, mark, percentage.
● *verb* **1 get**, gain, chalk up, achieve, make, record, rack up, notch up; *informal* bag, knock up. **2 arrange**, set, adapt, orchestrate, write, compose. **3 scratch**, cut, notch, incise, scrape, nick, gouge.
□ **score out/through** cross out, strike out, delete, put a line through, obliterate.

scorn *noun* **contempt**, derision, disdain, mockery, sneering.
- OPPOSITES admiration, respect.
● *verb* **1 deride**, treat with contempt, mock, scoff at, sneer at, jeer at, laugh at. **2 spurn**, rebuff, reject, ignore, shun, snub.
- OPPOSITES admire, respect.

scornful *adjective* **contemptuous**, derisive, withering, mocking, sneering, jeering, scathing, snide, disparaging, supercilious, disdainful.
- OPPOSITES admiring.

scour[1] *verb* **scrub**, rub, clean, polish, buff, shine, burnish, grind, abrade.

scour[2] *verb* **search**, comb, hunt through, rummage through, look high and low in, ransack, turn upside-down.

scourge *noun* **affliction**, bane, curse, plague, menace, evil, misfortune, burden, blight, cancer, canker.

scout *noun* **1 lookout**, outrider, spy. **2 reconnaissance**, reconnoitre, survey, exploration, search; *informal* recce; *Brit. informal* shufti.
● *verb* **1** *I scouted around for some logs* **search**, look, hunt, ferret around, root around. **2** *a patrol was sent to scout out the area* **reconnoitre**, explore, inspect, investigate, spy out, survey, scan, study; *informal* check out, case.

scowl *verb* **glower**, frown, glare, grimace, lour, look daggers.
- OPPOSITES smile.

scramble *verb* **1 clamber**, climb, crawl, claw your way, scrabble, struggle; *N. Amer.* shinny. **2 muddle**, confuse, mix up, jumble (up), disarrange, disorganize, disorder, disturb, mess up.
● *noun* **1 clamber**, climb. **2** *the scramble for a seat* **struggle**, jostle, scrimmage, scuffle, tussle, free-for-all, jockeying, competition, race.

scrap *noun* **1 fragment**, piece, bit, snippet, oddment, remnant, morsel, sliver. **2** *not a scrap of evidence* **bit**, shred, speck, iota, particle, ounce, jot. **3 waste**, rubbish, refuse, debris; *N. Amer.* garbage, trash; *informal* junk.
● *verb* **1 throw away**, throw out, dispose of, get rid of, discard, dispense with, bin, decommission, break up, demolish; *informal* chuck (away/out), ditch, dump, junk; *Brit. informal* get shot of; *N. Amer. informal* trash. **2 abandon**, drop, abolish, withdraw, do away with, put an end to, cancel, axe; *informal* ditch, dump, junk.
- OPPOSITES keep.

scrape *verb* **1 rub**, scratch, scour, grind, sand, sandpaper, abrade, file. **2 grate**, creak, rasp, scratch. **3 graze**, scratch, scuff, rasp, skin, cut, lacerate, bark, chafe.
● *noun* **1 grating**, creaking, rasp, scratch. **2 graze**, scratch, abrasion, cut, laceration, wound.

scratch *verb* **scrape**, abrade, graze, score, scuff, skin, cut, lacerate, bark, chafe.
● *noun* **abrasion**, graze, scrape, cut, laceration, wound, mark, line.
□ **up to scratch** good enough, up to the mark, up to standard, up to par, satisfactory, acceptable, adequate, passable, sufficient, all right; *informal* OK.

scream *verb* & *noun* **shriek**, screech, yell, howl, bawl, yelp, squeal, wail, squawk.

screen *noun* **1 partition**, divider, windbreak. **2 display**, monitor, visual display

unit. **3 mesh**, net, netting. **4 buffer**, protection, shield, shelter, guard.
● *verb* **1 partition**, divide, separate, curtain. **2 conceal**, hide, veil, shield, shelter, shade, protect. **3** *all blood is screened for the virus* **check**, test, examine, investigate, vet; *informal* check out. **4 show**, broadcast, transmit, televise, put out, air.

screw *noun* **1 bolt**, fastener. **2 propeller**, rotor.
● *verb* **1 tighten**, turn, twist, wind. **2 fasten**, secure, fix, attach. **3** *(informal)* **extort**, force, extract, wrest, wring, squeeze; *informal* bleed.
□ **screw up 1** wrinkle, pucker, crumple, crease, furrow, contort, distort, twist. **2** *(informal)* wreck, ruin, destroy, damage, spoil, mess up; *informal* louse up, foul up, scupper.

scribble *verb* **scrawl**, scratch, dash off, jot (down), doodle, sketch.
● *noun* **scrawl**, squiggle(s), jottings, doodle, doodlings.

script *noun* **1 handwriting**, writing, hand. **2 text**, screenplay, libretto, score, lines, dialogue, words.

scrounge *verb* **beg**, borrow; *informal* cadge, sponge, bum, touch someone for; *N. Amer. informal* mooch; *Austral./NZ informal* bludge.

scrounger *noun* **beggar**, parasite, cadger; *informal* sponger, freeloader; *N. Amer. informal* mooch; *Austral./NZ informal* bludger.

scrub *verb* **1 brush**, scour, rub, clean, cleanse, wash. **2** *(informal)* **abandon**, scrap, drop, cancel, call off, axe; *informal* ditch, dump, junk.

scruffy *adjective* **shabby**, worn, down at heel, ragged, tattered, mangy, dirty, untidy, unkempt, bedraggled, messy, dishevelled, ill-groomed; *informal* tatty.
- OPPOSITES smart.

scruples *plural noun* **qualms**, compunction, hesitation, reservations, second thoughts, doubt(s), misgivings, uneasiness, reluctance.

scrupulous *adjective* **careful**, meticulous, painstaking, thorough, assiduous,

sedulous, attentive, conscientious, punctilious, searching, close, rigorous, strict.
- OPPOSITES careless.

scrutinize *verb* **examine**, inspect, survey, study, look at, peruse, investigate, explore, probe, enquire into, go into, check.

sculpture *noun* **carving**, statue, statuette, figure, figurine, effigy, bust, head, model.

scum *noun* **film**, layer, covering, froth, filth, dross, dirt.

scupper *verb* (*Brit. informal*) **ruin**, wreck, destroy, sabotage, torpedo, spoil.

scurrilous *adjective* **defamatory**, slanderous, libellous, scandalous, insulting, offensive, abusive, malicious; *informal* bitchy.

sea *noun* **1 ocean**, waves; *informal* the drink; *Brit. informal* the briny; *literary* the deep. **2** *a sea of roofs* **expanse**, stretch, area, tract, sweep, carpet, mass.
● *adjective* **marine**, ocean, oceanic, maritime, naval, nautical.
□ **at sea** confused, perplexed, puzzled, baffled, mystified, bemused, bewildered, nonplussed, dumbfounded, at a loss, lost; *informal* flummoxed, fazed.

seal *noun* **1 sealant**, adhesive, mastic. **2 emblem**, symbol, insignia, badge, crest.
● *verb* **1 stop up**, seal up, cork, stopper, plug, make watertight. **2 clinch**, secure, settle, conclude, complete, finalize, confirm.
□ **seal off** close off, shut off, cordon off, fence off, isolate.

seam *noun* **1 join**, stitching, joint. **2 layer**, stratum, vein, lode.

seaman *noun* **sailor**, seafarer, mariner, boatman, hand, merchant seaman.
- OPPOSITES landlubber.

sear *verb* **1 scorch**, burn, singe, char, dry up, wither. **2 flash-fry**, seal, brown.

search *verb* **1 hunt**, look, seek, forage, look high and low, ferret about, root about, rummage. **2** *he searched the house* **look through**, scour, go

through, sift through, comb, turn upside down, ransack, rifle through; *Austral./NZ informal* fossick through. **3 examine**, inspect, check, frisk.
● *noun* **hunt**, look, quest, examination, exploration.

searching *adjective* **penetrating**, piercing, probing, keen, shrewd, sharp, intent.

seaside *noun* **coast**, shore, seashore, beach, sand, sands.

season *noun* **period**, time, time of year, spell, term.
● *verb* **flavour**, add salt/pepper to, spice.

seasoned *adjective* **experienced**, practised, well versed, knowledgeable, established, veteran, hardened.
- OPPOSITES inexperienced.

seasoning *noun* **flavouring**, salt and pepper, herbs, spices, condiments.

seat *noun* **1 chair**, bench, stool; (**seats**) seating. **2 headquarters**, base, centre, nerve centre, hub, heart, location, site. **3 residence**, ancestral home, mansion.
● *verb* **1 position**, put, place, ensconce, install, settle. **2 have room for**, contain, take, sit, hold, accommodate.

secluded *adjective* **sheltered**, private, concealed, hidden, unfrequented, sequestered, tucked away, remote, isolated, off the beaten track.

second[1] *adjective* **1 next**, following, subsequent. **2 additional**, extra, alternative, another, spare, backup; *N. Amer.* alternate. **3 secondary**, subordinate, subsidiary, lesser, inferior.
- OPPOSITES first.
● *noun* **assistant**, attendant, helper, aide, supporter, auxiliary, second in command, number two, deputy, understudy; *informal* sidekick.
● *verb* **support**, vote for, back, approve, endorse.

second[2] *noun* **moment**, bit, little while, instant, flash; *informal* sec, jiffy; *Brit. informal* mo, tick.

secondary *adjective* **1 less important**, subordinate, lesser, minor, peripheral,

incidental, subsidiary, ancillary. **2 accompanying**, attendant, concomitant, consequential, resulting, resultant.
- OPPOSITES primary, main.

second-hand *adjective* **used**, old, worn, pre-owned, nearly new, handed-down, hand-me-down, cast-off.
- OPPOSITES new, direct.
● *adverb* **indirectly**; *informal* on the grapevine.
- OPPOSITES directly.

secondly *adverb* **furthermore**, also, moreover, second, in the second place, next.

secrecy *noun* **confidentiality**, privacy, mystery, concealment, stealth.

secret *adjective* **1 confidential**, top secret, classified, undisclosed, unknown, private, under wraps; *Military* black; *informal* hush-hush. **2 hidden**, concealed, disguised, camouflaged. **3 clandestine**, covert, undercover, underground, surreptitious, stealthy, cloak-and-dagger, furtive, conspiratorial.
- OPPOSITES public, open.
□ **in secret** secretly, in private, behind closed doors, under cover, furtively, stealthily, on the quiet, covertly; *formal* sub rosa.

secretive *adjective* **uncommunicative**, secret, unforthcoming, playing your cards close to your chest, reticent, tight-lipped.
- OPPOSITES open, communicative.

secretly *adverb* **in secret**, in private, privately, behind closed doors, under cover, furtively, stealthily, on the quiet, covertly.

sect *noun* **group**, cult, denomination, order, splinter group, faction, camp.

sectarian *adjective* **factional**, separatist, partisan, doctrinaire, dogmatic, illiberal, intolerant, bigoted, narrow-minded.

section *noun* **1 part**, bit, portion, segment, compartment, module, element, unit. **2 passage**, subsection, chapter, subdivision, clause. **3 department**, area, division.

s

sector noun **1 part**, branch, arm, division, area, department, field, sphere. **2 district**, quarter, section, zone, region, area, belt.

secular adjective **non-religious**, lay, temporal, civil, worldly, earthly, profane.
- OPPOSITES sacred, religious.

secure adjective **1 fastened**, fixed, secured, done up, closed, shut, locked. **2 safe**, protected, safe and sound, out of harm's way, in safe hands, invulnerable, undamaged, unharmed. **3** his position as leader was secure **certain**, assured, settled, stable, not at risk. **4 unworried**, at ease, relaxed, happy, confident.
- OPPOSITES loose, insecure.
● verb **1 fasten**, close, shut, lock, bolt, chain, seal. **2 obtain**, acquire, gain, get, get hold of, come by; informal land.

security noun **1 safety**, protection. **2 safety measures**, safeguards, surveillance, defence, policing. **3 guarantee**, collateral, surety, pledge, bond.

sedate[1] verb **tranquillize**, put under sedation, drug.

sedate[2] adjective **1 slow**, steady, dignified, unhurried, relaxed, measured, leisurely, slow-moving, easy, gentle. **2 calm**, placid, tranquil, quiet, uneventful, staid, boring, dull.
- OPPOSITES fast, exciting.

sediment noun **dregs**, grounds, lees, residue, deposit, silt.

seduce verb **1 attract**, allure, lure, tempt, entice, beguile, inveigle, manipulate. **2 have your (wicked) way with**, take advantage of.

seductive adjective **tempting**, inviting, enticing, alluring, beguiling, attractive.

see verb **1 discern**, detect, perceive, spot, notice, catch sight of, glimpse, make out, pick out, distinguish, spy; informal clap eyes on, clock; literary behold, espy, descry. **2 watch**, look at, view, catch. **3 inspect**, view, look round, tour, survey, examine, scrutinize. **4 understand**, grasp, comprehend, follow, realize, appreciate, recognize, work out, fathom; informal get, latch on to, tumble to, figure out; Brit. informal twig, suss (out). **5** see what he's up to **find out**, discover, learn, ascertain, determine, establish. **6** see that no harm comes to him **ensure**, make sure/certain, see to it, take care, mind. **7** I see trouble ahead **foresee**, predict, forecast, prophesy, anticipate, envisage. **8 consult**, confer with, talk to, have recourse to, call in, turn to. **9 go out with**, date, take out, be involved with; informal go steady with; dated court.
□ **see to** attend to, deal with, see about, take care of, look after, sort out, organize, arrange.

seed noun **pip**, stone, kernel.

seek verb **1 search for**, try to find, look for, be after, hunt for. **2 ask for**, request, solicit, call for, appeal for, apply for. **3 try**, attempt, endeavour, strive, work, do your best.

seem verb **appear (to be)**, have the appearance/air of being, give the impression of being, look, sound, come across as, strike someone as.

seep verb **ooze**, trickle, exude, drip, dribble, flow, leak, drain, bleed, filter, percolate, soak.

seethe verb **1 teem**, swarm, boil, swirl, churn, surge, bubble, heave. **2 be angry**, be furious, be enraged, rage, be incensed, be beside yourself, boil, rant, fume; informal be livid, foam at the mouth.

segment noun **piece**, bit, section, part, portion, division, slice, wedge.

segregate verb **separate**, set apart, keep apart, isolate, quarantine, partition, divide, discriminate against.
- OPPOSITES integrate.

seize verb **1 grab**, grasp, snatch, take hold of, clutch, grip. **2 capture**, take, overrun, occupy, conquer, take over. **3 confiscate**, impound, commandeer, requisition, appropriate, expropriate, sequestrate. **4 kidnap**, abduct, take captive, take prisoner, take hostage,

hijack; *informal* snatch.
- OPPOSITES release.

seizure *noun* **1 capture**, takeover, annexation, invasion, occupation. **2 confiscation**, appropriation, expropriation, sequestration. **3 kidnap**, abduction, hijack. **4 convulsion**, fit, spasm, paroxysm.

seldom *adverb* **rarely**, infrequently, hardly (ever), scarcely (ever); *informal* once in a blue moon.
- OPPOSITES often.

select *verb* **choose**, pick (out), single out, opt for, decide on, settle on, sort out, take, adopt.
● *adjective* **1 choice**, prime, hand-picked, top-quality, first-class, A-list; *informal* top-flight. **2 exclusive**, elite, privileged, wealthy; *informal* posh.
- OPPOSITES inferior.

selection *noun* **1 choice**, pick, option, preference. **2 range**, array, diversity, variety, assortment, mixture. **3 anthology**, assortment, collection, assemblage, miscellany, medley.

selective *adjective* **discerning**, discriminating, exacting, demanding, particular; *informal* choosy, picky.
- OPPOSITES indiscriminate.

self-centred *adjective* **egocentric**, egotistic, self-absorbed, self-obsessed, self-seeking, self-serving, narcissistic, vain, inconsiderate, thoughtless; *informal* looking after number one.

self-confidence *noun* **self-assurance**, assurance, confidence, composure, aplomb, poise, sangfroid.

self-conscious *adjective* **embarrassed**, uncomfortable, uneasy, ill at ease, nervous, awkward, shy, diffident, timid.
- OPPOSITES confident.

selfish *adjective* **egocentric**, egotistic, self-centred, self-absorbed, self-obsessed, self-seeking, wrapped up in yourself, mean, greedy; *informal* looking after number one.
- OPPOSITES unselfish, altruistic.

selfless *adjective* **unselfish**, altruistic, considerate, compassionate, kind,

noble, generous, magnanimous, ungrudging.
- OPPOSITES selfish, inconsiderate.

self-righteous *adjective* **sanctimonious**, holier-than-thou, pious, self-satisfied, smug, priggish, complacent, moralizing, superior, hypocritical; *informal* goody-goody.
- OPPOSITES humble.

sell *verb* **put up for sale**, put on the market, auction (off), trade in, deal in, retail, market, traffic in, peddle, hawk.
- OPPOSITES buy.

seller *noun* **vendor**, dealer, retailer, trader, merchant, agent, hawker, pedlar, purveyor, supplier, stockist.
- OPPOSITES buyer.

semblance *noun* **(outward) appearance**, air, show, facade, front, veneer, guise, pretence.

seminar *noun* **1 conference**, symposium, meeting, convention, forum, summit. **2 study group**, workshop, tutorial, class.

send *verb* **1 dispatch**, post, mail, email, consign, forward, transmit, convey, communicate, broadcast, radio. **2 propel**, project, eject, deliver, discharge, spout, fire, shoot, release, throw, fling, cast, hurl. **3 *you're sending me crazy* make**, drive, turn.
- OPPOSITES receive.
□ **send for** call, summon, ask for, request, order. **send up** *(informal)* satirize, ridicule, make fun of, parody, lampoon, mock, caricature, imitate, ape; *informal* take off, spoof, take the mickey out of.

send-off *noun* **farewell**, goodbye, adieu, leave-taking, departure.

senior *adjective* **1 older**, elder. **2 superior**, higher-ranking, more important; *N. Amer.* ranking.
- OPPOSITES junior, subordinate.

sensation *noun* **1 feeling**, sense, perception, impression. **2 commotion**, stir, uproar, furore, scandal, impact; *informal* splash, to-do.

S

sensational *adjective* **1 shocking**, scandalous, fascinating, exciting, thrilling, interesting, dramatic, momentous, historic, newsworthy. **2 overdramatized**, melodramatic, exaggerated, sensationalist, graphic, explicit, lurid; *informal* shock-horror, juicy. **3** (*informal*) **gorgeous**, stunning, wonderful, superb, excellent, first-class; *informal* great, terrific, tremendous, fantastic, fabulous, out of this world; *Brit. informal* smashing.
- OPPOSITES dull, unremarkable.

sense *noun* **1 feeling**, faculty, awareness, sensation, recognition, perception. **2 appreciation**, awareness, understanding, comprehension. **3 wisdom**, common sense, wit, reason, intelligence, judgement, brain(s), sagacity; *informal* gumption, nous, horse sense, savvy; *N. Amer. informal* smarts. **4 purpose**, point, use, value, advantage, benefit. **5 meaning**, definition, denotation, nuance, drift, gist, thrust, tenor, message.
- OPPOSITES stupidity.
● *verb* **detect**, feel, observe, notice, recognize, pick up, be aware of, distinguish, make out, perceive, discern, divine, intuit; *informal* catch on to.

senseless *adjective* **pointless**, futile, useless, needless, meaningless, absurd, foolish, insane, stupid, idiotic, mindless, illogical.
- OPPOSITES wise.

sensible *adjective* **practical**, realistic, responsible, reasonable, commonsensical, rational, logical, sound, nononsense, level-headed, down-to-earth, wise.
- OPPOSITES foolish.

sensitive *adjective* **1** *she's sensitive to changes in temperature* **responsive to**, reactive to, sensitized to, aware of, conscious of, susceptible to, affected by, vulnerable to. **2 delicate**, fragile, tender, sore. **3 tactful**, careful, thoughtful, diplomatic, delicate, subtle, kid-glove. **4 touchy**, oversensitive, hypersensitive, easily offended, thin-skinned, defensive, paranoid, neurotic. **5 difficult**, delicate, tricky, awkward, problematic, ticklish, controversial, emotive.
- OPPOSITES insensitive, resilient.

sensitivity *noun* **1 responsiveness**, sensitiveness, reactivity, susceptibility. **2 tact**, diplomacy, delicacy, subtlety, understanding, soft skills. **3 touchiness**, oversensitivity, hypersensitivity, defensiveness. **4 delicacy**, trickiness, awkwardness, ticklishness.

sensual *adjective* **1 physical**, carnal, bodily, fleshly, animal. **2 passionate**, sexual, physical, tactile, hedonistic.
- OPPOSITES spiritual.

sensuous *adjective* **1 rich**, sumptuous, luxurious. **2 voluptuous**, sexy, seductive, luscious, lush, ripe.

sentence *noun* **1 judgement**, ruling, decision, verdict. **2** *a long sentence* **punishment**, prison term; *informal* time, stretch.
● *verb* **condemn**, doom, punish, convict.

sentiment *noun* **1 view**, feeling, attitude, thought, opinion, belief. **2 sentimentality**, emotion, tenderness, softness; *informal* schmaltz; *Brit. informal* soppiness.

sentimental *adjective* **1 nostalgic**, emotional, affectionate, loving, tender. **2 mawkish**, overemotional, romantic, hearts-and-flowers; *Brit.* twee; *informal* schmaltzy, corny; *Brit. informal* soppy; *N. Amer. informal* sappy.

separate *adjective* **1 unconnected**, unrelated, different, distinct, discrete, detached, divorced, disconnected, independent. **2 set apart**, detached, cut off, segregated, isolated, freestanding, self-contained.
● *verb* **1 disconnect**, detach, disengage, uncouple, split, sunder, sever. **2 partition**, divide, stand between, come between, keep apart, isolate, section off. **3 part (company)**, go their separate ways, split up, disperse, scatter. **4 split up**, break up, part, become estranged, divorce.
- OPPOSITES unite, join.

s

separately *adverb* **individually**, one by one, one at a time, singly, severally, apart, independently, alone, by yourself, on your own.

separation *noun* **1 disconnection**, splitting, division, breaking-up. **2 break-up**, split, estrangement, divorce; *Brit. informal* bust-up.

septic *adjective* **infected**, festering, suppurating, putrid, putrefying, poisoned; *Medicine* purulent.

sequel *noun* **continuation**, further episode, follow-up.

sequence *noun* **1 succession**, order, course, series, chain, train, progression, chronology, pattern, flow. **2 excerpt**, clip, extract, section.

serene *adjective* **calm**, composed, tranquil, peaceful, placid, untroubled, relaxed, at ease, unperturbed, unruffled, unworried; *chiefly US* centred; *informal* together, unflappable, chilled.
- OPPOSITES agitated.

series *noun* **succession**, sequence, string, chain, run, round, spate, wave, rash, course, cycle, row.

serious *adjective* **1 solemn**, earnest, grave, sombre, unsmiling, stern, grim, humourless, stony, dour, poker-faced, long-faced. **2 important**, significant, momentous, weighty, far-reaching, consequential. **3 intellectual**, highbrow, heavyweight, deep, profound, literary, learned, scholarly; *informal* heavy. **4** *a serious injury* **severe**, grave, bad, critical, acute, terrible, dire, dangerous, grievous. **5 sincere**, earnest, genuine, wholehearted, committed, resolute, determined.
- OPPOSITES light-hearted, trivial, minor.

sermon *noun* **address**, homily, talk, speech, lecture.

servant *noun* **attendant**, domestic, maid, housemaid, retainer, flunkey, minion, slave, lackey, drudge; *informal* skivvy.

serve *verb* **1 work for**, obey, do the bidding of. **2** *this job serves the community* **benefit**, help, assist, aid, make a contribution to. **3** *he served a six-month apprenticeship* **carry out**, perform, do, fulfil, complete, discharge, spend. **4 present**, give out, distribute, dish up, provide, supply. **5 attend to**, deal with, see to, assist, help, look after. **6** *a saucer serving as an ashtray* **act as**, function as, do duty.

service *noun* **1 work**, employment, labour. **2** *he has done us a service* **favour**, kindness, good turn, helping hand. **3 ceremony**, ritual, rite, sacrament. **4 overhaul**, check, maintenance, servicing, repair. **5** *a range of local services* **amenity**, facility, resource, utility, solution. **6 (armed) forces**, military, army, navy, air force.
● *verb* **overhaul**, check, go over, maintain, repair.

serviceable *adjective* **1 in working order**, working, functioning, operational, usable, workable, viable. **2 functional**, utilitarian, sensible, practical, hard-wearing, durable, tough, robust.

session *noun* **1 meeting**, sitting, assembly, conclave; *N. Amer. & NZ* caucus. **2 period**, time, term.

set¹ *verb* **1 put (down)**, place, lay, deposit, position, settle, leave, stand, plant; *informal* stick, dump, park, plonk, pop. **2 fix**, embed, insert, mount. **3** *set the table* **lay**, prepare, arrange. **4** *he set us some work* **assign**, allocate, give, allot. **5 arrange**, schedule, fix (on), decide on, settle on, choose, agree on, determine, designate, appoint, name, specify, stipulate. **6 adjust**, regulate, synchronize, calibrate, put right, correct. **7 solidify**, harden, stiffen, thicken, gel, cake, congeal, coagulate, clot.
□ **set off/out** set out, start out, sally forth, leave, depart, embark, set sail; *informal* hit the road. **set up 1** erect, put up, construct, build. **2** establish, start, begin, institute, found, create. **3** arrange, organize, fix (up), schedule, timetable, line up.

set² *noun* **1 series**, collection, group, batch, arrangement, array, assortment, selection. **2 group**, circle, crowd, crew, band, fraternity, company, ring, camp, school, clique, faction; *informal* gang, bunch.

set³ *adjective* **1 fixed**, established, scheduled, specified, appointed, arranged, settled, decided, agreed, predetermined, hard and fast, unvarying, unchanging, invariable, rigid, inflexible. **2 ready**, prepared, organized, equipped, primed; *informal* geared up, psyched up.
- OPPOSITES variable, unprepared.

setback *noun* **problem**, difficulty, hitch, issue, complication, upset, blow; *informal* glitch, hiccup.
- OPPOSITES breakthrough.

setting *noun* **surroundings**, position, situation, environment, background, backdrop, spot, place, location, locale, site, scene.

settle *verb* **1 resolve**, sort out, clear up, end, fix, work out, iron out, set right, reconcile; *informal* patch up. **2 put in order**, sort out, tidy up, arrange, organize, order, clear up, straighten out. **3 decide on**, set, fix, agree on, name, establish, arrange, choose, pick. **4** *I've settled the bill* **pay**, square, clear. **5 make your home**, set up home, take up residence, put down roots, establish yourself, live, move to. **6** *a drink will settle your nerves* **calm**, quieten, quiet, soothe, relax. **7 land**, come to rest, alight, perch.

settlement *noun* **1 agreement**, deal, arrangement, conclusion, resolution, understanding, pact. **2 community**, colony, outpost, encampment, post, village.

settler *noun* **colonist**, frontiersman, pioneer, immigrant, newcomer, incomer.

sever *verb* **1 cut off**, chop off, detach, separate, amputate. **2 cut (through)**, rupture, split, pierce. **3 break off**, discontinue, suspend, end, cease, dissolve.
- OPPOSITES join.

several *adjective* **some**, a number of, a few, various, assorted.

severe *adjective* **1 acute**, very bad, serious, grave, critical, dire, dangerous,

life-threatening. **2** *severe storms* **fierce**, violent, strong, powerful, intense, forceful. **3 cold**, freezing, icy, arctic, harsh, bitter. **4** *severe criticism* **harsh**, scathing, sharp, strong, fierce, savage, devastating, withering. **5** *a severe expression* **stern**, dour, grim, forbidding, disapproving, unsmiling, unfriendly, sombre, stony, cold, frosty. **6 plain**, simple, austere, spartan, unadorned, stark, clinical, uncluttered, minimalist, functional.
- OPPOSITES minor, gentle, mild.

sew *verb* **stitch**, tack, seam, hem, embroider.

sex *noun* **1 sexual intercourse**, lovemaking, making love, sexual relations, mating, copulation; *formal* fornication, coitus. **2 gender.**

> **WORD LINKS**
> **carnal** relating to sexual activity

sexuality *noun* **1 sensuality**, sexiness, seductiveness, eroticism, physicality, sexual appetite, passion, desire, lust. **2 sexual orientation**, sexual preference, leaning, persuasion.

sexy *adjective* **1 sexually attractive**, seductive, desirable, alluring; *informal* fanciable, hot; *Brit. informal* fit; *N. Amer. informal* foxy. **2 erotic**, sexually explicit, titillating, naughty, X-rated, rude, pornographic, crude; *informal* raunchy, steamy; *euphemistic* adult.

shabby *adjective* **1 run down**, scruffy, dilapidated, in disrepair, ramshackle, tumbledown, dingy; *Brit. informal* grotty. **2 scruffy**, old, worn out, threadbare, ragged, frayed, tattered, battered, faded, moth-eaten, the worse for wear; *informal* tatty; *N. Amer. informal* raggedy. **3 mean**, unkind, unfair, shameful, shoddy, unworthy, contemptible, despicable, discreditable, ignoble; *informal* rotten.
- OPPOSITES smart.

shack *noun* **hut**, cabin, shanty, lean-to, shed, hovel; *Scottish* bothy.

shackle *verb* **1 chain**, fetter, manacle, secure, tie (up), bind, tether, hobble, put in chains, clap in irons, handcuff. **2 restrain**, restrict, limit, constrain, handicap, hamstring, hamper, hinder, impede, obstruct, inhibit.

shade noun **1 shadow**, shadiness, shelter, cover. **2 colour**, hue, tone, tint, tinge. **3 nuance**, gradation, degree, difference, variation, variety, nicety, subtlety, undertone, overtone. **4 little**, bit, trace, touch, modicum, tinge; *informal* tad, smidgen. **5 blind**, curtain, screen, cover, covering, awning, canopy.
- OPPOSITES light.
● *verb* **cast a shadow over**, shadow, shelter, cover, screen.

shadow noun **1 silhouette**, outline, shape, contour, profile. **2 shade**, darkness, twilight, gloom.
● *verb* **follow**, trail, track, stalk, pursue; *informal* tail, keep tabs on.

shady adjective **1 shaded**, shadowy, dim, dark, sheltered, leafy. **2** (*informal*) **suspicious**, suspect, questionable, dubious, irregular, underhand; *informal* fishy, murky; *Brit. informal* dodgy; *Austral./NZ informal* shonky.
- OPPOSITES bright, honest.

shaft noun **1 pole**, stick, rod, staff, shank, handle, stem. **2** *a shaft of light* **ray**, beam, gleam, streak, pencil. **3 tunnel**, passage, hole, bore, duct, well, flue, vent.

shake verb **1 vibrate**, tremble, quiver, quake, shiver, shudder, judder, wobble, rock, sway, convulse. **2 jiggle**, joggle, jerk, agitate; *informal* wiggle, waggle. **3 brandish**, wave, flourish, swing, wield. **4 upset**, distress, disturb, unsettle, disconcert, discompose, unnerve, throw off balance, agitate, fluster, shock, alarm, scare, worry; *informal* rattle.
● *noun* **judder**, trembling, quivering, quake, tremor, shiver, shudder, wobble.

shaky adjective **1 unsteady**, unstable, rickety, wobbly; *Brit. informal* wonky. **2 faint**, dizzy, light-headed, giddy, weak, wobbly, in shock. **3 unreliable**, untrustworthy, questionable, dubious, doubtful, tenuous, suspect, flimsy,

weak; *informal* iffy; *Brit. informal* dodgy.
- OPPOSITES steady, stable.

shallow adjective **superficial**, trivial, facile, insubstantial, lightweight, empty, trifling, surface, skin-deep, frivolous, foolish, silly.
- OPPOSITES profound.

sham noun **pretence**, fake, act, simulation, fraud, lie, counterfeit, humbug.
● *adjective* **fake**, pretended, feigned, simulated, false, artificial, bogus, insincere, affected, make-believe; *informal* pretend, put-on, phoney.
- OPPOSITES genuine.
● *verb* **pretend**, fake, malinger; *informal* put it on; *Brit. informal* swing the lead.

shambles noun **1 chaos**, muddle, jumble, confusion, disorder, havoc; *Brit. informal* omnishambles. **2 mess**, pigsty; *informal* disaster area; *Brit. informal* tip.

shame noun **1 guilt**, remorse, contrition. **2 humiliation**, embarrassment, indignity, loss of face, mortification, disgrace, dishonour, discredit, ignominy, disrepute, infamy, scandal. **3** *it's a shame she never married* **pity**, sad thing, bad luck; *informal* crime, sin.
- OPPOSITES pride, honour.
● *verb* **1 disgrace**, dishonour, discredit, blacken, drag through the mud. **2 humiliate**, embarrass, humble, take down a peg or two, cut down to size, show up.
- OPPOSITES honour.

shamefaced adjective **ashamed**, abashed, sheepish, guilty, contrite, sorry, remorseful, repentant, penitent, regretful, rueful, apologetic; *informal* with your tail between your legs.
- OPPOSITES unrepentant.

shameful adjective **1 disgraceful**, deplorable, despicable, contemptible, discreditable, unworthy, reprehensible, shabby, shocking, scandalous, outrageous, abominable, atrocious, appalling, inexcusable, unforgivable. **2 embarrassing**, mortifying, humiliating, ignominious.
- OPPOSITES admirable.

S

shameless *adjective* **flagrant**, blatant, barefaced, overt, brazen, undisguised, unconcealed, unabashed, unashamed, unblushing, unrepentant.

shape *noun* **1 form**, appearance, configuration, structure, contours, lines, outline, silhouette, profile. **2 guise**, likeness, semblance, form, appearance, image. **3 condition**, health, trim, fettle, order; *Brit. informal* nick.
● *verb* **1 form**, fashion, make, mould, model. **2** *events which shaped the course of her life* **determine**, form, influence, affect.

shapeless *adjective* **1 formless**, amorphous, unformed, indefinite. **2 baggy**, saggy, ill-fitting, oversized, unstructured, badly cut.

shapely *adjective* **well proportioned**, curvaceous, voluptuous, full-figured, attractive, sexy; *informal* curvy.

share *noun* **portion**, part, division, quota, allowance, ration, allocation; *informal* cut, slice; *Brit. informal* whack.
● *verb* **1 split**, divide, go halves on; *informal* go fifty-fifty on. **2 apportion**, divide up, allocate, portion out, measure out, carve up; *Brit. informal* divvy up. **3 participate**, take part, play a part, be involved, have a hand.

sharp *adjective* **1 keen**, razor-edged, sharpened, well honed. **2 intense**, acute, severe, agonizing, excruciating, stabbing, shooting, searing. **3 tangy**, piquant, acidic, acid, sour, tart, pungent, vinegary. **4 cold**, chilly, icy, bitter, biting, brisk, keen, penetrating. **5 harsh**, bitter, cutting, caustic, scathing, barbed, spiteful, hurtful, unkind, cruel, malicious. **6** *a sharp increase* **sudden**, abrupt, unexpected, rapid, steep. **7 astute**, intelligent, bright, incisive, keen, quick-witted, shrewd, canny, perceptive, smart, quick; *informal* on the ball, quick on the uptake, genius; *N. Amer. informal* heads-up.
- OPPOSITES blunt, mild.
● *adverb* **precisely**, exactly, prompt, promptly, punctually; *informal* on the dot; *N. Amer. informal* on the button.

sharpen *verb* **hone**, whet, strop, grind, file.

shatter *verb* **1 smash**, break, splinter, crack, fracture, fragment, disintegrate. **2 destroy**, wreck, ruin, dash, crush, devastate, demolish, torpedo, scotch; *informal* do for, put paid to; *Brit. informal* scupper.

shave *verb* **1 cut off**, crop, trim, barber. **2 plane**, pare, whittle, scrape, shear.

sheath *noun* **covering**, cover, case, casing, sleeve, scabbard.

shed[1] *noun* **hut**, lean-to, outhouse, outbuilding, cabin, shack.

shed[2] *verb* **1 drop**, scatter, spill. **2 throw off**, cast off, discard, slough off, moult. **3 take off**, remove, discard, climb out of, slip out of; *Brit. informal* peel off. **4** *the moon shed a faint light* **cast**, radiate, emit, give out.

sheen *noun* **shine**, lustre, gloss, patina, burnish, polish, shimmer.

sheer *adjective* **1 utter**, complete, absolute, total, thorough, pure, downright, out-and-out, unqualified, unmitigated, unalloyed. **2 steep**, abrupt, sharp, precipitous, vertical. **3 thin**, fine, gauzy, diaphanous, transparent, see-through, flimsy, filmy, translucent.

sheet *noun* **1 layer**, covering, blanket, coat, film, veneer, crust, skin, surface, stratum. **2 pane**, panel, slab, plate, piece. **3 page**, leaf, folio. **4** *a sheet of water* **expanse**, area, stretch, sweep.

shell *noun* **1 pod**, hull, husk. **2 body**, case, casing, framework, hull, fuselage, hulk.
● *verb* **1 pod**, hull, husk; *N. Amer.* shuck. **2 bombard**, fire on, attack, bomb, blitz.

shelter *noun* **1 protection**, cover, shade, safety, security, refuge. **2 sanctuary**, refuge, home, haven, safe house.
- OPPOSITES exposure.
● *verb* **1 protect**, shield, screen, cover, shade, defend, cushion, guard, insulate, cocoon. **2 take shelter**, take refuge, take cover; *informal* hole up.
- OPPOSITES expose.

sheltered *adjective* **1 shady**, shaded, protected, still, tranquil. **2 protected**, cloistered, isolated, secluded, cocooned, insulated, secure, safe, quiet.

shelve *verb* **postpone**, put off, delay, defer, put back, reschedule, hold over/off, put to one side, suspend, stay, mothball; *N. Amer.* put over, table; *informal* put on ice, put on the back burner.

shepherd *verb* **usher**, steer, herd, lead, take, escort, guide, conduct, marshal, walk.

shield *noun* **protection**, guard, defence, cover, screen, shelter.
● *verb* **protect**, guard, defend, cover, screen, shade, shelter.
- OPPOSITES expose.

shift *verb* **1 move**, transfer, transport, switch, relocate, reposition, rearrange. **2** *the wind shifted* **veer**, alter, change, turn.
● *noun* **1 change**, alteration, adjustment, variation, modification, revision, reversal, rowback, U-turn. **2 stint**, stretch, spell.

shimmer *verb* **glint**, glisten, twinkle, sparkle, flash, gleam, glow, glimmer, wink.
● *noun* **glint**, twinkle, sparkle, flash, gleam, glow, glimmer, lustre, glitter.

shine *verb* **1 beam**, gleam, radiate, glow, glint, glimmer, sparkle, twinkle, glitter, glisten, shimmer, flash. **2 polish**, burnish, buff, rub up, brush, clean. **3 excel**, stand out.
● *noun* **polish**, gleam, gloss, lustre, sheen, patina.

shiny *adjective* **glossy**, bright, glassy, polished, gleaming, satiny, lustrous.
- OPPOSITES matt.

ship *noun* **boat**, vessel, craft.
● *verb* **deliver**, send, dispatch, transport, carry, distribute.

> **WORD LINKS**
> **maritime, nautical** relating to ships

shirk *verb* **evade**, dodge, avoid, get out of, sidestep, shrink from, shun, skip,

neglect; *informal* duck (out of), cop out of; *Brit. informal* skive off; *N. Amer. informal* cut.

shiver *verb* **tremble**, quiver, shake, shudder, quake.
● *noun* **shudder**, twitch, start.

shock¹ *noun* **1 blow**, upset, surprise, revelation, bolt from the blue, rude awakening, eye-opener. **2 fright**, scare, start; *informal* turn. **3 trauma**, collapse, breakdown, post-traumatic stress disorder. **4 vibration**, reverberation, shake, jolt, impact, blow.
● *verb* **appal**, horrify, outrage, scandalize, disgust, traumatize, distress, upset, disturb, stun, rock, shake.
- OPPOSITES delight.

shock² *noun* **mass**, mane, mop, thatch, head, bush, tangle, cascade, halo.

shocking *adjective* **appalling**, horrifying, horrific, dreadful, awful, terrible, scandalous, outrageous, disgraceful, abominable, atrocious, disgusting, distressing, upsetting, disturbing, startling.

shoddy *adjective* **poor-quality**, inferior, second-rate, tawdry, jerry-built, cheapjack, gimcrack; *informal* tatty.

shoot *verb* **1 gun down**, mow down, pick off, hit, wound, injure, kill. **2 fire**, open fire, snipe, let fly, bombard, shell, discharge, launch. **3 race**, speed, flash, dash, rush, hurtle, streak, whizz, zoom, career, fly; *informal* belt, tear, zip, whip; *Brit. informal* bomb; *N. Amer. informal* hightail it, barrel. **4 film**, photograph, record.
● *noun* **sprout**, bud, runner, tendril, offshoot, cutting.

shop *noun* **store**, retail outlet, boutique, emporium, department store, supermarket, hypermarket, superstore, chain store; *N. Amer.* mart.

shore *noun* **seashore**, beach, sand(s), shoreline, coast; *literary* littoral.

short *adjective* **1 small**, little, petite, tiny, diminutive, elfin; *Scottish* wee; *informal* pint-sized, knee-high to a grasshopper. **2 concise**, brief, succinct, to the point, compact, pithy, abridged,

S

abbreviated, condensed. **3 brief**, fleeting, short-lived, momentary, passing, lightning, quick, rapid, cursory. **4 scarce**, scant, meagre, sparse, insufficient, deficient, inadequate, lacking. **5 curt**, sharp, abrupt, blunt, brusque, terse, offhand.
- OPPOSITES tall, long, plentiful.
● *adverb she stopped short* **abruptly**, suddenly, sharply, all of a sudden, unexpectedly, without warning.
□ **short of** deficient in, lacking, in need of, low on, short on, missing; *informal* strapped for, pushed for, minus.

shortage *noun* **scarcity**, dearth, poverty, insufficiency, deficiency, inadequacy, famine, lack, deficit, shortfall.
- OPPOSITES abundance.

shortcoming *noun* **fault**, defect, flaw, imperfection, deficiency, limitation, failing, drawback, weakness, weak point.
- OPPOSITES strength.

shorten *verb* **abbreviate**, abridge, condense, contract, compress, reduce, shrink, diminish, cut (down), trim, pare (down), prune, curtail, truncate.
- OPPOSITES lengthen.

shortly *adverb* **soon**, presently, in a little while, at any moment, in a minute, in next to no time, before long, by and by; *N. Amer.* momentarily; *informal* anon, any time now, in a jiffy; *Brit. informal* in a mo.

shot *noun* **1 report**, crack, bang, blast; (**shots**) gunfire, firing. **2** *the winning shot* **stroke**, hit, strike, kick, throw. **3 marksman**, markswoman, shooter. **4 photograph**, photo, snap, snapshot, picture, print, slide, still.

shoulder *verb* **1 take on (yourself)**, undertake, accept, assume, bear, carry. **2 push**, shove, thrust, jostle, force, bulldoze, bundle.

shout *verb* **yell**, cry (out), call (out), roar, howl, bellow, bawl, raise your voice; *informal* holler.
- OPPOSITES whisper.
● *noun* **yell**, cry, call, roar, howl, bellow, bawl; *informal* holler.

shove *verb* **push**, thrust, propel, drive, force, ram, knock, elbow, shoulder, jostle.

show *verb* **1 be visible**, be seen, be in view, be obvious. **2 display**, exhibit, put on show, put on display, put on view. **3** *he showed his frustration* **manifest**, exhibit, reveal, convey, communicate, make known, express, make plain, make obvious, disclose, evince, betray. **4 demonstrate**, explain, describe, illustrate, teach, instruct. **5 prove**, demonstrate, confirm, substantiate, corroborate, verify, bear out. **6** *she showed them to their seats* **escort**, accompany, take, conduct, lead, usher, guide, direct.
- OPPOSITES conceal.
● *noun* **1 display**, array, sight, spectacle. **2 exhibition**, display, fair, exposition, festival, parade; *N. Amer.* exhibit. **3 programme**, broadcast, presentation, production. **4 appearance**, outward appearance, image, pretence, (false) front, guise, pose, affectation, semblance.
□ **show off 1** (*informal*) put on airs, put on an act, swank, strut, grandstand, posture, draw attention to yourself. **2 display**, show to advantage, exhibit, demonstrate, parade, draw attention to, flaunt. **show up 1** be visible, be obvious, be seen, be revealed, appear. **2** (*informal*) turn up, appear, arrive, come, get here/there, put in an appearance, materialize. **3** (*informal*) humiliate, embarrass, shame, put someone to shame, mortify. **4** expose, reveal, make obvious, highlight, emphasize, draw attention to.

showdown *noun* **confrontation**, clash, face-off.

shower *noun* **1 fall**, drizzle, sprinkling, flurry. **2 volley**, hail, salvo, barrage.
● *verb* **1 rain**, fall, hail. **2 deluge**, flood, inundate, swamp, overwhelm, snow under.

show-off *noun* (*informal*) **exhibitionist**, extrovert, poser, poseur, swaggerer, self-publicist.

showy adjective **ostentatious**, flamboyant, gaudy, garish, brash, vulgar, loud, fancy, ornate; informal flash, flashy.
- OPPOSITES restrained.

shred noun **1 tatter**, ribbon, rag, fragment, sliver, snippet, remnant. **2 scrap**, bit, speck, particle, ounce, jot, crumb, fragment, grain, drop, trace.
● verb **grate**, cut up, tear up.

shrewd adjective **astute**, sharp, smart, intelligent, clever, canny, perceptive; informal on the ball.
- OPPOSITES stupid.

shriek verb & noun **scream**, screech, squeal, squawk, roar, howl, shout, yelp; informal holler.

shrill adjective **high-pitched**, piercing, high, sharp, ear-piercing, ear-splitting, penetrating.

shrink verb **1 get smaller**, contract, diminish, lessen, reduce, decrease, dwindle, decline, fall off. **2 recoil**, shy away, flinch, be averse, be afraid, hesitate.
- OPPOSITES expand, increase.

shrivel verb **wither**, shrink, wilt, dry up, dehydrate, parch, frazzle.

shroud noun **covering**, cover, cloak, mantle, blanket, layer, cloud, veil, winding sheet.
● verb **cover**, envelop, veil, cloak, blanket, screen, conceal, hide, mask, obscure.

shudder verb **shake**, shiver, tremble, quiver, judder.
● noun **shake**, shiver, tremor, trembling, quivering, judder, vibration.

shuffle verb **1 shamble**, hobble, limp, drag your feet. **2 mix (up)**, rearrange, jumble (up), reorganize.

shun verb **avoid**, steer clear of, give a wide berth to, have nothing to do with; informal freeze out; Brit. informal send to Coventry.
- OPPOSITES welcome.

shut verb **close**, pull to, push to, slam, fasten, put the lid on, lock, secure.
- OPPOSITES open.
□ **shut down** close (down), cease

trading; informal fold, flatline. **shut up** be quiet, keep quiet, stop talking, hold your tongue; informal keep mum, pipe down, belt up; N. Amer. informal can it.

shuttle verb **commute**, run, ply, go/travel back and forth, ferry.

shy adjective **bashful**, diffident, timid, reserved, introverted, retiring, self-effacing, withdrawn.
- OPPOSITES confident.
□ **shy away from** flinch, recoil, hang back, be loath, be reluctant, baulk at, be unwilling, be disinclined, hesitate.

sick adjective **1 ill**, unwell, poorly, ailing, indisposed, out of sorts; informal under the weather, laid up; Austral./NZ informal crook. **2 nauseous**, queasy, bilious, green about the gills. **3** I'm sick of this music **fed up**, bored, tired, weary, jaded. **4** (informal) **macabre**, tasteless, ghoulish, morbid, black, gruesome, perverted, cruel.
- OPPOSITES well.
□ **be sick** (Brit.) vomit, heave, retch; informal puke (up), throw up, spew (up); N. Amer. informal barf, upchuck.

sicken verb **1 nauseate**, make sick, turn someone's stomach, disgust, revolt, repel, appal; N. Amer. informal gross out. **2 fall ill**, become infected, be stricken.

sickening adjective **nauseating**, stomach-turning, repulsive, revolting, disgusting, offensive, off-putting, distasteful, obscene, gruesome, grisly; N. Amer. vomitous; informal gross.

sickly adjective **1 unhealthy**, in poor health, delicate, frail, weak. **2 pale**, wan, pasty, sallow, pallid, ashen, anaemic. **3 sentimental**, mawkish, cloying, sugary, syrupy, saccharine; informal slushy, schmaltzy, cheesy, corny; Brit. informal soppy.
- OPPOSITES healthy.

sickness noun **1 illness**, disease, ailment, infection, malady, infirmity; informal bug, virus; Brit. informal lurgy. **2 nausea**, biliousness, queasiness, vomiting, retching; informal throwing up, puking.

S

side *noun* **1 edge**, border, verge, boundary, margin, rim, fringe(s), flank, bank, perimeter, extremity, periphery, limit(s). **2 district**, quarter, area, region, part, neighbourhood, sector, zone. **3 surface**, face. **4 point of view**, viewpoint, perspective, opinion, standpoint, position, outlook, slant, angle, aspect, facet. **5 faction**, camp, bloc, party, wing. **6 team**, squad, line-up.
- OPPOSITES centre, end.
  ● *adjective* **1 lateral**, wing, flanking. **2 subordinate**, secondary, minor, peripheral, incidental, subsidiary.
- OPPOSITES front, central.
  □ **side with** support, take someone's part, stand by, back, be loyal to, defend, champion, ally yourself with.

sidetrack *verb* **distract**, divert, deflect, draw away.

sideways *adverb* **1 to the side**, laterally. **2 edgewise**, edgeways, side first, end on.
  ● *adjective* **1 lateral**, sideward, on the side, side to side. **2 indirect**, oblique, sidelong, surreptitious, furtive, covert, sly.

sift *verb* **1 sieve**, strain, screen, filter. **2 we sift out unsuitable applications separate out**, filter out, sort out, weed out, get rid of, remove. **3 sifting through the data search**, look, examine, inspect, scrutinize.

sigh *verb* **1 breathe (out)**, exhale, groan, moan. **2 rustle**, whisper, murmur.

sight *noun* **1 eyesight**, vision, eyes. **2 view**, glimpse, glance, look. **3 landmark**, place of interest, monument, spectacle, marvel, wonder.
  ● *verb* **glimpse**, catch sight of, see, spot, spy, make out, pick out, notice, observe.

> **WORD LINKS**
> **optical**, **visual** relating to sight

sign *noun* **1 indication**, signal, symptom, pointer, suggestion, intimation, mark, manifestation, demonstration, token. **2 warning**, omen, portent, threat, promise. **3 notice**, board, placard, signpost. **4 symbol**, figure, emblem, device, logo, character.
  ● *verb* **1 write your name on**, autograph, initial, countersign. **2 endorse**, validate, agree to, approve, ratify, adopt. **3 write**, inscribe, pen.

signal *noun* **1 gesture**, gesticulation, sign, wave, cue, indication, warning, prompt, reminder. **2 indication**, sign, symptom, hint, pointer, clue, demonstration, evidence, proof.
  ● *verb* **1 gesture**, gesticulate, sign, indicate, motion, wave, beckon, nod. **2** *his death signals the end of an era* **mark**, signify, mean, indicate, be a sign of, be evidence of.

significance *noun* **importance**, import, consequence, seriousness, gravity, weight, magnitude.

significant *adjective* **1 notable**, noteworthy, remarkable, important, of consequence, momentous. **2 large**, considerable, sizeable, appreciable, conspicuous, obvious, sudden. **3 meaningful**, expressive, eloquent, suggestive, knowing, telling.

signify *verb* **mean**, denote, designate, represent, symbolize, stand for.

silence *noun* **1 quietness**, quiet, still, stillness, hush, tranquillity, peace, peacefulness. **2 failure to speak**, dumbness, muteness, reticence, taciturnity.
- OPPOSITES noise, loquacity.
  ● *verb* **1 quieten**, quiet, hush, still, muffle. **2 gag**, muzzle, censor.

silent *adjective* **1 quiet**, still, hushed, noiseless, soundless, inaudible. **2 speechless**, quiet, unspeaking, dumb, mute, taciturn, uncommunicative, tight-lipped. **3 unspoken**, wordless, tacit, unvoiced, unexpressed, implied, implicit, understood.
- OPPOSITES audible, loquacious.

silhouette *noun* **outline**, contour(s), profile, form, shape.
  ● *verb* **outline**, define.

silly *adjective* **1 foolish**, stupid, inane, feather-brained, bird-brained, frivolous,

immature, childish, empty-headed, scatterbrained; *informal* dotty, scatty. **2 unwise**, imprudent, thoughtless, foolish, stupid, unintelligent, rash, reckless, foolhardy, irresponsible, hare-brained; *informal* crazy, barmy; *Brit. informal* daft. **3** *he brooded about silly things* **trivial**, trifling, petty, small, insignificant, unimportant.
- OPPOSITES sensible.

similar *adjective* **alike**, like, much the same, comparable, corresponding, equivalent, parallel, analogous, kindred; *informal* much of a muchness.
- OPPOSITES different, dissimilar.

similarity *noun* **resemblance**, likeness, comparability, correspondence, parallel, equivalence, uniformity.

similarly *adverb* **likewise**, comparably, correspondingly, in the same way, by the same token.

simmer *verb* **1 boil gently**, cook gently, bubble, stew, poach. **2 seethe**, fume, smoulder.

simple *adjective* **1 straightforward**, easy, uncomplicated, uninvolved, undemanding, elementary; *informal* child's play, a cinch, a piece of cake, like falling off a log. **2 clear**, plain, lucid, straightforward, unambiguous, understandable, comprehensible, accessible; *informal* user-friendly. **3 plain**, unadorned, basic, unsophisticated, no-frills, classic, understated, uncluttered, restrained. **4 unpretentious**, unsophisticated, ordinary, unaffected, unassuming, natural, straightforward.
- OPPOSITES difficult, complex, ornate.

simplicity *noun* **1 straightforwardness**, ease. **2 clarity**, plainness, lucidity, intelligibility, comprehensibility, accessibility. **3 austerity**, plainness, spareness, clean lines. **4 plainness**, modesty, naturalness.
- OPPOSITES complexity.

simplify *verb* **make simpler**, clarify, put into words of one syllable, streamline; *informal* dumb down.
- OPPOSITES complicate.

simply *adverb* **1 straightforwardly**, directly, clearly, plainly, intelligibly, lucidly, unambiguously. **2 plainly**, soberly, unfussily, without clutter, classically. **3 merely**, just, purely, solely, only.

simulate *verb* **1 feign**, pretend, fake, affect, put on. **2 replicate**, reproduce, imitate, mimic.

simultaneous *adjective* **concurrent**, happening at the same time, contemporaneous, coinciding, coincident, synchronized.
- OPPOSITES separate.

simultaneously *adverb* **at the same time**, at one and the same time, at once, concurrently, (all) together, in unison, in concert, in chorus.

sin *noun* **1 wrong**, act of wickedness, transgression, crime, offence, misdeed; *old use* trespass. **2 wickedness**, wrongdoing, evil, immorality, iniquity, vice, crime.
- OPPOSITES virtue.
  ● *verb* **transgress**, do wrong, misbehave, err, go astray; *old use* trespass.

sincere *adjective* **1 heartfelt**, wholehearted, profound, deep, true, honest, earnest, fervent. **2 honest**, genuine, truthful, direct, frank, candid; *informal* straight, on the level, upfront; *N. Amer. informal* on the up and up.

sincerely *adverb* **genuinely**, honestly, really, truly, truthfully, wholeheartedly, earnestly.

sincerity *noun* **genuineness**, honesty, truthfulness, integrity, directness, openness, candour.

sinful *adjective* **immoral**, wicked, (morally) wrong, evil, bad, iniquitous, ungodly, irreligious, sacrilegious.
- OPPOSITES virtuous.

sing *verb* **1 chant**, trill, intone, croon, chorus. **2 trill**, warble, chirp, chirrup, cheep.

singe *verb* **scorch**, burn, sear, char.

singer *noun* **vocalist**, songster, songstress, soloist, chorister, cantor.

S

single *adjective* **1 sole**, one, lone, solitary, unaccompanied, alone. **2 individual**, separate, particular, distinct. **3 unmarried**, unwed, unattached, free.
- OPPOSITES double, multiple.
  □ **single out** select, pick out, choose, decide on, target, earmark, mark out, separate out, set apart.

single-handed *adverb* **by yourself**, alone, on your own, solo, unaided, unassisted, without help.

single-minded *adjective* **determined**, committed, unswerving, unwavering, resolute, purposeful, devoted, dedicated, uncompromising, tireless, tenacious, persistent, dogged.
- OPPOSITES half-hearted.

singly *adverb* **one by one**, one at a time, one after the other, individually, separately.
- OPPOSITES together.

sinister *adjective* **1 menacing**, threatening, forbidding, baleful, frightening, alarming, disturbing, ominous. **2 evil**, wicked, criminal, nefarious, villainous; *informal* shady.
- OPPOSITES innocent.

sink *verb* **1 submerge**, founder, capsize, go down, be engulfed. **2 scuttle**; *Brit.* scupper. **3 fall**, drop, descend, plunge, plummet, slump. **4 embed**, insert, drive, plant.
- OPPOSITES float, rise.

sinner *noun* **wrongdoer**, evil-doer, transgressor, miscreant, offender, criminal; *old use* trespasser.

sip *verb* **drink**, taste, sample, nip.
● *noun* **mouthful**, swallow, drink, drop, dram, nip; *informal* swig.

sit *verb* **1 take a seat**, sit down, be seated, perch, ensconce yourself, flop; *informal* take the load off your feet; *Brit. informal* take a pew. **2 be placed**, be positioned, be situated, be set, rest, stand, perch. **3 be in session**, meet, be convened. **4** *she sits on the tribunal* **serve on**, have a seat on, be a member of.
- OPPOSITES stand.

site *noun* **location**, place, position, situation, locality, whereabouts.
● *verb* **place**, put, position, situate, locate.

situation *noun* **1 circumstances**, state of affairs, affairs, state, condition, case, predicament, plight. **2 location**, position, spot, site, setting, environment. **3 post**, position, job, employment.

size *noun* **dimensions**, measurements, proportions, magnitude, largeness, area, expanse, breadth, width, length, height, depth.
□ **size up** *(informal)* assess, appraise, get the measure of, judge, take stock of, evaluate; *Brit. informal* suss out.

sizeable *adjective* **large**, substantial, considerable, respectable, significant, goodly.
- OPPOSITES small.

sizzle *verb* **crackle**, fizzle, sputter, hiss, spit.

sketch *noun* **drawing**, outline, draft, diagram, design, plan; *informal* rough.
● *verb* **draw**, make a drawing of, pencil, rough out, outline.

sketchy *adjective* **incomplete**, patchy, fragmentary, scrappy, cursory, perfunctory, scanty, vague, inadequate, insufficient.
- OPPOSITES detailed.

skilful *adjective* **expert**, accomplished, skilled, masterly, talented, deft, dexterous, handy; *informal* mean, crack, ace, genius; *N. Amer. informal* crackerjack.
- OPPOSITES incompetent.

skill *noun* **expertise**, accomplishment, skilfulness, mastery, talent, deftness, dexterity, prowess, competence, artistry.
- OPPOSITES incompetence.

skim *verb* **1** *skim off the fat* **remove**, scoop off, separate. **2 glide**, move lightly, slide, sail, skate. **3** *she skimmed through the paper* **glance**, flick, flip, leaf, thumb, scan, run your eye over.

skin *noun* **1 hide**, pelt, fleece. **2 peel**, rind. **3 film**, layer, membrane, crust, covering, coating.

S

● *verb* **1 peel**, pare. **2 graze**, scrape, abrade, bark, rub raw, chafe.

> **WORD LINKS**
>
> **cutaneous** relating to the skin
> **dermatology** branch of medicine concerning the skin

skinny *adjective* **thin**, underweight, scrawny, bony, gaunt, emaciated, skeletal, wasted, pinched, spindly, gangly; *informal* anorexic.

skip *verb* **1 caper**, prance, trip, dance, bound, bounce, gambol. **2 omit**, leave out, miss out, dispense with, pass over, skim over, disregard; *informal* give something a miss.

skirt *verb* **1 go round**, walk round, circle. **2 border**, edge, flank, line. **3** *he skirted round the subject* **avoid**, evade, sidestep, dodge, pass over, gloss over; *informal* duck.

skull *noun* cranium.

> **WORD LINKS**
>
> **cranial** relating to the skull

sky *noun* *literary* the heavens, the firmament, the ether, the (wide) blue yonder.

> **WORD LINKS**
>
> **celestial** relating to the sky

slab *noun* **piece**, block, hunk, chunk, lump, cake, tablet, brick, panel, plate, sheet.

slack *adjective* **1 limp**, loose. **2 sagging**, flabby, flaccid, loose, saggy. **3 sluggish**, slow, quiet, slow-moving, flat, depressed, stagnant. **4 lax**, negligent, careless, slapdash, slipshod; *informal* sloppy.
- OPPOSITES taut, firm.
● *verb* (*Brit. informal*) **idle**, shirk, be lazy, be indolent, waste time, lounge about; *Brit. informal* skive; *N. Amer. informal* goof off.

slam *verb* **bang**, thump, crash, smash, plough, run, bump, collide with, hit, strike, ram; *N. Amer.* impact.

slanderous *adjective* **defamatory**, denigratory, disparaging, libellous,

pejorative, false, misrepresentative, scurrilous, scandalous, malicious.

slant *verb* **1 slope**, tilt, incline, be at an angle, tip, lean, dip, pitch, shelve, list, bank. **2 bias**, distort, twist, skew, weight.
● *noun* **1 slope**, incline, tilt, gradient, pitch, angle, camber. **2 point of view**, viewpoint, standpoint, stance, angle, perspective, approach, view, attitude, position, bias, spin.

slap *verb* **smack**, strike, hit, cuff, clip, spank; *informal* whack.
● *noun* **smack**, blow, cuff, clip, spank; *informal* whack.

slash *verb* **1 cut**, gash, slit, lacerate, knife. **2** (*informal*) **reduce**, cut, lower, bring down, mark down.
● *noun* **cut**, gash, slit, laceration, incision, wound.

slaughter *verb* **1 kill**, butcher, cull, put down. **2 massacre**, murder, butcher, kill, exterminate, wipe out, put to death, execute; *literary* slay.
● *noun* **massacre**, (mass) murder, (mass) killing, (mass) execution, extermination, carnage, bloodshed, bloodletting, bloodbath; *literary* slaying.

slave *noun* **servant**, lackey, drudge; *Brit. informal* skivvy, dogsbody; *historical* serf, vassal.
- OPPOSITES master.
● *verb* **toil**, labour, sweat, work like a Trojan/dog, work your fingers to the bone; *informal* sweat blood, slog away; *Brit. informal* graft.

> **WORD LINKS**
>
> **servile** like a slave

slavery *noun* **enslavement**, servitude, serfdom, bondage, captivity.
- OPPOSITES freedom.

sleazy *adjective* **1 corrupt**, immoral, ignoble, dishonourable. **2 squalid**, seedy, seamy, sordid, insalubrious.

sleek *adjective* **1 smooth**, glossy, shiny, shining, lustrous, silken, silky. **2 streamlined**, elegant, graceful.
- OPPOSITES scruffy.

sleep noun **nap**, doze, siesta, catnap; *informal* snooze, forty winks, shut-eye; *Brit. informal* kip; *literary* slumber.
● *verb* **be asleep**, doze, take a siesta, take a nap, catnap; *informal* snooze, get some shut-eye; *Brit. informal* kip; *literary* slumber.
- OPPOSITES wake up.
  □ **go to sleep** fall asleep, get to sleep; *informal* drop off, nod off, drift off, crash out, flake out; *N. Amer. informal* sack out.

> **WORD LINKS**
> **sedative, soporific** causing sleep

sleepy adjective **1 drowsy**, tired, somnolent, heavy-eyed; *informal* dopey. **2 quiet**, peaceful, tranquil, placid, slow-moving, dull, boring.
- OPPOSITES awake, alert.

slender adjective **1 slim**, lean, willowy, svelte, lissom, graceful, slight, thin, skinny. **2 faint**, remote, tenuous, fragile, slim, small, slight.
- OPPOSITES plump, strong.

slice noun **1 piece**, portion, slab, wedge, rasher, sliver, wafer. **2 share**, part, portion, tranche, percentage, proportion, allocation; *informal* cut, whack.
● *verb* **cut**, carve, divide.

slick adjective **1 efficient**, smooth, smooth-running, polished, well organized, well run, streamlined. **2 glib**, polished, assured, self-assured, smooth-talking, plausible; *informal* smarmy.
● *verb* **smooth**, plaster, sleek, grease, oil, gel.

slide verb **glide**, slip, slither, skim, skate, skid, slew.

slight adjective **1 small**, tiny, minute, negligible, insignificant, minimal, remote, slim, faint. **2 slim**, slender, delicate, dainty, fragile.
- OPPOSITES large, plump.
  ● *verb* **insult**, snub, rebuff, spurn, give someone the cold shoulder, cut (dead), take no notice of, scorn, ignore.
  ● *noun* **insult**, affront, snub, rebuff; *informal* put-down, slap in the face.

slightly adverb **a little**, a bit, somewhat, faintly, vaguely, a shade.
- OPPOSITES very.

slim adjective **1 slender**, lean, thin, willowy, sylphlike, svelte, lissom, slight, trim. **2** *a slim chance* **slight**, small, slender, faint, remote.
- OPPOSITES fat.
  ● *verb* **lose weight**, diet, go on a diet; *N. Amer.* slenderize.

slimy adjective **slippery**, slithery, greasy, sticky, viscous; *informal* slippy.

sling verb **1 hang**, suspend, string, swing. **2** *(informal)* **throw**, toss, fling, hurl, cast, pitch, lob, flip; *informal* chuck, heave, bung.

slip verb **1 slide**, skid, slither, fall (over), lose your balance, lose your footing, tumble. **2 creep**, steal, sneak, slide, sidle, slope, slink, tiptoe.
● *noun* **1 false step**, slide, skid, fall, tumble. **2 mistake**, error, blunder, gaffe, oversight, miscalculation, omission, lapse; *informal* slip-up, boo-boo, howler; *Brit. informal* boob, clanger, bloomer; *N. Amer. informal* goof, blooper.
  □ **slip up** *(informal)* make a mistake, blunder, get something wrong, miscalculate, make an error, err; *informal* make a boo-boo; *Brit. informal* boob, drop a clanger; *N. Amer. informal* goof up.

slippery adjective **1 slithery**, greasy, oily, icy, glassy, smooth, slimy, wet; *informal* slippy. **2 sneaky**, sly, devious, crafty, cunning, tricky, evasive, scheming, unreliable, untrustworthy; *informal* shady, shifty; *Brit. informal* dodgy; *Austral./NZ informal* shonky.

slit noun **1 cut**, incision, split, slash, gash. **2 opening**, gap, chink, crack, aperture, slot.
● *verb* **cut**, slash, split open, slice open.

slither verb **slide**, slip, glide, wriggle, crawl, skid.

sliver noun **splinter**, shard, chip, flake, shred, scrap, shaving, paring, piece, fragment.

slobber *verb* **drool**, slaver, dribble, salivate.

slogan *noun* **catchphrase**, catchline, motto, jingle; *N. Amer. informal* tag line.

slope *noun* **tilt**, pitch, slant, angle, gradient, incline, inclination, fall, camber; *N. Amer.* grade.
● *verb* **tilt**, slant, incline, lean, drop/fall away, descend, shelve, camber, rise, ascend, climb.

sloping *adjective* **slanting**, leaning, inclined, angled, cambered, tilted.
- OPPOSITES level.

sloppy *adjective* **1 runny**, watery, liquid, mushy; *informal* gloopy. **2 careless**, slapdash, slipshod, disorganized, untidy, slack, slovenly; *informal* slap-happy.

slot *noun* **1 aperture**, slit, crack, hole, opening. **2 time**, spot, period, niche, space; *informal* window.
● *verb* **insert**, slide, fit, put, place.

slovenly *adjective* **1 scruffy**, untidy, messy, unkempt, ill-groomed, dishevelled, bedraggled, rumpled, frowzy. **2 careless**, slapdash, slipshod, haphazard, hit-or-miss, untidy, messy, negligent, lax, lackadaisical, slack; *informal* sloppy, slap-happy.
- OPPOSITES tidy, careful.

slow *adjective* **1 unhurried**, leisurely, steady, sedate, measured, ponderous, sluggish, plodding. **2 lengthy**, time-consuming, long-drawn-out, protracted, prolonged, gradual. **3 stupid**, unintelligent, obtuse; *informal* dense, dim, thick, slow on the uptake, dumb, dopey; *Brit. informal* dozy.
- OPPOSITES fast, quick.
● *verb* **1 reduce speed**, go slower, decelerate, brake. **2 hold back**, hold up, delay, retard, set back, check, curb.
- OPPOSITES accelerate.

slowly *adverb* **1 unhurriedly**, without hurrying, steadily, at a leisurely pace, at a snail's pace. **2 gradually**, bit by bit, little by little, slowly but surely, step by step.
- OPPOSITES quickly.

sluggish *adjective* **lethargic**, listless, lacking in energy, lifeless, inactive, slow, torpid, enervated.
- OPPOSITES vigorous.

slum *noun* **hovel**; (**slums**) ghetto, shanty town.

slump *verb* **1 sit heavily**, flop, collapse, sink; *informal* plonk yourself. **2 fall**, plummet, tumble, collapse, drop; *informal* crash, nosedive.
● *noun* **1 fall**, drop, tumble, downturn, downswing, slide, decline, decrease; *informal* nosedive. **2 recession**, decline, depression, slowdown.
- OPPOSITES rise, boom.

slur *verb* **mumble**, speak unclearly, garble.
● *noun* **insult**, slight, slander, smear, allegation, imputation.

sly *adjective* **1 cunning**, crafty, clever, wily, artful, tricky, scheming, devious, underhand, sneaky. **2 roguish**, mischievous, impish, playful, wicked, arch, knowing. **3 surreptitious**, furtive, stealthy, covert.
- OPPOSITES open, straightforward.

smack *noun* **slap**, blow, cuff, clip, spank; *informal* whack.
● *verb* **slap**, strike, hit, cuff, clip, spank; *informal* whack.
● *adverb* (*informal*) **exactly**, precisely, straight, right, directly, squarely, dead, plumb; *informal* slap, bang; *N. Amer. informal* smack dab.

small *adjective* **1 little**, tiny, short, petite, diminutive, elfin, miniature, mini, minute, toy, baby, undersized, poky, cramped; *Scottish* wee; *informal* teeny, tiddly, pint-sized; *Brit. informal* titchy. **2 slight**, minor, unimportant, trifling, trivial, insignificant, inconsequential, negligible, inappreciable; *informal* piffling.
- OPPOSITES big, large.

smarmy *adjective* (*informal*) **unctuous**, ingratiating, slick, oily, greasy, obsequious, sycophantic, fawning; *informal* slimy.

smart *adjective* **1 well dressed**, well turned out, stylish, chic, fashionable,

S

modish, elegant, dapper; *N. Amer.* trig; *informal* natty, snappy. **2** *a smart restaurant* **fashionable**, stylish, high-class, exclusive, chic, fancy; *Brit.* upmarket; *N. Amer.* high-toned; *informal* trendy, classy, swanky; *Brit. informal* swish; *N. Amer. informal* swank. **3** (*informal*) **clever**, bright, intelligent, quick-witted, shrewd, astute, perceptive; *informal* brainy, quick on the uptake, genius. **4** *a smart pace* **brisk**, quick, fast, rapid, lively, energetic, vigorous; *informal* cracking.
- OPPOSITES scruffy, stupid.
● *verb* **1** sting, burn, tingle, prickle, hurt. **2** *she smarted at the accusation* **feel hurt**, feel upset, take offence, feel aggrieved, feel indignant, be put out.

smash *verb* **1** break, shatter, splinter, crack; *informal* bust. **2** *he smashed into a wall* **crash**, smack, slam, plough, run, bump, hit, strike, ram, collide with; *N. Amer.* impact.
● *noun* **crash**, collision, accident; *N. Amer.* wreck; *informal* pile-up; *Brit. informal* shunt.

smattering *noun* bit, little, modicum, touch, soupçon, rudiments, basics; *informal* smidgen, smidge, tad.

smear *verb* **1** spread, rub, daub, slap, cover, coat, smother, plaster. **2** smudge, streak, mark. **3** sully, tarnish, blacken, drag through the mud, damage, defame, malign, slander, libel; *N. Amer.* slur.
● *noun* **1** streak, smudge, daub, dab, spot, patch, blotch, mark; *informal* splodge. **2** accusation, lie, untruth, slur, slander, libel, defamation.

smell *noun* **1** odour, aroma, fragrance, scent, perfume, bouquet, nose. **2** stink, stench, reek; *Brit. informal* pong, whiff.
● *verb* **1** scent, sniff, get a sniff of, detect. **2** stink, reek; *Brit. informal* pong, hum.

> **WORD LINKS**
> **olfactory** relating to the sense of smell

smelly *adjective* **foul-smelling**, stinking, reeking, rank, fetid, malodorous, pungent; *literary* noisome.

smile *verb* **beam**, grin (from ear to ear), smirk, simper, leer.
- OPPOSITES frown.
● *noun* **beam**, grin, smirk, simper, leer.

smirk *verb* **sneer**, simper, snigger, leer, grin.

smitten *adjective* **1** struck down, laid low, suffering, affected, afflicted. **2** infatuated, besotted, in love, obsessed, head over heels, enamoured, captivated, enchanted, under someone's spell; *informal* bowled over, swept off your feet.

smoke *verb* **1** smoulder; *old use* reek. **2** puff on, draw on, pull on, inhale; *informal* drag on.
● *noun* **fumes**, exhaust, gas, vapour, smog.

smoky *adjective* **smoke-filled**, sooty, smoggy, hazy, foggy, murky, thick; *Brit. informal* fuggy.

smooth *adjective* **1** even, level, flat, plane, unwrinkled, glassy, glossy, silky, polished. **2** creamy, fine, velvety. **3** calm, still, tranquil, undisturbed, unruffled, even, flat, like a millpond. **4** steady, regular, uninterrupted, unbroken, easy, effortless, trouble-free. **5** suave, urbane, sophisticated, polished, debonair, courteous, gracious, persuasive, glib, slick, smooth-tongued; *informal* smarmy.
- OPPOSITES uneven, rough.
● *verb* **1** flatten, level (out/off), even out/off, press, roll, iron, plane. **2** ease, facilitate, expedite, help, assist, aid, pave the way for.
- OPPOSITES roughen, hinder.

smother *verb* **1** suffocate, asphyxiate, stifle, choke. **2** extinguish, put out, snuff out, douse, stamp out. **3** smear, daub, spread, cover, plaster. **4** *she smothered a giggle* **stifle**, muffle, strangle, suppress, hold back, fight back, swallow, conceal.

smudge *noun* streak, smear, mark, stain, blotch, blob, dab; *informal* splotch, splodge.

● *verb* **streak**, mark, dirty, soil, blotch, blacken, smear, blot, daub, stain; *informal* splotch, splodge.

smug *adjective* **self-satisfied**, conceited, complacent, superior, pleased with yourself.

snack *noun* **light meal**, sandwich, refreshments, nibbles, titbit(s); *informal* bite (to eat).

snag *noun* **complication**, difficulty, catch, hitch, obstacle, pitfall, problem, issue, setback, disadvantage, drawback.

● *verb* **catch**, hook, tear.

snake *noun* serpent.

● *verb the road snakes inland* **twist**, wind, meander, zigzag, curve.

snap *verb* **1 break**, fracture, splinter, split, crack; *informal* bust. **2 bark**, snarl, growl, retort; *informal* jump down someone's throat.

● *noun* **photograph**, picture, photo, shot, snapshot, print, slide.

snare *noun* **trap**, gin, wire, net, noose.

● *verb* **trap**, catch, net, bag, ensnare, hook.

snatch *verb* **1 grab**, seize, take hold of, take, pluck, grasp at, clutch at. **2 steal**, take, thieve, make off with; *informal* swipe, nab, lift; *Brit. informal* nick, pinch, whip. **3 kidnap**, abduct, take as hostage.

sneak *verb* **creep**, slink, steal, slip, slide, sidle, tiptoe, pad.

sneaking *adjective* **1 secret**, private, hidden, concealed, unvoiced, unexpressed. **2** *a sneaking suspicion* **niggling**, nagging, insidious, lingering, persistent.

sneaky *adjective* **sly**, crafty, cunning, wily, scheming, devious, deceitful, underhand.

sneer *verb* **1 smirk**, snigger, curl your lip. **2 scoff**, laugh, scorn, disdain, be contemptuous, mock, ridicule, deride, jeer, jibe.

● *noun* **1 smirk**, snigger. **2 jeer**, jibe, insult; *informal* dig.

sniff *verb* **1 inhale**, snuffle. **2 smell**, scent, get a whiff of.

● *noun* **1 snuffle**, snort. **2 smell**, scent, whiff, lungful.

□ **sniff out** (*informal*) detect, find, discover, bring to light, track down, dig up, root out, uncover, unearth.

snigger *verb & noun* **giggle**, titter, snicker, chortle, laugh, sneer, smirk.

snippet *noun* **piece**, bit, scrap, fragment, particle, shred, excerpt, extract.

snivel *verb* **sniffle**, snuffle, whimper, whine, weep, cry; *Scottish* greet; *informal* blubber; *Brit. informal* grizzle.

snobbish, **snobby** *adjective* **elitist**, superior, supercilious, arrogant, condescending, pretentious, affected; *informal* snooty, high and mighty, la-di-da, stuck-up; *Brit. informal* toffee-nosed.

snoop *verb* (*informal*) **pry**, spy, be a busybody, poke your nose into, root about, ferret about; *informal* be nosy; *Austral. informal* stickybeak.

snub *verb* **rebuff**, spurn, cold-shoulder, cut (dead), ignore, insult, slight; *informal* freeze out; *N. Amer. informal* stiff.

● *noun* **rebuff**, slap in the face; *informal* brush-off, put-down.

snug *adjective* **1 cosy**, comfortable, warm, sheltered, secure; *informal* comfy. **2 tight**, skintight, close-fitting, figure-hugging.

- OPPOSITES loose.

snuggle *verb* **nestle**, curl up, huddle (up), cuddle up, nuzzle, settle; *N. Amer.* snug down.

soak *verb* **1 dip**, immerse, steep, submerge, douse, marinate, souse. **2 drench**, wet through, saturate. **3** *water soaked through the carpet* **permeate**, penetrate, impregnate, percolate, seep, spread. **4 absorb**, suck up, blot, mop up.

soaking *adjective* **drenched**, wet (through), soaked (through), sodden, soggy, waterlogged, saturated, sopping, dripping, wringing.

- OPPOSITES parched.

soar *verb* **1 rise**, ascend, climb. **2 glide**, plane, float, hover. **3 increase**, escalate, shoot up, spiral, rocket; *informal* go through the roof, skyrocket.
- OPPOSITES plummet.

sob *verb* **weep**, cry, snivel, whimper; *Scottish* greet; *informal* blubber; *Brit. informal* grizzle.

sober *adjective* **1 clear-headed**, teetotal, abstinent, dry; *informal* on the wagon. **2 serious**, solemn, sensible, staid, sedate, quiet, dignified, grave, level-headed, down-to-earth. **3 sombre**, subdued, restrained, austere, severe, drab, plain, dark.
- OPPOSITES drunk.

so-called *adjective* **supposed**, alleged, presumed, inappropriately named, ostensible, reputed, self-styled.

sociable *adjective* **friendly**, amicable, affable, companionable, gregarious, cordial, warm, genial.
- OPPOSITES unfriendly.

social *adjective* **1 communal**, community, collective, general, popular, civil, public, civic. **2 recreational**, leisure, entertainment.
● *noun* **party**, gathering, function, get-together, celebration; *informal* do.

socialize *verb* **interact**, converse, be sociable, mix, mingle, get together, meet, fraternize, consort; *informal* hobnob, hang out.

society *noun* **1 the community**, the (general) public, the people, the population, civilization, humankind, mankind, the world at large. **2** *an industrial society* **culture**, community, civilization, nation. **3 high society**, polite society, the upper classes, the gentry, the elite, the smart set, the beau monde; *informal* the upper crust. **4 club**, association, group, circle, institute, guild, lodge, league, union, alliance. **5 company**, companionship, fellowship, friendship.

> **WORD LINKS**
> **sociology** study of society

sofa *noun* **settee**, couch, divan, chaise longue, chesterfield.

soft *adjective* **1 mushy**, squashy, pulpy, squishy, doughy, spongy, springy, elastic, pliable, pliant; *informal* gooey; *Brit. informal* squidgy. **2 swampy**, marshy, boggy, muddy, squelchy. **3 smooth**, velvety, fleecy, downy, furry, silky, silken. **4 dim**, low, faint, subdued, muted, subtle. **5 quiet**, low, gentle, faint, muted, subdued, muffled, hushed, whispered. **6 lenient**, easy-going, tolerant, forgiving, forbearing, indulgent, liberal, lax.
- OPPOSITES hard, firm, harsh.

soften *verb* *the compensation should soften the blow* **ease**, alleviate, relieve, soothe, take the edge off, cushion, lessen, diminish, blunt, deaden.

soggy *adjective* **mushy**, squashy, pulpy, slushy, squelchy, swampy, marshy, boggy, soaking, wet, saturated, drenched; *Brit. informal* squidgy.

soil[1] *noun* **1 earth**, dirt, clay, ground, loam. **2 territory**, land, region, country, domain, dominion.

soil[2] *verb* **dirty**, stain, smear, smudge, spoil, foul.

soldier *noun* **fighter**, trooper, serviceman/woman, warrior; *US* GI; *Brit. informal* squaddie.

> **WORD LINKS**
> **military** relating to soldiers

sole *adjective* **only**, one, single, solitary, lone, unique, exclusive.

solely *adverb* **only**, simply, purely, just, merely, uniquely, exclusively, entirely, wholly, alone.

solemn *adjective* **1 dignified**, ceremonial, stately, formal, majestic, imposing, splendid, magnificent, grand. **2 serious**, grave, sober, sombre, unsmiling, stern, grim, dour, humourless. **3 sincere**, earnest, honest, genuine, firm, heartfelt, wholehearted, sworn.
- OPPOSITES frivolous, light-hearted.

solicit *verb* **1 ask for**, request, seek, apply for, put in for, call for, beg for, plead for. **2 ask**, approach, appeal to, lobby, petition, importune, call on, press.

solid adjective **1 hard**, rock-hard, rigid, firm, solidified, set, frozen, compact, compressed, dense. **2** solid gold **pure**, unadulterated, genuine. **3 well built**, sound, substantial, strong, sturdy, durable, stout. **4 well founded**, valid, sound, logical, authoritative, convincing, cogent. **5** solid support **unanimous**, united, consistent, undivided.
- OPPOSITES liquid, flimsy, untenable.

solidarity noun **unanimity**, unity, agreement, team spirit, accord, harmony, consensus; formal concord.

solidify verb **harden**, set, thicken, stiffen, congeal, cake, freeze, ossify, fossilize, petrify.
- OPPOSITES liquefy.

solitary adjective **1 lonely**, unaccompanied, by yourself, on your own, alone, friendless, unsociable, withdrawn, reclusive; N. Amer. lonesome. **2 isolated**, remote, lonely, out of the way, in the back of beyond, outlying, off the beaten track, secluded; N. Amer. in the backwoods. **3 single**, lone, sole, only, one, individual.
- OPPOSITES sociable.

solitude noun **loneliness**, solitariness, isolation, seclusion, privacy, peace.

solution noun **1 answer**, result, resolution, key, explanation. **2 mixture**, blend, emulsion, compound.

solve verb **answer**, resolve, work out, puzzle out, fathom, decipher, decode, clear up, straighten out, get to the bottom of, unravel, explain; informal figure out, crack; Brit. informal suss out.

sombre adjective **1 dark**, drab, dull, dingy, restrained, sober, funereal. **2 solemn**, earnest, serious, grave, sober, unsmiling, gloomy, sad, mournful, melancholy, lugubrious, cheerless.
- OPPOSITES bright, cheerful.

somehow adverb **one way or another**, no matter how, by fair means or foul, by hook or by crook, come what may.

sometimes adverb **occasionally**, from time to time, now and then, every so often, once in a while, on occasion, at times, off and on.

song noun **air**, strain, ditty, chant, number, track, melody, tune.

sonorous adjective **resonant**, rich, full, round, booming, deep, clear, mellow, strong, resounding, reverberant.

soon adverb **shortly**, presently, in the near future, before long, in a little while, in a minute, in a moment; Brit. informal in a tick.

sooner adverb **1 earlier**, before now. **2 rather**, preferably, given the choice.

soothe verb **1 calm (down)**, pacify, comfort, hush, quiet, settle (down), appease, mollify; Brit. quieten (down). **2 ease**, alleviate, relieve, take the edge off, allay, lessen, reduce.
- OPPOSITES agitate, aggravate.

soothing adjective **relaxing**, restful, calm, calming, tranquil, peaceful.

sophisticated adjective **1 advanced**, state-of-the-art, the latest, up-to-the-minute, cutting-edge, complex. **2 worldly**, worldly-wise, experienced, cosmopolitan, urbane, cultured, cultivated, polished, refined.
- OPPOSITES crude, naive.

sophistication noun **worldliness**, experience, urbanity, culture, polish, refinement, elegance, style, poise, finesse, savoir faire.

sordid adjective **1 sleazy**, seedy, seamy, unsavoury, tawdry, cheap, disreputable, discreditable, ignominious, shameful, wretched, despicable. **2 squalid**, slummy, dirty, filthy, shabby, scummy; informal scuzzy; Brit. informal grotty.
- OPPOSITES respectable.

sore adjective **1 painful**, hurting, aching, throbbing, smarting, stinging, inflamed, sensitive, tender, raw, wounded, injured. **2** (N. Amer. informal) **upset**, angry, annoyed, cross, disgruntled, dissatisfied, irritated; informal aggravated, miffed, peeved; Brit. informal narked, not best pleased; N. Amer. informal ticked off.

S

sorrow *noun* **1 sadness**, unhappiness, misery, despondency, regret, despair, desolation, heartache, grief. **2** *the sorrows of life* **trouble**, difficulty, problem, woe, affliction, trial, tribulation, misfortune.
- OPPOSITES joy.

sorry *adjective* **1 regretful**, apologetic, remorseful, contrite, repentant, rueful, penitent, guilty, shamefaced, ashamed. **2** *he felt sorry for her* **full of pity**, sympathetic, compassionate, moved, concerned. **3** *I was sorry to hear about the accident* **sad**, sorrowful, distressed.
- OPPOSITES glad, unrepentant.

sort *noun* **type**, kind, variety, class, category, style, form, genre, species, breed, make, model, brand.
● *verb* **1 classify**, class, group, organize, arrange, order, grade, catalogue. **2** *the problem was soon sorted out* **resolve**, settle, solve, fix, work out, straighten out, deal with, put right, set right, rectify, iron out.

soul *noun* **1 spirit**, psyche, (inner) self. **2 feeling**, emotion, passion, animation, intensity, warmth, energy, vitality, spirit.

sound[1] *noun* **1 noise**, din, racket, row, resonance, reverberation. **2 utterance**, cry, word, noise, peep.
- OPPOSITES silence.
● *verb* **1 make a noise**, resonate, resound, reverberate, go off, ring, chime, ping. **2** *sound the horn* **blow**, blast, toot, ring, use, operate, activate, set off. **3 appear**, look (like), seem, give every indication of being, strike someone as.

> **WORD LINKS**
> **acoustic**, **sonic** relating to sound

sound[2] *adjective* **1 healthy**, in good condition/shape, fit, hale and hearty, in fine fettle, undamaged, unimpaired. **2 well built**, solid, substantial, strong, sturdy, durable, stable, intact. **3 well founded**, valid, reasonable, logical, weighty, authoritative, reliable. **4 reliable**, dependable, trustworthy, fair, good. **5 solvent**, debt-free, in the black, in credit, creditworthy, secure. **6 deep**, undisturbed, uninterrupted, untroubled, peaceful.
- OPPOSITES unhealthy, unsafe.

sour *adjective* **1 acid**, acidic, tart, bitter, sharp, vinegary, pungent. **2 bad**, off, turned, curdled, rancid, high, fetid. **3 embittered**, resentful, jaundiced, bitter, cross, crabby, crotchety, cantankerous, bad-tempered, disagreeable, unpleasant; *informal* grouchy.
- OPPOSITES sweet, fresh.
● *verb* **spoil**, mar, damage, harm, impair, upset, poison, blight.

source *noun* **1 spring**, wellspring, wellhead, origin. **2 origin**, derivation, starting point, start, beginning, fountainhead, root, author, originator.

souvenir *noun* **memento**, keepsake, reminder, memorial, trophy.

sovereign *noun* **ruler**, monarch, potentate, overlord, king, queen, emperor, empress, prince, princess.
● *adjective* **autonomous**, independent, self-governing, self-determining, non-aligned, free.

sovereignty *noun* **1 power**, rule, supremacy, dominion, jurisdiction, ascendancy, domination, authority, control. **2 autonomy**, independence, self-rule, self-government, home rule, self-determination, freedom.

sow *verb* **plant**, scatter, disperse, strew, broadcast, seed.

space *noun* **1 room**, capacity, latitude, margin, leeway, play, elbow room, clearance. **2 area**, expanse, stretch, sweep, tract, footprint. **3 gap**, interval, opening, aperture, cavity, niche, interstice. **4 blank**, gap, box. **5 period**, span, time, duration, stretch, course, interval, gap. **6 outer space**, deep space, the universe, the galaxy, the solar system.
● *verb* **position**, arrange, range, array, spread, lay out, set.

spacious *adjective* **roomy**, capacious, commodious, voluminous, sizeable, generous.
- OPPOSITES cramped.

span *noun* **1 extent**, length, width, reach, stretch, spread, distance, range. **2 period**, space, time, duration, course, interval.
● *verb* **1 bridge**, cross, traverse, pass over. **2 last**, cover, extend, spread over.

spare *adjective* **1 extra**, supplementary, additional, second, other, alternative, emergency, reserve, backup, relief, substitute; *N. Amer.* alternate. **2 surplus**, superfluous, excess, leftover, redundant, unnecessary, unwanted; *informal* going begging. **3** *your spare time* **free**, leisure, unoccupied. **4 slender**, lean, willowy, svelte, lissom, thin, skinny, gaunt, lanky, spindly.
● *verb* **1 afford**, manage, part with, give, provide, do without. **2 pardon**, let off, forgive, have mercy on, reprieve, release, free.

sparing *adjective* **thrifty**, economical, frugal, careful, prudent, cautious.
- OPPOSITES lavish, extravagant.

spark *noun* **flash**, glint, twinkle, flicker, flare.
● *verb* *the arrest sparked off riots* **cause**, give rise to, occasion, bring about, start, precipitate, prompt, trigger (off), provoke, stimulate, stir up.

sparkle *verb & noun* **glitter**, glint, glisten, twinkle, flicker, flash, shimmer.

sparkling *adjective* **1 effervescent**, fizzy, carbonated, aerated. **2 brilliant**, dazzling, scintillating, coruscating, exciting, exhilarating, stimulating, invigorating, vivacious, lively, vibrant.
- OPPOSITES still, dull.

sparse *adjective* **scant**, scanty, scattered, scarce, infrequent, few and far between, meagre, paltry, limited, in short supply.
- OPPOSITES abundant.

spartan *adjective* **austere**, harsh, hard, frugal, rigorous, strict, severe, ascetic, self-denying, abstemious, bleak, bare, plain.
- OPPOSITES luxurious.

spate *noun* **series**, succession, run, cluster, string, rash, epidemic, outbreak, wave, flurry.

speak *verb* **1 talk**, converse, communicate, chat, have a word, gossip, commune, say something; *informal* chew the fat. **2 say**, utter, state, declare, voice, express, pronounce, articulate, enunciate, verbalize. **3 give a speech**, talk, lecture, hold forth; *informal* spout, sound off.

speaker *noun* **speech-maker**, lecturer, talker, orator, spokesperson, spokesman/woman, reader, commentator, broadcaster, narrator.

special *adjective* **1 exceptional**, unusual, remarkable, out of the ordinary, outstanding, unique. **2 distinctive**, distinct, individual, particular, specific, peculiar. **3 momentous**, significant, memorable, important, historic, red-letter.
- OPPOSITES ordinary, general.

specialist *noun* **expert**, authority, pundit, professional, connoisseur, master, maestro; *informal* buff.

speciality *noun* **strength**, strong point, forte, métier, strong suit, party piece, pièce de résistance, claim to fame.

species *noun* **type**, kind, sort, breed, strain, variety, class, classification, category.

specific *adjective* **1 particular**, specified, fixed, set, determined, distinct, definite. **2 detailed**, explicit, express, clear-cut, unequivocal, precise, exact.
- OPPOSITES general, vague.

specification *noun* *a shelter built to their specifications* **instruction**, guideline, parameter, stipulation, requirement, condition, order, detail.

specify *verb* **state**, name, identify, define, set out, itemize, detail, list, enumerate, spell out, stipulate, lay down.

specimen *noun* **sample**, example, model, instance, illustration, demonstration.

spectacle *noun* **1 display**, show, pageantry, performance, exhibition, pomp and circumstance, extravaganza, spectacular. **2 sight**, vision, scene, prospect, picture.

S

spectacular *adjective* **impressive**, magnificent, splendid, dazzling, sensational, stunning, dramatic, outstanding, memorable, unforgettable, striking, picturesque, eye-catching, breathtaking, glorious; *informal* out of this world.
- OPPOSITES dull, unimpressive.

spectator *noun* **watcher**, viewer, observer, onlooker, bystander, witness.

spectre *noun* **ghost**, phantom, apparition, spirit, wraith, presence; *informal* spook.

speculate *verb* **1 conjecture**, theorize, hypothesize, guess, surmise, wonder, muse. **2 gamble**, venture, wager, invest, play the market.

speculative *adjective* **1 conjectural**, suppositional, theoretical, hypothetical, tentative, unproven, unfounded, groundless, unsubstantiated. **2 risky**, hazardous, unsafe, uncertain, unpredictable; *informal* chancy.

speech *noun* **1 speaking**, talking, verbal communication, conversation, dialogue, discussion. **2 diction**, elocution, articulation, enunciation, pronunciation, delivery, words. **3 talk**, address, lecture, discourse, oration, presentation, sermon. **4 language**, parlance, tongue, idiom, dialect, vernacular; *informal* lingo.

> **WORD LINKS**
> **oral**, **phonetic**, **phonic** relating to speech

speechless *adjective* **lost for words**, dumbstruck, struck dumb, tongue-tied, inarticulate, mute, dumb, voiceless, silent.

speed *noun* **1 rate**, pace, tempo, momentum, velocity; *informal* lick. **2 rapidity**, swiftness, promptness, alacrity, briskness, haste, hurry; *old use* celerity.
- OPPOSITES slowness.
● *verb* **1 hurry**, rush, dash, race, sprint, career, shoot, hurtle, hare, fly, zoom, hasten; *informal* tear, belt, pelt; *Brit. informal* bomb. **2** *a holiday will speed his*

recovery **hasten**, accelerate, advance, further, promote, boost, stimulate, aid, assist, facilitate.
- OPPOSITES slow, hinder.
□ **speed up** hurry up, accelerate, go faster, get a move on, put a spurt on, pick up speed; *informal* step on it.

speedy *adjective* **fast**, swift, quick, rapid, expeditious, prompt, immediate, brisk, hasty, hurried, precipitate, rushed.
- OPPOSITES slow.

spell¹ *verb* **signal**, signify, mean, amount to, add up to, constitute.
□ **spell out** explain, make clear, clarify, specify, detail.

spell² *noun* **1 charm**, incantation, magic formula, curse; *N. Amer.* hex; (**spells**) magic, sorcery, witchcraft. **2 influence**, charm, magnetism, charisma, magic.
□ **put a spell on** bewitch, enchant, entrance, curse, jinx; *N. Amer.* hex.

spell³ *noun* **1 period**, time, interval, season, stretch, run; *Brit. informal* patch. **2 bout**, fit, attack.

spellbound *adjective* **enthralled**, fascinated, rapt, riveted, transfixed, gripped, captivated, bewitched, enchanted, mesmerized, hypnotized.

spend *verb* **1 pay out**, expend, disburse; *informal* lay out, blow, splurge. **2 pass**, occupy, fill, take up, while away.

sphere *noun* **1 globe**, ball, orb, bubble. **2** *his sphere of influence* **area**, field, compass, orbit, range, scope, extent. **3 domain**, realm, province, field, area, territory, arena, department.

spice *noun* **1 seasoning**, flavouring, condiment. **2 excitement**, interest, colour, piquancy, zest, an edge.

spicy *adjective* **hot**, tangy, peppery, piquant, spiced, highly seasoned, pungent.
- OPPOSITES bland.

spike *noun* **prong**, pin, barb, point, skewer, stake, spit.

spill *verb* **1 knock over**, tip over, upset, overturn. **2 overflow**, brim over, run over, pour, slop, slosh, splash, leak.

spin verb **1 revolve**, rotate, turn, go round, whirl, twirl, gyrate. **2** *she spun round to face him* **whirl**, wheel, turn, swing, twist, swivel, pivot.
● noun **1 rotation**, revolution, turn, whirl, twirl, gyration. **2 slant**, angle, twist, bias. **3 trip**, jaunt, outing, excursion, journey, drive, ride, run, turn; *informal* tootle.

spine noun **1 backbone**, spinal column, back. **2 needle**, quill, bristle, barb, spike, prickle, thorn.

> **WORD LINKS**
> **vertebral** relating to the spine

spiral adjective **coiled**, helical, curling, winding, twisting.
● noun **coil**, curl, twist, whorl, scroll, helix, corkscrew.
● verb *smoke spiralled up* **coil**, wind, swirl, twist, snake.

spirit noun **1 soul**, psyche, inner self, mind. **2 ghost**, phantom, spectre, apparition, presence. **3 mood**, frame/ state of mind, humour, temper, morale, esprit de corps. **4 ethos**, essence, atmosphere, mood, feeling, climate. **5 enthusiasm**, energy, verve, vigour, dynamism, dash, sparkle, exuberance, gusto, fervour, zeal, fire, passion; *informal* get-up-and-go.
- OPPOSITES body, flesh.

spirited adjective **lively**, energetic, enthusiastic, vigorous, dynamic, passionate; *informal* feisty, gutsy; *N. Amer. informal* peppy.
- OPPOSITES apathetic, lifeless.

spiritual adjective **1 inner**, mental, psychological, incorporeal, non-material. **2 religious**, sacred, divine, holy, devotional.
- OPPOSITES physical, secular.

spit verb **expectorate**, hawk; *Brit. informal* gob.
● noun **spittle**, saliva, sputum, slobber, dribble.

spite noun **malice**, malevolence, ill will, vindictiveness, meanness, nastiness; *informal* bitchiness, cattiness.
● verb **upset**, hurt, wound.

- OPPOSITES please.
□ **in spite of** despite, notwithstanding, regardless of, in defiance of, in the face of.

spiteful adjective **malicious**, malevolent, vindictive, vengeful, mean, nasty, hurtful, mischievous, cruel, unkind; *informal* bitchy, catty.
- OPPOSITES benevolent.

splash verb **1 sprinkle**, spatter, splatter, spray, shower, wash, squirt, slosh, slop. **2 wash**, break, lap, pound. **3 paddle**, wade, wallow.

splendid adjective **1 magnificent**, sumptuous, grand, imposing, superb, spectacular, resplendent, rich, lavish, ornate, gorgeous, glorious, dazzling, handsome, beautiful; *informal* plush; *Brit. informal* swish. **2** *(informal)* **excellent**, wonderful, marvellous, superb, glorious, lovely, delightful, first-class; *informal* super, great, amazing, fantastic, terrific, tremendous; *Brit. informal* smashing, brilliant.
- OPPOSITES simple, modest, inferior.

splendour noun **magnificence**, sumptuousness, grandeur, resplendence, richness, glory, majesty.
- OPPOSITES simplicity.

splinter noun **sliver**, chip, shard, fragment, shred; *Scottish* skelf.
● verb **shatter**, smash, break into smithereens, fracture, split, crack, disintegrate.

split verb **1 break**, cut, burst, snap, crack, splinter, fracture, rupture, come apart. **2 tear**, rip, slash, slit. **3 share**, divide up, distribute, dole out, parcel out, carve up, slice up, apportion. **4 fork**, divide, branch, diverge. **5** *the band split up last year* **break up**, separate, part, part company, go their separate ways.
- OPPOSITES join, unite, converge.
● noun **1 crack**, fissure, cleft, crevice, break, fracture, breach. **2 rip**, tear, cut, rent, slash, slit. **3 division**, rift, breach, schism, rupture, separation, estrangement. **4 break-up**, split-up, separation, parting, estrangement, rift.
- OPPOSITES merger.

S

spoil verb **1 damage**, ruin, impair, blemish, disfigure, blight, deface, harm, destroy, wreck. **2** *rain spoiled my plans* **upset**, mess up, ruin, wreck, undo, sabotage, scotch, torpedo; *informal* muck up, screw up, do for; *Brit. informal* scupper. **3 overindulge**, pamper, indulge, mollycoddle, cosset, wait on someone hand and foot. **4 go bad**, go off, go rancid, turn, go sour, rot, decompose, decay, perish.
- OPPOSITES improve, enhance.

spoilsport noun **killjoy**, dog in the manger, misery; *informal* wet blanket, party-pooper.

spoken adjective **verbal**, oral, vocal, unwritten, word-of-mouth.

spokesperson, **spokesman**, **spokeswoman** noun **representative**, voice, mouthpiece, agent, official; *informal* spin doctor.

sponsor noun **backer**, patron, promoter, benefactor, supporter, contributor.
● verb **finance**, fund, subsidize, back, promote, support, contribute to; *N. Amer. informal* bankroll.

spontaneous adjective **1 unplanned**, unpremeditated, impulsive, impromptu, spur-of-the-moment, unprompted; *informal* off-the-cuff. **2 natural**, uninhibited, relaxed, unselfconscious, unaffected.

sporadic adjective **occasional**, infrequent, irregular, periodic, scattered, patchy, isolated, odd, intermittent, spasmodic, fitful, desultory, erratic, unpredictable.
- OPPOSITES frequent, continuous.

sport noun **game**, physical recreation.
● verb **wear**, have on, dress in, show off, parade, flaunt.

sporting adjective **sportsmanlike**, generous, considerate, fair; *Brit. informal* decent.

sporty adjective (*informal*) **athletic**, fit, active, energetic.

spot noun **1 mark**, patch, dot, fleck, smudge, smear, stain, blotch, splash; *informal* splotch, splodge. **2 pimple**, pustule, blackhead, boil, blemish; *informal* zit; *Scottish informal* plook; (**spots**) acne, rash. **3 place**, site, position, situation, setting, location, venue.
● verb **see**, notice, observe, catch sight of, detect, make out, discern, recognize, identify, locate; *Brit. informal* clock; *literary* espy, descry.

spotless adjective **clean**, pristine, immaculate, shining, shiny, gleaming, spick and span.
- OPPOSITES filthy.

spotlight noun **attention**, glare of publicity, limelight, public eye.

spotted adjective **spotty**, dotted, polka-dot, freckled, mottled.

spotty adjective **1 polka-dot**, spotted, dotted. **2** (*Brit.*) **pimply**, pimpled, acned; *Scottish informal* plooky.

spouse noun **partner**, husband, wife, mate, consort; *informal* better half; *Brit. informal* other half.

sprawl verb **stretch out**, lounge, loll, slump, flop, slouch.

spray noun **1 shower**, sprinkle, jet, squirt, mist, spume, foam, froth, spindrift. **2 aerosol**, vaporizer, atomizer, sprinkler.
● verb **1 sprinkle**, dribble, drizzle, water, soak, douse, drench. **2 spout**, jet, gush, spurt, shoot, squirt.

spread verb **1 lay out**, open out, unfurl, unroll, roll out, straighten out, fan out, stretch out, extend. **2** *the landscape spread out below* **extend**, stretch, sprawl. **3 scatter**, strew, disperse, distribute. **4 circulate**, broadcast, put about, publicize, propagate, repeat. **5 travel**, move, be borne, sweep, diffuse, reproduce, be passed on, be transmitted. **6 smear**, daub, plaster, apply, rub.
● noun **1 expansion**, proliferation, dissemination, diffusion, transmission, propagation. **2 span**, width, extent, stretch, reach.

spree noun **bout**, orgy; *informal* binge, splurge.

spring *verb* **leap**, jump, bound, vault, hop.
● *noun* **springiness**, bounce, resilience, elasticity, flexibility, stretch, stretchiness, give.
□ **spring from** originate from, have its origins in, derive from, arise in, stem from, emanate from, evolve from.

> **WORD LINKS**
> **vernal** relating to the season of spring

sprinkle *verb* **splash**, trickle, drizzle, spray, shower, drip, scatter, strew, dredge, dust.

sprint *verb* **run**, race, rush, dash, bolt, fly, charge, shoot, speed; *informal* hotfoot it, leg it.
- OPPOSITES stroll.

sprout *verb* **1 germinate**, put/send out shoots, bud. **2 spring**, come up, grow, develop, appear.

spruce *adjective* **neat**, well groomed, well turned out, well dressed, smart, trim, dapper; *informal* natty, snazzy.
- OPPOSITES dishevelled.
□ **spruce up** smarten up, tidy up, clean, groom; *informal* do up, titivate; *Brit. informal* tart up; *N. Amer. informal* gussy up.

spur *noun* **stimulus**, incentive, encouragement, inducement, impetus, motivation.
- OPPOSITES disincentive.
● *verb* **stimulate**, encourage, prompt, prod, impel, motivate, move, galvanize, inspire, drive.
- OPPOSITES discourage.

spurious *adjective* **bogus**, fake, false, fraudulent, sham, artificial, imitation, simulated, feigned; *informal* phoney.
- OPPOSITES genuine.

spurn *verb* **reject**, rebuff, scorn, turn down, treat with contempt, disdain, look down your nose at; *informal* turn your nose up at.
- OPPOSITES welcome, accept.

spurt *verb* **squirt**, shoot, jet, erupt, gush, pour, stream, pump, surge, spew, course, well, spring, burst, spout.
● *noun* **squirt**, jet, gush, stream, rush, surge, flood, cascade, torrent.

spy *noun* **agent**, mole, plant; *N. Amer. informal* spook.
● *verb* **notice**, observe, see, spot, sight, catch sight of, glimpse, make out, discern, detect.
□ **spy on** observe, keep under surveillance, eavesdrop on, watch, bug.

spying *noun* **espionage**, intelligence gathering, surveillance, infiltration.

squabble *noun* **quarrel**, disagreement, row, argument, dispute, wrangle, clash, altercation; *informal* tiff, set-to, run-in, scrap, dust-up; *Brit. informal* barney, ding-dong.
● *verb* **quarrel**, row, argue, bicker, disagree; *informal* scrap.

squad *noun* **1 team**, crew, gang, force. **2 detachment**, detail, unit, platoon, battery, troop, patrol, squadron, commando.

squalid *adjective* **1 dirty**, filthy, dingy, grubby, grimy, wretched, miserable, mean, seedy, shabby, sordid, insalubrious; *Brit. informal* grotty. **2 improper**, sordid, unseemly, unsavoury, sleazy, cheap, base, low, corrupt, dishonest, dishonourable, disreputable, discreditable, contemptible, shameful.
- OPPOSITES clean.

squander *verb* **waste**, throw away, misuse, misspend, fritter away, spend like water; *informal* blow, run through, splurge, pour down the drain.
- OPPOSITES save.

square *noun* **piazza**, plaza, quadrangle.
● *adjective* **level**, even, drawn, equal, tied, level pegging; *informal* even-steven(s).

squash *verb* **1 crush**, squeeze, mash, pulp, flatten, compress, distort, pound, trample. **2 force**, ram, thrust, push, cram, jam, stuff, pack, squeeze, wedge.

squeak *noun & verb* **peep**, cheep, squeal, tweet, yelp, whimper.

squeeze *verb* **1 compress**, press, crush, squash, pinch, nip, grasp, grip, clutch. **2 extract**, press, force, express.

3 force, thrust, cram, ram, jam, stuff, pack, wedge, press, push, squash, crush, crowd, force your way.
● noun **1 press**, pinch, nip, grasp, grip, clutch, hug. **2 crush**, jam, squash, congestion.

squirm verb **1 wriggle**, wiggle, writhe, twist, slither, fidget, twitch, toss and turn. **2 wince**, shudder.

squirt verb **1 spurt**, shoot, spray, jet, erupt, gush, rush, pump, surge, stream, spew, well, issue, emanate. **2 splash**, spray, shower, sprinkle.

stab verb **knife**, run through, skewer, spear, gore, spike, impale.
● noun **1** a stab of pain **twinge**, pang, throb, spasm, cramp, prick. **2** (informal) **attempt**, try, endeavour, effort; informal go, shot, crack, bash.

stability noun **1 firmness**, solidity, steadiness. **2 balance (of mind)**, (mental) health, sanity, reason. **3 strength**, durability, lasting nature, permanence.

stable adjective **1 firm**, solid, steady, secure. **2 well balanced**, well adjusted, of sound mind, compos mentis, sane, normal, rational, reasonable, sensible. **3** a stable relationship **secure**, solid, strong, steady, firm, sure, steadfast, established, enduring, lasting.
- OPPOSITES unstable.

stack noun **heap**, pile, mound, mountain, pyramid, tower.
● verb **1 heap (up)**, pile (up), assemble, put together, collect. **2 load**, fill (up), pack, charge, stuff, cram, stock.

staff noun **1 employees**, workers, workforce, personnel, human resources, manpower, labour. **2 stick**, stave, pole, rod.
● verb **man**, people, crew, work, operate.

stage noun **1 phase**, period, juncture, step, point, level. **2 part**, section, portion, stretch, leg, lap, circuit. **3 platform**, dais, stand, rostrum, podium.

stagger verb **1 lurch**, reel, sway, teeter, totter, stumble. **2 amaze**, astound, astonish, surprise, stun, confound;

daze, take aback; informal flabbergast; Brit. informal knock for six.

stagnant adjective **1 still**, motionless, standing, stale, dirty, brackish. **2 inactive**, sluggish, slow-moving, static, flat, depressed, moribund, dead, dormant.
- OPPOSITES flowing.

staid adjective **sedate**, respectable, serious, steady, conventional, traditional, unadventurous, set in your ways, sober, formal, stuffy, stiff; informal starchy, stick-in-the-mud.
- OPPOSITES frivolous.

stain verb **1 discolour**, soil, mark, spot, spatter, splatter, smear, splash, smudge, begrime. **2 colour**, tint, dye, paint.
● noun **1 mark**, spot, blotch, smudge, smear. **2 blemish**, taint, blot, smear, slur, stigma.

stake[1] noun **post**, pole, stick, spike, upright, support, cane.

stake[2] noun **1 bet**, wager, ante. **2 share**, interest, investment, involvement, concern.
● verb **bet**, wager, lay, put on, gamble, risk.

stale adjective **1 old**, past its best, off, dry, hard, musty, mouldy, rancid. **2 stuffy**, musty, fusty, stagnant. **3 overused**, hackneyed, tired, worn out, overworked, threadbare, banal, clichéd, trite, unimaginative, uninspired, flat; informal old hat; N. Amer. played out.
- OPPOSITES fresh.

stalemate noun **deadlock**, impasse, stand-off, gridlock.

stalk verb **1 trail**, follow, shadow, track, go after, hunt; informal tail. **2 strut**, stride, march, flounce, storm, stomp, sweep.

stall noun **1 stand**, table, counter, booth, kiosk. **2 pen**, coop, sty, corral, enclosure, compartment.
● verb **1 delay**, play for time, procrastinate, hedge, drag your feet, filibuster, stonewall. **2 hold off**, stave off, keep at bay, evade, avoid.

stalwart *adjective* **staunch**, loyal, faithful, committed, devoted, dedicated, dependable, reliable.
- OPPOSITES disloyal.

stamina *noun* **endurance**, staying power, energy, toughness, determination, tenacity, perseverance, grit.

stammer *verb* **stutter**, stumble over your words, hesitate, falter, pause, splutter.

stamp *verb* **1 trample**, step, tread, tramp, stomp, stump, clump, crush, squash, flatten. **2 imprint**, print, impress, punch, inscribe, emboss.
● *noun* **mark**, hallmark, sign, seal, sure sign, smack, savour, air.
□ **stamp out** put an end to, end, stop, crush, put down, curb, quell, suppress, extinguish, stifle, abolish, get rid of, eliminate, eradicate, destroy, wipe out.

stance *noun* **1 posture**, body position, pose, attitude. **2 attitude**, opinion, standpoint, position, approach, policy, line.

stand *verb* **1 rise**, get to your feet, get up, pick yourself up. **2 be situated**, be located, be positioned, be sited. **3 put**, set, erect, place, position, prop, install, arrange; *informal* park. **4 remain in force**, remain in operation, hold, hold good, apply, be the case, exist, prevail. **5 withstand**, endure, bear, put up with, take, cope with, handle, sustain, resist, stand up to. **6** (*informal*) **put up with**, endure, tolerate, accept, take, abide, stand for, support, countenance; *formal* brook.
- OPPOSITES sit, lie down.
● *noun* **1 attitude**, stance, opinion, standpoint, position, approach, policy, line. **2 opposition**, resistance. **3 base**, support, platform, stage, dais, rest, plinth, tripod, rack, trivet. **4 stall**, counter, booth, kiosk.
□ **stand by 1** wait, be prepared, be ready for action, be on full alert, wait in the wings. **2** support, stick with/by, remain loyal to, stand up for, back up, defend, stick up for. **3** abide by, keep (to), adhere to, hold to, stick to,

observe, comply with. **stand for** mean, be short for, represent, signify, denote, symbolize. **stand in** deputize, act, substitute, fill in, take over, cover, hold the fort, step into the breach, replace, relieve. **stand out** be noticeable, be visible, be obvious, be conspicuous, stick out, attract attention; *informal* stick/ stand out a mile, stick/stand out like a sore thumb.

standard *noun* **1 quality**, level, calibre, merit, excellence. **2 guideline**, norm, yardstick, benchmark, gauge, measure, criterion, guide, touchstone, model, pattern. **3 principle**, ideal; (**standards**) morals, code of behaviour, ethics. **4 flag**, banner, ensign, colour(s).
● *adjective* **1 normal**, usual, average, typical, stock, common, ordinary, customary, conventional, established. **2 definitive**, classic, recognized, accepted, approved, authoritative.
- OPPOSITES unusual, special.

standing *noun* **1 status**, ranking, position, reputation, stature. **2 prestige**, rank, eminence, seniority, repute, stature, esteem, importance, account.

staple *adjective* **main**, principal, chief, major, primary, leading, foremost, first, most important, predominant, dominant, basic, prime; *informal* number-one.

star *noun* **1 heavenly body**, celestial body. **2 principal**, leading lady/man, lead, hero, heroine. **3 celebrity**, superstar, famous name, household name, leading light, VIP, personality, luminary; *informal* celeb, big shot, megastar.
● *adjective* **1 outstanding**, exceptional. **2 top**, leading, greatest, foremost, major, pre-eminent.

WORD LINKS

astral, stellar relating to stars
astronomy study of stars

---

stare *verb* **gaze**, gape, goggle, glare, ogle, peer; *informal* gawk; *Brit. informal* gawp.

stark *adjective* **1 sharp**, sharply defined, crisp, distinct, clear, clear-cut.

2 desolate, bare, barren, empty, bleak, dreary, depressing, grim.
- OPPOSITES indistinct, ornate.
● *adverb* stark naked **completely**, totally, utterly, absolutely, entirely, wholly, fully, quite, altogether, thoroughly.

start *verb* **1 begin**, commence, get under way, get going, go ahead, make a start; *informal* kick off, get the ball rolling, get the show on the road. **2 come into being**, begin, arise, originate, develop. **3 establish**, set up, found, create, bring into being, institute, initiate, inaugurate, introduce, open, launch. **4 activate**, switch/turn on, start up, fire up, boot up. **5 flinch**, jerk, jump, twitch, wince.
- OPPOSITES end, finish, stop.
● *noun* **1 beginning**, commencement, inception, onset, inauguration, dawn, birth, emergence; *informal* kick-off. **2 lead**, head start, advantage. **3 jerk**, twitch, spasm, jump.
- OPPOSITES end.

startle *verb* **surprise**, frighten, scare, alarm, shock, give someone a fright, make someone jump.

starving *adjective* **hungry**, undernourished, malnourished, starved, ravenous, famished.
- OPPOSITES full.

state¹ *noun* **1 condition**, shape, position, situation, circumstances, state of affairs, predicament, plight. **2 country**, nation, land, kingdom, realm, power, republic. **3 government**, parliament, administration, regime. **4 state of anxiety**, panic, fluster; *informal* flap, tizzy.

state² *verb* **express**, voice, utter, put into words, declare, announce, make known, put across/over, communicate, air.

stately *adjective* **dignified**, majestic, ceremonious, courtly, imposing, solemn, regal, grand.
- OPPOSITES undignified.

statement *noun* **declaration**, expression, affirmation, assertion,

announcement, utterance, communication, bulletin, communiqué.

static *adjective* **1 unchanged**, fixed, stable, steady, unchanging, unvarying, constant. **2 stationary**, motionless, immobile, unmoving, still, at a standstill.
- OPPOSITES variable, dynamic.

station *noun* **1 establishment**, base, camp, post, depot, mission, site, facility, installation. **2 office**, depot, base, headquarters. **3 channel**, wavelength.
● *verb* base, post, establish, deploy, garrison.

stationary *adjective* **static**, parked, motionless, immobile, still, stock-still, at a standstill, at rest.
- OPPOSITES moving.

stature *noun* **1 height**, size, build. **2 reputation**, repute, standing, status, position, prestige, distinction, eminence, prominence, importance.

status *noun* **1 standing**, rank, position, level, place. **2 prestige**, kudos, cachet, standing, stature, esteem, image, importance, authority, fame.

staunch¹ *adjective* **stalwart**, loyal, faithful, committed, devoted, dedicated, reliable.
- OPPOSITES disloyal, unfaithful.

staunch² *verb* **stem**, stop, halt, check, curb; *N. Amer.* stanch.

stay *verb* **1 remain (behind)**, wait, linger, stick, be left, hold on, hang on; *informal* hang around; *Brit. informal* hang about; *old use* tarry. **2 continue (to be)**, remain, keep, carry on being. **3 visit**, stop (off/over), holiday, lodge; *N. Amer.* vacation.
- OPPOSITES leave.
● *noun* visit, stop, stopover, break, holiday; *N. Amer.* vacation; *literary* sojourn.

steady *adjective* **1 stable**, firm, fixed, secure. **2 still**, motionless, static, stationary, unmoving. **3** a steady gaze **fixed**, intent, unwavering, unfaltering. **4** steady breathing **constant**, consistent, regular, even, rhythmic. **5 continuous**, continual, unceasing, ceaseless,

perpetual, unremitting, endless.
6 regular, settled, firm, committed,
long-term.
- OPPOSITES unstable, shaky, fluctuating.
● *verb* **1 stabilize**, hold steady, brace,
support, balance, rest. **2 calm**, soothe,
quieten, compose, settle, subdue,
quell.

steal *verb* **1 take**, thieve, help yourself
to, pilfer, embezzle; *informal* swipe, lift,
filch; *Brit. informal* nick, pinch, knock
off; *N. Amer. informal* heist. **2 plagiarize**, copy, pirate; *informal* rip off, lift,
pinch, crib; *Brit. informal* nick. **3 creep**,
sneak, slink, slip, glide, tiptoe, slope.

> **WORD LINKS**
> **kleptomania** compulsion to steal

stealth *noun* **furtiveness**, secretiveness,
secrecy, surreptitiousness.

stealthy *adjective* **furtive**, secretive,
secret, surreptitious, sneaky, sly;
Military black.
- OPPOSITES open.

steep *adjective* **1 sheer**, precipitous,
abrupt, sharp, perpendicular, verti-
cal. **2** *a steep increase* **sharp**, sudden,
dramatic, precipitate.
- OPPOSITES gentle, gradual.

steeped *adjective*
□ **steeped in** imbued with, filled with,
permeated with, suffused with, soaked
in, pervaded by.

steer *verb* **guide**, direct, manoeuvre,
drive, pilot, navigate.

stem[1] *noun* **stalk**, shoot, trunk.
□ **stem from** come from, arise from,
originate from, have its origins in,
spring from, derive from.

stem[2] *verb* **stop**, staunch, halt, check,
curb; *N. Amer.* stanch.

stench *noun* **stink**, reek; *Brit. informal*
niff, pong, whiff; *N. Amer. informal* funk;
literary miasma.

step *noun* **1 pace**, stride, footstep,
footfall, tread, tramp. **2 stair**, tread;
(**steps**) stairs, staircase, flight of
stairs. **3 action**, act, course of action,
measure, move, operation, procedure.
4 advance, development, move,

movement, breakthrough. **5 stage**,
level, grade, rank, degree, phase.
● *verb* **walk**, move, tread, pace, stride.
□ **step down** resign, stand down, give
up your post/job, bow out, abdicate;
informal quit. **step in** intervene,
become involved, intercede. **step up**
increase, intensify, strengthen, escalate, speed up, accelerate; *informal* up,
crank up.

stereotype *noun* **conventional idea**,
standard image, cliché, formula.
● *verb* **typecast**, pigeonhole, conven-
tionalize, categorize, label, tag.

sterile *adjective* **1 unproductive**,
infertile, unfruitful, barren. **2 hygienic**,
clean, pure, uncontaminated, sterilized,
disinfected, germ-free, antiseptic.
- OPPOSITES fertile.

sterilize *verb* **1 disinfect**, fumigate,
decontaminate, sanitize, clean, cleanse,
purify. **2 neuter**, castrate, spay, geld;
N. Amer. & Austral. alter; *Brit. informal*
doctor.
- OPPOSITES contaminate.

stern *adjective* **1 unsmiling**, frown-
ing, serious, severe, forbidding, grim,
unfriendly, austere, dour. **2 strict**,
severe, stringent, harsh, drastic, hard,
tough, extreme, draconian.
- OPPOSITES genial, lax.

stick[1] *noun* **1 branch**, twig, switch.
2 walking stick, cane, staff, crutch.
3 post, pole, cane, stake, rod.

stick[2] *verb* **1 thrust**, push, insert, jab,
poke, dig, plunge. **2 pierce**, penetrate,
puncture, prick, stab. **3 adhere**, cling.
4 *stick the stamp there* **attach**, fasten,
affix, fix, paste, glue, gum, tape. **5 jam**,
get jammed, catch, get caught, get
trapped. **6** (*Brit. informal*) **tolerate**, put
up with, take, stand, stomach, endure,
bear, abide.
□ **stick out 1** protrude, jut (out),
project, stand out, extend, poke out,
bulge. **2** be conspicuous, be obvious,
stand out, leap out; *informal* stick out
a mile. **stick to** abide by, keep, adhere
to, hold to, comply with, fulfil, stand by.
stick up for support, take someone's

S

side, take someone's part, side with, stand by, stand up for, defend.

sticky *adjective* **1 adhesive**, self-adhesive, gummed. **2 tacky**, gluey, gummy, treacly, glutinous, viscous; *informal* gooey. **3 humid**, muggy, close, sultry, steamy, sweaty, sweltering, oppressive. **4 awkward**, difficult, tricky, ticklish, delicate, embarrassing, sensitive; *informal* hairy.
- OPPOSITES dry, fresh, cool.

stiff *adjective* **1 rigid**, hard, firm, inelastic, unyielding, brittle. **2 thick**, firm, viscous, semi-solid. **3 aching**, achy, painful, arthritic; *informal* creaky. **4 formal**, reserved, wooden, forced, strained, stilted; *informal* starchy, uptight. **5** *stiff penalties* **harsh**, severe, heavy, stringent, drastic, draconian; *Brit.* swingeing. **6** *they put up a stiff resistance* **vigorous**, determined, strong, spirited, resolute, tenacious, dogged, stubborn. **7 difficult**, hard, arduous, tough, strenuous, laborious, exacting, tiring, demanding. **8 strong**, potent, alcoholic.
- OPPOSITES flexible, soft, limp.

stifle *verb* **1 smother**, check, restrain, keep back, hold back, hold in, withhold, choke back, muffle, suppress, curb. **2 suppress**, quash, quell, put an end to, put down, stop, extinguish, stamp out, crush, subdue, repress. **3 suffocate**, smother, asphyxiate, choke.

stigma *noun* **shame**, disgrace, dishonour, ignominy, humiliation, stain, taint.
- OPPOSITES honour.

still *adjective* **1 motionless**, unmoving, stock-still, immobile, rooted to the spot, transfixed, static, stationary. **2 quiet**, silent, calm, peaceful, serene, windless, noiseless, undisturbed, flat, smooth, like a millpond.
- OPPOSITES moving, noisy.
- ● *adverb* **1 even now**, yet. **2 nevertheless**, nonetheless, all the same, even so, but, however, despite that, in spite of that.
- ● *verb* **quieten**, quiet, silence, hush, calm, settle, pacify, subdue.

stimulate *verb* **encourage**, prompt, motivate, trigger, spark, spur on, galvanize, fire, inspire, excite; *N. Amer.* light a fire under.
- OPPOSITES discourage.

stimulating *adjective* **thought-provoking**, interesting, inspiring, inspirational, lively, exciting, provocative.
- OPPOSITES uninspiring, boring.

stimulus *noun* **motivation**, encouragement, impetus, prompt, spur, inducement, incentive, inspiration, fillip; *informal* shot in the arm.
- OPPOSITES deterrent.

sting *noun* **1 prick**, wound, injury. **2 pain**, pricking, smarting, soreness, hurt, irritation.
- ● *verb* **1 prick**, wound. **2 smart**, burn, hurt, be irritated, be sore. **3** *the criticism stung her* **upset**, wound, hurt, distress, pain, mortify.

stink *verb* **reek**, smell.
- ● *noun* **stench**, reek; *Brit. informal* pong; *N. Amer. informal* funk.

stint *noun* **spell**, stretch, turn, session, term, time, shift, tour of duty.

stipulate *verb* **specify**, set out, lay down, demand, require, insist on.

stir *verb* **1 mix**, blend, beat, whip, whisk, fold in; *N. Amer.* muddle. **2 move**, get up, get out of bed, rise, rouse yourself, bestir yourself. **3 disturb**, rustle, shake, move, agitate. **4** *the war stirred him to action* **spur**, drive, rouse, prompt, propel, motivate, encourage, urge, impel, provoke, goad.
- ● *noun* **commotion**, disturbance, fuss, excitement, sensation; *informal* to-do, hoo-ha.

stock *noun* **1 merchandise**, goods, wares. **2 store**, supply, stockpile, reserve, hoard, cache, bank. **3 animals**, livestock, beasts, flocks, herds. **4 descent**, ancestry, origin(s), lineage, birth, extraction, family, blood, pedigree.
- ● *adjective* **usual**, routine, predictable, set, standard, staple, customary, familiar, conventional, traditional, stereotyped, clichéd, hackneyed,

unoriginal, formulaic.
- OPPOSITES unusual, original.
● *verb* **sell**, carry, keep (in stock), offer, supply, provide, furnish.

stockpile *noun* **stock**, store, supply, collection, reserve, hoard, cache; *informal* stash.
● *verb* **store up**, amass, accumulate, stock up on, hoard, cache, collect, lay in, put away, put/set aside, put by, stow away, save; *informal* salt away, stash away.

stocky *adjective* **thickset**, sturdy, heavily built, chunky, burly, strapping, brawny, solid, heavy, hefty, beefy.
- OPPOSITES slender.

stomach *noun* **1 abdomen**, middle, belly, gut, paunch; *informal* tummy, insides, pot, spare tyre. **2 appetite**, taste, inclination, desire, wish.
● *verb* **tolerate**, put up with, take, stand, endure, bear; *informal* hack, abide; *Brit. informal* stick.

> **WORD LINKS**
> **gastric** relating to the stomach

stone *noun* **1 rock**, pebble, boulder. **2 gem**, gemstone, jewel; *informal* rock, sparkler. **3 kernel**, seed, pip, pit.

> **WORD LINKS**
> **lapidary** relating to stone

stoop *verb* **bend**, lean, crouch, bow, duck.

stop *verb* **1 end**, halt, finish, terminate, wind up, bring to a stop/halt, discontinue, cut short, interrupt, nip in the bud, shut down. **2** *he stopped smoking* **cease**, refrain from, discontinue, desist from, break off, give up, abandon, cut out; *informal* quit, pack in; *Brit. informal* jack in. **3 pull up**, draw up, come to a stop/halt, come to rest, pull in/over. **4** *the music stopped* **come to an end**, draw to a close, end, cease, halt, finish, be over, conclude. **5 prevent**, obstruct, impede, block, bar, preclude, dissuade from.
- OPPOSITES start, begin, continue.
● *noun* **1 halt**, end, finish, cessation, close, conclusion, termination, stand-

still. **2 break**, stopover, stop-off, stay, visit; *literary* sojourn. **3 stopping place**, station, halt.

store *noun* **1 stock**, supply, stockpile, hoard, cache, reserve, bank, pool; *informal* stash. **2 storeroom**, storehouse, repository, stockroom, depot, depository, warehouse. **3** *ship's stores* **supplies**, provisions, stocks, food, rations, materials, equipment, hardware. **4 shop**, emporium, (retail) outlet, boutique, department store, supermarket, hypermarket, superstore, megastore; *N. Amer.* mart.
● *verb* **keep**, stockpile, stock up with, lay in, set aside, put aside, put away/by, save, collect, accumulate, amass, hoard; *informal* squirrel away, salt away, stash.
- OPPOSITES use, discard.

storehouse *noun* **warehouse**, depository, repository, store, storeroom, depot.

storm *noun* **1 tempest**, squall, gale, hurricane, tornado, cyclone, typhoon, thunderstorm, rainstorm, monsoon, hailstorm, snowstorm, blizzard. **2 uproar**, outcry, fuss, furore, rumpus, trouble; *informal* to-do, hoo-ha, ructions, stink; *Brit. informal* row.
● *verb* **1 stride**, march, stomp, stamp, stalk, flounce, fling. **2 attack**, charge, rush, swoop on.

stormy *adjective* **1 blustery**, squally, windy, gusty, blowy, thundery, wild, violent, rough, foul. **2 angry**, heated, fierce, furious, passionate, acrimonious.
- OPPOSITES calm, peaceful.

story *noun* **1 tale**, narrative, account, history, anecdote, saga; *informal* yarn. **2 plot**, storyline, scenario. **3 news**, report, item, article, feature, piece. **4 rumour**, whisper, allegation, speculation, gossip.

stout *adjective* **1 fat**, big, plump, portly, rotund, dumpy, corpulent, thickset, burly, bulky; *informal* tubby; *Brit. informal* podgy; *N. Amer. informal* zaftig, corn-fed. **2 strong**, sturdy, solid, robust, tough, durable, hard-wearing.

3 determined, vigorous, forceful, spirited, committed, brave, fearless, valiant, gallant, bold, plucky; *informal* gutsy.
- OPPOSITES thin, flimsy.

straight adjective **1 direct**, linear, unswerving, undeviating. **2 level**, even, in line, aligned, square, vertical, upright, perpendicular, horizontal. **3 in order**, tidy, neat, shipshape, spick and span, orderly, organized, arranged, sorted out, straightened out. **4 honest**, direct, frank, candid, truthful, sincere, forthright, straightforward, plain-spoken, blunt, unambiguous; *informal* upfront. **5 undiluted**, neat, pure; *N. Amer. informal* straight up.
- OPPOSITES winding, crooked.
● adverb **1 right**, directly, squarely, full; *informal* smack, (slap) bang; *N. Amer. informal* smack dab. **2 frankly**, directly, candidly, honestly, forthrightly, plainly, point-blank, bluntly, flatly; *Brit. informal* straight up. **3 logically**, rationally, clearly, lucidly, coherently, cogently.
□ **straight away** at once, right away, (right) now, this/that (very) minute, this/that instant, immediately, instantly, directly, forthwith, then and there; *N. Amer.* in short order; *informal* straight off, pronto; *N. Amer. informal* lickety-split.

straighten verb **1 put straight**, adjust, put in order, arrange, rearrange, tidy, neaten. **2** *we must straighten things out with him* **put right**, sort out, clear up, settle, resolve, rectify, remedy; *informal* patch up.

straightforward adjective **1 uncomplicated**, easy, simple, plain sailing, elementary, undemanding. **2 honest**, frank, candid, open, truthful, sincere, on the level, forthright, plain-speaking, direct; *informal* upfront; *N. Amer. informal* on the up and up.
- OPPOSITES complicated, devious.

strain¹ verb **1 overtax**, overwork, overextend, overreach, overdo it, exhaust, wear out; *informal* knacker, knock yourself out. **2 injure**, damage,

pull, wrench, twist, sprain. **3 sieve**, sift, filter, screen.
● noun **1 tension**, tightness, tautness. **2 injury**, sprain, wrench, twist. **3 pressure**, demands, burdens, stress; *informal* hassle. **4 stress**, (nervous) tension, exhaustion, fatigue, pressure, overwork.

strain² noun **variety**, kind, type, sort, breed, genus.

strained adjective **1 awkward**, tense, uneasy, uncomfortable, edgy, difficult, troubled. **2 forced**, unnatural, artificial, insincere, false, affected, put-on.

strait noun **1 channel**, sound, narrows, stretch of water. **2 (straits) difficulty**, trouble, crisis, mess, predicament, plight; *informal* hot water, jam, hole, fix, scrape.

strand noun **thread**, filament, fibre, length.

stranded adjective **1 shipwrecked**, wrecked, marooned, grounded, aground, beached. **2 helpless**, abandoned, forsaken, left high and dry, left in the lurch.

strange adjective **1 unusual**, odd, curious, peculiar, funny, queer, bizarre, weird, uncanny, surprising, unexpected, anomalous, atypical; *informal* fishy. **2 unfamiliar**, unknown, new, novel.
- OPPOSITES ordinary, familiar.

stranger noun **newcomer**, new arrival, visitor, guest, outsider, foreigner.

strangle verb **throttle**, choke, garrotte, asphyxiate.

strap noun **belt**, tie, band, thong.
● verb **tie**, lash, secure, fasten, bind, make fast, truss.

strapping adjective **big**, strong, well built, brawny, burly, muscular; *informal* beefy.

strategic adjective **planned**, calculated, deliberate, tactical, judicious, prudent, shrewd.

strategy noun **plan**, grand design, game plan, policy, programme, scheme.

stray verb **1 wander off**, go astray, get separated, get lost, drift away. **2 digress**, deviate, wander, get sidetracked, go off at a tangent, get off the subject.
● adjective **1 homeless**, lost, abandoned, feral. **2** a stray bullet **random**, chance, freak, unexpected, isolated.

streak noun **1 band**, line, strip, stripe, vein, slash, ray, smear. **2 element**, vein, strain, touch. **3 period**, spell, stretch, run; Brit. informal patch.
● verb **1 stripe**, band, fleck, smear, mark. **2 race**, speed, flash, shoot, dash, rush, hurtle, whizz, zoom, career, fly; informal belt, tear, zip, whip; Brit. informal bomb; N. Amer. informal barrel.

stream noun **1 brook**, rivulet, tributary; Scottish & N. English burn; N. English beck; S. English bourn; N. Amer. & Austral./NZ creek. **2 jet**, flow, rush, gush, surge, torrent, flood, cascade. **3 succession**, series, string.
● verb **1 flow**, pour, course, run, gush, surge, flood, cascade, spill. **2 pour**, surge, flood, swarm, pile, crowd.

streamlined adjective **1 aerodynamic**, smooth, sleek, elegant. **2 efficient**, smooth-running, well run, well oiled, slick.

street noun **road**, thoroughfare, avenue, drive, boulevard, lane; N. Amer. highway.

strength noun **1 power**, muscle, might, brawn, muscularity, robustness, sturdiness, vigour, stamina. **2 fortitude**, resilience, spirit, backbone, courage, bravery, pluck, grit; informal guts. **3** strength of feeling **intensity**, vehemence, force, depth. **4** the strength of their argument **force**, weight, power, persuasiveness, soundness, cogency, validity. **5 strong point**, advantage, asset, forte, aptitude, talent, skill, speciality.
- OPPOSITES weakness.

strengthen verb **1 make strong**, make stronger, build up, harden, toughen. **2 grow strong**, grow stronger, gain strength, intensify, pick up.

3 reinforce, support, back up, bolster, authenticate, confirm, substantiate, corroborate.
- OPPOSITES weaken.

strenuous adjective **1 difficult**, arduous, hard, tough, taxing, demanding, exacting, exhausting, tiring, gruelling, back-breaking; Brit. informal knackering. **2 vigorous**, energetic, forceful, strong, spirited, intense, determined, resolute, dogged.
- OPPOSITES easy, half-hearted.

stress noun **1 strain**, pressure, (nervous) tension, worry, anxiety, trouble, difficulty; informal hassle. **2 emphasis**, importance, weight, accent, accentuation.
● verb **1 emphasize**, draw attention to, underline, underscore, point up, highlight, accentuate. **2 overstretch**, overtax, pressurize, pressure, push to the limit, worry, harass; informal hassle.
- OPPOSITES play down.

stressful adjective **demanding**, trying, taxing, difficult, hard, tough, fraught, traumatic, tense, frustrating.
- OPPOSITES relaxing.

stretch verb **1 expand**, give, be elastic, be stretchy, be tensile. **2 pull (out)**, draw out, extend, lengthen, elongate, expand. **3 bend**, strain, distort, exaggerate, embellish. **4** she stretched out her arm **reach out**, hold out, extend, straighten (out). **5** I stretched out on the sofa **lie down**, recline, lean back, sprawl, lounge, loll. **6 extend**, spread, continue, go on.
- OPPOSITES shorten, contract.
● noun **1 expanse**, area, tract, belt, sweep, extent. **2 period**, time, spell, run, stint, session, shift.

strict adjective **1 precise**, exact, literal, faithful, accurate, careful, scrupulous, meticulous, punctilious. **2 stringent**, rigorous, severe, harsh, hard, stern, rigid, tough, uncompromising, authoritarian, firm. **3** in strict confidence **absolute**, utter, complete, total.
- OPPOSITES loose, liberal.

stride verb & noun **step**, pace, march.

strife noun **conflict**, friction, discord, disagreement, dissension, dispute, argument, quarrelling.
- OPPOSITES peace.

strike verb **1 hit**, slap, smack, thump, punch, beat, bang; informal clout, wallop, belt, whack, thwack, bash, clobber, bop, biff; Austral./NZ informal quilt. **2 crash into**, collide with, hit, run into, bump into, smash into; N. Amer. impact. **3 occur to**, come to (mind), dawn on someone, hit, spring to mind, enter your head. **4** you strike me as intelligent **seem to**, appear to, give someone the impression of being. **5 take industrial action**, go on strike, down tools, walk out.
● noun **1 industrial action**, walkout. **2 attack**, assault, bombing.

striking adjective **1 noticeable**, obvious, conspicuous, visible, distinct, marked, unmistakable, strong, remarkable. **2 impressive**, imposing, magnificent, spectacular, breathtaking, marvellous, wonderful, stunning, sensational, dramatic.
- OPPOSITES unremarkable.

string noun **1 twine**, cord, yarn, thread. **2 series**, succession, chain, sequence, run, streak. **3 queue**, procession, line, file, column, convoy, train, cavalcade. **4 (strings) conditions**, qualifications, provisions, provisos, caveats, stipulations, riders, limitations, restrictions; informal catches.
● verb **hang**, suspend, sling, stretch, run, thread, loop, festoon.

stringent adjective **strict**, firm, rigid, rigorous, severe, harsh, tough, tight, exacting, demanding.
- OPPOSITES lax.

strip[1] verb **1 undress**, strip off, take your clothes off, disrobe. **2 dismantle**, disassemble, take to bits/pieces, take apart. **3 empty**, clear, clean out, plunder, rob, burgle, loot, pillage, ransack, sack.

strip[2] noun **(narrow) piece**, band, belt, ribbon, slip, shred, stretch.

strive verb **try (hard)**, attempt, endeavour, aim, make an effort, exert yourself, struggle, do your best, do all you can, do your utmost, labour, work, toil, strain; informal go all out, give it your best shot.

stroke noun **1 blow**, hit, slap, smack, thump, punch. **2 movement**, action, motion. **3 mark**, line. **4 thrombosis**, embolism, seizure; dated apoplexy.
● verb **caress**, fondle, pat, pet, touch, rub, massage, soothe.

stroll verb & noun **walk**, amble, wander, meander, ramble, promenade, saunter; informal mosey.

strong adjective **1 powerful**, sturdy, robust, athletic, fit, tough, rugged, strapping, well built, muscular, brawny, lusty, healthy. **2 forceful**, determined, spirited, assertive, self-assertive, tough, formidable, strong-minded, redoubtable; informal gutsy, feisty. **3 secure**, solid, well built, durable, hard-wearing, heavy-duty, tough, sturdy, well made, long-lasting. **4** a strong supporter **keen**, passionate, fervent, zealous, enthusiastic, eager, dedicated, loyal. **5** strong feelings **intense**, vehement, passionate, ardent, fervent, deep-seated. **6 forceful**, compelling, powerful, convincing, persuasive, sound, valid, cogent, well founded. **7 intense**, bright, brilliant, vivid, vibrant, dazzling, glaring. **8 highly flavoured**, mature, ripe, piquant, tangy, spicy. **9 concentrated**, undiluted. **10 alcoholic**, intoxicating, hard, stiff.
- OPPOSITES weak, gentle, mild.

stronghold noun **1 fortress**, fort, castle, citadel, garrison. **2** a Tory stronghold **bastion**, centre, hotbed.

structure noun **1 building**, edifice, construction, erection. **2 construction**, organization, system, arrangement, framework, form, formation, shape, composition, anatomy, make-up.
● verb **arrange**, organize, design, shape, construct, build.

struggle verb **1 strive**, try hard, endeavour, make every effort, exert yourself, do your best, do your utmost. **2 fight**, battle, grapple, wrestle, scuffle.

● noun **1 striving**, endeavour, effort, exertion, campaign, battle, drive, push. **2 fight**, scuffle, brawl, tussle, fracas; *informal* bust-up, set-to. **3** *a power struggle* **contest**, competition, fight, clash, rivalry, friction, feuding, conflict.

strut verb **swagger**, prance, parade, stride, sweep, flounce; *N. Amer. informal* sashay.

stubborn adjective **1 obstinate**, headstrong, wilful, strong-willed, pig-headed, mulish, inflexible, uncompromising, unbending, unyielding, obdurate, intractable, recalcitrant; *informal* stiff-necked. **2 indelible**, permanent, persistent, tenacious, resistant.

stuck adjective **1 fixed**, fastened, attached, glued, pinned. **2 jammed**, immovable. **3 baffled**, beaten, at a loss; *informal* stumped, up against a brick wall.

student noun **1 undergraduate**, scholar, pupil, schoolchild, schoolboy, schoolgirl. **2 trainee**, apprentice, probationer, novice, learner.

studio noun **workshop**, workroom, atelier.

studious adjective **scholarly**, academic, bookish, intellectual, erudite, learned, donnish; *informal* brainy.

study noun **1 learning**, education, schooling, scholarship, tuition, research. **2 investigation**, enquiry, research, examination, analysis, review, survey. **3 office**, workroom, studio.
● verb **1 work**, revise; *informal* swot, cram, mug up. **2 learn**, read up on, be taught. **3 investigate**, research, inquire into, look into, examine, analyse, survey. **4 scrutinize**, examine, inspect, consider, regard, look at, observe, watch, survey.

stuff noun **1 material**, substance, fabric, matter. **2 items**, articles, objects, goods, belongings, possessions, effects, paraphernalia; *informal* gear, kit, things, bits and pieces, odds and ends; *Brit. informal* clobber.
● verb **1 fill**, pack, pad, upholster. **2 shove**, thrust, push, ram, cram, squeeze, force, jam, pack, pile.

stuffing noun **padding**, wadding, filling, packing.

stuffy adjective **1 airless**, close, musty, stale, unventilated. **2 staid**, sedate, sober, priggish, strait-laced, conformist, conservative, old-fashioned; *informal* straight, starchy, fuddy-duddy.
- OPPOSITES airy.

stumble verb **1 trip**, lose your balance, lose your footing, slip. **2 stagger**, totter, blunder, hobble.
□ **stumble across/on** find, chance on, happen on, light on, come across/upon, discover, unearth, uncover; *informal* dig up.

stump verb *(informal)* **baffle**, perplex, puzzle, confound, defeat, put at a loss; *informal* flummox, fox, throw, floor.

stun verb **1 daze**, stupefy, knock out, lay out. **2 astound**, amaze, astonish, dumbfound, stupefy, stagger, shock, take aback; *informal* flabbergast, knock sideways.

stunning adjective **beautiful**, lovely, glorious, wonderful, marvellous, magnificent, superb, sublime, spectacular, fine, delightful; *informal* fantastic, terrific, tremendous, sensational, heavenly, divine, gorgeous, fabulous, awesome.
- OPPOSITES ordinary.

stunt noun **feat**, exploit, trick.

stunted adjective **small**, undersized, underdeveloped, diminutive.

stupid adjective **1 unintelligent**, dense, obtuse, foolish, idiotic, slow, simple-minded, brainless, mindless; *informal* thick, dim, dumb, dopey, dozy, moronic, cretinous; *Brit. informal* daft. **2 foolish**, silly, senseless, idiotic, ill-advised, ill-considered, unwise, nonsensical, ludicrous, ridiculous, laughable, fatuous, asinine, lunatic; *informal* crazy, half-baked, cockeyed, hare-brained, crackbrained; *Brit. informal* potty.
- OPPOSITES intelligent, sensible.

sturdy adjective **1 strapping**, well built, muscular, strong, hefty, brawny,

S

powerful, solid, burly; *informal* beefy.
2 robust, strong, well built, solid,
stout, tough, durable, long-lasting,
hard-wearing.
- OPPOSITES feeble.

stutter *verb* **stammer**, stumble, falter,
hesitate.

style *noun* **1 manner**, way, technique,
method, methodology, approach,
system, mode. **2 flair**, elegance,
stylishness, chic, taste, grace, poise,
polish, sophistication, suavity, urbanity;
informal class. **3 kind**, type, variety,
sort, design, pattern, genre. **4 fashion**,
trend, vogue, mode.
● *verb* **design**, fashion, tailor, cut.

stylish *adjective* **fashionable**, modern,
up to date, modish, smart, sophisticated, elegant, chic, dapper, dashing;
informal trendy, natty; *N. Amer. informal*
kicky, tony.
- OPPOSITES unfashionable.

subdue *verb* **conquer**, defeat, vanquish,
overcome, overwhelm, crush, beat,
subjugate, suppress.

subdued *adjective* **1 sombre**, downcast,
sad, dejected, depressed, gloomy,
despondent. **2 hushed**, muted, quiet,
low, soft, faint, muffled, subtle, indistinct, dim, unobtrusive.
- OPPOSITES cheerful, loud, bright.

subject *noun* **1 theme**, subject matter,
topic, issue, thesis, question, concern.
2 branch of study, discipline, field.
3 citizen, national, resident, taxpayer,
voter.
● *verb* **expose to**, submit to, treat with,
put through.
□ **subject to** conditional on, contingent on, dependent on.

subjective *adjective* **personal**, individual, emotional, biased, intuitive.
- OPPOSITES objective.

submerge *verb* **1 go under (water)**,
dive, sink, plunge, plummet.
2 immerse, dip, plunge, duck, dunk.
3 *the farmland was submerged* **flood**,
deluge, swamp, overwhelm, inundate.

submission *noun* **1 yielding**,
capitulation, surrender, resignation,

acceptance, consent, compliance,
acquiescence, obedience, subjection,
subservience, servility. **2 proposal**,
suggestion, proposition, tender, presentation. **3 argument**, assertion, contention, statement, claim, allegation.
- OPPOSITES defiance.

submissive *adjective* **compliant**,
yielding, acquiescent, passive, obedient, dutiful, docile, pliant, tractable,
biddable, malleable, meek, unassertive;
informal under someone's thumb.

submit *verb* **1 yield**, give in/way, back
down, cave in, capitulate, surrender,
acquiesce. **2** *he refused to submit to
their authority* **be governed by**, abide
by, comply with, accept, be subject
to, agree to, consent to, conform to.
3 put forward, present, offer, tender,
propose, suggest, enter, put in, send in.
4 contend, assert, argue, state, claim,
allege.
- OPPOSITES resist.

subordinate *adjective* **inferior**, junior,
lower-ranking, lower, supporting.
● *noun* **junior**, assistant, second (in
command), number two, deputy, aide,
underling, minion.
- OPPOSITES superior, senior.

subscribe *verb* **contribute**, donate,
give, pay.
□ **subscribe to** support, endorse,
agree with, accept, go along with.

subscription *noun* **membership fee**,
dues, annual payment, charge.

subsequent *adjective* **following**, ensuing, succeeding, later, future, coming,
to come, next.
- OPPOSITES previous.

subsequently *adverb* **later (on)**, at a
later date, afterwards, in due course,
following this/that, eventually; *formal*
thereafter.

subside *verb* **1 abate**, let up, quieten
down, calm, slacken (off), ease (up),
relent, die down, diminish, decline.
2 recede, ebb, fall, go down, get
lower. **3 sink**, settle, cave in, collapse,
give way.
- OPPOSITES intensify, rise.

S

subsidiary *adjective* **subordinate**, secondary, subservient, supplementary, peripheral, auxiliary.
- OPPOSITES principal.
- ● *noun* **branch**, division, subdivision, derivative, offshoot.

subsidize *verb* **finance**, fund, support, contribute to, give money to, underwrite, sponsor; *informal* shell out for; *N. Amer. informal* bankroll.

subsidy *noun* **finance**, funding, backing, support, grant, sponsorship, allowance, contribution, handout.

substance *noun* **1 material**, compound, matter, stuff. **2 significance**, importance, import, validity, foundation. **3 content**, subject matter, theme, message, essence. **4 wealth**, fortune, riches, affluence, prosperity, money, means.

substantial *adjective* **1 considerable**, real, significant, important, major, valuable, useful, sizeable, appreciable. **2 sturdy**, solid, stout, strong, well built, durable, long-lasting, hard-wearing.
- OPPOSITES insubstantial.

substitute *noun* **replacement**, deputy, relief, proxy, reserve, surrogate, cover, stand-in, understudy; *informal* sub.
- ● *verb* **1 exchange**, swap, use instead of, use as an alternative to, use in place of, replace with. **2** *I found someone to substitute for me* **deputize for**, stand in for, cover for, fill in for, take over from.

subtle *adjective* **1 understated**, muted, subdued, delicate, soft, low-key, toned-down. **2 gentle**, slight, gradual. **3** *a subtle distinction* **fine**, fine-drawn, nice, tenuous.
- OPPOSITES gaudy, crude.

suburban *adjective* **1 residential**, commuter-belt. **2 dull**, boring, uninteresting, conventional, ordinary, unsophisticated, provincial, parochial, bourgeois, middle-class.

subversive *adjective* **disruptive**, troublemaking, insurrectionary, seditious, dissident.
- ● *noun* **troublemaker**, dissident, agitator, renegade.

succeed *verb* **1 triumph**, achieve success, be successful, do well, flourish, thrive; *informal* make it, make the grade. **2 be successful**, turn out well, work (out), be effective; *informal* come off, pay off. **3 replace**, take over from, follow, supersede.
- OPPOSITES fail, precede.

success *noun* **1 victory**, triumph. **2 prosperity**, affluence, wealth, riches, opulence. **3 best-seller**, sell-out, winner, triumph; *informal* hit, smash, sensation.
- OPPOSITES failure.

successful *adjective* **1 prosperous**, affluent, wealthy, rich, famous, eminent, top, respected. **2 flourishing**, thriving, booming, buoyant, profitable, moneymaking, lucrative.

succession *noun* **sequence**, series, progression, chain, string, train, line, run.

successive *adjective* **consecutive**, in a row, sequential, in succession, running; *informal* on the trot.

succinct *adjective* **concise**, short (and sweet), brief, compact, condensed, crisp, laconic, terse, to the point, pithy.
- OPPOSITES verbose.

succulent *adjective* **juicy**, moist, luscious, soft, tender, choice, mouth-watering, appetizing, flavoursome, tasty, delicious; *informal* scrumptious, scrummy.
- OPPOSITES dry.

succumb *verb* **yield**, give in/way, submit, surrender, capitulate, cave in, fall victim.
- OPPOSITES resist.

suck *verb* **sip**, sup, slurp, drink, siphon.

sudden *adjective* **unexpected**, unforeseen, immediate, instantaneous, instant, precipitous, abrupt, rapid, swift, quick.

suddenly *adverb* **all of a sudden**, all at once, abruptly, swiftly, unexpectedly, without warning, out of the blue.
- OPPOSITES gradually.

sue *verb* **take legal action**, go to court, take to court, litigate.

S

suffer verb **1 hurt**, ache, be in pain, be in distress, be upset, be miserable. **2** *he suffers from asthma* **be afflicted by**, be affected by, be troubled with, have. **3 undergo**, experience, be subjected to, receive, sustain, endure, face, meet with.

suffering noun **hardship**, distress, misery, adversity, pain, agony, anguish, trauma, torment, torture, hurt, affliction.
- OPPOSITES pleasure, joy.

sufficient adjective & determiner **enough**, adequate, plenty of, ample.
- OPPOSITES inadequate.

suggest verb **1 propose**, put forward, recommend, advocate, advise. **2 indicate**, lead someone to the belief, give the impression, demonstrate, show. **3 hint**, insinuate, imply, intimate.

suggestion noun **1 proposal**, proposition, recommendation, advice, counsel, hint, tip, clue, idea. **2 hint**, trace, touch, suspicion, ghost, semblance, shadow, glimmer. **3 insinuation**, hint, implication.

suggestive adjective **1 redolent**, evocative, reminiscent, characteristic, indicative, typical. **2 provocative**, titillating, sexual, sexy, risqué, **indecent**, indelicate, improper, unseemly, smutty, dirty.

suit noun **1 outfit**, ensemble. **2 legal action**, lawsuit, (court) case, action, (legal/judicial) proceedings, litigation.
● verb **1 look attractive on**, look good on, become, flatter. **2 be convenient for**, be acceptable to, be suitable for, meet the requirements of; *informal* fit. **3** *recipes suited to students* **be appropriate**, tailor, fashion, adjust, adapt, modify, fit, gear, design.

suitable adjective **1 acceptable**, satisfactory, convenient. **2 appropriate**, apposite, apt, fitting, fit, suited, tailor-made, in keeping, ideal; *informal* right up someone's street. **3 proper**, right, seemly, decent, appropriate, fitting, correct, due.
- OPPOSITES unsuitable.

suite noun **apartment**, flat, rooms.

sullen adjective **surly**, sulky, morose, resentful, moody, grumpy, bad-tempered, unsociable, uncommunicative, unresponsive.
- OPPOSITES cheerful.

sum noun **1 amount**, quantity, price, charge, fee, cost. **2 total**, sum total, grand total, tally, aggregate. **3 entirety**, totality, total, whole, beginning and end. **4 calculation**, problem; (**sums**) arithmetic, mathematics; *Brit. informal* maths; *N. Amer. informal* math.
□ **sum up** summarize, make/give a summary of, encapsulate, put in a nutshell, precis, outline, recapitulate, review, recap.

summarize verb **sum up**, abridge, condense, outline, put in a nutshell, precis.

summary noun **synopsis**, precis, résumé, abstract, outline, rundown, summing-up, overview.

summit noun **1 (mountain) top**, peak, crest, crown, apex, tip, cap, hilltop. **2 meeting**, conference, talk(s).
- OPPOSITES base.

summon verb **1 send for**, call for, request the presence of, ask, invite. **2 convene**, call, assemble, rally, muster, gather together. **3 summons**, subpoena.

sumptuous adjective **lavish**, luxurious, opulent, magnificent, resplendent, gorgeous, splendid; *informal* plush; *Brit. informal* swish.
- OPPOSITES plain.

sun noun **sunshine**, sunlight, daylight, light, warmth.

> **WORD LINKS**
> **solar** relating to the sun

sundry adjective **various**, varied, miscellaneous, assorted, mixed, diverse, diversified, several, numerous, many, manifold, multifarious, multitudinous; *literary* divers.

sunny adjective **1 bright**, sunlit, clear, fine, cloudless. **2 cheerful**, cheery, happy, bright, merry, bubbly, jolly,

good-natured, good-tempered, optimistic, upbeat.
- OPPOSITES dull, cloudy.

sunrise noun **dawn**, crack of dawn, daybreak, break of day, first light, early morning; N. Amer. sunup.

sunset noun **nightfall**, twilight, dusk, evening; N. Amer. sundown.

superb adjective **excellent**, first-class, outstanding, marvellous, wonderful, splendid, admirable, fine, exceptional, glorious; informal great, fantastic, fabulous, terrific, super, awesome, ace; Brit. informal brilliant, smashing.
- OPPOSITES poor, unimpressive.

supercilious adjective **arrogant**, haughty, conceited, disdainful, overbearing, pompous, condescending, superior, patronizing, imperious, proud, snobbish, smug, scornful, sneering; informal high and mighty, snooty, stuck-up.

superficial adjective **1 surface**, exterior, external, outer, slight. **2 cursory**, perfunctory, casual, sketchy, desultory, token, slapdash, offhand, rushed, hasty, hurried. **3 apparent**, seeming, outward, ostensible, cosmetic, slight. **4 facile**, shallow, flippant, empty-headed, trivial, frivolous, silly, inane.
- OPPOSITES deep, thorough.

superfluous adjective **surplus**, redundant, unneeded, unnecessary, excess, extra, (to) spare, remaining, unused, left over, waste.
- OPPOSITES necessary.

superhuman adjective **extraordinary**, phenomenal, prodigious, stupendous, exceptional, immense, heroic, Herculean.

superior adjective **1 senior**, higher-ranking, higher. **2 better**, finer, higher quality, top-quality, choice, select, prime, excellent. **3 condescending**, supercilious, patronizing, haughty, disdainful, lordly, snobbish; informal high and mighty, snooty, toffee-nosed.
- OPPOSITES junior, inferior.
● noun **manager**, chief, supervisor,

senior, controller, foreman; informal boss.
- OPPOSITES subordinate.

superiority noun **supremacy**, advantage, lead, dominance, primacy, ascendancy, eminence.

supernatural adjective **1 paranormal**, psychic, magic, magical, occult, mystic, mystical. **2 ghostly**, phantom, spectral, other-worldly, unearthly.

supersede verb **replace**, take the place of, take over from, succeed, supplant.

supervise verb **oversee**, be in charge of, superintend, preside over, direct, manage, run, look after, be responsible for, govern, keep an eye on, observe, monitor, mind.

supervisor noun **manager**, director, overseer, controller, superintendent, governor, chief, head, foreman; informal boss; Brit. informal gaffer.

supple adjective **1 lithe**, lissom, willowy, flexible, agile, acrobatic, nimble. **2 pliable**, flexible, soft, bendy, workable, stretchy, springy.
- OPPOSITES stiff, rigid.

supplement noun **1 extra**, add-on, accessory, adjunct. **2 surcharge**, addition, increase, increment. **3 appendix**, addendum, postscript, addition, coda. **4 pull-out**, insert.
● verb **add to**, augment, increase, boost, swell, amplify, enlarge, top up.

supplementary adjective **additional**, supplemental, extra, more, further, add-on, subsidiary, auxiliary, ancillary.

supply verb **1 provide**, give, furnish, equip, contribute, donate, grant, confer, dispense. **2 satisfy**, meet, fulfil, cater for.
● noun **1 stock**, store, reserve, reservoir, stockpile, hoard, cache, fund, bank. **2** we're running out of supplies **provisions**, stores, rations, food, necessities.

support verb **1 hold up**, bear, carry, prop up, keep up, brace, shore up, underpin, buttress, reinforce. **2 provide for**, maintain, sustain, keep,

S

take care of, look after. **3 stand by**, defend, back, stand/stick up for, take someone's side, side with. **4 back up**, substantiate, bear out, corroborate, confirm, verify. **5 help**, aid, assist, contribute to, back, subsidize, fund, finance; *N. Amer. informal* bankroll. **6 back**, champion, favour, be in favour of, advocate, encourage, promote, endorse, espouse.
- OPPOSITES contradict, oppose.
● *noun* **1 pillar**, post, prop, upright, brace, buttress, foundation, underpinning. **2 encouragement**, friendship, backing, endorsement, help, assistance, comfort. **3 contributions**, donations, money, subsidy, funding, funds, finance, capital.

supporter *noun* **1 advocate**, backer, adherent, promoter, champion, defender, upholder, campaigner. **2 contributor**, donor, benefactor, sponsor, backer, patron, subscriber, well-wisher. **3 fan**, follower, enthusiast, devotee, admirer.

supportive *adjective* **encouraging**, caring, sympathetic, reassuring, understanding, concerned, helpful.

suppose *verb* **1 assume**, presume, surmise, expect, imagine, dare say, take it, take as read, suspect, guess, conjecture. **2 hypothesize**, postulate, posit.

supposed *adjective* **alleged**, reputed, rumoured, claimed, purported.

supposition *noun* **belief**, conjecture, speculation, assumption, presumption, inference, theory, hypothesis, feeling, idea, notion, guesswork.

suppress *verb* **1 subdue**, crush, quell, quash, squash, stamp out, crack down on, clamp down on, put an end to. **2 restrain**, repress, hold back, control, stifle, smother, check, keep in check, curb, contain, bottle up. **3 censor**, redact, keep secret, conceal, hide, hush up, gag, withhold, cover up, stifle.
- OPPOSITES encourage, reveal.

supremacy *noun* **control**, power, rule, sovereignty, dominance, superiority, predominance, primacy, dominion,

authority, mastery, ascendancy.

supreme *adjective* **1 highest**, chief, head, top, foremost, principal, superior, premier, first, prime. **2 extraordinary**, remarkable, phenomenal, exceptional, outstanding, incomparable, unparalleled. **3** *the supreme sacrifice* **ultimate**, greatest, highest, extreme, final, last.
- OPPOSITES subordinate.

sure *adjective* **1 certain**, positive, convinced, confident, definite, satisfied, persuaded, assured, free from doubt. **2 guaranteed**, unfailing, infallible, unerring, foolproof, certain, reliable, dependable, trustworthy, trusty; *informal* sure-fire.
- OPPOSITES uncertain, unlikely.

surface *noun* **1 outside**, exterior, top, side, finish. **2 outward appearance**, facade, veneer.
- OPPOSITES inside, interior.
● *verb* **1 come to the surface**, come up, rise. **2 emerge**, arise, appear, come to light, crop up, materialize, spring up.

surge *noun* **1 gush**, rush, outpouring, stream, flow. **2** *a surge in demand* **increase**, rise, growth, upswing, upsurge, escalation, leap.
● *verb* **1 gush**, rush, stream, flow, burst, pour, cascade, spill, sweep, roll. **2 increase**, rise, grow, leap.

surly *adjective* **sullen**, sulky, moody, morose, unfriendly, unpleasant, scowling, unsmiling, bad-tempered, grumpy, gruff, churlish, ill-humoured.
- OPPOSITES friendly.

surmise *verb* **guess**, conjecture, suspect, deduce, infer, conclude, theorize, speculate, assume, presume, suppose, understand, gather.

surmount *verb* **overcome**, prevail over, triumph over, beat, vanquish, conquer, get the better of.

surpass *verb* **excel**, exceed, transcend, outdo, outshine, outstrip, outclass, eclipse, improve on, top, trump, cap, beat, better, outperform.

surplus *noun* **excess**, surfeit, superfluity, oversupply, glut, remainder, residue, remains, leftovers.

- OPPOSITES dearth.

● *adjective* **excess**, leftover, unused, remaining, extra, additional, spare, superfluous, redundant, unwanted, unneeded, dispensable.
- OPPOSITES insufficient.

surprise *noun* **1 astonishment**, amazement, wonder, bewilderment, disbelief. **2 shock**, bolt from the blue, bombshell, revelation, rude awakening, eye-opener.

● *verb* **1 astonish**, amaze, startle, astound, stun, stagger, shock, take aback; *informal* bowl over, floor, flabbergast; *Brit. informal* knock for six. **2 take by surprise**, catch unawares, catch off guard, catch red-handed.

surprised *adjective* **astonished**, amazed, astounded, startled, stunned, staggered, nonplussed, shocked, taken aback, dumbfounded, speechless, thunderstruck; *informal* bowled over, flabbergasted.

surprising *adjective* **unexpected**, unforeseen, astonishing, amazing, startling, astounding, staggering, incredible, extraordinary.

surrender *verb* **1 give up**, give yourself up, give in, cave in, capitulate, concede (defeat), submit, lay down your arms/weapons. **2 give up**, relinquish, renounce, cede, abdicate, forfeit, sacrifice, hand over, turn over, yield.
- OPPOSITES resist.

● *noun* **1 capitulation**, submission, yielding. **2 relinquishing**, renunciation, abdication, resignation.

surreptitious *adjective* **secret**, secretive, stealthy, clandestine, sneaky, sly, furtive, covert; *Military* black.
- OPPOSITES blatant.

surround *verb* **encircle**, enclose, encompass, ring, hem in, confine, cut off, besiege, trap.

surrounding *adjective* **neighbouring**, enclosing, nearby, near, local, adjoining, adjacent.

surroundings *plural noun* **environment**, setting, background, backdrop, vicinity, locality, habitat.

surveillance *noun* **observation**, scrutiny, watch, view, inspection, supervision, spying, espionage.

survey *verb* **1 look at**, look over, view, contemplate, regard, gaze at, stare at, eye, scrutinize, examine, inspect, scan, study, assess, appraise, take stock of; *informal* size up. **2 interview**, question, canvass, poll, investigate, research.

● *noun* **1 study**, review, overview, examination, inspection, assessment, appraisal. **2 poll**, investigation, enquiry, study, probe, questionnaire, census, research.

survive *verb* **1 remain alive**, live, sustain yourself, pull through, hold out, make it. **2 continue**, remain, persist, endure, live on, persevere, abide, go on, carry on. **3 outlive**, outlast, remain alive after.

susceptible *adjective* **impressionable**, credulous, gullible, innocent, ingenuous, naive, easily led, defenceless, vulnerable.
□ **susceptible to** liable to, prone to, subject to, inclined to, predisposed to, open to, vulnerable to, an easy target for.

suspect *verb* **1 have a suspicion**, have a feeling, feel, be inclined to think, fancy, reckon, guess, conjecture, surmise, have a hunch, fear. **2 doubt**, distrust, mistrust, have misgivings about, have qualms about, be suspicious of, be sceptical about.

● *adjective* **suspicious**, dubious, doubtful, untrustworthy; *informal* fishy, funny; *Brit. informal* dodgy.

suspend *verb* **1 adjourn**, interrupt, break off, cut short, discontinue; *N. Amer.* table. **2 exclude**, debar, remove, expel, eject, rusticate. **3 hang**, sling, string, swing, dangle.

suspense *noun* **tension**, uncertainty, doubt, anticipation, excitement, anxiety, strain.

suspicion *noun* **1 intuition**, feeling, impression, inkling, hunch, fancy, notion, idea, theory, premonition; *informal* gut feeling. **2 misgiving**,

doubt, qualm, reservation, hesitation, scepticism.
- OPPOSITES trust.

suspicious adjective **1 doubtful**, unsure, dubious, wary, chary, sceptical, mistrustful. **2 suspect**, dubious, unsavoury, disreputable; informal shifty, shady; Brit. informal dodgy. **3** suspicious circumstances **strange**, odd, questionable, irregular, funny, doubtful, mysterious; informal fishy.
- OPPOSITES trusting, innocent.

sustain verb **1 comfort**, help, assist, encourage, support, give strength to, buoy up. **2 continue**, carry on, keep up, keep alive, maintain, preserve. **3 nourish**, feed, nurture, keep alive. **4 suffer**, experience, undergo, receive. **5 confirm**, corroborate, substantiate, bear out, prove, authenticate, back up, uphold.

sustained adjective **continuous**, ongoing, steady, continual, constant, prolonged, persistent, non-stop, perpetual, relentless.
- OPPOSITES sporadic.

sustenance noun **nourishment**, food, nutrition, provisions, rations; informal grub, chow; Brit. informal scoff; literary viands; dated victuals.

swagger verb **strut**, parade, stride, prance; informal sashay.

swallow verb **eat**, drink, gulp down, consume, devour, put away, quaff, slug; informal swig, swill, down; Brit. informal scoff.

swamp noun **marsh**, bog, fen, quagmire, morass.
● verb **1 flood**, inundate, deluge, fill. **2** fans swamped her website with messages **overwhelm**, engulf, snow under, overload, inundate, deluge.

swap verb **exchange**, trade, barter, switch, change, replace.

swarm noun **1 hive**, flock. **2 crowd**, horde, mob, throng, mass, army, herd, pack.
● verb **flock**, crowd, throng, surge, stream.

swathe verb **wrap**, envelop, bandage, cover, shroud, drape, wind, enfold.

sway verb **1 swing**, shake, undulate, move to and fro. **2 stagger**, wobble, rock, lurch, reel, roll. **3 influence**, affect, manipulate, bend, mould.
● noun **1 swing**, roll, shake, undulation. **2 power**, rule, government, sovereignty, dominion, control, jurisdiction, authority.

swear verb **1 promise**, vow, pledge, give your word, undertake, guarantee. **2 insist**, declare, proclaim, assert, maintain, emphasize, stress. **3 curse**, blaspheme, use bad language; informal cuss, eff and blind.

swearing noun **bad language**, cursing, blaspheming, obscenities, expletives, swear words; informal effing and blinding, four-letter words.

sweat verb **1 perspire**, drip with sweat. **2 work**, labour, toil, slog, slave, work your fingers to the bone.

WORD LINKS
sudorific causing sweating

sweep verb **brush**, clean (up), clear (up).

sweeping adjective **1 extensive**, wide-ranging, broad, comprehensive, far-reaching, thorough, radical. **2 wholesale**, blanket, general, unqualified, indiscriminate, oversimplified.
- OPPOSITES limited.

sweet adjective **1 sugary**, sweetened, sugared, honeyed, syrupy, sickly, cloying. **2 fragrant**, aromatic, perfumed. **3 musical**, melodious, dulcet, tuneful, soft, harmonious, silvery, mellifluous. **4 likeable**, appealing, engaging, amiable, pleasant, agreeable, kind, nice, thoughtful, considerate, delightful, lovely. **5 cute**, lovable, adorable, endearing, charming, winsome.
- OPPOSITES sour, savoury, disagreeable.
● noun (Brit.) **1 confectionery**, bonbon; N. Amer. candy; old use sweetmeat. **2 dessert**, pudding; Brit. informal afters, pud.

sweeten verb **1 make sweet**, add sugar to, sugar. **2 mollify**, placate, soothe, soften up, pacify, appease, win over.

sweetheart noun **lover**, love, girlfriend, boyfriend, beloved, beau; informal steady, squeeze; literary swain.

swell verb **1 expand**, bulge, distend, inflate, dilate, bloat, blow up, puff up, balloon, fatten, fill out. **2 grow**, enlarge, increase, expand, rise, escalate, multiply, proliferate, snowball, mushroom.
- OPPOSITES shrink, decrease.

swelling noun **bump**, lump, bulge, protuberance, protrusion, distension.

swerve verb **veer**, deviate, diverge, weave, zigzag, change direction; Sailing tack.

swift adjective **fast**, rapid, quick, speedy, expeditious, prompt, brisk, immediate, instant, hasty, hurried, sudden, abrupt.
- OPPOSITES slow, leisurely.

swindle verb **defraud**, cheat, trick, dupe, deceive, fool, hoax, hoodwink, bamboozle; informal fleece, do, con, diddle, rip off, take for a ride, pull a fast one on, put one over on; N. Amer. informal stiff.
● noun **fraud**, trick, deception, cheat, racket, sharp practice; informal con, fiddle, diddle, rip-off.

swindler noun **fraudster**, fraud, (confidence) trickster, cheat, rogue, charlatan, impostor, hoaxer; informal con man, shark, hustler, phoney, crook.

swing verb **1 sway**, move back and forth, oscillate, wave, rock, swivel, pivot, turn, rotate. **2 brandish**, wave, flourish, wield. **3 curve**, bend, veer, turn, bear, wind, twist, deviate, slew. **4 change**, fluctuate, waver, see-saw.
● noun **1 oscillation**, sway, wave. **2 change**, move, turnaround, turnabout, reversal, fluctuation, variation.

swirl verb **whirl**, eddy, billow, spiral, twist, twirl, circulate, revolve, spin.

switch noun **1 button**, lever, control. **2 change**, move, shift, transition, transformation, reversal, turnaround, rowback, U-turn, changeover, transfer, conversion.

● verb **1 change**, shift; informal chop and change. **2 exchange**, swap, interchange, change round, rotate.

swollen adjective **distended**, bulging, inflated, dilated, bloated, puffed up, puffy, tumescent, inflamed.

swoop verb **dive**, descend, pounce, sweep down, plunge, drop down.

sycophant noun **toady**, creep, flatterer; informal bootlicker, yes-man.

sycophantic adjective **obsequious**, servile, subservient, grovelling, toadying, fawning, ingratiating, unctuous; informal smarmy, bootlicking.

symbol noun **1 representation**, token, sign, emblem, figure, image, metaphor, allegory. **2 sign**, character, mark, letter. **3 logo**, emblem, badge, stamp, trademark, crest, insignia, coat of arms, seal, device, monogram, hallmark, motif.

symbolic adjective **1 emblematic**, representative, typical, characteristic, symptomatic. **2 figurative**, metaphorical, allegorical.
- OPPOSITES literal.

symbolize verb **represent**, stand for, be a sign of, denote, signify, mean, indicate, convey, express, embody, epitomize, encapsulate, personify.

symmetrical adjective **regular**, uniform, consistent, even, equal, balanced, proportional.

sympathetic adjective **1 compassionate**, caring, concerned, understanding, sensitive, supportive, empathetic, kind-hearted, warm-hearted. **2 likeable**, pleasant, agreeable, congenial, companionable.
- OPPOSITES unsympathetic.

sympathize verb **commiserate**, show concern, offer condolences; (**sympathize with**) pity, feel sorry for, feel for, identify with, understand, relate to.

sympathy noun **compassion**, care, concern, commiseration, pity, condolence.
- OPPOSITES indifference.

symptom noun **indication**, indicator, manifestation, sign, mark, feature, trait, clue, hint, warning, evidence, proof.

S

symptomatic *adjective* **indicative**, characteristic, suggestive, typical, representative, symbolic.

synthesis *noun* **combination**, union, amalgam, blend, mixture, compound, fusion, composite, alloy.

synthetic *adjective* **artificial**, fake, imitation, mock, simulated, man-made, manufactured; *informal* pretend.
- OPPOSITES natural.

system *noun* **1 structure**, organization, arrangement, order, network; *informal* set-up. **2 method**, methodology, modus operandi, technique, procedure, means, way, scheme, plan, policy, programme, formula, solution, routine. **3 (the system) the establishment**, the administration, the authorities, the powers that be, bureaucracy, officialdom.

systematic *adjective* **structured**, methodical, organized, orderly, planned, regular, routine, standardized, standard, logical, coherent, consistent.
- OPPOSITES disorganized.

Tt

table *noun* **chart**, diagram, figure, graphic, graph, plan, list.

tablet *noun* **1 slab**, stone, panel, plaque, plate, sign. **2 pill**, capsule, lozenge, pastille, drop. **3 bar**, cake, slab, brick, block.

taboo *noun* **prohibition**, proscription, veto, ban, interdict.
● *adjective* **forbidden**, prohibited, vetoed, banned, proscribed, outlawed, off limits, beyond the pale, unmentionable, unspeakable; *informal* no go.
- OPPOSITES acceptable.

tacit *adjective* **implicit**, understood, implied, inferred, hinted, suggested, unspoken, unstated, unsaid, unexpressed, unvoiced, taken for granted, taken as read.
- OPPOSITES explicit.

tack *noun* **pin**, nail, staple, rivet.
● *verb* **pin**, nail, staple, fix, fasten, attach, secure.
□ **tack something on** add, append, attach, join on, tag on.

tackle *noun* **1 equipment**, apparatus, kit, implements, paraphernalia; *informal* gear, clobber. **2 interception**, challenge, block, attack.
● *verb* **1 deal with**, take care of, attend to, see to, handle, manage, get to grips with, address. **2 confront**, face up to, take on, challenge, attack, grab, struggle with, intercept, block, stop, bring down, floor, fell, rugby-tackle; *informal* have a go at.

tacky[1] *adjective* **sticky**, wet, gluey, viscous, gummy; *informal* gooey.

tacky[2] *adjective* **tawdry**, tasteless, kitsch, vulgar, crude, garish, gaudy, trashy, cheap; *informal* cheesy; *Brit. informal* naff.
- OPPOSITES tasteful.

tactful *adjective* **diplomatic**, discreet, considerate, sensitive, understanding, thoughtful, delicate, judicious, subtle.

tactic *noun* **1 scheme**, plan, manoeuvre, method, trick, ploy. **2 (tactics) strategy**, policy, campaign, game plan, planning, manoeuvres, logistics.

tactical *adjective* **calculated**, planned, strategic, prudent, politic, diplomatic, judicious, shrewd.

tactless *adjective* **insensitive**, inconsiderate, thoughtless, indelicate, undiplomatic, indiscreet, unsubtle, inept, gauche, blunt.

tag *noun* **label**, ticket, badge, mark, tab, sticker, docket.
● *verb* **label**, mark, ticket, identify, flag, indicate.

tail *noun* **rear**, end, back, extremity, bottom.
- OPPOSITES head, front.
● *verb (informal)* **follow**, shadow, stalk, trail, track, keep under surveillance.

tailor *noun* **outfitter**, couturier, costumier, dressmaker, fashion designer.
● *verb* **customize**, adapt, adjust, modify, change, convert, alter, mould, gear, fit, shape, tune.

> **WORD LINKS**
> **sartorial** relating to tailoring

taint *verb* **1 contaminate**, pollute, adulterate, infect, blight, spoil, soil, ruin. **2 tarnish**, sully, blacken, stain, blot, damage.

take *verb* **1** *she took his hand* **grasp**, get hold of, grip, clasp, clutch, grab. **2** *he took an envelope from his pocket* **remove**, pull, draw, withdraw, extract, fish. **3 capture**, seize, catch, arrest, apprehend, take into custody, carry off, abduct. **4 steal**, remove, appropriate, make off with, pilfer, purloin; *informal* filch, swipe, snaffle; *Brit. informal* pinch, nick. **5** *take four from the total* **subtract**, deduct, remove, discount; *informal*

knock off, minus. **6 occupy**, use, utilize, fill, hold, reserve, engage; *informal* bag. **7 write**, note (down), jot (down), scribble, scrawl, record, register, document, minute. **8 bring**, carry, bear, transport, convey, move, transfer, shift, ferry; *informal* cart, tote. **9 escort**, accompany, help, assist, show, lead, guide, see, usher, convey. **10 travel on/by**, journey on, go via, use. **11** *I can't take much more* **endure**, bear, tolerate, stand, put up with, abide, stomach, accept, allow, countenance, support, shoulder; *formal* brook.
- OPPOSITES give, add.
□ **take after** resemble, look like, remind someone of. **take apart** dismantle, take to pieces, disassemble, break up. **take in 1** deceive, delude, hoodwink, mislead, trick, dupe, fool, cheat, defraud, swindle; *informal* con. **2** comprehend, understand, grasp, follow, absorb; *informal* get. **take off 1** become airborne, take to the air, leave the ground, lift off, blast off. **2** succeed, do well, become popular, catch on, prosper, flourish. **take on 1** compete against, oppose, challenge, confront, face. **2** engage, hire, employ, sign up. **3** undertake, accept, assume, shoulder, acquire. **take over** assume control of, take charge of, take command of, seize, hijack, commandeer. **take up 1** begin, start, commence, engage in, practise. **2** consume, fill, absorb, use, occupy. **3** resume, recommence, restart, carry on, continue, pick up, return to. **4** accept, say yes to, agree to, adopt.

takeover *noun* **buyout**, purchase, acquisition, amalgamation, merger.

takings *plural noun* **proceeds**, returns, receipts, earnings, winnings, pickings, spoils, profit, gain, income, revenue.

tale *noun* **story**, narrative, anecdote, account, history, legend, fable, myth, saga; *informal* yarn.

talent *noun* **flair**, aptitude, facility, gift, knack, technique, bent, ability, forte, genius, brilliance.

talented *adjective* **gifted**, skilful, accomplished, brilliant, expert, consummate, able, proficient; *informal* ace.
- OPPOSITES inept.

talk *verb* **1 speak**, chat, chatter, gossip, jabber, prattle; *informal* yak; *Brit. informal* natter, rabbit. **2** *they were able to talk in peace* **converse**, communicate, speak (to one another), confer, consult, negotiate, parley; *informal* have a confab.
● *noun* **1 chatter**, gossip, prattle, jabbering; *informal* yak; *Brit. informal* nattering. **2 conversation**, chat, discussion, tête-à-tête, heart-to-heart, dialogue; *informal* confab, gossip; *Austral. informal* convo. **3** (**talks**) **negotiations**, discussions, conference, summit, meeting, consultation, dialogue. **4 lecture**, speech, address, discourse, oration, presentation, report, sermon.

talkative *adjective* **chatty**, garrulous, loquacious, voluble, communicative; *informal* mouthy.
- OPPOSITES taciturn.

tall *adjective* **1** *a tall man* **big**, large, huge, giant, lanky, gangling. **2** *tall buildings* **high**, big, lofty, towering, sky-high, gigantic, colossal.
- OPPOSITES short, low.

tally *noun* **running total**, count, record, reckoning, register, account, roll.
● *verb* **correspond**, agree, accord, concur, coincide, match, fit, be consistent, conform, equate, parallel; *informal* square.
- OPPOSITES disagree.

tame *adjective* **1 domesticated**, docile, trained, gentle, mild, pet. **2 unexciting**, uninteresting, uninspiring, uninspired, dull, bland, flat, pedestrian, humdrum, boring.
- OPPOSITES wild.
● *verb* **1 domesticate**, break in, train. **2** *she learned to tame her emotions* **subdue**, curb, control, calm, master, moderate, discipline, overcome.

tamper *verb* **interfere**, meddle, monkey around, tinker, fiddle; *informal* mess about; *Brit. informal* muck about.

tangible *adjective* **real**, actual, physical, solid, palpable, material, substantial, concrete, visible, definite, perceptible, discernible.
- OPPOSITES abstract, theoretical.

tangle *verb* **entangle**, snarl, catch, entwine, twist, knot, mat.
- ● *noun* **1 snarl**, mass, knot, mesh. **2 muddle**, jumble, mix-up, confusion, shambles.

tank *noun* **container**, receptacle, vat, cistern, repository, reservoir, basin.

tantalize *verb* **tease**, torment, torture, tempt, entice, lure, beguile, excite, fascinate, titillate, intrigue.

tantrum *noun* **fit of temper**, fit of rage, outburst, pet, paroxysm, frenzy; *informal* paddy, wobbly; *N. Amer. informal* hissy fit.

tap[1] *noun* **valve**, stopcock; *N. Amer.* faucet, spigot.
- ● *verb* **1 bug**, wiretap, monitor, eavesdrop on. **2 draw on**, exploit, milk, mine, use, utilize, turn to account.

tap[2] *verb* **knock**, rap, strike, beat, pat, drum.

tape *noun* **1 binding**, ribbon, string, braid, band. **2 cassette**, recording, video.
- ● *verb* **1 bind**, stick, fix, fasten, secure, attach. **2 record**, tape-record, video.

taper *verb* **narrow**, thin (out), come to a point, attenuate.
- OPPOSITES thicken.
- □ **taper off** decrease, lessen, dwindle, diminish, reduce, decline, die down, peter out, wane, ebb, slacken (off), fall off, let up, thin out.

target *noun* **1 objective**, goal, aim, mark, end, plan, intention, aspiration, ambition. **2 victim**, butt, recipient, focus, object, subject.
- ● *verb* **1 pick out**, single out, earmark, fix on, attack, aim at, fire at. **2** *a product targeted at women* **aim**, direct, level, intend, focus.

tariff *noun* **1 tax**, duty, toll, excise, levy, charge, rate, fee. **2 price list**, menu.

tarnish *verb* **1 discolour**, rust, oxidize, corrode, stain, dull, blacken. **2 sully**, blacken, stain, blemish, ruin, disgrace, mar, damage, harm, drag through the mud.
- ● *noun* **discoloration**, oxidation, rust, verdigris.

tart[1] *noun* **pastry**, flan, quiche, tartlet, vol-au-vent, pie.

tart[2] *(informal) verb* **1 dress up**, smarten up; *informal* doll yourself up, titivate yourself. **2 decorate**, renovate, refurbish, redecorate, smarten up; *informal* do up, fix up.

tart[3] *adjective* **1 sour**, sharp, acidic, zesty, tangy, piquant. **2 scathing**, sharp, biting, cutting, sarcastic, hurtful, spiteful.
- OPPOSITES sweet, kind.

task *noun* **job**, duty, chore, charge, assignment, detail, mission, engagement, occupation, undertaking, exercise.

taste *noun* **1 flavour**, savour, relish, tang, smack. **2 mouthful**, morsel, drop, bit, sip, nip, touch, soupçon, dash. **3** *a taste for adventure* **liking**, love, fondness, fancy, desire, penchant, partiality, inclination, appetite, stomach, palate, thirst, hunger. **4** *his first taste of opera* **experience**, impression, exposure to, contact with, involvement with. **5 judgement**, discrimination, discernment, refinement, elegance, grace, style. **6 sensitivity**, decorum, propriety, etiquette, nicety, discretion.
- ● *verb* **1** *I tasted the wine* **sample**, test, try, savour. **2** *he could taste blood* **perceive**, discern, make out, distinguish.

> **WORD LINKS**
> **gustatory** relating to the sense of taste

tasteful *adjective* **stylish**, refined, cultured, elegant, smart, chic, exquisite.
- OPPOSITES tasteless.

tasteless *adjective* **1 flavourless**, bland, insipid, unappetizing, watery, weak, thin. **2 vulgar**, crude, tawdry, garish, gaudy, loud, trashy, showy, ostentatious, cheap;

informal flash, tacky, kitsch; *Brit. informal* naff. **3 crude**, indelicate, uncouth, crass, tactless, undiplomatic, indiscreet, inappropriate, offensive.
- OPPOSITES tasty, tasteful.

tasty *adjective* **delicious**, palatable, luscious, mouth-watering, delectable, appetizing, tempting; *informal* yummy, scrumptious, moreish.
- OPPOSITES bland.

taunt *noun* **jeer**, jibe, sneer, insult, barb; *informal* dig, put-down; (**taunts**) teasing, provocation, goading, derision, mockery.
● *verb* **jeer at**, sneer at, scoff at, poke fun at, make fun of, get at, insult, tease, torment, ridicule, deride, mock; *N. Amer.* ride; *informal* rib, needle.

taut *adjective* **tight**, stretched, rigid, flexed, tensed.
- OPPOSITES slack.

tawdry *adjective* **gaudy**, flashy, showy, garish, loud, tasteless, vulgar, trashy, cheapjack, shoddy, shabby, gimcrack; *informal* rubbishy, tacky, kitsch.
- OPPOSITES tasteful.

tax *noun* **duty**, excise, customs, dues, levy, tariff, toll, tithe, charge.
● *verb* **strain**, stretch, overburden, overload, overwhelm, try, wear out, exhaust, sap, drain, weary, weaken.

> **WORD LINKS**
> **fiscal** relating to tax

teach *verb* **educate**, instruct, school, tutor, inform, coach, train, drill.

> **WORD LINKS**
> **educational** relating to teaching

teacher *noun* **educator**, tutor, instructor, schoolteacher, master, mistress, schoolmarm, governess, coach, trainer, lecturer, professor, don, guide, mentor, guru.

team *noun* **group**, squad, company, party, crew, troupe, band, side, line-up; *informal* bunch, gang.
● *verb* *ankle boots teamed with jeans* **match**, coordinate, complement, pair up.

□ **team up** join (forces), collaborate, work together, unite, combine, cooperate, link, ally, associate, club together.

tear *verb* **1 rip**, split, slit, pull apart, pull to pieces, shred, rupture, sever. **2 lacerate**, cut (open), gash, slash, scratch, hack, pierce, stab. **3 snatch**, grab, seize, rip, wrench, wrest, pull, pluck; *informal* yank.
● *noun* **rip**, hole, split, slash, slit, ladder, snag.

tearful *adjective* **1 close to tears**, emotional, upset, distressed, sad, unhappy, in tears, crying, weeping, sobbing, snivelling; *informal* weepy, blubbing; *formal* lachrymose. **2 emotional**, upsetting, distressing, sad, heartbreaking, sorrowful, poignant, moving, touching, tear-jerking.
- OPPOSITES cheerful.

tease *verb* **make fun of**, laugh at, deride, mock, ridicule, guy, make a monkey (out) of, taunt, bait, goad, pick on; *informal* take the mickey out of, rag, have on, pull someone's leg; *Brit. informal* wind up.

technical *adjective* **1 practical**, scientific, technological, high-tech. **2 specialist**, specialized, scientific, complex, complicated, esoteric.

technique *noun* **1 method**, approach, procedure, system, way, manner, means, strategy, solution. **2 skill**, ability, proficiency, expertise, artistry, craftsmanship, adroitness, deftness, dexterity.

tedious *adjective* **boring**, dull, monotonous, repetitive, unrelieved, unvaried, uneventful, lifeless, uninteresting, unexciting, uninspiring, lacklustre, dreary, soul-destroying; *informal* deadly; *N. Amer. informal* dullsville.
- OPPOSITES exciting.

teenager *noun* **adolescent**, youth, young person, minor, juvenile; *informal* teen.

teetotal *adjective* **abstinent**, abstemious, sober, dry; *informal* on the wagon.

telephone *noun* **phone**, handset, receiver; *informal* blower; *N. Amer.*

informal horn.

● *verb* **phone**, call, dial; *Brit.* ring (up); *informal* call up, give someone a buzz, get on the blower to; *Brit. informal* give someone a bell, give someone a tinkle; *N. Amer. informal* get someone on the horn.

television *noun* **TV**; *informal* the small screen; *Brit. informal* telly, the box; *N. Amer. informal* the tube.

tell *verb* **1** *why didn't you tell me?* **inform**, notify, let know, make aware, acquaint with, advise, put in the picture, brief, fill in, alert, warn; *informal* clue in/up. **2** *she told the story slowly* **relate**, recount, narrate, report, recite, describe, sketch. **3** **instruct**, order, command, direct, charge, enjoin, call on, require. **4** *it was hard to tell what he meant* **ascertain**, determine, work out, make out, deduce, discern, perceive, see, identify, recognize, understand, comprehend; *informal* figure out; *Brit. informal* suss out. **5** *he couldn't tell one from the other* **distinguish**, differentiate, discriminate. **6** *the strain began to tell on him* **take its toll**, leave its mark, affect.

telling *adjective* **revealing**, significant, weighty, important, meaningful, influential, striking, potent, powerful, compelling.
- OPPOSITES insignificant.

temper *noun* **1** *he walked out in a temper* **rage**, fury, fit of pique, tantrum, bad mood, pet, sulk, huff; *Brit. informal* strop, paddy; *N. Amer. informal* hissy fit. **2** *a display of temper* **anger**, fury, rage, annoyance, irritation, pique, petulance; *Brit. informal* stroppiness. **3** *she struggled to keep her temper* **composure**, self-control, self-possession, calm, good humour; *informal* cool.
● *verb* *their idealism is tempered with realism* **moderate**, modify, modulate, mitigate, alleviate, reduce, weaken, lighten, soften.
□ **lose your temper** get angry, fly into a rage, erupt; *informal* go mad, go bananas, have a fit, see red, fly off the handle, blow your top, hit the roof, lose your rag; *Brit. informal* go spare, throw a wobbly.

temperament *noun* **character**, nature, disposition, personality, make-up, constitution, temper.

temperamental *adjective* **volatile**, excitable, emotional, unpredictable, hot-headed, quick-tempered, impatient, touchy, moody, sensitive, highly strung.
- OPPOSITES placid.

tempestuous *adjective* **turbulent**, wild, stormy, violent, emotional, passionate, impassioned, fiery, intense, uncontrolled, unrestrained.
- OPPOSITES calm.

temple *noun* **place of worship**, shrine, sanctuary, church, cathedral, mosque, synagogue, mandir, gurdwara.

temporarily *adverb* **1** **for the time being**, for the moment, for now, for the present, provisionally, pro tem, in the interim. **2** **briefly**, for a short time, momentarily, fleetingly.
- OPPOSITES permanently.

temporary *adjective* **1** **provisional**, short-term, interim, makeshift, stopgap, acting, fill-in, stand-in, caretaker. **2** **brief**, short-lived, momentary, fleeting, passing, ephemeral.
- OPPOSITES permanent, lasting.

tempt *verb* **entice**, persuade, convince, inveigle, induce, cajole, coax, lure, attract, appeal to, tantalize, whet the appetite of, seduce; *informal* sweet-talk.
- OPPOSITES discourage, deter.

temptation *noun* **1** **desire**, urge, itch, impulse, inclination. **2** **lure**, allure, enticement, attraction, draw, pull.

tempting *adjective* **enticing**, alluring, attractive, appealing, inviting, seductive, beguiling, fascinating, mouth-watering.
- OPPOSITES uninviting.

tenable *adjective* **defensible**, justifiable, supportable, sustainable, arguable, able to hold water, reasonable, rational, sound, viable, plausible, credible,

believable, conceivable.
- OPPOSITES untenable.

tenacious *adjective* **persevering**, persistent, determined, dogged, strong-willed, indefatigable, tireless, resolute, patient, purposeful, unflagging, staunch, steadfast, untiring, unwavering, unswerving, unshakeable; *formal* pertinacious.

tenant *noun* **occupant**, resident, inhabitant, leaseholder, lessee, lodger; *Brit.* occupier.

tend[1] *verb* **be inclined**, be apt, be disposed, be prone, be liable, be likely, have a tendency.

tend[2] *verb* **look after**, take care of, minister to, attend to, see to, watch over, keep an eye on, mind, protect, guard.
- OPPOSITES neglect.

tendency *noun* **inclination**, propensity, proclivity, proneness, aptness, likelihood, bent, leaning, liability.

tender[1] *adjective* **1** *a gentle, tender man* **caring**, kind, kind-hearted, soft-hearted, compassionate, sympathetic, warm, gentle, mild, benevolent. **2** *a tender kiss* **affectionate**, fond, loving, romantic, emotional; *informal* lovey-dovey. **3 soft**, succulent, juicy, melt-in-the-mouth. **4 sore**, sensitive, inflamed, raw, painful, hurting, aching, throbbing. **5** *the tender age of fifteen* **young**, youthful, impressionable, inexperienced; *informal* wet behind the ears.
- OPPOSITES hard-hearted, callous, tough.

tender[2] *verb* **offer**, proffer, put forward, present, propose, suggest, advance, submit, hand in.
● *noun* **bid**, offer, quotation, quote, estimate, price.

tense *adjective* **1 taut**, tight, rigid, stretched, strained, stiff. **2 anxious**, nervous, on edge, edgy, strained, stressed, ill at ease, uneasy, restless, worked up, keyed up, overwrought, jumpy, nervy; *informal* a bundle of nerves, jittery, twitchy, uptight. **3 nerve-racking**, stressful, anxious, worrying, fraught, charged, strained,

nail-biting.
- OPPOSITES relaxed, calm.
● *verb* **tighten**, tauten, flex, contract, brace, stiffen.
- OPPOSITES relax.

tension *noun* **1 tightness**, tautness, rigidity, pull. **2 strain**, stress, anxiety, pressure, worry, nervousness, jumpiness, edginess, restlessness, suspense, uncertainty. **3 strained relations**, strain, ill feeling, friction, antagonism, antipathy, hostility.

tentative *adjective* **1** *a tentative arrangement* **provisional**, unconfirmed, preliminary, exploratory, experimental. **2** *a few tentative steps* **hesitant**, uncertain, cautious, timid, hesitating, faltering, shaky, unsteady, halting.
- OPPOSITES definite, confident.

tenuous *adjective* **slight**, insubstantial, flimsy, weak, doubtful, dubious, questionable, suspect, vague, nebulous, hazy.
- OPPOSITES convincing.

tepid *adjective* **1 lukewarm**, warmish. **2 unenthusiastic**, apathetic, half-hearted, indifferent, cool, lukewarm, uninterested.

term *noun* **1 word**, expression, phrase, name, title, designation, label, description. **2** *the terms of the contract* **condition**, stipulation, specification, provision, proviso, restriction, qualification. **3 period**, length of time, spell, stint, duration, stretch, run, session.
● *verb* **call**, name, entitle, title, style, designate, describe as, dub, label, tag.

terminal *adjective* **1 incurable**, untreatable, inoperable, fatal, lethal, mortal, deadly. **2 final**, last, concluding, closing, end.
● *noun* **1 station**, last stop, end of the line, depot; *Brit.* terminus. **2 workstation**, VDU, visual display unit.

terminate *verb* **bring to an end**, end, bring to a close, close, conclude, finish, stop, wind up, discontinue, cease, cut short, abort, axe; *informal* pull the plug on.
- OPPOSITES begin.

terminology *noun* **phraseology**, terms, expressions, words, language, parlance, vocabulary, nomenclature, usage, idiom, jargon; *informal* lingo, geekspeak.

terrain *noun* **land**, ground, territory, topography, landscape, countryside, country.

terrestrial *adjective* **earthly**, worldly, mundane, earthbound.

terrible *adjective* **1** *a terrible crime* **dreadful**, awful, appalling, horrific, horrible, horrendous, atrocious, monstrous, sickening, heinous, vile, gruesome, unspeakable. **2** *terrible pain* **severe**, extreme, intense, excruciating, agonizing, unbearable. **3** *a terrible film* **very bad**, dreadful, awful, frightful, atrocious, execrable; *informal* pathetic, pitiful, useless, lousy, appalling; *Brit. informal* chronic.
- OPPOSITES minor, slight, excellent.

terrific *adjective* **1** **tremendous**, huge, massive, gigantic, colossal, mighty, considerable; *informal* mega, whopping; *Brit. informal* ginormous. **2** *(informal)* **marvellous**, wonderful, sensational, outstanding, superb, excellent, first-rate, dazzling, out of this world, breathtaking; *informal* great, fantastic, fabulous, super, ace, wicked, awesome; *Brit. informal* brilliant.

terrify *verb* **frighten**, horrify, petrify, scare, strike terror into, paralyse, transfix.

territory *noun* **1** **region**, area, enclave, country, state, land, dependency, colony, dominion. **2** *mountainous territory* **terrain**, land, ground, countryside.

terror *noun* **fear**, dread, horror, fright, alarm, panic, shock.

terrorize *verb* **persecute**, victimize, torment, tyrannize, intimidate, menace, threaten, bully, browbeat, scare, frighten, terrify, petrify; *Brit. informal* put the frighteners on.

terse *adjective* **brief**, short, to the point, concise, succinct, crisp, pithy, incisive, laconic, elliptical, brusque, abrupt, curt, clipped, blunt.
- OPPOSITES long-winded, polite.

test *noun* **1** **trial**, experiment, check, examination, assessment, evaluation, appraisal, investigation. **2** **exam**, examination; *N. Amer.* quiz.
● *verb* **try out**, trial, put through its paces, experiment with, check, examine, assess, evaluate, appraise, investigate, sample.

testify *verb* **swear**, attest, give evidence, state on oath, declare, assert, affirm.

testimonial *noun* **reference**, letter of recommendation, commendation.

testimony *noun* **evidence**, sworn statement, attestation, affidavit, statement, declaration, assertion.

testing *adjective* **difficult**, challenging, tough, hard, demanding, taxing, stressful.
- OPPOSITES easy.

text *noun* **1** **book**, work, textbook. **2** *the pictures relate well to the text* **words**, content, body, wording, script, copy.

textiles *plural noun* **fabrics**, cloths, materials.

texture *noun* **feel**, touch, appearance, finish, surface, grain, consistency.

thank *verb* **express your gratitude to**, say thank you to, show your appreciation to.

thankful *adjective* **grateful**, relieved, pleased, glad.

thankless *adjective* **unenviable**, difficult, unpleasant, unrewarding, unappreciated, unrecognized, unacknowledged.
- OPPOSITES rewarding.

thanks *plural noun* **gratitude**, appreciation, acknowledgement, recognition, credit.
□ **thanks to** as a result of, owing to, due to, because of, through, on account of, by virtue of.

thaw *verb* **melt**, unfreeze, defrost, soften, liquefy.
- OPPOSITES freeze.

t

theatre noun **1 playhouse**, auditorium, amphitheatre. **2 acting**, the stage, drama, dramaturgy, show business; informal showbiz. **3** a lecture theatre **hall**, room, auditorium.

theatrical adjective **1 stage**, dramatic, thespian, show-business; informal showbiz. **2 exaggerated**, ostentatious, stagy, melodramatic, showy, affected, overdone; informal hammy.

theft noun **robbery**, stealing, larceny, shoplifting, burglary, embezzlement, raid, hold-up; informal smash-and-grab; N. Amer. informal heist.

theme noun **1 subject**, topic, argument, idea, thrust, thread, motif, keynote. **2 melody**, tune, air, motif, leitmotif.

theoretical adjective **hypothetical**, speculative, academic, conjectural, suppositional, notional, unproven.
- OPPOSITES actual.

theory noun **1 hypothesis**, thesis, conjecture, supposition, speculation, postulation, proposition, premise, opinion, view, belief, contention. **2** modern economic theory **ideas**, concepts, philosophy, ideology, thinking, principles.

therapeutic adjective **healing**, curative, remedial, medicinal, restorative, health-giving.

therapist noun **psychologist**, psychotherapist, analyst, psychoanalyst, psychiatrist, counsellor; informal shrink.

therapy noun **1 treatment**, remedy, cure. **2** he's currently in therapy **psychotherapy**, psychoanalysis, counselling.

therefore adverb **consequently**, because of that, for that reason, that being the case, so, as a result, hence, accordingly.

thesis noun **1 theory**, contention, argument, proposal, proposition, premise, assumption, supposition, hypothesis. **2 dissertation**, essay, paper, treatise, composition, study; N. Amer. theme.

thick adjective **1 broad**, wide, deep, stout, bulky, hefty, chunky, solid, plump. **2** the station was thick with

people **crowded**, full, packed, teeming, seething, swarming, crawling, crammed, thronged, bursting at the seams, solid, overflowing; informal jampacked, chock-a-block, stuffed; Austral./NZ informal chocker. **3 plentiful**, abundant, profuse, luxuriant, bushy, rich, riotous, exuberant, rank, rampant, dense; informal jungly. **4 semi-solid**, firm, stiff, heavy, viscous, gelatinous. **5** thick fog **dense**, heavy, opaque, impenetrable, soupy, murky.
- OPPOSITES thin, slender, sparse.

thicken verb **stiffen**, condense, solidify, set, gel, congeal, clot, coagulate.

thief noun **robber**, burglar, housebreaker, shoplifter, pickpocket, mugger, kleptomaniac; informal crook.

thieve verb **steal**, take, purloin, help yourself to, snatch, pilfer, embezzle, misappropriate; informal rob, swipe, nab, lift; Brit. informal nick, pinch, knock off; N. Amer. informal heist.

thin adjective **1 narrow**, fine, attenuated. **2 lightweight**, light, fine, delicate, flimsy, diaphanous, gauzy, gossamer, sheer, filmy, transparent, see-through. **3 slim**, lean, slender, willowy, svelte, sylphlike, spare, slight, skinny, underweight, scrawny, scraggy, bony, gaunt, emaciated, skeletal, lanky, spindly, gangly; informal anorexic. **4 watery**, weak, runny, sloppy.
- OPPOSITES thick, broad, fat.
● verb **1 dilute**, water down, weaken. **2** the crowds thinned out **disperse**, dissipate, scatter.
- OPPOSITES thicken.

thing noun **1 object**, article, item, artefact, commodity; informal doodah, whatsit; Brit. informal gubbins. **2** (**things**) **belongings**, possessions, stuff, property, worldly goods, goods and chattels, effects, paraphernalia, bits and pieces, luggage, baggage; informal gear, junk; Brit. informal clobber. **3** (**things**) **equipment**, apparatus, gear, kit, tackle, stuff, implements, tools, utensils, impedimenta, accoutrements.

think *verb* **1 believe**, be of the opinion, be of the view, be under the impression, expect, imagine, anticipate, suppose, guess, fancy; *informal* reckon, figure. **2** *his family was thought to be rich* **consider**, judge, hold, reckon, deem, presume, estimate, regard as, view as. **3 ponder**, reflect, deliberate, consider, meditate, contemplate, muse, ruminate, brood; *formal* cogitate. **4** *she thought of all the visits she had made* **recall**, remember, recollect, call to mind, imagine, picture, visualize, envisage.
□ **think up** devise, dream up, come up with, invent, create, concoct, make up, hit on; *informal* cook up.

thinker *noun* **intellectual**, philosopher, scholar, sage, ideologist, theorist, intellect, mind; *informal* brain.

thinking *adjective* **intelligent**, sensible, reasonable, rational, logical, analytical, thoughtful.
● *noun* **reasoning**, idea(s), theory, thoughts, philosophy, beliefs, opinion(s), view(s).

thirst *noun* *his thirst for knowledge* **craving**, desire, longing, yearning, hunger, hankering, eagerness, lust, appetite; *informal* yen, itch.
□ **thirst for** crave, want, covet, desire, hunger for, lust after, hanker after, wish for, long for.

thirsty *adjective* **longing for a drink**, dry, dehydrated; *informal* parched, gasping.

thorn *noun* **prickle**, spike, barb, spine.

thorny *adjective* **1 prickly**, spiky, barbed, spiny, sharp. **2 problematic**, tricky, ticklish, delicate, controversial, awkward, difficult, knotty, tough, complicated, complex, involved, intricate, vexed; *informal* sticky.

thorough *adjective* **1** *a thorough investigation* **rigorous**, in-depth, exhaustive, minute, detailed, close, meticulous, methodical, careful, complete, comprehensive. **2** *he's slow but thorough* **meticulous**, scrupulous, assiduous, conscientious, painstaking, punctilious, methodical, careful. **3 utter**, downright, absolute, complete, total, out-and-out, real, perfect, proper; *Brit. informal* right; *Austral./NZ informal* fair.
- OPPOSITES superficial, cursory.

thought *noun* **1 idea**, notion, opinion, view, impression, feeling, theory. **2 thinking**, contemplation, musing, pondering, consideration, reflection, rumination, deliberation, meditation; *formal* cogitation. **3** *have you no thought for others?* **consideration**, understanding, regard, sensitivity, care, concern, compassion, sympathy.

thoughtful *adjective* **1 pensive**, reflective, contemplative, musing, meditative, ruminative, introspective, philosophical, preoccupied, in a brown study. **2 considerate**, caring, attentive, understanding, sympathetic, solicitous, concerned, helpful, obliging, accommodating, kind, compassionate.
- OPPOSITES thoughtless.

thoughtless *adjective* **1 inconsiderate**, uncaring, insensitive, uncharitable, unkind, tactless, undiplomatic, indiscreet, careless. **2 unthinking**, heedless, careless, unmindful, absent-minded, injudicious, ill-advised, ill-considered, imprudent, unwise, foolish, silly, stupid, reckless, rash, precipitate, negligent, neglectful, remiss.
- OPPOSITES thoughtful.

thrash *verb* **1 hit**, beat, strike, batter, thump, hammer, pound; *informal* belt. **2** *he was thrashing around in pain* **flail**, writhe, thresh, jerk, toss, twist, twitch.

thread *noun* **1 cotton**, yarn, fibre, filament. **2 train of thought**, drift, direction, theme, tenor.
● *verb* *she threaded her way through the tables* **weave**, inch, squeeze, navigate, negotiate.

threadbare *adjective* **worn**, old, holey, moth-eaten, mangy, ragged, frayed, tattered, decrepit, shabby, scruffy; *informal* tatty, the worse for wear.

threat *noun* **1 threatening remark**, warning, ultimatum. **2** *a possible threat to aircraft* **danger**, peril, hazard, menace, risk. **3** *the company faces the threat of liquidation* **possibility**, chance, probability, likelihood, risk.

threaten *verb* **1 menace**, intimidate, browbeat, bully, terrorize. **2 endanger**, jeopardize, imperil, put at risk. **3 herald**, bode, warn of, presage, foreshadow, indicate, point to, be a sign of, signal.

threshold *noun* **1 doorstep**, entrance, entry, gate, portal. **2 start**, beginning, commencement, brink, verge, dawn, inception, day one, opening, debut.

thrifty *adjective* **frugal**, economical, sparing, careful with money, provident, prudent, abstemious, parsimonious, penny-pinching.
- OPPOSITES extravagant.

thrill *noun* **excitement**, stimulation, pleasure, tingle; *informal* buzz, kick; *N. Amer. informal* charge.
- OPPOSITES boredom.
● *verb* **excite**, stimulate, arouse, rouse, inspire, delight, exhilarate, intoxicate, stir, electrify, move; *informal* give someone a buzz/kick; *N. Amer. informal* give someone a charge.
- OPPOSITES bore.

thrilling *adjective* **exciting**, stimulating, stirring, action-packed, rip-roaring, gripping, electrifying, riveting, fascinating, dramatic, hair-raising.
- OPPOSITES boring.

thrive *verb* **flourish**, prosper, burgeon, bloom, blossom, do well, advance, succeed, boom.
- OPPOSITES decline, wither.

thriving *adjective* **flourishing**, prospering, growing, developing, blooming, healthy, successful, booming, profitable; *informal* going strong.
- OPPOSITES declining.

throb *verb* **pulsate**, beat, pulse, palpitate, pound, thud, thump, drum, judder, vibrate, quiver.
● *noun* **pulsation**, beat, pulse, palpitation, pounding, thudding, thumping, drumming, juddering, vibration, quivering.

throng *noun* **crowd**, horde, mass, army, herd, flock, drove, swarm, sea, troupe, pack; *informal* bunch, gaggle, gang.
● *verb* **1** *pavements thronged with tourists* **fill**, crowd, pack, cram, jam. **2** *visitors thronged round him* **flock**, crowd, cluster, mill, swarm, congregate, gather.

throttle *verb* **choke**, strangle, garrotte.

through *preposition* **1 by means of**, by way of, by dint of, via, using, thanks to, by virtue of, as a result of, as a consequence of, on account of, owing to. **2 throughout**, for the duration of, until/to the end of, all.

throughout *preposition* **1 all over**, in every part of, everywhere in. **2 all through**, for the duration of, for the whole of, until the end of, all.

throw *verb* **1 hurl**, toss, fling, pitch, cast, lob, launch, bowl; *informal* chuck, heave, sling, bung. **2** *he threw the door open* **push**, thrust, fling, bang. **3 cast**, send, give off, emit, radiate, project. **4 disconcert**, unnerve, fluster, ruffle, put off, throw off balance, unsettle, confuse; *informal* rattle, faze.
● *noun* **lob**, toss, pitch, bowl.
□ **throw away/out** discard, dispose of, get rid of, scrap, dump, jettison; *informal* chuck (away/out), ditch, bin, junk; *Brit. informal* get shot of. **throw out** expel, eject, evict, drive out, force out, oust, remove, get rid of, depose, topple, unseat, overthrow; *informal* boot out, kick out; *Brit. informal* turf out.

thrust *verb* **1 shove**, push, force, plunge, stick, drive, ram, lunge. **2** *fame had been thrust on him* **force**, foist, impose, inflict.
● *noun* **1 shove**, push, lunge, poke. **2 advance**, push, drive, attack, assault, onslaught, offensive. **3 force**, propulsion, power, impetus. **4 gist**, substance, drift, message, import, tenor.

thug *noun* **ruffian**, hooligan, bully boy, hoodlum, gangster, villain; *informal* tough, bruiser, heavy; *Brit. informal* rough, bovver boy; *N. Amer. informal* hood, goon.

thump verb **1 hit**, beat, punch, strike, smack, batter, pummel; *informal* whack, wallop, bash, biff, clobber, clout; *Brit. informal* slosh; *N. Amer. informal* slug. **2 throb**, pound, beat, thud, hammer.

thunder noun **rumble**, boom, roar, pounding, crash, reverberation.
● verb **1 rumble**, boom, roar, pound, crash, resound, reverberate. **2** *'Answer me!' he thundered* **shout**, roar, bellow, bark, bawl.

thwart verb **foil**, frustrate, forestall, stop, check, block, prevent, defeat, impede, obstruct, derail, snooker; *informal* put paid to, do for, stymie; *Brit. informal* scupper.
- OPPOSITES help.

ticket noun **1 pass**, authorization, permit, token, coupon, voucher. **2 label**, tag, sticker, tab, slip, docket.

tickle verb **1 stroke**, pet. **2 stimulate**, interest, appeal to, amuse, entertain, divert, please, delight.

tide noun **1 current**, flow, stream, ebb. **2** *the tide of history* **course**, movement, direction, trend, current, drift, run.

tidy adjective **1** *a tidy room* **neat**, orderly, in good order, well kept, in apple-pie order, shipshape, spick and span, spruce, uncluttered, straight. **2** *a tidy person* **organized**, neat, methodical, meticulous, systematic.
- OPPOSITES untidy.
● verb **put in order**, clear up, sort out, straighten (up), clean up, spruce up, smarten up.

tie verb **1 bind**, tie up, tether, hitch, strap, truss, fetter, rope, make fast, moor, lash. **2 do up**, lace, knot. **3 restrict**, restrain, limit, tie down, constrain, cramp, hamper, handicap, hamstring, encumber, shackle. **4 link**, connect, couple, relate, join, marry. **5 draw**, be equal, be even.
● noun **1 lace**, string, cord, fastening. **2 bond**, connection, link, relationship, attachment, affiliation. **3 restriction**, constraint, curb, limitation, restraint,

hindrance, encumbrance, handicap, obligation, commitment. **4 draw**, dead heat.

tier noun **1 row**, rank, bank, line, layer, level. **2 grade**, gradation, echelon, rung on the ladder.

tight adjective **1 firm**, secure, fast. **2 taut**, rigid, stiff, tense, stretched, strained, clenched. **3 close-fitting**, narrow, figure-hugging, skintight; *informal* sprayed on. **4** *a tight mass of fibres* **compact**, compressed, dense, solid. **5 small**, tiny, narrow, limited, restricted, confined, cramped, constricted. **6** *tight security* **strict**, rigorous, stringent, tough.
- OPPOSITES slack, loose.

tighten verb **1 stretch**, tauten, strain, stiffen, tense. **2 strengthen**, increase, make stricter.
- OPPOSITES loosen, slacken.

tilt verb **slope**, tip, lean, list, bank, slant, incline, pitch, cant, angle.
● noun **slope**, list, camber, gradient, bank, slant, incline, pitch, cant, bevel, angle.

timber noun **1 wood**; *N. Amer.* lumber. **2 beam**, spar, plank, batten, lath, board, joist, rafter.

time noun **1 moment**, point (in time), occasion, instant, juncture, stage. **2** *he worked there for a time* **while**, spell, stretch, stint, interval, period, length of time, duration, phase. **3 era**, age, epoch, aeon, period, years, days.
● verb **schedule**, arrange, set, organize, fix, book, line up, timetable, plan; *N. Amer.* slate.
☐ **all the time** constantly, around the clock, day and night, {morning, noon, and night}, {day in, day out}, always, without a break, ceaselessly, endlessly, incessantly, perpetually, permanently, continuously, continually, eternally; *informal* 24-7. **at times** occasionally, sometimes, from time to time, now and then, every so often, once in a while, on occasion, off and on, at intervals, periodically.

WORD LINKS
chronological, temporal relating to time

timeless *adjective* **lasting**, enduring, classic, ageless, permanent, perennial, abiding, unchanging, unvarying, never-changing, eternal, everlasting.
- OPPOSITES ephemeral.

timely *adjective* **opportune**, well timed, convenient, appropriate, expedient, seasonable, propitious.
- OPPOSITES ill-timed.

timetable *noun* **schedule**, programme, agenda, calendar, diary.
● *verb* **schedule**, arrange, programme, organize, fix, time, line up; *Brit.* diarize; *N. Amer.* slate.

timid *adjective* **fearful**, afraid, faint-hearted, timorous, nervous, scared, frightened, shy, diffident.
- OPPOSITES bold.

tinge *verb* **tint**, colour, stain, shade, wash.
● *noun* **1 tint**, colour, shade, tone, hue. **2 trace**, note, touch, suggestion, hint, flavour, element, streak, suspicion, soupçon.

tingle *verb* **prickle**, prick, sting, itch, tickle.
● *noun* **prickle**, pricking, tingling, sting, itch, pins and needles.

tinker *verb* **fiddle**, play about, mess about, adjust, try to mend; *Brit. informal* muck about.

tint *noun* **1 shade**, colour, tone, hue, tinge, cast, flush, blush. **2 dye**, colourant, colouring, wash.
● *verb* **dye**, colour, tinge.

tiny *adjective* **minute**, minuscule, microscopic, very small, mini, diminutive, miniature, baby, toy, fun-size, dwarf; *Scottish* wee; *informal* teeny, tiddly; *Brit. informal* titchy.
- OPPOSITES huge.

tip¹ *noun* **1 point**, end, extremity, head, spike, prong, nib. **2 peak**, top, summit, apex, crown, crest, pinnacle.
● *verb* **cap**, top, crown, surmount.

tip² *verb* **1 overturn**, turn over, topple (over), fall (over), keel over, capsize, roll over. **2 lean**, tilt, list, slope, bank, slant, incline, pitch, cant. **3 pour**, empty, drain, dump, discharge, decant.
● *noun* (*Brit.*) **dump**, rubbish dump, landfill site.

tip³ *noun* **1 gratuity**, baksheesh, present, gift, reward. **2 piece of advice**, suggestion, word of advice, pointer, hint; *informal* wrinkle.

tirade *noun* **diatribe**, harangue, rant, attack, polemic, broadside, fulmination, tongue-lashing; *informal* blast.

tire *verb* **1 get tired**, weaken, flag, droop. **2 fatigue**, tire out, exhaust, wear out, drain, weary, enervate; *informal* knock out, take it out of; *Brit. informal* knacker.

tired *adjective* **1 exhausted**, worn out, weary, fatigued, ready to drop, drained, enervated; *informal* all in, dead beat, shattered, done in; *Brit. informal* knackered, whacked; *N. Amer. informal* pooped, tuckered out; *Austral./NZ informal* stonkered. **2** *I'm tired of him* **fed up with**, weary of, bored with/by, sick (and tired) of; *informal* up to here with. **3 hackneyed**, overused, stale, clichéd, predictable, unimaginative, unoriginal, dull, boring; *informal* corny.
- OPPOSITES energetic, fresh.

tiresome *adjective* **1 wearisome**, laborious, wearing, tedious, boring, monotonous, dull, uninteresting, unexciting, humdrum, routine. **2 troublesome**, irksome, vexatious, irritating, annoying, exasperating, trying; *informal* aggravating, pesky.
- OPPOSITES interesting, pleasant.

tiring *adjective* **exhausting**, wearying, taxing, draining, hard, arduous, strenuous, onerous, gruelling; *informal* killing; *Brit. informal* knackering.

title *noun* **1 heading**, label, inscription, caption, subheading, legend. **2 name**, designation, form of address, rank, office, position; *informal* moniker, handle. **3** *an Olympic title* **championship**, crown, first place.

toast *verb* **drink (to) the health of**, salute, honour, pay tribute to; *old use* pledge.

toddle *verb* **totter**, teeter, wobble, falter, waddle, stumble.

together *adverb* **1 with each other**, in conjunction, jointly, in cooperation, in collaboration, in partnership, in combination, in league, side by side; *informal* in cahoots. **2 simultaneously**, at the same time, at once, concurrently, as a group, in unison, in chorus.
- OPPOSITES separately.
● *adjective (informal)* **level-headed**, well adjusted, sensible, practical, realistic, mature, stable, full of common sense, well organized, efficient, methodical, self-confident, self-assured; *informal* unflappable.

toil *verb* **1 work**, labour, slave, strive; *informal* slog, beaver; *Brit. informal* graft. **2 struggle**, drag yourself, trudge, slog, plod; *N. Amer. informal* schlep.
● *noun* **hard work**, labour, exertion, slaving, drudgery, effort, {blood, sweat, and tears}; *informal* slog, elbow grease; *Brit. informal* graft; *old use* travail.

toilet *noun* **lavatory**, WC, (public) convenience, cloakroom, powder room, latrine, privy, urinal; *N. Amer.* bathroom, washroom, rest room, men's/ladies' room, comfort station; *Brit. informal* loo, bog, the Ladies, the Gents; *N. Amer. informal* can, john; *Austral./NZ informal* dunny.

token *noun* **1 symbol**, sign, emblem, badge, representation, indication, mark, expression, demonstration. **2 memento**, souvenir, keepsake, reminder. **3 voucher**, coupon, note.
● *adjective token resistance* **symbolic**, nominal, perfunctory, slight, minimal, superficial.

tolerable *adjective* **1 bearable**, endurable, supportable, acceptable. **2 fairly good**, fair, passable, adequate, all right, acceptable, satisfactory, average, run-of-the-mill, mediocre, middling, ordinary, unexceptional; *informal* OK, so-so, no great shakes.

- OPPOSITES intolerable.

tolerance *noun* **1 toleration**, acceptance, open-mindedness, broad-mindedness, forbearance, patience, charity, understanding, lenience. **2 endurance**, resilience, resistance, immunity.

tolerant *adjective* **open-minded**, forbearing, broad-minded, liberal, unprejudiced, unbiased, patient, long-suffering, understanding, charitable, lenient, easy-going, indulgent, permissive.

tolerate *verb* **1 allow**, permit, condone, accept, swallow, countenance; *formal* brook. **2** *he couldn't tolerate her moods any longer* **endure**, put up with, bear, take, stand, support, stomach, abide; *Brit. informal* stick.

toll[1] *noun* **1 charge**, fee, payment, levy, tariff, tax. **2 number**, count, tally, total, sum. **3** *the toll on the environment has been high* **harm**, damage, injury, detriment, adverse effect, cost, price, loss.

toll[2] *verb* **ring**, sound, clang, chime, strike, peal.

tomb *noun* **burial chamber**, vault, crypt, catacomb, sepulchre, mausoleum, grave.

> **WORD LINKS**
> **sepulchral** relating to a tomb

tone *noun* **1 sound**, timbre, voice, colour, tonality, intonation, inflection, modulation. **2 mood**, air, feel, flavour, note, attitude, character, spirit, vein. **3 shade**, colour, hue, tint, tinge.
● *verb* **harmonize**, go, blend, coordinate, team, match, suit, complement.
□ **tone down** moderate, modify, temper, soften, modulate, lighten, subdue.

tonic *noun* **stimulant**, boost, restorative, refresher, fillip; *informal* shot in the arm, pick-me-up, bracer.

too *adverb* **1 excessively**, overly, unduly, immoderately, inordinately, unreasonably, extremely, very. **2 also**, as well, in addition, into the bargain, besides, furthermore, moreover.

tool noun **implement**, utensil, instrument, device, apparatus, gadget, appliance, machine, contrivance, contraption; *informal* gizmo.

tooth noun **fang**, tusk; *informal* gnasher.

> **WORD LINKS**
> **dental** relating to teeth

top noun **1 summit**, peak, pinnacle, crest, crown, brow, head, tip, apex, apogee. **2 lid**, cap, cover, stopper, cork. **3** *he was at the top of his career* **height**, peak, pinnacle, zenith, culmination, climax, prime.
- OPPOSITES bottom, base.
● *adjective* **1 highest**, topmost, uppermost. **2 foremost**, chief, leading, principal, pre-eminent, greatest, best, finest, elite, premier, prime, superior, select, five-star, grade A, A-list. **3 maximum**, greatest, utmost.
- OPPOSITES lowest, minimum.
● *verb* **1 exceed**, surpass, go beyond, better, beat, outstrip, outdo, outshine, eclipse, transcend. **2 lead**, head, be at the top of. **3** *mousse topped with cream* **cover**, cap, coat, finish, garnish.
□ **top up** fill, refill, refresh, freshen, replenish, recharge, resupply.

topic noun **subject**, theme, issue, matter, point, question, concern, argument, thesis.

topical *adjective* **current**, up to date, up to the minute, contemporary, recent, relevant, in the news.
- OPPOSITES out of date.

topple verb **1 fall**, tumble, tip, overbalance, overturn, keel over, lose your balance. **2 knock over**, upset, push over, tip over, upend. **3 overthrow**, oust, unseat, overturn, bring down, defeat, get rid of, dislodge, eject.

torment noun **agony**, suffering, torture, pain, anguish, misery, distress, trauma.
● *verb* **1 torture**, afflict, rack, harrow, plague, haunt, distress, agonize.
2 tease, taunt, bait, provoke, harass, bother, persecute; *informal* needle.

torn *adjective* **1 ripped**, rent, cut, slit, ragged, tattered. **2 wavering**, vacillating, irresolute, dithering, uncertain, unsure, undecided, in two minds.

tornado noun **whirlwind**, cyclone, typhoon, storm, hurricane; *N. Amer. informal* twister.

torrent noun **1** *a torrent of water* **flood**, deluge, spate, cascade, rush. **2** *a torrent of abuse* **outburst**, outpouring, stream, flood, volley, barrage, tide.
- OPPOSITES trickle.

tortuous *adjective* **1 twisting**, winding, zigzag, sinuous, snaky, meandering, serpentine. **2 convoluted**, complicated, complex, labyrinthine, involved, Byzantine, lengthy.
- OPPOSITES straight.

torture noun **1 abuse**, ill-treatment, mistreatment, maltreatment, persecution, cruelty, atrocity. **2 torment**, agony, suffering, pain, anguish, misery, distress, heartbreak, trauma.
● *verb* **1 abuse**, ill-treat, mistreat, maltreat, persecute. **2 torment**, rack, afflict, harrow, plague, distress, trouble.

toss verb **1 throw**, hurl, fling, sling, pitch, lob, launch; *informal* heave, chuck, bung. **2** *he tossed a coin* **flip**, flick, spin. **3 pitch**, lurch, rock, roll, plunge, reel, sway.

total *adjective* **1 entire**, complete, whole, full, combined, aggregate, gross, overall. **2 utter**, complete, absolute, thorough, perfect, downright, out-and-out, outright, sheer, unmitigated, unqualified, unalloyed.
- OPPOSITES partial.
● *noun* **sum**, aggregate, whole, entirety, totality.
● *verb* **1 add up to**, amount to, come to, run to, make. **2** *he totalled up his score* **add**, count, reckon, tot up, compute, work out.

totalitarian *adjective* **autocratic**, undemocratic, one-party, dictatorial, tyrannical, despotic, fascist, oppressive, authoritarian, absolutist.
- OPPOSITES democratic.

totally *adverb* **completely**, entirely, wholly, thoroughly, fully, utterly, absolutely, perfectly, unreservedly,

unconditionally, downright.
- OPPOSITES partly.

touch *verb* **1 contact**, meet, brush, graze, come up against, be in contact with, border, abut. **2 feel**, pat, tap, stroke, fondle, caress, pet, handle. **3** *sales touched £20,000* **reach**, attain, come to, make, rise to, soar to; *informal* hit. **4 compare with**, be on a par with, equal, match, rival, measure up to, better, beat; *informal* hold a candle to. **5 handle**, hold, pick up, move, use, meddle with, play about with, fiddle with, interfere with, tamper with, disturb. **6 affect**, move, stir, make an impression on.
● *noun* **1 tap**, pat, contact, stroke, caress. **2 skill**, expertise, dexterity, deftness, adroitness, adeptness, ability, talent, flair, facility, proficiency, knack. **3 trace**, bit, suggestion, suspicion, hint, scintilla, tinge, dash, taste, spot, drop, dab, soupçon. **4** *the gas lights are a nice touch* **detail**, feature, point, element, addition. **5** *are you in touch with him?* **contact**, communication, correspondence.
□ **touch on** refer to, mention, comment on, remark on, bring up, raise, broach, allude to, cover, deal with.

> **WORD LINKS**
> **tactile** relating to touch

touching *adjective* **moving**, affecting, heart-warming, emotional, emotive, poignant, sad, tear-jerking.

touchy *adjective* **1 sensitive**, oversensitive, hypersensitive, easily offended, thin-skinned, highly strung, tense, irritable, tetchy, testy, crotchety, peevish, querulous, bad-tempered, petulant; *informal* snappy, ratty; *N. Amer. informal* cranky. **2 delicate**, sensitive, tricky, ticklish, embarrassing, awkward, difficult, contentious, controversial.

tough *adjective* **1 durable**, strong, resilient, sturdy, rugged, solid, stout, robust, hard-wearing, long-lasting, heavy-duty, well built, made to last. **2 chewy**, leathery, gristly, stringy, fibrous. **3 strict**, stern, severe, stringent, rigorous, hard, firm, hard-hitting, uncompromising. **4** *the training was pretty tough* **difficult**, hard, strenuous, onerous, gruelling, exacting, arduous, demanding, taxing, tiring, exhausting, punishing. **5** *tough questions* **difficult**, hard, knotty, thorny, tricky.
- OPPOSITES weak, lenient, easy.
● *noun* **ruffian**, thug, hoodlum, hooligan, bully boy; *informal* heavy, bruiser; *Brit. informal* yob.

toughen *verb* **1 strengthen**, fortify, reinforce, harden, temper, anneal. **2** *measures to toughen up discipline* **make stricter**, make more severe, stiffen, tighten up.

tour *noun* **1 trip**, excursion, journey, expedition, jaunt, outing, trek. **2** *a tour of the factory* **visit**, inspection, walkabout.
● *verb* **travel round**, visit, explore, holiday in, go round.

tourist *noun* **holidaymaker**, traveller, sightseer, visitor, backpacker, globetrotter, tripper; *N. Amer.* vacationer.
- OPPOSITES local.

tournament *noun* **competition**, contest, championship, meeting, event.

tow *verb* **pull**, haul, drag, draw, tug, lug.

tower *verb* **soar**, rise, rear, overshadow, overhang, hang over, dominate.

town *noun* **city**, metropolis, conurbation, municipality; *Brit.* borough; *Scottish* burgh.
- OPPOSITES country.

> **WORD LINKS**
> **urban, municipal** relating to towns

toxic *adjective* **poisonous**, dangerous, harmful, injurious, noxious, pernicious, deadly, lethal, environmentally unfriendly, polluting.
- OPPOSITES harmless.

toy *noun* **plaything**, game.
● *adjective* **model**, imitation, replica, miniature.
□ **toy with 1** think about, consider, flirt with, entertain the possibility of; *informal* kick around. **2** fiddle with, play

with, fidget with, twiddle, finger.

trace *verb* **1 track down**, find, discover, detect, unearth, turn up, hunt down, ferret out, run to ground. **2 draw**, outline, mark.
● *noun* **1 sign**, mark, indication, evidence, clue, vestige, remains, remnant. **2 bit**, touch, hint, suggestion, suspicion, shadow, dash, tinge; *informal* smidgen, tad.

track *noun* **1 path**, footpath, lane, trail, route, way. **2 course**, racecourse, racetrack, velodrome; *Brit.* circuit. **3** *the tracks of a fox* **traces**, marks, prints, footprints, trail, spoor. **4** *the railway tracks* **rail**, line. **5 song**, recording, number, piece.
● *verb* **follow**, trail, pursue, shadow, stalk; *informal* tail.
□ **track down** discover, find, detect, hunt down, unearth, uncover, turn up, dig up, ferret out, run to ground.

trade *noun* **1 dealing**, buying and selling, commerce, traffic, business. **2 occupation**, work, craft, job, career, profession, business, line (of work), métier.
● *verb* **1 deal**, do business, bargain, negotiate, traffic, buy and sell, merchandise. **2** *I traded the car for a newer model* **swap**, exchange, barter, part-exchange.

> **WORD LINKS**
> **mercantile** relating to trade

trader *noun* **dealer**, merchant, buyer, seller, vendor, purveyor, supplier, trafficker.

tradition *noun* **custom**, practice, convention, ritual, observance, way, usage, habit, institution, unwritten law; *formal* praxis.

traditional *adjective* **customary**, long-established, time-honoured, classic, wonted, accustomed, standard, regular, normal, conventional, habitual, ritual, age-old.

tragedy *noun* **disaster**, calamity, catastrophe, cataclysm, misfortune, adversity.

tragic *adjective* **1 disastrous**, calamitous, catastrophic, cataclysmic, devastating, terrible, dreadful, awful, appalling, horrendous, fatal. **2 sad**, unhappy, pathetic, moving, distressing, painful, harrowing, heart-rending, sorry.
- OPPOSITES fortunate, happy.

trail *noun* **1** *a trail of clues* **series**, string, chain, succession, sequence. **2 track**, spoor, path, scent, traces, marks, signs, prints, footprints. **3 path**, way, footpath, track, route.
● *verb* **1 drag**, sweep, be drawn, dangle. **2** *roses trailed over the banks* **hang**, droop, fall, spill, cascade. **3 follow**, pursue, track, shadow, stalk, hunt; *informal* tail. **4 lose**, be down, be behind, lag behind.

train *verb* **1 instruct**, teach, coach, tutor, school, educate, prime, drill, ground. **2 study**, learn, prepare, take instruction. **3 exercise**, work out, get into shape, practise. **4 aim**, point, direct, level, focus.
● *noun* **chain**, string, series, set, sequence, succession, course.

trainer *noun* **coach**, instructor, teacher, tutor, handler.

trait *noun* **characteristic**, attribute, feature, quality, habit, mannerism, idiosyncrasy, peculiarity.

traitor *noun* **betrayer**, back-stabber, double-crosser, renegade, Judas, quisling, fifth columnist, turncoat, defector; *informal* snake in the grass.

tramp *verb* **trudge**, plod, stamp, trample, lumber, trek, walk, slog, hike; *informal* traipse; *N. Amer. informal* schlep.
● *noun* **1 vagrant**, vagabond, homeless person, down-and-out, traveller, drifter; *N. Amer.* hobo; *N. Amer. informal* bum. **2 tread**, step, footstep, footfall. **3 trek**, walk, hike, slog, march, roam, ramble; *N. Amer. informal* schlep.

trample *verb* **tread**, stamp, walk, squash, crush, flatten.

trance *noun* **daze**, stupor, hypnotic state, dream, reverie.

tranquil *adjective* **peaceful**, calm, restful, quiet, still, serene, relaxing, undistributed.
- OPPOSITES busy, excitable.

tranquillizer *noun* **sedative**, barbiturate, calmative, narcotic, opiate; *informal* downer.
- OPPOSITES stimulant.

transaction *noun* **deal**, bargain, agreement, undertaking, arrangement, negotiation, settlement.

transcend *verb* **go beyond**, rise above, exceed, surpass, excel, outstrip.

transfer *verb* **move**, take, bring, shift, convey, remove, carry, transport, relocate.

transform *verb* **change**, alter, convert, revolutionize, overhaul, reconstruct, rebuild, reorganize, rearrange, rework.

transformation *noun* **change**, alteration, conversion, metamorphosis, revolution, overhaul, reconstruction, rebuilding, reorganization, rearrangement, reworking.

transient *adjective* **transitory**, temporary, short-lived, short-term, ephemeral, impermanent, brief, short, momentary, fleeting, passing.
- OPPOSITES permanent.

transition *noun* **change**, passage, move, transformation, conversion, metamorphosis, alteration, changeover, shift, switch.

transitional *adjective* **1** *a transitional period* **intermediate**, interim, changeover, changing, fluid, unsettled. **2** *a transitional government* **interim**, temporary, provisional, pro tem, acting, caretaker.

translate *verb* **interpret**, convert, render, put, change, express, decipher, reword, decode, gloss, explain.

translation *noun* **interpretation**, rendition, conversion, change, alteration, adaptation.

transmission *noun* **1 transfer**, communication, passing on, conveyance, dissemination, spread, circulation, relaying. **2 broadcasting**, televising, airing. **3 broadcast**, programme, show, telecast, videocast, podcast.

transmit *verb* **1 transfer**, communicate, pass on, hand on, convey, impart, channel, carry, relay, dispatch, disseminate, spread, circulate. **2 broadcast**, send out, air, televise, telecast, videocast, podcast.

transparent *adjective* **1 clear**, translucent, limpid, crystal clear, crystalline, pellucid. **2 see-through**, sheer, filmy, gauzy, diaphanous. **3 obvious**, blatant, unambiguous, unequivocal, clear, plain, apparent, unmistakable, manifest, conspicuous, patent.
- OPPOSITES opaque, obscure.

transport *verb* **convey**, carry, take, transfer, move, shift, send, deliver, bear, ship, ferry; *informal* cart.
● *noun* **conveyance**, carriage, delivery, shipping, freight, shipment, haulage.

trap *noun* **1 snare**, net, mesh, gin; *N. Amer.* deadfall. **2 trick**, ploy, ruse, deception, subterfuge; *informal* set-up.
● *verb* **1 snare**, entrap, capture, catch, ambush. **2 confine**, cut off, corner, shut in, pen in, hem in, imprison. **3 trick**, dupe, deceive, fool, hoodwink.

trash *noun* **1** (*N. Amer.*) **rubbish**, refuse, waste, litter, junk; *N. Amer.* garbage. **2** (*informal*) **nonsense**, rubbish, trivia, pulp fiction, pap; *informal* drivel.

trauma *noun* **1 shock**, upheaval, distress, stress, strain, pain, anguish, suffering, upset, ordeal. **2 injury**, damage, wound.

traumatic *adjective* **disturbing**, shocking, distressing, upsetting, painful, agonizing, hurtful, stressful, devastating, harrowing.

travel *verb* **journey**, tour, take a trip, voyage, go sightseeing, globetrot, backpack, trek.
● *noun* **travelling**, journeys, expeditions, trips, tours, excursions, voyages, treks, wanderings, jaunts.

traveller *noun* **tourist**, tripper, holidaymaker, sightseer, globetrotter, backpacker, passenger, commuter; *N. Amer.* vacationer.

treacherous adjective **1 traitorous**, disloyal, unfaithful, duplicitous, deceitful, false, back-stabbing, double-crossing, two-faced, untrustworthy, unreliable, apostate, renegade. **2 dangerous**, hazardous, perilous, unsafe, precarious, risky; informal dicey, hairy.
- OPPOSITES loyal, faithful.

tread verb **1 walk**, step, stride, pace, march, tramp, plod, stomp, trudge. **2 crush**, flatten, press down, squash, trample on, stamp on.
● noun **step**, footstep, footfall, tramp.

treason noun **treachery**, disloyalty, betrayal, sedition, subversion, mutiny, rebellion.

treasure noun **1 riches**, valuables, jewels, gems, gold, silver, precious metals, money, cash, wealth, fortune. **2 masterpiece**, gem, pearl, jewel.
● verb **cherish**, hold dear, prize, set great store by, value greatly.

treasury noun **storehouse**, repository, treasure house, exchequer, fund, mine, bank, coffers, purse.

treat verb **1 behave towards**, act towards, use, deal with, handle. **2** police are treating the fires as arson **regard**, consider, view, look on, put down as. **3 deal with**, tackle, handle, discuss, explore, investigate. **4 tend**, nurse, attend to, give medical attention to. **5 cure**, heal, remedy. **6** he treated her to lunch **buy**, take out for, stand, give, pay for, entertain, wine and dine; informal foot the bill for. **7** the crowd was treated to a superb display **entertain with**, regale with, fete with.
● noun **1 celebration**, entertainment, amusement, surprise. **2 present**, gift, titbit, delicacy, luxury, indulgence, extravagance; informal goody. **3 pleasure**, delight, thrill, joy.

treatment noun **1 behaviour**, conduct, handling, management, dealings. **2 medical care**, therapy, nursing, ministrations, medication, medicament, drugs. **3 discussion**, handling, investigation, exploration, consideration, study, analysis.

treaty noun **agreement**, settlement, pact, deal, entente, concordat, accord, protocol, compact, convention; formal concord.

tree noun

> **WORD LINKS**
> **arboreal** relating to trees

trek noun **journey**, trip, expedition, safari, hike, march, tramp, walk.

tremble verb **shake**, quiver, shudder, judder, vibrate, wobble, rock, move, sway.

tremendous adjective **1 huge**, enormous, immense, colossal, massive, cosmic, prodigious, stupendous; informal whopping, astronomical; Brit. informal ginormous. **2 excellent**, first-class, outstanding, marvellous, wonderful, splendid, superb, admirable; informal great, fantastic, fabulous, terrific, super, awesome, ace; Brit. informal brilliant, smashing.

trench noun **ditch**, channel, trough, excavation, furrow, rut, conduit.

trend noun **1 tendency**, movement, drift, swing, shift, course, current, direction, inclination, leaning. **2 fashion**, vogue, style, mode, craze, mania, rage; informal fad, thing.

trespass verb **intrude**, encroach, invade, enter without permission.

trial noun **1 case**, lawsuit, hearing, tribunal, litigation, proceedings. **2 test**, experiment, pilot study, examination, check, assessment, audition, evaluation, appraisal; informal dry run. **3 trouble**, affliction, ordeal, tribulation, difficulty, problem, misfortune, mishap.

tribe noun **ethnic group**, people, family, clan, race, dynasty, house, nation.

tribunal noun **court**, board, panel, committee.

tribute noun **accolade**, praise, commendation, salute, testimonial, homage, congratulations, compliments, plaudits.
- OPPOSITES criticism.

trick noun **1 stratagem**, ploy, ruse, scheme, device, manoeuvre, dodge, subterfuge, swindle, fraud; *informal* con, set-up, scam, sting. **2 practical joke**, hoax, prank; *informal* leg-pull, spoof, put-on. **3 knack**, skill, technique, secret, art.

● verb **deceive**, delude, hoodwink, mislead, take in, dupe, fool, gull, cheat, defraud, swindle; *informal* con, diddle, take for a ride, pull a fast one on; *N. Amer. informal* sucker.

trickle verb **dribble**, drip, ooze, leak, seep, spill, exude, percolate.
- OPPOSITES pour, gush.
● noun **dribble**, drip, thin stream, rivulet.

tricky adjective **1 difficult**, awkward, problematic, delicate, ticklish, sensitive; *informal* sticky. **2 cunning**, crafty, wily, devious, sly, scheming, calculating, deceitful.
- OPPOSITES straightforward.

trifle noun **triviality**, thing of no consequence, bagatelle, inessential, nothing, technicality; (**trifles**) trivia, minutiae.

trifling adjective **trivial**, unimportant, insignificant, inconsequential, petty, minor, of no account, footling, incidental; *informal* piffling.
- OPPOSITES important.

trigger verb **start**, set off, initiate, spark (off), activate, touch off, provoke, precipitate, prompt, stir up, cause, give rise to, lead to, set in motion, bring about.

trim verb **1 cut**, crop, bob, shorten, clip, snip, shear, dock, lop off, prune, shave, pare. **2 decorate**, adorn, ornament, embellish, edge, border, fringe.
● noun **1 decoration**, ornamentation, adornment, embellishment, border, edging, piping, fringe, frill. **2 haircut**, cut, clip, snip.
● adjective **1 neat**, tidy, orderly, uncluttered, well kept, well maintained, immaculate, spick and span, spruce, dapper. **2 slim**, slender, lean, sleek, willowy.
- OPPOSITES untidy.

□ **in trim** fit, in good health, in fine fettle, slim, in shape.

trimming noun **1 decoration**, ornamentation, adornment, borders, edging, piping, fringes, frills. **2 (trimmings) accompaniments**, extras, frills, accessories, accoutrements, trappings, paraphernalia.

trio noun **threesome**, three, triumvirate, triad, troika, trinity, trilogy.

trip verb **1 stumble**, lose your footing, catch your foot, slip, fall (down), tumble. **2 skip**, dance, prance, bound, spring, scamper.
● noun **1 excursion**, outing, jaunt, holiday, break, visit, tour, journey, expedition, voyage, drive, run; *informal* spin. **2 stumble**, slip, fall, misstep.

triple adjective **threefold**, tripartite, three-way, three times, treble.

triumph noun **1 victory**, win, conquest, success, achievement. **2 jubilation**, exultation, elation, delight, joy, happiness, glee, pride, satisfaction.
- OPPOSITES defeat, disappointment.
● verb **win**, succeed, come first, be victorious, carry the day, prevail.
- OPPOSITES lose.
□ **triumph over** defeat, beat, conquer, trounce, vanquish, overcome, overpower, overwhelm, get the better of; *informal* lick; *US informal* own.

triumphant adjective **1 victorious**, successful, winning, conquering. **2 jubilant**, exultant, celebratory, elated, joyful, delighted, gleeful, proud, cock-a-hoop.
- OPPOSITES defeated, despondent.

trivial adjective **unimportant**, insignificant, inconsequential, minor, of no account, of no importance, petty, trifling, footling, negligible; *informal* piffling.
- OPPOSITES important, significant.

troop noun **1 group**, party, band, gang, body, company, troupe, crowd, squad, unit. **2 (troops) soldiers**, armed forces, soldiery, servicemen, servicewomen.
● verb **walk**, march, file, flock, crowd, throng, stream, swarm.

trophy noun **1 cup**, medal, prize, award. **2 souvenir**, memento, keepsake, spoils, booty.

tropical adjective **hot**, sweltering, humid, sultry, steamy, sticky, oppressive, stifling.
- OPPOSITES cold.

trot verb **run**, jog, scuttle, scurry, bustle, scamper.

trouble noun **1 difficulty**, problems, issues, bother, inconvenience, worry, anxiety, distress, stress, agitation, harassment, unpleasantness; informal hassle. **2** she poured out all her troubles **problem**, misfortune, difficulty, trial, tribulation, woe, grief, heartache, misery, affliction, suffering. **3** he's gone to a lot of trouble **bother**, inconvenience, fuss, effort, exertion, work, labour. **4 nuisance**, bother, inconvenience, irritation, problem, trial, pest; informal headache, pain, drag. **5** you're too gullible, that's your trouble **shortcoming**, weakness, failing, fault. **6 disease**, illness, sickness, ailment, complaint, problem, disorder, disability. **7 malfunction**, failure, breakdown. **8 disturbance**, disorder, unrest, fighting, scuffles, breach of the peace.
● verb **1 worry**, bother, concern, disturb, upset, agitate, distress, perturb, annoy, nag, prey on someone's mind; informal bug. **2 afflict**, burden, suffer from, be cursed with. **3** I'm sorry to trouble you **inconvenience**, bother, impose on, disturb, put out, disoblige; informal hassle.

troublesome adjective **1 annoying**, irritating, exasperating, maddening, infuriating, bothersome, tiresome, nagging, difficult, awkward; N. Amer. informal pesky. **2 difficult**, awkward, uncooperative, rebellious, unmanageable, unruly, obstreperous, disruptive, disobedient, naughty, attention-seeking, recalcitrant.

truant noun **absentee**; Brit. informal skiver; Austral./NZ informal wag.
□ **play truant** stay away from school, truant; Brit. informal skive (off), bunk off; N. Amer. informal play hookey; Austral./NZ informal play the wag.

truce noun **ceasefire**, armistice, cessation of hostilities, peace.

true adjective **1 correct**, truthful, accurate, right, verifiable, the case; formal veracious. **2 genuine**, authentic, real, actual, bona fide, proper, legitimate; informal kosher. **3 sincere**, genuine, real, unfeigned, heartfelt. **4 loyal**, faithful, constant, devoted, trustworthy, reliable, dependable, staunch. **5** a true reflection **accurate**, faithful, telling it like it is, realistic, factual, lifelike.
- OPPOSITES false, untrue.

trumpet verb **proclaim**, announce, declare, noise abroad, shout from the rooftops.

trunk noun **1 stem**, bole, stock, stalk. **2 torso**, body. **3 proboscis**, nose, snout. **4 chest**, box, crate, coffer, case, portmanteau.

trust noun **confidence**, belief, faith, certainty, assurance, conviction, credence, reliance.
● verb **1 have faith in**, have (every) confidence in, believe in, pin your hopes/faith on. **2 rely on**, depend on, bank on, count on, be sure of. **3 hope**, expect, take it, assume, presume. **4 entrust**, consign, commit, give, hand over, turn over, assign.
- OPPOSITES distrust, mistrust.

trusting adjective **trustful**, unsuspecting, unquestioning, naive, innocent, childlike, ingenuous, wide-eyed, credulous, gullible, easily taken in.
- OPPOSITES distrustful, suspicious.

trustworthy adjective **reliable**, dependable, honest, as good as your word, above suspicion; informal on the level.
- OPPOSITES unreliable.

truth noun **1 accuracy**, correctness, authenticity, veracity, verity, truthfulness. **2 fact(s)**, reality, real life, actuality.
- OPPOSITES lies, fiction, falsehood.

truthful adjective **true**, accurate, correct, factual, faithful, reliable.
- OPPOSITES deceitful, untrue.

try *verb* **1 attempt**, endeavour, make an effort, exert yourself, strive, do your best, do your utmost, aim, seek; *informal* have a go/shot/crack/stab, go all out. **2 test**, put to the test, sample, taste, inspect, investigate, examine, appraise, evaluate, assess; *informal* check out. **3** *she tried his patience* **tax**, strain, test, stretch, sap, drain, exhaust, wear out.
● *noun* **attempt**, effort, endeavour; *informal* go, shot, crack, stab, bash.

trying *adjective* **1 stressful**, taxing, demanding, difficult, challenging, frustrating, fraught; *informal* hellish. **2 annoying**, irritating, exasperating, maddening, infuriating, tiresome, troublesome, irksome, vexatious.

tuck *verb* **push**, insert, slip, thrust, stuff, stick, cram; *informal* pop.

tug *verb* **1** *he tugged at her sleeve* **pull**, pluck, tweak, twitch, jerk, catch hold of; *informal* yank. **2 drag**, pull, lug, draw, haul, heave, tow, trail.

tuition *noun* **instruction**, teaching, coaching, tutoring, tutelage, lessons, education, schooling, training.

tumble *verb* **1 fall over**, fall down, topple over, go head over heels, lose your balance, take a spill, trip (up), stumble. **2** *oil prices tumbled* **plummet**, plunge, dive, nosedive, drop, slump, slide; *informal* crash.
- OPPOSITES rise.

tumour *noun* **cancer**, growth, lump, malignancy; *Medicine* carcinoma, sarcoma.

> **WORD LINKS**
> **oncology** branch of medicine concerning tumours

tune *noun* **melody**, air, strain, theme, song, jingle, ditty.
● *verb* **attune**, adapt, adjust, regulate.

tunnel *noun* **underground passage**, underpass, subway, shaft, burrow, hole, warren, labyrinth.
● *verb* **dig**, burrow, mine, bore, drill.

turbulent *adjective* **tempestuous**, stormy, unstable, unsettled, tumultuous, chaotic, anarchic, lawless.
- OPPOSITES peaceful.

turmoil *noun* **confusion**, upheaval, turbulence, tumult, disorder, disturbance, ferment, chaos, mayhem.
- OPPOSITES peace, order.

turn *verb* **1 go round**, revolve, rotate, spin, roll, circle, wheel, whirl, twirl, gyrate, swivel, pivot. **2 change direction**, change course, make a U-turn, turn about/round, wheel round. **3 bend**, curve, wind, twist, meander, snake, zigzag. **4** *he turned pale* **become**, go, grow, get. **5 (go) sour**, go off, curdle, become rancid, go bad, spoil.
● *noun* **1 rotation**, revolution, spin, whirl, twirl, gyration, swivel. **2 bend**, corner, junction, twist, dog-leg; *Brit.* hairpin bend. **3 opportunity**, chance, say, stint, time, try; *informal* go, shot, stab, crack. **4** *she did me some good turns* **service**, deed, act, favour, kindness.
□ **turn down 1** reject, spurn, rebuff, refuse, decline. **2** reduce, lower, decrease, lessen, mute. **turn into 1** become, develop into, turn out to be, be transformed into, change into, metamorphose into. **2** convert, change, transform, make, adapt, modify. **turn off/out** switch off, shut off, put off, extinguish, deactivate; *informal* kill, cut. **turn on** switch on, put on, start up, activate, trip. **turn out 1** come, be present, attend, appear, turn up, arrive, assemble, gather; *informal* show up. **2** transpire, emerge, come to light, become apparent. **3** happen, occur, come about, develop, work out, come out, end up; *informal* pan out. **turn up 1** be found, be discovered, be located, reappear. **2** arrive, appear, present yourself; *informal* show (up). **3** present itself, occur, happen, crop up. **4** increase, raise, amplify, intensify. **5** discover, uncover, unearth, find, dig up, expose.

turning *noun* **junction**, turn-off, side road, exit; *N. Amer.* turnout.

turning point *noun* **watershed**, critical moment, decisive moment, moment of truth, crossroads, crisis.

turnout noun **1 attendance**, audience, house, congregation, crowd, gate, gathering. **2 outfit**, clothing, dress, garb, attire, ensemble; *informal* get-up.

turnover noun **1 gross revenue**, income, yield, sales, business. **2** *staff turnover* **rate of replacement**, change, movement.

tutor noun **teacher**, instructor, coach, educator, lecturer, trainer, mentor.
● verb **teach**, instruct, educate, school, coach, train, drill.

twig noun **stick**, sprig, shoot, offshoot, stem, branchlet.

twilight noun **1 dusk**, sunset, sundown, nightfall, evening, close of day. **2 half-light**, semi-darkness, gloom.

> **WORD LINKS**
> **crepuscular** resembling twilight

twin noun **duplicate**, double, carbon copy, likeness, mirror image, replica, lookalike, clone, match, pair; *informal* spitting image, dead ringer.
● adjective **1 matching**, identical, paired. **2 twofold**, double, dual, related, linked, connected, parallel, complementary.
● verb **combine**, join, link, couple, pair.

twinge noun **pain**, spasm, ache, throb, cramp, stitch, pang.

twinkle verb & noun **glitter**, sparkle, shine, glimmer, shimmer, glint, gleam, glisten, flicker, flash, wink.

twist verb **1 crumple**, crush, buckle, mangle, warp, deform, distort, contort. **2 sprain**, wrench, turn, rick, crick. **3** *she twisted her hair round her finger* **wind**, twirl, coil, curl, wrap. **4** *the wires were twisted together* **intertwine**, interlace, weave, plait, braid, coil, wind. **5** *the road twisted and turned* **wind**, bend, curve, turn, meander, weave, zigzag, snake.
● noun **bend**, curve, turn, zigzag, dog-leg.

twitch verb **jerk**, convulse, have a spasm, quiver, tremble, shiver, shudder.
● noun **spasm**, convulsion, quiver, tremor, shiver, shudder, tic.

tycoon noun **magnate**, mogul, businessman, captain of industry, industrialist, financier, entrepreneur; *informal, derogatory* fat cat.

type noun **1 kind**, sort, variety, class, category, set, genre, species, order, breed, ilk. **2 print**, typeface, characters, lettering, font; *Brit.* fount.

typical adjective **1 representative**, characteristic, classic, quintessential, archetypal. **2 normal**, average, ordinary, standard, regular, routine, run-of-the-mill, conventional, unremarkable; *informal* bog-standard.
– OPPOSITES unusual, exceptional.

typify verb **epitomize**, exemplify, characterize, embody, be representative of, personify, symbolize.

tyranny noun **despotism**, absolute power, autocracy, dictatorship, totalitarianism, fascism, oppression, repression, subjugation, enslavement.

tyrant noun **dictator**, despot, autocrat, authoritarian, oppressor, slave-driver, martinet, bully.

Uu

ubiquitous *adjective* **everywhere**, omnipresent, all over the place, all-pervasive, universal, worldwide, global.
- OPPOSITES rare.

ugly *adjective* **1 unattractive**, unsightly, ill-favoured, hideous, plain, unprepossessing, horrible, ghastly, repellent, grotesque; *N. Amer.* homely; *Brit. informal* no oil painting. **2 unpleasant**, nasty, disagreeable, alarming, dangerous, perilous, threatening, menacing, hostile, ominous, sinister.
- OPPOSITES beautiful.

ulterior *adjective* **underlying**, undisclosed, undivulged, concealed, hidden, covert, secret, unapparent.
- OPPOSITES overt.

ultimate *adjective* **1 eventual**, final, concluding, terminal, end. **2 fundamental**, basic, primary, elementary, absolute, central, crucial, essential. **3 best**, ideal, greatest, quintessential, supreme.

ultimately *adverb* **1 eventually**, in the end, in the long run, at length, finally, in time, one day. **2 fundamentally**, basically, primarily, essentially, at heart, deep down.

umpire *noun* **referee**, judge, line judge, linesman, adjudicator, arbitrator, moderator; *informal* ref.

unable *adjective* **incapable**, powerless, impotent, inadequate, incompetent, unqualified, unfit.

unacceptable *adjective* **unsatisfactory**, inadmissible, inappropriate, unsuitable, undesirable, unreasonable, insupportable, intolerable, objectionable, distasteful; *informal* out of order.
- OPPOSITES satisfactory.

unanimous *adjective* **in agreement**, of one mind, in accord, united, undivided, with one voice.
- OPPOSITES split.

unarmed *adjective* **defenceless**, unprotected, unguarded.

unassuming *adjective* **modest**, self-effacing, humble, meek, reserved, diffident, unobtrusive, unostentatious, unpretentious, unaffected, natural.

unauthorized *adjective* **unofficial**, unsanctioned, unaccredited, unlicensed, unwarranted, unapproved, disallowed, prohibited, banned, forbidden, outlawed, illegal, illicit, proscribed.
- OPPOSITES official.

unaware *adjective* **ignorant**, oblivious, unconscious, unwitting, unsuspecting, uninformed, unenlightened, innocent; *informal* in the dark.
- OPPOSITES aware.

unbelievable *adjective* **incredible**, inconceivable, unthinkable, unimaginable, unconvincing, far-fetched, implausible, improbable; *informal* hard to swallow.

unbiased *adjective* **impartial**, unprejudiced, neutral, non-partisan, disinterested, detached, dispassionate, objective, even-handed, fair.

unborn *adjective* **expected**, embryonic, fetal, in utero.

unbroken *adjective* **1 undamaged**, unharmed, unscathed, untouched, sound, intact, whole. **2 uninterrupted**, continuous, endless, constant, unremitting, ongoing. **3 unbeaten**, undefeated, unsurpassed, unrivalled, unmatched, supreme.

uncanny *adjective* **1 eerie**, unnatural, unearthly, other-worldly, ghostly, strange, abnormal, weird; *informal* creepy, spooky. **2** *an uncanny resemblance* **striking**, remarkable, extraordinary, exceptional, incredible.

uncertain *adjective* **1** *the effects are uncertain* **unknown**, debatable, open

to question, in doubt, in the balance, up in the air, unpredictable, unforeseeable, undetermined; *informal* iffy. **2** *he was uncertain about the decision* **unsure**, doubtful, dubious, undecided, irresolute, hesitant, vacillating, vague, unclear, ambivalent, in two minds.
- OPPOSITES certain, sure.

unclear *adjective* **uncertain**, unsure, unsettled, up in the air, in doubt, ambiguous, equivocal, indefinite, vague, mysterious, obscure, hazy, nebulous.
- OPPOSITES clear, evident.

uncomfortable *adjective* **1** painful, awkward, lumpy, confining, cramped. **2 uneasy**, ill at ease, awkward, nervous, tense, edgy, restless, embarrassed, anxious; *informal* rattled, twitchy.
- OPPOSITES comfortable, relaxed.

uncommon *adjective* **unusual**, abnormal, rare, atypical, exceptional, unconventional, unfamiliar, strange, extraordinary, peculiar, scarce, few and far between, isolated, infrequent.

unconditional *adjective* **unquestioning**, unqualified, unreserved, unlimited, unrestricted, wholehearted, complete, total, entire, full, absolute, unequivocal.

unconscious *adjective* **1 knocked out**, senseless, comatose, inert, stunned; *informal* out cold, out for the count. **2 subconscious**, instinctive, involuntary, uncontrolled, subliminal; *informal* gut. **3 unaware**, oblivious, ignorant, in ignorance, heedless.
- OPPOSITES aware.

uncouth *adjective* **uncivilized**, uncultured, rough, coarse, crude, loutish, boorish, rude, discourteous, disrespectful, bad-mannered, ill-bred.
- OPPOSITES civilized.

uncover *verb* **1 expose**, reveal, lay bare, unwrap, unveil, strip. **2 discover**, detect, come across, stumble on, chance on, find, turn up, unearth, dig up.

under *preposition* **1 below**, beneath, underneath. **2 less than**, lower than, below. **3 subordinate to**, answerable

to, responsible to, subject to, junior to, inferior to.
- OPPOSITES above, over.

undercover *adjective* **secret**, covert, clandestine, underground, surreptitious, furtive, cloak-and-dagger, stealthy; *Military* black; *informal* hush-hush.
- OPPOSITES overt.

underestimate *verb* **underrate**, undervalue, miscalculate, misjudge, do an injustice to.
- OPPOSITES overestimate.

undergo *verb* **experience**, go through, submit to, face, be subjected to, receive, endure, brave, bear, withstand, weather.

underground *adjective* **1 subterranean**, buried, sunken. **2 secret**, clandestine, surreptitious, covert, undercover, closet, cloak-and-dagger, resistance, subversive; *Military* black.
● *noun* **metro**; *N. Amer.* subway; *Brit. informal* tube.

underline *verb* **1 underscore**, mark, pick out, emphasize, highlight. **2 emphasize**, stress, highlight, accentuate, accent, focus on, spotlight.

underlying *adjective* **fundamental**, basic, primary, central, essential, principal, elementary, initial.

undermine *verb* **weaken**, diminish, reduce, impair, mar, spoil, ruin, damage, sap, shake, threaten, subvert, compromise, sabotage.
- OPPOSITES strengthen.

understand *verb* **1 comprehend**, grasp, take in, see, apprehend, follow, make sense of, fathom; *informal* work out, figure out, make head or tail of, get; *Brit. informal* twig, suss. **2 know**, realize, recognize, acknowledge, appreciate, be aware of, be conscious of. **3 believe**, gather, take it, hear (tell), notice, see, learn.

understandable *adjective* **1 comprehensible**, intelligible, clear, plain, unambiguous, transparent, straightforward, explicit, coherent. **2 unsurprising**, expected, predictable, inevitable,

u

reasonable, acceptable, logical, rational, normal, natural, justifiable, excusable, pardonable, forgivable.
- OPPOSITES incomprehensible.

understanding noun **1 comprehension**, grasp, mastery, appreciation, knowledge, awareness, skill, expertise, proficiency; informal know-how. **2 intellect**, intelligence, brainpower, judgement, insight, intuition, acumen, sagacity, wisdom; informal nous. **3 belief**, perception, view, conviction, feeling, opinion, intuition, impression. **4 sympathy**, compassion, pity, feeling, concern, consideration, kindness, sensitivity, decency, goodwill. **5 agreement**, arrangement, deal, bargain, settlement, pledge, pact.
- OPPOSITES ignorance.
● adjective **sympathetic**, compassionate, sensitive, considerate, kind, thoughtful, tolerant, patient, forbearing, lenient, forgiving.

understate verb **play down**, underrate, underplay, trivialize, minimize, diminish, downgrade, brush aside, gloss over.
- OPPOSITES exaggerate.

undertake verb **1 set about**, embark on, go about, engage in, take on, be responsible for, get down to, get to grips with, tackle, attempt; informal have a go at. **2 promise**, pledge, vow, give your word, swear, guarantee, contract, give an assurance, commit yourself.

undertaker noun **funeral director**; N. Amer. mortician.

undertaking noun **1 enterprise**, venture, project, campaign, scheme, plan, operation, endeavour, effort, task. **2 promise**, pledge, agreement, oath, covenant, vow, commitment, guarantee, assurance.

underwater adjective **submerged**, sunken, undersea, submarine.

underwear noun **underclothes**, undergarments, underthings, lingerie; informal undies; Brit. informal smalls.

underwrite verb **sponsor**, support, back, insure, indemnify, subsidize, pay for, finance, fund; N. Amer. informal bankroll.

undesirable adjective **unpleasant**, disagreeable, nasty, unwelcome, unwanted, unfortunate.
- OPPOSITES pleasant.

undo verb **1 unfasten**, unbutton, unhook, untie, unlace, unlock, unbolt, loosen, detach, free, open. **2 cancel**, reverse, overrule, overturn, repeal, rescind, countermand, revoke, annul, invalidate, negate. **3 ruin**, undermine, overturn, scotch, sabotage, spoil, impair, mar, destroy, wreck; informal blow; Brit. informal scupper.
- OPPOSITES fasten.

undoubtedly adverb **doubtless**, indubitably, unquestionably, indisputably, undeniably, incontrovertibly, without (a) doubt, clearly.

undue adjective **excessive**, immoderate, intemperate, inordinate, disproportionate, uncalled for, unnecessary, unwarranted, unjustified, unreasonable, inappropriate, unmerited, unsuitable, improper.
- OPPOSITES appropriate.

unearth verb **1 dig up**, excavate, exhume, disinter, root out. **2** I unearthed an interesting fact **discover**, find, come across, hit on, bring to light, expose, turn up.

uneasy adjective **1 worried**, anxious, troubled, disturbed, nervous, nervy, tense, edgy, on edge, apprehensive, fearful, uncomfortable, unsettled, ill at ease; informal jittery. **2** an uneasy peace **tense**, awkward, strained, fraught, precarious, unstable, insecure.
- OPPOSITES calm.

unemployed adjective **jobless**, out of work, unwaged, redundant, laid off, on benefit; Brit. signing on; N. Amer. on welfare; Brit. informal on the dole, resting.

uneven adjective **1 bumpy**, rough, lumpy, stony, rocky, rutted. **2 irregular**, crooked, lopsided, askew, asymmetrical. **3 inconsistent**, variable,

u

fluctuating, irregular, erratic, patchy, fitful.
- OPPOSITES flat, regular.

unfair adjective **1 unjust**, prejudiced, biased, discriminatory, one-sided, unequal, uneven, unbalanced, partisan. **2 undeserved**, unmerited, unreasonable, unjustified; Brit. informal out of order. **3 unsporting**, dirty, underhand, dishonourable, dishonest.
- OPPOSITES just, justified.

unfasten verb **undo**, open, disconnect, untie, unbutton, unzip, loosen, free, unlock, unbolt.

unfit adjective **1** the film is unfit for children **unsuitable**, inappropriate, not designed. **2** unfit for duty **incapable of**, not up to, not equal to, unequipped, inadequate, unprepared; informal not cut out for. **3 unhealthy**, out of condition/shape, debilitated.
- OPPOSITES suitable, healthy.

unfold verb **1 open out**, spread out, flatten, straighten out, unroll, unfurl. **2 develop**, evolve, happen, take place, occur.

unfortunate adjective **1 unlucky**, hapless, ill-starred, star-crossed, wretched, poor, pitiful; informal down on your luck. **2 unwelcome**, disadvantageous, unfavourable, unlucky, adverse, unpromising, inauspicious. **3 regrettable**, inappropriate, unsuitable, tactless, injudicious.
- OPPOSITES lucky.

unfriendly adjective **hostile**, disagreeable, antagonistic, aggressive, unpleasant, surly, uncongenial, inhospitable, unneighbourly, unwelcoming, unsociable, cool, cold, aloof, distant; informal stand-offish.

ungainly adjective **awkward**, clumsy, graceless, inelegant, gawky, gauche, uncoordinated.
- OPPOSITES graceful.

unhappy adjective **1 sad**, miserable, sorrowful, dejected, despondent, disconsolate, morose, heartbroken, down, dispirited, downhearted, depressed, melancholy, mournful, gloomy, glum; informal down in the mouth, fed up, blue. **2** I was very unhappy with the service **dissatisfied**, displeased, discontented, disappointed, disgruntled; Brit. informal narked, not best pleased. **3 unfortunate**, unlucky, ill-starred, ill-fated, doomed; informal jinxed.
- OPPOSITES happy, pleased.

unhealthy adjective **1 harmful**, detrimental, destructive, injurious, damaging, noxious, poisonous. **2 sick**, poorly, ill, unwell, unfit, ailing, weak, frail, infirm, washed out, run down. **3 abnormal**, morbid, macabre, twisted, unwholesome, warped, depraved, unnatural; informal sick.

uniform adjective **1 constant**, consistent, steady, invariable, unchanging, stable, static, regular, fixed, even. **2 identical**, matching, similar, equal, same, like, consistent.
- OPPOSITES variable.
● noun **costume**, outfit, suit, ensemble, livery, regalia; informal get-up, rig, gear.

unify verb **unite**, combine, bring together, join, merge, fuse, amalgamate, coalesce, consolidate.
- OPPOSITES separate.

uninteresting adjective **boring**, dull, unexciting, tiresome, tedious, dreary, lifeless, humdrum, colourless, bland, insipid, banal, dry.
- OPPOSITES exciting.

union noun **1 unification**, joining, merger, fusion, amalgamation, coalition, combination, synthesis, blend. **2 association**, league, guild, confederation, federation.
- OPPOSITES separation.

unique adjective **1 distinctive**, individual, special, particular, specific, idiosyncratic, single, sole, lone, unrepeated, solitary, exclusive; informal one-off. **2 remarkable**, special, notable, unequalled, unparalleled, unmatched, unsurpassed, incomparable.
- OPPOSITES common.

unit noun **1 component**, part, section, segment, element, module, constituent, subdivision. **2 quantity**, measure, denomination. **3 group**, detachment, contingent, division, cell, faction, department, office, branch.

unite verb **1 unify**, join, link, connect, combine, amalgamate, fuse, weld, bond, bring together. **2 join together**, join forces, combine, band together, ally, cooperate, collaborate, work together, team up. **3 merge**, mix, blend, mingle, combine.
- OPPOSITES divide.

unity noun **1 union**, unification, integration, amalgamation, coalition, federation, confederation. **2 harmony**, accord, cooperation, collaboration, agreement, consensus, solidarity. **3 oneness**, singleness, wholeness, uniformity, homogeneity.
- OPPOSITES disunity.

universal adjective **general**, common, widespread, ubiquitous, comprehensive, global, worldwide, international.

universally adverb **always**, without exception, by everyone, in all cases, everywhere, worldwide, globally, internationally, commonly, generally.

universe noun **cosmos**, macrocosm, space, infinity, nature, all existence.

> **WORD LINKS**
> **cosmic** relating to the universe

unkind adjective **unpleasant**, disagreeable, nasty, mean, cruel, vicious, spiteful, malicious, callous, unsympathetic, uncharitable, harsh, hard-hearted, heartless, cold-hearted; informal bitchy, catty.

unknown adjective **1 undisclosed**, unrevealed, secret, undetermined, undecided. **2 unexplored**, uncharted, unmapped, undiscovered, untravelled. **3 unidentified**, unnamed, anonymous, nameless. **4 obscure**, unfamiliar, unheard of, unsung, minor, undistinguished.
- OPPOSITES familiar.

unlikely adjective **improbable**, doubtful, dubious, questionable, unconvincing, implausible, far-fetched, unrealistic, incredible, unbelievable, inconceivable.
- OPPOSITES probable, likely.

unload verb **unpack**, empty, clear, remove, offload.

unlucky adjective **1 unfortunate**, hapless, luckless, down on your luck, unsuccessful, ill-fated, ill-starred, jinxed. **2 unfavourable**, inauspicious, unpropitious, ominous.
- OPPOSITES lucky, fortunate.

unnatural adjective **1 abnormal**, unusual, uncommon, extraordinary, strange, unorthodox, exceptional, irregular, untypical. **2 artificial**, man-made, synthetic. **3 affected**, artificial, stilted, forced, false, fake, insincere, contrived, mannered, self-conscious; informal put on, phoney.
- OPPOSITES natural.

unnecessary adjective **unneeded**, inessential, not required, uncalled for, unwarranted, dispensable, optional, extraneous, expendable, redundant.

unpleasant adjective **1** an unpleasant situation **disagreeable**, distressing, nasty, horrible, terrible, awful, dreadful, invidious, objectionable. **2** an unpleasant man **unlikeable**, unlovable, disagreeable, bad-tempered, unfriendly, rude, impolite, obnoxious, nasty, spiteful, mean, objectionable, annoying, irritating. **3 unappetizing**, unpalatable, unsavoury, unappealing, disgusting, revolting, nauseating, sickening.
- OPPOSITES pleasant, agreeable.

unpopular adjective **disliked**, friendless, unloved, unwelcome, avoided, ignored, rejected, shunned, out of favour.

unravel verb **1 untangle**, disentangle, separate out, unwind, untwist. **2 solve**, resolve, clear up, puzzle out, get to the bottom of, explain, clarify; informal figure out.
- OPPOSITES entangle.

unreal adjective **imaginary**, fictitious, pretend, make-believe, made-up, dreamed-up, mock, false, illusory,

u

mythical, fanciful, hypothetical, theoretical; *informal* phoney.

unrest *noun* **disturbance**, trouble, turmoil, disruption, disorder, chaos, anarchy, dissatisfaction, dissent, strife, agitation, protest, rebellion, uprising, rioting.
- OPPOSITES peace.

unsafe *adjective* **1 dangerous**, risky, hazardous, high-risk, treacherous, insecure, unsound, harmful, injurious, toxic. **2 unreliable**, open to doubt, questionable, doubtful, dubious, suspect; *informal* iffy; *Brit. informal* dodgy.
- OPPOSITES safe.

unsatisfactory *adjective* **disappointing**, displeasing, inadequate, unacceptable, poor, bad, substandard, weak, mediocre, not up to par, defective, deficient; *informal* leaving a lot to be desired.

unscrupulous *adjective* **dishonest**, deceitful, devious, underhand, unethical, immoral, shameless, exploitative, corrupt, unprincipled, dishonourable, disreputable; *informal* crooked, shady.

unsettle *verb* **disturb**, disconcert, unnerve, upset, disquiet, perturb, alarm, dismay, trouble, bother, agitate, fluster, ruffle, shake (up), throw; *informal* rattle, faze.

unsightly *adjective* **unattractive**, ugly, unprepossessing, hideous, horrible, repulsive, revolting, offensive, grotesque.
- OPPOSITES attractive.

unsociable *adjective* **unfriendly**, uncongenial, unneighbourly, unapproachable, introverted, reserved, withdrawn, retiring, aloof, distant, remote, detached; *informal* stand-offish.

unstable *adjective* **1 unsteady**, rocky, wobbly, rickety, shaky, unsafe, insecure, precarious. **2 changeable**, volatile, variable, fluctuating, irregular, unpredictable, erratic. **3 unbalanced**, of unsound mind, mentally ill, deranged, demented, disturbed, unhinged; *Brit.* sectionable.
- OPPOSITES steady, firm.

unsuccessful *adjective* **1 failed**, abortive, ineffective, fruitless, profitless, unproductive, vain, futile. **2 unprofitable**, loss-making.

unsuitable *adjective* **1 inappropriate**, ill-suited, inapposite, inapt, unacceptable, unfitting, incompatible, out of place, out of keeping, incongruous, unseemly. **2** *an unsuitable moment* **inopportune**, badly timed, unfortunate, difficult, infelicitous.
- OPPOSITES appropriate.

unsure *adjective* **1 undecided**, uncertain, irresolute, dithering, in two minds, in a quandary, dubious, doubtful, sceptical, unconvinced. **2 unconfident**, unassertive, insecure, hesitant, diffident, anxious, apprehensive.
- OPPOSITES sure, certain.

untangle *verb* **disentangle**, unravel, unsnarl, straighten out, untwist, unknot, sort out.

unthinkable *adjective* **unimaginable**, inconceivable, unbelievable, incredible, implausible, out of the question, impossible, unconscionable, unreasonable.

untidy *adjective* **1 disordered**, messy, disorganized, cluttered, in chaos, haywire, in disarray, disorderly, topsy-turvy, at sixes and sevens, jumbled; *informal* higgledy-piggledy. **2 scruffy**, dishevelled, unkempt, messy, rumpled, bedraggled.
- OPPOSITES neat, tidy.

untoward *adjective* **unexpected**, unforeseen, surprising, unusual, inappropriate, inconvenient, unwelcome, unfavourable, adverse, unfortunate, infelicitous.

untrue *adjective* **false**, invented, made up, fabricated, concocted, trumped up, erroneous, wrong, incorrect, inaccurate.
- OPPOSITES true, correct.

unusual *adjective* **1** *an unusual sight* **uncommon**, abnormal, atypical, unexpected, surprising, unfamiliar, different, strange, odd, curious, extraordinary, unorthodox, unconventional, peculiar, queer, unwonted; *informal* weird,

offbeat. **2** *a man of unusual talent* **remarkable**, extraordinary, exceptional, particular, outstanding, notable, noteworthy, distinctive, striking, significant, special, unique, unparalleled, prodigious.
- OPPOSITES common.

unwarranted *adjective* **1 unjustified**, indefensible, inexcusable, unforgivable, unpardonable, uncalled for, unnecessary, unjust, groundless.
2 unauthorized, unsanctioned, unapproved, uncertified, unlicensed, illegal, unlawful, illicit, illegitimate, criminal, actionable.
- OPPOSITES justified.

unwieldy *adjective* **awkward**, unmanageable, unmanoeuvrable, cumbersome, clumsy, massive, heavy, hefty, bulky.

unwilling *adjective* **1 reluctant**, unenthusiastic, hesitant, resistant, grudging, involuntary, forced. **2** *he was unwilling to go* **disinclined**, reluctant, averse, loath, not in the mood; (**be unwilling to do something**) baulk at, demur at, shy away from, flinch from, shrink from, have qualms about, have misgivings about, have reservations about.
- OPPOSITES willing.

upbeat *adjective* **cheerful**, optimistic, cheery, positive, confident, hopeful, sanguine, bullish, buoyant.
- OPPOSITES pessimistic.

upbringing *noun* **childhood**, early life, formative years, teaching, instruction, rearing.

update *verb* **1 modernize**, upgrade, improve, overhaul. **2 brief**, bring up to date, inform, fill in, tell, notify, keep posted; *informal* clue in, put in the picture, bring/keep up to speed.

upgrade *verb* **improve**, modernize, update, reform.
- OPPOSITES downgrade.

upheaval *noun* **disturbance**, disruption, trouble, turbulence, disorder, confusion, turmoil.

uphill *adjective* **1 upward**, rising, ascending, climbing. **2 difficult**, hard,
tough, demanding, arduous, taxing, exacting, stiff, gruelling, onerous.
- OPPOSITES downhill.

uphold *verb* **1 confirm**, endorse, sustain, approve, support, back (up). **2 maintain**, sustain, continue, preserve, protect, keep, hold to, keep alive, keep going.
- OPPOSITES oppose.

upkeep *noun* **1 maintenance**, repair(s), servicing, care, preservation, conservation, running. **2 (financial) support**, maintenance, keep, subsistence, care.

uplifting *adjective* **inspiring**, stirring, inspirational, rousing, moving, touching, affecting, cheering, heartening, encouraging.

upper *adjective* **1 higher**, superior, top. **2 senior**, superior, higher-level, higher-ranking, top.
- OPPOSITES lower.

upper-class *adjective* **aristocratic**, noble, patrician, titled, blue-blooded, high-born, elite; *Brit.* county; *informal* upper-crust, top-drawer; *Brit. informal* posh.

upright *adjective* **1 vertical**, perpendicular, plumb, straight (up), erect, on end, on your feet. **2 honest**, honourable, upstanding, respectable, high-minded, law-abiding, worthy, righteous, decent, good, virtuous, principled.
- OPPOSITES flat, horizontal.

uprising *noun* **rebellion**, revolt, insurrection, mutiny, revolution, insurgence, rioting, coup.

uproar *noun* **1 commotion**, disturbance, rumpus, disorder, confusion, chaos, tumult, mayhem, pandemonium, bedlam, noise, din, clamour, hubbub, racket; *Brit.* row; *informal* hullabaloo. **2 outcry**, furore, fuss, commotion, hue and cry, rumpus; *Brit.* row; *informal* hullabaloo, stink, ructions.
- OPPOSITES calm.

upset *verb* **1 distress**, trouble, perturb, dismay, sadden, grieve, disturb, unsettle, disconcert, disquiet, worry, bother, agitate, fluster, throw, ruffle, unnerve,

u

shake. **2 knock over**, overturn, upend, tip over, topple, spill. **3 disrupt**, interfere with, disturb, throw into confusion, mess up.
- OPPOSITES calm.
● noun **1 distress**, trouble, dismay, disquiet, worry, bother, agitation, hurt, grief. **2** a stomach upset **disorder**, complaint, ailment, illness, sickness; informal bug; Brit. informal lurgy.
● adjective **1 distressed**, troubled, perturbed, dismayed, disturbed, unsettled, disconcerted, worried, bothered, anxious, agitated, flustered, ruffled, unnerved, shaken, saddened, grieved; informal cut up, choked; Brit. informal gutted. **2** an upset stomach **disturbed**, unsettled, queasy, bad, poorly; informal gippy.
- OPPOSITES calm.

upside down adjective **1 upturned**, upended, wrong side up, overturned, inverted, capsized. **2 in disarray**, in disorder, jumbled up, in a muddle, untidy, disorganized, in chaos, in confusion, topsy-turvy, at sixes and sevens; informal higgledy-piggledy.

up to date adjective **1 modern**, contemporary, the latest, state-of-the-art, new, up-to-the-minute, advanced. **2 informed**, up to speed, in the picture, in touch, au fait, conversant, familiar, knowledgeable, acquainted.
- OPPOSITES out of date, old-fashioned.

urban adjective **town**, city, municipal, metropolitan, built-up, inner-city, suburban.
- OPPOSITES rural.

urge verb **1 encourage**, exhort, press, entreat, implore, call on, appeal to, beg, plead with. **2 advise**, counsel, advocate, recommend.
● noun his urge to travel **desire**, wish, need, compulsion, longing, yearning, hankering, craving, hunger, thirst; informal yen, itch.

urgent adjective **pressing**, acute, dire, desperate, critical, serious, grave, intense, crying, burning, compelling, extreme, high-priority, life-and-death.

usage noun **1** energy usage **consumption**, use. **2** the usage of equipment **use**, utilization, operation, manipulation, running, handling. **3 language**, expression, phraseology, parlance, idiom.

use verb **1 utilize**, employ, avail yourself of, work, operate, wield, ply, apply, put into service. **2 exercise**, employ, bring into play, practise, apply. **3 take advantage of**, exploit, manipulate, take liberties with, impose on, abuse, capitalize on, profit from, trade on, milk; informal cash in on, walk all over. **4** we have used up our funds **consume**, get/go through, exhaust, deplete, expend, spend.
● noun **1 utilization**, application, employment, operation, manipulation. **2 exploitation**, manipulation, abuse. **3** what is the use of that? **advantage**, benefit, good, point, object, purpose, sense, reason, service, utility, help, gain, avail, profit, value, worth.

used adjective **second-hand**, pre-owned, nearly new, old, worn, hand-me-down, cast-off.
□ **used to** accustomed to, no stranger to, familiar with, at home with, in the habit of, experienced in, versed in, conversant with, acquainted with.

useful adjective **1** a useful tool **functional**, practical, handy, convenient, utilitarian, serviceable, of service; informal nifty. **2** a useful experience **beneficial**, advantageous, helpful, worthwhile, profitable, rewarding, productive, constructive, valuable, fruitful.
- OPPOSITES useless.

useless adjective **1 futile**, pointless, to no avail, vain, to no purpose, unavailing, hopeless, ineffectual, fruitless, unprofitable, unproductive, abortive. **2** (informal) **incompetent**, inept, ineffective, incapable, inadequate, hopeless, bad; informal a dead loss.
- OPPOSITES useful, beneficial.

usher verb **escort**, accompany, take, show, see, lead, conduct, guide.
● noun **guide**, attendant, escort.

usual *adjective* **normal**, customary, accustomed, wonted, habitual, routine, regular, standard, typical, established, set, stock, conventional, traditional, expected, familiar.
- OPPOSITES exceptional.

usually *adverb* **normally**, generally, habitually, customarily, routinely, typically, ordinarily, commonly, as a rule, in general, more often than not, mainly, mostly.

utensil *noun* **implement**, tool, instrument, device, apparatus, gadget, appliance, contrivance, contraption; *informal* gizmo.

utility *noun* **usefulness**, use, benefit, value, advantage, help, practicality, effectiveness, service.

utilize *verb* **use**, employ, avail yourself of, press into service, bring into play, deploy, draw on, exploit.

utmost *adjective* **greatest**, highest, maximum, most, extreme, supreme, paramount.

utter[1] *adjective* **complete**, total, absolute, thorough, perfect, downright, out-and-out, outright, sheer, arrant, positive, prize, pure, unmitigated, unadulterated, unqualified, unalloyed.

utter[2] *verb* **say**, speak, voice, mouth, express, articulate, pronounce, enunciate, emit, let out, give, produce.

utterance *noun* **remark**, comment, statement, observation, declaration, pronouncement.

Vv

vacancy noun **opening**, position, post, job, opportunity.

vacant adjective **1 empty**, unoccupied, not in use, free, available, unfilled, uninhabited, untenanted; informal up for grabs. **2 blank**, expressionless, unresponsive, emotionless, impassive, vacuous, empty, glazed.
- OPPOSITES full, occupied.

vacate verb **1 leave**, move out of, evacuate, quit, depart from. **2 resign from**, leave, stand down from, give up, bow out of, relinquish, retire from; informal quit.
- OPPOSITES occupy.

vacation noun **holiday**, trip, tour, break, leave, time off, recess.

vagrant noun **tramp**, drifter, down-and-out, beggar, itinerant, wanderer; N. Amer. hobo; N. Amer. informal bum.

vague adjective **1 indistinct**, indefinite, indeterminate, unclear, ill-defined, hazy, fuzzy, misty, blurry, out of focus, shadowy, obscure. **2 imprecise**, rough, approximate, inexact, non-specific, ambiguous, hazy, uncertain. **3 absent-minded**, forgetful, dreamy, abstracted; informal with your head in the clouds, scatty, not with it.
- OPPOSITES clear, definite.

vaguely adverb **1 slightly**, a little, a bit, somewhat, rather, in a way, faintly, obscurely; informal sort of, kind of. **2 absent-mindedly**, abstractedly, vacantly.

vain adjective **1 conceited**, narcissistic, proud, arrogant, boastful, cocky, egotistical, immodest; informal big-headed. **2 futile**, useless, pointless, ineffective, unavailing, fruitless, unproductive, unsuccessful, failed, abortive.
- OPPOSITES modest, successful.
□ **in vain** unsuccessfully, to no avail, to no purpose, fruitlessly.

valiant adjective **brave**, courageous, plucky, intrepid, heroic, gallant, bold, fearless, daring, unflinching, unafraid, undaunted, doughty, indomitable, stout-hearted; informal game, gutsy.
- OPPOSITES cowardly.

valid adjective **1 well founded**, sound, reasonable, rational, logical, justifiable, defensible, cogent, credible, forceful. **2 legally binding**, lawful, official, in force, in effect.

validate verb **ratify**, endorse, approve, agree to, accept, authorize, legalize, legitimize, warrant, license, certify, recognize.

valley noun **dale**, vale, hollow, gully, gorge, ravine, canyon, rift; Brit. combe; Scottish glen.

valuable adjective **1 precious**, costly, high-priced, expensive, dear, priceless. **2 useful**, helpful, beneficial, advantageous, invaluable, productive, worthwhile, worthy, important.
- OPPOSITES worthless.

valuables plural noun **precious items**, costly items, prized possessions, treasures.

value noun **1 price**, cost, worth, market price. **2 worth**, usefulness, advantage, benefit, gain, profit, good, help. **3 (values) principles**, ethics, morals, standards, code of behaviour.
● verb **1 evaluate**, assess, estimate, appraise, price. **2 think highly of**, have a high opinion of, rate highly, esteem, set great store by, respect.
- OPPOSITES despise.

vanish verb **disappear**, be lost to sight, become invisible, recede from view, fade (away), evaporate, melt away, end, cease to exist.
- OPPOSITES appear.

vanity noun **conceit**, narcissism, self-love, self-admiration, egotism, pride,

arrogance, boastfulness, cockiness; *informal* big-headedness.
- OPPOSITES modesty.

variable *adjective* **changeable**, shifting, fluctuating, irregular, inconstant, inconsistent, fluid, unstable; *informal* up and down.
- OPPOSITES constant.

variant *noun* **variation**, version, form, alternative, adaptation, alteration, modification.
● *adjective* **alternative**, other, different, divergent.

variation *noun* **1** *regional variations* **difference**, dissimilarity, disparity, contrast, discrepancy, imbalance. **2** *there was little variation from the pattern* **deviation**, variance, divergence, departure, fluctuation, change, alteration, modification.

varied *adjective* **diverse**, assorted, miscellaneous, mixed, sundry, wide-ranging, disparate, heterogeneous, motley.

variety *noun* **1 diversity**, variation, diversification, change, difference. **2 assortment**, miscellany, range, array, collection, selection, mixture, medley. **3 sort**, kind, type, class, category, style, form, make, model, brand, strain, breed.
- OPPOSITES uniformity.

various *adjective* **diverse**, different, differing, varied, assorted, mixed, sundry, miscellaneous, disparate, heterogeneous, motley.

varnish *noun & verb* **lacquer**, shellac, japan, enamel, glaze, polish.

vary *verb* **1 differ**, be dissimilar, disagree, be at variance. **2 fluctuate**, rise and fall, go up and down, change, alter, shift, swing.

vast *adjective* **huge**, extensive, broad, wide, boundless, enormous, immense, great, massive, colossal, gigantic, mammoth, giant, mountainous; *informal* mega, whopping.
- OPPOSITES tiny.

vault[1] *noun* **1 cellar**, basement, crypt, undercroft, catacomb, burial chamber. **2 strongroom**, safe deposit.

vault[2] *verb* **jump**, leap, spring, bound, clear.

veer *verb* **turn**, swerve, swing, weave, wheel, change direction, change course, deviate.

vehement *adjective* **passionate**, forceful, ardent, impassioned, heated, spirited, urgent, fervent, fierce, strong, forcible, powerful, emphatic, vigorous, intense, earnest, keen, enthusiastic, zealous.
- OPPOSITES mild.

vehicle *noun* **1 means of transport**, transportation, conveyance. **2 channel**, medium, means, agent, instrument, mechanism, organ, apparatus.

> **WORD LINKS**
> **automotive** relating to vehicles

veil *noun* **covering**, screen, curtain, mantle, cloak, mask, blanket, shroud, canopy, cloud, pall.
● *verb* **cover**, surround, swathe, enfold, envelop, conceal, hide, obscure, screen, shield, cloak, blanket, shroud.

vein *noun* **1 blood vessel**, capillary. **2 layer**, seam, lode, stratum, deposit.

> **WORD LINKS**
> **vascular**, **venous** relating to veins

velocity *noun* **speed**, pace, rate, tempo, rapidity.

veneer *noun* **1 surface**, lamination, layer, overlay, facing, covering, finish, exterior. **2 facade**, front, show, outward display, appearance, impression, semblance, guise, mask, pretence, cover, camouflage.

vengeance *noun* **revenge**, retribution, retaliation, requital, reprisal, an eye for an eye.
- OPPOSITES forgiveness.

venomous *adjective* **poisonous**, toxic, dangerous, deadly, lethal, fatal.
- OPPOSITES harmless.

V

vent noun **outlet**, **inlet**, opening, aperture, hole, gap, orifice, space, duct, flue, shaft, well, passage, airway.
● verb **let out**, release, pour out, utter, express, air, voice.

ventilate verb **air**, aerate, oxygenate, freshen, cool.

venture noun **enterprise**, undertaking, project, scheme, operation, endeavour, speculation.
● verb **1 put forward**, advance, proffer, offer, air, suggest, volunteer, submit, propose. **2 dare**, be so bold as, presume, have the audacity, have the nerve, take the liberty of.

verbal adjective **oral**, spoken, word-of-mouth, stated, said, unwritten.

verbose adjective **wordy**, loquacious, garrulous, talkative, voluble, long-winded, lengthy, prolix, circumlocutory, rambling.
- OPPOSITES succinct.

verdict noun **judgement**, adjudication, decision, finding, ruling, sentence.

verge noun **1 edge**, border, margin, side, brink, rim, lip, fringe, boundary, perimeter. **2** I was on the verge of tears **brink**, threshold, edge, point.
☐ **verge on** approach, border on, be close/near to, resemble, be tantamount to, tend towards, approximate to.

verify verb **confirm**, prove, substantiate, corroborate, back up, bear out, justify, support, uphold, testify to, validate, authenticate.
- OPPOSITES refute.

versatile adjective **1** a versatile player **adaptable**, flexible, all-round, multi-talented, resourceful. **2** a versatile device **adjustable**, adaptable, multi-purpose, all-purpose.

verse noun **1 poetry**, lyrics. **2 poem**, lyric, rhyme, ditty, limerick. **3 stanza**, canto.

version noun **1 account**, report, statement, description, record, story, rendering, interpretation, explanation, understanding, reading, impression, side. **2 edition**, translation, impression.

3 type, sort, kind, form, equivalent, variety, variant, design, model, style.

vertical adjective **upright**, erect, perpendicular, plumb, on end, standing.
- OPPOSITES flat, horizontal.

very adverb **extremely**, exceedingly, exceptionally, extraordinarily, tremendously, immensely, acutely, singularly, decidedly, highly, remarkably, really; informal awfully, terribly, seriously, mega, ultra; Brit. informal well, dead, jolly; N. Amer. informal real, mighty.
- OPPOSITES slightly.

vessel noun **1 boat**, ship, craft. **2 container**, receptacle, basin, bowl, pan, pot, jug.

vestige noun **remnant**, fragment, relic, echo, trace, mark, legacy, reminder.

vet verb **check up on**, screen, investigate, examine, scrutinize, inspect, look over, assess, evaluate, appraise; informal check out.

veteran noun **old hand**, past master, doyen, doyenne; informal old-timer; N. Amer. informal vet.
- OPPOSITES novice.
● adjective **long-serving**, seasoned, old, hardened, practised, experienced; informal battle-scarred.

veto noun **rejection**, dismissal, prohibition, proscription, embargo, ban, interdict.
● verb **reject**, turn down, throw out, dismiss, prohibit, forbid, proscribe, disallow, embargo, ban, rule out; informal kill, give the thumbs down to.
- OPPOSITES approve.

viable adjective **feasible**, workable, practicable, practical, realistic, achievable, attainable; informal doable.
- OPPOSITES impracticable.

vibrant adjective **1 spirited**, lively, energetic, vigorous, dynamic, passionate, fiery; informal feisty. **2 vivid**, bright, striking, brilliant, glowing, strong, rich.
- OPPOSITES lifeless, pale.

vibrate verb **shake**, tremble, shiver, quiver, shudder, throb, pulsate.

vice *noun* **1 immorality**, wrongdoing, wickedness, evil, iniquity, villainy, corruption, misconduct, sin, depravity. **2 fault**, failing, flaw, defect, shortcoming, weakness, deficiency, foible, frailty.
- OPPOSITES virtue.

vicious *adjective* **1 brutal**, ferocious, savage, violent, ruthless, merciless, heartless, callous, cruel, cold-blooded, inhuman, barbaric, bloodthirsty. **2 malicious**, spiteful, vindictive, venomous, cruel, bitter, acrimonious, hostile, nasty; *informal* catty.
- OPPOSITES gentle.

victim *noun* **sufferer**, injured party, casualty, fatality, loss, survivor.

victimize *verb* **persecute**, pick on, bully, abuse, discriminate against, exploit, take advantage of; *informal* have it in for.

victorious *adjective* **triumphant**, conquering, vanquishing, winning, champion, successful.
- OPPOSITES unsuccessful.

victory *noun* **success**, triumph, conquest, win, coup; *informal* walkover.
- OPPOSITES defeat, loss.

vie *verb* **compete**, contend, struggle, fight, battle, jockey.

view *noun* **1 outlook**, prospect, panorama, vista, scene, scenery, landscape. **2 opinion**, viewpoint, belief, judgement, thinking, notion, idea, conviction, persuasion, attitude, feeling, sentiment. **3** *the church came into view* **sight**, perspective, vision, visibility.
● *verb* **1 look at**, observe, eye, gaze at, contemplate, regard, scan, survey, inspect, scrutinize; *informal* check out; *N. Amer. informal* eyeball. **2 consider**, regard, look on, see, perceive, judge, deem, reckon.

viewer *noun* **watcher**, spectator, onlooker, observer; (**viewers**) audience, crowd.

vigilant *adjective* **watchful**, observant, attentive, alert, eagle-eyed, on the lookout, on your guard; *informal* beady-eyed.
- OPPOSITES inattentive.

vigorous *adjective* **1 robust**, healthy, hale and hearty, strong, sturdy, fit, hardy, tough, energetic, lively, active. **2 strenuous**, powerful, forceful, spirited, determined, aggressive, passionate; *informal* punchy, feisty.
- OPPOSITES weak, feeble.

vigorously *adverb* **strenuously**, strongly, powerfully, forcefully, energetically, heartily, all out, fiercely, hard; *informal* like mad; *Brit. informal* like billy-o.

vigour *noun* **health**, strength, robustness, energy, life, vitality, spirit, passion, determination, dynamism, drive; *informal* oomph, get-up-and-go.
- OPPOSITES lethargy.

vile *adjective* **foul**, nasty, unpleasant, bad, horrid, repulsive, disgusting, hateful, nauseating; *informal* gross.
- OPPOSITES pleasant.

villain *noun* **criminal**, lawbreaker, offender, felon, miscreant, wrongdoer, rogue, scoundrel, reprobate; *informal* crook, baddy.

vindicate *verb* **1 acquit**, clear, absolve, exonerate; *informal* let off. **2 justify**, warrant, substantiate, confirm, corroborate, prove, defend, support, back, endorse.
- OPPOSITES incriminate.

vintage *adjective* **1 high-quality**, quality, choice, select, superior. **2 classic**, ageless, timeless, old, antique, historic.

violate *verb* **1 contravene**, breach, infringe, break, transgress, disobey, defy, flout, disregard, ignore. **2 desecrate**, profane, defile, degrade, debase, damage, vandalize, deface, destroy.
- OPPOSITES respect.

violation *noun* **1 contravention**, breach, infringement, transgression, defiance, flouting, disregard. **2 desecration**, defilement, damage, vandalism, destruction.

violence *noun* **1 brutality**, savagery, cruelty, barbarity. **2 force**, power, strength, might, ferocity, intensity, vehemence.

v

violent *adjective* **1 brutal**, vicious, savage, rough, aggressive, threatening, fierce, ferocious, bloodthirsty. **2 powerful**, forceful, hard, sharp, smart, strong, vigorous, mighty, hefty. **3 intense**, extreme, strong, powerful, fierce, unbridled, uncontrollable, ungovernable, consuming, passionate.
- OPPOSITES gentle, mild.

virtual *adjective* **effective**, near (enough), essential, practical, to all intents and purposes, in all but name, implied, unacknowledged.

virtually *adverb* **effectively**, all but, more or less, practically, almost, nearly, close to, verging on, just about, as good as, essentially, to all intents and purposes.

virtue *noun* **1 goodness**, righteousness, morality, integrity, dignity, rectitude, honour, probity. **2 good point**, good quality, strong point, asset, forte, attribute, strength, merit, advantage, benefit; *informal* plus.
- OPPOSITES vice.

visible *adjective* **observable**, perceptible, noticeable, detectable, discernible, in sight, in view, on display, evident, apparent, manifest, plain.

vision *noun* **1 eyesight**, sight, observation, eyes, view, perspective. **2 apparition**, spectre, phantom, ghost, wraith, manifestation, hallucination, illusion, mirage. **3 dream**, reverie, plan, hope, fantasy, pipe dream. **4 imagination**, creativity, inventiveness, inspiration, intuition, perception, insight.

> **WORD LINKS**
> **visual, optic** relating to vision

visit *verb* **call on**, go to see, look in on, stay with, holiday with, stop by, drop by; *informal* pop/drop in on, look up.
● *noun* (**social**) **call**, stay, stopover, trip, holiday, vacation; *literary* sojourn.

visitor *noun* **1 guest**, caller, company. **2 tourist**, traveller, holidaymaker, tripper, vacationer, sightseer.

vista *noun* **view**, scene, prospect, panorama, sight, scenery, landscape.

visual *adjective* **1 optical**, ocular. **2 visible**, observable, perceptible, discernible.

visualize *verb* **envisage**, conjure up, picture, call to mind, see, imagine, dream up.

vital *adjective* **1 essential**, critical, crucial, indispensable, all-important, imperative, mandatory, high-priority, key, life-and-death. **2 lively**, energetic, active, sprightly, spirited, vivacious, exuberant, dynamic, vigorous; *informal* full of beans.
- OPPOSITES unimportant.

vitality *noun* **life**, energy, spirit, vivacity, exuberance, dynamism, vigour, passion, drive; *informal* get-up-and-go.

vivid *adjective* **1 bright**, colourful, brilliant, radiant, vibrant, strong, bold, deep, intense, rich, warm. **2 graphic**, realistic, lifelike, faithful, authentic, striking, evocative, arresting, colourful, dramatic, memorable, powerful, stirring, moving, haunting.
- OPPOSITES dull, vague.

vocal *adjective* **1 spoken**, said, voiced, uttered, articulated, oral. **2 vociferous**, outspoken, forthright, plain-spoken, blunt, frank, candid, passionate, vehement, vigorous.

vocation *noun* **calling**, life's work, mission, purpose, profession, occupation, career, job, employment, trade, craft, line (of work).

vogue *noun* **fashion**, trend, fad, fancy, craze, rage, enthusiasm, passion.

voice *noun* **opinion**, view, feeling, wish, desire, vote.
● *verb* **express**, communicate, declare, state, vent, utter, say, speak, articulate, air; *informal* come out with.

> **WORD LINKS**
> **vocal** relating to the human voice

void *noun* **vacuum**, emptiness, nothingness, blankness, (empty) space, gap, cavity, chasm, gulf.
● *adjective* **1 empty**, vacant, blank, bare, clear, free. **2 invalid**, null (and

void), ineffective, worthless.
- OPPOSITES full, valid.

volatile *adjective* **1 unpredictable**, temperamental, capricious, fickle, impulsive, emotional, excitable, turbulent, erratic, unstable. **2** *a volatile situation* **tense**, strained, fraught, uneasy, uncomfortable, charged, explosive, inflammatory, turbulent.
- OPPOSITES stable.

volley *noun* **barrage**, cannonade, battery, bombardment, salvo, burst, storm, hail, shower, deluge, torrent.

volume *noun* **1 book**, publication, tome, work, title. **2 capacity**, mass, bulk, extent, size, dimensions. **3 quantity**, amount, mass, bulk, measure. **4 loudness**, sound, amplification.

voluntarily *adverb* **of your own free will**, of your own volition, by choice, by preference, spontaneously, willingly, readily, freely.

voluntary *adjective* **1 optional**, discretionary, at your discretion, elective, non-compulsory. **2 unpaid**, unsalaried, for free, honorary.
- OPPOSITES compulsory.

volunteer *verb* **1 offer**, tender, proffer, put forward, put up, venture. **2 offer your services**, present yourself, make yourself available, come forward.

vomit *verb* **be sick**, spew, heave, retch, gag; *informal* throw up, puke; *N. Amer. informal* barf.

vote *noun* **1 ballot**, poll, election, referendum, plebiscite, show of hands. **2** (**the vote**) **suffrage**, franchise, voting rights.

> **WORD LINKS**
> **psephology** study of trends in voting

voucher *noun* **coupon**, token, ticket, pass, chit, slip, stub, docket; *Brit. informal* chitty.

vow *noun* **promise**, pledge, oath, bond, covenant, commitment, word (of honour).
● *verb* **promise**, pledge, swear, undertake, make a commitment, give your word, guarantee.

voyage *noun* **journey**, trip, cruise, passage, sail, crossing, expedition, odyssey.

vulgar *adjective* **1 rude**, crude, dirty, filthy, smutty, naughty, indecent, obscene, coarse, risqué; *informal* blue. **2 tasteless**, crass, tawdry, ostentatious, flamboyant, showy, gaudy, garish; *informal* flash, tacky. **3 impolite**, ill-mannered, boorish, uncouth, unsophisticated, unrefined.
- OPPOSITES tasteful.

vulnerable *adjective* **1 in danger**, in peril, in jeopardy, at risk, unprotected, undefended, unguarded, open to attack, exposed, defenceless, an easy target. **2 helpless**, weak, sensitive, thin-skinned.
- OPPOSITES invulnerable.

Ww

waddle *verb* **toddle**, totter, wobble, shuffle.

wag *verb* **1 swing**, swish, switch, sway, shake; *informal* waggle. **2 shake**, wave, wiggle, flourish, brandish.

wage *noun* **pay**, salary, stipend, fee, remuneration, income, earnings.
● *verb* **engage in**, carry on, conduct, execute, pursue, prosecute, proceed with.

wail *noun* & *verb* **howl**, cry, bawl, moan, groan, yowl, whine, lament.

wait *verb* **1** *we waited in the airport* **stay (put)**, remain, rest, stop, linger, loiter; *informal* stick around; *old use* tarry. **2** *she had to wait until her bags arrived* **stand by**, hold back, bide your time, mark time, kill time, waste time, kick your heels, twiddle your thumbs; *informal* hold on, hang around, sit tight.
● *noun* **delay**, hold-up, interval, interlude, pause, break, suspension, stoppage, halt, interruption, lull, gap.

waiter, **waitress** *noun* **server**, steward, stewardess, attendant, butler, servant; *N. Amer.* waitperson.

waive *verb* **1 give up**, abandon, renounce, relinquish, surrender, sacrifice, turn down. **2 disregard**, ignore, overlook, set aside, forgo.

wake[1] *verb* **awake**, waken, wake up, stir, come to, come round, rouse.
● *noun* **vigil**, watch, funeral.

wake[2] *noun* **backwash**, slipstream, trail, path, track.
□ **in the wake of** in the aftermath of, after, subsequent to, following, as a result of, as a consequence of, on account of, because of.

walk *verb* **1 stroll**, saunter, amble, trudge, plod, hike, tramp, trek, march, stride, troop, wander, ramble, promenade, traipse; *informal* mosey, hoof it. **2 accompany**, escort, guide, show,

see, take, usher.
● *noun* **1 ramble**, hike, tramp, march, stroll, promenade, constitutional, turn. **2 gait**, step, stride, tread. **3 path**, pathway, footpath, track, walkway, promenade, footway, pavement, trail, towpath.

walker *noun* **rambler**, hiker, trekker, stroller, pedestrian.

wall *noun* **fortification**, rampart, barricade, bulwark, partition.

wallet *noun* **purse**, case, pouch, holder; *N. Amer.* billfold, pocketbook.

wallow *verb* **1 roll**, loll about, lie around, splash about. **2 luxuriate**, bask, take pleasure, take satisfaction, indulge (yourself), delight, revel, glory.

wan *adjective* **pale**, ashen, white, grey, anaemic, colourless, waxen, pasty, peaky, sickly, washed out, ghostly.

wander *verb* **1 stroll**, amble, saunter, walk, potter, ramble, meander, roam, range, drift; *informal* traipse, mosey. **2 stray**, depart, diverge, deviate, digress, drift, get sidetracked.

wane *verb* **decline**, diminish, decrease, dwindle, shrink, tail off, ebb, fade, lessen, peter out, fall off, recede, slump, weaken, wither, evaporate, die out.
– OPPOSITES grow.

want *verb* **desire**, wish for, hope for, fancy, care for, like, long for, yearn for, crave, hanker after, hunger for, thirst for, cry out for, covet; *informal* have a yen for, be dying for.
● *noun* **1 lack**, absence, non-existence, dearth, deficiency, inadequacy, insufficiency, paucity, shortage, scarcity. **2 need**, austerity, privation, deprivation, poverty, destitution. **3** *her wants would be taken care of* **wish**, desire, demand, longing, fancy, craving, need, requirement; *informal* yen.

wanting *adjective* **deficient**, inadequate, lacking, insufficient, imperfect, flawed, unsound, substandard, inferior, second-rate.

wanton *adjective* **deliberate**, wilful, malicious, gratuitous, unprovoked, motiveless, arbitrary, unjustifiable, senseless.

war *noun* **1 conflict**, warfare, combat, fighting, action, bloodshed, fight, campaign, hostilities. **2 campaign**, crusade, battle, fight, struggle.
- OPPOSITES peace.
  ● *verb* **fight**, battle, combat, wage war, take up arms, feud, quarrel, struggle, contend, wrangle, cross swords.

> **WORD LINKS**
> **martial** relating to war
> **belligerent** engaged in a war

ward *noun* **1 room**, department, unit, area. **2 district**, constituency, division, quarter, zone, parish. **3 dependant**, charge, protégé.

warden *noun* **1 superintendent**, caretaker, porter, steward, custodian, watchman, concierge, doorman, commissionaire. **2 prison officer**, guard, jailer, warder, keeper; *informal* screw.

warehouse *noun* **storeroom**, depot, depository, stockroom; *informal* lock-up.

wares *plural noun* **goods**, merchandise, products, produce, stock, commodities.

warfare *noun* **fighting**, war, combat, conflict, action, hostilities.

warm *adjective* **1** *a warm kitchen* **hot**, cosy, snug. **2** *a warm day* **balmy**, summery, sultry, hot, mild, temperate. **3** *warm water* **tepid**, lukewarm, heated. **4** *a warm sweater* **thick**, chunky, thermal, woolly. **5** *a warm welcome* **friendly**, cordial, amiable, genial, kind, pleasant, fond, welcoming, hospitable, hearty.
- OPPOSITES cold, chilly.

warmth *noun* **1 heat**, cosiness, snugness. **2 friendliness**, amiability, geniality, cordiality, kindness, tenderness, fondness.

warn *verb* **1 inform**, notify, tell, alert, apprise, make someone aware, remind; *informal* tip off. **2 advise**, exhort, urge, counsel, caution.

warning *noun* **1 (advance) notice**, alert, hint, signal, sign, alarm bells; *informal* a tip-off. **2 caution**, notification, information, exhortation, advice. **3 omen**, premonition, foreboding, prophecy, prediction, forecast, token, portent, signal, sign. **4** *his sentence is a warning to other drunk drivers* **example**, deterrent, lesson, caution, message, moral. **5 reprimand**, caution, remonstrance, admonition, censure; *informal* dressing-down, talking-to, telling-off.

warp *verb* **1 buckle**, twist, bend, distort, deform, curve, bow, contort. **2 corrupt**, twist, pervert, deprave.

warrant *noun* **1 authorization**, order, writ, mandate, licence, permit, summons. **2 voucher**, chit, slip, ticket, coupon, pass.
  ● *verb* **1 justify**, deserve, vindicate, call for, sanction, permit, authorize, excuse, account for, legitimize, support, license, merit, qualify for, rate. **2 guarantee**, promise, affirm, swear, vouch, vow, pledge, undertake, declare, testify.

warranty *noun* **guarantee**, assurance, promise, commitment, undertaking, pledge, agreement, covenant.

warrior *noun* **fighter**, soldier, serviceman, combatant.

wary *adjective* **1 cautious**, careful, circumspect, on your guard, chary, alert, on the lookout, attentive, heedful, watchful, vigilant, observant. **2** *we are wary of strangers* **suspicious**, chary, leery, careful, distrustful.
- OPPOSITES inattentive, trustful.

wash *verb* **1 clean yourself**, bathe, shower. **2 clean**, cleanse, scrub, wipe, shampoo, launder, lather, sluice, swill, douse, swab, disinfect. **3** *she washed off the blood* **remove**, expunge, eradicate, sponge off, scrub off, wipe off, rinse off.

4 splash, lap, dash, break, beat, surge, ripple, roll.
● *noun* **1 laundry**, washing. **2 backwash**, wake, trail, path.
□ **wash away** erode, abrade, wear away, eat away.

waste *verb* **1 squander**, misspend, misuse, fritter away, throw away, lavish, dissipate; *informal* blow, splurge. **2** *she is wasting away* **grow weak**, grow thin, wilt, fade, deteriorate.
- OPPOSITES conserve.
● *adjective* **1 unwanted**, excess, superfluous, left over, scrap, unusable, unprofitable. **2 uncultivated**, barren, desert, arid, bare, desolate.
● *noun* **1 misuse**, misapplication, abuse, extravagance, lavishness. **2 rubbish**, refuse, litter, debris, junk, sewage, effluent; *N. Amer.* garbage, trash. **3** (**wastes**) **desert**, wasteland, wilderness, emptiness, wilds.

wasteful *adjective* **prodigal**, profligate, uneconomical, extravagant, lavish, excessive, imprudent, improvident, spendthrift.
- OPPOSITES frugal.

watch *verb* **1 observe**, view, look at, eye, gaze at, peer at, contemplate, inspect, scrutinize, scan; *informal* check out, get a load of, recce, eyeball. **2 spy on**, keep in sight, keep under surveillance, track, monitor, tail; *informal* keep tabs on, stake out. **3 guard**, mind, protect, look after, keep an eye on, take care of, shield, defend.
- OPPOSITES ignore.
● *noun* **1 wristwatch**, timepiece, chronometer. **2 guard**, vigil, lookout, observation, surveillance.

watchdog *noun* **ombudsman**, monitor, scrutineer, inspector, supervisor.

watchful *adjective* **observant**, alert, vigilant, attentive, aware, sharp-eyed, eagle-eyed, on the lookout, wary, cautious, careful.

water *verb* **1 sprinkle**, moisten, dampen, wet, spray, splash, hose, douse. **2 salivate**, become wet, moisten.

□ **water down 1** dilute, thin (out), weaken, adulterate. **2** tone down, temper, mitigate, moderate, soften, tame.

> **WORD LINKS**
> **aquatic**, **aqueous** relating to water

waterfall *noun* **falls**, cascade, cataract, rapids.

watertight *adjective* **1 impermeable**, impervious, (hermetically) sealed, waterproof. **2 indisputable**, unquestionable, incontrovertible, irrefutable, unassailable, foolproof, sound, flawless, conclusive.
- OPPOSITES leaky.

wave *verb* **1 flap**, wag, shake, swish, swing, brandish, flourish, wield. **2 ripple**, flutter, undulate, stir, flap, sway, shake, quiver. **3 gesture**, signal, beckon, motion.
● *noun* **1 signal**, sign, motion, gesture. **2 breaker**, roller, comber, boomer, ripple; (**waves**) swell, surf. **3** *a wave of planning applications* **spate**, surge, flow, flood, stream, torrent. **4** *a wave of emotion* **surge**, rush, tide, upsurge, sudden feeling.

waver *verb* **1** *the candlelight wavered* **flicker**, quiver. **2** *his voice wavered* **falter**, wobble, tremble, quaver. **3 hesitate**, dither, be irresolute, be undecided, vacillate, blow hot and cold; *Brit.* haver, hum and haw; *informal* shilly-shally, sit on the fence.

way *noun* **1 method**, process, procedure, technique, system, plan, strategy, scheme, solution, means, mechanism, approach. **2 manner**, style, fashion, mode. **3** *I've changed my ways* **practice**, wont, habit, custom, convention, routine, trait, attribute, peculiarity, idiosyncrasy, conduct, behaviour. **4 route**, course, direction, track, path, access, gate, exit, entrance, door. **5 distance**, length, stretch, journey. **6** *April is a long way away* **time**, stretch, term, span, duration. **7 direction**, bearing, course, orientation, line, tack. **8** *in some ways, he may be better off* **respect**, regard, aspect, facet, sense, detail, point, particular. **9** *the country is in a bad way*

w

state, condition, situation, circumstances, position, predicament, plight; *informal* shape.
❑ **give way 1** yield, back down, surrender, concede defeat, give in, submit; *informal* throw in the towel/sponge, cave in. **2** collapse, give, cave in, fall in, come apart, crumple.

waylay *verb* **1** ambush, hold up, attack, pounce on; *informal* mug. **2 accost**, detain, intercept; *informal* buttonhole.

wayward *adjective* **wilful**, headstrong, stubborn, obstinate, perverse, contrary, disobedient, undisciplined, rebellious, defiant, recalcitrant, unruly, wild; *formal* refractory.

weak *adjective* **1 feeble**, frail, delicate, fragile, infirm, ailing, debilitated, decrepit, exhausted, enervated; *informal* weedy. **2 inadequate**, poor, defective, faulty, deficient, imperfect, substandard. **3 unconvincing**, tenuous, implausible, unsatisfactory, poor, inadequate, lame, feeble, flimsy, hollow; *informal* pathetic. **4** *a weak bridge* **fragile**, rickety, insubstantial, wobbly, unstable, ramshackle, jerry-built, shoddy. **5 spineless**, craven, cowardly, timid, irresolute, indecisive, ineffectual, meek, tame, soft, faint-hearted; *informal* yellow, gutless. **6** *a weak voice* **indistinct**, muffled, muted, hushed, faint, low. **7 watery**, dilute, diluted, watered down, thin, tasteless.
- OPPOSITES strong.

weaken *verb* **1 enfeeble**, debilitate, incapacitate, sap, tire, exhaust. **2 decrease**, dwindle, diminish, wane, ebb, subside, peter out, fizzle out, tail off, decline, falter. **3 impair**, undermine, compromise, lessen.
- OPPOSITES strengthen, bolster.

weakness *noun* **1 frailty**, feebleness, fragility, delicacy, debility, incapacity, decrepitude; *informal* weediness. **2 fault**, flaw, defect, deficiency, failing, shortcoming, imperfection, Achilles heel. **3** *a weakness for champagne* **fondness**, liking, partiality, love, penchant, predilection, inclination, taste.

4 timidity, cravenness, cowardliness, indecision, irresolution, ineffectuality, ineffectiveness, impotence.

wealth *noun* **1 affluence**, prosperity, riches, means, fortune, money, cash, capital, treasure, finance, wherewithal, deep pockets; *informal* dough, bread. **2 abundance**, profusion, plethora, mine, store; *informal* lot, load, mountain, stack, ton; *Brit. informal* shedload.
- OPPOSITES poverty, dearth.

wealthy *adjective* **rich**, affluent, moneyed, well off, well-to-do, prosperous; *informal* well heeled, rolling in it, made of money, loaded, flush.
- OPPOSITES poor.

wear *verb* **1 be dressed in**, be clothed in, have on, sport. **2 bear**, show, display, exhibit, give, put on, assume. **3 erode**, abrade, rub away, grind away, wash away, crumble (away), eat away (at). **4 last**, endure, hold up, bear up.
● *noun* **1 use**, service, value; *informal* mileage. **2 clothes**, garments, dress, attire, garb, wardrobe; *informal* get-up, gear, togs; *Brit. informal* kit, clobber. **3 damage**, friction, abrasion, erosion.
❑ **wear off** fade, diminish, lessen, dwindle, decrease, wane, peter out, fizzle out, pall, disappear, vanish. **wear out 1** deteriorate, become worn, fray, become threadbare. **2** tire out, fatigue, weary, exhaust, drain, sap, enervate; *informal* whack, poop, shatter, do in; *Brit. informal* knacker.

wearing *adjective* **tiring**, exhausting, wearying, fatiguing, enervating, draining, sapping, demanding, exacting, taxing, gruelling, punishing.

weary *adjective* **1 tired**, worn out, exhausted, fatigued, sapped, spent, drained; *informal* done in, ready to drop, shattered, bushed; *Brit. informal* knackered, whacked; *N. Amer. informal* pooped. **2 tiring**, exhausting, fatiguing, enervating, draining, sapping, demanding, taxing, arduous, gruelling.
- OPPOSITES energetic.

weather *noun* **conditions**, climate, elements, forecast, outlook.

● *verb* **survive**, come through, ride out, pull through, withstand, endure, rise above; *informal* stick out.

weave[1] *verb* **1 entwine**, lace, twist, knit, braid, plait. **2 invent**, make up, fabricate, construct, create, spin.

weave[2] *verb he had to weave his way through the crowds* **thread**, wind, wend, dodge, zigzag.

web *noun* **1 mesh**, net, lattice, lacework, gauze, gossamer. **2 network**, nexus, complex, tangle, chain.

wedded *adjective* **1 married**, matrimonial, marital, conjugal, nuptial. **2** *he is wedded to his work* **dedicated**, devoted, attached, fixated.

wedding *noun* **marriage (service)**, nuptials, union.

wedge *noun* **triangle**, segment, slice, section, chunk, lump, slab, hunk, block, piece.
● *verb* **squeeze**, cram, jam, ram, force, push, shove; *informal* stuff, bung.

weep *verb* **cry**, shed tears, sob, snivel, whimper, wail, bawl, keen; *Scottish* greet; *informal* boohoo, blub.

weigh *verb* **1 measure the weight of**, put on the scales. **2 have a weight of**, tip the scales at. **3** *he weighed up the possibilities* **consider**, contemplate, think about, mull over, chew over, reflect on, ruminate about, muse on, assess, examine, review, explore, take stock of. **4** *they need to weigh benefit against risk* **balance**, evaluate, compare, juxtapose, contrast.

weight *noun* **1 mass**, heaviness, load, burden. **2 influence**, force, leverage, sway, pull, power, authority; *informal* clout. **3 burden**, load, millstone, trouble, worry. **4** *the weight of the evidence is against him* **most**, bulk, majority, preponderance, body, lion's share.

weird *adjective* **1 uncanny**, eerie, unnatural, supernatural, unearthly, other-worldly, ghostly, mysterious, strange, abnormal, unusual; *informal* creepy, spooky, freaky. **2 bizarre**, odd, curious, strange, quirky, outlandish, eccentric, unconventional, unorthodox, idiosyncratic, surreal, crazy, absurd, grotesque, peculiar; *informal* wacky, freaky; *N. Amer. informal* wacko.
– OPPOSITES normal, conventional.

welcome *noun* **greeting**, salutation, reception, hospitality, the red carpet.
● *verb* **1 greet**, salute, receive, meet, usher in. **2 be pleased by**, be glad about, approve of, applaud, appreciate, embrace.
– OPPOSITES resent.
● *adjective* **pleasing**, good, agreeable, encouraging, gratifying, heartening, promising, favourable, pleasant.

weld *verb* **fuse**, bond, stick, join, attach, seal, splice, melt, solder.

welfare *noun* **1 well-being**, health, comfort, security, safety, protection, success, interest, good. **2 social security**, benefit, public assistance, pension, credit, support, sick pay, unemployment benefit; *Brit. informal* the dole.

well[1] *adverb* **1 satisfactorily**, nicely, correctly, properly, fittingly, suitably, appropriately. **2 skilfully**, ably, competently, proficiently, adeptly, deftly, expertly, excellently. **3** *they speak well of him* **admiringly**, highly, approvingly, favourably, appreciatively, warmly, enthusiastically, in glowing terms.
– OPPOSITES badly.
● *adjective* **1 healthy**, fine, fit, robust, strong, vigorous, blooming, thriving, in fine fettle; *informal* in the pink. **2 satisfactory**, all right, fine, in order, as it should be, acceptable; *informal* OK, hunky-dory.
– OPPOSITES unwell, unsatisfactory.
□ **as well** too, also, in addition, into the bargain, besides, furthermore, moreover, to boot.

well[2] *noun* **borehole**, spring, waterhole, shaft.
● *verb* **flow**, spill, stream, gush, roll, cascade, flood, spout, burst, issue.

well built *adjective* **sturdy**, strapping, brawny, burly, hefty, muscular, strong, rugged; *informal* hunky, beefy.
– OPPOSITES puny.

w

well known *adjective* **1 familiar**, popular, common, everyday, established. **2 famous**, famed, prominent, notable, renowned, distinguished, eminent, illustrious, acclaimed.
- OPPOSITES unknown.

wet *adjective* **1 damp**, moist, soaked, drenched, saturated, sopping, dripping, soggy, waterlogged, squelchy. **2 rainy**, pouring, teeming, showery, drizzly. **3 sticky**, tacky.
● *verb* **dampen**, moisten, sprinkle, spray, splash, soak, saturate, flood, douse, drench.
- OPPOSITES dry.

wharf *noun* **quay**, pier, dock, berth, landing, jetty, harbour, dockyard.

wheel *verb* **1 push**, trundle, roll. **2** *gulls wheeled overhead* **turn**, go round, circle, orbit.

wheeze *verb* **gasp**, whistle, hiss, rasp, croak, pant, cough.

whereabouts *noun* **location**, position, site, situation, spot, point, home, address, neighbourhood.

while *noun* *we chatted for a while* **time**, spell, stretch, stint, span, interval, period; *Brit. informal* patch.
● *verb* *tennis helped to while away the time* **pass**, spend, occupy, use up, kill.

whim *noun* **impulse**, urge, notion, fancy, inclination, caprice, vagary.

whimper *verb* **whine**, cry, sob, moan, snivel, wail, groan; *Brit. informal* grizzle.

whimsical *adjective* **fanciful**, playful, mischievous, waggish, quaint, curious, droll, eccentric, quirky, idiosyncratic, unconventional.

whine *verb* **1 wail**, whimper, cry, mewl, moan, howl, yowl; *informal* grizzle. **2 complain**, grouse, grouch, grumble, moan, carp; *informal* gripe, bellyache, whinge.

whip *noun* **lash**, scourge, strap, belt.
● *verb* **1 flog**, lash, flagellate, cane, belt, thrash, beat; *informal* tan someone's hide. **2 whisk**, beat. **3 rouse**, stir up, excite, galvanize, electrify, stimulate, inspire, fire up, inflame, provoke.

whirl *verb* **rotate**, circle, wheel, turn, revolve, orbit, spin, twirl, pirouette, gyrate.

whirlpool *noun* **eddy**, vortex, maelstrom.

whirlwind *noun* **tornado**, hurricane, typhoon, cyclone, vortex; *N. Amer. informal* twister.
● *adjective* **rapid**, lightning, headlong, impulsive, breakneck, meteoric, sudden, swift, fast, quick, speedy.

whisk *verb* **1 speed**, hurry, rush, sweep, hurtle, shoot. **2 pull**, snatch, pluck, tug, jerk; *informal* whip, yank. **3 whip**, beat, mix.
● *noun* *an egg whisk* **beater**, mixer, blender.

whisper *verb* **murmur**, mutter, mumble, speak softly, breathe, say sotto voce.
● *noun* **1 murmur**, mutter, mumble, low voice, undertone. **2 rumour**, story, report, gossip, speculation, suggestion, hint; *informal* buzz.
- OPPOSITES shout.

white *adjective* **pale**, pallid, wan, ashen, chalky, pasty, peaky, washed out, ghostly, deathly.

whole *adjective* **1 entire**, complete, full, unabridged, uncut. **2 intact**, in one piece, unbroken, undamaged, flawless, unmarked, perfect.
- OPPOSITES incomplete.
● *noun* **1 entity**, unit, body, ensemble. **2** *the whole of the year* **all**, every part, the lot, the sum.
□ **on the whole** overall, all in all, all things considered, for the most part, in the main, in general, by and large, normally, usually, almost always, typically, ordinarily.

wholehearted *adjective* **unqualified**, unreserved, unconditional, complete, full, total, absolute.
- OPPOSITES half-hearted.

wholesale *adjective* **extensive**, widespread, large-scale, wide-ranging, comprehensive, total, mass, indiscriminate, sweeping.
- OPPOSITES partial.

w

wholesome adjective **1 healthy**, health-giving, good, nutritious, nourishing, natural, organic. **2 moral**, ethical, good, clean, virtuous, pure, innocent, chaste, uplifting, edifying.

wholly adverb **completely**, totally, absolutely, entirely, fully, thoroughly, utterly, downright, in every respect; informal one hundred per cent.

wicked adjective **1 evil**, sinful, immoral, wrong, bad, iniquitous, corrupt, base, vile, villainous, criminal, nefarious; informal crooked. **2 mischievous**, playful, naughty, impish, roguish, puckish, cheeky.
- OPPOSITES virtuous.

wide adjective **1 broad**, extensive, spacious, vast, spread out. **2 comprehensive**, ample, broad, extensive, wide-ranging, large, exhaustive, all-inclusive, expansive, all-embracing, encyclopedic, catholic. **3 off target**, off the mark, inaccurate.
- OPPOSITES narrow.

widen verb **broaden**, open up/out, expand, extend, enlarge.

widespread adjective **general**, extensive, universal, common, global, worldwide, omnipresent, ubiquitous, across the board, predominant, prevalent, rife, broad.
- OPPOSITES limited.

width noun **breadth**, thickness, span, diameter, girth.

wield verb **1 brandish**, flourish, wave, swing, use, employ, handle. **2** he wields enormous power **exercise**, exert, hold, maintain, command, control.

wife noun **spouse**, partner, mate, consort, bride; informal better half, missus; Brit. informal other half.

> **WORD LINKS**
> **uxorious** very fond of your wife

wild adjective **1 untamed**, undomesticated, feral, fierce, ferocious, savage. **2 uncultivated**, native, indigenous. **3 uninhabited**, unpopulated, uncultivated, rugged, rough, inhospitable, desolate, barren. **4 stormy**, squally,

tempestuous, turbulent, blustery. **5 uncontrolled**, unrestrained, undisciplined, attention-seeking, unruly, rowdy, disorderly, riotous, out of control, unbridled. **6** a wild scheme **foolish**, ridiculous, ludicrous, stupid, foolhardy, idiotic, madcap, absurd, silly, impractical, impracticable, unworkable; informal crazy, crackpot. **7** a wild guess **random**, arbitrary, haphazard, uninformed.
- OPPOSITES tame, cultivated, calm, disciplined.

wilderness noun **wilds**, wastes, desert, wasteland.

wiles plural noun **tricks**, ruses, ploys, schemes, dodges, manoeuvres, subterfuges, guile, artfulness, cunning.

wilful adjective **1 deliberate**, intentional, premeditated, planned, conscious, calculated. **2 headstrong**, strong-willed, obstinate, stubborn, pig-headed, recalcitrant; Brit. informal bloody-minded, bolshie.
- OPPOSITES accidental.

will noun **1 determination**, strength of character, resolve, single-mindedness, drive, commitment, dedication, doggedness, tenacity, staying power. **2** they stayed against their will **desire**, wish, preference, inclination, intention. **3** it was God's will **wish**, desire, decision, choice, decree, command.
● verb **1 want**, wish, please, see fit, think fit/best, like, choose, prefer. **2 decree**, order, ordain, command.

willing adjective **1 ready**, prepared, disposed, inclined, minded, happy, glad, pleased, agreeable, amenable; informal game. **2 readily given**, ungrudging.
- OPPOSITES reluctant.

willingly adverb **voluntarily**, of your own free will, of your own accord, readily, without reluctance, ungrudgingly, cheerfully, happily, gladly, with pleasure.
- OPPOSITES reluctantly.

willingness noun **readiness**, inclination, will, wish, desire.
- OPPOSITES reluctance.

w

wilt *verb* **1 droop**, sag, become limp, flop. **2 languish**, flag, droop, become listless, fade.
- OPPOSITES flourish.

wily *adjective* **shrewd**, clever, sharp, astute, canny, smart, crafty, cunning, artful, sly, scheming, calculating, devious; *informal* foxy.
- OPPOSITES naive.

win *verb* **1 come first**, be victorious, carry/win the day, come out on top, succeed, triumph, prevail. **2 earn**, gain, secure, collect, pick up, walk away/off with, carry off; *informal* land, net, bag, scoop.
- OPPOSITES lose.
● *noun* **victory**, triumph, conquest.
- OPPOSITES defeat.

wince *verb* **grimace**, pull a face, flinch, blench, start.

wind[1] *noun* **1 breeze**, current of air, gale, hurricane, gust, draught; *informal* blow; *literary* zephyr. **2 breath**; *informal* puff.

wind[2] *verb* **1 twist (and turn)**, bend, curve, loop, zigzag, weave, snake. **2 wrap**, furl, entwine, lace. **3 coil**, roll, twist, twine.
□ **wind up 1** conclude, bring to an end/close, terminate; *informal* wrap up. **2** close (down), dissolve, put into liquidation.

windfall *noun* **bonanza**, jackpot, pennies from heaven, godsend.

windy *adjective* **breezy**, blowy, fresh, blustery, gusty, wild, stormy, squally.
- OPPOSITES still.

wing *noun* **1 part**, section, side, annexe, extension. **2 faction**, camp, caucus, arm, branch, group, section, set.
● *verb* **1 fly**, glide, soar. **2 wound**, graze, hit.

wink *verb* **1 blink**, flutter, bat. **2 sparkle**, twinkle, flash, glitter, gleam, shine, scintillate.

winner *noun* **victor**, champion, conqueror, medallist; *informal* champ, top dog.
- OPPOSITES loser.

winning *adjective* **1 victorious**, successful, triumphant, undefeated, conquering, first, top. **2 engaging**, charming, appealing, endearing, sweet, cute, winsome, attractive, prepossessing, fetching, disarming, captivating.

winnings *plural noun* **prize money**, gains, booty, spoils, proceeds, profits, takings, purse.

wintry *adjective* **bleak**, cold, chilly, frosty, freezing, icy, snowy, arctic, glacial, bitter, raw; *informal* nippy; *Brit. informal* parky.
- OPPOSITES warm.

wipe *verb* **1 rub**, mop, sponge, swab, clean, dry, polish. **2** *he wiped off the marks* **rub off**, clean off, remove, erase, efface.

wisdom *noun* **1 understanding**, intelligence, sagacity, sense, common sense, shrewdness, astuteness, judgement, prudence, circumspection, logic, rationale, soundness, advisability. **2 knowledge**, learning, erudition, scholarship, philosophy, lore.
- OPPOSITES folly.

wise *adjective* **sage**, sagacious, intelligent, clever, learned, knowledgeable, enlightened, astute, smart, shrewd, sharp-witted, canny, knowing, sensible, prudent, discerning, perceptive.
- OPPOSITES foolish.

wish *verb* **want**, desire, feel inclined, feel like, care, choose, please, think fit.
● *noun* **1 desire**, longing, yearning, whim, craving, hunger, hope, aspiration, aim, ambition, dream; *informal* hankering, yen. **2** *her parents' wishes* **request**, requirement, bidding, instruction, direction, demand, order, command, want, desire, will.
□ **wish for** desire, want, hope for, covet, dream of, long for, yearn for, crave, hunger for, aspire to, set your heart on, seek, fancy, hanker after; *informal* have a yen for.

wistful *adjective* **nostalgic**, yearning, longing, forlorn, melancholy, sad, mournful, pensive, reflective, contemplative.

w

wit noun **1** *he needed all his wits to escape* **intelligence**, shrewdness, astuteness, cleverness, canniness, sense, judgement, acumen, insight, brains, mind; *informal* nous. **2 wittiness**, humour, drollery, repartee, badinage, banter, wordplay, jokes, witticisms, quips, puns. **3 comedian**, humorist, comic, joker; *informal* wag.

witch noun **sorceress**, enchantress, hex.

witchcraft noun **sorcery**, (black) magic, wizardry, spells, incantations, necromancy, Wicca.

withdraw verb **1 remove**, extract, pull out, take out, take back. **2 abolish**, cancel, lift, set aside, end, stop, remove, reverse, revoke, rescind, repeal, annul. **3 retract**, take back, go back on, recant, repudiate, renounce, back down, climb down, backtrack, back-pedal, do a U-turn, row back, eat your words. **4 retreat**, pull out of, evacuate, quit, leave. **5 retire**, retreat, adjourn, decamp, leave, depart, absent yourself; *formal* repair.
- OPPOSITES insert, enter.

withdrawal noun **1 removal**, abolition, cancellation, discontinuation, termination, elimination. **2 departure**, pull-out, exit, exodus, evacuation, retreat.

withdrawn adjective **introverted**, unsociable, inhibited, uncommunicative, unforthcoming, quiet, reticent, reserved, retiring, private, reclusive, distant, shy, timid.
- OPPOSITES outgoing.

wither verb **1 shrivel (up)**, dry up, wilt, droop, go limp, fade, perish. **2 waste (away)**, shrivel (up), shrink, atrophy. **3 diminish**, dwindle, shrink, lessen, fade, wane, evaporate, disappear.
- OPPOSITES thrive.

withering adjective **scornful**, contemptuous, scathing, stinging.

withhold verb **1 hold back**, keep back, refuse to give, retain, hold on to, hide, conceal, keep secret; *informal* sit on. **2 suppress**, repress, hold back, fight back, choke back, control, check, restrain, contain.
- OPPOSITES release.

withstand verb **resist**, weather, survive, endure, cope with, stand, tolerate, bear, defy, brave, hold out against.

witness noun **observer**, onlooker, eyewitness, spectator, viewer, watcher, bystander, passer-by.
● verb **1 see**, observe, watch, view, notice, spot, be present at, attend. **2 countersign**, sign, endorse, validate.

witty adjective **humorous**, amusing, droll, funny, comic, jocular, sparkling, scintillating, entertaining, clever, quick-witted.

wizard noun **1 sorcerer**, warlock, magus, (black) magician, enchanter. **2 genius**, expert, master, virtuoso, maestro, marvel; *informal* hotshot, whizz-kid; *Brit. informal* dab hand; *N. Amer. informal* maven.

wobble verb **1 rock**, sway, see-saw, teeter, jiggle, shake. **2 teeter**, totter, stagger, lurch, waddle. **3** *her voice wobbled* **tremble**, shake, quiver, quaver, waver.

wobbly adjective **1 unsteady**, unstable, shaky, rocky, rickety, unsafe, precarious; *informal* wonky. **2 shaky**, quivery, weak, unsteady; *informal* like jelly.
- OPPOSITES stable.

woe noun **1 misery**, sorrow, distress, sadness, unhappiness, heartache, heartbreak, despair, adversity, misfortune, disaster, suffering, hardship. **2** *financial woes* **trouble**, difficulty, problem, trial, tribulation, misfortune, setback, reverse.
- OPPOSITES joy.

woeful adjective **1 sad**, unhappy, sorrowful, miserable, gloomy, doleful, plaintive, wretched. **2 dreadful**, awful, terrible, atrocious, disgraceful, deplorable, hopeless, lamentable; *informal* rotten, appalling, pathetic, pitiful, lousy, abysmal, dire; *Brit. informal* duff, chronic.
- OPPOSITES cheerful, excellent.

woman noun **lady**, female; *Scottish & N. English* lass; *Irish* colleen; *informal* chick; *N. Amer. informal* sister, dame, broad; *Austral./NZ informal* sheila; *literary* damsel.

> **WORD LINKS**
> **female, feminine** relating to women
> **gynaecology** branch of medicine concerning women
> **misogyny** hatred of women

womanly *adjective* **1 feminine**, female. **2 voluptuous**, curvaceous, shapely, ample, buxom, full-figured; *informal* curvy, busty.
- OPPOSITES manly, boyish.

wonder *noun* **1 awe**, admiration, fascination, surprise, astonishment, amazement. **2** *the wonders of nature* **marvel**, miracle, phenomenon, sensation, spectacle, beauty, curiosity.
● *verb* **1 ponder**, think about, meditate on, reflect on, muse on, speculate about, conjecture, be curious about. **2 marvel**, be amazed, be astonished, stand in awe, be dumbfounded; *informal* be flabbergasted.

wonderful *adjective* **marvellous**, magnificent, superb, glorious, sublime, lovely, delightful; *informal* super, great, fantastic, terrific, tremendous, sensational, fabulous, awesome, magic, wicked; *Brit. informal* smashing, brilliant; *N. Amer. informal* peachy, dandy, neat; *Austral./NZ informal* beaut, bonzer.

woo *verb* **1 pay court to**, pursue, chase; *dated* court, romance, seek the hand of. **2 seek**, pursue, curry favour with, try to win, try to attract, try to cultivate. **3 entice**, tempt, coax, persuade, wheedle, seduce; *informal* sweet-talk.

wood *noun* **1 timber**, planks, logs; *N. Amer.* lumber. **2 forest**, woodland, trees, copse, coppice, grove; *Brit.* spinney.

> **WORD LINKS**
> **ligneous** relating to wood

wooded *adjective* **forested**, afforested, tree-covered; *literary* sylvan.

wooden *adjective* **1 wood**, timber. **2 stilted**, stiff, unnatural, awkward, flat, clumsy, graceless, inelegant. **3 expressionless**, impassive, poker-faced, emotionless, blank, vacant, unresponsive, lifeless.

wool *noun* **fleece**, hair, coat.

woolly *adjective* **1 woollen**, wool. **2 fleecy**, shaggy, hairy, fluffy. **3 vague**, ill-defined, hazy, unclear, fuzzy, indefinite, confused, muddled.

word *noun* **1 term**, name, expression, designation. **2 remark**, comment, observation, statement, utterance. **3 script**, lines, lyrics, libretto. **4** *I give you my word* **promise**, assurance, guarantee, undertaking, pledge, vow, oath, bond. **5 talk**, conversation, chat, tête-à-tête, heart-to-heart, one-to-one, discussion; *informal* confab. **6** *there's no word from the hospital* **news**, information, communication, intelligence, message, report, communiqué, dispatch, bulletin; *literary* tidings.
● *verb* **phrase**, express, put, couch, frame, formulate, style.

> **WORD LINKS**
> **verbal, lexical** relating to words

wording *noun* **phrasing**, phraseology, language, words, expression, terminology.

wordy *adjective* **long-winded**, verbose, lengthy, rambling, garrulous, voluble; *informal* windy; *Brit. informal* waffly.
- OPPOSITES succinct.

work *noun* **1 labour**, toil, slog, drudgery, exertion, effort, industry; *informal* grind, sweat; *Brit. informal* graft; *old use* travail. **2 employment**, job, post, position, situation, occupation, profession, career, vocation, calling. **3 tasks**, jobs, duties, assignments, projects, chores. **4 composition**, piece, creation, opus; (**works**) oeuvre, canon.
- OPPOSITES leisure.
● *verb* **1 labour**, toil, exert yourself, slave (away); *informal* slog (away), beaver away; *Brit. informal* graft. **2 be employed**, have a job, earn your living, do business. **3 function**, go, run, operate. **4 operate**, use, handle, control,

run, manipulate. **5 succeed**, turn out well, go as planned, get results, be effective; *informal* come off, pay off, do the trick. **6 achieve**, accomplish, bring about, produce, perform.
- OPPOSITES rest, fail.
▢ **work out 1** calculate, compute, reckon up, determine. **2** understand, comprehend, puzzle out, sort out, make sense of, get to the bottom of, make head or tail of, unravel, decipher, decode; *informal* figure out; *Brit. informal* suss out. **3** devise, formulate, draw up, put together, develop, construct, arrange, organize, contrive, concoct.

worker *noun* **employee**, member of staff, workman, labourer, hand, operator, operative, agent, wage-earner, breadwinner, proletarian.

workshop *noun* **1 workroom**, studio, factory, works, plant, industrial unit. **2 study group**, discussion group, seminar, forum, class.

world *noun* **1 earth**, globe, planet, sphere. **2 sphere**, society, circle, arena, milieu, province, domain, preserve, realm, field. **3 (the world) everyone**, people, mankind, humankind, humanity, the public, all and sundry.

worldly *adjective* **1 earthly**, terrestrial, temporal, mundane, mortal, human, material, physical. **2 sophisticated**, experienced, worldly-wise, knowledgeable, knowing, enlightened, mature, seasoned, cosmopolitan, urbane, cultured.
- OPPOSITES spiritual, naive.

worldwide *adjective* **global**, international, intercontinental, universal, ubiquitous.
- OPPOSITES local.

worn *adjective* **shabby**, worn out, threadbare, in tatters, falling to pieces, ragged, frayed, moth-eaten, scruffy, having seen better days.
- OPPOSITES new, smart.

worried *adjective* **anxious**, troubled, bothered, concerned, uneasy, fretful, agitated, nervous, edgy, tense, apprehensive, fearful, afraid, frightened; *Brit.*

informal in a stew, in a flap.
- OPPOSITES carefree.

worry *verb* **1 be anxious**, be concerned, fret, agonize, brood, panic, lose sleep, get worked up; *informal* get in a flap, get in a state. **2 trouble**, bother, make anxious, disturb, distress, upset, concern, unsettle, perturb, scare, prey on someone's mind; *informal* bug, get to.
● *noun* **1 anxiety**, distress, concern, unease, disquiet, nerves, agitation, edginess, tension, apprehension, fear, misgiving. **2 problem**, cause for concern, nuisance, pest, trial, trouble, bane, bugbear; *informal* pain, headache, hassle.

worsen *verb* **1 aggravate**, add to, intensify, increase, compound, magnify, heighten, inflame, exacerbate. **2 deteriorate**, degenerate, decline; *informal* go downhill.
- OPPOSITES improve.

worship *noun* **1 reverence**, veneration, adoration, glorification, exaltation, devotion, praise, thanksgiving, homage, honour. **2 service**, rite, prayer, praise, devotion, observance.
● *verb* **1 revere**, pray to, pay homage to, honour, adore, venerate, praise, glorify, exalt. **2 love**, cherish, treasure, hold dear, esteem, adulate, idolize, deify, hero-worship, lionize; *informal* put on a pedestal.

worth *noun* **1 value**, price, cost, valuation, estimate. **2 benefit**, good, advantage, use, value, virtue, desirability, sense.

worthless *adjective* **1 valueless**, of no value; *informal* trashy. **2 useless**, pointless, meaningless, senseless, inconsequential, ineffective, ineffectual, fruitless, unproductive, unavailing, valueless. **3 good-for-nothing**, ne'er-do-well, useless, despicable, contemptible, degenerate; *informal* no-good, lousy.
- OPPOSITES valuable, useful.

worthwhile *adjective* **valuable**, useful, of service, beneficial, rewarding, advantageous, positive, helpful, profitable,

w

gainful, fruitful, productive, constructive, effective.

worthy *adjective* **good**, righteous, virtuous, moral, ethical, upright, respectable, upstanding, high-minded, principled, reputable, decent.
- OPPOSITES disreputable.
● *noun* **dignitary**, personage, grandee, VIP, notable, pillar of society, luminary, leading light; *informal* bigwig.

would-be *adjective* **aspiring**, budding, promising, prospective, potential, hopeful, keen, eager, ambitious; *informal* wannabe.

wound *noun* **1 injury**, cut, gash, laceration, graze, scratch, abrasion, puncture, lesion; *Medicine* trauma. **2 insult**, blow, slight, offence, affront, hurt, damage, injury.
● *verb* **1 injure**, hurt, harm, lacerate, cut, graze, gash, stab, slash. **2** *her words wounded him* **hurt**, offend, affront, distress, grieve, pain.

wrap *verb* **1 enclose**, enfold, envelop, encase, cover, fold, wind, swathe, bundle, swaddle. **2 pack**, package, parcel up, bundle (up), gift-wrap.
● *noun* **shawl**, stole, cloak, cape, mantle, scarf.

wrath *noun* **anger**, rage, temper, fury, outrage, spleen, resentment, (high) dudgeon, indignation; *literary* ire.
- OPPOSITES happiness.

wreath *noun* **garland**, circlet, chaplet, crown, festoon, lei, ring, loop, circle.

wreathe *verb* **1 festoon**, garland, drape, cover, deck, decorate, ornament, adorn. **2 spiral**, coil, loop, wind, curl, twist, snake.

wreck *noun* **1 shipwreck**, sunken ship, hull. **2 wreckage**, debris, ruins, remains, burnt-out shell.
● *verb* **1 destroy**, break, demolish, crash, smash up, write off; *N. Amer. informal* trash, total. **2 ruin**, spoil, disrupt, undo, put a stop to, frustrate, blight, crush, dash, destroy, scotch, shatter, devastate, sabotage; *informal* mess up, screw up, put paid to, stymie; *Brit. informal* scupper.

wrench *verb* **1 tug**, pull, jerk, wrest, heave, twist, force, prise; *N. Amer.* pry; *informal* yank. **2 sprain**, twist, turn, strain, rick, crick.

wrestle *verb* **grapple**, fight, struggle, scuffle, tussle, brawl; *informal* scrap.

wretched *adjective* **1 miserable**, unhappy, sad, heartbroken, grief-stricken, distressed, desolate, devastated, disconsolate, downcast, dejected, depressed, melancholy, forlorn. **2 harsh**, hard, grim, difficult, poor, pitiful, piteous, pathetic, tragic, miserable, bleak, cheerless, hopeless, sorry, sordid; *informal* crummy.
- OPPOSITES cheerful, comfortable.

wriggle *verb* **squirm**, writhe, wiggle, thresh, flounder, flail, twitch, twist and turn, snake, worm.
□ **wriggle out of** avoid, shirk, dodge, evade, sidestep, escape; *informal* duck.

wrinkle *noun* **crease**, fold, pucker, line, crinkle, furrow, ridge, groove; *informal* crow's feet.
● *verb* **crease**, pucker, gather, crinkle, crumple, rumple, ruck up, scrunch up.

write *verb* **1 put in writing**, put down, jot down, note (down), take down, record, inscribe, sign, scribble, scrawl, pen, pencil. **2 compose**, draft, think up, formulate, compile, pen, dash off, produce. **3 correspond**, communicate, get in touch, keep in contact; *informal* drop someone a line.

writer *noun* **author**, wordsmith; *informal* scribbler, scribe, pen-pusher, hack.

writhe *verb* **squirm**, wriggle, thrash, flail, toss, twist.

writing *noun* **1 handwriting**, hand, script, calligraphy, lettering, print, printing; *informal* scribble, scrawl. **2 written work**, compositions, books, publications, papers, articles, essays, oeuvre.

> **WORD LINKS**
> **graphology** study of handwriting

wrong *adjective* **1 incorrect**, mistaken, erroneous, inaccurate, wide of the mark, inexact, imprecise; *informal* off

w

beam, out. **2 inappropriate**, unsuitable, ill-advised, ill-considered, ill-judged, unwise, infelicitous; *informal* out of order. **3 bad**, dishonest, illegal, unlawful, illicit, criminal, corrupt, unethical, immoral, wicked, sinful, iniquitous, nefarious, reprehensible; *informal* crooked. **4 amiss**, awry, out of order, not right, defective, faulty.
- OPPOSITES right, correct.
● *adverb* **incorrectly**, wrongly, inaccurately, erroneously, mistakenly.
● *noun* **1 immorality**, sin, wickedness, evil, illegality, unlawfulness, crime, corruption, villainy, dishonesty, injustice, misconduct, transgression. **2 misdeed**, offence, injury, crime, transgression, sin, injustice, outrage, atrocity.
- OPPOSITES right.
● *verb* **mistreat**, ill-use, ill-treat, do an injustice to, abuse, harm, hurt, injure.
wrongdoer *noun* **offender**, lawbreaker, criminal, felon, delinquent, villain, culprit, evil-doer, sinner, transgressor, malefactor, miscreant, rogue, scoundrel; *informal* crook, wrong 'un.

yank *verb & noun (informal)* **jerk**, pull, tug, wrench.

yardstick *noun* **standard**, measure, gauge, scale, guide, guideline, indicator, test, touchstone, barometer, criterion, benchmark.

yarn *noun* **thread**, cotton, wool, fibre, filament.

yawning *adjective* **gaping**, wide, cavernous, deep, huge, vast.

yearly *adverb* **annually**, once a year, per annum, each/every year.

yearn *verb* **long**, pine, crave, desire, want, wish, hanker, covet, hunger, thirst, ache; *informal* itch.

yell *verb* **shout**, cry out, howl, wail, scream, shriek, screech, yelp, squeal, roar, bawl; *informal* holler.

yellow *adjective* golden, gold, blonde, fair, flaxen, lemon, primrose, mustard.

yes *adverb* **certainly**, very well, of course, by all means, sure, all right, absolutely, indeed, affirmative, agreed, roger; *Scottish & N. English* aye; *informal* yeah, yep; *Brit. informal* righto.
- OPPOSITES no.

yield *verb* **1 produce**, bear, give, provide, afford, return, bring in, earn, realize, generate, deliver, pay out.
2 surrender, capitulate, submit, admit defeat, back down, give in, cave in, raise the white flag, throw in the towel, give up the struggle.
- OPPOSITES withhold, resist.

● *noun* **profit**, gain, return, dividend, earnings.

yob, yobbo *noun (Brit. informal)* **lout**, thug, hooligan, tearaway, vandal, ruffian, troublemaker; *Austral.* larrikin; *informal* tough, bruiser, yahoo; *Brit. informal* lager lout; *Scottish informal* ned.

yokel *noun* **rustic**, bumpkin, peasant, provincial; *N. Amer. informal* hayseed, hillbilly, hick.

young *adjective* **1 youthful**, juvenile, junior, adolescent, teenage, in your salad days. **2 immature**, childish, inexperienced, naive, green, wet behind the ears. **3** *a young industry* **new**, fledgling, developing, budding, in its infancy, emerging, in the making.
- OPPOSITES old, mature.
● *noun* **offspring**, progeny, family, babies, litter, brood.

youngster *noun* **child**, teenager, adolescent, youth, juvenile, minor, junior, boy, girl; *Scottish & N. English* lass, lassie; *informal* lad, kid, whippersnapper, teen.

youth *noun* **1 early years**, teens, adolescence, boyhood, girlhood, childhood, minority. **2 young man**, boy, juvenile, teenager, adolescent, junior, minor; *informal* lad, kid.

youthful *adjective* **young**, boyish, girlish, fresh-faced, young-looking, spry, sprightly, vigorous, active.
- OPPOSITES elderly.

Zz

zany *adjective* **eccentric**, odd, unconventional, bizarre, weird, mad, crazy, comic, madcap, quirky, idiosyncratic; *informal* wacky, oddball, off the wall; *Brit. informal* daft; *N. Amer. informal* kooky.
- OPPOSITES conventional.

zeal *noun* **enthusiasm**, passion, ardour, fervour, fervency, fire, devotion, gusto, vigour, energy, vehemence, intensity, eagerness, fanaticism.
- OPPOSITES apathy.

zealot *noun* **fanatic**, enthusiast, extremist, radical, diehard, activist, militant.

zealous *adjective* **ardent**, fervent, passionate, impassioned, enthusiastic, devoted, committed, dedicated, eager, keen, avid, vehement, intense, fierce, fanatical.
- OPPOSITES apathetic.

zenith *noun* **high point**, crowning point, height, top, acme, peak, pinnacle, apex, apogee, crown, crest, summit, culmination, climax.
- OPPOSITES nadir.

zero *noun* **nought**, nothing, nil, 0; *informal* zilch; *old use* naught.

zest *noun* **enthusiasm**, gusto, relish, appetite, eagerness, keenness, zeal, passion, energy, liveliness.

zigzag *verb* **twist**, meander, snake, wind, weave, swerve.

zone *noun* **area**, sector, section, belt, stretch, region, territory, district, quarter, neighbourhood.

zoom *verb (informal)* **hurry**, rush, dash, race, speed, sprint, career, shoot, hurtle, hare, fly; *informal* tear, belt, whizz; *Brit. informal* bomb.

Oxford Quick Reference

The Concise Oxford Companion to English Literature
Dinah Birch and Katy Hooper

Based on the best-selling *Oxford Companion to English Literature*, this is
an indispensable guide to all aspects of English literature.

Review of the parent volume:
'the foremost work of reference in its field'

Literary Review

A Dictionary of Shakespeare
Stanley Wells

Compiled by one of the best-known international authorities on the
playwright's works, this dictionary offers up-to-date information on all
aspects of Shakespeare, both in his own time and in later ages.

The Oxford Dictionary of Literary Terms
Chris Baldick

A best-selling dictionary, covering all aspects of literature, this is an
essential reference work for students of literature in any language.

A Dictionary of Critical Theory
Ian Buchanan

The invaluable multidisciplinary guide to theory, covering movements,
theories, and events.

'an excellent gateway into critical theory'

Literature and Theology

Oxford Companions

'Opening such books is like sitting down with a knowledgeable friend. Not a bore or a know-all, but a genuinely well-informed chum ... So far so splendid.'

Sunday Times [of *The Oxford Companion to Shakespeare*]

For well over 60 years Oxford University Press has been publishing Companions that are of lasting value and interest, each one not only a comprehensive source of reference, but also a stimulating guide, mentor, and friend. There is a wide range of Oxford Companions available at any one time, covering topics such as music, art, and literature, as well as history, warfare, religion, and wine.

Titles include:

The Oxford Companion to English Literature
Edited by Dinah Birch
'No guide could come more classic.'

Malcolm Bradbury, *The Times*

The Oxford Companion to Music
Edited by Alison Latham
'probably the best one-volume music reference book going'

Times Educational Supplement

The Oxford Companion to Theatre and Performance
Edited by Dennis Kennedy
'A work that everyone who is serious about the theatre should have at hand'

British Theatre Guide

The Oxford Companion to Food
Alan Davidson
'the best food reference work ever to appear in the English language'

New Statesman

The Oxford Companion to Wine
Edited by Jancis Robinson
'the greatest wine book ever published'

Washington Post

OXFORD

More Literature titles from OUP

The Oxford Companion to Charles Dickens
edited by Paul Schlicke

Reissued to celebrate the bicentenary of Charles Dickens's birth, this companion draws together an unparalleled diversity of information on one of Britain's greatest writers; covering his life, his works, his reputation, and his cultural context.

Reviews from previous edition:
'comes about as close to perfection as humanly possible'

Dickens Quarterly

'will prove invaluable to scholars, readers and admirers of Dickens'

Peter Ackroyd, *The Times*

The Oxford Companion to the Brontës
Christine Alexander and Margaret Smith

This Companion brings together a wealth of information about the fascinating lives and writings of the Brontë sisters.

'This book is a must ... a treasure trove of a book'

Irish Times

The Oxford Companion to Classical Literature
edited by M. C. Howatson

A broad-ranging and authoritative guide to the classical world and its literary heritage.

Reviews from previous edition:
'a volume for all seasons ... indispensable'

Times Educational Supplement

'A necessity for any seriously literary household.'

History Today

OXFORD

Oxford Quick Reference

The Kings and Queens of Britain
John Cannon and Anne Hargreaves

A detailed, fully-illustrated history ranging from mythical and pre-conquest rulers to the present House of Windsor, featuring regional maps and genealogies.

A Dictionary of World History

Over 4,000 entries on everything from prehistory to recent changes in world affairs. An excellent overview of world history.

A Dictionary of British History
Edited by John Cannon

An invaluable source of information covering the history of Britain over the past two millennia. Over 3,000 entries written by more than 100 specialist contributors.

Review of the parent volume
'the range is impressive ... truly (almost) all of human life is here'
Kenneth Morgan, *Observer*

The Oxford Companion to Irish History
Edited by S. J. Connolly

A wide-ranging and authoritative guide to all aspects of Ireland's past from prehistoric times to the present day.

'packed with small nuggets of knowledge'   *Daily Telegraph*

The Oxford Companion to Scottish History
Edited by Michael Lynch

The definitive guide to twenty centuries of life in Scotland.
'exemplary and wonderfully readable'

Financial Times

OXFORD

Oxford Quick Reference

A Dictionary of Chemistry

Over 4,700 entries covering all aspects of chemistry, including physical chemistry and biochemistry.

'It should be in every classroom and library ... the reader is drawn inevitably from one entry to the next merely to satisfy curiosity.'

School Science Review

A Dictionary of Physics

Ranging from crystal defects to the solar system, 4,000 clear and concise entries cover all commonly encountered terms and concepts of physics.

A Dictionary of Biology

The perfect guide for those studying biology — with over 5,500 entries on key terms from biology, biochemistry, medicine, and palaeontology.

'lives up to its expectations; the entries are concise, but explanatory'

Biologist

'ideally suited to students of biology, at either secondary or university level, or as a general reference source for anyone with an interest in the life sciences'

Journal of Anatomy

OXFORD

Oxford Quick Reference

The Concise Oxford Dictionary of Quotations
SIXTH EDITION
Edited by Susan Ratcliffe

Based on the highly acclaimed seventh edition of *The Oxford Dictionary of Quotations*, this dictionary provides extensive coverage of literary and historical quotations, and contains completely up-to-date material. A fascinating read and an essential reference tool.

Oxford Dictionary of Quotations by Subject
Edited by Susan Ratcliffe

The ideal place to discover what's been said about what, the dictionary presents quotations on nearly 600 areas of special interest and concern in today's world.

The Oxford Dictionary of Humorous Quotations
Edited by Ned Sherrin

From the sharply witty to the downright hilarious, this sparkling collection will appeal to all senses of humour.

The Oxford Dictionary of Political Quotations
Edited by Antony Jay

This lively and illuminating dictionary from the writer of 'Yes Minister' presents a vintage crop of over 4,000 political quotations. Ranging from the pivotal and momentous to the rhetorical, the sincere, the bemused, the tongue-in-cheek, and the downright rude, examples include memorable words from the old hands as well as from contemporary politicians.

'funny, striking, thought-provoking and incisive ... will appeal to those browsing through it at least as much as to those who wish to use it as a work of reference'
Observer

OXFORD